May 14–19, 2017
Chicago, IL, USA

Association for
Computing Machinery

Advancing Computing as a Science & Profession

PODS'17

Proceedings of the 36th ACM SIGMOD-SIGACT-SIGAI Symposium on

Principles of Database Systems

Sponsored by:

ACM SIGMOD, ACM SIGACT, and ACM SIGAI

Supported by:

Microsoft, Oracle, Amazon, Facebook, Google, Huawei, IBM, mongoDB, Recruit Institute of Technology, SAP, Vertica, Cloudera, Intel, LogicBlox, MEMSQL, Snowflake, Workday, Morgan & Claypool, Elsevier, and Springer

Association for
Computing Machinery

Advancing Computing as a Science & Profession

The Association for Computing Machinery
2 Penn Plaza, Suite 701
New York, New York 10121-0701

ISBN: 978-1-4503-4198-1 (Digital)

ISBN: 978-1-4503-5475-2 (Print)

Additional copies may be ordered prepaid from:

ACM Order Department
PO Box 30777
New York, NY 10087-0777, USA

Phone: 1-800-342-6626 (USA and Canada)
+1-212-626-0500 (Global)
Fax: +1-212-944-1318
E-mail: acmhelp@acm.org
Hours of Operation: 8:30 am – 4:30 pm ET

Printed in the USA

PODS 2017 General & Program Chair's Welcome Message

It is our great pleasure to welcome you to the 36th ACM SIGMOD-SIGACT-SIGAI Symposium on Principles of Database Systems (PODS 2017), held in Chicago, Illinois, USA, on May 14 – May 19, 2017, in conjunction with the 2017 ACM SIGMOD International Conference on Management of Data.

Since the first edition of the symposium in 1982, the PODS papers are distinguished by a rigorous approach to widely diverse problems in data management, often bringing to bear techniques from a variety of different areas, including computational logic, finite model theory, computational complexity, algorithm design and analysis, programming languages, and artificial intelligence.

The PODS Symposia study data management challenges in a variety of application contexts, including more recently probabilistic data, parallel computation, streaming data, graph data, information retrieval, ontology and semantic web, and data-driven processes and systems. PODS has a tradition of being the premier international conference on the theoretical and foundational aspects of data management, and the interested reader is referred to the web page https://databasetheory.org/pods for information on the history of this conference series.

This year's symposium continues this tradition and continues to explicitly invite for submission papers providing original, substantial contributions in one or more of the following categories:

a) Deep theoretical exploration of topical areas central to data management;

b) New formal frameworks that aim at providing the basis for deeper theoretical investigation of important emerging issues in data management; and

c) Validation of theoretical approaches from the lens of practical applicability in data management. Apart from validating the practical applicability of existing theoretical approaches, submissions in this category are expected to provide a clear message to the database theory community as to which aspects need further theoretical investigation, based on the experimental findings.

This volume contains the proceedings of PODS 2017, which include a paper for the keynote address by Susan Davidson (University of Pennsylvania, USA), abstracts based on two invited tutorials by Lise Getoor (University of California Santa Cruz, USA) and Dan Suciu (University of Washington, USA), and 29 contributions that were selected by the Program Committee for presentation at the symposium.

In addition, this volume also contains papers from our two "Gems of PODS" speakers, Alon Halevy (Recruit Institute of Technology, USA) and Val Tannen (University of Pennsylvania, USA). The Gems of PODS is an event, started in 2016, where the goal is to promote understanding of past seminal PODS results to the general audience. The Gems of PODS papers were selected by the Gems of PODS committee consisting of Floris Geerts (chair), Christoph Koch and Pierre Senellart.

This year, PODS continued with two submission cycles that were introduced two years ago. The first cycle allowed for the possibility for papers to be revised and resubmitted. For the first cycle, 28 papers were submitted, 3 of which were directly selected for inclusion in the proceedings, and 13 were invited for a resubmission after a revision. The quality of most of the revised papers increased substantially with respect to the first submission, and 9 of 13 revised papers were selected for the proceedings. For the second cycle, 73 papers were submitted, 17 of which were selected, resulting in 29 papers selected overall from a total number of 101 submissions.

With respect to the three categories mentioned above, of the 101 submissions (resp., 29 accepted papers), 66 (resp., 22) were classified by the authors in category (a), 9 (resp., 1) in category (b), 2 (resp., 0) in category (c), 14 (resp., 4) in categories (a)&(b), 7 (resp., 1) in categories (a)&(c), and 3 (resp., 1) in categories (b)&(c). The authors were asked to select the most appropriate categories for their papers at submission time.

An important task for the Program Committee has been the selection of the PODS 2017 Best Paper Award. The committee selected the paper

- "Dichotomies in Ontology-Mediated Querying with the Guarded Fragment" by André Hernich, Carsten Lutz, Fabio Papacchini and Frank Wolter.

This year, the Program Committee also selected a PODS 2017 Best Student Paper Award. The following paper is selected.

- "Tight Space-Approximation Tradeoff for the Multi-Pass Streaming Set Cover Problem" by Sepehr Assadi.

On behalf of the committee, we would like to extend our sincere congratulations to the authors!

Since 2008, PODS assigns the ACM PODS Alberto O. Mendelzon Test-of-Time Award to a paper or a small number of papers published in the PODS proceedings ten years prior that had the most impact over the intervening decade. This year's committee, consisting of Leonid Libkin (chair) and Moshe Vardi, selected the following paper. Our warmest congratulations to the authors!

- "Provenance Semirings" by Todd J. Green, Grigoris Karvounarakis, and Val Tannen.

We thank all authors who submitted papers to the symposium.

We would also like to thank all members of the Program Committee and all external referees for the enormous amount of work they have done. The two submission cycles, with the revision round for the first cycle, placed an extra burden on all of them. The program committee did not meet in person, but carried out extensive discussions during the electronic program committee meeting, relying on the EasyChair System.

Our thanks go also to the members of the PODS Executive Committee for their support. Special thanks go to Emanuel Sallinger, our Proceedings Chair of PODS 2017 and Paolo Guagliardo, our Publicity Chair of PODS 2017. We are also grateful to the SIGMOD 2017 General Chairs, Rada Chirkova and Jun Yang for their excellent coordination of the overall SIGMOD/PODS 2017 conference and their flexibility with regards to the special circumstances related to the change of location.

We also would like to thank the SIGMOD 2017 PC Chair, Dan Suciu, for the excellent coordination between SIGMOD and PODS. For the preparation of this volume, we also thank Lisa Tolles from Sheridan Communication Inc. Finally, we thank all our sponsors, in particular the ACM Special Interest Groups on Management of Data, on Algorithms and Computation Theory, and on Artificial Intelligence, for their invaluable support.

We wish you a profitable and enjoyable stay in Chicago, and we hope that you will find the PODS 2017 program informative, exciting, and thought provoking, in the best tradition of the PODS Symposium.

Jan Van den Bussche
PODS General Chair

Floris Geerts
PODS 2017 Program Chair

Table of Contents

PODS Session 6: Best Student Paper Award, Streaming and Sketches

Session Chair: Yufei Tao *(University of Queensland)*

PODS Session 7: Dependencies, Graphs and Query Evaluation

Session Chair: Angela Bonifati *(Université de Lyon)*

PODS 2017 Symposium Organization

General Chair: Jan Van den Bussche *(Hasselt University, Belgium)*

Program Chair: Floris Geerts *(University of Antwerp, Belgium)*

Proceedings Chair: Emanuel Sallinger *(University of Oxford, United Kingdom)*

Publicity Chair: Paolo Guagliardo *(University of Edinburgh, United Kingdom)*

Program Committee:
Leopoldo Bertossi *(Carleton University, Canada)*
Meghyn Bienvenu *(CNRS, University of Montpellier, France)*
Angela Bonifati *(Université de Lyon, France)*
Andrea Calì *(University of London, United Kingdom)*
Rada Chirkova *(NC State University, USA)*
Giuseppe De Giacomo *(Sapienza Università di Roma, Italy)*
Ting Deng *(Beihang University, China)*
Diego Figueira *(CNRS, France)*
Floris Geerts *(University of Antwerp, Belgium)*
Georg Gottlob *(Oxford University, United Kingdom)*
Paraschos Koutris *(University of Wisconsin-Madison, USA)*
Andrew McGregor *(University of Massachusetts, USA)*
Gerome Miklau *(University of Massachusetts, USA)*
Jeff Phillips *(University of Utah, USA)*
Andreas Pieris *(University of Edinburgh, United Kingdom)*
Juan L. Reutter *(Pontificia Universidad Católica, Chile)*
Thomas Schwentick *(Universität Dortmund, Germany)*
Francesco *Silvestri (IT University of Copenhagen, Denmark)*
Yufei Tao *(University of Queensland, Australia)*
Stijn Vansummeren *(Université Libre de Bruxelles, Belgium)*
Jef Wijsen *(Université de Mons, Belgium)*
Qin Zhang *(Indiana University Bloomington, USA)*

Alberto O. Mendelzon Test-of-Time Award Committee:
Leonid Libkin (Chair) *(University of Edinburgh, United Kingdom)*
Moshe Vardi *(Rice University, USA)*

Gems of PODS Committee:
Floris Geerts (Chair) *(University of Antwerp, Belgium)*
Christoph Koch *(EPFL, Switzerland)*
Pierre Senellart *(École normale supérieure, France)*

Additional reviewers:

Mahmoud Abo Khamis
Mario Alviano
Abdallah Arioua
Albert Atserias
Martin Aumüller
Luca Becchetti
Véronique Benzaken
Pierre Bourhis
Vladimir Braverman
Marco Calautti
Alessandro Campi
Samir Datta
Shaleen Deep
Stefania Dumbrava
George H. L. Fletcher
Marco Gaboardi
Wolfgang Gatterbauer
Matteo Ceccarello
T-H. Hubert Chan
Jiecao Chen
Radu Ciucanu
Edith Cohen
Pawel Gawrychowski
Gaetano Geck
Aristides Gionis
Michael Goodrich
Gianluigi Greco
Kasper Green Larsen
Paolo Guagliardo
Xiaocheng Hu
Zengfeng Huang
Ioana Ileana
Mark Kaminski
Kristian Kersting
Bas Ketsman
Benny Kimelfeld
George Kollios
Domenico Lembo
Yi Li
Paolo Liberatore
Leonid Libkin
Davide Martinenghi
Maarten Marx
Samuel Mccauley
Ryan McKenna
Loizos Michael
Marco Montali
Danupon Nanongkai
Dan Olteanu
Magdalena Ortiz
Reinhard Pichler
Antonella Poggi
Miguel Romero Orth
Riccardo Rosati
Emanuel Sallinger
Francesco Scarcello
Michele Schimd
Thomas Schneider
Chris Schwiegelshohn
Luc Segoufin
Cheng Sheng
Jesper Sindahl Nielsen
Frank Staals
Dan Suciu
Bernhard Thalheim
Ioan Todinca
Szymon Toruńczyk
Martin Ugarte
Jan Van den Bussche
Nils Vortmeier
Gottfried Vossen
Domagoj Vrgoc
Yue Wang
Zhewei Wei
Grigory Yaroslavtsev
Wei Yu
Norbert Zeh
Thomas Zeume
Dan Zhang
Dongfang Zhao
Peilin Zhong

PODS 2017 Sponsors and Supporters

Sponsors:

Platinum Supporters:

Gold Supporters:

Silver Supporters:

Platinum Publisher:

Silver Publishers:

Data Citation: a Computational Challenge

[Extended Abstract]

Susan B. Davidson
University of Pennsylvania
Philadelphia, PA
susan@cis.upenn.edu

Peter Buneman
University of Edinburgh
Edinburgh, UK
opb@inf.ed.ac.uk

Daniel Deutch
Tel Aviv University
Tel Aviv, Israel
danielde@post.tau.ac.il

Tova Milo
Tel Aviv University
Tel Aviv, Israel
milo@post.tau.ac.il

Gianmaria Silvello
University of Padua
Padua, Italy
silvello@dei.unipd.it

ABSTRACT

Data citation is an interesting computational challenge, whose solution draws on several well-studied problems in database theory: query answering using views, and provenance. We describe the problem, suggest an approach to its solution, and highlight several open research problems, both practical and theoretical.

Keywords

Data citation; Data provenance; Query answering using views

1. THE PROBLEM

Citation is essential to traditional scholarship. It helps identify the cited material so that it can be retrieved, gives credit to the creator of the material, dates it, and so on. In the context of printed materials, such as books and journals, citation is well understood. However, the world is now digital, and an increasing amount of information is being collected in structured and evolving curated databases, driving database owners, publishers and standards groups to consider how such data should be cited.

Currently, several databases describe (in English) what "snippets" of information are to be included in a citation for information displayed as web page views of the database. Three such examples are eagle-i[1], an RDF dataset built to facilitate translational science research which allows researchers to share information about resources such as cell lines and software; Reactome[2], an open-source, curated and peer reviewed pathway relational database; and Drugbank[3], a relational database combining chemical, pharmacological and pharmaceutical data with sequence, structure, and pathway information. Instructions are given on which snippets of information on the web page view of the resource should be included in a citation to the resource. However, generating the citation is left to the user.

Another interesting example is the IUPHAR/BPS Guide to Pharmacology [4] (GtoPdb). The content of GtoPdb represents the effort of a large number of members of the scientific community. Different portions of the database, with varying granularity, are contributed and/or curated by different subgroups of these individuals. While GtoPdb as a whole can be treated as a traditional publication and cited accordingly, citations to many web page views of the database include the people who provided the relevant content, along with an identifier for the view and the version of the database. Views are generated on the fly from the database, and citations are generated at the same time.[5] Thus, GtoPdb automatically generates citations, but only for *some* queries.

The question then is: How can we generate citations for *general queries* over the database, i.e. those which do not correspond to web page views of the database? The problem is that, unlike traditional publications which have a fixed granularity to which citations can be attached – e.g. a conference proceedings, or a paper in a conference proceedings – the *granularity* of the material to be cited varies. Since there are a potentially infinite number of queries, each accessing and generating different subsets of the database, we cannot hope to explicitly attach a citation to every possible result set and/or query. Instead, we must find ways of using citations for some portions of the database to automatically construct citations for more general queries. Thus data citation is a *computational* problem, as argued in [4].

The approach we propose next draws inspiration from results in two areas that have been extensively studied by the database theory community: *query answering using views* (e.g. [9, 3, 10]) and *database provenance* (e.g. [8, 5]). In particular, we leverage the fact that citations and provenance are both forms of *annotation* that are manipulated through queries. We give an overview of the approach next; details can be found in [6].

[1] https://www.eagle-i.net/
[2] http://www.reactome.org/
[3] http://www.drugbank.ca/

[4] http://www.guidetopharmacology.org/
[5] Since versioning is not enabled, re-executing the query brings back the current version which may be different from the version seen when cited.

PODS'17 May 14-19, 2017, Chicago, IL, USA

ACM ISBN 978-1-4503-4198-1/17/05.
DOI: http://dx.doi.org/10.1145/3034786.3056123

2. AN APPROACH

We start with a set of *view queries* that are specified by the database owner, representing the web-page views or portions of the database for which citations are understood. Each view query V is associated with one or more *citation queries* and a *citation function*, which are also specified by the database owner. The citation queries pulls snippets of information from the database to be included in the citation; the citation function takes the output of the citation queries as input and outputs a citation in some appropriate format (e.g. human readable, BibTex, RIS or XML). The citation becomes an *annotation* on every tuple t in the view.

View and citation queries are expressed as Conjunctive Queries [2] that are optionally *parameterized* by one or more variables. The parameters must appear in the head of the queries, and be consistent across the view and associated citation queries. In a parameterized view, subsets of tuples which agree on all parameter values will have the same citation, which is based on the output of the citation query when its parameters are instantiated with these values. Consequently, tuples which disagree on some parameter value may have different citations. We denote by $C_{\mathtt{V}}(p_1, ..., p_n)$ the citation for the tuples in the result of a view V parameterized with $p_1, ..., p_n$.

For example, suppose we have the following relations where the keys are underlined.[6] For each `Family` tuple, the `Committee` relation associates the names of committee members responsible for the content (`Desc`) of a particular family. The `FamilyIntro` relation contains additional information (`Text`) about a particular family, which may be contributed by people other than committee members (details omitted):

```
Family(FID, FName,Desc)
Committee(FID, PName)
FamilyIntro((FID, Text)
```

The following view query is parameterized by `FID`, and therefore creates a separate citation for each tuple in `Family`. The associated citation query pulls the names of committee members from the `Committee` relation for the family tuple, in addition to its `FID` and `FName` from the `Family` relation:

```
λ FID. V1(FID,FName,Desc):- Family(FID,FName,Desc)
λ FID.C_V1(FID,FName,PName):- Family(FID,FName,Desc),
                               Committee(FID,PName)
```

However, in the following (unparameterized) view all tuples in `Family` have the same citation, indicated by the associated citation query:

```
V2(FID,FName,Desc):- Family(FID,FName,Desc)
C_V2(D):- D="IUPHAR/BPS Guide to PHARMACOLOGY..."
```

Our approach to constructing the citation to a general query is to *rewrite* it to a set of equivalent queries using the views, and combine the citations for these views to construct a citation to the general query. To do this, we leverage the fact that citations and provenance are both forms of *annotation* that are manipulated through queries [5]. In particular, the *joint* ($\cdot$) and *alternative* ($+$) use of annotations within a rewriting are modeled using the *semirings* approach of [8].

Given a query Q and set of views $\mathcal{V}$ together with their associated citations, consider the set of minimal equivalent rewritings, $\{Q_1, ..., Q_n\}$. In the rewritings, parameters are ignored.

For example, consider the query

$\mathtt{Q(FName)} : -\mathtt{Family(FID, FName, Desc), FamilyIntro(FID, Text)}$

and an additional (unparameterized) view `V3` and associated citation query:

```
V3(FID,Text):- FamilyIntro(FID,Text)
C_V3(D):- D="IUPHAR/BPS Guide to PHARMACOLOGY..."
```

`Q` can be rewritten in terms of `V1` and `V3`, or `V2` and `V3`:

```
Q1(FName):- V1(FID,FName,Desc),V3(FID,Text)
Q2(FName):- V2(FID,FName,Desc),V3(FID,Text)
```

To define the citation for a tuple in the result of the query, we start by defining a citation for a *single binding* of a *single rewriting* of the query. This dictates a single output tuple, and a particular valuation to the parameters of the views. We define the citation of the output tuple as the joint use of citations for the views and the parameter valuations, denoted by "$\cdot$".

DEFINITION 2.1. *Let Q be a query and let V be a set of citation views, such that $C_{\mathtt{Vi}}$, F_{Vi} are respectively a citation query and citation function associated with Vi. Further let Q' be a (partial) rewriting of Q using $V1, ..., Vn \in V$. Further let B be a binding to the variables of Q', yielding an output tuple t. The citation for t w.r.t. Q, Q', V, B, denoted $cite(t, Q, Q', V, B)$, is defined as*

$cite(t,Q,Q',V,B)= F_{V1}(C_{\mathtt{V1}}(B1)) \cdot \ldots \cdot F_{Vn}(C_{\mathtt{Vn}}(Bn))$
where Bi is the result of applying B to the variables occurring in an atom involving Vi in Q'.

Multiple bindings lead to multiple *alternative* citations, which we capture using $+$.

DEFINITION 2.2. *Let Q, V, Q' be as in Definition 2.1, and let β_t be the set of all bindings for Q' that yield a tuple t. The citation for t w.r.t. Q, Q' (denoted $cite(t, Q, Q', V)$) is defined as*

$$cite(t, Q, Q', V) = \Sigma_{B \in \beta_t} cite(t, Q, Q', V, B).$$

As noted earlier, a query may have multiple rewritings, each leading to a possibly different citation for a tuple. These are again alternatives, but the function used to combine the citations for them may be different than the one used for multiple bindings for a single rewriting. We therefore use $+^R$ ("+ for rewritings") to denote this function. Note that this is a formal semantics, not a means of computation: going through all rewritings would be impractical.

Returning to our example, suppose that there are two families that share the name 'Calcitonin' and therefore two sets of bindings for the result tuple (Calcitonin):

```
{FID=11, FName='Calcitonin', Desc='C1', Text='1st'}
{FID=12, FName='Calcitonin', Desc='C2', Text='2nd'}
```

Using rewriting `Q1`, the citation for the result tuple 'Calcitonin' would be $C_{\mathtt{V1}}\mathtt{(11)}\cdot C_{\mathtt{V3}}+C_{\mathtt{V1}}\mathtt{(12)}\cdot C_{\mathtt{V3}}$, where 11 and 12 are the parameters passed to `V1`. Using rewriting `Q2`, the citation would be $C_{\mathtt{V2}}\cdot C_{\mathtt{V3}}$.

The resulting citation for result tuple 'Calcitonin' would therefore be:

[6]The example is drawn from GtoPdb, and `Family` refers to families of drug targets.

$$(C_{\texttt{V1}}\texttt{(11)}\cdot C_{\texttt{V3}}+C_{\texttt{V1}}\texttt{(12)}\cdot C_{\texttt{V3}})+^{R}(C_{\texttt{V2}}\cdot C_{\texttt{V3}})$$

Finally, to obtain a citation for the query answer, the citations for its member tuples must be combined. We denote this abstract function as *Agg*.

The abstract functions "·" , "+", $+^R$ and *Agg* are *policies* to be specified by the database owner. There are many interpretations that could be used for these functions. For "·", "+" and *Agg*, union or join are natural. For $+^R$, the "minimum" in some ordering would also be natural. The ordering could reflect how "precise" or "comprehensive" the rewritings are relative to each other, or the "size" of the resulting citation.

As a final step in our example, suppose we use union for "·", "+" and *Agg*, and $+^R$ as the (estimated) minimum size. Since `V1` is parameterized, $C_{\texttt{V1}}$ will be different for every tuple. In contrast, $C_{\texttt{V2}}$ and $C_{\texttt{V3}}$ will be the same for every tuple. The estimated size of the citation using `Q1` would therefore be proportional to the size of `Family`, whereas the estimated size of the citation using `Q2` would be 1 (recall that *Agg* is union). The final citation for `Q` would therefore be the citation leading to the minimum size, which is the one using `Q2` ($C_{\texttt{V2}}\cdot C_{\texttt{V3}}$).

3. DISCUSSION AND OPEN PROBLEMS

A number of interesting research questions arise from this approach, both practical and theoretical.

Calculating citations. While we have defined a model for citations for query results, we have not given an efficient means for computing them. In particular, it is infeasible both in terms of run time and the size of the resulting citation to go through all rewritings and all assignments within each of them, pointing to the need for cost functions to reduce the search space (somewhat analogous to e.g. [9, 3, 10]). It may also be possible to do some of the reasoning at the schema level, and impose the views that are retained at this level over tuple-level annotations.

Defining citations. As described, views represent the web-page views or common queries against the database for which citations are understood. From a practical perspective, the database owner must first ensure that the database includes the snippets of information to be included in the citation queries. They must then specify the view and citation queries in terms of the database schema, as well as the policies for combining citations ("·", "+" and *Agg*, and $+^R$). This could easily be overwhelming for a non-expert, and therefore designing a user-friendly interface with appropriate defaults is essential. Note that once the view and citation queries have been specified, the system should take care of the annotation tracking rather than relying on the database owner to modify the database schema.

From a theoretical perspective, there are interesting questions around defining and efficiently deciding whether these views represent the "best" ones given an expected query workload, i.e. the ones that "cover" the expected queries, and give concise and unambiguous results.

Fixity. One of the "core principles" of data citation [1, 7] is *fixity*: data may evolve over time, and a citation should bring back the data as seen at the time it was cited. Thus the citation must include a mechanism of obtaining the data, in addition to snippets of information useful for human understanding. One approach is for the database to support versioning, and citations to include a timestamp or version number along with the query (or some means of recovering the query) used to obtain the data. (A prototype system for relational databases which pursues these ideas can be found in [11].)

Size of citations. An obvious concern is that, since views may be parameterized, the size of a citation may be proportional to the size of the query result. In contrast, conventional citations are small – for example, when there is an extended author list (more than 3 authors), we use "et al" to abbreviate – and much of this is driven by wanting a reasonable size for the bibliography section of conventional publications. How does this change when we are talking about digital objects? In particular, should the citation object returned be an encoding of or reference to an extended citation which is a searchable object?

Citation evolution. The views or the citations associated with views may change over time, either in response to a change in query workload or evolving standards in data citation. This can be captured in our model by including a "timestamp" attribute in base relations, with lambda variables in views corresponding to this attribute. Citations could then depend on the timestamp. An intriguing computational challenge is how to compute citations in an incremental manner in this setting.

Other models. Conjunctive queries are a core for many different models and languages, and the idea of citation views is useful beyond relational systems, e.g. XML and RDF. However, do we need to go beyond conjunctive queries? In particular, for several of the RDF systems we have examined the citation depends on the *class* of resource and determining the class of the resource involves reasoning over an ontology. What extensions to the language are needed, or are there other approaches that might be useful for RDF systems?

4. ACKNOWLEDGMENTS

This work has been partially funded by NSF IIS 1302212, NSF ACI 1547360, and NIH 3-U01-EB-020954-02S1; by the European Research Council under the FP7, ERC grant MoDaS, agreement 291071; by the Israeli Science Foundation (1636/13); and by a grant from the Blavatnik Interdisciplinary Cyber Research Center.

5. REFERENCES

[1] *Out of Cite, Out of Mind: The Current State of Practice, Polocy, and Technology for the Citation of Data*, volume 12. CODATA-ICSTI Task Group on Data Citation Standards and Practices, September 2013.

[2] S. Abiteboul, R. Hull, and V. Vianu. *Foundations of Databases*. Addison-Wesley, 1995.

[3] F. N. Afrati, C. Li, and J. D. Ullman. Using views to generate efficient evaluation plans for queries. *J. Comput. Syst. Sci.*, 73(5):703–724, 2007.

[4] P. Buneman, S. Davidson, and J. Frew. Why data citation is a computational problem. *CACM*, 59, 2016.

[5] J. Cheney, L. Chiticariu, and W. C. Tan. Provenance in databases: Why, how, and where. *Foundations and Trends in Databases*, 1(4):379–474, 2009.

[6] S. B. Davidson, D. Deutch, T. Milo, and G. Silvello. A model for fine-grained data citation. In *CIDR 2017,*

8th Biennial Conference on Innovative Data Systems Research, Chaminade, CA, USA, January 8-11, 2017, Online Proceedings, 2017.

[7] FORCE-11. *Data Citation Synthesis Group: Joint Declaration of Data Citation Principles.* FORCE11, San Diego, CA, USA, 2014.

[8] T. J. Green, G. Karvounarakis, and V. Tannen. Provenance semirings. In *PODS*, pages 31–40, 2007.

[9] A. Y. Halevy. Answering queries using views: A survey. *VLDB J.*, 10(4):270–294, 2001.

[10] L. Popa and V. Tannen. An equational chase for path-conjunctive queries, constraints, and views. In *Database Theory - ICDT '99, 7th International Conference, Jerusalem, Israel, January 10-12, 1999, Proceedings.*, pages 39–57, 1999.

[11] S. Pröll and A. Rauber. Scalable data citation in dynamic, large databases: Model and reference implementation. In *Proc. of the 2013 IEEE International Conference on Big Data*, pages 307–312, 2013.

A Relational Framework for Classifier Engineering

Benny Kimelfeld
Technion – Israel Institute of Technology
Haifa 32000, Israel
bennyk@cs.technion.ac.il

Christopher Ré
Stanford University
Stanford, CA 94305, USA
chrismre@cs.stanford.edu

ABSTRACT

In the design of analytical procedures and machine-learning solutions, a critical and time-consuming task is that of feature engineering, for which various recipes and tooling approaches have been developed. In this framework paper, we embark on the establishment of database foundations for feature engineering. We propose a formal framework for classification in the context of a relational database. The goal of this framework is to open the way to research and techniques to assist developers with the task of feature engineering by utilizing the database's modeling and understanding of data and queries, and by deploying the well studied principles of database management. As a first step, we demonstrate the usefulness of this framework by formally defining three key algorithmic challenges. The first challenge is that of separability, which is the problem of determining the existence of feature queries that agree with the training examples. The second is that of evaluating the VC dimension of the model class with respect to a given sequence of feature queries. The third challenge is identifiability, which is the task of testing for a property of independence among features that are represented as database queries. We give preliminary results on these challenges for the case where features are defined by means of conjunctive queries, and in particular we study the implication of various traditional syntactic restrictions on the inherent computational complexity.

CCS Concepts

•**Information systems** → **Relational database model;** Data analytics; •**Computing methodologies** → **Feature selection;** *Supervised learning by classification;* Supervised learning; •**Theory of computation** → Machine learning theory;

Keywords

Feature engineering; relational databases; machine learning; classifiers; conjunctive queries

PODS'17, May 14-19, 2017, Chicago, Illinois, USA
© 2017 ACM. ISBN 978-1-4503-4198-1/17/05...$15.00
DOI: http://dx.doi.org/10.1145/3034786.3034797

1. INTRODUCTION

In the design of analytics and machine-learning solutions, a critical and time-consuming task is feature engineering [24, 37]. Given its importance, recipes and tooling have been developed for practioners [1,21]. With the advent of frameworks like SAS, Cloudera's IBIS, Oracle's ORE, feature engineering is often carried out over relational data. Thus, a pressing challenge is to understand how to merge these new analytics with traditional database management techniques. In this paper we propose a relational framework for classification, a simple and popular analytic task.

1.1 Feature Engineering

The task of *feature engineering* is that of generating inputs (or *signals*) from available data, in order to improve the performance of the underlying model in solving a target problem. This target problem is typically classification (predict an unknown category of a given entity), or regression (predict the value of an unknown function over the entity). The model makes its prediction based on various properties, called *features*, of the given entity. We focus here on *parametric models*, where the model has a pre-determined structure with numerical parameters that are tuned by fitting into training examples, a process termed *learning*.

Naturally, the choice of features has a major impact on the resulting model. A suboptimal set of features may lead to *overfitting* (where the learned model does not well generalize beyond the training examples), or to *underfitting* (the model is incapable of capturing the target function due to lack of information or expressiveness) [21]. Another consideration is that of *execution cost*, as costly features may cast the model impractical [37]. There are also legal and moral considerations when decision makers are required to practice fairness and lack of discrimination [14,36].

As an example, consider a scenario where the security branch of a credit-card company wishes to make an educated guess on whether an incoming transaction is an unauthorized purchase (i.e., made on a stolen card), and if so to take action such as inactivating the card and notifying the owner. To make such guess, the company uses its available information in the database, such as whether there were similar transactions in the past, whether the purchase is made in the same state of the owner's mailing address, or in the same country, the amount being paid, and so on. An employed engineer then selects a machine-learning library and learns a classifier, which can be trained based on past data on fraudulent activity. The classifier is simply a function that maps a vector of numbers into a yes/no decision; in turn, these numbers, called *features*, encode relevant pieces of information (e.g., $f = +1/-1$ depending on whether or not the transaction is in the country of the owner). The machine-learning library typically tunes parameters (or weights) of the classifier by fitting them to the examples. In our scenario, high quality is crucial: false positives disrupt legitimate business, and false negatives cause financial losses and customer distress. So, the engineer produces additional features to consider by phrasing different questions (*feature queries*) about the transaction at stake, until she is satisfied with the results. This activity is referred to as *feature engineering*.

Analysts typically spend the bulk of their time on feature engineering [20, 24, 37]. This process includes a lot of trial and error, and stepwise addition or deletion of features [21]. We argue that involving the database semantics in feature engineering has the potential of automating some important tasks, and by that assist the engineer. For instance, the engineer may ask whether some class of simple feature queries (e.g., select-project-join) suffices to properly capture (i.e., achieve good classification of) the training data, or otherwise that more expressiveness is in need. This motivates the *separability* problem that we later discuss. She may also ask the complement question, which is whether the current set of feature queries is too detailed and allows the learning algorithm to *overfit* the examples and poorly generalize to future transactions. A traditional way to measure overfitting potential is to compute the *Vapnik-Chervonenkis* (*VC*) dimension, and we later discuss the version of this problem in our setup, referred to as *VC dimensionality*.

The engineer may also encounter the common technical challenge where the machine-learning library fails due to incompatible data, as it requires the matrix of training data to be of a full (column) degree. Partial degree (column dependence) may be an artifact of the training examples; but it may also be an inherent error in the feature design. As an example, for US owners the features "payment is in the US" "payment is in the owner's state" and "payment is in a different US state" have an inherent linear dependence among them: the first minus the second equals the third. We could use the database to detect such problems. This leads to the problem that we later refer to as *identifiability*.

We remark that the trend of *deep learning* [9] aims at eliminating the need for feature engineering by providing the model with sufficient expressive power to handle arbitrary *raw* data (or *core features*). This paradigm has a remarkable success, yet currently in a handful of domains [26].

1.2 Proposed Framework

The framework we propose aims to lead the way to novel research and techniques for utilizing the database's intimate understanding of raw data and queries, in order to fundamentally assist in the process of feature engineering. More precisely, our goal is to establish the first steps in a theory that embeds the automation of core tasks in the process of feature selection. After presenting the basic definitions, we illustrate the potential value of this framework by showing an analysis of tasks in the context of classification with features phrased as conjunctive queries; these tasks relate to underfitting (*separability*), overfitting (*VC dimensionality*), and algebraic coherence (*identifiability*).

Our framework is based on an *entity schema*, which is simply a relational schema with a distinguished relation symbol that represents *entities*. A *database instance* over an entity schema represents a collection of entities, along with additional (direct or indirect) knowledge about these entities. A *feature query* selects entities with a certain property, and a *statistic* is a sequence of feature queries. The central goal in classification is to train and apply a *classifier* (or a *classifier model*), which is a function that takes as input the *statistic* of an entity (i.e., the vector obtained by applying each feature query) and outputs a $+1/-1$ decision. The task of *training* a classifier is the following: given a set of entities labeled with $+1/-1$, produce a classifier from a predefined class of classifiers (the *model class*). A linear classifier, for example, is encoded as a vector of weights over the features in the statistic. In our framework, the collection of training examples is represented simply by an instance over the entity schema, along with a labeling function that maps each entity of the instance to $+1/-1$.

For illustration, Figure 1(a) shows an entity schema $\mathbf{S}$ where entities are people (identified by a social security number), and Figure 1(b) shows a statistic Π over $\mathbf{S}$ with two feature queries π_1 and π_2. Figure 2 shows the training workflow in our framework: an instance I over $\mathbf{S}$ with a labeling of the entities (people) is transformed into a $(+1/-1)$-matrix (consisting of the row of feature values for every entity), which in turn is used for building a classifier h. This classifier is then used for predicting the labels in a new instance, as illustrated in Figure 3.

The features, as defined above, are based on boolean properties of the entities: if the entity satisfies the property (i.e., it is "selected"), then the feature value is $+1$, and otherwise -1. Boolean features are highly important in practice, and in fact, we are aware of quite a few deployments where numerical values are translated into booleans ones (e.g., by means of *bucketing*, or *binning*, numbers into intervals). The more general case is where the feature query associates a numerical value with each entity. We defer the general case to future work, as our preliminary analysis applies to conjunctive queries, which are boolean, and we establish nontrivial results already there. Moreover, numerical values would substantially complicate the basic model, as we would need to argue about schema constraints that guarantee inclusion and functional dependencies in query answers (i.e., each feature associates a unique value with each entity); we find it an interesting and important aspect, but too far from the investigation of this paper.

After developing the framework, we turn to phrasing computational problems that are motivated by the practice of feature engineering where one aims to design a "good" statistic. We discuss three foundational problems for analytics that we can ask in this framework: *separability*—whether a perfect separator exists for a training set; *identifiability*—testing for a statistical property guaranteeing that the classifier model is uniquely defined given enough data; and *VC dimensionality*—computing a fundamental measure of the complexity of a classifier class [34].

1.3 Vision

This framework paper aims to initiate a research effort of the theoretical database research community on the important task of feature engineering, and in particular, promote a future investigation that will contribute to this task the benefits of deep understanding of data and query fundamentals. Such an effort has already began in the system community of database research [37]. The preliminary results and analysis we present do not aim to cover the ultimate use cases, but rather to instantiate and illustrate the vision in simple cases that we well understand (e.g., conjunctive queries). In particular, we focus on classification over boolean features that are represented as simple database queries that select entities. Future extensions should consider more expressive query languages, numerical features, and regression tasks beyond classification. (A discussion on possible future directions is in the concluding section.) Even in the restricted scope of this paper, our complexity results imply mainly intractability, and future work should seek tractable cases. Our results illustrate how the framework gives rise to relevant computational problems that one can formally define and explore, and these require some nontrivial analyses. Furthermore, the computational hardness emphasizes the need for fundamental research within the framework, which is what we hope to stir up.

1.4 Organization

The rest of the paper is organised as follows. In Section 2 we give preliminary definitions and notation. We present the framework in Section 3, and the associated computational problems in Section 4. Then, we investigate the problems of separability, VC dimensionality and identifiability for CQs in Sections 5, 6 and 7, respectively. We discuss related work in Section 8, and conclude in Section 9 where we also propose directions for future work.

2. PRELIMINARIES

In this section we give the basic definitions and terminology that we use throughout the paper.

2.1 Relational Databases

Our relational terminology is as follows. A *schema* is a collection of *relation symbols*. Each relation symbol R has an associated *arity* k, and we use the conventional notation R/k to compactly denote that R is a relation symbol of arity k. We assume an infinite set Const of *constants*. An *instance* I over a schema $\mathbf{S}$ associates with every k-ary relation symbol $R \in \mathbf{S}$ a finite subset of Const^k. We denote by R^I the relation that I associates with the relation symbol R. The *active domain* of an instance I, denoted $adom(I)$, is the set of all the constants in Const that are mentioned in the tuples of I. Two instances I and I' are *domain disjoint* if $adom(I)$ and $adom(I')$ are disjoint. A *fact* over a schema $\mathbf{S}$ is an expression of the form $R(c_1, \dots, c_k)$, where $R/k \in \mathbf{S}$ and $c_1, \dots, c_k$ are constants. We say that the fact $R(c_1, \dots, c_k)$ *belongs to* an instance I over $\mathbf{S}$ if R^I contains the tuple $(c_1, \dots, c_k)$. By a slight abuse of notation, we view an instance as the set of its facts. So, for example, given two instances I and I' over a schema $\mathbf{S}$, their union $I \cup I'$ is the instance J such that $R^J = R^I \cup R^{I'}$ for all $R \in \mathbf{S}$.

COMMENT 2.1. While schema *constraints* are important for our framework, the results we later give are either oblivious to constraints or do not support them. Hence, to simplify the presentation we exclude constraints to begin with. Supporting constraints is an important future direction that we discuss in Section 9. □

Let I and J be two instances over the same schema $\mathbf{S}$. A *homomorphism* from I to J is a mapping $\mu : adom(I) \to adom(J)$ such that for every fact $f \in I$ we have $\mu(f) \in J$; here, $\mu(f)$ is the fact that is obtained from f by replacing each constant a with the constant $\mu(a)$. An *endomorphism* over I is a homomorphism from I to itself.

2.2 Queries

Let $\mathbf{S}$ be schema. A *query* (*over* $\mathbf{S}$) is a function Q that is associated with an arity k, and that maps every instance I over $\mathbf{S}$ into a finite subset $Q(I)$ of Const^k. A query Q' *contains* a query Q, in notation $Q \subseteq Q'$, if $Q(I) \subseteq Q'(I)$ for all instances I over $\mathbf{S}$. If $Q \subseteq Q'$ and $Q' \subseteq Q$ then Q and Q' are said to be *equivalent*. We will often be interested in *unary* queries Q (i.e., where $k = 1$); in that case we may abuse the notation and view $Q(I)$ as a set of constants a rather than a set of tuples (a).

In this paper we consider conjunctive queries *without constants*. Formally, here a Conjunctive Query (CQ) over a schema $\mathbf{S}$ is a logical formula $q(\mathbf{x})$ that has the form

$$\exists \mathbf{y}[\phi_1(\mathbf{x}, \mathbf{y}) \wedge \cdots \wedge \phi_m(\mathbf{x}, \mathbf{y})]$$

where $\mathbf{x}$ and $\mathbf{y}$ are disjoint sequences of variables and each ϕ_i is an atomic query over $\mathbf{S}$ (i.e., a formula that consists of a single relation symbol and no logical operators).[1] The atomic formula ϕ_i is called an *atom* of q. We use the conventional notation of

$$q(\mathbf{x}) \leftarrow \phi_1(\mathbf{x}, \mathbf{y}), \cdots, \phi_m(\mathbf{x}, \mathbf{y})$$

to denote a CQ. We assume that the variables of q come from a fixed, countably infinite set Vars, and that Const and Vars are disjoint. The left side $q(\mathbf{x})$ is called the *head* and the right side $\phi_1(\mathbf{x}, \mathbf{y}), \cdots, \phi_m(\mathbf{x}, \mathbf{y})$ is called the *body*. We require each variable in the head to occur at least once in the body. We may refer to a CQ by mentioning only its head $q(\mathbf{x})$ or even just q.

Let $\mathbf{S}$ be a schema, let q be a CQ over $\mathbf{S}$, and let I be an instance over $\mathbf{S}$. A *homomorphism* from q to I is a mapping from the variables of q to $adom(I)$, such that for every atom ϕ of q, the fact $\mu(\phi)$ belongs to I; here, $\mu(\phi)$ is the fact that is obtained from ϕ by replacing each variable z with the constant $\mu(z)$. The result of applying the CQ $q(\mathbf{x})$ to the instance I is the relation that consists of all the tuples $\mu(\mathbf{x})$, where μ is a homomorphism from q to I and $\mu(\mathbf{x})$ is obtained from $\mathbf{x}$ by replacing every variable x_i with $\mu(x_i)$. We denote this relation by $q(I)$.

The *incidence graph* [12] of a CQ q is the bipartite graph that has the variables of q on one side, the atoms on the other side, and an edge between an atom α and a variable x whenever α contains x. We use $\mathcal{G}_q$ to denote the incidence graph of the CQ q.

We will consider CQs with special properties, which we define as follows. Consider a CQ q.

- q is *connected* if $\mathcal{G}_q$ is connected.
- q is *self-join free* if it does not have two distinct atoms with the same relation symbol.

We will also mention CQs with *negation*, that is, CQs of the form $q(\mathbf{x}) \leftarrow \phi_1(\mathbf{x}, \mathbf{y}), \cdots, \phi_m(\mathbf{x}, \mathbf{y})$ where each $\phi_i(\mathbf{x}, \mathbf{y})$ is either an atomic query (positive atom) or a negated atomic query (negative atom). We require such CQs to be *safe* in the sense that every variable occurs in at least one positive

[1] Note that in this paper CQs do not contain built-in relations such as $x > y$; we use this assumption in our analysis.

Table 1: Main symbols

h	hypothesis/classifier $\{-1,1\}^n \to \{-1,1\}$
$\mathbf{H}$	hypothesis class
Lin	the class of linear classifiers
$\mathbf{S}$	relational/entity schema
η, $\eta_{\mathbf{S}}$	entity relation (unary)
I, J	database instance
η^I, $\eta_{\mathbf{S}}^I$	entity set of the instance I
e	entity in $\eta_{\mathbf{S}}^I$
$\mathbf{QL}$	query language
CQ	the class of CQs (without constants)
π	feature query (unary)
$\pi^I(e)$	$+1$ if $e \in \pi(I)$ and -1 if $e \notin \pi(I)$
Π	statistic $(\pi_1, \dots, \pi_n)$
λ	labeling function $\eta_{\mathbf{S}}^I \to \{-1,1\}$

atom. A negated atom has the classical (first-order-logic) semantics: the corresponding fact is *not* in the database instance. The definitions of *connected* and *self-join free* remain the same, while simply ignoring the negation symbols. Throughout the paper, we assume that CQs are without negation, unless explicitly stated otherwise.

We denote by CQ the class of CQs (as defined here, i.e., without constants), and by $\mathsf{CQ}^{\neg}$ the class of CQs with negation. We also use the subscript sjf to denote the restriction to CQs without self joins, and the subscript con to denote the restriction to connected CQs. For example, $\mathsf{CQ}^{\neg}_{\mathsf{sjf}}$ is the class of CQs with negation and without self joins.

2.3 Classifiers and Learning

In this work, a *classifier* is a function of the form

$$h : \{-1,1\}^n \to \{-1,1\}$$

where n is a natural number that we call the *arity* of h. A *hypothesis class* is a (possibly infinite) family $\mathbf{H}$ of classifiers, and a classifier in $\mathbf{H}$ is referred to as a *hypothesis*. We denote by $\mathbf{H}_n$ the restriction of $\mathbf{H}$ to the n-ary hypotheses in $\mathbf{H}$. An n-ary *training collection* is a multiset T of pairs $\langle \mathbf{x}, y\rangle$ where $\mathbf{x} \in \{-1,1\}^n$ and $y \in \{-1,1\}$. We denote by $\mathbf{T}_n$ the class of all n-ary training collections. A *cost function* for a hypothesis class $\mathbf{H}$ is a function of the form

$$c : \left(\cup_n (\mathbf{H}_n \times \mathbf{T}_n)\right) \to \mathbb{R}_{\geq 0}$$

where $\mathbb{R}_{\geq 0}$ is the set of nonnegative numbers. Given a training collection T and two hypotheses h_1 and h_2, the inequality $c(h_1, T) > c(h_2, T)$ implies that h_2 is preferred to h_1 according to c. In the context of a fixed hypothesis class $\mathbf{H}$ and a cost function c, *learning* a classifier is the task of finding a hypothesis $h \in \mathbf{H}_n$ that minimizes $c(h, T)$, given a training collection $T \in \mathbf{T}_n$.

It is importnat to allow T to be a multiset in order to enable the scoring function to account for the frequency (rather than only existence) of examples. For the scope of this paper, though, being a multiset does not play any role, and the reader may view T simply as a set.

We illustrate the above definitions on the important class of *linear classifiers*. An n-ary linear classifier is parameterized by a vector $\mathbf{w} = (w_0, \dots, w_n) \in \mathbb{R}^{n+1}$, denoted by $\Lambda_{\mathbf{w}}$, and defined as follows for all $\mathbf{a} \in \{-1,1\}^n$.

$$\Lambda_{\mathbf{w}}(\mathbf{a}) \stackrel{\text{def}}{=} \begin{cases} 1 & \text{if } \mathbf{a} \cdot \mathbf{w}' \geq w_0; \\ -1 & \text{otherwise.} \end{cases}$$

where $\mathbf{w}' = (w_1, \dots, w_n)$ and "$\cdot$" denotes the operation of dot product. By Lin we denote the class of linear classifiers. An example of a cost function is the *least square* cost that is given by

$$lsq(\Lambda_{\mathbf{w}}, T) \stackrel{\text{def}}{=} \sum_{\langle \mathbf{x}, y\rangle \in T} \left(\mathbf{x} \cdot \mathbf{w}' - w_0 - y\right)^2$$

for the arguments $\Lambda_{\mathbf{w}} \in \mathsf{Lin}_n$ and $T \in \mathbf{T}_n$.

More background on the basic theory of machine-learning classifiers, as well as the relevant linear algebra discussed in the next section, can be found in standard machine-learning textbooks, such as Shalev-Shwartz and Ben-David [31].

2.4 Matrix Independence

We denote by $\mathbf{0}^n$ the vector of n zeroes, and by $\mathbf{1}^n$ the vector of n ones. Let M be an $n \times m$ real matrix (consisting of n rows and m columns). A *linear column dependence* in M is a vector $\mathbf{w} \in \mathbb{R}^m$ such that $\mathbf{w} \neq \mathbf{0}^m$ and $M \cdot \mathbf{w} = \mathbf{0}^n$. A linear column dependence $\mathbf{w}$ in M is an *affine dependence* in M if $\mathbf{w} \cdot \mathbf{1}^m = 0$ (i.e., the components of $\mathbf{w}$ sum up to 0). If M does not have any linear column dependence, then we say that M is *linearly column independent.* And if M does not have any affine column dependence, then we say that M is *affinely column independent.* Note that linear independence implies affine independence, but the other direction is not necessarily true.

3. FRAMEWORK

We now present our formal framework. A central notion in this framework is that of an *entity schema*, which is simply an ordinary relational schema with a distinguished relation symbol for representing *entities.* For simplicity, we assume that an entity is represented by a single constant (an identifier), hence the corresponding relation is unary. Formally, an entity schema is a pair $(\mathbf{S}, \eta)$, where $\mathbf{S}$ is a schema and η is a unary relation symbol in $\mathbf{S}$. An *instance* over an entity schema $(\mathbf{S}, \eta)$ is simply an instance over $\mathbf{S}$. In the remainder of this paper all the schemas we consider are entity schemas. So, to simplify the presentation we refer to the entity schema $(\mathbf{S}, \eta)$ simply as $\mathbf{S}$, and refer to η as $\eta_{\mathbf{S}}$.

Let I be an instance over an entity schema $\mathbf{S}$. An *entity* of I is a constant a such that $\eta_{\mathbf{S}}(a) \in I$. Hence, I represents a set of entities along with information about the entities; this information is contained in the remaining relations, which can be joined with $\eta_{\mathbf{S}}$. By a slight abuse of notation, we use $\eta_{\mathbf{S}}^I$ to represent the set of all the entities of I.

EXAMPLE 3.1. We use a running example that instantiates the credit-card scenario from the introduction. Figure 1(a) depicts the entity schema $\mathbf{S}$ of the example, with one unary relation Txn, which is $\eta_{\mathbf{S}}$, and two quaternary relations $\mathsf{TxnInfo}$ and Card. The box on the top of Figure 3 contains an instance I' over $\mathbf{S}$. The entities are the transaction identifiers $\mathsf{5}$, $\mathsf{6}$ and $\mathsf{7}$, and these are the members of $\eta_{\mathbf{S}}^{I'} = \{\mathsf{5}, \mathsf{6}, \mathsf{7}\}$. □

Let $\mathbf{S}$ be an entity schema, and let I be an instance over $\mathbf{S}$. A *feature query* (*over* $\mathbf{S}$) is a unary query π over the schema

Txn = $\eta_{\mathbf{S}}$

id

TxnInfo

txn	*card*	*country*	*state*

Card

id	*ssn*	*country*	*state*

(a) An entity schema **S**

$$\pi_1(s) \leftarrow \mathsf{TxnInfo}(t, n, c, s), \mathsf{Card}(n, c, s)$$

$$\pi_2(s) \leftarrow \mathsf{TxnInfo}(t, n, c, s), \mathsf{Card}(n, c, s')$$

(b) A statistic $\Pi = (\pi_1, \pi_2)$ over **S**

Figure 1: An entity schema and a statistic

Txn

id	λ
1	1
2	1
3	-1
4	1

TxnInfo

txn	*card*	*country*	*state*
1	100	US	GA
2	100	US	NY
3	101	BR	RJ
4	102	US	CA

Card

id	*ssn*	*country*	*state*
100	200	US	GA
101	201	US	FL
102	202	BR	SP

Training instance (I, λ)

$\Rightarrow$

$\Pi^I(e)$		$\lambda(e)$
1	1	-1
-1	1	1
-1	-1	-1
-1	-1	-1

Training collection T

$\Rightarrow$

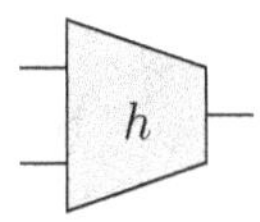

Classifier (model) $h : \{-1, 1\}^2 \rightarrow \{-1, 1\}$

Figure 2: The training process

S. We will always be interested in only the entities that are selected by a feature query, and we will be interested in cases where π is represented in a query language **QL** (e.g., CQ); we then say that π is *in* **QL**.

EXAMPLE 3.2. Figure 1(b) shows two feature queries in CQ: π_1 selects all transactions that took place in the same country and state of the owner's maling address, and π_2 selects all the ones that took place in the same country (but not necessarily same state) of the owner. □

Let π be a feature query over an entity schema **S**. We say that π is *selective* on an entity instance I if at least one entity of I is missing from $\pi(I)$. We say that π is *selective* if it is selective on at least one instance over **S** (or in other words, π is not logically contained in $\eta_{\mathbf{S}}$).

Let **S** be an entity schema, let I be an instance over **S**, and let π be a feature query. We denote by π^I the function from $\eta^I_{\mathbf{S}}$ to $\{-1, 1\}$ where

$$\pi^I(es) = \begin{cases} 1 & \text{if } e \in \pi(I); \\ -1 & \text{otherwise.} \end{cases}$$

Txn

id
5
6
7

TxnInfo

txn	*card*	*country*	*state*
5	105	US	AK
6	105	US	NY
7	110	BR	RJ

Card

id	*ssn*	*country*	*state*
105	200	US	AK
110	201	BR	SP

Instance I' over **S**

$\Rightarrow$

$\Pi^{I'}(e)$	
1	1
-1	1
-1	1

$\rightarrow$

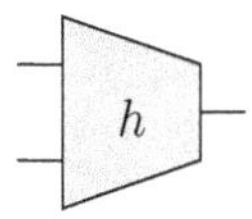

$\rightarrow$

-1
1
1

$\Rightarrow$

Txn

id	prediction
5	-1
6	1
7	1

Figure 3: The prediction process

Let **S** be an entity schema. A *statistic* (over **S**) is a sequence $\Pi = (\pi_1, \ldots, \pi_n)$ of feature queries. We say that Π is in a query language **QL** if each π_i is in **QL**. Given an instance I over **S**, we denote by Π^I the function $(\pi_1^I, \ldots, \pi_n^I)$ from $\eta^I_{\mathbf{S}}$ to $\{-1, 1\}^n$ that maps every entity $e \in \eta^I_{\mathbf{S}}$ to the sequence $(\pi_1^I(e), \ldots, \pi_n^I(e))$.

EXAMPLE 3.3. Figure 1(b) shows the statistic $\Pi = (\pi_1, \pi_2)$ over the schema **S** of Figure 1(a). The middle layer of Figure 3 contains (on its left) the tuples $\Pi^{I'}(e)$ for the entities e in the instance I' of the top box in this figure. For example, the top row corresponds to $\Pi^{I'}(5) = (1, 1)$, which is due to the fact Transaction 5 took place in the same country and state of the card holder. □

Let **S** be an entity schema. A *labeling* of an instance I over **S** is a function

$$\lambda : \eta^I_{\mathbf{S}} \rightarrow \{-1, 1\}$$

that partitions the entities into *negative examples* (i.e., e where $\lambda(e) = -1$) and *positive examples* (i.e., e where $\lambda(e) = 1$). A *training instance* over **S** is a pair (I, λ), where I is an instance over **S** and λ is a labeling of I.

Given an entity schema **S**, a statistic Π and a training instance (I, λ) together define a training collection, namely, the one that consists of the tuple $\langle \Pi^I(e), \lambda(e) \rangle$ for every entity $e \in \eta^I_{\mathbf{S}}$.

EXAMPLE 3.4. Continuing our running example, Figure 2 shows a training instance (I, λ) over the entity schema **S** of Figure 1(a), where λ is represented in the Txn relation. With the statistic Π of Figure 1(b) we then get the training collection in the left bottom part of Figure 2. From this training instance a classifier h is learned, and is applied for prediction on future instances, as illustrated in Figure 3 for the instance I' that we referred to in the previous examples. □

4. COMPUTATIONAL PROBLEMS

We now describe three computational problems that are motivated by the design of machine-learning solutions, and in particular feature engineering.

4.1 Separability

Separability is perhaps the most basic notion of learning. The traditional presentation of learning theory typically begins with the "noise free" case where the labeled examples are required to be perfectly separated by the features. In our framework *separability* refers to the following task: given a training instance over an entity schema, determine whether there is statistic and a classifier that agree with (i.e., classify precisely as) the example labels. It is, of course, a simplification of the practically motivated problem, where some noise is allowed (and say, $(1-\epsilon)$ of the examples are required to be correctly satisfied). We adopt the simplified (textbook) task as a first step, and show that it already leads to nontrivial insights within our framework.

The problem is parameterized by two important components: the family of classifiers in consideration, and the query language used for phrasing feature queries. The formal defintion of the problem is as follows.

Let $\mathbf{S}$ be a schema, Π a statistic over $\mathbf{S}$, and $\mathbf{H}$ a hypothesis class. A training instance (I, λ) is $\mathbf{H}$*-separable* with respect to (w.r.t.) Π if there exists a hypothesis $h \in \mathbf{H}$ that fully agrees with λ; that is, h and Π have the same arity, and $h(\Pi^I(e)) = \lambda(e)$ for every $e \in \eta^I_{\mathbf{S}}$.

PROBLEM 1 (SEPARABILITY). *For a hypothesis class* $\mathbf{H}$ *and a query language* $\mathbf{QL}$*, the problem* $(\mathbf{H}, \mathbf{QL})$-separability *is the following. Given an entity schema* $\mathbf{S}$ *and a training instance* (I, λ) *over* $\mathbf{S}$*, determine whether there exists a statistic* Π *in* $\mathbf{QL}$ *such that* (I, λ) *is* $\mathbf{H}$*-separable w.r.t.* Π.

EXAMPLE 4.1. We continue with our running example, and consider the training instance (I, λ) of Figure 2. Suppose that $\mathbf{H}$ is the class Lin of linear classifiers, and that $\mathbf{QL}$ is the class CQ. Then (I, λ) is a "yes" instance of the separability problem, and a witness is the statistic $\Pi = (\pi_1, \pi_2)$ of Figure 1(b) with the classifier $\pi_2 - \pi_1 \geq 1$. Now suppose that we add an entity 5, the tuple (5, 102, US, AL) to TxnInfo, and the labeling $\lambda(5) = -1$. The new training instance then becomes a "no" instance of the separability problem since, intuitively, there is no way to distinguish between 4 and 5 using $\mathbf{QL}$ over I, and yet, λ labels 4 and 5 differently. We make this point precise in Section 5. □

We remark that a problem similar to separability is that of separating graphs by tree patterns [13, 25].

4.2 VC Dimensionality

The *Vapnik-Chervonenkis (VC)* dimension is a measure of complexity of a hypothesis class, and is a de facto complexity measure for learnability. Bounds for *generalization* (how well a learned classifier does on unseen data) typically depend on the VC dimension. It measures the capacity of the classifier class, and is a key indicator of how much data one needs to reliably train the classifier: if this amount is low with respect to the VC dimension, then the classifier may overfit. If the amount of training data is high with respect to the VC dimension, we may be missing opportunities to devise a more accurate classifier.

As an example, the class of *polynomial* classifiers is more expressive than that of the *linear* classifiers, so there is a higher capability of a polynomial-classifier learner to overfit (i.e., exploit specific properties that are exhibited scarcely in the training examples but are not representative of the general population). Similarly, a *deep* decision tree might be constructed to handle every individual example, while a *shallow* one will have to utilize common properties, and hence, intuitively, to better apply to the behavior in the general population. VC dimension is a mathematical measure that aims to capture this expressive power in a manner that is uniform across model classes. In particular, high VC dimension implies a complicated classifier space that has a high ability to overfit its training data, and so, a high volume of training data is required for effective learning.

In our framework, VC dimension is not only a function of the hypothesis class, but also that of the statistic that translates entities into feature vectors. We give the formal definition next.

Let $\mathbf{S}$ be a schema, Π a statistic over $\mathbf{S}$, and $\mathbf{H}$ a hypothesis class. An instance I over $\mathbf{S}$ is *shattered by* $\mathbf{H}$ *w.r.t.* Π if for every labeling λ of I there exists a hypothesis $h \in \mathbf{H}$ that fully agrees with λ; that is, h and Π have the same arity, and $h(\Pi^I(e)) = \lambda(e)$ for every $e \in \eta^I_{\mathbf{S}}$.

The *VC dimension of* $\mathbf{H}$ *w.r.t.* Π is the maximal number m such that there exists an instance I over $\mathbf{S}$ where I has m entities and I is shattered by $\mathbf{H}$ w.r.t. Π. The *dimensionality problem* is defined as follows.

PROBLEM 2 (DIMENSIONALITY). *Let* $\mathbf{H}$ *be a hypothesis class and* $\mathbf{QL}$ *a query language. The computational problem* $(\mathbf{H}, \mathbf{QL})$-dimensionality *is the following. Given an entity schema* $\mathbf{S}$ *and a statistic* Π *in* $\mathbf{QL}$*, compute the VC dimension of* $\mathbf{H}$ *w.r.t.* Π.

EXAMPLE 4.2. Recall $\mathbf{S}$ and Π of our running example (Figure 1). Computing the VC dimension of Lin w.r.t. Π is an instance of (Lin, CQ)-dimensionality. Our results in Section 6 show that this dimension is 3. Hence, there exists an instance I with three entities, such that we can find a perfect linear classifier for every labeling λ for I. Yet, no such instance exists with four or more entities. □

4.3 Statistic Identifiability

Identifiability is a classical task that asks whether it is possible for one to learn the parameters of the given classifier model *unambiguously* from *some* data set. Here, the question refers to a given statistic, and we consider the case where training is done by means of optimization via linear algebra; we ask whether the space of solutions is bounded. More formally, this problem boils down to deciding, given a statistic, whether there exists any training instance such that the resulting feature matrix is of full column dimension (i.e., the columns are linearly independent). We also consider the variant where linear independence is relaxed to affine independence. (See Section 2 for the formal definitions.) Next, we give the formal definition.

Let $\mathbf{S}$ be an entity schema, Π a statistic over $\mathbf{S}$, and I an instance of $\mathbf{S}$. We fix an arbitrary order over the entities of I, and denote by $[\![\Pi^I]\!]$ the matrix that consists of the rows $\Pi^I(e)$ for every $e \in \eta^I_{\mathbf{S}}$ in order. We say that Π is *linearly identifiable* if there exists an instance I over $\mathbf{S}$ such that the matrix $[\![\Pi^I]\!]$ is linearly column independent. We say that Π is *affinely identifiable* if there exists an instance I over $\mathbf{S}$ such that the matrix $[\![\Pi^I]\!]$ is affinely column independent. Recall that if $[\![\Pi^I]\!]$ is linearly independent, then it is also affinely independent. Hence, we get the following fact, which we record here for later reference.

FACT 4.3. *Let Π be a statistic. If Π is linearly identifiable, then Π is affinely identifiable.*

Both types of identifiability are important properties in the design of machine-learning solutions [27]. Particularly, in the case of the hypothesis class Lin and the cost function *lsq* (defined in Section 2.3), linear independence implies that there is a single optimal hypothesis, whereas its absence implies that the space of optimal solutions is unbounded. Affine independence likewise arises in different cost functions such as *maximum entropy* [35]. The corresponding computational problem is formally defined as follows.

PROBLEM 3 (IDENTIFIABILITY). *Let* **QL** *be a query language. The computational problem of* linear *(respectively,* affine*)* **QL**-identifiability *is that of testing, given an entity schema* **S** *and a statistic Π over* **S**, *whether Π is linearly (respectively, affinely) identifiable.*

EXAMPLE 4.4. Consider again **S** and Π of our running example (Figure 1). Then **S** and Π form a "yes" instance of the linear (and affine) CQ-identifiability problem. Indeed, Π is linearly (and affinely) identifiable, and a witness instance is the instance I of Figure 2 with Txn restricted to the entities 1 and 2 (or 3 and 2, but not 1 and 3). In Section 7 we will show that under certain conditions (that hold in our case), a statistic that consists of CQ feature queries is always identifiable, unless two or more of the feature queries are equivalent. □

5. SEPARABILITY W.R.T. CQS

We now discuss the complexity of separability in the case where feature queries are from the class of CQs. We first state the complexity results of this section.

5.1 Complexity Results

Our first result states coNP-hardness in the case where feature queries are CQs without self joins, and the hypothesis class is that of linear classifiers. For illustration, we refer the reader to the "yes" and "no" instances of Example 4.1.

THEOREM 5.1. *(Lin, CQ)-separability is a* coNP*-complete problem. Moreover, there exists a fixed entity schema* **S** *such that (Lin, CQ)-separability is coNP-hard over* **S**.

We prove the theorem later in this section. In the proof of hardness we construct CQs over a fixed schema, but self joins are allowed. Next, we consider the case of self-join-free CQs. Interestingly, restricting the problem to simpler CQs (by disallowing self joins) does not make the problem easier; in fact, under conventional complexity assumptions it is harder!

THEOREM 5.2. *(Lin, $\mathbf{QL}_{\mathsf{sjf}}$)-separability is Σ_2^{P}-complete.*

The proof of Theorem 5.2 is in the appendix. Intuitively, the reason for the increased complexity is that self joins allow us to (efficiently) formulate a single statistic Π of representative ("canonical") feature CQs that captures the entire space of statistics; that is, if any statistic provides separation, then so does Π. In particular, with self joins the problem boils down to deciding on the existence of a homomorphism. Yet, without self joins it appears that we cannot do better than to inspect an exponential space of statistics, and solve the homomorphism problem in each. Finally, we remark that fixing the schema **S** in the case of $\mathbf{QL}_{\mathsf{sjf}}$ would make the separability problem solvable in polynomial time, since the number of possible statistics (without equivalent feature queries) is bounded by a fixed constant, and each feature query can be evaluated in polynomial time.

COMMENT 5.3. For CQs with constants, the separability problem is trivial and not interesting, since the positive examples can be hardcoded into (i.e., completely overfitted by) the statistic. In Figure 2, for instance, we could encode each of the first, second, and third tuples of TxnInfo (and even their join with Card) in a CQ that selects precisely the corresponding transactions. It would, however, be interesting to enforce restrictions on the usage of constants (e.g., limit their number), and we leave that for future work. (See further discussion in Section 9.) □

5.2 Proof of Theorem 5.1

We now prove Theorem 5.1. We need to prove membership in coNP and coNP-hardness.

The easier part is the proof of hardness, and it is given in the appendix. The proof constructs a reduction from the maximum-clique problem over graphs. Our fixed schema is $\mathbf{S}_0$ and it consists of the relation symbols $G/3$ and $\eta/1$, where $\eta_{\mathbf{S}} = \eta$. The lemma applies to *every* hypothesis class **H** (including Lin), under the very basic assumption that **H** contains the unary classifier $h(x) = x$; in that case we say that **H** *allows copying.*

LEMMA 5.4. *Let* **H** *be a hypothesis class that allows copying. The problem* **(H, CQ)***-separability is coNP-hard already over the schema $\mathbf{S}_0$ and for two entities.*

We now turn to proving membership in coNP. Let I be an instance of an entity schema **S**. Define a unique variable x_c for every constant c in $adom(I)$. For every fact f of I, let ϕ_f denote the atomic formula obtained from f by replacing every constant c with the variable x_c. Let Φ_I denote the conjunction of the atoms ϕ_f over all facts f in I. For an entity e of I, the *canonical CQ* of e (w.r.t. I), denoted Q_e^I, is the CQ defined by $Q_e^I(x_e) \leftarrow \Phi_I$. Following is an easy proposition.

PROPOSITION 5.5. *Let* **S** *be an entity schema, I an instance of* **S**, *and e and e' be two entities of I. The following are equivalent.*

1. *$e' \in Q_e^I(I)$.*
2. *For every feature query π in* CQ, *if $e \in \pi(I)$ then $e' \in \pi(I)$.*

Let I be an instance of an entity schema **S**. We denote by $\preceq_I$ the binary relation over $\eta_{\mathbf{S}}^I$ such that $e \preceq_I e'$ if and only if $e' \in Q_e^I(I)$. The following proposition follows immediately from Proposition 5.5.

PROPOSITION 5.6. *Let* **S** *be an entity schema, and I an instance of* **S**. *The order $\preceq_I$ is a preorder, that is, $\preceq_I$ is reflexive and transitive.*

Let (I, λ) be a training instance of an entity schema $\mathbf{S}$. Recall that an *equivalence class* of a preorder $\preceq$ is an equivalence class of the equivalence relation "$x \preceq y$ and $y \preceq x$." In the case of $\preceq_I$, an equivalence class E is a set of entities.

PROPOSITION 5.7. *Let* $\mathbf{S}$ *be an entity schema, and* I *an instance of* $\mathbf{S}$. *Let* $E_1, \dots, E_m$ *be the equivalence classes of the preorder* $\preceq_I$. *There is a statistic* $\Pi = (\pi_1, \dots, \pi_m)$ *in* CQ *with the following properties.*

- *Every entity* $e \in E_i$ *satisfies* $e \in \pi_i(I)$.
- $e \notin \pi_j(I)$ *for all* i *and* j *such that* $1 \leq i < j \leq m$ *and* $e \in E_i$.

PROOF. For each E_i, select a member entity e_i and denote by π'_i the CQ $Q^I_{e_i}(I)$. We extend $\preceq_I$ to the CQs π'_i naturally, by defining $\pi'_i \preceq_I \pi'_j$ if and only if $e_i \preceq_I e_j$. Observe that $\preceq_I$ is a partial order over the π'_i, and in particular, $\preceq_I$ is acyclic. We then take as $\pi_1, \dots, \pi_m$ the sequence that consists of $\pi'_1, \dots, \pi'_m$, sorted in a topological order according to $\preceq_I$; that is, if $i \neq j$ and $\pi_i \preceq_I \pi_j$, then $i < j$. □

An equivalence class E of $\preceq_I$ is said to be *consistent with* λ if $\lambda(e) = \lambda(e')$ for every two entities e and e' in E. Following is a key lemma for this section.

LEMMA 5.8. *Let* (I, λ) *be a training instance of an entity schema* $\mathbf{S}$. *The following are equivalent.*

1. *There exists a statistic* Π *in* CQ *such that* (I, λ) *is* Lin-*separable w.r.t.* Π.
2. *Every equivalence class of* $\preceq_I$ *is consistent with* λ.

PROOF. We prove each direction separately.

1 → 2. This direction is a straightforward consequence of Proposition 5.5. In particular, if e and e' are two entities such that $e \preceq_I e'$ and $e' \preceq_I e$, then from Proposition 5.5 it follows that every statistic Π in CQ gives precisely the same feature values for e and e', and in particular, if $\lambda(e) \neq \lambda(e')$ then λ is not $\mathbf{H}$-separable w.r.t. Π.

2 → 1. We now assume that every equivalence class of $\preceq_I$ is consistent with λ. Let $\Pi = (\pi_1, \dots, \pi_m)$ be the statistic of Proposition 5.7. We will construct a linear classifier h over Π, such that h perfectly fits λ. Hence, the existence of Π and h provides the required proof. The classifier h is defined as

$$\delta_1 + \cdots + \delta_m \geq 0$$

where the δ_j are defined as follows for $j = 1, \dots, m$:

$$\delta_j \stackrel{\mathsf{def}}{=} w_j \cdot (1 + \pi^I_j)$$

where:

$$w_j \stackrel{\mathsf{def}}{=} \frac{1}{2}\left(\lambda(e_j) - \sum_{k=1}^{j-1} \delta_k(e_j)\right)$$

To complete the proof, we need to prove that h classifies every entity e according to λ. Let $e \in \eta_{\mathbf{S}}(I)$ be given, and suppose that e belongs to E_i. Then, by assumption we have $\lambda(e) = \lambda(e_i)$. Moreover, due to Proposition 5.5 we have $\Pi(e) = \Pi(e_i)$. Therefore, it suffices to prove that h classifies e_i according to λ. First, we break the sum $\sum_{j=1}^m \delta_j(e_i)$.

$$\sum_{j=1}^{m} \delta_j(e_i) = \left(\sum_{j=1}^{i-1} \delta_j(e_i)\right) + \delta_i(e_i) + \left(\sum_{j=i+1}^{m} \delta_j(e_i)\right) \quad (1)$$

We have the following.

$$\delta_i(e_i) = w_i \cdot (1 + \pi^I_i(e_i)) = w_i \cdot (1+1) = 2w_i$$
$$= \lambda(e_i) - \left(\sum_{j=1}^{i-1} \delta_j(e_i)\right) \quad (2)$$

Moreover, as Π is the statistic of Proposition 5.7, for $j > i$ we have $\pi^I_j(e_i) = -1$, and therefore,

$$\delta_j(e_i) = w_i \cdot (1-1) = 0\,.$$

Hence, from (1) and (2) we get the following.

$$\sum_{j=1}^{m} \delta_j(e_i) = \left(\sum_{j=1}^{i-1} \delta_j(e_i)\right) + \lambda(e_i) - \left(\sum_{j=1}^{i-1} \delta_j(e_i)\right) = \lambda(e_i)$$

In particular we have $\sum_{j=1}^m \delta_j(e_i) > 0$ when $\lambda(e_i) = 1$, and $\sum_{j=1}^m \delta_j(e_i) < 0$ when $\lambda(e_i) = -1$, as required. □

From Lemma 5.8 we conclude the required membership in coNP.

LEMMA 5.9. (Lin, CQ)*-separability is in coNP.*

PROOF. From Lemma 5.8 we conclude that as an evidence of non-separability it suffices to show two entities e and e' with $\lambda(e) \neq \lambda(e')$, a homomorphism μ_1 from Q^I_e to I with $\mu_1(x_e) = e'$, and a homomorphism μ_2 from $Q^I_{e'}$ to I with $\mu_2(x_{e'}) = e$. □

6. VC DIMENSIONALITY W.R.T. CQS

Next, we investigate the problem of VC dimensionality for the query language of connected CQs, and the class of linear classifiers. Intuitively, the need for connectivity is due to the fact that with disconnected CQs, it may be the case that CQs are not equivalent, but they cannot distinguish between entities in any training instance. We illustrate it in Comment 6.2. We prove the following.

THEOREM 6.1. *Let* Π *be a statistic in* $\mathbf{QL}_{\mathsf{con}}$ *such that every feature query* π *in* Π *is selective. The VC dimension of* Lin *w.r.t.* Π *is* $d+1$*, where* d *is equal to the number of equivalence classes*[2] *among the queries in* Π.

PROOF. We first show that the dimension is at least $d+1$. We need to construct an instance I over $\mathbf{S}$ such that I has $d+1$ entities, and for every labeling λ of I we can find a linear classifier that is consistent with λ. Let $q_1, \dots, q_d$ be representatives of the d equivalence classes of the feature queries in Π. We denote by q_0 the CQ $Q(x) \leftarrow \eta_{\mathbf{S}}(x)$. Note that no two CQs in $q_0, \dots, q_d$ are equivalent. Let $r_0, \dots, r_d$ be an ordering of $q_0, \dots, q_d$ in a topological order, so that if $r_i \subseteq r_j$ and $i \neq j$, then $i > j$. For $i = 0, \dots, d$, we define the instance I_i to be a canonical instance of r_i, so that different I_i have disjoint active domains. We add to each I_i the entity e_i, which is the constant that corresponds to the head variable of r_i. The following hold for every $i = 0, \dots, d$.

1. $e_i \in r_i(I_i)$.
2. $e_j \notin r_i(I_j)$ if $i > j$.

[2]Query equivalence, as defined in Section 2.2.

The reason for the second item is well known in the theory of CQs [11]: $e_j \in r_i(I_j)$ implies a homomorphism from r_i to I_j that maps the head to e_j, and since I_j is the canonical instance of r_j this homomorphism can also be viewed as a homomorphism $\mu_{i,j}$ from r_i to r_j that preserves the head variable. So, every assignment $\mu_{j,J}$ from r_j to any instance J can be composed with $\mu_{i,j}$ to form a homomorphism $\mu = \mu_{j,J} \circ \mu_{i,j}$ from r_i to J so that $\mu(x) = \mu_{j,J}(x)$ for the head variable x, hence $r_j \subseteq r_i$, contradicting $i > j$.

We then define I as $I_0 \cup \cdots \cup I_d$. Observe that I has $d+1$ entities, namely $e_0, \dots, e_d$. Since each r_i is connected and constant free, for every entity e_j it is the case that $e_j \in r_i(I)$ if and only if $e_j \in r_i(I_j)$, since any homomorphism from r_i to I must be a homomorphism into a single I_k. From here on we continue similarly to Lemma 5.8. Specifically, let λ be a labeling of I. We need to construct a linear classifier h that is consistent with λ. The classifier h is defined as

$$\delta_0 + \delta_1 + \cdots + \delta_d \geq 0$$

where and δ_j are defined as follows for $j = 0, \dots, m$:

$$\delta_j \overset{\text{def}}{=} \frac{1}{2}\left(\lambda(e_j) - \sum_{k=1}^{j-1} \delta_k(e_j)\right)(1 + r_j^I)$$

The proof that h is consistent with λ is as in the proof of Lemma 5.8. Observe that $\delta_0(e_i)$ is always 1, since r_0 is the CQ q_0 that selects all the entities. Hence, δ_0 can be replaced by a constant, and so, it is indeed a classifier over Π.

We now need to prove that the VC dimension of Lin w.r.t. Π is at most $d+1$. Assume, by way of contradiction, that I is an instance over $\mathbf{S}$ such that I has $d+2$ entities, and Lin shatters I w.r.t. Π. To establish a contradiction, we will construct a sequence S of $d+2$ vectors in $\{-1,1\}^d$ such that S is shattered by Lin_d. It is well known that no such set S exists [33], and hence, we get a contradiction. So, in the remainder of this section we construct S.

Denote Π as $(\pi_1, \dots, \pi_m)$. If $i < j$ are such that π_i is equivalent to π_j, then every $\Pi^I(e)$ has the same value in the ith and jth positions. Therefore, every linear function over Π can be transformed into a linear function over Π', where Π' is obtained from Π by removing π_j, while preserving the output values. Therefore, I is shattered by Π' as well. We can continue to remove queries from Π until we obtain a statistic Π_d of arity d. Let $e_1, \dots, e_{d+2}$ be the entities of I. Then we define S to be the sequence $\Pi_d^I(e_1), \dots, \Pi_d^I(e_{d+2})$. By our assumption, the sequence S is shattered by Lin. □

Note that Theorem 6.1 implies that that computing the VC dimension considered class of CQs is not harder than computing equivalence. It is also not easier, since query equivalence can (quite straightforwardly) be reduced to computing the number of equivalence classes.

COMMENT 6.2. In Theorem 6.1, the assumption that Π contains only selective feature queries is necessary. As an example, consider the statistic Π that consists of *only* $q(x) \leftarrow \eta_{\mathbf{S}}(x)$. Then $\Pi^I(e) = 1$ for every instance I and entity e in I, and hence, no hypothesis class can shatter more than a single entity, and the VC dimension is 1 (rather than 2). Moreover, the assumption that Π consists of connected CQs is also necessary. As an example, consider the statistic Π that consists of the CQs $q(x) \leftarrow \eta_{\mathbf{S}}(x), R(x), P(y)$ and $q(x) \leftarrow \eta_{\mathbf{S}}(x), R(x), Q(z)$. Then two entities in R will have the same features, and two entities outside of R will have the same features; hence, the VC dimension is 2 (and not 3). We defer to future work the extension to the general case that avoids these assumptions. □

7. IDENTIFIABILITY WITH CQS

We now investigate the identifiability problem in the case where feature queries are given as CQs. We first consider connected CQs, and prove two results: (1) if negation is allowed, then affine identifiability and linear identifiability are different properties (i.e., linear identifiability is strictly more restrictive than affine identifiability, cf. Fact 4.3), and (2), without negation, the two types of identifiability converge, and their identification is coNP-complete. In the second part, we generalize by lifting the restriction of connectivity, but there our characterization becomes more complicated, and our analysis requires the assumption of selectivity of every feature query.

7.1 Connected CQs

Recall Fact 4.3. The following shows that the opposite direction does not always hold for CQs with negation (even if we assume lack of self joins).

THEOREM 7.1. *There is a statistic in $\mathsf{CQ}^{\neg}_{\mathsf{sjf}}$ that is affinely identifiable but not linearly identifiable.*

PROOF. We construct an entity schema $\mathbf{S}$ and a statistic Π over $\mathbf{S}$. The schema $\mathbf{S}$ contains three unary relation symbols η, R and S, with η being $\eta_{\mathbf{S}}$. We then define Π as (π_1, π_2, π_3) where:

$$\pi_1(x) \leftarrow \eta(x), R(x)$$
$$\pi_2(x) \leftarrow \eta(x), \neg R(x)$$
$$\pi_3(x) \leftarrow \eta(x), R(x), S(x)$$

We will show that Π is affinely identifiable but not linearly identifiable. We first prove that Π is not linearly identifiable. Let I be an instance over $\mathbf{S}$, and let C_1 and C_2 be the leftmost and middle columns of $[\![\Pi^I]\!]$, respectively. Then for every entity $e \in \eta_{\mathbf{S}}(I)$ we have $e \in \pi_1(x)$ if and only if $e \notin \pi_2(x)$. Therefore, it holds that $C_1 = -C_2$, and so we have a linear dependence.

To show that Π is affinely identifiable, we construct a specific instance I with three entities e_1, e_2 and e_3, such that the R-facts of I consist of $R(e_1)$ and $R(e_3)$, and the S-facts of I consist of only $S(e_3)$. And so, the matrix M is the following.

$$M = \begin{bmatrix} +1 & -1 & -1 \\ -1 & +1 & -1 \\ +1 & -1 & +1 \end{bmatrix}$$

Let C_1, C_2 and C_3 be the columns of M from left to right, respectively. Suppose that a, b and c are real numbers such that $aC_1 + bC_2 + cC_3 = \mathbf{0}^3$ and $a + b + c = 0$. We need to show that $a = b = c = 0$. We have the following.

$$a - b - c = 0$$
$$-a + b - c = 0$$
$$a - b + c = 0$$

From the first two equations we conclude that $c = 0$. Therefore, $a = b$. And from $a + b + c = 0$ we conclude that $a = b = c = 0$, as claimed. □

In the remainder of this section we show that in the case of CQs (without negation), the two types of identifiability converge, and they amount to query equivalence. We begin with connected CQs. A statistic Π is said to have *redundancy* if it contains two distinct feature queries that are equivalent.

THEOREM 7.2. *Let Π be a statistic in $\mathsf{CQ}_{\mathsf{con}}$. The following hold.*

1. *If Π has redundancy, then Π is not affinely identifiable (hence, also not linearly identifiable).*
2. *If Π has no redundancy, then Π is linearly identifiable (hence, also affinely identifiable).*

PROOF. Part 1 is straightforward: if Π has redundancy then every matrix $[\![\Pi^I]\!]$ has two identical columns. We will prove Part 2.

Let $\Pi = (\pi_1, \dots, \pi_n)$ be given. We assume that Π has no redundancy. We will construct an instance I over $\mathbf{S}$, and we will prove that the degree of $[\![\Pi^I]\!]$ is n (hence, its columns are independent).

The instance I is the union of $n+1$ instances $I_0, \dots, I_n$, where every two have disjoint active domains. We construct the I_i as follows. Without loss of generality, assume that no variable is shared among two or more π_i. For $i = 1, \dots, n$, we define I_i to be a canonical instance of π_i. Hence, I_i is obtained from π_i by replacing every variable x with a unique constant c_x. For each i, let e_i be the tuple of constants that corresponds to the variable sequence in the head of π_i. We insert e_i to the entity relation of η_I. Finally, we define I_0 to be an isomorphic copy of $I_1 \cup \dots \cup I_n$, where all the e_i are replaced with a new entity e_0 (using fresh new constants), and we add e_0 to the entity relation of I_0.

It remains to prove that $[\![\Pi^I]\!]$ has n independent rows. Let $r_0, \dots, r_n$ be the rows that correspond to the entities $e_0, \dots, e_n$. We will show that there are n independent rows among $r_0, \dots, r_n$. For that, it suffices to prove that the rows $r_1 + r_0, \dots, r_n + r_0$ are independent, and this is what we do. Observe that r_0 is a vector of 1s. Hence, $r_i + r_0$ is the vector $(v_1^i, \dots, v_n^i)$ where:

$$v_j^i = \begin{cases} 2 & \text{if } e_j \in \pi_i(I); \\ 0 & \text{otherwise.} \end{cases}$$

For $i = 1, \dots, n$, let r_i' be the vector $r_i + r_0$. Suppose that $a_1, \dots, a_k$ are real numbers satisfying

$$\sum_{i=1}^{n} a_i r_i' = 0$$

We need to show that $a_i = 0$ for all $i = 1, \dots, n$. Consider the containment binary relation $\subseteq$ among the π_is. Since no two π_is are equivalent, the relation $\subseteq$ is a preorder. Without loss of generality (as no order was assumed between the π_i), assume that π_n is a minimal element in the $\subseteq$ relationship. Then there is no π_i such that $i < n$ and $\pi_i \subseteq \pi_n$. If for some $i < n$ we have $e_i \in \pi_n(I)$, then we have $\pi_i \subseteq \pi_n$ due to the fact that all π_js are connected, and that our construction is based on canonical instances. Therefore, for $i < n$ we have $e_i \notin \pi_n(I)$. In particular, for $i < n$ we have that r_i' contains 0 in its nth component. And of course, r_n' contains 2 in its nth component. We then conclude that $a_n = 0$.

It then follows that $\sum_{i=1}^{n-1} a_i r_i' = 0$, and we can continue iteratively and prove that each a_i is zero. This concludes the proof. □

By applying the NP-completeness of CQ containment and equivalence [11] we get that identifiability is coNP-complete in the case of connected CQs.

COROLLARY 7.3. *Both linear and affine $\mathsf{CQ}_{\mathsf{con}}$-identifiability are* coNP*-complete.*

Next, we show that the assumptions of lack of constants (that we make throughout the paper) and connectivity are necessary for the correctness of Theorem 7.2. We begin with the lack of constants.

EXAMPLE 7.4. Let $\mathbf{S}$ be an entity schema with $\eta_{\mathbf{S}} = \eta$ and $\Pi = (\pi_1, \pi_2, \pi_3, \pi_4)$ be the statistic defined as follows.

$$\pi_1(x) \leftarrow \eta(x), S(x, \texttt{'a'})$$
$$\pi_2(x) \leftarrow \eta(x), S(x, \texttt{'a'}), S(x, y), T(y, z)$$
$$\pi_3(x) \leftarrow \eta(x), W(x, z), T(\texttt{'a'}, z)$$
$$\pi_4(x) \leftarrow \eta(x), V(x, z), T(\texttt{'a'}, z)$$

Note that these feature queries are connected, but *not* in $\mathsf{CQ}_{\mathsf{con}}$, since we do not allow constants in $\mathsf{CQ}_{\mathsf{con}}$. No two feature queries in Π are equivalent, but we will show that Π is not affinely identifiable. Let I be an instance over $\mathbf{S}$. We consider two cases.

- Case 1: No entity satisfies π_3 and π_4. Then in this case, the matrix $[\![\Pi^I]\!]$ has two identical columns (namely, the third and fourth).
- Case 2: At least one entity satisfies π_3 or π_4. Then in this case, we know that I contains $T(\texttt{'a'}, z)$ for some z, and hence, every entity x satisfies π_1 if and only if it satisfies π_2. Therefore, $[\![\Pi^I]\!]$ again contains two identical columns (namely the first and the second).

We conclude that $[\![\Pi^I]\!]$ contains two identical columns, and therefore, has an affine (and linear) dependency. □

The next example shows that Theorem 7.2 is not necessarily true if we avoid the assumption of connectivity.

EXAMPLE 7.5. Let $\mathbf{S}$ be an entity schema with $\eta_{\mathbf{S}} = \eta$ and the relation symbols $S/1$, $T/1$ and $W/1$, and $\Pi = (\pi_1, \pi_2, \pi_3, \pi_4)$ be the statistic defined as follows.

$$\pi_1(x) \leftarrow S(x)$$
$$\pi_2(x) \leftarrow S(x), T(y)$$
$$\pi_3(x) \leftarrow W(x), T(x)$$
$$\pi_4(x) \leftarrow V(x), T(x)$$

Observe that no two features in Π are equivalent. Nevertheless, Π is not affinely identifiable, and this can be shown using the same arguments of Example 7.4. □

7.2 Disconnected CQs

We now extend Theorem 7.2 to handle disconnected CQs. For that, we need some notation. Let π be a CQ feature query. We denote π as

$$\pi(x) \leftarrow \exists \mathbf{y}, \mathbf{z}[\phi(\mathbf{y}) \wedge \psi(\mathbf{z})]$$

where $\phi(\mathbf{y})$ is the conjunction of atoms that consists of the connected component of x, the vectors $\mathbf{y}$ and $\mathbf{z}$ are disjoint, and $\psi(\mathbf{z})$ is the conjunction of the remaining atoms. We denote by π^c and π^d the restrictions of π to ϕ and ψ, respectively. Hence, π^c is a feature query, and π^d is a Boolean query. Finally, we use π^b to denote the Boolean version of π, namely "there exists x such that $\pi(x)$." More formally, we have defined the following three CQs.

$$\pi^c(x) \leftarrow \exists \mathbf{y}\left[\phi(\mathbf{y})\right]$$
$$\pi^d() \leftarrow \exists \mathbf{z}\left[\psi(\mathbf{z})\right]$$
$$\pi^b() \leftarrow \exists x, \mathbf{y}, \mathbf{z}\left[\phi(\mathbf{y}) \wedge \psi(\mathbf{z})\right]$$

DEFINITION 7.6. *Let $\Pi = (\pi_1, \ldots, \pi_n)$ be a statistic in* CQ. *We say that Π is* weakly redundant *if one of the following holds.*

1. *There are two or more distinct pairs of equivalent queries among $\pi_1^c, \ldots, \pi_n^c$.*
2. *π_i^c and π_j^c are equivalent for some $1 \leq i < j \leq n$ and both of the following hold.*
   - *π_i^d is logically entailed by the conjunction of the π_l^b for $l \neq i$.*
   - *π_j^d is logically entailed by the conjunction of the π_l^b for $l \neq j$.*

We can now state the main theorem for this section.

THEOREM 7.7. *Let* **S** *be an entity schema, and let Π be a statistic in* CQ *such that π_i^c is selective for all π in Π.*

1. *If Π has weak redundancy, then Π is not affinely identifiable (hence, also not linearly identifiable).*
2. *If Π has no weak redundancy, then Π is linearly identifiable (hence, also affinely identifiable).*

The proof of Theorem 7.7 is in the appendix. We conclude the following.

COROLLARY 7.8. *Under the assumption that every feature query π is such that π^c is selective, both linear and affine* CQ*-identifiability are* coNP*-complete.*

Let us now remark on the assumption made in Theorem 7.7 that every π^c is selective. Consider the statistic $\Pi = (\pi_1, \pi_2)$ that is defined as follows.

$$\pi_1(x) \leftarrow \eta_{\mathbf{S}}(x) \qquad \pi_2(x) \leftarrow \eta_{\mathbf{S}}(x), T(y)$$

It is easy to see that Π is not linearly identifiable, since in every $[\![\Pi^I]\!]$ each column will be a either $\mathbf{1}^2$ or $-\mathbf{1}^2$. However, Π is affinely identifiable, since the instance I with two entities and an empty T satisfies

$$[\![\Pi^I]\!] = \begin{bmatrix} +1 & -1 \\ +1 & -1 \end{bmatrix}$$

which is column affinely independent. Hence, a more careful analysis should be made in the case where non-selective feature queries are allowed.

8. RELATED WORK

The task of feature engineering has been widely studied for decades [10, 20–23]. Our approach borrows heavily from the feature-engineering process identified in Guyon's seminal book [21] and those we have observed in practice. Feature engineering has received some attention from the database community [2, 3, 32, 37]. That work has made algorithmic or tooling contributions to better support feature engineering, but they do not answer the fundamental questions for which our framework is designed.

Frameworks and query languages that fuse logic with probabilistic semantics, to simplify the design of machine-learning models, have been proposed and developed in past decades. Examples of these include Probabilistic Relation Models pioneered by Koller and Friedman [18], PRISM [30], BLOG [28], Markov Logic Networks [29], and the recent *Probabilistic-Programming Datalog* [7]. However, these approaches focus on orthogonal formal questions: the semantics of the models and the complexity of the associated inference tasks. In contrast, we consider the interplay of the logical rules and learning properties. In particular, to the best of our knowledge this work is the first to consider separability, identifiability, and VC dimensionality in machine-learning models that are defined over database queries. Another related approach is *Probabilistic Soft Logic* (PSL) where Getoor et al. [6] modify the way in which the objective function is constructed for the task to preserve convexity, which is desirable for the sake of efficiency. All of our classifier models are convex, but this does not obviate the need to understand identifiability and VC dimension, which are finer information about the model.

Our formal framework draws inspiration from previous approaches to combining logical reasoning to probabilistic reasoning, which is a classical topic [5, 15], but is distinct in its goal. Our focus is on the process of feature engineering, which motivates the computational problems that occur during this loop. On the machine-learning side, we build on the conditions for identifiability described in Wainwright and Jordan's survey [35].

There has been a lot of work in the Machine Learning community on learnability aspects of First Order formulas. For instance, Arias and Khardon [4] have considered such aspects (including VC dimension) in the context of Horn clauses, where they establish bounds that are based on syntactic properties of the clauses (e.g., number of variables, literals, clauses, etc.). Such a setup is quite different from ours, since there the goal is to classify a whole interpretation (database) based on a single formula (to be learned), while we consider classification of entities within a single database and focus on *feature engineering* rather than the engineering of the classifier. More technically, our focus here is not on the syntactic properties of queries, but rather on the relationship among different feature queries. Finally, while the bounds of Arias and Khardon [4] are based on syntactic properties of Horn clauses, ours are based on equivalences. In particular, our proof techniques are quite different and draw the connection to traditional database theory.

9. CONCLUDING REMARKS

We have developed a framework for feature engineering towards programming machine-learning solutions, while focusing on the important task of classification. Our framework is based on simple additions to the relational data and query model, where an *entity schema* allows to represent entities along with their associated information, and where feature engineering is the task of designing a *statistic* when given a training instance over the entity schema. This framework enables us to formalize realistic problems in a manner that allows for nontrivial analysis and, consequently, insights and solutions. In particular, we have formalized three important computational problems within our framework: separability, identifiability, and VC dimensionality. These problems are parameterized by the hypothesis class in use and the query language deployed for feature extraction.

We have presented insights and complexity results on the three problems, while focusing on features definable by conjunctive queries and on linear hypotheses. We have drawn connections between these problems and those of query containment and equivalence. These connections have several important consequences. First, there is a tight relationship between the computational complexity of our problems and that of query containment: it is both necessary and sufficient to solve CQ containment in order to solve our problems. Second, the fact that identifiability "comes for free" (up to redundancy) gives a formal indication of the suitability of CQs as a language for feature engineering. It also motivates the challenge of finding other natural query languages that are likewise suitable.

We view the analysis we have done in this paper as providing preliminary results and a baseline for future research within our proposed framework and extensions thereof. We conclude this paper with a number of proposed directions and extensions for such future research. These fall in two main categories: *logical analysis* and *statistical questions.*

Logical Analysis

Further expressiveness. We have focused on the simple class of conjunctive queries for defining statistics, and on the classifier class of linear hypotheses. An obvious future direction would be to consider more expressive classes, such as queries with additional logical operators (and in particular deepen the exploration of non-monotonic features), and aggregate functions.

Schema constraints. Some of the tasks we have considered in this paper would be greatly impacted if we allowed for schema constraints. In particular, in the identifiability problem column independence would need to be realized by an instance that satisfies the constraints, and not by any instance of the signature (as our proofs assumed). The problem of VC dimensionality would be similarly impacted. We view this direction as an important opportunity of incorporating the database's rich modeling of data into the task of feature engineering.

Text analysis. An area where machine-learning classification is crucial for even simple tasks is that of text analysis, and in particular when the text is natural language from open domains such as Web and social media [32]. Consequently, we belive that a direction of a high potential impact is that of applying our framework to domains that allows queries over text, such as the *document spanners* of Fagin et al. [16,17] that construct and manipulate relations over text spans (intervals) using extractors (e.g., regular expressions). In particular, the computational challenges will involve queries with both relational and textual operations.

Statistical Questions

Generalized learning tasks. Our features in this work were all Boolean (± 1), and it is desirable to study the natural extension of the framework to numerical features, where numbers are either directly copied from the database or indirectly computed via queries. Moreover, our framework can be easily generalized to other prediction tasks, such as multilabel classification (e.g., predict the age group of a person) and numerical regression (e.g., predict the actual age of the person). It is important to understand how the challenges we considered are affected by such generalizations.

Separability relaxation. The separability problem, as defined in this paper, can be extended by allowing for an *approximate* agreement with the training examples (e.g., the hypothesis h should agree with the labeling λ on at least $(1-\epsilon)$ of the entities, or at most k entities should be misclassified). This is a practical and crucial relaxation in practical scenarios. For one, the training data may be noisy. Moreover, our hypothesis class may be too simple to precisely cover the examples, but can do so with only a small error.

Model complexity. In parallel to extending the expressiveness of queries, it is of high importance to find the proper restrictions on the engineered statistics (a.k.a. *regularization*), in order to reduce the *model complexity* and, consequently, reduce the risk of overfitting to the training samples (and, orthogonally, gain more efficient machine-leaning solutions). The common regularization limits the length of the statistic; in our framework, we can consider restrictions on the feature queries (e.g., size, depth, number of constants/variables, etc.). The ultimate goal is to find settings that properly balance between overfitting, underfitting, inference (classification) complexity and learning (training) complexity.

The vast literature on machine learning gives rise to many more directions for our framework to extend, such as notions of capacity beyond VC dimension (e.g., *Rademacher* and *Gaussian* complexities [8]) and the implications of the "transductive" learning environments, where we know to begin with what entities we will need to predict upon [19]. We believe that our framework can contribute to many of these directions the important angle of data and query modelling.

Acknowledgments

The authors are grateful to Stephen Bach and Alex Ratner for valuable suggestions on this work and on its presentation in this paper. Benny Kimelfeld is a Taub Fellow, supported by the Taub Foundation. His research is also supported by the Israeli Science Foundation, Grants 1295/15 and 1308/15. The research of Christopher Ré is supported by DARPA's projects XDATA (FA8750-12-2-0335), DEFT (FA8750-13-2-0039), MEMEX, and SIMPLEX. His research is also supported by NSF Career Award IIS-1353606, ONR Awards N000141210041 and N000141310129, NIH Grant U54EB-02005 (awarded by NIBIB through funds provided by the trans-NIH BD2K initiative), the Sloan Research Fellowship, the Moore Foundation, American Family Insurance, Google, and Toshiba. Any opinions, findings, and conclusions or recommendations expressed in this material are those of the authors and do not necessarily reflect the views of DARPA, AFRL, NSF, ONR, NIH, or the U.S. government.

10. REFERENCES

[1] *SAS Report on Analytics.* sas.com/reg/wp/corp/23876.

[2] M. Anderson, D. Antenucci, V. Bittorf, M. Burgess, M. Cafarella, A. Kumar, F. Niu, Y. Park, C. Ré, and C. Zhang. Brainwash: A Data System for Feature Engineering. In *CIDR*, 2013.

[3] M. R. Anderson, M. J. Cafarella, Y. Jiang, G. Wang, and B. Zhang. An integrated development environment for faster feature engineering. *PVLDB*, 7(13):1657–1660, 2014.

[4] M. Arias and R. Khardon. Complexity parameters for first order classes. *Machine Learning*, 64(1-3):121–144, 2006.

[5] F. Bacchus, A. J. Grove, J. Y. Halpern, and D. Koller. From statistical knowledge bases to degrees of belief. *CoRR*, cs.AI/0307056, 2003.

[6] S. H. Bach, M. Broecheler, B. Huang, and L. Getoor. Hinge-loss markov random fields and probabilistic soft logic. *CoRR*, abs/1505.04406, 2015.

[7] V. Bárány, B. ten Cate, B. Kimelfeld, D. Olteanu, and Z. Vagena. Declarative probabilistic programming with datalog. In *ICDT*, volume 48 of *LIPIcs*, pages 7:1–7:19. Schloss Dagstuhl - Leibniz-Zentrum fuer Informatik, 2016.

[8] P. L. Bartlett and S. Mendelson. Rademacher and gaussian complexities: Risk bounds and structural results. In *COLT*, pages 224–240, 2001.

[9] Y. Bengio and A. C. Courville. Deep learning of representations. In *Handbook on Neural Information Processing*, volume 49 of *Intelligent Systems Reference Library*, pages 1–28. Springer, 2013.

[10] D. E. Boyce. *Optimal Subset Selection: Multiple Regression, Interdependence, and Optimal Network Algorithms* . Springer-Verlag, 1974.

[11] A. K. Chandra and P. M. Merlin. Optimal implementation of conjunctive queries in relational data bases. In J. E. Hopcroft, E. P. Friedman, and M. A. Harrison, editors, *STOC*, pages 77–90. ACM, 1977.

[12] C. Chekuri and A. Rajaraman. Conjunctive query containment revisited. *Theor. Comput. Sci.*, 239(2):211–229, 2000.

[13] S. Cohen and Y. Y. Weiss. Learning tree patterns from example graphs. In *ICDT*, pages 127–143, 2015.

[14] C. Dwork, M. Hardt, T. Pitassi, O. Reingold, and R. S. Zemel. Fairness through awareness. In *ITCS*, pages 214–226. ACM, 2012.

[15] R. Fagin, J. Y. Halpern, and N. Megiddo. A logic for reasoning about probabilities. *Inf. Comput.*, 87(1/2):78–128, 1990.

[16] R. Fagin, B. Kimelfeld, F. Reiss, and S. Vansummeren. Spanners: a formal framework for information extraction. In *PODS*, pages 37–48, 2013.

[17] R. Fagin, B. Kimelfeld, F. Reiss, and S. Vansummeren. Document spanners: A formal approach to information extraction. *J. ACM*, 62(2):12, 2015.

[18] N. Friedman, L. Getoor, D. Koller, and A. Pfeffer. Learning probabilistic relational models. In *IJCAI*, pages 1300–1309, 1999.

[19] A. Gammerman, K. S. Azoury, and V. Vapnik. Learning by transduction. In *UAI*, pages 148–155. Morgan Kaufmann, 1998.

[20] I. Guyon and A. Elisseeff. An introduction to variable and feature selection. *Journal of Machine Learning Research*, 3:1157–1182, 2003.

[21] I. Guyon, S. Gunn, M. Nikravesh, and L. A. Zadeh. *Feature Extraction: Foundations and Applications (Studies in Fuzziness and Soft Computing).* Springer-Verlag New York, Inc., Secaucus, NJ, USA, 2006.

[22] T. Hastie, R. Tibshirani, and J. Friedman. *The Elements of Statistical Learning: Data mining, inference, and prediction.* Springer, 2001.

[23] G. H. John, R. Kohavi, and K. Pfleger. Irrelevant features and the subset selection problem. In *Machine Learning: Proceedings of the Eleventh International Conference*, pages 121–129, 1994.

[24] S. Kandel, A. Paepcke, J. M. Hellerstein, and J. Heer. Enterprise data analysis and visualization: An interview study. *IEEE Trans. Vis. Comput. Graph.*, 18(12):2917–2926, 2012.

[25] B. Kimelfeld and P. G. Kolaitis. The complexity of mining maximal frequent subgraphs. *ACM Trans. Database Syst.*, 39(4):32:1–32:33, 2014.

[26] Y. LeCun, Y. Bengio, and G. Hinton. Deep learning. *Nature*, 521(7553):436–444, 2015.

[27] E. L. Lehmann and G. Casella. *Theory of point estimation*, volume 31. Springer, 1998.

[28] B. Milch, B. Marthi, S. J. Russell, D. Sontag, D. L. Ong, and A. Kolobov. Blog: Probabilistic models with unknown objects. In *IJCAI*, pages 1352–1359, 2005.

[29] M. Richardson and P. Domingos. Markov logic networks. *Mach. Learn.*, 62(1-2):107–136, 2006.

[30] T. Sato and Y. Kameya. PRISM: A language for symbolic-statistical modeling. In *IJCAI*, pages 1330–1339, 1997.

[31] S. Shalev-Shwartz and S. Ben-David. *Understanding Machine Learning: From Theory to Algorithms.* Cambridge University Press, 2014.

[32] J. Shin, S. Wu, F. Wang, C. D. Sa, C. Zhang, and C. Ré. Incremental knowledge base construction using DeepDive. *PVLDB*, 8(11):1310–1321, 2015.

[33] V. Vapnik. An overview of statistical learning theory. *IEEE Transactions on Neural Networks*, 10(5):988–999, 1999.

[34] V. N. Vapnik and A. Y. Chervonenkis. On the uniform convergence of relative frequencies of events to their probabilities. *Theory of Probability and its Applications*, 16(2):264–280, 1971.

[35] M. J. Wainwright and M. I. Jordan. Graphical models, exponential families, and variational inference. *Foundations and Trends in Machine Learning*, 1(1-2):1–305, 2008.

[36] R. S. Zemel, Y. Wu, K. Swersky, T. Pitassi, and C. Dwork. Learning fair representations. In *ICML*, volume 28 of *JMLR Proceedings*, pages 325–333. JMLR.org, 2013.

[37] C. Zhang, A. Kumar, and C. RÃľ. Materialization optimizations for feature selection workloads. In *SIGMOD Conference*, pages 265–276, 2014.

APPENDIX

A. ADDITIONAL PROOFS

A.1 Proof of Theorem 5.2

We now prove Theorem 5.2. The following lemma states membership in Σ_2^{P}.

LEMMA A.1. $(\mathsf{Lin}, \mathsf{CQ}_{\mathsf{sjf}})$*-separability is in* Σ_2^{P}.

PROOF. Given an entity schema $\mathbf{S}$ and a training instance (I, λ) over $\mathbf{S}$, an evidence for separability can be a statistic $\Pi = (\pi_1, \dots, \pi_n)$ in $\mathsf{CQ}_{\mathsf{sjf}}$ where $n = |\eta_{\mathbf{S}}^I|$, such that there is a linear separation between the negative $\Pi(e)$ and the positive $\Pi(e)$. Proving every $+1$ in $\Pi(e)$ amounts to showing a homomorphism from the corresponding π_i to I, and so is refuting every -1. Observe that each π_i is of linear size in $\mathbf{S}$, since π_i does not have self joins. Determining whether there is a linear separator can be done in polynomial time by translation to Linear Programming (with both strict and non-strict inequalities). So, we get the following Σ_2^{P} representation of the problem: There exist a statistic Π and vectors $v_1, \dots, v_m \in \{-1, 1\}^n$ corresponding to $\Pi(e_1), \dots, \Pi(e_n)$, a linear separation between the positive and negative points, and a suitable homomorphism for every 1 in the v_j, such that for every -1 in the v_j and for every function μ from the corresponding π_j to I, the function μ is *not* a suitable homomorphism. This shows membership in Σ_2^{P}, as claimed. □

We now prove Σ_2^{P}-hardness. Our proof is by a reduction from the Π_2^{P}-complete problem QCNF_2 to the complement of separability. The problem QCNF_2 is defined as follows. Given a 3-CNF formula $\varphi(\mathbf{x}, \mathbf{y})$, determine whether it is the case that for every truth assignment to $\mathbf{x}$ there exists a truth assignment to $\mathbf{y}$ such that the two assignments satisfy φ.

Reduction. Let $\varphi(\mathbf{x}, \mathbf{y})$ be given. We will construct an entity schema $\mathbf{S}$ and a training instance (I, λ) with two entities a and b, such that $\lambda(a) = 1$ and $\lambda(b) = -1$, and show that a can be separated from b by a CQ in $\mathsf{CQ}_{\mathsf{sjf}}$ if and only if there exists an assignment to $\mathbf{x}$ such that $\varphi(\mathbf{x}, \mathbf{y})$ is violated by any assignment to $\mathbf{y}$.

We use the following notation. Recall that the input is $\varphi(\mathbf{x}, \mathbf{y})$. We assume $\mathbf{x} = (x_1, \dots, x_k)$ and $\mathbf{y} = (y_1, \dots, y_l)$. We denote φ as $c_1 \wedge \dots \wedge c_m$, where each c_i is a disjunction of three atomic formulas over $(\mathbf{x}, \mathbf{y})$. Each occurence of an atomic formula α_j in a clause $c_i = \alpha_1 \vee \alpha_2 \vee \alpha_3$ is associated with a unique *position* that we denote by $p = (i, j)$. We denote the atomic formula at position p by α_p and the variable in α_p as v_p. Two positions p and p' are *in agreement* if $\alpha_p = \alpha_{p'}$.

We construct the entity schema $\mathbf{S}$ with the following relation symbols.

- $\eta/1$ is the entity relation symbol.
- $\gamma/2$; a fact $\gamma(e, r)$ states that the r is a *branch* of the entity e.
- $C_i/4$ for each clause c_i; a fact $C_i(r, g_1, g_2, g_3)$ denotes an assignment (g_1, g_2, g_3) to the three variables of c_i, respectively, and this assignment is associated with the branch r.
- $X^{x,d}/1$ for each variable x in $\mathbf{x}$ and $d \in \{0, 1\}$; the fact $X^{x,d}(g)$ denotes that g represents an assignment of d to x.

We now construct the instance I over $\mathbf{S}$, as follows. There are precisely two entities a and b in I (and those occur in the relation η^I). We construct instances I_a and I_b over $\mathbf{S}$. We further construct an instance $I_b^{p,p'}$ for every pair p and p' of positions in agreement. The active domains of these instances are pairwise disjoint, except that I_b and $I_b^{p,p'}$ share the entity b. Finally, we define I as the union of I_a, I_b and all of the $I_b^{p,p'}$.

To construct the instance I_a, we define a fresh constant $g_a^{v,d}$ for every variable v in $(\mathbf{x}, \mathbf{y})$ and $d \in \{0, 1\}$. We then add to I_a the following facts:

- $\eta(a)$.
- $\gamma(a, a)$.
- $C_i(a, g_a^{v_1,d_1}, g_a^{v_2,d_2}, g_a^{v_3,d_3})$ for the variables v_1, v_2 and v_3 at positions $(i, 1)$, $(i, 2)$ and $(i, 3)$, respectively, and for all d_1, d_2 and d_3 in $\{0, 1\}$. In particular, I_a contains 8 facts of C_i.
- $X^{x,d}(g_a^{x,d})$ for all x in $\mathbf{x}$ and $d \in \{0, 1\}$.

The instance I_b is constructed in the same way as I_a, except for the following differences.

- Every occurence of a becomes b (hence, I_a and I_b are domain disjoint).
- We do not add the fact $C_i(b, g_b^{v_1,d_1}, g_b^{v_2,d_2}, g_b^{v_3,d_3})$ if it represents an assignment that violates the clause c_i. In particular, I_b contains 7 facts of C_i.

Similarly, the instance $I_b^{p,p'}$ is constructed in the same way as I_a, except for the following differences.

- Every occurence of a becomes b.
- The fact $\gamma(a, a)$ is replaced by $\gamma(b, \langle p, p' \rangle)$.
- Every occurrence of a constant $g_a^{v,d}$ becomes $g_{b,p,p'}^{v,d}$, which is a fresh new constant.
- If $p = (i, j)$, then we do not add any fact of the form $C_i(b, g_{b,p,p'}^{v_1,d_1}, g_{b,p,p'}^{v_2,d_2}, g_{b,p,p'}^{v_3,d_3})$ with $d_j = 1$.
- If $p' = (i', j')$, then we do not add any fact of the form $C_i(b, g_{b,p,p'}^{v_1,d_1}, g_{b,p,p'}^{v_2,d_2}, g_{b,p,p'}^{v_3,d_3})$ with $d_{j'} = 0$.

We have defined $\mathbf{S}$ and I. As said above, we define λ by $\lambda(a) = 1$ and $\lambda(b) = -1$. This completes the description of the reduction.

Correctness. We need to show that there is a CQ in $\mathsf{CQ}_{\mathsf{sjf}}$ that separates a from b if and only if $\varphi(\mathbf{x}, \mathbf{y})$ is a "no" instance. Hence, we prove the following lemmas.

LEMMA A.2. *Suppose that there is an assignment for* $\mathbf{x}$ *such that no assignment for* $\mathbf{y}$ *satisfies* φ. *Then there is a CQ* π *in* $\mathsf{CQ}_{\mathsf{sjf}}$ *such that* π *separates* a *from* b.

PROOF. Let $\tau : \mathbf{x} \to \{0, 1\}$ be an assignment for $\mathbf{x}$ as defined in the lemma. We denote $\tau(x_i)$ by d_i. We define the following CQ π, using $\mathbf{x}$ and $\mathbf{y}$ as variables.

$$\begin{aligned}\pi_0(z) \leftarrow & \gamma(z, r), X^{x_1,d_1}(x_1), \dots, X^{x_k,d_k}(x_k), \\ & C_1(r, v_{(1,1)}, v_{(1,2)}, v_{(1,3)}), \dots, \\ & C_m(r, v_{(m,1)}, v_{(m,2)}, v_{(m,3)})\end{aligned}$$

Note that $v_{(i,j)}$ is the variable at position (i, j), and so, different C_i may share variables. The CQ $\pi_0(z)$ states that there is an assignment to $(\mathbf{x}, \mathbf{y})$ that agrees with τ on $\mathbf{x}$ and can be matched in the C_i with the entity z. For $z = r = a$, the corresponding facts in C_i match against every possible assignment, and in particular, such an assignment to $(\mathbf{x}, \mathbf{y})$ necessarily exists. We conclude that $a \in \pi_0(I)$.

We now need to show that $b \notin \pi_0(I)$. Suppose, by way of contradiction, that μ is a homomorphism from π_0 to I, such that $\mu(z) = b$. From our construction of I and the fact that Q is connected it follows that μ is a homomorphism to either I_b or one of the $I_b^{p,p'}$. Now, μ cannot be a homomorphism into $I_b^{p,p'}$ since μ maps the same variable to every pair of attributes in agreement, and our construction of $I_b^{p,p'}$ guarantees that p and p' do not have the same value in $I_b^{p,p'}$. It thus follows that μ is a homomorphism into I_b. But then, μ represents a legal assignment that agrees with τ (due to $X^{x_1,d_1}(x_1), \dots, X^{x_k,d_k}(x_k)$). Moreover, the construction of I_b implies that this legal assignment is actually a satisfying assignment of φ. We therefore get a contradiction to the assumption of the lemma. □

LEMMA A.3. *Suppose that for each assignment for* $\mathbf{x}$ *there is an assignment for* $\mathbf{y}$ *that satisfies* φ. *Then no CQ* π *in* $\mathsf{CQ_{sjf}}$ *separates* a *from* b.

PROOF. Let $\pi(z)$ be a feature query in $\mathsf{CQ_{sjf}}$. We need to show that $a \in \pi(I)$ if and only if $b \in \pi(I)$. If π is not connected, then its part that is disconnected from z must be satisfied, unless neither a nor b are in $\pi(I)$ and we are done. So the question is about whether or not there is a homomorphism from the part that is connected to z. Therefore, we will assume that π is connected to begin with.

The "if" direction. Suppose that μ is a homomorphism from π to I such that $b \in \pi(I)$. Then, due to the fact that π is connected and has no self joins, we get that π is necessarily a homomorphism into either I_b or some $I_b^{p,p'}$. From our construction of these instances it follows that there is a homomorphism from I_b to I_a and from each $I_b^{p,p'}$ to I_a. Hence, there is a homomorphism μ' from π to I_a. And since such a homomorphism must map the head variable z into a we get that $a \in \pi(I)$.

The "only if" direction. Suppose that μ is a homomorphism from π to I such that $a \in \pi(I)$. Again, π is necessarily a homomorphism into I_a. We can view μ as a mapping of occurrences of variables in $\varphi(\mathbf{x}, \mathbf{y})$ into values. For example, if π contains $C_i(r, x, y, z)$ and π maps x to $g_a^{v_j,d_j}$, then we get the assignment $v_j \to d_j$. Nevertheless, this assignment need not be consistent (i.e., v_j may be mapped to 1 in one place, and to 0 in another place). If that is the case, then let p and p' be positions that give rise to inconsistency. Then, from the construction of $I_b^{p,p'}$ we can change μ to be a homomorphism to either $I_b^{p,p'}$ or $I_b^{p',p}$ (depending on whether the value at p is 0 or 1, respectively).

We now assume that μ represents a consistent assignment. We can replace every pair of variables in π to a new common variable whenever these are in positions that correspond to the same variable of φ. (Note that π cannot use the same variable for two different variables of φ, since I_a has different values in the corresponding positions.) We can further assume that the variables have the same names as used in the feature query π_0 defined in the proof of Lemma A.2. And we can add to π all the C_i atoms of π_0. Every atom $X^{x_i,d_i}(w)$ in π needs to be connected to some C_i atom (as π is connected), and since μ exists, d_i must be the value assigned to x by the consistent assignment. We can then add to π the missing $X^{x_i,d_i}(w)$ in π_0 defined in the proof of Lemma A.2. After this extension, we get that there a homomorphism from π to I_b if and only if there is a satisfying assignment τ for φ, such that τ agrees with the assignments defined by the $X^{x_i,d_i}(w)$ that occur in π. Hence, a homomorphism from π to I_b exists due to the assumption of the lemma. And since the head variable of such an assignment must be mapped to b, we conclude that $b \in \pi(I)$. (And thus, $b \in \pi(I)$ held true before we added new atoms to π.) □

A.2 Proof of Lemma 5.4

LEMMA 5.4. *Let* $\mathbf{H}$ *be a hypothesis class that allows copying. The problem* $(\mathbf{H}, \mathsf{CQ})$*-separability is coNP-hard already over the schema* $\mathbf{S}_0$ *and for two entities.*

PROOF. Let G and k be input for the maximum-clique problem, where G is an undirected graph and k is a natural number. The goal is to determine whether G contains a subgraph isomorphic to K_k (i.e., the complete graph over k nodes).

We construct two new graphs, each with a set of nodes that is disjoint from that of G. The first graph is G', which is simply an isomorphic copy of G. The second is a copy K of K_k.

We construct an instance I over $\mathbf{S}_0$, as follows. We fix two entities e_G and e_K, which are simply two distinct constants. The instance I is the union of two subinstances I_G and I_K, where:

- I_G contains the fact $\eta(e_G)$ and, for every edge $\{v_1, v_2\}$ of G, the fact $G(v_1, v_2, e_G)$.
- I_K contains the fact $\eta(e_K)$ and, for every edge $\{u_1, u_2\}$ of either G' or K_k, the fact $G(u_1, u_2, e_K)$.

We assume that the sets of nodes of I_G and I_K are disjoint. In particular, I_G and I_K consist of disjoint sets of facts. As said above, the instance I is $I_G \cup I_K$. Note that η_I consists of the two entities e_G and e_K. The function λ is defined by $\lambda(e_G) = 1$ and $\lambda(e_K) = -1$. Hence, we have defined the training instance (I, λ) over the entity schema $\mathbf{S}_0$.

We will prove there exists a statistic Π in CQ such that (I, λ) is $\mathbf{H}$-separable w.r.t. Π if and only if that G does not contain a clique of size k.

The "if" direction. Suppose that G does not contain any clique of size k. We will construct a statistic that separates e_G from e_K. We define the following CQ.

$$q(x) \leftarrow \bigwedge_{1 \le i < j \le k} G(y_i, y_j, x)$$

Then $q(x)$ states that the graph associated with x contains a clique of size k. Hence, we have that $e_G \notin q(I)$ and $e_K \in q(I)$, and the statistic $\Pi = (q)$ provides the required separation.

The "only if" direction. We now assume that G contains a clique of size k. We will construct an endomorphism $\mu_{GK} : I \to I$ and an endomorphism $\mu_{KG} : I \to I$ such that $\mu_{GK}(e_G) = e_K$ and $\mu_{KG}(e_K) = e_G$. This suffices to prove the "only if" direction, as the existence of μ_{KG} and μ_{GK} implies that for every q in CQ we have that $e_G \in q(I)$ if and only if $e_K \in q(I)$; therefore, every statistic Π in CQ satisfies $\Pi(e_G) = \Pi(e_K)$.

So, we complete the proof by constructing the endomorphisms μ_{GK} and μ_{KG}. Let C be a set of nodes in G such that $|C| = k$ and the subgraph induced by C is a clique. Let ξ be an arbitrary one-to-one mapping from the nodes of K to those in C, and let κ be the mapping of the nodes of G to their copies in G'. We define μ_{GK} as follows.

$$\mu_{GK}(x) = \begin{cases} e_K & \text{if } x \in \{e_G, e_K\} \\ x & \text{if } x \text{ is a node of } G' \text{ or } K \\ \kappa(x) & \text{if } x \text{ is a node of } G \end{cases}$$

And we define μ_{KG} as follows.

$$\mu_{KG}(x) = \begin{cases} e_G & \text{if } x \in \{e_G, e_K\} \\ x & \text{if } x \text{ is a node of } G \\ \kappa(x) & \text{if } x \text{ is a node of } G' \\ \xi(x) & \text{if } x \text{ is a node of } K \end{cases}$$

It remains to prove that μ_{GK} and μ_{KG} are indeed endomorphisms, which is straightforward. □

A.3 Proof of Theorem 7.7

THEOREM 7.7. *Let* $\mathbf{S}$ *be an entity schema, and let* Π *be a statistic in* CQ *such that* π_i^c *is selective for all* π *in* Π.

1. *If* Π *has weak redundancy, then* Π *is not affinely identifiable (hence, also not linearly identifiable).*
2. *If* Π *has no weak redundancy, then* Π *is linearly identifiable (hence, also affinely identifiable).*

PROOF. Throughout this proof we assume that Π is represented as $(\pi_1, \ldots, \pi_n)$, where each π_i is a CQ where π^c does not contain in $\eta_{\mathbf{S}}(x)$.

Part 1. We assume that Π has weak redundancy. Let I be an instance over $\mathbf{S}$. We need to show that $[\![\Pi^I]\!]$ has an affine column dependency. Let $C_1, \ldots, C_n$ be the columns of the matrix $[\![\Pi^I]\!]$.

Consider first the case where there are two or more equivalences among $\pi_1^c, \ldots, \pi_n^c$, then there are two options.

1. There are $i < j < k$ such that π_i^c, π_j^c and π_k^c are equivalent. If at least two of π_i^d, π_j^d and π_k^d are true, then at least two of C_i, C_j and C_k are the same (since the connected parts are equivalent). If at least two of π_i^d, π_j^d and π_k^d are false, then again at least two of C_i, C_j and C_k are the same (all -1). Hence, in any case, M has an affine column dependency.
2. There are four distinct indices $i < j$ and $k < l$ such that π_i^c is equivalent to π_j^c and π_k^c is equivalent to π_l^c. If at least two of π_i^d, π_j^d, π_k^d and π_l^d are false, at least two of C_i, C_j, C_k and C_l are the same. And if at most one of π_i^d, π_j^d, π_k^d and π_l^d is false, then either $C_i = C_j$ or $C_k = C_l$. Hence, in any case, M has an affine column dependency.

Consider now the case where there is exactly one equivalence among the $\pi_1^c, \ldots, \pi_n^c$. So, we assume now the feature queries π_i and π_j as defined in Definition 7.6. In particular, the only equivalence among $\pi_1^c, \ldots, \pi_n^c$ is that between π_i^c and π_j^c. We consider several options.

1. If both π_i^d and π_j^d are false in I, then $C_i = C_j$ and M has an affine column dependency.
2. Similarly, if both π_i^d and π_j^d are true in I, then $C_i = C_j$ (since π_i^c and π_j^c equivalent), and then again M has an affine column dependency.
3. If π_i^d is false and some π_l^b is false for $l \neq i$, then $C_i = C_l$ and M has an affine column dependency.
4. Similarly, if π_j^d is false and some π_l^b is false for $l \neq j$, then has an affine column dependency.

Eliminating all of the above cases, we have that exactly one of π_i^d and π_j^d is false in I. Suppose, without loss of generality, is π_i^d is false in I. So π_l^b is true for every $l \neq i$. But this is impossible, since π_i^d is logically entailed by the conjunction of the π_l^b for $l \neq i$.

Part 2. We assume that Π has no weak redundancy, and we will construct an instance I over $\mathbf{S}$ such that $[\![\Pi^I]\!]$ has degree n. We consider two cases.

In the first case, we assume that no two CQs among $\pi_1^c, \ldots, \pi_n^c$ are equivalent. In this case, we proceed as in the proof of Theorem 7.2. In particular, note that we satisfy each π_i^d by facts of an active domain that is disjoint from that of the remaining database. The reader can verify that, due to this disjointness, that proof holds in this case as well.

In the second case, we assume (without loss of generality) that there is exactly one equivalence among $\pi_1^c, \ldots, \pi_n^c$, and it is between π_{n-1}^c and π_n^c. Moreover, we assume that π_n^d is not logically entailed by the conjunction of the π_l^b for $l < n$. In this case, we construct the instance I as follows. For $i = 1, \ldots, n-1$, we define I_i as a canonical instance for π_i, using a fresh set of constants. For $i = 1, \ldots, n-1$, let e_i be the entity introduced for π_i. For π_n we do not introduce any new fact, besides the new entity e_n. Since we have used pairwise-disjoint canonical instances, we have that π_n^d is false in I. We conclude by showing that $[\![\Pi^I]\!]$ is linearly column independent. Let $C_1, \ldots, C_n$ be the columns of the matrix $[\![\Pi^I]\!]$, and let $r_1, \ldots, r_n$ be its rows. Then we have the following.

- C_n consists of only -1, because is π_n is false in I.
- r_n consists of only -1, because no π_i^c is equivalent to $\eta_{\mathbf{S}}$ (hence, $e_n \notin \pi_i^c(I)$ and $e_n \notin \pi_i(I)$).

So we will now continue like the proof of Theorem 7.2, but restrict ourselves to the rows $r_1, \ldots, r_{n-1}$, and use $r_0 = -r_n$. So, we have n rows that are a linear combination of the rows of M. For $1 \leq i < n-1$ we have that $r_i' = r_i - r_n$ is such that the nth column is 0, and so, all the arguments of that proof still hold and we have that $a_i = 0$ for $i = 1, \ldots, n-1$. And of course, we then have $a_n = 0$ since the nth element of r_0 is nonzero. □

Querying Probabilistic Preferences in Databases

Batya Kenig
Technion
Haifa, Israel
batyak@cs.technion.ac.il

Benny Kimelfeld
Technion
Haifa, Israel
bennyk@cs.technion.ac.il

Haoyue Ping
Drexel University
Philadelphia, USA
hp354@drexel.edu

Julia Stoyanovich
Drexel University
Philadelphia, USA
stoyanovich@drexel.edu

ABSTRACT

We propose a novel framework wherein probabilistic preferences can be naturally represented and analyzed in a probabilistic relational database. The framework augments the relational schema with a special type of a relation symbol—a preference symbol. A deterministic instance of this symbol holds a collection of binary relations. Abstractly, the probabilistic variant is a probability space over databases of the augmented form (i.e., probabilistic database). Effectively, each instance of a preference symbol can be represented as a collection of parametric preference distributions such as Mallows. We establish positive and negative complexity results for evaluating Conjunctive Queries (CQs) over databases where preferences are represented in the Repeated Insertion Model (RIM), Mallows being a special case. We show how CQ evaluation reduces to a novel inference problem (of independent interest) over RIM, and devise a solver with polynomial data complexity.

CCS Concepts

•**Mathematics of computing** → **Probabilistic inference problems;** •**Information systems** → *Database design and models;*

Keywords

Probabilistic Databases; Probabilistic Preferences; Ranking Distributions; Repeated Insertion Model

1. INTRODUCTION

Preferences are statements about the relative quality or desirability of items. Ever larger amounts of preference information are being collected and analyzed in a variety of domains, including recommendation systems [4, 31, 33] and polling and election analysis [10, 15, 16, 29]. Preference datasets are also abundant in bioinformatics, where information about the relative expression levels of genes in a cell may provide evidence that groups of genes are involved in a common biological pathway [1, 22, 34].

Preferences are often inferred from indirect input (e.g., a ranked list may be inferred from individual choices), and are therefore uncertain in nature. This motivates a rich body of work on uncertain preference models in the statistics literature; see Marden [28] for a comprehensive reference. More recently, the machine learning community has been developing methods for effective modeling and efficient inference over preferences [3, 7, 11, 15, 17, 19, 23–25], with the Mallows model [27] receiving particular attention [11, 12, 25, 32].

In this paper, we take the position that preference modeling and analysis should be accommodated within a general-purpose probabilistic database framework. The framework presented here is based on a deterministic concept that we proposed in a past vision paper [18]. There, a *preference schema* is a relational schema with some relation symbols marked as *preference symbols* (and others as *ordinary symbols*). Figure 1 gives an example of an instance of a preference database, with the ordinary symbols **Candidates** and **Voters** and the preference symbol **Polls**. An instance (table) over a preference symbol represents a collection of preference relations, called *sessions*, over a set of elements, called *items*. The signature (attribute list) of a preference symbol distinguishes between the session identifier, the left-hand-side item and the right-hand-side item. For example, the tuple (`Ann`, `Oct-5`; `Sanders`; `Clinton`) in **Polls** denotes that in the session of the voter Ann on October 5th, the candidate Sanders is preferred to the candidate Clinton.

In our past proposal [18] we focused on representing deterministic preferences, and emphasized the importance of scalable and usable support for operations on preference data. These include relational operators and common analytics such as rank aggregation, clustering, and transitive closure, which we called "preference-to-preference functions." In the present work we focus on a different angle of the story—handing *uncertain* preferences. We develop a probabilistic representation of preferences within a *probabilistic preference database*, or *PPD* for short.

A PPD may store the probability space explicitly, or it may represent it compactly using a parametric model. The PPD framework leads to novel theoretical problems and algorithms, as we illustrate in a specific kind of PPDs, where each session is represented as an independent *Repeated Insertion Model* (RIM) [12]. RIM specifies a probabilistic ranking (linear order) via a generative process that reorders

PODS'17, May 14-19, 2017, Chicago, IL, USA
© 2017 ACM. ISBN 978-1-4503-4198-1/17/05...$15.00
DOI: http://dx.doi.org/10.1145/3034786.3056111

a *reference ranking* by repeatedly inserting the items into the random ranking in a left-to-right scan. RIM generalizes various distributions over rankings, such as the well-known *Mallows* model [27], the *generalized Mallows* model [13] and the *multistage ranking* model [14].

In the PPD representations we explore, termed **RIM**-PPD, each session is associated with the parameters of a RIM model—the reference ranking and the dispersion parameter that determine the insertion probabilities. A **RIM**-PPD represents a probability space over preference databases, where a possible world is obtained by independently sampling a preference from the model of each session. Figure 2 gives an example of an instance of a **MAL**-PPD, which is a particular kind of a **RIM**-PPD. This representation compactly encodes the probability space of each session in **Polls** from Figure 1 by associating it with a Mallows model.

We study the data complexity of evaluating Conjunctive Queries (CQs) over **RIM**-PPDs. We focus on CQs to which we refer as *itemwise*. Intuitively, these are CQs where items are connected only through preferences. We first show a natural fragment of CQs where the itemwise CQs are *precisely* the CQs in which query evaluation can be done in polynomial time (under standard complexity assumptions). Here, *query evaluation* is meant in the sense of *probabilistic databases* [35], where the task is to compute the marginal probability of every possible answer. In the fragment we consider, we prove that every query that is *not* itemwise is actually #P-hard, and therefore, we establish a dichotomy in complexity.

The main analytical contribution of this paper is a polynomial-time algorithm for evaluating itemwise CQs. Interestingly, such CQs translate into a natural (and novel) inference problem over RIM. In this problem, every item is associated with one or more labels (e.g., "democratic" party or "comedy" genre), and the goal is to compute the probability that a graph pattern (or equivalently a partial order) over these labels *matches* the random ranking; that is, there exists a mapping from the nodes of the pattern to the items of the ranking such that labels (pattern nodes) and preferences (pattern edges) are preserved. The algorithm deploys dynamic programming, following a sequence of nontrivial reductions. We further describe how this algorithm can be extended to support claims about minimal and maximal indices of labels, and therefore compute the probabilities of events such as "the top-3 preferred movies include a Hitchcock movie" and "every young democratic candidate is preferred to every republican one." We are motivated by queries for recommendations that seek rankings subject to constraints on diversity.

As we illustrate in the paper, our labeled RIM model, and in particular our inference algorithm, are of interest independently from the PPD framework. We share motivation with recent research on probabilistic preferences, where the goal is in general to reason about distributions over rankings [8,25,26]. Existing inference algorithms apply to queries expressed as a partial order over individual items (e.g., compute the probability that `Sanders` is preferred to both `Clinton` and `Trump`, and that `Clinton` is preferred to `Trump`), but give only limited insight into preferences over groups of items (that we capture by labels). More recently, ranking distributions over labeled items have been introduced [17, 30] with the goal of using labels to enrich the expressiveness of distribution models.

There is a large body of work on supporting preference operators, such as top-k and partial orders, in relational databases. For example, Kießling [21] proposes to extend relational algebra with richer preference specifications than is supported by "ORDER BY" and "LIMIT", while Arvantis and Koutrika [2] demonstrate that preference operators can be implemented efficiently in scope of an RDBMS. In a nutshell, the goal of their work is to elegantly express and efficiently compute user preferences over the results of relational queries. In contrast, we focus on representing and querying databases in which preferences appear as data.

To summarize, in this paper we make the following contributions. First, we develop the framework of a probabilistic preference database. Second, we give a dichotomy in complexity for a fragment of CQs over **RIM**-PPDs. Third, we present an algorithm for evaluating itemwise CQs over **RIM**-PPDs. Fourth, we embark on the analysis of a novel and natural inference problem over RIM with labels. Lastly, we present an inference algorithm for querying labeled RIM.

2. PRELIMINARIES

In this section we set the basic terminology and notation that we use throughout the paper.

2.1 Database Model

A *relation signature* is a finite sequence α of distinct *attributes*. When there is no risk of ambiguity, we view α as a *set*, rather than *sequence*, of attributes. A *tuple* t over a relation signature α is a mapping from (the attribute set of) α to atomic values (e.g., numbers and strings). If $\alpha = (A_1, \dots, A_k)$, then we identify a tuple t over α with the sequence $(t(A_1), \dots, t(A_k))$. An *instance* over α is a finite set of tuples over α. A *relational schema* (or just *schema* for short) is a finite set $\mathbf{S}$ of *relation symbols*, where every relation symbol R is associated with a relation signature that we denote by $sig(R)$. We say that R is k*-ary* if $sig(R)$ consists of k attributes. A *database* D over a schema $\mathbf{S}$ associates with each relation symbol R an instance over $sig(R)$; we denote this instance by R^D.

A *query* Q over a schema $\mathbf{S}$ is associated with a relation signature that we denote by $sig(Q)$, and it maps every database D over $\mathbf{S}$ into an instance over $sig(Q)$; we denote this instance by $Q(D)$. A query Q is k*-ary* if $sig(Q)$ is of length k. A query Q of arity 0 is said to be *Boolean*, and in this case the result $Q(D)$ is either empty, corresponding to **false**, or the singleton $\{()\}$, corresponding to **true**. The statements $Q(D) = \{()\}$ and $Q(D) = \emptyset$ are also written as $D \models Q$ and $D \not\models Q$, respectively.

As a special case of a query, a *Conjunctive Query* (*CQ*) is represented by an expression of the form

$$Q(\mathbf{x}) \leftarrow \varphi_1(\mathbf{x}, \mathbf{y}), \dots, \varphi_m(\mathbf{x}, \mathbf{y})$$

where $\mathbf{x}$ and $\mathbf{y}$ are disjoint sequences of distinct variables, and each $\varphi_i(\mathbf{x}, \mathbf{y})$ is an atomic formula. Here, an *atomic formula* (or just *atom* for short) has the form $R(t_1, \dots, t_k)$, where R is a k-ary relation symbol, and each t_i, called *term*, is a variable (from $\mathbf{x}$ or $\mathbf{y}$) or a constant. The right hand side $\varphi_1(\mathbf{x}, \mathbf{y}), \dots, \varphi_m(\mathbf{x}, \mathbf{y})$ is called the *body* of Q. We make the requirement that each variable of Q occurs at least once in the body. A *homomorphism* from Q to a database D (over the same schema) is a function h that maps every variable of Q to a constant, such that for each atom $R(t_1, \dots, t_k)$, the tuple $(t_1, \dots, t_k)$ is in R^D once each variable z is replaced with $h(z)$. The signature $sig(Q)$ is $\mathbf{x}$ (hence, variables act as attributes). The set $Q(D)$ consists of the restrictions of all homomorphisms to $\mathbf{x}$; that is, if $\mathbf{x} = (x_1, \ldots, x_k)$ then $Q(D)$ is the set of all tuples $(h(x_1), \ldots, h(x_k))$ such that h is a homomorphism from Q to D.

2.2 Probability Spaces

All the probability spaces we refer to are discrete (and even finite). Formally, a *probability space* is a pair (Ω, π), where Ω is a countable set, called the *sample space*, and $\pi : \Omega \to [0, 1]$, called the *probability mass function*, is such that $\sum_{o \in \Omega} \pi(o) = 1$. Each element in the sample space is called a *sample*. Let $\mathcal{P} = (\Omega, \pi)$ be a probability space. As conventional, if $\psi : \Omega \to \{\mathbf{true}, \mathbf{false}\}$ is a Boolean condition over samples, then $\Pr(\psi(\mathcal{P}))$ denotes the sum of $\pi(o)$ over all the samples $o \in \Omega$ with $\psi(o) = \mathbf{true}$. (Note that this is a slight abuse of notation, as in $\psi(\mathcal{P})$ the symbol $\mathcal{P}$ denotes a random element from the sample space Ω and not the probability space.)

2.3 Orders and Rankings

A binary relation $\succ$ over a set $I = \{\sigma_1, \ldots, \sigma_n\}$ of *items* is a (strict) *partial order* if it is irreflexive and transitive; that is for all i, j and k we have $\sigma_i \not\succ \sigma_i$, and $\sigma_i \succ \sigma_j$ and $\sigma_j \succ \sigma_k$ imply $\sigma_i \succ \sigma_k$. A *linear* (or *total*) order is a partial order where every two items are comparable. By a slight abuse of notation, we often identify a linear order $\sigma_1 \succ \cdots \succ \sigma_n$ with the sequence $\langle \sigma_1, \ldots, \sigma_n \rangle$, and we call it a *ranking over* $\{\sigma_1, \ldots, \sigma_n\}$, or just *ranking* if the set of items is clear from the context. We denote by $rnk(I)$ the set of all rankings over I. If $\boldsymbol{\sigma} = \langle \sigma_1, \ldots, \sigma_n \rangle$ is a ranking, then $\text{items}(\boldsymbol{\sigma})$ denotes the set $\{\sigma_1, \ldots, \sigma_n\}$, and $\succ_{\boldsymbol{\sigma}}$ denotes the order that $\boldsymbol{\sigma}$ stands for; that is, $\sigma_i \succ_{\boldsymbol{\sigma}} \sigma_j$ whenever $i < j$. Finally, $\boldsymbol{\sigma}(\tau)$ denotes the position of an item τ in a ranking $\boldsymbol{\sigma}$; that is, if $\boldsymbol{\sigma} = \langle \sigma_1, \ldots, \sigma_n \rangle$ and $\tau = \sigma_i$, then $\boldsymbol{\sigma}(\tau) = i$.

EXAMPLE 2.1. Our running example is on individual preferences among US presidential candidates. Let I be the set $\{\texttt{Clinton}, \texttt{Rubio}, \texttt{Sanders}, \texttt{Trump}\}$. The ranking

$$\boldsymbol{\tau} = \langle \texttt{Clinton}, \texttt{Rubio}, \texttt{Sanders}, \texttt{Trump} \rangle$$

is an example member of $rnk(I)$. We have $\text{items}(\boldsymbol{\tau}) = I$ and $\succ_{\boldsymbol{\tau}}$ is the linear order given by

$$\texttt{Clinton} \succ_{\boldsymbol{\tau}} \texttt{Rubio} \succ_{\boldsymbol{\tau}} \texttt{Sanders} \succ_{\boldsymbol{\tau}} \texttt{Trump}.$$

In particular, we have $\texttt{Clinton} \succ_{\boldsymbol{\tau}} \texttt{Trump}$. □

2.4 The Repeated Insertion Model (RIM)

The *Repeated Insertion Model* [12], or *RIM* for short, is a generative process that gives rise to a family of distributions over rankings (linear orders over an itemset). RIM is a generalization of some well known statistical models for rankings such as *Mallows* [27] (defined later in this section), *generalized Mallows* [13], and *multistage ranking* [14].

A RIM model has two parameters, $\boldsymbol{\sigma}$ and Π, and is denoted by $\mathsf{RIM}(\boldsymbol{\sigma}, \Pi)$. The first parameter is a ranking $\boldsymbol{\sigma} = \langle \sigma_1, \ldots, \sigma_m \rangle$ referred to as a *reference ranking*. The model defines a probability distribution over the rankings of the items, or more formally, over the sample space $rnk(\text{items}(\boldsymbol{\sigma}))$. The probability of each ranking is defined by a generative insertion process that we describe below, using the second parameter. This parameter, Π, is called an *insertion probability function* (or just *insertion function* for short) and it maps every pair (i, j) of integers, with $1 \leq i \leq m$ and $1 \leq j \leq i$, into a probability $\Pi(i, j) \in [0, 1]$, so that for all $i = 1, \ldots, m$ we have $\sum_{j=1}^{i} \Pi(i, j) = 1$. (In particular, $\Pi(1, 1) = 1$.)

Semantically, in $\mathsf{RIM}(\boldsymbol{\sigma}, \Pi)$ a ranking in $rnk(\text{items}(\boldsymbol{\sigma}))$ is generated by the following randomized process. Suppose that $\boldsymbol{\sigma} = \langle \sigma_1, \ldots, \sigma_m \rangle$. We begin with the empty ranking, and scan the items $\sigma_1, \ldots, \sigma_m$ in order, starting with σ_1. Each σ_i is inserted into a *random position* $j \in \{1, \ldots, i\}$ inside the current series $\langle \tau_1, \ldots, \tau_{i-1} \rangle$, pushing $\tau_j, \ldots, \tau_{i-1}$ forward, and resulting in the series

$$\langle \tau_1, \ldots, \tau_{j-1}, \sigma_i, \tau_j, \ldots, \tau_{i-1} \rangle.$$

An important property of this process is that the insertion position of each σ_i is probabilistically independent of the positions of the previous items $\sigma_1, \ldots, \sigma_{i-1}$. Moreover, an easy observation is that every insertion sequence gives rise to a unique ranking.

The above process defines a probability for each ranking $\boldsymbol{\tau}$ over $\text{items}(\boldsymbol{\sigma})$, and we denote this probability by $\Pi_{\boldsymbol{\sigma}}(\boldsymbol{\tau})$. The resulting probability space is (Ω, π), where Ω is $rnk(\text{items}(\boldsymbol{\sigma}))$ and π is $\Pi_{\boldsymbol{\sigma}}$. We denote this probability space by $[\![\mathsf{RIM}(\boldsymbol{\sigma}, \Pi)]\!]$.

EXAMPLE 2.2. Continuing with our running example, consider a model $\mathsf{RIM}(\boldsymbol{\sigma}, \Pi)$, where

$$\boldsymbol{\sigma} = \langle \texttt{Clinton}, \texttt{Sanders}, \texttt{Rubio}, \texttt{Trump} \rangle.$$

The following is a possible random execution of the generative process, where the result is the ranking $\boldsymbol{\tau}$ of Example 2.1. We begin with $\boldsymbol{\tau}$ being the empty ranking $\langle\rangle$, and insert items (candidates) as follows.

1. $\boldsymbol{\tau} = \langle \texttt{Clinton} \rangle$ (with probability $\Pi(1, 1) = 1$);
2. $\boldsymbol{\tau} = \langle \texttt{Clinton}, \texttt{Sanders} \rangle$ (with probability $\Pi(2, 2)$);
3. $\boldsymbol{\tau} = \langle \texttt{Clinton}, \texttt{Rubio}, \texttt{Sanders} \rangle$ (with probability $\Pi(3, 2)$);
4. $\boldsymbol{\tau} = \langle \texttt{Clinton}, \texttt{Rubio}, \texttt{Sanders}, \texttt{Trump} \rangle$ (with probability $\Pi(4, 4)$).

Therefore, the probability of $\boldsymbol{\tau}$ is given by $\Pi_{\boldsymbol{\sigma}}(\boldsymbol{\tau}) = \Pi(1, 1) \times \Pi(2, 2) \times \Pi(3, 2) \times \Pi(4, 4)$. □

An important and well known special case of RIM is the Mallows model, which we define next.

2.4.1 The Mallows Model

A *Mallows* model [27] is parameterized by a reference ranking $\boldsymbol{\sigma} = \langle \sigma_1, \ldots, \sigma_m \rangle$ and a *dispersion parameter* $\phi \in (0, 1]$, and is denoted by $\mathsf{MAL}(\boldsymbol{\sigma}, \phi)$. The model $\mathsf{MAL}(\boldsymbol{\sigma}, \phi)$ assigns to every ranking $\boldsymbol{\tau} \in rnk(\text{items}(\boldsymbol{\sigma}))$ a non-zero probability defined by

$$\Pr(\boldsymbol{\tau} \mid \boldsymbol{\sigma}, \phi) \stackrel{\text{def}}{=} \frac{1}{Z} \phi^{d(\boldsymbol{\tau}, \boldsymbol{\sigma})}.$$

Here, $d(\boldsymbol{\tau}, \boldsymbol{\sigma})$ is *Kendall's tau* [20] distance between $\boldsymbol{\tau}$ and $\boldsymbol{\sigma}$ that counts the disagreements between $\boldsymbol{\tau}$ and $\boldsymbol{\sigma}$, and is formally given by

$$d(\boldsymbol{\tau}, \boldsymbol{\sigma}) \stackrel{\text{def}}{=} \sum_{1 \leq i < j \leq m} \mathbb{1}[\boldsymbol{\tau}(\sigma_j) < \boldsymbol{\tau}(\sigma_i)].$$

Candidates (o)

cand	party	sex	edu
Trump	R	M	BS
Clinton	D	F	JD
Sanders	D	M	BS
Rubio	R	M	JD

Voters (o)

voter	edu	sex	age
Ann	BS	F	25
Bob	BS	M	35
Cat	MS	F	40
Dave	MS	M	45
Eve	BS	F	55
Fred	JD	M	35

Polls (p)

voter	date	lcand	rcand
Ann	Oct-5	Sanders	Clinton
Ann	Oct-5	Sanders	Rubio
Ann	Oct-5	Sanders	Trump
Ann	Oct-5	Clinton	Rubio
Ann	Oct-5	Clinton	Trump
Ann	Oct-5	Rubio	Trump
Bob	Oct-5	Sanders	Rubio
Bob	Oct-5	Sanders	Clinton
Bob	Oct-5	Sanders	Trump
Bob	Oct-5	Rubio	Clinton
Bob	Oct-5	Rubio	Trump
Bob	Oct-5	Clinton	Trump
Dave	Nov-5	Clinton	Rubio
Dave	Nov-5	Clinton	Sanders
Dave	Nov-5	Clinton	Trump
Dave	Nov-5	Rubio	Sanders
Dave	Nov-5	Rubio	Trump
Dave	Nov-5	Sanders	Trump

Figure 1: An example of a preference database

The indicator function $\mathbb{1}$ assigns 1 to true statements and 0 to false ones. The *normalization constant* Z is the sum of $\phi^{d(\boldsymbol{\tau},\boldsymbol{\sigma})}$ over all $\boldsymbol{\tau} \in rnk(\text{items}(\boldsymbol{\sigma}))$.

Intuitively, the higher the distance of a ranking $\boldsymbol{\tau}$ is from the reference ranking $\boldsymbol{\sigma}$, the lower its probability under the Mallows model. Lower values of ϕ concentrate most of the probability mass around $\boldsymbol{\sigma}$, while $\phi = 1$ corresponds to the uniform probability distribution over $rnk(\text{items}(\boldsymbol{\sigma}))$.

Doignon [12] has shown that $\mathsf{MAL}(\boldsymbol{\sigma}, \phi)$ can be represented as the insertion model $\mathsf{RIM}(\boldsymbol{\sigma}, \Pi)$ where

$$\Pi(i,j) \stackrel{\text{def}}{=} \frac{\phi^{i-j}}{1+\phi+\cdots+\phi^{i-1}}.$$

The reader can verify that Π is, indeed, an insertion function for RIM, as previously defined.

Example 2.3. Figure 2 depicts three Mallows models, aligned with the rows of the table (that we later discuss). The model in the top row, for instance, is $\mathsf{MAL}(\boldsymbol{\sigma}, \phi)$ where $\boldsymbol{\sigma} = \langle$`Clinton`, `Sanders`,`Rubio`,`Trump`$\rangle$ and $\phi = 0.3$. □

3. PROBABILISTIC PREFERENCE DATABASES

In this section we define the central concept of our framework—the *probabilistic preference database*. The definition builds on the concept of a "preference relation" that we introduced in a past vision paper [18]. We will illustrate the concepts of this section with our running example of a probabilistic preference database describing polling in a presidential election.

3.1 Preference Databases

Intuitively, a preference relation stores a collection of binary relations (called *preferences*) among a set of items, where each such binary relation is called a *session*. A preference relation instantiates a special relation symbol with a signature that distinguishes between three kinds of attributes: one corresponds to the session identifier, one to the left item, and one to the right item.

Formally, a *preference signature* is a relation signature of the form β, A_l, A_r (i.e., the concatenation of β, A_l and A_r from left to right), where β is a relation signature that we call the *session signature*, and A_l and A_r are attributes that we call the *left-hand-side* (*lhs*) attribute and *right-hand-side* (*rhs*) attribute, respectively. For presentation sake, we use semicolon (;) to distinguish between the different parts and write $(\beta; A_l; A_r)$.

Example 3.1. In our running example we use the preference signature $(\mathsf{voter}, \mathsf{date}; \mathsf{lcand}; \mathsf{rcand})$. Here the components β, A_l and A_r are $(\mathsf{voter}, \mathsf{date})$, lcand, and rcand, respectively. □

Let $(\beta; A_l; A_r)$ be a preference signature, and let r be an instance over $(\beta; A_l; A_r)$. Every value that occurs in either the lhs attribute or rhs attribute of r is called an *item*, and we denote by items(r) the set of items of r. Hence, items(r) can be identified with $\pi_{A_l}(r) \cup \pi_{A_r}(r)$. A *session* of an instance r is the β part of a tuple; that is, a tuple in the projection $\pi_\beta(r)$. We denote $\pi_\beta(r)$ by sessions(r). Observe that β can be empty, and then an instance r can store at most one session. Semantically, r maps every $\mathbf{s} \in$ sessions(r) into an order $\succ$ over items(r), where $\sigma \succ \tau$ if and only if r contains the tuple $(\mathbf{s}; \sigma; \tau)$.

Example 3.2. The table **Polls** of Figure 1 is an instance of the preference signature of Example 3.1. This instance contains three sessions:

- The session (`Ann`, `Oct-5`) is associated with the ranking $\langle$`Sanders`, `Clinton`, `Rubio`, `Trump`$\rangle$;
- The session (`Bob`, `Oct 5`) is associated with the ranking $\langle$`Sanders`, `Rubio`, `Clinton`, `Trump`$\rangle$;
- The session (`Dave`, `Nov 5`) is associated with the ranking $\langle$`Clinton`, `Rubio`, `Sanders`, `Trump`$\rangle$.

Polls represents each ranking explicitly, as an order, by listing all pairwise preferences. This is a conceptual representation and, in effect, when the orders are rankings (linear orders) a compact physical representation can be used, as we do later on in this paper. □

A *preference schema* **S** is a relational schema with two types of relation symbols: *ordinary* relation symbols R that are associated with ordinary signatures $sig(R)$, and *preference relation symbols* P that are associated with preference signatures $sig(P)$. For clarity and brevity, we refer to an ordinary and a preference relation symbol as an *o-symbol* and

Polls^E

voter	date	*Preference model* $\mathbf{MAL}(\boldsymbol{\sigma}, \phi)$
Ann	Oct-5	$\langle$`Clinton`, `Sanders`, `Rubio`, `Trump`$\rangle$, 0.3
Bob	Oct-5	$\langle$`Trump`, `Rubio`, `Sanders`, `Clinton`$\rangle$, 0.3
Dave	Nov-5	$\langle$`Clinton`, `Sanders`, `Rubio`, `Trump`$\rangle$, 0.5

Figure 2: A **MAL**-instance over the p-symbol **Polls**

a *p-symbol*, respectively. A database D over a preference schema, called a *preference database*, associates with each o-symbol R an instance over $sig(R)$, and with each p-symbol P an instance over $sig(P)$; we call the former an *o-instance* and the latter a *p-instance*.

EXAMPLE 3.3. Our running example uses a preference schema **S** with three relation symbols:

- o-symbol **Candidates**(candidate, party, sex, edu) for information about political candidates.
- o-symbol **Voters**(voter, edu, sex, age) for information on individual voters.
- p-symbol **Polls**(voter, date; lcand; rcand) for polls of voters on specific dates.

Figure 1 depicts a preference database over **S**. We write "(o)" and "(p)" next to each relation symbol to stress that it is an o-symbol or a p-symbol, respectively. □

In our running example so far, we assumed that we had exact information about voters' opinions on the candidates on specific dates. In the next section, we will make this knowledge probabilistic, interpreting the preference database of Figure 1 as one *possible world*.

3.2 Probabilistic Preference Databases

Let **S** be a preference schema. A *Probabilistic Preference Database* (abbrv. *PPD*) over **S** is a probability space over preference databases over **S**. A PPD can be represented by explicitly specifying the entire sample space; however, we wish to allow for standard compact representations of preferences such as RIM and Mallows. In the remainder of this section we discuss a specific representation of this sort.

A *probabilistic preference model* is a (finite and typically compact) representation M of a probability space over partial orders $\succ$ over a finite set of items; we denote this probability space by $[\![M]\!]$. A *probabilistic preference model family*, or just *model family* for short, is a collection $\mathcal{M}$ of probabilistic preference models. As prominent examples, we define two model families.

- **RIM** is the family of RIM models $\mathsf{RIM}(\boldsymbol{\sigma}, \Pi)$.
- **MAL** is the family of Mallows models $\mathsf{MAL}(\boldsymbol{\sigma}, \phi)$.

Let **S** be a preference schema, and let $\mathcal{M}$ be a model family. Let P be a p-symbol of **S** and suppose that $sig(P) = (\beta; A_l; A_r)$. An *$\mathcal{M}$-instance* over P is a pair (r, μ), where r is an instance over β, and μ maps every tuple $\mathbf{s} \in r$ into a probabilistic preference model $M \in \mathcal{M}$. Each tuple in r is, as usual, referred to as a *session*.

EXAMPLE 3.4. Let **S** be the preference schema of Figure 1, as described in Example 3.3. Figure 2 depicts a **MAL**-instance (r, μ) over the p-symbol **Polls**. Note that r is an instance of the signature $\beta =$ (voter, date), and in the figure it is the table on the left. The model $\mu(\mathbf{s})$ for each $\mathbf{s} \in r$ is shown to the right of $\mathbf{s}$. For example, the model $\mu(\texttt{Ann}, \texttt{Oct-5})$ is the one we discussed previously in Example 2.3. □

A *session-independent $\mathcal{M}$-PPD*, or just *$\mathcal{M}$-PPD* for short, over a preference schema **S** is a mapping that associates with each o-symbol R an instance over $sig(R)$, and with each p-symbol P an $\mathcal{M}$-instance over P; we denote these instances by R^E and P^E, respectively. An $\mathcal{M}$-PPD E over **S** defines a PPD over **S** by viewing each session as an independent probabilistic preference model. We denote this PPD by $[\![E]\!]$. More precisely, a sample (or *possible world*) D of $[\![E]\!]$ is constructed by the following generative process.

```
for all o-symbols R of S do
  R^D := R^E
for all p-symbol P of S do
  P^D := an empty p-instance over P
  let (r, μ) be the M-instance P^E
  for all sessions s ∈ r do
    sample a partial order ≻ from [[μ(s)]]
    P^D := P^D ∪ {(s; σ; τ) | σ ≻ τ}
```

EXAMPLE 3.5. Let D be the preference database of Figure 1. We define the **MAL**-PPD E as the one that consists of the following:

- The o-instances **Candidates**^{D} and **Voters**^{D} of Figure 1, now referred to as **Candidates**^{E} and **Voters**^{E}, respectively.
- The **MAL**-instance **Polls**^{E} of Figure 2, and we denote it as (r, μ).

Then D is a possible world of $[\![E]\!]$. Let $\mathbf{s}_1$, $\mathbf{s}_2$ and $\mathbf{s}_3$ be the three sessions of r, top down ($\mathbf{s}_1 = (\texttt{Ann}, \texttt{Oct-5})$, and so on). The probability of D in $[\![E]\!]$ is the product $p_1 \times p_2 \times p_3$, where p_1 is the probability of $\succ_{\mathbf{s}_1}$ in the model $\mu(\mathbf{s}_1)$, which is $\mathsf{MAL}(\boldsymbol{\sigma}, 0.3)$ for $\boldsymbol{\sigma} = \langle \texttt{Clinton}, \texttt{Sanders}, \texttt{Rubio}, \texttt{Trump} \rangle$, and p_2 and p_3 defined analogously for the sessions $\mathbf{s}_2$ and $\mathbf{s}_3$, respectively. □

3.3 Querying PPDs

We adopt the semantics of probabilistic databases [35] for query evaluation. Specifically, let **S** be a schema, let Q be a query, and let $\mathcal{D} = (\Omega, \pi)$ be a PPD. A *possible answer* for Q is a tuple $\mathbf{a}$ over $sig(Q)$ such that $\mathbf{a} \in Q(D)$ for some sample D of $\mathcal{D}$. We denote by $PosAns(Q, \mathcal{D})$ the set of all possible answers. Note that $PosAns(Q, \mathcal{D})$ is finite, since $\mathcal{D}$ is a finite probability space. The *confidence* of a possible answer $\mathbf{a} \in PosAns(Q, \mathcal{D})$, denoted $conf_Q(\mathcal{D}, \mathbf{a})$, is the probability of having $\mathbf{a}$ as an answer when querying a sample of $\mathcal{D}$:

$$conf_Q(\mathcal{D}, \mathbf{a}) \stackrel{\text{def}}{=} \Pr(\mathbf{a} \in Q(\mathcal{D}))$$

As a special case, if Q is Boolean then $conf_Q(\mathcal{D})$ denotes the probability of true; that is,

$$conf_Q(\mathcal{D}) \stackrel{\text{def}}{=} \Pr(Q(\mathcal{D}) = \textbf{true}).$$

In particular, if E is an $\mathcal{M}$-PPD for some model class $\mathcal{M}$, then *evaluating Q on E* is the task of computing the following (finite) set.

$$Q(E) \stackrel{\text{def}}{=} \{(\mathbf{a}, conf_Q([\![E]\!], \mathbf{a})) \mid \mathbf{a} \in PosAns([\![E]\!])\}$$

When Q is Boolean, the evaluation of Q boils down to computing the number $conf_Q([\![E]\!])$.

EXAMPLE 3.6. We now present several Boolean CQs for our running example. We will refer to these queries in later sections of the paper. For clarity, we refer to every relational symbol by its first letter (e.g., C for **Candidates**). We also follow the convention of using underscore (_) instead of variables that occur only once in the query; however, we index the underscores by subscripts for later reference. Recall the preference schema in Figure 1: $C(\mathsf{cand}, \mathsf{party}, \mathsf{sex}, \mathsf{edu})$, $V(\mathsf{voter}, \mathsf{edu}, \mathsf{sex}, \mathsf{age})$ and $P(\mathsf{voter}, \mathsf{date}, \mathsf{lcand}, \mathsf{rcand})$.

The query Q_1 asks whether there is a voter with a BS degree who prefers a male Democratic candidate to a female Democratic candidate.

$$Q_1() \leftarrow P(v, \_1; l; r), V(v, \mathtt{BS}, \_2, \_3), \\ C(l, \mathtt{D}, \mathtt{M}, \_4), C(r, \mathtt{D}, \mathtt{F}, \_5)$$

The query Q_2 asks whether there is a voter who prefers a male candidate to a female candidate such that both candidates are of the same political party.

$$Q_2() \leftarrow P(\_1, \_2; l; r), C(l, p, \mathtt{M}, \_3), C(r, p, \mathtt{F}, \_4)$$

The query Q_3 asks whether there is a voter who prefers a female candidate to both Trump and Sanders.

$$Q_3() \leftarrow P(v, d; l; \mathtt{Trump}), P(v, d; l; \mathtt{Sanders}), \\ C(l, \_1, \mathtt{F}, \_2)$$

Finally, the query Q_4 asks whether there is a voter who prefers a candidate of the same gender to a candidate of the same education.

$$Q_4() \leftarrow P(v, \_1; l; r), V(v, \_2, s, \_3), V(v, e, \_4, \_5) \\ C(l, \_6, s, \_7), C(r, \_8, \_9, e)$$

Note that we can combine the atoms $V(v, \_2, s, \_3)$ and $V(v, e, \_4, \_5)$ into a single atom if we make the (natural) assumption that v is a key. We choose to use this phrasing to illustrate definitions from the next section.

When evaluating the above Boolean queries over a PPD, such as the **MAL**-PPD of Example 3.5, the goal is to compute the probability that the query evaluates to **true**. For example, by posing Q_1 we wish to compute the probability that at least one voter with a BS degree prefers a male Democratic candidate to a female Democratic candidate. □

4. CQ EVALUATION ON RIM-PPDS

In this section we establish preliminary complexity results on querying **RIM**-PPDs with CQs. All our results are on *data complexity*, where the schema and query are considered fixed. Recall that query evaluation entails computing the probability of every possible tuple in the result. Given that, it suffices to consider only *Boolean CQs* (for both lower and upper bounds), as the complexity of a general CQ can be determined by considering the Boolean CQ that is obtained by replacing the head variables with constant values.

4.1 Tractability of Itemwise CQs

In this section we define the notion of an *itemwise* CQ over a preference schema, and give a positive complexity result on their evaluation over **RIM**-PPDs. To define an itemwise CQ, we need some terminology.

Let $\mathbf{S}$ be a preference schema, and let Q be a CQ over $\mathbf{S}$. An atomic formula of Q is called a *p-atom* if it is over a p-symbol, and an *o-atom* if it is over an o-symbol. The *Gaifman graph* (or *primal graph*) of Q, denoted $\mathcal{G}_Q$, is the graph that has the variables of Q as the nodes, and an edge between two variables x and y whenever x and y are different variables that occur in the same atomic formula of Q. The *Gaifman o-graph* of Q, denoted $\mathcal{G}_Q^{\circ}$, is defined similarly to $\mathcal{G}_Q$, except that edges due to p-atoms are avoided—there is an edge between x and y whenever x and y are different variables that occur in the same o-atom of Q.

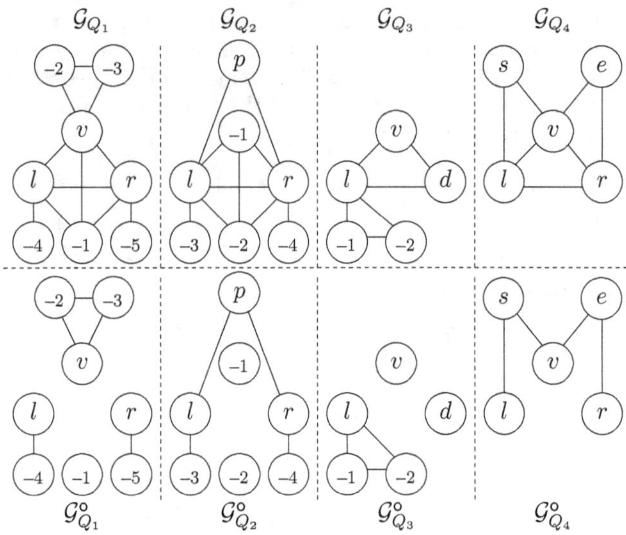

Figure 3: Gaifman graphs (top) and Gaifman o-graphs of the CQs of Example 3.6

EXAMPLE 4.1. Figure 3 depicts the Gaifman graphs $\mathcal{G}_Q$ and the Gaifman o-graphs $\mathcal{G}_Q^{\circ}$ for the CQs Q of Example 3.6. To see the definition of $\mathcal{G}_Q^{\circ}$ in action, consider the leftmost Gaifman o-graph, $\mathcal{G}_{Q_1}$. The variable v is connected by an edge to the variable l in $\mathcal{G}_{Q_1}$, but not in $\mathcal{G}_{Q_1}^{\circ}$, since the only atom that contains both v and l is the p-atom $P(v, \_1; l; r)$. To simplify the figure, in $\mathcal{G}_{Q_4}$ and $\mathcal{G}_{Q_4}^{\circ}$ we do not include the underscore variables, since they do not impact the definitions that follow. □

Let $P(s_1, \ldots, s_k; t_l; t_r)$ be p-atom of Q. Each term s_i for $i = 1, \ldots, k$ is said to occur in a *session position*, and each of t_l and t_r is said to occur in an *item position*. A *session variable* of Q is a variable that occurs in a session position, and an *item variable* of Q is a variable that occurs in an item position. We say that Q is *sessionwise* if all p-atoms of Q refer to the same session; that is, if $P(s_1, \ldots, s_k; t_l; t_r)$ and $P'(s'_1, \ldots, s'_l; t'_l; t'_r)$ are p-atoms of Q, then $P = P'$ and $(s_1, \ldots, s_k) = (s'_1, \ldots, s'_l)$.

EXAMPLE 4.2. All of the CQs of Example 3.6 are sessionwise. Indeed, queries Q_1, Q_2 and Q_4 involve a single p-atom (hence, they are sessionwise by definition), and in Q_3 both atoms have (v, d) in their session parts. □

Finally, let g be an undirected graph, and let U and W be sets of nodes of g. We say that U *completely separates* W if every path between two different nodes of W visits at least one node of U. We can now define an itemwise CQ.

DEFINITION 1 (ITEMWISE CQ). *A CQ Q over a preference schema is* itemwise *if Q is sessionwise and the set of session variables completely separates the set of item variables in $\mathcal{G}_Q^{\circ}$.*

Intuitively, in an itemwise CQ the joins between item variables occur only inside the p-atoms, or through session variables. Put differently, in an itemwise CQ with a constant session, the o-atoms state properties of individual items but do not draw connections between the items.

EXAMPLE 4.3. We consider again the CQs of Example 3.6, and their Gaifman o-graphs in Figure 3. Recall from Example 4.2 that the CQs are all sessionwise. The CQ Q_1 is itemwise since there is no path between l and r in $\mathcal{G}^{\circ}_{Q_1}$. The CQ Q_3 is itemwise since there is a single item variable (namely l). The CQ Q_4 is itemwise since there is a single path between l and r in $\mathcal{G}^{\circ}_{Q_4}$, and that path visits the session variable v. Finally, Q_2 is *not* itemwise since the path l—p—r does not visit any session variable. □

We later prove the following theorem, which states that every itemwise Boolean CQ can be evaluated in polynomial time (under data complexity).

THEOREM 4.4. *Let* **S** *be a preference schema, and let* Q *be a Boolean CQ over* **S**. *If* Q *is itemwise, then* Q *can be evaluated in polynomial time on* **RIM**-*PPDs over* **S**.

We discuss the evaluation algorithm in Section 4.4.

4.2 Hardness

The following theorem shows a restricted (yet natural) class of Boolean CQs where itemwise CQs are *precisely* the tractable ones (among the queries in the class), under conventional complexity assumptions. In other words, every Boolean CQ (in the class) that is not itemwise is necessarily hard to evaluate, and therefore, we establish a dichotomy.

THEOREM 4.5. *Let* **S** *be a preference schema, and let* Q *be a Boolean CQ over* **S** *such that* Q *has no self joins and* Q *has a single p-atom. If* Q *is not itemwise, then the evaluation of* Q *on* **RIM**-*PPDs over* **S** *is* $\mathrm{FP}^{\#\mathrm{P}}$*-hard.*

Recall that a *self join* of a CQ is a pair of distinct atoms with the same relation symbol. Also recall that $\mathrm{FP}^{\#\mathrm{P}}$ is the class of functions that are efficiently computable using an oracle to some function in #P. A function f is $\mathrm{FP}^{\#\mathrm{P}}$-hard if there is a polynomial-time *Turing reduction*[1] (or *Cook reduction*) from every function in $\mathrm{FP}^{\#\mathrm{P}}$ to f.

The proof of Theorem 4.5 is in the appendix. The proof technique is similar to that of Dalvi and Suciu [9]. We first prove hardness of the simplest intractable CQ, which is the following.

$$Q_{\mathsf{h}}() \leftarrow R(x,y), P(x;y)$$

Here, R is an o-symbol and P is a p-symbol.

LEMMA 4.6. *The evaluation of* Q_{h} *on a given* **RIM**-*PPD is* $\mathrm{FP}^{\#\mathrm{P}}$*-hard.*

We then reduce the evaluation of Q_{h} to the evaluation of every other CQ in the intractability side. We note in the proof of Lemma 4.6 we explain that the lower bound holds even for **MAL**-PPDs (using the same proof). Hence, Theorem 4.5 applies to **MAL**-PPDs, and so is the dichotomy in complexity.

[1]Using an oracle to a #P-hard (or $\mathrm{FP}^{\#\mathrm{P}}$-hard) function, one can solve in polynomial time every problem in the polynomial hierarchy [36].

4.3 Pattern Matching in Labeled Models

Our algorithm for evaluating itemwise CQs (Theorem 4.4) is a reduction to a certain type of inference over a generalized RIM model. In this section we introduce this generalized model and the type of queries we support, and in the next section we describe the reduction. In Section 5 we present an efficient algorithm for inference.

We assume an infinite set $\mathbf{\Lambda}$ of *item labels*. A *labeled RIM model* extends RIM by associating with each item a finite set of labels. More formally, labeled RIM is parameterized by $\boldsymbol{\sigma}$, Π and λ, where $\mathsf{RIM}(\boldsymbol{\sigma},\Pi)$ is a RIM model and λ is a labeling function that maps every item σ_i in $\boldsymbol{\sigma}$ to a finite set $\lambda(\sigma_i)$ of labels in $\mathbf{\Lambda}$. We denote this model by $\mathsf{RIM}_{\mathsf{L}}(\boldsymbol{\sigma},\Pi,\lambda)$. A *label pattern* (or just *pattern* for short) is a directed graph g where every node of g is a label in $\mathbf{\Lambda}$. We denote by $\mathrm{nodes}(g)$ and $\mathrm{edges}(g)$ the sets of nodes and edges of g, respectively.

Let $\boldsymbol{\tau} = \langle \tau_1,\dots,\tau_m\rangle$ be a random ranking of a model $\mathsf{RIM}_{\mathsf{L}}(\boldsymbol{\sigma},\Pi,\lambda)$, and let g be a pattern. Recall that $\succ_{\boldsymbol{\tau}}$ is the linear order that corresponds to $\boldsymbol{\tau}$; that is, $\tau_i \succ_{\boldsymbol{\tau}} \tau_j$ if and only if $i<j$. A *matching* of g in $\boldsymbol{\tau}$ (w.r.t. λ) is a function $\gamma : \mathrm{nodes}(g) \to \mathrm{items}(\boldsymbol{\sigma})$ that satisfies the following conditions.

1. Labels match: $l \in \lambda(\gamma(l))$ for all nodes l of g;
2. Edges match: for all edges $l \to l'$ of g it holds that $\gamma(l) \succ_{\boldsymbol{\tau}} \gamma(l')$.

The ranking $\boldsymbol{\tau}$ *matches* g (w.r.t. λ), denoted $(\boldsymbol{\tau},\lambda) \models g$, if there is at least one matching of g in $\boldsymbol{\tau}$. We denote by $\Gamma(g,\boldsymbol{\tau})$ the set of all the matchings of g in $\boldsymbol{\tau}$.

EXAMPLE 4.7. Consider the model $\mathsf{RIM}_{\mathsf{L}}(\boldsymbol{\sigma},\Pi,\lambda)$ for

$$\boldsymbol{\sigma} \stackrel{\text{def}}{=} \langle \texttt{Sanders},\texttt{Clinton},\texttt{Rubio},\texttt{Trump},\texttt{Stein}\rangle\,.$$

The labeling λ is given alongside the pattern g of Figure 4a: next to each label v the candidates with the corresponding label are mentioned (e.g., $\lambda(\texttt{Trump}) = \{l_{\mathsf{R}}, l_{\mathsf{BS}}\}$). The label l_{R} corresponds to "Republican," l_{F} to "Female," and l_{BS} to the "BS" academic degree. Consider the ranking $\boldsymbol{\tau}$ given by

$$\boldsymbol{\tau} \stackrel{\text{def}}{=} \langle \texttt{Rubio},\texttt{Clinton},\texttt{Sanders},\texttt{Trump},\texttt{Stein}\rangle\,.$$

Then, $\Gamma(g,\boldsymbol{\tau})$ contains the following matchings:

- $\gamma_1 \stackrel{\text{def}}{=} \{l_{\mathsf{R}} \mapsto \texttt{Rubio}, l_{\mathsf{BS}} \mapsto \texttt{Sanders}, l_{\mathsf{F}} \mapsto \texttt{Stein}\}$
- $\gamma_2 \stackrel{\text{def}}{=} \{l_{\mathsf{R}} \mapsto \texttt{Trump}, l_{\mathsf{BS}} \mapsto \texttt{Sanders}, l_{\mathsf{F}} \mapsto \texttt{Stein}\}$
- $\gamma_3 \stackrel{\text{def}}{=} \{l_{\mathsf{R}} \mapsto \texttt{Trump}, l_{\mathsf{BS}} \mapsto \texttt{Trump}, l_{\mathsf{F}} \mapsto \texttt{Stein}\}$

Note that in γ_3 two labels are mapped to Trump. □

The problem of *pattern matching* on labeled RIM models is the following. Given a model $\mathsf{RIM}_{\mathsf{L}}(\boldsymbol{\sigma},\Pi,\lambda)$ and a pattern g, compute the probability that a random ranking matches g; more formally, the goal is to compute $\Pr(g \mid \boldsymbol{\sigma},\Pi,\lambda)$ that we define as follows.

$$\Pr(g \mid \boldsymbol{\sigma},\Pi,\lambda) \stackrel{\text{def}}{=} \sum_{\substack{\boldsymbol{\tau}\in rnk(\mathrm{items}(\boldsymbol{\sigma}))\\ (\boldsymbol{\tau},\lambda)\models g}} \Pi_{\boldsymbol{\sigma}}(\boldsymbol{\tau}) \qquad (1)$$

Note that this expression does not lend itself immediately to an efficient computation, since the number of possible rankings $\boldsymbol{\tau}$ to consider can be factorial in m. In Section 5 we will present an algorithm for computing this probability, where the time is polynomial under data complexity (i.e., the pattern g is assumed fixed).

4.4 From CQs to Label Patterns

We now describe the reduction from evaluating an itemwise CQ on a **RIM**-PPD to computing the probability of pattern matching over labeled RIM. Throughout this section we fix a preference schema **S**, an itemwise CQ Q over **S**, and a **RIM**-PPD E.

Since Q is itemwise, it uses a single p-symbol (possibly multiple times), and we denote this p-symbol by P. We assume and that each p-atom has the session terms $t_1, \ldots, t_k$. Denote the **RIM**-instance P^E by (r, μ). Hence, μ maps every session $\mathbf{s} \in r$ to a RIM model, and we denote it by $\mathsf{RIM}(\boldsymbol{\sigma}^{\mathbf{s}}, \Pi^{\mathbf{s}})$. Recall that our goal is to compute the probability $\Pr([\![E]\!] \models Q)$.

Let r_Q be the set of tuples in r that can be obtained from $t_1, \ldots, t_k$ by assigning values to variables. For $\mathbf{s} = (a_1, \ldots, a_k) \in r_Q$, let $Q^{\mathbf{s}}$ be the CQ that is obtained from Q by replacing the terms $t_1, \ldots, t_k$ with the constants $a_1, \ldots, a_k$, respectively. The following proposition follows from the assumption that Q is sessionwise. The proof of the proposition is straightforward.

LEMMA 4.8. *The following hold.*

1. $\Pr([\![E]\!] \models Q) = \Pr\left(\bigvee_{\mathbf{s} \in r_Q} ([\![E]\!] \models Q^{\mathbf{s}})\right)$.
2. *No two item variables of $Q^{\mathbf{s}}$ belong to the same connected component of $\mathcal{G}^{\circ}_{Q^{\mathbf{s}}}$.*

Lemma 4.8 has several important consequences. From Part 1 we have the following due to probabilistic independence of the sessions.

$$\Pr([\![E]\!] \models Q) = 1 - \Pr\left(\wedge_{\mathbf{s} \in r_Q} ([\![E]\!] \not\models Q^{\mathbf{s}})\right) =$$
$$1 - \prod_{\mathbf{s} \in r_Q} \Pr([\![E]\!] \not\models Q^{\mathbf{s}}) = 1 - \prod_{\mathbf{s} \in r_Q} (1 - \Pr([\![E]\!] \models Q^{\mathbf{s}}))$$

Therefore, to compute $\Pr([\![E]\!] \models Q)$ it suffices to compute the probabilities $\Pr([\![E]\!] \models Q^{\mathbf{s}})$. Now, all p-atoms of Q use the same session terms, so to compute $\Pr([\![E]\!] \models Q^{\mathbf{s}})$ we can assume that P^E contains a single RIM model, namely $\mathsf{RIM}(\boldsymbol{\sigma}^{\mathbf{s}}, \Pi^{\mathbf{s}})$, since any other RIM model does not have its session matched in $Q^{\mathbf{s}}$.

We now consider Part 2 of Lemma 4.8. We split $Q^{\mathbf{s}}$ into several CQs. Denote by $Q^{\mathbf{s}}_p$ the CQ that consists of (all and only) the p-atoms of $Q^{\mathbf{s}}$, and by $Q^{\mathbf{s}}_o$ the CQ that consists of the remaining atoms (i.e., the o-atoms of $Q^{\mathbf{s}}$). Consider the graph G that contains the atoms of $Q^{\mathbf{s}}_o$ as nodes, and edges between every two atoms that share one or more variables. Let $C_1, \ldots, C_k$ be the connected components of G. For $i = 1, \ldots, k$ we denote by $Q^{\mathbf{s}}_i$ the CQ that consists of the atoms in C_i. Part 2 of Lemma 4.8 implies that each $Q^{\mathbf{s}}_i$ contains at most one item variable. Let x be an item variable of some $Q^{\mathbf{s}}_i$, and let $\sigma \in \text{items}(\boldsymbol{\sigma}^{\mathbf{s}})$. We say that σ is a *potential match* for x if at least one homomorphism from $Q^{\mathbf{s}}_i$ to E maps x to σ. In addition, σ is a *potential match* for an item variable y if y occurs only in p-atoms of $Q^{\mathbf{s}}$.

From the above development we get the following. A random ranking $\boldsymbol{\tau}$ of $\mathsf{RIM}(\boldsymbol{\sigma}^{\mathbf{s}}, \Pi^{\mathbf{s}})$ corresponds to a database D over **S** with $D \models Q^{\mathbf{s}}$ if and only if both of the following conditions hold.

1. There is a homomorphism from $Q^{\mathbf{s}}_i$ to D for all $i = 1, \ldots, k$.
2. There is a homomorphism μ from $Q^{\mathbf{s}}_p$ to P^D such that for all item variables x, the item $\mu(x)$ is a potential match for x.

So, we first check whether the first condition holds. If not, then $\Pr([\![E]\!] \models Q^{\mathbf{s}})$ is zero. Otherwise, we construct a labeling function λ over $\boldsymbol{\sigma}^{\mathbf{s}}$. The labels in the range of λ are the terms in the item positions of $Q^{\mathbf{s}}$. For each item variable x, we include the label x in $\lambda(\sigma_i)$ if σ_i is a potential match for x. And for every constant τ, we include the label τ in $\lambda(\sigma_i)$ if $\sigma_i = \tau$. Next, we construct the label pattern g, where (as expected) the nodes of g are the terms in the item positions of $Q^{\mathbf{s}}$. The pattern g contains an edge $t_1 \to t_2$ for every p-atom of $Q^{\mathbf{s}}$ of the form $(t'_1, \ldots, t'_k; t_1; t_2)$, having t_1 and t_2 on the lhs and rhs attributes, respectively. It follows from Condition 2 that $\Pr([\![E]\!] \models Q^{\mathbf{s}})$ is equal to the probability that $\mathsf{RIM_L}(\boldsymbol{\sigma}^{\mathbf{s}}, \Pi^{\mathbf{s}}, \lambda)$ matches g.

EXAMPLE 4.9. Let Q be the query Q_3 of Example 3.6. We consider the model $\mathsf{RIM}(\boldsymbol{\sigma}^{\mathbf{s}}, \Pi^{\mathbf{s}})$ defined from the model $\mathsf{MAL}(\boldsymbol{\sigma}^{\mathbf{s}}, 0.3)$ for the session $\mathbf{s} = (\texttt{Ann}, \texttt{Oct-5})$ in the **MAL**-instance of Figure 2. The query $Q^{\mathbf{s}}$ is the following.

$$Q^{\mathbf{s}}_3() \leftarrow P(\texttt{Ann}, \texttt{Oct-5}; l; \texttt{Trump}),$$
$$P(\texttt{Ann}, \texttt{Oct-5}; l; \texttt{Sanders}), C(l, \_1, \texttt{F}, \_2)$$

The terms in the item positions are l, `Trump` and `Sanders`. Moreover, only `Clinton` is a potential match for l, since l stands for a female candidate. Hence, we translate the evaluation of $Q^{\mathbf{s}}$ into $\mathsf{RIM_L}(\boldsymbol{\sigma}^{\mathbf{s}}, \Pi^{\mathbf{s}}, \lambda)$, where λ is defined as follows.

$$\lambda(\sigma) \stackrel{\text{def}}{=} \begin{cases} \{\texttt{Trump}\} & \text{if } \sigma = \texttt{Trump}; \\ \{\texttt{Sanders}\} & \text{if } \sigma = \texttt{Sanders}; \\ \{\texttt{l}\} & \text{if } \sigma = \texttt{Clinton}; \\ \emptyset & \text{otherwise.} \end{cases}$$

Finally, the label pattern g is the one of Figure 4b, which asks for the existence of an l-item before both `Trump` and `Sanders`.

Now let Q be the query Q_4 of Example 3.6, and let $\mathbf{s}$ be the above session. The query $Q^{\mathbf{s}}$ is the following.

$$Q^{\mathbf{s}}_4() \leftarrow P(\texttt{Ann}, \texttt{Oct-5}; l; r), V(\texttt{Ann}, \_2, s, \_3),$$
$$V(\texttt{Ann}, e, \_4, \_5), C(l, \_6, s, \_7), C(r, \_8, \_9, e)$$

There are two terms in item positions: l and r. The potential matches of l are those that match the subquery

$$V(\texttt{Ann}, \_2, s, \_3), C(l, \_6, s, \_7)$$

(i.e., the same gender as `Ann`), and there is only one such candidate, namely `Clinton`. Similarly, the potential matches of r are those that match the subquery

$$V(\texttt{Ann}, e, \_4, \_5), C(r, \_8, \_9, e)$$

(i.e., the same education as `Ann`), namely `Trump` and `Sanders`. We construct $\mathsf{RIM_L}(\boldsymbol{\sigma}^{\mathbf{s}}, \Pi^{\mathbf{s}}, \lambda)$, where λ is

$$\lambda(\sigma) \stackrel{\text{def}}{=} \begin{cases} \{l\} & \text{if } \sigma = \texttt{Clinton}; \\ \{r\} & \text{if } \sigma \in \{\texttt{Trump}, \texttt{Sanders}\}; \\ \emptyset & \text{otherwise.} \end{cases}$$

Finally, g is simply the graph given by $l \to r$. $\square$

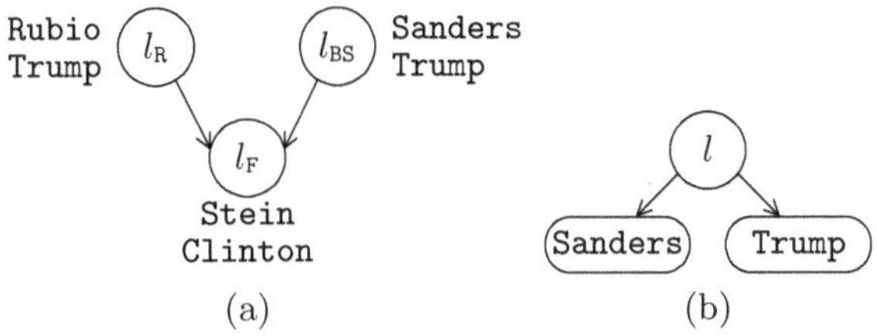

Figure 4: Examples of label patterns

Observe that the size of the pattern g we generated is determined by Q, and is independent of the **RIM**-PPD E. Hence, we establish Theorem 4.4 if we can efficiently compute the probability that a random sample of $\mathsf{RIM_L}(\boldsymbol{\sigma}, \Pi, \lambda)$ matches a pattern g of a fixed size. We devise an algorithm for this task in the next section.

5. INFERENCE ON LABELED RIM

In this section we fix a model $\mathsf{RIM_L}(\boldsymbol{\sigma}, \Pi, \lambda)$ and a pattern g, where $\boldsymbol{\sigma} = \langle \sigma_1, \dots, \sigma_m \rangle$. We devise an algorithm for computing $\Pr(g \mid \boldsymbol{\sigma}, \Pi, \lambda)$, as defined in (1).

5.1 Top Matchings

Naturally, the challenge in computing $\Pr(g \mid \boldsymbol{\sigma}, \Pi, \lambda)$ is that the number of rankings in our space (and in particular those that match g) can be factorial in m. We are able to overcome this challenge by *partitioning* the space of all rankings $\boldsymbol{\tau} \in rnk(\boldsymbol{\sigma})$ into (pairwise-disjoint) subspaces, using the notion of a *top match* that we define next. The number of partitions is polynomial in m (assuming g is fixed), and hence, it will suffice to compute the probability of each partition. We then devise an algorithm for computing this probability.

Let $\boldsymbol{\tau}$ be a random ranking. For two matchings γ_1 and γ_2 in $\Gamma(g, \boldsymbol{\tau})$, we denote by $\gamma_1 \succeq_{\boldsymbol{\tau}} \gamma_2$ the fact that $\gamma_1(l) \succ_{\boldsymbol{\tau}} \gamma_2(l)$ for all nodes l of g for which $\gamma_1(l) \neq \gamma_2(l)$. A matching $\gamma \in \Gamma(g, \boldsymbol{\tau})$ is said to be a *top matching of* g *in* $\boldsymbol{\tau}$ if $\gamma \succeq_{\boldsymbol{\tau}} \gamma'$ for all matchings $\gamma' \in \Gamma(g, \boldsymbol{\tau})$.

EXAMPLE 5.1. Consider the model $\mathsf{RIM_L}(\boldsymbol{\sigma}, \Pi, \lambda)$ of Example 4.7, and the pattern g of Figure 4a. The example also defines a ranking $\boldsymbol{\tau}$ and two matchings γ_1 and γ_2 in $\Gamma(g, \boldsymbol{\tau})$. Then we have $\gamma_1 \succeq_{\boldsymbol{\tau}} \gamma_2$ and, in fact, γ_1 is a top matching of g in $\boldsymbol{\tau}$. □

EXAMPLE 5.2. Consider the model $\mathsf{RIM_L}(\boldsymbol{\sigma}^{\mathtt{s}}, \Pi^{\mathtt{s}}, \lambda)$ constructed in Example 4.9, and let g be the label pattern of Figure 4b. Let $\boldsymbol{\tau}$ be given by

$$\boldsymbol{\tau} \stackrel{\text{def}}{=} \langle \texttt{Clinton}\,\texttt{Trump}, \texttt{Rubio}, \texttt{Sanders} \rangle .$$

Then a top matching of g in $\boldsymbol{\tau}$ is the following:

$$\{l \mapsto \texttt{Clinton}\,, \texttt{Trump} \mapsto \texttt{Trump}\,, \texttt{Sanders} \mapsto \texttt{Sanders}\}$$

We denote this matching by γ_0 for later reference. □

The following lemma shows that if there is any matching of g in $\boldsymbol{\tau}$, then there is a *unique* top matching. Recall that $(\boldsymbol{\tau}, \lambda) \models g$ denotes that $\Gamma(g, \boldsymbol{\tau})$ is nonempty.

LEMMA 5.3. *For all random rankings* $\boldsymbol{\tau}$, *if* $(\boldsymbol{\tau}, \lambda) \models g$ *then there is precisely one top matching of* g *in* $\boldsymbol{\tau}$.

Intuitively, Lemma 5.3 allows us to partition the set of rankings that match g according to their top match. This enables us to reduce the inference task to the one of calculating the probability of the set of possible top matchings.

5.2 Strategy

For a function $\gamma : \text{nodes}(g) \to \text{items}(\boldsymbol{\sigma})$ we denote by $rnk(\boldsymbol{\sigma}, \gamma)$ the set of all rankings $\boldsymbol{\tau} \in rnk(\boldsymbol{\sigma})$ such that $(\boldsymbol{\tau}, \lambda) \models g$ and γ is the top matching of g in $\boldsymbol{\tau}$. By Lemma 5.3 we have that

$$\Pr(g \mid \boldsymbol{\sigma}, \Pi, \lambda) = \sum_{\substack{\gamma:\text{nodes}(g)\to \\ \text{items}(\boldsymbol{\sigma})}} \; \sum_{\substack{\boldsymbol{\tau}\in \\ rnk(\boldsymbol{\sigma},\gamma)}} \Pi_{\boldsymbol{\sigma}}(\boldsymbol{\tau}) . \tag{2}$$

As there is only a polynomial number of functions from nodes(g) to items$(\boldsymbol{\sigma})$, it suffices to be able to efficiently compute $\sum_{\boldsymbol{\tau} \in rnk(\boldsymbol{\sigma}, \gamma)} \Pi_{\boldsymbol{\sigma}}(\boldsymbol{\tau})$, which we denote by p_γ.

$$p_\gamma \stackrel{\text{def}}{=} \sum_{\boldsymbol{\tau} \in rnk(\boldsymbol{\sigma},\gamma)} \Pi_{\boldsymbol{\sigma}}(\boldsymbol{\tau}) \tag{3}$$

In the rest of this section we show how to compute p_γ. Hence, we fix $\gamma : \text{nodes}(g) \to \text{items}(\boldsymbol{\sigma})$, and present an algorithm for computing p_γ. To shorten the notation, in the remainder of this section we will denote $rnk(\boldsymbol{\sigma}, \gamma)$ by $\mathcal{P}$.

We assume that g is acyclic, and that all nodes of g are labels that occur in the image of λ; otherwise, $p_\gamma = 0$. Let l be a node of g. A *child* of l is a node l' such that g has the edge $l \to l'$, and a *parent* of l is a node l' such that g has the edge $l' \to l$. We denote by $ch_g(l)$ and $pa_g(l)$ the sets of all children and all parents of l, respectively.

Denote by $img(\gamma)$ the item set $\{\gamma(l) \mid l \in \text{nodes}(g)\}$. The position of the items in $img(\gamma)$ within a random ranking is described by a mapping $\delta \colon \text{nodes}(g) \to [1, m]$, where $\delta(l)$ represents the position of item $\gamma(l)$ in the ranking. We say that δ is *consistent with* g (or just consistent) if for all edges $l' \to l$ of g we have that $\delta(l') < \delta(l)$. We denote by $\mathcal{R}$ the set of all mappings that are consistent with g. We say that δ is *realized* in a ranking $\boldsymbol{\tau}$, or that $\boldsymbol{\tau}$ *realizes* δ, if $\delta(l) = \boldsymbol{\tau}(\gamma(l))$ for every $l \in \text{nodes}(g)$.

The algorithm is based on the following lemma.

LEMMA 5.4. *For all* $\boldsymbol{\tau} \in rnk(\boldsymbol{\sigma})$ *we have* $\boldsymbol{\tau} \in \mathcal{P}$ *if and only if there exists a consistent mapping* δ *such that:*

1. $\boldsymbol{\tau}$ *realizes* δ;
2. *For every* $l \in \text{nodes}(g)$ *and* $\sigma \in \text{items}(\boldsymbol{\tau})$, *if* $l \in \lambda(\sigma)$ *and* $\boldsymbol{\tau}(\sigma) < \delta(l)$, *then* $pa_g(l) \neq \emptyset$ *and*

$$\boldsymbol{\tau}(\sigma) < \max_{l' \in pa_g(l)} \delta(l') .$$

In particular, if $pa_g(l) = \emptyset$ then $\gamma(l)$ is the highest ranking item of type l in $\boldsymbol{\tau}$, that is, $\gamma(l) \succ_{\boldsymbol{\tau}} \sigma$ for all σ such that $l \in \lambda(\sigma)$.

EXAMPLE 5.5. Consider again the $\mathsf{RIM_L}(\boldsymbol{\sigma}^{\mathtt{s}}, \Pi^{\mathtt{s}}, \lambda)$ model constructed in Example 4.9. Let g be the label pattern of Figure 4b. Recall the top matching γ_0 of g in $\boldsymbol{\tau}$ from Example 5.2, and assume that γ is γ_0. Let δ be the mapping $\{l \mapsto 1, \texttt{Trump} \mapsto 2, \texttt{Sanders} \mapsto 4\}$. Then δ is consistent with g, and δ is realized in $\boldsymbol{\tau}$. The reader can verify that Lemma 5.4 holds with respect to $\boldsymbol{\tau}$ and δ. □

We denote by $p(\delta)$ the probability that the generated random ranking $\boldsymbol{\tau}$ is such that $\boldsymbol{\tau} \in \mathcal{P}$ and $\boldsymbol{\tau}$ realizes δ:

$$p(\delta) \stackrel{\text{def}}{=} \sum_{\substack{\boldsymbol{\tau}\in\mathcal{P},\\ \boldsymbol{\tau} \text{ realizes } \delta}} \Pi_{\boldsymbol{\sigma}}(\boldsymbol{\tau}) \tag{4}$$

Then, from Lemma 5.3 we conclude that

$$p_\gamma = \sum_{\delta\in\mathcal{R}} p(\delta)\,. \tag{5}$$

Next, we describe an algorithm for computing the $p(\delta)$ for all $\delta \in \mathcal{R}$. The algorithm follows the stochastic insertion process of RIM, with the following twist. We begin the RIM process not with the empty ranking, but rather with one that contains $img(\gamma)$ in an ordering that is consistent with g. Since there can be multiple such orderings, we track all of them simultaneously.

For a formal description, some notation is needed. For $t = 0,\dots,m$ we denote by the cardinality of the item set $\{\sigma_1,\dots,\sigma_t\}\cup img(\gamma)$ by s_t, and the set of all consistent mappings $\delta\colon \text{nodes}(g) \to [1, s_t]$ by $\mathcal{R}_t$. In particular, $s_m = m$ and $\mathcal{R}_m = \mathcal{R}$. As usual, the algorithm iterates through the items of $\boldsymbol{\sigma}$ in order, from σ_1 to σ_m. At iteration t, it inserts σ_t into a prefix that contains $\{\sigma_1,\dots,\sigma_{t-1}\} \cup img(\gamma)$ and realizes a consistent mapping in $\mathcal{R}_{t-1}$, thereby generating a new prefix that realizes a mapping in $\mathcal{R}_t$. If σ_t happens to be in $img(\gamma)$, then the insertion is avoided.

Next, we denote by $\widehat{\mathcal{P}}_t$ the set of all rankings $\boldsymbol{\tau}$ over $\{\sigma_1,\dots,\sigma_t\} \cup img(\gamma)$ such that for some $\delta \in \mathcal{R}_t$ the two conditions of Lemma 5.4 are satisfied. For $\boldsymbol{\tau} \in \widehat{\mathcal{P}}_t$, we denote by $\boldsymbol{\tau}_{|t}$ the projection of $\boldsymbol{\tau}$ onto $\{\sigma_1,\dots,\sigma_t\}$. In other words, $\boldsymbol{\tau}_{|t}$ is obtained from $\boldsymbol{\tau}$ by removing the items σ_i of $img(\gamma)$ with $i > t$. In particular, $\boldsymbol{\tau}_{|m} = \boldsymbol{\tau}$.

Finally, for $\delta \in \mathcal{R}_t$ we denote by $\widehat{p}_t(\delta)$ the sum of probabilities given by the (classic) RIM distribution function to all rankings in $\widehat{\mathcal{P}}_t$ that realize δ, projected onto the members of $\{\sigma_1,\dots,\sigma_t\}$. Formally:

$$\widehat{p}_t(\delta) \stackrel{\text{def}}{=} \sum_{\substack{\boldsymbol{\tau}\in\widehat{\mathcal{P}}_t,\\ \boldsymbol{\tau} \text{ realizes } \delta}} \Pi^t_{\boldsymbol{\sigma}}(\boldsymbol{\tau}_{|t}) \tag{6}$$

where $\Pi^t_{\boldsymbol{\sigma}}(\boldsymbol{\tau}')$ is the probability of generating the ranking $\boldsymbol{\tau}' \in rnk(\{\sigma_1,\dots,\sigma_t\})$ at time t (i.e., the product of the corresponding insertion probabilities).

From the definition of $p(\delta)$ in Equation (4), the above discussion, and the definition of $\widehat{p}_t(\delta)$ in Equation (6) we conclude that

$$p(\delta) = \widehat{p}_m(\delta)\,. \tag{7}$$

Our algorithm computes $\widehat{p}_t(\delta)$ for all $t \in \{1,\dots,m\}$ and $\delta \in \mathcal{R}_t$; in particular, the algorithm computes $\widehat{p}_m(\delta)$, and hence the required $p(\delta)$.

5.2.1 *Summary*

So far we proved that every ranking that matches g has a unique top matching, hence computing $\Pr(g \mid \boldsymbol{\sigma}, \Pi, \lambda)$ reduces, by (2), to computing the probability that a given mapping γ is a top matching for a random ranking $\boldsymbol{\tau}$, denoted p_γ (3). Next, in Lemma 5.4 we translated having γ as a top matching into consistency conditions over the function δ that maps $img(\gamma)$ into specific indices. That allowed us to reduce the computation of p_γ, by (5), to the computation of $p(\delta)$, which the probability that δ is realized in the random $\boldsymbol{\tau}$ (4). Finally, we defined in (6) the function $\widehat{p}_t(\delta)$ that tracks insertions over a series augmented with $img(\gamma)$, so that $p(\delta)$ is precisely $\widehat{p}_m(\delta)$. Hence, computing $p(\delta)$ reduces to computing $\widehat{p}_t(\delta')$ for every $\delta' \in \mathcal{R}_t$. Our algorithm, described in the next section, accomplishes this task and returns p_γ.

5.3 Algorithm Description

We begin by defining the insertion probability function $\Upsilon[i,j,\delta]$ for our algorithm, which returns the probability of inserting item σ_i into index j of a subranking containing items $\{\sigma_1,\dots,\sigma_{i-1}\}\cup img(\gamma)$, where the members of $img(\gamma)$ are positioned as in $\delta \in \mathcal{R}_{i-1}$. We denote by $img_{>t}(\gamma)$ the items in $img(\gamma)$ with an index larger than t, that is:

$$img_{>t}(\gamma) \stackrel{\text{def}}{=} img(\gamma) \cap \{\sigma_{t+1},\dots,\sigma_m\}$$

Intuitively, our insertion function accounts only for inconsistencies that arise between item σ_i and those with a lower index in $\boldsymbol{\sigma}$. Therefore, we can ignore all items of $img_{>i}(\gamma)$ in the subranking by appropriately adjusting the insertion index as follows:

$$\Upsilon[i,j,\delta] \stackrel{\text{def}}{=} \Pi\left(i, j - |\{\gamma(l) \in img_{>i}(\gamma) \mid \delta(l) < j\}|\right) \tag{8}$$

That is, $\Upsilon[i,j,\delta]$ is the probability $\Pi[i,j']$, returned by the classic RIM insertion function, for inserting item σ_i into the modified index j' that accounts only for those items whose index is smaller than i.

Recall that $\Pi^t_{\boldsymbol{\sigma}}(\boldsymbol{\tau})$ denotes the probability that RIM generated the subranking $\boldsymbol{\tau}$, at time t. Analogously, we denote by $\Upsilon^t_{\boldsymbol{\sigma}}(\boldsymbol{\tau})$ the probability of the ranking $\boldsymbol{\tau}$ induced by the new insertion function (8). For every consistent mapping $\delta \in \mathcal{R}_t$, we compute the probability

$$q_t(\delta) = \sum_{\substack{\boldsymbol{\tau}\in\mathcal{P}_t,\\ \boldsymbol{\tau} \text{ realizes } \delta}} \Upsilon^t_{\boldsymbol{\sigma}}(\boldsymbol{\tau})\,.$$

The algorithm TopProb (Figure 5) constructs the sets of consistent mappings $\mathcal{R}_1,\dots,\mathcal{R}_m$ by extending the set of consistent mappings from the previous iteration. The initial set $\mathcal{R}_0$ is simply the set of all rankings over $img(\gamma)$ that are consistent with g, and for every $\delta \in \mathcal{R}_0$, we define $q_0(\delta) = 1$.

At iteration t, a consistent mapping $\delta \in \mathcal{R}_{t-1}$ is extended by inserting item σ_t into every possible *legal* position, as defined by the second condition of Lemma 5.4 (line 3). The subroutine Range implements this constraint based on the values in δ (lines 5-7).

In the case where $\sigma_t \in img(\gamma)$ (that is, $\gamma(l) = \sigma_t$ for some $l \in \text{nodes}(g)$), there is only a single legal position for σ_t, namely $\delta(l)$. Therefore, the mapping does not change (i.e., $\delta' = \delta$). Otherwise, the mapping is updated according to the insertion position j as follows. We denote by δ_{+j} the assignment obtained from δ by inserting an item into index j in the random prefix; that is, $\delta_{+j}(l) = \delta(l) + 1$ whenever $\delta(l) \geq j$, and otherwise $\delta_{+j}(l) = \delta(l)$. The probability of the resulting mapping δ', combining the previous mapping δ and the insertion position j, is calculated in line 8.

In the following section we show that for every consistent mapping $\delta \in \mathcal{R}_t$ it holds that $q_t(\delta) = \widehat{p}_t(\delta)$, proving that the algorithm indeed computes $\widehat{p}_m(\delta)$, and thus $p(\delta)$, for every $\delta \in \mathcal{R}_m$. This allows us to compute p_γ (Eq. (5)).

Algorithm $\mathsf{TopProb}(\mathsf{RIM_L}(\boldsymbol{\sigma},\Pi,\lambda),g,\gamma)$

for $i = 1,\dots,m$ **do**
  for all $\delta \in \mathcal{R}_{i-1}$ **do**
    for all $j \in \mathsf{Range}(\delta,g,\gamma,\sigma_i)$ **do**
      if $\sigma_i \in \mathit{img}(\gamma)$ **then**
        $\delta' := \delta$
      else
        $\delta' := \delta_{+j}$
      $q_i(\delta') \mathrel{+}= q_{i-1}(\delta) \times \Upsilon(i,j,\delta)$
      $\mathcal{R}_i := \mathcal{R}_i \cup \{\delta'\}$
return $\sum_{\delta\in\mathcal{R}_m} q_m(\delta)$

Subroutine $\mathsf{Range}(\delta,g,\gamma,\sigma_i)$

if $\sigma_i \in \mathit{img}(\gamma)\colon \sigma_i = \gamma(l)$ **then**
  return $\delta(l)$
$s_i := i + |\mathit{img}_{>i}(\gamma)|$ {prefix size}
range $:= \{1,\dots,s_i\}$
for all $\{l \in \lambda(\sigma_i)\}$ **do**
  $l_p := \arg\max_{l'\in pa_g(l)} \delta(l')$
  range $:=$ range $\setminus \{\delta(l_p)+1,\dots,\delta(l)\}$
return range

Figure 5: An algorithm for computing p_γ

5.4 Correctness

Let $t > 1$ be a position in $\boldsymbol{\sigma}$, and let $\boldsymbol{\tau} \in \widehat{\mathcal{P}}_{t-1}$. Then $\boldsymbol{\tau}_{+j}$ is the ranking that results from inserting σ_t into index j. If $\sigma_t \in \mathit{img}(\gamma)$ then $\boldsymbol{\tau}_{+j}$ is simply $\boldsymbol{\tau}$. Otherwise, $\boldsymbol{\tau}_{+j}[i] = \boldsymbol{\tau}[i-1]$ for all $i > j$, $\boldsymbol{\tau}_{+j}[j] = \sigma_t$, and $\boldsymbol{\tau}_{+j}[i] = \boldsymbol{\tau}[i]$ in case $i < j$. As before, $\boldsymbol{\tau}_{|t}$ is the ranking projected onto the items with index at most t. We begin with the following lemma.

Lemma 5.6. *The following hold for all iterations t of* TopProb.

1. *For all legal indices j returned by* Range *and $\boldsymbol{\tau} \in \widehat{\mathcal{P}}_{t-1}$ we have $\boldsymbol{\tau}_{+j} \in \widehat{\mathcal{P}}_t$.*
2. *For every $\boldsymbol{\tau} \in \widehat{\mathcal{P}}_t$ there exists a ranking $\boldsymbol{\tau}' \in \widehat{\mathcal{P}}_{t-1}$ and a legal index j returned by* Range *such that $\tau'_{+j} = \boldsymbol{\tau}$.*

Lemma 5.6 implies that the algorithm correctly constructs the $\mathcal{R}_t$. The lemma is needed for the next one.

Lemma 5.7. *In the execution of* TopProb *we have $q_i(\delta) = \widehat{p}_i(\delta)$ for all $i \in \{1,\dots,m\}$ and $\delta \in \mathcal{R}_i$.*

From Lemma 5.7 we conclude that $q_m(\delta) = \widehat{p}_m(\delta) = p(\delta)$ for all $\delta \in \mathcal{R}$. Therefore, from (5) we get the desired probability, as stated in the following theorem.

Theorem 5.8. *Algorithm* TopProb *returns p_γ (Eq. (5)).*

Finally, the following theorem gives an upper bound on the execution cost of the algorithm.

Theorem 5.9. *(Complexity) Algorithm* TopProb *runs in time $O(m^{|\mathsf{nodes}(g)|+2})$.*

Proof. The number of consistent mappings that the algorithm processes is in $O(m^{|\mathsf{nodes}(g)|})$. For each mapping, all possible insertion positions are inspected, and this is repeated for every index $i \in \{1,\dots,m\}$, overall the complexity of the algorithm is $O(m^{|\mathsf{nodes}(g)|+2})$. □

Therefore, we establish the main result of this section.

Theorem 5.10. *For every fixed label pattern g, the probability $\Pr(g \mid \boldsymbol{\sigma},\Pi,\lambda)$ can be computed in polynomial time on a given $\mathsf{RIM_L}(\boldsymbol{\sigma},\Pi,\lambda)$ model.*

In particular, from the reduction of Section 4.4 and Theorem 5.10 we get the correctness of Theorem 4.4.

5.5 Incorporating Min/Max Conditions

Consider a labeled RIM model $\mathsf{RIM_L}(\boldsymbol{\sigma},\Pi,\lambda)$. We now describe an extension of the algorithm TopProb to handle conditions over the *minimal* and *maximal* index where a label occurs in the random ranking. In the context of our running example, this allows us to compute probabilities of the following kinds of events.

1. Every Democratic candidate is preferred to every Republican candidate.
2. Every female Republican is preferred to every male Democrat.
3. Hillary Clinton is among the top 3 choices.
4. A Libertarian is among the bottom 3 choices.
5. Every Green candidate is ranked higher than every Republican and lower than every Democrat.

We support such queries as follows. Let $\mathsf{RIM_L}(\boldsymbol{\sigma},\Pi,\lambda)$ be a labeled RIM model. We denote by $\boldsymbol{\Lambda}_\lambda$ the (finite) set of all labels that occur in the image of λ. The positions of the minimal and maximal items associated with label $l \in \boldsymbol{\Lambda}_\lambda$, within a random ranking, is described by the following pair of mappings:

$$\alpha\colon \boldsymbol{\Lambda}_\lambda \to [1,m] \tag{9}$$

$$\beta\colon \boldsymbol{\Lambda}_\lambda \to [1,m] \tag{10}$$

That is, $\alpha(l)$ and $\beta(l)$ represent the positions of the highest and lowest ranked items of type l in a random ranking, respectively. We say that α and β are *realized* in a ranking $\boldsymbol{\tau}$, or that $\boldsymbol{\tau}$ *realizes* α and β, if for every $l \in \boldsymbol{\Lambda}_\lambda$:

$$\alpha(l) = \min\{i \mid l \in \lambda(\tau_i)\}$$

$$\beta(l) = \max\{i \mid l \in \lambda(\tau_i)\}$$

To phrase the above examples as conditions over minimal and maximal indices of labels, suppose that the labels l_D, l_G, l_L and l_R stand for Democratic, Green, Libertarian and Republican parties, respectively. The first event states that $\beta(l_D) < \alpha(l_R)$, the fourth event states that $\beta(l_L) \geq m-2$ (m being the number of candidates), and the fifth event states that $\alpha(l_R) > \beta(l_G)$ and $\alpha(l_G) > \beta(l_D)$.

For a fixed number of labels, there is only a polynomial number of possible mappings α and β (see (9) and (10)). Our extension of the algorithm TopProb computes the marginal probability of each pair of such mappings. Hence, the algorithm can evaluate *every* fixed condition over these mappings, as long as the numerical operations are assumed to

Algorithm TopProbMinMax($\mathsf{RIM_L}(\boldsymbol{\sigma}, \Pi, \lambda), g, \gamma, \varphi$)

1: **for** $i = 1, \dots, m$ **do**
2:   **for all** $\langle \delta, \alpha, \beta \rangle \in \mathcal{R}_{i-1}$ **do**
3:     **for all** $j \in \mathsf{Range}(\delta, g, \gamma, \sigma_i)$ **do**
4:       **if** $\sigma_i \in img(\gamma)$ **then**
5:         $\langle \delta', \alpha', \beta' \rangle := \langle \delta, \alpha, \beta \rangle$
6:       **else**
7:         $\langle \delta', \alpha', \beta' \rangle := \langle \delta_{+j}, \alpha_{+j}, \beta_{+j} \rangle$
8:         $q_i(\langle \delta', \alpha', \beta' \rangle) \mathrel{+}= q_{i-1}(\langle \delta, \alpha, \beta \rangle) \times \Upsilon(i, j, \delta)$
9:         $\mathcal{R}_i := \mathcal{R}_i \cup \langle \delta', \alpha', \beta' \rangle$
10:       **for all** $l \in \boldsymbol{\Lambda}_\lambda \mid l \in \lambda(\sigma_i)$ **do**
11:         $\alpha'(l) := \min(\alpha'(l), j)$
12:         $\beta'(l) := \max(\beta'(l), j)$
13: **return** $\sum_{\{\langle \delta, \alpha, \beta \rangle \in \mathcal{R}_m \mid \langle \alpha, \beta \rangle \models \varphi\}} q_m(\langle \delta, \alpha, \beta \rangle)$

Figure 6: A dynamic programming algorithm for computing $p_{\gamma,\varphi}$

take constant time, as in the *Real RAM* model [5]. (And for ordinary Turing machines, the complexity should be adjusted to incorporate bitwise operations.)

We now state the formal conclusion. Let $\boldsymbol{\Lambda}_\lambda = \{l_1, \dots, l_k\}$. By *computable min/max condition* we refer to any Boolean recursive (computable) condition $\varphi(x_1, \dots, x_k, y_1, \dots, y_k)$ over the natural numbers where x_i and y_i represent the values of $\alpha(l_i)$ and $\beta(l_i)$ respectively. The mappings α and β are essentially an *assignment* to the variables of φ. We say that the mappings α and β *satisfy* a min/max condition φ, denoted $\langle \alpha, \beta \rangle \models \varphi$ if substituting the values of these mappings to the corresponding variables causes φ to evaluate to true.

Given a label pattern g, we denote by $\Pr(g \wedge \varphi \mid \boldsymbol{\sigma}, \Pi, \lambda)$ the probability that a random ranking $\boldsymbol{\tau}$ matches g (i.e., $(\boldsymbol{\tau}, \lambda) \models g$), and realizes a pair of mappings α and β that satisfy φ (i.e., $\langle \alpha, \beta \rangle \models \varphi$). In particular, we denote by $p_{\gamma,\varphi}$ the probability that γ is the top matching of g in a random ranking (see (3)) that also realizes a pair of mappings α and β, which satisfy φ.

THEOREM 5.11. *For every fixed label pattern g and fixed computable min/max condition φ, the probability $\Pr(g \wedge \varphi \mid \boldsymbol{\sigma}, \Pi, \lambda)$ is computable in polynomial time on Real RAM for given labeled RIM models $\mathsf{RIM_L}(\boldsymbol{\sigma}, \Pi, \lambda)$.*

Theorem 5.11 is realized by the dynamic programming algorithm TopProbMinMax (Figure 6), which is an extension of the algorithm TopProb (Figure 5), and explained below.

The constraints defined by a min/max condition φ are incorporated into the dynamic programming algorithm (Figure 6) as follows. We extend the set of mappings maintained by the algorithm to a triple $\langle \delta, \alpha, \beta \rangle$ where δ remains unchanged (recall that $\delta\colon \text{nodes}(g) \mapsto [1, m]$ represents the position of the item $\gamma(l)$ in a random ranking), and mappings α and β are as previously described (see (9) and (10)). A triple $\langle \delta, \alpha, \beta \rangle$ is *consistent* if δ is consistent (that is, for all edges $l' \to l$ of g the inequality $\delta(l') < \delta(l)$ holds).

The new algorithm TopProbMinMax, supporting min/max conditions is depicted in Figure 6. The subroutine Range is the same as in algorithm TopProb, and is therefore omitted. The updating of the values in mappings α and β, for each label $l \in \boldsymbol{\Lambda}_\lambda$, is performed in lines 10-12. The rest of the algorithm follows in a straightforward manner from algorithm TopProb.

The extended algorithm maintains and processes a larger state space, leading to increased complexity. Nevertheless, the number of possible consistent mappings $\langle \delta, \alpha, \beta \rangle$ is limited to $O(m^{3|\boldsymbol{\Lambda}_\lambda|})$. While larger than the space maintained by the original algorithm (TopProb), this is still exponential only in the size of the query, preserving the polynomial data complexity.

6. CONCLUDING REMARKS

In our past vision paper [18] we made the case for incorporating preferences into the relational model, to allow for queries that involve popular operations over preferences. In this paper we proposed a novel angle to this framework—querying probabilistic preferences by utilizing the expressive power of the relational model. Our investigation of **RIM-PPDs** illustrates that our framework gives rise to new challenges in two domains: databases and statistical inference. In particular, we showed how the evaluation of CQs leads to a novel and natural inference problem over RIM models, and we presented a nontrivial algorithm for solving this problem. We conclude this paper by proposing several directions for future research.

Theoretical directions include the generalization of our results in various directions: more general query languages (e.g., larger fragments of FO), a more general dichotomy in the complexity of CQs, approximate query evaluation (e.g., PTAS on Boolean CQ evaluation), and additional statistical models of preferences (e.g., Choi et al. [8]). Furthermore, it is important to establish general conditions where tractability can be attained under *combined* (i.e., query-and-data) complexity.

Practical directions are, naturally, abundant. While our algorithm provides the guarantee of polynomial time, translating it into a practical implementation over preferences of realistic volumes presents significant challenges. Our long-term goal is to build a database system that incorporates preferences in the PPD model, and allows for both nontrivial preference-specific operations (e.g., rank aggregation) and statistical inference.

Towards this goal, we will propose efficient physical representations of preferences. Further, we will develop efficient algorithms for exact answering of probabilistic preference queries that leverage CPU parallelism and data parallelism in distributed architectures. Finally, we will explore performance optimization opportunities that can be derived from approximate query answering. Our ongoing and future systems work will build on the theoretical insights developed in this paper.

Acknowledgments

This work was supported in part by the US National Science Foundation (NSF) Grants No. 1464327 and 1539856, by the US-Israel Binational Science Foundation (BSF) Grant No. 2014391, and by the Israel Science Foundation (ISF) Grant No. 1295/15. Benny Kimelfeld is a Taub Fellow, supported by the Taub Foundation.

7. REFERENCES

[1] S. Aerts, D. Lambrechts, S. Maity, P. V. Loo, B. Coessens, F. D. Smet, L.-C. Tranchevent, B. D. Moor, P. Marynen, B. Hassan, P. Carmeliet, and Y. Moreau. Gene prioritization through genomic data fusion. *Nature Biotechnology*, 24(5):537–544, 2006.

[2] A. Arvanitis and G. Koutrika. Prefdb: Supporting preferences as first-class citizens in relational databases. *IEEE Trans. Knowl. Data Eng.*, 26(6):1430–1446, 2014.

[3] P. Awasthi, A. Blum, O. Sheffet, and A. Vijayaraghavan. Learning mixtures of ranking models. In *NIPS*, pages 2609–2617, 2014.

[4] S. Balakrishnan and S. Chopra. Two of a kind or the ratings game? adaptive pairwise preferences and latent factor models. *Frontiers of Computer Science*, 6(2):197–208, 2012.

[5] L. Blum, M. Shub, and S. Smale. On a theory of computation and complexity over the real numbers: *np*- completeness, recursive functions and universal machines. *Bull. Amer. Math. Soc. (N.S.)*, 21(1):1–46, 07 1989.

[6] G. R. Brightwell and P. Winkler. Counting linear extensions is #P-complete. In *STOC*, pages 175–181, 1991.

[7] L. M. Busse, P. Orbanz, and J. M. Buhmann. Cluster analysis of heterogeneous rank data. In *ICML*, pages 113–120, 2007.

[8] A. Choi, G. V. den Broeck, and A. Darwiche. Tractable learning for structured probability spaces: A case study in learning preference distributions. In *IJCAI*, pages 2861–2868. AAAI Press, 2015.

[9] N. N. Dalvi and D. Suciu. Efficient query evaluation on probabilistic databases. In *VLDB*, pages 864–875. Morgan Kaufmann, 2004.

[10] P. Diaconis. A generalization of spectral analysis with applications to ranked data. *Annals of Statistics*, 17(3):949–979, 1989.

[11] W. Ding, P. Ishwar, and V. Saligrama. Learning mixed membership mallows models from pairwise comparisons. *CoRR*, abs/1504.00757, 2015.

[12] J.-P. Doignon, A. Pekeč, and M. Regenwetter. The repeated insertion model for rankings: Missing link between two subset choice models. *Psychometrika*, 69(1):33–54, 2004.

[13] M. A. Fligner and J. S. Verducci. Distance based ranking models. *Journal of the Royal Statistical Society. Series B (Methodological)*, 48(3):359–369, 1986.

[14] M. A. Fligner and J. S. Verducci. Multistage ranking models. *Journal of the American Statistical Association*, 83(403):892–901, 1988.

[15] I. C. Gormley and T. B. Murphy. A latent space model for rank data. In *ICML*, 2006.

[16] I. C. Gormley and T. B. Murphy. A mixture of experts model for rank data with applications in election studies. *The Annals of Applied Statistics*, 2(4):1452–1477, 12 2008.

[17] J. Huang, A. Kapoor, and C. Guestrin. Riffled independence for efficient inference with partial rankings. *J. Artif. Intell. Res. (JAIR)*, 44:491–532, 2012.

[18] M. Jacob, B. Kimelfeld, and J. Stoyanovich. A system for management and analysis of preference data. *PVLDB*, 7(12):1255–1258, 2014.

[19] T. Kamishima and S. Akaho. Supervised ordering by regression combined with thurstone's model. *Artif. Intell. Rev.*, 25(3):231–246, 2006.

[20] M. G. Kendall. A new measure of rank correlation. *Biometrika*, 30(1/2):81–93, 1938.

[21] W. Kießling. Foundations of preferences in database systems. In *VLDB*, pages 311–322, 2002.

[22] R. Kolde, S. Laur, P. Adler, and J. Vilo. Robust rank aggregation for gene list integration and meta-analysis. *Bioinformatics*, 28(4):573–580, 2012.

[23] G. Lebanon and J. D. Lafferty. Cranking: Combining rankings using conditional probability models on permutations. In *ICML*, pages 363–370, 2002.

[24] G. Lebanon and Y. Mao. Non-parametric modeling of partially ranked data. *Journal of Machine Learning Research*, 9:2401–2429, 2008.

[25] T. Lu and C. Boutilier. Effective sampling and learning for mallows models with pairwise-preference data. *J. Mach. Learn. Res.*, 15(1):3783–3829, Jan. 2014.

[26] T. Lukasiewicz, M. V. Martinez, D. Poole, and G. I. Simari. Probabilistic models over weighted orderings: Fixed-parameter tractable variable elimination. In *KR*, pages 494–504. AAAI Press, April 2016.

[27] C. L. Mallows. Non-null ranking models. i. *Biometrika*, 44(1-2):114–130, June 1957.

[28] J. I. Marden. *Analyzing and Modeling Rank Data.* Chapman & Hall, 1995.

[29] G. McElroy and M. Marsh. Candidate gender and voter choice: Analysis from a multimember preferential voting system. *Political Research Quarterly*, 63(4):pp. 822–833, 2010.

[30] C. Meek and M. Meila. Recursive inversion models for permutations. In *NIPS*, pages 631–639. Curran Associates, Inc., 2014.

[31] A. D. Sarma, A. D. Sarma, S. Gollapudi, and R. Panigrahy. Ranking mechanisms in twitter-like forums. In *WSDM*, pages 21–30, 2010.

[32] J. Stoyanovich, L. Ilijasic, and H. Ping. Workload-driven learning of mallows mixtures with pairwise preference data. In *WebDB*, page 8, 2016.

[33] J. Stoyanovich, M. Jacob, and X. Gong. Analyzing crowd rankings. In *WebDB*, pages 41–47, 2015.

[34] J. M. Stuart, E. Segal, D. Koller, and S. K. Kim. A gene-coexpression network for global discovery of conserved genetic modules. *Science*, 302:249–255, 2003.

[35] D. Suciu, D. Olteanu, C. Ré, and C. Koch. *Probabilistic Databases.* Synthesis Lectures on Data Management. Morgan & Claypool Publishers, 2011.

[36] S. Toda and M. Ogiwara. Counting classes are at least as hard as the polynomial-time hierarchy. *SIAM Journal on Computing*, 21(2), 1992.

APPENDIX

A. ADDITIONAL PROOFS

A.1 Proof of Lemma 4.6

LEMMA 4.6. *The evaluation of Q_{h} on a given* **RIM**-*PPD is* $\mathrm{FP}^{\#\mathrm{P}}$-*hard.*

PROOF. The proof is by reduction from the problem of counting the number of linear extensions of a partial order. The input for this problem consists of a set $A = \{\sigma_1, \dots, \sigma_m\}$ of items and a partial order $\succ$ over A. The goal is to compute $|rnk(A|\succ)|$, where $rnk(A|\succ)$ is the set of all rankings $\boldsymbol{\sigma} \in rnk(A)$ that satisfy $\sigma_i \succ_{\boldsymbol{\sigma}} \sigma_j$ whenever $\sigma_i \succ \sigma_j$. This problem is known to be #P-complete [6]. Given the input A and $\succ$, we construct the following **RIM**-PPD E. The relation R^E is the inverse of $\succ$, that is, it consists of all the pairs (σ_j, σ_i) where $\sigma_i \succ \sigma_j$. The single model of P^E is $\mathsf{RIM}(\boldsymbol{\sigma}, \Pi)$, where $\boldsymbol{\sigma}$ is the ranking $\langle \sigma_1, \dots, \sigma_m \rangle$ and Π is the insertion function that defines a uniform distribution over the permutations of A; that is: $\Pi(i,j) = \frac{1}{i}$ whenever $1 \leq i \leq m$ and $1 \leq j \leq i$. Note that $\mathsf{RIM}(\boldsymbol{\sigma}, \Pi)$ is the same as $\mathsf{MAL}(\boldsymbol{\sigma}, 1)$.

Observe that every possible world W of the PPD $[\![E]\!]$ consists of R^W, which is the same as R^E, and a linear order over A that is encoded in P^W. Also note that a possible world satisfies Q_{h} if and only if P^W shares at least one pair with R^W. From the construction of R^W it follows that W satisfies Q_{h} if and only if P^W is *not* a linear extension of $\succ$. Finally, we observe that every possible world W has the same probability, namely $\frac{1}{m!}$ (where m is the number of items in A). Therefore:

$$conf_{Q_{\mathsf{h}}}([\![E]\!]) = \frac{m! - |rnk(A|\succ)|}{m!} .$$

In particular, we can compute $|rnk(A|\succ)|$ by multiplying $1 - conf_{Q_{\mathsf{h}}}([\![E]\!])$ by $m!$. □

A.2 Proof of Theorem 4.5

THEOREM 4.5. *Let* **S** *be a preference schema, and let Q be a Boolean CQ over* **S** *such that Q has no self joins and Q has a single p-atom. If Q is not itemwise, then the evaluation of Q on* **RIM**-*PPDs over* **S** *is* $\mathrm{FP}^{\#\mathrm{P}}$-*hard.*

PROOF. We will prove the hardness of evaluating Q over RIM-PPDs by a reduction from the evaluation of the CQ $Q_{\mathsf{h}}() \leftarrow R(x,y), P(x;y)$, which is shown to be $\mathrm{FP}^{\#\mathrm{P}}$-hard in Lemma 4.6. Let E_h be an input **RIM**-PPD instance over the schema of Q_{h}. Then E_h maps R to an instance R^{E_h} over R, and P to a **RIM**-instance that consists of a single **RIM**-model, which we denote by M_h.

Let $P_Q(\beta; A_l; A_r)$ be the single p-symbol that appears in Q, and let $P_Q(s_1, \dots, s_k; x_Q; y_Q)$ be the single p-atom of Q. Observe that x_Q and y_Q must be distinct, and neither is a session variable; otherwise, Q is itemwise by definition, contradicting our assumption. We fix a constant $\mathtt{c}$, and denote by $(c_1, \dots, c_k)$ the tuple that is obtained from $(s_1, \dots, s_k)$ by replacing every variable with $\mathtt{c}$. Hence, the tuple $(c_1, \dots, c_k)$ consists of the constants in $\{s_1, \dots, s_k\}$ and, possibly, the constant $\mathtt{c}$.

We now construct a **RIM**-instance E over the schema of Q. The **RIM**-model P_Q^E is the pair (r, μ), where the relation r consists of the single tuple $(c_1, \dots, c_k)$ defined above, and μ maps this tuple to the above model M_h. The o-instances of E are constructed by the following procedure. For each tuple (a,b) of R^{E_h} and o-atom $S(t_1, \dots, t_n)$ of Q, we add to the S-instance of E the tuple $(d_1, \dots, d_n)$, where for $i = 1, \dots, n$ we have:

$$d_i = \begin{cases} t_i & \text{if } t_i \text{ is a constant;} \\ \mathtt{c} & \text{if } t_i \text{ is a session variable;} \\ a & \text{if } t_i = x_Q; \\ b & \text{otherwise.} \end{cases}$$

Observe that every variable z of Q that is neither x_Q nor a session variable is replaced with b. In particular, y_Q is replaced with b. Let p be a path of $\mathcal{G}_Q^{\circ}$ that does not visit any session variable. The existence of p is guaranteed, since Q is not itemwise. Then all the variables along p are replaced with b, except for x_Q that is replaced with a. In particular, there is an edge in p such that one incident node is replaced with a and one with b.

This completes the construction of E. To complete the proof, we will show that

$$\Pr(Q([\![E]\!]) = \mathbf{true}) \;=\; \Pr(Q_{\mathsf{h}}([\![E_h]\!]) = \mathbf{true}) . \qquad (11)$$

Let Q_o be the CQ that is obtained from Q by removing the single p-atom. From the construction of E we get the following.

1. For every tuple (a,b) of R^{E_h} there is a homomorphism from Q_o to E that maps x_Q and y_Q to a and b, respectively.
2. For every homomorphism from Q_o to E that maps x_Q and y_Q to a and b, respectively, the tuple (a,b) is in R^{E_h}.

We mention here that the second item uses the fact that there are no self joins, and is not necessarily true otherwise.

Finally, from the construction of P_Q^E it follows that there is a bijection φ between the possible worlds of $[\![E_h]\!]$ and $[\![E]\!]$ such that for every possible world D of $[\![E_h]\!]$ we have that $Q_{\mathsf{h}}(D) = Q(\varphi(D))$, and moreover, D and $\varphi(D)$ have the same probability. Hence, Equation (11) immediately follows, as required. □

A.3 Proof of Lemma 5.3

LEMMA 5.3. *For all random rankings $\boldsymbol{\tau}$, if $(\boldsymbol{\tau}, \lambda) \models g$ then there is precisely one top matching of g in $\boldsymbol{\tau}$.*

PROOF. If $(\boldsymbol{\tau}, \lambda) \models g$ then there exists a matching of g in $\boldsymbol{\tau}$. This means that there is a mapping from the nodes of g to the items of $\boldsymbol{\tau}$ that is consistent with the edges of g. Since $\boldsymbol{\tau}$ defines a total order over its items and in particular over the items mapped by the matching, then g must be acyclic.

We prove the claim by induction on $|\mathrm{nodes}(g)|$. If g contains a single node l, then $\gamma^*(l) = \tau_k$ where $k = \min\{i \in \{1, \dots, m\} \mid l \in \lambda(\tau_i)\}$. Since $\boldsymbol{\tau}$ matches g, then k exists, and by the minimality condition is unique.

Assume correctness for patterns with n nodes, and we prove the claim for a pattern with $n+1$ nodes. Consider a node $l \in \mathrm{nodes}(g)$ with no outgoing edges in g. Since g is acyclic such a node must exist. Now consider the pattern induced by $\mathrm{nodes}(g) \setminus \{l\}$ (i.e., without l and its incoming edges), defined over n nodes. Since $\boldsymbol{\tau}$ matches g it must also match the pattern induced by $\mathrm{nodes}(g) \setminus \{l\}$, denoted g^n. By the induction hypothesis, $\boldsymbol{\tau}$ has a single, unique top matching γ_n^* corresponding to g^n. Let τ_k be an item in $\boldsymbol{\tau}$

that is associated with l (i.e., $l \in \lambda(\tau_k)$). We define k as follows. If $pa_g(l) \neq \emptyset$ then τ_k is the highest ranked item of type l that appears after $\gamma_n^*(u)$ for each $u \in pa_g(l)$:

$$k = \min\left\{i > \max_{u \in pa_g(l)} \boldsymbol{\tau}(\gamma_n^*(u)) \mid l \in \lambda(\tau_i)\right\} \quad (12)$$

Recall that $\boldsymbol{\tau}(a)$ denotes the index of item a in the ranking. Otherwise, if $pa_g(l) = \emptyset$, then:

$$k = \min\{i > 0 \mid l \in \lambda(\tau_i)\}$$

Since $\boldsymbol{\tau}$ matches g, such an index k must exist, and due to the minimality condition, is unique. Define the matching γ_{n+1} as follows:

$$\gamma_{n+1}(u) = \begin{cases} \gamma_n^*(u) & \text{if } u \neq l \\ \tau_k & \text{otherwise} \end{cases}$$

We now show that γ_{n+1} is both minimum and unique. By the induction hypothesis γ_n^* is both minimum and unique for the pattern g excluding the node l. Therefore, the top matching for g must be identical to γ_n^* for all nodes in nodes$(g) \setminus \{l\}$. By the minimality and uniqueness of the index k, we get that γ_{n+1} is also minimum and unique, as required. □

A.4 Proof of Lemma 5.4

LEMMA 5.4. *For all $\boldsymbol{\tau} \in rnk(\boldsymbol{\sigma})$ we have $\boldsymbol{\tau} \in \mathcal{P}$ if and only if there exists a consistent mapping δ such that:*

1. *$\boldsymbol{\tau}$ realizes δ;*
2. *For every $l \in$ nodes(g) and $\sigma \in$ items$(\boldsymbol{\tau})$, if $l \in \lambda(\sigma)$ and $\boldsymbol{\tau}(\sigma) < \delta(l)$, then $pa_g(l) \neq \emptyset$ and*

$$\boldsymbol{\tau}(\sigma) < \max_{l' \in pa_g(l)} \delta(l').$$

PROOF. We prove each direction separately.

The "only if" direction. Let $\boldsymbol{\tau} \in \mathcal{P}$. Hence, γ is a top matching for g in $\boldsymbol{\tau}$. We will show that there exists a consistent mapping δ such that $\boldsymbol{\tau}$ and δ meet the conditions of the lemma. Define the mapping δ: nodes$(g) \to [1, m]$ such that $\delta(l)$ is $\boldsymbol{\tau}(\gamma(l))$, that is, the index of $\gamma(l)$ in $\boldsymbol{\tau}$. By this definition, $\boldsymbol{\tau}$ clearly realizes δ, and δ is consistent with g.

Assume, by way of contradiction, that the second item of the lemma is not met. That is, there exists a label $l \in$ nodes(g), and an item τ_i such that *(a)* $l \in \lambda(\tau_i)$, *(b)* $\tau_i \succ_{\boldsymbol{\tau}} \gamma(l)$, *and (c)* either $pa_g(l) = \emptyset$ or $i > \max_{l' \in pa_g(l)} \delta(l')$. In this case, the mapping γ': nodes$(g) \to [1, m]$ defined as:

$$\gamma'(v) = \begin{cases} \gamma(v) & \text{if } v \neq l \\ \tau_i & \text{otherwise} \end{cases}$$

is a matching for $\boldsymbol{\tau}$ (i.e., $\gamma' \in \Gamma(g, \boldsymbol{\tau})$), and $\gamma' \succeq_{\boldsymbol{\tau}} \gamma$. Therefore, we arrive at a contradiction that γ is a top matching for g in $\boldsymbol{\tau}$.

The "if" direction. Now assume that $\boldsymbol{\tau}$ realizes a consistent mapping δ such that $\boldsymbol{\tau}$ and δ meet the conditions of the lemma. We will show that $\boldsymbol{\tau} \in \mathcal{P}$. The fact that $\boldsymbol{\tau}$ realizes δ means that δ maps the items of $img(\gamma)$ to their positions in $\boldsymbol{\tau}$. Therefore, the matching γ is defined by $\gamma(l) = \boldsymbol{\tau}(\delta(l))$. Since δ is consistent, we get that γ is a matching of g in $\boldsymbol{\tau}$ (i.e., $\gamma \in \Gamma(g, \boldsymbol{\tau})$).

Assume, by way of contradiction, that there exists a matching γ' of g in $\boldsymbol{\tau}$ such that $\gamma' \neq \gamma$ and $\gamma' \succeq_{\boldsymbol{\tau}} \gamma$. (Recall from Lemma 5.3 that the top matching is unique.) This means that there exists a label $l \in$ nodes(g) such that $\gamma'(l) \succ_{\boldsymbol{\tau}} \gamma(l)$. We can assume that g is acyclic, since otherwise $\Gamma(g, \boldsymbol{\tau})$ is empty. Let $l \in$ nodes(g) be the smallest node in some topological order over g, for which $\gamma'(l) \succ_{\boldsymbol{\tau}} \gamma(l)$.

If $pa_g(l) = \emptyset$, then we immediately arrive at a contradiction of the second condition of the lemma. So, we assume that $pa_g(l) \neq \emptyset$. Since γ' is a matching, it holds that $\gamma'(l)$ appears after all items $\gamma'(l_p)$ where $l_p \in pa_g(l)$. Moreover, the fact that l was chosen to be first in some topological order over g implies that $\gamma'(l_p) = \gamma(l_p)$ for every node $l_p \in pa_g(l)$. Therefore, the label l and the item $\sigma = \gamma'(l)$ are in violation of the second condition of the lemma, proving the claim. □

A.5 Proof of Lemma 5.6

We denote by $\boldsymbol{\tau}_{-j}$ the ranking that results from removing item $\boldsymbol{\tau}[j]$ from the ranking $\boldsymbol{\tau}$. Specifically, $\boldsymbol{\tau}_{-j}[i] = \boldsymbol{\tau}[i]$ for all $i < j$, and $\boldsymbol{\tau}_{-j}[i] = \boldsymbol{\tau}[i+1]$ otherwise.

LEMMA 5.6. *The following hold for all iterations t of* TopProb.

1. *For all legal indices j returned by* Range *and $\boldsymbol{\tau} \in \widehat{\mathcal{P}}_{t-1}$ we have $\boldsymbol{\tau}_{+j} \in \widehat{\mathcal{P}}_t$.*
2. *For every $\boldsymbol{\tau} \in \widehat{\mathcal{P}}_t$ there exists a ranking $\boldsymbol{\tau}' \in \widehat{\mathcal{P}}_{t-1}$ and a legal index j returned by* Range *such that $\boldsymbol{\tau}'_{+j} = \boldsymbol{\tau}$.*

PROOF. We recall that $\widehat{\mathcal{P}}_t$ is the set of all rankings $\boldsymbol{\tau}$ over $\{\sigma_1, \ldots, \sigma_t\} \cup img(\gamma)$ such that for some $\delta \in \mathcal{R}_t$ the two conditions of Lemma 5.4 are satisfied.

We first prove the claim for the case where $\sigma_t \in img(\gamma)$. In this case, the rankings of both $\widehat{\mathcal{P}}_{t-1}$ and $\widehat{\mathcal{P}}_t$ are defined over the items in $\{\sigma_1, \ldots, \sigma_t\} \cup img_{>t}(\gamma)$. For this reason we also have that $\mathcal{R}_{t-1} = \mathcal{R}_t$. Hence, we get that $\widehat{\mathcal{P}}_{t-1} = \widehat{\mathcal{P}}_t$, proving both claims. In the remainder of the proof we assume that $\sigma_t \notin img(\gamma)$.

We first prove Part 1. Assume that $\boldsymbol{\tau} \in \widehat{\mathcal{P}}_{t-1}$, and let $\delta \in \mathcal{R}_{t-1}$ be the mapping realized by $\boldsymbol{\tau}$. Then for every legal index j returned by Range, $\boldsymbol{\tau}_{+j}$ realizes the mapping δ_{+j}, which is consistent because δ is consistent. Therefore, $\delta_{+j} \in \mathcal{R}_t$. Furthermore, according to Range, the position j is guaranteed to ensure the second condition of Lemma 5.4 with respect to the mapping δ_{+j}. Therefore, by definition of $\widehat{\mathcal{P}}_t$ we get that $\boldsymbol{\tau}_{+j} \in \widehat{\mathcal{P}}_t$.

We now prove Part 2. Assume that $\boldsymbol{\tau} \in \widehat{\mathcal{P}}_t$, and let $\delta \in \mathcal{R}_t$ such that $\boldsymbol{\tau}$ realizes δ. Therefore, every item in $\boldsymbol{\tau}$ is in a legal position with respect to δ. In particular, σ_t is in a legal position j of $\boldsymbol{\tau}$ (i.e., $\tau_j = \sigma_t$). We consider the ranking $\boldsymbol{\tau}_{-j}$. Since $\boldsymbol{\tau} \in \widehat{\mathcal{P}}_t$ realizes $\delta \in \mathcal{R}_t$, then $\boldsymbol{\tau}_{-j}$ realizes the mapping δ_{-j}, which is consistent because δ is consistent, thus $\delta_{-j} \in \mathcal{R}_{t-1}$. Since $\boldsymbol{\tau}$ and $\delta \in \mathcal{R}_t$ meet the conditions of Lemma 5.4, then $\boldsymbol{\tau}_{-j}$ and $\delta_{-j} \in \mathcal{R}_{t-1}$ do so as well, because the $-j$ operator cannot cause a violation of the lemma's second condition. From that, we get that $\boldsymbol{\tau}_{-j} \in \widehat{\mathcal{P}}_{t-1}$. □

A.6 Proof of Lemma 5.7

LEMMA 5.7. *In the execution of* TopProb *we have $q_i(\delta) = \widehat{p}_i(\delta)$ for all $i \in \{1, \ldots, m\}$ and $\delta \in \mathcal{R}_i$.*

PROOF. The proof of the lemma follows an inductive argument on the index i. As the basis of the induction, consider any consistent mapping $\delta \in \mathcal{R}_1$. The probability calculated by the algorithm (line 8) is

$$q_1(\delta) = q_0(\delta_0) \times \Upsilon(1, j, \delta) = 1$$

for any $j \in \{1, \ldots, |img(\gamma)| + 1\}$. This is because $q_0(\delta_0) = 1$ by definition, and $\Upsilon(1, j, \delta) = \Pi(1, 1) = 1$ for any $j \in \{1, \ldots, |img(\gamma)|+1\}$ (see (8)). We now show that $\widehat{p}_1(\delta) = 1$, proving the basis. Let $\boldsymbol{\tau} \in \widehat{\mathcal{P}}_1$. Since $\boldsymbol{\tau}_{|1} = \langle\sigma_1\rangle$, we get, by (6), that $\widehat{p}_1(\delta) = \Pi^1_{\boldsymbol{\sigma}}(\boldsymbol{\tau}_{|1}) = 1$. This proves that $q_1(\delta) = \widehat{p}_1(\delta)$ as required.

We now assume correctness for $i - 1$, and prove that $q_i(\delta) = \widehat{p}_i(\delta)$. Assume that $\sigma_i \in img(\gamma)$. In this case, let $l \in \text{nodes}(g)$ be such that $\sigma_i = \gamma(l)$. Therefore, σ_i is inserted into position $\delta(l)$ (line 2 of Range), and the resulting realization $\delta' \in \mathcal{R}_i$ is identical to $\delta \in \mathcal{R}_{i-1}$ (line 5 of TopProb). Therefore,

$$q_i(\delta) = q_{i-1}(\delta) \times \Upsilon(i, \delta(l), \delta)\,.$$

By the induction hypothesis $q_{i-1}(\delta) = \widehat{p}_{i-1}(\delta)$, and combined with (6), we get that

$$\begin{aligned} q_i(\delta) &= \widehat{p}_{i-1}(\delta) \times \Upsilon(i, \delta(l), \delta) \\ &= \sum_{\substack{\boldsymbol{\tau}\in\widehat{\mathcal{P}}_{i-1},\\ \boldsymbol{\tau} \text{ realizes } \delta}} \Pi^{i-1}_{\boldsymbol{\sigma}}(\boldsymbol{\tau}_{|i-1}) \times \Upsilon(i, \delta(l), \delta)\,. \end{aligned} \tag{13}$$

Now, consider any ranking $\boldsymbol{\tau}_{|i-1}$, where $\boldsymbol{\tau} \in \widehat{\mathcal{P}}_{i-1}$. Since $\sigma_i \in img(\gamma)$ is positioned at index $\delta(l)$ of $\boldsymbol{\tau}$, the ranking that results from inserting item σ_i into position $\delta(l)$ in the ranking $\boldsymbol{\tau}_{|i-1}$ is exactly $\boldsymbol{\tau}_{|i}$. Therefore,

$$\Pi^i_{\boldsymbol{\sigma}}(\boldsymbol{\tau}_{|i}) = \Pi^{i-1}_{\boldsymbol{\sigma}}(\boldsymbol{\sigma}, \boldsymbol{\tau}_{|i-1}) \times \Upsilon(i, \delta(l), \delta)\,. \tag{14}$$

Furthermore, since $\sigma_i \in img(\gamma)$, $\widehat{\mathcal{P}}_{i-1}$ and $\widehat{\mathcal{P}}_i$ are defined over the same set of items $\{\sigma_1, \ldots, \sigma_i\} \cup img_{>i}(\gamma)$, and for the same reason $\mathcal{R}_{i-1} = \mathcal{R}_i$. Therefore, $\widehat{\mathcal{P}}_{i-1} = \widehat{\mathcal{P}}_i$, and in particular,

$$\{\boldsymbol{\tau} \in \widehat{\mathcal{P}}_{i-1} \mid \boldsymbol{\tau} \text{ realizes } \delta\} = \{\boldsymbol{\tau} \in \widehat{\mathcal{P}}_i \mid \boldsymbol{\tau} \text{ realizes } \delta'\}\,. \tag{15}$$

Substituting (14) and (15) into (13) proves the inductive step.

For the second case we assume that $\sigma_i \notin img(\gamma)$. Note that in this case, for every ranking $\boldsymbol{\tau} \in \widehat{\mathcal{P}}_{i-1}$ we have that $\boldsymbol{\tau}_{|i-1}$ is identical to $\boldsymbol{\tau}_{|i}$. We denote by $I(i, \delta)$ the set of legal indexes returned by the procedure Range$(\delta, g, \gamma, \sigma_i)$. Finally, for brevity, we denote by $\widehat{\mathcal{P}}_t(\delta)$ to be the set of rankings in $\widehat{\mathcal{P}}_t$ that realize δ. We start by expressing the probability $q_i(\delta)$ computed by TopProb.

$$q_i(\delta) = \sum_{\delta'\in\mathcal{R}_{i-1}} q_{i-1}(\delta') \sum_{\substack{j\in I(i,\delta),\\ \delta'_{+j}=\delta}} \Upsilon(i, j, \delta) \tag{16}$$

By the induction hypothesis we have that $q_{i-1}(\delta') = \widehat{p}_{i-1}(\delta')$, and therefore,

$$q_i(\delta) = \sum_{\delta'\in\mathcal{R}_{i-1}} \widehat{p}_{i-1}(\delta') \sum_{\substack{j\in I(i,\delta),\\ \delta'_{+j}=\delta}} \Upsilon(i, j, \delta)\,. \tag{17}$$

We substitute the exact definition of $\widehat{p}_{i-1}(\delta')$ by (6) and get the following.

$$q_i(\delta) = \sum_{\delta'\in\mathcal{R}_{i-1}} \sum_{\boldsymbol{\tau}\in\widehat{\mathcal{P}}_{i-1}(\delta')} \Pi^{i-1}_{\boldsymbol{\sigma}}(\boldsymbol{\tau}_{|i-1}) \sum_{\substack{j\in I(i,\delta),\\ \delta'_{+j}=\delta}} \Upsilon(i, j, \delta) \tag{18}$$

As we remarked, since $\sigma_t \notin img(\gamma)$, then $\boldsymbol{\tau}_{|i-1} = \boldsymbol{\tau}_{|i}$. Therefore, we can write:

$$q_i(\delta) = \sum_{\delta'\in\mathcal{R}_{i-1}} \sum_{\boldsymbol{\tau}\in\widehat{\mathcal{P}}_{i-1}(\delta')} \sum_{\substack{j\in I(i,\delta),\\ \delta'_{+j}=\delta}} \Pi^{i-1}_{\boldsymbol{\sigma}}(\boldsymbol{\tau}_{|i}) \cdot \Upsilon(i, j, \delta) \tag{19}$$

According to (8), $\Upsilon(i, j, \delta) = \Pi(i, j')$, where j' is the modified index that considers only the items $\{\sigma_1, \ldots, \sigma_{i-1}\}$. That is, j' is the index that corresponds to j for the ranking $\boldsymbol{\tau}_{|i}$. By the definition of $\boldsymbol{\tau}_{+j}$, we have that

$$\Pi^{i-1}_{\boldsymbol{\sigma}}(\boldsymbol{\tau}_{|i}) \cdot \Upsilon(i, j, \delta) = \Pi^i_{\boldsymbol{\sigma}}((\boldsymbol{\tau}_{|i})_{+j})\,.$$

By substituting and reversing the summation order we get that

$$q_i(\delta) = \sum_{\delta'\in\mathcal{R}_{i-1}} \sum_{\substack{j\in I(i,\delta),\\ \delta'_{+j}=\delta}} \sum_{\boldsymbol{\tau}\in\widehat{\mathcal{P}}_{i-1}(\delta')} \Pi^i_{\boldsymbol{\sigma}}((\boldsymbol{\tau}_{|i})_{+j})\,. \tag{20}$$

So now, we only need to show that the set of rankings aggregated in (20) is precisely $\widehat{\mathcal{P}}_i(\delta)$. We denote this set of rankings by $\widehat{\mathcal{Q}}_i(\delta)$ and express it as follows.

$$\widehat{\mathcal{Q}}_i(\delta) = \{\boldsymbol{\tau} \mid \boldsymbol{\tau} \text{ realizes } \delta \text{ and } \exists j \in I(i, \delta) \text{ s.t. } \boldsymbol{\tau}_{-j} \in \mathcal{P}_{i-1}\}$$

From Lemma 5.6 we conclude that $\widehat{\mathcal{Q}}_i(\delta) = \widehat{\mathcal{P}}_i(\delta)$, as required. □

Benchmarking the Chase

Michael Benedikt [1] George Konstantinidis [1] Giansalvatore Mecca [2]
Boris Motik [1] Paolo Papotti [3] Donatello Santoro [2]
Efthymia Tsamoura [1]

[1] University of Oxford
Oxford, UK

[2] University of Basilicata
Potenza, Italy

[3] Arizona State University
Phoenix, AZ, USA

ABSTRACT

The chase is a family of algorithms used in a number of data management tasks, such as data exchange, answering queries under dependencies, query reformulation with constraints, and data cleaning. It is well established as a theoretical tool for understanding these tasks, and in addition a number of prototype systems have been developed. While individual chase-based systems and particular optimizations of the chase have been experimentally evaluated in the past, we provide the first comprehensive and publicly available benchmark—test infrastructure and a set of test scenarios—for evaluating chase implementations across a wide range of assumptions about the dependencies and the data. We used our benchmark to compare chase-based systems on data exchange and query answering tasks with one another, as well as with systems that can solve similar tasks developed in closely related communities. Our evaluation provided us with a number of new insights concerning the factors that impact the performance of chase implementations.

1. INTRODUCTION

The chase [25] is a long-standing technique developed by the database community for reasoning with constraints, also known as *dependencies*, expressed as universal implications possibly containing existential quantification in the conclusion. When applied to a set of dependencies and a set of facts, the chase extends the facts in a forward-chaining manner to satisfy the dependencies.

The chase has been intensively studied as a theoretical tool, but over the last decade practical aspects, such as developing optimizations of the chase algorithms and building chase-based systems for various tasks, have also been considered. Although algorithms for chasing source-to-target dependencies have shown promise in practice, with target dependencies scalability has been achieved only in quite restricted cases. The performance of chase implementations on large sets of complex dependencies and large datasets remains unknown. This suggests that it is time to evaluate the extent to which computing the chase is practically feasible.

The chase is closely related to and can be seen as a special case of theorem proving calculi such as tableaux and resolution, and it can also be seen as a generalization of standard query evaluation in databases. But while the theorem proving and the database communities have a long history of creating benchmarks and detailed evaluation methodologies (e.g., SMTLib [37] and TPTP [40] in the former, the TPC family [39] in the latter), there is little corresponding infrastructure to support experimental validation of techniques such as the chase that combine reasoning and data management.

This paper aims to take a major step in changing this situation. We present a new benchmark for chase systems covering a wide range of scenarios. Since the systems in the literature support different kinds of dependencies, we have developed dependency sets with different structural properties, and datasets of varying sizes.

We also define example tasks for two main applications of the chase: (i) data exchange, which involves materializing an instance of a target schema satisfying a given set of dependencies with respect to an instance of a source schema; and (ii) computing certain answers to conjunctive queries over databases with dependencies.

We then analyze a variety of publicly available systems on our benchmark in order to answer the following questions:

- How do existing chase-related systems fare in absolute terms on these tasks? That is, to what extent can they be considered as proof that the chase-based approaches to solving these tasks are practically feasible?
- What algorithmic and architectural choices are most critical for the performance of chase-related systems?
- Are there other approaches or other kinds of systems that can perform these same tasks and, if so, how do they compare to tools that use the chase?

In an attempt to answer these questions, we considered a number of systems that implement the chase as a component, including systems motivated from data exchange, data cleaning, query reformulation, and query answering.

We mentioned above that many communities have looked at techniques similar to the chase, and at problems similar to data exchange and query answering. To better understand the connection with the related communities, we also applied our benchmark to systems that are not specifically "branded" as chase systems, but that can nonetheless perform some of the tasks that the chase addresses. In particular, we looked at Datalog engines that support function symbols as they can solve both data exchange and query answering problems, as well as a leading theorem prover that can solve various query answering problems.

Organization. In the rest of this paper, we first present some background about the chase (Sections 2 and 3). Next, we describe our test systems (Section 4), and discuss our testing infrastructure and test scenarios (Section 5). Then, we present the system comparison results (Section 6), followed by a discussion of the insights gained (Section 7) and the future challenges that emerged from our study (Section 8). Finally, we close with a discussion of the re-

PODS'17, May 14-19, 2017, Chicago, Illinois, USA

 ISBN 978-1-4503-4198-1/17/05...$15.00
DOI: http://dx.doi.org/10.1145/3034786.3034796

lated work and conclusions (Sections 9 and 10). We emphasize that *full details regarding the systems under test, our test infrastructure, and our scenarios are available on the benchmark Web page* (http://dbunibas.github.io/chasebench).

2. BACKGROUND

Database basics. Let Const, Nulls, and Vars be mutually disjoint, infinite sets of *constant values*, *labeled nulls*, and *variables*, respectively. Intuitively, constant values are unique; labeled nulls represent unknown values; and variables are used in dependencies and queries. A *value* is a constant value or a labeled null, and a *term* is a value or a variable. We often abbreviate an n-tuple of terms $t_1, \ldots, t_n$ as $\vec{t}$, and we often treat it as a set and write $t_i \in \vec{t}$.

A *schema* is a set of *relation names* (or just *relations*), each associated with a nonnegative integer called *arity*. An *instance* I of a schema assigns to each n-ary relation R in the schema a (possibly infinite) set $I(R)$ of n-tuples of values. The *active domain* of I is the set of all values occurring in a tuple of some $I(R)$. A *relational atom* has the form $R(\vec{t})$ where R is an n-ary relation and $\vec{t}$ is an n-tuple of terms. An *equality atom* has the form $t_1 = t_2$ where t_1 and t_2 are terms. A *fact* is an atom that does not contain variables. An instance can equivalently be seen as a set of relational facts, so we use notation $R(\vec{t}) \in I$ and $\vec{t} \in I(R)$ interchangeably. An atom (resp. an instance) is *null-free* if it does not contain null values.

Term mappings. A *term mapping* σ is a partial mapping of terms to terms; we write $\sigma = \{t_1 \mapsto s_1, \ldots, t_n \mapsto s_n\}$ to denote that $\sigma(t_i) = s_i$ for $1 \le i \le n$. For α a term, an atom, a conjunction of atoms, or a set of atoms, $\sigma(\alpha)$ is obtained by replacing each occurrence of a term t in α that also occurs in the domain of σ with $\sigma(t)$ (i.e., terms outside the domain of σ remain unchanged). The *composition* of σ with a term mapping μ is the term mapping $\sigma \circ \mu$ whose domain is the union of the domains of σ and μ, and it is defined by $(\sigma \circ \mu)(t) = \sigma(\mu(t))$. A *substitution* σ is a term mapping whose domain contains only variables and whose range contains only values; moreover, σ is *null-free* if its range contains only constants; finally, σ is a *homomorphism* of a conjunction of atoms $\rho = \bigwedge_i A_i$ into an instance I if the domain of σ is the set of all variables occurring in ρ and $\sigma(\rho) \subseteq I$.

Dependencies and solutions. Semantic relationships between relations can be described using *dependencies*, which come in two forms. A *Tuple Generating Dependency* (TGD) is a logical sentence of the form (1), where $\lambda(\vec{x})$ and $\rho(\vec{x}, \vec{y})$ are conjunctions of relational, null-free atoms whose free variables are contained in $\vec{x}$, and $\vec{x} \cup \vec{y}$ correspondingly.

$$\forall \vec{x}\, \lambda(\vec{x}) \to \exists \vec{y}\, \rho(\vec{x}, \vec{y}) \tag{1}$$

An *Equality Generating Dependency* (EGD) is a logical sentence of the form (2), where $\lambda(\vec{x})$ is a conjunction of relational, null-free atoms over variables $\vec{x}$, and $\{x_i, x_j\} \subseteq \vec{x}$.

$$\forall \vec{x}\, \lambda(\vec{x}) \to x_i = x_j \tag{2}$$

The left-hand side of a TGD or an EGD (i.e., the conjunction $\lambda(\vec{x})$) is the *body* of the dependency, and the right-hand side is the *head*. A dependency is *linear* if it has exactly one atom in the body. By a slight abuse of notation, we often treat heads and bodies as sets of atoms, and we commonly omit the leading universal quantifiers.

Let I be an instance and let τ be a TGD of the form (1) or an EGD of the form (2). The notion of dependency τ *holding* in I (or I *satisfying* τ, written $I \models \tau$) is given by first-order logic, and it can be restated using homomorphisms as follows. A *trigger* for τ in I is a homomorphism h of $\lambda(\vec{x})$ into I. Moreover, an *active trigger* for τ in I is a trigger h for τ in I such that, if τ is a TGD, then no extension of h to a homomorphism of $\rho(\vec{x}, \vec{y})$ into I exists, and if τ is an EGD, then $h(x_i) \neq h(x_j)$. Finally, dependency τ is satisfied in I if there does not exist an active trigger for τ in I.

Let Σ be a set of dependencies and let I be a finite, null-free instance. Instance J is a *solution* for Σ and I if $I \subseteq J$ and $J \models \tau$ for each $\tau \in \Sigma$. A solution J for Σ and I is *universal* if, for each solution J' for Σ and I, a term mapping μ from the active domain of J to the active domain of J' exists such that $\mu(J) \subseteq J'$ and $\mu(c) = c$ holds for each constant value $c \in$ Const. Solutions for Σ and I are not unique, but universal solutions are unique up to homomorphism.

Queries. A *conjunctive query* (CQ) is a formula of the form $\exists \vec{y} \bigwedge_i A_i$, where A_i are relational, null-free atoms. A substitution σ is an *answer* to Q on instance I if the domain of σ is precisely the free variables of Q, and if σ can be extended to a homomorphism of $\bigwedge_i A_i$ in I. By choosing a canonical ordering for the free variables $\vec{x}$ of Q, we often identify σ with an n-tuple $\sigma(x_1), \ldots, \sigma(x_n)$. The *output* of Q on I is the set $Q(I)$ of all answers to Q on I.

Answering queries under dependencies. Let Σ be a set of dependencies, let I be a finite, null-free instance, and let Q be a CQ. A substitution σ is a *certain answer* to Q on Σ and I if σ is an answer to Q on each solution J for Σ and I. The task of finding all certain answers to Q on Σ and I is called *query answering under dependencies*, and we often abbreviate it to just *query answering*. The following fundamental result connects universal solutions and query answering: *for each substitution σ and each universal solution J for Σ and I, substitution σ is a certain answer to Q on Σ and I if and only if σ is a null-free answer to Q on J* [15].

The chase. The chase modifies an instance by a sequence of *chase steps* until all dependencies are satisfied. Let I be an instance, let τ be a TGD or an EGD of the form (1) or (2), and let h be a trigger for τ in I. If τ is a TGD, applying the chase step for τ and h to I extends I with facts of the conjunction $h'(\rho(\vec{x}, \vec{y}))$, where h' is a substitution such that $h'(x_i) = h(x_i)$ for each variable $x_i \in \vec{x}$, and $h'(y_j)$, for each $y_j \in \vec{y}$, is a fresh labeled null that does not occur in I. Moreover, if τ is an EGD, applying the chase step for τ and h to I *fails* if $h(x_i) \neq h(x_j)$ and $\{h(x_i), h(x_j)\} \subseteq$ Const, and otherwise it computes $\mu(I)$ where $\mu = \{h(x_j) \mapsto h(x_i)\}$ if $h(x_i) \in$ Const, and $\mu = \{h(x_i) \mapsto h(x_j)\}$ if $h(x_i) \notin$ Const.

For Σ a set of TGDs and EGDs and I a finite, null-free instance, a *chase sequence* for Σ and I is a (possibly infinite) sequence $I_0, I_1, \ldots$ such that $I = I_0$ and, for each $i > 0$, instance I_i (if it exists) is obtained from I_{i-1} by applying a successful chase step to a dependency $\tau \in \Sigma$ and an active trigger h for τ in I_{i-1}. The sequence must be *fair*: for each $\tau \in \Sigma$, each $i \ge 0$, and each active trigger h for τ in I_i, some $j > i$ must exist such that h is not an active trigger for τ in I_j (i.e., no chase step should be postponed indefinitely). The *result* of a chase sequence is the (possibly infinite) instance $I_\infty = \bigcup_{i \ge 0} \bigcap_{j \ge i} I_j$. Since EGD chase steps can fail, a chase sequence for a given Σ and I may not exist. Moreover, chase steps can be applied in an arbitrary order so a chase sequence for Σ and I is not unique. Finally, EGD steps are not monotonic (i.e., $I_{i-1} \not\subseteq I_i$ holds when I_i is obtained by applying an EGD step to I_{i-1}), and so I_∞ is not uniquely determined by Σ and I. Still, each result I_∞ of a chase sequence for Σ and I is a universal solution for Σ and I [15].

A finite chase sequence is *terminating*. A set of dependencies Σ *has terminating chase* if, for each finite, null-free instance I, each chase sequence for Σ and I is terminating. For such Σ, the chase provides an effective approach to computing certain answers to a CQ Q on Σ and I: we compute (any) chase I_∞ of Σ and I, we compute the output $Q(I_\infty)$, and finally remove all substitutions that are not null-free. Checking if a set of dependencies Σ has terminating chase is undecidable [13]. *Weak acyclicity* [15] was the first suffi-

Algorithm 1 RESTRICTED-CHASE(Σ, I)

1: $\Delta I := I$
2: **while** $\Delta I \neq \emptyset$ **do**
3: $\quad N := \emptyset, \quad \mu := \emptyset$
4: $\quad$**for each** $\tau \in \Sigma$ with body $\lambda(\vec{x})$ **do**
5: $\quad\quad$**for each** trigger h for τ in I such that $h(\lambda(\vec{x})) \cap \Delta I \neq \emptyset$ **do**
6: $\quad\quad\quad$**if** h is an active trigger for τ in $\mu(N \cup I)$ **then**
7: $\quad\quad\quad\quad$**if** $\tau = \forall \vec{x}\, \lambda(\vec{x}) \rightarrow \exists \vec{y}\, \rho(\vec{x}, \vec{y})$ is a TGD **then**
8: $\quad\quad\quad\quad\quad h' := h \cup \{\vec{y} \mapsto \vec{v}\}$ where $\vec{v} \subseteq$ Nulls is fresh
9: $\quad\quad\quad\quad\quad N := N \cup h'(\rho(\vec{x}, \vec{y}))$
10: $\quad\quad\quad\quad$**else if** $\tau = \forall \vec{x}\, \lambda(\vec{x}) \rightarrow x_i = x_j$ is an EGD **then**
11: $\quad\quad\quad\quad\quad$**if** $\{h(x_i) \neq h(x_j)\} \subseteq$ Const **then fail**
12: $\quad\quad\quad\quad\quad \omega := \{\max(h(x_i), h(x_j)) \mapsto \min(h(x_i), h(x_j))\}$
13: $\quad\quad\quad\quad\quad \mu := \mu \circ (\omega \circ \mu)$
14: $\quad \Delta I := \mu(N \cup I) \setminus I$
15: $\quad I := \mu(I) \cup \Delta I$

cient polynomial-time condition for checking if Σ has terminating chase. Stronger sufficient (not necessarily polynomial-time) conditions have been proposed subsequently [20, 32].

Data exchange. In relational-to-relational *data exchange* [15], a transformation of an arbitrary instance of a *source schema* into an instance of a *target schema* is described using

- a set Σ_{st} of *s-t* (source-to-target) TGDs where all body atoms use relations of the source schema and all head atoms use relations of the target schema, and
- a set Σ_t of *target dependencies* (i.e., TGDs or EGDs) whose atoms use relations of the target schema.

Given a finite, null-free instance I of the source schema, the objective of data exchange is to compute a universal solution to the set of dependencies $\Sigma = \Sigma_{st} \cup \Sigma_t$ and I. If Σ has terminating chase, then a universal solution can be computed using the chase, and it can be used to answer queries [15].

3. IMPLEMENTING THE CHASE

In this section we discuss the main challenges that chase implementations must address. Our discussion is largely independent of the specific technology, but we discuss briefly how these issues impact RDBMS-based implementations.

General structure. Computing the chase is naturally expressed as a fixpoint computation. Algorithm 1 achieves this by following the definition of a chase sequence from Section 2: in each iteration (lines 2–15), the algorithm examines each dependency τ (line 4) and trigger h (line 5), checks whether h is active (line 6), and, if so, applies the chase step (lines 8–9 for TGDs and lines 11–13 for EGDs). Although chase implementations may and do depart from the specifics of Algorithm 1, the algorithm is useful because it allows us to discuss the following issues, which each implementation must address in one form or another.

- To avoid an important source of inefficiency, we must ensure that each relevant trigger for τ and I is considered in line 5 at most once.
- Applying chase steps should not interfere with the enumeration of triggers.
- The EGD chase steps are complex and require care.
- Checking whether a trigger is active can be expensive.

Identifying triggers. Let τ be a TGD or an EGD of the form (1) or (2), respectively, and let I be a finite instance. Clearly, substitution h is a trigger for τ and I if and only if h is an answer to $\lambda(\vec{x})$ on I. Hence, the triggers for τ can be determined in line 5 by evaluating $\lambda(\vec{x})$ as a CQ over I. The latter can be solved using any known join algorithm, and an RDBMS-based implementation can translate $\lambda(\vec{x})$ into SQL in a straightforward manner. However, evaluating $\lambda(\vec{x})$ in each iteration "from scratch" would be very inefficient since it would repeatedly consider triggers from all previous iterations. Algorithm 1 thus uses *seminaïve* evaluation [1]. It maintains an auxiliary set ΔI of "newly derived facts" from the most recent iteration, and it requires at least one atom of $h(\lambda)$ in line 5 to be contained in ΔI. As a consequence, each combination of τ and h is considered at most once during algorithm's execution.

Applying chase steps. An important consideration is how query $\lambda(x)$ is evaluated over I in line 5: we must ensure that we do not miss any applicable triggers, and that we retrieve each such trigger once. One possibility is to compute and store the result in a temporary relation, but this can impose a significant overhead. It is therefore often preferable to evaluate $\lambda(x)$ over I in a "streaming" mode, where a trigger h is returned as soon as it is computed; but then, set I should not change in lines 4–13 or the modifications to I could affect the enumeration of triggers in line 5. To ensure this, the chase steps in Algorithm 1 do not modify I directly. Instead, all changes are accumulated in an auxiliary set N and a term mapping μ; after each iteration, ΔI contains the "newly derived subset" of N (line 14), which is propagated to I (line 15). The algorithm terminates when ΔI becomes empty in line 2 since another iteration then cannot derive new facts.

Handling EGDs. Applying a chase step to an EGD τ of the form (2) and trigger h poses several problems. A minor issue is that, when $h(x_i)$ and $h(x_j)$ are both labeled nulls, we can replace either value with the other. To make this choice deterministic, one can totally order all values so that all constant values are smaller than all labeled nulls, and then always replace the larger value with the smaller one (line 12). Constant values are thus never replaced with labeled nulls, and this also ensures uniqueness of the chase for a specific chase variant that we discuss shortly.

A more complex issue is to ensure that I does not change in lines 5–13. To achieve this, Algorithm 1 uses a term mapping μ that accumulates all the required changes to I (line 13): at the end of each iteration, $\mu(v)$ is defined for each labeled null v that is to be replaced with $\mu(v)$. The expression in line 13 ensures that μ is correctly updated when several EGD steps are applied in single iteration. For example, consider $\mu = \{v_1 \mapsto v_2, v_3 \mapsto v_4\}$ and $\omega = \{v_2 \mapsto v_3\}$; then, $\omega \circ \mu = \{v_1 \mapsto v_3, v_2 \mapsto v_3, v_3 \mapsto v_4\}$ "normalizes" μ with ω, and $\mu \circ (\omega \circ \mu) = \{v_1 \mapsto v_4, v_2 \mapsto v_4, v_3 \mapsto v_4\}$ reflects the cumulative effects of all EGDs.

At the end of each iteration (lines 14–15), the facts in both I and N may require updating, and all facts newly derived in the iteration most be added to ΔI to correctly further trigger dependencies.

Checking active triggers. Assume that h is a trigger for a dependency τ in an instance I, and consider checking whether h is an active trigger for τ in $\mu(N \cup I)$ in line 6. It should be clear that h is a trigger for τ in $\mu(N \cup I)$ if and only if $\mu(h(x)) = h(x)$ for each variable x from the domain of h. In other words, we simply check whether "h up-to-date with μ." Thus, to complete the active trigger check, if τ is of the form (2), we check whether $h(x_i) \neq h(x_j)$ holds; and if τ is of the form (1), we check $\gamma(I) = \emptyset$ where $\gamma = \exists \vec{y}\, \rho(h(\vec{x}), \vec{y})$ is a boolean CQ. The latter can be implemented using standard query evaluation techniques, and RDBMS-based systems can simply extend the CQ from line 5 with a `NOT EXISTS (SELECT * WHERE ...)` condition. In the rest of this section and in Section 7 we discuss several theoretical and practical drawbacks of checking for active triggers and present alternatives.

Chase variants. The chase variant given in Algorithm 1 is called the *restricted chase* to stipulate that triggers are restricted only to the active ones (cf. line 6). A drawback of the restricted chase is that the chase solution is not unique (even up to isomorphism of labeled nulls), as Example 1 shows.

EXAMPLE 1. *Let* Σ *and* I *be as in* (3) *and* (4).

$$R(x_1,x_2) \to \exists y\, R(x_1,y) \land A(y) \land A(x_2) \tag{3}$$

$$I = \{\, R(a,b), R(b,b) \,\} \tag{4}$$

Dependencies in Σ *are weakly acyclic [15] so the restricted chase terminates on all finite instances, but the chase solution depends on the ordering of chase steps. Triggers* $h_1 = \{x_1 \mapsto a, x_2 \mapsto b\}$ *and* $h_2 = \{x_1 \mapsto b, x_2 \mapsto b\}$ *for* (3) *are both active in* I*. Applying the TGD step to* h_1 *makes* h_2 *inactive by deriving* $R(a,v_1)$, $A(v_1)$, *and* $A(b)$*. In contrast, applying the TGD step to* h_2 *makes* h_1 *inactive by deriving* $R(b,v_1)$, $A(v_1)$, *and* $A(b)$.

The chase can be optimized by *normalizing* TGDs prior to applying the chase: for each TGD $\tau \in \Sigma$ of the form (1) such that $\rho(\vec{x},\vec{y})$ can be rewritten as $\rho_1(\vec{x}_1,\vec{y}_1) \land \rho_2(\vec{x}_2,\vec{y}_2)$ so that $\vec{y}_1 \cap \vec{y}_2 = \emptyset$, we replace τ in Σ with $\forall \vec{x}\, \lambda(\vec{x}) \to \exists \vec{y}_i\, \rho_i(\vec{x}_i,\vec{y}_i)$ for $i \in \{1,2\}$. Example 2 shows how normalization can lead to smaller instances.

EXAMPLE 2. *Normalizing TGD* (3) *produces* (5) *and* (6)*. Now by applying* (6) *to* I *from Example 1 we derive* $A(b)$*, which makes triggers* h_1 *and* h_2 *for* (5) *both inactive.*

$$R(x_1,x_2) \to \exists y\, R(x_1,y) \land A(y) \tag{5}$$

$$R(x_1,x_2) \to A(x_2) \tag{6}$$

Checking whether trigger h is active (line 6) can be difficult in practice, particularly for a test against $\mu(N \cup I)$; we discuss these issues in detail in Section 7. Furthermore, the dependence on the ordering of chase steps can make the chase more difficult to analyze from a theoretical point of view. This motivates several variants in which the check in line 6 is either eliminated or weakened.

The *unrestricted* (or *oblivious*) *chase* simply eliminates line 6. Such a simple solution removes the overhead of checking active triggers and the dependence on the ordering of chase steps. But, as Example 3 shows, the unrestricted chase does not necessarily terminate even for weakly acyclic TGDs.

EXAMPLE 3. *For* Σ *and* I *defined as in Example 1, the unrestricted chase derives the following infinite set of facts.*

$$R(a,v_1),\ A(v_1),\ R(a,v_2),\ A(v_2),\ \dots$$

$$A(b), R(b,w_1), A(w_1), R(b,w_2), A(w_2), \dots$$

The *unrestricted Skolem chase* [26, 38, 28] also eliminates line 6, but it also skolemizes TGDs: in each TGD τ of the form (1), each existentially quantified variable $y \in \vec{y}$ is replaced with a function term $f(\vec{z})$ where f is a fresh function symbol and $\vec{z}$ contains all variables occurring in both the head and the body of τ. The chase then proceeds as in Algorithm 1, but without line 6 and by using the preprocessed τ in line 7. The result of the Skolem chase is unique (if the EGD steps are determinized as in line 8). Although cases exist where the restricted chase terminates but the Skolem chase does not, the known acyclicity conditions [20] ensure termination of both. Example 4 illustrates the Skolem chase.

EXAMPLE 4. *Normalizing and then skolemizing TGD* (3) *produces* (7) *and* (8).

$$R(x_1,x_2) \to R(x_1,f(x_1)) \land A(f(x_1)) \tag{7}$$

$$R(x_1,x_2) \to A(x_2) \tag{8}$$

Applying TGDs (7) *and* (8) *to the set of facts* I *from Example 1 produces facts* $R(a,f(a))$, $A(f(a))$, $A(b)$, $R(b,f(b))$, *and* $A(f(b))$, *after which the chase terminates: functional term* $f(x_1)$ *in* (7) *captures the fact that the fresh null depends only on* x_1*, and so applying* (7) *to* $R(a,f(a))$ *and* $R(b,f(b))$ *does not introduce more nulls as in Example 3. Normalization is very important since it eliminates variables within Skolem terms; for example, skolemizing* (3) *directly produces* (9)*, and applying* (9) *to* I does not *terminate.*

$$R(x_1,x_2) \to R(x_1,f(x_1,x_2)) \land A(f(x_1,x_2)) \land A(x_2) \tag{9}$$

Since functional terms provide canonical "names" for labeled nulls, a global counter of labeled nulls is not required, which may simplify implementation. For example, deriving the first atom of (7) can be implemented using the SQL query (10), which does not interact with other TGDs.

```
INSERT INTO R(a,b)
SELECT DISTINCT R.a, append('_Sk_f(',R.a,')') FROM R        (10)
```

The *parallel chase* [13] weakens line 6 so that it checks whether h is active in I, rather than in $\mu(N \cup I)$; since I is fixed in an iteration, this can make checking active triggers much easier to implement. Known acyclicity conditions [20] ensure termination of the parallel chase, and the solution is deterministic, although it may be larger than the one produced by the restricted chase. Example 5 illustrates the parallel chase.

EXAMPLE 5. *Let* Σ, I, h_1, *and* h_2 *be as in Example 1. Both* h_1 *and* h_2 *are active for* I*, so the parallel chase applies the TGD step to both triggers independently and derives* $R(a,v_1)$, $A(v_1)$, $A(b)$, $R(a,w_1)$, *and* $A(w_1)$*. No active triggers exist after this step so the parallel chase terminates.*

The *single-TGD-parallel* (or *1-parallel*) *chase* checks active triggers w.r.t. all facts derived thus far apart from the ones derived by the TGD τ currently considered in line 4. As with the parallel chase, implementing this variant can be much easier than for the restricted chase (see Section 7).

While the check in line 6 is not needed with skolemized TGDs, it can still be used, in which case we obtain the *restricted* (or *parallel* or *1-parallel*) *Skolem chase*: each of these two chase variants never produces more facts than the original variant, and in certain cases it can produce fewer facts.

The *frugal chase* [22] further considers triggers that are only partially active. Let τ be a TGD τ of the form (1) such that $\rho(\vec{x},\vec{y})$ can be rewritten as $\rho_1(\vec{x}_1,\vec{y}_1) \land \rho_2(\vec{x}_2,\vec{y}_2)$ where $\vec{x}_1$ and $\vec{x}_2$, and $\vec{y}_1$ and $\vec{y}_2$ are not necessarily disjoint, and let h be a trigger for τ in an instance I. Then, h is *partially active* for τ in I if h can be extended to a homomorphism h' such that (i) $\rho_1(h'(\vec{x}_1),h'(\vec{y}_1)) \subseteq I$, (ii) $h'(\vec{y}_1)$ contains only labeled nulls, and (iii) for each fact $P(\vec{w}) \in I$ such that $\vec{w} \cap h'(\vec{y}_1) \neq \emptyset$, we have $P(\vec{w}) \in \rho_1(h'(\vec{x}_1),h'(\vec{y}_1))$ (i.e., each atom in I that joins "existentially" with the image of ρ_1 is contained in the image of ρ_1). Since ρ_1 is already satisfied, the frugal chase satisfies the TGD τ by extending I with $\rho_2(h''(\vec{x}_2),h''(\vec{y}_2))$, where h'' is a homomorphism that extends (one such) h' by mapping the variables in $\vec{y}_2 \setminus \vec{y}_1$ to fresh labeled nulls.

EXAMPLE 6. *Let* Σ *contain the TGD* (5) *from Example 2 and TGD* (11)*, and let* I *be as in* (12).

$$B(x) \to \exists y\, R(x,y) \tag{11}$$

$$I = \{\, B(a) \,\} \tag{12}$$

Assume now that the frugal chase first applies (11) *and thus extends* I *with fact* $R(a,v_1)$*. Then,* $h = \{x_1 \mapsto a, x_2 \mapsto v_1\}$ *is a partially active trigger for TGD* (5)*: we can decompose the head of* (5) *such that* $\rho_1 = R(x_1,y)$ *and* $\rho_2 = A(y)$*, and we can extend* h *to*

$h' = \{x_1 \mapsto a, x_2 \mapsto v_1, y \mapsto v_1\}$ *such that* $h'(\rho_1)$ *is contained in the current instance, and* $h'(y) = v_1$ *does not occur in the instance outside of* $h'(\rho_1)$. *Hence, the frugal chase satisfies* (5) *by adding* $A(v_1)$ *to the instance, instead of introducing a fresh labelled null.*

The *core chase* [13] omits the active trigger check completely; however, after each iteration it replaces the current instance with its *core* [16]—the smallest subset of I that is homomorphically equivalent to I. The core chase produces a smallest finite solution whenever one exists, but efficient computation of the core on instances of nontrivial sizes is an open problem.

4. THE SYSTEMS TESTED

As we explained in Section 1, our objectives are to determine whether existing chase implementations can support data exchange and query answering on nontrivial inputs, and to identify the implementation decisions most relevant to performance. To answer these questions, we used nine publicly available systems shown in Table 1. We group the systems based on their primary motivation.

Systems motivated by data exchange. DEMO [34] was one of the first data exchange engines. It implements the restricted chase for s-t TGDs and target TGDs and EGDs; moreover, upon termination, it computes the core of the solution using the algorithm by Gottlob and Nash [19]. The system runs on top of PostgreSQL or HSQLDB, and we used the former in our experiments.

CHASEFUN [12] is a more recent data exchange system. It supports only s-t TGDs and functional dependencies, and it implements a variant of the unrestricted Skolem chase that orders TGD and EGD chase steps to reduce the size of the intermediate chase results. We used an implementation that runs on top of PostgreSQL.

Systems motivated by data cleaning. LLUNATIC [18] was initially developed for data cleaning, but has since been redesigned as an open-source data exchange system. It handles s-t TGDs and target TGDs and EGDs, and it can also compute certain query answers over the target instance. It implements the 1-parallel Skolem chase (the default), the unrestricted and restricted Skolem chase, and the restricted chase with fresh nulls (i.e., without Skolem terms). The system runs on top of PostgreSQL.

Systems motivated by query reformulation. Three of our test systems use the chase for query reformulation.

PEGASUS [29] is a system for finding minimal queries equivalent to a given query with respect to a set of TGDs and EGDs. It uses the Chase & Backchase method of Deutsch, Popa, and Tannen [14], which internally uses the restricted chase implemented in RAM.

PDQ [10, 11] takes a query, a set of integrity constraints, and a set of interface descriptions (e.g., views or access methods), and it produces an equivalent query that refers only to the interfaces and whose cost is minimal according to a preselected cost function. By extending the Chase & Backchase method, PDQ reduces query reformulation to checking query containment under TGDs and/or EGDs, and the latter problem is solved using an implementation of the restricted chase on top of PostgreSQL.

Systems motivated by query answering. GRAAL [7] is an open-source toolkit developed for computing certain answers to queries under dependencies. Although the system was not originally designed for chase computation, it uses a "saturation algorithm" that can be seen as variant of the standard chase. GRAAL can be used both in an RAM and on secondary storage, such an RDBMS, a triple store, or a graph database. We used the RAM-based version as we found it to be faster.

Chase-related systems. A prominent goal of our work was to investigate how chase implementations fare against systems from other communities that either (i) implement algorithms related to the chase, or (ii) can answer queries over dependencies using very different approaches. Many systems satisfy these requirements, so we decided to restrict our attention to several prominent representatives. In particular, we considered Datalog engines in the former, and a resolution-based theorem prover in the latter category.

DLV [24] is a mature disjunctive Datalog system supporting a range of features such nonmonotonic negation, aggregates, and user-defined functions. The system comes in several flavors: a RAM-based version that supports function symbols in the rules, another RAM-based version with native support for TGDs [23], and an RDBMS-based version that supports neither function symbols nor TGDs. The latter is not applicable to our setting, and we used the version with function symbols since it proved to be more stable. We implemented a preprocessing skolemization step, allowing DLV to support the unrestricted Skolem chase for TGDs; however, the system does not support EGDs [33]. The system can be used without a query, in which case it computes and outputs the chase solution. If a query is provided, the system evaluates the query over the chase and outputs the result. To obtain certain answers, we externally postprocess the query output to remove functional terms.

RDFOX [30] is a high-performance RAM-based Datalog engine. It was originally designed for Datalog with EGDs over the RDF data model and without the unique name assumption. To support the chase, RDFOX was extended as follows. First, a builtin function was added that produces a labeled null unique for the function's arguments, which emulates Skolem terms. Second, a builtin function was added that checks whether a CQ is not satisfied in the data, thus enabling both the restricted and the unrestricted chase variants. Third, a mode was implemented that handles EGDs under unique name assumption. Fourth, to support relations of arbitrary arity, a preprocessor was implemented that shreds n-tuples into RDF triples and rewrites all dependencies accordingly.

E [36] is a state of the art first-order theorem prover that has won numerous competitions. It takes as input a set of axioms $\mathscr{F}$ and a conjecture H, and it decides the unsatisfiability of $\bigwedge \mathscr{F} \wedge \neg H$. E implements the paramodulation with selection [31] calculus, of which the unrestricted Skolem chase is an instance: each inference of the Skolem chase is an inference of paramodulation (but not vice versa). Paramodulation requires $\mathscr{F}$ to be represented as a set of clauses—that is, first-order implications without existential quantifiers but possibly containing function symbols and the equality predicate. Thus, $\mathscr{F}$ can capture EGDs and the result of preprocessing TGDs as described in Section 3. Moreover, E can also be used in a mode where $\mathscr{F}$ contains arbitrary first-order formulas, thus capturing TGDs directly without any preprocessing; however, this approach proved less efficient, so we did not use it in our experiments. Finally, conjecture H can contain free variables, in which case E outputs each substitution σ that makes $\bigwedge \mathscr{F} \wedge \neg\sigma(H)$ unsatisfiable; thus, E is interesting as it can answer queries without computing the chase in full. Ordered paramodulation targets first-order logic, which is undecidable; hence, E is not guaranteed to terminate on all inputs, not even if $\mathscr{F}$ encodes dependencies on which the unrestricted Skolem chase terminates. The system's behavior can be configured using many parameters, and we used the values suggested by the system's author.

5. THE BENCHMARK

Our CHASEBENCH benchmark consists of two distinct parts. The first part is described in Section 5.1 and it comprises several tools that allow the generation and processing of test data in a common format. The second part is described in Section 5.2 and it comprises a number of *test scenarios*, each consisting of a (i) schema

System	s-t TGDs	t TGDs	EGDs	Cert. Ans.	Engine	Strategy	Sources
Explicit chase implementations							
ChaseFun	✓		FDs only		RDBMS	unrestricted skolem chase	
DEMo	✓	✓	✓		RDBMS	restricted chase + core computation	
Graal	✓	✓		✓	RAM	restricted chase	✓
Llunatic	✓	✓	✓	✓	RDBMS	restr./unrestr./1-parallel skolem/fresh-nulls chase	✓
PDQ	✓	✓	✓	✓	RDBMS	restricted chase	✓
Pegasus	✓	✓	✓		RAM	restricted chase	✓
Chase-related systems							
DLV	✓	✓		✓	RAM	unrestricted skolem chase	
E	✓	✓	✓	✓	RAM	paramodulation	✓
RDFox	✓	✓	✓	✓	RAM	restricted/unrestricted skolem chase	✓

Table 1: Summary of the tested systems

description, (ii) a source instance, (iii) sets of s-t TGDs, target TGDs, and/or target EGDs, and (iv) possibly a set of queries. We used existing resources whenever possible; for example, we repurposed scenarios produced by iBench [4], as well as instances of varying sizes produced by the instance-generation tool ToXGene [8]. We divide our scenarios into the following two groups.

Correctness scenarios were designed to verify that the systems correctly produce universal solutions. Checking homomorphisms between solutions is computationally challenging so these scenarios generate very small solutions. Moreover, these scenarios do not contain queries, as correctness of query answering can be verified by simply comparing the certain answers on larger scenarios.

Data exchange and query answering scenarios aim to test the performance of computing the target instance and of answering queries over the target instance in data exchange. These scenarios vary the data size and the complexity of the dependencies to simulate different workloads.

5.1 Test Infrastructure

1. The common format. In their "native" versions, the systems from Section 4 take a wide range of input formats. For example, RDBMS-based systems expect the source instance to be preloaded into a relational database, whereas RAM-based systems typically read their input from files. Moreover, the structure of the inputs varies considerably; for example, RDFox expects data to be represented as triples, and E expects data to be encoded as first-order sentences in the TPTP format. The translation between various input formats is often straightforward, but in certain cases (e.g., if schema shredding or the transformation of TGDs is required) it involves choices that can significantly affect a system's performance.

To allow for an automated and fair comparison of all systems regardless of their implementation details, we standardized the input structure for all systems. Theorem-proving formats such as TPTP can express first-order sentences and can thus represent dependencies and queries, but such formats are difficult to read for humans and so we found them inappropriate for ChaseBench. We thus developed our own "common format" for describing all parts of a scenario (i.e., the schema description, the source instance, the dependencies, and the queries). We also wrote a parser for the common format, which was used to develop wrappers for the systems. The wrapper was provided by the system designers whenever possible, but for E, DLV, and Pegasus we developed the wrappers ourselves. Our tests required each system to read the scenarios in the common format, so our test results cover all times necessary to parse and transform the inputs.

2. The instance repair tool. Generating scenarios with EGDs and large source instances is complex since, due to the size of the source instance, it is difficult to ensure that no EGD chase step fails. For example, ToXGene does not necessarily generate instances that are consistent with a collection of TGDs and EGDs, and in fact the chase failed on all instances initially produced by ToXGene so this problem is not merely hypothetical. Thus, we developed a simple instance repair tool. Given a set of dependencies Σ and an instance I on which the chase of Σ fails, the tool proceeds as follows. First, it computes the chase of Σ and I without the unique name assumption: when equating two distinct constant values, one value is selected as *representative* and the other one as *conflicting*, the latter is replaced with the former, and the chase continues. Second, the tool removes from I all facts containing a conflicting value encountered in the previous step. The chase of Σ and the subset of I produced in this way is guaranteed to succeed. This strategy proved very effective in practice: on average it removed slightly more than 1% of the facts from I, and so the size and the distribution of the source instance remain largely unaffected.

3. The target TGD generator. In addition to generating large source instances, generating scenarios with a significant number of s-t TGDs, target TGDs, and target EGDs was critical for adequately evaluating the performance of the tested systems. One of our goals was to push the systems to their limit by testing them on *deep chase scenarios* that generate very large instances using long chase sequences. To this end, we developed a custom target TGD generator that can generate weakly acyclic TGDs while controlling their depth and complexity. In our experiments we used the generator to develop scenarios from scratch, but the generator can also be used to increase the difficulty of existing scenarios.

Our generator is based on our earlier approach [22] for generating linear dependencies, which we extended to support an arbitrary number of body atoms. The generator creates a predicate name space of a certain required size, and it uniformly chooses a (parameterized) number of predicates to populate a conjunction of atoms (which can become a query or a dependency). A parameter is used to control the maximum number of repeated relations in this formula, and another parameter is used to determine the arity of the atoms. The generator can create "chain" conjunctions (the last variable of an atom is joined with the first one of the next atom), "star" conjunctions (the first variable of all atoms also occurs in a designated "center" atom that has a different arity than the other atoms), and "random" ones in which variables are chosen out of a variable name space and are distributed in a conjunction (the larger the variable name space, the fewer joins are introduced). Each dependency is generated by first creating a conjunction and then selecting the subset of atoms that make up the head. The size of the dependencies' bodies can be fixed; for example, this parameter was 1 in our Deep scenarios, thus producing linear TGDs. The generator maintains a weakly-acyclic dependency graph and tests each generated dependency against the ones there were created previous; if the newly created dependency violates weak acyclicity, it is discarded and a new dependency is produced.

4. The query generator. To evaluate the performance of computing certain answers, nontrivial queries over the target schema are required. Existing benchmarks such as LUBM [21] come with several manually curated queries, which we incorporated into our scenarios. To obtain queries for scenarios where the target schema is automatically generated, we developed a new query generator. The tool is given a desired number of joins in the output query N_J, the desired number of selections conditions in the output query N_S, the percentage of attributes that will be projected P, and a set of tables of the target schema. It first identifies a set of joinable attribute pairs from the tables of the source and target schema by analyzing the dependencies. Two attributes are considered joinable if they join either in the head or the body of the rule; moreover, if a variable is passed from the body to the head of the rule, then the attributes that map to these variables are considered joinable as well; and finally, the joinable attributes are transitively closed. Next, the algorithm iteratively creates N_J join conditions by choosing at random a table T and attribute a from the schema and then choosing a random table and attribute that is joinable with $T.a$. The algorithm then proceeds analogously to create N_S selections by first choosing an attribute that does not appear in a join condition and then a introducing randomly selected value from the attribute's domain. Finally, the algorithm randomly projects P attributes. By focusing on joinable attributes, the algorithm is more likely to produce a query with a nonempty output, but does not guarantee it; therefore, we discarded and regenerated each query that produced an empty output on the target instance as long as needed.

5. The homomorphism checker. Checking correctness of computing certain query answers is easy: certain answers are unique for the query so the systems' outputs can be compared syntactically. Checking correctness of the chase is more involved since the result of the restricted chase is not unique and, even with the unrestricted Skolem chase, it is unique only up to the renaming of Skolem functions. Hence, to verify the correctness of the systems, we developed a tool that can check the existence of homomorphisms, mutual homomorphisms, and isomorphisms between instances. The tool enumerates all candidate homomorphisms using brute force, so it can be used only on relatively small instances (i.e., few thousands facts). Consequently, we designed our correctness scenarios so that they produce small solutions.

5.2 Test Scenarios

Our benchmark consists of a total of 23 scenarios, each comprising a source and target schema, a source instance, a set of dependencies, and possibly a set of queries; all dependencies in all scenarios are weakly acyclic. We classify the scenarios into five families, as shown in Table 2. The first family contains six small scenarios for testing correctness of data exchange, whereas all other families are aimed at testing the performance of computing the target instance and the certain answers. The IBENCH and the LUBM families were derived from the well established benchmarks in the database and the Semantic Web communities, respectively. Finally, we developed the MANUALLY CURATED and the DEEP families ourselves to test specific aspects of the chase. We identify each scenario using a unique identifier; for DOCTORS and LUBM scenarios, the identifier is obtained by combining the scenario name with the source instance size, such as LUBM-90k. We discuss next the main features of our scenario families.

a. Correctness tests. As we explained in Section 5.1, our homomorphism checker can handle only small instances. We thus prepared six scenarios that produce small chase results, while aiming to cover exhaustively the different combinations of various features. All scenarios contain s-t TGDs and test different combinations such as joins over the source schema, vertical partitioning, and self-joins both in the source and in the target schemas. The scenarios cover standard examples from some of the prior papers and surveys on the chase (e.g., [32, 27]), including cases where TGDs and EGDs interact, where the chase fails, and where various acyclicity conditions are used to ensure chase termination.

b. Manually curated scenarios. Our scenarios from this family are based on the DOCTORS data integration task from the schema mapping literature [17]. These scenarios are relatively small in terms of the number of relations, attributes, and dependencies (cf. Table 2), but we believe that they represent a useful addition to the benchmark for two reasons. First, these scenarios are based on schemas inspired by real databases about medical data. Second, they simulate a common use case for data exchange: take two databases from the same domain but with different schemas and bring them to a unified target representation. We used TOXGENE to generate instances of the source schema of 10 k, 100 k, 500 k, and 1 M facts. DOCTORS contains EGDs that refer to more than one relation in the body, which cannot be handled by all systems in our evaluation. Hence, we also generated a simplified version, called DOCTORSFD, that contains only EGDs corresponding to functional dependencies. Consequently, the manually curated family contains eight scenarios. We also used the query generator described in Section 5.1 to generate nine queries covering most of the possible joins among the three target relations.

c. LUBM scenarios. LUBM [21] is a popular benchmark in the Semantic Web community. It does not simulate a data exchange task, but it is useful as it comes with nontrivial target TGDs and queries designed to test various aspects of query answering. Using the LUBM data generator we produced instances with 90 k, 1 M, 12 M, and 120 M facts and transformed them as follows.

- The LUBM generator produces data as RDF triples, which we converted into a source instance using vertical partitioning: a triple $\langle s,p,o\rangle$ is transformed into a unary fact $o_{src}(s)$ if $p = rdf{:}type$, and into a binary fact $p_{src}(s,o)$ otherwise.
- For each unary relation o_{src} from the previous step, we added the s-t TGD $\forall x\, o_{src}(x) \to o(x)$, and similarly for each binary relation. Thus, the s-t TGDs simply copy the source instance into the target instance.
- The dependencies in LUBM are encoded using an ontology, which we converted into target TGDs using vertical partitioning and the known correspondences between description logics and first-order logic [5].
- We manually converted all SPARQL queries into CQs; this was possible for all queries.

As a consequence of these transformations, the source and the target schemas of LUBM contain only unary and binary relations. Also, the source instance of LUBM-120M is much larger than any other source instance in our scenarios.

d. IBENCH scenarios. IBENCH [4] is a tool for generating dependencies whose properties can be finely controlled using a wide range of parameters. For our purpose, we selected two existing sets of dependencies [4, Section 5] that consist of second-order TGDs, primary keys, and foreign keys. To obtain dependencies compatible with most of our systems, we modified a parameter in the IBENCH scripts to generate ordinary s-t TGDs instead of second-order TGDs, thus obtaining two scenarios of the IBENCH family.

- STB-128, derived from an earlier ST-benchmark [3], is the smaller scenario of the family.
- ONT-256, a scenario motivated by ontologies, has several times larger source instance.

Scenario		Source Schema		Target Schema		s-t	t TGDs		EGDs		Qrs	Source Instance Facts
Family	Name	Rel	Attr	Rel	Attr	TGDs	Tot	Inc.Dep	Tot	FDs		
CORR.	EMPDEPT	1	3	2	5	1	2	2	0	0	0	1
CORR.	TGDS-A	1	3	5	12	2	5	5	0	0	0	1
CORR.	TGDS-B	2	8	3	9	5	2	1	0	0	0	8
CORR.	EGDS	1	2	1	2	1	0	0	1	1	0	3
CORR.	TGDSEGDS-A	1	3	5	12	3	5	5	4	4	0	4
CORR.	TGDSEGDS-B	1	3	5	12	6	5	5	4	4	0	80
MAN.C.	DOCTORSFD	3	24	5	17	5	0	0	8	8	9	10 k, 100 k, 500 k, 1 M
MAN.C.	DOCTORS	3	24	5	17	5	0	0	10	8	9	10 k, 100 k, 500 k, 1 M
LUBM	LUBM	30	76	74	179	30	106	91	0	0	14	90 k, 1 M, 12 M, 120 M
IBENCH	STB-128	111	535	176	832	128	39	39	193	193	20	150 k
IBENCH	ONT-256	218	1210	444	1952	256	273	273	921	921	20	1 M
DEEP	DEEP100	1000	5000	299	1495	1000	100	50	0	0	20	1 k
DEEP	DEEP200	1000	5000	299	1495	1000	200	100	0	0	20	1 k
DEEP	DEEP300	1000	5000	299	1495	1000	300	150	0	0	20	1 k

Table 2: Summary of the test scenarios

For both of these scenarios, we used the integration of IBENCH and TOXGENE to generate 1 k facts per source relation. Next, we used our instance repair tool from Section 5.1 to ensure that the chase does not fail. Finally, we generated 20 queries for each scenario using our query generator.

e. The DEEP scenarios. The final family of scenarios was developed as a "pure stress" test. We used our target TGD generator to generate three scenarios with 1000 source relations, 299 target relations, 1000 linear s-t TGDs, and increasing numbers (100, 200, and 300) of linear target TGDs. Moreover, to generate the source instance, we globally fixed a substitution σ that maps each variable $x \in \mathsf{Vars}$ into a distinct constant value $\sigma(x) \in \mathsf{Const}$; then, for each linear s-t TGD with $R(\vec{x})$ in the body, we added $\sigma(R(\vec{v}))$ to the source instance. Thus, all source instances contain just one fact per relation; however, the TGDs are very complex so they produce over 500 M facts on the largest DEEP300 scenario.

The TGDs were taken from previous work [22] and they have the following structure. All TGD heads have three relations joined in a chain. Each atom has arity four and each dependency can have up to three repeated relations. The three head predicates and the body predicate have been chosen randomly out of a space of 300 predicates. We generated 10% of all TGDs from a smaller subset of predicates of size 60. Also, around 10% of the s-t TGD heads were constructed by getting the body and two (out of three) head atoms of a target TGD. This causes some target TGDs to almost map entirely to these particular s-t TGDs. After generating each dependency, a weak acyclicity test was used to discard the dependency if acyclicity was violated.

6. SYSTEM COMPARISON

We ran a total of 40 tests per system: 6 correctness tests, 17 chase computation tests, and 17 query answering tests. Our correctness tests revealed a number of errors in the systems, most of which were corrected by the system authors during the evaluation period. All systems eventually passed all correctness tests, except for PEGASUS which failed two correctness tests but could not be updated. Complete results of the performance tests, including a breakdown of all times, are given in the appendix and on the benchmark Web site. Figure 1 summarizes some results that we discuss next.

Hardware configuration. We ran all tests on a server with six physical 1.9 GHz Xeon v3 cores, 16 GB of RAM, and a 512 GB SSD, running Ubuntu v16. Our configuration is thus not very far from that of a high-end laptop.

Test Setup. All systems apart from E and DLV (as we discuss shortly) were required to perform the following steps:

1. load the source instance from .csv files on disk;
2. load the dependencies in the common format;
3. run the chase of the s-t TGDs;
4. run the chase of the target dependencies;
5. save the target instance to .csv files on disk; and
6. run each query and save its results to .csv files on disk.

For each scenario, each system was allowed three hours to complete all of these tasks; if the system ran out of time or memory, we count the scenario in question as failure and report no results (not even the loading times). In order to analyze the relative contribution of all the steps, we captured the times for all steps independently whenever the systems supported such time measurements. We also repeated the experiments with s-t TGDs only.

Figure 1 shows (I) the *chase execution times* (steps 3+4), (II) the *source import and target export times* (steps 1+5), (III) the *s-t TGDs chase times* (step 3), (IV) the total chase times (steps 1+2+3+4), and (V) the *query execution times* (step 6) for the scenarios where the results vary significantly between different system configurations. Figure 1 shows the results only for the 1-parallel Skolem chase for LLUNATIC and the unrestricted Skolem chase for RDFOX. All results for all scenarios and all chase variants supported by the systems are given in the appendix. The data sizes in the STB-128 and ONT-256 scenarios do not vary so we report our results as a single bar chart; for all other scenarios we use line charts that show scaling with the data size. Test coverage of different systems is reported separately.

E and DLV do not report any intermediate times so we treated them differently. The reasoning strategy of DLV is closely related to the Skolem chase so we report its "total chase time"; however, we found no reasonable analogous time for E. Moreover, to compare E and DLV with the other systems, in Figure 1.VI we show the query evaluation times measured in a different way: (i) for DLV and E, we report the total time needed to answer all queries; and (ii) for all other systems we report the import and chase times multiplied by the number of queries (thus compensating for the fact that, for each query, DLV and E load the dataset and perform reasoning from scratch), plus the sum of all query times.

A "db-to-db" test protocol, where the source and the target instances are stored in an RDBMS, might have been more natural for RDBMS-based systems. Our "file-to-file" test protocol, however, has two advantages. First, even in RDBMS-based systems importing the data may require indexing or building supporting data structures (e.g., we discuss the dictionary encoding in Section 7), which

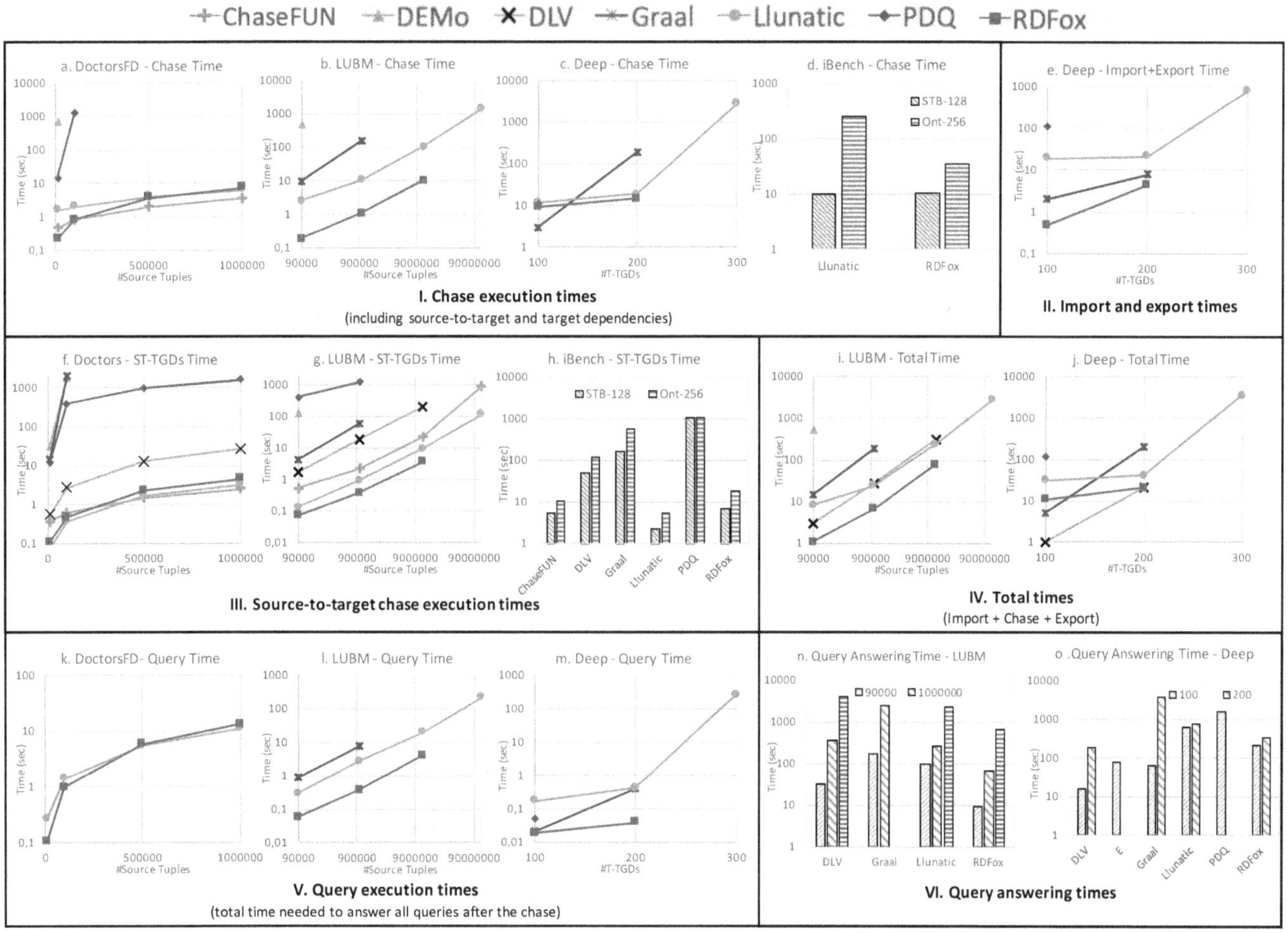

Figure 1: Experimental results for scenarios where times vary significantly between system configurations

can incur overheads; thus, reporting the import and the chase times separately allows us to investigate these issues. Second, reporting the cumulative times allows us to take DLV and E into account.

Test coverage. On some tests, certain systems did not support all required features, they terminated with an exception, or did not finish in three hours; such tests are not shown in Figures 1. Table 3 summarizes test coverage for all tested systems. For each system and each of the three test categories, we report the number of tests that the system was applicable to and the number of successfully completed tests; furthermore, we report the causes of failures (if any). Note that for most systems a failure in data exchange on a test scenario implies failure in the corresponding query answering tests, and we count such failures only once in the table.

As one can see, LLUNATIC was the only system that completed all tests, closely followed by RDFOX which ran out of memory on LUBM-120M and DEEP300. DEMO and the systems that use chase for query reformulation exhibited low coverage; for example, PDQ completed only five out of the 17 data exchange tests. CHASEFUN completed all tests that it was applicable to.

7. LESSONS LEARNED

Our tests should not be misunderstood as aiming primarily for a performance competition: the tested systems were designed under completely different assumptions, often targeting tasks currently not covered by our benchmark. A key feature of our benchmark is that it covers a range of scenarios, which allowed us to answer the questions we posed in Section 1. Specifically, we could observe the behavior of the chase on a diverse set of systems and inputs, which allowed us to derive many general conclusions about the tradeoffs in implementing different chase variants (see Section 3). Moreover, we could compare the effectiveness of the systems specifically designed for the chase with that of the systems that tackle related problems. We summarize our findings in the rest of this section.

Restricted vs. unrestricted vs. parallel chase. A major decision facing a chase system designer is whether to implement the active trigger check (line 6 of Algorithm 1). By analyzing the performance of different chase variants implemented in LLUNATIC and RDFOX on our scenarios (Table 4 shows some, and Table 7 in the appendix shows all results), we obtained several important insights. Interestingly, the tradeoffs associated with this question are quite different for RDBMS- and RAM-based systems.

Implementing the restricted chase in RDBMS-based systems is quite challenging. Triggers are retrieved in such systems using SQL queries, so it is natural to embed the active trigger check into these queries. For example, query (13) attempts to retrieve the active triggers for TGD (3) from Example 1.

```
SELECT DISTINCT R.a FROM R WHERE NOT EXISTS
  (SELECT * FROM R AS R1, A AS A1, A AS A2        (13)
   WHERE R.a=R1.a AND R1.b=A1.a AND R.b=A2.a)
```

System	Tests Run				Tests Completed				Failures	
	Corr.	Chase	Query	Total	Corr.	Chase	Query	Total	Timeouts	Memory
Explicit chase implementations										
CHASEFUN	1	4	0	**5**	1	4	0	**5**	0	0
DEMO	6	17	0	**23**	6	3	0	**9**	11	3
GRAAL	3	7	7	**17**	3	4	4	**11**	0	3
LLUNATIC	6	17	17	**40**	6	17	17	**40**	0	0
PDQ	6	17	17	**40**	6	5	5	**16**	12	0
PEGASUS	6	17	0	**23**	4	0	0	**4**	17	0
Chase-related systems										
DLV	3	7	7	**17**	3	5	5	**13**	2	0
E	6	0	17	**23**	6	0	3	**9**	14	0
RDFOX	6	17	17	**40**	6	15	15	**36**	0	2

Table 3: Test coverage

	LUBM-90k			DEEP200		
	Ch.Time	# Facts	Query T.	Ch.Time	# Facts	Query T.
LLUNATIC 1-Parallel	2.67	141,213	0.29	19.25	902,636	0.41
LLUNATIC Unrest	6.37	177,738	0.31	33.35	926,324	0.44
LLUNATIC Rest	2196.00	141,213	0.23	7521.00	893,990	0.36
RDFOX Unrest	0.19	177,738	0.06	15.23	926,324	0.03
RDFOX Rest	0.21	141,213	0.06	24.02	892,516	0.03

Table 4: Results for variants of the chase

RDBMSs, however, evaluate queries fully before any updates, so query (13) cannot detect that applying a chase step to one trigger makes another trigger inactive (as in Example 1). To properly implement the restricted chase, we must check triggers one-by-one using independent queries; for example, we can add `LIMIT 1` to (13) and run one query per trigger, but this is very slow on large instances in most RDBMSs. Table 7 confirms this: with both the 1-parallel and the unrestricted Skolem chase, LLUNATIC runs orders of magnitude faster than with the restricted Skolem chase, and some of the latter tests timed out.

Query (13), however, can be used to implement the 1-parallel chase, which can even eliminate a common source of overhead: by combining `DISTINCT` and the active triggers check, the query never produces duplicate answers, so separate duplicate elimination is not needed. Indeed, as Table 7 shows, LLUNATIC is faster with the 1-parallel Skolem chase than with the unrestricted Skolem chase.

In contrast, RAM-based systems can more efficiently interleave queries with updates, which can make the active triggers check easier. For example, RDFOX identifies active triggers using a subquery similar to (13), but its optimized RAM-based indexes [30] can efficiently answer the `NOT EXISTS` subqueries while taking into account the result of all concurrent updates. Thus, as Table 7 shows, the performance of the restricted and the unrestricted Skolem chase in RDFOX differs by only a couple of seconds.

Solution sizes and getting to the core. Another question to consider is the impact of the chase variant on the size of the universal solution. Our benchmark again allowed us to investigate this issue: Table 4 shows the solution sizes obtained by the chase variants in LLUNATIC and RDFOX (Table 7 in the appendix shows all results). As one can see, solutions produced by the restricted chase can be between 4% and 21% smaller than those produced by the unrestricted chase; however, we did not observe any significant impact on the performance of query answering. Thus, we conclude that the choice of the chase variant can be mainly driven by the ease of implementation, rather than the solution size.

An interesting question is whether computing the core can further reduce solution sizes. To this end, we ran DEMO to compute the core of the universal solutions for scenarios in our benchmark. DEMO computed the core for DOCTORS-10k and LUBM-90k; the computation failed on all other scenarios, and the core was in both cases of the same size as the result of the restricted chase. We were not able to test the impact of computing the core on most of our scenarios: as we discuss in Section 8, computing the core of large instances is an important open problem. We could, however, answer this question partially: a set Σ of s-t TGDs can be rewritten into a set Σ' such that the restricted chase of Σ' returns the core of the universal solution for Σ [28]. We ran this experiment on the DOCTORS scenario and only s-t TGDs; full results are shown in Table 8 in the appendix. On the 10k and 100k scenarios, the core target instances were 18% smaller then the ones produced using unrestricted Skolem chase, suggesting that scalable methods for core computation in a more general setting could be practically relevant.

Implementing EGDs. In order to apply the EGDs, a system typically first retrieves and deletes all affected facts, applies μ, and inserts the result back into the instance. These operations require mass updates that are much more expensive in an RDBMS-based than a RAM-based system, which makes supporting EGDs in an RDBMS very challenging. Our benchmark results offer evidence for this observation: the chase times of LLUNATIC were considerably higher than of RDFOX on the ONT-256 scenario, which had the largest and most complex set of EGDs (see Figure 1.I.d).

Representing labeled nulls. Chase systems must consistently distinguish labeled nulls from constant values, which turned out to be a source of complexity in RDBMS-based systems. We noticed two common solutions to this problem.

RDBMS-based systems represent labeled nulls using a suitable encoding, which is often string-based; for example, string values are encoded in query (10) using the `'_Sk_'` prefix. Each attribute is thus represented using just one relation column, so join conditions are expressed naturally. Nevertheless, value decoding requires pattern matching; for example, to compute certain answers, LLUNATIC filters string-typed labeled nulls using `NOT LIKE '_Sk_'` in the `WHERE` clause. This is a considerable source of overhead, for two reasons. First, pattern matching is costly. Second, this kind of conditions are not handled nicely by the query planner: as usual, the optimizer pushes selections down towards the scans, but this forces the database engine to apply pattern matching to most facts in the target relations. In most cases, filtering out labeled nulls as a last step of the query would be faster, since the number of facts to analyze is much smaller. This effect can be observed in the query times of LLUNATIC on DEEP300, one of our very large scenarios: the system answers Query 16 in 147 s, but of these, 118 s (80%) are used to filter out labeled nulls; similarly, Query 20 takes 44 s, of which 30 s (68%) are used to filter out labeled nulls.

There are no obvious solutions to this issue. One could implement an alternative query execution strategy that forces the query planner to materialize the intermediate result of the query and then filter labeled nulls at the very end, but this incurs a materialization overhead. An alternative is to adopt a multi-column representation of labeled nulls. For example, DEMO represents labeled nulls using three columns per attribute of the target relation: one boolean column determines whether the attribute contains a constant value or a labeled null, one column stores constant values, and one column stores labels of labeled nulls. This cleanly separates labeled nulls from constant values; however, it triples the size of the database, and it greatly complicates join conditions, which also often confuses the query optimizer.

In summary, our benchmark allowed us to examine the drawbacks of both approaches, to the point that we consider the development of new, performance-oriented representations of labeled nulls an interesting open research question.

Query execution and query characteristics. All systems that successfully computed the chase also successfully evaluated all relevant queries. Most queries can be answered very quickly (typically in under 1 s). Query evaluation was slowest on DEEP300 and LUBM-120M because the target instances of that scenario are much larger than in the case of other scenarios.

We analyzed the queries in our benchmark to detect a possible correlation between execution times and various complexity parameters, such as the number of variables in the head and the body, the number of joins and so on; the parameters for all queries are shown on the benchmark Web site. We observed no clear correlation between the query parameters and the query answering times. Moreover, we found removing duplicates and filtering out labeled nulls to be significant sources of overhead for query answering, and these have no clear connection to the shape and size of the query.

Dictionary encoding. Columnar databases often compress data using a *dictionary encoding*, which can be applied in the chase setting using the following steps:

- one fixes an invertible mapping e of values to integers;
- the set of dependencies Σ and the input instance I are encoded as $\Sigma_e = e(\Sigma)$ and $I_e = e(I)$, respectively;
- the encoded chase J_e of Σ_e and I_e is computed; and
- J_e is decoded as $J = e^{-1}(J_e)$ by inverting the mapping.

Clearly, J is the chase of Σ and I. This process improves performance in a number of ways. First, the encoded instance is usually much smaller than the original. Second, comparing integers is faster than comparing strings. Third, data access structures such as indexes are smaller so joins are faster. Fourth, dictionary encoding removes a problem specific to the Skolem chase: target TGDs may produce very "deep" Skolem terms that can be expensive to manage, but dictionary encoding reduces the depth of such terms.

DLV, GRAAL, and RDFOX all use a variant of this idea as they load the input, and E achieves similar benefits using term indexing [35]. Dictionary encoding is less common in RDBMS-based systems, but it is even more useful as it reduces the amount of data to be transferred from secondary storage, and we were again able to evaluate the impact of this optimization using the benchmark. To this end, we ran LLUNATIC with and without the encoding on LUBM-120M and DEEP300. To isolate the impact of the encoding, the source instance was available (but not encoded) in the RDBMS. First, we measured the chase time on the unencoded instance. Second, we measured the total time needed to encode the source instance, run the chase, and decode the solution. Despite the overhead of the encoding process, the execution with dictionary encoding was 46% faster on LUBM-120M and 58% faster on DEEP300. In our performance comparison, LLUNATIC was configured to turn on the encoding on all scenarios with target TGDs.

Chase vs. first-order theorem proving. E answered all queries in less than a minute on the DOCTORS-10k and DOCTORSFD-10k scenarios, but it was not as efficient on the remaining scenarios (all times are given in the appendix): it took more than an hour for DOCTORS-100k and DOCTORSFD-100k, and it ran out of memory on LUBM-1M, LUBM-12M, and LUBM-120M. Nevertheless, although E was not specifically designed for answering queries over dependencies, it could still process nontrivial scenarios. Note that the Skolem chase is actually an instance of the theorem proving calculus used in E, so the performance gap between E and the other systems is most likely due to the generality of the former.

This generality can actually be beneficial in some cases. As Figure 1.VI.o shows, E performed very well on DEEP100 by answering each query in several seconds, so we analyzed the saturated set of clauses produced by E. We noticed that, by a combination of forward and backward reasoning, the system derived many intermediate clauses (i.e., "lemmas"). Some lemmas were obtained by composing s-t TGDs with target TGDs to obtain new s-t TGDs, which introduced "shortcuts" in proofs and thus sped up query answering. In fact, queries over weakly-acyclic linear dependencies (i.e., dependencies with just one atom in the body, which covers all DEEP scenarios) can always be answered fully using such an approach [2]. Thus, E "discovered" this method using a general first-order theorem proving technique.

Query reformulation vs. query answering. Systems that use chase to support query reformulation (i.e., PEGASUS and PDQ) fared badly on all tests. The chase implementation in these systems is optimized for small instances obtained from the queries being reformulated, rather than for sizes found in data exchange.

Maturity of the chase. Despite the increasing complexity of the test scenarios, some consisting of over 1000 dependencies and generating up to 500 M facts, several systems successfully completed most tests on mainstream hardware (a CPU with 6 cores, 16 GB of RAM, and a 512 GB SSD). In addition, some systems were able to complete the chase and answer the queries in the majority of the tests within a few minutes. Thus, our results suggest that applying the chase to tasks of nontrivial sizes is practically feasible.

8. FUTURE CHALLENGES

Our experiments also gave us some insight regarding directions for future work in the community.

Modular implementations. While a good benchmark should provide a range of workloads for testing the chase, systems with a more modular architecture are needed in order to test hypotheses about the performance of chase. A prominent example of this kind is comparing RDBMS- and RAM-based systems: one would ideally use a system that can work either in RAM or on top of an RDBMS, and it would allow one to measure the impact of this choice independently of the myriad of other implementation factors; however, no such system exists at present. A more modular chase implementation would also be beneficial in practice since many design choices (including the one above) are appropriate for some scenarios and not for others.

Understanding the chase with EGDs. The handling of EGDs in the chase is an area in need of much further study, both in terms of theory (e.g., termination guarantees and static analysis) and implementation. Equality reasoning has been studied extensively in the theorem-proving community (e.g., [6]), and thus a first step would be to better understand the applicability of these techniques to the chase with EGDs.

Computing the core. An open question is to what extent can computing the core reduce the size of the target instance. We investigated this for s-t TGDs, but to answer this question more generally scalable techniques for computing the core in the presence of target dependencies are needed.

Alternative approaches to query answering. The chase is often used for computing the certain answers to queries—a task that, in some cases, can also be tackled using radically different reasoning techniques such as theorem provers. In this paper we took a first look at comparing the chase to the other approaches, but more work is needed to further compare and possibly even combine the chase with the related approaches. The classical chase procedure is particularly well-suited for use cases where the certain answers for many queries must be computed for the same instance. For comparison with other approaches, it might be appropriate to consider a more dynamic setting, as well as possibly develop a set of complexity measures appropriate to such a setting.

Answering queries without materializing the chase. As our experiments show, the chase can be very large so computing and maintaining it can be impractical. It can sometimes thus be desirable to answer queries without first materializing the chase. A lot of work has already been invested in *query rewriting*, where a query is transformed to take into account the effect of dependencies so that the transformed query can be evaluated directly over the source instance. This, however, is feasible only with simple dependencies such as linear TGDs, and answering queries in cases where query rewriting is not applicable remains an open problem. Goal-oriented query answering techniques from Datalog such as *magic sets* [9] provide a promising starting point for this investigation.

Ordering of steps. We found considerable evidence in our experiments that ordering chase steps is important in practice; for example, the good performance of CHASEFUN is due to its careful ordering of EGD and TGD steps. More research is needed to understand the impact of the ordering: even with TGDs only, a particular order can make the active triggers check more effective.

9. RELATED WORK

Experimental evaluations of many chase based systems have already been conducted [34, 28, 27, 17, 22, 12]. In many cases we reused and extended systems from these earlier studies, but our work differs in several important ways. First, previous studies have involved a limited number of systems, typically one or two. To the best of our knowledge, this is the first attempt to compare a large number of a very different, yet related systems. Second, earlier studies have considered only a narrow range of scenarios closely related to the function of the tested systems. We evaluate the systems on over 20 scenarios covering a wide range of assumptions, testing both correctness and scalability, covering a broad spectrum of steps related to the chase from data loading to query execution. Finally, the systems, datasets, and scenarios from the earlier studies have not been made available to the community—an important step towards advancing the experimental culture of the community.

Previous efforts that are more similar in spirit to our work include ST-Benchmark [3] and iBench [4]. ST-Benchmark is concerned with evaluating tools for generating *schema mappings*. It consists of a number of mapping tasks, where each task comprises two schemas, possibly in different data models, and a description of a transformation between them. In addition, ST-Benchmark provides a generator for mapping specifications themselves. It also modifies TOXGENE—a generator of schema instances with certain properties. The tests reported in [3] focus on common transformations on a nested relational model, as opposed to relational data exchange. The ST-Benchmark suite of tools is no longer available, so we could not reuse it. However, several pieces of the infrastructure used in the ST-benchmark, such as TOXGENE and IBENCH (a successor of the specification generator from the ST-benchmark), play a prominent role in our work.

IBENCH [4] is a tool for generating metadata for benchmarking mapping scenarios. It can generate source and target schemas, s-t TGDs, and target EGDs. It is publicly available, it provides some support for data generation via TOXGENE, and it has already been used for testing schema mapping tools. We complemented IBENCH with a number of additional tools, as discussed in Section 5.

10. CONCLUSIONS

Our work provides the first broad look at the performance of chase systems. Our contributions include a new benchmark that comprises test infrastructure and many test scenarios, experimental results for nine prominent systems, and insights about aspects of the systems' implementation. We intend to maintain and extend our infrastructure for benchmarking the chase presented in this paper as new systems appear and as existing systems are improved. We feel that our work can be easily extended to support new classes of dependencies and other chase-related tasks, such as query reformulation with respect to dependencies.

We hope that our infrastructure will have an impact beyond the specific techniques examined here. As mentioned in the introduction, many automated reasoning communities, from SMT solving to description logics, have invested enormous effort in evaluation in the past years. In contrast, while the research literature on extending database systems with reasoning capabilities is extensive, evaluation methodologies are much less developed. A major contribution of this work, beyond its results on the chase, is as a preliminary step in addressing this gap. Evaluation infrastructure is not just a matter of providing synthetic data and dependency generators: it includes common formats, common test harnesses, and much more (see Section 5). We hope that some of our infrastructure and methods will spur activity in other evaluation tasks around reasoning in database systems.

Finally, in this work we took an initial step in comparing reasoning systems produced by the database community with the systems developed by other related communities.

11. ACKNOWLEDGMENTS

The work by Benedikt, Motik, and Konstantinidis was funded by the EPSRC grants PDQ (EP/M005852/1), ED^3 (EP/N014359/1), DBOnto (EP/L012138/1), and $MaSI^3$ (EP/K00607X/1).

12. REFERENCES

[1] S. Abiteboul, R. Hull, and V. Vianu. *Foundations of Databases*. Addison-Wesley, 1995.

[2] F. N. Afrati and N. Kiourtis. Computing certain answers in the presence of dependencies. *Inf. Syst.*, 35(2):149–169, 2010.

[3] B. Alexe, W.-C. Tan, and Y. Velegrakis. STBenchmark: towards a benchmark for mapping systems. In *VLDB*, 2008.

[4] P. C. Arocena, B. Glavic, R. Ciucanu, and R. J. Miller. The iBench integration metadata generator. In *VLDB*, 2015.

[5] F. Baader, D. Calvanese, D. McGuinness, D. Nardi, and P. F. Patel-Schneider, editors. *The Description Logic Handbook: Theory, Implementation and Applications*. Cambridge University Press, 2007.

[6] Franz Baader and Tobias Nipkow. *Term Rewriting and All That*. Cambridge University Press, 1998.

[7] J.-F. Baget, M. Leclère, M.-L. Mugnier, S. Rocher, and C. Sipieter. Graal: A toolkit for query answering with existential rules. In *RuleML*, 2015.

[8] D. Barbosa, A. Mendelzon, and K. Keenleyside, J.and Lyons. ToXgene: A template-based data generator for XML. In *SIGMOD*, 2002.

[9] C. Beeri and R. Ramakrishnan. On the power of magic. In *PODS*, pages 269–283, 1987.

[10] M. Benedikt, J. Leblay, and E. Tsamoura. PDQ: Proof-driven query answering over web-based data. In *VLDB*, 2014.

[11] M. Benedikt, J. Leblay, and E. Tsamoura. Querying with access patterns and integrity constraints. In *VLDB*, 2015.

[12] A. Bonifati, I. Ileana, and M. Linardi. Functional Dependencies Unleashed for Scalable Data Exchange. In *SSDBM*, 2016.

[13] A. Deutsch, A. Nash, and J. Remmel. The chase revisited. In *PODS*, 2008.

[14] A. Deutsch, L. Popa, and V. Tannen. Query reformulation with constraints. *SIGMOD Record*, 35(1):65–73, 2006.

[15] R. Fagin, P.G. Kolaitis, R.J. Miller, and L. Popa. Data Exchange: Semantics and Query Answering. *TCS*, 336(1):89–124, 2005.

[16] R. Fagin, P.G. Kolaitis, and L. Popa. Data Exchange: Getting to the Core. *TODS*, 30(1):174–210, 2005.

[17] F. Geerts, G. Mecca, P. Papotti, and D. Santoro. Mapping and Cleaning. In *ICDE*, 2014.

[18] F. Geerts, G. Mecca, P. Papotti, and D. Santoro. That's All Folks! LLUNATIC Goes Open Source. In *VLDB*, 2014.

[19] G. Gottlob and A. Nash. Efficient Core Computation in Data Exchange. *J. of the ACM*, 55(2):1–49, 2008.

[20] B. Cuenca Grau, I. Horrocks, M. Krötzsch, C. Kupke, D. Magka, B. Motik, and Z. Wang. Acyclicity notions for existential rules and their application to query answering in ontologies. *JAIR*, 47:741–808, 2013.

[21] Y. Guo, Z. Pan, and J. Heflin. LUBM: A benchmark for OWL knowledge base systems. *Web Semantics: Science, Services and Agents on the World Wide Web*, 3(2-3), 2011.

[22] G. Konstantinidis and J. L. Ambite. Optimizing the chase: Scalable data integration under constraints. In *VLDB*, 2015.

[23] N. Leone, M. Manna, G. Terracina, and P. Veltri. Efficiently computable Datalog$^{\exists}$ programs. In *KR*, 2012.

[24] N. Leone, G. Pfeifer, W. Faber, T. Eiter, G. Gottlob, S. Perri, and F. Scarcello. The DLV system for knowledge representation and reasoning. *TOCL*, 7(3):499–562, 2006.

[25] D. Maier, A. O. Mendelzon, and Y. Sagiv. Testing implications of data dependencies. *TODS*, 4(4):455–469, 1979.

[26] B. Marnette. Generalized Schema Mappings: From Termination to Tractability. In *PODS*, 2009.

[27] B. Marnette, G. Mecca, and P. Papotti. Scalable Data Exchange with Functional Dependencies. In *VLDB*, 2010.

[28] G. Mecca, P. Papotti, and S. Raunich. Core Schema Mappings: Scalable Core Computations in Data Exchange. *Inf. Systems*, 37(7):677–711, 2012.

[29] M. Meier. The backchase revisited. *VLDB J.*, 23(3):495–516, 2014.

[30] B. Motik, Y. Nenov, R. Piro, I. Horrocks, and D. Olteanu. Parallel Materialisation of Datalog Programs in Centralised, Main-Memory RDF Systems. In *AAAI*, 2014.

[31] R. Nieuwenhuis and A. Rubio. Paramodulation-Based Theorem Proving. In *Handbook of Automated Reasoning*, volume I. Elsevier, 2001.

[32] A. Onet. The chase procedure and its applications in data exchange. In *DEIS*, pages 1–37, 2013.

[33] S. Perri, F. Scarcello, G. Catalano, and N. Leone. Enhancing DLV instantiator by backjumping techniques. *Ann. Math. Art. Int.*, 51(2-4):195–228, 2007.

[34] R. Pichler and V. Savenkov. DEMo: Data Exchange Modeling Tool. In *VLDB*, 2009.

[35] I. V. Ramakrishnan, R. Sekar, and A. Voronkov. Term Indexing. In *Handbook of Automated Reasoning*. Elsevier, 2001.

[36] Stephan Schulz. System Description: E 1.8. In *LPAR*, 2013.

[37] SMT-LIB. http://smtlib.cs.uiowa.edu/.

[38] B. ten Cate, L. Chiticariu, P. Kolaitis, and W. C. Tan. Laconic Schema Mappings: Computing Core Universal Solutions by Means of SQL Queries. In *VLDB*, 2009.

[39] TPC. http://www.tpc.org/.

[40] TPTP. http://www.cs.miami.edu/~tptp/.

APPENDIX

A. FULL EXPERIMENTAL RESULTS

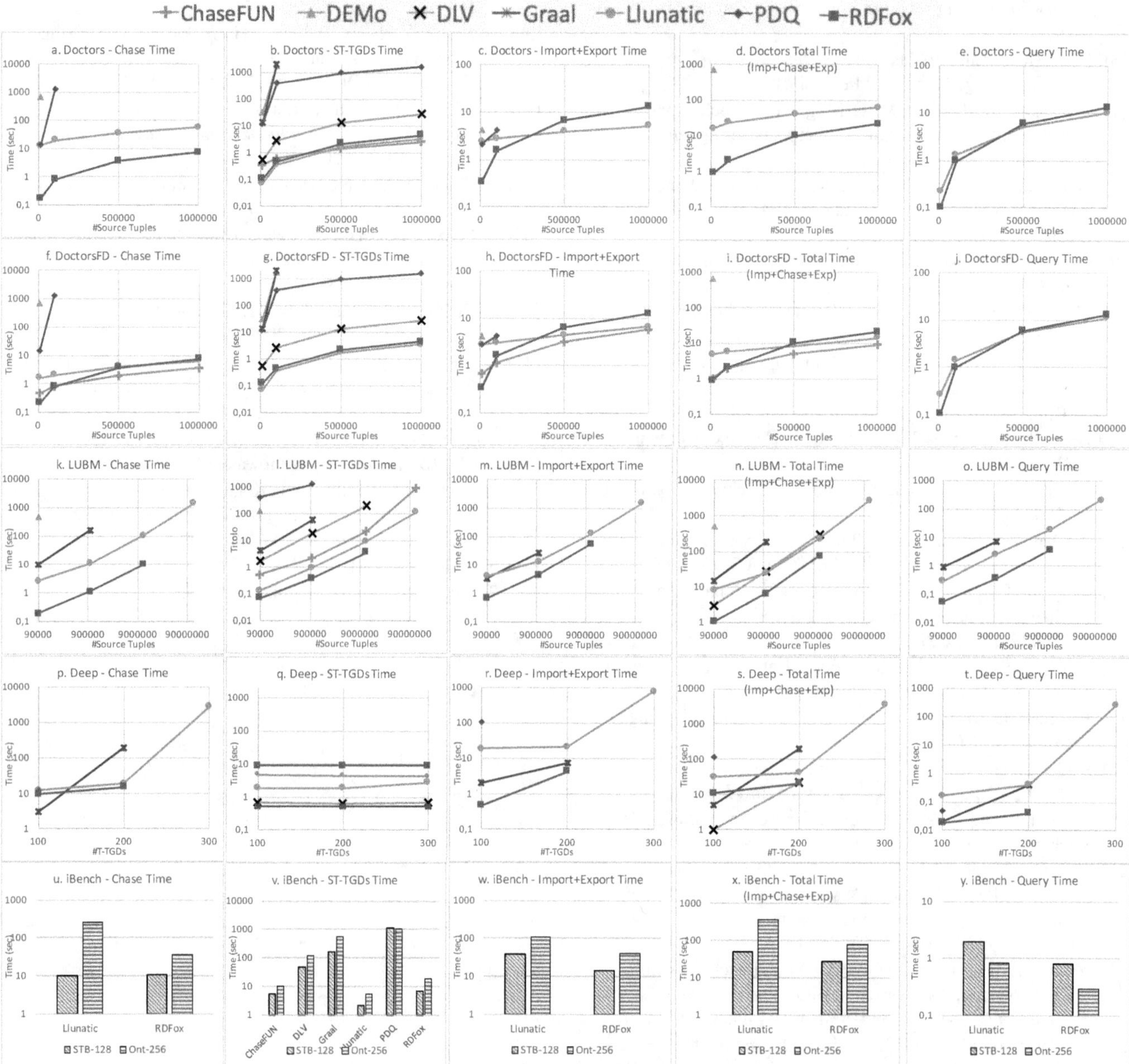

Figure 2: Full charts of the chase experiments

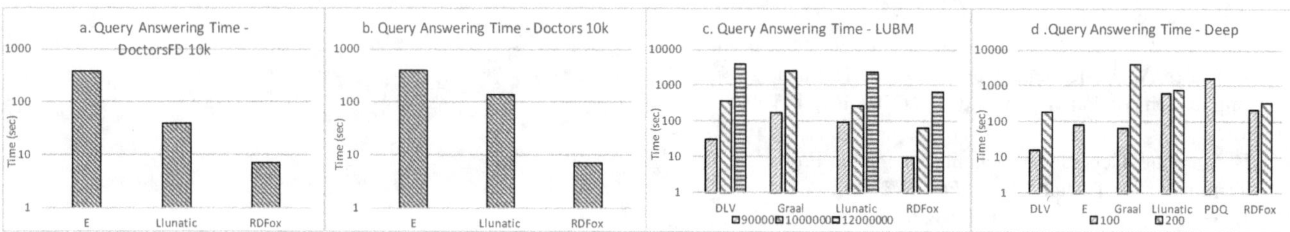

Figure 3: Full charts of the query answering experiments

Chase Times

Doctors

	10k					100k				
	Chase	Chase ST-TGDs	Import/Exp	Total time	Query	Chase	Chase ST-TGDs	Import/Exp	Total time	Query
	10000	10000	10000	10000	10000	100000	100000	100000	100000	100000
ChaseFUN		0,35					0,62			
DEMo	686,00	31,00	4,14	691,00			1777,00			
DLV		0,54					2,68			
Graal		13,71					1936,96			
Llunatic	12,63	0,08	2,37	15,78	0,22	19,56	0,35	2,75	23,70	1,30
PDQ	13,55	12,00	2,06			1220,00	388,00	4,06		
RDFox	0,18	0,11	0,33	0,90	0,10	0,81	0,46	1,53	2,03	0,97

	500k					1m				
	Chase	Chase ST-TGDs	Import/Exp	Total time	Query	Chase	Chase ST-TGDs	Import/Exp	Total time	Query
	500000	500000	500000	500000	500000	1000000	1000000	1000000	1000000	1000000
ChaseFUN		1,49					2,58			
DEMo										
DLV		13,06					26,98			
Graal										
Llunatic	34,76	1,64	3,86	39,82	5,18	55,96	3,32	5,11	62,00	10,00
PDQ		977,00					1622,00			
RDFox	3,73	2,26	6,57	10,12	5,88	7,53	4,57	13,01	21,59	13,41

DoctorsFD

	10k					100k				
	Chase	Chase ST-TGDs	Import/Exp	Total time	Query	Chase	Chase ST-TGDs	Import/Exp	Total time	Query
	10000	10000	10000	10000	10000	100000	100000	100000	100000	100000
ChaseFUN	0,46		0,66	1,00		0,83		1,14	2,00	
DEMo	658,00	31,00	4,09	665,00			1777,00			
DLV		0,56					2,69			
Graal		13,71					1936,96			
Llunatic	1,60	0,07	2,73	4,74	0,26	2,02	0,37	3,04	5,59	1,41
PDQ	14,50	12,00	2,66			1258,00	388,00	4,14		
RDFox	0,21	0,13	0,33	0,90	0,10	0,81	0,46	1,60	2,03	0,97

	500k					1m				
	Chase	Chase ST-TGDs	Import/Exp	Total time	Query	Chase	Chase ST-TGDs	Import/Exp	Total time	Query
	500000	500000	500000	500000	500000	1000000	1000000	1000000	1000000	1000000
ChaseFUN	1,97		3,17	5,00		3,55		5,75	9,00	
DEMo										
DLV		13,03					27,05			
Graal										
Llunatic	3,99	1,77	4,32	8,46	5,54	6,48	3,52	6,64	13,78	11,22
PDQ		977,00					1622,00			
RDFox	3,73	2,27	6,39	10,15	5,85	7,49	4,56	12,67	20,77	13,23

LUBM

	001					010				
	Chase	Chase ST-TGDs	Import/Exp	Total time	Query	Chase	Chase ST-TGDs	Import/Exp	Total time	Query
	90000	90000	90000	90000	90000	1000000	1000000	1000000	1000000	1000000
ChaseFUN		0,54					2,29			
DEMo	503,00	127,00	3,44	512,00						
DLV		1,78		3,00			19,04		28,00	
Graal	9,73	4,44	3,37	14,90	0,90	162,00	59,02	27,00	188,56	7,44
Llunatic	2,67	0,13	4,03	8,29	0,29	10,79	0,95	13,13	24,31	2,69
PDQ		410,00					1276,00			
RDFox	0,19	0,07	0,68	1,06	0,06	1,12	0,39	4,59	6,63	0,37

	100					01k				
	Chase	Chase ST-TGDs	Import/Exp	Total time	Query	Chase	Chase ST-TGDs	Import/Exp	Total time	Query
	12000000	12000000	12000000	12000000	12000000	120000000	120000000	120000000	120000000	120000000
ChaseFUN		22,17					906,51			
DEMo										
DLV		197,10		304,00						
Graal										
Llunatic	107,35	9,47	129,21	237,44	19,56	1415,53	117,82	1543,17	2739,29	214,71
PDQ										
RDFox	10,34	3,65	57,03	77,04	3,96					

iBench

	STB-128					Ont-256				
	Chase	Chase ST-TGDs	Import/Exp	Total time	Query	Chase	Chase ST-TGDs	Import/Exp	Total time	Query
	STB-128	STB-128	STB-128	STB-128	STB-128	Ont-256	Ont-256	Ont-256	Ont-256	Ont-256
ChaseFUN		5,46					10,23			
DLV		48,59					118,01			
Graal		160,38					566,46			
Llunatic	10,10	2,16	39,31	50,08	1,92	257,12	5,34	108,55	366,18	0,82
PDQ		1088,00					1045,00			
RDFox	10,73	6,65	14,22	27,19	0,81	35,27	18,73	40,87	82,71	0,29

Deep

	100,00					200,00					300,00				
	Chase	Chase ST-TGDs	Import/Exp	Total time	Query	Chase	Chase ST-TGDs	Import/Exp	Total time	Query	Chase	Chase ST-TGDs	Import/Exp	Total time	Query
	100	100	100	100	100	200	200	200	200	200	300	300	300	300	300
ChaseFUN		4,73					4,50					4,31			
DLV		0,67		1,00			0,65		22,00			0,67			
Graal	2,98	0,53	2,00	4,98	0,02	192,00	0,52	7,61	199,61	0,39		0,52			
Llunatic	12,13	1,90	18,96	31,83	0,17	19,25	1,86	21,51	41,59	0,41	2805,48	2,79	770,15	3576,85	253,16
PDQ	11,82		106,51	118,33	0,05										
RDFox	9,49	8,93	0,47	10,98	0,02	15,23	9,03	4,41	20,96	0,04		8,86			

Unsupported
Timeout

Table 5: Full results of the chase experiments

Query Answering Times

	Doctors	DoctorsFD
	10k	10k
E	399,00	383,00
Llunatic	138,05	38,63
RDFox	6,96	7,02

LUBM

	001	010	100
DLV	31,00	356,00	3960,00
Graal	176,32	2479,28	
Llunatic	95,42	267,31	2393,79
RDFox	9,26	66,47	653,21

Deep

	100	200
DLV	16,00	184,00
E	79,00	
Graal	62,82	3843,99
Llunatic	609,39	783,85
PDQ	1566,79	
RDFox	212,64	333,78

Table 6: Full results of the query answering experiments

	Doctors								
	10k			100k			500k		
	Chase Time	#Target Tuples	Query Time	Chase Time	#Target Tuples	Query Time	Chase Time	#Target Tuples	Query Time
Llunatic - 1-Parallel	12,63	9.734	0,22	19,56	81.000	1,30	34,76	397.000	5,18
Llunatic - Unrestricted	15,40	9.734	0,21	20,69	81.000	1,38	44,91	397.000	5,60
Llunatic - Restricted	69,12	9.734	0,21	3948,14	81.000	2,83			
RDFox - Unrestricted	0,18	9.734	0,10	0,81	81.000	0,97	3,73	397.000	5,88
RDFox - Restricted	0,14	9.734	0,11	0,67	81.000	0,98	2,92	397.000	5,75

	LUBM					
	001			010		
	Chase Time	#Target Tuples	Query Time	Chase Time	#Target Tuples	Query Time
Llunatic - 1-Parallel	2,67	141.213	0,29	10,79	1.779.697	2,69
Llunatic - Unrestricted	6,37	177.738	0,31	32,99	2.246.699	1,69
Llunatic - Restricted	2196,80	141.213	0,23			
RDFox - Unrestricted	0,19	177.738	0,06	1,12	2.246.699	0,45
RDFox - Restricted	0,21	141.213	0,06	0,94	1.779.697	0,42

	iBench					
	STB-128			Ont-256		
	Chase Time	#Target Tuples	Query Time	Chase Time	#Target Tuples	Query Time
Llunatic - 1-Parallel	10,10	1.918.178	1,92	257,12	5.673.830	0,82
Llunatic - Unrestricted	34,04	1.918.217	1,40	307,13	5.674.103	0,73
Llunatic - Restricted						
RDFox - Unrestricted	10,73	1.918.217	0,81	35,27	5.674.103	0,29
RDFox - Restricted	10,87	1.918.178	0,78	36,83	5.673.830	0,30

	Deep					
	100			200		
	Chase Time	#Target Tuples	Query Time	Chase Time	#Target Tuples	Query Time
Llunatic - 1-Parallel	12,13	18.386	0,17	19,25	902.636	0,41
Llunatic - Unrestricted	15,89	19.537	0,22	33,35	926.324	0,44
Llunatic - Restricted	22,23	18.347	0,17	7521,92	893.990	0,36
RDFox - Unrestricted	9,49	19.537	0,02	15,23	926.324	0,03
RDFox - Restricted	18,86	18.385	0,02	24,02	892.516	0,03

Table 7: Impact of the chase variants

	Doctors (S-T tgds only)									
	Unrestricted		Restricted Less Favorable		Restricted Random		Restricted Favorable		Core	
	Chase Time	# Tuples	Chase Time	# Tuples	Chase Time	# Tuples	Chase Time	# Tuples	Chase Time	# Tuples
10k	0,17	11.808	79,40	10.208	89,33	9.867	87,96	9.734	0,25	9.734
100k	1,14	97.500	12404,00	95.634	11340,00	85.168	103720,00	81.000	0,73	81.000

Table 8: Impact of the core

Efficient and Provable Multi-Query Optimization

Tarun Kathuria
Microsoft Research
tarunkathuria@gmail.com

S. Sudarshan
Indian Institute of Technology Bombay
sudarsha@cse.iitb.ac.in

ABSTRACT

Complex queries for massive data analysis jobs have become increasingly commonplace. Many such queries contain common subexpressions, either within a single query or among multiple queries submitted as a batch. Conventional query optimizers do not exploit these subexpressions and produce sub-optimal plans. The problem of multi-query optimization (MQO) is to generate an optimal *combined* evaluation plan by computing common subexpressions once and reusing them. Exhaustive algorithms for MQO explore an $\mathcal{O}(n^n)$ search space. Thus, this problem has primarily been tackled using various heuristic algorithms, without providing any theoretical guarantees on the quality of their solution.

In this paper, instead of the conventional cost minimization problem, we treat the problem as maximizing a linear transformation of the cost function. We propose a greedy algorithm for this transformed formulation of the problem, which under weak, intuitive assumptions, provides an approximation factor guarantee for this formulation. We go on to show that this factor is optimal, unless $\mathsf{P} = \mathsf{NP}$. Another noteworthy point about our algorithm is that it can be easily incorporated into existing transformation-based optimizers. We finally propose optimizations which can be used to improve the efficiency of our algorithm.

Keywords

Approximation algorithms; hardness of approximation; Multi-query optimization

1. INTRODUCTION

Modern data analytics platforms frequently have to run scripts that contain a large number of complex queries. Often, these queries contain common subexpressions due to the nature of the analysis performed. These subexpressions may occur within a single complex query which i) contains multiple correlated nested subqueries or ii) if the database contains many materialized views which are referenced multiple times in the query. A more interesting case where common subexpressions arise is when a batch of related queries are being executed together.

Conventional query optimizers are not suited for such scenarios since they do not exploit these subexpressions and instead produce locally optimal plans for each query. These plans can be globally sub-optimal since they do not make use of the shared subexpressions while generating the plans. The goal of multi-query optimization (MQO) is to generate query plans where these subexpressions are executed once and their results used by multiple consumers. The best plan is selected in a completely cost-based manner.

We now present an example to illustrate the MQO problem and how locally optimal plans may be globally sub-optimal for multiple queries in the presence of common subexpressions.

Example 1. (Example 1.1 in [25]) Consider a batch consisting of two queries $(A \bowtie B \bowtie C)$ and $(B \bowtie C \bowtie D)$ whose locally optimal plans (i.e., individual best plans) are $(A \bowtie B) \bowtie C$ and $(B \bowtie C) \bowtie D$ respectively. The individual best plans for the two queries do not have any common subexpressions. However, consider a locally sub-optimal plan for the first query $A \bowtie (B \bowtie C)$. It is clear that $(B \bowtie C)$ is a common subexpression and can be computed once and used by both queries.

Consider the following instantiation of the various costs for the two queries shown in Figure 1. Suppose the base relations A, B, C and D each have a scan cost of 10 units. Each of the joins have a cost of 100 units, giving a total evaluation cost of 460 units for the locally optimal plans shown in Figure 1a. On the other hand, in the plan shown in Figure 1b, the common subexpression $(B \bowtie C)$ is first computed and materialized on the disk at a cost of 10. Then, it is scanned twice - the first time to join with A in order to compute the first query, and the second time to join it with D in order to compute the second - at a cost of 10 per scan. Each of these joins have a cost of 100 units. Thus, the total cost of this consolidated plan is 370 units, which is lesser than the cost of the locally optimal plan in Figure 1a.

It should be noted that blindly sharing a subexpression may not always lead to a globally optimal strategy. For example, there may be cases where the cost of joining the subexpression $(B \bowtie C)$ with A is very large compared to the cost of the plan $(A \bowtie B) \bowtie C$; in such cases it may make no sense to reuse $(B \bowtie C)$ even if it were available. □

The benefits of a good algorithm for MQO are not just restricted to multiple queries in a batch but can also be used to find better plans for a single complex query. Consider an example of a large query consisting of multiple subqueries

PODS'17, May 14-19, 2017, Chicago, Illinois, USA

DOI: http://dx.doi.org/10.1145/3034786.3034792

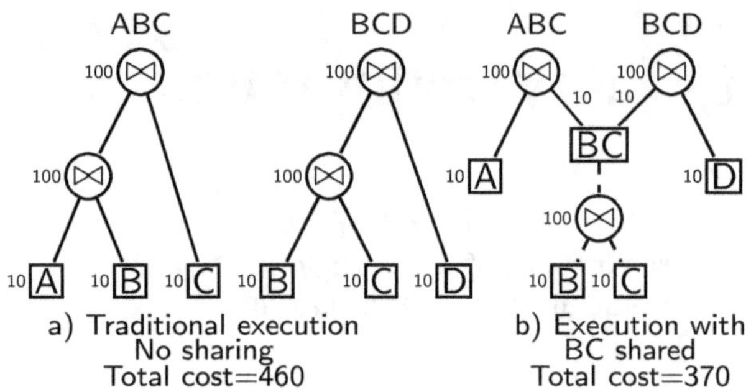

Figure 1: MQO example (from [25]) illustrating benefit of sharing subexpressions

with a common subexpression between two subqueries. Traditional query optimizers do not consider such sharing, but multi-query optimization techniques have been developed to find the best plans taking such sharing into account, such as [26, 27, 25, 32, 28] . While the early work on multi-query optimization, e.g. [26, 27], focused on queries with only selections and joins, later work, e.g. [25, 32, 28], which are based on the Volcano/Cascades query optimization framework [9, 10] use an AND-OR DAG representation of the query plan space to handle arbitrary queries.

Dynamic-programming techniques for join order enumeration, as well as transformation-rule based optimization techniques based on the Volcano/Cascades framework with optimizations described in [21], run in time $\mathcal{O}(3^n)$ for a query that computes the join of n relations, when all join orders are considered.

However, when these techniques are extended to handle multi-query optimization, they need to consider all subexpressions that are potentially shared by multiple query plans, or multiple parts of the same query plan. The number of such common subexpressions can be $\mathcal{O}(2^n)$ when we consider join queries involving n relations. An optimal plan for the set of queries may materialize and share up to n of these common subexpressions. A naive exhaustive algorithms for MQO would consider all such subsets of cardinality n, leading to a very high cost. The best known exhaustive algorithm takes $\mathcal{O}(n^n)$ time [31], which is infeasible for even moderate numbers of relations. Thus, work in this area relies on heuristics to restrict the space of alternatives considered [25, 28, 32]. While such algorithms seems to work well in practice, to the best of our knowledge there has been no work that provides theoretical guarantees on the quality of solution obtained by such heuristics.

Thus, an open question is

Can we devise an algorithm which runs in time polynomial in the number of shared nodes (common subexpressions) which provides us with theoretical guarantees on the quality of the solution obtained as compared to the optimal? If so, what is the best possible polynomial-time approximation algorithm?

As a first step towards answering this question, we propose a reformulation of the MQO problem, the motivation for which is stated next.

The canonical multi-query optimization problem is concerned with minimizing cost of the query plan for a set of queries by choosing a set of nodes to materialize (say M) and then finding the optimal plan exploiting nodes in M. Another way to look at this problem is to maximize the "materialization-benefit" we get by materializing M *with respect to* a naive execution plan which is locally optimal and does not exploit any common subexpressions. More formally, this corresponds to maximizing the difference of the cost of the best plan in which the set of materialized nodes is M from the latter. As this is just a linear transformation of the cost function, it is clear that the maximizer of the materialization-benefit will be the minimizer of the cost.

Roy et al. [25] assume a property on the cost function that they call the "monotonicity heuristic". This essentially corresponds to assuming the supermodularity of the cost function defined on the set of nodes to be materialized. In [25], this assumption is used to speed up their greedy algorithm via a heap-based argument which exploits the supermodularity. This is similar to the LazyGreedy algorithm described in [16] for speeding up monotone submodular function maximization subject to cardinality constraints via the well-known greedy algorithm, which is also used by [25]. On the queries used in their experiments, it was observed that the plan obtained with or without assuming supermodularity led to the same plan. This seems to imply that the supermodularity assumption may be a reasonable one and may hold in practice.

1.1 Our contribution

The contributions of this paper are as follows

- Motivated by [25], we proceed with the "monotonicity heuristic" assumption (which implies the submodularity of the materialization benefit function). *Under this assumption*, we propose an approximation algorithm for the *underlying problem* of unconstrained, normalized submodular maximization (UNSM). Note that we allow the submodular function to take negative values, which has not been considered previously and poses a significant challenge[1]. Our algorithm runs in time $\mathcal{O}(u^2)$, where u is the size of the universe. In the MQO setting, where u is the number of shared nodes, this translates to a $\mathcal{O}(2^{2n})$ time algorithm instead of the exhaustive $\mathcal{O}(n^n)$ algorithm.
- We then present a hardness of approximation proof for the UNSM problem, which matches that obtained by our algorithm, assuming $\mathsf{P} \neq \mathsf{NP}$.
- We present optimizations to our algorithm to improve the running time of the algorithm, without sacrificing any theoretical guarantees.
- We also consider a special case of the problem of submodular maximization under cardinality constraints.
  - A natural extension to our greedy algorithm for this problem is presented. We further propose a pruning strategy to reduce the search space before running our greedy algorithm, by exploiting this cardinality constraint.
  - While, at this point, we do not formally prove any theoretical guarantees on the approximation factor for this constrained problem, we show that the answer obtained by our greedy algorithm is the same when run with or without this pruning.

[1]Inapproximability results when the submodular function may be unnormalized are well known [8].

- We compare our algorithm against the Greedy algorithm and stand-alone Volcano (without MQO) on queries from the TPCD benchmark and show significant benefits.

It is important to note that our approximation guarantees are for the benefit-maximization problem, under the submodularity assumption, and do not imply a multiplicative factor approximation to the cost minimization problem. However, results in our experimental section shows that our proposed algorithm performs as well as or better than the Greedy heuristic of [25].

Our techniques for the problem of multi-query optimization are presented in the context of query optimizers based on the Volcano/Cascades framework [10, 9]. This framework for optimizing queries uses transformation rules which makes it inherently extensible, and has been implemented in several widely-used commercial database systems such as Microsoft SQL Server. It should be noted, however, that our algorithm is agnostic to the query optimization framework, and can be easily extended to other frameworks as well.

Organization. In Section 2, we present a detailed overview of multi-query optimization in the context of the Volcano framework which was presented in [25] along with how submodular maximization arises in this context. Section 3 presents our greedy algorithm for unconstrained, normalized submodular maximization with the proof of its approximation factor guarantee. In Section 4, we prove the hardness of approximation of the unconstrained, normalized submodular maximization which rules out better approximation factors than the one attained by our algorithm, under the assumption of $\mathsf{P} \neq \mathsf{NP}$. Section 5 presents ways to speed up our algorithm. We present experimental results on benchmark queries in Section 6. Related work in the areas of MQO and submodular maximization is presented in Section 7. We conclude and discuss directions for future work in Section 8.

2. PRELIMINARIES

This section presents some relevant background in (Multi)-Query Optimization in the Volcano framework followed by some preliminaries of submodular maximization and finally ends with how submodular maximization arises in MQO. Readers well-versed in MQO techniques in Volcano may skip to the Section 2.3 directly.

2.1 Query Optimization in Volcano

The Volcano/Cascades query optimization framework [10, 9] is based on a system of equivalence rules, which specify that the result of a particular transformation of a query tree is the same as the result of the original query tree. The key aspect of this framework is the efficient implementation of the transformation rule-based approach.

The Volcano framework uses the AND-OR DAG representation [10, 23] for compactly representing the given query and its alternative query plans. An AND-OR DAG is a directed acyclic graph whose nodes can be divided into AND-nodes and OR-nodes; the AND-nodes have only OR-nodes as children and the OR-nodes have only AND-nodes as children. An AND-node corresponds to an algebraic operator, such as the join operator ($\bowtie$) or a select operator (σ). It represents the expression defined by the operator and its inputs. An OR-node represents a set of logical expressions

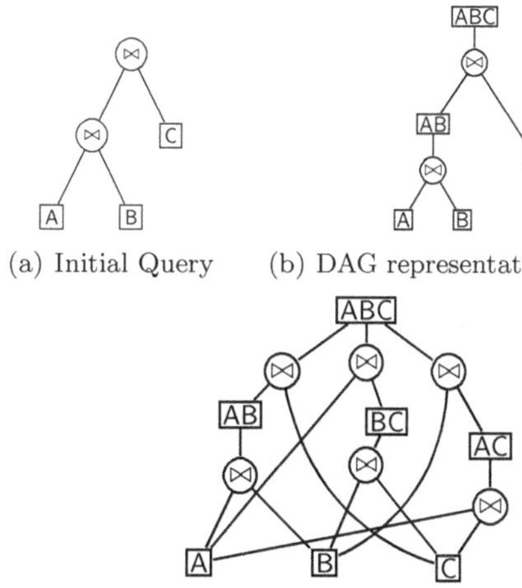

(a) Initial Query (b) DAG representation of query

(c) Expanded LQDAG after transformation (Commutativity not shown explicitly)

Figure 2: Initial Query and LQDAG Representation

that generate the same result set; the set of such expressions is defined by the children AND nodes of the OR node, and their inputs. Hereafter, we refer to the OR-nodes and AND-nodes as equivalence nodes and operator nodes respectively.

The given query tree is initially represented in the AND-OR DAG formulation. For example, the query tree of Figure 2a is initially represented in the AND-OR DAG formulation, as shown in Figure 2b. Equivalence nodes are shown as boxes, while operator nodes are shown in circles.

The initial AND-OR DAG is then expanded by applying all possible logical transformations on every node of the initial DAG created from the given query. Suppose the only possible transformations are join associativity and commutativity. Then the plans $A \bowtie (B \bowtie C)$ and $(A \bowtie C) \bowtie B$, as well as several plans equivalent to these, modulo commutativity, can be obtained by transformations on the initial AND-OR DAG of Figure 2b. These are represented in the DAG shown in Figure 2c. The AND-OR DAG representation after applying all the logical tranformations is called the (expanded) Logical Query DAG (or LQDAG).

Each operator node can have different physical implementations; for example, a join operator can be implemented as a hash join, a nested loop join or as a merge join. Once the LQDAG has been generated, physical implementation rules are applied on the logical operators to generate the physical AND-OR DAG, which is called the Physical Query DAG or PQDAG for short.

Properties of the results of an expression, such as sort order, that do not form part of the logical data model are called physical properties [10]. The importance of exploiting physical properties such as sort order and partitioning of result sets is well known in traditional query optimization. The DAG is actually built and stored using a "memo" structure, a concise data structure used in the Volcano/Cascades framework to represent the entire space of equivalent query evaluation plans succintly. The AND-OR DAG representation considered for MQO actually works on the PQDAG but we present our algorithms to work at the LQDAG level for brevity.

2.2 Multi-Query Optimization in Volcano

This subsection primarily focuses on the techniques presented in [25] for MQO in the Volcano framework. In order

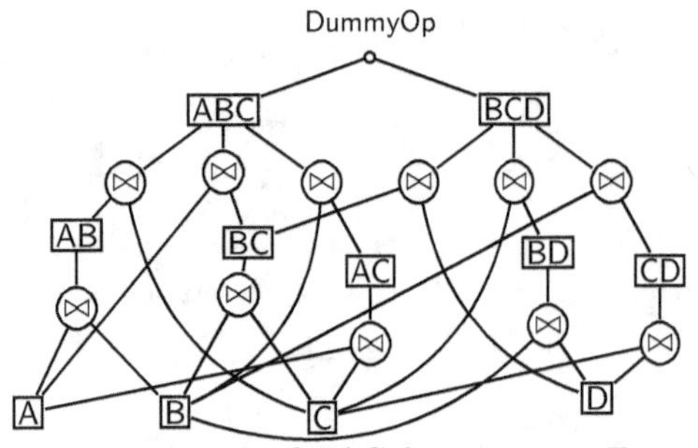

Figure 3: Combined LQDAG for queries in Example 1

to extend the Volcano AND-OR DAG generation for MQO on a batch of queries to be jointly optimized, the queries are represented together in a single DAG, sharing subexpressions. The DAG is converted to a rooted DAG by adding a dummy operation node, which does nothing, but has the root equivalence nodes of all the queries as its inputs.

The two main challenges for a multi-query optimizer are :

1. Recognizing possibilities of shared computation by identifying common subexpressions.
2. Finding a globally optimal evaluation plan exploiting the common subexpressions identified.

Roy et al. [25] present an efficient hashing-based algorithm that identifies the set of all common subexpressions, including subqueries that are syntactically different but semantically equivalent, in a single bottom-up traversal of the LQDAG by using the "memo" structure; for details see [25]. This is similar to the "expression fingerprinting" used to identify the common subexpressions in [28]. The combined LQDAG for the queries of Example 1 is shown in Figure 3. This step takes exponential time as the size of the DAGs may itself be exponential and is unavoidable, even in single-query optimization.

Similar to the single query optimization done by Volcano, in a single-pass, one can annotate each node in the DAG with its estimated cost. Note that the cost estimator functions are taken as input to the optimizer, i.e., the optimizer algorithm is agnostic to the cost estimates. Indeed, this is one of the reasons why the Volcano query optimizer framework is widely used. It is important to note that in the single query optimization as well as the multi query optimization setting, one assumes that the cost estimates provided to us are correct for any guarantees to hold. Thus, we also work under the assumption that the cost estimates are correct. After the common subexpressions are identified and the cost of each node computed, the next task is to find the best consolidated plan for the queries exploiting the subexpressions.

In this paper, we are primarily concerned with the optimization philosophy adopted by the Greedy algorithm in [25] which is presented next. For a set of equivalence nodes S, let $bestCost(Q, S)$ (for brevity, $bc(S)$) denote the cost of the optimal plan for Q given that nodes in S are to be materialized (this includes the cost of computing and materializing nodes in S). Here Q is the combined query DAG with the dummy root operator node with inputs being the DAGs of $Q_1, \dots, Q_k$, as described above. The $bc(S)$ function, of course, depends on the cost estimates and is treated as a black-box for the MQO algorithms. Given a set of nodes S to be materialized, [25] present an efficient scheme to find the best plan and the best cost, $bc(S)$ (this includes the cost of materializing S, which may be done in multiple ways and is figured out by the optimizer in [25] as well).

Now, we just need to identify the subset S of nodes in the AND-OR DAG for which $bestCost(Q, S)$ is minimum. However, an exhaustive algorithm which enumerates all possible subsets S will take time exponential in the size of the AND-OR DAG, which itself may be exponential in the number of relations. In [25], an intuitive greedy algorithm is proposed, which iteratively picks which node to materialize. At each iteration, the node x that gives the maximum reduction in the cost, if materialized, is chosen to be added to the current set of materialized nodes X. While this greedy algorithm is shown to work well in practice, [25] does not provide any theoretical guarantees on the quality of solution obtained via this algorithm. The algorithm is presented below for completeness.

Algorithm 1 Greedy Algorithm of [25]

```
X = ∅
Y = Set of shareable equivalence nodes in the DAG
while Y ≠ ∅ do
    Pick x ∈ Y which minimizes bc(X ∪ {x})
    if bc(X) > bc(X ∪ {x}) then
        X = X ∪ {x}, Y = Y \ {x}
    else
        Y = ∅
    end if
end while
return X
```

As noted in [25], the nodes materialized in the globally optimal plan are just a subset of the ones that are shared in some plan for the query. It is, thus, sufficient to search only over the set of *shareable* equivalence nodes, instead of searching over the entire set of equivalence nodes in the DAG.

Clearly, some assumptions on the cost function have to be made in order to give theoretical guarantees for any algorithm. Furthermore, it is desirable to make assumptions which may hold in practice. Roy et al. [25] make an additional assumption which they call the "monotonicity heuristic".

Define $benefit(x, X)$ as $bc(X) - bc(X \cup \{x\})$. The assumption is that

$$\forall\, Y \subseteq X,\ \forall\, x \notin X,\ benefit(x, X) \leq benefit(x, Y).$$

They [25] make this assumption in order to improve the running time of their greedy algorithm via a heap-based argument which corresponds to the LazyGreedy algorithm [16] for faster monotone, submodular maximization. Their experiments, however, show that the plans obtained with and without the assumption had exactly the same cost. While the assumption may not always hold, their experiments seem to indicate that the assumption may be a reasonable one, in practice. Thus, in this paper, we work under this assumption to devise an algorithm *with theoretical guarantees* on its performance for maximizing the "materialization benefit".

2.3 Submodular Maximization

Let U be a universe of $n = |U|$ elements, let $f : 2^U \to \mathbb{R}$ be a function. For simplicity, we use the notation $f'(u, S)$ to denote the incremental value in f of adding u to S, i.e., $f'(u, S) = f(S \cup \{u\}) - f(S)$.

Definition 1. *(Submodular Functions)*
A function $f : 2^U \rightarrow \mathbb{R}$ is called submodular if

$$\forall\ A \subseteq B \subseteq U,\ \forall\ u \in U \setminus B, \textit{we have } f'(u, A) \geq f'(u, B).$$

Definition 2. *(Supermodular Functions)*
A function $f : 2^U \rightarrow \mathbb{R}$ is called supermodular if

$$\forall\ A \subseteq B \subseteq U,\ \forall\ u \in U \setminus B, \textit{we have } f'(u, A) \leq f'(u, B).$$

Definition 3. *(Additive Functions)*
A function $c : 2^U \rightarrow \mathbb{R}$ is called additive if it is of the form $c(S) = \sum_{e \in S} c(\{e\})$.

Definition 4. *(Monotone Functions)*
A function $f : 2^U \rightarrow \mathbb{R}$ is said to be monotone if

$$\forall A \subseteq B \subseteq U, \textit{we have } f(A) \leq f(B).$$

Definition 5. *(Normalized Functions)*
A function $f : 2^U \rightarrow \mathbb{R}$ is called normalized if $f(\emptyset) = 0$.

Given a normalized submodular function $f : 2^U \rightarrow \mathbb{R}$, the unconstrained, normalized submodular maximization (UNSM) problem is to find a set $S \subseteq U$ which maximizes the value of f, i.e., $\arg\max_{S \subseteq U} f(S)$.

Since submodular maximization problems are in general NP-hard and can only be approximated, a simple additive scaling of the function by a large constant to make the function non-negative and running an algorithm like [2] suffers in the approximation factor and moreover does not guarantee a multiplicative approximation.

It is well-known that any non-monotone submodular function f, with the constraint that $f(\emptyset) = 0$, can be written as the difference of a non-negative monotone submodular function f_M and an additive "cost" function c. However, multiple such decompositions are possible and as we will show, there is one particular decomposition (the decomposition in Proposition 1) which will give us the best approximation ratio and a matching hardness of approximation.

Proposition 1. *Any normalized, non-monotone (which may take negative values) submodular function f can be decomposed as*

$$f(S) = f_M(S) - c(S) \quad ,\forall\ S \subseteq U$$

where f_M is a monotone submodular function and c is an additive cost function. In particular, one possible decomposition is

$$f^*_M(S) = f(S) + \sum_{e \in S}(f(U \setminus \{e\}) - f(U))$$

$$c^*(S) = \sum_{e \in S}(f(U \setminus \{e\}) - f(U))$$

Proof. The proof is provided in Appendix A. □

Since our approximation ratio depends on the decomposition and owing to the importance of the decomposition in Proposition 1, we refer to it as f^*_M and c^*.

2.4 Multi-Query Optimization and UNSM

We now describe the changes to the MQO formulation of [25] and show the role submodularity plays in the same. As defined above, *bestCost*(Q, S) includes the cost of computing and materializing the set of PQDAG nodes to be materialized S. Consider a scenario where S was already materialized and we just have to find the optimal plan which *may or may not* use the materialized nodes in S. However, no further nodes may be chosen to be materialized. The cost of the optimal plan can be thought of as the *best use cost* and the function is thus called *bestUseCost*(Q, S). This function is monotonically decreasing since as more nodes are materialized, we will exploit the additional nodes only if they lead to a reduction in cost. Of course, the cost of materializing S needs to be taken into account and we call that function $c(S)$. Clearly, *bestCost*(Q, S) = *bestUseCost*$(Q, S) + c(S)$. For brevity, we refer to *bestUseCost*(Q, S) as *buc*(S).

The MQO problem can be thought of as maximizing the "materialization-benefit" (*mb*(S) for brevity) we get in the plan cost by exploiting common subexpressions over a naive execution plan which is just locally optimal and does not exploit subexpressions. Clearly the cost of the latter is $bc(\emptyset) = buc(\emptyset)$. Mathematically, *mb*$(S)$ is defined as

$$\begin{aligned} mb(S) &= bc(\emptyset) - bc(S) \\ &= buc(\emptyset) - (buc(S) + c(S)) \\ &= (buc(\emptyset) - buc(S)) - c(S) \end{aligned}$$

The function in parenthesis in the last line is a monotonically increasing function since *buc*(S) is a monotonically decreasing function. Also, if the set of materialized nodes S are "far apart" in the PQDAG, the cost of computing and materializing a node $e \in S$ can be thought of as being independent of the other nodes in S. This motivates us to assume that the c function is additive. Of course, this assumption need not be true. For example, if two of the equivalence nodes in S are just below each other, we can significantly benefit by computing the "lower" node and then just reading it from disk to compute the "upper" node. As proved in Proposition 1, under the assumption of submodularity, *mb* can always be decomposed into a difference of monotone, submodular function and an additive function[2]. Observe that

$$\forall X,\ \forall x \notin X, benefit(x, X) = -bc'(x, X)$$

Thus, the "monotonicity heuristic" assumption is essentially that the *bestCost* function is supermodular. This implies that *mb* is submodular. Note that *mb* is normalized. Thus, the problem is essentially the UNSM problem with *mb* as the submodular function. The reason why materialization benefit for a particular set of nodes may be negative is due to the fact that there may be certain nodes which may have very high materialization cost but may not have high benefit.

3. THE MARGINAL GREEDY ALGORITHM

In this section, we propose a greedy algorithm for the UNSM problem for which we prove an approximation guarantee. A proof of a matching hardness of approximation, under the assumption of P ≠ NP is presented in the next section.

Given a decomposition of a non-monotone, normalized submodular function f, let the monotone submodular and

[2]The decomposition in Proposition 1 does not actually correspond to the cost of materializing nodes but parallels are drawn for intuition

additive functions be denoted by f_M and c. Thus, the problem we want to solve is as follows

$$\max_{S \subseteq U} f(S) = \max_{S \subseteq U} f_M(S) - c(S)$$

The MarginalGreedy algorithm (Algorithm 2) has been proposed before [30], albeit for non-negative, *monotone* submodular maximization under knapsack constraints. At each iteration, the algorithm greedily selects the element with the highest use-benefit to cost ratio from those elements which satisfy a knapsack constraint. In our case, however, there is no knapsack constraint and instead we add elements as long as it leads to an increase in the value of f. We emphasize that the problem in our case is considerably different than this problem and highlight the differences in subsection 3.1.

Algorithm 2 MarginalGreedy Algorithm

```
X = ∅
Y = Set of shareable equivalence nodes in the DAG
while Y ≠ ∅ do
    Pick x ∈ Y which maximizes r(x, X) = f'_M(x,X) / c({x})
    if r(x, X) > 1 then
        X = X ∪ {x}, Y = Y \ {x}
    else
        Y = ∅
    end if
end while
return X
```

The MarginalGreedy algorithm also finally adds all elements with negative c values. This was also done in Sviridenko's case [30] as one can only increase the value of the function without increasing the budget. This is fine for us as well and can only raise the value of the function f. This is because f_M is monotone so including more elements only raises its value and we are subtracting off some negative c values which can only raise the value of f. If the decomposition used is the one given in Proposition 1, we can compute the term in the summation for each element once and store it. This can be done in just $n+1$ $bc(S)$ invocations (for the sets U and for $U \setminus \{e_i\}$ $\forall e_i \in V$). We note that while Algorithm 2 is presented referencing shared nodes in the DAG, the algorithm works for any instance of UNSM with an arbitrary universe of elements U.

3.1 Approximation Factor of Marginal Greedy

Let Θ be an optimal solution. Let X_i denote the set of nodes selected by Algorithm 2 just after the ith iteration. Define $\Delta_{f_M}(E, S) = f_M(S \cup E) - f_M(S)$, where E and S are subsets of U.

We state the main theorem of this section which mentions the approximation guarantee Algorithm 2 provides. The approximation factor is not a constant and instead depends on the value of the f and c functions at optimal.

Theorem 1. *The answer obtained by the MarginalGreedy algorithm (X) satisfies the following inequality*

$$f(X) \geq \left[1 - \frac{c(\Theta)}{f(\Theta)} \ln(1 + \frac{f(\Theta)}{c(\Theta)})\right] f(\Theta).$$

We prove the theorem after presenting a lemma and its corollary which are central to the proof. At a high level, the lemma states that upto a certain point in the execution of the algorithm, there exists an element that can be picked and has a marginal-benefit to cost ratio which is at least the marginal-benefit to cost ratio we would get if we picked all remaining elements in the optimal solution.

Lemma 1. *At any iteration $i+1 < n$ in the execution of the MarginalGreedy algorithm, if $f_M(X_i) < f(\Theta)$, then there exists some element $e \in \Theta \setminus X_i$ that satisfies*

$$\frac{\Delta_{f_M}(\{e\}, X_i)}{c(\{e\})} \geq \frac{\Delta_{f_M}(\Theta, X_i)}{c(\Theta)}.$$

Proof. Firstly, note that if

$$f_M(X_i) < f(\Theta) = f_M(\Theta) - c(\Theta) \leq f_M(\Theta),$$

then $\Theta \setminus X_i \neq \emptyset$. This is because f_M is monotonically increasing. Also, note that if S is fixed, $\Delta_{f_M}(E, S)$ is a submodular function in E, due to submodularity of f_M.

We consider two cases. Since the f_M function is monotonically increasing, the numerators on both sides of the inequality are non-negative.

Case 1. $\Delta_{f_M}(\Theta, X_i) = 0$
In this case, the RHS of the inequality is 0. Since the f_M function is monotonically increasing, $\forall e' \in \Theta \setminus X_i$, we have

$$\frac{\Delta_{f_M}(e', X_i)}{c(\{e'\})} \geq \frac{\Delta_{f_M}(\Theta, X_i)}{c(\Theta)}.$$

Since $\Theta \setminus X_i \neq \emptyset$, any element $e' \in \Theta \setminus X_i$ satisfies the required inequality.

Case 2. $\Delta_{f_M}(\Theta, X_i) > 0$
We first show that there exists some element $e \in \Theta$ for which the inequality holds. Assume the contradiction, i.e.,

$$\forall e \in \Theta, \frac{\Delta_{f_M}(\{e\}, X_i)}{c(e)} < \frac{\Delta_{f_M}(\Theta, X_i)}{c(\Theta)}.$$

$$\therefore c(e)(\Delta_{f_M}(\Theta, X_i)) > c(\Theta)(\Delta_{f_M}(\{e\}, X_i)).$$

Summing up over all $e \in \Theta$, we get

$$\sum_{e \in \Theta} c(e)(\Delta_{f_M}(\Theta, X_i)) > \sum_{e \in \Theta} c(\Theta)(\Delta_{f_M}(\{e\}, X_i))$$

$$\Longrightarrow (\Delta_{f_M}(\Theta, X_i)) \sum_{e \in \Theta} c(e) > c(\Theta) \sum_{e \in \Theta} (\Delta_{f_M}(\{e\}, X_i))$$

$$\Longrightarrow (\Delta_{f_M}(\Theta, X_i)) c(\Theta) > c(\Theta) \sum_{e \in \Theta} (\Delta_{f_M}(\{e\}, X_i))$$

$$\Longrightarrow \Delta_{f_M}(\Theta, X_i) > \sum_{e \in \Theta} (\Delta_{f_M}(\{e\}, X_i)).$$

Since X_i is fixed, $\Delta_{f_M}(E, X_i)$ is a submodular function in E. Thus, we have

$$\Delta_{f_M}(\Theta, X_i) \leq \sum_{e \in \Theta} (\Delta_{f_M}(\{e\}, X_i)).$$

This leads to a contradiction. Thus, there exists some element $e' \in \Theta$ for which the required inequality holds.

Now, observe that the RHS of the required inequality in this case is strictly positive and $\forall e \in X_i$, the LHS of the inequality is 0. Hence, $e' \notin X_i$ and we are done. □

Corollary 1. *When the conditions of Lemma 1 hold,*

$$\frac{\Delta_{f_M}(\{e\}, X_i) - c(\{e\})}{\Delta_{f_M}(\{e\}, X_i)} \geq \frac{\Delta_{f_M}(\Theta, X_i) - c(\Theta)}{\Delta_{f_M}(\Theta, X_i)}.$$

PROOF. From Lemma 1, we have

$$\frac{\Delta_{f_M}(\{e\}, X_i)}{c(\{e\})} \geq \frac{\Delta_{f_M}(\Theta, X_i)}{c(\Theta)}.$$

Since f_M is monotonically increasing, it implies

$$\frac{\Delta_{f_M}(\{e\}, X_i) - c(\{e\})}{\Delta_{f_M}(\{e\}, X_i)} \geq \frac{\Delta_{f_M}(\Theta, X_i) - c(\Theta)}{\Delta_{f_M}(\Theta, X_i)},$$

and we are done. □

PROOF. (of Theorem 1) Say the MarginalGreedy algorithm runs for $l \leq n$ iterations. Define $\alpha(X_i)$ to be the rate of increase of f with respect to f_M just after the ith iteration (and thus the current chosen set of elements is X_i). Further, let $e \in U \setminus X_i$ be the next element that will be chosen by the MarginalGreedy algorithm. Note that e is actually a function of X_i and, thus, once X_i is fixed, so is e. Mathematically,

$$\alpha(X_i) = \frac{f(X_i \cup \{e\}) - f(X_i)}{\delta(f_M(X_i))}$$

where $\delta(f_M(X_i)) = f_M(X_i \cup \{e\}) - f_M(X_i)$.

Let $j \leq l$ be the maximal index such that $f_M(X_j) < f(\Theta)$. The rate of increase at iteration i of the algorithm is at least as large as choosing the element from $\Theta \setminus X_i$ with the rate presented in LHS of Corollary 1.

The corollary also implies that while $f_M(X_i) < f(\Theta)$, the greedy algorithm has an element that it can pick. This implies that $j < l$. Thus, we have

$$f(X_l) = \sum_{i=0}^{l-1} \alpha(X_i)\delta(f_M(X_i)).$$

Using Corollary 1,

$$\begin{aligned} f(X_l) &\geq \sum_{i=0}^{l-1} \left(\frac{f_M(\Theta) - f_M(X_i) - c(\Theta)}{f_M(\Theta) - f_M(X_i)}\right)\delta(f_M(X_i)) \\ &\geq \sum_{i=0}^{l-1} \left(1 - \frac{c(\Theta)}{f_M(\Theta) - f_M(X_i)}\right)\delta(f_M(X_i)). \end{aligned}$$

Since the term in the parenthesis in the last line is a decreasing function of $f_M(X_i)$, we get

$$\begin{aligned} f(X_l) &\geq \int_0^{f_M(X_l)} \left(1 - \frac{c(\Theta)}{f_M(\Theta) - u}\right) du \\ &\geq \int_0^{f(\Theta)} \left(1 - \frac{c(\Theta)}{f_M(\Theta) - u}\right) du \\ &= \Big[u + c(\Theta)\ln(f_M(\Theta) - u)\Big]_0^{f(\Theta)} \\ &= f(\Theta) + c(\Theta)\ln\left(\frac{f_M(\Theta) - f(\Theta)}{f_M(\Theta)}\right) \\ &= f(\Theta) + c(\Theta)\ln\left(\frac{c(\Theta)}{f(\Theta) + c(\Theta)}\right) \\ &= f(\Theta) - c(\Theta)\ln\left(\frac{c(\Theta) + f(\Theta)}{c(\Theta)}\right) \\ &= f(\Theta) - c(\Theta)\ln\left(1 + \frac{f(\Theta)}{c(\Theta)}\right) \\ &= \left[1 - \frac{c(\Theta)}{f(\Theta)}\ln\left(1 + \frac{f(\Theta)}{c(\Theta)}\right)\right] f(\Theta). \end{aligned}$$

This concludes our proof and gives us our required approximation factor of $\left[1 - \frac{c(\Theta)}{f(\Theta)}\ln\left(1 + \frac{f(\Theta)}{c(\Theta)}\right)\right]$. □

Since the approximation ratio depends on the decomposition (specifically the function c), it is natural to ask whether different decompositions can lead to different solutions and approximation ratios. This is indeed the case; given a decomposition f_M and c, we can add a positive linear function $d(S) = \sum_{i \in S} d_i$ to both f_M and c, we still have a valid decomposition and the approximation factor has become smaller. This is because $f(\Theta)$ is fixed but $c(\Theta)$ becomes larger and clearly, the ratio is a decreasing function of c. Since this is the case, one may ask what is the "best" decomposition for this problem? We now show that the decomposition in Proposition 1, f_M^* and c^*, is indeed the best decomposition. This is done by first improving the ratio for an arbitrary decomposition and then showing that the improvement procedure for f_M^* and c^* does not lead to any improvement. In fact, in the next section, we will show a hardness of approximation which matches the ratio provided by this decomposition.

First we show how to obtain from an arbitrary decomposition f_M and c, another decomposition $\widetilde{f}_M$ and $\widetilde{c}$ such that the ratio improves. This happens if we can subtract a linear term from f_M and c while preserving monotonicity of f_M based on the above argument. And then we show that for f_M^* and c^*, this improvement procedure returns f_M^* and c^*

Proposition 2. *Given an arbitrary decomposition f_M and c of a normalized submodular function f, i.e., $f(S) = f_M(S) - c(S)$ $\forall$ $S \subseteq V$ with monotone f_M and consider another decomposition*

$$\widetilde{f}_M(S) = f_M(S) - \sum_{i \in S} (f_M(U) - f_M(U \setminus i))$$

$$\widetilde{c}(S) = c(S) - \sum_{i \in S} (f_M(U) - f_M(U \setminus i))$$

Then, $\widetilde{f}_M$ is monotone. Furthermore, for the decomposition in Proposition 1, f_M^* and c^*, $\widetilde{f}_M^* = f_M^*$ and $\widetilde{c}^* = c^*$.

PROOF. The proof is provided in Appendix A. □

We now remark on certain aspects of the algorithm and its analysis. Since the algorithm is inspired by [30], one may ask whether running that algorithm for multiple values of the budget in the knapsack constraint leads to the same answer. Indeed, this is the case with the budget being the value of $c(\Theta)$. However, since we do not apriori know $c(\Theta)$, we would have to potentially try out a large number of budget values which is not feasible. Furthermore, our analysis of the approximation ratio crucially uses the fact that we are actually running the algorithm on this decomposition of f in order to maximize f itself, and not maximizing a monotone submodular function subject to knapsack constraints.

4. INAPPROXIMABILITY OF UNSM

In this section, we prove a hardness of approximation result for the UNSM problem, when the size of the universe is part of the input, which matches the approximation factor given by the MarginalGreedy algorithm in Theorem 1 when the decomposition used is f_M^* and c^* as defined in Proposition 1.

Theorem 2. *For any $\varepsilon > 0$, it is NP-hard to approximate the unconstrained, normalized submodular maximization problem to a factor of at least*

$$\left(1 - \frac{\ln(1+\gamma)}{\gamma} + \varepsilon\right).$$

Here, $\gamma = \frac{f(\Theta)}{c^*(\Theta)}$ and Θ is an optimal solution to the UNSM problem.

This approximation factor depends on the value at optimal (which may go to 0), implying that a constant factor approximation to the UNSM problem is unlikely.

Before proving Theorem 2, we first present a separation result of the Max Coverage problem which is central to the proof of Theorem 2.

4.1 Inapproximability of Max Coverage

An instance $\mathcal{I} = (X, \mathcal{S})$ of the Set Cover problem is defined as follows: we are given the ground set $X = \{e_1, e_2, \ldots, e_n\}$ and $\mathcal{S} = \{S_1, S_2, \ldots, S_m\} \subseteq 2^X$. The goal is to choose the minimum number of sets $\mathcal{O} \subseteq \mathcal{S}$ such that $\bigcup_{S_i \in \mathcal{O}} S_i = X$. Feige [7] showed that for any $\varepsilon > 0$, there is no $(1-\varepsilon)\ln n$-approximation polynomial time algorithm for this problem unless $\mathsf{NP} \subseteq \mathsf{DTIME}(n^{O(\log\log n)})$. The hardness was later proved under the weaker assumption of $\mathsf{P} \neq \mathsf{NP}$ by [18, 5].

A problem closely related to the Set Cover problem is the Max Coverage problem. An instance of the Max Coverage problem consists of an instance $\mathcal{I} = (X, \mathcal{S}, l)$ where X is the ground set, $\mathcal{S}$ is a collection of subsets of X, and $l \leq m$ is an integer specifying the budget. The goal is to select l sets $S_{i_1}, S_{i_2} \ldots, S_{i_l}$ and cover as many elements of the ground set as possible. Feige [7] shows that it is NP-hard to approximate this problem to a factor better than $1 - 1/e$. Krishnaswamy and Sviridenko [14] prove the following separation result (which is an extension of the Max Coverage hardness stated above) which is of interest to us.

Theorem 3. *(Theorem 2.2 in [14]) Suppose there exists a polynomial algorithm, which for some constants $B \geq 1$ and $0 < \varepsilon < e^{-B}$ has the following property : Given any instance $(X, \mathcal{S}, l)$ of Max Coverage with optimal value equal to $|X|$ (i.e., there exist l sets that cover the ground set X completely), the algorithm picks a collection of βl sets for some $\beta \in [0, B]$ which can cover $(1 - e^{-\beta} + \varepsilon)n$ elements. Then $\mathsf{P} = \mathsf{NP}$. Note that we allow the algorithm to pick different values of β for different instances of the problem.*

Theorem 2.2 in [14] is actually stated under the stronger assumption of $\mathsf{NP} \not\subseteq \mathsf{DTIME}(n^{O(\log\log n)})$. Their reduction relies on the hardness of Set Cover which, at the time of that paper, was known only under this stronger assumption. Leveraging the set cover hardness result by [18, 5] under the weaker assumption of $\mathsf{P} \neq \mathsf{NP}$, we arrive at Theorem 3 without any changes to the proof provided in [14].

Note that the coverage function $f(\mathcal{A}) = \left|\bigcup_{S \in \mathcal{A}} S\right|$ is a monotone, submodular function. The proof of Theorem 2 proceeds by considering a special case of UNSM where for a Max Coverage instance, $f_M(\mathcal{A})$ is taken to be a scaling of the coverage function and the additive cost function $c(\mathcal{A})$ is a scaling of the cardinality of the chosen set of subsets $\mathcal{A}$. We call this the Profitted Max Coverage problem.

Problem 1. *(The Profitted Max Coverage problem) An instance of this problem consists of an instance $\mathcal{I} = (X, \mathcal{S}, l)$ like the Max Coverage problem. Consider γ to be a constant for this problem whose value will be revealed later.*

Let $f_M(\mathcal{A}) = \frac{(\gamma+1)}{\gamma} \frac{\left|\bigcup_{S \in \mathcal{A}} S\right|}{n}$ and $c(\mathcal{A}) = \frac{1}{\gamma}\frac{|\mathcal{A}|}{l}$. The goal is to maximize

$$\begin{aligned} f(\mathcal{A}) &= f_M(\mathcal{A}) - c(\mathcal{A}) \\ &= \frac{(\gamma+1)}{\gamma} \frac{\left|\bigcup_{S \in \mathcal{A}} S\right|}{n} - \frac{1}{\gamma}\frac{|\mathcal{A}|}{l} \end{aligned}$$

Proof. (of Theorem 2) We want to show that if there exists a polynomial time algorithm which approximates the Profitted Max Coverage problem to a ratio better than

$$1 - \frac{\ln(\gamma+1)}{\gamma} + \varepsilon\frac{(\gamma+1)}{\gamma},$$

then $\mathsf{P} = \mathsf{NP}$.

We consider a hard instance $\mathcal{I} = (X, \mathcal{S}, l)$ of the Max Coverage problem such that the optimal value is n (i.e., there exist l sets to cover the entire ground set X). Now, let functions f, f_M and c be defined as in Problem 1.

[*Completeness*] Let us take a collection of l sets $\mathcal{G} = \{S_{i_1}, S_{i_2}, \ldots, S_{i_l}\}$ that cover the ground set X (such a collection exists because $\mathcal{I}$ is a Max Coverage instance with optimal value n). The optimal value of the corresponding Profitted Max Coverage instance occurs when exactly the sets in $\mathcal{G}$ are chosen.

$$\begin{aligned} f(\mathcal{G}) &= \frac{(\gamma+1)}{\gamma}\frac{n}{n} - \frac{1}{\gamma}\frac{l}{l} \\ &= \frac{(\gamma+1)}{\gamma} - \frac{1}{\gamma} \\ &= 1. \end{aligned}$$

Observe that $\frac{f(\mathcal{G})}{c(\mathcal{G})} = \gamma$.

[*Soundness*] It is easy to see that we will never choose more than $(\gamma+1)l$ sets as the function f will take negative values in those cases.

For any set, say $\mathcal{F}$, of βl (where $\beta \in [0, \gamma+1]$) subsets from $\mathcal{S}$ which cover at most $(1 - e^{-\beta} + \varepsilon)n$ elements, the value of the Profitted Max Coverage instance in this case is at most:

$$\begin{aligned} f(\mathcal{F}) &\leq \frac{(\gamma+1)}{\gamma}\frac{(1-e^{-\beta}+\varepsilon)n}{n} - \frac{1}{\gamma}\frac{\beta l}{l} \\ &= \frac{(\gamma+1)}{\gamma}(1 - e^{-\beta} + \varepsilon) - \frac{1}{\gamma}\beta \\ &= \frac{(\gamma+1)(1-e^{-\beta}+\varepsilon) - \beta}{\gamma}. \end{aligned}$$

Differentiating the expression in the last line w.r.t β and setting the derivative to 0, we get

$$\begin{aligned} &\frac{\gamma+1}{\gamma}(e^{-\beta}) - \frac{1}{\gamma} = 0 \\ &\implies e^{\beta} = (\gamma+1) \\ &\implies \beta = \ln(\gamma+1) \leq (\gamma+1). \end{aligned}$$

Thus, the value $f(\mathcal{F})$ is always less than the value attained for that value of β and is

$$f(\mathcal{F}) \leq 1 - \frac{\ln(\gamma+1)}{\gamma} + \varepsilon\frac{(\gamma+1)}{\gamma}.$$

Now, if there exists a polynomial time algorithm (say Alg) which solves the Profitted Max Coverage problem to a factor better than $1-\frac{\ln(\gamma+1)}{\gamma}+\varepsilon\frac{(\gamma+1)}{\gamma}$, then on any input instance of the Max Coverage problem such that the optimal value is n, Alg will output a set $\mathcal{F}$ such that $f(\mathcal{F}) > 1-\frac{\ln(\gamma+1)}{\gamma}+\varepsilon\frac{(\gamma+1)}{\gamma}$ (since the optimal value is 1). Thus, $\mathcal{F}$ covers strictly more than $(1-e^{-\beta}+\varepsilon)n$ elements with $\beta = \frac{|\mathcal{F}|}{l}$ (by contrapositivity). By Theorem 3, we have P = NP.

The above argument establishes the hardness for $\gamma = \frac{f(\Theta)}{c(\Theta)}$ for the function c defined in Problem 1. Since the factor depends only on $c(\Theta)$, if we can show that $c(\Theta) = c^*(\Theta)$ for these hard instances, we would be done. This can be shown by considering the expression for $c^*(\Theta)$ in this case :

$$\begin{aligned}
c^*(\Theta) &= \sum_{i\in\Theta} \left(f(U\setminus\{i\}) - f(U)\right) \\
&= \sum_{i\in\Theta} \left(f_M(U\setminus\{i\}) - f_M(U) - c(U\setminus\{i\}) + c(U)\right) \\
&= \sum_{i\in\Theta} \left(c(U) - c(U\setminus\{i\})\right) + \sum_{i\in\Theta} \left(f_M(U\setminus\{i\}) - f_M(U)\right) \\
&= c(\Theta) + \sum_{i\in\Theta} \left(f_M(U\setminus\{i\}) - f_M(U)\right) \\
&= c(\Theta) + \frac{(\gamma+1)}{\gamma\cdot n}\sum_{i\in\Theta}\left[\left|\bigcup_{S\in U\setminus\{i\}} S\right| - \left|\bigcup_{S\in U} S\right|\right]
\end{aligned}$$

Note that all the hard instances of SetCover and Max Coverage are derived from the construction of [15]. All such instances are such that each element has multiple subsets which may cover it (intuitively if there is only one subset which covers a particular element in any hard instance, then we will pick it and get a smaller, easier instance of the problem). Since the union of all subsets of the given instance is n and so is the union of all but one of the available subsets in the hard instance, each term in the above summation is 0. This implies that $c^*(\Theta) = c(\Theta)$ and we are done. □

5. SPEEDING UP THE MARGINAL GREEDY

In the worst case, the MarginalGreedy algorithm runs in $\mathcal{O}(n^2 \cdot \text{EO})$ time, where n is the number of shareable nodes and EO is the time to evaluate $bc(S)$, i.e., the time to optimize the batch of queries given the set of nodes S, to be materialized. This makes the algorithm expensive since n itself may be exponential in the worst case. Thus, we would like to reduce the time taken by the algorithm without sacrificing on the theoretical guarantees on the quality of the solution proved in Section 3. In this section, we present some optimizations to our algorithm to improve its running time.

5.1 Basic Optimizations

We first note that two optimizations presented in [25] can be used for our algorithm as well. Their first observation is about searching only over all the shareable nodes. As noted above, this can be directly used by us since our algorithm just presents a different heuristic for choosing which nodes to materialize. Their second optimization presents a way to incrementally update the *bestCost* function for various sets that exploits the result of earlier cost computations to incrementally compute the new plan. Since the *mb* function is just a linear transformation of the *bestCost* function and our greedy algorithm (at least when the decomposition presented in the proof of Proposition 1 is used) is also concerned with just successive differences in the values of the *bestCost* function, their optimization can also be used to speed up our algorithm; for details see [25].

Another optimization (not in [25]) that can be made is based on a simple observation of the greedy algorithm and by exploiting submodularity. In the ith iteration, the MarginalGreedy algorithm needs to compute the maximum benefit to cost ratio $\frac{f'_M(e,X_{i-1})}{c(\{e\})}$. Thus, if while scanning elements to compute the maximum, we encounter an element that has the marginal-benefit to cost ratio less than 1, we can remove it from the set Y of elements to be searched over as it will never be picked by the MarginalGreedy algorithm in the future iterations either. This is because f_M is also submodular and the size of X_i always increases as i increases so the value of the marginal-benefit to cost ratio only decreases as the algorithm proceeds and will never become greater than 1. A similar optimization for the simple greedy algorithm used for monotone, submodular maximization under cardinality constraints is also possible.

5.2 The Lazy Marginal Greedy algorithm

The third optimization in [25] essentially leverages supermodularity to improve the running time of the greedy algorithm. The argument is similar to that used by [16] for the LazyGreedy algorithm. We observe that a similar argument as the ones presented in these two papers may be used for the MarginalGreedy algorithm and is presented next.

As noted previously, in each iteration i, the MarginalGreedy algorithm must identify the element e with the maximum marginal-benefit to cost ratio $\frac{f'_M(e,X_{i-1})}{c(\{e\})}$. For each element e, the denominator is fixed and the marginal benefits are monotonically nonincreasing during the iterations of the algorithm, i.e., $f'_M(e,X_i) \geq f'_M(e,X_j)$ whenever $i \leq j$. Thus, instead of recomputing $\frac{f'_M(e,X_{i-1})}{c(\{e\})}$ for each element $e \in V$, which requires $\mathcal{O}(n)$ computations of f, the LazyMarginalGreedy algorithm maintains a list of upper bounds $u(e)$ (initialized to a large value) on the marginal-benefit to cost ratio sorted in decreasing order (using a heap).

In each iteration, the algorithm extracts the element with largest $u(e)$ from the ordered list of remaining elements and add its to the current solution. If, after this update, $u(e) \geq u(e')$ $\forall e' \neq e$, then submodularity guarantees that $\frac{f'_M(e,X_{i-1})}{c(\{e\})} \geq \frac{f'_M(e',X_{i-1})}{c(\{e\})}$ $\forall e' \neq e$, and therefore the algorithm has identified the element with the largest marginal benefit to cost ratio without computing the ratio for a potentially large number of elements e'.

5.3 Universe Reduction under size constraints

We may sometimes want to consider a cardinality constraint (say k) on the number of nodes to be materialized. This may arise due to storage constraints which only allow materialization of a few subexpressions. We adapt our greedy algorithm for this constraint by simply stopping after k elements are picked.

While, at this point, we do not show any theoretical approximation guarantees for this problem, there is a way to leverage this cardinality constraint to prune out certain elements from the ground set U. This preprocessing step may be used to reduce the size of the set of PQDAG nodes U on which the algorithm will be run.

We show that the algorithm run on this reduced set is the same as that obtained when the algorithm runs on the full set. This check is useful only when there is a cardinality constraint of $k < n$, as we will show.

Theorem 4. *Let $U = \{e_1, \ldots, e_n\}$ be the set of all shareable PQDAG nodes ordered as*

$$\frac{f'_M(e_1, U \setminus \{e_1\})}{c(\{e_1\})} \geq \ldots \geq \frac{f'_M(e_n, U \setminus \{e_n\})}{c(\{e_n\})}.$$

Furthermore, let

$$U' = \{e \in U | \frac{f_M(e)}{c(\{e\})} \geq \frac{f'_M(e_k, U \setminus \{e_k\})}{c(\{e_k\})}\} \text{ for } k < n.$$

The output of the MarginalGreedy algorithm (with cardinality constraint of k) when it runs on U is the same as the output when it runs on U'.

PROOF. The proof is provided in Appendix A. □

It is important to note that this strategy may not always lead to a reduction in the ground set but it may lead to pruning in certain cases.

Note that this pruning procedure can be modified to work for the simple greedy algorithm for monotone, submodular maximization under cardinality constraints. The proof is also along similar lines as those stated above.

6. EXPERIMENTAL SECTION

We now describe our experimental setup and findings. We worked with the original C++ code of Pyro which implemented the Greedy algorithm [25]. We extended it by implementing the Marginal Greedy algorithm. All the optimizations discussed in Section 5 are implemented with the exception of the one discussed in subsection 5.3 as we are mainly interested in the best plan without imposing any cardinality constraints.

The optimizer rule set consists of select push down, join commutativity and associativity (to generate bushy join trees), and select and aggregate subsumption. The physical operators included sort-based aggregation, merge join, nested loop join, indexed selection and relation scan. The implementation includes handling physical properties (sort order and presence of indices) on base and intermediate relations, unification and subsumption during DAG generation (see [25] for details).

The block size was taken as 4KB and our cost functions assume 6MB is available to each operator during execution (we also conducted experiments with memory sizes of 128MB). Standard techniques were used for estimating costs, using statistics about relations. The cost estimates are of the standard resource consumption estimates (see Appendix C of Roy's thesis [24] for details) which contain an I/O component and a CPU component, with seek time as 10 msec, transfer time of 2 msec/block for read and 4 msec/block for write, and CPU cost of 0.2 msec/block of data processed.

We assume that intermediate results are pipelined to the next input, using an iterator model as in Volcano; they are saved to disk only if the result is to be materialized for sharing. The materialization cost is the cost of writing out the results sequentially. The tests were performed on a 2.4 GHz Intel i7 processor laptop with 8GB memory running Linux. We compare Marginal Greedy with Greedy and stand-alone Volcano (no MQO). The optimization time of our Marginal Greedy algorithm was very close to that of the Greedy algorithm in [25]. The optimization times are measured as CPU time.

6.1 Experiment 1 (Batched TPCD Queries)

The workload for the first experiment models a system where several TPCD queries are executed as a batch. The workload consists of subsequences of the queries Q3, Q5, Q7, Q8, Q9 and Q10. Each query was repeated twice with different selection constants. Composite query BQi consists of the first i of the above queries, and we used composite queries BQ1 to BQ6 in our experiments. The TPCD database is used at a scale of 1 (1 GB total size), with a clustered index on the primary keys for all the base relations. We also ran the queries in this experiment and the next at a scale of 100 (total size 100GB).

Note that although a query is repeated with two different values for a selection constant, we found that the selection operator generally lands up at the bottom of the best Volcano plan tree, and the two best plan trees may not have common subexpressions.

The results on the two workloads (1GB and 100 GB total sizes) are shown in Figure 4. The number on top of the bars for Greedy and Marginal Greedy denotes the number of materialized nodes. Greedy does substantially better than Volcano (without MQO) by upto 57%. Marginal Greedy always does as well as or better than Greedy. In fact, the results are the same only for BQ1 where both chose to materialize the two nodes which lead to benefit. For all other queries in the experiment with 1GB Total Size, the improvement of Marginal Greedy is always between 12% and 25%. This is primarily due to the number of materialized nodes by Marginal Greedy being more than that by Greedy. BQ5 is especially interesting in Figure 4a as the number of materialized nodes is the same yet there is almost a 20% improvement over Greedy. In fact, for queries from BQ4 to BQ6, the intersection in the materialized nodes by the two algorithms had an overlap of 1 or 2 only.

In the experiment with 100GB Total Size (Figure 4b), as mentioned, the nodes chosen to be materialized for BQ1 are the same for both algorithms. For the rest of the queries, the number of materialized nodes is much larger than in the 1GB size dataset. While the relative gains in this dataset might seem comparable or slightly lesser than those observed in the smaller dataset, the actual gains in these cases are substantial due to large costs coming from these large data sizes. In these queries, there were 1 or 2 nodes which had substantially more benefit and got picked by both Greedy and Marginal Greedy. While Greedy picked a few more nodes which seemed benefical initially, Marginal Greedy picked many more nodes, each of which had moderate benefit but lead to an overall decrease in the cost. This behaviour was particularly observed in BQ5 and BQ6 and we conjecture for larger sets of queries on larger data sets, this behavior may be more pronounced.

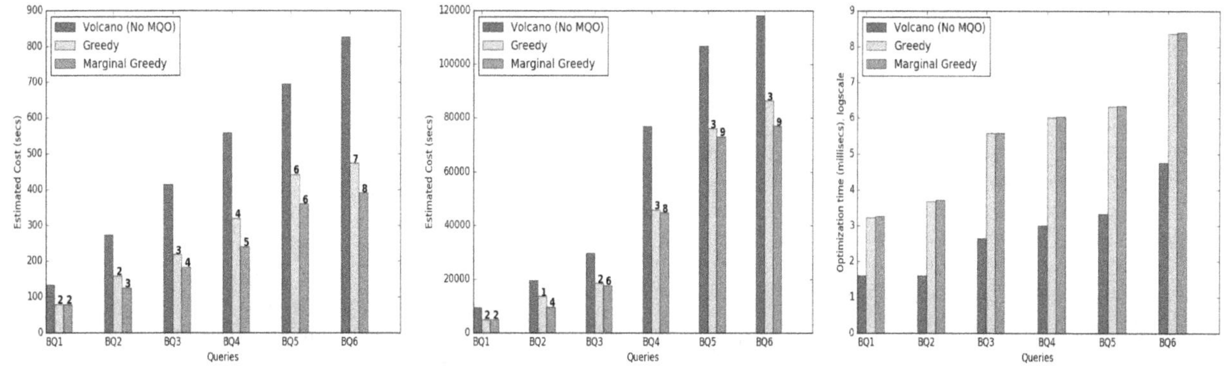

(a) 1GB Total Size (b) 100GB Total Size (c) Optimization Time (logscale)

Figure 4: Results for batched TPCD queries (Experiment 1)

The optimization times for the queries are shown in Figure 4c. Since the values for Greedy and Marginal Greedy were very close to each other, we present the results in logscale. As can be seen, the optimization times are very close to each other. We stress that while the execution cost of a query depends on the size of the underlying data, the cost of optimization does not.

6.2 Experiment 2 (Stand-Alone TPCD Queries)

Roy et al. [25] also had an experiment consisting of four individual queries based on TPCD using the same data sizes (1GB and 100GB) and the same indices. These queries had common subexpressions within themselves and benefitted from MQO to optimize just those queries individually. However, in each of these queries only one node was beneficial and hence, both algorithms found that node and resulted in the same answer. We present the results here for completeness. We explain these queries themselves and the actual results are presented in Figure 5 in Appendix B.

TPCD query Q2 has a large nested query, and repeated invocations of the nested query in a correlated evaluation could benefit from reusing some of the intermediate results. Greedy and Marginal Greedy gave a plan with an estimated cost of 79 seconds for the smaller data set and 1929 seconds for the larger one. Decorrelation is an alternative to correlated evaluation and Q2-D is a (manually) decorrelated version of Q2 (due to decorrelation, Q2-D is actually a batch of queries). Multi-query optimization also gives substantial gains on the decorrelated query Q2-D, results in a plan of estimated cost 46 and 2059 for the two data sizes respectively, by both algorithms. We next considered the TPCD queries Q11 and Q15, both of which have common subexpressions, and hence make a case for multi-query optimization. For Q11, both the greedy algorithms lead to a plan of approximately half the cost as that returned by Volcano. The improvements for Q15 are similar but more pronounced for the smaller data set.

The conclusion based on the experiments seems to be that when there are multiple possible nodes that can be materialized, Greedy chooses the nodes which result in considerable improvements early on but Marginal Greedy is more global and chooses to materialize more nodes which might have moderate benefit individually but can result in overall benefits.

7. RELATED WORK

We now present the related work in the areas of multi-query optimization and submodular maximization.

7.1 Multi-Query Optimization

The MQO problem has received significant attention in the past [26, 20, 27, 22, 29]. Initial work [26, 20, 22, 27] proposed solutions that were not fully integrated with the query optimizer and were primarily exhaustive.

Subramanian and Venkataraman [29] consider sharing only among the best plans of the query; this approach can be implemented as an efficient, post-optimization phase in existing systems, but can be highly suboptimal.

To choose the set of nodes to be materialized, Roy et al. [25] use a greedy algorithm discussed in detail in Section 2. Dalvi et al. [4] explores the possibility of sharing intermediate results by pipelining, avoiding unnecessary materializiations. Thomas et al. [31] consider the MQO problem in Volcano taking scheduling and caching into account. They present an exhaustive algorithm which takes $\mathcal{O}(n^n)$ time, which is clearly infeasible.

Zhou et al. [32] propose a framework to use common subexpressions for MQO and materialized view selection in a query optimizer based on the Cascades framework [9]. The focus however is on "covering" subexpressions at the LQDAG level and they do not take into account competing physical properties like sort orders and partitioning properties from different consumers.

Silva et al. [28] consider physical properties in a cost-based fashion. However, their solution is also based on heuristics which materializes *every* common subexpression at the LQDAG level. The best physical property for each subexpression is chosen and all consumers are forced to use the same physical property, which can be sub-optimal. Even with this heuristic, their approach can be very expensive when there are many potential physical properties for each subexpression.

7.2 Submodular Maximization

Submodular maximization has received a significant amount of attention in optimization [3, 19, 2] with wide applicability in machine learning, computer vision and information retrieval [11, 12, 1, 13]. In this problem, we are given a submodular function f and a universe U, with the goal of selecting a subset $S \subseteq U$ which maximizes $f(S)$.

Typically, S must satisfy additional feasibility constraints such as cardinality, knapsack or matroid constraints.

This problem is NP-hard even for the simplest problems which involve only *cardinality constraints* and monotone functions. Nemhauser et al. [19] show that a simple greedy algorithm gives a $(1 - 1/e)$ approximation for monotone submodular maximization under cardinality constraints. They further show that it is NP-hard to obtain a better approximation guarantee. Sviridenko [30] presents a modified greedy algorithm for monotone submodular function maximization under knapsack constraints and is the main motivation for our algorithm.

Buchbinder et al. [2] gave a $1/2$-approximation algorithm for unconstrained non-monotone submodular maximization, for which there is a matching hardness result. However, all these results assume non-negativity of the function f. Mittal and Shulz [17] show that a constant factor approximation for non-negative supermodular minimization is NP-hard. Inapproximability of non-monotone submodular maximization (with possibly negative values) is also well known. More specfically, it is NP-hard to even decide whether the optimum is non-negative or not for a general non-monotone submodular function (which may take negative values). We were able to sidestep this hardness as we already knew that the optimum is greater than or equal to zero due to the normalized assumption. To the best of our knowledge, ours is the first work which, under the assumption of $f(\emptyset) = 0$, provides an approximation algorithm with a matching hardness of approximation result for unconstrained non-monotone submodular maximization when the function may take negative values. Since the hardness of approximation factor depends on the optimal (and may go to 0), this rules out constant factor approximations for the problem even in the restricted setting of $f(\emptyset) = 0$.

8. CONCLUSIONS AND FUTURE WORK

In this paper, we have presented a reformulation of the well-studied MQO problem. Under the assumption of supermodularity of the *bestCost* function, we propose a greedy algorithm for the maximization problem and provide an approximation factor guarantee for our algorithm. We then showed that obtaining a better approximation factor than the one attained by our greedy algorithm is NP-hard. Such a theoretical guarantee on the quality of any heuristic has not been presented before. Since the underlying problem solved in this paper is the unconstrained, normalized submodular maximization problem, with possibly negative values, we believe our results can be useful beyond just MQO.

One area of future work is the problem of *non-negative*, non-monotone submodular maximization problem under cardinality constraints and more generally, matroid constraints. This is an open problem and even the most recent work [6] has a considerable gap in the approximation ratio and the hardness of approximation known. We would like to see if ideas in this paper like the "best decomposition" can be used to devise algorithms with better guarantees for that problem.

9. ACKNOWLEDGMENTS

We would like to thank Sebastien Tavenas, Amit Deshpande, Deeparnab Chakrabarty and Ravishankar Krishnaswamy for comments on the paper.

10. REFERENCES

[1] Y. Boykov and M. Jolly. Interactive graph cuts for optimal boundary and region segmentation of objects in N-D images. In *ICCV*, pages 105–112, 2001.

[2] N. Buchbinder, M. Feldman, J. Naor, and R. Schwartz. A tight linear time (1/2)-approximation for unconstrained submodular maximization. In *53rd Annual IEEE Symposium on Foundations of Computer Science, FOCS*, pages 649–658, 2012.

[3] G. Călinescu, C. Chekuri, M. Pál, and J. Vondrák. Maximizing a monotone submodular function subject to a matroid constraint. *SIAM J. Comput.*, 40(6):1740–1766, 2011.

[4] N. N. Dalvi, S. K. Sanghai, P. Roy, and S. Sudarshan. Pipelining in multi-query optimization. *J. Comput. Syst. Sci.*, 66(4):728–762, 2003.

[5] I. Dinur and D. Steurer. Analytical approach to parallel repetition. In *Symposium on Theory of Computing, STOC*, pages 624–633, 2014.

[6] A. Ene and H. L. Nguyen. Constrained submodular maximization: Beyond 1/e. In *IEEE 57th Annual Symposium on Foundations of Computer Science, FOCS*, pages 248–257, 2016.

[7] U. Feige. A threshold of ln n for approximating set cover. *J. ACM*, 45(4):634–652, 1998.

[8] U. Feige, V. S. Mirrokni, and J. Vondrák. Maximizing non-monotone submodular functions. *SIAM J. Comput.*, 40(4):1133–1153, 2011.

[9] G. Graefe. The Cascades framework for query optimization. *IEEE Data Eng. Bull.*, 18(3):19–29, 1995.

[10] G. Graefe and W. J. McKenna. The Volcano optimizer generator: Extensibility and efficient search. In *Proceedings of the Ninth International Conference on Data Engineering*, pages 209–218, 1993.

[11] S. Jegelka and J. A. Bilmes. Submodularity beyond submodular energies: Coupling edges in graph cuts. In *The 24th IEEE Conference on Computer Vision and Pattern Recognition, CVPR*, pages 1897–1904, 2011.

[12] D. Kempe, J. M. Kleinberg, and É. Tardos. Maximizing the spread of influence through a social network. In *Proceedings of the Ninth ACM SIGKDD International Conference on Knowledge Discovery and Data Mining*, pages 137–146, 2003.

[13] P. Kohli, M. P. Kumar, and P. H. S. Torr. P3 & beyond: Solving energies with higher order cliques. In *IEEE Computer Society Conference on Computer Vision and Pattern Recognition (CVPR)*, 2007.

[14] R. Krishnaswamy and M. Sviridenko. Inapproximability of the multi-level uncapacitated facility location problem. In *Proceedings of the Twenty-Third Annual ACM-SIAM Symposium on Discrete Algorithms, SODA*, pages 718–734, 2012.

[15] C. Lund and M. Yannakakis. On the hardness of approximating minimization problems. *J. ACM*, 41(5):960–981, 1994.

[16] M. Minoux. Accelerated greedy algorithms for maximizing submodular set functions. *Optimization Techniques*, pages 234–243, 1977.

[17] S. Mittal and A. S. Schulz. An FPTAS for optimizing a class of low-rank functions over a polytope. *Math. Program.*, 141(1-2):103–120, 2013.

[18] D. Moshkovitz. The projection games conjecture and the NP-hardness of ln n-approximating set-cover. *Theory of Computing*, 11:221–235, 2015.

[19] G. L. Nemhauser, L. A. Wolsey, and M. L. Fisher. An analysis of approximations for maximizing submodular set functions - I. *Math. Program.*, 14(1):265–294, 1978.

[20] J. Park and A. Segev. Using common subexpressions to optimize multiple queries. In *Proceedings of the Fourth International Conference on Data Engineering (ICDE)*, pages 311–319, 1988.

[21] A. Pellenkoft, C. A. Galindo-Legaria, and M. L. Kersten. The complexity of transformation-based join enumeration. In *VLDB*, pages 306–315, 1997.

[22] A. Rosenthal and U. S. Chakravarthy. Anatomy of a mudular multiple query optimizer. In *Fourteenth International Conference on Very Large Data Bases (VLDB)*, pages 230–239, 1988.

[23] N. Roussopoulos. View indexing in relational databases. *ACM Trans. Database Syst.*, 7(2):258–290, 1982.

[24] P. Roy. *Multi Query Optimization and Applications.* Ph.d. thesis, Indian Institute of Technology, Bombay, 2001.

[25] P. Roy, S. Seshadri, S. Sudarshan, and S. Bhobe. Efficient and extensible algorithms for multi query optimization. In *Proceedings of the 2000 ACM SIGMOD International Conference on Management of Data*, pages 249–260, 2000.

[26] T. K. Sellis. Multiple-query optimization. *ACM Trans. Database Syst.*, 13(1):23–52, 1988.

[27] K. Shim, T. K. Sellis, and D. S. Nau. Improvements on a heuristic algorithm for multiple-query optimization. *Data Knowl. Eng.*, 12(2):197–222, 1994.

[28] Y. N. Silva, P. Larson, and J. Zhou. Exploiting common subexpressions for cloud query processing. In *IEEE 28th International Conference on Data Engineering (ICDE)*, pages 1337–1348, 2012.

[29] S. N. Subramanian and S. Venkataraman. Cost-based optimization of decision support queries using transient views. In *SIGMOD 1998, Proceedings ACM SIGMOD International Conference on Management of Data*, pages 319–330, 1998.

[30] M. Sviridenko. A note on maximizing a submodular set function subject to a knapsack constraint. *Oper. Res. Lett.*, 32(1):41–43, 2004.

[31] D. Thomas, A. A. Diwan, and S. Sudarshan. Scheduling and caching in multiquery optimization. In *Proceedings of the 13th International Conference on Management of Data (COMAD)*, pages 150–153, 2006.

[32] J. Zhou, P. Larson, J. C. Freytag, and W. Lehner. Efficient exploitation of similar subexpressions for query processing. In *Proceedings of the ACM SIGMOD International Conference on Management of Data*, pages 533–544, 2007.

APPENDIX

A. ADDITIONAL PROOFS

We now present the missing proofs. We reproduce the theorem statements for convenience.

Proposition 1. (in the main paper) Any normalized, non-monotone (which may take negative values) submodular function f can be decomposed as

$$f(S) = f_M(S) - c(S) \quad ,\forall\ S \subseteq U$$

where f_M is a monotone submodular function and c is an additive cost function. In particular, one possible decomposition is

$$f^*_M(S) = f(S) + \sum_{e \in S}(f(U \setminus \{e\}) - f(U))$$
$$c^*(S) = \sum_{e \in S}(f(U \setminus \{e\}) - f(U))$$

PROOF. It is easy to see that c is additive and that

$$\forall\ S \subseteq X, \text{ we have } f(S) = f_M(S) - c(S)$$

Since c is additive and f is submodular, f_M is also submodular since for arbitrary $S_1 \subset S_2 \subset U$ and an arbitrary $e \in U \setminus S_2$,

$$\begin{aligned}
&f_M(S_1 \cup \{e\}) - f_M(S_1)\\
&= f(S_1 \cup \{e\}) - c(S_1 \cup \{e\}) - f(S_1) + c(S_1)\\
&= f(S_1 \cup \{e\}) - f(S_1) - c(\{e\}) \ \text{ (by linearity of } c)\\
&\geq f(S_2 \cup \{e\}) - f(S_2) - c(\{e\}) \ \text{ (by submodularity of } f)\\
&= f(S_2 \cup \{e\}) - f(S_2) - c(S_2 \cup \{e\}) + c(S_2) \ \text{ (by linearity)}\\
&= f_M(S_2 \cup \{e\}) - f_M(S_2).
\end{aligned}$$

Now we just have to show that f_M is monotone. Consider an arbitrary $S \subset U$ and an arbitrary $e \in U \setminus S$. Let us consider the expression

$$\begin{aligned}
& f_M(S \cup \{e\}) - f_M(S)\\
=\ & f(S \cup \{e\}) - f(S) + (f(U \setminus \{e\}) - f(U))\\
=\ & (f(S \cup \{e\}) - f(S)) - (f(U) - f(U \setminus \{e\}))\\
\geq\ & 0
\end{aligned}$$

The inequality in the last line follows from the fact that $S \subseteq U \setminus \{e\}$ and the submodularity of f. The terms in the summation can be suitably scaled to ensure that c is zero only at $\emptyset$ and positive everywhere else. □

Proposition 2. (in the main paper) Given an arbitrary decomposition f_M and c of a normalized submodular function f, i.e., $f(S) = f_M(S) - c(S)\ \forall\ S \subseteq V$ with monotone f_M and consider another decomposition

$$\widetilde{f}_M(S) = f_M(S) - \sum_{i \in S}\left(f_M(U) - f_M(U \setminus i)\right)$$
$$\widetilde{c}(S) = c(S) - \sum_{i \in S}\left(f_M(U) - f_M(U \setminus i)\right)$$

Then, $\widetilde{f}_M$ is monotone. Furthermore, for the decomposition in Proposition 1, f^*_M and c^*, $\widetilde{f}^*_M = f^*_M$ and $\widetilde{c}^* = c^*$.

PROOF. To show monotonicity of $\widetilde{f}_M$, it is enough to show $\forall j \in U,\ \forall S \subseteq U \setminus \{j\}, \widetilde{f}_M(S \cup \{j\}) - \widetilde{f}_M(S) \geq 0$.

$$\begin{aligned}
&\widetilde{f}_M(S \cup \{j\}) - \widetilde{f}_M(S)\\
&= f_M(S \cup \{j\}) - f_M(S) - \left(f_M(U) - f_M(U \setminus \{j\})\right)\\
&\geq 0 \ \text{ (by submodularity of } f_M)
\end{aligned}$$

For the second part, we just expand the expressions to get the desired result.

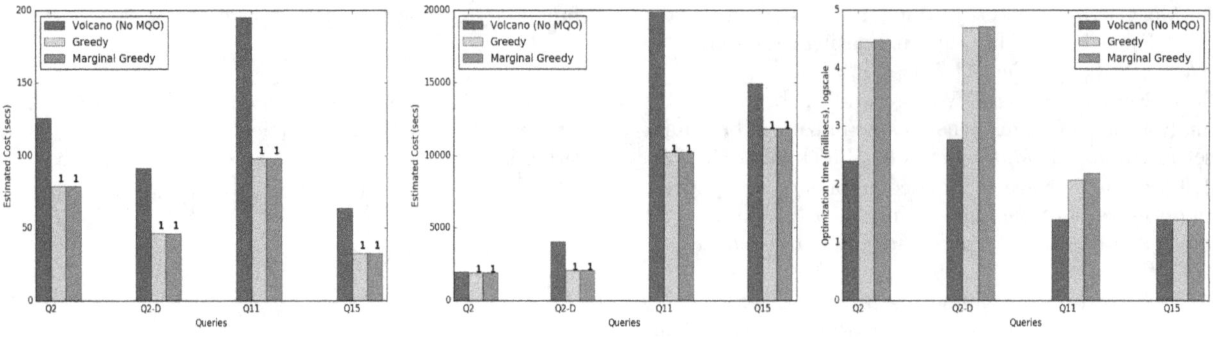

(a) 1GB Total Size (b) 100GB Total Size (c) Optimization Times (logscale)

Figure 5: Results for stand-alone TPCD queries (Experiment 2)

$$
\begin{aligned}
\widetilde{c}^*(S) &= c^*(S) - \sum_{i \in S} \left(f_M^*(U) - f_M^*(U \setminus \{i\})\right) \\
&= c^*(S) - \sum_{i \in S} f(U) - f(U \setminus \{i\}) + \left(f(U \setminus \{i\}) - f(U)\right) \\
&= c^*(S)
\end{aligned}
$$

The computation for $\widetilde{f}_M^*(S)$ proceeds similarly. □

Theorem 4. (in the main paper) Let the set of all shareable PQDAG nodes $U = \{e_1, \ldots, e_n\}$ be ordered as

$$\frac{f_M'(e_1, U \setminus \{e_1\})}{c(\{e_1\})} \geq \ldots \geq \frac{f_M'(e_n, U \setminus \{e_n\})}{c(\{e_n\})}.$$

Furthermore, let

$$U' = \{e \in U | \frac{f_M(e)}{c(\{e\})} \geq \frac{f_M'(e_k, U \setminus \{e_k\})}{c(\{e_k\})}\} \text{ for } k < n.$$

The output of the MarginalGreedy algorithm (with cardinality constraint of k) when it runs on U is the same as the output when it runs on U'.

PROOF. Without loss of generality, assume that the algorithm, when run on U', terminates after the full k steps. Let the sequence of chosen elements, in order of inclusion, be $\{s_1, s_2, \ldots, s_k\}$ and for all $i \in [k]$, let $X_i = \{s_1, s_2, \ldots, s_i\}$, as before. Clearly, $\emptyset = X_0 \subset X_1 \subset X_2 \subset \ldots \subset X_k$.

Case 1. $k = n$

This is a simple case in which all elements are chosen and, thus, U' should be equal to U which is shown as follows $\forall e \in U$, we have

$$
\begin{aligned}
\frac{f_M(\{e\})}{c(\{e\})} &= \frac{f_M'(e, \emptyset)}{c(\{e\})} \\
&\geq \frac{f_M'(e, U \setminus \{e\})}{c(\{e\})} \qquad \text{(by submodularity)} \\
&\geq \frac{f_M'(e_k, U \setminus \{e_k\})}{c(\{e_k\})}.
\end{aligned}
$$

Hence, all elements of U are going to be in U' since they all satisfy the condition to be in U'. In this case, the check is clearly wasteful since the ground set has no reduction and a lot of functional calls are made. In the MQO context, this corresponds to invoking a lot of *bestCost*(Q, S) calls, each of which are moderately expensive. Thus, in this case, the preprocessing step should just check if $k = n$ and if so, directly pass the full ground set to the greedy algorithm.

Case 2. $k < n$ & $X_k = \{e_1, e_2, \ldots, e_k\}$.

In this case, the theorem follows trivially since U' will contain all elements in X_k, along with some other elements.

Case 3. $k < n$ & $X_k \neq \{e_1, e_2, \ldots, e_k\}$.

We first make a claim which we will prove later.

Claim 1. *For all $i \in \{1, 2, \ldots, k\}$, we have*

$$\frac{f_M'(s_i, X_{i-1})}{c(\{s_i\})} \geq \frac{f_M'(e_i, U \setminus \{e_i\})}{c(\{e_i\})}.$$

The claim is used to show that elements in $U \setminus U'$ will never be picked by the MarginalGreedy algorithm. Intuitively, for any element $e \notin U'$, the $\frac{f_M'(e, X_i)}{c(\{e\})}$ ratio of picking it is largest in the first iteration (by submodularity) and that itself is less than the element with the smallest ratio of the elements selected by the greedy algorithm. So, it is guaranteed that the greedy algorithm does not pick any element which is not in U'. This is easy to see and is as follows

For all $e \in U \setminus U'$, we have

$$\frac{f_M'(e, \emptyset)}{c(\{e\})} = \frac{f_M(e)}{c(\{e\})} < \frac{f_M'(e_k, U \setminus \{e_k\})}{c(\{e_k\})}.$$

By Claim 1,

$$
\begin{aligned}
& \frac{f_M'(s_k, X_{k-1})}{c(\{s_k\})} \geq \frac{f_M'(e_k, U \setminus \{e_k\})}{c(\{e_k\})} \\
\implies & \frac{f_M'(s_k, X_{k-1})}{c(\{s_k\})} > \frac{f_M'(e, \emptyset)}{c(\{e\})}.
\end{aligned}
$$

We now present the proof of Claim 1.

PROOF. (of Claim 1) The case of $e_i \notin X_{i-1}$ is trivial due to submodularity and the greedy algorithm.

Thus, we just have to prove for the case when $e_i \in X_{i-1}$ Since $|X_{i-1}| = i - 1$, X_{i-1} cannot include all elements from the set $\{e_1, e_2, \ldots, e_i\}$. Thus, there exists some element, say, $e_z \in e_1, e_2, \ldots, e_i$ such that $e_z \notin X_{i-1}$.

$$
\begin{aligned}
\text{Thus, we have } & \frac{f_M'(s_i, X_{i-1})}{c(\{s_i\})} \\
&= \max_{e \in U \setminus X_{i-1}} \frac{f_M'(e, X_{i-1})}{c(\{e\})} \\
&\geq \frac{f_M'(e_z, X_{i-1})}{c(\{e_z\})} \\
&\geq \frac{f_M'(e_z, U \setminus \{e_z\})}{c(\{e_z\})} \quad \text{(by submodularity)}
\end{aligned}
$$

$$\geq \frac{f'_M(e_i, U \setminus \{e_i\})}{c(\{e_i\})}$$

□

This concludes our proof.

B. RESULTS OF EXPERIMENT 2

In this section, we present the results of Experiment 2 (Stand-alone TPCD). The results are shown in Figure 5.

Write-Optimized Skip Lists

Michael A. Bender*
Stony Brook University

Martín Farach-Colton†
Rutgers University

Rob Johnson*
Stony Brook University

Simon Mauras‡
ENS Lyon

Tyler Mayer*
Stony Brook University

Cynthia A. Phillips§
Sandia National Laboratories

Helen Xu¶
MIT

ABSTRACT

The skip list is an elegant dictionary data structure that is commonly deployed in RAM. A skip list with N elements supports searches, inserts, and deletes in $O(\log N)$ operations with high probability (w.h.p.) and range queries returning K elements in $O(\log N + K)$ operations w.h.p.

A seemingly natural way to generalize the skip list to external memory with block size B is to "promote" with probability $1/B$, rather than $1/2$. However, there are practical and theoretical obstacles to getting the skip list to retain its efficient performance, space bounds, and high-probability guarantees.

We give an external-memory skip list that achieves write-optimized bounds. That is, for $0 < \varepsilon < 1$, range queries take $O(\log_{B^\varepsilon} N + K/B)$ I/Os w.h.p. and insertions and deletions take $O((\log_{B^\varepsilon} N)/B^{1-\varepsilon})$ amortized I/Os w.h.p.

Our write-optimized skip list inherits the virtue of simplicity from RAM skip lists. Moreover, it matches or beats the asymptotic bounds of prior write-optimized data structures such as B^ε trees or LSM trees. These data structures are deployed in high-performance databases and file systems.

The main technical challenge in proving our bounds comes from the fact that there are so few levels in the skip list, an aspect of the data structure that is essential to getting strong external-memory bounds. We use extremal-graph coloring to show that it is possible to decompose paths in the skip list into uncorrelated groups, regardless of the insertion/deletion pattern. Thus, we achieve our bounds by averaging over these uncorrelated paths rather than by averaging over uncorrelated levels, as in the standard skip list.

*Department of Computer Science, Stony Brook University, Stony Brook, NY 11794-2424 USA. Email: {bender, rob}@cs.stonybrook.edu.
Department of Applied Mathematics and Statistics, Stony Brook University, Stony Brook, NY 11794-3600 USA. Email: tyler.mayer@stonybrook.edu.

†Department of Computer Science, Rutgers University, Piscataway, NJ 08854 USA. Email: farach@cs.rutgers.edu.

‡École Normale Supérieure de Lyon, Lyon, France. Email: simon.mauras@ens-lyon.fr.

§MS 1326, PO Box 5800, Albuquerque, NM 87185 USA. Email: caphill@sandia.gov.

¶Computer Science and Artificial Intelligence Laboratory, Massachusetts Institute of Technology, Cambridge, MA, 02139 USA. Email: hjxu@mit.edu.

PODS'17, May 14-19, 2017, Chicago, IL, USA

DOI: http://dx.doi.org/10.1145/3034786.3056117

1. INTRODUCTION

The skip list [39] is an elegant randomized dictionary data structure built from cascading linked lists of geometrically decreasing sizes.

A skip list with N elements supports searches, inserts, and deletes in $O(\log N)$ operations with high probability[1] (w.h.p.) and range queries returning K elements in $O(\log N + K)$ operations w.h.p. [18, 28, 36]. Skip lists have found broad application [3, 5, 6, 19, 21, 25, 26, 35, 43], and they are widely deployed in production [29, 37, 42].

In this paper, we propose a ***write-optimized skip list***. The write-optimized skip list is a randomized ***external-memory*** dictionary that offers asymptotically optimal point-query and insertion performance in the external-memory model while inheriting many of the practical and theoretical advantages of a traditional skip list.

By external-memory, we mean that our data structure resides on a large external storage device, such as a disk or SSD. The external storage device is accessed via I/Os that transfer blocks of size B to a smaller cache (e.g. RAM) of size M.

By write-optimized, we mean that the data structure has asymptotically better insertion performance than a B-tree [7] and query performance at or near that of a B-tree. In practice, the best write-optimized dictionaries match B-trees in terms of query speed while performing insertions and deletions one or two orders-of-magnitude faster. Over the past two decades, researchers have developed write-optimized dictionaries for databases and file systems [4, 9–11, 13–15, 22, 23, 27, 30, 34, 40, 41, 48], several of which have been shown to be asymptotically optimal [14, 48].

Skip list structure. A skip list consists of $h = O(\log N)$ lists $\{\mathcal{L}_0, \mathcal{L}_1, .., \mathcal{L}_h\}$, called ***levels***, where the base level $\mathcal{L}_0$ is a linked list of all items of the set, in sorted order. Each item in level $\mathcal{L}_i$ also appears in (i.e., ***is promoted to***) level $\mathcal{L}_{i+1}$ with probability 1/2. All elements that have been promoted to $\mathcal{L}_{i+1}$ are ***pivots*** with respect to $\mathcal{L}_i$ because they partition $\mathcal{L}_i$ into ranges for searches.

[1] An event E_n on a problem of size n occurs ***with high probability*** if $\Pr[E_n] \geq 1 - 1/n^c$ for some constant c.

An element promoted to level $\mathcal{L}_{i+1}$ has a pointer to its successor in level $\mathcal{L}_{i+1}$ as well as a pointer to its own occurrence in level $\mathcal{L}_i$ (see Figure 1).

A query for element y begins at the first node on level $\mathcal{L}_h$ and ends on level $\mathcal{L}_0$ at the smallest element no greater than y. At level i, the search performs a sequential scan until it finds the last element, e, that is less than or equal to y in $\mathcal{L}_i$. At that point, the search follows the pointer to e in level $\mathcal{L}_{i-1}$ and resumes its sequential scan from that point.

An insertion of element e first performs coin tosses to compute the height h_e of e. The insertion then searches for e and inserts it into lists $\mathcal{L}_0, \ldots, \mathcal{L}_{h_e}$, with appropriate pointer adjustments.

Inheriting the desirable properties of skip lists. Skip lists have desirable algorithmic properties, which our write-optimized skip list inherits.

For example, it is an advantage to be built from a collection of linked lists. Practitioners generally like to make concurrent lock-free dictionaries as lock-free skip lists [19,24,38,46,47] because it is attractive to build on top of existing, production-quality lock-free linked lists [31,32,45].

Moreover, skip lists are elegant and have an easy-to-understand randomized balancing mechanism. Finally, skip-lists are weight balanced [33] in a probabilistic sense, which makes them useful as an algorithmic tool.

It is these desirable properties that makes us particularly excited to have another optimal write-optimized data structure at our disposal, even though (a few) other optimal structures already exist [9,13–15,48].

See Section 7 for our speculation how a write-optimized skip list may make it easier to implement concurrency and perhaps lock-freedom. Given that the community is only now exploring how to make full-featured, scalable, acid-compliant, write-optimized indexing structures, it is worth having many options in an implementer's arsenal.

Adapting to External Memory

We now articulate the subtleties in adapting skip lists to work in external memory. We review the external-memory model, which is used to analyze disk-resident indexing structures in databases and file systems.

External-memory model. The external-memory or disk-access model (DAM) [2] consists of two levels of memory: a fast memory (RAM) of size M and a slow arbitrarily large external memory, such as a disk. Block transfers, or I/Os, between disk and RAM occur in blocks of size B. Performance is measured in terms of the number of I/Os.

External-memory skip lists. Given the success of the skip list in internal memory, it is natural to extend it to external memory. Indeed, such a data structure exists and is called a B-skip list [1,8, 12,16,17,20].

The straightforward way to extend the skip list to external memory is to promote elements with probability $1/B$ rather than $1/2$. At a given level, each promoted element is stored in a contiguous chunk along with the run of nonpromoted elements that follow it. These chunks define the ***nodes*** of the B-skip-list. Since disk blocks have size B, each node consumes at least B space, regardless of how many elements it contains (see Figure 1).

This B-skip list retains the simplicity of the original RAM skip list but unfortunately has optimal search performance only in expectation, not with high probability [8]. Each node has an expected $\Theta(B)$ elements, but w.h.p. there exist nodes with as many as $\Theta(B \log N)$ elements and nodes with as few as $\Theta(B/\log N)$ elements. Large nodes cause problems because we want searches to take $O(\log_B N)$ I/Os, but performing a linear scan of a node of size $\Theta(B \log N)$ requires $\Theta(\log N)$ I/Os.

We can obtain high-probability bounds on the cost of searches by changing the promotion probability to $1/\sqrt{B}$, rather than $1/B$ [8]. Even with this larger promotion probability, there are only $O(\log_{\sqrt{B}} N) = O(\log_B N)$ levels. Each node now has $\sqrt{B}$ elements in expectation, with the actual number of elements ranging from $\Theta(\sqrt{B}/\log N)$ to $\Theta(\sqrt{B}\log N)$ w.h.p. No matter how big B is relative to $\log N$, this version of the skip list has a search cost of $O(\log_B N)$.

However, now most nodes are mostly empty, so this version wastes space.

Write-Optimized Skip List

Our write-optimized skip list uses the random and variable amount of extra space in each node to store a buffer, similar to a B$^\varepsilon$-tree [10, 14]. By buffering elements within nodes, we can move (or "flush") inserted items down the skip list in batches. This speeds up insertions on average, similar to buffer use in other write-optimized data structures. However, unlike deterministic write-optimized structures, the number of pivots in a node can vary by a factor of as much as $O(\log^2 N)$, which changes the effectiveness of the buffer substantially, and threatens the attainability of optimal high-probability amortized insert bounds.

The main contribution of the paper lies in the analysis. We show that the write-optimized skip list has an asymptotically optimal search-insert tradeoff [14, 48], similar to the B$^\varepsilon$-tree [14, 15, 27], the COLA [9], or the xdict [13]. Our search-insert bounds hold both in expectation and with high probability.

Our write-optimized skip list has an additional technical complication at the leaves to ensure good range-queries and space consumption. We promote with probability $1/B^{1-\varepsilon}$ at the leaf level and $1/B^\varepsilon$ at all other levels. We delay the promotion of elements from buffers at the leaf level as a simple mechanism to guarantee that leaf nodes remain $\Theta(B)$ full.

Challenges in attaining high-probability bounds. A particularly troublous aspect of this data structure is that the ratio of a node's buffer size to number of children can vary by a factor of $\Theta(\log^2 N)$. For example, the root itself might be one of these outlier nodes, an $O(\log N)$ factor larger than average. In that case, the large number of pivots (and low amortized per-child buffer size) would affect all insertions.

In data structures with depth $O(\log N)$ such local variation would even out, both on average and w.h.p. But, our data structure has only $O(\log_B N)$ depth, which is insufficient to overcome unlucky coin tosses. The surprising result is that this buffered skip list meets the desired I/O goals.

To prove high-probability bounds, we need to find, for any workload, sets of $\Omega(\log B^\varepsilon)$ insert paths whose I/O complexity is uncorrelated. This appears to be challenging for some workloads. For example, in a sequential-insert workload, any insert path lies on the rightmost spine of the data structure. Furthermore, since all insertions pass through the top level of the data structure, a large node at the top of the skip list can affect the I/O performance of a substantial fraction of insertions.

Fortunately, we are operating in external memory: we can assume that the top few levels of the data structure are cached. Traversing cached levels incurs no I/Os. We show that the remaining levels of the tree offer enough disjoint root-to-leaf paths so that

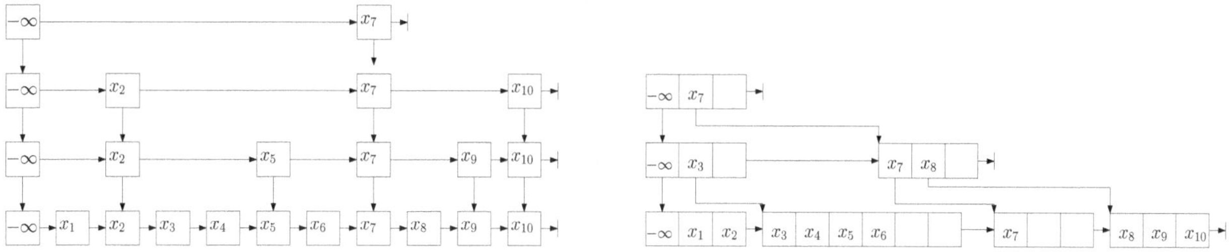

(a) RAM skip list. (b) B-skip list.

Figure 1: An in-memory (RAM) skip list (a) and external-memory B-skip list (b). In the B-skip list, the node size varies by a factor of $O(\log^2 N)$. While the B-skip list achieves asymptotically better bounds than the RAM skip list in expectation, they both achieve the same high-probability bounds [8]. In contrast, the write-optimized skip list has better bounds than the B-skip list both in expectation and w.h.p.

we can prove the desired bounds for write optimization. Indeed, even if all insert paths seem to follow the same root-to-leaf path (e.g., the rightmost spine), the insert path changes structure sufficiently frequently that we can find disjoint root-to-leaf paths.

This proof assumes an optimal paging algorithm. However, our performance bounds still hold in systems that use LRU, since LRU with constant resource augmentation is constant competitive with the optimal paging algorithm.

For ease of presentation, we first give a proof of high-probability bounds that applies when there are insertions, but no deletions. Our proof relies on a coloring argument of the insert paths.

Deletions destroy this first proof: paths that are independent at some point can be moved together by deletions of intervening elements so that they become correlated. We show, via an extremal graph-coloring argument, that there is always a good partitioning of the paths into uncorrelated sets, no matter what the deletion pattern is. This allows us to prove high-probability bounds under any mix of insertions and deletions.

Results

We prove the following theorem establishing the performance of write-optimized skip lists.

THEOREM 1. *Consider an N-element write-optimized skip list running in external memory. Let memory-hierarchy parameters B and M obey the "tall-cache" assumption that $M = \Omega(B^2 \log^4 B)$. Let the block size B be large enough that $\min\{B^\varepsilon, B^{1-\varepsilon}\} \geq \log N$.*

A write-optimized skip list that performs insertions, deletions, and queries achieves the following I/O bounds for tunable performance parameter $0 < \varepsilon < 1$:

- *Insertions and deletions take $O((\log_{B^\varepsilon} N)/(B^{1-\varepsilon}))$ amortized I/Os in expectation and w.h.p.*
- *Range queries returning K elements take $O(\log_{B^\varepsilon} N + K/B)$ I/Os in expectation and w.h.p. (Point queries are range queries with $K = 1$.)*
- *The structure takes $O(N)$ space, in expectation and w.h.p.*

The write-optimized skip list's guarantees (like those of a regular skip list) are based on an oblivious adversary. The oblivious adversary can issue arbitrary insert and delete operations, but does not have access to the heights of the elements in the structure (i.e., the random tosses).

Organization. In Section 2, we explain how to build and use the write-optimized skip list. In Section 3 we prove several structural properties of the write-optimized skip list. In Section 4 we prove performance bounds for point queries and range queries whp. We also prove bounds on insertion and deletion in expectation. In Section 5 we prove amortized insertions bounds w.h.p. and in Section 6 we adjust the argument to include deletions w.h.p. We conclude with some extensions and implementation issues in Section 7.

2. STRUCTURE AND OPERATIONS OF A WRITE-OPTIMIZED SKIP LIST

In this section we explain how to build the write-optimized skip list. This section also sets up notation that will be used throughout the rest of the paper.

Overall Structure. The write-optimized skip list has pointer structure similar to that of the B-skip list [8, 20]. It is composed of a sequence of hierarchical ***levels*** $\mathcal{L}_0, \mathcal{L}_1, \ldots, \mathcal{L}_h$, where h is the height of the data structure. We will show $h = O(\log_{B^\varepsilon} N)$ w.h.p.

Each level consists of a linked list of ***nodes*** (which will have size $\Theta(B)$ w.h.p.), where each node is partially filled with ***pivots***. Nodes at level 0 are ***leaves***. Each pivot element e on level $\mathcal{L}_{i\geq 1}$ has a pointer to the ***child*** node containing its occurrence on level $\mathcal{L}_{i-1}$. (We will see that sometimes there may temporarily be no node that contains e on level $\mathcal{L}_{i-1}$; in this case, the pointer points to the node that would contain e based on the sort order.) The smallest pivot in a node is called its ***leader***. Each node at level i contains a pointer to the next node at that level (see Figure 2).

Write-optimized skip list nodes are similar to nodes in a B^ε-tree [10, 14] in that each node also contains a ***buffer***. All the elements in a node's buffer are greater than or equal to the node's leader and smaller than the leader of the next node on that level. Inserted items are stored in nodes' buffers and are ***flushed*** in batches from parents to children. Thus, all elements move towards $\mathcal{L}_0$, where they remain (until they are deleted).

Randomized balancing. Each element e in the data structure has an integer ***height*** h_e determined by a sequence of biased coin flips. Coin flips are implemented by hashing e, meaning that even if an element is inserted, deleted, and reinserted, h_e does not change. To determine h_e, flip a biased coin until the first tail and set h_e to the length of the run of heads. For the first flip, the probability of heads is $1/B^{1-\varepsilon}$, and on subsequent flips the probability of heads is $1/B^\varepsilon$. We say that an element e has been ***promoted*** to level $i > 0$ if $h_e \geq i$.

The promotion probabilities are set such that each node on levels $\mathcal{L}_{i\geq 1}$ has $\Theta(B^\varepsilon)$ pivot elements in expectation and each node on level $\mathcal{L}_0$ has $\Theta(B^{1-\varepsilon})$ elements in expectation. The variable (random) amount of extra space in each node serves as the buffer space in our insertion algorithm and enables us to achieve amortized high-probability write-optimized update bounds, as discussed in Section 5 and Section 6.

As with a regular skip list, to ensure that there is a root for the entire structure, there is a special element $-\infty$ that is defined to have the largest height of any element.

Insertions and deletions. When a new element is inserted, store it qin the root's buffer. When an element e is deleted, store a ***tombstone*** $\bar{e}$ in the root's buffer.

Buffer-flushing mechanism. When the buffer in node D at level $\mathcal{L}_{i\geq 1}$ becomes full (i.e., it ***overflows***), perform a ***flush*** operation. During a flush, distribute the elements in D's buffer among the buffers of D's children. This may require an I/O per child to bring the children nodes into main memory.

Whenever any one child has $B^{1-\varepsilon}$ delete messages destined for it, flush those delete messages to the appropriate child immediately. (This extra rule for flushing deletes helps us achieve the desired range-query bounds; see Theorem 9).

Pivots and leaders. When an element e gets flushed out of the buffer of a node D of height $i \leq h_e$, e becomes a pivot of D in addition to being flushed to the buffer of one of D's children. This new pivot will point to the node to which e is being flushed. This means that D now has two (or more) pivots that point to the same child.

If $i < h_e$, then split D into two nodes D' and D'', making the current leader of D the leader of D' and e the leader of D''. Since D may have multiple pivots pointing to the same child, splitting D may result in some of D's children having more than one parent.

Whenever a node D that has multiple parents is split, update all of D's parents to point to the newly created nodes. Splitting a node D will not change the size of any of D's parents so that, unlike a B-tree, splitting can proceed in a purely top-to-bottom fashion. This is because, whenever a node D is split to create a new node D'' with leader e, element e must already be a pivot in D's parents.

When a delete message $\bar{e}$ is flushed from a node, delete e as a pivot of that node, if it happens to be one. If e is also the leader of that node, then merge that node with its predecessor on that level. Thus, merges are the reverse of splits.

Leaves require special handling. Whenever there is a flush from a parent D at level 1 to all of its leaves, rebalance all the leaves as follows: greedily choose the breaks between leaves so that each leaf approximately fills a block and each leaf begins with a pivot of D (but not every pivot of D begins a leaf).

Queries. To search for element e, traverse the root-to-leaf path to e, and retain all these nodes in memory until the query is done. Our assumptions on the size of memory imply that $M > B \log_{B^\varepsilon} N$, so that a complete root-to-leaf path fits in memory.

The leaf may or may not contain e itself. Insertions and deletions of e may reside in buffers on the root-to-leaf path. Find the messages in the highest buffer that affects e: if it is an insert, then e is present. If it is a delete, then e is absent. The I/O complexity is $O(\log_{B^\varepsilon} N)$ w.h.p.

Each buffer could be checked on the way down, until the first message that affects e is found. But the above method generalizes to richer queries. Consider finding the successor of e. First, find the successor of e in every root-to-leaf buffer and return the min-value of these that is currently in the dictionary. A trivial way to do this is to sort all the messages in all the buffers under consideration by (f, i, t), where f is the key, i is the height, and t is the type (insertion or deletion), then to remove all but the first occurrence of each key. This yields the current state of each key. Finally, search for e's successor by finding the smallest $f > e$ and then scanning to the first insertion.

There is one missing detail. If e is the largest element in its leaf and is larger than everything in the root-to-leaf buffers, then the successor of e will reside in the root-to-leaf path of the successor leaf. This does not increase the I/O complexity of successor, which is $O(\log_{B^\varepsilon} N)$.

A range query is implemented by repeated successor queries. Once the beginning of the range is found, successive leaves contain $\Theta(B)$ values in the range, and the I/Os for fetching internal nodes is dominated by that of fetching leaves. Thus, a K-element range query takes $O(K/B + \log_{B^\varepsilon} N)$ I/Os.

Top-down splits and merges: another advantage of write-optimized skip lists. Splits, merges, and promotions are performed in a *top-to-bottom* fashion. As we describe briefly in Section 7, this artifact of using a randomized rebalancing scheme may, in fact, turn out to be another hidden advantage of the write-optimized skip list over other data structures.

In particular, it may make it easier to implement concurrent write-optimized skip lists. There may be advantages both for lock-based implementations as well as well as lock-free versions. See Section 7 for details.

3. STRUCTURAL BOUNDS

In this section we establish structural properties of the write-optimized skip list, establishing both expected and high-probability bounds.

We assume throughout that $\min\{B^\varepsilon, B^{1-\varepsilon}\} \geq \log N$.

3.1 Local Structure

LEMMA 2 (PIVOTS IN AN INTERNAL NODE). *An internal node has B^ε pivots in expectation. and $O(B^\varepsilon \log N) = O(B)$ pivots w.h.p.*

PROOF. By construction, we begin a new internal node when we see a promotion to the next level. Therefore, the number of pivots in each internal node can be modeled as the number X of tails before the first heads in a sequence of independent coin flips with a head probability of $B^{-\varepsilon}$. The expectation of X is B^ε. The high probability bounds follow from the Chernoff bounds. □

The following lemma implies that accessing any node requires $O(1)$ I/Os w.h.p.

LEMMA 3 (NODE SIZE). *For $0 < \varepsilon < 1$, a node is comprised of $O(1)$ blocks w.h.p.*

PROOF. For levels greater than 0, nodes contain pivots and $\Theta(B)$ buffer space. By Lemma 2, nodes have $O(B)$ pivots w.h.p., so the total size of an internal node is $O(1)$ disk blocks.

By the same argument, even though the promotion probability at the leaves is $1/B^{1-\varepsilon}$, every run of $\Theta(B)$ elements at the leaf level has a promoted element w.h.p. Thus, when packing elements at the leaf level into blocks, we can create a new leaf every $\Theta(B)$ blocks w.h.p. Hence, every node at level 0 consumes $O(1)$ blocks w.h.p. □

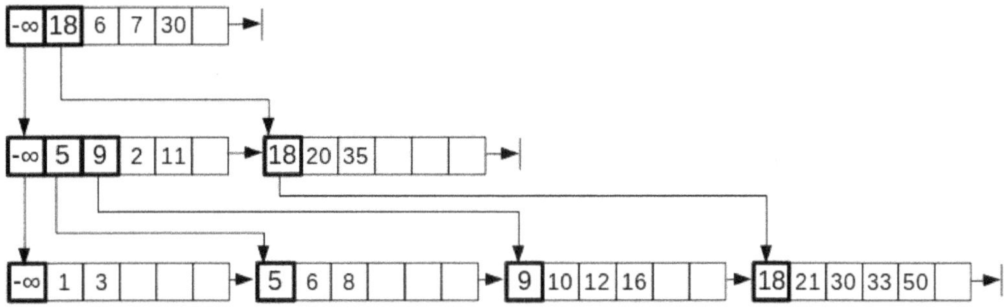

Figure 2: Structure of a write-optimized B-skip list with block size $B = 6$. We illustrate the pointer structure of the skip list as well as the pivot and buffer structure of nodes. Each node has size $O(B)$ w.h.p. Any extra space in the nodes is used as buffer space. The number of children at any (internal nonroot) node varies by an $O(\log^2 N)$ factor, meaning that the contribution to the amortized I/O cost for insertions and deletions from that node also varies by an $O(\log^2 N)$ factor. This large variation is an obstacle for designing external-memory skip lists with high-probability performance bounds.

The following lemma bounds the number of neighbors—parents, children, successors and predecessors—of a node. This will help us bound the cost of performing flushes, since flushes may have to access all of a node's neighbors.

LEMMA 4 (NEIGHBOR BOUNDS). *Let D be a node at height at least 1. The number of parents of D is $O(1)$ w.h.p. The expected number of children of D is $O(B^\varepsilon)$. If the height of D is exactly 1, then D has $O(\log N) = O(B^\varepsilon)$ children w.h.p.*

PROOF. The bound on children breaks into two cases:

- If D is at level $i > 1$ then, by Lemma 2, its expected number of pivots is $O(B^\varepsilon)$, and therefore so is the expected number of children.
- Nodes at level 1 are split whenever an element is promoted to level 2. Each element in level 0 has a $1/B$ chance of being promoted to level 2. By Chernoff bounds, any run of $\Omega(B \log N)$ elements at level 0 has at least 1 element promoted to level 2 w.h.p. Thus, w.h.p. no node at level 1 has more than $O(B \log N)$ elements in its children. Since each child has $\Theta(B)$ elements, nodes at level 1 have $O(\log N) = O(B^\varepsilon)$ children w.h.p.

The number of parents of D is at most the number of messages in D's buffer that have height at least 2 larger than the height of D. Since D has height at least 1, the probability that any particular item in D's buffer has height 2 greater than the height of D is at most $1/B^{1+\varepsilon}$. Since D's buffer contains $O(B)$ items, the expected number of such elements in D's buffer is $O(1/B^\varepsilon)$. Thus, by the Chernoff bounds, the number of such elements is $O((\log N)/B^\varepsilon)$ w.h.p. Since $\log N < B^\varepsilon$, the number of such elements, and hence the number of parents of D, is $O(1)$. □

3.2 Global Structure

THEOREM 5 (LINEAR SPACE). *A write-optimized skip list on N elements uses $O(N/B)$ blocks in expectation and w.h.p.*

PROOF. Each leaf holds $\Theta(B)$ items by construction and from Lemma 3 consumes $O(1)$ blocks w.h.p. Thus, the total space consumed by leaves is $O(N/B)$ w.h.p.

The number of blocks at $\mathcal{L}_1$ is also $O(N/B)$ since it is not more than the number of leaves.

For levels 2 and above, the space consumption follows the same analysis as the B-skip list. □

The following two lemmas help us bound the I/O costs of queries and inserts.

LEMMA 6 (HEIGHT UPPER BOUND). *For constant $0 < \varepsilon < 1$, the height of the write-optimized skip list is $O(\log_{B^\varepsilon} N)$ both in expectation and w.h.p.*

PROOF. The probability that any given element has height at least $h \geq 1$ is $1/B^{1-\varepsilon+(h-1)\varepsilon}$.

Let $c \geq 2$ be a constant. The probability that a given element has height at least $h = 1 + c \log_{B^\varepsilon} N$ is at most

$$\frac{1}{B^{1+(h-2)\varepsilon}} \leq \frac{1}{B^{\varepsilon(h-1)}} \leq \frac{1}{B^{\varepsilon c \log_{B^\varepsilon} N}}.$$

The probability that any given element has height at least $1 + c \log_{B^\varepsilon} N$ is at most $1/N^c$. By the union bound, the probability that any of the N elements has height at least $1 + c \log_{B^\varepsilon} N$, is at most $1/N^{c-1}$. □

LEMMA 7 (PIVOTS ON A SEARCH PATH). *The total number of pivots at level 2 or higher touched by any root-to-leaf search path in the data structure is $O(B^\varepsilon \log N)$ w.h.p.*

PROOF. Consider the search path "backwards." That is, start from the element x_i in the leaf level, and consider the unique trajectory from x_i back to the root following pointers backwards. The search path is comprised of some number of horizontal pointers (point to pivots on the same level) and $O(\log_{B^\varepsilon} N)$ vertical pointers (from Lemma 6).

We can model the length of this search path mathematically as the number of coin flips until $O(\log_{B^\varepsilon} N)$ heads have been seen with high probability. At levels 1 and above, the probability of a head is $1/B^\varepsilon$. Using Chernoff bounds, one can prove that $O(B^\varepsilon \log N)$ coin flips are enough to go back from level 1 to the root w.h.p. □

4. SIMPLE RUNTIME BOUNDS

This section gives high-probability bounds on the query performance. It also gives expected bounds on the amortized cost of insertion and deletion.

The amortization in the insertion bound is similar to the analysis of flushes in a B^ε-tree [14]. One interesting difference is that, with B^ε-trees, one must analyze the cost of splitting separately from the cost of flushes, since splitting is a non-local operation. In the write-optimized skip list, on the other hand, splitting and merging is performed locally as part of flushing, so we can bound its cost as part of the analysis of the flushing cost.

4.1 Query Performance

Next, we show bounds for point queries with constant tunable performance parameter ε.

THEOREM 8 (POINT QUERIES). *A point query has a worst case I/O complexity $O(\log_{B^\varepsilon} N)$ w.h.p.*

PROOF. From Lemma 7, each search path contains $O(B^\varepsilon \log N)$ elements w.h.p. Furthermore, the height of the tree is $O(\log_{B^\varepsilon} N)$ w.h.p. (from Lemma 6). For any search path, we must pay at most a single random I/O each time we descend a level. However, elements of the same level are stored contiguously in blocks (nodes), therefore we can make a linear scan over a level reading $O(B)$ elements per I/O.

Thus, the cost to read all elements in a particular search path is $O(\log_{B^\varepsilon} N + (B^\varepsilon \log N)/B) = O(\log_{B^\varepsilon} N)$ w.h.p. □

THEOREM 9 (RANGE QUERIES). *The I/O complexity of range queries is $O(\log_{B^\varepsilon} N + K/B)$ w.h.p. where K is the number of elements in the requested interval.*

PROOF. The cost for range queries can be analyzed using the search paths of the left and right ends of the requested interval. The complexity of a range query is bounded by the number of leaf nodes holding the elements in the range plus $O(\log_{B^\varepsilon} N)$ (the cost of a point query w.h.p.). Between the two search paths is a small write-optimized skip list of the K items returned by the range query. By Theorem 5, the total space consumed by the nodes in this mini skip list is $O(K/B)$ w.h.p. □

4.2 Insert and Delete Bounds in Expectation

THEOREM 10 (WRITE-OPTIMIZED UPDATES). *For $0 < \varepsilon < 1$, the amortized cost of inserting or deleting an element in the data structure is $O((\log_{B^\varepsilon} N)/B^{1-\varepsilon})$ in expectation.*

PROOF. We first analyze the expected cost of a flush. A flush of a node D must access all the children and parents of D, in addition to writing any new nodes that result from splitting or merging D. By Lemma 4, there are $O(B^\varepsilon)$ parents and children in expectation. If we do a merge, we may have to access D's predecessor and its parents, but this is $O(1)$ additional nodes in expectation. Thus, the total number of nodes accessed during a flush is $O(B^\varepsilon)$ in expectation. From Lemma 3, each node fits in $O(1)$ blocks w.h.p., so the total number of I/Os required by a flush is $O(B^\varepsilon)$ in expectation.

We now analyze the expected amortized insertion/deletion cost. By Lemma 6, Each element (or tombstone) must be flushed $O(\log_B N)$ times w.h.p. Thus, the total number of element flushes we must perform during any sequence of N insertions and deletions is $O(N \log_B N)$ with high probability. Each flush performs $\Theta(B)$ element-flushes with high probability. Thus, the total number of flushes performed is $O((N \log_B N)/B)$ with high probability. Since each flush costs $O(B^\varepsilon)$ I/Os in expectation, the amortized insertion cost is $O((\log_B N)/B^{1-\varepsilon})$ I/Os in expectation. □

5. HIGH PROBABILITY INSERTION-ONLY BOUNDS

This section establishes expected and high-probability bounds on the amortized insertion cost for a write optimized skip list that only handles insertions. We prove these bounds for a skip list that also handles deletes in Section 6.

Unfortunately, Theorem 10 does not obviously generalize to give matching high probability bounds on the amortized insertion cost. This is because, although there are many node flushes, many are not independent, preventing us from applying Chernoff bounds. We may flush a node many times before it gets split or merged with one of its siblings.

To overcome this problem, we partition the elements inserted into the skip list into ***color classes***, where all the elements of the same color follow (mostly) disjoint flushing paths. As a result, all the flushes (and flushing costs) involving these elements are independent. As long as the number of elements in a color class is large enough, we can use Chernoff bounds on the total cost of all the flushes of all the elements in that class.

The main challenge is that we are not guaranteed enough disjoint paths near the root of the skip list.

We use caching to address this problem. Flushes between nodes in cache incur no I/O, and hence can be ignored. As long as enough levels at the top of the skip list are cached, we can find large classes of elements that all follow disjoint paths through the uncached portion of the skip list.

5.1 Caching Assumptions and Structural Bounds

Caching Assumptions. Our high-probability bounds assume that the top $\Omega(1)$ levels of this data structure (those closest to the root) are permanently pinned in cache. An optimal cache-replacement policy will outperform these results, but an optimal policy requires prescience, rendering it unimplementable. However, the LRU (least-recently used) cache-replacement strategy is a 2-approximation to optimal, given a cache of twice the size [44], implying that our bounds still hold asymptotically with LRU. We account for the doubled memory in the asymptotics of our tall cache assumption.

For the analysis of the skip list assuming only insertions, we need the cache size to be $\Omega(B^2 \log^2 B)$; for the analysis with insertions and deletions, $\Omega(B^2 \log^4 B)$. Therefore, we generalize the analysis to a cache of size $M = \Omega(B^2 X)$.

Structural Properties. We now establish preliminary lemmas about the ***cached region*** (i.e., levels stored in cache).

We first give a lower bound on the number of levels that can be cached and the size of the largest cached level.

LEMMA 11 (HEIGHT OF CACHED REGION). *Suppose that internal memory has size $M = \Omega(XB^2)$ and let h' be the height of the lowest level with $O(XB^\varepsilon \log N)$ nodes. Then every node in level at least h' fits in memory w.h.p.*

PROOF. The number of nodes at level h' is $O(XB^\varepsilon \log N)$. Each node requires $\Theta(B)$ space w.h.p. The amount of space for all nodes at height h' is order the following:

$$BXB^\varepsilon \log N \le XB^{1+\varepsilon} B^{1-\varepsilon} = XB^2.$$

Thus, the size needed to store nodes of level h' is $O(XB^2)$ w.h.p. By Chernoff bounds, the number of nodes in higher levels decreases exponentially. Once the expected number of elements at a level is at most $\log N$, w.h.p, that level consumes at most one block. So the total number of nodes in all levels at or above h' is $O(XB^\varepsilon \log N + \log_{B^\varepsilon} N)$. Given the tall cache assumption that $M = \Omega(XB^2)$, there is sufficient space to store all levels with height at least h'. □

LEMMA 12 (PIVOTS IN LAST LEVEL CACHED). *With a cache of size $\Omega(B^2 X)$, the lowest level that fits in cache has $\omega(X \log N)$ pivots with separate children w.h.p.*

PROOF. Let h be the height of the highest level that does not fit into internal memory. (Since $M < N$, h exists.) Then, from Lemma 11, the number of nodes at that level is $\omega(XB^{\varepsilon} \log N)$. This means that the number of pivots at level $h + 1$ that have separate children is $\omega(XB^{\varepsilon} \log N)$. □

The following theorem will help us argue the existence of independent paths through the disk-resident region.

THEOREM 13 (CACHED ELEMENT FREQUENCY). *If $M = \Omega(XB^2)$, then, in any set of $\Omega(N/X)$ contiguous distinct elements at least one element is promoted into a cached level w.h.p.*

PROOF. Let p be the probability that an element has been promoted to the cached region. Using Lemma 12, $p \geq (cX \log N)/N$ with high probability for all constants $c > 0$.

Now, let q be the probability that no element is promoted to the cached region in a group of $\Omega(N/X)$ elements.

$$\begin{aligned} q = (1-p)^{\Omega(N/X)} &= \exp\left(\Omega\left(\frac{N}{X}\right)\log(1-p)\right) \\ &\leq \exp\left(-\Omega\left(\frac{pN}{X}\right)\right) \\ &\leq \exp\left(-\Omega\left(\frac{cNX\log N}{NX}\right)\right) \\ &= \frac{1}{\Omega(N^c)}. \end{aligned}$$

Thus, in any such such group of $\Omega(N/X)$ elements, w.h.p. at least one element is promoted to a cached level. □

5.2 Element Coloring Algorithm and Analysis

We use the aforementioned bounds on the size of the cached region and the frequency of cached elements to present an element coloring algorithm for insertion analysis.

We describe why normal Chernoff-bound analysis is insufficient and then use a coloring argument on disjoint root-to-leaf paths in a skip list with a large enough cache to establish the amortized cost of insert operations w.h.p.

The obstacle to using Chernoff bounds as above is that insertions that pass through the same node of the skip list will have correlated flushing costs. However, flushes between nodes in cache require no I/Os. Thus, if enough levels at the top of the tree are cached, then many insertions will follow independent paths through the uncached levels of the skip list enabling us to use Chernoff bounds to bound their overall cost.

The ***rank*** of an element is its position in the sorted list of all elements in the data structure regardless of whether or not it has reached the leaves. That is, the ith smallest element in the data structure has rank i, even if it is still making its way through the internal nodes due to the buffer-flushing scheme described earlier.

The insertion paths of two elements a, b are ***independent*** if they are node-disjoint in the part of the skip list that is not cached in memory. The following lemma proves the existence of a coloring of elements into such independence classes.

LEMMA 14. *There exists a coloring of elements inserted in the data structure such that elements in the same color class experience disjoint root-to-leaf paths w.h.p.*

PROOF. The following algorithm colors elements such that after every operation, the difference in rank between any two elements of the same color is at least $N/2X$.

Coloring Algorithm:

- Insert the first N/X elements with distinct colors, establishing the set of colors C.
- When a new element e is inserted at rank k, let C_I be the set of colors of the elements at ranks $[k - N/2X, k + N/2X]$. Assign e the color in $C \setminus C_I$ that currently has the fewest elements.

If the difference in rank between two elements a and b (where $a < b$) is $\Omega(N/X)$, then there exists at least one element (greater than a and at most b) between them promoted into the cached region w.h.p. (from Theorem 13). This element will be a leader at every level not cached in internal memory. The presence of such an element is enough to isolate the insertion paths of a and b.

Later insertions in the data structure do not affect this property, because the difference in rank between two elements can only increase over time. □

Now we prove, using the above coloring scheme, that the expected amortized cost of insertions holds w.h.p. We use the union bound on the amortized insertion costs for each color class as described in Theorem 15.

THEOREM 15. *The amortized insertion cost for $\Omega(\log B)$ elements with independent insertion paths in the data structure is $O((\log_{B^{\varepsilon}} N)/B^{1-\varepsilon})$ w.h.p.*

PROOF. We show that the amortized cost of flushes is $O((\log_{B^{\varepsilon}} N)/B^{1-\varepsilon})$ w.h.p. Recall from Lemma 4 that the amortized cost of flushes from level 1 to level 0 is $O(1/B^{1-\varepsilon})$ I/Os w.h.p. Thus, we need to bound the amortized cost of flushing elements only to levels 1 and above.

As an element moves down the $\log_{B^{\varepsilon}} N$ levels, there is a flush at each level. Each flush moves $\Theta(B)$ elements down one level. The total number of I/Os for all these flushes is the total number of pivots on the path, since each pivot has a child at the next lower level which could receive elements in a flush. Lemma 7 shows that the total number of pivots on levels 1 and above along any root-to-leaf search path of length $\log_{B^{\varepsilon}} N$ is $O(B^{\varepsilon} \log N)$ w.h.p., not matching the expected bounds.

For the amortized analysis to hold w.h.p., we need $\Theta(B^{\varepsilon} \log_{B^{\varepsilon}} N)$ pivots at levels two and above per path when averaged over all paths. At a high level, when we only consider one path there are not enough trials for us to avoid paying an additional asymptotic cost.

By identifying $\Omega(\log B)$ disjoint paths through the above coloring scheme, we can "concatenate" them. We model the total number of pivots at level 2 and above along this grouped search path mathematically as the number of coin flips needed until $\Omega(\log N)$ heads have been seen with high probability.

By Chernoff bounds, we need $O(B^{\varepsilon} \log N)$ coin flips in total for $\Omega(\log B)$ heads. Therefore, the amortized number of pivots at level 2 or above per path is $O((B^{\varepsilon} \log N)/\log B) = O(B^{\varepsilon} \log_{B^{\varepsilon}} N)$ w.h.p.

Since we transfer B elements with each I/O, the amortized cost of inserting an element along each of these disjoint paths is $O((B^{\varepsilon} \log_{B^{\varepsilon}} N)/B) = O((\log_{B^{\varepsilon}} N)/B^{1-\varepsilon})$. □

Recall our "tall cache" assumption that the size of memory $M = \Omega(XB^2)$ for some memory parameter X. We now show that $X = \Omega(\log^2 B)$ is sufficient to achieve the desired write-optimized bounds in an insert-only data structure.

THEOREM 16 (WRITE-OPTIMIZED INSERTIONS). *If the size of memory $M = \Omega(XB^2) = \Omega(B^2 \log^2 B)$ in an insert-only skip list, the insertion cost per element is $O((\log_{B^\varepsilon} N)/B^{1-\varepsilon})$ w.h.p.*

PROOF. After an insertion sequence, the elements have been divided into color classes. Consider the following two cases for the color classes:

Case 1: A color class has at least $\log B$ elements in it. We can apply the Chernoff bound analysis for concatenated paths and obtain $O((\log_{B^\varepsilon} N)/B^{1-\varepsilon})$ amortized insert cost per element w.h.p.

Case 2: A color class has fewer than $\log B$ elements in it. If $X = \Omega(\log^2 B)$, there are $O(N/X) = O(N/\log^2 B)$ color classes by construction. Therefore, there are at most $O(N/\log^2 B)$ "bad" color classes for which we cannot apply Chernoff bounds to acquire the same asymptotic bound w.h.p. as in Theorem 15. Furthermore, there are strictly fewer than $\log B$ elements in each of these "bad" classes. Therefore, there are at most $O(N/\log B)$ "bad" elements. For a "bad" element we may have to pay the naïve (single path analysis) cost of $(\log N)/B^{1-\varepsilon}$ (w.h.p.). However, the total cost amortized for these elements is at most $O((N \log_{B^\varepsilon} N)/B^{1-\varepsilon})$ w.h.p.

Finally, we calculate the amortized insertion cost per element over N inserts. That is,

$$\left(O(N)\frac{\log_{B^\varepsilon} N}{B^{1-\varepsilon}} + O\left(\frac{N}{\log B}\right)\frac{\log N}{B^{1-\varepsilon}}\right)/N$$
$$= O\left(\frac{\log_{B^\varepsilon} N}{B^{1-\varepsilon}}\right).$$

□

6. HIGH PROBABILITY BOUNDS WITH INSERTIONS AND DELETIONS

The previously described coloring scheme allows us to build groups of $\Omega(\log B)$ independent paths. However, we cannot perform delete operations, because the proofs do not allow the difference in rank between elements to decrease.

As the coloring algorithm is only a theoretical tool, we can assume that the adversary has no knowledge of the chosen colors. Equivalently, we can assume that we know all the requests from the beginning creating an "offline" coloring problem. We show that this allows us to extend the w.h.p. update bounds to include deletes.

We begin by describing a modified coloring scheme based on building a conflict graph of keys less than X apart in rank. Next, we show that this analysis technique allows us to prove the desired write-optimized bounds for both insertions and deletions.

Specifically, we describe a scheme to color $\Theta(N)$ updates on a skip list of size N. We introduce an undirected graph $G = (V, E)$, with the set of vertices V being the keys in the skip list. An edge $\{u, v\}$ is added to E if and only if at some point the difference in rank between keys u and v is smaller than N/X.

- When inserting an element at rank k, we add at most $2N/X$ edges to the graph, binding all the keys for which the difference in rank with k is smaller than N/X not to be of the same color.
- When removing an element at rank k, we add at most N/X edges between the key of rank $k + i - N/X - 1$ and key of rank $k + i$ for $0 \le i \le N/X$.

The total number of edges is therefore $O(N^2/X)$. We will use this information with Lemma 17.

Recall from Theorem 13 that if $M = \Omega(B^2 X)$, then at least one element is promoted into the cached region in a block of N/X elements w.h.p.

Therefore, two elements with the same color will have at least one "splitting element" between them that causes them to have disjoint paths outside of the cached region.

At a high level, assume that we have a write-optimized skiplist with some N active elements. In the very beginning (startup stage), allow the data structure to fill to some chosen constant size $C_{\min}$—all operations in this stage therefore have constant cost. We set this as our first N in the following analysis.

We build a conflict graph for some sequence of N' operations such that even if all N' operations are deletes, we still have $\Theta(N)$ active elements in the data structure for our amortized analysis. Thus, N' is some constant fraction of N, e.g., $N/4$. We also stop the sequence if the size of the data structure falls below $C_{\min}$.

Coloring the conflict graph. The analysis of the update cost based on the conflict graph is done in stages, or **epochs**, based on the length of the sequence of operations. At the beginning of a sequence we have N active elements. After N' operations, we have some N_0 active elements such that $N_0 = \Theta(N)$. At the end of this epoch, we set N_0 as the new N and repeat.

LEMMA 17. *Given an undirected graph $G = (V, E)$, let $\chi(G)$ be the smallest number of colors needed to color the vertices (chromatic number). Then $\chi(G) = O(\sqrt{|E|})$.*

PROOF. Assume that we have fewer than $\binom{\chi(G)}{2}$ edges. There must be two colors that can be merged together, contradicting the fact that $\chi(G)$ is optimal. Therefore, $\chi(G) = O(\sqrt{|E|})$. □

We can therefore color the keys using $O(N/\sqrt{X})$ colors.

Analysis using color classes. The analysis is similar to the proof of Theorem 16. We use the grouping technique again with the coloring of the conflict graph and bound the number of color classes with fewer than $\log B$ elements.

If a color class has at least $\log B$ elements, we can do the analysis using Chernoff bounds within this color.

We can bound the number of elements for which the "grouped" analysis is not feasible by $O((N \log B)/\sqrt{X})$. For those elements, we can apply Chernoff bounds naïvely for a total cost of $O\left(\frac{N \log B}{\sqrt{X}} \cdot \frac{\log N}{B^{1-\varepsilon}}\right)$.

Since $X = \Omega(\log^4 B)$, the amortized complexity for the "bad" elements is $O((\log_{B^\varepsilon} N)/B^{1-\varepsilon})$.

At the end of each epoch, start a new conflict graph from scratch. That is, start with a vertex for each of the N'' keys currently in the data structure and add edges between each pair of keys whose ranks differ by at most N/X. Now repeat the analysis process with $N = N''$. We thus obtain the following:

THEOREM 18 (WRITE-OPTIMIZED INSERTS/DELETES). *If the size of memory $M = \Omega(B^2 \log^4 B)$ in a skip list with inserts and deletes, then with high probability, the amortized insertion and deletion cost per element is $O((\log_{B^\varepsilon} N)/B^{1-\varepsilon})$ w.h.p.*

7. CONCLUSION

The write-optimized skip list achieves the asymptotically optimal I/O bounds of the best write-optimized data structure while retaining the elegance and simplicity of skip lists. The high probability bounds are established via extremal graph-coloring arguments based on the elements' root-to-leaf paths through the data structure.

We are hopeful that the skip list's randomized rebalancing will have practical (as well as theoretical) impact in the burgeoning area of write-optimization (e.g., as a basis for full-featured production data structures). We briefly try to articulate why we are so hopeful.

Regular skip lists have formed the basis for concurrent and lock-free production dictionaries. Part of the reason why is that they have simpler implementations because they are built out of regular linked lists.

We believe that write-optimized skip lists will benefit from these advantages as well. Consider, for example, the node-splitting mechanisms in write-optimized skip lists versus a B-tree or B^{ε}-tree. In a write-optimized skip list, node splits and merges are triggered "on the way down," i.e., as insert and delete messages make their way deeper into the structure.

In contrast, in B-trees and B^{ε}-trees, splits are triggered "on the way up," once inserts and deletes have reached the leaves. In a concurrent data structure based on locks, it is important to grab locks according to a prespecified partial order in order to avoid deadlock. Naïve "hand-over-hand" locking (grab and release locks as you walk down the tree to avoid throttling concurrency) is insufficient to design concurrent B-trees or B^{ε}-trees. If an insert reaches a leaf and triggers some splits higher up in the tree, the data structure no longer has the necessary locks higher up in the tree. Industrial B-trees and B^{ε}-trees generally deal with this concurrency issue by implementing delayed splitting mechanisms.

For example, when we built TokuDB, we built a mechanism for delaying splits, letting node sizes grow, and letting future inserts or deletes take care of the splits. Clearly, this locking issue is a solvable problem, but the coding seems simpler in a write-optimized skip list.

Similarly, skip lists have been the data structure of choice for theoretically good, in-production lock-free dictionaries. This is not only because they are built out of separate linked lists, but also because of other structural properties (such as level pointers along the entire level). Perhaps write-optimized skip lists will become the easiest-to-implement lock-free write-optimized data structures.

In future research, we will perform an implementation study to explore whether the theoretical advantages revealed in this paper can lead to benefits for implementers and users.

Acknowledgments

This work is supported by the Laboratory Directed Research and Development program at Sandia National Laboratories, a multi-program laboratory managed and operated by Sandia Corporation, a wholly owned subsidiary of Lockheed Martin Corporation, for the U.S. Department of Energy's National Nuclear Security Administration under contract DE-AC04-94AL85000.

This research was also supported by NSF grants CCF 1617618, IIS 1247726, IIS 1251137, CNS 1408695, and CCF 1439084, CNS 1408782, IIS 1247750, by NIH grant CA198952-01, and by EMC, Inc and NetApp, Inc.

We thank Jon Berry of Sandia National Laboratories for helpful comments.

8. REFERENCES

[1] I. Abraham, J. Aspnes, and J. Yuan. Skip B-trees. In *Proc. 9th Annual International Conference on Principles of Distributed Systems (OPODIS)*, page 366, 2006.

[2] A. Aggarwal and J. S. Vitter. The input/output complexity of sorting and related problems. *Communications of the ACM*, 31(9):1116–1127, Sept. 1988.

[3] A. Anagnostopoulos, M. Goodrich, and R. Tamassia. Persistent authenticated dictionaries and their applications. *Information Security*, pages 379–393, 2001.

[4] L. Arge. The buffer tree: A technique for designing batched external data structures. *Algorithmica*, 37(1):1–24, 2003.

[5] L. Arge, D. Eppstein, and M. T. Goodrich. Skip-webs: efficient distributed data structures for multi-dimensional data sets. In *Proc. 24th Annual ACM Symposium on Principles of Distributed Computing (PODC)*, pages 69–76, 2005.

[6] J. Aspnes and G. Shah. Skip graphs. *ACM Transactions on Algorithms*, 3(4):37, 2007.

[7] R. Bayer and E. M. McCreight. Organization and maintenance of large ordered indexes. *Acta Informatica*, 1:173–189, 1972.

[8] M. A. Bender, J. W. Berry, R. Johnson, T. M. Kroeger, S. McCauley, C. A. Phillips, B. Simon, S. Singh, and D. Zage. Anti-persistence on persistent storage: History-independent sparse tables and dictionaries. In *Proc. 35th ACM SIGMOD-SIGACT-SIGAI Symposium on Principles of Database Systems (PODS)*, pages 289–302, 2016.

[9] M. A. Bender, M. Farach-Colton, J. T. Fineman, Y. R. Fogel, B. C. Kuszmaul, and J. Nelson. Cache-oblivious streaming B-trees. In *Proc. 19th Annual ACM Symposium on Parallelism in Algorithms and Architectures (SPAA)*, pages 81–92, 2007.

[10] M. A. Bender, M. Farach-Colton, W. Jannen, R. Johnson, B. C. Kuszmaul, D. E. Porter, J. Yuan, and Y. Zhan. An introduction to B^{ε}-trees and write-optimization. *:login; magazine*, 40(5):22–28, October 2015.

[11] M. A. Bender, M. Farach-Colton, R. Johnson, R. Kraner, B. C. Kuszmaul, D. Medjedovic, P. Montes, P. Shetty, R. P. Spillane, and E. Zadok. Don't thrash: How to cache your hash on flash. *Proc. of the VLDB Endowment (PVLDB)*, 5(11):1627–1637, 2012.

[12] M. A. Bender, J. T. Fineman, S. Gilbert, and B. C. Kuszmaul. Concurrent cache-oblivious B-trees. In *Proc. 17th Annual ACM Symposium on Parallelism in Algorithms and Architectures (SPAA)*, pages 228–237, 2005.

[13] G. S. Brodal, E. D. Demaine, J. T. Fineman, J. Iacono, S. Langerman, and J. I. Munro. Cache-oblivious dynamic dictionaries with update/query tradeoffs. In *Proc. 21st Annual ACM-SIAM Symposium on Discrete Algorithms (SODA)*, pages 1448–1456, 2010.

[14] G. S. Brodal and R. Fagerberg. Lower bounds for external memory dictionaries. In *Proc. 14th Annual ACM-SIAM Symposium on Discrete Algorithms (SODA)*, pages 546–554, 2003.

[15] A. L. Buchsbaum, M. Goldwasser, S. Venkatasubramanian, and J. R. Westbrook. On external memory graph traversal. In *Proc. 11th Annual ACM-SIAM Symposium on Discrete Algorithms (SODA)*, pages 859–860, 2000.

[16] P. Callahan, M. T. Goodrich, and K. Ramaiyer. Topology B-trees and their applications. In *Proc. 4th International Workshop on Algorithms and Data Structures (WADS)*, pages 381–392, 1995.

[17] V. Ciriani, P. Ferragina, F. Luccio, and S. Muthukrishnan. Static optimality theorem for external memory string access. In *Proc. 43rd Annual IEEE Symposium on Foundations of Computer Science (FOCS)*, pages 219–227, 2002.

[18] L. Devroye. A limit theory for random skip lists. *The Annals of Applied Probability*, pages 597–609, 1992.

[19] M. Fomitchev and E. Ruppert. Lock-free linked lists and skip lists. In *Proc. 23rd Annual ACM Symposium on Principles of Distributed Computing (PODC)*, pages 50–59, 2004.

[20] D. Golovin. The B-skip-list: A simpler uniquely represented alternative to B-trees. *arXiv preprint arXiv:1005.0662*, 2010.

[21] M. T. Goodrich and R. Tamassia. Efficient authenticated dictionaries with skip lists and commutative hashing. *US Patent App*, 10(416,015), 2000.

[22] G. Graefe. Write-optimized B-trees. In *Proc. 30th International Conference on Very Large Data Bases (VLDB)*, pages 672–683, 2004.

[23] G. Graefe. B-tree indexes for high update rates. *SIGMOD Rec.*, 35(1):39–44, Mar. 2006.

[24] M. Herlihy, Y. Lev, V. Luchangco, and N. Shavit. A provably correct scalable concurrent skip list. In *Proc. Conference On Principles of Distributed Systems (OPODIS)*, 2006.

[25] M. Herlihy, Y. Lev, V. Luchangco, and N. Shavit. A simple optimistic skiplist algorithm. *Proc. 14th Annual Colloquium on Structural Information and Communication Complexity (SIROCCO)*, page 124, 2007.

[26] R. Jacob, A. Richa, C. Scheideler, S. Schmid, and H. Täubig. A distributed polylogarithmic time algorithm for self-stabilizing skip graphs. In *Proc. 28th ACM Symposium on Principles of Distributed Computing (PODC)*, pages 131–140, 2009.

[27] C. Jermaine, A. Datta, and E. Omiecinski. A novel index supporting high volume data warehouse insertion. In M. P. Atkinson, M. E. Orlowska, P. Valduriez, S. B. Zdonik, and M. L. Brodie, editors, *Proc. 25th International Conference on Very Large Data Bases (VLDB)*, pages 235–246, 1999.

[28] P. Kirschenhofer and H. Prodinger. The path length of random skip lists. *Acta Informatica*, 31(8):775–792, 1994.

[29] G. Korland, N. Shavit, and P. Felber. Noninvasive concurrency with Java STM. In *Third Workshop on Programmability Issues for Multi-Core Computers (MULTIPROG)*, 2010.

[30] Y. Li, B. He, Q. Luo, and K. Yi. Tree indexing on flash disks. In *Proc. 2009 IEEE International Conference on Data Engineering (ICDE)*, pages 1303–1306, 2009.

[31] P. A. Martin. Method and apparatus for implementing a lock-free skip list that supports concurrent accesses, Dec. 11 2007. US Patent 7,308,448.

[32] M. M. Michael. High performance dynamic lock-free hash tables and list-based sets. In *Proc. 14th Annual ACM Symposium on Parallel Algorithms and Architectures (SPAA)*, pages 73–82, 2002.

[33] J. Nievergelt and E. M. Reingold. Binary search trees of bounded balance. *SIAM Journal on Computing*, 2(1):33–43, 1973.

[34] P. O'Neil, E. Cheng, D. Gawlic, and E. O'Neil. The log-structured merge-tree (LSM-tree). *Acta Informatica*, 33(4):351–385, 1996.

[35] R. Oshman and N. Shavit. The SkipTrie: low-depth concurrent search without rebalancing. In *Proc. 32nd Annual ACM Symposium on Principles of Distributed Computing (PODC)*, pages 23–32, 2013.

[36] T. Papadakis, J. I. Munro, and P. V. Poblete. Analysis of the expected search cost in skip lists. In *Proc. 2nd Scandinavian Workshop on Algorithm Theory (SWAT)*, pages 160–172, 1990.

[37] T. Peierls, B. Goetz, J. Bloch, J. Bowbeer, D. Lea, and D. Holmes. ConcurrentSkipList. In *Java concurrency in practice*. Pearson Education, 2006.

[38] W. Pugh. Concurrent maintenance of lists. Technical report, Dept. of Computer Science, University of Maryland, College Park, 1990.

[39] W. Pugh. Skip lists: a probabilistic alternative to balanced trees. *Communications of the ACM*, 33(6):668–676, 1990.

[40] R. Sears, M. Callaghan, and E. A. Brewer. Rose: compressed, log-structured replication. *Proc. of the VLDB Endowment*, 1(1):526–537, 2008.

[41] R. Sears and R. Ramakrishnan. bLSM: a general purpose log structured merge tree. In *Proc. ACM SIGMOD International Conference on Management of Data (SIGMOD)*, pages 217–228, 2012.

[42] N. Shamgunov. The MemSQL in-memory database system. In *Proc. 2nd International Workshop on In Memory Data Management and Analytics (IMDM)*, 2014.

[43] N. Shavit and I. Lotan. Skiplist-based concurrent priority queues. In *Proc. 14th International Parallel and Distributed Processing Symposium (IPDPS)*, pages 263–268, 2000.

[44] D. D. Sleator and R. E. Tarjan. Amortized efficiency of list update and paging rules. *Communications of the ACM*, 28(2):202–208, Feb. 1985.

[45] G. L. Steele Jr, A. T. Garthwaite, P. A. Martin, N. N. Shavit, M. S. Moir, and D. L. Detlefs. Lock-free implementation of concurrent shared object with dynamic node allocation and distinguishing pointer value, Nov. 30 2004. US Patent 6,826,757.

[46] H. Sundell and P. Tsigas. Scalable and lock-free concurrent dictionaries. In *Proc. 2004 ACM Symposium on Applied Computing (SAC)*, pages 1438–1445, 2004.

[47] J. D. Valois. Lock-free linked lists using compare-and-swap. In *Proc. 14th Annual ACM Symposium on Principles of Distributed Computing (PODC)*, pages 214–222, 1995.

[48] K. Yi. Dynamic indexability and the optimality of b-trees. *Journal of the ACM*, 59(4):21:1–21:19, Aug. 2012.

Output-optimal Parallel Algorithms for Similarity Joins*

Xiao Hu
HKUST

Yufei Tao
University of Queensland

Ke Yi
HKUST

ABSTRACT

Parallel join algorithms have received much attention in recent years, due to the rapid development of massively parallel systems such as MapReduce and Spark. In the database theory community, most efforts have been focused on studying worst-optimal algorithms. However, the worst-case optimality of these join algorithms relies on the hard instances having very large output sizes. In the case of a two-relation join, the hard instance is just a Cartesian product, with an output size that is quadratic in the input size.

In practice, however, the output size is usually much smaller. One recent parallel join algorithm by Beame et al. [8] has achieved *output-optimality*, i.e., its cost is optimal in terms of both the input size and the output size, but their algorithm only works for a 2-relation equi-join, and has some imperfections. In this paper, we first improve their algorithm to true optimality. Then we design output-optimal algorithms for a large class of similarity joins. Finally, we present a lower bound, which essentially eliminates the possibility of having output-optimal algorithms for any join on more than two relations.

Categories and Subject Descriptors

F.2.2 [**Analysis of algorithms and problem complexity**]: Nonnumerical Algorithms and Problems

Keywords

Parallel computation, similarity joins, output-sensitive algorithms

1. INTRODUCTION

The similarity join problem is perhaps one of the most extensively studied problems in the database and data mining literature. Numerous variants exist, depending on the metric space and the distance function used. Let dist$(\cdot,\cdot)$ be a distance function. Given two point sets R_1 and R_2 and a threshold $r \geq 0$, the similarity join problem asks to find all pairs of points $x \in R_1, y \in R_2$, such that $\text{dist}(x,y) \leq r$. In this paper, we will be mostly interested in the ℓ_1, ℓ_2, and ℓ_∞ distances, although some of our results (the one based on LSH) can be extended to other distance functions as well.

1.1 The computation model

Driven by the rapid development of massively parallel systems such as MapReduce [14], Spark [29], and many other systems that adopt very similar architectures, there have also been resurrected interests in the theoretical computer science community to study algorithms in such massively parallel models. One popular model that has often been used to study join algorithms in particular, is the *massively parallel computation* model (MPC) [1, 2, 3, 7, 8, 20, 21, 22].

In the MPC model, data is initially partitioned arbitrarily across p servers that are connected by a complete network. Computation proceeds in rounds. In each round, each server first receives messages from other servers (sent in a previous round, if there is one), does some local computation, and then sends messages to other servers, which will be received by them at the beginning of the next round. The complexity of the algorithm is measured first by the number of rounds, then the *load*, denoted L, which is the maximum message size received by any server in any round. Initial efforts were mostly spent on understanding what can be done in a single round of computation [2, 7, 8, 21, 22], but recently, more interests have been given to multi-round (but still a constant) algorithms [1, 3, 20, 21], since new main memory based systems, such as Spark, tend to have much lower overhead per round than previous systems like Hadoop. Meanwhile, this puts more emphasis on minimizing the load, to ensure that the local memory at each server is never exceeded.

One thing that we want to point out, which was never explicitly stated in the prior work on the MPC model, is that the MPC model is essentially the same as Valiant's *bulk synchronous processing* model (BSP) [28]. More precisely, it is the same as the CREW version of the BSP [15], where a server may broadcast a message to multiple servers. The incoming message size at each server is still limited in the CREW BSP model, as in the MPC model.

The MPC model, as well as the CREW BSP model, allows broadcasts. This is often justified by the fact that in some systems, broadcasts may indeed be more efficient than sending the message to each destination individually. Very recently, it has been shown [18] that any algorithm in the

*Xiao Hu and Ke Yi are supported by HKRGC under grants GRF-16211614 and GRF-16200415.

PODS'17, May 14-19, 2017, Chicago, IL, USA

 ISBN 978-1-4503-4198-1/17/05...$15.00

DOI: http://dx.doi.org/10.1145/3034786.3056110

CREW BSP model can be simulated in the standard BSP model without using any broadcasts by just increasing the number of rounds and the load by a constant factor, provided that $\text{IN} > p^{1+\epsilon}$, where IN is the input size and $\epsilon > 0$ is any small constant. This provides a stronger justification of using broadcasts.

1.2 Previous join algorithms in the MPC model

All prior work on join algorithms in the MPC model has focused on equi-joins, and has mostly been concerned with the worst case. Notably, the *hypercube* algorithm [2] computes the equi-join between two relations of size N_1 and N_2, respectively, with load $L = \tilde{O}(\sqrt{N_1 N_2/p})$[1]. Note that this is optimal in the worst case, as the output size can be as large as $N_1 N_2$, when all tuples share the same join key and the join degenerates into a Cartesian product. Since each server can only produce $O(L^2)$ join results in a round[2] if the load is limited to L, all the p servers can produce at most $O(pL^2)$ join results in a constant number of rounds. Thus, producing $N_1 N_2$ results needs at least a load of $L = \Omega(\sqrt{N_1 N_2/p})$. Note that this lower bound argument is assuming *tuple-based* join algorithms, i.e., the tuples are atomic elements that must be processed and communicated in their entirety. They can be copied but cannot be broken up or manipulated with bit tricks. To produce a join result, all tuples (or their copies) that make up the join result must reside at the same server when the join result is output. However, the server does not have to do any further processing with the result, such as sending it to another server. The same model has also been used in [7, 8, 21].

However, on most realistic data sets, the join size is nowhere near the worst case. Suppose the join size is OUT. Applying the same argument as above, one would hope to get a load of $\tilde{O}(\sqrt{\text{OUT}/p})$. Such a bound would be *output-optimal.* Of course, this is not entirely possible, as OUT can even be zero, so a more reasonable target would be $L = \tilde{O}(\sqrt{\text{OUT}/p} + \text{IN}/p)$, where $\text{IN} = N_1 + N_2$ is the total input size. This is exactly the goal of this work, although in some cases, we have not achieved this ideal input-dependent term $\tilde{O}(\text{IN}/p)$ exactly. Note that we are still doing worst-case analysis, i.e., we do not make any assumptions on the input data and how it is distributed on the p servers initially. We merely use OUT as an additional parameter to measure the complexity of the algorithm.

There are some previous join algorithms that use both IN and OUT to measure the complexity. Afrati et al. [1] gave an algorithm with load $O(\text{IN}^w/\sqrt{p} + \text{OUT}/\sqrt{p})$, where w is the *width* of the join query, which is 1 for any acyclic query, including a two-relation join. However, both terms $O(\text{OUT}/\sqrt{p})$ or $O(\text{IN}/\sqrt{p})$ are far from optimal.

Beame et al. [8] classified the join values into being heavy and light. For a join value v, let $R_i(v)$ be the set of tuples in R_i with join value v. Then a join value v is *heavy* if $|R_1(v)| \geq N_1/p$ or $|R_2(v)| \geq N_2/p$. Then they gave an algorithm with load

$$\tilde{\Theta}\left(\sqrt{\frac{\sum_{\text{heavy } v} |R_1(v)| \cdot |R_2(v)|}{p}} + \frac{\text{IN}}{p}\right). \quad (1)$$

In fact, this bound can be equivalently written as $\tilde{\Theta}(\sqrt{\text{OUT}/p} + \text{IN}/p)$. Note that

$$\begin{aligned}\text{OUT} &= \sum_v |R_1(v)| \cdot |R_2(v)| \\ &= \sum_{\text{heavy } v} |R_1(v)| \cdot |R_2(v)| + \sum_{\text{light } v} |R_1(v)| \cdot |R_2(v)|,\end{aligned}$$

so (1) is upper bounded by $\tilde{O}(\sqrt{\text{OUT}/p} + \text{IN}/p)$. Meanwhile, it is also lower bounded by $\tilde{\Omega}(\sqrt{\text{OUT}/p} + \text{IN}/p)$: First, it is clearly in $\tilde{\Omega}(\text{IN}/p)$. Second, it is also in $\tilde{\Omega}(\sqrt{\text{OUT}/p})$ since

$$\sum_{\text{light } v} |R_1(v)| \cdot |R_2(v)| \leq \frac{N_1 N_2}{p} \leq \frac{\text{IN}^2}{p},$$

hence

$$\begin{aligned}(1) &= \tilde{\Omega}\left(\sqrt{\frac{\text{OUT} - \text{IN}^2/p}{p}} + \frac{\text{IN}}{p}\right) \\ &= \tilde{\Omega}\left(\sqrt{\frac{\text{OUT} - \text{IN}^2/p}{p} + \frac{\text{IN}^2}{p^2}}\right) = \tilde{\Omega}(\sqrt{\text{OUT}/p}).\end{aligned}$$

Therefore, their algorithm is output-optimal, but up to a polylog factor, due to the use of hashing (the hidden polylog factor is $O(\log^2 p)$). Their analysis relies on the uniform hashing assumption, i.e., the hash function distributes each distinct key to the servers uniformly and independently. It is not clear whether more realistic hash functions, such as universal hashing, could still work. They also assume that each server knows the entire set of heavy join values and their frequencies, namely, all the $|R_i(v)|$'s that are larger than N_i/p, for $i = 1, 2$.

Note that equi-join is a special case of similarity joins with $r = 0$. There are previously no algorithms in the MPC model for similarity joins with $r > 0$, except computing the full Cartesian product of the two relations with load $O(\sqrt{N_1 N_2/p})$, which is not output-optimal.

As a remark, there exists a general reduction [21] that converts MPC join algorithms into I/O-efficient counterparts under the *enumerate version* [26] of the external memory model [4], where each result tuple only needs to be seen in memory, as opposed to being reported in the disk. A nice application of the reduction has been demonstrated for the *triangle enumeration problem,* where an MPC algorithm [21] is shown to imply an EM algorithm matching the I/O lower bound of [26] up to a logarithmic factor.

1.3 Our results

We start with an improved algorithm for computing the equi-join between two relations, i.e., a degenerated similarity join with $r = 0$. We improve upon the algorithm of Beame et al. [8] in the following aspects: (1) Our algorithm does not assume any prior statistical information about the data, such as the heavy join values and their frequencies. (2) The load of our algorithm is exactly $O(\sqrt{\text{OUT}/p} + \text{IN}/p)$ tuples, without any extra logarithmic factors. (3) Our algorithm is deterministic. The only price we pay is that the number of rounds increases from 1 to $O(1)$. This algorithm is described in Section 3.

While the $O(\sqrt{\text{OUT}/p})$ term is optimal by the tuple-based argument above, prior work did not show why the input-dependent term $O(\text{IN}/p)$ is necessary. In fact, the load

[1] The $\tilde{O}$ notation suppresses polylogarithmic factors.

[2] Technically, this is true under the condition $L = \Omega(\frac{N_1+N_2}{p})$, but as will be proved in this paper, the condition indeed holds even just to decide whether the join result is empty.

has often been written in form of $O(\text{IN}/p^{1-\delta})$ for $\delta \in [0,1]$, implicitly assuming that $O(\text{IN}/p)$ is the best load possible, i.e., every tuple has to be communicated at least once. Indeed, if OUT is not a parameter, the worst-case input is always when the output size is maximized, i.e., a full Cartesian product for two-relation joins, or the AGM bound [6] for multi-way joins. In this case, the simple tuple-based argument above already leads to a lower bound higher than $\Omega(\text{IN}/p)$, so this is not an issue. However, when the output size is restrained to be a parameter OUT, these worst-case constructions do not work anymore; and it is not clear why $O(\text{IN}/p)$ load is necessary. Indeed, if OUT $= 1$, then the tuple-based argument above yields a meaningless lower bound of $\Omega(1/p)$. To complete the picture, we provide a lower bound showing that even if OUT $= O(1)$, computing the equi-join between two relations requires $\Omega(\text{IN}/p)$ load, by resorting to strong results from communication complexity.

The main results in this paper, however, are on similarity joins with $r > 0$. In this regard, We achieve the following results under various distance functions.

1. For ℓ_1/ℓ_∞ distance in constant dimensions, we give a deterministic algorithm with load
$$O\left(\sqrt{\frac{\text{OUT}}{p}} + \frac{\text{IN}}{p} \cdot \log^{O(1)} p\right),$$
i.e., the output-dependent term is optimal, while the input-dependent term is away from optimal by a polylogarithmic factor, which depends on the dimensionality.

2. For ℓ_2 distance in d dimensions, we give a randomized algorithm with load
$$O\left(\sqrt{\frac{\text{OUT}}{p}} + \text{IN}/p^{\frac{d}{2d-1}} + p^{\frac{d}{2d-1}} \log p\right).$$
Again, the term $O\left(\sqrt{\frac{\text{OUT}}{p}}\right)$ is output-optimal. The input-dependent term $O(\text{IN}/p^{\frac{d}{2d-1}})$ is worse than the ℓ_1/ℓ_∞ case, due to the non-orthogonal nature of the ℓ_2 metric, but it is always better than $O(\text{IN}/\sqrt{p})$, which is the load for computing the full Cartesian product.

3. In high dimensions, we provide an LSH-based algorithm with load
$$O\left(\sqrt{\frac{\text{OUT}}{p^{1/(1+\rho)}}} + \sqrt{\frac{\text{OUT}(cr)}{p}} + \frac{\text{IN}}{p^{1/(1+\rho)}}\right),$$
where $\text{OUT}(cr)$ is the output size if the distance threshold is enlarged to cr for some constant $c > 1$, and $0 < \rho < 1$ is the quality measure of the hash function used, which depends only on c and the distance function. Similarly, the term $O(\text{IN}/p^{1/(1+\rho)})$ is always better than that for computing the Cartesian product, although output-optimality here is only with respect to $\text{OUT}(cr)$ instead of OUT, due to the approximation nature of LSH.

All the algorithms run in $O(1)$ rounds, under the mild assumption IN $> p^{1+\epsilon}$, where $\epsilon > 0$ is any small constant. Note that the randomized output-optimal algorithm in [8] for equi-joins has an implicit assumption that IN $\geq p^2$, since there are $\Theta(p)$ heavy join values, so each server has load at least $\Omega(p)$ to store these values and their frequencies. We acknowledge that in practice, IN $\geq p^2$ is a very reasonable assumption. Our desire to relax this to IN $> p^{1+\epsilon}$ is more from a theoretical point of view, namely, achieving the minimum requirement for solving these problem in $O(1)$ rounds and optimal load. Indeed, Goodrich [15] has shown that, if IN $= p^{1+o(1)}$, then even computing the "or" of IN bits requires $\omega(1)$ rounds under load $O(\text{IN}/p)$.

Finally, we turn to multi-way joins. The only known multi-way equi-join algorithm in the MPC model that has a term related to OUT is the algorithm in [1] mentioned in Section 1.2. However, that term is $O(\text{OUT}/\sqrt{p})$, which is almost quadratically larger than the output-optimal term $O(\sqrt{\text{OUT}/p})$ we have achieved above. We show that, unfortunately, such an output-optimal term is not achievable, even for the simplest multi-way equi-join, a 3-relation chain join $R_1(A,B) \bowtie R_2(B,C) \bowtie R_3(C,D)$. More precisely, in Section 7 we show that if any tuple-based algorithm computing this join has a load in the form of
$$L = O\left(\frac{\text{IN}}{p^\alpha} + \sqrt{\frac{\text{OUT}}{p}}\right),$$
for some constant α, then we must have $\alpha \leq 1/2$, provided IN $\log^2$ IN $= \Omega(p^3)$. On the other hand, the algorithm in [21] can already compute any 3-relation chain join with $\tilde{O}(\text{IN}/\sqrt{p})$ load. This means that it is meaningless to introduce the output-dependent term $O(\sqrt{\text{OUT}/p})$.

2. PRELIMINARIES

We first introduce the following primitives in the MPC model. We will assume IN $> p^{1+\epsilon}$ where $\epsilon > 0$ is any small constant.

2.1 Sorting

The sorting problem in the MPC model is defined as follows. Initially, IN elements are distributed arbitrarily on p servers, which are labeled $1, 2, \ldots, p$. The goal is to redistribute the elements so that each server has IN$/p$ elements in the end, while any element at server i is smaller than or equal to any element at server j, for any $i < j$. By realizing that the MPC model is the same as the BSP model, we can directly invoke Goodrich's optimal BSP sorting algorithm [15]. His algorithm has load $L = \Theta(\text{IN}/p)$ and runs in $O(\log_L \text{IN}) = O(\log_L(pL)) = O(\log_L p)$ rounds. When IN $> p^{1+\epsilon}$, this is $O(1)$ rounds.

2.2 Multi-numbering

Suppose each tuple has a key. The goal of the *multi-numbering* problem is, for each key, assign consecutive numbers $1, 2, 3, \ldots$ to all the tuples with the same key.

We solve this problem by reducing it to the *all prefix-sums* problem: Given an array of elements $A[1], \ldots, A[\text{IN}]$, compute $S[i] = A[1] \oplus \cdots \oplus A[i]$ for all $i = 1, \ldots, \text{IN}$, where $\oplus$ is any associative operator. Goodrich et al. [16] gave an algorithm in the BSP model for this problem that uses $O(\text{IN}/p)$ load and $O(1)$ rounds.

To see how the multi-numbering problem reduces to the all prefix-sums problem, we first sort all tuples by their keys; ties are broken arbitrarily. The i-th tuple in the sorted order will produce a pair (x, y), which will act as $A[i]$. For each tuple that is the first of its key in the sorted order, we produce the pair $(0,1)$; otherwise, we produce $(1,1)$. Note that we need another round of communication to determine whether each tuple is the first of its key, in case that its predecessor resides on another server.

Then we define the operator $\oplus$ as

$$(x_1, y_1) \oplus (x_2, y_2) = (x_1 x_2, y),$$

where

$$y = \begin{cases} y_1 + y_2, & \text{if } x_2 = 1; \\ y_2, & \text{if } x_2 = 0. \end{cases}$$

Consider any $(x, y) = A[i] \oplus \cdots \oplus A[j]$. Intuitively, $x = 0$ indicates that $A[i], \ldots, A[j]$ contain at least one tuple that is the first of its key, while y counts the number of tuples in $A[i], \ldots, A[j]$ whose key is the same as that of $A[j]$. It is an easy exercise to check that $\oplus$ is associative, and after solving the all prefix-sums problem, $S[i]$ is exactly the number of tuples in front of the i-th tuple that has the same key (including the i-th tuple itself), which solves the multi-numbering problem as desired.

2.3 Sum-by-key

Suppose each tuple is associated with a key and a weight. The goal of the *sum-by-key* problem is to compute, for each key, the total weight of all the tuples with the same key.

This problem can be solved using essentially the same approach as for the multi-numbering problem. First sort all the N tuples by their keys. As above, each tuple will produce a pair (x, y). Now, x still indicates whether this tuple is the first of its key, but we just set y to be the weight associated with the tuple. After we have solved the all prefix-sums problem on these pairs, the last tuple of each key has the total weight for this key. Again, we need another round to identify the last tuple of each key, by checking each tuple's successor.

After the algorithm above finishes, for each key, exactly one tuple knows the total weight for the key, i.e., the last one in the sorted order. In some cases, we also need every tuple to know the total weight for the tuple's own key. To do so, we invoke the multi-numbering algorithm, so that the last tuple of each key also knows the number of tuples with that key. From this number, we can compute exactly the range of servers that hold all the tuples with this key. Then we broadcast the total weight to these servers.

2.4 Multi-search

The *multi-search* problem is defined as follows. Given N_1 distinct keys and N_2 queries, where $\text{IN} = N_1 + N_2$, for each query, find its predecessor, i.e., the largest key that is no larger than the query. The multi-search algorithm given by Goodrich et al. [16] is randomized, with a small probability exceeding $O(\text{IN}/p)$ load. In fact, this problem can also be solved using all prefix-sums, which results in a deterministic algorithm with load $O(\text{IN}/p)$: We first sort all the keys and queries together. Then for each key k, define its corresponding $A[i]$ as itself; for each query, define its $A[i] = -\infty$; define $\oplus = \max$. Then it should be obvious that $S[i]$ is the predecessor of the corresponding query.

2.5 Cartesian product

The hypercube algorithm [2, 8] is a randomized algorithm that computes the Cartesian product of two sets R_1 and R_2. Suppose the two sets have size N_1 and N_2, respectively. This algorithm has a load of $O((\sqrt{N_1 N_2/p} + \text{IN}/p)\log^2 p)$ with probability $1 - 1/p^{O(1)}$. The extra log factors are due to the use of hashing. We observe that if the elements in each set are numbered as $1, 2, 3, \ldots,$ then we can achieve deterministic and perfect load balancing.

Without loss of generality, assume $N_1 \le N_2$. As in the standard hypercube algorithm, we arrange the p servers into a $d_1 \times d_2$ grid such that $d_1 d_2 = p$. If an element in R_1 gets assigned a number x, then we send it to all servers in the $(x \mod d_1)$-th row of the grid; for an element in R_2, we send it to all servers in the $(x \mod d_2)$-th column of the grid. Each server then produces all pairs of elements received. By setting (1) $d_1 = \sqrt{\frac{pN_1}{N_2}}, d_2 = \sqrt{\frac{pN_2}{N_1}}$, if $N_2 \le pN_1$; or (2) $d_1 = 1$, $d_2 = p$, if $N_2 > pN_1$, the load is $O(\sqrt{N_1 N_2/p} + \text{IN}/p)$.

2.6 Server allocation

In many of our algorithms, we decompose the problem into up to p subproblems, and allocate the p servers appropriately, with subproblem j having $p(j)$ servers, where $\sum_j p(j) \le p$. Thus, each subproblem needs to know which servers have been allocated to it. This is trivial if $\text{IN} \ge p^2$, as we can collect all the $p(j)$'s to one server, do a central allocation, and broadcast the allocation results to all servers, as is done in [8]. When we only have $\text{IN} \ge p^{1+\epsilon}$, some more work is needed to ensure $O(\text{IN}/p)$ load.

More formally, in the *server allocation* problem, each tuple has a subproblem id j, which identifies the subproblem it belongs to (the j's do not have to be consecutive), and $p(j)$, which is the number of servers allocated to subproblem j. The goal is to attach each tuple a range $[p_1(j), p_2(j)]$, such that the ranges of different subproblems are disjoint and $\max_j p_2(j) \le p$.

We again resort to all prefix-sums. First sort all tuples by their subproblem id. For each tuple, define its corresponding $A[i] = p(j)$ if it is the first tuple of subproblem j, and 0 otherwise. After running all prefix-sums, for each tuple, we set its $p_2(j) = S[i]$, and $p_1(j) = S[i] - p(j) + 1$.

3. EQUI-JOIN

We start by revisiting the equi-join problem between 2 relations, $R_1 \bowtie R_2$. Let N_1 and N_2 be the sizes of R_1 and R_2, respectively; set $\text{IN} = N_1 + N_2$. First, if $N_1 > pN_2$ or $N_2 > pN_1$, the problem can be trivially solved by broadcasting the smaller relation to all servers, incurring a load of $O(\min\{N_1, N_2\})$. Below, we assume $N_1 \le N_2 \le pN_1$, and describe an algorithm that achieves the following result.

THEOREM 1. *There is a deterministic algorithm that computes the equi-join between 2 relations in $O(1)$ rounds with load $O\left(\sqrt{\frac{\text{OUT}}{p}} + \frac{\text{IN}}{p}\right)$. It does not assume any prior statistical information about the data.*

3.1 The algorithm

Our algorithm can be seen as an MPC version of sort-merge-join.

Step (1) Computing OUT

Consider each distinct join value v. Let $R_i(v)$ be the set of tuples in R_i with join value v; let $N_i(v) = |R_i(v)|$. Note that

OUT $= \sum_v N_1(v)N_2(v)$. We first use the sum-by-key algorithm to compute all the $N_i(v)$'s, i.e., each tuple in $R_i(v)$ is considered to have key v and weight 1. Recall that after the sum-by-key algorithm, for each v, exactly one tuple knows $N_i(v)$. We sort all such tuples by the key v. Then we add up all the $N_1(v)N_2(v)$'s, which can also be done by sum-by-key (just that the key is the same for all tuples).

Step (2) Computing $R_1 \bowtie R_2$

Next, we compute the join, i.e., the Cartesian products $R_1(v) \times R_2(v)$ for all v. Sort all tuples in both R_1 and R_2 by the join value. Consider each join value v. If all tuples in $R_1(v) \cup R_2(v)$ land on the same server, their join results can be emitted directly, so we only need to deal with the case when they land on 2 or more servers. There are at most p such v's. For each such v, we allocate

$$p_v = \left\lceil p \cdot \frac{N_1(v)}{N_1} + p \cdot \frac{N_2(v)}{N_2} + p \cdot \frac{N_1(v)N_2(v)}{\text{OUT}} \right\rceil$$

servers and compute the Cartesian product $R_1(v) \times R_2(v)$. Note that we need a total of $O(p)$ servers; scaling down the initial p can ensure that at most p servers are needed. Here, we also need the server allocation primitive to allocate servers to these subproblems accordingly. Finally, to be able to use the deterministic version of the hypercube algorithm, the elements in each $R_i(v)$ need to be assigned consecutive numbers, which can be achieved by running the multi-numbering algorithm, treating each distinct join value v as a key. It can be easily verified that the load is $O\left(\sqrt{\frac{N_1(v)N_2(v)}{p_v}} + \frac{N_1(v)}{p_v} + \frac{N_2(v)}{p_v}\right) = O\left(\sqrt{\frac{\text{OUT}}{p}} + \frac{N_1}{p} + \frac{N_2}{p}\right)$.

3.2 A matching lower bound

As argued in Section 1.2, the term $O(\sqrt{\text{OUT}/p})$ is optimal for any tuple-based algorithm. Below we show that the term $O(\text{IN}/p)$ is also necessary, even when OUT $= O(1)$.

THEOREM 2. *Any randomized algorithm that computes the equi-join between 2 relations in $O(1)$ rounds with a success probability more than 3/4 must incur a load of at least $\Omega(\min\{N_1, N_2, \frac{\text{IN}}{p}\})$ bits.*

PROOF. We use a reduction from the *lopsided set disjointness* problem studied in communication complexity: Alice has $\le n$ elements and Bob has $\le m$ elements with $m > n$, both from a universe of size m, and the goal is to decide whether they have an element in common. It has been proved that in any multi-round communication protocol, either Alice has to send $\Omega(n)$ bits to Bob, or Bob has to send $\Omega(m)$ bits to Alice [27]. This holds even for randomized algorithms with a success probability larger than 3/4. We also note that in the hard instances used in [27], the intersection size of Alice's and Bob's sets is either 0 or 1.

The reduction works as follows. Without loss of generality, we assume $N_1 \le N_2$. Given a hard instance of lopsided set disjointness, we create R_1 with $N_1 = n$ tuples, whose join values are the elements of Alice's set; create R_2 with $N_2 = m$ tuples, whose join values are the elements of Bob's set. Then solving the join problem also determines whether the two sets intersect or not, while OUT can only be 1 or 0.

Recall that in the MPC model, the adversary can allocate the input arbitrarily. We allocate R_1 and R_2 to the p servers as follows.

If $N_2 \le p \cdot N_1$, we allocate Alice's set to $\frac{pN_2}{\text{IN}}$ servers and Bob's set to $\frac{pN_1}{\text{IN}}$ servers. Then Alice's servers must send $\Omega(N_1)$ bits to Bob's servers, which incurs a total load (across all rounds) of $\Omega(\text{IN}/p)$ bits per server, or Bob's servers must send $\Omega(N_2)$ bits to Alice's servers, also incurring a total load of $\Omega(\text{IN}/p)$ bits per server.

If $N_2 > p \cdot N_1$, then we allocate Bob's set to one server, and Alice's set to the other $p-1$ servers. Then Alice's servers will send $\Omega(N_1)$ bits to Bob's server, or receive $\Omega(N_2)$ bits, so the load is $\Omega(\min(N_1, N_2/p)) = \Omega(N_1)$. □

4. SIMILARITY JOIN UNDER ℓ_1/ℓ_∞

In this section, we study similarity joins under the ℓ_1 or the ℓ_∞ metric. We will actually study a more general problem, namely the *rectangles-containing-points* problem. Here we are given a set R_1 of N_1 points and a set R_2 of N_2 orthogonal rectangles. The goal is to return all pairs $(x, y) \in R_1 \times R_2$ such that $x \in y$. Note that a similarity join with ℓ_∞ metric is equivalent to a rectangles-containing-points problem where each side of the rectangles has length $2r$. A similarity join with ℓ_1 metric in d dimensions can be reduced to a similarity join with ℓ_∞ metric in 2^{d-1} dimensions, by noticing that for any vector $(x_1, \ldots, x_d) \in \mathbb{R}^d$,

$$\sum_{i=1}^{d} |x_i| = \max_{(z_2,\ldots,z_d)\in\{-1,1\}^{d-1}} |x_1 + z_2x_2 + \cdots + z_dx_d|.$$

In this section and the next, we will assume constant dimensions, so that 2^{d-1} is still a constant. We deal with the high-dimensional case in Section 6.

4.1 One dimension

We start by considering the one-dimensional case, i.e., the *intervals-containing-points* problem. We are given a set of N_1 points and a set of N_2 intervals. Set IN $= N_1 + N_2$. The goal to report all (point, interval) pairs such that the point is inside the interval. Below we describe how to solve this problem in $O(\sqrt{\text{OUT}/p} + \text{IN}/p)$ load. Note that as with the equi-join case, if $N_1 > p \cdot N_2$ or $N_2 > p \cdot N_1$, then the problem can be trivially and optimally solved with $O(\min(N_1, N_2))$ load.

Step (1) Computing OUT

As with the equi-join algorithm, we start by computing the value of OUT. First, we sort all the points and number them consecutively in the sorted order. Then, for each interval $I = [x, y]$, we find the predecessor points of x and y (multi-search). Taking the difference of the numbers assigned to the two predecessors will give us the number of points inside I. Finally, we add up all these counts to get OUT (special case of sum-by-key).

Step (2) Partially covered slabs

By setting $b = \sqrt{\text{OUT}/p} + \text{IN}/p$, we will ensure that the load of the remaining steps is $O(b)$. We sort all the points and divide them into *slabs* of size b. Note that there are at most p slabs. Consider each interval I in R_2. All the points inside I can be classified into two cases: (1) points that fall in a slab partially covered by I, and (2) points that fall in a slab fully covered by I. For example, in Figure 1, the join between I_1 and the points in the leftmost and the rightmost slab is considered under case (1), while the join between I_1 and the points in the two middle slabs is considered under case (2). Note that if an interval falls inside a slab completely, its join with the points in that slab is also considered under case (1), such as I_2 in Figure 1.

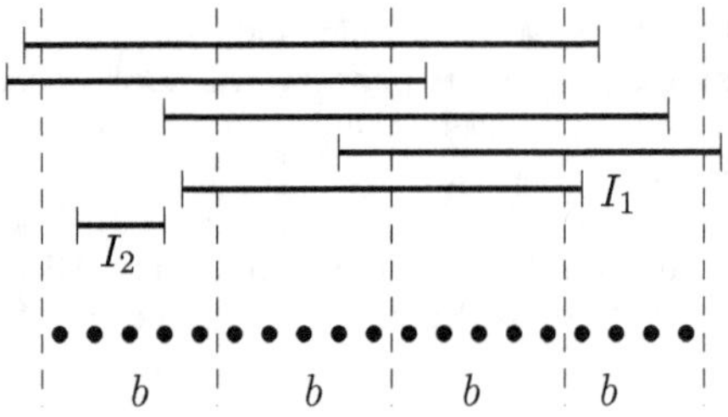

Figure 1: Partially covered and fully covered slabs.

In this step, we deal with the partially covered slabs. For each interval endpoint, we find which slab it falls into (multi-search). Then, for each slab, we compute the number of endpoints falling inside (sum-by-key). Consider each slab i. Suppose it contains $P(i)$ endpoints. We allocate $\lceil p \cdot \frac{P(i)}{N_2} \rceil$ servers to compute the join between the b points in the slab and the intervals with these $P(i)$ endpoints (note that we need $O(p)$ servers). We simply evenly allocate the $P(i)$ intervals to these servers (use multi-numbering to ensure balance), and broadcast all the b points to them. The load is thus

$$O\left(b + \frac{P(i)}{pP(i)/N_2}\right) = O(b).$$

Step (3) Fully covered slabs

Let $F(i)$ be the number of intervals fully covering a slab i. We can compute all the $F(i)$'s using all prefix-sums algorithm, as follows. If an interval fully covers slabs $i, \dots, j$, we generate two pairs $(i, 1)$ and $(j+1, -1)$. For each slab i, we generate a pair $(i + 0.5, 0)$. Then we sort all these (i, v) pairs by i and compute the prefix-sums on the v's.

Now, the full slabs can be dealt with using essentially the same algorithm. We allocate $p_i = \lceil p \cdot \frac{bF(i)}{\mathrm{OUT}} \rceil$ servers to compute the join (full Cartesian product) of the b points in slab i and the $F(i)$ intervals fully covering the slab. Since $\sum_i bF(i) \le \mathrm{OUT}$, this requires at most $O(p)$ servers. We simply evenly allocate the $F(i)$ intervals to these servers and broadcast all the b points to them. The load is thus

$$O\left(b + \frac{F(i)}{pbF(i)/\mathrm{OUT}}\right) = O\left(b + \frac{\mathrm{OUT}}{pb}\right) = O(b).$$

THEOREM 3. *There is a deterministic algorithm for the intervals-containing-points problem that runs in $O(1)$ rounds with $O\left(\sqrt{\frac{\mathrm{OUT}}{p}} + \frac{\mathrm{IN}}{p}\right)$ load.*

4.2 Two and higher dimensions

Next, we generalize the algorithm above to two dimensions. Here we are given a set of N_1 points in 2D and a set of N_2 rectangles. Set $\mathrm{IN} = N_1 + N_2$. The goal is to report all (point, rectangle) pairs such that the point is inside the rectangle.

Step (1) Computing OUT

The first step is still to compute the output size OUT. We first sort all the x-coordinates, including those of the points and those of the left and right sides of the rectangles. Then each server defines a vertical slab, containing $O(\mathrm{IN}/p)$ x-coordinates. All joining (point, rectangle) pairs that land on the same server can be counted and output easily. For example, in Figure 2, the join results between σ_1 and all the points in slab 1 and slab 7 can be found by those two servers easily. This also includes rectangles that completely fall inside a slab, such as σ_2.

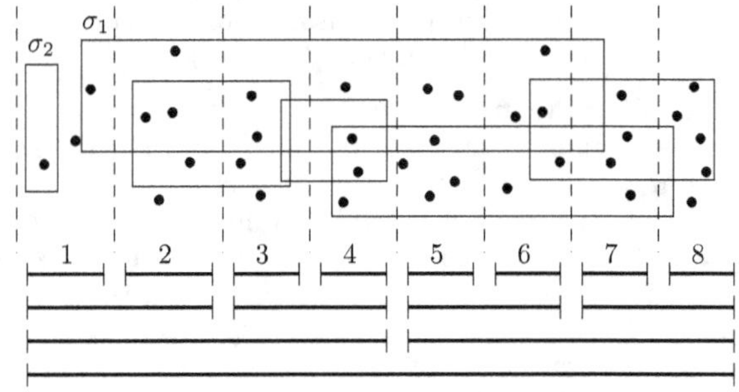

Figure 2: Rectangles-joining-points.

So we are left to count the joining pairs such that the x-projection of the rectangle fully spans the slab containing the point. We impose a binary hierarchy on the p slabs, and decompose each rectangle into $O(\log p)$ canonical slabs. For example, σ_1 in Figure 2 fully spans slabs 2–6, and it is decomposed into 3 canonical slabs: 2, 3–4, 5–6.

This results in a total of $O(N_2 \log p)$ canonical rectangles, each of which corresponds to one canonical slab. For each canonical slab s, we count its output size $\mathrm{OUT}(s)$, using step (1) of the 1D algorithm. To run all these instances in parallel, we allocate the servers as follows. For a canonical slab s that has $N_2(s)$ canonical rectangles and consists of $k(s)$ atomic slabs, we allocate $p_s = \left\lceil p \cdot \frac{k(s)\mathrm{IN}/p + N_2(s)}{\mathrm{IN} \log p} \right\rceil$ servers. As each atomic slab is covered by $O(\log p)$ canonical slabs, we have $\sum_s k(s) = O(p \log p)$. This step uses $O(p)$ servers, with each server having load $O(\frac{k(s)\mathrm{IN}/p + N_2(s)}{p_s}) = O(\frac{\mathrm{IN}}{p} \log p)$. To count the $N_2(s)$'s, we first count $F(i)$, the number of rectangles fully covering an atomic slab i. This is the same as the $F(i)$'s in the 1D case, can be counted with $O(\mathrm{IN}/p)$ load. Then for each atomic slab i, we produce $O(\log p)$ pairs $(s, F(i))$, one for each canonical slab s that contains i. This generates $O(p \log p)$ such pairs. Finally, we run sum-by-key on these pairs (using s as the key) to compute $N_2(s)$, with load $O(p \log p/p) = O(\log p) = O(\mathrm{IN}/p)$.

Note that this step always has load $O(\frac{\mathrm{IN}}{p} \log p)$ regardless of how large OUT is.

Step (2) Reduction to the 1D case

In this step, we compute, for each rectangle σ, all the result pairs produced by σ and the points in the slabs fully spanned by σ. We follow the same approach as in step (1), but will also need to take into account the output size of each canonical slab, i.e., $\mathrm{OUT}(s)$, when allocating the servers. More precisely, for a canonical slab s that has $N_2(s)$ canonical rectangles and consists of $k(s)$ contiguous slabs, we allocate

$$p_s = \left\lceil p \cdot \frac{\mathrm{OUT}(s)}{\mathrm{OUT}} + p \cdot \frac{k(s)\mathrm{IN}/p + N_2(s)}{\mathrm{IN} \log p} \right\rceil$$

servers, and invoke step (2) and (3) of the 1D algorithm (since $\mathrm{OUT}(s)$ is already computed) for all the canonical slabs in parallel. Note that a point knows which canonical slabs it falls into, hence which 1D instances it should participate in, from just its own slab number. For each canonical slab s, denote the size of its derived instance as $\text{IN}(s) = k(s)\text{IN}/p + N_2(s)$. Plugging $\text{OUT} = \text{OUT}(s), \text{IN} = \text{IN}(s), p = p_s$ into Theorem 3 yields the following result.

THEOREM 4. *There is a deterministic algorithm for the rectangles-containing-points problem in 2D that runs in $O(1)$ rounds with $O\left(\sqrt{\frac{\text{OUT}}{p}} + \frac{\text{IN}}{p}\log p\right)$ load.*

The algorithm can also be extended to higher dimensions using similar ideas, with an extra $O(\log p)$ factor for each dimension higher. We give the following result without proof.

THEOREM 5. *There is a deterministic algorithm for the rectangles-containing-points problem in d dimensions that runs in $O(1)$ rounds with $O\left(\sqrt{\frac{\text{OUT}}{p}} + \frac{\text{IN}}{p}\log^{d-1} p\right)$ load.*

5. SIMILARITY JOIN UNDER ℓ_2

In this section, we consider the similarity join between two point sets R_1 and R_2 under the ℓ_2 distance in d dimensions. We first use the *lifting transformation* [13] to convert the problem to the *halfspaces-containing-points* problem in $d+1$ dimensions. Consider any two points $(x_1, \ldots, x_d) \in R_1$ and $(y_1, \ldots, y_d) \in R_2$. The two points join under the ℓ_2 distance if

$$(x_1 - y_2)^2 + \cdots + (x_d - y_d)^2 \leq r^2,$$

or

$$x_1^2 + y_1^2 + \cdots + x_d^2 + y_d^2 - 2x_1y_1 - \cdots - 2x_dy_d - r^2 \geq 0.$$

We map the point $(x_1, \ldots, x_d)$ to a point in $d+1$ dimensions: $(x_1, \ldots, x_d, x_1^2 + \cdots + x_d^2)$, and the point $(y_1, \ldots, y_d)$ to a halfspace in $d+1$ dimensions (z_i's are the parameters):

$$-2y_1z_1 - \cdots - 2y_dz_d + z_{d+1} + y_1^2 + \cdots + y_d^2 - r^2 \geq 0.$$

We see that the two d-dimensional points join if and only if the corresponding $(d+1)$-dimensional halfspace contains the $(d+1)$-dimensional point.

Thus, in the following, we will study the halfspaces-containing-points problem. Given a set of N_1 points and a set of N_2 halfspaces in d dimensions, report all the (point, halfspace) pairs such that the point is inside the halfspace.

A key challenge in this problem, compared with the ℓ_1/ℓ_∞ case, is that there is no easy way to compute OUT, due to the non-orthogonal nature of the problem. Knowing the value of OUT is crucial in the previous algorithms, which is used to determine the right slab size, which in turn decides the load.

Our way to get around this problem is based on the observation that the load is determined by the output-dependent term only when OUT is sufficiently large. But in this case, a constant-factor approximation of OUT suffices to guarantee the optimal load asymptotically, and random sampling can be used to estimate OUT. Random sampling will not be effective when OUT is small (it is known that to decide whether $\text{OUT} = 1$ or 0 by sampling requires us to essentially sample the whole data set), but in that case, the input-dependent term will dominate the load, and we do not need to know the value of OUT anyway.

The following notion of a *θ-thresholded approximation* captures our needs, which will be used in the development of the algorithm.

DEFINITION 1. *A θ-thresholded approximation of x is an estimate $\hat{x}$ such that: (1) if $x \geq \theta$, then $\frac{x}{2} < \hat{x} < 2x$; (2) if $x < \theta$, then $\hat{x} < 2\theta$.*

5.1 Useful tools from computational geometry

We will need the following tools from computational geometry. The first relates thresholded approximations with random sampling.

THEOREM 6 ([23, 17]). *For any $q > 1$, let S be a random sample from a set P of n points with $|S| = O(q\log(q/\delta))$. Then with probability at least $1-\delta$, $n \cdot \frac{|\Delta \cap S|}{|S|}$ is a $\frac{n}{q}$-thresholded approximation of $|\Delta \cap P|$ for every simplex Δ.*

Next, we introduce the *partition tree*. In particular, we make use of the *b-partial partition tree* of Chan [11].

A b-partial partition tree on a set of points is a tree T with constant fanout, where each leaf stores at most b points, and each point is stored in exactly one leaf. Each node $v \in T$ (both internal nodes and leaf nodes) stores a cell $\Delta(v)$, which is a simplex that encloses all the points stored at the leaves below v. For any v, the cells of its children do not overlap. In particular, this implies that all the leaf cells are disjoint. Chan [11] presented an algorithm to construct a b-partial partition tree with the following properties.

THEOREM 7 ([11]). *Given n points in $\mathbb{R}^d$ and a parameter $b < n/\log^{\omega(1)} n$, we can build a b-partial partition tree with $O(n/b)$ nodes, such that any hyperplane intersects $O((n/b)^{1-1/d})$ cells of the tree.*

Chan's construction only guarantees that each leaf cell contains at most b points but offers no lower bound, while we will need each leaf cell to have $\Theta(b)$ points. This can be easily achieved, though. Suppose Chan's b-partial partition tree has at most $c \cdot n/b$ leaves for some constant c. A leaf cell is *big* if it contains at least $b/2c$ points; otherwise *small*. Observe that there must be at least $n/2b$ big leaf cells. Then, we simply combine $O(1)$ small leaf cells with each of the big leaf cells. This will eliminate all small leaf cells, while each merged cell consists of a constant number of the original cells.

5.2 The algorithm

Let q be a parameter such that $1 < q < p$. The value of q will be determined later.

Step (1) Constructing a partition tree

Randomly sample $\Theta(q\log p)$ points, and send all the sampled points to one server. The server builds a $\Theta(\log p)$-partial partition tree on the sampled points. By Theorem 6 and 7, this tree has $O(q)$ nodes, and with probability $1 - 1/p^{O(1)}$, every leaf cell contains $O(N_1/q)$ points in the original data set, and any hyperplane intersects $O(q^{1-\frac{1}{d}})$ cells. Then we perform the merging process described after Theorem 7. Since each merged cell consists of $O(1)$ leaf cells, each merged cell has constant description complexity and still contains $O(N_1/q)$ points. Note that the merging process does not increase the total cell count and the number of cells intersected by any hyperplane.

We broadcast these merged cells to all servers. This step incurs a load of $O(q\log p)$. Henceforth, a "cell" will refer to such a merged cell.

Similar to the intervals-containing-points algorithm, we consider the following two cases for all points inside a halfspace: (1) those in cells partially covered by the halfspace, and (2) those in cells fully covered by the halfspace.

Step (2) Partially covered cells

For each halfspace, we find all the cells Δ such that its bounding halfplane intersects Δ. There are $O(q^{1-\frac{1}{d}})$ such intersecting cells, by Theorem 7. For each cell Δ, we compute the number of halfspaces whose bounding halfplane intersects Δ, denoted as $P(\Delta)$. Note that $\sum_\Delta P(\Delta) = O(N_2 \cdot q^{1-\frac{1}{d}})$, so this is a sum-by-key problem on a total of $O(N_2 \cdot q^{1-\frac{1}{d}})$ key-value pairs. The load is thus

$$O\left(\frac{N_2}{p} \cdot q^{1-\frac{1}{d}}\right). \tag{2}$$

For each cell Δ, we allocate $p_\Delta = \left\lceil p \cdot \frac{P(\Delta)}{N_2 \cdot q^{1-\frac{1}{d}}} \right\rceil$ servers to compute the join between the $\Theta(N_1/q)$ points in the cell and these $P(\Delta)$ halfspaces that partially cover Δ. The total number of servers needed is $O(p)$. Invoking the hypercube algorithm to compute their Cartesian product incurs a load of

$$O\left(\sqrt{\frac{\frac{N_1}{q} \cdot P(\Delta)}{p_\Delta}} + \frac{\frac{N_1}{q} + P(\Delta)}{p_\Delta}\right)$$
$$= O\left(\sqrt{\frac{N_1 N_2}{p q^{\frac{1}{d}}}} + \frac{N_1}{q} + \frac{N_2 q^{1-\frac{1}{d}}}{p}\right). \tag{3}$$

Choosing $q = p^{\frac{d}{2d-1}}$ balances the terms in (2) and (3), and the load becomes

$$O\left(\frac{\text{IN}}{q}\right) = O\left(\frac{\text{IN}}{p^{d/(2d-1)}}\right).$$

Step (3): Fully covered cells

In the intervals-containing-points algorithm, fully covered cells are dealt in a way similar to the partially covered cells, but that is because we can compute OUT and set the right slab size. In this algorithm, we may have used a cell size (i.e., IN$/q$) that is too small in relation to OUT. This would result in too many join results to be produced for the fully covered cells, exceeding the load target. Our strategy is thus to first estimate the join size for the fully covered cells (which is easier than computing OUT), and then rectify the mistake by restarting the whole algorithm with the right cell size, if needed.

Step (3.1): Join size estimation

For each cell Δ, let $F(\Delta)$ be the number of halfspaces fully covering it, and let $K = \sum_\Delta F(\Delta)$. Since every point inside Δ joins with every halfspace fully covering Δ, $K \cdot N_1/q$ is (a constant-factor approximation of) the remaining output size, and we will be able to estimate K easily.

We first compute an $(\frac{N_2}{q})$-thresholded approximation of $F(\Delta)$ for each Δ. This can be done by sampling $O(q \log p)$ halfspaces and collecting them on one server. For each cell Δ, we count the number of sampled halfspaces fully covering it, and scale up appropriately. Standard Chernoff type of analysis shows that with probability $1 - 1/p^{O(1)}$, we get an $(\frac{N_2}{q})$-thresholded approximation for every $F(\Delta)$. We use these approximate $F(\Delta)$'s to compute $\widehat{K}$, which is then an N_2-thresholded approximation of the true value of K.

Step (3.2): If $\widehat{K} < \frac{\text{IN}\cdot p}{q}$

Since we have chosen $q = o(p)$, if $\widehat{K} < \frac{\text{IN}\cdot p}{q}$ and $\widehat{K}$ is an N_2-thresholded approximation of K, then we must have $K = O(\frac{\text{IN}\cdot p}{q})$. In this case, we just break up each halfspace that fully covers k cells into k small pieces, which results in a total of K pieces. Now every piece covers exactly one cell, thus joins with all the points in that cell. The problem now reduces to an equi-join on two relations of size N_1 and K. Invoking the hypercube algorithm, the load is

$$O\left(\sqrt{\frac{\text{OUT}}{p}} + \frac{K + N_1}{p}\right) = O\left(\sqrt{\frac{\text{OUT}}{p}} + \frac{\text{IN}}{q}\right).$$

Step (3.3): If $\widehat{K} > \frac{\text{IN}\cdot p}{q}$

In this case, we cannot afford to reduce the problem to an equi-join, since the halfspaces cover too many cells. This means we have used a cell size too small. Now, we restart the whole algorithm, but with a new $q' = \sqrt{\frac{\text{IN}\cdot pq}{\widehat{K}}} < q$. In the re-execution of the algorithm, we further merge every $O(q/q')$ cells into a bigger cell containing $\Theta(N_1/q')$ points. Now, each newly merged cell has non-constant description complexity, but since there are only a total of $O(q)$ cells, the entire mapping from these cells to the newly merged cells can be broadcast to all servers. Each server can still identify, for each of its points, which newly merged cell contains it.

Meanwhile, note that if $\widehat{K}$ is an N_2-thresholded approximation and $\widehat{K} > \frac{\text{IN}\cdot p}{q}$, then $\widehat{K}$ must be a constant-factor approximation of K and we have $q' = \Theta\left(\sqrt{\frac{\text{IN}\cdot pq}{K}}\right)$.

With the new q', step (1) has load $O(q' \log p) = O(q \log p)$; step (2) has load

$$O\left(\frac{\text{IN}}{q'}\right) = O\left(\sqrt{\frac{\text{IN} \cdot K}{pq}}\right) = O\left(\sqrt{\frac{\text{OUT}}{p}}\right),$$

where the second step uses the fact that $KN_1/q \le K \cdot \text{IN}/q$ is the output size for the fully covered cells in the first attempt of the algorithm, so must be no larger than OUT.

In the re-execution of the algorithm, let $F'(\Delta)$ be the number of halfspaces covering a newly merged cell Δ, and let $K' = \sum_\Delta F(\Delta)$. Observe that each newly merged cell consists of $\Theta(q/q')$ old cells. This means that we have $K' = O(Kq'/q)$, since any halfspace fully covering one newly merged cell must cover $\Theta(q/q')$ old cells (but not vice versa).

We argue that in the re-execution, we will always have $\widehat{K}' = O(\frac{\text{IN}\cdot p}{q'})$, thus always reaching step (3.2), whose load is $O\left(\sqrt{\frac{\text{OUT}}{p}} + \frac{\text{IN}}{q'}\right) = O\left(\sqrt{\frac{\text{OUT}}{p}}\right)$. Indeed, we have

$$\begin{aligned}
\widehat{K}' &= O(K' + \text{IN}) \\
&\qquad (\widehat{K}' \text{ is a } N_2\text{-thresholded approximation of } K') \\
&= O\left(K \cdot \frac{q'}{q} + \text{IN}\right) \\
&= O\left(\frac{\text{IN}\cdot pq}{(q')^2} \cdot \frac{q'}{q} + \text{IN}\right) = O\left(\frac{\text{IN}\cdot p}{q'}\right).
\end{aligned}$$

Therefore, the re-execution, if it takes place, must have load $O\left(\sqrt{\frac{\text{OUT}}{p}}\right)$. Combining with the load of the first execution, we obtain the following result.

THEOREM 8. *There is a randomized algorithm that solves the halfspaces-containing-points problem in $O(1)$ rounds and load*

$$O\left(\sqrt{\frac{\text{OUT}}{p}} + \text{IN}/p^{\frac{d}{2d-1}} + p^{\frac{d}{2d-1}} \log p\right).$$

The algorithm succeeds with probability at least $1 - 1/p^{O(1)}$.

6. SIMILARITY JOIN IN HIGH DIMENSIONS

So far we have assumed that the dimensionality d is a constant. The load for both the ℓ_1/ℓ_∞ algorithm and the ℓ_2 algorithm hides constant factors that depend on d exponentially in the big-Oh notation. For the ℓ_2 algorithm, even for constant d, the term $O(\mathrm{IN}/p^{\frac{d}{2d-1}})$ approaches $O(\mathrm{IN}/\sqrt{p})$ as d grows, which is the load for computing the full Cartesian product.

In this section, we present an algorithm for high-dimensional similarity joins based on *locality sensitive hashing* (LSH), where d is not considered a constant. The nice thing about the LSH-based algorithm is that its load is independent of d (we still measure the load in terms of tuples; if measured in words, then there will be an extra factor of d). The downside is that its output-dependent term will not depend on OUT exactly; instead, it will depend on $\mathrm{OUT}(cr)$, which is the output size when the distance threshold of the similarity join is made c times larger, for some constant $c > 1$. LSH is known to be an approximate solution for nearest neighbor search, as it may return a neighbor whose distance is c times larger than the true nearest neighbor. In the case of similarity joins, all answers returned are truly within a distance of r (since this can be easily verified), but its cost will depend on $\mathrm{OUT}(cr)$ instead of OUT. It is also an approximate solution, in the sense that it approximates the optimal cost. The same notion of approximation has also been used for LSH-based similarity joins in the external memory model [25].

Let $\mathrm{dist}(\cdot,\cdot)$ be a distance function. For $c > 1, p_1 > p_2$, recall that a family $\mathcal{H}$ of hash functions is (r, cr, p_1, p_2)-sensitive, if for any uniformly chosen hash function $h \in \mathcal{H}$, and any two tuples x, y, we have (1) $\Pr[h(x) = h(y)] \geq p_1$ if $\mathrm{dist}(x, y) \leq r$; and (2) $\Pr[h(x) = h(y)] \leq p_2$ if $\mathrm{dist}(x, y) \geq cr$. In addition, we require $\mathcal{H}$ to be *monotone*, i.e., for a randomly chosen $h \in \mathcal{H}$, $\Pr[h(x) = h(y)]$ is a non-increasing function of $\mathrm{dist}(x, y)$. This requirement is not in the standard definition of LSH, but the LSH constructions for most metric spaces satisfy this property, include Hamming [19], ℓ_1 [12], ℓ_2 [5, 12], Jaccard [9], etc.

The quality of a hash function family is measured by $\rho = \frac{\log p_1}{\log p_2} < 1$, which is bounded by a constant that depends only on c, but not the dimensionality, and $\rho \approx 1/c$ for many common distance functions [19, 12, 5]. In a standard hash family $\mathcal{H}$, p_1 and p_2 are both constants, but by concatenating multiple hash functions independently chosen from $\mathcal{H}$, we can make p_1 and p_2 arbitrarily small, while $\rho = \frac{\log p_1}{\log p_2}$ is kept fixed, or equivalently, $p_2 = p_1^{1/\rho}$.

In the description of our algorithm below, we leave p_1, p_2 unspecified, which will be later determined in the analysis.

The algorithm proceeds in the following 3 steps:

(1) Choose $1/p_1$ hash functions $h_1, \ldots, h_{1/p_1} \in \mathcal{H}$ randomly and independently, and broadcast them to all servers.

(2) For each tuple x, make $1/p_1$ copies, and attach the pair $(i, h_i(x))$ to each of these copies, for $i = 1, \ldots, 1/p_1$.

(3) Perform an equi-join on all the copies of tuples, treating the pair $(i, h_i(x))$ as the join value, i.e., two tuples x, y join if $h_i(x) = h_i(y)$ for some i. For two joined tuples x, y, output them if $\mathrm{dist}(x, y) \leq r$.

THEOREM 9. *Assume there is a monotone (r, cr, p_1, p_2)-sensitive LSH family with $\rho = \frac{\log p_1}{\log p_2}$. Then there is a randomized similarity join algorithm that runs in $O(1)$ rounds and with expected load*

$$O\left(\sqrt{\frac{\mathrm{OUT}}{p^{1/(1+\rho)}}} + \sqrt{\frac{\mathrm{OUT}(cr)}{p}} + \frac{\mathrm{IN}}{p^{1/(1+\rho)}}\right).$$

The algorithm reports each join result with at least constant probability.

PROOF. Correctness of the algorithm follows from standard LSH analysis: For any two tuples x, y with $\mathrm{dist}(x, y) \leq r$, the probability that they join on one h_i is at least p_1. Across $1/p_1$ independently hash functions, we have constant probability that they join on at least one of them.

Below we analyze the load. Step (1) has load $O(1/p_1)$; step (2) is local computation. So we only need to analyze step (3).

The total number of tuples generated in step (2) is $O(N/p_1)$, which is the input size to the equi-join. The expected output size is at most

$$\mathrm{OUT}/p_1 + \mathrm{OUT}(cr) + \mathrm{IN}^2/p_1^{1-1/\rho}.$$

The first term is for all pairs (x, y) such that $\mathrm{dist}(x, y) \leq r$. They could join on every h_i. The second term is for (x, y)'s such that $r < \mathrm{dist}(x, y) \leq cr$. There are $\mathrm{OUT}(cr)$ such pairs, and each pair has probability at most p_1 to join on each h_i, so each pair joins exactly once in expectation. The last term is for all (x, y)'s such that $\mathrm{dist}(x, y) > cr$. There are N^2 such pairs, and each pair joins with probability at most p_2 on each h_i, so they contribute the term $\mathrm{IN}^2 p_2/p_1 = \mathrm{IN}^2/p_1^{1-\rho}$ in expectation.

Plugging these into Theorem 1, and using Jensen's inequality $E[\sqrt{X}] \leq \sqrt{E[X]}$, the expected load can be bounded by (the big-Oh of)

$$\frac{\sqrt{\mathrm{OUT}/p_1 + \mathrm{OUT}(cr) + \mathrm{IN}^2/p_1^{1-1/\rho}}}{\sqrt{p}} + \frac{\mathrm{IN}}{pp_1}$$
$$\leq \sqrt{\frac{\mathrm{OUT}}{pp_1}} + \sqrt{\frac{\mathrm{OUT}(cr)}{p}} + \mathrm{IN}\sqrt{\frac{1}{pp_1^{1-1/\rho}}} + \frac{\mathrm{IN}}{pp_1}.$$

Setting $p_1 = 1/p^{\frac{\rho}{1+\rho}}$ balances the last two terms, and we obtain the claimed bound in the theorem. □

Remark. Note that since $0 < \rho < 1$, the input-dependent term is always better than performing a full Cartesian product. The output-term $O\left(\sqrt{\frac{\mathrm{OUT}(cr)}{p}}\right)$ is also the best we can achieve for any LSH-based algorithm, by the following intuitive argument: Due to its approximation nature, LSH cannot tell whether the distance between two tuples are smaller than r or slightly above r. A worst-case scenario is all the $\mathrm{OUT}(cr)$ pairs of tuples have distance slightly above r but none of them actually joins. Unfortunately, since the hash functions cannot distinguish the two cases, any LSH-based algorithm will have to check all the $\mathrm{OUT}(cr)$ pairs to make sure that it does not miss any true join results. Finally, the term $O\left(\sqrt{\frac{\mathrm{OUT}}{p^{1/(1+\rho)}}}\right)$ is also worse than the bound $O\left(\sqrt{\frac{\mathrm{OUT}}{p}}\right)$ we achieved in earlier sections. This is perhaps the best one can hope for as well, if $O(1)$ rounds are required: In order to capture all joining pairs, $1/p_1$ repetitions are necessary, and two very close tuples may join in all these repetitions, introducing the extra $1/p_1$ factor in the output size. If we want to perform all of them in parallel, there seems to be no way to eliminate the redundancy beforehand. Of course, this is just an intuitive argument, not a formal proof.

7. A LOWER BOUND ON 3-RELATION CHAIN JOIN

In this section, we consider the possibility of designing output-optimal algorithms for multi-way joins. We show that, unfortunately, this is not possible, even for the simplest multi-way join, a 3-relation equi-join, $R_1(A,B) \bowtie R_2(B,C) \bowtie R_3(C,D)$.

The first question is how an output-optimal term would look like for a 3-relation join. Applying the tuple-based argument in Section 1.2, each server can potentially produce $O(L^3)$ join results in a single round, hence $O(pL^3)$ results over all p servers in a constant number of round. Thus, an $O((\text{OUT}/p)^{1/3})$ term is definitely output-optimal.

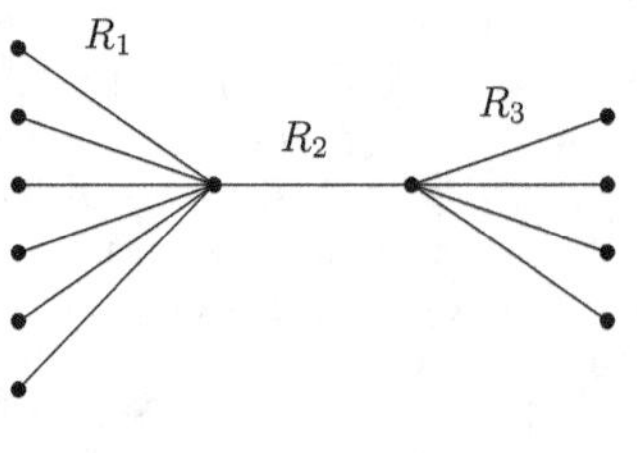

Figure 3: An instance of a 3-relation chain join.

However, consider the instance shown in Figure 3, where we use vertices to represent attribute values, and edges for tuples. On such an instance, the 3-relation join degenerates into the Cartesian product of R_1 and R_3. Each server can produce at most $O(L^2)$ pairs of tuples in one round, one from R_1 and one from R_3, so we must have $O(pL^2) = \Omega(\text{OUT})$, or $L = \Omega(\sqrt{\text{OUT}/p})$. This means that the best possible output-dependent term is still $O(\sqrt{\text{OUT}/p})$. Below we show that this is not possible, either, assuming any meaningful input-dependent term.

THEOREM 10. *For any tuple-based algorithm computing a 3-relation chain join, if its load is in the form of*

$$L = O\left(\frac{\text{IN}}{p^{\alpha}} + \sqrt{\frac{\text{OUT}}{p}}\right),$$

for some constant α, then we must have $\alpha \le 1/2$, provided $\text{IN}/\log^2 \text{IN} > cp^3$ for some sufficiently large constant c.

Note that there is an algorithm for the 3-relation chain join with load $\tilde{O}(\text{IN}/\sqrt{p})$ [21], without any output-dependent term. This means that it is meaningless to introduce the output-dependent term $O(\sqrt{\text{OUT}/p})$.

PROOF. Suppose there is an algorithm with a claimed load L in the form stated above. We will construct a hard instance on which we must have $\alpha \le 1/2$. Our construction is probabilistic, and we will show that with high probability, the constructed instance satisfies our needs.

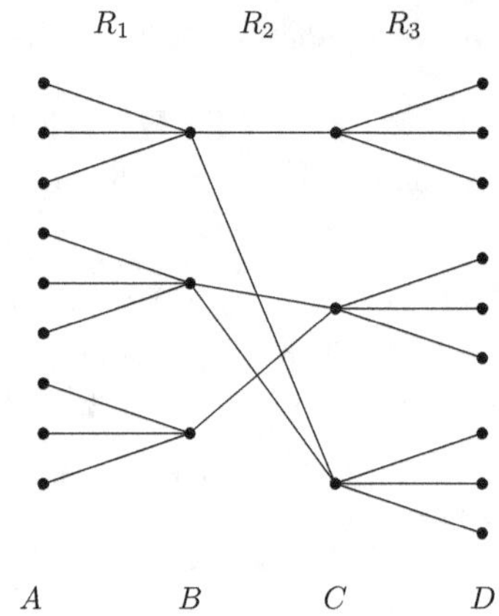

Figure 4: A randomly constructed hard instance.

The construction is illustrated in Figure 4. More precisely, attributes B and C each have $\frac{N}{\sqrt{L}}$ distinct values. Each distinct value of B appears in $\sqrt{L}$ tuples in R_1, and each distinct value in C appears in $\sqrt{L}$ tuples in R_3. Each distinct value of B and each distinct value of C have a probability of $\frac{L}{N}$ to form a tuple in R_2. Note that R_1 and R_3 are deterministic and always have N tuples, while R_2 is probabilistic with N tuples in expectation, so $E[\text{IN}] = 3N$. The output size is expected to be $E[\text{OUT}] = NL$. By the Chernoff inequality, the probability that IN or OUT deviates from their expectations by more than a constant fraction is $\exp(-\Omega(N))$.

We allow all servers to access R_2 for free, and only charge the algorithm for receiving tuples from R_1 and R_3. More precisely, we bound the maximum number of join results a server can produce in a round, if it only receives L tuples from R_1 and L tuples from R_3. Then we multiply this number by p, which must be larger than OUT. Note that this is purely a counting argument; if the same join result is produced at two or more servers, it is counted multiple times.

First we argue that a server should load R_1 and R_3 in whole groups in order to maximize its output size. Here, a group means all tuples sharing the same value on B (or C). Without loss of generality, suppose two groups in R_1 are not loaded in full by a server, say, g_1 and g_2. If g_1 joins more tuples from R_3 that have been loaded by the same server than g_2, then we can always shift tuples from g_2 to g_1 so as to produce more (at least not less) join results.

Thus, each server in each round loads $\sqrt{L}$ groups from R_1 and $\sqrt{L}$ groups from R_3. Below we show that, on a random instance constructed as above, with high probability, not many pairs of groups can join, no matter which subset of $2\sqrt{L}$ groups are loaded. Consider any subset of $\sqrt{L}$ groups from R_1 and any subset of $\sqrt{L}$ groups from R_3. There are L possible pairs of groups, and each pair has probability $\frac{L}{N}$ to join, so we expect to see $\frac{L^2}{N}$ pairs to join. By Chernoff bound, the probability that more than $2\frac{L^2}{N}$ pairs join is at most $\exp(-\Omega(\frac{L^2}{N}))$. There are $O\left(\left(N/\sqrt{L}\right)^{2\sqrt{L}}\right)$ different choices of $\sqrt{L}$ groups from R_1 and $\sqrt{L}$ groups from R_3. So, the probability that one of them yields more than $2\frac{L^2}{N}$

joining groups is at most

$$O\left(\left(\frac{N}{\sqrt{L}}\right)^{2\sqrt{L}}\right)\cdot\exp\left(-\Omega\left(\frac{L^2}{N}\right)\right)$$
$$=\exp\left(-\Omega\left(\frac{L^2}{N}\right)-O\left(\sqrt{L}\cdot\log N\right)\right).$$

This probability is exponentially small if

$$\frac{L^2}{N}>c_1\sqrt{L}\cdot\log N,$$

for some sufficiently large constant c_1. Rearranging, we get

$$N\log N<\frac{1}{c_1}\cdot L^{\frac{3}{2}}.$$

By Theorem 2, we always have $L=\Omega(N/p)$, so this is true as long as

$$N\log N<\frac{1}{c_2}\cdot\left(\frac{N}{p}\right)^{\frac{3}{2}},$$

for some sufficiently large constant c_2, or $N/\log^2 N>c_2p^3$.

By a union bound, we conclude that with high probability, a randomly constructed instance has $\text{IN}=\Theta(N)$, $\text{OUT}=\Theta(NL)$, and on this instance, no matter which groups are chosen, no more than $\frac{2L^2}{N}$ pairs of groups can join. Since each pair of joining groups produces L results, the p servers in total produce $O\left(\frac{L^3p}{N}\right)$ results in a constant number of rounds. So we have

$$\frac{L^3p}{N}=\Omega(NL),$$

i.e.,

$$L=\Omega\left(\frac{N}{\sqrt{p}}\right).$$

Suppose an algorithm has a load in the form as stated in the theorem, then with $\text{OUT}=\Theta(NL)$, we have

$$\frac{N}{p^\alpha}+\sqrt{\frac{NL}{p}}=\Omega\left(\frac{N}{\sqrt{p}}\right).$$

If $\alpha>1/2$, we must have

$$\sqrt{\frac{NL}{p}}=\Omega\left(\frac{N}{\sqrt{p}}\right),$$

or $L=\Omega(N)$, which is an even higher lower bound. Thus we must have $\alpha\le 1/2$. □

8. CONCLUDING REMARKS

Our negative result has ruled out the possibility of having output-optimal algorithms for any join on 3 or more relations. However, there is still hope if we sacrifice the output optimality slightly. For example, what can be done if the output-dependent term is to be $\tilde{O}(\sqrt{\text{OUT}/p^{1-\delta}})$ for some small δ?

More broadly, using OUT as a parameter to measure the complexity falls under the realm of parameterized complexity, or beyond-worst-case analysis in general. This type of analyses often yields more insights for problems where worst-case scenarios are rare in practice, such as joins. While OUT is considered the most natural additional parameter to introduce, other possibilities exist, such as assuming that the data follows certain parameterized distributions, or the degree (i.e., maximum number of tuples a tuple can join) is bounded [10, 24], etc.

9. REFERENCES

[1] F. Afrati, M. Joglekar, C. Ré, S. Salihoglu, and J. D. Ullman. Gym: A multiround join algorithm in mapreduce. *arXiv preprint arXiv:1410.4156*, 2014.

[2] F. N. Afrati and J. D. Ullman. Optimizing multiway joins in a map-reduce environment. *IEEE Transactions on Knowledge and Data Engineering*, 23(9):1282–1298, 2011.

[3] P. K. Agarwal, K. Fox, K. Munagala, and A. Nath. Parallel algorithms for constructing range and nearest-neighbor searching data structures. In *Proc. ACM Symposium on Principles of Database Systems*, 2016.

[4] A. Aggarwal and J. Vitter. The input/output complexity of sorting and related problems. *Communications of the ACM*, 31(9):1116–1127, 1988.

[5] A. Andoni and P. Indyk. Near-optimal hashing algorithms for approximate nearest neighbor in high dimensions. In *Proc. IEEE Symposium on Foundations of Computer Science*, 2006.

[6] A. Atserias, M. Grohe, and D. Marx. Size bounds and query plans for relational joins. In *Proc. IEEE Symposium on Foundations of Computer Science*, pages 739–748, 2008.

[7] P. Beame, P. Koutris, and D. Suciu. Communication steps for parallel query processing. In *Proc. ACM Symposium on Principles of Database Systems*, 2013.

[8] P. Beame, P. Koutris, and D. Suciu. Skew in parallel query processing. In *Proc. ACM Symposium on Principles of Database Systems*, 2014.

[9] A. Z. Broder, S. C. Glassman, M. S. Manasse, and G. Zweig. Syntactic clustering of the web. *Computer Networks*, 29(8-13):1157–1166, 1997.

[10] Y. Cao, W. Fan, T. Wo, and W. Yu. Bounded conjunctive queries. In *Proc. International Conference on Very Large Data Bases*, 2014.

[11] T. M. Chan. Optimal partition trees. *Discrete & Computational Geometry*, 47(4):661–690, 2012.

[12] M. Datar, N. Immorlica, P. Indyk, and V. S. Mirrokni. Locality sensitive hashing scheme based on p-stable distributions. In *Proc. Annual Symposium on Computational Geometry*, 2004.

[13] M. De Berg, M. Van Kreveld, M. Overmars, and O. C. Schwarzkopf. Computational geometry. In *Computational geometry*, pages 1–17. Springer, 2000.

[14] J. Dean and S. Ghemawat. MapReduce: Simplified data processing on large clusters. In *Proc. Symposium on Operating Systems Design and Implementation*, 2004.

[15] M. T. Goodrich. Communication-efficient parallel sorting. *SIAM Journal on Computing*, 29(2):416–432, 1999.

[16] M. T. Goodrich, N. Sitchinava, and Q. Zhang. Sorting, searching and simulation in the mapreduce framework. In *Proc. International Symposium on Algorithms and Computation*, 2011.

[17] S. Har-Peled and M. Sharir. Relative (p,

ε)-approximations in geometry. *Discrete & Computational Geometry*, 45(3):462–496, 2011.

[18] X. Hu, P. Koutris, and K. Yi. The relationships among coarse-grained parallel models. Technical report, HKUST, 2016.

[19] P. Indyk and R. Motwani. Approximate nearest neighbors: Towards removing the curse of dimensionality. In *Proc. ACM Symposium on Theory of Computing*, 1998.

[20] B. Ketsman and D. Suciu. A worst-case optimal multi-round algorithm for parallel computation of conjunctive queries. In *Proc. ACM Symposium on Principles of Database Systems*, 2017.

[21] P. Koutris, P. Beame, and D. Suciu. Worst-case optimal algorithms for parallel query processing. In *Proc. International Conference on Database Theory*, 2016.

[22] P. Koutris and D. Suciu. Parallel evaluation of conjunctive queries. In *Proc. ACM Symposium on Principles of Database Systems*, 2011.

[23] Y. Li, P. M. Long, and A. Srinivasan. Improved bounds on the sample complexity of learning. *Journal of Computer and System Sciences*, 62(3):516–527, 2001.

[24] C. R. Manas Joglekar. It's all a matter of degree: Using degree information to optimize multiway joins. In *Proc. International Conference on Database Theory*, 2016.

[25] R. Pagh, N. Pham, F. Silvestri, and M. Stöckel. I/O-efficient similarity join. In *Proc. European Symposium on Algorithms*, 2015.

[26] R. Pagh and F. Silvestri. The input/output complexity of triangle enumeration. In *Proc. ACM Symposium on Principles of Database Systems*, 2014.

[27] M. Pătraşcu. Unifying the landscape of cell-probe lower bounds. *SIAM Journal on Computing*, 40(3), 2011.

[28] L. G. Valiant. A bridging model for parallel computation. *Communications of the ACM*, 33(8):103–111, 1990.

[29] M. Zaharia, M. Chowdhury, T. Das, A. Dave, J. Ma, M. McCauley, M. J. Franklin, S. Shenker, and I. Stoica. Resilient distributed datasets: A fault-tolerant abstraction for in-memory cluster computing. In *Proc. USENIX conference on Networked Systems Design and Implementation*, 2012.

2017 ACM PODS Alberto O. Mendelzon Test-of-Time Award

In 2007, the PODS Executive Committee established a Test-of-Time Award, named after the late Alberto O.Mendelzon, in recognition of his scientific legacy and his service and dedication to the database community. Mendelzon was an international leader in database theory, whose pioneering and fundamental work has inspired and influenced both database theoreticians and practitioners, and continues to be applied in a variety of advanced settings. He served the database community in many ways: he served as both the Program and the General Chair of the PODS conference, and was instrumental in bringing SIGMOD and PODS together. He was an outstanding educator, who guided the research of numerous doctoral students and postdoctoral fellows. The Award is to be given each year to a paper or a small number of papers published in the PODS proceedings ten years prior, that had the most impact (in terms of research, methodology, or transfer of practice) over the intervening decade. The decision was approved by SIGMOD and ACM. The funds for the Award were contributed by IBM Toronto. The PODS Executive Committee has appointed us to serve as the Award Committee for 2017. After careful consideration and having solicited external nominations and advice, we have decided to select the following paper as the award winner for 2017:

"Provenance Semirings"

by Todd J. Green, Gregory Karvounarakis, and Val Tannen.

Citation. In the mid-1990s, Stefano Bistarelli, Ugo Montanari, and Francesca Rossi discovered an elegant framework for constraint solving based on assigning constraints values in a semiring; it accounted, in a uniform way, for several hitherto different approaches to constraint solving. In their PODS 2007 paper, titled "Provenance Semirings", Green, Karvounarakis, and Tannen demonstrated, via a collection of well-chosen examples, that the same idea is applicable in database theory: they used the semiring approach to capture in a uniform way a variety of scenarios where unions of conjunctive queries or datalog queries are posed over relational databases. These included incomplete and probabilistic databases, and computing provenance of tuples by using well known and studied semirings. After the publication of PODS 2007 paper, the semiring approach was adopted by the database community; it was extended to more expressive queries and was used in provenance applications as well as in applications related to incomplete and probabilistic data and causality in databases. The paper has gathered over 500 citations, giving evidence to its broad impact.

Leonid Libkin
University of Edinburgh, UK

Moshe Y. Vardi
Rice University, USA

The Alberto O. Mendelzon Test-of-Time Award Committee for 2017

The Semiring Framework for Database Provenance

Todd J. Green
LogicBlox Inc.
todd.green@logicblox.com

Val Tannen
Computer and Information Science Department
University of Pennsylvania
val@cis.upenn.edu

This paper does not offer a survey of the semiring framework. Rather, it is intended to bring forward, with the benefit of 20/20 (well, at least 15/20) hindsight, a couple of insights that were not emphasized in the papers that constitute the core of the framework's development. These insights do not even pertain to all the technical aspects of the framework, leaving out, most notably, Datalog. We have also tried to collect a reasonably large set of relevant references. Most of all, we hope to make the reader intrigued enough to follow up with additional reading and perhaps examine further research questions.

Data provenance.

Imagine a computational process that uses a complex input consisting of multiple items. The granularity and nature of "input item" can vary significantly. It can be a single tuple, a database table, or a whole database. It can a spreadsheet describing an experiment, a laboratory notebook entry, or another form of capturing annotation by humans in software. It can also be a file, or a storage system component. It can be a parameter used by a module in a scientific workflow. It can also be a configuration rule used in software-defined routing or in a complex network protocol. Or it can be a configuration decision made by a distributed computation scheduler (think map-reduce). *Provenance analysis* allows us to understand how these different input items affect the output of the computation. When done appropriately, such analysis can be further used, for example,

A1: to figure out how much to trust the output, assuming that we may trust some input items more than others;

A2: to minimize the cost of obtaining the output, assuming that one has to pay for the input items;

A3: to figure out the clearance level required for accessing the output, assuming that we know the clearance levels for the input items;

A4: to compute the probabilistic distribution of the output, assuming that we know the distributions of the input items;

A5: to figure out if the output might change (and therefore whether output *maintenance* is necessary) when certain input items change; or

A6: to track back and find the input items at fault, assuming the output is somehow wrong.

We shall have occasion below to refer to the applications A1-A6 just listed. In practice, a computational process will produce a collection of output items and the applications above become more interesting when we realize that we may get different analyses for each output item.

Now, observe that these applications should not rely on just a trace, or a log, of a specific execution of the computational process itself. [1] Some approach to applications A3 and A5 could probably be devised using just execution traces, but we should still worry whether repeating the execution with the same input items but with a differently optimized execution platform will produce the same provenance. At the same time, we cannot simply peg provenance as a kind of static analysis of the underlying program since it will also depend on the input items themselves. This dual static-dynamic nature makes provenance analysis particularly interesting, especially so for database computations.

Database provenance.

Provenance analysis for queries, views, database ETL tools, and schema mappings takes advantage of their declarative nature. An early approach for RDBMS [18, 19], let's call it *which-provenance*, produces a set of tuple ids that answer the question *" which tuples in the input database contributed to obtaining a particular output tuple?"*. When an output tuple can be derived in multiple ways, which-provenance collects the contributing tuples in each of these ways but then puts them all in the same set. This yields a (workable, but not completely satisfactory) solution for applications A3, A5, and A6, however it does not help with any of the other applications. This work was followed by a seminal contribution: the *why-provenance* of [14] which collects contributing input tuples separately for each derivation of an output tuple. The result is a set of *witnesses*, each witness being a set of input tuples. We illustrate the difference between which- and why-provenance in Figure 1 where we

[1]Although in many existing approaches provenance collection consists of just adding entries to a log.

PODS'17, May 14 - 19, 2017, Chicago, IL, USA

ISBN 978-1-4503-4198-1/17/05...15.00
DOI: http://dx.doi.org/10.1145/3034786.3056125

R

A B C	*tid*
a b c	p
d b c	r

$\pi_{B}(\pi_{AC} R \bowtie \pi_{BC} R)$

B	*which*	*why*	*bag-why*
b	$\{p, r\}$	$\{\{p\}, \{p, r\}, \{r\}\}$	$\{[p, p], [p, r], [r, r]\}$

Figure 1: Which, why, or bag-why provenance

also use an important perspective cemented by [14]: provenance as *data annotation.* The query shown there has three distinct witnesses: $\{p\}, \{p, r\}$ and $\{r\}$. Each of these witnesses can lead to different reasoning about trust, cost, and probabilistic events.

The kind of provenance that works properly for probabilistic reasoning is, not surprisingly, given by boolean expressions (see, e.g., [44]). Motivated by conjunctive query equivalence, rather than by probabilistic reasoning, [14] also developed *minimal witness* provenance. For example, in the why-provenance $\{\{p\}, \{p, r\}, \{r\}\}$ the minimal witnesses are $\{p\}$ and $\{r\}$: either of them "absorbs" the witness $\{p, r\}$. Interestingly, it was realized later (see [30]) that minimal witness provenance is isomorphic to positive boolean expression provenance.

And yet, neither why-provenance nor boolean provenance is appropriate for A1 or A2 (trust or cost). The reason for this is that an input tuple might be used more than once in the derivation of an output. If so, the cost of that tuple should be doubled (and as we shall see, the trust/confidence can be squared). Therefore we need to track how many times each input item is used. With the hindsight afforded by the development of the semiring framework, an appropriate provenance here could be a variant of why- in which the witnesses are *bags* rather than sets. In Figure 1 we gave the local ad-hoc name *bag-why-provenance* to this approach. It collects $\{[p, p], [p, r], [r, r]\}$ where, for example, $[p, p]$ is the bag with two copies of p. [2] If, say, the tuple p costs 1$ and the tuple r costs 2$ then I wish to only pay 2$ to run this query since I can get the answer using just two copies of p as the bag-witness $[p, p]$ attests.

The approaches discussed so far are appropriate for set semantics but they do not capture bag semantics, specifically, not the multiplicity of output tuples. The semiring framework does.

Joint and alternative use of data.

In [34] a careful analysis of information flow through the operators of the positive relational algebra is performed. The result identifies two fundamental ways in which tuples are used: *jointly* as in cartesian product, join, selection, and intersection, and *alternatively* as in projection and union.

[2]In fact, these sets of bags are isomorphic to the polynomials with boolean coefficients introduced in [30]. There is a corresponding minimal-witness version for bag witnesses, the absorptive polynomials introduced in [24].

This leads naturally to consider a space of provenance annotations instrumented by two *abstract* binary operations: $+$ for alternative use, and $\cdot$ for joint use. The provenance space will also contain the annotations of the input tuples. More flexibility is gained if we do not think of them as tuple ids. We use the term *provenance tokens* and allow multiple tuples (e.g., all the tuples in the same table) to be annotated with the same token if useful.

For the query in Figure 1 the annotation of the output, so far, is $p \cdot (p + r) + r \cdot (p + r)$.

We think of $\sigma_P R$ as intersecting R with a virtual relation W_R that consists of all the possible tuples over the active domain of R. We postulate two constant provenance annotations, 0 and 1, and we annotate those tuples in W_R that satisfy P with 1 and those which do not with 0. So, for example, for the relation R in Figure 1 and the query $\pi_B \sigma_{A=d}(\pi_{AC} R \bowtie \pi_{BC} R)$ the annotation of the output, so far, is $(p \cdot (p + r)) \cdot 0 + (r \cdot (p + r)) \cdot 1$.

As shown in [34] the algebraic identities that we may desire for the algebra of annotated relations determine a specific structure on the space K of annotations: $(K, +, \cdot, 0, 1)$ is a **commutative semiring**.

Now we can use the semiring laws to revisit the examples given before. For the query in Figure 1 the annotation of the output can be written as a multivariate polynomial in indeterminates p and r: $p^2 + 2pr + r^2$ while for the query $\pi_B \sigma_{A=d}(\pi_{AC} R \bowtie \pi_{BC} R)$ we have $pr + r^2$. These *provenance polynomials* are called *how-provenance* in [16]. They can also be seen as bags of bag-witnesses.

Commutative semirings.

$(K, +, \cdot, 0, 1)$ with $0 \neq 1$, is a *semiring* when $(K, +, 0)$ is a commutative monoid, $(K, \cdot, 1)$ is a monoid, $\cdot$ distributes over $+$ and $0 \cdot a = a \cdot 0 = 0$. The semiring is *commutative* when $\cdot$ is commutative. The semiring is *idempotent* when $+$ is idempotent.

Any distributive lattice is an idempotent commutative semiring. Here are some commutative semirings of interest to us:

1. $\mathbb{B} = (\mathbb{B}, \vee, \wedge, \perp, \top)$ is the standard habitat of logical truth. It is a distributive lattice and it corresponds to *set semantics* in databases.
2. $\mathbb{N} = (\mathbb{N}, +, \cdot, 0, 1)$ is used for *bag semantics* and can also be used for *counting derivations.*
3. $\mathbb{T} = (\mathbb{R}_+^\infty, \min, +, \infty, 0)$, is called the *tropical* semiring and is idempotent but not a distributive lattice. Its elements and operations appear in *min-cost* interpretations (e.g., shortest paths) and it plays a surprising role in connecting certain dynamic programming algorithms in statistics with certain methods of algebraic geometry [43] (see also next item).
4. $\mathbb{V} = ([0, 1], \max, \cdot, 0, 1)$ is called the *Viterbi* semiring and is isomorhic to $\mathbb{T}$ via $x \mapsto e^{-x}$ and $y \mapsto -\ln y$. When interpreted as probabilities, its elements and operations appear in *statistical model* interpretations (e.g., maximum probability trajectories in Hidden Markov Models). We can think of the elements of $\mathbb{V}$ as *confidence scores*, and use them in a quantitative approach to trust.
5. $\mathbb{F} = ([0, 1], \max, \min, 0, 1)$, is called the *fuzzy* semiring. It is a distributive lattice.

6. $\mathbb{A} = (\{\mathsf{P} < \mathsf{C} < \mathsf{S} < \mathsf{T} < 0\}, \min, \max, 0, \mathsf{P})$ is the *access control* semiring
P is "public"
C is "confidential"
S is "secret"
T is "top secret"
0 is "so secret that nobody can access it!"
This is a distributive lattice (beware! the lattice order is the opposite of the one we used in the definition). This is a just an illustrative example of clearance levels. Any finite distributive lattice would do. Interestingly, non-distributive lattices may lead to wrong permissions depending on optimizations performed by the DBMS.

7. $\mathbb{N}[X] = (\mathbb{N}[X], +, \cdot, 0, 1)$, denoted $\mathbb{N}[X]$, consist of multivariate polynomials in indeterminates from X and with coefficients from $\mathbb{N}$. This is the commutative semiring freely generated by the set X. It's used for a general form of provenance: the provenance polynomials.

8. $(\mathsf{PosBool}(X), \vee, \wedge, \bot, \top)$, denoted $\mathsf{PosBool}(X)$, whose elements are classes of equivalent positive (monotone) boolean expressions with boolean variables from X (its elements are in bijection with the positive boolean expressions in irredundant disjunctive normal form). This is the distributive lattice freely generated by the set X. Also used for provenance, e.g., in probabilistic databases.

K-sets and linear (semi)algebra.

In what follows we fix a commutative semiring $(K, +, \cdot, 0, 1)$. For a set D and a function $A : D \to K$ we define the *support* of A

$$\mathsf{supp}(A) \;=\; \{x \in D \mid A(x) \neq 0\}$$

We now define a K-**set** with elements from D to be a function $D \to K$ that has *finite support*. The straightforward definition of addition of K-sets

$$(A + B)(x) \;=\; A(x) + B(x)$$

determines a commutative monoid structure on K-sets with $0(x) = 0$. Notice that $\mathbb{B}$-sets are ordinary sets whose addition is union while $\mathbb{N}$-sets are bags with bag union. For a finite arity r we can define [34] a K-*relation* to be a $\mathbb{D}^r$-set where $\mathbb{D}$ is a database domain.

In addition to forming a commutative monoid, the K-sets also can be "multiplied" by elements of K, an operation similar to multiplication by scalars in a vector space. For any $k \in K$ and any K-set A we define:

$$(k * A)(x) \;=\; k \cdot A(d)$$

This puts a K-**semimodule** structure (see [8, 47]) on K-sets. In the semimodule of K-sets the singletons form a *basis*. Indeed, for each $d \in D$ define $\{d\} : D \to K$

$$\{d\}(x) \;=\; \textit{if } x = d \textit{ then } 1 \textit{ else } 0$$

Then, any K-set A such that $\mathsf{supp}(A) = \{d_1, \ldots, d_n\}$ can be written as a linear combination of singletons

$$A \;=\; A(d_1) * \{d_1\} + \cdots + A(d_n) * \{d_n\}$$

Now the definition of cross-product of K-relations (similar to [34]) is forced by a postulate that requires $\times$ to be *bilinear*, together with

$$(k * \{r\}) \times (l * \{s\}) = (k \cdot l) * \{\langle r, s\rangle\}$$

which follows from $k \cdot l$ corresponding to joint use.

With 20/20 hindsight, regarding K-sets as linear combinations also explains the extension of the semiring framework from flat to nested relational query languages [27]. It can also partially explain the extension to aggregation [8]. There, aggregation domains are commutative monoids with operations such as min, max or summation. Regarding these monoids as semimodules is an essential insight. The other important component of the aggregation work is the *tensor product* construction $K \otimes M$ which extends any commutative monoid M to a K-semimodule. Similar to the K-sets, the elements of $K \otimes M$ can be expressed as a linear combination

$$k_1 * \iota(m_1) + \cdots + k_n * \iota(m_n)$$

where $\iota : M \to K \otimes M$ maps the elements of M to tensors that generate the entire space (M represents a basis when ι is injective). This gives us a general idea of K-*annotated aggregations* that also covers "sums" of K-sets as a particular case. See [47] for more details and note also the interesting connections with [38].

Semiring homomorphisms and query equivalence.

K-relations give a whole family of standard ($K = \mathbb{B}$ and $K = \mathbb{N}$) and nonstandard (all other K of interest) semantics for relational query languages and beyond. For each K, such a K-**semantics** yields a corresponding notion of *query equivalence.* [3] Pleasingly (even sanely), K-semantics for many query languages satisfies the following **fundamental property**. We state it for the positive relational queries [34] but it also holds for Datalog [34], for the Nested Relational Calculus and its extension to trees [27], for unordered XQuery [27], for extension to aggregates [8], and for FOL model checking [48].

Given two commutative semirings and a homomorphism between them $h : K_1 \to K_2$ we lift h to map K_1-relations, and even K_1-databases, to K_2-relations, respectively K_2-databases: simply by replacing an annotation $k \in K_1$ with $h(k) \in K_2$. Then, for any positive relational query (SPJRU or UCQ), Q the following diagram commutes:

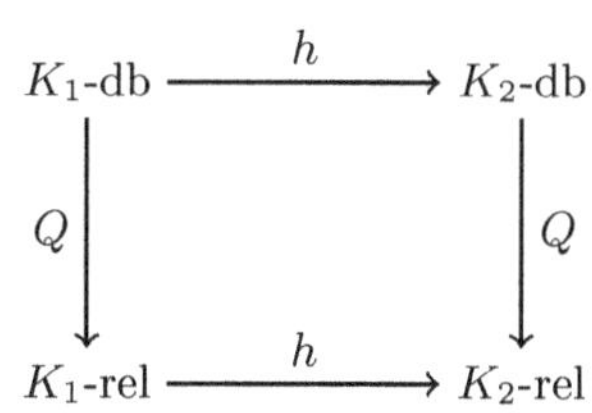

Equivalence of positive relational queries (in the form of UCQs—unions of conjunctive queries) for various K was studied in [30, 31].

Of particular interest are the cases when K is used for capturing provenance. We have already mentioned two such semirings: $\mathbb{N}[X]$, the semiring of provenance polynomials,

[3] And, it turns out, also of *query containment*. However, the latter relies on *naturally ordered* semirings, a topic we shall not discuss here.

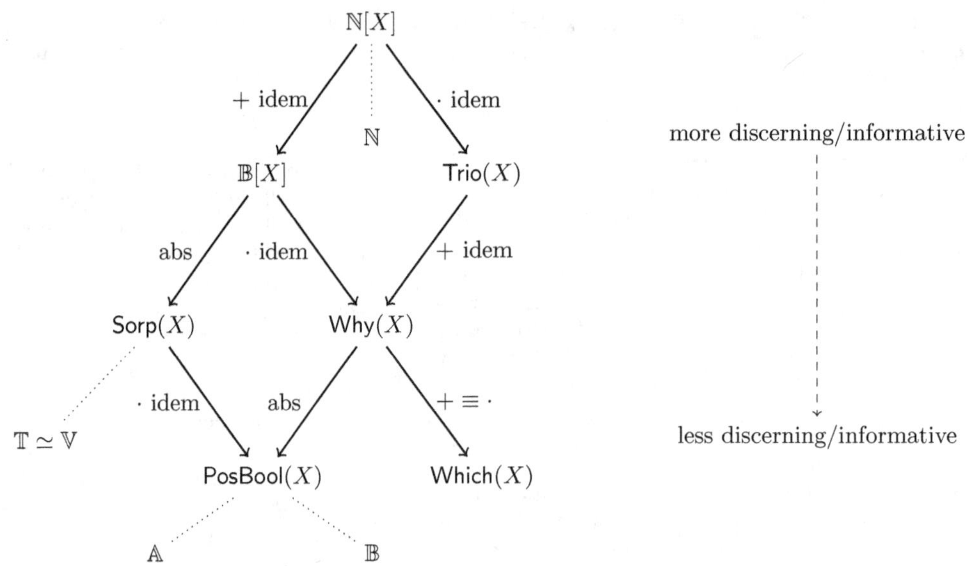

Figure 2: A hierarchy of provenance semirings

and (PosBool(X), the semiring of positive boolean expressions (modulo equivalence). The former captures the most general form of provenance available in the semiring framework while the latter captures provenance that suffices for the applications A3 and A4 and for certain aspects of the applications A5 and A6 (A1-A6 are mentioned at the beginning of this paper). A couple of other commutative semrings have been deemed useful for expressing provenance. For example, it is shown in [30, 31] how to capture the which-provenance, the why-provenance, and the bag-why-provenance (recall Figure 1) in specific commutative semirings (called there Lin(X), Why(X) and respectively $\mathbb{B}[X]$, the latter consisting of polynomials similar to those in $\mathbb{N}[X]$, except with boolean coefficients). An appropriate semiring, Trio(X), is also described for the provenance defined in [9]. [4] Another semiring, Sorp(X) consists of the *absorptive* polynomials and is the absorptive commutative semiring freely generated by X (the absorption law is $a + a \cdot b = a$). It was introduced in [24] and while it does not support bag semantics, it is nicely appropriate for applications A1-A6 above, consisting of minimal bag-witnesses.

We shall say that two relational queries are K**-equivalent** if they give the same result when applied to databases consisting of K-relations. It is a consequence of the fundamental property shown above that when we have a *surjective* homomorphism $h : K_1 \to K_2$ then K_1-equivalence of UCQs implies their K_2-equivalence. Thus, surjective homomorphisms offer a tool for comparing semirings to understand (to some extent) how *discerning* the various K-semantics are. Their presence means "at least as discerning" (but not necessarily "strictly more discerning"), see [30, 31]. We show this in Figure where the solid arrows indicate the presence of a surjective homomorphism. Moreover, these homomorphisms preserves the provenance tokens and all the digrams shown commute. The arrows are labeled with the algebraic laws whose addition characterizes the passage from a more discerning to a less discerning provenance semiring. For example, making both $+$ and $\cdot$ idempotent gives us Why(X). This semiring can be shown to be the commutative, $+$-idempotent, and $\cdot$-idempotent semiring generated by X. Further adding absorption gives the free distributive lattice PosBool(X). As expected less discerning corresponds to less "informative" provenance. Here is an example polynomial mapped along two paths of DAG of surjective homomorphisms (the mappings not shown can be deduced):

$$\begin{aligned} 2p^2r + pr + 5r^2 + ps \in \mathbb{N}[X] &\mapsto p^2r + pr + r^2 + ps \in \mathbb{B}[X] \\ &\mapsto pr + r^2 + ps \in \mathsf{Sorp}(X) \\ &\mapsto r + ps \in \mathsf{PosBool}(X) \end{aligned}$$

and

$$\begin{aligned} 2p^2r + pr + 5r^2 + ps \in \mathbb{N}[X] &\mapsto 3pr + 5r + ps \in \mathsf{Trio}(X) \\ &\mapsto pr + r + ps \in \mathsf{Why}(X) \\ &\mapsto prs \in \mathsf{Which}(X) \end{aligned}$$

For more details, a study of query containment and complexity results see [30, 31].

Finally, the dotted arrows in Figure connect the "application" semirings, $\mathbb{B}, \mathbb{A}, \mathbb{T}, \mathbb{V}$ and $\mathbb{N}$ with the least informative provenance semiring that can still be used for their application. For example, any assignment of values in, say, $\mathbb{V}$ to provenance tokens in X extends uniquely to an (evaluation) homomorphism from Sorp(X) to $\mathbb{V}$.

Some relevant papers.

Here are some useful surveys of provenance and its impact in several domains: [21, 16, 17, 3].

The original motivation for the semiring framework came from the need to manage trust in data sharing as formulated by Z. Ives et al. [36]. The first paper [34] dealt with the positive relational algebra and Datalog. It was followed by investigations into provenance for nested relations/complex values (objects) as well as XQuery (for unordered XML) [27],

[4]We should warn the reader against a possible confusion with the terminology in this field. Which-provenance is called *lineage* in [18, 19], but lineage was used in [9] for a different kind of provenance, and yet again in [44] for what we called here PosBool(X)-provenance.

SQL aggregates [8], workflows with map-reduce modules [4], and languages for data-centric (data-dependent) processes [25], SemanticWeb's SPARQL [29], and even matrix operations [51].

The semiring approach has been successfully implemented in two software systems, Orchestra [33, 35] and Propolis [25]. In addition, access control in Facebook's search feature uses a provenance-based scheme very similar in spirit to the semiring approach [20]. Importantly, space-efficient implementations of semiring provenance use the graph representations nicely described in [26]. The design and implementation of a language for querying provenance graphs was presented in [37]. The size of provenance information has been an early and continuous concern for the semiring framework, both theoretically [5, 6, 24], and practically [2, 1].

The core theoretical underpinnings of the semiring framework (query containment and equivalence properties, constructions of semirings, fixed points, semimodules, and tensor products) have been developed mostly in [34, 27, 30, 8, 32, 47, 25]. The reader may have noticed that the bulk of this work was concerned with *positive* query languages. Indeed, trying to add to the commutative semiring structure operations that capture negation or difference of relations has led to interesting but divergent approaches [28, 32, 8, 7, 29] and a somewhat puzzling state of affairs. Recent work done by E. Grädel and the second author [48] deals with negation syntactically, via *negation normal forms* and thus supports full duality, and, for example, tuple insertion, and why-not provenance.

We note the interesting line of work on *where-provenance* which tracks the input items that get copied as part of the output [14, 13]. Tuple-level annotations will not, in general, be able to track the copying of individual field values. However, a more flexible annotation scheme combined with semiring provenance can [46].

The use of Datalog extensions to specify network configuration rules [40] has already led to many applications of provenance in this area, e.g. [54, 53, 50, 49, 15]. Similarly, the use of Datalog in formal verification [52, 41] is likely to benefit from provenance analysis [42].

The semiring framework has also played a role in motivating recent work on "what-if analysis" [23, 12], "query-by-explanation" [22], and "missing data" [45].

There exists a well-known tight connection between conjunctive queries in databases and constraint satisfaction problems in AI [39]. In this light, and despite a number of technical differences, there exists an interesting connection (that needs more exploration) between the semiring provenance framework applied to conjunctive queries and the semiring framework for *soft constraint satisfaction* [11, 10].

Acknowledgements.

None of this would have been possible without the crucial contributions of our closest collaborators (so far, and in chronological/alphabetical order): Zack Ives, Grigoris Karvounarakis, Nate Foster, Yael Amsterdamer, Daniel Deutch, Tova Milo, Sudeepa Roy, Yuval Moskovitch, Allen Yan, and Erich Grädel. We are also very grateful to others with whom we have collaborated on papers with related topics: Susan Davidson, Julia Stoyanovich, Sanjeev Khanna, Shan Shan Huang, Boon Thau Loo, Molham Aref, Vittorio Perduca, Sepehr Assadi, Yang Li, Jeff Naughton, Bruhathi Sundarmurthy, and Paris Koutris. Val Tannen was partially supported by NSF 1302212 and 1547360, by NIH U01EB020954-01 as well as by the Simons Institute for the Theory of Computing.

1. REFERENCES

[1] E. Ainy, P. Bourhis, S. B. Davidson, D. Deutch, and T. Milo. Approximated summarization of data provenance. In *Proceedings of the 24th ACM International Conference on Information and Knowledge Management, CIKM 2015, Melbourne, VIC, Australia, October 19 - 23, 2015*, pages 483–492, 2015.

[2] E. Ainy, S. B. Davidson, D. Deutch, and T. Milo. Approximated provenance for complex applications. In *6th Workshop on the Theory and Practice of Provenance, TaPP'14, Cologne, Germany, June 12-13, 2014*, 2014.

[3] I. Altintas, M. K. Anand, D. Crawl, S. Bowers, A. Belloum, P. Missier, B. Ludäscher, C. A. Goble, and P. M. A. Sloot. Understanding collaborative studies through interoperable workflow provenance. In *Provenance and Annotation of Data and Processes - Third International Provenance and Annotation Workshop, IPAW 2010, Troy, NY, USA, June 15-16, 2010. Revised Selected Papers*, pages 42–58, 2010.

[4] Y. Amsterdamer, S. B. Davidson, D. Deutch, T. Milo, J. Stoyanovich, and V. Tannen. Putting lipstick on pig: Enabling database-style workflow provenance. *PVLDB*, 5(4):346–357, 2011.

[5] Y. Amsterdamer, D. Deutch, T. Milo, and V. Tannen. On provenance minimization. In *Proceedings of the 30th ACM SIGMOD-SIGACT-SIGART Symposium on Principles of Database Systems, PODS 2011, June 12-16, 2011, Athens, Greece*, pages 141–152, 2011.

[6] Y. Amsterdamer, D. Deutch, T. Milo, and V. Tannen. On provenance minimization. *ACM Trans. Database Syst.*, 37(4):30, 2012.

[7] Y. Amsterdamer, D. Deutch, and V. Tannen. On the limitations of provenance for queries with difference. In *3rd Workshop on the Theory and Practice of Provenance, TaPP'11, Heraklion, Crete, Greece, June 20-21, 2011*, 2011. See also CoRR abs/1105.2255.

[8] Y. Amsterdamer, D. Deutch, and V. Tannen. Provenance for aggregate queries. In *Proceedings of the 30th ACM SIGMOD-SIGACT-SIGART Symposium on Principles of Database Systems, PODS 2011, June 12-16, 2011, Athens, Greece*, pages 153–164, 2011. See also CoRR abs/1101.1110.

[9] O. Benjelloun, A. D. Sarma, A. Y. Halevy, and J. Widom. ULDBs: Databases with uncertainty and lineage. In *VLDB*, pages 953–964, 2006.

[10] S. Bistarelli. *Semirings for Soft Constraint Solving and Programming*, volume 2962 of *Lecture Notes in Computer Science*. Springer, 2004.

[11] S. Bistarelli, U. Montanari, and F. Rossi. Semiring-based constraint satisfaction and optimization. *J. ACM*, 44(2):201–236, 1997.

[12] P. Bourhis, D. Deutch, and Y. Moskovitch. Analyzing data-centric applications: Why, what-if, and how-to. In *32nd IEEE International Conference on Data Engineering, ICDE 2016, Helsinki, Finland, May 16-20, 2016*, pages 779–790, 2016.

[13] P. Buneman, J. Cheney, and S. Vansummeren. On the expressiveness of implicit provenance in query and update languages. In *Database Theory - ICDT 2007, 11th International Conference, Barcelona, Spain, January 10-12, 2007, Proceedings*, pages 209–223, 2007.

[14] P. Buneman, S. Khanna, and W. C. Tan. Why and where: A characterization of data provenance. In *ICDT*, pages 316–330, 2001.

[15] A. Chen, Y. Wu, A. Haeberlen, B. T. Loo, and W. Zhou. Data provenance at internet scale: Architecture, experiences, and the road ahead. In *Conference on Innovative Data Systems Research (CIDR'17)*, Jan. 2017.

[16] J. Cheney, L. Chiticariu, and W. C. Tan. Provenance in databases: Why, how, and where. *Foundations and Trends in Databases*, 1(4), 2009.

[17] J. Cheney, S. Chong, N. Foster, M. I. Seltzer, and S. Vansummeren. Provenance: a future history. In *Companion to the 24th Annual ACM SIGPLAN Conference on Object-Oriented Programming, Systems, Languages, and Applications, OOPSLA 2009, October 25-29, 2009, Orlando, Florida, USA*, pages 957–964, 2009.

[18] Y. Cui and J. Widom. Practical lineage tracing in data warehouses. In *ICDE*, pages 367–378, 2000.

[19] Y. Cui, J. Widom, and J. L. Wiener. Tracing the lineage of view data in a warehousing environment. *ACM Trans. Database Syst.*, 25(2):179–227, 2000.

[20] M. Curtiss, I. Becker, T. Bosman, S. Doroshenko, L. Grijincu, T. Jackson, S. Kunnatur, S. B. Lassen, P. Pronin, S. Sankar, G. Shen, G. Woss, C. Yang, and N. Zhang. Unicorn: A system for searching the social graph. *PVLDB*, 6(11):1150–1161, 2013.

[21] S. B. Davidson, S. C. Boulakia, A. Eyal, B. Ludäscher, T. M. McPhillips, S. Bowers, M. K. Anand, and J. Freire. Provenance in scientific workflow systems. *IEEE Data Eng. Bull.*, 30(4):44–50, 2007.

[22] D. Deutch and A. Gilad. Qplain: Query by explanation. In *32nd IEEE International Conference on Data Engineering, ICDE 2016, Helsinki, Finland, May 16-20, 2016*, pages 1358–1361, 2016.

[23] D. Deutch, Z. G. Ives, T. Milo, and V. Tannen. Caravan: Provisioning for what-if analysis. In *CIDR*, 2013.

[24] D. Deutch, T. Milo, S. Roy, and V. Tannen. Circuits for datalog provenance. In *Proc. 17th International Conference on Database Theory (ICDT), Athens, Greece, March 24-28, 2014.*, pages 201–212, 2014.

[25] D. Deutch, Y. Moskovitch, and V. Tannen. Provenance-based analysis of data-centric processes. *VLDB J.*, 24(4):583–607, 2015.

[26] A. Doan, A. Y. Halevy, and Z. G. Ives. *Principles of Data Integration.* Morgan Kaufmann, 2012.

[27] J. N. Foster, T. J. Green, and V. Tannen. Annotated XML: queries and provenance. In *Proceedings of the Twenty-Seventh ACM SIGMOD-SIGACT-SIGART Symposium on Principles of Database Systems, PODS 2008, June 9-11, 2008, Vancouver, BC, Canada*, pages 271–280, 2008.

[28] F. Geerts and A. Poggi. On database query languages for k-relations. *J. Applied Logic*, 8(2):173–185, 2010.

[29] F. Geerts, T. Unger, G. Karvounarakis, I. Fundulaki, and V. Christophides. Algebraic structures for capturing the provenance of SPARQL queries. *J. ACM*, 63(1):7:1–7:63, 2016.

[30] T. J. Green. Containment of conjunctive queries on annotated relations. In *Database Theory - ICDT 2009, 12th International Conference, St. Petersburg, Russia, March 23-25, 2009, Proceedings*, pages 296–309, 2009.

[31] T. J. Green. Containment of conjunctive queries on annotated relations. *Theory Comput. Syst.*, 49(2):429–459, 2011.

[32] T. J. Green, Z. G. Ives, and V. Tannen. Reconcilable differences. *Theory Comput. Syst.*, 49(2):460–488, 2011.

[33] T. J. Green, G. Karvounarakis, Z. G. Ives, and V. Tannen. Update exchange with mappings and provenance. In *Proceedings of the 33rd International Conference on Very Large Data Bases, University of Vienna, Austria, September 23-27, 2007*, pages 675–686, 2007.

[34] T. J. Green, G. Karvounarakis, and V. Tannen. Provenance semirings. In *Proceedings of the Twenty-Sixth ACM SIGACT-SIGMOD-SIGART Symposium on Principles of Database Systems, June 11-13, 2007, Beijing, China*, pages 31–40, 2007.

[35] Z. G. Ives, T. J. Green, G. Karvounarakis, N. E. Taylor, V. Tannen, P. P. Talukdar, M. Jacob, and F. C. N. Pereira. The ORCHESTRA collaborative data sharing system. *SIGMOD Record*, 37(3):26–32, 2008.

[36] Z. G. Ives, N. Khandelwal, A. Kapur, and M. Cakir. ORCHESTRA: rapid, collaborative sharing of dynamic data. In *CIDR 2005, Second Biennial Conference on Innovative Data Systems Research, Asilomar, CA, USA, January 4-7, 2005, Online Proceedings*, pages 107–118, 2005.

[37] G. Karvounarakis, Z. G. Ives, and V. Tannen. Querying data provenance. In *Proceedings of the ACM SIGMOD International Conference on Management of Data, SIGMOD 2010, Indianapolis, Indiana, USA, June 6-10, 2010*, pages 951–962, 2010.

[38] C. Koch. Incremental query evaluation in a ring of databases. In *Proceedings of the Twenty-Ninth ACM SIGMOD-SIGACT-SIGART Symposium on Principles of Database Systems, PODS 2010, June 6-11, 2010, Indianapolis, Indiana, USA*, pages 87–98, 2010.

[39] P. G. Kolaitis and M. Y. Vardi. Conjunctive-query containment and constraint satisfaction. *J. Comput. Syst. Sci.*, 61(2):302–332, 2000.

[40] B. T. Loo, T. Condie, M. Garofalakis, D. E. Gay, J. M. Hellerstein, P. Maniatis, R. Ramakrishnan, T. Roscoe, and I. Stoica. Declarative networking. *Comm. ACM*, 52(11):87–95, 2009.

[41] R. Mangal, X. Zhang, A. V. Nori, and M. Naik. A user-guided approach to program analysis. In *Proceedings of the 2015 10th Joint Meeting on Foundations of Software Engineering, ESEC/FSE 2015, Bergamo, Italy, August 30 - September 4, 2015*, pages 462–473, 2015.

[42] M. Naik. Private communication.

[43] L. Pachter and B. Sturmfels. *Algebraic Statistics for Computational Biology.* Cambridge University Press,

2005.

[44] D. Suciu, D. Olteanu, C. Ré, and C. Koch. *Probabilistic Databases.* Synthesis Lectures on Data Management. Morgan & Claypool Publishers, 2011.

[45] B. Sundarmurthy, P. Koutris, W. Lang, J. Naughton, and V. Tannen. m-tables: Representing missing data. In *ICDT*, 2017. To appear.

[46] V. Tannen. Provenance for database transformation. 2010 EDBT/ICDT Keynote slides `www.cis.upenn.edu/~val/EDBTkeynoteLausanne.pdf`.

[47] V. Tannen. Provenance propagation in complex queries. In *In Search of Elegance in the Theory and Practice of Computation - Essays Dedicated to Peter Buneman*, pages 483–493, 2013.

[48] V. Tannen. Provenance analysis for FOL model checking (Semantics Column, Mike Mislove, ed.). *ACM SIGLOG News*, 4(1):24–36, 2017.

[49] Y. Wu, A. Chen, A. Haeberlen, W. Zhou, and B. T. Loo. Automated network repair with meta provenance. In *Proceedings of the 14th USENIX Symposium on Networked Systems Design and Implementation (NSDI'17)*, Mar. 2017.

[50] Y. Wu, M. Zhao, A. Haeberlen, W. Zhou, and B. T. Loo. Diagnosing missing events in distributed systems negative provenance. In *Proceedings of ACM SIGCOMM 2014*, Aug. 2014.

[51] Z. Yan, V. Tannen, and Z. G. Ives. Fine-grained provenance for linear algebra operators. In *8th USENIX Workshop on the Theory and Practice of Provenance (TaPP 16)*, 2016.

[52] X. Zhang, R. Mangal, R. Grigore, M. Naik, and H. Yang. On abstraction refinement for program analyses in datalog. In *ACM SIGPLAN Conference on Programming Language Design and Implementation, PLDI '14, Edinburgh, United Kingdom - June 09 - 11, 2014*, pages 239–248, 2014.

[53] W. Zhou, L. Ding, A. Haeberlen, Z. Ives, and B. T. Loo. TAP: Time-aware provenance for distributed systems. In *Proceedings of the 3rd USENIX Workshop on the Theory and Practice of Provenance (TaPP'11)*, June 2011.

[54] W. Zhou, Q. Fei, A. Narayan, A. Haeberlen, B. T. Loo, and M. Sherr. Secure Network Provenance. In *Proc. SOSP*, 2011.

Data Integration: After the Teenage Years

Behzad Golshan Alon Halevy George Mihaila Wang-Chiew Tan

Recruit Institute of Technology
{behzad, alon, george, wangchiew}@recruit.ai

ABSTRACT

The field of data integration has expanded significantly over the years, from providing a uniform query and update interface to structured databases within an enterprise to the ability to search, exchange, and even update, structured or unstructured data that are within or external to the enterprise.

This paper describes the evolution in the landscape of data integration since the work on rewriting queries using views in the mid-1990's. In addition, we describe two important challenges for the field going forward. The first challenge is to develop good open-source tools for different components of data integration pipelines. The second challenge is to provide practitioners with viable solutions for the long-standing problem of systematically combining structured and unstructured data.

Keywords

data integration; views; open-source; structured and unstructured data

1. INTRODUCTION

The field of data integration has expanded in many directions as the technology landscape evolved in recent years. At the outset, the goal of data integration was to build systems that provide a uniform query (and for the ambitious, update) interface to multiple databases within an enterprise. As the Web came into prominence, data integration addressed challenges such as incorporating data from external business partners, data exchange between multiple sources, peer-to-peer data sharing architectures, and querying multiple deep-web data sources. The field also had to consider semi-structured data such as XML and unstructured textual data. When personal data management came to the forefront, researchers developed methods for integrating data from streams available to a single user. Most recently, the focus has shifted to integrating extremely large data sets, and extremely large numbers of data sets, such as the collection of HTML tables on the Web.

Data integration has also been a field that pushed on the combination of techniques from data management and artificial intelligence. Initially, the contribution of AI was to propose knowledge representation formalisms as a mechanism for describing the contents of heterogeneous data sources. With time, AI techniques became even more critical to the field, since data integration operators need to handle uncertainty, need to extract facts from text, need to learn from previous experience, and often, they need to do all of the above at the same time.

PODS'17, May 14 - 19, 2017, Chicago, IL, USA

ISBN 978-1-4503-4198-1/17/05...$15.00

DOI: http://dx.doi.org/10.1145/3034786.3056124

This paper accompanies a PODS 2017 Gems talk describing the evolution of data integration since the work on rewriting queries using views in the mid-1990's. The paper can also be considered to be a follow on to the paper "Data Integration: the Teenage Years" published in 2006 [25]. We begin by describing the role that views had in the work on data integration (Section 2) and surveying some of the subsequent developments (Section 3). Like its predecessor [25], the paper is *not* meant to be a comprehensive survey of the field (see [14, 16] for recent textbooks).

We then turn to the main focus of the paper, where we describe two important challenges for the field. The first challenge (Section 4) is that progress of data integration and its application in practice are hindered by the fact that there are very few quality tools with which practitioners and researchers can freely experiment. As a result, the progress on research does not accumulate in the form of open-source tools available for use. We describe an attempt to address this challenge, the BigGorilla open-source platform for data integration in Python. One of the important aspects of BigGorilla is that it offers powerful tools for data integration operators that are needed in practice, and each of them can be used by itself in a data pipeline without requiring the others. We hope that the community will contribute to the platform and improve it with time.

The second challenge we discuss (Section 5) is the current-day version of the long-standing challenge to combine structured and unstructured data. We argue that despite the multiple efforts to address this problem, we still do not offer practitioners viable solutions.

2. VIEWS IN DATA INTEGRATION

Data integration systems provide a uniform query interface to multiple heterogeneous data sources. To provide that interface, they introduce the abstraction of a *global schema* (often called a *mediated schema*). Users pose queries against the global schema, rather than having to know the details of each of the source schemas. Early work on data integration focused on modeling the contents and capabilities of heterogeneous data sources and mapping them to the global schema.

There were two predominant approaches to modeling data sources. *Global-as-view* (GAV) modeled the global schema as a set of view definitions over the schemas of the data sources. In contrast, *local-as-view* (LAV) proposed to model the contents of a data source as a view over the global schema. The approach known as *Global-local-as-view* (GLAV) combined the two formalisms, where a view over the data sources is defined as a view over the global schema. The GLAV formalism is also known as tuple-generating dependencies [5] and is used widely in the study of data integration and exchange [2, 17, 30, 33]. In the GAV approach, reformulating a query that is posed over the global schema into a query on the data sources is conceptually straightforward–the query is unfolded using the view definitions. In the LAV approach, reformulating a query posed over the global schema is trickier and amounts to the problem of rewriting queries using views.

The problem of rewriting queries using views received additional attention at the time because there was also a natural application of the techniques in query optimization [12, 21, 32, 40, 41]: if query plans can use materialized views instead of base tables, they can be significantly more efficient.

It is also interesting to note that LAV was a subtle introduction of AI techniques (or more specifically, knowledge representation) into the modeling of data sources (a much less subtle introduction was made earlier in [10]). A view definition is a simple form of knowledge representation, and rewriting queries using views is a reasoning algorithm whose properties are relatively attractive compared to proposals based on description logics that were also discussed at the time. The main benefits of the LAV approach were that it was easier to add data sources as they became available and that it was possible to describe the contents of the data sources more precisely.

The tradeoffs between different schema mapping formalisms (GAV, LAV, or GLAV), the expressive power of queries and of the views provided a rich area of exploration. Some of the main directions included data exchange (defined as the problem of mapping the actual contents of an origin database into a target database with a different schema), adapting the formalisms for tree and graph data, and answering queries from views without necessarily constructing a rewritten query as an intermediate step. A few years later, the area of model management [6] took a comprehensive look at operations that can be performed on database schemas (e.g., merging, composition and inversion of schema mappings, matching schemas). In addition, there was quite a bit of work on building efficient data integration systems and on algorithms for semi-automatically finding matchings and mappings between heterogeneous schemas [7] and work on benchmarking data integration systems [1, 3]. Some of these developments are described in more detail in [25].

3. THE LANDSCAPE CHANGES

To appreciate the developments in data integration in subsequent years, it is important to understand the typical assumptions made by early data integration systems. These assumptions were perfectly reasonable at the time, but they broke down in later years when the applications of data integration expanded. We will refer to the early work as the *classic* data integration paradigm. The assumptions they made were the following.

A1: The global schema is of reasonable size and can be built with modest effort.

A2: The data sources are structured (or at least semi-structured) and have well-defined schemas.

A3: There is a need to integrate all the data sources at hand.

A4: All data integration functionality should be part of an end-to-end data integration system.

A5: The data in the data sources is mostly correct and consistent across data sources (and if not, then getting it into that state is a matter of standard data cleaning).

The fundamental reasons that the assumptions of the classic paradigm break down are the scale and nature of the data sources. Early applications of data integration handled tens of data sources and often less, and they only had to model well-defined domains (e.g., customer support, supply-chain management, certain scientific databases). While it may be easy for a data owner to arrive at a global schema of the data sources she owns, it is often difficult for different data owners to agree on how the global schema of all their data sources should be represented and which sources are more authoritative. To make matters worse, data sources are rarely static in their lifetime. For this reason, collaborative data sharing architectures, such as [28], have been proposed. Today, data integration applications need to consider data sources on the Web and large collections of data sets in enterprises.

The number of structured data sources on the Web is vast. Work from Google and Microsoft report that the number of high-quality HTML tables is in the hundreds of millions [4, 11]. Due to progress on data integration, these HTML tables are now routinely included in responses to queries posed to Web search engines. Earlier work estimated the number of deep web sources to be in the tens of millions [35]. But even within enterprises the number of datasets is enormous. As a somewhat extreme example, [24] reported that the Google dataset search system had 26 billion datasets in its index. In fact, search for datasets is becoming so important that each of the cloud service providers are now starting to support search over datasets.

When you have this number of data sources it is impossible to build a global schema, and hence assumption A1 breaks down. The data sources will also be much more diverse, and therefore assumption A2 does not hold anymore either. In the relatively simple case of modeling all the data in an enterprise, building a global schema would involve understanding every aspect of your enterprise and all the operations it runs. In the case of the Web, structured data covers all domains that are of interest to mankind. Hence, building a global schema involves a Herculean effort of modeling all possible domains, doing it in over 100 languages, and taking into consideration cultural nuances. Even Freebase, the broadest schema, has been shown to cover only a small fraction of the attributes used in HTML tables [23].

If you cannot build a global schema, the question of whether it is really necessary to integrate all the available data arises. In fact, sometimes data integration involves a great deal of human effort as (external) facts have to be carefully verified before they can be merged into a database [9]. In the ideal world it would be nice to be able to answer any question over these vast data collections. In practice, however, you can get by with less lofty goals, putting into question assumption A3. Instead of integrating the data, the focus shifts to building a system that provides useful search services over data sources. That does not mean that integration will never happen – when the benefit of fully integrating a smaller number of data sources arises, then it is the time to expend the effort. In practice, this trend has led to the rise of two complimentary types of systems: data lakes (often referred to as *dataspaces* [20]), and search systems over the collection of datasets in a data lake.

The key idea of data lakes is *pay-as-you-go* data management. Given the collection of data sources available in the lake, the system should offer several useful services. The first such service is to locate sources that are relevant to a particular query. Given a specific data source, the data lake should provide as much useful information about it, such as usage statistics and provenance infor-

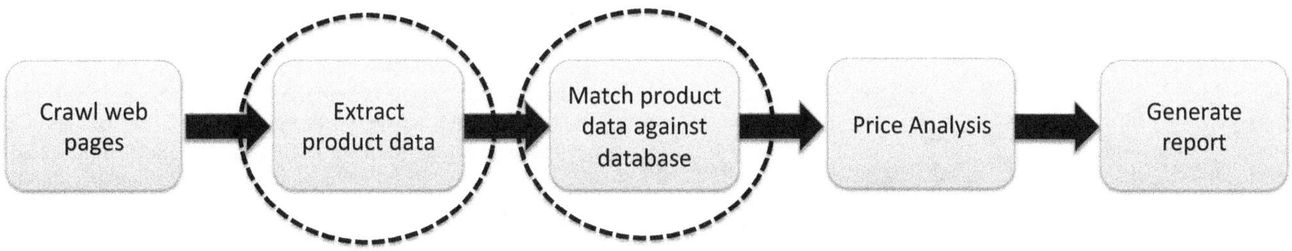

Figure 1: A data pipeline for comparing the prices of products with one's competitor. The pipeline starts by crawling the competitor's site, then extracts the product's attributes from each product page. Next, the pipeline matches products across the two databases, and finally the price comparison is performed. The first, second, and third steps of the pipeline are data integration operators.

mation (which data sources it depends on, and which data sources depend on it). The system should also monitor the data source as it is updated and send an alert when something unusual happens that may indicate a problem.

The data lake should also help a user find similar data sources, including sources that could be joined or unioned with a given data source. When a collection of related data sources are found, the tools of the data lake should help to build an integrated global view over them.

The above discussion should make it clear that even though the focus has shifted from integration to looser federation architectures, the technical challenges in both cases have many similarities. A good search system still needs to understand the semantics of the underlying data sources, needs to be able to find matches between schemas of disparate datasets and needs to find how entities in one dataset correspond to those in another. Hence, we see that the value of the basic data integration operators, such as schema matching and merging, data matching and merging, schema mappings, that were developed in the context of classic data integration are useful in isolation as well, leading to questioning assumption A4. We return to this point in detail in Section 4.

Finally, assumption A5 breaks down when there is such a large number of data sources from independent organizations. In such a case, there are likely to be more inconsistencies between data sources [18, 27] and cases where the actual truth is a matter of perspective [15].

4. MAKING IT ON OUR OWN

As we have alluded to above, data integration operators are useful as standalone services, not just as part of a complete data integration system. In particular, operations such as data matching, schema matching, and data transformation arise in common scenarios such as data-analysis pipelines and data-lake services. Consider the example in Figure 1.

The example describes a pipeline used by an online merchant (e.g., Walmart or Amazon) who wants to periodically compare its prices with the corresponding prices of a competitor. The pipeline begins by crawling the competitor's Web site and extracting from every product page a structured description of the product including the price. Once the pipeline created a database of the competitor's products, the next task is to match the competitor's products with the vendor's own product database so a direct comparison of prices can be performed. After the correspondence between the product databases is found, the actual analysis can begin and the appropriate reports can be generated.

The second, and third steps of the pipeline (structured product extraction and matching across databases) are prototypical data integration operators. It would be highly beneficial to the data scientists or engineers if they can simply plug existing tools into the appropriate stages of their pipeline. In general, a data pipeline is typically more complex than what is depicted in the figure. Also, some operators may be invoked repeatedly for different purposes. In any case, significant time is almost always involved to collect and integrate data before a data scientist can apply her favorite algorithm for analysis [34].

The above example illustrates an important overarching challenge our community faces, namely, that data integration problems are not recognized as such when practitioners encounter them. Specifically, if an engineer is building a pipeline as the one described above, and she needs to match data records from two sources, she probably would not even realize that data matching is an example of a bigger set of tasks known collectively as data integration. Even if she does recognize the problem, she will not consider buying a data integration product to solve her problem, because it is probably too expensive for the problem at hand. More importantly, the data integration system will not provide a module that fits into the existing pipeline. One of the causes of this recognition problem is that data integration operators have always been part of a comprehensive data management solution, and we have never tried to go at it on our own. To emphasize, we describe the problem not because we lack professional pride or yearn for more recognition for our work as a community. Our goal is to considerably expand the impact we can have in practice.

In response to this challenge, we and others have started developing an open-source platform for data integration and preparation (learning some of the lessons from a previous attempt [37]). BigGorilla[1] exposes data integration and preparation operators as modules in Python [8]. BigGorilla currently uses Python because it is the easiest environment for data scientists to quickly perform experiments. However, as the project develops, implementations in other programming languages will be encouraged. Currently, BigGorilla has modules for string matching, entity matching [31], and a simple schema matcher that considers both schema attributes and data if available. In addition, it has consolidated open-source tools for other modules such as acquisition, extraction, and workflow management. New modules are being added as they are required by applications. BigGorilla also aims to enrich its repository of data pipelines, which can serve as instructive examples for the development of other pipelines, over time.

Though BigGorilla focuses on data integration operators, we do

[1]Data integration is a big, dirty, and hairy problem. Hence, BigGorilla. http://www.biggorilla.org

Figure 2: Google's answer to the query "speaker of the house" circa Fall, 2016.

acknowledge the important role and benefits arising from building end-to-end systems, recent examples of which include Data Tamer [39], Deepdive [36], High-level Integration Language [26], Data Civilizer [13] and also integration and visualization systems such as [22, 29].

5. COMBINING STRUCTURED AND UNSTRUCTURED DATA

Combining structured data and unstructured data is a long-standing challenge to the data management community and to the data integration community in particular. However, like other long-standing challenges, its importance only increases.

The challenge arises because the content that data integration systems manage is both structured and unstructured and because they need to answer queries that can be formulated using both keywords and structured query languages. Web search engines have faced this challenge for a while, but it has become more acute in recent years because they try to answer some of their queries using structured data stored in their knowledge graph [38]. The challenge is faced also by vertical search engines, such as search for jobs, beauty salons or houses, and enterprise data lakes. Even narrower applications such as tracking the sentiment towards a company's products on social media face this challenge head on.

On the query side, users have gotten use to simple keyword search engines and expect every system to offer such an interface. For certain query fields, such as location and date ranges, users still provide structured data in their queries.

On the content side the data may simply be unstructured, such as a stream of social media comments, or a collection of Web documents. However, even when the primary organization of the content is structured, salient aspects of the content may still end up in unstructured text fields. Consider the example of a search engine for beauty salons (e.g., treatwell.com). Each beauty salon is a record in a structured database. To register with the search service, the owner of a beauty salon will fill out a questionnaire with a few fields, such as address and opening hours. However, some of the nuanced content describing the salon is more detailed than the schema of the search service. For example, the owner may want to describe some of the skills and experience of particular hair stylists, or some culturally specific names for the services they offer.

In summary, a data integration system needs to understand unstructured queries, translate them into a structured query when possible, and then find answers from content that may be partially structured and partially in text. There are many facets to this challenge. In the following example we highlight a particularly important facet, that of combining data to produce query answers.

Consider the query *who is speaker of the house*, posed to Google. Figure 2 shows the answer given sometime in the Fall of 2016 (Google answers change constantly for many reasons, including locale, time of day, and device from which the query is issued, and numerous changes to the search engine algorithms). To those not familiar with American politics, or rightfully skeptical about them at this point in time, at the time of writing, the answer to this query is Paul Ryan. Ryan was preceded by John Boehner who was preceded by Nancy Pelosi. The speaker of the house is the head of the U.S. Congress and would become president if both the sitting president and vice-president are unable to fulfill their duties.

As can be seen from the screenshot, Google provides answers from three sources, and in this example, they are all different. The top result, John Boehner, comes from a system that performs information extraction from Web documents. Since Paul Ryan was relatively new on the job at the time of the query, the number of Web documents supporting him may have been considerably smaller than those supporting his predecessor and therefore Boehner was chosen. The second answer (the HTML table) has the correct data, but that is apparent only to a human looking at the table who can interpret the meaning of the order of rows in the table. Finally, the third part of the page (which is not strictly speaking a direct answer to the query, but only a visual adornment to the answer), the image of Nancy Pelosi comes from image search. The three algorithms are independently contributing to the displayed result and are inconsistent with each other. Amusingly, the ad on the top of the search result page refers to the correct answer.

Abstracting from the example, the challenge is the following (see Figure 3). We have developed many techniques to extract structured data from unstructured data, such as the algorithm yielding John Boehner above. We also have algorithms for finding good structured data in the sea of unstructured Web documents, such as the table above. However, we have no principled way to combine the results of different algorithms. Google's case is a relatively extreme one since there are many algorithms at play, and as seen above, there is no attempt to try to reconcile them. But even in less complex query engines, engineers struggle with this challenge. In the current state of the art, the algorithm for combining results is hardwired somewhere in the code of the search engine. As a result, it's hard to know how the engine works, hard to modify it, and impossible to explain to users.

Our community has spent quite a bit of effort addressing this challenge. One of the main lines of research has been on probabilistic databases and more generally, reasoning with uncertainty. However, these techniques have had limited impact in practice because of the difficulty of coming up with reliable probabilities and interpreting them in practical settings. Work on tracing provenance/lineage has a potential of contributing to the solution, because combining evidence often has to do with where they come from. However, provenance is only one component of the solution.

Though we are actively thinking about this challenge, we are not yet in a position to describe a solution. We believe, however, that there are two principles that should guide the solution. First, it should be possible to declaratively specify the combination of structured and unstructured data using an appropriate language. A

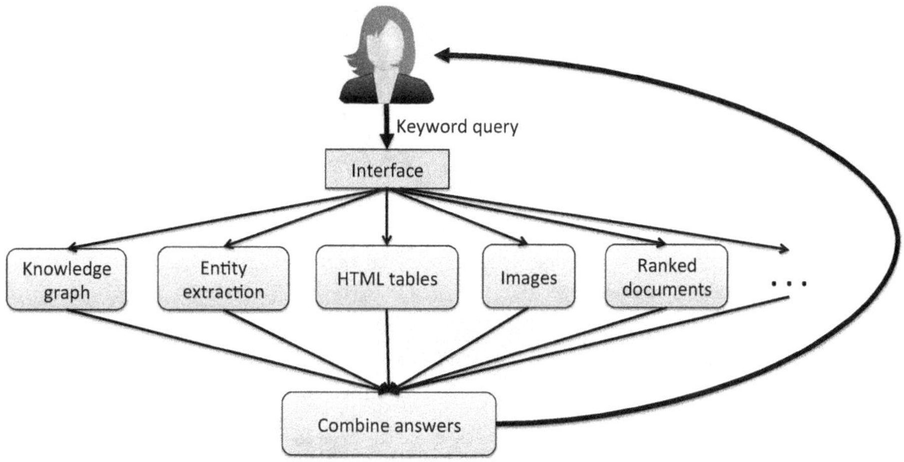

Figure 3: Different algorithms are consulted when answering a query to the search engine. Some of these algorithms consult structured data and others find responses from unstructured data. The challenge we face is to develop a principled method to *combine* the results of all these algorithms into a coherent answer to the user.

declarative specification would enable engineers to easily inspect their systems, debug the outcome, modify them when necessary, and possibly expand the scope of the search as needed [19]. At the same time, that does *not* mean that the rules for the combination need to always be written manually. In particular, some of the rules can be inferred with machine learning techniques.

The second principle is the original data should be accessible at all levels of the system. For example, in the query above, once we realize that extraction of John Boehner may not be consistent with the HTML table, we may want to inspect the documents from which Boehner was extracted to see if they're earlier than those of Ryan. However, if all we have access to is the final result of the extraction algorithm, even if it is a ranked list of names with probabilities, we cannot reason any deeper. In practice, we may have to approximate this principle, and keep around, as much as possible, the context of the original data.

6. CONCLUSION

As computing continues to deepen its impact on every aspect of our lives, new application scenarios create novel data integration challenges. The basic operations that data integration research has addressed since its inception have withstood the test of time and continue to appear in different variants in the new contexts. We believe that it is time for data integration operators to break free of end-to-end data integration systems and be available in the open source to speed up adoption and progress. With the rise of speech and natural language interfaces to our mobile devices, it also becomes critical that we find effective solutions to combining structured and unstructured data. The exciting golden age of data integration is still in front of us.

7. REFERENCES

[1] B. Alexe, W. C. Tan, and Y. Velegrakis. Stbenchmark: towards a benchmark for mapping systems. *PVLDB*, 1(1):230–244, 2008.

[2] M. Arenas, P. Barceló, L. Libkin, and F. Murlak. *Foundations of Data Exchange*. Cambridge University Press, 2014.

[3] P. C. Arocena, B. Glavic, R. Ciucanu, and R. J. Miller. The ibench integration metadata generator. *PVLDB*, 9(3):108–119, 2015.

[4] S. Balakrishnan, A. Y. Halevy, B. Harb, H. Lee, J. Madhavan, A. Rostamizadeh, W. Shen, K. Wilder, F. Wu, and C. Yu. Applying webtables in practice. In *CIDR*, 2015.

[5] C. Beeri and M. Vardi. A proof procedure for data dependencies. *Journal of the ACM*, 31(4):718–741, 1984.

[6] P. A. Bernstein. Applying model management to classical meta-data problems. In *CIDR*, 2003.

[7] P. A. Bernstein and L. M. Haas. Information integration in the enterprise. *Commun. ACM*, 51(9):72–79, 2008.

[8] Biggorilla: Data integration and data preparation in python. http://www.biggorilla.org, 2017.

[9] P. Buneman, J. Cheney, W. C. Tan, and S. Vansummeren. Curated databases. In *Proc. of PODS*, pages 1–12, 2008.

[10] T. Catarci and M. Lenzerini. Representing and using interschema knowledge in cooperative information systems. *Journal of Intelligent and Cooperative Information Systems*, pages 55–62, 1993.

[11] K. Chakrabarti, S. Chaudhuri, Z. Chen, K. Ganjam, and Y. He. Data services leveraging bing's data assets. *IEEE Data Eng. Bull.*, 39(3):15–28, 2016.

[12] S. Chaudhuri, R. Krishnamurthy, S. Potamianos, and K. Shim. Optimizing queries with materialized views. In *Proc. of ICDE*, pages 190–200, Taipei, Taiwan, 1995.

[13] D. Deng, R. C. Fernandez, Z. Abedjan, S. Wang, M. Stonebraker, A. K. Elmagarmid, I. F. Ilyas, S. Madden, M. Ouzzani, and N. Tang. The data civilizer system. In *CIDR*, 2017.

[14] A. Doan, A. Y. Halevy, and Z. G. Ives. *Principles of Data Integration*. Morgan Kaufmann, 2012.

[15] X. Dong, L. Berti-Equille, Y. Hu, and D. Srivastava. SOLOMON: seeking the truth via copying detection. *PVLDB*, 3(2):1617–1620, 2010.

[16] X. L. Dong and D. Srivastava. *Big Data Integration*. Synthesis Lectures on Data Management. Morgan & Claypool Publishers, 2015.

[17] R. Fagin, P. G. Kolaitis, R. J. Miller, and L. Popa. Data exchange: semantics and query answering. *Theor. Comput. Sci.*, 336(1):89–124, 2005.

[18] W. Fan and F. Geerts. *Foundations of Data Quality Management*. Synthesis Lectures on Data Management. Morgan & Claypool Publishers, 2012.

[19] G. H. L. Fletcher, J. V. den Bussche, D. V. Gucht, and S. Vansummeren. Towards a theory of search queries. *ACM Trans. Database Syst.*, 35(4):28:1–28:33, 2010.

[20] M. Franklin, A. Halevy, and D. Maier. From databases to dataspaces: A new abstraction for information management. *Sigmod Record*, 34(4):27–33, 2005.

[21] J. Goldstein and P.-A. Larson. Optimizing queries using materialized

views: a practical, scalable solution. In *Proc. of ACM SIGMOD*, pages 331–342, 2001.

[22] P. J. Guo, S. Kandel, J. M. Hellerstein, and J. Heer. Proactive wrangling: mixed-initiative end-user programming of data transformation scripts. In *UIST*, pages 65–74, 2011.

[23] R. Gupta, A. Y. Halevy, X. Wang, S. E. Whang, and F. Wu. Biperpedia: An ontology for search applications. *PVLDB*, 7(7):505–516, 2014.

[24] A. Y. Halevy, F. Korn, N. F. Noy, C. Olston, N. Polyzotis, S. Roy, and S. E. Whang. Managing google's data lake: an overview of the goods system. *IEEE Data Eng. Bull.*, 39(3):5–14, 2016.

[25] A. Y. Halevy, A. Rajaraman, and J. J. Ordille. Data integration: The teenage years. In *VLDB*, 2006.

[26] M. Hernández, G. Koutrika, R. Krishnamurthy, L. Popa, and R. Wisnesky. Hil: A high-level scripting language for entity integration. In *Proc. of EDBT*, pages 549–560, 2013.

[27] I. F. Ilyas and X. Chu. Trends in cleaning relational data: Consistency and deduplication. *Foundations and Trends in Databases*, 5(4):281–393, 2015.

[28] Z. G. Ives, T. J. Green, G. Karvounarakis, N. E. Taylor, V. Tannen, P. P. Talukdar, M. Jacob, and F. C. N. Pereira. The ORCHESTRA collaborative data sharing system. *SIGMOD Record*, 37(3):26–32, 2008.

[29] S. Kandel, A. Paepcke, J. M. Hellerstein, and J. Heer. Wrangler: interactive visual specification of data transformation scripts. In *CHI*, pages 3363–3372, 2011.

[30] P. Kolaitis. Schema mappings, data exchange, and metadata management. In *Proc. of ACM PODS*, pages 61–75, 2005.

[31] P. Konda, S. Das, P. S. G. C., A. Doan, A. Ardalan, J. R. Ballard, H. Li, F. Panahi, H. Zhang, J. F. Naughton, S. Prasad, G. Krishnan, R. Deep, and V. Raghavendra. Magellan: Toward building entity matching management systems. *PVLDB*, 9(12):1197–1208, 2016.

[32] P. A. Larson and H. Yang. Computing queries from derived relations. In *Proc. of VLDB*, pages 259–269, 1985.

[33] M. Lenzerini. Data Integration: A Theoretical Perspective. In *Proc. of ACM PODS*, 2002.

[34] S. Lohr. For Big-Data Scientists, 'Janitor Work' is Key Hurdle to Insights. New York Times, 2014.

[35] J. Madhavan, D. Ko, L. Kot, V. Ganapathy, A. Rasmussen, and A. Halevy. Google's deep-web crawl. In *Proc. of VLDB*, pages 1241–1252, 2008.

[36] C. D. Sa, A. Ratner, C. Ré, J. Shin, F. Wang, S. Wu, and C. Zhang. Deepdive: Declarative knowledge base construction. *SIGMOD Record*, 45(1):60–67, 2016.

[37] L. Seligman, P. Mork, A. Y. Halevy, K. P. Smith, M. J. Carey, K. Chen, C. Wolf, J. Madhavan, A. Kannan, and D. Burdick. Openii: an open source information integration toolkit. In *Proc. of ACM SIGMOD*, pages 1057–1060, 2010.

[38] A. Singhal. Introducing the knowledge graph: things, not strings. *Official google blog*, 2012.

[39] M. Stonebraker, D. Bruckner, I. F. Ilyas, G. Beskales, M. Cherniack, S. B. Zdonik, A. Pagan, and S. Xu. Data curation at scale: The data tamer system. In *CIDR*, 2013.

[40] O. G. Tsatalos, M. H. Solomon, and Y. E. Ioannidis. The GMAP: A versatile tool for physical data independence. *VLDB Journal*, 5(2):101–118, 1996.

[41] H. Z. Yang and P. A. Larson. Query transformation for PSJ-queries. In *Proc. of VLDB*, pages 245–254, 1987.

How Fast can a Distributed Transaction Commit?

Rachid Guerraoui
École Polytechnique Fédérale de Lausanne
Station 14, CH-1015
Lausanne, Switzerland
rachid.guerraoui@epfl.ch

Jingjing Wang
École Polytechnique Fédérale de Lausanne
Station 14, CH-1015
Lausanne, Switzerland
jingjing.wang@epfl.ch

ABSTRACT

The atomic commit problem lies at the heart of distributed database systems. The problem consists for a set of processes (database nodes) to agree on whether to commit or abort a transaction (*agreement* property). The commit decision can only be taken if all processes are initially willing to commit the transaction, and this decision must be taken if all processes are willing to commit *and* there is no failure (*validity* property). An atomic commit protocol is said to be *non-blocking* if every correct process (a database node that does not fail) eventually reaches a decision (commit or abort) even if there are failures elsewhere in the distributed database system (*termination* property).

Surprisingly, despite the importance of the atomic commit problem, little is known about its complexity. In this paper, we present, for the first time, a systematic study on the time and message complexity of the problem. We measure complexity in the executions that are considered the most frequent in practice, i.e., failure-free, with all processes willing to commit. In other words, we measure *how fast a transaction can commit.* Through our systematic study, we close many open questions like the complexity of synchronous non-blocking atomic commit. We also present optimal protocols which may be of independent interest. In particular, we present an effective protocol which solves what we call *indulgent atomic commit* that tolerates practical distributed database systems which are synchronous "most of the time".

Keywords

Atomic commit; time and message complexity; indulgent atomic commit

1. INTRODUCTION

The use of transactions to ensure the consistency of distributed databases systems despite concurrency and failures dates back to the 70's [1, 2, 3], and is still prominent today. Many modern distributed information systems are transactional, including HP's Sinfonia [4], Yahoo's PNUTS [5], Google's Percolator [6] and Spanner [7], Clock-SI [8] and Yesquel [9].

PODS'17, May 14-19, 2017, Chicago, Illinois, USA

DOI: http://dx.doi.org/10.1145/3034786.3034799

At the heart of those distributed transaction processing systems lies the fundamental *atomic commit* problem [2]. To illustrate the nature of the problem, consider a distributed database system that ensures the serializability of transactions by tracking their concurrency conflicts across datacenters (nodes) as in Helios [10]. In short, each datacenter $\mathcal{D}$ votes to abort every transaction tx that causes a conflict at $\mathcal{D}$. Transaction tx is committed if no datacenter detects any conflict involving tx. To orchestrate the termination of tx, coordination is necessary among datacenters: all have to agree on whether to commit or abort tx, despite failures, and tx cannot be committed if at least one datacenter votes to abort. This coordination is called a distributed commit protocol and its complexity impacts the performance of the entire distributed database system [10].

1.1 Problem statement

More specifically, the atomic commit problem consists for a set of nodes of the distributed database system (we simply call them *processes*) to decide whether to *abort* or *commit* a transaction. The decision is based on the *vote* of each process about the local faith of the transaction. A process votes "no" if the transaction did not execute correctly at that process (due to a full disk, a concurrency control problem, etc.). A process votes "yes" (willingness to commit) if the transaction did execute correctly at that process. The processes (a) commit the transaction *only* if all vote to commit, and (b) *have to* commit the transaction if all vote to commit and there is no failure. This property is usually called *validity* [11, 12, 13, 14, 15]. All processes need to agree on the same decision. This property is called *agreement* [11, 12, 13, 14, 15]. If one additionally stipulates that correct processes (those that do not crash) need to eventually decide (commit or abort) despite failures (e.g., crashes of other processes), then this property is called *termination* [14, 15], and the resulting problem, where processes need to ensure validity, agreement as well as termination, is called *non-blocking atomic commit* (NBAC) [16]. NBAC has been investigated since the 70's by the database and distributed system communities [16, 17, 18, 11, 19, 12, 20, 21].

In this paper, we present a systematic study of the time and message complexity of the atomic commit problem and study the exact tradeoff between robustness and *best-case* complexity (in the sense of Lamport [22]), i.e., the complexity of any failure-free execution where all processes vote to commit. Such executions, called *nice* executions in this paper, are arguably the most frequent in practice and are those for which protocols are usually optimized.

Not surprisingly, this complexity depends on *robustness*, i.e., on which property (validity, agreement, termination) is required in which executions (including less likely executions with failures). The most robust form of atomic commit protocol is, roughly speaking, the one that tolerates both *crash failures* (i.e., some process crashes) and *network failures* (e.g., a network partition occurs and later recovers), i.e., all executions with such failures have to solve NBAC. However, by the impossibility result of consensus [23, 24], this most robust form has infinite complexity. On the contrary, the least robust form of atomic commit, of which only *failure-free* executions are required to solve NBAC, is clearly easy to solve in finite complexity. Although there is obviously a tradeoff between robustness and complexity, the exact tradeoff was not clear. Furthermore, between the least and most robust forms of atomic commit, the situation is more complicated and the complexity results harder to obtain.

We exhaustively study complexity in the cases between two extremes, assuming certain robustness of an atomic commit protocol. More precisely, we determine the optimal number of message delays/messages in nice executions of a protocol π assuming that, in π, (1) every *crash-failure* execution satisfies X and (2) every *network-failure* execution satisfies Y, where X and Y are subsets of these three properties: agreement, validity, and termination. With two kinds of failure-prone executions (crash-failure and network-failure) and three properties, we end up with $(2^3)^2 = 64$ possibilities, as shown in Table 1. Since a property satisfied in every network-failure execution is also satisfied in every crash-failure execution, the 64 possibilities reduce to 27 different cases, the non-empty cells in Table 1.

1.2 Previous results

Many distributed database systems (Sinfonia [4], Percolator [6], Spanner [7], Clock-SI [8] and Yesquel [9], for instance) guarantee validity and agreement in crash-failure executions through a two-phase commit (2PC) protocol [2]. 2PC induces two communication rounds among processes. Although efficient, 2PC does not solve NBAC in crash-failure executions since it does not guarantee termination. However, NBAC can actually be solved in crash-failure executions (by a three-phase commit protocol [16], which has only finite complexity).

Except for some results on the number of messages necessary for synchronous NBAC protocols (which solve NBAC in every crash-failure execution) [17, 25, 26], the fundamental question of the complexity of synchronous NBAC has actually been open for more than three decades [16, 17]. In fact, only the lower bound of $2n-2$ messages in the face of $n-1$ crashes [17] was known until the present paper. Although important, little was known on the complexity of atomic commit (e.g., when network failures are also considered) or its tradeoff with robustness, which we address in this paper.

1.3 Our results

Table 1 summarizes our results for the 27 atomic commit problems considered. Besides the tradeoff between complexity and robustness (which properties are required in which execution), we also highlight a tradeoff between time and message complexity. We prove that in 18 out of 27 problem variants, the optimal number of message delays and the optimal number of messages cannot be achieved at the same time.

Among the 27 variants, the most robust one, which we call *indulgent atomic commit*, is particularly appealing.[1] Indulgent atomic commit captures the best robustness of a distributed commit protocol, i.e., despite failures, agreement, validity and termination are still satisfied. We propose a protocol, which we denote by INBAC, that matches the lower bound of two message delays of indulgent atomic commit. Moreover, we prove that INBAC is optimal in the number of messages among all delay-optimal indulgent atomic commit protocols. Thus, in practical distributed database systems that are synchronous "most of the time" [34][2], and where practitioners consider violations of timeouts (e.g., due to network failures), if rare, to be acceptable, INBAC tolerates such violations and is also optimal in complexity for the arguably most frequent executions. Comparing our INBAC protocol with the popular 2PC protocol, we show, interestingly, that (1) INBAC has the same best-case message delay as 2PC if all processes start spontaneously, and (2) in the special case where at most one process can crash (among n processes), INBAC and 2PC use $2n$ and $2n-2$ messages respectively. In this sense, INBAC may be of independent interest, as a more robust yet efficient alternative to 2PC for implementing distributed transactions.

At the same time, we close the question of the complexity of synchronous NBAC (which is one among the 27 cases we consider). We show, for the first time, that for synchronous NBAC, one message delay is optimal. We also generalize Dwork and Skeen's lower bound of $2n-2$ messages [17] to $n-1+f$ messages in the face of f crashes and propose a matching message-optimal synchronous NBAC protocol.

1.4 Techniques

We denote a cell in Table 1 by a property pair (X, Y). (X, Y) is less robust than another pair (U, V) if $X \subseteq U$ and $Y \subseteq V$. Then our proof goes through two main steps. First, we group the pairs (X, Y) that give the same number of message delays/messages in Table 1 and prove the lower bound for the least robust pair in each group. To design matching protocols, by symmetry, we look for "the most robust pair" in each group. However, as shown in Table 1, in some groups, there is no "most robust pair". Thus, our second step is to choose, in each group, the pairs that are locally maximal in robustness and present a protocol that matches the lower bound for each local maximum.

Three techniques are key to our results.

1. To prove our lower bounds, we introduce and leverage the notion of "process reachability", the arrival of a message m at process Q that makes Q know process P's vote, which is necessary in the context of a network-failure execution. (Dwork and Skeen [17] used "process coloring" in proving lower bounds for synchronous NBAC. Compared with our notion, theirs does not distinguish the arrival from the departure of

[1]We define indulgent atomic commit in the same vein as indulgent consensus [27, 28] protocols like Paxos [29], CHT [15] and others [30, 31, 32, 33].

[2]It was experimentally shown, e.g., in [34], that the latency of a communication round is below some seconds (most of the time) if the link does not lose too many messages.

Table 1: Complexity of Atomic Commit. NF = network-failure executions; CF = crash-failure executions; A = agreement; V = validity; T = termination. Fraction d/m in a cell (X, Y) means that the tight lower bounds are d message delays, m messages respectively if (1) every failure-free execution solves NBAC, (2) every crash-failure execution satisfies a set X of properties and (3) every network-failure execution satisfies a set Y of properties. For every empty cell (X, Y), there exists a non-empty cell (Z, Y) such that $X \cup Y = Z$.

NF \ CF	$\emptyset$	A	V	T	AV	AT	VT	AVT
$\emptyset$	$1/0$	$1/0$	$1/n-1+f$	$1/0$	$1/n-1+f$	$1/0$	$1/n-1+f$	$1/n-1+f$
A		$1/0$			$1/n-1+f$	$1/0$		$2/2n-2+f$
V			$1/2n-2$		$1/2n-2$		$1/2n-2$	$1/2n-2$
T				$1/0$		$1/0$	$1/n-1+f$	$1/n-1+f$
AV					$1/2n-2$			$2/2n-2+f$
AT						$1/0$		$2/2n-2+f$
VT							$1/2n-2$	$1/2n-2$
AVT								$2/2n-2+f$

a message, since they solely focus on crash-failure executions, featuring bounded message delays.)

2. To design our optimal protocols, we introduce and leverage "implicit" votes for the willingness to commit. For example, to achieve 0-message protocols, instead of receiving a message telling process P process Q's vote, P may know that Q votes 1 by *not* receiving a certain message. We support an optimal nice execution by a complex failure-free execution that aborts.

3. Another technique we use is "helping". To reach the smallest number of messages or message delays in any nice execution, if some failure occurs, then processes must ask for help. To enable helping, backing up votes at other processes is necessary while sometimes a message of acknowledgement (that confirms the success of the backup) is also necessary. Both are key ideas behind INBAC.

The rest of the paper is organized as follows. Section 2 presents the distributed database models we consider and defines the non-blocking atomic commit problem. Section 3 establishes our lower bounds. Section 4 describes atomic commit protocols that meet the lower bounds. Section 5 presents indulgent atomic commit, an overview of our protocol INBAC and a proof of its optimality (with details in Appendix A and Appendix B respectively). Section 6 discusses related work. For space limitation, we put the details of other protocols, as well as some of our proofs, in our full version [35].

2. MODELS AND DEFINITIONS

2.1 Processes and channels

We consider a set Ω of n processes $P_1, P_2, \ldots, P_n$ (sometimes also denoted by O, P, Q, R). Here processes represent database nodes. Processes communicate by exchanging messages, through the network.

We assume that no process deviates from its specification and at most $f, 1 \leq f \leq n-1$ processes can *crash*. After a process crashes, it does not send any message. If a process does not crash, it is said to be *correct*.

Communication channels do not modify, inject, duplicate or lose messages. Every message sent is eventually received.

2.2 Failures and executions

We assume *synchronous computation*: there is a known upper bound on the time to execute a local step, which includes the delivery of a message by a process, its local processing by that process, as well as the sending of a message as a consequence of that processing.

Communication is said to be *synchronous* if there is a known upper bound on message transmission delays. Communication is said to be *eventually synchronous* if the delay on message transmission might be unbounded but only until some, possibly unknown, *global stabilization time* (after which there is a known upper bound on delays).[3] We accordingly consider two kinds of system models (or simply systems): a synchronous system [17] and an eventually synchronous system [36], based on their respective assumptions on communication.

An execution of a synchronous system is either *failure-free* or has *crash failures*: either all processes are correct, or some process crashes, while all message transmission delays are smaller than some known upper bound which we denote by U. If, in some execution, some message transmission delay is greater than U, then the system is no longer synchronous: we say that a *network failure* occurs. An execution of an eventually synchronous system can be failure-free, has crash failures, or network failures. We call a *failure-free* execution an execution where no failure occurs, a *crash-failure* execution one execution of a synchronous system (where only crash failures are possible) and a *network-failure* execution one execution of an eventually synchronous system (where network failures are also possible). We accordingly call a synchronous system and an eventually synchronous system, a crash-failure system and a network-failure system, respectively.

2.3 Non-blocking atomic commit

We consider the problem of non-blocking atomic commit (NBAC) in the classical sense of Skeen [16], which was later refined in [14, 15].

Definition 1 (NBAC [14, 15, 16]). A protocol π is an atomic commit protocol if π is defined by two events:

[3] Recall that, in an *asynchronous* system, without any communication bound, agreement problems like consensus and NBAC are impossible [24].

- *Propose*: $P_i, i = 1, 2, \ldots, n$ proposes value $v = 1$ (vote "yes") or $v = 0$ (vote "no").
- *Decide*: $P_i, i = 1, 2, \ldots, n$ outputs the decided value.

An execution of π solves NBAC if it satisfies the following three properties:[4]

- *Validity*: A process decides 0 only if some process proposes 0 or a failure occurs. A process decides 1 only if no process proposes 0.
- *Termination*: Every correct process eventually decides.
- *Agreement*: No two processes decide differently.

Given a system $\mathcal{S}$ (crash-failure or network-failure), π solves NBAC in $\mathcal{S}$ if every execution of π in $\mathcal{S}$ solves NBAC.

(Later in the paper, in Section 5, we will introduce our new variant of the problem: *indulgent atomic commit.*)

A comparison with previous definitions from the literature is now in order. A synchronous NBAC protocol [16, 17] is a protocol which solves NBAC in a crash-failure system (and thus the complexity is covered by our study). In previous impossibility results [14, 37, 38, 27, 28], the definition of validity depended on which failure may occur. *(Strong) validity* was considered in the only case of crash failures, whereas a weak form of validity, *weak validity*,[5] was distinguished if a failure could be a network failure. Definition 1 unifies validity and weak validity for presentation clarity and consistency with previous impossibility results.

2.4 Complexity measures

We define a *nice execution* of an atomic commit protocol as a failure-free execution in which every process proposes 1. We study in this paper *best-case complexity*, i.e., the complexity over nice executions (which are arguably the most frequent in practice). We consider two complexity measures: the number of messages and the number of message delays. Here (as in Lamport [22, 39]), for any message m, one message delay is a period of time between two events: the sending of m and the reception of m [22, 39]. Thus if local computation is instantaneous (negligible), and every message is received exactly one unit of time after it was sent, then the number of message delays of an execution is the number of units of time of that execution [22].

3. LOWER BOUNDS

In this section, we establish lower bounds on the number of message delays, and then lower bounds on the number of messages. For each lower bound, we prove by contradiction some necessary messages in every nice execution and then count the number. We show that assuming a nice execution E that does not contain some of such necessary messages, we can construct a crash-failure (or network-failure) execution indistinguishable from E that violates a certain property.

[4]An execution of an atomic commit protocol also satisfies a property called *integrity*, i.e., no process decides twice in any execution. This is immediate to satisfy in our context so we omit it for presentation simplicity.

[5]Weak validity allows processes to abort a transaction (decide 0) even if none of them crashes and all of them vote to commit (propose 1), as long as there is a network failure.

3.1 Message delays

As shown in Table 1, there are two possibilities for the lower bound on the number of message delays: 1 and 2. There are four non-empty cells in Table 1 of which the lower bound is 2: (AVT, A), (AVT, AV), (AVT, AT), and (AVT, AVT). Among them, (AVT, A) is the least robust. The rest of the non-empty cells have 1 as the lower bound, among which ($\emptyset$, $\emptyset$) is the least robust. Thus we need only to prove lower bounds for two cells: ($\emptyset$, $\emptyset$), (AVT, A) respectively, as summarized in Theorem 1.

Theorem 1 (Lower bound on message delays). *Let $\mathcal{P}_1$ and $\mathcal{P}_2$ be any two subsets of $\mathcal{P} = \{agreement, validity, termination\}$. Let π be any protocol that (a) solves NBAC in every failure-free execution, (b) satisfies $\mathcal{P}_1$ in every crash-failure execution and (c) satisfies $\mathcal{P}_2$ in every network-failure execution. Let d be the smallest number of message delays among all nice executions of π. If for π, $\mathcal{P}_1 = \mathcal{P}_2 = \emptyset$, then $d \geq 1$. If for π, $\mathcal{P}_1 = \mathcal{P}$ and $\mathcal{P}_2 = \{agreement\}$, then $d \geq 2$.*

The proof of the first part of Theorem 1 is immediate: to satisfy validity in every failure-free execution, no process can decide immediately; i.e., the process has to wait for at least one message delay to know other processes' votes.

The proof of the second part is less obvious, and goes through an intermediary lemma. This lemma makes use of the notion of "process reachability", which we introduce here and use in all our lower bound proofs.

Definition 2 (Reaching a process). If a protocol instructs a process src to send a message m to another process $dest$, then we say that src is the *source* of m and $dest$, the *destination* of m. Let E be any execution. In E, if src sends m at time t, then we may interchangeably say that m *leaves* from src (for $dest$) at t; if at time t, $dest$ receives m, then we may interchangeably say that m *arrives* at $dest$ at t.

Let $\underline{m} = \{m_1, m_2, \ldots, m_l\}$ be a sequence of messages such that (a) the source of m_1 is P, (b) the destination of m_l is $Q, Q \neq P$, (c) the source src_i of m_i is the destination of m_{i-1} for $i = 2, 3, \ldots, l$, and (d) m_i leaves from src_i later than or at the time at which m_{i-1} arrives at src_i for $i = 2, 3, \ldots, l$. If $\underline{m}$ exists for two processes P, Q and $l \geq 1$ in E, then we say that P *reaches* Q in E.

If m_l arrives at Q at time t or earlier and $\underline{m}$ is the earliest sequence of messages for P (according to t) to reach Q in E, then we say that P *has reached* Q at time t in E.

By Definition 2, if a process P reaches another process Q, it is possible that, by a sequence of messages, P *backs up* P's vote at Q. The intuition of the lower bound in question, captured by Lemma 1 below, is then that (the arrival of) the messages by which P backups P's vote precede (the departure of) the message by which P decides.

Lemma 1 (Backups). *Let π be any protocol that solves NBAC in every crash-failure execution and ensures agreement in every network-failure execution. Let E be any nice execution of π. Let P decide at time t_1 in E. Among the messages whose destination is P, let $\mathcal{M}$ be the set of messages that arrive at P before or at t_1. For each $m \in \mathcal{M}$, let t_m be the time at which m leaves from its source and let $t_2 = \max_{m \in \mathcal{M}} t_m$.*

Then at t_2, P has reached at least f processes.

Proof. By contradiction. Suppose that at t_2, P has reached at most $f - 1$ processes. To show a contradiction, we first construct a crash-failure execution E_0 where these $f-1$ processes as well as P (denoted by Φ) crash and every correct process R decides 0. We then construct a network-failure execution E_{async} that is indistinguishable from E to P, and also indistinguishable from E_0 to R; then P and R decide differently in E_{async}, which breaks *agreement*, contradictory to the definition of π.

We first construct E_0. For any process $Q \in \Phi \backslash \{P\}$, denote by τ_Q the time at which P reaches Q. In E_0, P crashes at time 0 (before sending any message). For Q, E_0 is the same as E until Q crashes at τ_Q (before possibly notifying P's crash). In addition, every message sent after t_2 arrives later than t_1. Let P propose 0, let every process other than P propose 1 and let no process in $\Omega \backslash \Phi$ crash. Then as $|\Phi| \leq f$ and $t_1 - t_2 \leq U$, E_0 is a legitimate crash-failure execution. Let R be the earliest correct process that decides. Denote by t_3 the time at which R decides. Since π solves NBAC in every crash-failure execution, R decides 0 in E_0.

We then build E_{async} based on E and E_0. In E_{async}, every process proposes 1 and no process crashes. We construct E_{async} such that E_{async} starts as E and:

a. Every message from P to a process in $\Omega \backslash \Phi$ arrives later than $\max(t_1, t_3)$;

b. Every message from Q to a process in $\Omega \backslash \Phi$ sent after or at time τ_Q arrives later than $\max(t_1, t_3)$;

c. Every message sent after t_2 arrives later than t_1.

Delays in (a) and (b) ensure that E_{async} is the same as E_0 for R before R decides: any process in Φ seems to have crashed. Delays in (c) ensure that E_{async} and E are indistinguishable for P before P decides: those messages and only those messages in $\mathcal{M}$ arrive for P's decision. □

Lemma 1 additionally shows that for P's vote, at least f backups are necessary. Using Lemma 1, we now prove the necessary number of message delays in Theorem 1.

Proof. (Proof of the second part of Theorem 1.) Let t_2 be defined as in Lemma 1 for the earliest process P that decides in any nice execution. Then for $f \geq 1$, by Lemma 1, at t_2, at least one message from P must have arrived while another message just leaves from its source for P. This, in total, gives at least two message delays before any process decides. □

3.2 Messages

As shown in Table 1, there are four possibilities for the lower bound on the number of messages: 0, $n-1+f$, $2n-2$ and $2n-2+f$. We group the cells in Table 1 with the same value, and then prove the lower bound for the least robust atomic commit in each group. Thus we need only to prove lower bounds for four cells in Table 1: (∅, ∅), (V, ∅), (V, V), and (AVT, A) respectively, as summarized in Theorem 2. While proving our lower bounds, we highlight the intuition behind the increasing lower bounds (from 0 to $2n-2+f$), and a tradeoff between time and message complexity (for the 14 variants of the atomic commit problem that have $n-1+f$ messages or $2n-2$ messages as lower bounds).

Theorem 2 (Lower bounds on messages). *Let $\mathcal{P}_1$ and $\mathcal{P}_2$ be any two subsets of $\mathcal{P} = \{$agreement, validity, termination$\}$. Let π be any protocol that (a) solves NBAC in every failure-free execution, (b) satisfies $\mathcal{P}_1$ in every crash-failure execution and (c) satisfies $\mathcal{P}_2$ in every network-failure execution. Let m be the smallest number of messages among all nice executions of π. If for π, $\mathcal{P}_1 = \mathcal{P}_2 = \emptyset$, then $m \geq 0$. If for π, $\mathcal{P}_1 = \{$validity$\}$ and $\mathcal{P}_2 = \emptyset$, then $m \geq n-1+f$. If for π, $\mathcal{P}_1 = \mathcal{P}_2 = \{$validity$\}$, then $m \geq 2n-2$. If for π, $\mathcal{P}_1 = \mathcal{P}$ and $\mathcal{P}_2 = \{$agreement$\}$, then $m \geq 2n-2+f$.*

The proof of 0 message for the cell (∅, ∅) is trivial and omitted. In what follows, we count the number of necessary messages in the other three cases separately.

Lower bound of $n-1+f$ messages. We generalize here the lower bound of $2n-2$ messages for synchronous NBAC from Dwork and Skeen [17]. As in their proof, we first present a preliminary lemma, Lemma 2, which we phrase here in terms of "process reachability". As Lemma 2 is a (straightforward) generalization of the preliminary lemma in Dwork and Skeen's proof, the proof of Lemma 2 is omitted.[6]

Lemma 2 (Validity despite crashes). *Let π be any protocol that (a) solves NBAC in every failure-free execution and (b) ensures validity in every crash-failure execution. Then in any nice execution of π, every process reaches at least f processes.*

Lemma 2 captures the intuition that at least f backups are necessary in the face of at most f crashes. This leads to $n-1+f$ messages as the lower bound for cell (V, ∅): by Lemma 2, every process has to reach at least f processes in every nice execution, and thus at least $n-1+f$ messages have to be exchanged.

Lower bound of $2n-2$ messages. Before counting the number of necessary messages for cell (V, V), we introduce a preliminary lemma.

Lemma 3 (Validity in every execution). *Let π be any protocol that that (a) solves NBAC in every failure-free execution and (b) ensures validity in every network-failure execution. Then in every nice execution of π, for any process Q, every other process P reaches Q before or when Q decides.*

Proof. By contradiction. Consider a nice execution E with two processes P and Q such that P has not reached Q when Q decides 1. In E, let Q decide at time t; let Φ be the set of processes which P has reached before or at t; for every $R \in \Phi$, let τ_R be the time at which P reaches R. To show a contradiction, we construct a network-failure execution E_{async} such that P crashes before sending any message and P votes 0, but for Q, E_{async} is indistinguishable from E (where Q decides 1). In E_{async}, every process (except P) votes 1; for them, E_{async} starts as E. In addition, for every $R \in \Phi$, every message from R sent at or after τ_R arrives later than t. Since in E, Q does not expect any message from R sent at or after τ_R and Q does not expect any message from P either, then Q does not distinguish E and E_{async} and thus decides 1 at t again in E_{async}, which violates validity. □

[6] We note, however, that the original preliminary lemma in [17] does not distinguish between the necessity of sending a message (before a certain point in time) and the necessity of receiving a message (before a certain point in time). It is thus only appropriate for a crash-failure execution (as after a message m is sent, it is predictable that m is received within some time period) and does not apply, as is, to the setting of a network-failure execution as we study in the rest of the paper. Hence the need to rephrase the preliminary lemma.

By Lemma 3, now every process P must know every vote *explicitly*, while in Lemma 2, some process Q's vote of 1 may be *implicit* (i.e., in a nice execution, P knows Q's vote of 1 by not receiving a certain message), which adds extra messages. This requirement of the explicit votes is due to the fact that here every execution satisfies validity. Thus for cell (V, V), we count the number of necessary messages as follows. Let R be the latest process that decides in a nice execution. By Lemma 3, before or when R decides, for any process Q, every other process $P \neq Q$ has reached Q. As a result, before or when R decides, at least $2n - 2$ messages are exchanged.

We note that for atomic commit problems with $n - 1 + f$ messages and $2n - 2$ messages as lower bounds, the lower bound on the number of message delays is 1. It is easy to show that the lower bound on the number of messages and that on the number of message delays cannot achieved at the same time: all those problems feature *validity* at least in every crash-failure execution and thus a 1-delay protocol must use at least $n(n - 1)$ messages. This shows that for those problems (14 cases among totally 27 ones which we consider), there is a tradeoff between the number of messages and that of message delays. (Later in Section 5, we show tradeoffs between time and message complexity for other 4 cases related to indulgent atomic commit.)

Lower bound of $2n-2+f$ messages. Before counting the number of necessary messages for cell (AVT, A), we again introduce a preliminary lemma.

Lemma 4 (Agreement in every execution). *Assume $f \geq 2$. Let π be any protocol that solves NBAC in every crash-failure execution and ensures agreement in every network-failure execution. Let E be any nice execution. Let P decide at time t_1 in E. Among the messages whose destination is P, let $\mathcal{M}$ be the set of messages that arrive at P before or at t_1. For each $m \in \mathcal{M}$, let t_m be the time at which m leaves from its source and $t_{2,P} = \max_{m \in \mathcal{M}} t_m$.*

Then at $t_{2,P}$ in E, every process has reached at least $f - 1$ processes.

Let Π denote the class of protocols considered in Lemma 4 above. This is the same class of protocols considered in Lemma 1. The proof of Lemma 4 is actually similar to that of Lemma 1, and thus omitted for space limitation. By the robust relation, Π is uncomparable with the class of protocols considered in Lemma 3 (with $2n - 2$ messages as the lower bound) but is more robust than the class of protocols considered in Lemma 2 (with $n - 1 + f$ messages as the lower bound). Thus we only show the increase from $n - 1 + f$ messages to the lower bound of Π. We actually compare Lemma 1 (which considers also Π) with Lemma 2. While both lemmas show that P backups at (at least) f processes, the former demonstrates that after P backups, some message just leaves for P, which accounts for (part of) the increase of the necessary messages.

We use Lemma 4 to count the exact number of necessary messages for cell (AVT, A). Let $t_{2,P}$ be defined as in the statement of Lemma 4 for any process P in any execution. Let $t_2 = \min_{P \in \Omega} t_{2,P}$. Then at and after t_2, at least n messages have to leave their sources respectively. Since at t_2, every process has reached at least $f - 1$ processes, then before or at t_2, at least $n - 2 + f$ messages have arrived at their destinations respectively. Therefore, at least $2n-2+f$ messages are exchanged in every nice execution.

Table 2: Delay-optimal Protocols. 1NBAC is a synchronous NBAC protocol. Each protocol achieves its lower bound in every nice execution.

Cell	AV, AV	AT, AT	AVT, VT	AVT, AVT
Prot.	avNBAC	0NBAC	1NBAC	INBAC

4. MATCHING PROTOCOLS

In this section, we prove the tightness of the lower bounds by presenting matching commit protocols. For each protocol, we describe first its nice executions and then sketch the executions that deviate from nice executions due to some vote of 0 or failure. We present matching protocols for the number of message delays and the number of messages separately.

4.1 Delay-optimal protocols

Recall that in Table 1, there are two possibilities for the lower bound on the number of message delays: 1 and 2. Recall also that there are four cells in Table 1 of which the lower bound is 2: (AVT, A), (AVT, AV), (AVT, AT), and (AVT, AVT), among which the last one is the most robust. The rest of the non-empty cells correspond to a lower bound of 1 delay, among which (AV, AV), (AT, AT) and (AVT, VT) are three local maximum by the relation of robustness. Thus we need only to present delay-optimal protocols for four cells, as summarized in Table 2 as well as in Theorem 3.

Theorem 3 (Delay-optimal protocols). *Let $\mathcal{P}_1$ and $\mathcal{P}_2$ be any two subsets of $\mathcal{P}$ = {agreement,validity,termination}. Let π be any protocol that (a) solves NBAC in every failure-free execution, (b) satisfies $\mathcal{P}_1$ in every crash-failure execution and (c) satisfies $\mathcal{P}_2$ in every network-failure execution. Let d be the smallest number of message delays among all nice executions of π. If $d = 1$, then it is possible that $\mathcal{P}_1 = \mathcal{P}_2$ = {agreement, validity}, or $\mathcal{P}_1 = \mathcal{P}_2$ = {agreement, termination}, or $\mathcal{P}_1 = \mathcal{P}$ and $\mathcal{P}_2$ = {validity, termination}. If $d = 2$, then it is possible that $\mathcal{P}_1 = \mathcal{P}_2 = \mathcal{P}$.*

Among the protocols of Table 2, INBAC solves what we call *indulgent atomic commit*, which we will discuss in Section 5. 0NBAC is an optimal protocol also for the number of messages, which we will discuss with other message-optimal protocols. For space limitation, we only sketch the other two protocols here.

1NBAC. During a failure-free execution of 1NBAC, a process (a) sends its vote to every process, (b) collects all n votes, (c) sends the logical AND of all n votes to every process, and then (d) decides. Thus in every failure-free execution (as well as in every nice execution), every process decides the logical AND of all n votes within one message delay.

In other executions, every process starts by sending its vote to every (other) process, but then since failures may occur, a process P may collect fewer than n votes at the end of the first message delay. If so, P waits for the logical AND of all n votes sent by another process for one message delay. (This is the key to agreement in any crash-failure execution, since in a crash-failure execution, if some process Q decides

Table 3: Message-optimal Protocols. Name avNBAC is abused as the meaning is clear in the context. Protocol (n-1+f)NBAC is a synchronous NBAC protocol. Each protocol achieves its lower bound in every nice execution.

Cell	AT, AT	AV, A	AVT, T
Prot.	0NBAC	aNBAC	(n-1+f)NBAC
Cell	AV, AV	AVT, VT	AVT, AVT
Prot.	avNBAC	(2n-2)NBAC	(2n-2+f)NBAC

at step (d), then Q's messages sent at step (c) must arrive at their receivers in one message delay.) Denoted by [D, d] a message that contains the logical AND, d, of all n votes. If P receives any [D, d] before or at the end of the second message delay, then P proposes d to consensus uc; otherwise, P proposes 0 to uc. Then P decides the same as uc. Here and later in this paper, we consider the consensus as defined in Definition 5 (which is deferred to Section 5).[7] By the *termination* property of consensus in a network-failure execution, uc eventually decides. The full description of 1NBAC and its full proof of correctness are in our full version [35].

avNBAC. As 1NBAC, avNBAC starts by having every process send its vote to every other process. Unlike 1NBAC, avNBAC does not require termination if a failure occurs; thus every process decides if and only if it collects all the votes at the end of the first message delay. The full description of avNBAC, which is similar to that of 1NBAC, is omitted.

4.2 Message-optimal protocols

As shown in Table 1, there are four lower bounds on the number of message delays: 0, $n-1+f$, $2n-2$, and $2n-2+f$. Similarly, we group the cells of which the lower bound takes the same value in Table 1, and find the most robust one or the local maximum in each group. Thus we need only to present message-optimal protocols for six cells, as summarized in Table 3 as well as in Theorem 4.

Theorem 4 (Message-optimal protocols). *Let $\mathcal{P}_1$ and $\mathcal{P}_2$ be any two subsets of $\mathcal{P} = \{$agreement, validity, termination$\}$. Let π be any protocol that (a) solves NBAC in every failure-free execution, (b) satisfies $\mathcal{P}_1$ in every crash-failure execution and (c) satisfies $\mathcal{P}_2$ in every network-failure execution. Let m be the smallest number of messages among all nice executions of π. If $m = 0$, then it is possible that $\mathcal{P}_1 = \mathcal{P}_2 = \{$agreement, termination$\}$. If $m = n-1+f$, then it is possible that $\mathcal{P}_1 = \{$agreement, validity$\}$ and $\mathcal{P}_2 = \{$agreement$\}$, or $\mathcal{P}_1 = \mathcal{P}$ and $\mathcal{P}_2 = \{$termination$\}$. If $m = 2n-2$, then it is possible that $\mathcal{P}_1 = \mathcal{P}_2 = \{$agreement, validity$\}$, or $\mathcal{P}_1 = \mathcal{P}$ and $\mathcal{P}_2 = \{$validity, termination$\}$. If $m = 2n-2+f$, then it is possible that $\mathcal{P}_1 = \mathcal{P}_2 = \mathcal{P}$.*

For space limitation, we sketch only 0NBAC, (n-1+f)-NBAC, and (2n-2)NBAC, since avNBAC is similar to (2n-2)NBAC while aNBAC and (2n-2+f)NBAC are close to (n-1+f)NBAC. As shown in the sketches below of the three protocols, 0NBAC, (n-1+f)NBAC, and (2n-2)NBAC, the primary technique to achieve an optimal number of messages is to support nice executions by complex executions that abort; namely, processes take complex steps before a decision of 0: they try to inform every other of this decision. The full descriptions of the protocols and their full proofs of correctness are in our full version [35].

0NBAC. During every nice execution, no process sends a message, and after one message delay, a process (who votes 1) decides 1 if it has received no message. In other executions, a process who votes 1 still sends no message at the beginning, while a process who votes 0 sends [V, 0] to every (other) process. Then after one message delay, n processes are divided into three categories: (1) those who vote 0, (2) those who vote 1 and receive [V, 0], and (3) those who vote 1 but do not receive any message. The last category decides 1 again immediately, while the other two later propose a value to consensus uc (and decide the same as uc). The second category now sends [B, 0] to every other process. Any receiver of [*, 0] who has not decided yet acknowledges to the sender. If a process in category (1) or (2) receives $n-1$ acknowledgements, then it proposes 0 to uc, and otherwise, 1. Clearly, both categories (1) and (2) may potentially decide 0 and thus they try to inform the others of this decision. The key to agreement here is to agree with the last category which may have already decided 1 (at the end of the first message delay). However, since by the protocol, the third category does not acknowledge to [*, 0], if the third category is non-empty, then all other processes must propose 1 to uc and decide 1, satisfying agreement.

For best-case complexity, it is easy to see that in every nice execution, no message is ever sent, and furthermore, every process decides after one message delay. 0NBAC achieves the lower bound on the number of messages and that on the number of message delays at the same time. As a result, for the 9 cases (among 27 cases) covered by this protocol (using the robustness relation), no tradeoff is necessary.

(n-1+f)NBAC. During every nice execution of this protocol, the communication steps among processes are totally ordered. The totally-ordered sequence is: $P_1, P_2, \ldots, P_n$ and subsequently $P_1, P_2, \ldots, P_f$. Then (a) P_1 starts by sending P_1's vote to P_2; (b) each process in the sequence, upon receiving its predecessor's message, sends the collection of the votes so far to its successor except P_f which is at the end of the sequence; (c) (after $n-1+f$ steps above) every process waits (i.e., does no-ops) for $f+1$ message delays; and (d) during step (c), a process does not receive any message and thus decides 1.

In other executions, for any process P, if P votes 0, then P sends no message to the successor (when P first occurs in the sequence). If P does not receive its predecessor's message, then P sends no message to its successor as well except that P is in the suffix $P_n, P_1, P_2, \ldots, P_f$. In the suffix, if P does not receive its predecessor's message or receives 0 from its predecessor, then P sends 0 to every other process. Subsequently, if any process receives a message of 0, then the process sends 0 as well to every other process. Every process decides at the same time as in a nice execution (i.e., step (d) in a nice execution). At the end, if a process has ever received a message of 0, then it decides 0 (and 1 otherwise).

The number of messages in any nice execution is thus $n-1+f$, matching the lower bound. To match the lower bound, in any nice execution, some process P decides 1 without being reached by every process: some votes of 1 are only

[7] Consensus in this sense is sometimes called *uniform consensus* in the literature [40].

implicit to P. In (n-1+f)NBAC, the decision at step (d) ensures that those who accept implicit votes (as votes of 1) can be notified of a decision of 0 in the face of at most f crashes in any crash-failure execution.

(2n-2)NBAC. During every nice execution, (a) every process sends its vote to P_n spontaneously, (b) then P_n sends the logical AND of all n votes to every process, and (c) every process waits for $f+1$ message delays, and then decides 1. When a failure occurs or some process votes 0, at step (b), P_n sends 0 to every process. Then at step (c), a process can receive no message from P_n or a message of 0 from P_n. If so, the process sends 0 to every process. Later, any process who receives a message of 0 also sends 0 to every process. Every process decides at the same time as in a nice execution (i.e., the end of step (c) in a nice execution). At the end, if a process has ever received a message of 0, it decides 0 (and 1 otherwise).

The number of messages in any nice execution is thus $2n-2$. Similar to (n-1+f)NBAC, here any process who decides 0 tries to inform every other process before the decision, while the decision at the end of step (c) ensures that at least one process succeeds in notifying every correct process of the potential decision of 0 in every crash-failure execution, to satisfy agreement.

5. INDULGENT ATOMIC COMMIT

In this section, we present our INBAC protocol. INBAC solves indulgent atomic commit as defined below. We believe this protocol to be of practical relevance for it is suited to practical distributed database systems which are synchronous "most of the time".

Definition 3 (Indulgent atomic commit). A protocol π solves *indulgent atomic commit* if it satisfies the following:

- Every network-failure execution of π solves NBAC.

Indulgent atomic commit is the most robust atomic commit problem in Table 1. For this problem, we show that our INBAC protocol is optimal in the number of message delays, as well as in the number of messages given that optimal number of message delays. To give the intuition behind the optimal protocol, we first prove the lower bounds on the number of messages, and then sketch the optimal protocol. For space limitation, the full description of our INBAC protocol is deferred to Appendix A.

5.1 Lower bounds

We prove a lower bound on the number of messages exchanged given two message delays (which is optimal as shown in Theorem 1) during any nice execution actually for a less robust problem (than indulgent atomic commit), as stated in the following theorem.

Theorem 5 (Lower bound on messages given fewer than three message delays). *Let π be any protocol that (a) solves NBAC in every crash-failure execution, and (b) satisfies agreement in every network-failure execution. Let E be any nice execution of π where every message is transmitted after an exact message delay U. W.l.o.g., E starts at time 0. If every process decides at or before $2U$ in E, then at least $2fn$ messages are exchanged in E.*

Note that for this less robust problem as well as indulgent atomic commit, $2n-2+f$ messages are optimal. Thus Theorem 5 also demonstrates the tradeoff between the number of messages and that of message delays for this less robust problem, indulgent atomic commit and other related problems (in total 4 cases out of 27 ones which we consider). As a result, including our tradeoff results obtained in Section 3, all atomic commit problems with nonzero messages as lower bounds (in total 18 out of 27 problem variants) highlight a tradeoff between time and message complexity.

To prove the lower bound of $2fn$ messages, we count the number of necessary messages for each of the n processes. In particular, we show in any nice execution, for any process P, there are two overlapping sets of f messages, Λ_1 and Λ_2, such that every message in Λ_1 precedes some message in Λ_2. To describe the relation between those messages precisely, we again apply the notion of "process reachability" introduced in Definition 2 and complete the terminology.

Definition 4 (Reaching a process: complete terminology). Let E be any execution. Let $\underline{m} = \{m_1, m_2, \dots, m_l\}$ be a sequence of messages in E such that (a) the source of m_1 is P, (b) the destination of m_l is $Q, Q \neq P$, (c) the source src_i of m_i is the destination of m_{i-1} for $i = 2, 3, \dots, l$, and (d) m_i leaves from src_i later than or at the time at which m_{i-1} arrives at src_i for $i = 2, 3, \dots, l$.

Recall that (as defined in Definition 2) if m_l arrives at Q at time t or earlier and $\underline{m}$ is the earliest sequence of messages for P (according to t) to reach Q in E, then we say that P *has reached* Q at time t in E.

For any two processes P and Q, if there are two sequences of messages $\underline{m}^1 = m_1^1, m_2^1, \dots, m_{l_1}^1$ and $\underline{m}^2 = m_1^2, m_2^2, \dots, m_{l_2}^2$ such that (a) the source of m_1^1 and the destination of $m_{l_2}^2$ is P, (b) the source of m_1^2 and the destination of $m_{l_1}^1$ is Q, (c) m_1^2 leaves from Q later than or at the time at which $m_{l_1}^1$ arrives at Q, and (d) $m_{l_2}^2$ arrives at some time t or earlier, then we say that P reaches Q and *subsequently* Q reaches P before time t (including t).

More generally, given three processes P, Q and R, if there are two sequences of messages $\underline{m}^1 = m_1^1, m_2^1, \dots, m_{l_1}^1$ and $\underline{m}^2 = m_1^2, m_2^2, \dots, m_{l_2}^2$ such that (a) the source of m_1^1 is R, (b) the destination of $m_{l_2}^2$ is P, (c) the source of m_1^2 and the destination of $m_{l_1}^1$ is Q, (d) m_1^2 leaves from Q later than or at the time at which $m_{l_1}^1$ arrives at Q, and (e) $m_{l_2}^2$ arrives at some time t or earlier, then we say that R reaches Q and *subsequently* Q reaches P before time t (including t).[8]

Recall that if a process P reaches another process Q, then it is possible that by a sequence of messages, P backs up P's vote at Q. (Lemma 1 actually captures the intuition of backups.) Similarly, if P reaches Q and subsequently Q reaches P, then it is possible that by a sequence of messages, Q *acknowledges* the backup of P's vote at Q. Then Lemma 5 below essentially says that at least f processes must send acknowledgements that confirm the success of the backup, the intuition for our proof of lower bound.

Lemma 5 (Quick acknowledgements). *Let π be any protocol that (a) solves NBAC in every crash-failure execution, and*

[8]The time t mentioned in Definition 4 is only for convenience of our proof: the time is assumed to be an accurate global clock, but no process necessarily has access to the global clock.

(b) satisfies agreement in every network-failure execution. Let E be any nice execution of π. Let P decide at some time t_1 in E. Let Θ be such set of processes that $\forall Q \in \Theta$, Q satisfies that before t_1 (including t_1) in E, P reaches Q, and subsequently Q reaches P. Among the messages whose destination is P, let $\mathcal{M}$ be the set of messages that arrive at P before or at t_1. For each $m \in \mathcal{M}$, let t_m be the time at which m leaves from its source and let $t_2 = \max_{m \in \mathcal{M}} t_m$.

If $t_2 \leq 2U$, then $|\Theta| \geq f$.

The sufficient condition in Lemma 5 is actually non-trivial: if P decides in *two or three message delays*, then f acknowledgements for one backup are necessary.[9]

Proof. (Proof sketch of Lemma 5. The full proof is in our full version [35].) The number of acknowledgements is closely related to how quickly P can decide in a nice execution. In a network-failure system, P may be incorrectly detected as having crashed, be unaware of the incorrect detection and still decide quickly. Suppose that only s, for some $s < f$, acknowledgements are sufficient for decision. Then P's quick decision might put agreement at risk, since if all those s processes as well as P crash, no process will be able to recover P's quick decision.

However, if P decides slowly and P expects a message from some process R in order to decide, then some process Q^- might notice the crash detection of P (or Q). (We consider the worst scenario where $n \geq 3$ here. If $n \leq 2$, then the proof could be easier.) Then Q^- might report it to P via R, and as a result, P may notice the incorrect crash detection of itself and wait for others (instead of taking a decision). If $t_2 \leq 2U$, then there is no guarantee for Q^- to inform P of this incorrect detection in time since Q^- notices the detection at the earliest at U, Thus $t_2 \leq 2U$ is indeed a sufficient condition for P to be considered quick to require f acknowledgements. □

Given Lemma 5, it is easy to see that certain messages do follow an order in any nice execution and because of the inherent order, there exist two non-overlapping sets of messages in any nice execution of a 2-delay protocol. We now prove our Theorem 5, the lower bound on the number of messages.

Proof. (Proof of Theorem 5.) Consider any process P and let t_1 be the time at which P decides. Among the messages whose destination is P, let $\mathcal{M}$ be the set of messages that arrive at P before or at t_1. For each $m \in \mathcal{M}$, let t_m be the time at which m leaves from its source and let $t_2 = \max_{m \in \mathcal{M}} t_m$. Then $t_2 = U$ and $t_1 = 2U$. By Lemma 1, at least f messages leave from P at time 0, and by Lemma 5, at least f messages arrive at P at time $2U$. This, in total, gives at least $2fn$ messages during any nice execution. □

5.2 Optimal protocol

We present here a protocol, which we denote INBAC, and which is delay-optimal as well as message-optimal given the optimal number of message delays.

[9]Yet the question whether f acknowledgements are necessary if a process decides after more than three message delays remains open. The reason why it may be possible to use fewer than f acknowledgements is also explained in the proof sketch of Lemma 5.

We start by looking at what happens in nice executions of INBAC (which actually follows Lemma 1 and Lemma 5); then we explain in other executions, how INBAC uses an underlying consensus module to solve agreement. The module solves consensus in a network-failure system [23, 36, 12], which we recall in Definition 5. Many solutions to consensus have been devised, e.g., Paxos and its variants [29, 41], but the correctness of INBAC or the best-case complexity of it does not rely on a particular algorithm. The modular approach (using consensus as a service) has been also taken in other distributed algorithms [21, 42].

The state transition of a process in both executions (nice or not) is illustrated in Figure 1. For space limitation, the detailed protocol and the proof of its correctness are deferred to Appendix A and Appendix B, respectively.

Definition 5 (Consensus [23]). A *consensus* protocol is defined by two events: *propose*, by which a process proposes a value $v = 0$ or 1, and *decide*, which outputs a decision to the process; furthermore, every execution satisfies the following properties: *termination*, *agreement* (similar to those properties of NBAC) and the following *validity* property:

- *Validity*: If a process decides v, then v was proposed by some process.

For simplicity, for time $2U$ or earlier in INBAC, every process sends a message or decides at multiples of U, i.e., at time 0, U or $2U$.

Overview of INBAC.
- Nice execution. Every nice execution E of INBAC starts by $P_1, P_2, \dots, P_n$ sending their votes simultaneously. At time 0, every process P sends P's vote to f processes. We say that those f processes are P's *backup processes*. At time U, each of P's backup processes sends P's vote back to P as an acknowledgement. INBAC chooses the set $\mathcal{B}_P$ of P's backup processes as follows: for $P \in \{P_{f+1}, P_{f+2}, \dots, P_n\}$, $\mathcal{B}_P = \{P_1, P_2, \dots, P_f\}$; for $P \in \{P_1, P_2, \dots, P_f\}$, $\mathcal{B}_P = \{P_1, P_2, \dots, P_{f+1}\} \backslash \{P\}$. Clearly, a process may backup more than one vote. In fact, at time U, P's backup process sends to P a set $\mathcal{V}$ of the votes received as an acknowledgement of the successful backup of each vote in $\mathcal{V}$. (This is a necessary design, which we summarize later in Lemma 6). Thus at time $2U$, P decides if P receives f correct acknowledgements (from P's f backup processes where a correct acknowledgement from process $B \in \mathcal{B}_P$ includes Q's vote for all Q such that $B \in \mathcal{B}_Q$). Obviously, in a nice execution, or more generally, in an execution where messages arrive in time, at $2U$, P knows every process's vote and is able to decide properly.
- Consensus to the rescue. Now in an execution E^- in which some process crashes, or some message is delayed, P can propose a value to consensus (we say that P may *cons-propose* a value) and wait for the decision of the consensus. We first explain when P cons-proposes a value and then explain which value P cons-proposes. Now, at $2U$, if P receives at least one acknowledgement from a process in $\{P_1, P_2, \dots, P_f\}$, then P cons-proposes a value immediately at $2U$. Otherwise, P asks $P_{f+1}, P_{f+2}, \dots, P_n$ for the acknowledgements which $P_{f+1}, P_{f+2}, \dots, P_n$ have received. To be more specific, if P is a process in $\{P_1, P_2, \dots, P_f\}$, then P can always cons-proposes a value at $2U$ in E^-. If not and if at $2U$, P indeed receives no acknowledgement from any process in $\{P_1, P_2, \dots, P_f\}$, then P eventually receives acknowledgement messages from $n - f$ out of n processes

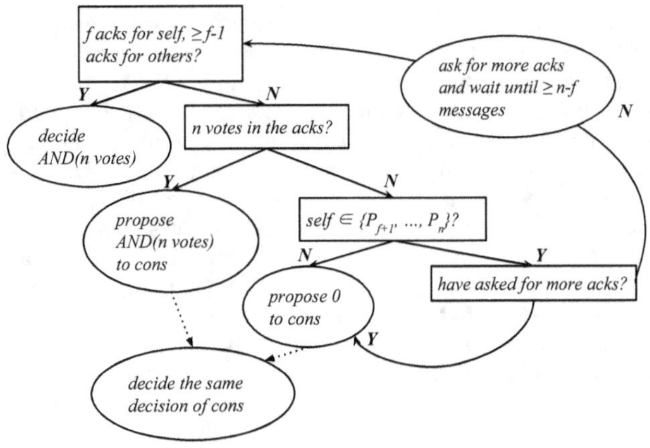

Figure 1: State transition after $2U$

and then may cons-propose a value. At the point when P is ready to cons-propose a value, P looks for every process's vote in the acknowledgement messages which P has received so far. If P finds that every process's vote is 1, then P cons-proposes 1; otherwise, P cons-proposes 0.

The state transition of P in E and in E^- is illustrated in Figure 1. We use there the following notations: AND denotes the logical AND of those 0's and 1's as votes; Y and N are the abbreviated for *yes* and *no* respectively; $self$ denotes P, the process in question; *ack* denotes an acknowledgement; *cons* denotes consensus (which is not invoked if no process crashes and every message arrives in time).

Some remarks on the protocol are in order. Clearly, the strategy of decisions of our INBAC protocol is independent of the underlying consensus algorithm. In addition, INBAC encourages processes to propose 1 to consensus by looking at every process's vote in the acknowledgements received.

Best-case complexity. We now count the number of messages and that of message delays. Since in every nice execution every process decides at $2U$, then the number of message delays meets the lower bound (Theorem 1). As for the number of messages in any nice execution, at time 0, for every process P, f messages leave from P; at time $2U$, exactly f messages arrive at the same process P.[10] (This is because in INBAC, a backup process sends the acknowledgement of several votes $\mathcal{V}$ in one message). Therefore, among n processes, $2fn$ messages are exchanged in E, which meets the lower bound on the number of messages in Theorem 5. This optimal result shows that both lower bounds are tight, as summarized in Theorem 6.

In the version as described above, the complexity of INBAC of a failure-free execution in which some process votes 0 is the same as the complexity of any nice execution. We remark that our protocol INBAC may accelerate such failure-free execution by doing the following: if a process P votes 0, then P sends its vote to every process and decides 0 at the very beginning (and in the meantime, a process $Q \neq P$ who receives one vote of 0 decides 0 immediately). Then a failure-free execution in which some process votes 0 can terminate at the end of the *first* message delay, which is faster than any nice execution.

Theorem 6 (Message-optimal indulgent atomic commit given two message delays)**.** *Given any protocol that solves consensus in a network-failure system, INBAC solves indulgent atomic commit, and during every nice execution of INBAC, (a) any process decides after two message delays, and (b) n processes exchange $2fn$ messages.*

Proof sketch of correctness. (The full proof is deferred to Appendix B.) Obviously, every execution of INBAC satisfies *validity*. Every network-failure execution also satisfies *termination* because, only a process in $\{P_{f+1}, P_{f+2}, \ldots, P_n\}$ might wait, but such wait eventually terminates given that at most f processes might crash. Thus as long as a consensus protocol satisfies *termination* in any network-failure system, INBAC also terminates in any network-failure system.

Every execution of INBAC satisfies *agreement* given that consensus satisfies *agreement* and *validity*. We can show that by contradiction. If two processes decide differently, then the one who decides 1 must receive all the acknowledgements which it expects at $2U$ while the one who decides 0 must have 0 as a decision of consensus. However, the one who decides 1 must have observed that (a) every process proposes 1, and (b) every process has f successful backups of its vote; thus as a result, no process can propose 0 to consensus. A contradiction.

Finally, as we claimed in the beginning of this section, we note a necessary design for the optimal protocol. We show in Lemma 6 that $f-1$ acknowledgements of other processes' votes are necessary. (Our INBAC adopts this design for optimality; for example, when P_{f+1} decides in a nice execution, P_{f+1} has received exactly $f-1$ acknowledgements of P_1's votes.) The proof of Lemma 6 is in our full version [35], which is similar to the proof of Lemma 5. As both Lemma 5 and Lemma 6 are necessary in designing message-optimal protocols, e.g., given three message delays, they may be of independent interest and worth mentioning here.

Lemma 6 (Quick acknowledgements of other votes)**.** *Let π be any indulgent atomic commit protocol. Let E be any nice execution of π. Let P decide at some time t_1 in E. Let process $R \neq P$. Let Θ be such set of processes that $\forall Q \in \Theta$, Q satisfies that before t_1 (including t_1) in E, R reaches Q, and subsequently Q reaches P. Among the messages whose destination is P, let $\mathcal{M}$ be the set of messages that arrives at P before or at t_1. For each $m \in \mathcal{M}$, let t_m be the time at which m leaves from its source and let $t_2 = \max_{m \in \mathcal{M}} t_m$.*

If $t_2 \leq 2U$, then $|\Theta| \geq f-1$.

6. RELATED WORK

6.1 Complexity of commit protocols

The formal study of atomic commit problems dates back to Skeen [16]. Later, substantial refinement [11, 14, 15] has been made, leading to the properties of NBAC we consider in this paper.

Complexity measures. We consider two measures of complexity: the classical notion of *number of messages*, and the *number of message delays*, following the complexity study by Lamport of consensus [22]. The use of this complexity

[10]A message whose source and destination is the same does not need to be sent over the network; such a message arrives immediately and is not counted in the messages exchanged among the n processes.

Table 4: Complexity of Indulgent Atomic Commit, and Synchronous NBAC with f Crashes

	Indulgent atomic commit (this paper)	Sync. NBAC (this paper)	Sync. NBAC [17, 25, 26, 40, 43]
#delays	2	1	-
#messages	$2n-2+f$ (for $f \geq 2$)	$n-1+f$	$2n-2$ (when $f=n-1$) [17, 25, 26]

Table 5: Complexity of INBAC, (n-1+f)NBAC, 1NBAC, 2PC, PaxosCommit and faster PaxosCommit

	1NBAC (this paper)	(n-1+f)NBAC (this paper)	INBAC (this paper)	2PC [2]	Paxos-Commit [21]	Faster Paxos-Commit [21]
#delays	1	$2f+n-1$	2	2	3	2
#messages	n^2-n	$f+n-1$	$2fn$	$2n-2$	$nf+2n-2$	$2fn+2n$ $-2f-2$
Atomic commit	Sync. NBAC	Sync. NBAC	Indulgent	Blocking	Indulgent	Indulgent

measure (message delays) is justified by the general context of an arbitrary (asynchronous) system (considering network-failure executions) in [22] and in this paper. Unlike [17, 18], we do not consider the *number of steps* as a measure of time. In [17, 18], steps were defined for synchronous systems and do not fit a general asynchronous setting. (In addition, since steps and message delays measure time differently, even for the special case of synchronous NBAC, the results on number of steps in [17, 18] and our results on message delays are uncomparable.)

Complexity results. The most closely related works to ours are (a) Dwork and Skeen's lower bound on the number of messages [17, 25, 26] and (b) Charron-Bost and Schiper's bound on the number of *rounds* [40] (of which the tightness was shown by Dutta et al. [43]). Both works focus on synchronous NBAC, while our study is for an arbitrary (asynchronous) system as well as an arbitrary combination of properties of NBAC. For the special case of synchronous NBAC, we are the first to present a tight lower bound on both the number of messages and that of message delays.

Compared with previous work, we generalize Dwork and Skeen's necessary and sufficient number of messages when at most $n-1$ processes may crash among n processes to an arbitrary number of crashes. Still for the special case of synchronous NBAC, we make Charron-Bost and Schiper's lower bound on time complexity more precise. They showed a lower bound of two rounds. In their model, one round consists of one send phase and one receive phase [40, 44]. Thus a lower bound of two rounds only says that the number of send phases *or* receive phases is at least two: it does not articulate which one. Combined with our tight lower bound of one message delay, we get a clear picture of the time complexity of synchronous NBAC protocols: a process can decide at the earliest by the end of the first message delay, and if so, it has to send messages before its decision. In other words, for any synchronous NBAC protocol, before any process decides, two send phases and one receive phase are necessary. (The tight two-round protocol of [43] needs at least two message delays and thus does not help to get such a picture.)

To the best of our knowledge, the present paper is the first to study the complexity of atomic commit problems in a systematic way. For indulgent atomic commit, the most robust among atomic commit problems we study, no (non-trivial) lower bound on the number of message delays or the number of messages was known until this paper.[11] Table 4 summarizes the complexity results of previous work and the present paper. The number of message delays for previous work is left blank.

6.2 Commit protocols

Two-phase commit (2PC) [2] distinguishes one process as the leader, which is a single point of failure in the sense that if it crashes, every other process is blocking in the fear of disagreement [16]. To circumvent this, Skeen [16] proposed three-phase commit (3PC), which adds one message delay and $2n-2$ messages over 2PC, along with a termination protocol. However, as several papers [19, 21] pointed out, 3PC (as well as many of its variants) does not solve the potential conflict between two backup leaders at the same time given by the termination protocol in crash-failure executions. Gray and Lamport [21] proposed *PaxosCommit* based on Paxos consensus [29] to solve the disagreement of non-unique leaders in network-failure executions. They also proposed *faster PaxosCommit* [21], an optimization of PaxosCommit, removing one message delay.[12] Both PaxosCommit [21] and faster PaxosCommit [21] solve indulgent atomic commit.

Table 5 summarizes the time and message complexity of our INBAC, our two optimal synchronous NBAC protocols: (n-1+f)NBAC and 1NBAC, 2PC, PaxosCommit, and faster PaxosCommit. To enable a fair comparison, we assume that each protocol starts when n processes send messages spontaneously.[13]

Clearly, our (n-1+f)NBAC and 1NBAC protocols are the best regarding messages and message delays respectively.

[11]Based on Charron-Bost and Schiper's two-round lower bound, Gray and Lamport [21] informally argued that two message delays should be optimal for indulgent atomic commit. However, by the model of rounds [40, 44], two rounds only imply a bound of one message delay.

[12]Gray and Lamport [21] pointed out a possible optimization (without details) for an atomic commit protocol, MD3PC, proposed in [20]. Then MD3PC achieves the same number of message delays and messages as faster PaxosCommit. As MD3PC and faster PaxosCommit are equally efficient in nice executions, MD3PC is omitted from the discussion.

[13]Thus 1 delay from 2PC and 2 delays from PaxosCommit and faster PaxosCommit are removed respectively, while $n-1$ messages are removed from the three protocols respectively from their original counting.

Among indulgent atomic commit protocols, in the special case of $f = 1$, INBAC performs the best regarding both messages and message delays (for $n \geq 2$), and performs almost as efficiently as 2PC. Still among indulgent atomic commit protocols, PaxosCommit and our INBAC protocol show a tradeoff between time and message complexity: for $f \geq 2, n \geq 3$, PaxosCommit is better in messages while our INBAC protocol is better in message delays. On satisfaction of properties, our (n-1+f)NBAC and 1NBAC protocols and 2PC show a tradeoff between agreement and termination. 2PC guarantees agreement in an arbitrary (asynchronous) system (considering a network-failure execution) but not termination even if only crash failures are possible. On the other hand, (n-1+f)NBAC and 1NBAC terminate despite f crashes but an execution in an arbitrary (asynchronous) system may violate *agreement* (due to the use of no-ops for (n-1+f)NBAC and due to the optimal delay for 1NBAC respectively).

On a technical level, while solving the same problem, faster PaxosCommit and our INBAC protocol differ significantly in how they achieve two message delays: the design of INBAC follows immediately the proof of the lower bounds (Lemma 1 and Lemma 5) and does not invoke consensus in any nice execution, while faster PaxosCommit uses Paxos consensus in a non-black-box way in every execution.

6.3 Low-latency commit protocols with weak semantics

As observed in [45], 1-delay commit protocols proposed in [46, 47] assumes that all processes propose 1 before an execution starts. Jiménez-Peris et al. proposed a commit service which has the same latency as 2PC but allows a process to decide twice and differently. MDCC [48] proposed a variant of Paxos to coordinate transactions assuming all processes vote the same. Replicated Commit [49] executed also the Paxos protocol to commit transactions, assuming here that the votes from a majority of processes are already sufficient to commit. All these protocols solve different (and weaker) problems than classical atomic commit.

Calvin [50] eliminated the explicit commit protocol by using a deterministic locking scheme, using only one message to notify the decision; in fact, NBAC is only solved in failure-free executions where one message delay is (not surprisingly) sufficient. Helios [10] commits a distributed transaction if no conflict involving the transaction is detected across datacenters. Helios considers both failure-free and network-failure executions. In failure-free executions, optimal commit latency is achieved. In network-failure executions, the scheme proposed is far from the optimal in terms of complexity. Our INBAC protocol may be adapted to the needs of Helios with better complexity.

7. CONCLUDING REMARKS

We present the first systematic study of the (time and message) complexity of atomic commit. We give a collection of lower bounds and matching protocols, by which we also close many questions on atomic commit. Some questions remain open. For example, for the tradeoff between time and message complexity, the optimal number of messages given greater than two message delays for indulgent atomic commit is not yet clear (although we close the question for two message delays).

8. ACKNOWLEDGEMENTS

We would like to thank Professor Giuliano Losa for helpful discussions. This work has been supported in part by the European ERC Grant 339539 - AOC.

9. REFERENCES

[1] K. P. Eswaran, J. N. Gray, R. A. Lorie, and I. L. Traiger, "The notions of consistency and predicate locks in a database system," *Commun. ACM*, vol. 19, no. 11, pp. 624–633, 1976.

[2] J. Gray, "Notes on data base operating systems," in *Operating Systems, An Advanced Course*, 1978, pp. 393–481.

[3] C. Mohan, B. Lindsay, and R. Obermarck, "Transaction management in the r* distributed database management system," *ACM Trans. Database Syst.*, vol. 11, no. 4, pp. 378–396, 1986.

[4] M. K. Aguilera, A. Merchant, M. Shah, A. Veitch, and C. Karamanolis, "Sinfonia: A new paradigm for building scalable distributed systems," *SIGOPS Oper. Syst. Rev.*, vol. 41, no. 6, pp. 159–174, 2007.

[5] B. F. Cooper, R. Ramakrishnan, U. Srivastava, A. Silberstein, P. Bohannon, H.-A. Jacobsen, N. Puz, D. Weaver, and R. Yerneni, "Pnuts: Yahoo!'s hosted data serving platform," *Proc. VLDB Endow.*, vol. 1, no. 2, pp. 1277–1288, 2008.

[6] D. Peng and F. Dabek, "Large-scale incremental processing using distributed transactions and notifications," in *OSDI '10*, pp. 1–15.

[7] J. C. Corbett, J. Dean, M. Epstein, A. Fikes, C. Frost, J. J. Furman, S. Ghemawat, A. Gubarev, C. Heiser, P. Hochschild, W. Hsieh, S. Kanthak, E. Kogan, H. Li, A. Lloyd, S. Melnik, D. Mwaura, D. Nagle, S. Quinlan, R. Rao, L. Rolig, Y. Saito, M. Szymaniak, C. Taylor, R. Wang, and D. Woodford, "Spanner: Google's globally distributed database," *ACM Trans. Comput. Syst.*, vol. 31, no. 3, pp. 8:1–8:22, 2013.

[8] J. Du, S. Elnikety, and W. Zwaenepoel, "Clock-si: Snapshot isolation for partitioned data stores using loosely synchronized clocks," in *SRDS '13*, pp. 173–184.

[9] M. K. Aguilera, J. B. Leners, and M. Walfish, "Yesquel: Scalable sql storage for web applications," in *SOSP '15*, pp. 245–262.

[10] F. Nawab, V. Arora, D. Agrawal, and A. El Abbadi, "Minimizing commit latency of transactions in geo-replicated data stores," in *SIGMOD '15*, pp. 1279–1294.

[11] V. Hadzilacos, "On the relationship between the atomic commitment and consensus problems," in *Proceedings of the Workshop on Fault-Tolerant Distributed Computing*, 1990, pp. 201–208.

[12] R. Guerraoui, "Revisiting the relationship between non-blocking atomic commitment and consensus," in *WDAG '95*, pp. 87–100.

[13] B. Charron-Bost, "Agreement problems in fault-tolerant distributed systems," in *SOFSEM '01*, pp. 10–32.

[14] R. Guerraoui, "Non-blocking atomic commit in asynchronous distributed systems with failure detectors," *Distrib. Comput.*, vol. 15, no. 1, pp. 17–25, 2002.

[15] R. Guerraoui, V. Hadzilacos, P. Kuznetsov, and S. Toueg, "The weakest failure detectors to solve quittable consensus and nonblocking atomic commit," *SIAM J. Comput.*, vol. 41, no. 6, pp. 1343–1379, 2012.

[16] D. Skeen, "Nonblocking commit protocols," in *SIGMOD '81*, pp. 133–142.

[17] C. Dwork and D. Skeen, "The inherent cost of nonblocking commitment," in *PODC '83*, pp. 1–11.

[18] K. V. S. Ramarao, "Complexity of distributed commit protocols," *Acta Informatica*, vol. 26, no. 6, pp. 577–595, 1989.

[19] I. Keidar and D. Dolev, "Increasing the resilience of atomic commit, at no additional cost," in *PODS '95*, pp. 245–254.

[20] R. Guerraoui, M. Larrea, and A. Schiper, "Reducing the cost for non-blocking in atomic commitment," in *ICDCS '96*, pp. 692–697.

[21] J. Gray and L. Lamport, "Consensus on transaction commit," *ACM Trans. Database Syst.*, vol. 31, no. 1, pp. 133–160, 2006.

[22] L. Lamport, "Lower bounds for asynchronous consensus," *Distrib. Comput.*, vol. 19, no. 2, pp. 104–125, 2006.

[23] L. Lamport, R. Shostak, and M. Pease, "The byzantine generals problem," *ACM Trans. Program. Lang. Syst.*, vol. 4, no. 3, pp. 382–401, 1982.

[24] M. J. Fischer, N. A. Lynch, and M. S. Paterson, "Impossibility of distributed consensus with one faulty process," *J. ACM*, vol. 32, no. 2, pp. 374–382, 1985.

[25] V. Hadzilacos, "A knowledge-theoretic analysis of atomic commitment protocols," in *PODS '87*, pp. 129–134.

[26] O. Wolfson and A. Segall, "The communication complexity of atomic commitment and of gossiping," *SIAM J. Comput.*, vol. 20, no. 3, pp. 423–450, 1991.

[27] R. Guerraoui, "Indulgent algorithms (preliminary version)," in *PODC '00*, pp. 289–297.

[28] R. Guerraoui and N. Lynch, "A general characterization of indulgence," *ACM Trans. Auton. Adapt. Syst.*, vol. 3, no. 4, pp. 20:1–20:19, 2008.

[29] L. Lamport, "The part-time parliament," *ACM Trans. Comput. Syst.*, vol. 16, no. 2, pp. 133–169, 1998.

[30] G. Taubenfeld, "Computing in the presence of timing failures," in *ICDCS '06*, pp. 16–16.

[31] P. Dutta and R. Guerraoui, "The inherent price of indulgence," *Distrib. Comput.*, vol. 18, no. 1, pp. 85–98, 2005.

[32] R. Guerraoui and M. Raynal, "The information structure of indulgent consensus," *IEEE Trans. Comput.*, vol. 53, no. 4, pp. 453–466, 2004.

[33] L. Sampaio and F. Brasileiro, "Adaptive indulgent consensus," in *DSN'05*, pp. 422–431.

[34] O. Bakr and I. Keidar, "Evaluating the running time of a communication round over the internet," in *PODC '02*, pp. 243–252.

[35] R. Guerraoui and J. Wang, "How fast can a distributed transaction commit?" Tech. Rep., 2017, http://infoscience.epfl.ch/record/225579.

[36] C. Dwork, N. Lynch, and L. Stockmeyer, "Consensus in the presence of partial synchrony," *J. ACM*, vol. 35, no. 2, pp. 288–323, 1988.

[37] T. D. Chandra and S. Toueg, "Unreliable failure detectors for reliable distributed systems," *J. ACM*, vol. 43, no. 2, pp. 225–267, 1996.

[38] T. D. Chandra, V. Hadzilacos, and S. Toueg, "The

weakest failure detector for solving consensus," *J. ACM*, vol. 43, no. 4, pp. 685–722, 1996.

[39] L. Lamport, "Time, clocks, and the ordering of events in a distributed system," *Commun. ACM*, vol. 21, no. 7, pp. 558–565, 1978.

[40] B. Charron-Bost and A. Schiper, "Uniform consensus is harder than consensus," *J. Algorithms*, vol. 51, no. 1, pp. 15 – 37, 2004.

[41] R. D. Prisco, B. Lampson, and N. Lynch, "Revisiting the paxos algorithm," *Theoretical Computer Science*, vol. 243, no. 1, pp. 35 – 91, 2000.

[42] R. Guerraoui and A. Schiper, "The generic consensus service," *IEEE Trans. Softw. Eng.*, vol. 27, no. 1, pp. 29–41, 2001.

[43] P. Dutta, R. Guerraoui, and B. Pochon, "Fast non-blocking atomic commit: an inherent trade-off," *Inform. Process. Lett.*, vol. 91, no. 4, pp. 195 – 200, 2004.

[44] N. A. Lynch, *Distributed Algorithms*. Morgan Kaufmann Publishers Inc., 1996.

[45] M. Abdallah, R. Guerraoui, and P. Pucheral, "One-phase commit: does it make sense?" in *ICPADS '98*, pp. 182–192.

[46] Y. J. Al-Houmaily and P. K. Chrysanthis, "An atomic commit protocol for gigabit-networked distributed database systems," *J. Syst. Architect.*, vol. 46, no. 9, pp. 809 – 833, 2000.

[47] J. W. Stamos and F. Cristian, "A low-cost atomic commit protocol," in *SRDS '90*, pp. 66–75.

[48] T. Kraska, G. Pang, M. J. Franklin, S. Madden, and A. Fekete, "Mdcc: Multi-data center consistency," in *EuroSys '13*, pp. 113–126.

[49] H. Mahmoud, F. Nawab, A. Pucher, D. Agrawal, and A. El Abbadi, "Low-latency multi-datacenter databases using replicated commit," *Proc. VLDB Endow.*, vol. 6, no. 9, pp. 661–672, 2013.

[50] A. Thomson, T. Diamond, S.-C. Weng, K. Ren, P. Shao, and D. J. Abadi, "Calvin: Fast distributed transactions for partitioned database systems," in *SIGMOD '12*, pp. 1–12.

[51] C. Cachin, R. Guerraoui, and L. Rodrigues, *Introduction to Reliable and Secure Distributed Programming*, 2nd ed. Springer Publishing Company, Incorporated, 2011.

APPENDIX

A. INBAC

We describe here our INBAC protocol in detail. Some preliminary remarks are in order. (a) We assume that every process knows its own ID stored in the local variable i of that process. (b) We assume that a message delivery event has a higher priority than a timeout event; i.e., if both events occur at a process, the process is first triggered by the delivery event and then the timeout event. (c) Sometimes a process is triggered by both the delivery of some message m and a logical condition ℓ; we assume that if m arrives earlier than when ℓ is satisfied, then m (as well as the delivery of m) is queued to wait for the satisfaction of ℓ. (d) This protocol satisfies some properties in every crash-failure execution and thus we assume that one unit at the timer at every process is set to the known upper bound of the message delay of a given crash-failure system. (Clearly, in a network-failure execution of the protocol, message delays might violate the upper bound, and as a result, although the timer timeouts, a process does not receive the message which it sets the timer to wait for.) (e) The timer starts at time 0 when every process proposes its value. (f) Sending messages and processing messages are considered negligible in time. For the other protocols, we do not repeat these remarks when they still apply.

The pseudo code which we use to describe INBAC (and all the other protocols described in the later sections) follows the approach of Cachin et al. [51]. The pseudo code uses "callbacks": an algorithm is described as a set of event handlers where a process reacts to incoming events by possibly triggering new events.

The communication channels are abstracted as a module called *PerfectPointToPointLinks*, denoted by *pl*. The module defines two events: <*pl*, Send|r, m> and <*pl*, Deliver|s, m>, where r is the receiver of the sending event, s is the sender of the message delivery event and m represents the message. The timer is abstracted as a module called *Timer*, denoted by *timer*. The module defines two events: <*timer*, Timeout> and **set** timer, where *timer* timeouts at the time set previously. A timer may be set several times at one process. The uniform consensus (defined in Definition 5, which terminates in every network-failure execution) is abstracted as a module called *IndulgentUniformConsensus*, denoted by *iuc*. The module defines two events: <*iuc*, Propose | v> and <*iuc*, Decide | d>, where v is the value proposed to *iuc* and d is the decision of *iuc*.

Finally, we also abstract indulgent atomic commit as a module called *IndulgentNonBlockingAtomicCommit*, denoted by *inbac*. The module defines two events (in addition to event <*inbac*, Init> which performs the initialization of the module once for all): <*inbac*, Propose | v> and <*inbac*, Decide | d> where v is the value proposed to indulgent atomic commit and d is the decision of indulgent atomic commit.

Note that the name of a module is considered as an identifier. The existence of multiple copies of the same module is possible in one algorithm. For example, later in protocol aNBAC, two timers are used and identified by different names.

Implements:
IndulgentNonBlockingAtomicCommit, **instance** *inbac*.

Uses:
PerfectPointToPointLinks, **instance** *pl*.
Timer, **instance** *timer*.
IndulgentUniformConsensus, **instance** *iuc*.

upon event <*inbac, Init*> **do**
phase := 0;
proposed := FALSE;
decided := FALSE;
collection0 := $\emptyset$;
collection1 := $\emptyset$;
collection_help := $\emptyset$;
wait := FALSE;
val := $\perp$;
decision := $\perp$;
proposal := $\perp$;
cnt := 0;

```
   cnt_help := 0;

upon event <inbac, Propose | v> do
   val := v;
   forall q ∈ {P_1, ..., P_f} do
      trigger <pl, Send | q, [V, v]>;
   if 1 ≤ i ≤ f then
      trigger <pl, Send | P_{f+1}, [V, v]>;
   if 1 ≤ i ≤ f+1 then
      set timer to 1;
   else
      set timer to 2;
      phase := 1;

upon event <pl, Deliver | p, [V, v]> and phase = 0 do
   collection0 := collection0 ∪ {(p, v)};

upon event <timer, Timeout> and phase = 0 and 1 ≤ i
≤ f do
   forall q ∈ Ω do
      trigger <pl, Send | q, [C, collection0]>;
   phase := 1;
   set timer to 2;

upon event <timer, Timeout> and phase = 0 and i
= f + 1 do
   forall q ∈ {P_1, P_2, ..., P_f} do
      trigger <pl, Send | q, [C, collection0]>;
   phase := 1;
   set timer to 2;

upon event <pl, Deliver | p, [C, collection]> do
   collection1 := collection1 ∪ {(p, collection)};
   cnt := cnt + 1;

upon event <timer, Timeout> and phase = 1 and not decided and not proposed and i ≥ f + 1 do
   phase := 2;
   collection_val := ⋃_{(p,c)∈ collection1} c;
  collection0 := collection0 ∪ collection_val ∪ {(self, val)};
   if collection1 = {(P_j, c_j) | 1 ≤ j ≤ f} where c_j =
   {(P_k, val_k) | 1 ≤ k ≤ n} for every j, 1 ≤ j ≤ f (with
   val_k being the proposal of P_k) then
      decision := AND_{1≤ k ≤ n} val_k;
      decided := TRUE;
      trigger <inbac, Decide | decision>;
   else if cnt ≥ 1 then
    if for every process P_k, 1 ≤ k ≤ n, ∃ val_k s.t. (P_k, val_k)
      ∈ ⋃_{(p,c)∈ collection1} c then
         proposal := AND_{1≤ k≤ n} val_k;
         proposed := TRUE;
         trigger <iuc, Propose | proposal>;
      else
         proposed := TRUE;
         trigger <iuc, Propose | 0>;
   else
      wait := TRUE;
      forall q ∈ {P_{f+1}, P_{f+2}, ..., P_n} do
         trigger < pl, Send | q, [HELP]>;

upon event <pl, Deliver | p, [HELP]> and phase = 2 and i
≥ f + 1 do
   trigger < pl, Send | p, [HELPED, collection0]>;

upon event <pl, Deliver | p, [HELPED, collection]> and
i ≥ f + 1 do
   collection_help := collection_help ∪ collection;
   cnt_help := cnt_help + 1;

upon cnt + cnt_help ≥ n − f and wait and not proposed and not decided and i ≥ f + 1 do
   wait := FALSE;
   if collection1 = {(P_j, c_j) | 1 ≤ j ≤ f} where c_j =
   {(P_k, val_k) | 1 ≤ k ≤ n} for every j, 1 ≤ j ≤ f (with
   val_k being the proposal of P_k) then
      decision := AND_{1≤ k≤ n} val_k;
      decided := TRUE;
      trigger <inbac, Decide | decision>;
   else if cnt ≥ 1 then
      if for every process P_k, 1 ≤ k ≤ n, ∃ val_k s.t. (P_k,
      val_k) ∈ ⋃_{(p,c)∈ collection1} c then
         proposal := AND_{1≤ k≤ n} val_k;
         proposed := TRUE;
         trigger <iuc, Propose | proposal>;
      else
         proposed := TRUE;
         trigger <iuc, Propose | 0>;
   else
    if collection_help = {(P_k, val_k) | 1 ≤ k ≤ n} where
      val_k is the proposal of P_k then
         proposal := AND_{1≤ k≤ n} val_k;
         proposed := TRUE;
         trigger <iuc, Propose | proposal>;
      else
         proposed := TRUE;
         trigger <iuc, Propose |0 >;

upon event <timer, Timeout> and phase = 1 and not decided and not proposed and 1 ≤ i ≤ f do
   if collection1 = {(P_j, c_j) | 1 ≤ j ≤ f+1} where c_j =
   {(P_k, val_k) | 1 ≤ k ≤ n} for every j, 1 ≤ j ≤ f and c_{f+1}
   = {(P_k, val_k) | 1 ≤ k ≤ f}
   (with val_k being the proposal of P_k) then
      decision := AND_{1≤ k≤ n} val_k;
      decided := TRUE;
      trigger <inbac, Decide | decision>;
      return;
   if for every process P_k, 1 ≤ k ≤ n, ∃ val_k s.t. (P_k, val_k)
   ∈ ⋃_{(p,c)∈ collection1} c then
      proposal := AND_{1≤ k≤ n} val_k;
      proposed := TRUE;
      trigger <iuc, Propose | proposal>;
   else
      proposed := TRUE;
      trigger <iuc, Propose | 0>;

upon event <iuc, Decide | v> and not decided do
   decided := TRUE;
   trigger <inbac, Decide | v>;
```

B. CORRECTNESS OF INBAC

Proof. (Proof of Theorem 6.) First, we prove that every execution of INBAC satisfies the *agreement* property.

Agreement. By contradiction. Suppose that in some execution E, two different processes P and Q decide differently. Suppose further that P decides 1 and Q decides 0. Given that consensus satisfies the *agreement* property, at least one of P and Q's decisions is *not* a result of the decision of the consensus.

If neither of P and Q's decisions is a result of the decision of the consensus, then either process decides the value of its local variable *decision*. Since *decision* is assigned as the AND of the n processes' votes to *inbac* at every process, P and Q must agree on their decisions, which contradicts our assumption. If P's decision is a result of the decision of the consensus, then by the *validity* property of consensus, some process R proposes 1 to *iuc*. Therefore R's local variable *proposal* is 1, which is equal to the AND of the n processes' votes to *inbac*. Now that Q's decision is equal to its local variable *decision*, which is the AND of the n processes' votes to *inbac*, P and Q must agree on their decisions, which contradicts our assumption.

As a result, Q's decision must be a result of the decision of the consensus while P's decision must not be. Now P's local variable *decision* is 1. Therefore, every process proposes 1 to *inbac* and at the same time, if any process assigns a value to its local variable *proposal* or *decision*, it can only assign a 1. Since Q's decision is a result of the consensus, by the *validity* property of consensus, some process R (not necessarily Q) proposes 0 to consensus. First, we assume that $P \in \{P_{f+1}, P_{f+2}, \ldots, P_n\}$ and examine whether R exists. As P decides 1, variable *collection0* at every process in $\{P_1, P_2, \ldots, P_f\}$ is $\{(P_k, val_k) | 1 \leq k \leq n\}$. Therefore, $R \notin \{P_1, P_2, \ldots, P_f\}$. I.e., $R \in \{P_{f+1}, P_{f+2}, \ldots, P_n\}$. Then variable *cnt* at R must be 0 and thus for R to propose 0, R must have *cnt_help* $= n - f$, i.e., every process in $\{P_{f+1}, P_{f+2}, \ldots, P_n\}$ has sent to R their variable *collection0*. As a result, P has also sent its *collection0*, which is updated to $\{(P_k, val_k) | 1 \leq k \leq n\}$ when *phase* $= 2$. This leads R to propose 1 to consensus. A contradiction.

Now we assume that $P \in \{P_1, P_2, \ldots, P_f\}$ and examine whether R exists. Similarly, variable *collection0* at every process in $\{P_1, P_2, \ldots, P_f\}$ is $\{(P_k, val_k) | 1 \leq k \leq n\}$. Moreover, variable *collection0* at P_{f+1} includes $\{(P_k, val_k) | 1 \leq k \leq f\}$ as a subset. Again, R must belong to $\{P_{f+1}, P_{f+2}, \ldots, P_n\}$. For R to propose 0, R must have *cnt_help* $= n - f$, i.e., every process in $\{P_{f+1}, P_{f+2}, \ldots, P_n\}$ has sent to R their updated variable *collection0*, the union of which is equal to $\{(P_k, val_k) | 1 \leq k \leq n\}$. (Variable *collection0* at every process in $\{P_{f+1}, P_{f+2}, \ldots, P_n\}$ is updated to include its own vote.) This again leads R to propose 1 to consensus. A contradiction.

Next, we prove that every network-failure execution of INBAC satisfies the *validity* property, and the *termination* property.

Validity. Clearly, the *validity* property can be separated into the *commit-validity* property: if a process decides 1, then every process proposes 1; and the *abort-validity* property: if a process decides 0, then some process proposes 0 or a failure occurs. The proof here (and the proofs for the correctness of protocols later) proves that the protocol satisfies the *commit-validity* property and the *abort-validity* property respectively.

Commit-Validity. Suppose that some process P decides 1. If P's decision is a result of the decision of the consensus, then since consensus satisfies the *validity* property, some process R (not necessarily P) must propose 1 to consensus. Since variable *proposal* at R is equal to the AND of the n votes, every process proposes 1 to *inbac*. If P's decision is not a result, then variable *decision* at P is equal to the AND of the n votes, which implies that every process proposes 1 to *inbac*.

Abort-Validity. Suppose that process P decides 0. If P's decision is equal to variable *decision* at P or variable *proposal* at some other process R, then some process must propose 0 to *inbac*. If not, then some process R (not necessarily P) must have proposed 0 to consensus in the case where some value is missing in variable *collection_help* or the collection $\bigcup_{(p,c) \in collection1} c$ at R. This indicates that some message does not arrive before the timer issues a timeout event, which is set to the upper bound of the message delay. Then, in a network-failure system, we can safely conclude that a failure occurs. Thus the *abort-validity* property is satisfied.

Termination. By contradiction. Suppose that some correct process P does not decide. P assigns *phase* to 1 in finite time. Then P is triggered by the event that the timer issues a timeout and *phase* $= 1$, when P has not proposed to consensus or decided in *inbac*. If $P \in \{P_1, P_2, \ldots, P_f\}$, then since consensus *iuc* satisfies the *termination* property in a network-failure system, P eventually decides in *inbac*. A contradiction. If $P \in \{P_{f+1}, P_{f+2}, \ldots, P_n\}$, then P assigns *phase* to 2 in finite time. In fact, every correct process in $\{P_{f+1}, P_{f+2}, \ldots, P_n\}$ assigns *phase* to 2 in finite time. Since P does not decide, thus by the *termination* property of *iuc* in a network-failure system, P must assign *wait* to TRUE and wait for the condition *cnt* + *cnt_help* $\geq n - f$ to satisfy. If the condition is satisfied and the corresponding event is triggered, then P eventually decides in *inbac*. In other words, for P to not decide, the condition should never be satisfied.

However, when *wait* is assigned to TRUE, *cnt* is 0. Only the message of [C, *] increments *cnt*. Since $P \in \{P_{f+1}, P_{f+2}, \ldots, P_n\}$, then the message of [C, *] that arrives at P can only be from a process in $\{P_1, P_2, \ldots, P_f\}$, each correct process of which must send [C, *] to P. On the other hand, *cnt_help* at P is incremented if a message from a process in $\{P_{f+1}, P_{f+2}, \ldots, P_n\}$ arrives. Every correct process in $\{P_{f+1}, P_{f+2}, \ldots, P_n\}$ also must send message [HELPED, *] to P. As at most f processes can crash and messages eventually arrive at their destinations respectively, *cnt*+*cnt_help* is eventually equal to or greater than $n - f$. In other words, the condition is eventually satisfied. A contradiction.

Finally, since consensus satisfies the *termination* property in an network-failure system (assuming a majority of correct processes), INBAC also satisfies the *termination* property in an network-failure system (assuming a majority of correct processes).

Therefore, given that consensus can be implemented for a network-failure system, protocol INBAC (i.e., instance *inbac*) solves indulgent atomic commit. □

JSON: Data model, Query languages and Schema specification

Pierre Bourhis
CNRS CRIStAL UMR9189,
Lille; INRIA Lille
pierre.bourhis@univ-lille1.fr

Juan L. Reutter
PUC Chile and Center for
Semantic Web Research
jreutter@ing.puc.cl

Fernando Suárez
PUC Chile and Center for
Semantic Web Research
fsuarez1@uc.cl

Domagoj Vrgoč
PUC Chile and Center for
Semantic Web Research
dvrgoc@ing.puc.cl

ABSTRACT

Despite the fact that JSON is currently one of the most popular formats for exchanging data on the Web, there are very few studies on this topic and there is no agreement upon a theoretical framework for dealing with JSON. Therefore in this paper we propose a formal data model for JSON documents and, based on the common features present in available systems using JSON, we define a lightweight query language allowing us to navigate through JSON documents. We also introduce a logic capturing the schema proposal for JSON and study the complexity of basic computational tasks associated with these two formalisms.

CCS Concepts

•**Information systems → Database design and models; Query languages;** *Web data description languages;* •**Theory of computation →** *Data modeling;*

Keywords

JSON; Schema languages; Navigation

1. INTRODUCTION

JavaScript Object Notation (JSON) [17, 11] is a lightweight format based on the data types of the JavaScript programming language. In their essence, JSON documents are dictionaries consisting of key-value pairs, where the value can again be a JSON document, thus allowing an arbitrary level of nesting. An example of a JSON document is given in Figure 1. As we can see here, apart from simple dictionaries, JSON also supports arrays and atomic types such as integers and strings. Arrays and dictionaries can again contain arbitrary JSON documents, thus making the format fully compositional.

PODS'17, May 14-19, 2017, Chicago, IL, USA

DOI: http://dx.doi.org/10.1145/3034786.3056120

```
{
  "name": {
     "first": "John",
     "last": "Doe"
     },
  "age": 32,
  "hobbies": ["fishing","yoga"]
}
```

Figure 1: A simple JSON document.

Due to its simplicity, and the fact that it is easily readable both by humans and by machines, JSON is quickly becoming one of the most popular formats for exchanging data on the Web. This is particularly evident with Web services communicating with their users through an Application Programming Interface (API), as JSON is currently the predominant format for sending API requests and responses over the HTTP protocol. Additionally, JSON format is much used in database systems built around the NoSQL paradigm (see e.g. [22, 2, 26]), or graph databases (see e.g. [32]).

Despite its popularity, the coverage of the specifics of JSON format in the research literature is very sparse, and to the best of our knowledge, there is still no agreement on the correct data model for JSON, no formalisation of the core query features which JSON systems should support, nor a logical foundation for JSON Schema specification. And while some preliminary studies do exist [23, 21, 8, 28], as far as we are aware, no attempt to describe a theoretical basis for JSON has been made by the research community. Therefore, the main objective of this paper is to formally define an appropriate data model for JSON, identify the key querying features provided by the existing JSON systems, and to propose a logic allowing us to specify schema constraints for JSON documents.

In order to define the data model, we examine the key characteristics of JSON documents and how they are used in practice. As a result we obtain a tree-shaped structure very similar to the ordered data-tree model of XML [7], but with some key differences. The first difference is that JSON trees are deterministic by design, as each key can appear at most once inside a dictionary. This has various implications at the time of querying JSON documents: on one hand we sometimes deal with languages far simpler than XML, but on the other hand this key restriction can make static analysis more complicated, even for simpler queries. Next, arrays are explicitly present in JSON, which is not the case in XML. Of course, the ordered structure of XML could be used to simulate arrays, but the defining feature of each JSON dictionary is that it is unordered, thus dictating the nodes of our tree to be typed accordingly. And finally, JSON values are again JSON objects, thus making equality comparisons much more complex than in case of XML, since we are now comparing subtrees, and not just atomic values. We cover all of these features of JSON in more detail in the paper, and we also argue that, while technically possible (albeit, in a very awkward manner), coding JSON documents using XML might not be the best solution in practice.

Next, we consider the problem of querying JSON. As there is currently no agreed upon query language in place, we examine an array of practical JSON systems, ranging from programming languages such as Python [13], to fully operational JSON databases such as MongoDB [22], and isolate what we consider to be key concepts for accessing JSON documents. As we will see, the main focus in many systems is on navigating the structure of a JSON tree, therefore we propose a navigational logic for JSON documents based on similar approaches from the realm of XML [12], or graph databases [3, 20]. We then show how our logic captures common use cases for JSON, extend it with additional features, and demonstrate that it respects the "lightweight nature" of the JSON format, since it can be evaluated very efficiently, and it also has reasonable complexity of main static tasks. Interestingly, sometimes we can reuse results devised for other similar languages such as XPath or Propositional Dynamic Logic, but the nature of JSON and the functionalities present in query languages also demand new approaches or a refinement of these techniques.

Another important aspect of working with any data format is being able to specify the structure of documents. A usual way to do this is through schema specification, and in the case of JSON, there is indeed a draft proposal for a schema language [18] (called JSON Schema), which has recently been formalised in [28]. Based on the formalisation of [28] we define a logic capturing the full formal specification of JSON Schema, show that it is essentially equivalent to the navigational language we propose for querying JSON, and study the complexity of its evaluation and static tasks. However, once we take into account the recursive functionalities of JSON Schema, we arrive at a powerful new formalism that is much more difficult to encompass inside well known frameworks.

Finally, since theoretical study of JSON is still in its early stages, we close with a series of open problems and directions for future research.

Organisation. We formally define JSON and some of its features in Section 2. The appropriate data model for JSON is discussed in Section 3, and its query language in Section 4. In Section 5 we define a logic capturing a schema specification for JSON. Our conclusions and the directions for future work are discussed in Section 6. Due to the lack of space most proofs are placed in the appendix to this paper.

2. PRELIMINARIES

JSON documents. We start by fixing some notation regarding JSON documents. The full JSON specification defines seven types of values: objects, arrays, strings, numbers and the values true, false and null [9]. However, to abstract from encoding details we assume our JSON documents are only formed by objects, arrays, strings and natural numbers.

Formally, denote by Σ the set of all unicode characters. JSON values are defined as follows. First, any natural number $n \geqslant 0$ is a JSON value, called a *number*. Furthermore, if `s` is a string in Σ^*, then `"s"` is a JSON value, called a *string*. Next, if $v_1, \dots, v_n$ are JSON values and $s_1, \dots, s_n$ are pairwise distinct string values, then $\{s_1 : v_1, \dots, s_n : v_n\}$ is a JSON value, called an *object*. In this case, each $s_i : v_i$ is called a key-value pair of this object. Finally, if $v_1, \dots, v_n$ are JSON values then $[v_1, \dots, v_n]$ is a JSON value called an *array*. In this case $v_1, \dots, v_n$ are called the *elements* of the array. Note that in the case of arrays and objects the values v_i can again be objects or arrays, thus allowing the documents an arbitrary level of nesting. A *JSON document* (or just document) is any JSON value. From now on we will use the term JSON document and JSON value interchangeably.

JSON navigation instructions. Arguably all systems using JSON base the extraction of information in what we call *JSON navigation instructions*. The notation used to specify JSON navigation instructions varies from system to system, but it always follows the same two principles:

- If J is a JSON object, then one should be able to access the JSON value in a specific key-value pair of this object.
- If J is a JSON array, then one should be able to access the i-th element of J.

In this paper we adopt the python notation for navigation instructions: If J is an object, then $J[key]$ is the value of J whose key is the string value `"key"`. Likewise, if J is an array, then $J[n]$, for a natural number n, contains the n-th element of J[1].

As far as we are aware, all JSON systems use JSON navigation instructions as a primitive for querying JSON documents, and in particular it is so for the systems we have reviewed in detail: Python and other programming languages [13], the mongoDB database [22], the JSON Path query language [14] and the SQL++ project that tries to bridge relational and JSON databases [24].

At this point it is important to note a few important consequences of using JSON navigation instructions, as these have an important role at the time of formalising this framework.

First, note that we do not have a way of obtaining the keys of JSON objects. For example, if `J` is the object `{"first":"John", "last":"Doe"}` we could issue the instructions $J[first]$ to obtain the value of the pair `"first":"John"`, which is the string value `"John"`. Or use $J[last]$ to obtain the value of the pair `"last":"Doe"`. However, there is no instruction that can retrieve the keys inside this document (i.e. `"first"` and `"last"` in this case).

Similarly, for the case of the arrays, the access is essentially a *random access*: we can access the i-th element of an array, and most of the time there are primitives to access the first or the last element of arrays. However, we can not reason about different elements of the array. For example, for the array K = `[12,5,22]` we can not retrieve, say, an element (or any element) which is greater than the first element of K. Some systems do feature FLWR expressions that

[1]Some JSON systems prefer using a *dot* notation, where J.key and J.n are the equivalents of J[key] and $J[n]$.

support iterating over all elements. But this iteration is itself treated as a series of random accesses, using commands such as For i in (0,n) print(J[i]).

3. DATA MODEL FOR JSON

In this section we propose a formal data model for JSON documents whose goal is to closely reflect the manner in which JSON is manipulated using JSON navigation instructions, and that will be used later on as the basis of our formalisation of JSON query and schema languages. We begin by introducing our formal model, called JSON trees. Afterwards we discuss the main differences between JSON trees and other well-studied tree formalisms such as data trees or XML.

3.1 JSON trees

JSON objects are by definition compositional: each JSON object is a set of key-value pairs, in which values can again be JSON objects. This naturally suggests using a tree-shaped structure to model JSON documents. However, this structure must preserve the compositional nature of JSON. That is, if each node of the tree structure represents a JSON document, then the children of each node must represent the documents nested within it. For instance, consider the following JSON document J.

```
{
  "name": {
    "first": "John",
    "last": "Doe"
    },
  "age": 32
}
```

as explained before, this document is a JSON *object* which contains two keys: "name" and "age". Furthermore, the value of the key "name" is another JSON document and the value of the key "age" is the integer 32. There are in total 5 JSON values inside this object: the complete document itself, plus the literals 32, "John" and "Doe", and the object "name": {"first":"John", "last":"Doe"}. So how should a tree representation of the document J look like? If we are to preserve the compositional structure of JSON, then the most natural representation is by using the following edge-labelled tree:

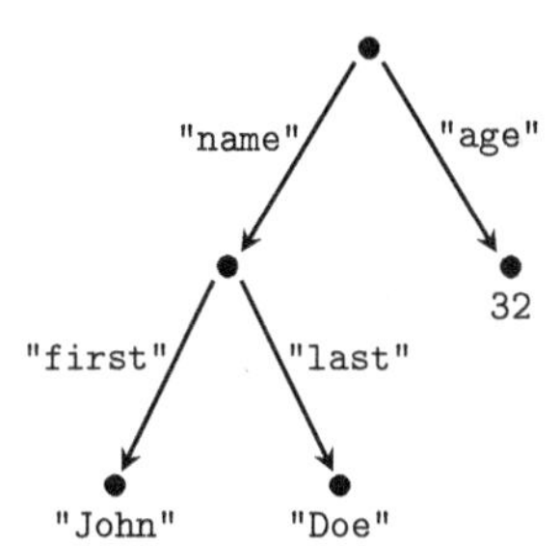

The root of tree represents the entire document. The two edges labelled "name" and "age" represent two keys inside this JSON object, and they lead to nodes representing their respective values. In the case of the key "age" this is just an integer, while in the case of "name" we obtain another JSON object that is represented as a subtree of the entire tree.

Finally, we need to enforce the property of JSON that no object can have two keys with the same name, thus making the model deterministic in some sense, since each node will have only one child reachable by an edge with a specific label. Let us briefly summarise the properties of our model so far.

Labelled edges. Edges in our model are labelled by the keys forming the key-value pairs of objects. This means that we can directly follow the label of edges when issuing JSON navigation instructions, and also means that information of keys is represented in a different medium than JSON values (labels for the former, nodes for the latter). This is inline with the way JSON navigation instructions work, as one can only retrieve values of key-value pairs, but not the keys themselves. To comply with the JSON standard, we disallow trees where a same edge label is repeated in two different edges leaving a node.

Compositional structure. One of the advantages of our tree representation is that any of its subtrees represent a JSON document themselves. In fact, the five possible subtrees of the tree above correspond to the five JSON values present in the JSON J.

Atomic values. Finally, some elements of a JSON document are actual values, such as integers or strings. For this reason leaf nodes corresponding to integers and strings will also be assigned a value they carry. Leaf nodes without a value represent empty objects: that is, documents of the form {}.

Although this model is simple and conceptually clear, we are missing a way of representing arrays. Indeed, consider again the document from Figure 1 (call this document J_2). In J_2 the value of the key "hobbies" is an array: another feature explicitly present in JSON that thus needs to be reflected in our model.

As arrays are ordered, this might suggest that we can have some nodes whose children form an ordered list of siblings, much like in the case of XML. But this would not be conceptually correct, for the following two reasons. First, as we have explained, JSON navigation instructions use random access to access elements in arrays. For example, the navigation instruction used to retrieve an element of an array is of the form $J_2[hobbies][i]$, aimed at obtaining the i-th element of the array under the key "hobbies". But more importantly, we do not want to treat arrays as a list because lists naturally suggest navigating through different elements of the list. On the contrary, none of the systems we reviewed feature a way of navigating from one element of the array to another element. That is, once we retrieve the first element of the array under the key "hobbies", we have no way of linking it to its siblings.

We choose to model JSON arrays as nodes whose children are accessed by axes labelled with natural numbers reflecting their position in the array. Namely, in the case of JSON document J_2 above we obtain the following representation:

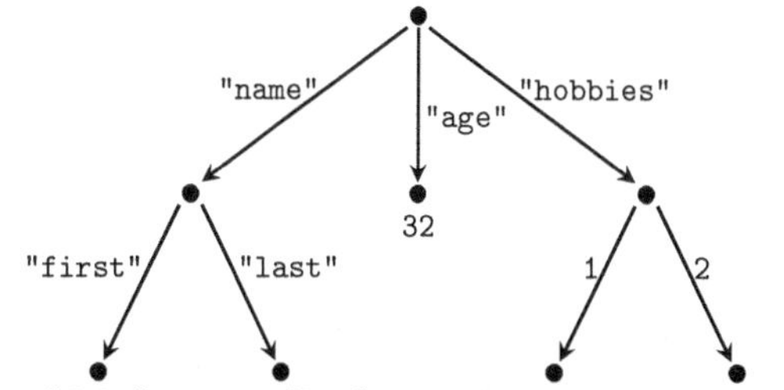

Having arrays defined in this way allows us still to treat the child edges of our tree as navigational axes: before we used a key such as "age" to traverse an edge, and now we use the number labelling the edge to traverse it and arrive at the child.

Formal definition. As our model is a tree, we will use tree domains as its base. A *tree domain* is a prefix-closed subset of $\mathbb{N}^*$. Without loss of generality we assume that for all tree domains D, if D contains a node $n \cdot i$, for $n \in \mathbb{N}^*$ then D contains all $n \cdot j$ with $0 \leqslant j < i$.

Let Σ be an alphabet. A **JSON tree** over Σ is a structure $J = (D, Obj, Arr, Str, Int, \mathcal{A}, \mathcal{O}, val)$, where D is a tree domain that is partitioned by *Obj*, *Arr*, *Str* and *Int*, $\mathcal{O} \subseteq Obj \times \Sigma^* \times D$ is the object-child relation, $\mathcal{A} \subseteq Arr \times \mathbb{N} \times D$ is the array-child relation, $val : Str \cup Int \rightarrow \Sigma^* \cup \mathbb{N}$ is the string and number *value* function, and where the following holds:

1 For each node $n \in Obj$ and child $n \cdot i$ of n, $\mathcal{O}$ contains one triple $(n, w, n \cdot i)$, for a word $w \in \Sigma^*$.

2 The first two components of $\mathcal{O}$ form a *key*: if $(n, w, n{\cdot}i)$ and $(n, w, n \cdot j)$ are in $\mathcal{O}$, then $i = j$.

3 For each node $n \in Arr$ and child $n \cdot i$ of n, $\mathcal{A}$ contains the triple $(n, i, n \cdot i)$.

4 If n is in *Str* or *Int* then D cannot contain nodes of form $n \cdot u$.

5 The value function assigns to each string node in *Str* a value in Σ^* and to each number node in *Int* a natural number,

The usage of a tree domain is standard, and we have elected to explicitly partition the domain into four types of nodes: *Obj* for objects, *Arr* for arrays, *Str* for strings and *Int* for integers. The first and second conditions specify that edges between objects and their children are labelled with words, but we can only use each label one time per each node. The third condition specifies that the edges between arrays and their children are labelled with the number representing the order of children. The fourth condition simply states that strings and numbers must be leaves in our trees, and the fifth condition describes the value function *val*. Note that we have explicitly distinguished the four type of JSON documents (objects, arrays, strings and integers). This is important when modelling schema definitions for JSON, as we shall show later.

Throughout this paper we will use the term JSON tree and JSON interchangeably; that is, when we are given a JSON document we will assume that it is represented as a JSON tree. As already mentioned above, one important feature of our model is that when looking at any node of the tree, a subtree rooted at this node is again a valid JSON. We can therefore define, for a JSON tree J and a node n in J, a function *json*(n) which returns the subtree of J rooted at n. Since this subtree is again a JSON tree, the value of *json*(n) is always a valid JSON.

3.2 JSON and XML

Before continuing we give a few remarks about differences and similarities between JSON and XML, and how are these reflected in their underlying data models. We start by summarising the differences between the two formats.

1. *JSON mixes ordered and unordered data.* JSON objects are completely without order, but for arrays we can do random access depending on their position. On the other hand, XML enforces a strict order between the children of each node. Coding JSON as XML would imply permitting sibling traversal for some nodes, but disallowing it for others. We can do that with XML with some ad-hoc rules, but this is precisely what we do in our model in a much cleaner way.
2. *JSON Arrays are neither lists nor sets.* As we have explained, we have random access, but we do not have the possibility of sibling traversal. Enforcing this in languages such as XPath is a very cumbersome task.
3. *JSON trees are deterministic.* The property of JSON tree which imposes that all keys of each object have to be distinct makes JSON trees deterministic in the sense that if we have the key name, there can be at most one node reachable through an edge labelled with this key. On the other hand, XML trees are nondeterministic since there are no labels on the edges, and a node can have multiple children. As we will see, the deterministic nature of JSON can make some problems more difficult than in the XML setting.
4. *Value is not just in the node, but is the entire subtree rooted at that node.* Another fundamental difference is that in XML when we talk about values we normally refer to the value of an attribute in a node. On the contrary, it is common for systems using JSON to allow comparisons of the full subtree of a node with a nested JSON document, or even comparing two nodes themselves in terms of their subtrees. To be fair, in XML one could also argue this to be true, but unlike in the case of XML, these "structural" comparisons are intrinsic in most JSON languages, as we discuss in the following sections.

On the other hand, it is certainly possible to code JSON documents using the XML data format. In fact, the model of ordered unranked trees with labels and attributes, which serves as the base of XML, was shown to be powerful enough to code some very expressive database formats, such as relational and even graph data. However, both models have enough differences to justify a study of JSON on its own. This is particularly evident when considering navigation through JSON documents, where keys in each object have to be unique, thus allowing us to obtain values very efficiently. On the other hand, coding JSON as XML would require us to have keys as node labels, thus forcing a scan of all of the node's children in order to retrieve the value.

4. NAVIGATIONAL QUERIES OVER JSON

As JSON navigation instructions are too basic to serve as a complete query language, most systems have developed different ways of querying JSON documents. Unfortunately, there is no standard, nor general guidelines, about how documents are accessed. As a result the syntax and operations between systems vary so much that it would be almost impossible to compare them. Hence, it would be desirable to identify a common core of functionalities shared between these systems, or at least a general picture of how such query languages look like. Therefore we begin this section by reviewing the most common operations available in current JSON systems.

Here we mainly focus on the subdocument selecting functionalities of JSON query languages. By subdocument selecting we mean functionalities that are capable of finding or highlighting specific parts within JSON documents, either to be returned immediately or to be combined as new JSON documents. As our work is not intended to be a survey, we have not reviewed all possible systems available to date. However, we take inspiration from MongoDB's query language (which arguably has served as a basis for many other systems as well, see e.g. [2, 26, 31]), and JSONPath [14]and SQL++ [24], two other query languages that have been proposed by the community.

Based on this, we propose a navigational logic that can serve as a common core to define a standard way of querying JSON. We then define several extensions of this logic, such as allowing nondeterminism or recursion, and study how these affect basic reasoning task such as evaluation and satisfiability.

4.1 Accessing documents in JSON databases

Here we briefly describe how JSON systems query documents.

Query languages inspired by FLWR or relational expressions. There are several proposals to construct query languages that can merge, join and even produce new JSON documents. Most of them are inspired either by XQuery (such as JSONiq [29]) or SQL (such as SQL++ [24]). These languages have of course a lot of intricate features, and to the best of our knowledge have not been formally studied. However, in terms of JSON navigation they all seem to support basic JSON navigation instructions and not much more.

MongoDB's find function. The basic querying mechanism of MongoDB is given by the *find* function [22], therefore we focus on this aspect of the system[2]. The find function receives two parameters, which are both JSON documents. Given a collection of JSON documents and these parameters, the find function then produces an array of JSON documents.

The first parameter of the find function serves as a *filter*, and its goal is to select some of the JSON documents from the input. The second parameter is the *projection*, and as its name suggests, is used to specify which parts of the filtered documents are to be returned. Since our goal is specifying a navigational logic, we will only focus on the filter parameter, and on queries that only specify the filter. We return to the projection in Section 6. For more details we refer the reader to the current version of the documentation [22].

The basic building block of filters are what we call *navigation condition*, which can be visualised as expressions of the form $P \sim J$, where P is a JSON navigation instruction, $\sim$ is a comparison operator (MongoDB allows all the usual $<, \leqslant, =, \geqslant, >$, and several others operators) and J is a JSON document.

Example 1. *Assume that we are dealing with a collection of JSON files containing information about people and that we want to obtain the one describing a person named Sue. In MongoDB this can be achieved using the following query* `db.collection.find({name: {$eq: "Sue"}},{})`. *The initial part* `db.collection` *is a system path to find the collection of JSON documents we want to query. Next,* `"name"` *is a simple navigation instruction used to retrieve the value under the key* `"name"`. *Last, the expression* `{$eq: "Sue"}` *is used to state that the JSON document retrieved by the navigation instruction is equal to the JSON* `"Sue"`. *Since we are not dealing with projection, the second parameter is simply the empty document* `{}`. *Using the notation above we could also write this navigation condition as* $J[name] =$`"Sue"`.

[2]For a detailed study of other functionalities MongoDB offers see e.g. [8]. Note that this work does not consider the find function though.

Finally, navigation conditions can be combined using boolean operations with the standard meaning. Also note that filters always return entire documents. If we want a part of a JSON file we need to use projection.

Query languages inspired by XPath or relational expressions. The languages we analysed thus far offer very simple navigational features. However, people also recognized the need to allow more complex properties such as nondetermnistic navigation, expression filters and allowing arbitrary depth nesting through recursion. As a result, an adaptation of the XML query language XPath to the context of JSON, called JSONPath [14] was introduced and implemented (see e.g. https://github.com/jayway/JsonPath).

Based on these features, we first introduce a logic capturing basic queries provided by navigation instructions and conditions, and then extend it with non-determinism and recursion resulting in a logic resembling similar approaches over XML.

4.2 Deterministic JSON logic

The first logic we introduce is meant to capture JSON navigation instructions and other deterministic forms of querying such as MongoDB's find function. We call this logic *JSON navigation logic*, or JNL for short. We believe that this logic, although not very powerful, is interesting in its own right, as it leads to very lightweight algorithms and implementations, which is one of the aims of the JSON data format.

As often done in XML [12] and graph data [20], we define ours in terms of unary and binary formulas.

Definition 1 (JSON navigational logic). *Unary formulas* φ, ψ *and binary formulas* α, β *of the* JSON navigational logic *are expressions satisfying the grammar*

$$\begin{aligned} \alpha, \beta \; &:= \; \langle \varphi \rangle \mid X_w \mid X_i \mid \alpha \circ \beta \mid \varepsilon \\ \varphi, \psi \; &:= \; \top \mid \neg \varphi \mid \varphi \wedge \psi \mid \varphi \vee \psi \mid [\alpha] \mid \\ & \qquad EQ(\alpha, A) \mid EQ(\alpha, \beta) \end{aligned}$$

where w *is a word in* Σ^*, i *is a natural number and* A *is an arbitrary JSON document.*

Intuitively, binary operators allow us to move through the document (they connect two nodes of a JSON tree), and unary formulas check whether a property is true at some point of our tree. For instance, X_w and X_i allow basic navigation by accessing the value of the key named w, or the ith element of an array respectively. They can subsequently be combined using composition or boolean operations to form more complex navigation expressions. Unary formulas serve as tests if some property holds at the part of the document we are currently reading. These also include the operator $[\alpha]$ allowing us to test if some binary condition is true starting at a current node (similarly, $\langle \varphi \rangle$ allows us to combine node tests with navigation). Finally, the comparison operators $EQ(\alpha, A)$ and $EQ(\alpha, \beta)$ simulate XPath style tests which check whether a current node can reach a node whose value is A, or if two paths can reach nodes with the same value. The difference with XML though, is that this value is again a JSON document and thus a subtree of the original tree.

The semantics of binary formulas is given by the relation $[\![\alpha]\!]_J$, for a binary formula α and a JSON J, and it selects pairs of nodes of J:

- $[\![\langle\varphi\rangle]\!]_J = \{(n, n) \mid n \in [\![\varphi]\!]_J\}$.
- $[\![X_w]\!]_J = \{(n, n') \mid (n, w, n') \in \mathcal{O}\}$.
- $[\![X_i]\!]_J = \{(n, n') \mid (n, i, n') \in \mathcal{A}\}$, for $i \in \mathbb{N}$.
- $[\![\alpha \circ \beta]\!]_J = [\![\alpha]\!]_J \circ [\![\beta]\!]_J$.
- $[\![\varepsilon]\!]_J = \{(n, n) \mid n$ is a node in $J\}$.

For the semantic of the unary operators, let us assume that D is the domain of J.

- $[\![\top]\!]_J = D$.
- $[\![\neg\varphi]\!]_J = D - [\![\varphi]\!]_J$.
- $[\![\varphi \wedge \psi]\!]_J = [\![\varphi]\!]_J \cap [\![\psi]\!]_J$.
- $[\![\varphi \vee \psi]\!]_J = [\![\varphi]\!]_J \cup [\![\psi]\!]_J$.
- $[\![[\alpha]]\!]_J = \{n \mid n \in D$ and there is a node n' in D such that $(n, n') \in [\![\alpha]\!]_J\}$
- $[\![EQ(\alpha, A)]\!]_J = \{n \mid n \in D$ and there is a node n_1 in D such that $(n, n_1) \in [\![\alpha]\!]_J$ and $json(n_1) = A\}$
- $[\![EQ(\alpha, \beta)]\!]_J = \{n \mid n \in D$ and there are nodes n_1, n_2 in D such that $(n, n_1) \in [\![\alpha]\!]_J$, $(n, n_2) \in [\![\beta]\!]_J$, and $json(n_1) = json(n_2)\}$.

Typically, most systems allow jumping to the last element of an array, or the j-th element counting from the last to the first. To simulate this we can allow binary expressions of the form X_i, for an integer $i < 0$, where -1 states the last position of the array, and $-j$ states the j-th position starting from the last to the first. Having this dual operator would not change any of our results, but we prefer to leave it out for the sake of readability.

Algorithmic properties of JNL. As promised, here we show that JNL is a logic particularly well behaved for database applications. For this we study the evaluation problem and satisfiability problem associated with JNL. The EVALUATION problem asks, on input a JSON J, a JNL unary expression φ and a node n of J, whether n is in $[\![\varphi]\!]_J$. The SATISFIABILITY problem asks, on input a JNL expression φ, whether there exists a JSON J such that $[\![\varphi]\!]_J$ is nonempty. We start with evaluation, showing that JNL indeed matches the "lightweight" spirit of the JSON format and can be evaluated very efficiently:

PROPOSITION 1. *The* EVALUATION *problem for JNL can be solved in time* $O(|J| \cdot |\varphi|)$.

For this result, we can reuse techniques for XPath evaluation (see e.g. [27, 15]). However, the presence of the $EQ(\alpha, \beta)$ operator forces us to refine these techniques in a non-trivial way. A straightforward way of incorporating this predicate into XPath algorithms is to pre-process all pairs of nodes to see which pairs have equal subtrees, but this only gives us a quadratic algorithm. Instead, we transform our JNL formula into an equivalent non recursive monadic datalog program with stratified negation [16], and show how to evaluate the latter by doing equality comparisons "online" as they appear.

Next, we move to satisfiability, showing that the complexity of the problem is optimal, considering that JNL can emulate propositional formulas.

PROPOSITION 2. *The* SATISFIABILITY *problem for JNL is* NP*-complete. It is* NP*-hard even for formulas neither using negation nor the equality operator.*

It might be somewhat surprising that the positive fragment without data comparisons is not trivially satisfiable. This holds due to the fact that each key in an object is unique, so a formula of the form $[X_a \circ \langle [X_1] \rangle] \wedge [X_a \circ \langle [X_b] \rangle]$ is unsatisfiable because it forces the value of the key a to be both an array and a string at the same time.

4.3 Extensions

Although the base proposal for JNL captures the deterministic spirit of JSON, it is somewhat limited in expressive power. Here we propose two natural extensions: the ability to non-deterministically select which child of a node is selected, and the ability to traverse paths of arbitrary length.

Non-determinism. The path operators X_w and X_i can be easily extended such that they return more than a single child; namely, we can permit matching of regular expressions and intervals, instead of simple words and array positions.

Formally, non-deterministic JSON logic extends binary formulas of JNL by the following grammar:

$$\alpha, \beta \;:=\; \langle\varphi\rangle \mid X_e \mid X_{i:j} \mid \alpha \circ \beta \mid \varepsilon$$

where e is a subset of Σ^* (given as a regular expression), and $i \leqslant j$ are natural numbers, or $j = +\infty$ (signifying that we want any element of the array following i). The semantics of the new path operators is as follows:

- $[\![X_e]\!]_J = \{(n, n') \mid$ there is $w \in L(e)$ such that $(n, w, n') \in \mathcal{O}\}$.
- $[\![X_{i:j}]\!]_J = \{(n, n') \mid$ there is $i \leqslant p \leqslant j$ such that the triple (n, p, n') is in $\mathcal{A}\}$.

Recursion. In order to allow exploring paths of arbitrary length we add the Kleene star to our logic. That is, recursive JNL allows $(\alpha)^*$ as a binary formula (as usual we normally omit the brackets when the precedence of operators is clear). The semantics of $(\alpha)^*$ is given by

$$[\![(\alpha)^*]\!] = [\![\varepsilon]\!]_J \cup [\![\alpha]\!]_J \cup [\![\alpha \circ \alpha]\!] \cup [\![\alpha \circ \alpha \circ \alpha]\!]_J \cup \ldots.$$

So what happens to the evaluation and satisfiability when we extend this logic? For the case of evaluation, we can easily show that the linear algorithm is retained as long as we do not have the binary equality operator $EQ(\alpha, \beta)$. Indeed, in this case, the evaluation can be done using the classical PDL model checking algorithm [1, 10] with small extensions which account for the specifics of the JSON format. However, we are not able to extend the linear algorithm for the full case, because an expression of the form $EQ(\alpha, \beta)$ might require checking all pairs of nodes in our tree for equality, resulting in a jump in complexity.

PROPOSITION 3. *The evaluation problem for JNL with non-determinism and recursion can be solved in time $O(|J|^3 \cdot |\varphi|)$, and in time $O(|J| \cdot |\varphi|)$ if the formula does not use the predicate $EQ(\alpha, \beta)$.*

For satisfiability the situation is radically different, as the combination of recursion, non-determinism and the binary equalities ends up being too difficult to handle.

PROPOSITION 4. *The* SATISFIABILITY *problem is undecidable for non-deterministic recursive JNL formulas, even if they do not use negation.*

However, if we rule out the equality operator we can show much better bounds. For the full non-deterministic, recursive JNL (without equalities) the satisfiability problem is the same as other similar fragments such as PDL. For (non-recursive) non-deterministic JNL the problem is slightly easier.

PROPOSITION 5. *The* SATISFIABILITY *problem is:*

- PSPACE-*complete for non-deterministic, non-recursive JNL without the $EQ(\alpha, \beta)$ operator.*
- EXPTIME-*complete for non-deterministic, recursive JNL without the $EQ(\alpha, \beta)$ operator.*

Note that PSPACE-hardness for satisfiability follows easily from the fact that we now allow regular expressions in our edges: Given a regular expression e, we have that the e is universal if and only if the query $[X_{\Sigma*}] \wedge \neg[X_e]$ is not satisfiable. However, in the proof of this proposition we in fact show that the problem remains PSPACE-hard even when the only regular expression which is not a word in a X_e axis is Σ^*. One can also show that PSPACE-hardness remains when one only considers JSON documents without object values.

5. SCHEMA DEFINITIONS FOR JSON

Having dealt with navigational primitives for querying JSON, our next task is to analyse JSON Schema definitions. We focus solely on the JSON Schema specification [17], which is, up to our best knowledge, the only attempt to define a general schema language for JSON documents. The JSON Schema specification is currently in its fourth draft, and on its way of becoming an IETF standard.

5.1 JSON Schema

As before, we first briefly present how JSON Schema works. We remark again that our intention is not to provide a full analysis for the specification, but rather show how the navigation works, with the aim of obtaining a logic that can capture JSON Schema. We thus concentrate on a core fragment that is equivalent to the full specification; we refer to [28] for more details and a full formalisation of this core.

Every JSON schema is JSON document itself. JSON Schema can specify that a document must be any of the different types of values (objects, arrays, strings or numbers); and for each of these types there are several keywords that help shaping and restricting the set of documents that a schema specifies. The most important keyword is the "type" keyword, as it determines the type of a value that has to be validated against the schema: a document of the form {`"type":"string"`, ...} specifies string values, {`"type":"number"`, ...} specifies number values, {`"type":"object"`, ...} specifies objects and {`"type":"array"`, ...} specifies arrays. In addition to the type keyword, each schema includes a number of other pairs that shape the documents they describe.

We now describe each of the four types of basic schemas. Table 1 contains a list of all keywords available for each of these schemas.

String schemas. String schemas are those featuring the `"type":"string"` pair. Additionally, they may include the pair `"pattern"`:"*regexp*", for *regexp* a regular expression over Σ, which validates only against those strings that belong to the language of this expression. For example, {`"type":"string"`} and {`"type":"string"`,`"pattern"`:"$(01)^+$"} are string schemas. The first schema validates against any string, and the second only against strings built from 0 or 1.

Number schemas. For numbers, we can use the pair `"minimum"`:i to specify that the number is at least i, `"maximum"`:i to specify that the number is at most i, and `"multipleOf"`:i to specify that a number must be a multiple of i. Thus for example {`"type":"number"`,`"maximum"`:12,`"multipleOf"`:4} describes numbers 0, 4, 8 and 12.

Object schemas. Besides the `"type":"object"` pair, object schemas may additionally have the following:

- Pairs `"minProperties":i` and `"maxProperties":j`, to specify that an object has to have at least i and/or at most j key-value pairs.

- a pair `"required"`:$[k_1, \ldots, k_n]$, where each k_i is a string value. This keyword mandates that the specified object values must contain pairs with keys $k_1, \ldots, k_n$.

- a pair `"properties"`:$\{k_1 : J_1, \ldots, k_m : J_m\}$, where each k_i is a string value and each J_i is itself a JSON Schema. This keyword states that the value of each pair with key k_i must validate against schema J_i.

- A pair `"patternProperties"`:{"e_1":$J_1, \ldots,$ "e_ℓ":J_ℓ}, where each e_i is a regular expression over Σ and each J_i is a JSON schema. This keyword works just like `properties`, but now any value under any key that conforms to the expression exp_i must satisfy J_i.

- finally, the pair `"additionalProperties"`:J, where J is a JSON schema. This keyword presents a schema that must be satisfied by all values whose keys do not appear neither in `properties` nor conform to the language of an expression in `patternProperties`. For example, the schema in the Figure 2 below specifies objects where the value under "name" must be a string, the value under any key of the form `a(b|c)a` must be an even number, and the value under any key which is neither "name" nor conforms to the expression above must always be the number 1.

Keywords for string schemas:	
- "type":"string"	- "pattern": exp

Keywords for number schemas:	
- "type":"number"	-"multipleOf": i
- "minimum": i	- "maximum": i

Keywords for array schemas:
- "items":$[J_1, \ldots, J_n]$
- "uniqueItems":true
- "additionalItems":J

Keywords for object schemas:	
- "type":"object"	- "required": $[k_1, \ldots, k_n]$
- "minProperties": i	- "maxProperties": i
- "properties":$\{k_1 : J_1, \ldots, k_m : J_m\}$	
- "patternProperties":$\{$"e_1":$J_1, \ldots,$ "e_ℓ":$J_\ell\}$	
- "additionalProperties": J	

Boolean combination and comparisons:	
- "anyOf": $[J_1, \ldots, J_n]$	- "allOf": $[J_1, \ldots, J_m]$
- "not": J	- "enum": $[A_1, \ldots, A_n]$

Table 1: The form for all keyords in JSON schema. Here i is always a natural number, J and each J_i are JSON schemas, $A_1, \ldots, A_n$ are JSON documents, each k_i is a string value (k stand for key); and exp and each exp_i are regular expressions over the alphabet Σ of strings.

```
{
   "type": "object",
   "properties": {
      "name": {"type":"string"},
      },
   "patternProperties: {
      "a(b|c)a": {"type":"number", "multipleOf": 2}
      },
   "additionalProperties: {
      "type": "number",
      "minimum": 1
      "maximum": 1
   }
}
```

Figure 2: Example of an object schema.

Array schemas. Array schemas are specified with the "type": "array" keyword. For arrays there are two ways of specifying what kind of documents we find in arrays. We can use a pair "items":$[J_1, \ldots, J_n]$ to specify a document with an array of n elements, where each i-th element must satisfy schema J_i. We can also use "additionalItems":J to specify that all elements in the array must satisfy schema J. If both keywords are used together, then we allow the array to have more values than those specified with items, as long as they agree with the schema specified in additionalItems. Finally, one can include the pair "uniqueItems":true to force arrays whose elements are all distinct from each other. For example, the following schema validates against arrays of at least 2 elements, where the first two are strings and the remaining ones, if they exists, are numbers.

```
{
   "type": "array",
   "items": [{"type":"string"}, {"type":"string"}],
   "additionalItems": {"type":"number"},
   "uniqueItems":true
}
```

Boolean combinations. The last feature in JSON Schema are boolean combinations. These allow us to specify that a document must validate against two schemas, against at least one schema, or that it must not validate against a schema. For example, the schema "not":{"type":"number","multipleOf":2} validates against any odd number, or any document which is not a number.

5.2 JSON Schema Logic

In order to capture the JSON Schema specification with a logical formalism, we isolate navigation and atomic tests into two different sets of operators. Let us start with atomic operations, which are basically a rewriting of most JSON Schema keywords into our framework. We allocate them in the set *NodeTests*.

Formally, *NodeTests* contains the predicates *Arr*, *Obj*, *Str*, *Int* and *Unique*, plus a predicate *Pattern*(e) for each regular expression e built from Σ, predicates *Min*(i) and *Max*(i) for each integer i, a predicate *MultOf*(i) for each $i \geqslant 0$, predicates *MinCh*(k) and *MaxCh*(k) for each $k \geqslant 0$ and a predicate $\sim(A)$ for each JSON document A. The semantics of these predicates is given by the relation $\models$, that states whether an atomic predicate holds for a given node n of a JSON J.

- $(J, n) \models Arr$ iff. $n \in Arr$. - $(J, n) \models Obj$ iff. $n \in Obj$.
- $(J, n) \models Str$ iff. $n \in Str$. - $(J, n) \models Int$ iff. $n \in Int$.
- $(J, n) \models Pattern(e)$ iff. $val(n)$ is a string in $L(e)$.
- $(J, n) \models Min(i)$ iff. $val(n)$ is a number greater than i.
- $(J, n) \models Max(i)$ iff. $val(n)$ is a number smaller than i.
- $(J, n) \models MultOf(i)$ iff. $val(n)$ is a multiple of i.
- $(J, n) \models MinCh(i)$ iff. n has at least i children.
- $(J, n) \models MaxCh(i)$ iff. n has at most i children.
- $(J, n) \models Unique$ iff. $n \in Arr$ and all of its children are different JSON values: for each $n' \neq n''$ such that (n, p, n') and (n, q, n'') belong to $\mathcal{A}$ we have that $json(n') \neq json(n'')$.
- $(J, n) \models \sim(A)$ iff. $json(n) = A$.

With *NodeTests* we cover all atomic features of JSON Schema. All that remains is the navigation, which in JSON Schema is given by the keywords properties, patternProperties, additionalProperties and required, for objects, and items and additionalItems for arrays. These forms of navigation suggest using existential and universal modalities. For instance, the keyword patternProperties specifies a schema that must be validated by *all* values whose keys satisfy a regular expression, and "required": $[w]$ demands that there must *exist* a children with key w. Thus, to fully define our logic, we augment our node tests with universal and existential modalities, as well as boolean combinations.

Definition 2. *Formulas in the* JSON schema logic *(JSL) are expressions satisfying the grammar*

$$\varphi, \psi \ := \ \top \mid \neg\varphi \mid \varphi \wedge \psi \mid \varphi \vee \psi \mid \psi \in \textit{NodeTests} \mid \Box_e \varphi \mid \Box_{i:j} \varphi \mid \Diamond_e \varphi \mid \Diamond_{i:j} \varphi$$

where e is a subset of Σ^* *(given as a regular expression),* $i \leqslant j$ *are natural numbers, or* $j = +\infty$ *(signifying that we want any element of the array following i).*

As with JSON navigational logic, we can also obtain a deterministic version of JSL by restricting the syntax to use only modal operators $\Box_w$ and $\Box_i$, and $\Diamond_w$ and $\Diamond_i$; for a word $w \in \Sigma^*$ and a natural number i.

The semantics is given by extending the relation $\models$.

- $(J, n) \models \top$ for every node n in J.
- $(J, n) \models \neg\varphi$ iff. $(J, n) \not\models \varphi$.
- $(J, n) \models \varphi \wedge \psi$ iff. $(J, n) \models \varphi$ and $(J, n) \models \psi$.
- $(J, n) \models \varphi \vee \psi$ iff. either $(J, n) \models \varphi$ or $(J, n) \models \psi$.
- $(J, n) \models \Diamond_e \varphi$ iff. there is a word $w \in L(e)$ and a node n' in J such that $(n, w, n') \in \mathcal{O}$ and $(J, n') \models \varphi$
- $(J, n) \models \Diamond_{i:j} \varphi$ iff. there is $i \leqslant p \leqslant j$ and a node n' in J such that $(n, p, n') \in \mathcal{A}$ and $(J, n') \models \varphi$
- $(J, n) \models \Box_e \varphi$ iff. $(J, n') \models \varphi$ for all nodes n' such that $(n, w, n') \in \mathcal{O}$ for some $w \in L(e)$.
- $(J, n) \models \Box_{i:j} \varphi$ iff. $(J, n') \models \varphi$ for all nodes n' such that $(n, p, n') \in \mathcal{A}$ for some $i \leqslant p \leqslant j$.

In order to present our results regarding JSL and JSON Schema, we abuse notation and write $J \models \psi$ whenever $(J, r) \models \psi$, where r is the root of J.

Expressive power. As promised we show that JSL can capture JSON schema. In order to present this result we informally speak of the validation relation of JSON Schema, and say that a JSON S validates against J whenever J is in accordance to all keywords present in S. We refer to [28] for more details on the semantics. As usual, we say that JSON Schema and JSL are equivalent in expressive power if for any JSON Schema S there exists a *JSL* formula ψ_S such that for every JSON document J we have that J validates against S if and only if $J \models \psi_S$; and conversely, for any JSL formula φ there exists a JSON Schema S_φ such that for every JSON document J we have that $J \models \varphi$ if and only if J validates against S_φ.

Theorem 1. *JSL and JSON Schema are equivalent in expressive power.*

Comparing JSL and JNL. Next, we consider how the navigation logic of Section 4 compares to the schema logic JSL. Even though the starting point of the two logics is different, we next show that the two logics are essentially the same, their expressivity differing simply because of the different atomic predicates. More precisely, we have:

Theorem 2. *Non-deterministic JNL not using the equality* $EQ(\alpha, \beta)$ *and non-deterministic JSL using only the node test* $\sim (A)$ *are equivalent in terms of expressive power. More precisely:*

- *For every formula* φ^S *in JSL there exists a unary formula* φ^N *in JNL such that for every JSON J:*

$$[\![\varphi^N]\!]_J = \{n \in J \mid (J, n) \models \varphi^S\}.$$

- *For every unary formula* φ^N *in JNL there exists a* φ^S *in JSL such that for every JSON J:*

$$[\![\varphi^N]\!]_J = \{n \in J \mid (J, n) \models \varphi^S\}.$$

In the proof above, we also show that going from JSL to JNL takes only polynomial time, while the transition in the other direction can be exponential. This implies that the upper bounds for JNL are valid for JSL, while the lower bounds transfer in the opposite direction (without taking into account node tests).

Algorithmic Properties. Since JSL is designed to be a schema logic to validate trees, we specify a boolean Evaluation problem: the input is a JSON J and a JSL expression φ, and we decide whether $J \models \varphi$.

Proposition 6. *The* Evaluation *problem for JSL can be solved in time* $O(|J|^2 \cdot |\varphi|)$, *and in* $O(|J| \cdot |\varphi|)$ *when* φ *does not use the Unique predicate.*

From Theorem 1 we obtain as a corollary that the validation problem for JSON Schema has the same bounds. This was already shown in [28]. Next, we study the Satisfiability problem, which receives a formula φ as input and consists of deciding whether there is any JSON tree J such that $J \models \varphi$. Here we need to be careful with the encoding we choose, as the interplay between *Unique* and $\Diamond_i \top$ immediately forces a node with exponentially many different children when i is given in binary. In terms of results, this means that our algorithms raise by one exponential, although we do not know if this increase is actually unavoidable.

Proposition 7. *The* Satisfiability *problem for JSL is in* Expspace, *and* Pspace*-complete for expressions without Unique.*

We remark that the Satisfiability problem is important in the context of JSON Schema. For example, the community has repeatedly stated the need for algorithms that can learn JSON Schemas from examples. We believe that understanding basic tasks such as satisfiability are the first steps to proceed in this direction.

5.3 Adding recursion

The JSON Schema specification also allows defining statements that will be reused later on. We have so far ignored this functionality, and to capture it we will need to define the same operator in our logic. As we will see, this lifts the expressive power of JSL away from even the recursive version of our navigational logic; and is very similar to certain forms of tree automata.

Let us explain first how recursion is added into JSON Schema. The idea is to allow to an additional keyword, of the form `{$ref: <path>}`, where `<path>` is a navigation instruction. This instruction is used within the same document to fetch other schemas that have been predefined in a reserved `definitions` section[3]. For example, the following schema validates against any JSON which is not a string following the specified pattern.

[3]Definitions and references can also be used to fetch schemas in different documents or even domains; here we just focus on the recursive functionality.

```
{
    "definitions": {
        "email": {
            "type": "string",
            "pattern": "[A-z]*@ciws.cl"
        }
    },
    "not": {"$ref": "#/definitions/email"}
}
```

As we have mentioned, different schemas are defined under the **definitions** section of the JSON document, and these definitions can be reused using the **$ref** keyword. In the example above, we use `{"$ref": "#/definitions/email"}` to retrieve the schema `{"type": "string", "pattern": "[A-z]*@ciws.cl"}`. These definitions can be nested within each other, but semantics is currently defined only for a fragment with limited recursion. We come back to this issue after we define a logic capturing these schemas.

Recursive JSL. The idea of this logic is to capture the recursive functionalities present in JSON Schema: there is a special section where one can define new formulas, which can be then re-used in other formulas.

Fix an infinite set $\Gamma = \{\gamma_1, \gamma_2, \gamma_3, \dots\}$ of symbols. A *recursive* JSL formula is an expression of the form

$$\begin{array}{rcl} \gamma_1 & = & \varphi_1 \\ \gamma_2 & = & \varphi_2 \\ & \vdots & \\ \gamma_m & = & \varphi_m \\ \psi & & \end{array} \qquad (1)$$

where each γ_i is a symbol in Γ and φ_i, ψ are JSL formulas over the extended syntax that allows $\gamma_1, \dots, \gamma_m$ as atomic predicates. Here each equality $\gamma_i = \varphi_i$ is called a definition, and ψ is called the base expression.

The intuition is that each γ_i is one of the references of JSON Schema. Before moving to the semantics, let us show the way recursive JSL formulas work.

EXAMPLE 2. *Consider the expression Δ given by*

$$\begin{array}{l} \gamma_1 = \Box_{\Sigma^*}\gamma_2 \\ \gamma_2 = (\Diamond_{\Sigma^*}\top) \wedge (\Box_{\Sigma^*}\gamma_1) \\ \gamma_1 \end{array}$$

Intuitively, γ_1 holds in a node n if n either has no children, or if γ_2 holds all of its children. On the other hand, γ_2 holds in a node n if this node has at least one child, and γ_1 holds in all children of n. Finally, the base expression simply states that γ_1 has to hold in the root of the document (recall that a schema statement is evaluated at the root). The intuition for Δ is, then, that it should hold on every tree such that each path from the root to the leaves is of even length.

Well-formed recursive JSL. As usual in formalisms that mix recursion and negation, giving a formal semantics for JSON Schema is not a straightforward task. As an example of the problems we face, consider the following JSL expression.

$$\begin{array}{l} \gamma_1 = \neg\gamma_1 \\ \gamma_1 \end{array}$$

Of course, we can always give a logical interpretation to this formula, but we argue that this expression does not specify any real restriction on JSON documents, and thus any semantics we establish will not be intuitive from the point of view of defining schemas for JSON.

The most straightforward way to avoid these issues is by imposing a strict acyclicity condition on definitions. However, we can in fact work with a much milder restriction that we call *well-formedness*. This restriction was introduced in [28] for the case of JSON Schema, but we can seemingly define well-formed recursive JSL expressions, which can then be shown to capture well-formed recursive JSON Schemas.

For a recursive JSL expression Δ of the form (1) defined above, we define the precedence graph of Δ as a graph whose nodes are $\gamma_1, \dots, \gamma_m$ and where there is an edge from γ_i to γ_j if γ_j appears in the expression φ_i of the definition $\gamma_i = \varphi_i$, but only if this appearance is *not under the scope of a modal operator*. We then say that Δ is *well-formed* if its precedence graph is acyclic.

EXAMPLE 3. *The definition $\gamma_1 = \neg\gamma_1$ clearly creates a cyclic precedence graph, as the construction mandates a self-loop in the node corresponding to γ_1. On the other hand, the recursive JSL expression in Example 2 is indeed well-formed. It does introduce cycles in the definitions, but no edges are added into the precedence graph of such expression because formula symbols are always under the scope of a modal operator.*

Semantics. How do we then define the semantics of well-formed expressions? If Δ is a recursive JSL expression that is completely acyclic, then we can simply replace the symbols in Γ by their respective definitions. But we cannot do this with every well-formed expression, because some of them can have cycles in the definitions (under a scope of a modal operator), and thus we would never stop replacing symbols. This is the case, for instance, in Example 2.

However, the key thing to notice is that we only need to do this as many times as the height of the JSON tree we are trying to validate. More precisely, let J be a JSON tree of height h and Δ a well-formed recursive JSL expression of the form (1). Construct a (non-recursive) JSL expression $unfold_J(\psi)$ by replacing each symbol γ_i in ψ by the corresponding definition φ_i, but stop once every symbol from Γ is under the scope of at least $h+1$ modal operators. Afterwards, replace all the remaining symbols γ_i for the symbol $\bot$ (shorthand for $\neg\top$). If Δ is well-formed, then this procedure is guaranteed to stop, because every time we come back to the same symbol γ when replacing, we know that this symbol has to be under the scope of at least one more modal operator. Then, we define the satisfaction relation based on the satisfaction of the constructed formula ψ, so that $J \models \Delta$ if and only if $J \models unfold_J(\psi)$.

EXAMPLE 4. *Suppose that we need to evaluate the expression in Example 2 over the tree J of height 4. Then we would only need to keep rewriting ψ until all of γ_1 and γ_2 are under at least 5 modal operators. The query obtained corresponds to*

$$\Box_{\Sigma^*}(\Diamond_{\Sigma^*}\top \wedge \Box_{\Sigma^*}\Box_{\Sigma^*}(\Diamond_{\Sigma^*}\top \wedge \Box_{\Sigma^*}\Box_{\Sigma^*}\gamma_2))$$

To finalise we create the formula $unfold_J(\gamma_1)$ by replacing the symbol γ_2 in the expression above for $\bot$. Now the evaluation of the original expression over J corresponds to the evaluation of $unfold_J(\gamma_1)$ over J.

Expressive Power. As promised, one can show that recursive JSL captures the recursive definition of JSON Schema. We use the same notation as for Theorem 1.

THEOREM 3. *Well-formed recursive JSL and well-formed recursive JSON Schema are equivalent in expressive power.*

Comparing JSL to navigational logic JNL, we can again show that different atomic predicates force them to have different expressive power: for instance JSL can not express the $EQ(\alpha, \beta)$ operator, while JNL can not cover unique items. On the other hand, if $EQ(\alpha, \beta)$ is not allowed, then we conjecture recursive non-deterministic JNL to be strictly less expressive than recursive JSL without unique items, due to the more powerful form of recursion available in the language.

We finish with a few remarks on the expressive power of recursive JSL expressions. First, let us note that, even if one would like to compare recursive JSL or JSON Schema against XML Schema definitions such as DTDs or XML Schema, or even to Monadic Second Order (MSO), we cannot do it in a direct way since the models of XML and JSON have several important differences, and it is not immediate to express JSON as a relational structure. However, just for the sake of establishing a comparison we can assume that the set Σ^* of possible keys is fixed and finite, and that we do not consider arrays. We can then just focus on a relational representation of JSON that has one binary relation $\mathcal{O}_w$ for each word w in our set of keys, plus all predicates specified in *NodeTests*. We can then show the following (as usual MSO is said be equivalent to JSL if for every JSL expression we can create a boolean MSO formula accepting the same trees, and vice-versa):

PROPOSITION 8. *Well-formed recursive JSL is equivalent to MSO, if the set Σ^* of possible keys is fixed and finite, and if we do not consider arrays.*

What about arrays? The first observation is that the presence of arrays introduces the atomic test *Unique*, which can express properties not definable in MSO:

EXAMPLE 5. *The following recursive JSL expression accepts only JSON documents representing complete binary trees:*

$$\gamma = \neg(\Diamond_1 \top) \vee (\mathit{MinCh}(2) \wedge \mathit{MaxCh}(2) \wedge \neg\, \mathit{Unique} \wedge \Box_{1:2}\gamma)$$

$$\gamma$$

Every node is an array with either no child or with two children both satisfying γ, and the $\neg$ Unique restriction forces the two children of each node to be equal.

Even if we rule out *Unique*, it is still not easy to exactly pinpoint what JSL can do. On one hand, JSON arrays are ordered, in the sense that the first item can be distinguished from the second. But on the other hand the reasoning between elements in arrays in JSON is very limited. For example, we cannot use JSL to specify that after an element satisfying a formula φ we must have an element satisfying another formula ψ.

Evaluation. The first thing to note is that the semantics for recursive JSL, as defined previously, leads to very inefficient evaluation algorithms: the rewriting $\mathit{unfold}_J(\psi)$ may well be of exponential size with respect to the original query, even if J contains a single node. However, we can show that evaluating recursive JSL expressions remains in PTIME in combined complexity, although the succinctness introduced by the possibility of reusing definitions makes the problem PTIME-hard. Our algorithm consists on evaluating all subtrees of J in a bottom-up fashion, proceeding to higher height levels of J only when all the previous levels have already been computed. The algorithm resembles the evaluation of Datalog programs with stratified negation.

PROPOSITION 9. *The* EVALUATION *problem for recursive JSL expressions over JSON trees is* PTIME*-complete in combined complexity.*

Satisfiability. The most common way of building a satisfiability algorithm in schema formalisms for trees is to show that they are equivalent to some class of tree automata whose non-emptiness problem can be shown to be decidable. We use the same ideas, albeit we need to introduce a specific model of automata that can capture our formalism. Interestingly, we show that the *Unique* predicate can also be handled in this case, albeit with an exponential blowup. To show this we encode *Unique* as a special local constraint, as done in e.g. [4, 19]. Again, we do not know if this blowup is unavoidable.

PROPOSITION 10. *The* SATISFIABILITY *problem for recursive JSL expressions is in* 2EXPTIME*, and* EXPTIME*-complete for expressions without the Unique predicate.*

6. FUTURE PERSPECTIVES

In this work we present a first attempt to formally study the JSON data format. To this end, we describe the underlying data model for JSON, and introduce logical formalisms which capture the way JSON data is accessed and controlled in practice. Through our results we emphasise how the new features present in JSON, affect classical results known from the XML context, and highlight that there is a need for developing new techniques to tackle main static tasks for JSON languages. And while some of these features have been consider in the past (e.g. comparing subtrees [5, 33], or an infinite number of keys [6]), it is still not entirely clear how these properties mix with the deterministic structure of JSON trees, thus providing an interesting ground for future work.

Apart from these fundamental problems that need to be tackled, there is also a series of practical aspects of JSON that we did not consider. In particular, we identify three areas that we believe warrant further study, and where the formal framework we propose could be of use in understanding the underlying problems.

MongoDB's projection. While we have presented a navigational logic that can capture the way MongoDB filters JSON documents within its find function, we have left out the second argument of the find function, known as projection. In its essence, the idea of the projection argument is to select only those subtrees of input documents that can be reached by certain navigation instructions, thus defining a JSON to JSON transformation. Although well-defined, the projection in MongoDB is quite limited in expressive power, and does not allow a lot of interaction between filtering and projecting. We believe that this is an interesting ground for future work, as there are many fundamental questions regarding the expressive power of these transformations, and their possible interactions with schema definitions.

Streaming. Another important line of future work is streaming. Indeed, the widespread use of JSON as a means of communicating information through the Web demands the usage of streaming techniques to query JSON documents or validate document against schemas. Streaming applications most surely will be related to APIs, either to be able to query data fetched from an API without resorting to store the data (for example if we are in a mobile environment) or to validate JSONs on-the-fly before they are received by APIs. In contrast with XML (see, e.g., [30], we suspect that our deterministic versions of both JNL and JSL might actually be shown to be evaluated in a streaming context with constant memory requirements when tree equality is excluded from the language.

Documenting APIs. One of the main uses of JSON Schema is the *Open API initiative* [25], an endeavour founded in early 2016 that intends to build an open documentation of RESTful APIs available worldwide. This initiative uses JSON Schema to specify the inputs and the outputs of a large number of APIs, and is trying to describe which parts of the API output actually come from the input. A formal perspective in these tasks will certainly be well appreciated by the community. Furthermore, there is also the problem of documenting how JSON APIs interact with real databases. For example, when large organisations expose data they sometimes use APIs instead of proper database views, even if it is for internal uses. This immediately raises the problem of exchanging data that may now not reside on real databases, but is exposed only by means of JSON. We believe these problems raise interesting questions for future work.

Acknowledgements

We would like to thank the anonymous reviewers for many helpful comments. Reutter, Suárez and Vrgoč were funded by the Millennium Nucleus Center for Semantic Web Research under Grant NC120004. Bourhis and Vrgoč were partially funded by the STIC AMSUD project Foundations of Graph Structured Data (Fog). Bourhis was partially funded by the DeLTA project (ANR-16-CE40-0007).

7. REFERENCES

[1] N. Alechina and N. Immerman. Reachability logic: An efficient fragment of transitive closure logic. *Logic Journal of the IGPL*, 8(3):325–337, 2000.

[2] AranbgoDB Inc. The ArangoDB database. https://www.arangodb.com/, 2016.

[3] Pablo Barceló, Jorge Pérez, and Juan L. Reutter. Relative expressiveness of nested regular expressions. In *Proceedings of the 6th Alberto Mendelzon International Workshop on Foundations of Data Management, Ouro Preto, Brazil, June 27-30, 2012*, pages 180–195, 2012.

[4] Bruno Bogaert and Sophie Tison. Equality and disequality constraints on direct subterms in tree automata. In *Annual Symposium on Theoretical Aspects of Computer Science*, pages 159–171. Springer, 1992.

[5] Bruno Bogaert and Sophie Tison. Equality and disequality constraints on direct subterms in tree automata. In *STACS 92, 9th Annual Symposium on Theoretical Aspects of Computer Science, Cachan, France, February 13-15, 1992, Proceedings*, pages 161–171, 1992.

[6] Adrien Boiret, Vincent Hugot, Joachim Niehren, and Ralf Treinen. Deterministic automata for unordered trees. In *Proceedings Fifth International Symposium on Games, Automata, Logics and Formal Verification, GandALF 2014, Verona, Italy, September 10-12, 2014.*, pages 189–202, 2014.

[7] Mikoaj Bojańczyk, Anca Muscholl, Thomas Schwentick, and Luc Segoufin. Two-variable logic on data trees and xml reasoning. *Journal of the ACM (JACM)*, 56(3):13, 2009.

[8] Elena Botoeva, Diego Calvanese, Benjamin Cogrel, Martin Rezk, and Guohui Xiao. A formal presentation of mongodb (extended version). *CoRR*, abs/1603.09291, 2016.

[9] Tim Bray. The JavaScript Object Notation (JSON) Data Interchange Format. 2014.

[10] R. Cleaveland and B. Steffen. A linear-time model-checking algorithm for the alternation-free modal mu-calculus. *Formal Methods in System Design*, 2(2):121–147, 1993.

[11] ECMA. The JSON Data Interchange Format. http://www.ecma-international.org/publications/standards/Ecma-404.htm, 2013.

[12] Diego Figueira. *Reasoning on words and trees with data. (Raisonnement sur mots et arbres avec données)*. PhD thesis, École normale supérieure de Cachan, France, 2010.

[13] Python Software Foundation. Python programming language. https://www.python.org/, 2016.

[14] Stefan Gössner and Stephen Frank. JSONPath. http://goessner.net/articles/JsonPath/, 2007.

[15] Georg Gottlob, Christoph Koch, and Reinhard Pichler. Efficient algorithms for processing xpath queries. *ACM Trans. Database Syst.*, 30(2):444–491, 2005.

[16] Georg Gottlob, Christoph Koch, and Klaus U. Schulz. Conjunctive queries over trees. *J. ACM*, 53(2):238–272, March 2006.

[17] Internet Engineering Task Force (IETF). The JavaScript Object Notation (JSON) Data Interchange Format. https://tools.ietf.org/html/rfc7159, March 2014.

[18] json-schema.org: The home of json schema. http://json-schema.org/.

[19] Wong Karianto and Christof Löding. Unranked tree automata with sibling equalities and disequalities. In *International Colloquium on Automata, Languages, and Programming*, pages 875–887. Springer, 2007.

[20] Leonid Libkin, Wim Martens, and Domagoj Vrgoč. Querying graphs with data. *J. ACM*, 63(2):14, 2016.

[21] Zhen Hua Liu, Beda Christoph Hammerschmidt, and Doug McMahon. JSON data management: supporting schema-less development in RDBMS. In *International Conference on Management of Data, SIGMOD 2014, Snowbird, UT, USA, June 22-27, 2014*, pages 1247–1258, 2014.

[22] MongoDB Inc. The MongoDB3.0 Manual. https://docs.mongodb.org/manual/, 2015.

[23] Nurzhan Nurseitov, Michael Paulson, Randall Reynolds, and Clemente Izurieta. Comparison of json and xml data interchange formats: A case study. *Caine*, 2009:157–162, 2009.

[24] Kian Win Ong, Yannis Papakonstantinou, and Romain Vernoux. The SQL++ semi-structured data model and query language: A capabilities survey of sql-on-hadoop, nosql and newsql databases. *CoRR*, abs/1405.3631, 2014.

[25] The Open API Initiative. https://openapis.org/, 2016.

[26] OrientDB LTD. The OrientDB database. http://orientdb.com/, 2016.

[27] Pawel Parys. Xpath evaluation in linear time with polynomial combined complexity. In *Proceedings of the Twenty-Eigth ACM SIGMOD-SIGACT-SIGART Symposium on Principles of Database Systems, PODS 2009, June 19 - July 1, 2009, Providence, Rhode Island, USA*, pages 55–64, 2009.

[28] Felipe Pezoa, Juan L. Reutter, Fernando Suarez, Martín Ugarte, and Domagoj Vrgoč. Foundations of JSON schema. In *Proceedings of the 25th International Conference on World Wide Web, WWW 2016, Montreal, Canada, April 11 - 15, 2016*, pages 263–273, 2016.

[29] Jonathan Robie, Ghislain Fourny, Matthias Brantner, Daniela Florescu, Till Westmann, and Markos Zaharioudakis. JSONiq: The JSON Query Language. http://www.jsoniq.org/, 2016.

[30] Luc Segoufin and Cristina Sirangelo. Constant-memory validation of streaming xml documents against dtds. In *International Conference on Database Theory*, pages 299–313. Springer, 2007.

[31] The Apache Software Foundation. Apache CouchDB. http://couchdb.apache.org/, 2015.

[32] The Neo4j Team. The Neo4j Manual v3.0. http://neo4j.com/docs/stable/, 2016.

[33] Karianto Wong and Christof Löding. Unranked tree automata with sibling equalities and disequalities. In *Automata, Languages and Programming, 34th International Colloquium, ICALP 2007, Wroclaw, Poland, July 9-13, 2007, Proceedings*, pages 875–887, 2007.

J-Logic: Logical Foundations for JSON Querying

Jan Hidders
Vrije Universiteit Brussel

Jan Paredaens
Universiteit Antwerpen

Jan Van den Bussche
Universiteit Hasselt

ABSTRACT

We propose a logical framework, based on Datalog, to study the foundations of querying JSON data. The main feature of our approach, which we call J-Logic, is the emphasis on paths. Paths are sequences of keys and are used to access the tree structure of nested JSON objects. J-Logic also features "packing" as a means to generate a new key from a path or subpath. J-Logic with recursion is computationally complete, but many queries can be expressed without recursion, such as deep equality. We give a necessary condition for queries to be expressible without recursion. Most of our results focus on the deterministic nature of JSON objects as partial functions from keys to values. Predicates defined by J-Logic programs may not properly describe objects, however. Nevertheless we show that every object-to-object transformation in J-Logic can be defined using only objects in intermediate results. Moreover we show that it is decidable whether a positive, nonrecursive J-Logic program always returns an object when given objects as inputs. Regarding packing, we show that packing is unnecessary if the output does not require new keys. Finally, we show the decidability of query containment for positive, nonrecursive J-Logic programs.

1. INTRODUCTION

JSON is a popular semistructured data model used in NoSQL systems and also integrated in relational systems. Proposals for expressive query languages for JSON include JSONiq [17, 18], which is based on XQuery, and SQL++ [29], which is based on SQL. Schema formalisms for JSON are also being investigated [31]. Hence the time is ripe to investigate the logical foundations of JSON querying, which is the goal of the present paper.

A JSON object is a partial function, mapping keys to values. Here, a value is either an atomic value or an object in turn. Hence, objects can be nested, and thus can be viewed as trees, similarly to XML documents. JSON trees have some special characteristics, however, which form the starting point of our work. A first difference with XML trees is that JSON trees are edge-labeled rather than node-labeled; the keys are the edge labels. More importantly, JSON trees are *deterministic* in the sense of Buneman, Deutsch and Tan [11, 33]. Specifically, since objects are functions, different edges from a common parent must have different labels.[1]

Determinism is convenient because paths starting in the root of a given tree can be identified with key sequences.[2] This suggests an alternative view of objects as sets of path–value pairs, where each path is a path from the root to a leaf, and the corresponding value is the atomic value of that leaf. We call such a set of path–value pairs an *object description*. Since paths are sequences of keys, we are led to the conclusion that to query JSON objects, we need a query language that can work with sets of sequences.

At the same time, the theory of query languages is solidly grounded in logic [2]. Datalog in particular is a convenient logic-based language with a long tradition in data management research and a wide variety of current applications [23, 15, 7, 20].

We are thus motivated to investigate the logical foundations for JSON querying within a Datalog language for sets of sequences. Such a language, called sequence Datalog, has already been introduced by Bonner and Mecca [9, 28, 10]. Bonner and Mecca were primarily interested in expressive sequence manipulation, of the kind needed in bioinformatics applications. They reported results on expressiveness, complexity of computations, and on ways to combine recursion with sequence concatenation while still guaranteeing termination or tractability.

In this paper, we focus more on questions motivated by JSON querying and deterministic semistructured data. To this end, we propose a new approach to sequence Datalog, called J-Logic. Moreover, J-Logic adds a feature for generating new keys, called *packing*. Key generation is necessary if we want the result of a query over objects to be again an object. Consider, for example, the Cartesian product of two objects that have N keys each. The result needs to be a object with N^2 keys. So, we cannot manage by just reusing the keys from the input; new keys must be generated.

The creation of new data elements (keys, identifiers, nodes, and so on) in the result of a query has already been considered in many contexts, such as highly expressive languages

PODS '17, May 14–19, 2017, Chicago, IL, USA.

 ISBN 978-1-4503-4198-1/17/05...$15.00
DOI: http://dx.doi.org/10.1145/3034786.3056106

[1]Buneman, Deutsch and Tan actually considered an extension of JSON where keys need not be atomic, but can be objects in turn.

[2]In JSON Schema [31], key sequences are called "JSON pointers".

$$T(\langle @x.@y\rangle.r.@x.\$x' : @u) \leftarrow R(@x.\$x' : @u), S(@y.\$y' : @v)$$
$$T(\langle @x.@y\rangle.s.@y.\$y' : @v) \leftarrow R(@x.\$x' : @u), S(@y.\$y' : @v)$$

Figure 1: J-Logic program defining T as the Cartesian product of R and S. Here, $@x$ and $@y$ are atomic variables, binding to the top-level atomic keys of R and S respectively; $\$x'$ and $\$y'$ are path variables, binding to the paths in the subobjects below $@x$ and $@y$ in R and S respectively. The variables $@u$ and $@v$ bind to atomic values stored in the leaves. The dot indicates concatenation. We also use constant keys r and s to indicate the R- and S-parts of each pair of the Cartesian product.

[4, 5], object databases [3, 22, 27], information integration [21], data exchange [6], and ontology based data access [32]. The popular languages XQuery and SPARQL both have node creation. In logic based approaches, element creation is typically achieved through the use of Skolem functions [24, 25].

In J-Logic, however, we can take advantage of having sequences in the language. We can generate new keys simply by *packing* a key sequence s into a new key $\langle s\rangle$. For example, consider two objects

$$R = \{a : o_1, b : o_2\} \text{ and } S = \{c : o_3, d : o_4\},$$

where o_1, o_2, o_3, and o_4 are subobjects. We can represent the Cartesian product of R and S by the object

$$\begin{aligned} T = \{&\langle a.c\rangle : \{r : \{a : o_1\}, s : \{c : o_3\}\},\\ &\langle a.d\rangle : \{r : \{a : o_1\}, s : \{d : o_4\}\},\\ &\langle b.c\rangle : \{r : \{b : o_2\}, s : \{c : o_3\}\},\\ &\langle b.d\rangle : \{r : \{b : o_2\}, s : \{d : o_4\}\}\}. \end{aligned}$$

The two J-Logic rules in Figure 1 accomplish this.

Packed keys should be seen as an intermediate construct. We envisage that any packed keys present in the final result of a query will be replaced by fresh identifiers, as in the ILOG approach [24]. For example, T above could be returned in the following form:

$$\begin{aligned} T = \{&t_1 : \{r : \{a : o_1\}, s : \{c : o_3\}\},\\ &t_2 : \{r : \{a : o_1\}, s : \{d : o_4\}\},\\ &t_3 : \{r : \{b : o_2\}, s : \{c : o_3\}\},\\ &t_4 : \{r : \{b : o_2\}, s : \{d : o_4\}\}\}. \end{aligned}$$

The aforementioned languages SQL++ and JSONiq do not have key generation: there, the Cartesian product can be computed as a bag (or sequence) of objects, but not as one object itself. Key generation can thus be seen as an alternative to adding an extra collection feature (like bags, or sequences if we agree on some way to order objects) to the query language. We admit that a bag of objects could be easily transformed into one object by generating fresh keys. Thus the two approaches (key generation, or bags that are eventually transformed into objects) are largely equivalent. In J-Logic we have chosen for key generation through packing, because it is a lightweight addition to sequence Datalog. Moreover, it allows us to work with just a single kind of collections, namely, objects (more precisely, object descriptions).

In this paper we will show the following results.

1. J-Logic programs may be recursive, but we are mostly interested in the nonrecursive case. Nonrecursive programs have polynomial-time data complexity, and due to the use of sequence variables, nonrecursive programs are already quite powerful. We give a necessary condition on queries computable by nonrecursive programs, which can serve as a tool to show that certain queries involving objects of unbounded depth require recursion. (Nonrecursive J-Logic over objects of bounded depth is essentially equivalent to relational algebra.)

2. We show the technical result that packing, while convenient and necessary in general, is not needed to compute queries from flat inputs to flat outputs. Here, *flat* means that no packed keys occur in the data. An open question is whether this can be done without recursion (our simulation of packing needs recursion). An affirmative answer would yield a result analogous to the "flat–flat theorem" for the nested relational algebra [30] or calculus [12].

3. In J-Logic, a JSON object is described as a mapping from root-to-leaf paths to atomic values. Accordingly, predicates defined by J-Logic rules are relations between paths and atomic values. Not every such relation properly describes a JSON object, however. Nevertheless, we show the "object–object theorem": every query from objects to objects, computable by a J-Logic program, is computable by a J-Logic program so that every intermediate relation is a proper object description.

4. The object–object theorem assumes a J-Logic program that maps objects to objects. But can we check this? We show that the object–object property is decidable for positive, nonrecursive programs. We do this by adapting the chase procedure for equality-generating dependencies, well known from relational databases [2]. In our model, however, the chase is not complete in general. We nevertheless can use it resolve our problem.

5. Finally, we show that the containment problem for positive, nonrecursive programs, over flat instances, is decidable. To the best of our knowledge, the containment problem was not yet addressed in the setting of sequence Datalog. We solve the problem in our setting by extending the known inclusion test for pattern languages over an infinite alphabet [19].

This paper is further organized as follows. In Section 2 we introduce our formalization of the JSON data model. In Section 3 we define J-Logic. In Section 4 we discuss the expressive power of nonrecursive J-Logic and state the flat–flat theorem. In Section 5 we discuss the problem of proper object descriptions, state the object–object theorem, and study the object–object decision problem. Section 6 is devoted to the containment problem. We conclude in Section 7.

2. A FORMAL DATA MODEL BASED ON JSON

We begin by defining our formalization of the JSON data model. From the outset we assume an infinite domain **dom** of atomic data elements, which we call *atomic keys*. In practice, these would be strings, numbers, or any other type of data that the database system treats as atomic. Now the sets of *values* and *objects* are defined as the smallest sets satisfying the following:

- Every atomic key is a value;
- Every object is a value;
- Every mapping from a finite set of atomic keys to values is an object.

Recall that a mapping is a set of pairs where no two pairs have the same first component. Thus, an object is a set of key–value pairs. It is customary to write a key–value pair (k, v) in the form $k : v$. For an object o and a key a, we sometimes use the notation $o.a$ for the a-value of o, i.e., for $o(a)$.

Example 2.1. Using strings such as 'name', 'age', 'anne', 'bob' and 'chris', and numbers such as 12, 18 and 24, as atomic keys, the following are three examples of objects:

$$o_1 = \{\text{name} : \text{anne}, \text{age} : 12\}$$
$$o_2 = \{\text{name} : \text{bob}, \text{age} : 18\}$$
$$o_3 = \{\text{name} : \text{chris}, \text{age} : 24\}$$

Since objects can be nested, the following is also an object:

$$o = \{\text{name} : \text{john}, \text{children} : \{1 : o_1, 2 : o_2, 3 : o_3\}\}$$

We have $o.\text{children}.2 = o_2$. Finally, note that the set $\{\text{name} : \text{anne}, \text{name} : \text{bob}\}$ is not an object since it is not a well-defined mapping. The set $\{\text{anne} : \text{name}, \text{bob} : \text{name}\}$, however, is perfectly allowed as an object. □

Remark 2.2. Some remarks are in order.

1. In the JSON standard [16], the keys in an object can only be strings, but values can be numbers. In our formalization we make no distinction between different types of atomic data, which explains the example above where we used the numbers 1, 2 and 3 as keys. In the language JavaScript, an array may be viewed as an object with numbers as keys. So, our approach is not too much at odds with reality.

2. Indeed, the JSON standard also has arrays besides objects. In this paper we focus on unordered objects. An extension of our approach, where a total order is assumed on atomic keys (and extended to packed keys, see later) seems feasible and would be able to model arrays.

3. The term "atomic *key*" is a bit misleading, as these elements may not only be used as keys, but also as values. Indeed, that keys can occur as data values, and vice versa, is a characteristic feature of JSON.

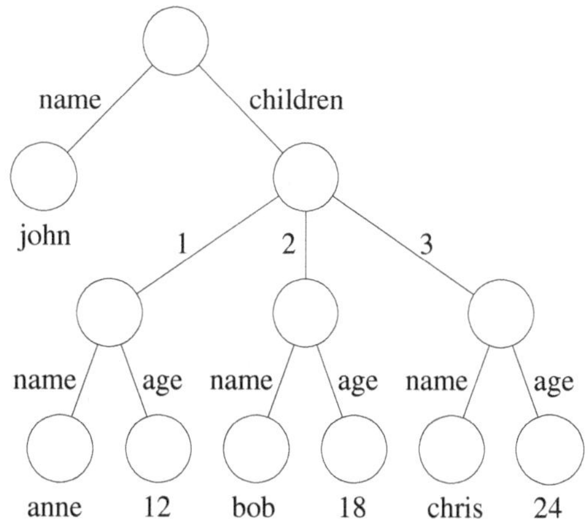

Figure 2: Object o from Example 2.1 as a tree.

Packed keys.

Until now we have defined an object as a mapping from atomic keys to values. Since these values can be objects in turn, we can use sequences of atomic keys to navigate deeper inside an object. Sequences of keys will be called paths. Moreover, we also introduce packed keys, as they can be created by J-Logic rules. Formally, the sets of *keys* and *paths* are defined as the smallest sets such that

- every atomic key is a key;
- if p is a path then $\langle p \rangle$ is a key, called a *packed key*;
- every nonempty finite sequence of keys is a path.

In our notation, we use dots to separate the elements of a sequence. At the same time, the dot will be used to denote concatenation of paths.

Example 2.3. Let a and b be atomic keys. Then $a.b$ is a path; $k = \langle a.b \rangle$ is a packed key; $p = b.b.k.a$ is again a path; and $\langle p \rangle$ is again a packed key. Note that $\langle a \rangle$ and $\langle \langle a \rangle \rangle$ are distinct paths. □

From now on we allow packed keys in objects. Thereto we generalize the notion of object by defining an object to be a mapping from a finite set of keys to values. Thus, keys need not be atomic but can also be packed. We already saw an example of an object with packed keys, T in the Introduction.

Object descriptions.

An object can be visualized as a tree, where edges are labeled with keys and leaves are labeled with *atomic values*: atomic keys or $\emptyset$ (the empty object). Thus, we can completely describe an object by listing all paths from the root to the leaves, and, for each such path, giving the label of the corresponding leaf.

Example 2.4. Recall the object o from Example 2.1. Figure 2 shows o as a tree. Its description as a set of path–value pairs is as follows:

name : john
children.1.name : anne
children.1.age : 12
children.2.name : bob
children.2.age : 18
children.3.name : chris
children.3.age : 24

□

Formally, we define an *object description* to be any set of pairs of the form $p : v$, where p is a path and v is an atomic value. If o is an object, the object description of o, denoted by $\mathrm{OD}(o)$, is defined inductively as follows:

- If o is $\emptyset$, or a singleton object of the form $\{k : b\}$ with b an atomic value, then $\mathrm{OD}(o) = o$.
- If o is a singleton object of the form $\{k : o'\}$, with o' an object, then
$$\mathrm{OD}(o) = \{k.p : b \mid (p : b) \in \mathrm{OD}(o')\}.$$
- If o is a non-singleton object, then
$$\mathrm{OD}(o) = \bigcup\{\mathrm{OD}(\{k : v\}) \mid (k : v) \in o\}.$$

Remark 2.5. Not every finite object description is the object description of some object; those that are, are called *proper*. Simple examples of improper object descriptions are $\{a : 1, a : 2\}$ and $\{a : 1, a.a : 1\}$. We will focus on proper object descriptions in Section 5. For now, we allow arbitrary object descriptions.

Vocabularies, instances, and queries.

We can finally define the fundamental notions of database instance and query in our data model. Just like a relational database instance is a finite collection of named relations, here we will define an instance as a finite collection of named object descriptions. Since object descriptions are binary relations (sets of pairs), we refer to their names as "relation names".

Formally, a *vocabulary* $\mathcal{V}$ is a finite set of relation names. An *instance* I over $\mathcal{V}$ assigns to each name $R \in \mathcal{V}$ an object description $I(R)$. Given two disjoint vocabularies $\mathcal{V}_{\mathrm{in}}$ and $\mathcal{V}_{\mathrm{out}}$, a *query from* $\mathcal{V}_{\mathrm{in}}$ *to* $\mathcal{V}_{\mathrm{out}}$ is a partial function from instances over $\mathcal{V}_{\mathrm{in}}$ to instances over $\mathcal{V}_{\mathrm{out}}$.

In database theory one often focuses on *generic* queries [2]. We can define a similar notion of genericity here. Let f be a permutation of **dom**. Then f can be extended to paths, packed keys, object descriptions, and instances, simply by applying f to every occurrence of an atomic key. Let C be a finite subset of **dom** (these are the atomic keys that would be explicitly mentioned in a program for the query). Then a query Q is called *C-generic* if for every permutation f of **dom** that is the identity on C, and for every instance I, we have $Q(f(I)) = f(Q(I))$. In particular, if $Q(I)$ is undefined, then $Q(f(I))$ must also be undefined.

3. J-LOGIC

In the syntax of J-Logic, we assume disjoint supplies of *atomic variables* (ranging over atomic keys) and *path variables* (ranging over paths). The set of all variables is also disjoint from **dom**. We indicate atomic variables as $@x$ and path variables as $\$x$.

Key expressions and *path expressions* are defined just like keys and paths, but with variables added in. Formally, we define the sets of key expressions and path expressions to be the smallest sets such that

- every atomic key is a key expression, called a *constant*;
- every atomic variable is a key expression; constants and atomic variables are also called *atomic key expressions*;
- if e is a path expression then $\langle e\rangle$ is a key expression, called a *packed key expression*;
- every nonempty finite sequence of key expressions and path variables is a path expression.

Recall that an atomic value is an atomic key or $\emptyset$. Now an *atomic term* is an atomic value or an atomic variable.

A *predicate* is an expression of the form $P(e : t)$, with P a relation name, e a path expression, and t an atomic term.

An *equality* is an expression of the form $e_1 = e_2$, with e_1 and e_2 path expressions.

Many of the following definitions adapt the standard definition of Datalog [2] to our data model.

An *atom* is a predicate or an equality. A *negated atom* is an expression of the form $\neg A$ with A an atom. A *literal* is an atom (also called a positive literal) or a negated atom (a negative literal).

A *body* is a finite set of literals.

A *rule* is an expression of the form $H \leftarrow B$, where H is a predicate, called the *head* of the rule, and B is a body. We define the *limited variables* of the rule as the smallest set such that

- every variable occurring in a positive predicate in B is limited; and
- if all variables occurring in one of the sides of a positive equality in B are limited, then all variables occurring in the other side are also limited.

A rule is called *safe* if all variables occurring in the rule are limited.

Finally, a *program* is a finite set of safe rules with stratified negation. We omit the definition of stratified negation, which is well known [2]. For our purposes in this paper, stratified negation suffices. A program is called *positive* if it does not use negation. We also assume familarity with the distinction between recursive and nonrecursive programs.

Semantics.

We have defined the notion of instance as an assignment of object descriptions to relation names. A convenient equivalent view of instances is as sets of *facts*. A fact is an expression of the form $R(p : v)$ with R a relation name, p a path, and v an atomic value. An instance I over vocabulary $\mathcal{V}$ is viewed as the set of facts
$$I = \{R(p : v) \mid R \in \mathcal{V} \text{ and } (p : v) \in I(R)\}.$$

A *valuation* is a function ν defined on a finite set of variables, that maps atomic variables to atomic keys and path variables to paths. We say that ν is *appropriate* for a syntactical construct (such as a path expression, a literal, or a rule) if ν is defined on all variables occurring in the construct. We can apply an appropriate valuation ν to a key or path expression e in the obvious manner: we substitute each variable by its image under ν and obtain a key or a path $\nu(e)$. Likewise, we can apply an appropriate valuation to a predicate and obtain a fact.

Let L be a literal, ν be a valuation appropriate for L, and I be an instance. The definition of when I, ν *satisfies* L is as expected: if L is a predicate, then the fact $\nu(L)$ must be in I; if L is an equality $e_1 = e_2$, then $\nu(e_1)$ and $\nu(e_2)$ must be the same path. If L is a negated atom $\neg A$, then I, ν must not satisfy A.

A body B is satisfied by I, ν if all its literals are. Now a rule $\mathbf{r} = H \leftarrow B$ is satisfied in I if for every valuation ν appropriate for $\mathbf{r}$ such that I, ν satisfies B, also I, ν satisfies H.

The notions of EDB and IDB relation names of a program are well known: the IDB relation names are the relation names used in the head of some rules; the other relation names are the EDB relation names. Given a vocabulary $\mathcal{V}_{\text{in}}$, a program is said to be *over* $\mathcal{V}_{\text{in}}$ if all its EDB relation names belong to $\mathcal{V}_{\text{in}}$, and its IDB relation names do not.

Now the semantics of programs with stratified negation is defined as usual [2]. Recall that a program is called semipositive if negative predicates only use EDB relation names. We first apply the first stratum, which is semipositive, and then apply each subsequent stratum as a semipositive program to the result of the previous stratum. So we only need to give semantics for semipositive programs.

Let $\mathbf{P}$ be a semipositive program over $\mathcal{V}_{\text{in}}$, and let I be an instance over $\mathcal{V}_{\text{in}}$. Let $\mathcal{V}$ be the set of IDB relation names of $\mathbf{P}$. Then $\mathbf{P}(I)$ is the smallest instance over $\mathcal{V}_{\text{in}} \cup \mathcal{V}$ that satisfies all the rules of $\mathbf{P}$, and that agrees with I on $\mathcal{V}_{\text{in}}$.

In the end, a program $\mathbf{P}$ over $\mathcal{V}_{\text{in}}$ can be used to compute a query Q from $\mathcal{V}_{\text{in}}$ to $\mathcal{V}_{\text{out}}$, for any designated subset $\mathcal{V}_{\text{out}}$ of the IDB relation names of $\mathbf{P}$. Here, $Q(I)$ simply equals the restriction of $\mathbf{P}(I)$ to $\mathcal{V}_{\text{out}}$.

Syntactic sugar.

We have kept the syntax of J-Logic minimal so as to keep the formal definitions as simple as possible. For writing practical programs, however, it is convenient to introduce some syntactic sugar:

- Variables of the form $\%u$ range over atomic values, i.e., atomic keys or $\emptyset$. We could always eliminate such a variable in a rule by splitting the rule in two: one in which we replace $\%u$ by a normal atomic variable $@u$, and one in which we replace $\%u$ by $\emptyset$ (and resolve equalities accordingly).
- Variables of the form $?z$ range over paths or the empty sequence (recall that paths are nonempty). As long as such a variable is only used concatenated with other path expressions, we could always eliminate it from a rule by splitting the rule in two: one in which we replace $?z$ by a normal path variable $\$z$, and one in which we simply delete all occurrences of $?z$ (resolving equalities accordingly).
- Variables of the form $\#z$ range over keys, atomic as well as packed. We could always eliminate such a variable in a rule by splitting the rule in one where we replace $\#z$ by an atomic variable $@z$, and one where we replace $\#z$ by a packed key expression $\langle \$z \rangle$.

Examples.

We aim to illustrate that J-Logic does not need recursion to express many useful queries involving deeply nested data. We begin, however, by illustrating why nonrecursive programs are desirable.

Example 3.1 (Nontermination). Due to the use of concatenation in heads of rules, the result of a recursive program applied to a finite instance may be infinite. A simple example is the following: (this program has no EDB relation names; the body of the first rule is empty)

$$S(a : \emptyset) \leftarrow$$
$$S(a.\$x : \emptyset) \leftarrow S(\$x : \emptyset)$$

We consider such programs to be nonterminating. For limited forms of recursion that guarantee termination or even tractability, we refer to the work of Bonner and Mecca [9, 28]. Nonrecursive programs clearly always terminate. □

Example 3.2 (Deep equality). The following nonrecursive program is applied to the object description R of an object o, assumed to have values $o.a$ and $o.b$. The program tests equality of $o.a$ and $o.b$; if so, it outputs the fact $Q(\text{yes} : \emptyset)$. Note that $o.a$ and $o.b$ may be atomic values (case handled by the first and last rule), or may be objects themselves. Thus, the other rules of the program test set equality of the object descriptions of $o.a$ and $o.b$. These rules derive an atomic key 'no' when one of the containments in the two directions needed for set equality fails.

$$T(\text{atomic} : \emptyset) \leftarrow R(a : \%u), R(b : \%v)$$
$$Q'(\text{no} : \emptyset) \leftarrow R(a.\$x : \%u), \neg R(b.\$x : \%u)$$
$$Q'(\text{no} : \emptyset) \leftarrow R(b.\$x : \%u), \neg R(a.\$x : \%u)$$
$$Q(\text{yes} : \emptyset) \leftarrow \neg T(\text{atomic} : \emptyset), \neg Q'(\text{no} : \emptyset)$$
$$Q(\text{yes} : \emptyset) \leftarrow R(a : \%u), R(b : \%u)$$

□

Example 3.3 (Unnesting). Let o be the object described by R. The following single-rule program retrieves all subobjects of o (at arbitrary depths, but not o itself) that have a 'name'-value equal to 'John'. These objects are returned as top-level elements of a result object S, with new keys generated by packing.

$$S(\langle \$x \rangle.\$y : \%u) \leftarrow R(\$x.\text{name} : \text{John}), R(\$x.\$y : \%u)$$

□

Example 3.4 (Key lookup, nesting). Like the previous example, the following program again considers subobjects, but now focuses on those that have a key 'ref' with an atomic key k as value. That key k is looked up and all values found for it are collected in a new subobject created under the 'ref' key (and k at that place is removed). As in the previous example, new keys (for the elements of the collection) are generated using packing. The output object S is thus obtained from the input object R by a process similar to dereferencing pointers.

$$T(\$x.\text{ref} : \emptyset) \leftarrow R(\$x.\text{ref} : @k)$$
$$S(\$x.\text{ref}.\langle \$y \rangle.?z : \%u) \leftarrow R(\$x.\text{ref} : @k), R(\$y.@k.?z : \%u)$$
$$S(\$x' : \%u) \leftarrow R(\$x' : \%u), \neg T(\$x' : \emptyset)$$

4. EXPRESSIVENESS AND COMPLEXITY

Nonrecursive J-Logic has polynomial-time data complexity. Since rules are safe, we can find valuations satisfying the body of a rule through finding valuations of predicates.

To find the valuations satisfying a predicate $P(e : t)$, note that the path expression e is a sequence of key expressions and path variables. Let k be the length of this sequence. Then we choose a pair $(p : v)$ from P; the number of possibilities is linear. We match t to the atomic value v in the obvious manner, and match e to the path p by splitting p in k pieces. The number of possible splits is polynomial of degree k. A piece corresponding to a path variable provides a binding for that path variable, or must be equal to an already existing binding. A piece corresponding to an atomic variable must be an atomic key. A piece corresponding to a constant must match the constant. Finally, a piece corresponding to a packed key expression $\langle e' \rangle$ must be a packed key $\langle p' \rangle$. Then e' is matched to p' in turn.

Using positive, recursive, programs we can already simulate Turing machines [9]. Using general programs, we are computationally complete: we can express any computable C-generic query from finite instances to finite instances. Using an encoding of instances as defined here by relational database instances, this can be proven following the known body of work on the computational completeness of query languages [14, 4, 3, 35, 13].

Nonrecursive programs, relational algebra, and practical languages.

Let us call a class of instances *bounded* if there is a fixed bound on the length of all paths occurring in the instances, as well as on the nesting depth of packed keys.

On a bounded class of inputs, nonrecursive J-Logic can be simulated by relational algebra. Indeed, due to the bound, there are only finitely many nonequivalent predicates, and each equivalence class can be described using atomic variables only. Thus, for each equivalence class of predicates we can keep the bindings in a fixed-arity relation. Given such a representation the evaluation of a rule can be expressed in relational algebra. Moreover, the application of a rule to a bounded instance produces again a bounded instance (with the new bound depending only on the old bound and the rule). In this way we can simulate nonrecursive J-Logic over bounded instances in relational algebra.

Conversely, it is quite clear that we can represent all relational database instances over some fixed schema as a bounded class of instances in our data model. There are various ways to do this. One approach is to represent a tuple as an object in the obvious way (each attribute is a key) and then represent a set of tuples as a set of objects, using tuple identifiers as top-level keys. Under such a representation we can easily simulate, say, the relational algebra, using nonrecursive J-Logic. We use packing to generate new tuple identifiers, as illustrated in the Introduction for Cartesian product.

Another approach is to use a (bounded-depth) trie representation for relations, as used, for example, in the Leapfrog Triejoin algorithm [36]. Such tries are naturally represented as JSON objects. We can then again simulate the relational algebra using nonrecursive J-Logic, and we would not even need packing.

Note that practical JSON query languages SQL++ [29] and JSONiq without recursive functions [18] are mainly oriented towards bounded-depth data. Apart from features such as aggregation and full-text search, these languages are fundamentally based on the nested relational algebra or calculus [12]. This calculus can be translated into nonrecursive J-Logic. As already mentioned in the Introduction, packing can be used to represent nested collections. The only caveat (which is also not really mentioned by SQL++ and JSONiq) is to do duplicate elimination on nested collections. It follows from known results [34] that a special set-oriented packing operator would need to be added for this purpose.

Moreover, we feel that the main contribution of J-Logic is as a language in which nonrecursive programs can also work well with unbounded inputs, i.e., deeply nested data.

Limitations of nonrecursive programs.

By the above discussion we readily obtain examples of queries not expressible by nonrecursive programs: any query over relational instances that is not expressible in the relational algebra will do, such as the transitive closure of a binary relation. That does not tell us anything about unbounded instances, however. In Proposition 4.2 we will give a general necessary condition on the output of nonrecursive programs.

Example 4.1. Let c be some constant and consider the query Q from $\{R\}$ to $\{S\}$ defined by

$$Q(I) = \{S(k_1.c.k_2.c \dots k_n.c : \emptyset) \mid R(k_1.k_2 \dots k_n : \emptyset) \in I\}$$

where n is not fixed but ranges over all possible lengths. Proposion 4.2 will imply that this query is not expressible by a nonrecursive program. □

Bonner and Mecca [9] have proposed mixing transducers with sequence Datalog, so that manipulations as in the above example can be easily expressed. They already noted informally that without recursion through concatenation, only a fixed number of concatenations can be performed. The following proposition formalizes this observation and adapts it to J-Logic.

In order to state the necessary condition, we introduce the following notations. For a set S of paths, $sub(S)$ denotes all subpaths of paths occurring in S (also paths occurring in packed keys). Also, $concat(S, i)$ denotes all paths that can be built up (using concatenation and packing) from the paths in S using a total of at most i concatenations. The set of paths of an instance J is denoted by $paths(J)$, so formally, $paths(J) = \{p \mid R(p : v) \in J \text{ for some } R \text{ and } v\}$.

Proposition 4.2. *Let* $\mathbf{P}$ *be a nonrecursive program. There exists a finite set* L *of paths and a natural number* i *such that for every instance* I*, we have*

$$paths(\mathbf{P}(I)) \subseteq concat(sub(paths(I) \cup L), i).$$

Proof. By induction on the number of strata. For the base case, assume $\mathbf{P}$ consists of a single stratum. By an obvious rewriting we may assume without loss of generality that the body of each rule only mentions EDB relation names. Consider an element $p \in paths(\mathbf{P}(I))$. Then p is produced by applying a valuation to a path expression, say e, in the head of some rule. Every variable is mapped to an element of $sub(paths(I))$. Let $\hat{e}$ denote the sequence obtained by removing all variables from e, as well as all opening and closing brackets of packed keys; we refer to these lexical elements as *separators*. Let i_e denote the number of separators; we can view e as chopping $\hat{e}$ in $i_e + 1$ pieces. Thus, $p \in concat(sub(paths(I) \cup \{\hat{e}\}), i_e + 1)$. Hence, we can set i to the maximum i_e, and we can set L to the set of $\hat{e}$.

Now assume $\mathbf{P}$ has at least two strata. Let $\mathbf{P}'$ be the part without the last stratum, which we denote by $\mathbf{P}''$. So, $\mathbf{P}$

is the composition of $\mathbf{P}''$ after $\mathbf{P}'$. By induction, we have i' and L' for $\mathbf{P}'$. Moreover, reasoning as in the base case, we have i'' and L'' for $\mathbf{P}''$ applied to $\mathbf{P}'(I)$. After some calculations we can see that we can now set $i = i' \cdot i''$ and $L = L' \cup L''$. □

Flat–flat queries.

An instance is called *flat* if no packed keys occur in it. A query Q is called *flat–flat* if for every flat instance I, if $Q(I)$ is defined then it is also flat. It may still be convenient to use packing in the computation of a flat–flat query, as illustrated next.

Example 4.3. The query from Example 4.1 is flat–flat. Over flat inputs, we can compute it by the following program:

$T(\langle @i \rangle.?y : \emptyset) \leftarrow R(@i.?y : \emptyset)$
$T(?x.@i.c.\langle @j \rangle.?y : \emptyset) \leftarrow T(?x.\langle @i \rangle.@j.?y : \emptyset)$
$S(?x.@i.c : \emptyset) \leftarrow T(?x.\langle @i \rangle : \emptyset)$

We see that packing is conveniently used as a cursor to run through the sequence. With more effort, however, we can also compute the query without using packing. The trick is to use some constant a and to look for the longest consecutive sequence of a's occurring in any path in R. Then a sequence of a's one longer than that can be used as a cursor. The program is as follows. Since all predicates in the program will be of the form $P(e : \emptyset)$, we abbreviate them as $P(e)$.

$Sub(a.?y) \leftarrow R(?x.a.?y.?z)$
$Subnota(\$x.@i.?y) \leftarrow Sub(\$x.@i.?y),\ @i \neq a$
$Suba(\$x) \leftarrow Sub(\$x), \neg Subnota(\$x)$
$A(a.\$x) \leftarrow Suba(\$x), \neg Suba(a.\$x)$
$T(\$a.\$x) \leftarrow R(\$x), A(\$a)$
$T(?x.@i.c.\$a.?y) \leftarrow T(?x.\$a.@i.?y), A(\$a)$
$S(\$x) \leftarrow T(\$x.\$a), A(\$a)$ □

The above example illustrates a general theorem:

Theorem 4.4 (Flat–flat theorem)**.** *For every J-Logic program computing a flat–flat query there is equivalent program without packing, over flat instances.*

Proof. (Sketch.) The proof would be easy if we could use two constants, say a and b, that are never used in any instance. Then a packed key expression $\langle e \rangle$ could be simulated using $a.e.b$, where we also would need to write additional rules checking that e matches a path with balanced a's and b's.

If we want a simulation that always works, without an assumption on the constants used in instances, we can encode a path $p = k_1.k_2 \dots k_n$ by its doubled version $p' = k_1.k_1.k_2.k_2 \dots k_n.k_n$. Then $\langle e \rangle$ can be simulated using the sequence $a.b.e'.b.a$. Doubling can be computed without packing using the technique illustrated in Example 4.3. When matching path variables, we make sure we always match a subpath beginning with $@i.@i$ or $a.b$ and ending with $@j.@j$ or $b.a$. □

The above proof needs recursion, even if the given program is nonrecursive. In general it is fair to say that the above flat–flat theorem is mainly of theoretical interest. Still it is an interesting open question whether for every nonrecursive program computing a flat–flat query, there is an equivalent *nonrecursive* program without packing, over all flat instances.

5. PROPER OBJECT DESCRIPTIONS AND OBJECT–OBJECT QUERIES

In Remark 2.5 we introduced the notion of proper object description as the object description of an actual object, as opposed to just any set of path–value pairs. Proper object descriptions can be characterized as follows.

Proposition 5.1. *A finite object description D is proper if and only if it satisfies the following two constraints:*

- *the functional dependency from paths to atomic values, i.e., if $(p : u) \in D$ and $(p : v) \in D$, then $u = v$.*
- *prefix-freeness, i.e., if p and q are paths, and $(p.q : u) \in D$ for some u, then $(p : v) \notin D$ for every v.*

Example 5.2. $D = \{a : 1, a.a : 1\}$ is not prefix-free and indeed D is not proper. In proof, suppose D would be the description of an object o. Then $o.a$ is the atomic value 1 by the first pair in D. But by the second pair, $o.a$ is an object with a-value 1, a contradiction. □

Remark 5.3. Only finite object descriptions can be proper, since objects are always finite. Still, the two constraints from the above proposition can be taken to be the *definition* of properness for infinite instances. Later in this paper, we will consider the object–object problem, the implication problem for jaegds (defined in Section 5), and the containment problem. These three problems ask a question about *all* instances. These problems do not change, however, if we restrict attention to finite instances. □

An instance is called proper if it assigns a proper object description to every relation name. A query Q is called *object–object* if for every proper instance I, if $Q(I)$ is defined then it is also proper.

The object–object property is practically important. In practice, a JSON processor may accept improper object descriptions, or object syntax that is not well-defined, such as $\{a : 1, a : 2\}$ or $\{a : 1, a : \{b : 2\}\}$. However, the processor will interpret such syntax in an unpredictable manner. Perhaps it will overwrite a previously read a-value by an a-value read later. Or, on the contrary, it may keep only the value that was read first. To avoid depending on such system-defined behavior, we better write queries having the object–object property.

One may go further and demand that also all intermediate relations generated by a J-Logic program hold proper object descriptions. This may be relevant, for example, if we implement the query language on top of a JSON store. We next show that this is always possible. We call the result the "object–object theorem", which may be a bit pompous, as it is proven by a simple trick using packing (thus again illustrating the utility of packing).

Theorem 5.4 (Object–object theorem)**.** *Let $\mathbf{P}$ be a program expressing an object–object query Q. Then there exists an equivalent program $\mathbf{P}'$ such that, on any proper input instance, all IDB relations of $\mathbf{P}'$ hold proper object descriptions. Program $\mathbf{P}'$ has the same number of strata as $\mathbf{P}$, and is recursive if and only if $\mathbf{P}$ is recursive.*

Proof. The idea is to encode arbitrary object descriptions by object descriptions that are always proper. Then the program is simulated using the encoding. At the end the output relations are decoded. Such an encoding is easy to do using packing.

Formally, fix an arbitrary atomic key b. For any input relation name R we introduce the following two encoding rules:

$R'(\langle \$x\rangle.\langle @u\rangle : \emptyset) \leftarrow R(\$x : @u)$
$R'(\langle \$x\rangle.\langle b.b\rangle : \emptyset) \leftarrow R(\$x : \emptyset)$

These rules are added to the first stratum of $\mathbf{P}$.

Furthermore, we modify $\mathbf{P}$ by replacing each atom (in bodies and in heads) of the form $P(e : t)$ by $P'(\langle e\rangle.\langle t\rangle : \emptyset)$ if t is not $\emptyset$, and by $P'(\langle e\rangle.\langle b.b\rangle : \emptyset)$ otherwise.

Finally for every output relation name S we add the following decoding rules to the last stratum:

$S(\$x : @u) \leftarrow S'(\langle \$x\rangle.\langle @u\rangle)$
$S(\$x : \emptyset) \leftarrow S'(\langle \$x\rangle.\langle b.b\rangle)$ □

Example 5.5. The following program begins by eliminating the top layer from an object R, which brings the second-level keys to the top level. This intermediate result R_1 may well be improper. We then throw away all "bad" paths (paths that violate properness). The result, S, is of course proper. Thus, this program computes an object–object query but is easiest to write using improper intermediate results. Yet, the object–object theorem assures us it can be rewritten using only proper intermediate results.

$R_1(\$y : \%u) \leftarrow R(\#x.\$y : \%u)$
$Bad(\$y : \%u) \leftarrow R_1(\$y : \%u), R_1(\$y : \%v), \%u \neq \%v$
$Bad(\$x.\$z : \%v) \leftarrow R_1(\$x : \%u), R_1(\$x.\$z : \%v)$
$S(\$y : \%u) \leftarrow R_1(\$y : \%u), \neg Bad(\$y : \%u)$ □

Remark 5.6. Our proof of the object–object theorem uses packing. Of course there is nothing wrong with packing; we think it is a versatile tool. Yet, theoretically one may wonder whether one can also do without. Indeed it turns out one can prove a combination of the flat–flat theorem and the object–object theorem. Specifically, for every program computing a flat–flat object–object query, we can find a program without packing that is equivalent over flat instances and that only works with proper intermediate results. The idea is to encode a path–value pair $a_1 \dots a_n : \emptyset$ by $b.a_1 \dots b.a_n.a.a.b : \emptyset$, and a path–value pair $a_1 \dots a_n : c$ by $b.a_1 \dots b.a_n.c.a.a.b : \emptyset$. It can be verified that an encoding of an object description is always proper. The program is then modified to work over encodings. As for the flat–flat theorem, the program without packing would need recursion. Again we leave open whether there is a nonrecursive version of the flat–flat object–object theorem.

5.1 Deciding the object–object property

The *object–object problem* is defined as follows: given a J-Logic program $\mathbf{P}$ and appropriate vocabularies $\mathcal{V}_{\text{in}}$ and $\mathcal{V}_{\text{out}}$, decide whether the query from $\mathcal{V}_{\text{in}}$ to $\mathcal{V}_{\text{out}}$ computed by $\mathbf{P}$ has the object–object property.

In general, this problem is of course undecidable. It is undecidable for positive recursive programs, because these can simulate Turing machines, and also for nonrecursive programs that can use negation, because these can express first-order logic (relational algebra).

In this subsection we show:

Theorem 5.7. *When restricted to positive, nonrecursive programs, the object–object problem is decidable in exponential time.*

Our starting point is to note that this problem has similarities with a problem known from relational databases. This problem is the FD–FD implication problem for (unions of) conjunctive queries (UCQs) [1, 2]. It is also called the view dependency problem [26]. This problem asks, given two sets Σ_1 and Σ_2 of functional dependencies (FDs) and a query Q, whether the result of Q, applied to an instance satisfying Σ_1, always satisfies Σ_2. The similarity lies in that properness involves satisfying an FD; moreover, positive nonrecursive J-Logic programs are the J-Logic analog of UCQs. Of course there are also differences: J-Logic has packing and path variables, and the notion of properness is not only about FDs but also about prefix-freeness.

The decidability of the FD–FD implication problem for UCQs follows readily from the decidability of the implication problem for equality-generating dependencies (egds), using the chase [2, 8]. Hence our approach is to introduce *J-Logic atomic equality-generating dependencies* or jaegds, and investigate the chase for these dependencies.

Syntactically, a *jaegd* is a rule σ of the form $B \rightarrow E$, where B is a positive body without equalities and E is an atomic equality, i.e., an equality of the form $u = v$ where u and v are atomic key expressions (atomic constants or atomic variables). If u or v is a variable, that variable must occur in B.

Semantically, note that B consists exclusively of positive predicates. Hence, for any instance I and valuation ν appropriate for B, we have that I, ν satisfies B if and only if $\nu(B) \subseteq I$. We denote this by $\nu : B \rightarrow I$ and call ν a *matching* of B in I. We now define that I satisfies a jaegd σ as above, denoted by $I \models \sigma$, if for every matching $\nu : B \rightarrow I$, the atomic keys $\nu(u)$ and $\nu(v)$ are identical.

Note that dependencies of the form $B \rightarrow a = b$, where a and b are distinct atomic keys, are allowed. Since $a = b$ is always false, this can be written more clearly as $B \rightarrow$ **false** or also $B \rightarrow \bot$. This is used to express a *denial constraint*: it is only satisfied in an instance I if there does not exist any matching of B in I.

Note that we also allow dependencies of the form $B \rightarrow u = u$. Obviously such dependencies are trivial (satisfied in any instance), but we allow them because they may be produced by the chase procedure.

Example 5.8. By Proposition 5.1, an object description D is proper if and only if it satisfies the jaegds δ_1–δ_6:

$\delta_1 : D(\$x : @i), D(\$x : @j) \rightarrow @i = @j$
$\delta_2 : D(\$x : \emptyset), D(\$x : @i) \rightarrow \bot$
$\delta_3 : D(\$x : @i), D(\$x.\$y : \emptyset) \rightarrow \bot$
$\delta_4 : D(\$x : @i), D(\$x.\$y : @j) \rightarrow \bot$
$\delta_5 : D(\$x : \emptyset), D(\$x.\$y : \emptyset) \rightarrow \bot$
$\delta_6 : D(\$x : \emptyset), D(\$x.\$y : @j) \rightarrow \bot$ □

For a set of dependencies Σ, we define $I \models \Sigma$ to mean that I satisfies every dependency in Σ. We say that Σ *logically implies* a dependency σ if every instance that satisfies Σ also satisfies σ. The *implication problem for jaegds* asks to decide, given a set of jaegds Σ and a jaegd σ, whether Σ logically implies σ. We actually do not know whether this problem is decidable in general. We will, however, solve a special case that is sufficient to solve the object–object problem.

The Chase.

We first need the notion of a *variable mapping*. This is a function defined on a finite set of variables that maps path variables to path expressions and atomic variables to atomic key expressions. Like valuations, we can apply a variable mapping to a predicate simply by applying it to every variable occurring in the predicate. The result is again a predicate. Thus, the result of applying a variable mapping to a body is again a body. A *homomorphism* h from a body B_1 in a body B_2, denoted by $h : B_1 \to B_2$, is a variable mapping appropriate for B_1 such that $h(B_1) \subseteq B_2$.

With this notion of homomorphism in place, the notion of *chasing a jaegd* σ *with a set of jaegds* Σ is defined entirely similarly to the well-known chase for egds in the relational model [2]. The chase provides a sound proof procedure for logical implication, as stated in the following proposition.

Proposition 5.9. *Assume that either chasing* σ *with* Σ *fails, or the chase succeeds and results in a jaegd whose consequent is a trivial equality. Then* Σ *logically implies* σ*.*

For egds in the relational model, the converse to the above proposition holds as well, showing the completeness of the chase as a proof procedure. In our model, however, the converse fails, as shown next.

Example 5.10. Consider Σ consisting of the following three denial constraints:

$$P(@x : \emptyset) \to \bot$$
$$P(\langle \$x \rangle : \emptyset) \to \bot$$
$$P(\$x.\$y : \emptyset) \to \bot$$

Then Σ is equivalent to the single denial constraint $\sigma \equiv P(\$x : \emptyset) \to \bot$, so certainly Σ logically implies σ. However, chasing σ with Σ does not fail. Actually, no chase step can be applied at all and the chase ends immediately on σ itself. Since the consequent $\bot$ is not a trivial equality, this shows that the converse of Proposition 5.9 fails. □

We can still get completeness of the chase in a special case, which we call *unambiguous*. We first define the notion of *weak variable mapping*. Recall that a variable mapping must map atomic variables to atomic key expressions. A weak variable mapping is like a variable mapping, except that atomic variables may also be mapped to path variables. A *weak morphism* from a body B_1 in a body B_2 is a weak variable mapping h such that $h(B_1) \subseteq B_2$.

Now consider an input (Σ, σ) to the implication problem for jaegds. We say that (Σ, σ) is *unambiguous* if either chasing σ with Σ fails, or the chase succeeds, and the following condition holds. Let B' be the body of the jaegd resulting from the chase. Then every weak morphism from a body in Σ to B' must actually be a variable mapping.

Example 5.11. Take Σ and σ from the previous example. We already noted that the chase succeeds immediately. We see there is a weak morphism from the body $\{P(@x : \emptyset)\}$ of the first dependency in Σ, to the body $\{P(\$x : \emptyset)\}$ of σ, namely the mapping $@x \mapsto \$x$. This is not a variable mapping. Hence (Σ, σ) is not unambiguous. □

Example 5.12. For another example, consider the set $\Delta = \{\delta_1, \dots, \delta_6\}$ from Example 5.8. Then (Δ, σ) is always unambiguous for any σ. Indeed, atomic variables occur only in the second component of predicates in Δ, i.e., after the : sign, and path variables can never occur after the : sign in any body. □

The notion of unambiguity captures the cases where the usual proof of completeness of the chase applies in our setting. So, we have the following result.

Proposition 5.13. *Assume* Σ *logically implies* σ*, and* (Σ, σ) *is unambiguous. Then chasing* σ *with* Σ *fails, or the chase succeeds and results in a jaegd whose consequent is a trivial equality.*

It follows that the unambiguous cases of the implication problem for jaegds are decidable by the chase. En route to solving the object–object problem, it is especially important that chasing from Δ is unambiguous, as we saw in Example 5.12.

Equality elimination.

There is one final hurdle to overcome. A discrepancy between bodies of jaegds and bodies of positive J-Logic rules is that the latter can have equalities. We next show, however, that equalities can always be removed.

Lemma 5.14. *Every J-Logic rule is equivalent to a finite set of equality-free rules. Also, every jaegd where we would allow equalities in the body, is equivalent to a finite set of ordinary jaegds.*

We are now ready for the

Proof of Theorem 5.7. Let $\mathbf{P}$ be a program that computes a query Q from $\mathcal{V}_{\text{in}}$ to $\mathcal{V}_{\text{out}}$. For the sake of simplicity we assume $\mathcal{V}_{\text{in}} = \{R\}$ and $\mathcal{V}_{\text{out}} = \{S\}$ consist of a single relation name. Then $\mathbf{P}$ is a set of rules with S in the head predicate and R as the only EDB relation.

Recall from Example 5.8 the set of six jaegds $\Delta = \{\delta_1, \dots, \delta_6\}$ that expresses properness. The main idea is that Q has the object–object property if and only if the "Δ–Δ implication problem" holds for Q. We then leverage the observation made in Example 5.12 that chasing from Δ is unambiguous.

More precisely, for a relation name P and each $i = 1, \dots, 6$, let δ_i^P be the version of δ_i where we substitute P for the name D. Let $\Delta^R = \{\delta_1^R, \dots, \delta_6^R\}$. Then for each each $i = 1, \dots, 6$ and every instance $I \models \Delta^R$, we want to check that $Q(I) \models \delta_i^S$.

Let us begin with δ_1^S. We consider every pair of rules $(\mathbf{r}_1, \mathbf{r}_2)$ from $\mathbf{P}$, where $\mathbf{r}_1$ and $\mathbf{r}_2$ can also be the same rule. Let the head of $\mathbf{r}_j$ be $S(e_j : t_j)$, for $j = 1, 2$. We apply a variable renaming ρ so that $\mathbf{r}_1$ and $\rho(\mathbf{r}_2)$ have no variables in common. Now construct a jaegd with equalities from δ_1, $\mathbf{r}_1$ and $\rho(\mathbf{r}_2)$ as follows. Using fresh variables $\$x$, $@i$ and $@j$, the body consists of the bodies of $\mathbf{r}_1$ and $\rho(\mathbf{r}_2)$, together with the equalities $\$x = e_1$, $\$x = \rho(e_2)$, $t_1 = @i$, and $\rho(t_2) = @j$. The head is $(@i = @j)$. By Lemma 5.14, this jaegd with equalities is equivalent to a finite set of jaegds, which we denote by $\Delta_1^{\mathbf{r}_1, \mathbf{r}_2}$. It is now clear that $Q(I) \models \delta_1^S$ for every $I \models \Delta^R$, if and only if every jaegd in $\Delta_1^{\mathbf{r}_1, \mathbf{r}_2}$ is logically implied by Δ^R. This is a unambiguous case of the implication problem, so it can be solved by the chase.

Checking implication for δ_2–δ_5 is similar. For example, from δ_3, $\mathbf{r}_1$ and $\rho(\mathbf{r}_2)$ and fresh variables $\$x$, $\$y$ and $@i$, we construct a denial constraint with equalities having as body the bodies of $\mathbf{r}_1$ and $\rho(\mathbf{r}_2)$ together with the equalities $e_1 = \$x$, $t_1 = @i$, and $\rho(e_2) = \$x.\$y$. □

Computational complexity.

Like the implication problem for egds in the relational model, the computational complexity of the unambiguous cases of the implication problem for jaegds is NP-complete. Note, however, that in the above proof we only need to chase jaegds from $\Delta_i^{\mathbf{r}_1,\mathbf{r}_2}$ with the fixed set of jaegds Δ^R. Hence each application of the chase would be polynomial, were it not for the following caveat. The caveat is that $\Delta_i^{\mathbf{r}_1,\mathbf{r}_2}$ is obtained after elimination of equalities, which can result in exponentially many rules, and these rules may be exponential in size due to the repeated doubling. Even when the given program has no equalities, there are still equalities to be eliminated in the jaegd constructed from $\mathbf{r}_1$ and $\mathbf{r}_2$. We thus can only conclude an exponential-time upper bound on the complexity of the object–object problem for positive nonrecursive J-Logic programs. We leave the exact complexity open.

6. THE CONTAINMENT PROBLEM OVER FLAT INSTANCES

Let $\mathbf{P}_1$ and $\mathbf{P}_2$ be J-Logic programs both expressing a query from $\mathcal{V}_{\text{in}}$ to $\mathcal{V}_{\text{out}}$; let Q_j be the query expressed by $\mathbf{P}_j$.

Let $\mathcal{F}$ be a family of instances. The *containment problem over* $\mathcal{F}$ asks, given $\mathbf{P}_1$, $\mathbf{P}_2$, $\mathcal{V}_{\text{in}}$ and $\mathcal{V}_{\text{out}}$ as above, whether $Q_1(I) \subseteq Q_2(I)$ for all instances I over $\mathcal{V}_{\text{in}}$ belonging to $\mathcal{F}$. Recall that an instance is *flat* if no packed keys occur in it. In this section we show:

Theorem 6.1. *Let $\mathcal{F}$ be the set of flat instances, and let $\mathcal{PF}$ be the set of proper flat instances. For positive nonrecursive programs, containment over $\mathcal{F}$ is decidable, and so is containment over $\mathcal{PF}$.*

Note that we restrict attention to flat instances. Indeed, our current solution does not work with packed keys in the inputs (see Remark 6.5). It is an interesting topic for further research to see whether our solution can be extended in the presence of packing.

To solve the containment problem over $\mathcal{F}$ one can take inspiration from the inclusion problem for *pattern languages* over an infinite alphabet [19]. The main additional aspect here is the distinction between atomic variables and path variables.

In the field of pattern languages, a pattern is a finite sequence of constants and path variables, so, in our terminology, a path expression without atomic variables and packed key expressions. The *language* of a pattern e is the set $L(e)$ of all flat paths p for which there exists a valuation h such that $h(e) = p$. Here, a flat path is a path in which no packed keys occur, i.e., a nonempty sequence of atomic keys. Note that this essentially interprets patterns over an infinite alphabet, since our universe **dom** of atomic keys is infinite. In this case it is known [19] that $L(e_1) \subseteq L(e_2)$ if and only if there exists a variable mapping h such that $h(e_2) = e_1$. When atomic variables come into play, however, this "homomorphism property" is no longer necessary for containment.

Example 6.2. Let us allow atomic variables in patterns. Then consider the following four patterns:

$$e_1 = \$x.\$y \qquad e_3 = @x.\$y.@z$$
$$e_2 = @x.\$y \qquad e_4 = \$u.@v.\$w$$

Then e_1 and e_2 describe the same language, namely all flat paths of length at least two. There is a variable mapping from e_1 to e_2 but not from e_2 to e_1, since a variable mapping cannot map an atomic variable (in this case $@x$) to a path variable (in this case $\$x$). Also e_3 and e_4 describe the same language, namely all flat paths of length at least three. Here there is neither a variable mapping from e_3 to e_4 nor one from e_4 to e_3.

The simplistic idea to just allow weak variable mappings does not work. For example, there is a weak variable mapping from $@x$ to $\$x$ but $L(\$x)$ is not contained in $L(@x)$. □

We next develop our general solution to the containment problem over flat instances. For simplicity, we always consider positive nonrecursive programs expressing a query from $\mathcal{V}_{\text{in}}$ to $\mathcal{V}_{\text{out}}$ where $\mathcal{V}_{\text{out}} = \{S\}$ is a single-relation vocabulary. Since the programs are not recursive, they can be rewritten as finite sets of rules with S in the head predicate and relation names from $\mathcal{V}_{\text{in}}$ in the bodies.

It is sufficient to solve the containment problem given programs $\mathbf{P}_1$ and $\mathbf{P}_2$ where $\mathbf{P}_1$ consists of a single rule $\mathbf{r}_1$ (since otherwise we can check containment for all rules of $\mathbf{P}_1$ separately). Moreover, we can make the following proviso:

Proviso. *The body of $\mathbf{r}_1$ and the bodies of rules in $\mathbf{P}_2$ do not have equalities. Moreover, these bodies are flat, i.e., do not use packing.*

The first part of the proviso is justified by Lemma 5.14. The second part is justified because we work over flat instances: non-flat bodies can never match anyway. The heads may still use packing.

We begin by noting that there *is* a simple homomorphism theorem when $\mathbf{r}_1$ does not have path variables.

Proposition 6.3. *Assume $\mathbf{r}_1$ does not have path variables. Then $\mathbf{r}_1$ is contained in $\mathbf{P}_2$ over $\mathcal{F}$ if and only if there exists a rule $\mathbf{r}_2 \in \mathbf{P}_2$ such that there is a homomorphism from B_2 to B_1, mapping H_2 to H_1. Here, B_i and H_i denote the body and the head of $\mathbf{r}_i$.*

Proof. The if-direction is straightforward. For the only-if direction, we view B_1 as a (flat) instance I by viewing each variable as an atomic key (called a frozen variable). We similarly view H_1 as a fact. Then clearly $H_1 \in \mathbf{r}_1(I)$, so also $H_1 \in \mathbf{P}_2(I)$. Hence there exists $\mathbf{r}_2 \in \mathbf{P}_2$ and a valuation ν such that $\nu(B_2) \subseteq B_1$ and $\nu(H_2) = H_1$. Since $\mathbf{r}_1$ does not have path variables, ν can map atomic variables only to constants or to (frozen) atomic variables. Hence, we can view ν as a homomorphism from $\mathbf{r}_2$ to $\mathbf{r}_1$. □

We now reduce the containment problem where $\mathbf{r}_1$ has path variables, to infinitely many calls to the containment problem where $\mathbf{r}_1$ does not have path variables. Thereto, we associate to every path variable $\$x$ an infinite sequence $@x^1$, $@x^2$, ... of atomic variables. Obviously, for distinct path variables $\$x$ and $\$y$ we assume $@x^i$ and $@y^j$ are distinct for all i and j.

A *variant* of $\mathbf{r}_1$ is a rule obtained from $\mathbf{r}_1$ as follows. For every path variable $\$x$ in $\mathbf{r}_1$, choose a natural number $n_{\$x}$. We call $n_{\$x}$ the *chosen length* for $\$x$. Now replace each occurrence of $\$x$ in $\mathbf{r}_1$ by the sequence $@x^1 \dots @x^{n_{\$x}}$. Thus, as soon as $\mathbf{r}_1$ has at least one path variable, there are infinitely many variants of $\mathbf{r}_1$.

The following is now clear:

Proposition 6.4. *$\mathbf{r}_1$ is equivalent, over $\mathcal{F}$, to the infinite union of its variants. In particular, $\mathbf{r}_1$ is contained in $\mathbf{P}_2$ over $\mathcal{F}$ if and only if every variant of $\mathbf{r}_1$ is contained in $\mathbf{P}_2$ over $\mathcal{F}$.*

Remark 6.5. The above proposition only works over flat instances. Consider, for example, the rules

$$\mathbf{r}_2 = S(c : \emptyset) \leftarrow R(@u.\$z : \emptyset)$$
$$\mathbf{r}_1 = S(c : \emptyset) \leftarrow R(\$x.\$y : \emptyset)$$

Rule $\mathbf{r}_2$ tests if R contains a path of length at least two, starting with an atomic key, and with the empty value at the leaf. If so, the fact $S(c : \emptyset)$ is returned (c is some constant). An example of a variant of $\mathbf{r}_1$, with 2 as chosen length for $\$x$ and 3 for $\$y$, is

$$S(c : \emptyset) \leftarrow R(@x^1.@x^2.@y^1.@y^2.@y^3 : \emptyset).$$

We see that this variant, and indeed every variant, of $\mathbf{r}_1$ is contained in $\mathbf{r}_2$. Nevertheless $\mathbf{r}_1$ is not contained in $\mathbf{r}_2$ over all instances, as witnessed by the instance $I = \{R(\langle a\rangle.b : \emptyset)\}$. □

The above proposition gives us infinitely many variant containments to check. Our final step reduces this to a finite number.

Proposition 6.6. *Let m be the number of atomic variables used in $\mathbf{P}_2$. Assume all variants of $\mathbf{r}_1$ with chosen lengths up to $m+1$ are contained in $\mathbf{P}_2$ over $\mathcal{F}$. Then every variant of $\mathbf{r}_1$ is contained in $\mathbf{P}_2$ over $\mathcal{F}$.*

Proof. By Proposition 6.3, it is sufficient to show the following claim. *Let $\mathbf{r}$ be a variant of $\mathbf{r}_1$ with a chosen length $k \geq m+1$ for some path variable $\$x$. Assume there is a homomorphism h from a rule $\mathbf{r}_2 \in \mathbf{P}_2$ to $\mathbf{r}$. Let $\mathbf{r}'$ be the same variant as $\mathbf{r}$, except that the chosen length for $\$x$ is increased to $k' > k$. Then there is still a homomorphism from $\mathbf{r}_2$ to $\mathbf{r}'$.*

We argue the claim as follows. Since $k > m$, one of the variant variables for $\$x$, say $@x^j$, is not in the image of h applied to any atomic variable from $\mathbf{r}_2$. Hence it only occurs in the images of some path variables. Each such path variable is mapped by h to a flat path expression in which $@x^j$ occurs. Now for each such variable $\$z$, modify $h(\$z)$ by inserting the sequence $@x^{k+1}\dots@x^{k'}$ behind each occurrence of $@x^j$. The resulting variable mapping h' gives us the desired homomorphism from $\mathbf{r}_2$ to $\mathbf{r}'$. (The only detail is that the variant sequence for $\$x$ is permuted a bit, instead of $@x^1\dots@x^{k'}$ it is now $@x^1\dots@x^j@x^{k+1}\dots@x^{k'}@x^{j+1}\dots@x^k$.) □

We conclude that containment of $\mathbf{r}_1$ in $\mathbf{P}_2$ over $\mathcal{F}$ is decidable with Π_2^{P} complexity. Indeed, instead of trying all variants of $\mathbf{r}_1$, as given by Proposition 6.4, it suffices to try all variants of $\mathbf{r}_1$ with chosen length bounds as given by Proposition 6.6. For each variant we test the existence of a homomorphism as given by Proposition 6.3. We leave open whether the problem is actually Π_2^{P}-hard.

Containment over proper flat instances.

For simplicity, let us assume that $\mathcal{V}_{\mathrm{in}}$ consists of a single relation name D. Recall from Example 5.8 the set Δ of jaegds that expresses properness. We can chase a rule with Δ in much the same way as we chase a jaegd. We establish:

Proposition 6.7. *$\mathbf{r}_1$ is contained in $\mathbf{P}_2$ over $\mathcal{PF}$ if and only if either chasing $\mathbf{r}_1$ with Δ fails, or it succeeds and results in a rule $\mathbf{r}$ such that $\mathbf{r}$ is contained in $\mathbf{P}_2$ over $\mathcal{F}$.*

Proof. For the if-direction, first assume the chase fails. Then $\mathbf{r}_1(I)$ is empty on all proper instances so containment holds trivially. Next assume the chase succeeds and results in the rule $\mathbf{r}$. Let I be a proper flat instance. By the soundness of the chase, we have $\mathbf{r}_1(I) = \mathbf{r}(I)$. By the given, $\mathbf{r}(I) \subseteq \mathbf{P}_2(I)$ and we are done.

For the only-if direction, suppose the chase succeeds and results in the rule $\mathbf{r} = H \leftarrow B$. By Proposition 6.4, we have to show that every variant $\mathbf{r}' = H' \leftarrow B'$ of $\mathbf{r}$ is contained in $\mathbf{P}_2$. We can view B as an instance I by viewing each variable as an atomic key (I is called a frozen body). Because chasing from Δ is unambiguous, we obtain as in the proof of Theorem 5.13 that $I \models \Delta$, i.e., I is proper.

But then I', the frozen variant body B', is also proper. Indeed, by replacing each frozen path variable by a sequence of frozen atomic variables, the functional dependency from paths to atomic values remains satisfied. Moreover, I' is also still prefix-free. In proof, suppose $D(p' : v) \in I'$. The last element s of p' is either a constant or a frozen atomic variable from $\mathbf{r}$, or a frozen atomic variable $@x^n$ coming from a path variable $\$x$ in $\mathbf{r}$. In the latter case, n must be the chosen length for $\$x$. Now suppose there would exists $D(p'.q' : u) \in I'$. Since the first symbol of q' follows the last symbol of p', it is either again a constant or frozen atomic variable from $\mathbf{r}$, or a frozen atomic variable y^1 coming from a path variable $\$u$ in $\mathbf{r}$. We conclude that the presence of $D(p' : v)$ and $D(p'.q' : u)$ in I' would imply the presence of some $D(p : v)$ and $D(p.q : u)$ in I, which is impossible because I is prefix-free.

Clearly, $H' \in \mathbf{r}'(I')$, so also $H' \in \mathbf{r}(I')$ since $\mathbf{r}'$ is a variant of $\mathbf{r}$. Furthermore, since $\mathbf{r}$ was obtained from $\mathbf{r}_1$ by applying chase steps, which are applications of homomorphisms, also $H' \in \mathbf{r}_1(I')$. By the given, then $H' \in \mathbf{P}_2(I')$. This means there exists $\mathbf{r}_2 \in \mathbf{P}_2$ and a matching $\nu : B_2 \to I'$ such that $\nu(B_2) \subseteq I'$ and $\nu(H_2) = H'$. Since $\mathbf{r}'$ does not have path variables, ν can be viewed as a homomorphism from $\mathbf{r}_2$ to $\mathbf{r}'$. Hence, $\mathbf{r}'$ is contained in $\mathbf{P}_2$ as desired. □

7. CONCLUSION

Thanks to the deterministic nature of JSON objects, it is very convenient to view objects as sets of key sequences paired with atomic values. We recommend the use of path variables, ranging over key sequences, in languages for JSON querying for accessing deeply nested data. While the data complexity is polynomial-time, it would be interesting to investigate practical query processing issues involving path variables.

Furthermore, packing is a versatile tool not only for expressive power and the generation of new keys, but also for marking parts of sequences, duplicate elimination, and other tricks. We recommend that practical JSON query processors support packed keys.

Our technical results have shown that the proposed approach is workable. Much further work can be done: Is there a nonrecursive flat–flat theorem? Is the implication problem for jaegds decidable in general? What is the exact complexity of the object–object problem for nonrecursive programs? Is the containment problem for nonrecursive programs decidable in the presence of packing? How does the complexity of the containment problem change when equalities are allowed in rules?

During our research we also encountered the following intriguing puzzle. Consider the extreme case where there exists only one atomic key, and there is no packing. Then J-Logic amounts to monadic Datalog with stratified negation over sets of sequences of a's, with path variables and atomic variables. This corresponds to monadic Datalog with stratified negation over sets of natural numbers, with natural number constants and variables, and addition as the only operation. Which functions on sets of natural numbers are expressible in this language?

Acknowledgments.

We thank Dominik Freydenberger and Georg Gottlob for helpful communications. We also thank the anonymous reviewers for their suggestions, which we will keep in mind when preparing a journal version of this paper.

8. REFERENCES

[1] S. Abiteboul and R. Hull. Data functions, datalog and negation. In H. Boral and P.A. Larson, editors, *1988 Proceedings SIGMOD International Conference on Management of Data*, pages 143–153. ACM Press, 1988.

[2] S. Abiteboul, R. Hull, and V. Vianu. *Foundations of Databases.* Addison-Wesley, 1995.

[3] S. Abiteboul and P.C. Kanellakis. Object identity as a query language primitive. *Journal of the ACM*, 45(5):798–842, 1998.

[4] S. Abiteboul and V. Vianu. Procedural languages for database queries and updates. *Journal of Computer and System Sciences*, 41(2):181–229, 1990.

[5] S. Abiteboul and V. Vianu. Datalog extensions for database queries and updates. *Journal of Computer and System Sciences*, 43(1):62–124, 1991.

[6] P.C. Arocena, B. Glavic, and R.J. Miller. Value invention in data exchange. In *Proceedings 2013 SIGMOD Conference*, pages 157–168. ACM, 2013.

[7] P. Barceló and R. Pichler, editors. *Datalog in Academia and Industry: Second International Workshop, Datalog 2.0*, volume 7494 of *Lecture Notes in Computer Science*. Springer, 2012.

[8] C. Beeri and M.Y. Vardi. A proof procedure for data dependencies. *Journal of the ACM*, 31(4):718–741, 1984.

[9] A. Bonner and G. Mecca. Sequences, Datalog, and transducers. *Journal of Computer and System Sciences*, 57:234–259, 1998.

[10] A.J. Bonner and G. Mecca. Querying sequence databases with transducers. *Acta Informatica*, 36:511–544, 2000.

[11] P. Buneman, A. Deutsch, and W.-C. Tan. A deterministic model for semi-structured data. http://users.soe.ucsc.edu/~tan/papers/1998/icdt.pdf. Presented at the Workshop on Query Processing for Semistructured Data and Non-standard Data Formats, Jerusalem, Israel, January 13, 1999.

[12] P. Buneman, S.A. Naqvi, V. Tannen, and L. Wong. Principles of programming with complex objects and collection types. *Theoretical Computer Science*, 149(1):3–48, 1995.

[13] L. Cabibbo. The expressive power of stratified logic programs with value invention. *Information and Computation*, 147(1):22–56, 1998.

[14] A.K. Chandra and D. Harel. Computable queries for relational data bases. *Journal of Computer and System Sciences*, 21(2):156–178, 1980.

[15] O. de Moor, G. Gottlob, T. Furche, and A. Sellers, editors. *Datalog Reloaded: First International Workshop, Datalog 2010*, volume 6702 of *Lecture Notes in Computer Science*. Springer, 2011.

[16] The JSON data interchange format. Standard ECMA-404, October 2013.

[17] D. Florescu and G. Fourny. JSONiq: The history of a query language. *IEEE Internet Computing*, 17(5):86–90, 2013.

[18] G. Fourny. JSONiq, the SQL of NoSQL. http://www.28.io/jsoniq-the-sql-of-nosql. Retrieved 25 November 2016.

[19] D.D. Freydenberger and D. Reidenbach. Bad news on decision problems for patterns. *Information and Computation*, 208(1):83–96, 2010.

[20] T. Furche, G. Gottlob, B. Neumayr, and E. Sallinger. Data wrangling for big data: Towards a lingua franca for data wrangling. In R. Pichler and A. Soares da Silva, editors, *Proceedings 10th Alberto Mendelzon International Workshop on Foundations of Data Management*, volume 1644 of *CEUR Workshop Proceedings*, 2016.

[21] H. Garcia-Molina, Y. Papakonstantinou, D. Quass, A. Rajaraman, Y. Sagiv, J. Ullman, V. Vassalos, and J. Widom. The TSIMMIS approach to mediation: data models and languages. *Journal of Intelligent Information Systems*, 8(2):117–132, 1997.

[22] M. Gyssens, J. Paredaens, J. Van den Bussche, and D. Van Gucht. A graph-oriented object database model. *IEEE Transactions on Knowledge and Data Engineering*, 6(4):572–586, 1994.

[23] S.S. Huang, T.J. Green, and B.T. Loo. Datalog and emerging applications: an interactive tutorial. In *Proceedings 2011 ACM SIGMOD International Conference on Management of Data*, pages 1213–1216. ACM Press, 2011.

[24] R. Hull and M. Yoshikawa. ILOG: Declarative creation and manipulation of object identifiers. In D. McLeod, R. Sacks-Davis, and H. Schek, editors, *Proceedings of the 16th International Conference on Very Large Data Bases*, pages 455–468. Morgan Kaufmann, 1990.

[25] M. Kifer and J. Wu. A logic for programming with complex objects. *Journal of Computer and System Sciences*, 47(1):77–120, 1993.

[26] A. Klug and R. Price. Determining view dependencies using tableaux. *ACM Transactions on Database Systems*, 7:361–380, 1982.

[27] G. Kuper and M. Vardi. The logical data model. *ACM Transactions on Database Systems*, 18(3):379–413, 1993.

[28] G. Mecca and A.J. Bonner. Query languages for sequence databases: Termination and complexity. *IEEE Transactions on Knowledge and Data Engineering*, 13(3):519–525, 2001.

[29] K.W. Ong, Y. Papakonstantinou, and R. Vernoux. The SQL++ query language: Configurable, unifying and semi-structured. arXiv:1405.3631, 2015.

[30] J. Paredaens and D. Van Gucht. Converting nested algebra expressions into flat algebra expressions. *ACM Transactions on Database Systems*, 17(1):65–93, 1992.

[31] F. Pezoa, J.L. Reutter, F. Suarez, M. Ugarte, and D. Vrgoč. Foundations of JSON Schema. In *Proceedings 25th International Conference on World Wide Web*, pages 263–273, 2016.

[32] A. Poggi et al. Linking data to ontologies. *Journal on Data Semantics*, 10:133–173, 2008.

[33] K. Tajima. Schemaless semistructured data revisited: Reinventing Peter Buneman's deterministic semistructured data model. In V. Tannen, L. Wong, et al., editors, *In Search of Elegance in the Theory and Practice of Computation*, volume 8000 of *Lecture Notes in Computer Science*, pages 466–482. Springer, 2013.

[34] J. Van den Bussche and J. Paredaens. The expressive power of complex values in object-based data models. *Information and Computation*, 120:220–236, 1995.

[35] J. Van den Bussche, D. Van Gucht, M. Andries, and M. Gyssens. On the completeness of object-creating database transformation languages. *Journal of the ACM*, 44(2):272–319, 1997.

[36] T.L. Veldhuizen. Leapfrog triejoin: A simple, worst-case optimal join algorithm. In *Proceedings 17th International Conference on Database Theory*, pages 96–106, 2014.

Reverse Engineering SPJ-Queries from Examples

Yaacov Y. Weiss
Rachel and Selim Benin School of Computer Science and Engineering
Hebrew University of Jerusalem
Jerusalem, Israel
yyweiss@cs.huji.ac.il

Sara Cohen
Rachel and Selim Benin School of Computer Science and Engineering
Hebrew University of Jerusalem
Jerusalem, Israel
sara@cs.huji.ac.il

ABSTRACT

This paper investigates the problem of *reverse engineering*, i.e., *learning*, select-project-join (SPJ) queries from a user-provided example set, containing positive and negative tuples. The goal is then to determine whether there exists a query returning all the positive tuples, but none of the negative tuples, and furthermore, to find such a query, if it exists. These are called the *satisfiability* and *learning* problems, respectively. The ability to solve these problems is an important step in simplifying the querying process for non-expert users.

This paper thoroughly investigates the satisfiability and learning problems in a variety of settings. In particular, we consider several classes of queries, which allow different combinations of the operators select, project and join. In addition, we compare the complexity of satisfiability and learning, when the query is, or is not, of bounded size. We note that bounded-size queries are of particular interest, as they can be used to avoid over-fitting (i.e., tailoring a query precisely to only the seen examples).

In order to fully understand the underlying factors which make satisfiability and learning (in)tractable, we consider different components of the problem, namely, the size of a query to be learned, the size of the schema and the number of examples. We study the complexity of our problems, when considering these as part of the input, as constants or as parameters (i.e., as in parameterized complexity analysis). Depending on the setting, the complexity of satisfiability and learning can vary significantly. Among other results, our analysis also provides new problems that are complete for $W[3]$, for which few natural problems are known. Finally, by considering a variety of settings, we derive insight on how the different facets of our problem interplay with the size of the database, thereby providing the theoretical foundations necessary for a future implementation of query learning from examples.

PODS'17, May 14-19, 2017, Chicago, IL, USA

DOI: http://dx.doi.org/10.1145/3034786.3056112

1. INTRODUCTION

Increasingly many datasets are publicly available, and can be freely accessed. Census data, US and European government data, geospatial datasets, bibliographic information, health-care statistics, human genetic information and NASA's database of satellite imagery of Earth, are just a few of such datasets. However, public datasets can be effectively leveraged only if users can formulate their queries of interest. Unfortunately, for naive users, formulating a query in SQL or in relational algebra can be a very challenging task.

One way to simplify the querying process is to allow users to provide a set of positive and negative examples, i.e., tuples they expect to appear in the result, and tuples they expect not to appear in the result. Then, a system could attempt to learn a query of interest to the user, which satisfies the given examples. This can be useful for users who are somewhat familiar with the query language, as the system would suggest a satisfying query, which could be adjusted by the user to derive his particular query of interest. Adjusting a given query may be easier than deriving a query from scratch. Second, and more importantly, for naive users who are not familiar with the query language at all, the system could learn a query satisfying the examples, and then present all of the query results to the user. Using an interactive process (as described in [2]), the user may mark additional tuples as positive and negative examples, thereby eventually finding data of interest. Such a system is useful even for languages for which precise learning of a concept is intractable [3, 4]. We do not describe an interactive system, rather consider the underlying single step of deriving a query from a set of examples.

This paper studies the problem of *learning*, i.e., reverse engineering, a select-project-join query satisfying a given set of positive and negative examples. To be more a bit more precise, given a database and an example set, we study the complexity of finding a query that returns all positive examples, but none of the negative examples, over the given database.[1] The complexity of this problem is highly dependent on the types of operators that are allowed in the query to be learned. An orthogonal issue is which components of the problem are part of the input, and which can be considered constants, or parameters (as in parameterized complexity analysis). We consider the size of the query to be

[1]This is different from the learnability problem, which focuses on the complexity of learning a specific query, e.g., [1]. We are simply interested in finding a candidate query satisfying the examples.

learned (for bounded sized queries), the size of the schema and the number of examples, as possible inputs, constants or parameters to our problems.

The following examples demonstrate some of the issues that arise when learning queries.

EXAMPLE 1.1 (UNBOUNDED SIZE QUERIES). *Consider the database $\mathcal{D}$ appearing in Figure 1, (while ignoring the "✓" and "✗"-marks), and an example set consisting of the positive tuple $t_p = \{A : 1, C : 2, E : 5\}$ and the negative tuple $t_n = \{A : 1, C : 2, E : 4\}$. When learning a query containing selections and projections, the query*

$$\pi_{A,C,E}(\sigma_{A=1}(\sigma_{C=2}(\sigma_{E=5}(R_6))))$$

satisfies the example set over $\mathcal{D}$ as it returns t_p, but not t_n. However, this query is rather restrictive, as it can return only t_p, and no other tuples. Thus, it suffers from over-fitting of the examples, and does not help us generalize beyond the user's examples. When bounding the size of the query to contain at most two operators, one satisfying query is

$$\pi_{A,C,E}(\sigma_{E\geq 5}(R_6)).$$

Clearly, such a query is of more interest. Hence, we will also study the problem of learning queries of bounded size. However, finding queries of bounded size will usually be more difficult (unless the bound is considered to be a constant).

EXAMPLE 1.2 (OPERATOR TYPES). *Another issue that affects the complexity of learning is the combinations of operators allowed in the query to be learned. For some combinations, simply determining whether a given query satisfies the example set can be intractable. This holds, e.g., for queries containing projection and natural join. Thus, even if we can identify a small number of candidate queries that must be considered in order to satisfy an example set, it still may be intractable to determine if there exists a satisfying query. To demonstrate, for the tuples t_p and t_n in Example 1.1, the query*

$$\pi_{A,C,E}(R_5 \bowtie R_6),$$

is satisfying. However, determining this in the general case is difficult.

In this case, assuming a constant bound on the query size makes learning tractable, as query evaluation, for constant sized queries, is in PTIME. In other cases, assuming a bound on the size of the schema, or the number of examples, can yield tractability. All such assumptions are natural, as the size of the query, schema, and example set, are likely to be significantly smaller than the size of the database.

EXAMPLE 1.3 (CONSTANTS VS. PARAMETERS). *While the size of the query, schema, and example set are likely to be not very large, they may also not be negligible. Therefore, an algorithm running in time $\mathcal{O}(|\mathcal{D}|^k)$, where k is one of the above parameters, will probably not be efficient enough in practice. Hence, it is of great interest to consider the parameterized complexity analysis of our problems.*

For example, consider the problem of learning a query of bounded size k, containing projection and selection, such as the query $\pi_{A,C,E}(\sigma_{E\geq 5}(R_6))$ from Example 1.1. This problem is in PTIME, when k is considered a constant. But, when k is a parameter to the problem, it becomes $W[3]$-complete. Therefore, it is unlikely for an algorithm to exist for this problem, that runs in time polynomial in $|\mathcal{D}|$ and exponential in k.

The main contribution of this paper is a full characterization of the complexity of learning a query from examples, as a function of the type of query to be learned, and the input parameters to the problem. This yields insight into how the various facets of our problem interplay with one another and provides the theoretical foundations necessary for a future implementation of query learning from examples. Among other results, our analysis also provides new problems that are complete for $W[3]$, for which few natural problems are known.

This paper is structured as follows. In Section 2, we discuss related work on learning queries from examples. Section 3 provides necessary notation and definitions, and formally defines our problems of interest. In Section 4 we consider the complexity of learning and satisfiability when no parameters are given. In Sections 5, 6 and 7 we study learning and satisfiability when the size of the query, size of the schema, and number of examples, respectively, are parameters. Finally, in Section 8, we conclude. We note that throughout the paper, we omit formal proofs, and provide intuition and examples, instead. Due to lack of space, we include only the proofs for our $W[3]$-completeness results in the appendix.

2. RELATED WORK

The problem of learning a concept from a set of examples, often called the *reverse engineering problem,* has been studied for decades, e.g., [16, 19] studied the problem of learning an automaton, based on examples. Within the area of databases, [10] consider learning XPath from XML examples, [11, 12] learn tree patterns from graph examples and [8] learn path queries from graphs. Recently, [5] study the problem of reverse engineering SPARQL queries from example triples. Due to the difference in the data models and languages, the above work does not imply results on learning relational algebra from queries. We note that SPARQL does share some characteristics with relational algebra. However, the setting of [5] is very different from ours, e.g., the schema is of constant width, queries are unbounded in size, and there is no projection or natural join.

Several papers have considered learning join queries from examples. In [24], the problem of reverse engineering join queries is considered. However, they assume that they are given the complete answer, and they must find a query (without selections) returning precisely this result. In addition to differences in the problem setting, [24] deals with practical aspects, and does not study the complexity of the problems. In [23], the focus is also on finding a query returning precisely a given result (or one that is approximately the same), while [22] studies the problem of refining a given query, to include additional results. In a recent work, [7] studies the complexity of learning queries from examples. They also do not allow selections, but they allow for arbitrary equijoins (unlike our setting which includes only natural join). When arbitrary equijoins are allowed, satisfying queries can be of exponential size, which is a major source of complexity in their setting. To overcome this problem, they consider queries with bounded tree width. In our paper, we only allow for natural joins, thus avoiding exponential size queries. (This is also the reason why we do not allow renaming of attributes in our queries.) This difference implies completely different complexity results.

Learnability of conjunctive queries was the focus of [9]. Learnability differs from the problem at hand as it studies

R_1		
A	C	D
1	1	1
1	2	2

R_2		
B	C	D
1	1	1
2	2	2

R_3		
A	B	D
1	1	1
1	2	2

	R_6				
	A	B	C	D	E
✓	1	2	3	4	5
✗	1	3	2	3	4
	2	4	4	1	3
	5	3	2	4	2
✗	4	2	3	1	2
	2	2	4	3	2
✓	1	1	2	1	5
✓	1	5	4	2	3

R_4		
A	C	D
1	1	1
1	1	2

R_5		
A	B	C
1	2	1
1	2	2
1	1	2

Figure 1: Database for a running example.

the complexity of the process of honing in on one specific query, while interactively receiving examples from the user, as opposed to simply finding an arbitrary candidate query satisfying all examples. (Satisfiability is also considered in [9], but there are significant differences between the query language considered there, and our language, e.g., [9] does not have selection, and has limited projection.) In [18], the focus is also in learnability, and it is shown that under cryptographic assumptions, learnability of acyclic conjunctive queries is hard.

It is also possible to view the problem at hand as a variation of the general question of the expressive power of relational algebra, studied in [6] and [21]. While several of the scenarios we consider can be formulated in these terms, the differences in the settings prevent results from [6,21] from being applicable in our settings. Intuitively, these papers consider the following problem. Given a database $\mathcal{D}$ and a relation R, does there exist a query in relational algebra that returns precisely R from $\mathcal{D}$. They consider different operators from those considered in this paper. In addition, they aim to find a query returning a precise relation, while our requirements on the relation to be returned are different—we only require inclusion and exclusion of a set of tuples. Thus, the results of [6,21] are not applicable in our setting. Placing our work in the wider framework of the expressive power of relational algebra can give rise to interesting future work, e.g., extensions of the style of [14] to the work of [6,21] can be considered for the problem we investigate.

Beyond the significant differences in settings between our work and previous work, no work to date has considered the parameterized complexity of learning queries from examples. Parameterized complexity provides a fine-grained analysis, which clearly delineates which factors give rise to intractability in practice. Parameterized complexity and the W-hierarchy was first introduced in [13]. A summary of results on parameterized complexity of query evaluation appears in [17]. The main result related to our work, is that of [20], which shows (among other results) that evaluation of conjunctive queries is $W[1]$-complete with respect to the size of the query. We utilize this result in several proofs.

3. DEFINITIONS

Relations, Databases and Schemas. A *tuple* is a set of pairs $t = \{A_1 : c_1, \ldots, A_n : c_n\}$, with $n \geq 1$, where A_i is an *attribute* and c_i is a value in a totally ordered domain. In addition, we require $A_i \neq A_j$, for all $i \neq j$. We use $ar(t)$ to denote the *arity* of t, i.e., n, and $schema(t)$ to denote the *schema* of t, i.e., $\{A_1, \ldots, A_n\}$.

A *relation* $R, S, \ldots$ is a named set of tuples, all of which have the same schema. We use $ar(R)$ and $schema(R)$ to denote the arity and schema of the tuples in R. We use $name(R)$ to denote the name of the relation R. A *database* is a set of relations $\mathcal{D} = \{R_1, \ldots, R_n\}$. We use $schema(\mathcal{D})$ to denote the set of pairs $\{name(R_i) : schema(R_i) \mid i \leq n\}$. We use $size(schema(\mathcal{D}))$ to denote the sum of arities of all relations in $schema(\mathcal{D})$. In particular, note that if $size(schema(\mathcal{D})) = k$, then $schema(\mathcal{D})$ contains at most k relations.

EXAMPLE 3.1. *The database instance $\mathcal{D}$ which appears in Figure 1 contains 6 relations, with a total of 19 tuples, and has a schema of size 20.*

Queries. We use Q, Q' to denote queries. Queries will be written in relational algebra, using the operations natural join, selection and projection, denoted $\bowtie, \sigma, \pi$, respectively. For queries with disjoint schemas, natural join is simply a Cartesian product. We use Θ to denote the set of comparison operators $\{=, \neq, \leq, \geq\}$. Conditions in a selection operation (abstractly denoted as ψ) are comparisons of attributes with constants, of the form $A_i \ \theta \ c$ where A_i is an attribute, c is a constant, and $\theta \in \Theta$. Each selection operation contains a single comparison. Sometimes we will restrict the discussion to subsets of Θ, such as $\Theta_{pos} = \Theta - \{\neq\}$. Note that we only consider natural join in this paper, and not arbitrary conditional joins. In addition, to simplify, we assume that join always precedes selection, which, in turn, precedes projection.

We use $Q(\mathcal{D})$ to denote the set of tuples derived by applying query Q to database $\mathcal{D}$. We use $ar(Q)$ to denote the arity of the results of Q and $schema(Q)$ to denote the schema of the result of Q, defined recursively as follows:

1. $schema(R)$, if $Q = R$, for some relation R;
2. $schema(Q')$, if $Q = \sigma_\psi(Q')$;
3. $\{A_1, \ldots, A_k\}$, if $Q = \pi_{A_1,\ldots,A_k}(Q')$;
4. $schema(Q') \cup schema(Q'')$, if $Q = Q' \bowtie Q''$.

EXAMPLE 3.2. *Consider the queries $Q_1 = \pi_{A,D}(R_1 \bowtie R_6)$ and $Q_2 = \sigma_{D \geq 2}(R_6)$. Then, we have*

$$schema(Q_1) = \{A, D\} \quad schema(Q_2) = \{A, B, C, D, E\}.$$

Example Sets. The result of applying a query to a database is a set of tuples. Hence, such tuples can be used as examples of what the user expects (or does not expect) to be returned by a query. Formally, an *example* e is a tuple. We say that e is a *positive example* if it is expected to appear in the output, and is a *negative example*, otherwise.

An *example set* E is a set of positive and negative examples, all having the same schema, denoted $schema(E)$. Given a database $\mathcal{D}$ and an example set E, we say that a query Q *satisfies* E if *(1)* $schema(E) = schema(Q)$ *and (2)* for all $e \in E$, it holds that $e \in Q(\mathcal{D})$ if and only if e is a positive example.

EXAMPLE 3.3. *Consider the database instance $\mathcal{D}$ from Figure 1 and the example set E containing as positive and negative examples all tuples marked with "✓" and "✗", respectively. Recall queries Q_1 and Q_2 from Example 3.2. Query Q_1 does not satisfy E over $\mathcal{D}$, because $schema(E) \neq schema(Q_1)$. Query Q_2 does not satisfy E over $\mathcal{D}$, because $Q_2(\mathcal{D})$ does not return the positive example*

$$\{A:1, B:1, C:2, D:1, E:5\}.$$

The query $\sigma_{A=1}(\sigma_{B\neq3}(R_6))$ satisfies E over $\mathcal{D}$, as it returns all the positive examples (and none of the negative examples) when applied to the database $\mathcal{D}$.

Query Classes. In this paper, we are interested in learning queries from example sets. The difficulty of this problem can depend on the operators allowed within the query, as well as on the type of example sets allowed. We use $\mathcal{Q}^O$, where O is a list of operators from $\{\bowtie, \sigma(f), \pi\}$, to denote a class of RA queries. The query class $\mathcal{Q}^O$ contains all queries using only the operators in O, where $f \subseteq \Theta$ lists the permitted selection operators. We note that we always assume that $f \neq \emptyset$, if O contains selection. In our queries, the operators $\bowtie, \sigma, \pi$ (when appearing) are evaluated in this order (i.e., joins, then selections, and finally projection).

We may sometimes be interested in bounding the size of a query. Learning queries of small, bounded, size is of interest, as such queries will avoid over-fitting of the given example set. They will also be simpler to understand, and thus, can be of more interest to the user. To formalize this notion, we define the *size* of a query Q, denoted $size(Q)$, recursively, as:

1. 1, if $Q = R$, for some relation R.
2. $size(Q') + 1$, if $Q = \pi_{A_1,\dots,A_n}(Q')$.
3. $size(Q') + 1$, if $Q = \sigma_\psi(Q')$;
4. $size(Q') + size(Q'')$, if $Q = Q' \bowtie Q''$;

Now, if $\mathcal{Q}^O$ is a class of queries, we use $\mathcal{Q}^O_k$ to denote the subset of $\mathcal{Q}^O$ that contains only queries Q such that $size(Q) \leq k$. We use $\mathcal{Q}$ as an abstract notation for a query class, if O, and possibly k, are not of importance.

EXAMPLE 3.4. *Recall the queries in Example 3.2. The query $Q_1 = \pi_{A,D}(R_1 \bowtie R_6)$ has size 3, as it joins 2 relations, and then performs a projection. Query $Q_2 = \sigma_{D=2}(R_6)$ has size 2.*

Problems of Interest. In this paper we will be interested in the complexity of determining whether there exists a satisfying query for an example set, as well as in finding such a query, if one exists. Thus, our two problems of interest are defined as follows.

PROBLEM 1 (SATISFIABILITY). *Given a query class $\mathcal{Q}$, the* satisfiability problem, *denoted* SAT($\mathcal{Q}$) *is defined as follows: Given an example set E and a database $\mathcal{D}$, determine whether there exists a query $Q \in \mathcal{Q}$ that satisfies E over $\mathcal{D}$.*

PROBLEM 2 (LEARNING). *Given a query class $\mathcal{Q}$, the* learning problem, *denoted* LEARN($\mathcal{Q}$) *is defined as follows: Given an example set E and a database $\mathcal{D}$, find a query $Q \in \mathcal{Q}$ that satisfies E over $\mathcal{D}$, or determine that such a query does not exist.*

We will be interested in a bounded variant of the above two problems, defined as follows.

PROBLEM 3 (BOUNDED SATISFIABILITY). *Given a query class $\mathcal{Q}$, the* bounded-query-size satisfiability problem, *denoted* BSAT($\mathcal{Q}$) *is defined as follows: Given an example set E, a database $\mathcal{D}$, and a value k, determine whether there exists a query $Q \in \mathcal{Q}$ that satisfies E over $\mathcal{D}$ such that the size of Q is bounded by k.*

The *bounded-query-size learning problem*, denoted BLEARN($\mathcal{Q}$) is defined similarly.

The complexity of these problems depends highly upon the types of example sets and queries allowed. Thus, we will study these problems for a variety of settings. We note that even when we can determine that if a satisfying query exists, it must be one among a small predetermined set of possible queries $Q_1, \dots, Q_k$, these problems may still be hard, since it may not be possible to determine in polynomial time whether tuples in the example set are in the result of evaluating some query Q_i over a given database instance $\mathcal{D}$.

Constants and Parameters. The complexity of satisfiability and learning will obviously depend on the size of the input. In our problems, there are many different natural components to the problem, whose size may be of interest:

1. *The number of tuples in the database, denoted $|\mathcal{D}|$:* Finding a satisfying query often involves evaluating a query Q over the database, to check for satisfaction of the example set. The size of the database will impact the time it takes to evaluate a query. In addition, the search for a satisfying query is sometimes driven by looking for tuples in the database, that can be used to derive positive tuples in the example set. If there are more tuples in the database, there will naturally be more candidate tuples of origin, and hence, more candidate queries.
2. *The size of the query to be learned, for bounded-sized queries:* The complexity of learning queries from a class $\mathcal{Q}_k$ (containing queries of size at most k), is obviously dependent on k. For larger values of k, there will be more queries to consider, and query evaluation will be more expensive.
3. *The size of the database schema, denoted $|schema(\mathcal{D})|$:* A satisfying query may join relations from the database,

or perform selections over attributes in the database. The maximum number of such joins will be determined by the number of relations in the database. The number of different selections considered may also be a function of the number of attributes in the database. Hence the size of the schema can directly affect the size of a query to be learned.

4. *The number of examples in the example set, denoted* $|E|$*:* As mentioned above, we may search for a satisfying query by looking for tuples that can (resp., cannot) be used to derive positive (resp., negative) examples. Hence, when there are more examples, it may be more difficult to find a satisfying query.

Among the four components considered above, the first component, i.e., $|\mathcal{D}|$, is likely to be the largest by far, in practice. Hence, we will never assume that the number of tuples is bounded in size. For each of the other three components, it is of interest to study the complexity of satisfiability and learning, when they may be bounded in size. We differentiate between two types of bounds on k, $|schema(\mathcal{D})|$ and $|E|$: *(1)* the component is assumed to be a constant or *(2)* the component is a parameter to the problem. For the former, we would say that an algorithm running in time $\mathcal{O}(|\mathcal{D}|^c)$, where c is one of k, $|schema(\mathcal{D})|$ or $|E|$, is in PTIME. For the latter, we consider parameterized complexity analysis, and thus, would consider an algorithm running in time $\mathcal{O}(p(|\mathcal{D}|) \cdot f(c))$, where p is a polynomial function over $|\mathcal{D}|$ and f is a (computable) function over c, to be fixed parameter tractable. Note that when $|\mathcal{D}|$ is large, and c is not negligible, an algorithm with the latter runtime will be asymptotically faster.

In light of the above discussion, we consider four flavors of our problems. In Section 4, we study satisfiability and learning when there are no bounded components to our problem. Then, in Section 5, we assume that the queries to be learned are of bounded size, i.e., in $\mathcal{Q}_k$, and study the complexity of our problems both when k is a constant, and when it is a parameter. Section 6 considers the size of the schema, and again, analyzes the complexity of our problem both when the schema size is a constant, and when it is a parameter. Finally, in Section 7 we consider the complexity of our problems when the number of examples is a constant, or a parameter.

REMARK 3.1. *It is important to note that throughout our paper, we consider learning both queries that are unbounded in size, and those that are in* $\mathcal{Q}_k$. *In all sections, other than Section 5, we assume that k is part of the input of the problem. Only in Section 5 do we assume that k is a constant, or a parameter of the problem. Note that even when the query to be learned is bounded in size, it can be natural to view k as part of the input. This is in the spirit of the well-known measure of combined complexity.*

4. NO PARAMETERS

In this section, we consider the complexity of learning queries from examples, when there are no parameters, i.e., all components of the problem are part of the input. In particular, we do not assume a constant bound on the size of the schema or example set. In addition, even when learning bounded-sized queries from a class $\mathcal{Q}$ (queries of size at most k), we do not consider k to be a constant in our complexity analysis (and thus, e.g., a runtime of $|\mathcal{D}|^k$ is not polynomial). This analysis is in the spirit of the standard notion of combined complexity.

We start by considering the class of queries $\mathcal{Q}^{\pi}$, i.e., queries containing only the project operator. Recall that example sets contain tuples, i.e., sets of the form $\{A_1 : c_1, \ldots, A_n : c_n\}$. Hence, the queries in $\mathcal{Q}^{\pi}$ that can satisfy a given example set E are of the form $\pi_{A_1,\ldots,A_n} R$, where R is a relation.[2] Clearly, given a relation R, one can determine in polynomial time whether $\pi_{A_1,\ldots,A_n} R$ satisfies E. Hence, in the remainder of the paper, we do not consider learning queries that contain only the project operation.

The following theorem summarizes the complexity of learning queries of unbounded size, for different combinations of operators. For tractable cases, we show how learning can be performed efficiently, while for intractable cases, we show that determining satisfiability is already hard.

THEOREM 4.1. *Let f be any nonempty subset of* Θ.

1. LEARN($\mathcal{Q}^{\sigma(f)}$), LEARN($\mathcal{Q}^{\bowtie}$) *and* LEARN($\mathcal{Q}^{\sigma(f),\bowtie}$) *are in PTIME;*
2. SAT($\mathcal{Q}^{\pi,\sigma(f)}$) *is NP-complete;*
3. SAT($\mathcal{Q}^{\pi,\bowtie}$) *and* SAT($\mathcal{Q}^{\pi,\sigma(f),\bowtie}$) *are both NP-hard and coNP-hard, and in DP.*

We explain the intuition behind these results, while formal proofs are omitted, due to lack of space. Tractability of LEARN($\mathcal{Q}^{\sigma(f)}$) follows from the fact that queries in $\mathcal{Q}^{\sigma(f)}$ can be evaluated in polynomial time, and a single most specific query, for a given set of examples, can be identified. This is demonstrated next.

EXAMPLE 4.2. *Consider the relation R_6 from Figure 1, as well as the example set containing as positive and negative examples, the tuples marked by "✓" and "✗", respectively. When learning a query in $\mathcal{Q}^{\sigma(f)}$, we can simply consider the single query containing the most restrictive conditions allowed by f, given the positive examples. For example, if $f = \Theta_{pos}$, this is the query*[3]

$$\sigma_{A=1}(\sigma_{1\leq B\leq 5}(\sigma_{2\leq C\leq 4}(\sigma_{1\leq D\leq 4}(\sigma_{3\leq E\leq 5}(R_6))))),$$

which does not satisfy the example set. Hence, no satisfying query exists in $\mathcal{Q}^{\sigma(\Theta_{pos})}$. When allowing $\neq$-comparisons, additional selections can be added, such as $\sigma_{B\neq 3}$, $\sigma_{D\neq 3}$ and $\sigma_{E\neq 4}$. Such selections will yield a satisfying query. As will be shown later, when the class of queries considered is bounded in size, satisfiability becomes intractable, as, intuitively, it is difficult to choose a small subset of selections that yield a satisfying query.

Interestingly, LEARN($\mathcal{Q}^{\bowtie}$) (Claim 1 of Theorem 4.1) is tractable, even though fully evaluating queries for this class of queries is intractable, as the query may return an exponential number of tuples. Intuitively, this follows from two observations. First, given a specific tuple t and a database

[2]Technically, one may also consider queries of the form $\pi_{A_1,\ldots,A_n}(\pi_{B_1,\ldots,B_m} R)$, where each A_i is among B_j. However, such queries may be safely ignored, as it only increases query size, but does not increase expressive power. Note also that the order in which attributes are listed in a projection operator is of no importance.

[3]We use $\sigma_{c_1\leq A\leq c_2}$ as a shorthand for $\sigma_{A\geq c_1}\sigma_{A\leq c_2}$.

	A_{x_1}	$A_{\bar{x}_1}$	A_{x_2}	$A_{\bar{x}_2}$	A_{x_3}	$A_{\bar{x}_3}$	A_1	A_2
$t^p_{x_1}$	1	0	0	0	0	0	x_1	0
$t^n_{x_1}$	0	1	0	0	0	0	x_1	0
$t^b_{x_1}$	1	1	0	0	0	0	0	1
$t^p_{x_2}$	0	0	1	0	0	0	x_2	0
$t^n_{x_2}$	0	0	0	1	0	0	x_2	0
$t^b_{x_2}$	0	0	1	1	0	0	0	1
$t^p_{x_3}$	0	0	0	0	1	0	x_3	0
$t^n_{x_3}$	0	0	0	0	0	1	x_3	0
$t^b_{x_3}$	0	0	0	0	1	1	0	1
$t^1_{\phi_1}$	0	1	0	0	0	0	ϕ_1	1
$t^2_{\phi_1}$	0	0	1	0	0	0	ϕ_1	1
$t^3_{\phi_1}$	0	0	0	0	0	1	ϕ_1	1
$t^1_{\phi_2}$	1	0	0	0	0	0	ϕ_2	1
$t^2_{\phi_2}$	0	0	1	0	0	0	ϕ_2	1
$t^3_{\phi_2}$	0	0	0	0	1	0	ϕ_2	1
t_0	0	0	0	0	0	0	0	0

Figure 2: Reduction from 3-SAT for Example 4.4.

$\mathcal{D}$, it is possible to determine in polynomial time whether t is returned by a query $Q \in \mathcal{Q}^{\bowtie}$, while avoiding full evaluation of $Q(\mathcal{D})$ (which may be exponential in size). Second, the result of a join query monotonically decreases when additional joins are added (as long as the new joins do not introduce new attributes). Thus, we can create a most specific query returning the positive examples, and then check (without full evaluation) whether the negative examples are returned. Tractability of LEARN($\mathcal{Q}^{\sigma(f),\bowtie}$) follows by combining the ideas for $\mathcal{Q}^{\bowtie}$ and for $\mathcal{Q}^{\sigma(f)}$.

EXAMPLE 4.3. *Consider the relations $R_1, \ldots, R_6$ from the database $\mathcal{D}$ appearing in Figure 1, and the example set E_1 containing a single positive example*

$$t_p = \{A{:}1, B{:}1, C{:}1, D{:}1\}$$

and a single negative example

$$t_n = \{A{:}1, B{:}1, C{:}2, D{:}1\}.$$

In order to learn a query in $\mathcal{Q}^{\bowtie}$ satisfying E_1, we first observe that R_6 cannot participate in a satisfying query, as it has an attribute not appearing in E_1. Next, we note that all remaining relations, other than R_5, can potentially be in a join query producing t_p. This follows, since for all R_i where $i < 5$, it holds that $\pi_{schema(R_i)}(\{t_p\}) \in R_i$. Hence, when there is no bound on the query size, there is a satisfying query if and only if $Q = R_1 \bowtie R_2 \bowtie R_3 \bowtie R_4$ is such a satisfying query. Since, $\pi_{schema(R_1)}(\{t_n\}) \notin R_1$, we can immediately conclude that Q is indeed satisfying (as it produces the positive example, but not the negative one).

Intractability of SAT($\mathcal{Q}^{\pi,\sigma(f)}$), i.e., Claim 2 of Theorem 4.1) can be shown by a reduction from 3-SAT, as demonstrated in the following example.

EXAMPLE 4.4. *Consider a 3-SAT formula, $\Phi = \phi_1 \wedge \phi_2$, where*

$$\phi_1 = x_1 \vee \neg x_2 \vee x_3 \qquad \phi_2 = \neg x_1 \vee \neg x_2 \vee \neg x_3 .$$

We create the relation R as in Figure 2. The relation R has columns A_{x_i} and $A_{\bar{x}_i}$, for every variable x_i, as well as columns A_1 and A_2. Observe that R has three tuples $t^p_{x_i}$, $t^n_{x_i}$ and $t^b_{x_i}$, for each variable x_i. In $t^p_{x_i}$ (resp. $t^n_{x_i}$) attribute A_1 has the value x_i (i.e., the name of the variable x_i) and attribute A_{x_i} (resp $A_{\bar{x}_i}$) has the value 1. In $t^b_{x_i}$, A_{x_i}, $A_{\bar{x}_i}$ and A_2 have the value 1. In addition, R has three tuples $t^1_{\phi_j}$, $t^2_{\phi_j}$, $t^3_{\phi_j}$ for each ϕ_j, with value ϕ_j (the name of the j-th clause) in attribute A_1. In addition, $t^k_{\phi_j}$ has the value 1 in the attribute corresponding to the negation of the k-th variable in ϕ_j. Finally, R also has a tuple containing only the value 0.

We create an example set, with a positive example for each variable, and for each clause, and a single negative example, as follows.

	A_1	A_2
✓	ϕ_1	*1*
✓	ϕ_2	*1*
✓	x_1	*0*
✓	x_2	*0*
✓	x_3	*0*
✓	*0*	*0*
✗	*0*	*1*

To simplify, consider only queries in $\mathcal{Q}^{\pi,\sigma(\{=\})}$. Clearly, a satisfying query must require exactly one of A_{x_i} or $A_{\bar{x}_i}$ to have the value 0. Otherwise, (1) if neither are required, the tuple $t^b_{x_i}$ will derive the negative example and (2) if both are required, we will not derive the positive example $\{A_1 : x_i, A_2 : 0\}$. Thus, a satisfying query Q corresponds to a truth assignment, in which we assign x_i true if and only if Q contains the selection $A_{x_i} = 0$. In addition, a satisfying query Q will derive each positive example $\{A_1 : \phi_j, A_2 : 1\}$. This implies satisfaction of ϕ_j by the truth assignment. Thus, for example, the satisfying truth assignment $x_1 = \top, x_2 = \bot, x_3 = \bot$ corresponds to the satisfying query

$$\pi_{A_1,A_2}(\sigma_{A_{x_1}=0}(\sigma_{A_{\bar{x}_2}=0}(\sigma_{A_{\bar{x}_3}=0}(R)))).$$

Finally, when both join and projection operators are permitted, as in Claim 3 of Theorem 4.1, a new difficulty arises. Not only can it be difficult to find a satisfying query, but given a specific query Q, it can be intractable to determine whether Q satisfies an example set. This contrasts with all previously considered cases, in which it is possible to efficiently decide satisfiability of a given query. For both SAT($\mathcal{Q}^{\pi,\bowtie}$) and SAT($\mathcal{Q}^{\pi,\sigma(f),\bowtie}$), NP-hardness and coNP-hardness follow from the fact that we must both determine that all positive answers are returned, and that no negative answers are returned. Determining whether a tuple is in a query result is NP-hard for these classes, while determining query emptiness is coNP-hard.

We now consider the complexity of learning queries of bounded size.

THEOREM 4.5. *Let f be any nonempty subset of Θ.*

1. BSAT($\mathcal{Q}^{\bowtie}$), BSAT($\mathcal{Q}^{\sigma(f)}$), BSAT($\mathcal{Q}^{\sigma(f),\bowtie}$), *and* BSAT($\mathcal{Q}^{\pi,\sigma(f)}$) *are NP-complete;*

2. BSAT($\mathcal{Q}^{\pi,\bowtie}$) *and* BSAT($\mathcal{Q}^{\pi,\sigma(f),\bowtie}$) *are both NP-hard and coNP-hard, and in DP.*

Bounding the size of the queries to be learned increases the complexity of satisfiability for query classes $\mathcal{Q}^{\bowtie}$, $\mathcal{Q}^{\sigma(f)}$ and $\mathcal{Q}^{\sigma(f),\bowtie}$. Satisfiability can be shown to be NP-complete, by different reductions from the set cover problem, where query size corresponds to cover size. For the remaining classes, determining satisfiability is the same as in the unbounded cases, i.e., as in Theorem 4.1.

We demonstrate the intuition behind NP-completeness of $\text{BSAT}(\mathcal{Q}^{\bowtie})$ in the following example.

EXAMPLE 4.6. *Consider a set $U = \{1,2,3,4,5\}$, and a collection of subsets $S = \{s_1, s_2, s_3, s_4\}$, where*

$$s_1 = \{1,2,3\} \qquad s_2 = \{2,4\}$$
$$s_3 = \{3,4\} \qquad s_4 = \{4,5\}.$$

Our goal is to find a subset C of S with at most k sets, such that the union of the sets in C is precisely U.

Consider the database $\mathcal{D}_1$, containing the following four relations:

$$R_{s_1} = \{\{A:4\},\{A:5\}\}$$
$$R_{s_2} = \{\{A:1\},\{A:3\},\{A:5\}\}$$
$$R_{s_3} = \{\{A:1\},\{A:2\},\{A:5\}\}$$
$$R_{s_4} = \{\{A:1\},\{A:2\},\{A:3\}\}.$$

Observe that R_{s_i} contains a tuple for each element that is not in s_i. Let E_1 be the example set containing no positive examples, and a negative example $\{A:v\}$, for every $v \in U$. Now, it is not difficult to see that there is a satisfying query in $\mathcal{Q}^{\bowtie}_k$ if and only if there is a cover of size at most k, for U. For example, the satisfying query $R_{s_1} \bowtie R_{s_4}$ corresponds to the set cover s_1, s_4.

The intuition behind NP-completeness of $\text{BSAT}(\mathcal{Q}^{\sigma(f)})$ is demonstrated in the following example.

EXAMPLE 4.7. *Consider again the set U, and the set of subsets S, from Example 4.6. Consider the database $\mathcal{D}_2$, containing the following single relation R, defined as:*

		A_{s_1}	A_{s_2}	A_{s_3}	A_{s_4}
✗	t_1	*0*	*1*	*1*	*1*
✗	t_2	*0*	*0*	*1*	*1*
✗	t_3	*0*	*1*	*0*	*1*
✗	t_4	*1*	*0*	*0*	*0*
✗	t_5	*1*	*1*	*1*	*0*
✓	t^1	*1*	*1*	*1*	*1*

where "✗" and "✓" are used to mark negative and positive tuples, respectively, in the example set. (Note that every tuple in R is either a negative or positive example.)

Observe that R contains an attribute A_{s_i} for each subset s_i. There is a tuple t_v corresponding to each element $v \in U$, with 0 (resp. 1) for A_{s_i} if $v \in s_i$ (resp. $v \notin s_i$), as well as a tuple t^1 containing 1 in all attributes. Now, by careful observation one can see that there is a satisfying query in $\mathcal{Q}^{\sigma(f)}_{k+1}$ if and only if there is a cover of size at most k. For example, the satisfying query $\sigma_{A_{s_1}=1}(\sigma_{A_{s_4}=1}(R))$ corresponds to the set cover s_1, s_4.

It is useful to note that both of these polynomial reductions are also fpt-reductions, with respect to parameter k. This will be used to show $W[2]$-hardness, in the next section, when k is parameterized.

5. BOUNDING THE QUERY SIZE

In this section, we consider the complexity of learning bounded-sized queries from a class $\mathcal{Q}$ from examples, where we consider the size of permitted queries, i.e., k, to be constant or a parameter.

When k is constant, there are always a polynomial number of possible queries to be considered. Moreover, the evaluation of constant sized join queries is also polynomial. Hence, we derive the following result.

THEOREM 5.1. *Let f be any nonempty subset of Θ and O be any subset of $\{\pi, \sigma(f), \bowtie\}$. Then $\text{BLEARN}(\mathcal{Q}^{O})$ is in PTIME when the query size bound is constant.*

Since Theorem 4.5 implies that satisfiability is hard when k is considered input, and Theorem 5.1 shows that learning is tractable when k is constant, it is of interest to determine the parameterized complexity of these problems with respect to k.

THEOREM 5.2. *Let f be any nonempty subset of Θ. When the query size bound is considered a parameter*

1. *$\text{BSAT}(\mathcal{Q}^{\bowtie})$, $\text{BSAT}(\mathcal{Q}^{\sigma(f)})$, and $\text{BSAT}(\mathcal{Q}^{\sigma(f),\bowtie})$ are $W[2]$-complete;*
2. *$\text{BSAT}(\mathcal{Q}^{\pi,\sigma(f)})$ is $W[3]$-complete;*
3. *$\text{BSAT}(\mathcal{Q}^{\pi,\bowtie})$ is both $W[2]$-hard and co$W[1]$-hard;*
4. *$\text{BSAT}(\mathcal{Q}^{\pi,\sigma(f),\bowtie})$ is both $W[3]$-hard and co$W[1]$-hard.*

For Claim 1, (queries without projection) $W[2]$-hardness can be shown using the reductions from set cover used in Theorem 4.5, which were also fpt-reductions. These reductions were demonstrated in Examples 4.6 and 4.7. Membership in $W[2]$ is shown by reductions from each of $\text{BSAT}(\mathcal{Q}^{\bowtie})$, $\text{BSAT}(\mathcal{Q}^{\sigma(f)})$, and $\text{BSAT}(\mathcal{Q}^{\sigma(f),\bowtie})$ to set cover. The idea behind one such reduction, that of $\text{BSAT}(\mathcal{Q}^{\bowtie})$, is demonstrated next.

EXAMPLE 5.3. *Consider the database $\mathcal{D}$ from Figure 1, and the example set E containing no positive examples, and three negative examples*

$$t_n^1 = \{A{:}1, B{:}1, C{:}2, D{:}1\} \quad t_n^2 = \{A{:}1, B{:}2, C{:}1, D{:}2\}$$
$$t_n^3 = \{A{:}2, B{:}2, C{:}2, D{:}2\}.$$

We define an instance of the set cover problem over $\{t_n^1, t_n^2, t_n^3, A, B, C, D\}$, with sets

$$s_1 = \{t_n^1, t_n^2, t_n^3, A, C, D\} \qquad s_2 = \{t_n^1, t_n^2, B, C, D\}$$
$$s_3 = \{t_n^3, A, B, D\} \qquad s_4 = \{t_n^1, t_n^3, A, C, D\}$$
$$s_5 = \{t_n^3, A, B, C\}$$

Intuitively, each set s_i contains the attributes of R_i, as well as all negative examples disqualified from the result by including R_i. Then, a cover of size k of $\{t_n^1, t_n^2, t_n^3, A, B, C, D\}$ can be shown to correspond to a satisfying join query of size k, e.g., the cover s_2, s_3 corresponds to the satisfying query $R_2 \bowtie R_3$. We note that in this example E contains only negative tuples. In our proof we also consider the case that E contains positive examples.

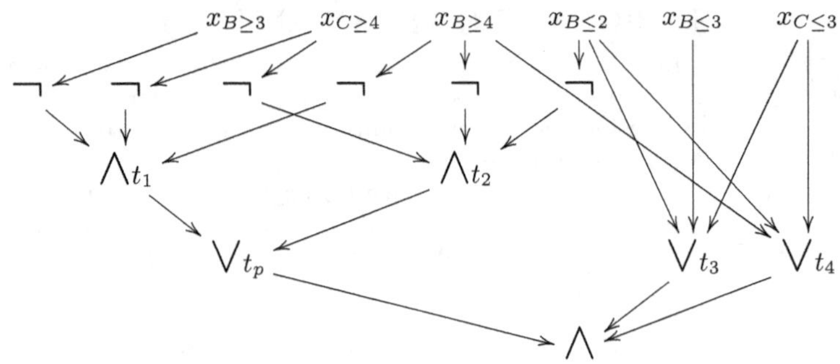

R

	A	B	C
t_1	1	2	3
t_2	1	3	3
t_3	1	4	4
t_4	1	3	4

E

		A	C
✓	t_p	1	3
✗	t_n	1	4

Figure 3: Circuit of weft 3.

Showing Claim 2 of Theorem 5.2, i.e., $W[3]$-completeness of $\text{BSAT}(\mathcal{Q}^{\pi,\sigma(f)})$, is more difficult as few natural complete problems for $W[3]$ are known. To show membership in $W[3]$, we give a reduction to the *weighted circuit satisfiability problem* with weft 3, a canonical complete problem for $W[3]$ (see [13]). To show $W[3]$-hardness, we give a reduction from the *weighted circuit anti-monotone normalized satisfiability problem* with weft 3, which is also complete for $W[3]$. The full details are deferred to the appendix, but in the following example, we demonstrate the idea behind our reduction showing membership in $W[3]$.

EXAMPLE 5.4. *We briefly review the weighted circuit satisfiability problem. In the weighted circuit satisfiability problem, we are given a Boolean circuit, with a single output gate, which is an AND gate. The circuit may contain both* small *gates of fan-in at most 2, and* large *AND/OR gates with arbitrary fan-in. The* weft *of a circuit is the maximum number of large gates on any path from an input to the output gate. Given a Boolean circuit, and a number k, the* weighted circuit satisfiability *problem is to determine whether there exists an input of Hamming weight at most k that is accepted by the circuit.*[4] *For circuits of weft t, this problem is $W[t]$-complete, given parameter k.*

Consider the database $\mathcal{D}$ containing the relation R from Figure 3, as well as the example set E depicted in this figure. To simplify, in this example, we assume that f is the set $\{\leq, \geq\}$, i.e., we reduce bounded satisfiability of $\mathcal{Q}^{\pi,\sigma(\{\leq,\geq\})}$ to the weighted circuit satisfiability problem. We construct a circuit of weft 3, as depicted in the same figure.

The input variables correspond to selections on the attributes. Now, observe that the two possible origins for t_p in the result of a query are t_1 and t_2. Hence, at least one of these two tuples must remain after the selections. Therefore, all variables corresponding to selections removing one of these tuples are negated and fed into an AND gate, and then these two AND gates are the input of an OR gate. This ensures that a satisfying assignment of the input will leave at least one of t_1 and t_2. Observe that there are two possible origins for t_n, namely t_3 and t_4. Both of these must be removed by the selections of the query. This is ensured by using OR gates that combine all selections removing the tuples. Finally, it is not difficult to see that an assignment of weight k corresponds to a query with k selections, and one projection (and one relation), i.e., to a query of size $k+2$.

[4]The classic weighted circuit satisfiability problem is to determine whether there exists an input of Hamming weight precisely k. The flavor of the problem considered here is also $W[3]$-complete.

The problem of $\text{BSAT}(\mathcal{Q}^{\pi,\bowtie})$, i.e., Claim 3 of Theorem 5.2 is both $W[2]$-hard and co$W[1]$-hard. Observe that $W[2]$-hardness follows immediately from Claim 1, which shows that $\text{BSAT}(\mathcal{Q}^{\bowtie})$ is $W[2]$-complete. The co$W[1]$-hardness comes from the difficulty of determining non-satisfiability of negative examples, even if the target query is known. Similarly, in Claim 4, i.e., $\text{BSAT}(\mathcal{Q}^{\pi,\sigma(f),\bowtie})$, we have co$W[1]$-hardness for the same reason, and $W[3]$-hardness immediately follows from Claim 2.

6. BOUNDING THE SCHEMA SIZE

In this section, we consider a bound on the size of the schema of the database. Thus, the number of tuples in the database is unbounded, but we assume that the number of relations, and the number of attributes per relation, is bounded. This is a natural assumption, as the schema will typically be significantly smaller than the actual data in a database.

For some query classes (in particular, those without "$\neq$"-selections), bounding the schema size also bounds the size of a query to be learned. For these classes, the complexity can only decrease in comparison to that in the previous section. In other cases, bounding the schema size does not imply a bound on the size of a query to be learned, and hence, new complexity bounds must be formulated. Note that, as in Section 4, even when learning bounded-sized queries from a class $\mathcal{Q}$ (queries of size at most k), we do not consider k to be a constant in our complexity analysis, but rather only consider the schema size to be a constant (or a parameter). Finally, we will not parameterize an input of a problem if the non-parameterized version of the problem is tractable.

We begin by considering queries that may contain any of the operators natural join, projection and *positive* selection, i.e., queries that may contain "=", "$\leq$" and "$\geq$", but do not contain "$\neq$". In this case, bounding the schema size effectually bounds the size of a query, as:

- the number of joins will be at most the size of the schema *and*
- for each attribute, there are at most three comparisons of interest (one each using the operators "=", "$\leq$" and "$\geq$").

Therefore, the following theorem follows immediately from Theorem 5.1, which considers queries of size bounded by a constant.

THEOREM 6.1. *Let f_{pos} be any nonempty subset of Θ_{pos} and O be any subset of $\{\pi, \sigma(f_{pos}), \bowtie\}$. Then,* $\text{LEARN}(\mathcal{Q}^{O})$

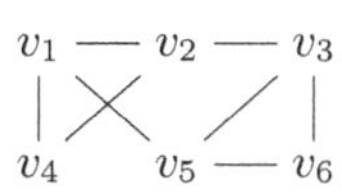

Figure 4: A graph of maximum degree 3.

and BLEARN($\mathcal{Q}^O$) *is in PTIME, if the schema is of constant size.*

Theorem 6.1 does not imply fixed parameter tractability for queries with positive selection. In particular, as shown in Section 5, determining satisfiability, for queries of bounded size, is not fixed parameter tractable, regardless of the operators allowed in the queries. Interestingly, bounding the schema size can sometimes lead to fixed parameter tractability, as shown in the following theorem.

THEOREM 6.2. *Let f_{pos} be any nonempty subset of Θ_{pos}. When the schema size is a parameter,*

1. BLEARN($\mathcal{Q}^{\bowtie}$), BLEARN($\mathcal{Q}^{\sigma(f_{pos})}$), BLEARN($\mathcal{Q}^{\sigma(f_{pos}),\bowtie}$), LEARN($\mathcal{Q}^{\pi,\sigma(\{=\})}$) *and* BLEARN($\mathcal{Q}^{\pi,\sigma(\{=\})}$) *are FPT;*
2. SAT($\mathcal{Q}^{\pi,\sigma(\{\leq,\geq\})}$) *and* BSAT($\mathcal{Q}^{\pi,\sigma(\{\leq,\geq\})}$) *are in* $W[3]$*;*
3. SAT($\mathcal{Q}^{\pi,\bowtie}$), BSAT($\mathcal{Q}^{\pi,\bowtie}$), SAT($\mathcal{Q}^{\pi,\sigma(f_{pos}),\bowtie}$), *and* BSAT($\mathcal{Q}^{\pi,\sigma(f_{pos}),\bowtie}$) *are W[1]-hard and co-W[1]-hard.*

As Theorem 6.2 shows, in the absence of projection, or when projection is combined with "="-selections, learning is fixed parameter tractable. Thus, Claim 1 is shown by a counting argument on the number of queries that must be considered. For Claim 2, observe that considering only "≤" and "≥"-selections effectually bounds the size of a query that must be considered, as there are at most two selections of interest per attribute. Hence, this result follows from Claim 2 of Theorem 5.2. Finally, Claim 3 can be shown to follow from the fact that it is $W[1]$-hard to determine whether a given tuple is in the result of a query, in these classes.

Finally, in the following theorem, we consider queries that can have "≠"-selections. Even when the schema is of constant size, satisfiability is NP-complete, for all classes that are not tractable in the absence of parameters.

THEOREM 6.3. *Let O be any subset of $\{\pi, \bowtie\}$ and let $O_{neg} = O \cup \{\sigma(\{\neq\})\}$. Suppose that the schema is of constant size.*

1. *If $\pi \in O_{neq}$ then* SAT($\mathcal{Q}^{O_{neq}}$) *is NP-complete.*
2. BSAT($\mathcal{Q}^{O_{neq}}$) *is NP-complete.*

For both claims, membership in NP is easily shown, since queries can be evaluated in polynomial time, when the size of the join is bound by a constant. Hardness is shown by a reduction from 3-SAT in Claim 1, and by a reduction from the degree-3 vertex cover problem in Claim 2. We demonstrate the latter reduction in the following example.

EXAMPLE 6.4. *Consider the undirected and connected graph G in Figure 4, in which each vertex has degree at most three. It is well known that such graphs have a chromatic number of no more than three (if they contain at least five vertices), and that a 3-coloring can be found in linear time. For example, the following is a 3-coloring of G:*

$$\text{Red} = \{v_4, v_6\} \quad \text{Blue} = \{v_1, v_3\} \quad \text{Green} = \{v_2, v_5\}$$

Our goal is to find a vertex cover of size at most k, for such a degree-3 graph. This problem is NP-complete [15].

We create a relation R containing the tuples:

$$\begin{array}{ll} \{r:0, b:v_1, g:v_2\} & \{r:v_4, b:v_1, g:0\} \\ \{r:0, b:v_1, g:v_5\} & \{r:0, b:v_3, g:v_2\} \\ \{r:v_4, b:0, g:v_2\} & \{r:0, b:v_3, g:v_5\} \\ \{r:v_6, b:v_3, g:0\} & \{r:v_6, b:0, g:v_5\} \\ \{r:0, b:0, g:0\} & \end{array}$$

Observe that each edge in the graph corresponds with a tuple in the relation, with the vertices appearing in the attribute corresponding to their color. In addition, observe that R also has a tuple containing only the value 0. The example set E contains all tuples associated with edges as negative examples, and the tuple with only 0-s as a positive example.

Now, it is not difficult to see that a vertex cover U corresponds to a satisfying query that has an inequality selection for each vertex in U. For example, the vertex cover $\{v_1, v_2, v_3, v_5\}$ corresponds to the satisfying query

$$\sigma_{b \neq v_1}(\sigma_{g \neq v_2}(\sigma_{b \neq v_3}(\sigma_{g \neq v_5}(R)))) .$$

Given the NP-completeness result of Theorem 6.3, it is interesting to consider the complexity of learning queries with "≠"-selections, when both the schema and query are bounded in size. Note that if the query is of bounded size, it is intractable to determine satisfiability of queries with selections, even if the query size is a parameter, as shown in Theorem 5.2. Interestingly, the following theorem shows that by considering both the schema size and the query size as parameters, we derive fixed parameter tractability.

THEOREM 6.5. *When both the size of the schema and the size of the query are parameters,* BLEARN($\mathcal{Q}^{\sigma(\{\neq\})}$), BLEARN($\mathcal{Q}^{\pi,\sigma(\{\neq\})}$) *and* BLEARN($\mathcal{Q}^{\sigma(\{\neq\}),\bowtie}$) *are in FPT.*

The cases of $\mathcal{Q}^{\sigma(\{\neq\})}$ and $\mathcal{Q}^{\pi,\sigma(\{\neq\})}$ follow from the following counting argument. Let $e_1, \ldots, e_n$ be the negative examples. For a given

$$e_i = \{A_1 : c_1, \ldots, A_s : c_s\},$$

there are s inequality conditions that can be used to disqualify e_i from the result of a query, namely $A_i \neq c_i$, for all $i \leq s$. Therefore, we can find a satisfying query, if one exists, by repeatedly choosing a negative example, considering each disqualifying selection, and then filtering out any other negative examples that are also disqualified by this process. As we must find a query of size at most k, this process will be continued up to a depth of k, thereby creating s^k queries to consider. Since s is bound by the schema size, which is a parameter, and k is also a parameter, this yields fixed parameter tractability.

The above argument can be adapted to the case of $\mathcal{Q}^{\sigma(\{\neq\}),\bowtie}$. Suppose that the schema is of size s. Then, there are at most 2^s join combinations that must be considered. For each such query, we must disqualify any remaining negative examples, as before. Again, given a negative example with at most s attributes, there are at most s inequality conditions that can be used to disqualify the tuple. Therefore, for each join query, we repeatedly choose a remaining negative example, and a disqualifying condition, and then filter out any other negative examples that are disqualified by this process. We continue this process up to a depth of k, yielding at most $2^s s^k$ queries to be considered. Since both s and k are parameters, this yields our desired FPT result.

7. BOUNDING NUMBER OF EXAMPLES

In this section we consider the complexity of satisfiability and learning queries, when the number of examples is considered to be constant or a parameter. Since the examples are provided by the users, the example set is likely to be significantly smaller than the size of the database.

We first consider query classes which include the join operator. The following theorem summarizes the complexity of satisfiability for all classes of queries with join, that are intractable when no parameters are given. Indeed, even when the number of examples is a constant, the complexity remains the same as when no parameters are available, i.e., as in Theorems 4.1 and 4.5. However, a new proof is required for Claim 1 of Theorem 7.1, as the proof of Theorem 4.5 used an unbounded number of examples to show NP-completeness of BSAT($\mathcal{Q}^{\bowtie}$).

THEOREM 7.1. *Let f be any nonempty subset of Θ. When the number of examples is a constant,*

1. *BSAT($\mathcal{Q}^{\bowtie}$) and BSAT($\mathcal{Q}^{\sigma(f),\bowtie}$) are NP-complete;*
2. *SAT($\mathcal{Q}^{\pi,\bowtie}$), SAT($\mathcal{Q}^{\pi,\sigma(f),\bowtie}$), BSAT($\mathcal{Q}^{\pi,\bowtie}$), and BSAT($\mathcal{Q}^{\pi,\sigma(f),\bowtie}$) are NP-hard, coNP-hard, and in DP.*

The following example demonstrates the reduction from set cover used to show that BSAT($\mathcal{Q}^{\bowtie}$) is NP-hard.

EXAMPLE 7.2. *Consider again the set $U = \{1,2,3,4,5\}$ and collection of subsets $S = \{s_1, s_2, s_3, s_4\}$, where*

$$s_1 = \{1,2,3\} \qquad s_2 = \{2,4\}$$
$$s_3 = \{3,4\} \qquad s_4 = \{4,5\}$$

from Example 4.6. We create a database with relations R_1, R_2, R_3, R_4, with the following tuples

$$R_1 = \{A_1:1, A_2:1, A_3:1\} \qquad R_2 = \{A_2:1, A_4:1\}$$
$$R_3 = \{A_3:1, A_4:1\} \qquad R_4 = \{A_4:1, A_5:1\}$$

Note that the attributes in relation R_i correspond to the elements in set s_i. We consider the example set containing a single positive example

$$\{A_1:1, A_2:1, A_3:1, A_4:1, A_5:1\}.$$

Now, it is easy to see that there is a satisfying query in $\mathcal{Q}^{\bowtie}_k$ if and only if there is a cover of size at most k, for U. For example, the satisfying query $R_1 \bowtie R_4$ corresponds to the set cover s_1, s_4.

We now consider the complexity of the learning and satisfiability problems for query classes which allow selection, but do not allow join. Recall that in the absence of projection, for unbounded queries, i.e., $\mathcal{Q}^{\sigma(f)}$, learning is in PTIME, even if there are no parameters given. Hence, we consider only the bounded satisfiability problem for the query class $\mathcal{Q}^{\sigma(f)}$, and both the bounded and unbounded variants for the class $\mathcal{Q}^{\pi,\sigma(f)}$.

THEOREM 7.3. *Let f be any nonempty subset of Θ. Let e be the number of examples in the example set.*

1. *BLEARN($\mathcal{Q}^{\sigma(f)}$) is in FPT when e is a parameter;*
2. *SAT($\mathcal{Q}^{\pi,\sigma(f)}$) is $W[3]$-complete when e is a parameter;*
3. *BSAT($\mathcal{Q}^{\pi,\sigma(f)}$) is NP-complete even when e is constant.*

Let k denote the query size bound in Claims 1 and 3. To show Claim 1, observe that at most one selection is required to remove each negative example. Thus, if a satisfying query exists, then there is one of size at most $e+1$. If $k \geq e+1$, then FPT complexity follows from the fact that LEARN($\mathcal{Q}^{\sigma(f)}$) is PTIME, in the absence of parameters (Claim 1 of Theorem 4.1). In this case, it is sufficient to learn any satisfying query (in PTIME), and then to remove redundant selections, until a query of size at most k is derived. If $k \leq e$, more care must be taken to prove the FPT complexity result. The proof involves dividing the negative examples into at most $k-1$ sets, where each set must be disqualified by a single selection, and then applying a similar process to find a satisfying query. We note that this yields FPT time, since e is a parameter, and the number of ways to divide e into sets is a function of e, and not of the database size.

We next consider Claim 2 of Theorem 7.3, i.e., $W[3]$-completeness of SAT($\mathcal{Q}^{\pi,\sigma(f)}$), when the number of examples is a parameter. Our proof of Claim 2 of Theorem 5.2 cannot be applied to show $W[3]$-completeness in the current case, as our problem considers queries of unbounded size, while Theorem 5.2 considered queries of bounded size, i.e., BSAT($\mathcal{Q}^{\pi,\sigma(f)}$). To show membership in $W[3]$, we give a reduction to the *weighted circuit satisfiability problem* with weft 3 and to show $W[3]$-hardness, we give a reduction from the *weighted circuit anti-monotone normalized satisfiability problem* with weft 3, as in Claim 2 of Theorem 5.2.

In the following example, we demonstrate the reduction for the $W[3]$-hardness result.

EXAMPLE 7.4. *In the* weighted circuit anti-monotone normalized satisfiability problem *with weft 3, all inputs are negated, and all paths from inputs to the root of the circuit tree pass through large AND gates, large OR gates, and a final large AND gate. Large gates can have arbitrary fan-in. The problem is to find a satisfying assignment of precisely Hamming weight k.*

For example, the following formula Ψ can be expressed using an anti-monotone circuit of weft 3. (In the interest of simplifying the example, we give small formulas, which could also be expressed using small gates. A larger formula would require the use of large gates.)

$$\phi_1 = \neg v_1 \wedge \neg v_2 \qquad \phi_2 = \neg v_3 \wedge \neg v_1$$
$$\phi_3 = \neg v_3 \wedge \neg v_4 \qquad \phi_4 = \neg v_1 \wedge \neg v_3$$
$$\Phi_1 = \phi_1 \vee \phi_2 \qquad \Phi_2 = \phi_3 \vee \phi_4$$
$$\Psi = \Phi_1 \wedge \Phi_2$$

The problem at hand is to find a satisfying assignment of weight precisely k. To simplify, in this example, we assume that $k = 2$.

We create a database with a single relation R, as in the left-hand side of Figure 5. Observe that R has an attribute A_{ϕ_i} for each formula ϕ_i and k attributes for each variable v_j, as well as two additional attributes B and C. The relation R has tuples, as follows:

	A_{ϕ_1}	A_{ϕ_2}	A_{ϕ_3}	A_{ϕ_4}	$A^1_{v_1}$	$A^1_{v_2}$	$A^1_{v_3}$	$A^1_{v_4}$	$A^2_{v_1}$	$A^2_{v_2}$	$A^2_{v_3}$	$A^2_{v_4}$	B	C
t_{Φ_1}	1	1	0	0	0	0	0	0	0	0	0	0	0	0
t_{Φ_2}	0	0	1	1	0	0	0	0	0	0	0	0	0	0
$t^1_{v_1}$	1	1	0	1	0	1	1	1	1	0	0	0	1	0
$t^1_{v_2}$	1	0	0	0	1	0	1	1	0	1	0	0	1	0
$t^1_{v_3}$	0	1	1	1	1	1	0	1	0	0	1	0	1	0
$t^1_{v_4}$	0	0	1	0	1	1	1	0	0	0	0	1	1	0
$t^2_{v_1}$	1	1	0	1	1	0	0	0	0	1	1	1	2	0
$t^2_{v_2}$	1	0	0	0	0	1	0	0	1	0	1	1	2	0
$t^2_{v_3}$	0	1	1	1	0	0	1	0	1	1	0	1	2	0
$t^2_{v_4}$	0	0	1	0	0	0	0	1	1	1	1	0	2	0
t^1	0	0	0	0	1	1	1	1	0	0	0	0	0	0
t^2	0	0	0	0	0	0	0	0	1	1	1	1	0	0
$t^{\{1,2\}}_{v_1}$	0	0	0	0	0	1	1	1	0	1	1	1	0	0
$t^{\{1,2\}}_{v_2}$	0	0	0	0	1	0	1	1	1	0	1	1	0	0
$t^{\{1,2\}}_{v_3}$	0	0	0	0	1	1	0	1	1	1	0	1	0	0
$t^{\{1,2\}}_{v_4}$	0	0	0	0	1	1	1	0	1	1	1	0	0	0
t_C	0	0	0	0	0	0	0	0	0	0	0	0	0	1

	B	C
✓	1	0
✓	2	0
✓	0	1
✗	0	0

Figure 5: Relation and example set created for weighted circuit anti-monotone normalized satisfiability problem in Example 7.4.

- *A tuple t_{Φ_j} for each Φ_j, containing 1 for each ϕ_i in its disjunction;*
- *k tuples t^m_n for each variable v_n, in which tuple t^m_n has (1) a value 1 for A_{ϕ_i} if v_n appears in ϕ_i, (2) a value 1 for every column corresponding to an attribute $A^{m'}_{v_{n'}}$ if both $m' = m$ and $n' \neq n$ or both $m' \neq m$ and $n' = n$ and (3) the value m in attribute B;*
- *a tuple t^m, for all $m \leq k$ that has 1 in the attributes corresponding to the m-the copies of the variables;*
- *tuples $t^{\{m,m'\}}_{v_n}$, for each variable v_n, where $1 \leq m < m' \leq k$ with 1 for every attribute corresponding to a variable other than v_n;*
- *a tuple with 1 in attribute C.*

Consider the example set E, containing $k+2$ tuples, appearing on the right-hand side of Figure 5. To understand how satisfying queries and satisfying assignments correlate, assume, to simplify, that all selections are equality constraints. Now, it is easy to observe that the only equality constraints that can appear in a satisfying query are of the form $A = 0$, where A is some attribute other than B or C.

A satisfying query for the example set will have 2 (in general, k) selections of the form $A^m_{v_n} = 0$ with different subscripts and different superscripts. Otherwise, we could not derive both of the first two positive examples, or we would derive the negative example, via t^1 or t^2 (if we use the same superscript) or via one of $t^{\{1,2\}}_{v_n}$ (if we use the same subscript). A satisfying condition must also contain a selection of the form $A_{\phi_i} = 0$, where $\phi_i \in \Phi_j$, for all j, since otherwise, one of the tuples t_{Φ_i} would agree with the selection condition, thereby deriving the negative tuple.

Thus, by careful consideration, it is possible to see that satisfying queries precisely correspond to satisfying assignments of weight k, e.g., the satisfying assignment assigning precisely v_2 and v_4 to true, which satisfies the formulas ϕ_2 and ϕ_4 corresponds to the satisfying query

$$\pi_{B,C}(\sigma_{A_{\phi_2}=0}(\sigma_{A_{\phi_4}=0}(\sigma_{A^1_{v_2}=0}(\sigma_{A^2_{v_4}=0}(R))))).$$

Finally, we consider Claim 3 of Theorem 7.3, i.e., NP-completeness of BSAT($\mathcal{Q}^{\pi,\sigma(f)}$), when the number of examples (or even only the number of positive examples) is a constant. Membership in NP is immediate. To show completeness, we show that for any database $\mathcal{D}$ and example set E containing at most two positive examples, and arbitrarily many negative examples, we can define a database $\mathcal{D}'$ and example set E', containing a constant number of examples, such that there is a satisfying query in $\mathcal{Q}^{\sigma(f)}_k$ for E over $\mathcal{D}$ if and only if there is a satisfying query in $\mathcal{Q}^{\pi,\sigma(f)}_{k+1}$ for E' over $\mathcal{D}'$. This will allow us to adapt the NP-hardness reduction used for Claim 1 of Theorem 4.5 (for BSAT($\mathcal{Q}^{\sigma(f)}$)), to show NP-hardness of BSAT($\mathcal{Q}^{\pi,\sigma(f)}$), when the number of examples is a constant. We demonstrate this construction next.

EXAMPLE 7.5. *Consider relation R_5 from Figure 1, and the example set E*

	A	*B*	*C*
✓	*1*	*2*	*2*
✗	*1*	*2*	*1*
✗	*1*	*1*	*2*

We create a relation R' as follows:

A	*B*	*C*	*X*	*Y*
1	*2*	*2*	*0*	*1*
1	*2*	*2*	*1*	*0*
1	*2*	*1*	*0*	*0*
1	*1*	*2*	*0*	*0*

	SAT			BSAT			
	None	Sch	Exmp	None	Qry	Sch	Exmp
π	P	-	-	P	-	-	-
$\bowtie$	P	-	-	NPC	P $W[2]C$	P FPT	NPC
σ	P	-	-	NPC	P $W[2]C$	$\{=\}: P$, $\{\neq\}: NPC$ $\{=\}: FPT$	P FPT
$\sigma, \bowtie$	P	-	-	NPC	P $W[2]C$	$\{=\}: P$, $\{\neq\}: NPC$ $\{=\}: FPT$	NPC
π, σ	NPC	$\{=\}: P$, $\{\neq\}: NPC$ $\{=\}: FPT$	P $W[3]C$	NPC	P $W[3]C$	$\{=\}: P$, $\{\neq\}: NPC$ $\{=\}: FPT$	NPC
$\pi, \bowtie$	DP	P $W[1]H$, co-$W[1]H$	DP	DP	P $W[2]H$, co-$W[1]H$	P $W[1]H$, co-$W[1]H$	DP
$\pi, \sigma, \bowtie$	DP	$\{=\}: P$, $\{\neq\}: NPC$ $\{=\}: W[1]H$, co-$W[1]H$	DP	DP	P $W[3]H$, co-$W[1]H$	$\{=\}: P$, $\{\neq\}: NPC$ $\{=\}: W[1]H$, co-$W[1]H$	DP

Table 1: Table summarizing complexity results. Columns labeled "None" contain complexity results when none of the input is considered a constant or a parameter. Columns with "Qry," "Sch," "Exmp" contain results when the query size, schema size or number of examples, respectively, is considered a constant or parameter. Within each such column, the results for constant input appear on the first line (per operator), and the results for parameterized input appear on the second line (per operator). For cases in which the complexity is dependent on the type of selection conditions, these are listed explicitly. (To simplify the table, we included only the complexity results for "=" and "≠," but not for "≤" or "≥".) Note that we list parameterized complexity only when the complexity for the constant case is polynomial.

Note that this relation contains two tuples derived from the positive example, and one each from the negative examples. (Some changes are required to the construction if E contains more or less positive examples.)

We define E' as the example set

	X	Y
✓	*0*	*1*
✓	*1*	*0*
✗	*0*	*0*

Now, it is easy to see that a satisfying query of E over R_5 corresponds to one for E' over R', e.g., as do Q and Q' in the following example

$$Q = \sigma_{B=2}(\sigma_{C=2}(R_5)) \quad Q' = \pi_{X,Y}(\sigma_{B=2}(\sigma_{C=2}(R'))) .$$

8. CONCLUSION

This paper presented a complete study of the complexity of learning SPJ-queries from positive and negative examples. We considered a variety of query classes, with different input parameters. We compare the complexity when input parameters are constant, in the spirit of data complexity, and when performing parameterized complexity analysis. The latter, in particular, helps to delineate between cases that can, and cannot, be solved efficiently, in practice. Thus, this work lays the theoretical foundation for a practical system that can learn a candidate query from given example sets. Our complexity results are summarized in Table 1.

In the future we intend to extend this work in several important directions. First, we will consider additional operators, namely union and minus, as well as queries with aggregate operators. Second, we will study the learnability problem, i.e., determining the number of examples necessary to learn a specific given query.

Acknowledgments

The authors were partially supported by the Israel Science Foundation (Grant 879/16).

9. REFERENCES

[1] Azza Abouzied, Dana Angluin, Christos Papadimitriou, Joseph M. Hellerstein, and Avi Silberschatz. Learning and verifying quantified boolean queries by example. In *PODS*, pages 49–60, New York, NY, USA, 2013. ACM.

[2] Dana Angluin. Learning regular sets from queries and counterexamples. *Inf. Comput.*, 75(2):87–106, November 1987.

[3] Dana Angluin. Queries and concept learning. *Machine Learning*, 2(4):319–342, April 1988.

[4] Dana Angluin. Negative results for equivalence queries. *Machine Learning*, 5(2):121–150, July 1990.

[5] Marcelo Arenas, Gonzalo I. Diaz, and Egor V. Kostylev. Reverse engineering sparql queries. In *Proceedings of the 25th International Conference on World Wide Web*, pages 239–249, 2016.

[6] François Bancilhon. On the completeness of query languages for relational data bases. In *Mathematical Foundations of Computer Science*, pages 112–123, Berlin, Heidelberg, 1978. Springer Berlin Heidelberg.

[7] Pablo Barceló and Miguel Romero. The complexity of reverse engineering problems for conjunctive queries. In *20th International Conference on Database Theory (ICDT 2017)*, 2017.

[8] Angela Bonifati, Radu Ciucanu, and Aurélien Lemay. Learning Path Queries on Graph Databases. In *18th International Conference on Extending Database Technology (EDBT)*, Bruxelles, Belgium, March 2015.

[9] Angela Bonifati, Radu Ciucanu, and Slawomir

Staworko. Learning join queries from user examples. *ACM Trans. Database Syst.*, 40:24, 2016.

[10] Sara Cohen and Yaacov Y. Weiss. Certain and possible xpath answers. In *Proceedings of the 16th International Conference on Database Theory*, ICDT '13, pages 237–248, New York, NY, USA, 2013. ACM.

[11] Sara Cohen and Yaacov Y. Weiss. Learning Tree Patterns from Example Graphs. In Marcelo Arenas and Martín Ugarte, editors, *18th International Conference on Database Theory (ICDT 2015)*, volume 31 of *Leibniz International Proceedings in Informatics (LIPIcs)*, pages 127–143, Dagstuhl, Germany, 2015. Schloss Dagstuhl–Leibniz-Zentrum fuer Informatik.

[12] Sara Cohen and Yaacov Y. Weiss. The complexity of learning tree patterns from example graphs. *ACM Trans. Database Syst.*, 41(2):14:1–14:44, May 2016.

[13] Rodney G. Downey and Michael R. Fellows. Fixed-parameter tractability and completeness I: basic results. *SIAM J. Comput.*, 24(4):873–921, 1995.

[14] George H. L. Fletcher, Marc Gyssens, Jan Paredaens, and Dirk Van Gucht. On the expressive power of the relational algebra on finite sets of relation pairs. *IEEE Trans. Knowl. Data Eng.*, 21(6):939–942, 2009.

[15] M.R. Garey, D.S. Johnson, and L. Stockmeyer. Some simplified NP-complete graph problems. *Theoretical Computer Science*, 1(3):237 – 267, 1976.

[16] E Mark Gold. Complexity of automaton identification from given data. *Information and Control*, 37(3):302 – 320, 1978.

[17] Martin Grohe. Parameterized complexity for the database theorist. *SIGMOD Rec.*, 31(4):86–96, December 2002.

[18] Kouichi Hirata. On the hardness of learning acyclic conjunctive queries. In *11th International Conference on Algorithmic Learning Theory*, pages 238–251, Berlin, Heidelberg, 2000. Springer Berlin Heidelberg.

[19] A. Nerode. Linear automaton transformations. *Proceedings of the American Mathematical Society*, 9(4):541–544, 1958.

[20] Christos H. Papadimitriou and Mihalis Yannakakis. On the complexity of database queries. *Journal of Computer and System Sciences*, 58(3):407 – 427, 1999.

[21] J. Paredaens. On the expressive power of the relational algebra. *Information Processing Letters*, 7(2):107 – 111, 1978.

[22] Quoc Trung Tran and Chee-Yong Chan. How to conquer why-not questions. In *Proceedings of the 2010 ACM SIGMOD International Conference on Management of Data*, SIGMOD '10, pages 15–26, New York, NY, USA, 2010. ACM.

[23] Quoc Trung Tran, Chee-Yong Chan, and Srinivasan Parthasarathy. Query by output. In *Proceedings of the 2009 ACM SIGMOD International Conference on Management of Data*, SIGMOD '09, pages 535–548, New York, NY, USA, 2009. ACM.

[24] Meihui Zhang, Hazem Elmeleegy, Cecilia M. Procopiuc, and Divesh Srivastava. Reverse engineering complex join queries. In *Proceedings of the 2013 ACM SIGMOD International Conference on Management of Data*, SIGMOD '13, pages 809–820, New York, NY, USA, 2013. ACM.

APPENDIX

A. PROOFS FOR W[3]-COMPLETENESS

PROPOSITION A.1. BSAT($Q^{\sigma(f),\pi}$) *is* $W[3]$*-complete, when the query size bound is considered a parameter, for any* $f \subseteq \Theta$.

PROOF. In order to show membership in $W[3]$, we present a reduction to the *weighted circuit satisfiability problem* with weft 3, a well known complete problem for $W[3]$ (see [13]). We briefly recall this problem.

In the weighted circuit satisfiability problem, we are given a Boolean circuit, with a single output gate, which is an AND gate. The circuit may contain both *small* gates of fan-in at most 2, and *large* AND/OR gates with arbitrary fan-in. The *weft* of a circuit is the maximum number of large gates on any path from an input to the output gate. Given a Boolean circuit, and a number k, the *weighted circuit satisfiability* problem is to determine whether there exists an input of Hamming weight at most k that is accepted by the circuit.[5] For circuits of weft t, this problem is $W[t]$-complete, given parameter k.

Let $\mathcal{D}$ be a database with a single relation R and E be an example set. We create a Boolean circuit, containing, for every attribute A in R, and every constant c associated with A in some tuple of R or in a negative example, variables (i.e., input gates) $x_{A\theta c}$, where $\theta \in f$. In addition,

- for each tuple t in R that can be a source of a positive example (i.e., that when projected yields a positive example), we create an AND-gate. For each condition $A\theta c$, with $\theta \in f$, such that t is disqualified when the selection $\sigma_{A\theta c}$ is applied, we connect variable $x_{A\theta c}$ to t using a NOT-gate.
- for each positive example $t^p \in E$, we create an OR-gate, which has as input all gates t such that t can be a source of t^p.
- for each tuple t in R that can be a source of a negative example, we create an OR-gate. For each condition $A\theta c$, with $\theta \in f$, such that t is disqualified when the selection $\sigma_{A\theta c}$ is applied, we connect variable $x_{A\theta c}$ to t.
- finally, all gates corresponding to positive examples, and to sources of negative examples feed into the output AND-gate.

Observe that the circuit constructed has weft 3. It is easy to see that a satisfying assignment of Hamming weight $k-2$ will correspond immediately to a satisfying query of size k (by including both the selections that were assigned true, and the final projection). We demonstrate this construction in Example 5.4, when $f = \{\leq, \geq\}$. Note that input gates that are unreachable from the output gate are omitted from the figure.

In order to show $W[3]$-hardness, we consider the more constrained *weighted circuit anti-monotone normalized satisfiability problem* with weft 3, which is also complete for $W[3]$ (see [13]). In this problem, all inputs are negated, and all paths from inputs to the root of the circuit tree pass through a large AND gate, a large OR gate, and another large AND gate. The problem is to determine whether there exists a

[5]The classic weighted circuit satisfiability problem is to determine whether there exists an input of Hamming weight precisely k. The flavor of the problem considered here is also $W[3]$-complete.

	A_1^1	A_2^1	A_3^1	A_4^1	A_1^2	A_2^2	A_3^2	A_4^2	A_Φ	A'
t_{ϕ_1}	1	1	0	0	1	1	0	0	Φ_1	0
t_{ϕ_2}	1	0	1	0	1	0	1	0	Φ_1	0
t_{ϕ_3}	0	0	1	1	0	0	1	1	Φ_2	0
t_{ϕ_4}	1	0	1	0	1	0	1	0	Φ_2	0
t_1	1	1	1	1	0	0	0	0	0	0
t_2	0	0	0	0	1	1	1	1	0	0
$t_1^{\{1,2\}}$	0	1	1	1	0	1	1	1	0	0
$t_2^{\{1,2\}}$	1	0	1	1	1	0	1	1	0	0
$t_3^{\{1,2\}}$	1	1	0	1	1	1	0	1	0	0
$t_4^{\{1,2\}}$	1	1	1	0	1	1	1	0	0	0
$t_{A'}$	0	0	0	0	0	0	0	0	0	1

	A_Φ	A'
✓	Φ_1	0
✓	Φ_2	0
✓	0	1
✗	0	0

Figure 6: Construction for $W[3]$-hardness in Proposition A.1 for the formula $((\neg v_1 \wedge \neg v_2) \vee (\neg v_3 \wedge \neg v_1)) \wedge ((\neg v_3 \wedge \neg v_4) \vee (\neg v_1 \wedge \neg v_3))$, with $p = 2$, as defined in Example 7.4.

satisfying assignment of weight precisely p. The constraint on the assignment weight is part of the problem definition. We will need to also take that into account when constructing a learning problem.

Let $\{x_1, \ldots, x_n\}$ be a set of input variables. Let formulas of the form $\phi_j = \bigwedge_i \neg x_{j,i}$ represent large AND gates which conjunct negated variables. These formulas are one level deep. Let formulas of the form $\Phi_j = \bigvee_i \phi_{j,i}$ represent large OR gates which disjunct formulas which themselves are one level deep conjunctions with all negative variables. These formulas are DNF formulas with only negative variables. Finally, let $\Psi = \bigwedge_i \Phi_{j,i}$ be a conjunction of formulas of the above form. The resulting circuit or formula is anti-monotone and normalized, with weft 3, and finding a satisfying assignment of weight p is $W[3]$ complete, when p is a parameter.

We next show how to convert this weighted satisfiability problem Ψ a query satisfiability problem $\text{SAT}(\mathcal{Q}_k^{\sigma(f),\pi})$, when the query size k is parameterized. We need to describe what each of the variables represents, what each gate in circuit represents, and how we require a satisfying query to represent a satisfying assignment of the right size.

In this construction, a weight parameter p, will correspond to a query size parameter of $k = p + 2$. (p selections, 1 for the relation with no selections, and 1 for the projection.)

The construction will have the following properties:

- Each formula Φ_i will be represented by a positive example e_i^+.
- Each formula ϕ (as part of a disjunction of Φ_i) will be converted into a tuple which can satisfy the positive example e_i^+.
- Each variable x_i will be represented by a possible selection.

Additional examples will be added in order to allow only appropriate selections, and require the right number of them. An assignment of weight p for Ψ will then correspond to a query with p selections, i.e., a query of size $p + 2 = k$. A satisfying assignment will clearly correspond to a satisfying query.

Let Ψ be a formula as above, for which we want to find a satisfying assignment with weight p. We build the following database $\mathcal{D}_\Psi$, with a single relation R, which has the following attributes:

- p attributes $A_i^1, \ldots, A_i^p$ for each variable x_i in Ψ. Intuitively, selections on an attribute A_i^j can be interpreted as saying that x_i is the jth positive variable in an assignment. These attributes will be projected out.
- An attribute A_Φ, which represents which positive example would be satisfied by selecting this tuple.
- An attribute A' which will be used to prevent selections on A_Φ. Selections will also be forbidden on this attribute, i.e., such selections will create a query that is not satisfying.

The rest of the construction will ensure that the only selections that will possibly derive a satisfying query will be on the attributes A_i^j, and only those which force their value to be 0.

The relation R will contain the following tuples: (In all tuples, all values not specifically mentioned are 0.)

- Each formula ϕ_j, which is a subformula of Φ_i, will be represented by a tuple t_{ϕ_j} where attributes representing variables in ϕ will get the value 1, and the attribute A_Φ will get the value Φ_i.
- For each $1 \leq j \leq p$, we add a tuple t_j where all attributes A_i^j get the value 1. These will be used to ensure that we choose p selections.
- For each variable x_m and each pair $1 \leq j_1 \neq j_2 \leq p$, we add a tuple $t_m^{\{j_1,j_2\}}$ in which all attributes $A_i^{j_1}$ and $A_i^{j_2}$ get the value 1, with the exception of the attributes $A_m^{j_1}$ and $A_m^{j_2}$ which receive the value 0. This will be used to ensure that we will not select the same variable twice.
- A tuple $t_{A'}$ where the attribute A' receives a value of 1. This will be used to prevent selections directly on A_Φ.

Finally, the example set will contain:

- A positive example $\{A_\Phi : \Phi_i, A' : 0\}$ for each subformula Φ_i in Ψ.
- A positive example $\{A_\Phi : 0, A' : 1\}$.
- A negative example $\{A_\Phi : 0, A' : 0\}$.

This construction is demonstrated in Figure 6.

We now need to show that the reduction is valid, i.e., that there is a satisfying query Q with a size no more than

$k = p + 2$ if and only if Ψ has a satisfying assignment with a weight of exactly p.

Consider a truth assignment μ that assigns $x_{s_1} \dots x_{s_p}$ to true, and all other variables to false. Then by construction, the query $Q = \pi_{A_{\Psi}, A'} \sigma_{A^1_{s_1}=0} \cdots \sigma_{A^p_{s_p}=0} R$ will satisfy the example set E over $\mathcal{D}$ if and only if μ satisfies Ψ. This holds because by construction selections remove tuples, corresponding to a ϕ clause in Ψ which are dissatisfied by positive variables. A positive example is satisfied by making sure at least one of its possible source tuples remains, which corresponds to a Φ clause being satisfied because at least one of its ϕ clauses is not dissatisfied. The size of Q is exactly $k = p + 2$ as required. It immediately follows that if Ψ has a satisfying assignment, then there is a query satisfying E over $\mathcal{D}$.

In the other direction, suppose Q satisfies E over $\mathcal{D}$. If Q has the form above, and each of the attributes represent different variables, satisfaction of Ψ is immediate. We also know from construction that Q may only include comparisons where attributes must equal 0. (Or equivalently, attributes must not be equal to 1, or not more than 0.) Suppose, on the other hand, that Q has a different form. If Q does not include a projection, the schema returned by Q and the schema of the example set will differ, preventing satisfaction. Since Q must include a projection operator, it may include at most p selections. Suppose Q includes less than p selections. Then there is some j, for which none of the attributes A^j_i are selected upon. It immediately follows that Q cannot satisfy, as it will return a negative example (using t_j). We therefore know that Q must include exactly p selections, as $p+1$ selections would already make the query too big. We immediately see that for each $1 \leq j \leq p$, there is exactly one attribute A^j_i upon which we select. Finally, suppose there is some $j_1 \neq j_2$ and some i such that Q selects upon both $A^{j_1}_i$ and $A^{j_2}_i$. In that case, one of the tuples described by the third bullet above will prevent satisfaction by Q, as each j can only have a single selection of the form A^j_i. It follows that if Q satisfies E over $\mathcal{D}$, it must have the form of the query mentioned above, which must correspond to a satisfying assignment over Ψ, as required. □

PROPOSITION A.2. *$\text{SAT}(Q^{\pi,\sigma(f)})$ is $W[3]$-complete when the number of examples is a parameter.*

PROOF. To show membership in $W[3]$, the same reduction used to prove Proposition A.1 cannot be applied, as we no longer have a limit on the size of the query. Hence, we provide a different modeling of the problem at hand as a Boolean circuit with weft 3. Let $\mathcal{D}$ be a database with a single relation R and E be an example set with e examples. We create a Boolean circuit with input gates x_t for each tuple t in R that is a possible source of a positive example from E. In addition,

- for each selection of interest $A\theta c$, where A is an attribute in R and $\theta \in f$, we create an AND-gate. An input gate x_t that is a possible source of a positive tuple is connected to this gate via a NOT-gate if t is disqualified by $A\theta c$.
- for each positive example $t^p \in E$, we create an OR-gate, which has as input all gates x_t such that t can be a source of t^p.
- for each tuple t in R that can be a source of a negative example, we create an OR-gate. For each condition $A\theta c$, with $\theta \in f$, such that t is disqualified when the selection $\sigma_{A\theta c}$ is applied, we connect variable $x_{A\theta c}$ to t.
- finally, all gates corresponding to positive examples, and to sources of negative examples feed into the output AND-gate.

Observe that the circuit constructed has weft 3. We demonstrate this construction in Figure 7, when $f = \{\leq, \geq\}$. Note that this circuit is easily derived from the circuit in Figure 3 by changing the direction of the arrows from the input variables to the gates representing selections (and then reassigning which gates are input and which are AND-gates appropriately).

It is easy to see that there is a query satisfying the example set E if and only if there is a satisfying assignment of Hamming weight at most e, as the source tuples for the positive examples will be assigned true (and it is sufficient to have e such source tuples), and the query itself can be read off the circuit by seeing which gates corresponding to selection have the value true.

In order to show $W[3]$-hardness, we again consider the *weighted circuit anti-monotone normalized satisfiability problem* with weft 3, using the same notation used for Proposition A.1. Recall that we have a formula Ψ, which is a conjunction of formulas called Φ, which are disjunctions of formulas called ϕ which are conjunction of negative literals.

In this construction, a weight parameter p, will correspond to a parameter $e = p + 2$, bounding the number of examples. (p positive examples corresponding to the formula, 1 negative example, and an additional positive example to prevent unwanted selections.)

The construction will have the following properties:

- Each formula Φ_i will be represented a tuple forbidden by the negative example.
- Each formula ϕ (as part of a disjunction of Φ_i) will be converted into a possible selection, which can remove the forbidden tuple which represents Φ_i.
- Each variable x_i will be represented by a tuple which can be removed by any of the selections representing formulas containing the variable.

Additional examples will be added in order to allow only appropriate selections. An assignment of weight p for Ψ will then correspond to a query which does not remove p chosen tuples. A satisfying assignment will clearly correspond to a satisfying query.

Let Ψ be a formula as above, for which we want to find a satisfying assignment with weight p. We build the following database $\mathcal{D}_\Psi$. $\mathcal{D}_\Psi$ will contain a single relation R with the following attributes.

- An attribute A_{ϕ_i} for each conjunction ϕ_i in Ψ. These attributes will be projected out.
- p attributes $A^1_i, \dots, A^p_i$ for each variable x_i in Ψ. Intuitively, selections on an attribute A^j_i can be interpreted as saying that x_i is the jth positive variable in an assignment. These attributes will also be projected out.
- An attribute B.
- An attribute C which will be used to prevent selections on B. Selections will also be forbidden on this attribute.

R			
	A	B	C
t_1	1	2	3
t_2	1	3	3
t_3	1	4	4
t_4	1	3	4

E			
		A	C
✓	t_p	1	3
✗	t_n	1	4

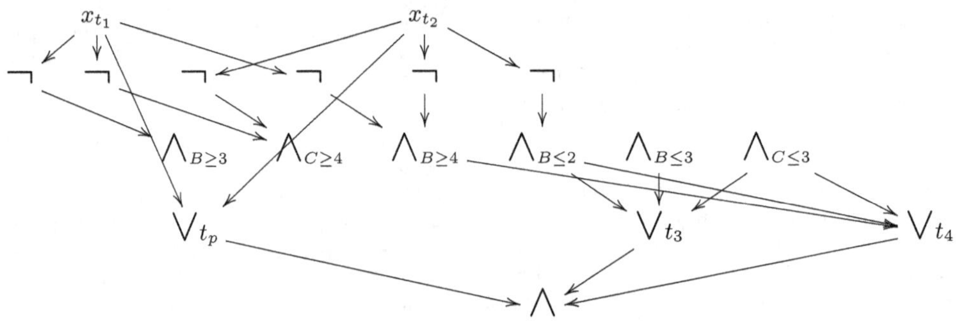

Figure 7: Reduction to $W[3]$ for Proposition A.2.

The only permitted selections will be on the attributes A_{ϕ_i} and A_i^j, and only those which force their value to be 0.

The relation R will contain the following tuples: (In all tuples, all values not specifically mentioned are 0.)

- Each formula Φ, represents a forbidden tuple, which will have the value 1 in each attribute A_{ϕ_i} when ϕ_i is a subformula of Φ.
- For each $1 \leq j \leq p$, and for each variable x_i, we add a tuple where the attribute B gets the value j. An attribute A_{ϕ_k} gets the value 1 if x_i is in ϕ_k. An attribute A_m^j gets the value 1 when $i \neq m$. An attribute A_i^m gets the value 1 when $m \neq j$. Intuitively, these tuples state that the jth variable is x_i.
- For each $1 \leq j \leq p$, we add a tuple with all attributes A_i^j getting the value 1. This will ensure we choose p satisfying tuples.
- For each variable x_m and each pair $1 \leq j_1 \neq j_2 \leq p$, we add a tuple with the attributes A_i^{j1} and A_i^{j2} getting the value 1, with the exception of the attributes A_m^{j1} and A_m^{j2} which receive the value 0. This ensures we don't select the same variable twice.
- A tuple where the attribute C receives a value of 1. This will be used to prevent selections directly on A_Φ.

Finally, the example set will contain:

- A positive example $\{B : j, C : 0\}$ for each $1 \leq j \leq p$.
- A positive example $\{B : 0, C : 1\}$.
- A negative example $\{B : 0, C : 0\}$.

This construction is demonstrated in Example 7.4.

We now need to show that the reduction is valid, i.e., that there is a query satisfying E over $\mathcal{D}_\Psi$, if and only if Ψ has a satisfying assignment with a weight of exactly p.

Consider a query q which satisfies E over $\mathcal{D}_\Psi$. It is clear that q must have the following properties:

- For each $1 \leq j \leq p$, there is a selection on some attribute A_i^j. (Otherwise negative example is not satisfied.)
- For each $1 \leq j \leq p$, there are no selections on more than one attribute A_i^j. (Positive example $\{B : j, C : 0\}$)
- No two $1 \leq j_1 \neq j_2 \leq p$ share the same i by selecting on both A_i^{j1} and A_i^{j2}. (Otherwise negative example is not satisfied.)

These selections completely determine which tuples satisfy which positive examples. These tuples correspond with variables in the weighted circuit satisfaction problem. A maximal selection can be found from such a base, by including all possible selections which do not prevent satisfaction of the positive examples. This provides a correspondence between assignments and queries.

The correspondence between satisfying assignments and satisfying queries is immediate, as satisfying Φ clauses by choosing a satisfying subformula ϕ, corresponds to choosing selections to remove unwanted tuples, while the variables prevent satisfaction of some ϕ clauses, as positive examples prevent usage of some selections. □

Private Incremental Regression

Shiva Prasad Kasiviswanathan
Samsung Research America
kasivisw@gmail.com

Kobbi Nissim*
Georgetown University
kobbi.nissim@georgetown.edu

Hongxia Jin
Samsung Research America
hongxia.jin@samsung.com

ABSTRACT

Data is continuously generated by modern data sources, and a recent challenge in machine learning has been to develop techniques that perform well in an incremental (streaming) setting. A variety of offline machine learning tasks are known to be feasible under differential privacy, where generic construction exist that, given a large enough input sample, perform tasks such as PAC learning, Empirical Risk Minimization (ERM), regression, etc. In this paper, we investigate the problem of private machine learning, where as common in practice, the data is not given at once, but rather arrives incrementally over time.

We introduce the problems of *private incremental ERM* and *private incremental regression* where the general goal is to always maintain a good empirical risk minimizer for the history observed under differential privacy. Our first contribution is a generic transformation of private batch ERM mechanisms into private incremental ERM mechanisms, based on a simple idea of invoking the private batch ERM procedure at some regular time intervals. We take this construction as a baseline for comparison. We then provide two mechanisms for the private incremental regression problem. Our first mechanism is based on privately constructing a noisy incremental gradient function, which is then used in a modified projected gradient procedure at every timestep. This mechanism has an excess empirical risk of $\approx \sqrt{d}$, where d is the dimensionality of the data. While from the results of Bassily *et al.* [2] this bound is tight in the worst-case, we show that certain geometric properties of the input and constraint set can be used to derive significantly better results for certain interesting regression problems. Our second mechanism which achieves this is based on the idea of projecting the data to a lower dimensional space using random projections, and then adding privacy noise in this low dimensional space. The mechanism overcomes the issues of adaptivity inherent with the use of random projections in online streams, and uses recent developments in high-dimensional estimation to achieve an excess empirical risk bound of $\approx T^{1/3}W^{2/3}$, where T is the length of the stream and W is the sum of the Gaussian widths of the input domain and the constraint set that we optimize over.

*Supported by a grant from the Sloan Foundation, a Simons Investigator grant to Salil Vadhan, and NSF grant CNS-1237235.

PODS'17, May 14-19, 2017, Chicago, Illinois, USA
© 2017 ACM. ISBN 978-1-4503-4198-1/17/05...$15.00
DOI: http://dx.doi.org/10.1145/3034786.3034795

1. INTRODUCTION

Most modern data such as documents, images, social media data, sensor data, and mobile data naturally arrive in a streaming fashion, giving rise to the challenge of incremental machine learning, where the goal is build and publish a model that evolves as data arrives. Learning algorithms are frequently run on sensitive data, such as location information in a mobile setting, and results of such analyses could leak sensitive information. For example, Kasiviswanathan *et al.* [30] show how the results of many convex ERM problems can be combined to carry out reconstruction attacks in the spirit of Dinur and Nissim [10]. Given this, a natural direction to explore, is whether, we can carry out incremental machine learning, without leaking any significant information about individual entries in the data. For example, a data scientist, might want to continuously update the regression parameter of a linear model built on a stream of user profile data gathered from an ongoing survey, but these updates should not reveal whether any one person participated in the survey or not.

Differential privacy [14] is a rigorous notion of privacy that is now widely studied in computer science and statistics. Intuitively, differential privacy requires that datasets differing in only one entry induce similar distributions on the output of a (randomized) algorithm. One of the strengths of differential privacy comes from the large variety of machine learning tasks that it allows. Good generic constructions exist for tasks such as PAC learning [4, 29] and Empirical Risk Minimization [39, 33, 24, 25, 46, 26, 2, 11, 49, 45]. These constructions, however, are typically focused on the batch (offline) setting, where information is first collected and then analyzed. Considering an incremental setting, it is natural to ask whether these tasks can still be performed with high accuracy, under differential privacy.

In this paper, we introduce the problem of private incremental empirical risk minimization (ERM) and provide algorithms for this new setting. Our particular focus will be on the problem of private incremental linear regression. Let us start with a description of the traditional batch convex ERM framework. Given a dataset and a constraint space $\mathcal{C}$, the goal in ERM is to pick a $\theta \in \mathcal{C}$ that minimizes the *em-*

pirical error (risk). Formally, given n datapoints $\mathbf{z}_1, \ldots, \mathbf{z}_n$ from some domain $\mathcal{Z}$, and a closed, convex set $\mathcal{C} \subseteq \mathbb{R}^d$, consider the optimization problem:

$$\min_{\theta \in \mathcal{C}} \mathcal{J}(\theta; \mathbf{z}_1, \ldots, \mathbf{z}_n) \text{ where } \mathcal{J}(\theta; \mathbf{z}_1, \ldots, \mathbf{z}_n) = \sum_{i=1}^{n} \jmath(\theta; \mathbf{z}_i). \tag{1}$$

The loss function $\mathcal{J} : \mathcal{C} \times \mathcal{Z}^n \to \mathbb{R}$ measures the fit of $\theta \in \mathcal{C}$ to the given data $\mathbf{z}_1, \ldots, \mathbf{z}_n$, the function $\jmath : \mathcal{C} \times \mathcal{Z} \to \mathbb{R}$ is the loss associated with a single datapoint and is assumed to be convex in the first parameter θ for every $\mathbf{z} \in \mathcal{Z}$. It is common to assume that the loss function has certain properties, e.g., positive valued. The *M-estimator* (true empirical risk minimizer) $\hat{\theta}$ associated with a given a function $\mathcal{J}(\theta; \mathbf{z}_1, \ldots, \mathbf{z}_n) \geq 0$ is defined as:[1]

$$\hat{\theta} \in \text{argmin}_{\theta \in \mathcal{C}} \mathcal{J}(\theta; \mathbf{z}_1, \ldots, \mathbf{z}_n) = \text{argmin}_{\theta \in \mathcal{C}} \sum_{i=1}^{n} \jmath(\theta; \mathbf{z}_i).$$

This type of program captures a variety of empirical risk minimization (ERM) problems, e.g., the MLE (Maximum Likelihood Estimators) for linear regression is captured by setting $\jmath(\theta; \mathbf{z}) = (y - \langle \mathbf{x}, \theta \rangle)^2$ in (1), where $\mathbf{z} = (\mathbf{x}, y)$ for $\mathbf{x} \in \mathbb{R}^d$ and $y \in \mathbb{R}$. Similarly, the MLE for logistic regression is captured by setting $\jmath(\theta; \mathbf{z}) = \ln(1 + \exp(-y\langle \mathbf{x}, \theta \rangle))$. Another common example is the support vector machine (SVM), where $\jmath(\theta; \mathbf{z}) = \text{hinge}(y\langle \mathbf{x}, \theta \rangle)$, where $\text{hinge}(a) = 1 - a$ if $a \leq 1$ and 0 otherwise.

The main focus of this paper will be on a particularly important ERM problem of linear regression. Linear regression is a popular statistical technique that is commonly used to model the relationship between the outcome (label) and the explanatory variables (covariates). Informally, in a linear regression, given n covariate-response pairs $(\mathbf{x}_1, y_1), \ldots, (\mathbf{x}_n, y_n) \in \mathbb{R}^d \times \mathbb{R}$, we wish to find a (regression) parameter vector $\hat{\theta}$ such that $\langle \mathbf{x}_i, \hat{\theta} \rangle \approx y_i$ for most i's. Specifically, let $\mathbf{y} = (y_1, \ldots, y_n) \in \mathbb{R}^n$ denote a vector of the responses, and let $X \in \mathbb{R}^{n \times d}$ be the design matrix where $\mathbf{x}_i^\top$ is the ith row. Consider the linear model: $\mathbf{y} = X\theta^\star + \mathbf{w}$, where $\mathbf{w}$ is the noise vector, the goal in linear regression is to estimate the unknown regression vector $\theta^\star$. Assuming that the noise vector $\mathbf{w} = (w_1, \ldots, w_n)$ follows a (sub)Gaussian distribution, estimating the vector $\theta^\star$ amounts to solving the "ordinary least squares" (OLS) problem:

$$\hat{\theta} \in \text{argmin}_{\theta} \sum_{i=1}^{n} (y_i - \langle \mathbf{x}_i, \theta \rangle)^2.$$

Typically, for additional guarantees such as sparsity, stability, etc., θ is constrained to be from a convex set $\mathcal{C} \subset \mathbb{R}^d$. Popular choices of $\mathcal{C}$ include the L_1-ball (referred to as *Lasso* regression) and L_2-ball (referred to as *Ridge* regression). In an incremental setting, the $(\mathbf{x}_i, y_i)$'s arrive over time, and the goal in incremental linear regression is to maintain over time (an estimate of) the regression parameter.

Incremental Setting. In an incremental setting the data arrives in a stream at discrete time intervals. The incremental setting is a variant of the traditional batch setting capturing the fact that modern data is rarely collected at one single time and more commonly data gathering and analysis may be interleaved. An incremental algorithm is modeled as follows: at each timestep the algorithm receives an input from the stream, computes, and produces outputs. Typically, constraints are placed on the algorithm in terms of some computational resource (such as memory, computation time) availability. In this paper, the challenge in this setting comes from the differential privacy constraint because frequent releases about the data can lead to privacy loss (see, e.g., [10, 30]).

We focus on the incremental ERM problem. In this problem setting, the data $\mathbf{z}_1, \ldots, \mathbf{z}_T \in \mathcal{Z}$ arrives one point at each timestep $t \in \{1, \ldots, T\}$. The goal of an incremental ERM algorithm is to release at each timestep t, an estimator that minimizes the risk measured on the data $\mathbf{z}_1, \ldots, \mathbf{z}_t$. In more concrete terms, the goal is to output $\hat{\theta}_t$ at every $t \in \{1, \ldots, T\}$, where:

$$\text{Incremental ERM:} \quad \hat{\theta}_t \in \text{argmin}_{\theta \in \mathcal{C}} \sum_{i=1}^{t} \jmath(\theta; \mathbf{z}_i).$$

The goal of *private incremental ERM* algorithm, is to (differential) privately estimate $\hat{\theta}_t$ at every $t \in \{1, \ldots, T\}$.[2] In this paper, we develop the first private incremental ERM algorithms.

There is a long line of work in designing differentially private algorithms for empirical risk minimization problems in the batch setting [39, 33, 25, 46, 26, 2, 11, 49, 45]. A naive approach to transform the existing batch techniques to work in the incremental model is by using them to recompute the outcome after each datapoint's arrival. However, for achieving an overall fixed level of differential privacy, this would result in an unsatisfactory loss in terms of utility. Precise statements can be obtained using composition properties of differential privacy (as in Theorem A.4), but informally if a differentially private algorithm is executed T times on the same input, then the privacy parameter (ϵ in Definition 4) degrades by a factor of $\approx \sqrt{T}$, and this affects the overall utility of this approach as the utility bounds typically depend inversely on the privacy parameter. Therefore, the above naive approach will suffer an additional multiplicative factor of $\approx \sqrt{T}$ over the risk bounds obtained for the batch case. Our goal is to obtain risk bounds in the incremental setting that are comparable to those in the batch setting, i.e., bounds that do not suffer from this additional penalty of $\sqrt{T}$.

Generalization. For the kind of problems we consider in this paper, if the process generating the data satisfies the conditions for *generalization* (e.g., if the data stream contains datapoints where each datapoint is sampled independent and identically from an unknown distribution), the incremental ERM would converge to the true risk on the distribution (via uniform convergence and other ideas, re-

[1] This formulation also captures *regularized* ERM, in which an additional convex function $R(\theta)$ is added to the loss function to penalize certain type of solutions, e.g., "penalize" for the "complexity" of θ. The loss function $\mathcal{J}(\theta; \mathbf{z}_1, \ldots, \mathbf{z}_n)$ then equals $\sum_{i=1}^{n} \jmath(\theta; \mathbf{z}_i) + R(\theta)$, which is same as replacing $\jmath(\theta; \mathbf{z}_i)$ by $\jmath(\theta; \mathbf{z}_i) + R(\theta)/n$ in (1).

[2] A point to note in the above description, while we have the privacy constraint, we have placed no computational constraints on the algorithm. In particular, the above description allows also those algorithms that at time t use the whole input history $\mathbf{z}_1, \ldots, \mathbf{z}_t$. However, as we will discuss in Sections 4 and 5, our proposed approaches for private incremental regression are also efficient in terms of their resource requirements.

fer to [51, 41, 2] for more details). In this case, the model learned in an incremental fashion will have a good predictive accuracy on unseen arriving data. If however, the data does not satisfy these conditions, then $\hat{\theta}_t$ can be viewed as a "summarizer" for the data seen so far. Generating these summaries could also be useful in many applications, e.g., the regression parameter can be used to explain the associations between the outcome (y_i's) and the covariates ($\mathbf{x}_i$'s). These associations are regularly used in domains such as public health, social sciences, biological studies, to understand whether specific variables are important (e.g., statistically significant) or unimportant predictors of the outcome. In practice, these associations would need to be constantly re-evaluated over time as new data arrives.

Comparison to Online Learning. Online learning (or sequential prediction) is another well-studied setting for learning when the data arrives in a sequential order. There are differences between the goals of incremental and online learning. In online ERM learning, the aim is to provide an estimator $\tilde{\theta}_t$ that can be used for future prediction. More concretely, at time t, an online learner, chooses $\tilde{\theta}_t$ and then the adversary picks $\mathbf{z}_t$ and the learner suffers loss of $\jmath(\tilde{\theta}_t; \mathbf{z}_t)$. Online learners try to minimize *regret* defined as the difference between the cumulative loss of the learner and the cumulative loss of the best fixed decision at the end of T rounds [40]. In an incremental setting, the algorithm gets to observe $\mathbf{z}_t$ before committing to the estimator, and the goal is to ensure at each timestep t, the algorithm maintains a *single* estimator that minimizes the risk on the history. There are strong lower bounds on the achievable regret for online ERM learning. In particular, even under the differential privacy constraint, the excess risk bounds on incremental learning that we obtain here have better dependence on T (stream length) than the regret lower bounds for online ERM. Incremental learning model should be viewed as a variant of batch (offline) learning model, where the data arrives over time, and the goal is to output intermediate results.

1.1 Our Results

Before stating our results, let us define how we measure success of our algorithms. As is standard in ERM, we measure the quality of our algorithm by the worst-case (over inputs) excess (empirical) risk (defined as the difference from the minimum possible risk over a function class). In an incremental setting, we want this excess risk to be always small for any sequence of inputs. The following definition captures this requirement. All our algorithms are randomized, and they take a confidence parameter β and produce bounds that hold with probability at least $1 - \beta$.

Definition 1. *A (randomized) incremental algorithm is an* (α, β)-estimator *for loss function* $\mathcal{J}$, *if with probability at least* $1 - \beta$ *over the coin flips of the algorithm, for each* $t \in \{1, \dots, T\}$, *after processing a prefix of the stream of length* t, *it generates an output* $\theta_t \in \mathcal{C}$ *that satisfies the following bound on excess (empirical) risk:*

$$\mathcal{J}(\theta_t; \mathbf{z}_1, \dots, \mathbf{z}_t) - \mathcal{J}(\hat{\theta}_t; \mathbf{z}_1, \dots, \mathbf{z}_t) \leq \alpha,$$

where $\hat{\theta}_t \in \text{argmin}_{\theta \in \mathcal{C}} \mathcal{J}(\theta; \mathbf{z}_1, \dots, \mathbf{z}_t)$ *is the true empirical risk minimizer. Here,* α *is referred to as the bound on the excess risk.*

In this paper, we propose incremental ERM algorithms that provide a differential privacy guarantee on data streams. Informally, differential privacy requires that the output of a data analysis mechanism is not overly affected by any single entry in the input dataset. In the case of incremental setting, we insist that this guarantee holds at each timestep for all outputs produced up to that timestep (precise definition in Section 2). This would imply that, an adversary is unable to determine whether a particular datapoint was present or not in the input stream by observing the output of the algorithm over time. Two parameters, ϵ and δ control the level of privacy. Very roughly, ϵ is an upper bound on the amount of influence an individual datapoint has on the outcome and δ is the probability that this bound fails to hold (for a precise interpretation, refer to [31]), so the definition becomes more stringent as $\epsilon, \delta \to 0$. Therefore, while parameters α, β measure the accuracy of an incremental algorithm, the parameters ϵ, δ represent its privacy risk. Our private incremental algorithms take ϵ, δ as parameters and satisfies: a) the differential privacy constraint with parameters ϵ, δ and b) (α, β)-estimator property (Definition 1) for every $\beta > 0$ and some α (parameter that the algorithm tries to minimize).

There is a trivial differentially private incremental ERM algorithm that completely ignores the input and outputs at every $t \in \{1, \dots, T\}$, any $\theta \in \mathcal{C}$ (this scheme is private as the output is always independent of the input). The excess risk of this algorithm is at most $2TL\|\mathcal{C}\|$, where L is the Lipschitz constant of $\jmath$ and $\|\mathcal{C}\|$ is the maximum attained norm in the convex set $\mathcal{C}$ (Definition 2). All bounds presented in this paper, as also true for all other existing results in the private ERM literature, are only interesting in the regime where they are less than this trivial bound.

For the purposes of this section, we make some simplifying assumptions and omit[3] dependence on all but key variables (dimension d and stream length T). Slightly more detailed bounds are stated in Table 1. All our algorithms run in time polynomial in d and T (exact bounds depend on the time needed for Euclidean projection onto the constraint set which will differ based on the constraint set). Additionally, our private incremental regression algorithms, which utilize the *Tree Mechanism* of [15, 6] have space requirement whose dependence on the stream length T is only logarithmic.

(1) **A Generic Transformation.** A natural first question is whether *non-trivial* private ERM algorithms exist in general for the incremental setting. Our first contribution is to answer this question in the affirmative – we present a simple generic transformation of private batch ERM algorithms into private incremental ERM algorithms. The construction idea is simple: rather than invoking the batch ERM algorithm every timestep, the batch ERM algorithm is invoked every τ timesteps, where τ is chosen to balance the excess risk factor coming from the stale risk minimizer (because of inaction) with the excess risk factor coming from the increased privacy noise due to reuse of the data. Using this idea along with recent results of Bassily *et al.* [2] for private batch ERM, we obtain an excess risk bound (α in Definition 1) of

[3]This includes parameters $\epsilon, \delta, \beta, \|\mathcal{C}\|$, and the Lipschitz constant of the loss function.

	Incremental ERM Problem Objective	Bound on the Excess (Empirical) Risk under (ϵ, δ)-Differential Privacy (α in Definition 1)
1	Convex Function (using a generic transformation)	$\frac{(Td)^{\frac{1}{3}} \log^{\frac{5}{2}}(1/\delta)}{\epsilon^{2/3}}$
2	Strongly Convex Function (using a generic transformation)	$\frac{\sqrt{d} \log^4(1/\delta)}{\nu^{1/2}\epsilon}$
3	Linear Regression	Mech 1: $\frac{\sqrt{d}\sqrt{\log(1/\delta)}}{\epsilon}$ Mech 2: $\frac{T^{\frac{1}{3}} W^{\frac{2}{3}} \sqrt{\log(1/\delta)}}{\epsilon} + T^{\frac{1}{6}} W^{\frac{1}{3}} \sqrt{\text{OPT}} + T^{\frac{1}{4}} W^{\frac{1}{2}} \sqrt[4]{\text{OPT}}$ (where $W = w(\mathcal{X}) + w(\mathcal{C})$ and OPT is the minimum empirical risk at timestep T)

Table 1: Summary of our results. The stream length is T and d is the dimensionality of the data (number of covariates in the case of regression). The bounds are stated for the setting where both the Lipschitz constant of the function and $\|\mathcal{C}\|$ are scaled to 1. The bounds ignore polylog factors in d and T, and the value in the table gives the bound when it is below T, i.e., the bounds should be read as $\min\{T, \cdot\}$. ν is the strong convexity parameter. For the regression problem, $\mathcal{X}$ is the domain from which the inputs (covariates) are drawn and $\mathcal{C}$ is the constraint space. OPT **stands for the minimum empirical risk at time T. The exact results are provided in Theorems 3.1, 4.2, and 5.7, respectively.**

$\tilde{O}(\min\{(Td)^{1/3}, T\})$.[4] Using this same framework, we also show that when the loss function is strongly convex the excess risk bound can be improved to $\tilde{O}(\min\{\sqrt{d}, T\})$.

A follow-up question is: how much worse is this private incremental ERM risk bound compared to best known private batch ERM risk bound (with a sample size of T datapoints)? In the batch setting, the results of Bassily *et al.* [2] establish that for any convex ERM problem, it is possible to achieve an excess risk bound of $\tilde{O}(\min\{\sqrt{d}, T\})$ (which is also tight in general). Therefore, our transformation from the batch to incremental setting, causes the excess risk to increase by at most a factor of $\approx \max\{T^{1/3}/d^{1/6}, 1\}$. Note that even for a low-dimensional setting (small d case), the factor increase in excess risk of $\approx T^{1/3}$ (as now $\max\{T^{1/3}/d^{1/6}, 1\} \approx T^{1/3}$) is much smaller than the factor increase of $\approx T^{1/2}$ for the earlier described naive approach based on using a private batch ERM algorithm at every timestep. The situation only improves for larger dimensional data.

(2) Private Incremental Regression Using Tree Mechanism. We show that we can improve the generic construction from **(1)** for the important problem of linear regression. We do so by introducing the notion of a *private gradient function* (Definition 5) that allows differentially private evaluation of the gradient at any $\theta \in \mathcal{C}$.[5] More formally, for any $\theta \in \mathcal{C}$, a private gradient function allows differentially private evaluation of the gradient at θ to within a small error (with high probability). Since the data arrives continually, our algorithm utilizes the *Tree Mechanism* of [15, 6] to continually update the private gradient function. Now given access to a private gradient function, we can use any first-order convex optimization technique (such as projected gradient descent) to privately estimate the regression parameter. The idea is, since these optimization techniques operate by iteratively taking steps in the direction opposite to the gradient evaluated at the current point, we can use a private gradient function for evaluating all the required gradients. Using this, we design a private regression algorithm for the incremental setting, that achieves an excess risk bound of $\tilde{O}(\min\{\sqrt{d}, T\})$. It is easy to observe, for private incremental linear regression, this result improves the bounds from the generic construction above for any choice of d, T (as $\min\{\sqrt{d}, T\} \leq \min\{(Td)^{1/3}, T\}$).[6]

Ignoring polylog factors, this worst-case bound matches the lower bounds on the excess risk for squared-loss in the batch case [2], implying that this bound cannot be improved in general (an excess risk upper bound for a problem in the incremental setting trivially holds for the same problem in the batch setting).

(3) Private Incremental Regression: Beyond Worst-Case. The noise added in our previous solution **(2)** grows approximately as the square root of the input dimension (for sufficiently large T), which could be prohibitive for a high-dimensional input. While in a worst-case setup this, as we discussed above, seems unavoidable, we investigate whether certain geometric properties of the input/output space could be used to obtain better results in certain interesting scenarios.

A natural strategy for reducing the dependence of the excess risk bounds on d is to use dimensionality reduction techniques such as the Johnson-Lindenstrauss (JL) transform: The server performing the computation can choose a random projection matrix $\Phi \in \mathbb{R}^{m \times d}$ which is then used for projecting all the $\mathbf{x}_i$'s onto a lower-dimensional space. The advantage being that, using the techniques from **(2)**, one could privately minimize the excess risk in the projected subspace, and in doing so, the dependence on the dimension in excess risk is reduced to $\approx \sqrt{m}$ (from $\approx \sqrt{d}$).[7] However, there are two significant challenges in implementing this idea for incremental regression, both of which we overcome using geometric techniques.

[4]For simplicity of exposition, the $\tilde{O}(\cdot)$ notation hides factors polynomial in $\log T$ and $\log d$.

[5]Intuitively, this would imply that for any $\theta \in \mathcal{C}$, the output of a private gradient function cannot be used to distinguish two streams that are almost the same (differential privacy guarantee).

[6]A linear regression instance typically does not satisfy strong convexity requirements.

[7]A point to note that this use of random projections for linear regression is different from its typical use in prior work [55], where they are used not for reducing dimensionality but rather for reducing the number of samples used in the regression computation.

The first one being that this only solves the problem in the projected subspace, whereas our goal is to produce an estimate to true empirical risk minimizer. To achieve this we would need to "lift" back the solution from the projected subspace to the original space. We do so by using recent developments in the problem of high dimensional estimation with constraints [52]. The *Gaussian width* of the constraint space $\mathcal{C}$ plays an important role in this analysis. Gaussian width is a well-studied quantity in convex geometry that captures the geometric complexity of any set of vectors.[8] The rough idea here being that a good estimation (lifting) can be done from few observations (small m) as long as the constraint set $\mathcal{C}$ has small Gaussian width. Many popular sets have low Gaussian width, e.g., the width of L_1-ball (B_1^d is $\Theta(\sqrt{\log d})$, and that of set of all sparse vectors in $\mathbb{R}^d$ with at most k non-zero entries is $\Theta(\sqrt{k \log(d/k)})$.

The next challenge comes from the incremental nature of input generation, because it allows for generation of $\mathbf{x}_i$'s after Φ is *fixed*. This is an issue as the guarantees of random projections only hold if the inputs on which it is applied are chosen before choosing the transformation. For example, given a random projection matrix $\Phi \in \mathbb{R}^{m \times d}$ with $m \ll d$, it is simple to generate $\mathbf{x}$ such that the norm on $\mathbf{x}$ is substantially different from the norm of $\Phi\mathbf{x}$.[9] Again to deal with these kind of adaptive choice of inputs, we rely on the geometric properties of problem. In particular, we use Gordon's theorem that states that one can embed a set of points S on a unit sphere into a lower-dimensional space $\mathbb{R}^m$ using a Gaussian random matrix[10] Φ such that, $\sup_{\mathbf{a} \in S} |\|\Phi\mathbf{a}\|^2 - \|\mathbf{a}\|^2|$ is small (with high probability), provided m is at least the square of the Gaussian width of S [20].

Using the above geometric ideas, and the *Tree Mechanism* to incrementally construct the private gradient function (as in **(2)**), we present our second private algorithm for incremental regression, with an

$$\tilde{O}(\min\{T^{\frac{1}{3}} W^{\frac{2}{3}} + T^{\frac{1}{6}} W^{\frac{1}{3}} \sqrt{\text{OPT}} + T^{\frac{1}{4}} W^{\frac{1}{2}} \sqrt[4]{\text{OPT}}, T\})$$

excess risk bound, where $W = w(\mathcal{X}) + w(\mathcal{C})$, $\mathcal{X} \subset \mathbb{R}^d$ is the domain from which the $\mathbf{x}_i$'s (covariates) are drawn, and OPT is the true minimum empirical risk at time T. As we discuss in Section 5, for many practically interesting regression instances, such as when $\mathcal{X}$ is a domain of sparse vectors, and $\mathcal{C}$ is bounded by an L_1-ball (as is the case of popular Lasso regression) or is a polytope defined by polynomial (in dimension) many vertices, $W \approx \text{polylog}(d)$, in which case the risk bound can be simplified to $\tilde{O}(\min\{T^{\frac{1}{3}} + T^{\frac{1}{6}} \sqrt{\text{OPT}} + T^{\frac{1}{4}} \sqrt[4]{\text{OPT}}, T\})$. In most practical scenarios, when the relationship between covariates and response satisfy a linear relationship, one would also expect OPT $\ll T$. These bounds show that, for certain instances, it is possible to design differentially private risk minimizers in the incremental setting with excess risk that depends only poly-logarithmically on the dimensionality of the data, a desired feature in a high-dimensional setting.

[8]For a set $S \subseteq \mathbb{R}^d$, Gaussian width is defined as $w(S) = \mathbb{E}_{\mathbf{g} \in \mathcal{N}(0,1)^d} [\sup_{\mathbf{a} \in S} \langle \mathbf{a}, \mathbf{g} \rangle]$.

[9]Note that this issue arises independent of the differential privacy requirements, and holds even in a non-private incremental setting.

[10]Recent results [5] have shown other distributions for generating $\Phi \in \mathbb{R}^{m \times d}$ also provide similar guarantees.

Organization. In Section 1.2, we discuss some related work. In Section 2, we present some preliminaries. Our generic transformation from a private batch ERM algorithm to a private incremental ERM algorithm is given in Section 3. We present techniques that improve upon these bounds for the problem of private incremental regression in Sections 4 and 5. The appendices contain some proof details and supplementary material. In Appendix C, we analyze the convergence rate of a noisy projected gradient descent technique, and in Appendix D, we present the *Tree Mechanism* of [15, 6].

1.2 Related Work

Private ERM. Starting from the works of Chaudhuri *et al.* [7, 8], private convex ERM problems have been studied in various settings including the low-dimensional setting [39, 33], high-dimensional sparse regression setting [33, 46], online learning setting [24, 47, 26, 36], local privacy setting [11], and interactive setting [25, 49].

Bassily *et al.* [2] presented algorithms that for a general convex loss function $\jmath(\theta; \mathbf{z})$ which is 1-Lipschitz for every $\mathbf{z}$, achieves an expected excess risk of $\approx \sqrt{d}$ under (ϵ, δ)-differential privacy and $\approx d$ under ϵ-differential privacy (ignoring the dependence on other parameters for simplicity).[11] We use their batch mechanisms in our generic construction to obtain risk bounds for incremental ERM problems (Theorem 3.1). They also showed that these bounds cannot be improved *in general*, even for the least-squares regression function. However, if the constraint space has low Gaussian width (such as with the L_1-ball), Talwar *et al.* [45, 44] recently showed that, under (ϵ, δ)-differential privacy, the above bound can be improved by exploiting the geometric properties of the constraint space. An analogous result under ϵ-differential privacy for the class of *generalized linear functions* (which includes linear, logistic regression) was recently obtained by Kasiviswanathan and Jin [28]. Our excess risk bounds based on Gaussian width (presented in Section 5) uses a lifting procedure similar to that used by Kasiviswanathan and Jin [28]. All of these above algorithms operate in the batch setting, and ours is the first work dealing with private ERM problems in an incremental setting.

Private Online Convex Optimization. Differentially private algorithms have also been designed for a large class of online (convex optimization) learning problems, in both the full information and bandit settings [24, 47, 26]. Adapting the popular *Follow the Approximate Leader* framework [22], Smith and Thakurta [47] obtained regret bounds for private online learning with nearly optimal dependence on T (though the dependence on the dimensionality d in these results is much worse than the known lower bounds). As discussed earlier, incremental learning is a variant of the batch learning, with goals different from online learning.

Private Incremental Algorithms. Dwork *et al.* [15] introduced the problem of counting under incremental (continual) observations. The goal is to monitor a stream of T bits, and continually release a counter of the number of 1's that have been observed so far, under differential privacy.

[11]Better risk bounds were achieved under strong convexity assumptions [2, 45].

The elegant *Tree Mechanism* introduced by Dwork *et al.* [15] and Chan *et al.* [6] solves this problem, under ϵ-differential privacy, with error roughly $\log^{5/2} T$. The versatility of this mechanism has been utilized in different ways in subsequent works [47, 16, 23]. We use the *Tree Mechanism* as a basic building block for computing the private gradient function incrementally. Dwork *et al.* [15] also achieve *pan-privacy* for their continual release (which means that the mechanism preserves differential privacy even when an adversary can observe snapshots of the mechanism's internal states), a property that we do not investigate in this paper.

Use of JL Transform for Privacy. The use of JL transform for achieving differential privacy with better utility has been well documented for a variety of computational tasks [56, 3, 32, 42, 50]. Blocki *et al.* [3] have shown that if $\Phi \in \mathbb{R}^{m\times n}$ is a Gaussian random matrix of appropriate dimension, then $\Phi X \in \mathbb{R}^{m\times d}$ is differentially private if the least singular value of the matrix $X \in \mathbb{R}^{n\times d}$ is "sufficiently" large. The bound on the least singular value was recently improved by Sheffet [42]. Here the privacy comes as a result of randomization inherent in the transform. However, these results require that the projection matrix is kept private, which is an issue in an incremental setting, where an adversary could learn about Φ over time. Kenthapadi et al. [32] use Johnson-Lindenstrauss transform to publish a private sketch that enables estimation of the distance between users. Their main idea is based on projecting a d-dimensional user feature vector into a lower m-dimensional space by first applying a random Johnson-Lindenstrauss transform and then adding Gaussian noise to each entry of the resulting vector. None of these above results deal with an incremental setting, where applying the JL transform is itself a challenge because of the adaptivity issues.

Traditional Streaming Algorithms. The literature on streaming algorithms is replete with various techniques that can solve linear regression and related problems on various streaming models of computation under various computational resource constraints. We refer the reader to the survey by Woodruff [55] for more details. However, incremental regression under differential privacy, poses a different challenge than that faced by traditional streaming algorithms. The issue is that the solution (regression parameter) at each timestep relies on all the datapoints observed in the past, and frequent releases about earlier points can lead to privacy loss.

2. PRELIMINARIES

Notation and Data Normalization. We denote $[n] = \{1,\dots,n\}$. Vectors are in column-wise fashion, denoted by boldface letters. For a vector $\mathbf{v}$, $\mathbf{v}^\top$ denotes its transpose, $\|\mathbf{v}\|$ it's Euclidean (L_2-) norm, and $\|\mathbf{v}\|_1$ it's L_1-norm. For a matrix M, $\|M\|$ denotes its spectral norm which equals its largest singular value, and $\|M\|_F$ its Frobenius norm. We use $\mathbf{0}$ to denote a d-dimensional vector of all zeros. The d-dimensional unit ball in L_p-norm centered at origin is denoted by B_p^d. $\mathbb{I}_d$ represents the $d\times d$ identity matrix. $\mathcal{N}(\mu,\Sigma)$ denotes the Gaussian distribution with mean vector μ and covariance matrix Σ. For a variable n, we use poly(n) to denote a polynomial function of n and polylog(n) to denote poly(log(n)).

We use standard definitions for function properties such as convexity, Lipschitzness, and strong convexity (see e.g., [40]). In our setting, for a loss function $\jmath(\theta;\mathbf{z})$, these properties are all defined with respect to the first argument θ. We use the notation $\nabla\jmath(\theta;\mathbf{z})$ to denote the gradient (if it exists) or any subgradient of function $\jmath(\cdot;\mathbf{z})$ at θ.

We assume all streams are of a fixed length T, which is known to the algorithm. We make this assumption for simplifying the discussion. In fact, in our presented generic transformation for incremental ERM this assumption can be straightforwardly removed. Whereas in the case of algorithms for private incremental regression this assumption can be removed by using a simple trick[12] introduced by Chan *et al.* [6]. For a stream Γ, we use Γ_t to denote the stream prefix of length t.

Throughout this paper, we use ℓ and $\mathcal{L}$ to indicate the least-squared loss on a single datapoint and a collection of datapoints, respectively. Namely,

$$\ell(\theta;(\mathbf{x},y)) = (y-\langle\mathbf{x},\theta\rangle)^2 \text{ and}$$
$$\mathcal{L}(\theta;(\mathbf{x}_1,y_1),\dots,(\mathbf{x}_n,y_n)) = \textstyle\sum_{i=1}^n \ell(\theta;(\mathbf{x}_i,y_i)).$$

For a set of vectors, we define its diameter as the maximum attained norm in the set.

Definition 2. *(Diameter of Set) The diameter $\|\mathcal{C}\|$ of a closed set $\mathcal{C} \subseteq \mathbb{R}^d$, is defined as $\|\mathcal{C}\| = \sup_{\theta\in\mathcal{C}}\|\theta\|$.*

For improving the worst-case dependence on dimension d, we exploit the geometric properties of the input and constraint space. We use the well-studied quantity of *Gaussian width* that captures the L_2-geometric complexity of a set $S \subseteq \mathbb{R}^d$.

Definition 3 (Gaussian Width). *Given a closed set $S \subseteq \mathbb{R}^d$, its Gaussian width $w(S)$ is defined as:*

$$w(S) = \mathbb{E}_{\mathbf{g}\in\mathcal{N}(0,1)^d}\,[\sup_{\mathbf{a}\in S}\langle\mathbf{a},\mathbf{g}\rangle].$$

In particular, $w(S)^2$ can be thought as the "effective dimension" of S. Many popular convex sets have low Gaussian width, e.g., the width of both the unit L_1-ball in $\mathbb{R}^d$ (B_1^d) and the standard d-dimensional probability simplex equals $\Theta(\sqrt{\log d})$, and the width of any ball B_p^d for $1 \le p \le \infty$ is $\approx d^{1-1/p}$. For a set $\mathcal{C}$ contained in the B_2^d, $w(\mathcal{C})$ is always $O(\sqrt{d})$. Another prominent set with low Gaussian width is that made up of sparse vectors. For example, the set of all k-sparse vectors (with at most k non-zero entries) in $\mathbb{R}^d$ has Gaussian width $\Theta(\sqrt{k\log(d/k)})$.

Differential Privacy on Streams. We will consider differential privacy on data streams [15]. A stream is a sequence of points from some domain set $\mathcal{Z}$. We say that two streams $\Gamma,\Gamma' \in \mathcal{Z}^*$ of the same length are neighbors if there exists a datapoint $\mathbf{z}\in\Gamma$ and $\mathbf{z}'\in\mathcal{Z}$ such that if we change $\mathbf{z}$ in Γ to $\mathbf{z}'$ we get the stream Γ'. The result of an algorithm processing a stream is a sequence of outputs.

Definition 4 (Event-level differential privacy [14, 15]). *Algorithm* Alg *is (ϵ,δ)-differentially private*[13] *if for all neigh-*

[12]Chan *et al.* [6] presented a scheme that provides a generic way for converting the *Tree Mechanism* that requires prior knowledge of T into a mechanism that does not. They also showed that this new mechanism (referred to as the *Hybrid Mechanism*) achieves asymptotically the same error guarantees as the *Tree Mechanism*. The same ideas work in our case too without affecting the asymptotic excess risk bounds.

[13]In the practice of differential privacy, we generally think of ϵ as a small non-negligible constant, and δ as a parameter that is cryptographically small.

Mechanism 1: PrivIncERM (ϵ, δ)

Input: A stream $\Gamma = \mathbf{z}_1, \ldots, \mathbf{z}_T$, where each $\mathbf{z}_t$ is from the domain $\mathcal{Z} \subseteq \mathbb{R}^d$, and $\tau \in \mathbb{N}$

Output: A differentially private estimate of $\hat{\theta}_t \in \operatorname{argmin}_{\theta \in \mathcal{C}} \sum_{i=1}^{t} \jmath(\theta; \mathbf{z}_i)$ at every timestep $t \in [T]$

1 Set $\epsilon' \leftarrow \frac{\epsilon}{\left(2\sqrt{\frac{2T}{\tau}\ln\left(\frac{2}{\delta}\right)}\right)}$ and $\delta' \leftarrow \frac{\delta\tau}{2T}$

2 $\theta_0^{\text{priv}} \leftarrow \mathbf{0}$

3 **for** *all* $t \in [T]$ **do**

4   **if** *t is a multiple of τ* **then**

5     $\theta_t^{\text{priv}} \leftarrow$ Output of an (ϵ', δ')-differentially private algorithm minimizing $\mathcal{J}(\theta; \mathbf{z}_1, \ldots, \mathbf{z}_t)$

6   **end**

7   **else**

8     $\theta_t^{\text{priv}} \leftarrow \theta_{t-1}^{\text{priv}}$

9   **end**

10   Return θ_t^{priv}

11 **end**

boring streams Γ, Γ' and for all sets of possible output sequences $\mathcal{R} \subseteq \mathbb{R}^{\mathbb{N}}$, we have

$$\Pr[\text{Alg}(\Gamma) \in \mathcal{R}] \leq \exp(\epsilon) \cdot \Pr[\text{Alg}(\Gamma') \in \mathcal{R}] + \delta,$$

where the probability is taken over the randomness of the algorithm. When $\delta = 0$, the algorithm Alg *is ϵ-differentially private.*

3. PRIVATE INCREMENTAL ERM: A GENERIC MECHANISM

We present a generic transformation for converting any private batch ERM algorithm into a private incremental ERM algorithm. We take this construction as a baseline for comparison for our private incremental regression algorithms. Missing proofs from this section are presented in Appendix B.

Mechanism PrivIncERM describes this simple transformation. At every timestep, Mechanism PrivIncERM outputs a θ_t^{priv}, a differentially private approximation of $\hat{\theta}_t \in \operatorname{argmin}_{\theta \in \mathcal{C}} \mathcal{J}(\theta; \mathbf{z}_1, \ldots, \mathbf{z}_t)$.

The idea is to perform "relevant" computations only every τ timesteps, thereby ensuring that no $\mathbf{z}_i$ is used in more than T/τ invocations of the private batch ERM algorithm (for simplicity, assume that T is a multiple of τ). In Theorem 3.1, the parameter τ is set to balance the increase in excess risk due to lack of updates on the estimator and the increase in the excess risk due to the change in the privacy risk parameter ϵ (which arises from multiple interactions with the data).

Mechanism PrivIncERM invokes a differentially private (batch) ERM algorithm for timesteps t which are a multiple of τ, and in all other timesteps it just outputs the result from the previous timestep. In Step 5 of Mechanism PrivIncERM any differentially private batch ERM algorithm can be used, and this step dominates the time complexity of this mechanism. Here we present excess risk bounds obtained by invoking Mechanism PrivIncERM with the differentially private ERM algorithms of Bassily *et al.* [2] and Talwar *et al.* [44]. As mentioned earlier, the bounds of Bassily *et al.* [2] are tight in the worst-case. But as shown by Talwar *et al.* [44], if the constraint space $\mathcal{C}$ has a small Gaussian width, then these bounds could be improved. The bounds of Talwar *et al.* depend on the curvature constant of $\jmath$ defined as:

$$C_\jmath = \sup_{\mathbf{z} \in \mathcal{Z}} \sup_{\theta_a, \theta_b \in \mathcal{C}, l \in (0,1], \theta_c = \theta_a + l(\theta_b - \theta_a)} \frac{2}{l^2}(\jmath(\theta_c; \mathbf{z}) - \jmath(\theta_a; \mathbf{z}) - \langle \theta_c - \theta_a, \nabla \jmath(\theta_a; \mathbf{z}) \rangle).$$

For linear regression where $\jmath(\theta; \mathbf{z}) = \ell(\theta; (\mathbf{x}, y)) = (y - \langle \mathbf{x}, \theta \rangle)^2$, then with $\|\mathbf{x}\| \leq 1$ and $|y| \leq 1$, it follows that $C_\ell \leq \|\mathcal{C}\|^2$ [9].

We now show that Mechanism PrivIncERM is event-level differentially private (Definition 4), and analyze its utility under various invocations in Step 5.

Theorem 3.1. PrivIncERM *is (ϵ, δ)-differentially private with respect to a single datapoint change in the stream Γ. Also,*

1. *(Using Theorem 2.4, Bassily* et al. *[2]). If the function $\jmath(\theta; \mathbf{z}) : \mathcal{C} \times \mathcal{Z} \to \mathbb{R}$ is a positive-valued function that is convex with respect to θ over the domain $\mathcal{C} \subseteq \mathbb{R}^d$. Then for any $\beta > 0$, with probability at least $1 - \beta$, for each $t \in [T]$, θ_t^{priv} generated by Mechanism* PrivIncERM *with $\tau = \lceil \frac{(Td)^{1/3}}{\epsilon^{2/3}} \rceil$ satisfies:*

$$\mathcal{J}(\theta_t^{\text{priv}}; \Gamma_t) - \min_{\theta \in \mathcal{C}} \mathcal{J}(\theta; \Gamma_t) = O(\min\{\frac{(Td)^{1/3} L \|\mathcal{C}\| \log^{5/2}(1/\delta)\, \textit{polylog}(T/\beta)}{\epsilon^{2/3}}, TL\|\mathcal{C}\|\}),$$

where L is the Lipschitz parameter of the function $\jmath$.

2. *(Using Theorem 2.4, Bassily* et al. *[2]). If the function $\jmath(\theta; \mathbf{z}) : \mathcal{C} \times \mathcal{Z} \to \mathbb{R}$ is a positive-valued function which is ν-strongly convex with respect to θ over the domain $\mathcal{C} \subseteq \mathbb{R}^d$. Then for any $\beta > 0$, with probability at least $1 - \beta$, for each $t \in [T]$, θ_t^{priv} generated by Mechanism* PrivIncERM *with $\tau = \lceil \frac{\sqrt{dL}}{(\nu^{1/2} \epsilon \|\mathcal{C}\|^{1/2})} \rceil$ satisfies:*

$$\mathcal{J}(\theta_t^{\text{priv}}; \Gamma_t) - \min_{\theta \in \mathcal{C}} \mathcal{J}(\theta; \Gamma_t) = O(\min\{\frac{\sqrt{d} L^{3/2} \|\mathcal{C}\|^{1/2} \log^4(1/\delta) \textit{polylog}(T/\beta)}{\nu^{1/2}\epsilon}, TL\|\mathcal{C}\|\}),$$

where L is the Lipschitz parameter of the function $\jmath$.

3. *(Using Theorem 2.6 of Talwar* et al. *[44]). If the function $\jmath(\theta; \mathbf{z}) : \mathcal{C} \times \mathcal{Z} \to \mathbb{R}$ is a positive-valued function that is convex with respect to θ over the domain $\mathcal{C} \subseteq \mathbb{R}^d$. Then for any $\beta > 0$, with probability at least $1 - \beta$, for each $t \in [T]$, θ_t^{priv} generated by Mechanism* PrivIncERM *with $\tau = \lceil \frac{\sqrt{Tw(\mathcal{C})} C_\jmath^{1/4}}{((L\|\mathcal{C}\|)^{1/4} \epsilon^{1/2})} \rceil$ satisfies:*

$$\mathcal{J}(\theta_t^{\text{priv}}; \Gamma_t) - \min_{\theta \in \mathcal{C}} \mathcal{J}(\theta; \Gamma_t) = O(\min\{\frac{\sqrt{Tw(\mathcal{C})} C_\jmath^{1/4} (L\|\mathcal{C}\|)^{3/4} \log^{7/3}(1/\delta)\, \textit{polylog}(T/\beta)}{\epsilon^{1/2}}, TL\|\mathcal{C}\|\}),$$

where L is the Lipschitz parameter and $C_\jmath$ is the curvature constant of the function $\jmath$.

4. PRIVATE INCREMENTAL LINEAR REGRESSION USING TREE MECHANISM

We now focus on the problem of private incremental linear regression. Our first approach for this problem is based on a private incremental computation of the gradient. The algorithm is particularly effective in the regime of large T and small d. Missing proofs from this section are presented in Appendix E.

A central idea in our approach is the construction of a *private gradient function* defined as follows.

Definition 5. *Let $\mathcal{C} \subseteq \mathbb{R}^d$. Algorithm* Alg *computes an (α, β)-accurate gradient of the loss function $\mathcal{J}(\theta; \mathbf{z}_1, \ldots, \mathbf{z}_t)$ with respect to $\theta \in \mathcal{C}$, if given $\mathbf{z}_1, \ldots, \mathbf{z}_t \in \mathcal{Z}$ it outputs a function $g_t : \mathcal{C} \to \mathbb{R}^d$ such that:*

(i) Privacy*: Alg is (ϵ, δ)-differentially private (as in Definition 4), i.e., for all neighboring streams $\Gamma, \Gamma' \in \mathcal{Z}^*$ and subsets $\mathcal{R} \subseteq \mathcal{C} \to \mathbb{R}^d$,*

$$\Pr[\mathrm{Alg}(\Gamma) \in \mathcal{R}] \leq \exp(\epsilon) \cdot \Pr[\mathrm{Alg}(\Gamma') \in \mathcal{R}] + \delta.$$

(ii) Utility*: The function g_t is an (α, β)-approximation to the true gradient, in that,*

$$\Pr_{\mathrm{Alg}}\left[\max_{\mathbf{z}_1,\ldots,\mathbf{z}_t \in \mathcal{Z}, \theta \in \mathcal{C}} \|g_t(\theta) - \nabla \mathcal{J}(\theta; \mathbf{z}_1, \ldots, \mathbf{z}_t)\| \geq \alpha\right] \leq \beta.$$

Note that the output of Alg in the above definition is a function g_t. The first requirement on Alg specifies that it satisfies the differential privacy condition (Definition 4). The second requirement on Alg specifies that for any $\theta \in \mathcal{C}$, it gives a "sufficiently" accurate estimate of the true gradient $\nabla \mathcal{J}(\theta; \mathbf{z}_1, \ldots, \mathbf{z}_t)$.

Let $\Gamma = (\mathbf{x}_1, y_1), \ldots, (\mathbf{x}_T, y_T)$ represent the stream of covariate-response pairs, we use Γ_t to denote $(\mathbf{x}_1, y_1), \ldots, (\mathbf{x}_t, y_t)$. Consider the gradient of the loss function $\mathcal{L}(\theta; \Gamma_t)$ where $X_t \in \mathbb{R}^{t \times d}$ is a matrix with rows $\mathbf{x}_1^\top, \ldots, \mathbf{x}_t^\top$ and $\mathbf{y}_t = (y_1, \ldots, y_t)$:

$$\nabla \mathcal{L}(\theta; \Gamma_t) = 2(X_t^\top X_t \theta - X_t^\top \mathbf{y}_t) = 2\left(\sum_{i=1}^{t} \mathbf{x}_i \mathbf{x}_i^\top \theta - \sum_{i=1}^{t} \mathbf{x}_i y_i\right). \quad (2)$$

A simple observation from the gradient form of (2) is that if we can maintain the streaming sum of $\mathbf{x}_1 y_1, \ldots, \mathbf{x}_T y_T$ and the streaming sum of $\mathbf{x}_1 \mathbf{x}_1^\top, \ldots, \mathbf{x}_T \mathbf{x}_T^\top$, then we can maintain the necessary ingredients needed to compute $\nabla \mathcal{L}(\theta; \Gamma_t)$ for any $t \in [T]$. We use this observation to construct a private gradient function $g_t : \mathcal{C} \to \mathbb{R}^d$ at every timestep t. The idea is to privately maintain $\sum_{i=1}^{T} \mathbf{x}_i \mathbf{x}_i^\top$ and $\sum_{i=1}^{T} \mathbf{x}_i y_i$ over the steam using the *Tree Mechanism* of [15, 6]. We present the entire construction of the *Tree Mechanism* in Appendix D. The rough idea behind this mechanism is to build a binary tree where the leaves are the actual inputs from the stream, and the internal nodes store the partial sums of all the leaves in its sub-tree. For a stream of vectors, $v_1, \ldots, v_T$ in the unit ball, the *Tree Mechanism* allows private estimation of $\sum_{i=1}^{t} v_i$, for every $t \in [T]$, with error roughly $\sqrt{d} \log^2 T$ (under (ϵ, δ)-differential privacy, ignoring other parameters).

Somewhat similar to our approach, Smith and Thakurta also use the *Tree Mechanism* to maintain the sum of gradients in their private online learning algorithm [47], however, unlike our approach, they do not construct a private gradient function.

Algorithm 2: PRIVINCREG$_1$ (ϵ, δ)

Input: A stream $\Gamma = (\mathbf{x}_1, y_1), \ldots, (\mathbf{x}_T, y_T)$, where each $(\mathbf{x}_t, y_t)$ in Γ is from the domain $\mathcal{X} \times \mathcal{Y}$ where $\mathcal{X} \subset \mathbb{R}^d$ with $\|\mathcal{X}\| \leq 1$ and $\mathcal{Y} \subset \mathbb{R}$ with $\|\mathcal{Y}\| \leq 1$

Output: A differentially private estimate of $\hat{\theta}_t \in \mathrm{argmin}_{\theta \in \mathcal{C}} \sum_{i=1}^{t} (y_i - \langle \mathbf{x}_i, \theta \rangle)^2$ at every timestep $t \in [T]$

1 Set $\epsilon' \leftarrow \frac{\epsilon}{2}$, $\delta' \leftarrow \frac{\delta}{2}$, $\kappa \leftarrow \frac{\log^{3/2}(T)\sqrt{\log(\frac{1}{\delta'})}}{\epsilon'}$, $\alpha' \leftarrow O(\kappa \|\mathcal{C}\| \sqrt{d})$, and $r \leftarrow \Theta\left(\left(1 + \frac{T\|\mathcal{C}\|}{\alpha'}\right)^2\right)$

2 **for** *all* $t \in [T]$ **do**

3     $\mathbf{q}_t \leftarrow$ output of TREEMECH $(\epsilon', \delta', 2)$ at t when invoked on the stream $\mathbf{x}_1 y_1, \ldots, \mathbf{x}_T y_T$

4     $Q_t \leftarrow$ output of TREEMECH $(\epsilon', \delta', 2)$ at t when invoked on the stream $\mathbf{x}_1 \mathbf{x}_1^\top, \ldots, \mathbf{x}_T \mathbf{x}_T^\top$ which can be viewed as d^2-dimensional vectors (the outputs are converted back to form $d \times d$ matrices)

5   Define a private gradient function, $g_t : \mathcal{C} \to \mathbb{R}^d$ as:

$$g_t(\theta) = 2(Q_t \theta - \mathbf{q}_t)$$

6     $\theta_t^{\mathrm{priv}} \leftarrow$ NOISYPROJGRAD$(\mathcal{C}, g_t, r)$ (described in Appendix C)

7   Return θ_t^{priv}

8 **end**

Once the private gradient function g_t is released, it could be used to obtain an approximation to the estimator $\hat{\theta}$ by using any traditional gradient-based optimization technique. In this paper, we use a variant of the classical *projected gradient descent* approach, described in Algorithm NOISYPROJGRAD (Appendix C). Algorithm NOISYPROJGRAD is an iterative algorithm that takes in the constraint set $\mathcal{C}$, private gradient function g_t, and a parameter r denoting the number of iterations, and returns back (θ_t^{priv}) a private estimate of regression parameter.

An important point to note is that evaluating the gradient function at different θ's, as needed for any gradient descent technique, does not affect the privacy parameters ϵ and δ. We analyze the convergence of Algorithm NOISYPROJGRAD in Appendix C. This convergence result (Corollary C.2) is used to set the parameter r in Algorithm PRIVINCREG$_1$.

Algorithm PRIVINCREG$_1$ is (ϵ, δ)-differentially private with respect to a single datapoint change in the stream Γ. This follows as the L_2-sensitivity of the stream in both the invocations (Steps 3 and 4) of Algorithm TREEMECH is less than 2 (because of the normalization on the $\mathbf{x}_i$'s and y_i's). Using the standard composition properties (Theorem A.3) of differential privacy gives that the Algorithm PRIVINCREG$_1$ is (ϵ, δ)-differentially private. The algorithm only requires $O(d^2 \log T)$ space (see Appendix D), therefore having only a logarithmic dependence on the length of the stream. The running time of the algorithm is dominated by Steps 4 and 6; at every timestep t, Step 4 has time complexity of $O(d^2 \log T)$, whereas the time complexity of Step 6 is r times the time complexity of projecting a datapoint onto $\mathcal{C}$ (the $P_\mathcal{C}$ operation defined in Appendix C). We now analyze the utility of this algorithm, using the error bound on *Tree Mechanism* from Proposition D.1.

Lemma 4.1. *For any $\beta > 0$, $\theta \in \mathcal{C}$, and $t \in [T]$, with probability at least $1-\beta$, the function g_t defined in Algorithm* PRIVINCREG$_1$ *satisfies:*

$$\|g_t(\theta) - \nabla\mathcal{L}(\theta;\Gamma_t)\| = O\left(\kappa\|\mathcal{C}\|(\sqrt{d}+\sqrt{\log(1/\beta)})\right).$$

Theorem 4.2. *Algorithm* PRIVINCREG$_1$ *is (ϵ,δ)-differentially private with respect to a single datapoint change in the stream Γ. For any $\beta > 0$, with probability at least $1-\beta$, for each $t \in [T]$, θ_t^{priv} generated by Algorithm* PRIVINCREG$_1$ *satisfies:*

$$\mathcal{L}(\theta_t^{\text{priv}};\Gamma_t) - \min_{\theta\in\mathcal{C}} \mathcal{L}(\theta;\Gamma_t) = O\left(\frac{\log^{3/2} T\sqrt{\log(1/\delta)}\|\mathcal{C}\|^2(\sqrt{d}+\sqrt{\log(T/\beta)})}{\epsilon}\right).$$

Remark 4.3. *For linear regression instances, which typically do not satisfy the strong convexity property, the $\approx \min\{(Td)^{1/3}, T\}$ risk bound obtained from Mechanism* PRIVINCERM *is substantially worse than the $\approx \min\{\sqrt{d}, T\}$ risk bound provided by Algorithm* PRIVINCREG$_1$.

The dependence on dimension d is tight in the worst-case; due to $\approx \sqrt{d}$ excess risk lower bounds established by Bassily et al. *[2].*

Remark 4.4. *The techniques developed in this section (based on Tree Mechanism) can be applied to any convex ERM problem whose gradient has a* linear *form, in which case we obtain an excess risk bound as in Theorem 4.2. It is an interesting open question to obtain similar bounds for general convex ERM problems in an incremental setting.*

5. PRIVATE INCREMENTAL LINEAR REGRESSION: BEYOND WORST-CASE

The noise added in Theorem 4.2 for privacy grows proportionately as $\sqrt{d}$. While this seems unavoidable in the worst-case, we ask whether it is possible to go beyond this worst-case bound under some realistic assumptions. An intuitive idea to overcome this curse of dimensionality is to project (compress) the data to a lower dimension, before the addition of noise. In this section, we use this and other geometric ideas to cope with the high-dependency on dimensionality in Theorem 4.2. The resulting bound will depend on the Gaussian width of the input and constraint space which for many interesting problem instances will be smaller than $\sqrt{d}$. We mention some specific instantiations and extensions of our result in Section 5.2 including a scenario when not all inputs are drawn from a domain with a "small" Gaussian width. Missing proofs from this section are presented in Appendix F.

Our general approach in this section will be based on this simple principle: reduce the dimensionality of the problem, solve it privately in the lower dimensional space, and then "lift" the solution back to the original space. Our lifting procedure is similar to that used by Kasiviswanathan and Jin [28] in their recent work on bounding excess risk for private ERM in a batch setting.

Fix t and consider solving the following projected least-squares problem, defined as:[14]

$$\mathcal{L}_{\text{proj}}(\theta;\Gamma_t;\Phi) = \sum_{i=1}^{t}\left(y_i - \frac{\|\mathbf{x}_i\|}{\|\Phi\mathbf{x}_i\|}\langle\Phi\mathbf{x}_i,\Phi\theta\rangle\right)^2, \quad (3)$$

where $\Phi \in \mathbb{R}^{m\times d}$ is a random projection matrix (to be defined later). The loss function, $\mathcal{L}_{\text{proj}}$ is also referred to as *compressed least-squares* in the literature [35, 19, 27].

As a first step, we investigate the relationship between $\mathcal{L}(\theta;\Gamma_t)$ and $\mathcal{L}_{\text{proj}}(\theta;\Gamma_t;\Phi)$. A fundamental tool in dimensionality reduction, the Johnson-Lindenstrauss (JL) lemma, states that for any set $S \subseteq \mathbb{R}^d$, given $\gamma > 0$ and $m = \Omega(\log|S|/\gamma^2)$, there exists a map that embeds the set into $\mathbb{R}^m$, distorting all pairwise distances within at most $1\pm\gamma$ factor. A simple consequence of the JL Lemma is that, for any set of n vectors $\mathbf{x}_1,\dots,\mathbf{x}_n \in \mathbb{R}^d$, $\theta \in \mathbb{R}^d$, $\gamma > 0$, and $\beta > 0$, if Φ is an $m\times d$ matrix with entries drawn i.i.d. from $\mathcal{N}(0,1/m)$ with $m = \Theta(\log(n/\beta)/\gamma^2)$, we get,

$$\Pr\left[|\langle\Phi\mathbf{x}_i,\Phi\theta\rangle - \langle\mathbf{x}_i,\theta\rangle| \geq \gamma\|\mathbf{x}_i\|\|\theta\| \text{ for all } i \in [n]\right] \leq \beta. \quad (4)$$

Using standard inequalities such as (4), establishing the relationship between $\mathcal{L}$ and $\mathcal{L}_{\text{proj}}$ is relatively straightforward in a batch setting. However, the incremental setting raises the challenge of dealing with adaptive inputs in JL transformation. The issue being that JL transformation is inherently non-adaptive, in that "success" of the JL transformation (properties such as (4)) depends on the fact that the inputs on which it gets applied are chosen before (independent of) fixing the transformation Φ.

To deal with this kind of adaptive generation of inputs, we use a generalization of JL lemma which yields similar guarantees but with a much smaller (than $\log|S|$) requirement on m, if the set S has certain geometric characteristics. For ease of exposition, in the rest of this section, we are going to assume that Φ is a matrix in $\mathbb{R}^{m\times d}$ with i.i.d. entries from $\mathcal{N}(0,1/m)$.[15] Gordon [20] showed that using a Gaussian random matrix, one can embed the set S into a lower-dimensional space $\mathbb{R}^m$, where m roughly scales as the square of Gaussian width of S. This result has found several interesting applications in high-dimensional convex geometry, statistics, and compressed sensing [38].

Theorem 5.1 (Gordon [20]). *Let $\tilde{\Phi}$ be an $m\times d$ random matrix, whose rows $\phi_1^\top,\dots,\phi_m^\top$ are i.i.d. Gaussian random vectors in $\mathbb{R}^d$ chosen according to the standard normal distribution $\mathcal{N}(\mathbf{0},\mathbb{I}_d)$. Let $\Phi = \tilde{\Phi}/\sqrt{m}$. Let S be a set of points in $\mathbb{R}^d$. There is a constant $C > 0$ such that for any $0 < \gamma, \beta < 1$,*

$$\Pr\left[\sup_{\mathbf{a}\in S}\left|\|\Phi\mathbf{a}\|^2 - \|\mathbf{a}\|^2\right| \geq \gamma\|\mathbf{a}\|^2\right] \leq \beta,$$

provided that $m \geq \frac{C}{\gamma^2}\max\left\{w(S)^2, \log\left(\frac{1}{\beta}\right)\right\}$.

[14] The scaling factor of $\frac{\|\mathbf{x}_i\|}{\|\Phi\mathbf{x}_i\|}$ is for simplicity of analysis only. One could omit it and still obtain the same results using a slightly different analysis. Also without loss of generality, we assume $\mathbf{x}_i \neq 0$ for all i.

[15] One could also use other (better) constructions of Φ, such as those that create sparse Φ matrix, using recent results by Bourgain *et al.* [5] extending Theorem 5.1 to other distributions.

Note that the $w(S)$ is defined for all sets, not just convex sets, a fact that we use below as the input domain $\mathcal{X}$ may not be convex. As a simple corollary to the above theorem it also follows that,

Corollary 5.2. *Under the setting of Theorem 5.1, there exists a constant $C' > 0$ such that for any $0 < \gamma, \beta < 1$,*

$$\Pr\left[\sup_{\mathbf{a},\mathbf{b}\in S} |\langle \Phi\mathbf{a}, \Phi\mathbf{b}\rangle - \langle \mathbf{a}, \mathbf{b}\rangle| \geq \gamma\|\mathbf{a}\|\|\mathbf{b}\|\right] \leq \beta,$$

provided that $m \geq \frac{C'}{\gamma^2}\max\left\{w(S)^2, \log\left(\frac{1}{\beta}\right)\right\}$.

Applying the above corollary to the set of vectors in $\mathcal{X} \cup \mathcal{C}$, and by noting that $w(\mathcal{X} \cup \mathcal{C}) \leq w(\mathcal{X}) + w(\mathcal{C})$, gives that if $m = \Theta((1/\gamma^2)\max\{(w(\mathcal{X}) + w(\mathcal{C}))^2, \log(1/\beta)\})$, then with probability at least $1 - \beta$,

$$\Pr\left[\sup_{\mathbf{x}\in\mathcal{X},\theta\in\mathcal{C}} |\langle \Phi\mathbf{x}, \Phi\theta\rangle - \langle \mathbf{x}, \theta\rangle| \geq \gamma\|\mathbf{x}\|\|\theta\|\right] \leq \beta. \quad (5)$$

5.1 Algorithm for the Streaming Setting

We now present a mechanism (Algorithm PrivIncReg$_2$) for private incremental linear regression based on minimizing the projected least-squares objective (3), under differential privacy. The idea is to again construct a private gradient function g_t, but of function $\mathcal{L}_{\text{proj}}$ (instead of $\mathcal{L}$ as done in Algorithm PrivIncReg$_1$).

Let X_t be a matrix with rows $\mathbf{x}_1^\top, \dots, \mathbf{x}_t^\top$, and $\tilde{X}_t \in \mathbb{R}^{n\times d}$ be a matrix with rows $\tilde{\mathbf{x}}_1^\top, \dots, \tilde{\mathbf{x}}_t^\top$. As before, let $\mathbf{y}_t$ be the vector $(y_1, \dots, y_t)$. Under these notation, $\mathcal{L}_{\text{proj}}(\theta; \Gamma_t; \Phi)$ from (3) can be re-expressed as:

$$\mathcal{L}_{\text{proj}}(\theta; \Gamma_t; \Phi) = \|\mathbf{y}_t - \tilde{X}_t\Phi^\top\Phi\theta\|^2.$$

The gradient of $\mathcal{L}_{\text{proj}}$ with respect to $\Phi\theta$ equals:

$$\nabla_{(\Phi\theta)}\mathcal{L}_{\text{proj}}(\theta; \Gamma_t; \Phi) = \frac{\partial\, \|\mathbf{y}_t - (\tilde{X}_t\Phi^\top)(\Phi\theta)\|^2}{\partial\, (\Phi\theta)}$$
$$= 2((\tilde{X}_t\Phi^\top)^\top(\tilde{X}_t\Phi^\top))(\Phi\theta) - 2(\tilde{X}_t\Phi^\top)^\top\mathbf{y}_t.$$

Note that $\nabla_{(\Phi\theta)}\mathcal{L}_{\text{proj}} \in \mathbb{R}^m$.

Let $\Phi\mathcal{C} = \{\vartheta \in \Phi\theta : \theta \in \mathcal{C}\}$. Note for a convex $\mathcal{C}$, $\Phi\mathcal{C} \subset \mathbb{R}^m$ is also convex. In Algorithm PrivIncReg$_2$, $\vartheta_t^{\text{priv}}$ is a private estimate of $\hat{\vartheta}_t$, where

$$\hat{\vartheta}_t \in \text{argmin}_{\vartheta\in\Phi\mathcal{C}} \sum_{i=1}^{t}\left(y_i - \frac{\|\mathbf{x}_i\|}{\|\Phi\mathbf{x}_i\|}\langle \Phi\mathbf{x}_i, \vartheta\rangle\right)^2.$$

Algorithm PrivIncReg$_2$ only requires $O(m^2\log T + \log d)$ space, therefore is slightly more memory efficient than Algorithm PrivIncReg$_1$ (as $m \leq d$). The time complexity can be analyzed as for Algorithm PrivIncReg$_1$.

Algorithm PrivIncReg$_2$ is (ϵ, δ)-differentially private with respect to a single datapoint change in the stream Γ. The L_2-sensitivity for both invocations of Algorithm TreeMech is 2. In Step 6, this holds because

$$\max_{\mathbf{x}_a,\mathbf{x}_b\in\mathcal{X}} \|(\Phi\tilde{\mathbf{x}}_a)(\Phi\tilde{\mathbf{x}}_a)^\top - (\Phi\tilde{\mathbf{x}}_b)(\Phi\tilde{\mathbf{x}}_b)^\top\|_F$$
$$\leq \|(\Phi\tilde{\mathbf{x}}_a)(\Phi\tilde{\mathbf{x}}_a)^\top\|_F + \|(\Phi\tilde{\mathbf{x}}_b)(\Phi\tilde{\mathbf{x}}_b)^\top\|_F$$
$$= \|\Phi\tilde{\mathbf{x}}_a\|^2 + \|\Phi\tilde{\mathbf{x}}_b\|^2 = \|\mathbf{x}_a\|^2 + \|\mathbf{x}_b\|^2 = 2,$$

the second to last equality follows as, for every $\mathbf{x} \in \mathcal{X}$, $\|\Phi\tilde{\mathbf{x}}\| = \|\mathbf{x}\|$ (by construction). Since $\Phi\mathbf{x}_i$'s are in the projected subspace ($\mathbb{R}^m$), the noise needed for differential privacy (in Steps 5 and 6) of Algorithm PrivIncReg$_2$ roughly scales as $\sqrt{m}$.

Algorithm 3: PrivIncReg$_2$ (ϵ, δ)

Input: A stream $\Gamma = (\mathbf{x}_1, y_1), \dots, (\mathbf{x}_T, y_T)$, where each $(\mathbf{x}_t, y_t)$ in Γ is from the domain $\mathcal{X} \times \mathcal{Y}$ where $\mathcal{X} \subset \mathbb{R}^d$ with $\|\mathcal{X}\| \leq 1$ and $\mathcal{Y} \subset \mathbb{R}$ with $\|\mathcal{Y}\| \leq 1$

Output: θ_t^{priv} a differentially private estimate of $\hat{\theta}_t \in \text{argmin}_{\theta\in\mathcal{C}} \sum_{i=1}^{t}(y_i - \langle \mathbf{x}_i, \theta\rangle)^2$ at every timestep $t \in [T]$

1 Set $\epsilon' \leftarrow \frac{\epsilon}{2}$, $\delta' \leftarrow \frac{\delta}{2}$, $\kappa \leftarrow \frac{\log^{3/2}(T)\sqrt{\log(\frac{1}{\delta'})}}{\epsilon'}$,
$\alpha' \leftarrow O(\kappa\|\mathcal{C}\|\sqrt{m})$, $r \leftarrow \Theta\left(\left(1 + \frac{T\|\mathcal{C}\|}{\alpha'}\right)^2\right)$,
$\gamma \leftarrow \frac{(w(\mathcal{X})+w(\mathcal{C}))^{1/3}}{T^{1/3}}$, and
$m \leftarrow \Theta\left(\frac{1}{\gamma^2}\max\{(w(\mathcal{X}) + w(\mathcal{C}))^2, \log(\frac{T}{\beta})\}\right)$

2 Let $\Phi \leftarrow m \times d$ random matrix with entries drawn i.i.d. from $\mathcal{N}(0, 1/m)$

3 **for** *all* $t \in [T]$ **do**

4 Let $\tilde{\mathbf{x}}_t \leftarrow \frac{\|\mathbf{x}_t\|}{\|\Phi\mathbf{x}_t\|}\mathbf{x}_t$

5 $\mathbf{q}_t \leftarrow$ output of TreeMech $(\epsilon', \delta', 2)$ at t when invoked on the stream $\Phi\tilde{\mathbf{x}}_1 y_1, \dots, \Phi\tilde{\mathbf{x}}_T y_T$

6 $Q_t \leftarrow$ output of TreeMech $(\epsilon', \delta', 2)$ at t when invoked on the stream $(\Phi\tilde{\mathbf{x}}_1)(\Phi\tilde{\mathbf{x}}_1)^\top, \dots, (\Phi\tilde{\mathbf{x}}_T)(\Phi\tilde{\mathbf{x}}_T)^\top$ which can be viewed as m^2-dimensional vectors (the outputs are converted back to form $m \times m$ matrices)

7 Define a private gradient function, $g_t : \Phi\mathcal{C} \to \mathbb{R}^m$ as:

$$g_t(\vartheta) = 2(Q_t\vartheta - \mathbf{q}_t)$$

8 $\vartheta_t^{\text{priv}} \leftarrow$ NoisyProjGrad$(\Phi\mathcal{C}, g_t, r)$ (described in Appendix C)

9 $\theta_t^{\text{priv}} \leftarrow \text{argmin}_{\theta\in\mathbb{R}^d} \|\theta\|_{\mathcal{C}}$ subject to $\Phi\theta = \vartheta_t^{\text{priv}}$ (can be solved using any convex optimization technique)

10 Return θ_t^{priv}

11 **end**

In Step 9 of Algorithm PrivIncReg$_2$, we lift $\vartheta_t^{\text{priv}}$ into the original d-dimensional constraint space $\mathcal{C}$. Since $\vartheta_t^{\text{priv}} \in \Phi\mathcal{C}$, we know that there exists a $\theta_t^{\text{true}} \in \mathcal{C}$, such that $\Phi\theta_t^{\text{true}} = \vartheta_t^{\text{priv}}$. Then the goal is to estimate θ_t^{true} from $\Phi\theta_t^{\text{true}}$. Again geometry of $\mathcal{C}$ (Gaussian width) plays an important role, as it controls the diameter of high-dimensional random sections of $\mathcal{C}$ (referred to as $M^\star$ bound [34, 52]). We refer the reader to the excellent tutorial by Vershynin [52] for more details.

We define Minkowski functional, as commonly used in geometric functional analysis and convex analysis.

Definition 6 (Minkowski functional)**.** *For any vector $\theta \in \mathbb{R}^d$, the Minkowski functional of $\mathcal{C}$ is the non-negative number $\|\theta\|_{\mathcal{C}}$ defined by the rule: $\|\theta\|_{\mathcal{C}} = \inf\{\rho \in \mathbb{R} : \theta \in \rho\mathcal{C}\}$.*

For the typical situation in ERM problems, where $\mathcal{C}$ is a symmetric convex body, $\|\cdot\|_{\mathcal{C}}$ defines a norm. The optimization problem solved in Step 9 of Algorithm PrivIncReg$_2$ is convex if $\mathcal{C}$ is convex, and hence can be efficiently solved. The existence of θ_t^{priv} follows from the following theorem.

Theorem 5.3. *[52] Let Φ be an $m \times d$ matrix, whose rows $\phi_1^\top, \dots, \phi_m^\top$ are i.i.d. Gaussian random vectors in $\mathbb{R}^d$ chosen* *according to the standard normal distribution $\mathcal{N}(0, \mathbb{I}_d)$. Let $\mathcal{C}$ be a convex set. Given $\mathbf{v} = \Phi\mathbf{u}$ and Φ, let $\hat{\mathbf{u}}$ be the solution to the following convex program: $\min_{\mathbf{u}' \in \mathbb{R}^d} \|\mathbf{u}'\|_{\mathcal{C}}$ subject to $\Phi\mathbf{u}' = \mathbf{v}$. Then for any $\beta > 0$, with probability at least $1-\beta$,*

$$\sup_{\mathbf{u}:\mathbf{v}=\Phi\mathbf{u}} \|\mathbf{u} - \hat{\mathbf{u}}\| = O\left(\frac{w(\mathcal{C})}{\sqrt{m}} + \frac{\|\mathcal{C}\|\sqrt{\log(1/\beta)}}{\sqrt{m}}\right).$$

The next thing to be verified is that θ_t^{priv} generated by Algorithm PrivIncReg$_2$ is in $\mathcal{C}$. This is simple as by definition of Minkowski functional, as any closed set $\mathcal{C} = \{\theta \in \mathbb{R}^d : \|\theta\|_{\mathcal{C}} \leq 1\}$. Hence, $\|\theta_t^{\text{true}}\|_{\mathcal{C}} \leq 1$. By choice of θ_t^{priv} in Step 9, ensures that $\|\theta_t^{\text{priv}}\|_{\mathcal{C}} \leq \|\theta_t^{\text{true}}\|_{\mathcal{C}} \leq 1$, which guarantees that $\theta_t^{\text{priv}} \in \mathcal{C}$. Finally, note that the lifting is a post-processing operation on a differentially private output $\vartheta_t^{\text{priv}}$, and hence does not affect the differential privacy guarantee.

Utility Analysis of Algorithm PrivIncReg$_2$. In Lemma 5.4, by using the fact that the Gaussian noise for privacy (in the *Tree Mechanism*) is added on a lower dimensional (m) instance, we show that the difference between $\mathcal{L}_{\text{proj}}(\theta_t^{\text{priv}}; \Gamma_t; \Phi)$ and $\mathcal{L}_{\text{proj}}(\hat{\theta}_t; \Gamma_t; \Phi)$ (the minimum empirical risk) roughly scales as $\sqrt{m}$, for sufficiently large m. The Lipschitz constant of the function $\mathcal{L}_{\text{proj}}(\theta; \Gamma_t; \Phi)$ is $O(\|\Phi\mathcal{C}\|)$, which by Theorem 5.1, with probability at least $1-\beta$ is $O(\|\mathcal{C}\|)$, when

$$m = \Theta((1/\gamma^2)\max\{(w(\mathcal{X}) + w(\mathcal{C}))^2, \log(T/\beta)\}).$$

Let $\mathcal{E}_0$ be the event that the above Lipschitz bound holds.

Lemma 5.4. *For any $\beta > 0$, with probability at least $1-\beta$, for each $t \in [T]$, θ_t^{priv} generated by Algorithm PrivIncReg$_2$ satisfies:*

$$\mathcal{L}_{\text{proj}}(\theta_t^{\text{priv}}; \Gamma_t; \Phi) - \mathcal{L}_{\text{proj}}(\hat{\theta}_t; \Gamma_t; \Phi) = O\left(\frac{\sqrt{m}\log^{3/2} T\sqrt{\log(1/\delta)}\|\mathcal{C}\|^2}{\epsilon}\right)$$

where $\hat{\theta}_t \in \operatorname{argmin}_{\theta \in \mathcal{C}} \sum_{i=1}^t (y_i - \langle \mathbf{x}_i, \theta\rangle)^2$.

Using properties of random projections, we now bound $\mathcal{L}_{\text{proj}}(\hat{\theta}_t; \Gamma_t; \Phi)$ in terms of $\mathcal{L}(\hat{\theta}_t; \Gamma_t)$.

Lemma 5.5. *Let Φ be a random matrix as defined in Theorem 5.1 with $m = \Theta((1/\gamma^2)\max\{(w(\mathcal{X})+w(\mathcal{C}))^2, \log(T/\beta)\})$, and let $\beta > 0$. Then with probability at least $1-\beta$, for each $t \in [T]$,*

$$\mathcal{L}_{\text{proj}}(\hat{\theta}_t; \Gamma_t; \Phi) \leq \mathcal{L}(\hat{\theta}_t; \Gamma_t) + 4\gamma^2\|\mathcal{C}\|^2 t + 2\gamma\|\mathcal{C}\|\sqrt{t\mathcal{L}(\hat{\theta}_t; \Gamma_t)} + 2\sqrt{2}\gamma^{3/2}\|\mathcal{C}\|^{3/2} t^{3/4}\mathcal{L}(\hat{\theta}_t; \Gamma_t)^{1/4}.$$

The next step is to lower bound $\mathcal{L}_{\text{proj}}(\theta_t^{\text{priv}}; \Gamma_t; \Phi)$ in terms of $\mathcal{L}(\theta_t^{\text{priv}}; \Gamma_t)$.

Lemma 5.6. *For any $\beta > 0$, with probability at least $1-\beta$, for each $t \in [T]$, θ_t^{priv} generated by Algorithm PrivIncReg$_2$ satisfies:*

$$\mathcal{L}(\theta_t^{\text{priv}}; \Gamma_t) \leq \mathcal{L}_{\text{proj}}(\theta_t^{\text{priv}}; \Gamma_t; \Phi) + 2\gamma\|\mathcal{C}\|\sqrt{T\mathcal{L}(\theta_t^{\text{priv}}; \Gamma_t)} + 2\sqrt{2}\gamma^{3/2}\|\mathcal{C}\|^{3/2} T^{3/4}\mathcal{L}(\theta_t^{\text{priv}}; \Gamma_t)^{1/4} + 4\gamma^2\|\mathcal{C}\|^2 T.$$

Putting together Lemmas 5.4, 5.5, and 5.6 and simple arithmetic manipulation gives: that with probability at least $1-\beta$, for each $t \in [T]$,

$$\mathcal{L}(\theta_t^{\text{priv}}; \Gamma_t) - \mathcal{L}(\hat{\theta}_t; \Gamma_t) = O\left(\frac{\sqrt{m}\log^{3/2} T\sqrt{\log(1/\delta)}\|\mathcal{C}\|^2}{\epsilon}\right) + 8\gamma^2\|\mathcal{C}\|^2 T + 2\gamma\|\mathcal{C}\|\sqrt{T\mathcal{L}(\hat{\theta}_t; \Gamma_t)} + 2\gamma\|\mathcal{C}\|\sqrt{T\mathcal{L}(\theta_t^{\text{priv}}; \Gamma_t)} + 2\sqrt{2}\gamma^{3/2}\|\mathcal{C}\|^{3/2} T^{3/4}\mathcal{L}(\theta_t^{\text{priv}}; \Gamma_t)^{1/4} + 2\sqrt{2}\gamma^{3/2}\|\mathcal{C}\|^{3/2} T^{3/4}\mathcal{L}(\hat{\theta}_t; \Gamma_t)^{1/4}. \quad (6)$$

To simplify (6) in terms of its dependence on $\mathcal{L}(\theta_t^{\text{priv}}; \Gamma_t)$, start by noting that it is of the form $p - a\sqrt{p} - a^{3/2}\sqrt[4]{p} - b - 2a^2 \geq 0$, where

$$p = \mathcal{L}(\theta_t^{\text{priv}}; \Gamma_t),$$
$$a = 2\gamma\|\mathcal{C}\|\sqrt{T}, \text{ and}$$
$$b = \mathcal{L}(\hat{\theta}_t; \Gamma_t) + O\left(\frac{\sqrt{m}\log^{3/2} T\sqrt{\log(1/\delta)}\|\mathcal{C}\|^2}{\epsilon}\right) + 2\gamma\|\mathcal{C}\|\sqrt{T\mathcal{L}(\hat{\theta}_t; \Gamma_t)} + 2\sqrt{2}\gamma^{\frac{3}{2}}\|\mathcal{C}\|^{\frac{3}{2}} T^{\frac{3}{4}}\mathcal{L}(\hat{\theta}_t; \Gamma_t)^{\frac{1}{4}}.$$

Solving for p from $p - a\sqrt{p} - a^{3/2}p^{1/4} - b - 2a^2 = 0$ (we use WolframAlpha solver [54]), and using that to simplify (6) yields, that with probability at least $1-\beta$, for each $t \in [T]$,

$$\mathcal{L}(\theta_t^{\text{priv}}; \Gamma_t) - \mathcal{L}(\hat{\theta}_t; \Gamma_t) = O(\frac{\sqrt{m}\log^{3/2} T\sqrt{\log(1/\delta)}\|\mathcal{C}\|^2}{\epsilon} + \gamma^2\|\mathcal{C}\|^2 T + \gamma\|\mathcal{C}\|\sqrt{T\mathcal{L}(\hat{\theta}_t; \Gamma_t)} + \gamma^{3/2}\|\mathcal{C}\|^{3/2} T^{3/4}\mathcal{L}(\hat{\theta}_t; \Gamma_t)^{1/4}). \quad (7)$$

Theorem 5.7. *Algorithm PrivIncReg$_2$ is (ϵ, δ)-differentially private with respect to a single datapoint change in the stream Γ. For any $\beta > 0$, with probability at least $1-\beta$, for each $t \in [T]$, θ_t^{priv} generated by Algorithm PrivIncReg$_2$ satisfies:*

$$\mathcal{L}(\theta_t^{\text{priv}}; \Gamma_t) - \mathcal{L}(\hat{\theta}_t; \Gamma_t) = O(\frac{T^{\frac{1}{3}} W^{\frac{2}{3}} \log^2 T\|\mathcal{C}\|^2\sqrt{\log(1/\delta)\log(1/\beta)}}{\epsilon} + T^{\frac{1}{6}} W^{\frac{1}{3}}\|\mathcal{C}\|\sqrt{\mathcal{L}(\hat{\theta}_t; \Gamma_t)} + T^{\frac{1}{4}} W^{\frac{1}{2}}\|\mathcal{C}\|^{\frac{3}{2}}\sqrt[4]{\mathcal{L}(\hat{\theta}_t; \Gamma_t)}),$$

where $\hat{\theta}_t \in \min_{\theta \in \mathcal{C}} \mathcal{L}(\theta; \Gamma_t)$ and $W = w(\mathcal{X}) + w(\mathcal{C})$.

Remark 5.8. *Since $\mathcal{L}$ is an non-decreasing function in t, in the above theorem $\mathcal{L}(\hat{\theta}_t; \Gamma_t)$ in the right-hand side could be replaced by $\mathcal{L}(\hat{\theta}_T; \Gamma_T)$ (defined as OPT in the introduction).*

5.2 Discussion about Theorem 5.7

We start this discussion by mentioning a few instantiations of Theorem 5.7. Let $\text{OPT} = \mathcal{L}(\hat{\theta}_T; \Gamma_T)$ (remember, that $\text{OPT} \leq T$). For simplicity, below we ignore dependence on the privacy and confidence parameters.

For arbitrary $\mathcal{X}$ and $\mathcal{C}$, with just an L_2-diameter assumption as in Theorem 4.2, $W = w(\mathcal{X}) + w(\mathcal{C}) = O(\sqrt{d})$, and therefore the excess risk bound provided by Theorem 5.7 (accounting for the trivial excess risk bound of T) equals $\tilde{O}(\min\{T^{1/3}d^{1/3} + T^{1/6}d^{1/6}\sqrt{\text{OPT}} + T^{1/4}d^{1/4}\sqrt[4]{\text{OPT}}, T\})$, which is worse than the $\tilde{O}(\min\{\sqrt{d}, T\})$ excess risk bound provided by Theorem 4.2. However, as we discuss below, for many interesting high-dimensional problems, one could get substantially better bounds using Theorem 5.7. This happens when W is "small".

In many practical regression instances, the input data is high-dimensional and sparse [37, 21] which leads to a small $w(\mathcal{X})$. For example, if the $\mathbf{x}_i$'s are k-sparse, then $w(\mathcal{X}) = O(\sqrt{k\log(d/k)})$. Another common scenario is to have the $\mathbf{x}_i$'s come from a bounded L_1-diameter ball, in which case $w(\mathcal{X}) = O(\sqrt{\log d})$. Now under any of these assumptions, let us look at different choices of constraint spaces ($\mathcal{C}$) that have a small Gaussian width.

- If $\mathcal{C} = \text{conv}\{\mathbf{a}_1, \dots, \mathbf{a}_l\}$ be convex hull of vectors $\mathbf{a}_i \in \mathbb{R}^d$, such that for all $i \in [d], \|\mathbf{a}_i\| \leq c$ with $c \in \mathbb{R}^+$, then $w(\mathcal{C}) = O(c\sqrt{\log l})$. A popular subcase of the above is the *cross-polytope* B_1^d (unit L_1-ball). For example, the popular Lasso formulation [48] used for high-dimensional linear regression is:

$$\hat{\theta}_t \in \text{argmin}_{\theta \in cB_1^d} \sum_{i=1}^{t} (y_i - \langle \mathbf{x}_i, \theta \rangle)^2.$$

  Another popular subcase is the probability simplex where, $\mathcal{C} = \{\theta \in \mathbb{R}^d : \sum_i \theta_i = 1, \forall i \in [d], \theta_i \geq 0\}$.
- Group/Block L_1-norm is another prominent sparsity inducing norm used in many applications [1]. For a vector $\theta \in \mathbb{R}^d$, and a parameter k, this norm is defined as:[16]

$$\|\theta\|_{k,L_{1,2}} = \sum_{i=1}^{\lceil d/k \rceil} \sqrt{\sum_{j=(i-1)k+1}^{\min\{ik,d\}} |\theta_j|^2}.$$

  If $\mathcal{C}$ denotes the convex set centered with radius one with respect to $\|\cdot\|_{k,L_{1,2}}$-norm then the Gaussian width of $\mathcal{C}$ is $O(\sqrt{k\log(d/k)})$ [45].
- L_p-balls ($1 < p < 2$) are another popular choice of constraint space. The regression problem in this case is defined as:

$$\hat{\theta}_t \in \text{argmin}_{\theta \in cB_p^d} \sum_{i=1}^{t} (y_i - \langle \mathbf{x}_i, \theta \rangle)^2,$$

  and $w(cB_p^d) = O(cd^{1-1/p})$.

As the reader may notice, in all of the above problem settings, W is much smaller than $\sqrt{d}$. As a comparison to the bound in Theorem 4.2, if $W = O(\text{polylog}(d))$, then Theorem 5.7 yields an excess risk bound of $\tilde{O}(T^{1/3} + T^{1/6}\sqrt{\text{OPT}} + T^{1/4}\sqrt[4]{\text{OPT}})$. This is significantly better than the $\tilde{O}(\sqrt{d})$ risk bound from Theorem 4.2 for many setting of T, d, and OPT, e.g., if $d \gg T^{4/3}$.

One could also compare the result from Theorem 5.7 to the bound obtained by applying the differentially private ERM algorithm of Talwar *et al.* [44] in the generic mechanism (Theorem 3.1, Part 3). It is hard to do a precise comparison because of the dependence on different parameters in these bounds. In general, when OPT is not very big (say $\ll T^{2/3}$) and $W = O(\text{polylog}(d))$ then the excess risk bound from Theorem 5.7 is significantly better than $\tilde{O}(\sqrt{T})$ risk bound obtained in Theorem 3.1, Part 3.

Extension to a case where not all inputs are drawn from a domain with small Gaussian Width. The previous analysis assumes that $w(\mathcal{X})$ is small (all inputs are drawn from a domain with small Gaussian Width). We now show that the techniques and results in the previous section extend to a more robust setting, where not all inputs are assumed to come from a domain with small Gaussian width.

In particular, we assume that there exists a set $\mathcal{G} \subseteq \mathcal{X}$, such that $w(\mathcal{G})$ is small, and only some inputs in the stream come from $\mathcal{G}$ (e.g., only a fraction of the covariates could be sparse). We also assume that the algorithm has access to an oracle which given a point $\mathbf{x} \in \mathcal{X}$, returns whether $\mathbf{x} \in \mathcal{G}$ or not. The goal of the algorithm is to perform private incremental linear regression on inputs from $\mathcal{G}$. In a non-private world, this is trivial as the algorithm can simply ignore when $\mathbf{x}_t$ is not in $\mathcal{G}$, but this operation is not private. However, a simple change to Algorithm PRIVINCREG2 can handle this scenario without a breach in the privacy. The idea is to check whether $\mathbf{x}_t \in \mathcal{G}$, if so $(\mathbf{x}_t, y_t)$ is used as currently in Algorithm PRIVINCREG2. Otherwise, $(\mathbf{x}_t, y_t)$ is replaced by $(\mathbf{0}, 0)$ before invoking Algorithm TREEMECH (in Steps 5 and 6 of Algorithm PRIVINCREG2). With this change, the resulting algorithm is (ϵ, δ)-differentially private, and with probability at least $1-\beta$, for each $t \in [T]$, its output θ_t^{priv} will satisfy:

$$\sum_{\mathbf{x}_i \in \mathcal{G}, i \in [t]} (y_i - \langle \mathbf{x}_i, \theta_t^{\text{priv}} \rangle)^2 - \sum_{\mathbf{x}_i \in \mathcal{G}, i \in [t]} (y_i - \langle \mathbf{x}_i, \hat{\theta}_t \rangle)^2$$
$$= O(\frac{T^{\frac{1}{3}} W^{\frac{2}{3}} \log^2 T \|\mathcal{C}\|^2 \sqrt{\log(1/\delta)\log(1/\beta)}}{\epsilon}$$
$$+ T^{\frac{1}{6}} W^{\frac{1}{3}} \|\mathcal{C}\| \sqrt{\mathcal{L}(\hat{\theta}_t; \Gamma_t)} + T^{\frac{1}{4}} W^{\frac{1}{2}} \|\mathcal{C}\|^{\frac{3}{2}} \sqrt[4]{\mathcal{L}(\hat{\theta}_t; \Gamma_t)}),$$

where $\hat{\theta}_t \in \min_{\theta \in \mathcal{C}} \sum_{\mathbf{x}_i \in \mathcal{G}, i \in [t]} (y_i - \langle \mathbf{x}_i, \theta \rangle)^2$ and $W = w(\mathcal{G}) + w(\mathcal{C})$.

6. REFERENCES

[1] F. Bach, R. Jenatton, J. Mairal, and G. Obozinski. Optimization with Sparsity-inducing Penalties. *Foundations and Trends in Machine Learning*, 2012.

[2] R. Bassily, A. Smith, and A. Thakurta. Differentially Private Empirical Risk Minimization: Efficient Algorithms and Tight Error Bounds. In *FOCS*. IEEE, 2014.

[3] J. Blocki, A. Blum, A. Datta, and O. Sheffet. The Johnson-Lindenstrauss Transform itself Preserves Differential Privacy. In *FOCS*. IEEE, 2012.

[4] A. Blum, C. Dwork, F. McSherry, and K. Nissim. Practical Privacy: The SuLQ Framework. In *PODS*. ACM, 2005.

[5] J. Bourgain, D. Sjoerd, and J. Nelson. Toward a Unified Theory of Sparse Dimensionality Reduction in Euclidean Space. In *STOC*. ACM, 2015.

[6] T.-H. H. Chan, E. Shi, and D. Song. Private and Continual Release of Statistics. *TISSEC*, 14(3), 2011.

[7] K. Chaudhuri and C. Monteleoni. Privacy-preserving Logistic Regression. In *NIPS*, 2009.

[8] K. Chaudhuri, C. Monteleoni, and A. D. Sarwate. Differentially Private Empirical Risk Minimization. *JMLR*, 12, 2011.

[9] K. L. Clarkson. Coresets, Sparse Greedy Approximation, and the Frank-Wolfe Algorithm. *TALG*, 6(4), 2010.

[16]There are generalizations of this norm that can handle different group (block) sizes.

[10] I. Dinur and K. Nissim. Revealing Information while Preserving Privacy. In *PODS*. ACM, 2003.

[11] J. C. Duchi, M. Jordan, and M. J. Wainwright. Local Privacy and Statistical Minimax Rates. In *FOCS*. IEEE, 2013.

[12] J. C. Duchi, M. I. Jordan, and M. J. Wainwright. Privacy Aware Learning. *JACM*, 61(6), 2014.

[13] C. Dwork, K. Kenthapadi, F. McSherry, I. Mironov, and M. Naor. Our Data, Ourselves: Privacy via Distributed Noise Generation. In *EUROCRYPT*. Springer, 2006.

[14] C. Dwork, F. McSherry, K. Nissim, and A. Smith. Calibrating Noise to Sensitivity in Private Data Analysis. In *TCC*. Springer, 2006.

[15] C. Dwork, M. Naor, T. Pitassi, and G. N. Rothblum. Differential Privacy under Continual Observation. In *STOC*. ACM, 2010.

[16] C. Dwork, M. Naor, O. Reingold, and G. Rothblum. Pure Differential Privacy for Rectangle Queries via Private Partitions. In *ASIACRYPT*, 2015.

[17] C. Dwork and A. Roth. The Algorithmic Foundations of Differential Privacy. *Theoretical Computer Science*, 9(3-4), 2013.

[18] C. Dwork, G. N. Rothblum, and S. Vadhan. Boosting and Differential Privacy. In *FOCS*. IEEE, 2010.

[19] M. M. Fard, Y. Grinberg, J. Pineau, and D. Precup. Compressed Least-Squares Regression on Sparse Spaces. In *AAAI*, 2012.

[20] Y. Gordon. *On Milman's Inequality and Random Subspaces which Escape through a Mesh in* $\mathbb{R}^n$. Springer, 1988.

[21] N. Halko, P.-G. Martinsson, and J. A. Tropp. Finding Structure with Randomness: Probabilistic Algorithms for Constructing Approximate Matrix Decompositions. *SIAM Review*, 53(2), 2011.

[22] E. Hazan, A. Kalai, S. Kale, and A. Agarwal. Logarithmic Regret Algorithms for Online Convex Optimization. In *COLT*. Springer, 2006.

[23] J. Hsu, Z. Huang, A. Roth, T. Roughgarden, and Z. S. Wu. Private Matchings and Allocations. In *STOC*. ACM, 2014.

[24] P. Jain, P. Kothari, and A. Thakurta. Differentially Private Online Learning. In *COLT*, 2012.

[25] P. Jain and A. Thakurta. Differentially Private Learning with Kernels. In *ICML*, 2013.

[26] P. Jain and A. G. Thakurta. (Near) Dimension Independent Risk bounds for Differentially Private Learning. In *ICML*, 2014.

[27] A. Kabán. New bounds on compressive linear least squares regression. In *AISTATS*, 2014.

[28] S. Kasiviswanathan and H. Jin. Efficient Private Empirical Risk Minimization for High-dimensional Learning. In *ICML*, 2016.

[29] S. P. Kasiviswanathan, H. K. Lee, K. Nissim, S. Raskhodnikova, and A. Smith. What can we learn privately? In *FOCS*, pages 531–540. IEEE, 2008.

[30] S. P. Kasiviswanathan, M. Rudelson, and A. Smith. The Power of Linear Reconstruction Attacks. In *SODA*. SIAM, 2013.

[31] S. P. Kasiviswanathan and A. Smith. On the'Semantics' of Differential Privacy: A Bayesian Formulation. *Journal of Privacy and Confidentiality*, 6(1), 2014.

[32] K. Kenthapadi, A. Korolova, I. Mironov, and N. Mishra. Privacy via the Johnson-Lindenstrauss Transform. *Journal of Privacy and Confidentiality*, 5(1), 2013.

[33] D. Kifer, A. Smith, and A. Thakurta. Private Convex Empirical Risk Minimization and High-dimensional Regression. In *COLT*, 2012.

[34] M. Ledoux and M. Talagrand. *Probability in Banach Spaces: Isoperimetry and Processes*, volume 23. Springer Science & Business Media, 2013.

[35] O. Maillard and R. Munos. Compressed Least-squares Regression. In *NIPS*, 2009.

[36] N. Mishra and A. Thakurta. (Nearly) Optimal Differentially Private Stochastic Multi-Arm Bandits. In *UAI*, 2015.

[37] J. Nelson and H. L. Nguyên. OSNAP: Faster Numerical Linear Algebra Algorithms via Sparser Subspace Embeddings. In *FOCS*. IEEE, 2013.

[38] G. E. Pfander. *Sampling Theory, a Renaissance*. Springer, 2015.

[39] B. I. Rubinstein, P. L. Bartlett, L. Huang, and N. Taft. Learning in a Large Function Space: Privacy-preserving Mechanisms for SVM Learning. *arXiv:0911.5708*, 2009.

[40] S. Shalev-Shwartz. Online Learning and Online Convex Optimization. *Foundations and Trends in Machine Learning*, 4(2), 2011.

[41] S. Shalev-Shwartz, O. Shamir, N. Srebro, and K. Sridharan. Learnability, Stability and Uniform Convergence. *The Journal of Machine Learning Research*, 11, 2010.

[42] O. Sheffet. Private Approximations of the 2nd-Moment Matrix Using Existing Techniques in Linear Regression. *arXiv:1507.00056*, 2015.

[43] S. Song, K. Chaudhuri, and A. D. Sarwate. Stochastic Gradient Descent with Differentially Private Updates. In *GlobalSIP*. IEEE, 2013.

[44] K. Talwar, A. Thakurta, and L. Zhang. Nearly Optimal Private Lasso. In *NIPS*, 2015.

[45] K. Talwar, A. Thakurta, and L. Zhang. Private Empirical Risk Minimization Beyond the Worst Case: The Effect of the Constraint Set Geometry. *arXiv:1411.5417,*, 2015.

[46] A. G. Thakurta and A. Smith. Differentially Private Feature Selection via Stability Arguments, and the Robustness of the Lasso. In *COLT*, 2013.

[47] A. G. Thakurta and A. Smith. (Nearly) Optimal Algorithms for Private Online Learning in Full-information and Bandit Settings. In *NIPS*, 2013.

[48] R. Tibshirani. Regression Shrinkage and Selection via the Lasso. *Journal of the Royal Statistical Society. Series B (Methodological)*, 1996.

[49] J. Ullman. Private Multiplicative Weights beyond Linear Queries. In *PODS*. ACM, 2015.

[50] J. Upadhyay. Randomness Efficient Fast-Johnson-Lindenstrauss Transform with Applications in Differential Privacy and Compressed Sensing. *arXiv:1410.2470*, 2014.

[51] V. Vapnik. *The Nature of Statistical Learning Theory.* Springer Science & Business Media, 2013.

[52] R. Vershynin. Estimation in High Dimensions: A Geometric Perspective. *arXiv:1405.5103*, 2014.

[53] O. Williams and F. McSherry. Probabilistic Inference and Differential Privacy. In *NIPS*, 2010.

[54] WolframAlpha. https://www.wolframalpha.com/examples/EquationSolving.html, 2016.

[55] D. P. Woodruff. Sketching as a Tool for Numerical Linear Algebra. *Foundations and Trends in Theoretical Computer Science*, 10, 2014.

[56] S. Zhou, K. Ligett, and L. Wasserman. Differential Privacy with Compression. In *ISIT*. IEEE, 2009.

APPENDIX

A. GAUSSIAN NORM BOUNDS

Let $\mathcal{N}(0,\sigma^2)$ denote the Gaussian (normal) distribution with mean 0 and variance σ^2. We use the following standard result on the spectral norm (largest singular value) of an i.i.d. Gaussian random matrix throughout this paper.

Proposition A.1. *Let A be an $N \times n$ matrix whose entries are independent standard normal random variables. Then for every $t > 0$, with probability at least $1-2\exp(-t^2/2)$ one has, $\|A\| = O(\sqrt{N}+\sqrt{n}+t)$. In particular, with probability at least $1-\beta$, $\|A\| = O(\sqrt{N}+\sqrt{n}+\sqrt{\log(1/\beta)})$.*

A.1 Background on Differential Privacy

In this section, we review some basic constructions in differential privacy. The literature on differential privacy is now rich with tools for constructing differentially private analyses, and we refer the reader to a survey by Dwork and Roth [17] for a comprehensive review of developments there.

One of the most basic technique, for achieving differential privacy is by adding noise to the outcome of a computed function where the noise magnitude is scaled to the *(global) sensitivity* of the function defined as:

Definition 7 (Sensitivity). *Let f be a function mapping streams $\Gamma \in \mathcal{Z}^*$ to $\mathbb{R}^d$. The L_2-sensitivity Δ_2 of f is the maximum of $\|f(\Gamma)-f(\Gamma')\|$ over neighboring streams Γ,Γ'.*

Theorem A.2 (Framework of Global Sensitivity [14]). *Let $f : \mathcal{Z}^* \to \mathbb{R}^d$ be a function with L_2-sensitivity Δ_2. The algorithm that on an input Γ outputs $f(\Gamma) + Y where Y \sim \mathcal{N}(0,(2\Delta_2^2\ln(2/\delta))/\epsilon^2)^d$ is (ϵ,δ)-differentially private.*

Composition theorems for differential privacy allow a modular design of privacy preserving algorithms based on algorithms for simpler sub tasks:

Theorem A.3 ([13]). *A mechanism that permits k adaptive interactions with mechanisms that preserves (ϵ,δ)-differential privacy (and does not access the database otherwise) ensures $(k\epsilon,k\delta)$-differential privacy.*

A stronger composition is also possible as shown by Dwork *et al.* [18].

Theorem A.4 ([18]). *Let $\epsilon,\delta,\delta^* > 0$ and $\epsilon \leq 1$. A mechanism that permits k adaptive interactions with mechanisms that preserves (ϵ,δ)-differential privacy (and does not access the database otherwise) ensures $(\epsilon\sqrt{2k\ln(1/\delta^*)}+2k\epsilon^2, k\delta+\delta^*)$-differential privacy.*

B. PROOF OF THEOREM 3.1

Proof of Theorem 3.1. **Privacy Analysis.** Each $\mathbf{z}_i$ is accessed at most T/τ times by the algorithm invoked in Step 5. Let $l = T/\tau$. By using the composition Theorem A.4 with $\delta^* = \delta/2$ it follows that the entire algorithm is $(\epsilon'\sqrt{2l\ln(2/\delta)}+2l\epsilon'^2, l\cdot(\delta/2l)+\delta/2)$-differentially private. We set ϵ' as $\epsilon/2 = \epsilon'\sqrt{2l\ln(2/\delta)}$. Note that with this setting of ϵ', $2l\epsilon'^2 \leq \epsilon/2$, therefore, $\epsilon'\sqrt{2l\ln(2/\delta)}+2l\epsilon'^2 \leq \epsilon$. Hence, Mechanism PrivIncERM is (ϵ,δ)-differentially private.
Utility Analysis. If $T < \tau$, algorithm does not access the data, and in that case, the excess risk can be bounded by $TL\|\mathcal{C}\|$. Now assume $T \geq \tau$. Note that the algorithm performs no computation when t is not a multiple of τ. Let Γ_t denote the prefix of stream Γ till time t. Let t lie in the interval of $[j\tau,(j+1)\tau]$ for some $j \in \mathbb{N}$. The total loss accumulated by the algorithm at time t can be split as:

$$\sum_{i=1}^{t} \jmath(\theta_t^{\mathrm{priv}};\mathbf{z}_i) = \sum_{i=1}^{j\tau} \jmath(\theta_{j\tau}^{\mathrm{priv}};\mathbf{z}_i) + \sum_{i=j\tau+1}^{t} \jmath(\theta_{j\tau}^{\mathrm{priv}};\mathbf{z}_i) \leq \sum_{i=1}^{j\tau} \jmath(\theta_{j\tau}^{\mathrm{priv}};\mathbf{z}_i) + \tau L\|\mathcal{C}\|,$$

as $\theta_t^{\mathrm{priv}} = \theta_{j\tau}^{\mathrm{priv}}$.

Let $\hat{\theta}_t \in \mathrm{argmin}_{\theta\in\mathcal{C}} \sum_{i=1}^{t} \jmath(\theta;\mathbf{z}_i)$. As $\jmath$ is positive-valued,

$$\sum_{i=1}^{t} \jmath(\hat{\theta}_t;\mathbf{z}_i) \geq \sum_{i=1}^{j\tau} \jmath(\hat{\theta}_t;\mathbf{z}_i) \geq \sum_{i=1}^{j\tau} \jmath(\hat{\theta}_{j\tau};\mathbf{z}_i).$$

Hence, we get,

$$\sum_{i=1}^{t} \jmath(\theta_t^{\mathrm{priv}};\mathbf{z}_i) - \sum_{i=1}^{t} \jmath(\hat{\theta}_t;\mathbf{z}_i) \leq \sum_{i=1}^{j\tau} \jmath(\theta_{j\tau}^{\mathrm{priv}};\mathbf{z}_i) - \sum_{i=1}^{j\tau} \jmath(\hat{\theta}_{j\tau};\mathbf{z}_i) + \tau L\|\mathcal{C}\|.$$

Using the results from Bassily *et al.* [2] or Talwar *et al.* [44] to bound $\sum_{i=1}^{j\tau} \jmath(\theta_{j\tau}^{\mathrm{priv}};\mathbf{z}_i) - \sum_{i=1}^{j\tau} \jmath(\hat{\theta}_{j\tau};\mathbf{z}_i)$, setting τ to balance the various opposing terms, and a final union bound provide the claimed bounds. □

C. NOISY GRADIENT DESCENT

In this section, we investigate the convergence rate of noisy projected gradient descent. Williams and McSherry first investigated gradient descent with noisy updates for probabilistic inference [53]; noisy stochastic variants of gradient descent have also been studied by [24, 11, 43, 2] in various private convex optimization settings. Other convex optimization techniques such as mirror descent [12, 45] and Frank-Wolfe scheme [45] have also been considered for designing private ERM algorithms.

For completeness, in this section, we present an analysis of the projected gradient descent procedure that operates with only access to a private gradient function (Definition 5). The analysis relies on standard ideas in convex optimization literature.

Consider the following constrained optimization problem,

$$\min_{\theta\in\mathcal{C}} f(\theta) \text{ where } \mathcal{C} \subseteq \mathbb{R}^d, \tag{8}$$

where $f : \mathbb{R}^d \to \mathbb{R}$ is a convex function and $\mathcal{C}$ is some non-empty closed convex set. Define projection of $\theta \in \mathbb{R}^d$ onto a convex set $\mathcal{C}$ as:

$$P_{\mathcal{C}}(\theta) = \operatorname{argmin}_{\mathbf{z} \in \mathcal{C}} \|\theta - \mathbf{z}\|^2.$$

Projected gradient descent algorithm uses the following update to solve (8)

$$\text{ProjGrad}(\mathcal{C}, r) : \text{Initialize } \theta_1 \in \mathcal{C}, \text{Repeat } r \text{ times:}$$

$$\theta_{k+1} = P_{\mathcal{C}}(\theta_k - \eta_k \nabla f(\theta_k)), \text{ Output } \bar{\theta} = \frac{1}{r}\sum_{i=1}^{r} \theta_i, \quad (9)$$

for some stepsize η_k. Here $P_{\mathcal{C}}(\theta)$ defines the projection of θ onto $\mathcal{C}$.

Let $g : \mathbb{R}^d \to \mathbb{R}^d$ be an (α, β)-approximation of the true gradient of f (as in Definition 5),

$$\Pr\left[\max_{\theta \in \mathcal{C}} \|g(\theta) - \nabla f(\theta)\| > \alpha\right] \leq \beta.$$

The noisy projected gradient descent is a simple modification of the projected gradient descent algorithm (9), where instead of the true gradient, a noisy gradient is used. In other words, noisy projected gradient descent takes the form,

$$\text{NoisyProjGrad}(\mathcal{C}, g, r) : \text{Initialize } \theta_1 \in \mathcal{C}, \text{Repeat } r \text{ times:}$$

$$\theta_{k+1} = P_{\mathcal{C}}(\theta_k - \eta_k g(\theta_k)), \text{ Output } \bar{\theta} = \frac{1}{r}\sum_{i=1}^{r} \theta_i. \quad (10)$$

The following proposition analyzes the convergence of the above NoisyProjGrad procedure assuming g is an (α, β)-approximation of the true gradient of f. The proof ideas are quite standard and we omit it in this extended abstract. Note that the proposition holds, even if f is not differentiable, in which case, $\nabla f(\theta)$ represents any subgradient of f at θ.

Proposition C.1. *Suppose f is convex and is L-Lipschitz. Let $\|\mathcal{C}\|$ be the diameter of $\mathcal{C}$. Let $g : \mathbb{R}^d \to \mathbb{R}^d$ be an (α, β)-approximation of the true gradient of f. Then after r steps of Algorithm* NoisyProjGrad, *starting with any $\theta_0 \in \mathcal{C}$ and constant stepsize of $\eta_k = \frac{\|\mathcal{C}\|}{\sqrt{r}(\alpha+L)}$, with probability at least $1 - r\beta$,*

$$f(\bar{\theta}) - f(\theta^*) \leq \frac{(\alpha + L)\|\mathcal{C}\|}{\sqrt{r}} + \alpha\|\mathcal{C}\|.$$

Corollary C.2. *By setting $r = \frac{(\alpha+L)^2\|\mathcal{C}\|^2}{\zeta^2}$, in Proposition C.1 gives that with probability at least $1 - r\beta$,*

$$f(\bar{\theta}) - f(\theta^*) \leq \zeta + \alpha\|\mathcal{C}\|.$$

If $\alpha > 0$, then we can set $r = \left(1 + \frac{L}{\alpha}\right)^2$ gives $f(\bar{\theta}) - f(\theta^*) \leq 2\alpha\|\mathcal{C}\|$.

After constructing the private gradient function, evaluating the gradient function at any θ can be done without affecting the privacy budget, as this is just a post-processing of private outputs.

D. TREE MECHANISM

Given a bit stream $b_1, \ldots, b_T \in \{0, 1\}$, the *private streaming counter* problem is to release at every timestep t, (an approximation to) $\sum_{i=1}^{t} b_i$ while satisfying differential privacy

Algorithm 4: TreeMech $(\epsilon, \delta, \Delta_2)$

Input: A stream $\Upsilon = v_1, \ldots, v_T$, where each v_t is from the domain $\mathcal{Z} \subseteq \mathbb{R}^d$, and $\Delta_2 = \max_{v,v' \in \mathcal{Z}} \|v - v'\|$

Output: A differentially private estimate of $\sum_{i=1}^{t} v_i$ at every timestep $t \in [T]$

for *all* $t \in [T]$ **do**

- Express $t = \sum_{j=0}^{\log t} 2^j \text{Bin}_j(t)$ (where $\text{Bin}_j(t)$ is the bit at the jth index in the binary representation of t)
- $i \leftarrow \min_{0 \leq j \leq \log T} \{\text{Bin}_j(t) \neq 0\}$
- $\mathbf{a}_i \leftarrow \sum_{j<i} \mathbf{a}_j + v_t$
- **for** $0 \leq j \leq i - 1$ **do**
  - $\mathbf{a}_j \leftarrow \mathbf{0}$ and $\mathbf{b}_j \leftarrow \mathbf{0}$
- **end**
- $\mathbf{b}_i \leftarrow \mathbf{a}_i + \mathcal{N}\left(\mathbf{0}, \frac{2\log^2(T)\Delta_2^2 \ln(2/\delta)\mathbb{I}_d}{\epsilon^2}\right)$
- $\mathbf{s}_t \leftarrow \sum_{j:\text{Bin}_j(t) \neq 0} \mathbf{b}_j$
- Return $\mathbf{s}_t$

end

(Definition 4). Chan *et al.* [6] and Dwork *et al.* [15] proposed an elegant differentially private mechanism (referred to as the *Tree Mechanism*) for this problem. We use this mechanism as a basic building block in our private incremental regression algorithms.[17]

For completeness, in Algorithm TreeMech, we present the entire *Tree Mechanism* as applied to a set of vectors. Given a data stream $\Upsilon = v_1, \ldots, v_T \in \mathcal{Z}$, the algorithm releases at each timestep t, (an approximation to) the sum function $\sum_{i=1}^{t} v_i$, while satisfying differential privacy.

Algorithm TreeMech can be viewed as releasing partial sums of different ranges at each timestep t and computing the final sum is simply a post-processing of the partial sums. At most $\log T$ partial sums are used for constructing each private sum. The following theorem follows by using the standard upper deviation inequality for Gaussian random variables (Proposition A.1) in the analysis of *Tree Mechanism* from [15, 6]. Another advantage of this mechanism is that it can be implemented with small memory, as only $O(\log t)$ partial sums are needed at any time t.

Proposition D.1. TreeMech *is (ϵ, δ)-differentially private with respect to a single datapoint change in the stream Υ. For any $\beta > 0$ and $t \in [T]$, with probability at least $1 - \beta$, $\mathbf{s}_t$ computed by Algorithm* TreeMech *satisfies:*

$$\left\|\mathbf{s}_t - \sum_{i=1}^{t} v_i\right\| = O\left(\frac{\Delta_2(\sqrt{d} + \sqrt{\log(1/\beta)}) \log^{3/2} T \sqrt{\log(1/\delta)}}{\epsilon}\right),$$

where Δ_2 is the L_2-sensitivity of the sum function from Definition 7.

[17]Dwork *et al.* [16] have recently improved the bounds for the private streaming counter problem in the case where the bit stream is *sparse*, i.e., have many fewer 1's than 0's.

E. MISSING PROOFS FROM SECTION 4

Proof of Lemma 4.1. Applying Proposition D.1, we know with probability at least $1-\beta$,

$$\|\mathbf{q}_t - \sum_{i=1}^t \mathbf{x}_i y_i\| = O\left(\kappa(\sqrt{d}+\sqrt{\log(1/\beta)})\right) \text{ and}$$
$$\|Q_t - \sum_{i=1}^t \mathbf{x}_i\mathbf{x}_i^\top\| = O\left(\kappa(\sqrt{d}+\sqrt{\log(1/\beta)})\right).$$

Therefore, we get with probability at least $1-\beta$,

$$\begin{aligned}&\|g_t(\theta) - \nabla\mathcal{L}(\theta;\Gamma_t)\| \\ &= \left\|2\left(Q_t - \sum_{i=1}^t \mathbf{x}_i\mathbf{x}_i^\top\right)\theta - 2\left(\mathbf{q}_t - \sum_{i=1}^t \mathbf{x}_i y_i\right)\right\| \\ &= O\left(\kappa\|\mathcal{C}\|(\sqrt{d}+\sqrt{\log(1/\beta)})\right),\end{aligned}$$

where we used the fact that $\|\theta\| \le \|\mathcal{C}\|$ for any $\theta \in \mathcal{C}$. □

Proof of Theorem 4.2. The (ϵ,δ)-differential privacy follows from the above discussed global sensitivity bound.

Fix any $t \in [T]$. Let $\hat{\theta}_t \in \operatorname{argmin}_{\theta\in\mathcal{C}} \sum_{i=1}^t (y_i - \langle \mathbf{x}_i,\theta\rangle)^2$. Combining Lemma 4.1 and Corollary C.2, with probability at least $1-r\beta'$

$$\mathcal{L}(\theta_t^{\text{priv}};\Gamma_t) - \mathcal{L}(\hat{\theta}_t;\Gamma_t) = O\left(\kappa\|\mathcal{C}\|^2(\sqrt{d}+\sqrt{\log(1/\beta')})\right).$$

Replacing β' by β/r, substituting for κ, and taking a union bound over all $t \in [T]$ gives the claimed result. □

F. MISSING PROOFS FROM SECTION 5

Proof of Lemma 5.4. Let us condition on event $\mathcal{E}_0$ to hold. By definition,

$$\min_{\vartheta\in\Phi\mathcal{C}} \sum_{i=1}^t \left(y_i - \frac{\|\mathbf{x}_i\|}{\|\Phi\mathbf{x}_i\|}\langle\Phi\mathbf{x}_i,\vartheta\rangle\right)^2 \equiv \min_{\theta\in\mathcal{C}} \sum_{i=1}^t \left(y_i - \frac{\|\mathbf{x}_i\|}{\|\Phi\mathbf{x}_i\|}\langle\Phi\mathbf{x}_i,\Phi\theta\rangle\right)^2.$$

Since the inputs are m-dimensional and $\vartheta_t^{\text{priv}} = \Phi\theta_t^{\text{priv}}$, using an analysis similar to Theorem 4.2 gives that, with probability at least $1-\beta$, for each $t \in [T]$,

$$\begin{aligned}&\sum_{i=1}^t \left(y_i - \frac{\|\mathbf{x}_i\|}{\|\Phi\mathbf{x}_i\|}\langle\Phi\mathbf{x}_i,\Phi\theta_t^{\text{priv}}\rangle\right)^2 \\ &\quad - \min_{\theta\in\mathcal{C}} \sum_{i=1}^t \left(y_i - \frac{\|\mathbf{x}_i\|}{\|\Phi\mathbf{x}_i\|}\langle\Phi\mathbf{x}_i,\Phi\theta\rangle\right)^2 \\ &= O\left(\frac{\log^{3/2} T\sqrt{\log(1/\delta)}\|\mathcal{C}\|^2(\sqrt{m}+\sqrt{\log(T/\beta)})}{\epsilon}\right).\end{aligned}$$

In other words, with probability at least $1-\beta$, for each $t \in [T]$,

$$\begin{aligned}&\mathcal{L}_{\text{proj}}(\theta_t^{\text{priv}};\Gamma_t;\Phi) - \min_{\theta\in\mathcal{C}} \mathcal{L}_{\text{proj}}(\theta;\Gamma_t;\Phi) \\ &= O\left(\frac{\log^{3/2} T\sqrt{\log(1/\delta)}\|\mathcal{C}\|^2(\sqrt{m}+\sqrt{\log(T/\beta)})}{\epsilon}\right).\end{aligned}$$

By noting that $\min_{\theta\in\mathcal{C}} \mathcal{L}_{\text{proj}}(\theta;\Gamma_t;\Phi) \le \mathcal{L}_{\text{proj}}(\hat{\theta}_t;\Gamma_t;\Phi)$ and removing the conditioning on $\mathcal{E}_0$ (by adjusting β), completes the proof. □

Proof of Lemma 5.5. Fix a $t \in [T]$. From Theorem 5.1, for the chosen value of m, with probability at least $1-\beta$,

$$\begin{aligned}&\mathcal{L}(\hat{\theta}_t;(\tilde{\mathbf{x}}_1,y_1),\dots,(\tilde{\mathbf{x}}_t,y_t)) = \sum_{i=1}^t (y_i - \langle\tilde{\mathbf{x}}_i,\hat{\theta}_t\rangle)^2 \\ &= \sum_{i=1}^t \left(y_i - \frac{\|\mathbf{x}_i\|}{\|\Phi\mathbf{x}_i\|}\langle\mathbf{x}_i,\hat{\theta}_t\rangle\right)^2 \\ &\le \sum_{i=1}^t (|y_i - \langle\mathbf{x}_i,\hat{\theta}_t\rangle| + \gamma\|\hat{\theta}_t\|)^2 \le \sum_{i=1}^t (|y_i - \langle\mathbf{x}_i,\hat{\theta}_t\rangle| + \gamma\|\mathcal{C}\|)^2 \\ &\le \mathcal{L}(\hat{\theta}_t;\Gamma_t) + \gamma^2\|\mathcal{C}\|^2 t + 2\gamma\|\mathcal{C}\|\sum_{i=1}^t |y_i - \langle\mathbf{x}_i,\hat{\theta}_t\rangle| \\ &\le \mathcal{L}(\hat{\theta}_t;\Gamma_t) + \gamma^2\|\mathcal{C}\|^2 t + 2\gamma\|\mathcal{C}\|\sqrt{t\mathcal{L}(\hat{\theta}_t;\Gamma_t)}. \qquad (11)\end{aligned}$$

Consider $\mathcal{L}_{\text{proj}}(\hat{\theta}_t;\Gamma_t;\Phi)$. From Corollary 5.2, for the chosen value of m, with probability at least $1-\beta$,

$$\begin{aligned}&\mathcal{L}_{\text{proj}}(\hat{\theta}_t;\Gamma_t;\Phi) = \sum_{i=1}^t (y_i - \langle\Phi\tilde{\mathbf{x}}_i,\Phi\hat{\theta}_t\rangle)^2 \\ &\le \sum_{i=1}^t (|y_i - \langle\tilde{\mathbf{x}}_i,\hat{\theta}_t\rangle| + \gamma\|\hat{\theta}_t\|)^2 \\ &\le \sum_{i=1}^t (|y_i - \langle\tilde{\mathbf{x}}_i,\hat{\theta}_t\rangle| + \gamma\|\mathcal{C}\|)^2 \\ &= \mathcal{L}(\hat{\theta}_t;(\tilde{\mathbf{x}}_1,y_1),\dots,(\tilde{\mathbf{x}}_t,y_t)) + \gamma^2\|\mathcal{C}\|^2 t \\ &\qquad + 2\gamma\|\mathcal{C}\|\sum_{i=1}^t |y_i - \langle\tilde{\mathbf{x}}_i,\hat{\theta}_t\rangle| \\ &\le \mathcal{L}(\hat{\theta}_t;(\tilde{\mathbf{x}}_1,y_1),\dots,(\tilde{\mathbf{x}}_t,y_t)) + \gamma^2\|\mathcal{C}\|^2 t \\ &\qquad + 2\gamma\|\mathcal{C}\|\sqrt{t\mathcal{L}(\hat{\theta}_t;(\tilde{\mathbf{x}}_1,y_1),\dots,(\tilde{\mathbf{x}}_t,y_t))},\end{aligned}$$

where the first inequality is by application of Corollary 5.2. Substituting the result from (11) and taking a union bound over all $t \in [T]$ (i.e., replacing β by β/T), completes the proof. □

Proof of Lemma 5.6. Fix a $t \in [T]$. For the chosen value of m,

$$\Pr\left[|\|\Phi\mathbf{x}_i\| - \|\mathbf{x}_i\|| \ge \gamma\|\mathbf{x}_i\| \text{ for all } i \in [t]\right] \le \beta.$$

Similarly for the chosen value of m by using (5),

$$\Pr\left[\left|\langle\Phi\mathbf{x}_i,\Phi\theta_t^{\text{priv}}\rangle - \langle\mathbf{x}_i,\theta_t^{\text{priv}}\rangle\right| \ge \gamma\|\mathbf{x}_i\|\|\theta_t^{\text{priv}}\| \text{ for all } i \in [t]\right] \le \beta.$$

Using arguments as in Lemma 5.5, but by focusing on the lower bounds, we get that with probability at least $1-\beta$,

$$\begin{aligned}\mathcal{L}_{\text{proj}}(\theta_t^{\text{priv}};\Gamma_t;\Phi) &\ge \mathcal{L}(\theta_t^{\text{priv}};\Gamma_t) - 2\gamma\|\mathcal{C}\|\sqrt{T\mathcal{L}(\theta_t^{\text{priv}};\Gamma_t)} \\ &\quad - 2\sqrt{2}\gamma^{3/2}\|\mathcal{C}\|^{3/2}T^{3/4}\mathcal{L}(\theta_t^{\text{priv}};\Gamma_t)^{1/4} - 4\gamma^2\|\mathcal{C}\|^2 T.\end{aligned}$$

Taking a union bound over all $t \in [T]$ completes the proof. □

Proof of Theorem 5.7. The (ϵ,δ)-differential privacy follows from the established global sensitivity bound.

For the utility analysis, we start from (7), and substitute $\gamma = (w(\mathcal{X}) + w(\mathcal{C}))^{1/3}/T^{1/3}$ to get the claimed bound. The value of γ is picked to balance the various opposing factors. □

Statistical Relational Learning: Unifying AI & DB Perspectives on Structured Probabilistic Models

Lise Getoor
UC Santa Cruz
getoor@ucsc.edu

ABSTRACT

Machine learning and database approaches to structured probabilistic models share many commonalities, yet exhibit certain important differences. Machine learning methods focus on learning probabilistic models from (certain) data and efficient learning and inference, whereas probabilistic database approaches focus on storing and efficiently querying uncertain data. Nonetheless, the structured probabilistic models that both use are often (almost) identical. In this tutorial, I will overview the field of statistical relational learning (SRL) [1] and survey common approaches. I'll make connections to work in probabilistic databases [2], and highlight commonalities and differences among them. I'll close by describing some of our recent work on probabilistic soft logic [3].

CCS Concepts

• **Computing methodologies~Statistical relational learning** • *Information systems~Uncertainty*

Keywords

Statistical relational learning; probabilistic databases; probabilistic models; probabilistic soft logic.

1. REFERENCES

[1] Getoor, L., and Taskar, B. 2007. Introduction to Statistical Relational Learning. MIT Press.

[2] Suciu, D, Olteanu, D, Ré, C., and Koch, C. 2011. Probabilistic Databases. Synthesis Lectures on Data Management. Morgan & Claypool Publishers.

[3] Bach, S, Broecheler, M., Huang, B, and Getoor, L. 2015. Hinge-Loss Markov Random Fields and Probabilistic Soft Logic. ArXiv:1505.04406 [cs.LG]

PODS'17, May 14-19, 2017, Chicago, IL, USA
ACM 978-1-4503-4198-1/17/05.
http://dx.doi.org/10.1145/3034786.3056450

Dichotomies in Ontology-Mediated Querying with the Guarded Fragment

André Hernich
University of Liverpool
United Kingdom
andre.hernich@liverpool.ac.uk

Carsten Lutz
University of Bremen
Germany
clu@informatik.uni-bremen.de

Fabio Papacchini
University of Liverpool
United Kingdom
fabio.papacchini@liverpool.ac.uk

Frank Wolter
University of Liverpool
United Kingdom
wolter@liverpool.ac.uk

ABSTRACT

We study the complexity of ontology-mediated querying when ontologies are formulated in the guarded fragment of first-order logic (GF). Our general aim is to classify the data complexity on the level of ontologies where query evaluation w.r.t. an ontology $\mathcal{O}$ is considered to be in PTIME if all (unions of conjunctive) queries can be evaluated in PTIME w.r.t. $\mathcal{O}$ and CONP-hard if at least one query is CONP-hard w.r.t. $\mathcal{O}$. We identify several large and relevant fragments of GF that enjoy a dichotomy between PTIME and CONP, some of them additionally admitting a form of counting. In fact, almost all ontologies in the BioPortal repository fall into these fragments or can easily be rewritten to do so. We then establish a variation of Ladner's Theorem on the existence of NP-intermediate problems and use this result to show that for other fragments, there is provably no such dichotomy. Again for other fragments (such as full GF), establishing a dichotomy implies the Feder-Vardi conjecture on the complexity of constraint satisfaction problems. We also link these results to Datalog-rewritability and study the decidability of whether a given ontology enjoys PTIME query evaluation, presenting both positive and negative results.

Keywords

Ontology-Based Data Access; Query Answering; Dichotomies

1. INTRODUCTION

In *Ontology-Mediated Querying*, incomplete data is enriched with an ontology that provides domain knowledge, enabling more complete answers to queries [47, 10, 34]. This paradigm has recently received a lot of interest, a significant fraction of the research being concerned with the (data) complexity of querying [46, 14] and, closely related, with the rewritability of ontology-mediated queries into more conventional database query languages [16, 26, 28, 31, 27]. A particular emphasis has been put on designing ontology languages that result in PTIME data complexity, and in delineating these from the CONP-hard cases. This question and related ones have given rise to a considerable array of ontology languages, including many description logics (DLs) [3, 37] and a growing number of classes of tuple-generating dependencies (TGDs), also known as Datalog$^{\pm}$ and as existential rules [13, 45]. A general and uniform framework is provided by the *guarded fragment (GF)* of first-order logic and extensions thereof, which subsume many of the mentioned ontology languages [5, 6].

PODS'17, May 14 – 19, 2017, Chicago, IL, USA.

ISBN 978-1-4503-4198-1/17/05...$15.00

DOI: http://dx.doi.org/10.1145/3034786.3056108

In practical applications, ontologies often need to use language features that are only available in computationally expensive ontology languages, but do so in a way such that one may hope for hardness to be avoided. This observation has led to a more fine-grained study of data complexity than on the level of ontology languages, initiated in [42], where the aim is to classify the complexity of individual ontologies while quantifying over the actual query: query evaluation w.r.t. an ontology $\mathcal{O}$ is in PTIME if every CQ can be evaluated in PTIME w.r.t. $\mathcal{O}$ and it is CONP-hard if there is at least one CQ that is CONP-hard to evaluate w.r.t. $\mathcal{O}$. In this way, one can identify tractable ontologies within ontology languages that are, in general, computationally hard. Note that an even more fine-grained approach is taken in [11], where one aims to classify the complexity of each pair $(\mathcal{O}, q)$ with $\mathcal{O}$ an ontology and q an actual query. Both approaches are reasonable, the first one being preferable when the queries to be answered are not fixed at the design time of the ontology; this is actually often the case because ontologies are typically viewed as general purpose artifacts to be used in more than a single application. In this paper, we follow the former approach.

The main aim of this paper is to *identify fragments of GF (and of extensions of GF with different forms of counting) that result in a dichotomy between* PTIME *and* CONP *when used as an ontology language and that cover as many real-world ontologies as possible, considering conjunctive queries (CQs) and unions thereof (UCQs) as the actual query language.* We also aim to provide insight into which fragments of GF (with and without counting) do *not* admit such a dichotomy, to understand the relation between PTIME data complexity and rewritability into Datalog (with inequality in rule bodies, in case we start from GF with equality or counting), and to clarify whether it is decidable whether a given ontology has PTIME data complexity. Note that we concentrate on *fragments* of GF because for the full guarded fragment, proving a dichotomy between PTIME and CONP implies the long-standing Feder-Vardi conjecture on constraint satisfaction problems [23] which indicates that it is very difficult to obtain (if it holds at all). In particular, we concentrate on the fragment of GF that is invariant under disjoint unions, which we call uGF, and on fragments thereof and their ex-

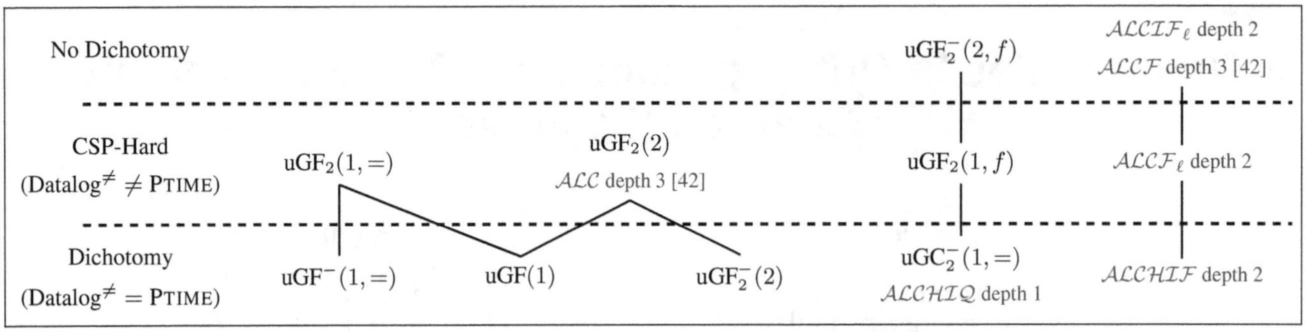

Figure 1: Summary of the results—Number in brackets indicates depth, f presence of partial functions, $\cdot_2$ restriction to two variables, $\cdot^-$ restricts outermost guards to be equality, $\mathcal{F}$ globally function roles, $\mathcal{F}_\ell$ concepts $(\leq 1\, R)$.

tension with forms of counting. Invariance under disjoint unions is a fairly mild restriction that is shared by many relevant ontology languages, and it admits a very natural syntactic characterization.

Our results are summarized in Figure 1. We first explain the fragments shown in the figure and then survey the obtained results. A uGF ontology is a set of sentences of the form $\forall \vec{x}(R(\vec{x}) \rightarrow \varphi(\vec{x}))$ where $R(\vec{x})$ is a guard (possibly equality) and $\varphi(\vec{x})$ is a GF formula that does not contain any sentences as subformulas and in which equality is not used as a guard. The *depth* of such a sentence is the quantifier depth of $\varphi(\vec{x})$ (and thus the outermost universal quantifier is not counted). A main parameter that we vary is the depth, which is typically very small in real world ontologies. In Figure 1, the depth is the first parameter displayed in brackets. As usual, the subscript $\cdot_2$ indicates the restriction to two variables while a superscript $\cdot^-$ means that the guard $R(\vec{x})$ in the outermost universal quantifier can only be equality, $=$ means that equality is allowed (in non-guard positions), f indicates the ability to declare binary relation symbols to be interpreted as partial functions, and GC_2 denotes the two variable guarded fragment extended with counting quantifiers, see [32, 48]. While guarded fragments are displayed in black, description logics (DLs) are shown in grey and smaller font size. We use standard DL names except that '$\mathcal{F}$' denotes globally functional roles while '$\mathcal{F}_\ell$' refers to counting concepts of the form $(\leq 1\, R)$. We do not explain DL names here, but refer to the standard literature [4].

The bottommost part of Figure 1 displays fragments for which there is a dichotomy between PTIME and CONP, the middle part shows fragments for which such a dichotomy implies the Feder-Vardi conjecture (from now on called CSP-hardness), and the topmost part is for fragments that provably have no dichotomy (unless PTIME = NP). The vertical lines indicate that the linked results are closely related, often indicating a fundamental difficulty in further generalizing an upper bound. For example, $uGF^-(1, =)$ enjoys a dichotomy while $uGF_2(1, =)$ is CSP-hard, which demonstrates that generalizing the former result by dropping the restriction that the outermost quantifier has to be equality (indicated by $\cdot^-$) is very challenging (if it is possible at all).[1] Our positive results are thus optimal in many ways. All results hold both when CQs and when UCQs are used as the actual query; in this context, it is interesting to note that there is a GF ontology (which is not an uGF ontology) for which CQ answering is in PTIME while UCQ-answering is CONP-hard. In the cases which enjoy a dichotomy, we also show that PTIME query evaluation coincides with rewritability into Datalog (with inequality in the rule bodies if we start from a fragment with equality or counting). In contrast, for all fragments that are CSP-hard or have no dichotomy, these two properties do provably not coincide. This is of course independent of whether or not the Feder-Vardi conjecture holds.

For $\mathcal{ALCHIQ}$ ontologies of depth 1, we also show that it is decidable and EXPTIME-complete whether a given ontology admits PTIME query evaluation (equivalently: rewritability into Datalog$^{\neq}$). For $uGC_2^-(1, =)$, we show a NEXPTIME upper bound. For $\mathcal{ALC}$ ontologies of depth 2, we establish NEXPTIME-hardness. The proof indicates that more sophisticated techniques are needed to establish decidability, if the problem is decidable at all (which we leave open).

To understand the practical relevance of our results, we have analyzed 411 ontologies from the BioPortal repository [52]. After removing all constructors that do not fall within $\mathcal{ALCHIF}$, an impressive 405 ontologies turned out to have depth 2 and thus belong to a fragment with dichotomy (sometimes modulo an easy complexity-preserving rewriting). For $\mathcal{ALCHIQ}$, still 385 ontologies had depth 1 and so belonged to a fragment with dichotomy. As a concrete and simple example, consider the two $uGC_2^-(1)$-ontologies

$$\mathcal{O}_1 = \{\forall x\,(\mathsf{Hand}(x) \rightarrow \exists^{=5} y\,\mathsf{hasFinger}(x, y))\}$$
$$\mathcal{O}_2 = \{\forall x\,(\mathsf{Hand}(x) \rightarrow \exists y\,(\mathsf{hasFinger}(x, y) \wedge \mathsf{Thumb}(y)))\}$$

which both enjoy PTIME query evaluation (and thus rewritability into Datalog$^{\neq}$), but where query evaluation w.r.t. the union $\mathcal{O}_1 \cup \mathcal{O}_2$ is CONP-hard. Note that such subtle differences cannot be captured when data complexity is studied on the level of ontology languages, at least when basic compositionality conditions are desired.

We briefly highlight some of the techniques used to establish our results. An important role is played by the notions of materializability and unraveling tolerance of an ontology $\mathcal{O}$. Materializability means that for every instance $\mathfrak{D}$, there is a universal model of $\mathfrak{D}$ and $\mathcal{O}$, defined in terms of query answers rather than in terms of homomorphisms (which, as we show, need not coincide in our context). Unraveling tolerance means that the ontology cannot distinguish between an instance and its unraveling into a structure of bounded treewidth. While non-materializability of $\mathcal{O}$ implies that query evaluation w.r.t. $\mathcal{O}$ is CONP-hard, unraveling tolerance of $\mathcal{O}$ implies that query evaluation w.r.t. $\mathcal{O}$ is in PTIME (in fact, even rewritable into Datalog). To establish dichotomies, we prove for the relevant fragments that materializability implies unraveling tolerance which, depending on the fragment, can be technically rather subtle. To prove CSP-hardness or non-dichotomies, very informally speaking, we need to express properties in the ontology that a (positive existential) query cannot 'see'. This is often very subtle and can often be achieved only partially. While the latter is not

[1] A tentative proof of the Feder-Vardi conjecture has very recently been announced in [49], along with an invitation to the research community to verify its validity.

a major problem for CSP-hardness (where we need to deal with CSPs that 'admit precoloring' and are known to behave essentially in the same way as traditional CSPs), it poses serious challenges when proving non-dichotomy. To tackle this problem, we establish a variation of Ladner's theorem on NP-intermediate problems such that instead of the word problem for NP Turing machines, it speaks about the run fitting problem, which is to decide whether a given partially described run of a Turing machine (which corresponds to a precoloring in the CSP case) can be extended to a full run that is accepting. Also our proofs of decidability of whether an ontology admits PTIME query evaluation are rather subtle and technical, involving e.g. mosaic techniques.

Due to space constraints, throughout the paper we defer proof details to the long version this paper available at http://cgi.csc.liv.ac.uk/~frank/publ/publ.html.

Related Work. Ontology-mediated querying has first been considered in [40, 15]; other important papers include [16, 12, 5]. It is a form of reasoning under integrity constraints, a traditional topic in database theory, see e.g. [9, 8] and references therein, and it is also related to deductive databases, see e.g. the monograph [44]. Moreover, ontology-mediated querying has drawn inspiration from query answering under views [17, 18]. In recent years, there has been significant interest in complete classification of the complexity of hard querying problems. In the context of ontology-mediated querying, relevant references include [42, 11, 41]. In fact, this paper closes a number of open problems from [42] such as that $\mathcal{ALCI}$ ontologies of depth two enjoy a dichotomy and that materializability (and thus PTIME complexity and Datalog-rewritability) is decidable in many relevant cases. Other areas of database theory where complete complexity classifications are sought include consistent query answering [36, 35, 24, 21], probabilistic databases [51], and deletion propagation [33, 25].

2. PRELIMINARIES

We assume an infinite set Δ_D of data constants, an infinite set Δ_N of labeled nulls disjoint from Δ_D, and a set Σ of relation symbols containing infinitely many relation symbols of any arity ≥ 1. A *(database) instance* $\mathfrak{D}$ is a non-empty set of *facts* $R(a_1, \ldots, a_k)$, where $R \in \Sigma$, k is the arity of R, and $a_1, \ldots, a_k \in \Delta_D$. We generally assume that instances are finite, unless otherwise specified. An *interpretation* $\mathfrak{A}$ is a non-empty set of *atoms* $R(a_1, \ldots, a_k)$, where $R \in \Sigma$, k is the arity of R, and $a_1, \ldots, a_k \in \Delta_D \cup \Delta_N$. We use $\mathsf{sig}(\mathfrak{A})$ and $\mathsf{dom}(\mathfrak{A})$ to denote the set of relation symbols and, respectively, constants and labelled nulls in $\mathfrak{A}$. We always assume that $\mathsf{sig}(\mathfrak{A})$ is finite while $\mathsf{dom}(\mathfrak{A})$ can be infinite. Whenever convenient, interpretations $\mathfrak{A}$ are presented in the form $(A, (R^{\mathfrak{A}})_{R \in \mathsf{sig}(\mathfrak{A})})$ where $A = \mathsf{dom}(\mathfrak{A})$ and $R^{\mathfrak{A}}$ is a k-ary relation on A for each $R \in \mathsf{sig}(\mathfrak{A})$ of arity k. An interpretation $\mathfrak{A}$ is a *model* of an instance $\mathfrak{D}$, written $\mathfrak{A} \models \mathfrak{D}$, if $\mathfrak{D} \subseteq \mathfrak{A}$. We thus make a strong open world assumption (interpretations can make true additional facts and contain additional constants and nulls) and also assume *standard names* (every constant in $\mathfrak{D}$ is interpreted as itself in $\mathfrak{A}$). Note that every instance is also an interpretation.

Assume $\mathfrak{A}$ and $\mathfrak{B}$ are interpretations. A *homomorphism* h from $\mathfrak{A}$ to $\mathfrak{B}$ is a mapping from $\mathsf{dom}(\mathfrak{A})$ to $\mathsf{dom}(\mathfrak{B})$ such that $R(a_1, \ldots, a_k) \in \mathfrak{A}$ implies $R(h(a_1), \ldots, h(a_k)) \in \mathfrak{B}$ for all $a_1, \ldots, a_k \in \mathsf{dom}(\mathfrak{A})$ and $R \in \Sigma$ of arity k. We say that h *preserves a set* D of constants and labelled nulls if $h(a) = a$ for all $a \in D$ and that h is an *isomorphic embedding* if it is injective and $R(h(a_1), \ldots, h(a_k)) \in \mathfrak{B}$ entails $R(a_1, \ldots, a_k) \in \mathfrak{A}$. An interpretation $\mathfrak{A} \subseteq \mathfrak{B}$ is a *subinterpretation* of $\mathfrak{B}$ if $R(a_1, \ldots, a_k) \in \mathfrak{B}$ and $a_1, \ldots, a_k \in \mathsf{dom}(\mathfrak{A})$ implies $R(a_1, \ldots, a_k) \in \mathfrak{A}$; if $\mathsf{dom}(\mathfrak{A}) = A$, we denote $\mathfrak{A}$ by $\mathfrak{B}_{|A}$ and call it *the subinterpretation of* $\mathfrak{B}$ *induced by* A.

Conjunctive queries (CQs) q *of arity* k take the form $q(\vec{x}) \leftarrow \phi$, where $\vec{x} = x_1, \ldots, x_k$ is the tuple of *answer variables* of q, and ϕ is a conjunction of *atomic formulas* $R(y_1, \ldots, y_n)$ with $R \in \Sigma$ of arity n and $y_1, \ldots, y_n$ variables. As usual, all variables in $\vec{x}$ must occur in some atom of ϕ. Any CQ $q(\vec{x}) \leftarrow \phi$ can be regarded as an instance $\mathfrak{D}_q$, often called the *canonical database of* q, in which each variable y of ϕ is represented by a unique data constant a_y, and that for each atom $R(y_1, \ldots, y_k)$ in ϕ contains the atom $R(a_{y_1}, \ldots, a_{y_k})$. A tuple $\vec{a} = (a_1, \ldots, a_k)$ of constants is an *answer to* $q(x_1, \ldots, x_k)$ *in* $\mathfrak{A}$, in symbols $\mathfrak{A} \models q(\vec{a})$, if there is a homomorphism h from $\mathfrak{D}_q$ to $\mathfrak{A}$ with $h(a_{x_1}, \ldots, a_{x_k}) = \vec{a}$. A *union of conjunctive queries (UCQ)* q takes the form $q_1(\vec{x}), \ldots, q_n(\vec{x})$, where each $q_i(\vec{x})$ is a CQ. The q_i are called *disjuncts* of q. A tuple $\vec{a}$ of constants is an *answer* to q in $\mathfrak{A}$, denoted by $\mathfrak{A} \models q(\vec{a})$, if $\vec{a}$ is an answer to some disjunct of q in $\mathfrak{A}$.

We now introduce the fundamentals of ontology-mediated querying. An *ontology language* $\mathcal{L}$ is a set of first-order sentences over signature Σ (that is, function symbols are not allowed) and an $\mathcal{L}$*-ontology* $\mathcal{O}$ is a finite set of sentences from $\mathcal{L}$. We introduce various concrete ontology languages throughout the paper, including fragments of the guarded fragment and descriptions logics. An interpretation $\mathfrak{A}$ is a *model of an ontology* $\mathcal{O}$, in symbols $\mathfrak{A} \models \mathcal{O}$, if it satisfies all its sentences. An instance $\mathfrak{D}$ is *consistent w.r.t.* $\mathcal{O}$ if there is a model of $\mathfrak{D}$ and $\mathcal{O}$.

An *ontology-mediated query (OMQ)* is a pair $(\mathcal{O}, q)$, where $\mathcal{O}$ is an ontology and q a UCQ. The semantics of an ontology-mediated query is given in terms of *certain answers*, defined next. Assume that q has arity k and $\mathfrak{D}$ is an instance. Then a tuple $\vec{a}$ of length k in $\mathsf{dom}(\mathfrak{D})$ is a *certain answer to* q *on an instance* $\mathfrak{D}$ *given* $\mathcal{O}$, in symbols $\mathcal{O}, \mathfrak{D} \models q(\vec{a})$, if $\mathfrak{A} \models q(\vec{a})$ for all models $\mathfrak{A}$ of $\mathfrak{D}$ and $\mathcal{O}$. The *query evaluation problem for an OMQ* $(\mathcal{O}, q(\vec{x}))$ is to decide, given an instance $\mathfrak{D}$ and a tuple $\vec{a}$ in $\mathfrak{D}$, whether $\mathcal{O}, \mathfrak{D} \models q(\vec{a})$.

We use standard notation for Datalog programs (a brief introduction is given in the appendix). An OMQ $(\mathcal{O}, q(\vec{x}))$ is called *Datalog-rewritable* if there is a Datalog program Π such that for all instances $\mathfrak{D}$ and $\vec{a} \in \mathsf{dom}(\mathfrak{D})$, $\mathcal{O}, \mathfrak{D} \models q(\vec{a})$ iff $\mathfrak{D} \models \Pi(\vec{a})$. *Datalog*$^{\neq}$*-rewritability* is defined accordingly, but allows the use of inequality in the body of Datalog rules. We are mainly interested in the following properties of ontologies.

Definition 1 *Let* $\mathcal{O}$ *be an ontology and* $\mathcal{Q}$ *a class of queries. Then*

- $\mathcal{Q}$-evaluation w.r.t. $\mathcal{O}$ is in PTIME *if for every* $q \in \mathcal{Q}$*, the query evaluation problem for* $(\mathcal{O}, q)$ *is in* PTIME.
- $\mathcal{Q}$-evaluation w.r.t. $\mathcal{O}$ is Datalog-rewritable *(resp.* Datalog$^{\neq}$-rewritable*) if for every* $q \in \mathcal{Q}$*, the query evaluation problem for* $(\mathcal{O}, q)$ *is Datalog-rewritable (resp. Datalog*$^{\neq}$*-rewritable).*
- $\mathcal{Q}$-evaluation w.r.t. $\mathcal{O}$ is CONP-hard *if there is a* $q \in \mathcal{Q}$ *such that the query evaluation problem for* $(\mathcal{O}, q)$ *is* CONP*-hard.*

2.1 Ontology Languages

As ontology languages, we consider fragments of the guarded fragment (GF) of FO, the two-variable guarded fragment of FO with counting, and DLs. Recall that GF formulas [1] are obtained by starting from atomic formulas $R(\vec{x})$ over Σ and equalities $x = y$ and then using the boolean connectives and *guarded quantifiers* of the form

$$\forall \vec{y}(\alpha(\vec{x}, \vec{y}) \rightarrow \varphi(\vec{x}, \vec{y})), \quad \exists \vec{y}(\alpha(\vec{x}, \vec{y}) \wedge \varphi(\vec{x}, \vec{y}))$$

where $\varphi(\vec{x}, \vec{y})$ is a guarded formula with free variables among $\vec{x}, \vec{y}$ and $\alpha(\vec{x}, \vec{y})$ is an atomic formula or an equality $x = y$ that contains all variables in $\vec{x}, \vec{y}$. The formula α is called the *guard of the quantifier*.

In ontologies, we only allow GF sentences φ that are *invariant under disjoint unions*, that is, for all families $\mathfrak{B}_i$, $i \in I$, of interpretations with mutually disjoint domains, the following holds: $\mathfrak{B}_i \models \varphi$ for all $i \in I$ if, and only if, $\bigcup_{i \in I} \mathfrak{B}_i \models \varphi$. We give a syntactic characterization of GF sentences that are invariant under disjoint unions. Denote by *openGF* the fragment of GF that consists of all (open) formulas whose subformulas are all open and in which equality is not used as a guard. The fragment *uGF* of GF is the set of sentences obtained from openGF by a *single guarded universal quantifier*: if $\varphi(\vec{y})$ is in openGF, then $\forall \vec{y}(\alpha(\vec{y}) \rightarrow \varphi(\vec{y}))$ is in uGF, where $\alpha(\vec{y})$ is an atomic formula or an equality $y = y$ that contains all variables in $\vec{y}$. We often omit equality guards in uGF sentences of the form $\forall y(y = y \rightarrow \varphi(y))$ and simply write $\forall y \varphi$. A *uGF ontology* is a finite set of sentences in uGF.

Theorem 1 *A GF sentence is invariant under disjoint unions iff it is equivalent to a uGF sentence.*

PROOF. The direction from right to left is straightforward. For the converse direction, observe that every GF sentence is equivalent to a Boolean combination of uGF sentences. Now assume that φ is a GF sentence and invariant under disjoint unions. Let cons(φ) be the set of all sentences χ in uGF with $\varphi \models \chi$. By compactness of FO it is sufficient to show that cons(φ) $\models \varphi$. If this is not the case, take a model $\mathfrak{A}_0$ of cons(φ) refuting φ and take for any sentence ψ in uGF that is not in cons(φ) an interpretation $\mathfrak{A}_{\neg\psi}$ satisfying φ and refuting ψ. Let $\mathfrak{A}_1$ be the disjoint union of all $\mathfrak{A}_{\neg\psi}$. By preservation of φ under disjoint unions, $\mathfrak{A}_1$ satisfies φ. By reflection of φ for disjoint unions, the disjoint union $\mathfrak{A}$ of $\mathfrak{A}_0$ and $\mathfrak{A}_1$ does not satisfy φ. Thus $\mathfrak{A}_1$ satisfies φ and $\mathfrak{A}$ does not satisfy φ but by construction $\mathfrak{A}$ and $\mathfrak{A}_1$ satisfy the same sentences in uGF. This is impossible since φ is equivalent to a Boolean combination of uGF sentences. □

The following example shows that some very simple Boolean combinations of uGF sentences are not invariant under disjoint unions.

Example 1 *Let*

$$\begin{aligned} \mathcal{O}_{UCQ/CQ} &= \{(\forall x(A(x) \vee B(x)) \vee \exists x E(x)\} \\ \mathcal{O}_{Mat/PTime} &= \{\forall x A(x) \vee \forall x B(x)\} \end{aligned}$$

Then $\mathcal{O}_{Mat/PTime}$ is not preserved under disjoint unions since $\mathfrak{D}_1 = \{A(a)\}$ and $\mathfrak{D}_2 = \{B(b)\}$ are models of $\mathcal{O}_{Mat/PTime}$ but $\mathfrak{D}_1 \cup \mathfrak{D}_2$ refutes $\mathcal{O}_{Mat/PTime}$; $\mathcal{O}_{UCQ/CQ}$ does not reflect disjoint unions since the disjoint union of $\mathfrak{D}'_1 = \{E(a)\}$ and $\mathfrak{D}'_2 = \{F(b)\}$ is a model of $\mathcal{O}_{UCQ/CQ}$ but $\mathfrak{D}'_2$ refutes $\mathcal{O}_{UCQ/CQ}$. We will use these ontologies later to explain why we restrict this study to fragments of GF that are invariant under disjoint unions.

When studying uGF ontologies, we are going to vary several parameters. The *depth* of a formula φ in openGF is the nesting depth of guarded quantifiers in φ. The *depth* of a sentence $\forall \vec{y}(\alpha(\vec{y}) \rightarrow \varphi(\vec{y}))$ in uGF is the depth of $\varphi(\vec{y})$, thus the outermost guarded quantifier is not counted. The *depth* of a uGF ontology is the maximum depth of its sentences. We indicate restricted depth in brackets, writing e.g. uGF(2) to denote the set of all uGF sentences of depth at most 2.

Example 2 *The sentence*

$$\forall xy(R(x, y) \rightarrow (A(x) \vee \exists z S(y, z)))$$

is in uGF(1) since the openGF formula $A(x) \vee \exists z S(y, z)$ has depth 1.

For every GF sentence φ, one can construct in polynomial time a conservative extension φ' in uGF(1) by converting into Scott normal form [29]. Thus, the satisfiability and CQ-evaluation problems for full GF can be polynomially reduced to the corresponding problem for uGF(1).

We use uGF$^-$ to denote the fragment of uGF where only equality guards are admitted in the outermost universal quantifier applied to an openGF formula. Thus, the sentence in Example 2 (1) is a uGF sentence of depth 1, but not a uGF$^-$ sentence of depth 1. It is, however, equivalent to the following uGF$^-$ sentence of depth 1:

$$\forall x(\exists y((R(y, x) \wedge \neg A(y)) \rightarrow \exists z S(x, z)))$$

An example of a uGF sentence of depth 1 that is not equivalent to a uGF$^-$ sentence of depth 1 is given in Example 3 below. Intuitively, uGF sentences of depth 1 can be thought of as uGF$^-$ sentences of 'depth 1.5' because giving up $\cdot^-$ allows an additional level of 'real' quantification (meaning: over guards that are not forced to be equality), but only in a syntactically restricted way.

The two-variable fragment of uGF is denoted with uGF$_2$. More precisely, in uGF$_2$ we admit only the two fixed variables x and y and disallow the use of relation symbols of arity exceeding two. We also consider two extensions of uGF$_2$ with forms of counting. First, uGF$_2(f)$ denotes the extension of uGF$_2$ with function symbols, that is, an uGF$_2(f)$ ontology is a finite set of uGF$_2$ sentences and of *functionality axioms* $\forall x \forall y_1 \forall y_2((R(x, y_1) \wedge R(x, y_2)) \rightarrow (y_1 = y_2))$ [29]. Second, we consider the extension uGC$_2$ of uGF$_2$ with counting quantifiers. More precisely, the language openGC$_2$ is defined in the same way as the two-variable fragment of openGF, but in addition admits *guarded counting quantifiers* [48, 32]: if $n \in \mathbb{N}$, $\{z_1, z_2\} = \{x, y\}$, and $\alpha(z_1, z_2) \in \{R(z_1, z_2), R(z_2, z_1)\}$ for some $R \in \Sigma$ and $\varphi(z_1, z_2)$ is in openGC$_2$, then $\exists^{\geq n} z_1(\alpha(z_1, z_2) \wedge \varphi(z_1, z_2))$ is in openGC$_2$. The ontology language uGC$_2$ is then defined in the same way as uGF$_2$, using openGC$_2$ instead of openGF$_2$. The *depth* of formulas in uGC$_2$ is defined in the expected way, that is, guarded counting quantifiers and guarded quantifiers both contribute to it.

The above restrictions can be freely combined and we use the obvious names to denote such combinations. For example, uGF$_2^-(1, f)$ denotes the two-variable fragment of uGF with function symbols and where all sentences must have depth 1 and the guard of the outermost quantifier must be equality. Note that uGF admits equality, although in a restricted way (only in non-guard positions, with the possible exception of the guard of the outermost quantifier). We shall also consider fragments of uGF that admit no equality at all except as a guard of the outermost quantifier. To emphasize that the restricted use of equality is allowed, we from now on use the equality symbol in brackets whenever equality is present, as in uGF(=), uGF$^-(1, =)$, and uGC$_2^-(1, =)$. Conversely, uGF, uGF$^-(1)$, and uGC$_2^-(1)$ from now on denote the corresponding fragments where equality is only allowed as a guard of the outermost quantifier.

Description logics are a popular family of ontology languages that are related to the guarded fragments of FO introduced above. We briefly review the basic description logic $\mathcal{ALC}$, further details on this and other DLs mentioned in this paper can be found in the appendix and in [4]. DLs generally use relations of arity one and two, only. An $\mathcal{ALC}$ *concept* is formed according to the syntax rule

$$C, D ::= A \mid \top \mid \bot \mid \neg C \mid C \sqcap D \mid C \sqcup D \mid \exists R.C \mid \forall R.C$$

where A ranges over unary relations and R over binary relations. An $\mathcal{ALC}$ *ontology* $\mathcal{O}$ is a finite set of *concept inclusions* $C \sqsubseteq D$, with C and D $\mathcal{ALC}$ concepts. The semantics of $\mathcal{ALC}$ concepts C can be given by translation to openGF formulas $C^*(x)$ with one free variable x and two variables overall. A concept inclusion $C \sqsubseteq D$ then translates to the uGF$_2^-$ sentence $\forall x(C^*(x) \rightarrow D^*(x))$. The *depth* of an $\mathcal{ALC}$ concept is the maximal nesting depth of $\exists R$ and $\forall R$. The *depth* on an $\mathcal{ALC}$ ontology is the maximum depth of concepts that occur in it. Thus, every $\mathcal{ALC}$ ontology of depth n is a uGF$_2^-$ ontology of depth n. When translating into uGF$_2$ instead of into uGF$_2^-$, the depth might decrease by one because one can exploit the outermost quantifier (which does not contribute to the depth). A more detailed description of the relationship between DLs and fragments of uGF is given in the appendix.

Example 3 *The $\mathcal{ALC}$ concept inclusion $\exists S.A \sqsubseteq \forall R.\exists S.B$ has depth 2, but is equivalent to the uGF$_2(1)$ sentence*

$$\forall xy(R(x, y) \rightarrow ((\exists S.A)^*(x) \rightarrow (\exists S.B)^*(y))$$

Note that for any ontology $\mathcal{O}$ in any DL considered in this paper one can construct in a straightforward way in polynomial time a conservative extension $\mathcal{O}^*$ of $\mathcal{O}$ of depth one. In fact, many DL algorithms for satisfiability or query evaluation assume that the ontology is of depth one and normalized.

We also consider the extensions of $\mathcal{ALC}$ with inverse roles R^- (denoted in the name of the DL by the letter $\mathcal{I}$), role inclusions $R \sqsubseteq S$ (denoted by $\mathcal{H}$), qualified number restrictions $(\geq n\ R\ C)$ (denoted by $\mathcal{Q}$), partial functions as defined above (denoted by $\mathcal{F}$), and local functionality expressed by $(\leq 1 R)$ (denoted by $\mathcal{F}_\ell$). The depth of ontologies formulated in these DLs is defined in the obvious way. Thus, $\mathcal{ALCHIQ}$ ontologies (which admit all the constructors introduced above) translate into uGC$_2^-$ ontologies, preserving the depth.

For any syntactic object O (such as an ontology or a query), we use $|O|$ to denote the number of symbols needed to write O, counting relation names, variable names, and so on as a single symbol and assuming that numbers in counting quantifiers and DL number restrictions are coded in unary.

2.2 Guarded Tree Decompositions

We introduce guarded tree decompositions and rooted acyclic queries [30]. A set $G \subseteq \text{dom}(\mathfrak{A})$ is *guarded* in the interpretation $\mathfrak{A}$ if G is a singleton or there are $R \in \Sigma$ and $R(a_1, \ldots, a_k) \in \mathfrak{A}$ such that $G = \{a_1, \ldots, a_k\}$. By $S(\mathfrak{A})$, we denote the set of all guarded sets in $\mathfrak{A}$. A tuple $(a_1, \ldots, a_k) \in A^k$ is *guarded* in $\mathfrak{A}$ if $\{a_1, \ldots, a_k\}$ is a subset of some guarded set in $\mathfrak{A}$. A *guarded tree decomposition* of $\mathfrak{A}$ is a triple (T, E, bag) with (T, E) an acyclic undirected graph and bag a function that assigns to every $t \in T$ a set $\text{bag}(t)$ of atoms such that $\mathfrak{A}_{|\text{dom}(\text{bag}(t))} = \text{bag}(t)$ and

1. $\mathfrak{A} = \bigcup_{t \in T} \text{bag}(t)$;
2. $\text{dom}(\text{bag}(t))$ is guarded for every $t \in T$;
3. $\{t \in T \mid a \in \text{dom}(\text{bag}(t))\}$ is connected in (T, E), for every $a \in \text{dom}(\mathfrak{A})$.

We say that $\mathfrak{A}$ is *guarded tree decomposable* if there exists a guarded tree decomposition of $\mathfrak{A}$. We call (T, E, bag) a *connected guarded tree decomposition (cg-tree decomposition)* if, in addition, (T, E) is connected (i.e., a tree) and $\text{dom}(\text{bag}(t)) \cap \text{dom}(\text{bag}(t')) \neq \emptyset$ for all $(t, t') \in E$. In this case, we often assume that (T, E) has a designated root r, which allows us to view (T, E) as a directed tree whenever convenient.

A CQ $q \leftarrow \phi$ is a *rooted acyclic query (rAQ)* if there exists a cg-tree decomposition (T, E, bag) of the instance $\mathfrak{D}_q$ with root r such that $\text{dom}(\text{bag}(r))$ is the set of answer variables of q. Note that, by definition, rAQs are non-Boolean queries.

Example 4 *The CQ*

$$q(x) \leftarrow \phi, \quad \phi = R(x, y) \wedge R(y, z) \wedge R(z, x)$$

is not an rAQ since $\mathfrak{D}_q$ is not guarded tree decomposable. By adding the conjunct $Q(x, y, z)$ to ϕ one obtains an rAQ.

We will frequently use the following construction: let $\mathfrak{D}$ be an instance and $\mathcal{G}$ a set of guarded sets in $\mathfrak{D}$. Assume that $\mathfrak{B}_G$, $G \in \mathcal{G}$, are interpretations such that $\text{dom}(\mathfrak{B}_G) \cap \text{dom}(\mathfrak{D}) = G$ and $\text{dom}(\mathfrak{B}_{G_1}) \cap \text{dom}(\mathfrak{B}_{G_2}) = G_1 \cap G_2$ for any two distinct guarded sets G_1 and G_2 in $\mathcal{G}$. Then the interpretation

$$\mathfrak{B} = \mathfrak{D} \cup \bigcup_{G \in \mathcal{G}} \mathfrak{B}_G$$

is called the *interpretation obtained from $\mathfrak{D}$ by hooking $\mathfrak{B}_G$ to $\mathfrak{D}$ for all $G \in \mathcal{G}$*. If the $\mathfrak{B}_G$ are cg-tree decomposable interpretations with $\text{dom}(\text{bag}(r)) = G$ for the root r of a (fixed) cg-tree decomposition of $\mathfrak{B}_G$, then $\mathfrak{B}$ is called a *forest model of $\mathfrak{D}$ defined using* $\mathcal{G}$. If $\mathcal{G}$ is the set of all maximal guarded sets in $\mathfrak{D}$, then we call $\mathfrak{B}$ simply a *forest model of* $\mathfrak{D}$. The following result can be proved using standard guarded tree unfolding [29, 30].

Lemma 1 *Let $\mathcal{O}$ be a uGF$(=)$ or uGC$_2(=)$ ontology, $\mathfrak{D}$ a possibly infinite instance, and $\mathfrak{A}$ a model of $\mathfrak{D}$ and $\mathcal{O}$. Then there exists a forest model $\mathfrak{B}$ of $\mathfrak{D}$ and $\mathcal{O}$ and a homomorphism h from $\mathfrak{B}$ to $\mathfrak{A}$ that preserves dom$(\mathfrak{D})$.*

3. MATERIALIZABILITY

We introduce and study materializability of ontologies as a necessary condition for query evaluation to be in PTIME. In brief, an ontology $\mathcal{O}$ is materializable if for every instance $\mathfrak{D}$, there is a model $\mathfrak{A}$ of $\mathcal{O}$ and $\mathfrak{D}$ such that for all queries, the answers on $\mathfrak{A}$ agree with the certain answers on $\mathfrak{D}$ given $\mathcal{O}$. We show that this sometimes, but not always, coincides with existence of universal models defined in terms of homomorphisms. We then prove that in uGF$(=)$ and uGC$_2(=)$, non-materializability implies CONP-hard query answering while this is not the case for GF. Using these results, we further establish that in uGF$(=)$ and uGC$_2(=)$, query evalution w.r.t. ontologies to be in PTIME, Datalog$^{\neq}$-rewritable, and CONP-hard does not depend on the query language, that is, all these properties agree for rAQs, CQs, and UCQs. Again, this is not the case for GF.

Definition 2 (Materializability) *Let $\mathcal{O}$ be an FO$(=)$-ontology, $\mathcal{Q}$ a class of queries, and $\mathcal{M}$ a class of instances. Then*

- *an interpretation $\mathfrak{B}$ is a* $\mathcal{Q}$-materialization *of $\mathcal{O}$ and an instance $\mathfrak{D}$ if it is a model of $\mathcal{O}$ and $\mathfrak{D}$ and for all $q(\vec{x}) \in \mathcal{Q}$ and $\vec{a}$ in dom$(\mathfrak{D})$, $\mathfrak{B} \models q(\vec{a})$ iff $\mathcal{O}, \mathfrak{D} \models q(\vec{a})$.*
- *$\mathcal{O}$ is* $\mathcal{Q}$-materializable for $\mathcal{M}$ *if for every instance $\mathfrak{D} \in \mathcal{M}$ that is consistent w.r.t. $\mathcal{O}$, there is a $\mathcal{Q}$-materialization of $\mathcal{O}$ and $\mathfrak{D}$.*

If $\mathcal{M}$ is the class of all instances, we simply speak of $\mathcal{Q}$-materializability of $\mathcal{O}$.

We first observe that the materializability of ontologies does not depend on the query language (although concrete materializations do).

Theorem 2 *Let $\mathcal{O}$ be a uGF$(=)$ or uGC$_2(=)$ ontology and $\mathcal{M}$ a class of instances. Then the following conditions are equivalent:*

1. *$\mathcal{O}$ is rAQ-materializable for $\mathcal{M}$;*

2. *$\mathcal{O}$ is CQ-materializable for $\mathcal{M}$;*

3. *$\mathcal{O}$ is UCQ-materializable for $\mathcal{M}$.*

PROOF. The only non-trivial implication is (1) $\Rightarrow$ (2). It can be proved by using Lemma 1 and showing that if $\mathfrak{A}$ is a rAQ-materialization of an ontology $\mathcal{O}$ and an instance $\mathfrak{D}$, then any forest model $\mathfrak{B}$ of $\mathcal{O}$ and $\mathfrak{D}$ which admits a homomorphism to $\mathfrak{A}$ that preserves $\mathsf{dom}(\mathfrak{D})$ is a CQ-materialization of $\mathcal{O}$ and $\mathfrak{D}$. $\square$

Because of Theorem 2, we from now on speak of *materializability* without reference to a query language and of *materializations* instead of UCQ-materializations (which are then also CQ-materializations and rAQ-materializations).

A notion closely related to materializations are (homomorphically) universal models as used e.g. in data exchange [22, 20]. A model of an ontology $\mathcal{O}$ and an instance $\mathfrak{D}$ is *hom-universal* if there is a homomorphism preserving dom($\mathfrak{D}$) into any model of $\mathcal{O}$ and $\mathfrak{D}$. We say that an ontology $\mathcal{O}$ *admits hom-universal models* if there is a hom-universal model for $\mathcal{O}$ and any instance $\mathfrak{D}$. It is well-known that hom-universal models are closely related to what we call UCQ-materializations. In fact, in many DLs and in $\text{uGC}_2(=)$, materializability of an ontology $\mathcal{O}$ coincides with $\mathcal{O}$ admitting hom-universal models (although for concrete models, being hom-universal is not the same as being a materialization). We show in the long version that this is not the case for ontologies in uGF(2) (with three variables). The proof also shows that admitting hom-universal models is not a necessary condition for query evaluation to be in PTIME (in contrast to materializability).

Lemma 2 *A $\text{uGC}_2(=)$ ontology is materializable iff it admits hom-universal models. This does not hold for uGF(2) ontologies.*

The following theorem links materializability to computational complexity, thus providing the main reason for our interest into this notion. The proof is by reduction of 2+2-SAT [50], a variation of a related proof from [42].

Theorem 3 *Let $\mathcal{O}$ be an FO(=)-ontology that is invariant under disjoint unions. If $\mathcal{O}$ is not materializable, then rAQ-evaluation w.r.t. $\mathcal{O}$ is CONP-hard.*

We remark that, in the proof of Theorem 3, we use instances and rAQs that use additional fresh (binary) relation symbols, that is, relation symbols that do not occur in $\mathcal{O}$.

The ontology $\mathcal{O}_{\text{Mat/PTime}}$ from Example 1 shows that Theorem 3 does not hold for GF ontologies, even if they are of depth 1 and use only a single variable. In fact, $\mathcal{O}_{\text{Mat/PTime}}$ is not CQ-materializable, but CQ-evaluation is in PTIME (which is both easy to see).

Theorem 4 *For all uGF(=) and $\text{uGC}_2(=)$ ontologies $\mathcal{O}$, the following are equivalent:*

1. *rAQ-evaluation w.r.t. $\mathcal{O}$ is in* PTIME*;*

2. *CQ-evaluation w.r.t. $\mathcal{O}$ is in* PTIME*;*

3. *UCQ-evaluation w.r.t. $\mathcal{O}$ is in* PTIME.

This remains true when 'in PTIME*' is replaced with 'Datalog$^{\neq}$-rewritable' and with 'CONP-hard' (and with 'Datalog-rewritable' if $\mathcal{O}$ is a uGF ontology).*

PROOF. By Theorem 3, we can concentrate on ontologies that are materializable. For the non-trivial implication of Point 3 by Point 1, we exploit materializability to rewrite UCQs into a finite disjunction of queries $q \wedge \bigwedge_i q_i$ where q is a "core CQ" that only needs to be evaluated over the input instance $\mathfrak{D}$ (ignoring labeled nulls) and each q_i is a rAQ. This is similar to squid decompositions in [12], but more subtle due to the presence of subqueries that are not connected to any answer variable of q. Similar constructions are used also to deal with Datalog$^{\neq}$-rewritability and with CONP-hardness. $\square$

The ontology $\mathcal{O}_{\text{UCQ/CQ}}$ from Example 1 shows that Theorem 4 does not hold for GF ontologies, even if they use only a single variable and are of depth 1 up to an outermost universal quantifier with an equality guard.

Lemma 3 *CQ-evaluation w.r.t. $\mathcal{O}_{UCQ/CQ}$ is in* PTIME *and UCQ-evaluation w.r.t. $\mathcal{O}_{UCQ/CQ}$ is* CONP*-hard.*

The lower bound essentially follows the construction in the proof of Theorem 3 and the upper bound is based on a case analysis, depending on which relations occur in the CQ and in the input instance.

4. UNRAVELLING TOLERANCE

While materializability of an ontology is a necessary condition for PTIME query evaluation in uGF(=) and $\text{uGC}_2(=)$, we now identify a sufficient condition called unravelling tolerance that is based on unravelling instances into cg-tree decomposable instances (which might be infinite). In fact, unravelling tolerance is even a sufficient condition of Datalog$^{\neq}$-rewritability and we will later establish our dichotomy results by showing that, for the ontology languages in question, materializability implies unravelling tolerance.

We start with introducing suitable forms of unravelling (also called guarded tree unfolding, see [30] and references therein). The *uGF-unravelling* $\mathfrak{D}^u$ of an instance $\mathfrak{D}$ is constructed as follows. Let $T(\mathfrak{D})$ be the set of all sequences $t = G_0 G_1 \cdots G_n$ where G_i, $0 \le i \le n$, are maximal guarded sets of $\mathfrak{D}$ and

(a) $G_i \neq G_{i+1}$,

(b) $G_i \cap G_{i+1} \neq \emptyset$, and

(c) $G_{i-1} \neq G_{i+1}$.

In the following, we associate each $t \in T(\mathfrak{D})$ with a set of atoms $\mathsf{bag}(t)$. Then we define $\mathfrak{D}^u$ as $\bigcup_{t \in T(\mathfrak{D})} \mathsf{bag}(t)$ and note that $(T(\mathfrak{D}), E, \mathsf{bag})$ is a cg-tree decomposition of $\mathfrak{D}^u$ where $(t, t') \in E$ if $t' = tG$ for some G.

Set $\mathsf{tail}(G_0 \cdots G_n) = G_n$. Take an infinite supply of *copies* of any $d \in \mathsf{dom}(\mathfrak{D})$. We set $e^{\uparrow} = d$ if e is a copy of d. We define $\mathsf{bag}(t)$ (up to isomorphism) proceeding by induction on the length of the sequence t. For any $t = G$, $\mathsf{bag}(t)$ is an instance whose domain is a set of copies of $d \in G$ such that the mapping $e \mapsto e^{\uparrow}$ is an isomorphism from $\mathsf{bag}(G)$ onto the subinstance $\mathfrak{D}_{|G}$ of $\mathfrak{D}$ induced by G. To define $\mathsf{bag}(t')$ for $t' = tG'$ when $\mathsf{tail}(t) = G$, take for any $d \in G' \setminus G$ a fresh copy d' of d and define $\mathsf{bag}(t')$ with domain $\{d' \mid d \in G' \setminus G\} \cup \{e \in \mathsf{bag}(t) \mid e^{\uparrow} \in G' \cap G)\}$ such that the mapping $e \mapsto e^{\uparrow}$ is an isomorphism from $\mathsf{bag}(t')$ onto $\mathfrak{D}_{|G'}$. The following example illustrates the construction of $\mathfrak{D}^u$.

Example 5 *(1) Consider the instance $\mathfrak{D}$ depicted below with the maximal guarded sets G_1, G_2, G_3. Then the unravelling $\mathfrak{D}^u$ of $\mathfrak{D}$ consists of three isomorphic chains (we depict only one such chain):*

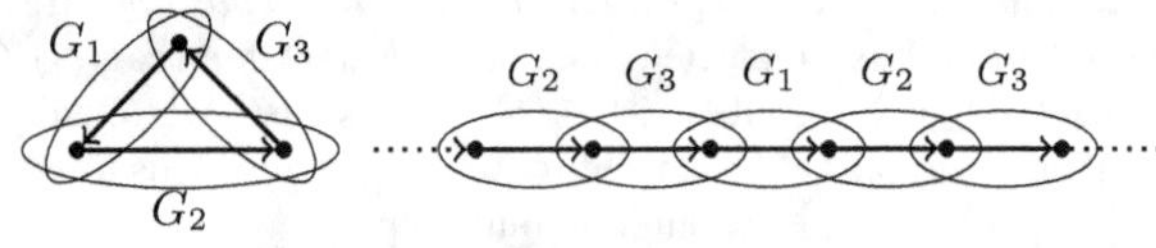

(2) Next consider the instance $\mathfrak{D}$ depicted below which has the shape of a tree of depth one with root a and has three maximal

guarded sets G_1, G_2, G_3. Then the unravelling $\mathfrak{D}^u$ of $\mathfrak{D}$ consists of three isomorphic trees of depth one of infinite outdegree (again we depict only one):

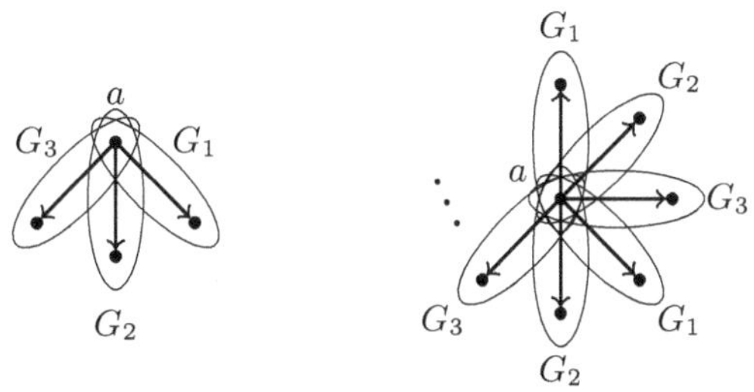

By construction, the mapping $h : e \mapsto e^\uparrow$ is a homomorphism from $\mathfrak{D}^u$ onto $\mathfrak{D}$ and the restriction of h to any guarded set G is an isomorphism. It follows that for any uGF(=) ontology $\mathcal{O}$, UCQ $q(\vec{x})$, and $\vec{a}$ in $\mathfrak{D}^u$, if $\mathcal{O}, \mathfrak{D}^u \models q(\vec{a})$, then $\mathcal{O}, \mathfrak{D} \models q(h(\vec{a}))$. This implication does not hold for ontologies in the guarded fragment with functions or counting. To see this, let

$$\mathcal{O} = \{\forall x(\exists^{\geq 4} y R(x,y) \rightarrow A(x))\}$$

Then $\mathcal{O}, \mathfrak{D}^u \models A(a)$ for the instance $\mathfrak{D}$ from Example 5 (2) but $\mathcal{O}, \mathfrak{D} \not\models A(a)$. For this reason the uGF-unravelling is not appropriate for the guarded fragment with functions or counting. By replacing Condition (c) by the stronger condition

(c′) $G_i \cap G_{i-1} \neq G_i \cap G_{i+1}$,

we obtain an unravelling that we call *uGC$_2$-unravelling* and that we apply whenever all relations have arity at most two. One can show that the uGC$_2$-unravelling of an instance preserves the number of R-successors of constants in $\mathfrak{D}$ and that, in fact, the implication '$\mathcal{O}, \mathfrak{D}^u \models q(\vec{a}) \Rightarrow \mathcal{O}, \mathfrak{D} \models q(h(\vec{a}))$' holds for every uGC$_2$(=) ontology $\mathcal{O}$, UCQ $q(\vec{x})$, and tuple $\vec{a}$ in the uGC$_2$-unravelling $\mathfrak{D}^u$ of $\mathfrak{D}$.

We are now ready to define unravelling tolerance. For a maximal guarded set G in $\mathfrak{D}$, the *copy in bag(G) of a tuple $\vec{a} = (a_1, \dots, a_k)$ in G* is the unique $\vec{b} = (b_1, \dots, b_k)$ in dom(bag(G)) such that $b_i^\uparrow = a_i$ for $1 \leq i \leq k$.

Definition 3 *A uGF(=) (resp. uGC$_2$(=)) ontology $\mathcal{O}$ is* unravelling tolerant *if for every instance $\mathfrak{D}$, every rAQ $q(\vec{x})$, and every tuple $\vec{a}$ in $\mathfrak{D}$ such that the set G of elements of $\vec{a}$ is maximally guarded in $\mathfrak{D}$ the following are equivalent:*

1. *$\mathcal{O}, \mathfrak{D} \models q(\vec{a})$;*
2. *$\mathcal{O}, \mathfrak{D}^u \models q(\vec{b})$ where $\vec{b}$ is the copy of $\vec{a}$ in bag(G)*

where $\mathfrak{D}^u$ is the uGF-unravelling (resp. the uGC$_2$-unravelling) of $\mathfrak{D}$.

We have seen above that the implication (2) $\Rightarrow$ (1) in Definition 3 holds for every uGF(=) and uGC$_2$(=) ontology and every UCQ. Note that it is pointless to define unravelling tolerance using the implication (1) $\Rightarrow$ (2) for UCQs or CQs that are not acyclic. The following example shows that (1) $\Rightarrow$ (2) does not always hold for rAQs.

Example 6 *Consider the uGF ontology $\mathcal{O}$ that contains the sentences*

$$\forall x(X(x) \rightarrow (\exists y(R(x,y) \land X(y)) \rightarrow E(x)))$$

with $X \in \{A, \neg A\}$ and

$$\forall x(E(x) \rightarrow ((R(x,y) \lor R(y,x)) \rightarrow E(y)))$$

For instances $\mathfrak{D}$ not using A, $\mathcal{O}$ states that $E(a)$ is entailed for all $a \in dom(\mathfrak{D})$ that are R-connected to some R-cycle in $\mathfrak{D}$ with an odd number of constants. Thus, for the instance $\mathfrak{D}$ from Example 5 (1) we have $\mathcal{O}, \mathfrak{D} \models E(a)$ for every $a \in dom(\mathfrak{D})$ but $\mathcal{O}, \mathfrak{D}^u \not\models E(a)$ for any $a \in dom(\mathfrak{D}^u)$.

We now show that, as announced, unraveling tolerance implies that query evaluation is Datalog$^{\neq}$-rewritable.

Theorem 5 *For all uGF(=) and uGC$_2$(=) ontologies $\mathcal{O}$, unravelling tolerance of $\mathcal{O}$ implies that rAQ-evaluation w.r.t. $\mathcal{O}$ is Datalog$^{\neq}$-rewritable (and Datalog-rewritable if $\mathcal{O}$ is formulated in uGF).*

Proof. We sketch the proof for the case that $\mathcal{O}$ is a uGF(=) ontology; similar constructions work for the other cases. Suppose that $\mathcal{O}$ is unravelling tolerant, and that $q(\vec{x})$ is a rAQ. We construct a Datalog$^{\neq}$ program Π that, given an instance $\mathfrak{D}$, computes the certain answers $\vec{a}$ of q on $\mathfrak{D}$ given $\mathcal{O}$, where w.l.o.g. we can restrict our attention to answers $\vec{a}$ such that the set G of elements of $\vec{a}$ is maximally guarded in $\mathfrak{D}$. By unravelling tolerance, it is enough to check if $\mathcal{O}, \mathfrak{D}^u \models q(\vec{b})$, where $\vec{b}$ is the copy of $\vec{a}$ in bag(G) and $\mathfrak{D}^u$ is the uGF-unravelling of $\mathfrak{D}$.

The Datalog$^{\neq}$ program Π assigns to each maximally guarded tuple $\vec{a} = (a_1, \dots, a_k)$ in $\mathfrak{D}$ a set of *types*. Here, a type is a maximally consistent set of uGF formulas with free variables in $x_1, \dots, x_k$, where the variable x_i represents the element a_i. It can be shown that we only need to consider types with formulas of the form ϕ or $\neg\phi$, where ϕ is obtained from a subformula of $\mathcal{O}$ or q by substituting a variable in $x_1, \dots, x_k$ for each of its free variables, or ϕ is an atomic formula in the signature of $\mathcal{O}, q$ with free variables in $x_1, \dots, x_k$. In particular, the set of all types is finite. We further restrict our attention to types θ that are realizable in some model of $\mathcal{O}$, i.e., there is a model $\mathfrak{B}(\theta)$ of $\mathcal{O}$ containing all elements of $\vec{a}$ that is a model of each formula in θ under the interpretation $x_i \mapsto a_i$. The Datalog$^{\neq}$ program Π ensures the following:

1. for any two maximally guarded tuples $\vec{a} = (a_1, \dots, a_k)$, $\vec{b} = (b_1, \dots, b_l)$ in $\mathfrak{D}$ that share an element, and any type θ assigned to $\vec{a}$ there is a type θ' assigned to $\vec{b}$ that is *compatible* to θ (intuitively, the two types agree on all formulas that only talk about elements shared by $\vec{a}$ and $\vec{b}$);
2. a tuple $\vec{a} = (a_1, \dots, a_k)$ is an answer to Π if all types assigned to $\vec{a}$ contain $q(x_1, \dots, x_k)$, or some maximally guarded tuple $\vec{b}$ in $\mathfrak{D}$ has no type assigned to it.

It can be shown that $\vec{a}$ is an answer to Π iff $\mathcal{O}, \mathfrak{D}^u \models q(\vec{a})$.

The interesting part is the "if" part. Suppose $\vec{a} = (a_1, \dots, a_k)$ is *not* an answer to Π. Then, each maximally guarded tuple $\vec{b}$ in $\mathfrak{D}$ is assigned to at least one type, and for some type θ^* assigned to $\vec{a}$ we have $q(x_1, \dots, x_k) \notin \theta^*$. We use this type assignment to label each maximally guarded tuple $\vec{b}$ of $\mathfrak{D}^u$ with a type $\theta_{\vec{b}}$ so that (1) for each maximally guarded tuple $\vec{c}$ of $\mathfrak{D}^u$ that shares an element with $\vec{b}$ the two types $\theta_{\vec{b}}$ and $\theta_{\vec{c}}$ are compatible; and (2) $\theta^* = \theta_{\vec{a}^*}$, where $\vec{a}^*$ is the copy of $\vec{a}$ in $G = \{a_1, \dots, a_k\}$. We can now show that the interpretation $\mathfrak{A}$ obtained from $\mathfrak{D}^u$ by hooking $\mathfrak{B}(\theta_{\vec{b}})$ to $\mathfrak{D}^u$, for all maximally guarded tuples $\vec{b}$ of $\mathfrak{D}^u$, is a model of $\mathcal{O}$ and $\mathfrak{D}^u$ with $\mathfrak{A} \not\models q(\vec{a}^*)$. □

5. DICHOTOMIES

We prove dichotomies between PTime and coNP for query evaluation in the five ontology languages displayed in the bottommost part of Figure 1. In fact, the dichotomy is even between

Datalog$^{\neq}$-rewritability and coNP. The proof establishes that for ontologies $\mathcal{O}$ formulated in any of these languages, CQ-evaluation w.r.t. $\mathcal{O}$ is Datalog$^{\neq}$-rewritable iff it is in PTIME iff $\mathcal{O}$ is unravelling tolerant iff $\mathcal{O}$ is materializable for the class of (possibly infinite) cg-tree decomposable instances iff $\mathcal{O}$ is materializable and that, if none of this is the case, CQ-evaluation w.r.t. $\mathcal{O}$ is coNP-hard. The main step towards the dichotomy result is provided by the following theorem.

Theorem 6 *Let $\mathcal{O}$ be an ontology formulated in one of uGF(1), uGF$^-(1,=)$, uGF$_2^-(2)$, uGC$_2^-(1,=)$, or an $\mathcal{ALCHIF}$ ontology of depth 2. If $\mathcal{O}$ is materializable for the class of (possibly infinite) cg-tree decomposable instances $\mathfrak{D}$ with sig$(\mathfrak{D}) \subseteq$ sig$(\mathcal{O})$, then $\mathcal{O}$ is unravelling tolerant.*

PROOF. We sketch the proof for uGF(1) and uGF$_2^-(2)$ ontologies $\mathcal{O}$ and then discuss the remaining cases. Assume that $\mathcal{O}$ satisfies the precondition from Theorem 6. Let $\mathfrak{D}$ be an instance and $\mathfrak{D}^u$ its uGF unravelling. Let $\vec{a}$ be a tuple in a maximal guarded set G in D and $\vec{b}$ be the copy in dom(bag(G)) of $\vec{a}$. Further let q be an rAQ such that $\mathcal{O}, \mathfrak{D}^u \not\models q(\vec{b})$. We have to show that $\mathcal{O}, \mathfrak{D} \not\models q(\vec{a})$. Using the condition that $\mathcal{O}$ is materializable for the class of cg-tree decomposable instances $\mathfrak{D}$ with sig$(\mathfrak{D}) \subseteq$ sig$(\mathcal{O})$, it can be shown that there exists a materialization $\mathfrak{B}$ of $\mathcal{O}$ and $\mathfrak{D}^u$.

By Lemma 1 we may assume that $\mathfrak{B}$ is a forest model which is obtained from $\mathfrak{D}^u$ by hooking cg-tree decomposable $\mathfrak{B}_{\text{bag}(t)}$ to maximal guarded bag(t) in $\mathfrak{D}^u$. Now we would like to obtain a model of $\mathcal{O}$ and the original $\mathfrak{D}$ by hooking for any maximal guarded G in $\mathfrak{D}$ the interpretation $\mathfrak{B}_{\text{bag}(G)}$ to $\mathfrak{D}$ rather than to $\mathfrak{D}^u$. However, the resulting model is then not guaranteed to be a model of $\mathcal{O}$. The following example illustrates this. Let $\mathcal{O}$ contain

$$\forall x \exists y (S(x,y) \land A(y)),$$

and for $\varphi(x) = \exists z (S(x,z) \land \neg A(z))$

$$\forall xy (R(x,y) \rightarrow (\varphi(x) \rightarrow \varphi(y))$$

Thus in every model of $\mathcal{O}$ each node has an S-successor in A and having an S-successor that is not in A is propagated along R. $\mathcal{O}$ is unravelling tolerant. Consider the instance $\mathfrak{D}$ from Example 5 (1) depicted here again with the maximal guarded sets G_1, G_2, G_3.

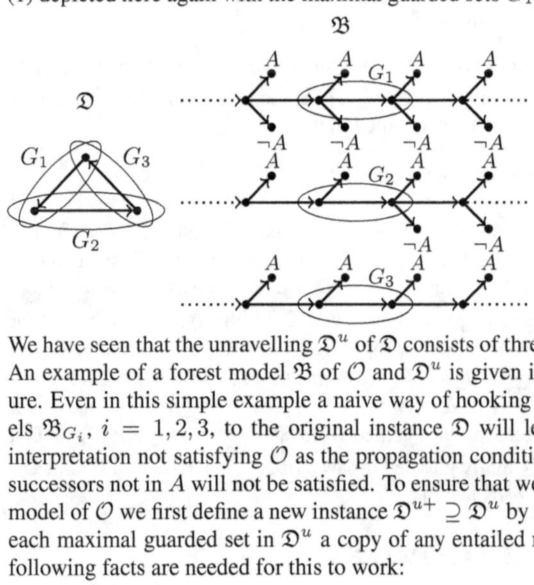

We have seen that the unravelling $\mathfrak{D}^u$ of $\mathfrak{D}$ consists of three chains. An example of a forest model $\mathfrak{B}$ of $\mathcal{O}$ and $\mathfrak{D}^u$ is given in the figure. Even in this simple example a naive way of hooking the models $\mathfrak{B}_{G_i}$, $i = 1,2,3$, to the original instance $\mathfrak{D}$ will lead to an interpretation not satisfying $\mathcal{O}$ as the propagation condition for S-successors not in A will not be satisfied. To ensure that we obtain a model of $\mathcal{O}$ we first define a new instance $\mathfrak{D}^{u+} \supseteq \mathfrak{D}^u$ by adding to each maximal guarded set in $\mathfrak{D}^u$ a copy of any entailed rAQ. The following facts are needed for this to work:

1. Automorphisms: for any $t, t' \in T(\mathfrak{D})$ with tail$(t) =$ tail(t') there is an automorphism $\hat{h}_{t,t'}$ of $\mathfrak{D}^u$ mapping bag(t) onto bag(t') and such that $\hat{h}_{t,t'}(a)^{\uparrow} = a^{\uparrow}$ for all $a \in$ dom$(\mathfrak{D}^u)$. (This is trivial in the example above.) It is for this property that we need that $\mathfrak{D}^u$ is obtained from $\mathfrak{D}$ using maximal guarded sets only and the assumption that $G_{i-1} \neq G_{i+1}$. It follows that if tail$(t) =$ tail(t') then the same rAQs are entailed at bag(t) and bag(t') in $\mathfrak{D}^u$.

2. Homomorphism preservation: if there is a homomorphism h from instance $\mathfrak{D}$ to instance $\mathfrak{D}'$ then $\mathcal{O}, \mathfrak{D} \models q(\vec{a})$ entails $\mathcal{O}, \mathfrak{D}' \models q(h(\vec{a}))$. Ontologies in uGF$(1)$ and uGF$_2^-(2)$ have this property as they do not use equality nor counting. Because of homomorphism preservation the answers in $\mathfrak{D}^u$ to rAQs are invariant under moving from $\mathfrak{D}^u$ to $\mathfrak{D}^{u+}$. Note that the remaining ontology languages in Theorem 6 do not have this property.

Now using that $\mathfrak{D}^{u+}$ is materializable w.r.t. $\mathcal{O}$ one can uniformize a materialization $\mathfrak{B}^{u+}$ of $\mathfrak{D}^{u+}$ that is a forest model in such a way that the automorphisms $\hat{h}_{t,t'}$ for tail$(t) =$ tail(t') extend to automorphisms of the resulting model $\mathfrak{B}^{u*}$ which also still satisfies $\mathcal{O}$. In the example, after uniformization all chains will behave in the same way in the sense that every node receives an S-successor not in A. We then obtain a forest model $\mathfrak{B}^*$ of $\mathfrak{D}$ by hooking the interpretations $\mathfrak{B}^{u*}_{\text{bag}(G)}$ to the maximal guarded sets G in $\mathfrak{D}$. $(\mathfrak{B}^*, \vec{a})$ and $(\mathfrak{B}^{u*}, \vec{b})$ are guarded bisimilar. Thus $\mathfrak{B}^*$ is a model of $\mathcal{O}$ and $\mathfrak{B}^* \not\models q(\vec{a})$, as required.

For uGF$^-(1,=)$ and uGC$_2^-(1,=)$ the intermediate step of constructing $\mathfrak{D}^{u+}$ is not required as sentences have smaller depth and no uniformization is needed to satisfy the ontology in the new model. For $\mathcal{ALCHIF}$ ontologies of depth 2 uniformization by constructing $\mathfrak{D}^{u+}$ is needed and has to be done carefully to preserve functionality when adding copies of entailed rAQs to $\mathfrak{D}^u$. □

We can now prove our main dichotomy result.

Theorem 7 *Let $\mathcal{O}$ be an ontology formulated in one of uGF(1), uGF$^-(1,=)$, uGF$_2^-(2)$, uGC$_2^-(1,=)$, or an $\mathcal{ALCHIF}$ ontology of depth 2. Then the following conditions are equivalent (unless* PTIME = NP*):*

1. *$\mathcal{O}$ is materializable;*

2. *$\mathcal{O}$ is materializable for the class of cg-tree decomposable instances $\mathfrak{D}$ with sig$(\mathfrak{D}) \subseteq$ sig$(\mathcal{O})$;*

3. *$\mathcal{O}$ is unravelling tolerant;*

4. *query evaluation w.r.t. $\mathcal{O}$ is Datalog$^{\neq}$-rewritable (and Datalog-rewritable if $\mathcal{O}$ is formulated in uGF);*

5. *query evaluation w.r.t. $\mathcal{O}$ is in* PTIME.

Otherwise, query evaluation w.r.t. $\mathcal{O}$ is coNP*-hard.*

PROOF. (1) $\Rightarrow$ (2) is not difficult to establish by a compactness argument. (2) $\Rightarrow$ (3) is Theorem 6. (3) $\Rightarrow$ (4) is Theorem 5. (4) $\Rightarrow$ (5) is folklore. (5) $\Rightarrow$ (1) is Theorem 3 (assuming PTIME $\neq$ NP). □

The qualification 'with sig$(\mathfrak{D}) \subseteq$ sig$(\mathcal{O})$' in Point 2 of Theorem 7 can be dropped without compromising the correctness of the theorem, and the same is true for Theorem 6. It will be useful, though, in the decision procedures developed in Section 8.

6. CSP-HARDNESS

We establish the four CSP-hardness results displayed in the middle part of Figure 1, starting with a formal definition of CSP-hardness. In addition, we derive from the existence of CSPs in PTIME that are not Datalog definable the existence of ontologies in any of these languages with PTIME query evaluation that are not Datalog$^{\neq}$ rewritability.

Let $\mathfrak{A}$ be an instance. The *constraint satisfaction problem* CSP($\mathfrak{A}$) is to decide, given an instance $\mathfrak{D}$, whether there is a homomorphism from $\mathfrak{D}$ to $\mathfrak{A}$, which we denote with $\mathfrak{D} \rightarrow \mathfrak{A}$. In this context, $\mathfrak{A}$ is called the *template* of CSP($\mathfrak{A}$). We will generally and w.l.o.g. assume that relations in sig($\mathfrak{A}$) have arity at most two and that the template $\mathfrak{A}$ *admits precoloring*, that is, for each $a \in \mathsf{dom}(\mathfrak{A})$, there is a unary relation symbol P_a such that $P_a(b) \in \mathfrak{A}$ iff $b = a$ [19]. It is known that for every template $\mathfrak{A}$, there is a template $\mathfrak{A}'$ of this form such that CSP($\mathfrak{A}$) is polynomially equivalent to CSP($\mathfrak{A}'$) [39]. We use coCSP($\mathfrak{A}$) to denote the complement of CSP($\mathfrak{A}$).

Definition 4 *Let $\mathcal{L}$ be an ontology language and $\mathcal{Q}$ a class of queries. Then $\mathcal{Q}$-evaluation w.r.t. $\mathcal{L}$ is* CSP-hard *if for every template $\mathfrak{A}$, there exists an $\mathcal{L}$ ontology $\mathcal{O}$ such that*

1. *there is a $q \in \mathcal{Q}$ such that coCSP($\mathfrak{A}$) polynomially reduces to evaluating the OMQ $(\mathcal{O}, q)$ and*

2. *for every $q \in \mathcal{Q}$, evaluating the OMQ $(\mathcal{O}, q)$ is polynomially reducible to coCSP($\mathfrak{A}$).*

It can be verified that a dichotomy between PTIME and CONP for $\mathcal{Q}$-evaluation w.r.t. $\mathcal{L}$ ontologies implies a dichotomy between PTIME and NP for CSPs, a notorious open problem known as the Feder-Vardi conjecture [23, 7], when $\mathcal{Q}$-evaluation w.r.t. $\mathcal{L}$ is CSP-hard. As noted in the introduction, a tentative proof of the conjecture has recently been announced, but at the time this article is published, its status still remains unclear.

The following theorem summarizes our results on CSP-hardness. We formulate it for CQs, but remark that due to Theorem 4, a dichotomy between PTIME and CONP for any of the mentioned ontology languages and any query language from the set {rAQ, CQ, UCQ} implies the Feder-Vardi conjecture.

Theorem 8 *For any of the following ontology languages, CQ-evaluation w.r.t. $\mathcal{L}$ is CSP-hard: $uGF_2(1,=)$, $uGF_2(2)$, $uGF_2(1,f)$, and the class of $\mathcal{ALCF}_\ell$ ontologies of depth 2.*

PROOF. We sketch the proof for $\mathrm{uGF}_2(1,=)$ and then indicate the modifications needed for $\mathrm{uGF}_2(1,f)$ and $\mathcal{ALCF}_\ell$ ontologies of depth 2. For $\mathrm{uGF}_2(2)$, the result follows from a corresponding result in [42] for $\mathcal{ALC}$ ontologies of depth 3.

Let $\mathfrak{A}$ be a template and assume w.l.o.g. that $\mathfrak{A}$ admits precoloring. Let R_a be a binary relation for each $a \in \mathsf{dom}(\mathfrak{A})$, and set

$$\begin{aligned}\varphi_a^{\neq}(x) &= \exists y(R_a(x,y) \wedge \neg(x=y))\\ \varphi_a^{=}(x) &= \exists y(R_a(x,y) \wedge (x=y))\end{aligned}$$

Then $\mathcal{O}$ contains

$$\begin{array}{ll}\forall x(\bigwedge_{a\neq a'} \neg(\varphi_a^{\neq}(x) \wedge \varphi_{a'}^{\neq}(x)) \wedge \bigvee_a \varphi_a^{\neq}(x)) & \\ \forall x(A(x) \rightarrow \neg\varphi_a^{\neq}(x)) & \text{when } A(a) \notin \mathfrak{A}\\ \forall xy(R(x,y) \rightarrow \neg(\varphi_a^{\neq}(x) \wedge \varphi_{a'}^{\neq}(y))) & \text{when } R(a,a') \notin \mathfrak{A}\\ \forall x \varphi_a^{=}(x) & \text{for all } a \in \mathsf{dom}(\mathfrak{A})\end{array}$$

where A and R range over symbols in sig($\mathfrak{A}$) of the respective arity. A formula $\varphi_a^{\neq}(x)$ being true at a constant c in an instance $\mathfrak{D}$ means that c is mapped to $a \in \mathsf{dom}(\mathfrak{A})$ by a homomorphism from $\mathfrak{D}$ to $\mathfrak{A}$. The first sentence in $\mathcal{O}$ thus ensures that every node in $\mathfrak{D}$ is mapped to exactly one node in $\mathfrak{A}$ and the second and third set of sentences ensure that we indeed obtain a homomorphism. The last set of sentences enforces that $\varphi_a^{=}(x)$ is true at every constant c. This makes the disjunction in the first sentence 'invisible' to the query (in which inequality is not available), thus avoiding that $\mathcal{O}$ is CONP-hard for trivial reasons. In the long version, we show that $\mathcal{O}$ satisfies Conditions 1 and 2 from Definition 4 where there query q used in Condition 1 is $q \leftarrow N(x)$ with N a fresh unary relation.

For $\mathrm{uGF}_2(1,f)$, state that a binary relation F is a function and that $\forall x F(x,x)$. Now replace in $\mathcal{O}$ the formulas $\varphi_a^{\neq}(x)$ by $\exists y(R_a(x,y) \wedge \neg F(x,y))$ and $\varphi_a^{=}(x)$ by $\exists y(R_a(x,y) \wedge F(x,y))$.

For $\mathcal{ALCF}_\ell$ of depth 2, replace in $\mathcal{O}$ the formulas $\varphi_a^{\neq}(x)$ by $\exists^{\geq 2} y R_a(x,y)$ and $\varphi_a^{=}(x)$ by $\exists y R_a(x,y)$. The resulting ontology is equivalent to a $\mathcal{ALCF}_\ell$ ontology of depth 2. □

It is known that for some templates $\mathfrak{A}$, CSP($\mathfrak{A}$) is in PTIME while coCSP($\mathfrak{A}$) is not Datalog$^{\neq}$-definable [23]. Then CQ-evaluation w.r.t. the ontologies $\mathcal{O}$ constructed from $\mathfrak{A}$ in the proof of Theorem 4 is in PTIME, but not Datalog$^{\neq}$-rewritable.

Theorem 9 *In any of the following ontology languages $\mathcal{L}$ there exist ontologies with* PTIME *CQ-evaluation which are not Datalog$^{\neq}$-rewritable: $uGF_2(1,=)$, $uGF_2(2)$, $uGF_2(1,f)$, and the class of $\mathcal{ALCF}_\ell$ ontologies of depth 2.*

The ontology languages in Theorem 5 thus behave provably different from the languages for which we proved a dichotomy in Section 5, since there PTIME query evaluation and Datalog$^{\neq}$-rewritability coincide.

7. NON-DICHOTOMY AND UNDECIDABILITY

We show that ontology languages that admit sentences of depth 2 as well as functions symbols tend to be computationally problematic as they do neither enjoy a dichotomy between PTIME and CONP nor decidability of meta problems such as whether query evaluation w.r.t. a given ontology $\mathcal{O}$ is in PTIME, Datalog$^{\neq}$-rewritable, or CONP-hard, and whether $\mathcal{O}$ is materializable. We actually start with these undecidability results.

Theorem 10 *For the ontology languages $uGF_2^-(2,f)$ and $\mathcal{ALCIF}_\ell$ of depth 2, it is undecidable whether for a given ontology $\mathcal{O}$,*

1. *query evaluation w.r.t. $\mathcal{O}$ is in* PTIME, *Datalog$^{\neq}$-rewritable, or* CONP*-hard (unless* PTIME = NP*);*

2. *$\mathcal{O}$ is materializable.*

PROOF. The proof is by reduction of the undecidable finite rectangle tiling problem. To establish both Points 1 and 2, it suffices to exhibit, for any such tiling problem $\mathfrak{P}$, an ontology $\mathcal{O}_\mathfrak{P}$ such that if $\mathfrak{P}$ admits a tiling, then $\mathcal{O}_\mathfrak{P}$ is not materializable and thus query evaluation w.r.t. $\mathcal{O}_\mathfrak{P}$ is CONP-hard and if $\mathfrak{P}$ admits no tiling, then query evaluation w.r.t. $\mathcal{O}_\mathfrak{P}$ is Datalog$^{\neq}$-rewritable and thus materializable (unless PTIME = NP).

The rectangle to be tiled is represented in input instances using the binary relations X and Y, and $\mathcal{O}_\mathfrak{P}$ declares these relations and their inverses to be functional. The main idea in the construction of $\mathcal{O}_\mathfrak{P}$ is to verify the existence of a properly tiled grid in the input instance by propagating markers from the top right corner to the lower left corner. During the propagation, one makes sure that grid cells close (that is, the XY-successor coincides with the

YX-successor) and that there is a tiling that satisfies the constraints in $\mathfrak{P}$. Once the existence of a properly tiled grid is completed, a disjunction is derived by $\mathcal{O}_\mathfrak{P}$ to achieve non-materializability and coNP-hardness. The challenge is to implement this construction such that when $\mathfrak{P}$ has no solution (and thus the verification of a properly tiled grid can never complete), $\mathcal{O}_\mathfrak{P}$ is Datalog$^{\neq}$-rewritable. In fact, achieving this involves a lot of technical subtleties.

A central issue is how to implement the markers (as formulas with one free variable) that are propagated through the grid during the verification. The markers must be designed in a way so that they cannot be 'preset' in the input instance as this would make it possible to prevent the verification of a (possibly defective) part of the input. In $\mathcal{ALCIF}_\ell$, we use formulas of the form $\exists^{=1} y P(x,y)$ while additionally stating in $\mathcal{O}_\mathfrak{P}$ that $\forall x \exists y P(x,y)$. Thus, the choice is only between whether a constant has exactly one P-successor (which means that the marker is set) or more than one P-successor (which means that the marker is not set). Clearly, this difference is invisible to queries and we cannot preset a marker in an input instance in the sense that we make it true at some constant. We can, however, easily make the marker false at a constant c by adding two P-successors to c in the input instance. It seems that this effect, which gives rise to many technical complications, can only be avoided by using marker formulas with higher quantifier depth which would result in $\mathcal{O}_\mathfrak{P}$ not falling within $\mathcal{ALCIF}_\ell$ depth 2. For uGF$_2^-(2,f)$ we work with $\neg\exists y(P(x,y) \wedge \neg F(x,y))$, where F is a function for which we state $\forall x F(x,x)$ (as in the CSP encoding).

Full proof details can be found in the long version. We only mention that closing of a grid cell is verified by using marker formulas as second-order variables. □

Theorem 11 *For the ontology languages uGF$_2^-(2,f)$ and $\mathcal{ALCIF}_\ell$ of depth 2, there is no dichotomy between* PTIME *and* coNP *(unless* PTIME = coNP*).*

By Ladner's theorem [38], there is a non-deterministic polynomial time Turing machine (TM) whose word problem is neither in PTIME nor NP-hard (unless PTIME = coNP). Ideally, we would like to reduce the word problem of such TMs to prove Theorem 11. However, this does not appear to be easily possible, for the following reason. In the reduction, we use a grid construction and marker formulas as in the proof of Theorem 10, with the grid providing the space in which the run of the TM is simulated and markers representing TM states and tape symbols. We cannot avoid that the markers can be preset either positively or negatively in the input (depending on the marker formulas we choose), which means that some parts of the run are not 'free', but might be predetermined or at least constrained in some way. We solve this problem by first establishing an appropriate variation of Ladner's theorem.

We consider non-deterministic TMs M with a single one-sided infinite tape. Configurations of M are represented by strings vqw, where q is the state, and v and w are the contents of the tape to the left and to the right of the tape head, respectively. A *partial configuration* of M is obtained from a configuration γ of M by replacing some or all symbols of γ by a wildcard symbol $\star$. A partial configuration $\tilde{\gamma}$ *matches* a configuration γ if it has the same length and agrees with γ on all non-wildcard symbols. A *partial run* of M is a finite sequence $\tilde{\gamma}_0, \dots, \tilde{\gamma}_m$ of partial configurations of M of the same length. It is a *run* if each $\tilde{\gamma}_i$ is a configuration, and it *matches* a run $\gamma_0, \dots, \gamma_n$ if $m = n$ and each $\tilde{\gamma}_i$ matches γ_i. A run is accepting if its last configuration has an accepting state. Note that runs need not start in any specific configuration (unless specified by a partial run that they extend). The *run fitting problem* for M is to decide whether a given partial run of M matches some accepting run of M. It is easy to see that for any TM M, the run fitting problem for M is in NP. We prove the following result in the long version by a careful adaptation of the proof of Ladner's theorem given in [2].

Theorem 12 *There is a non-deterministic Turing machine whose run fitting problem is neither in* PTIME *nor* NP*-hard (unless* PTIME = NP*).*

Now Theorem 11 is a consequence of the following lemma.

Lemma 4 *For every Turing machine M, there is a uGF$_2^-(2,f)$ ontology $\mathcal{O}$ and an $\mathcal{ALCIF}_\ell$ ontology $\mathcal{O}$ of depth 2 such that the following hold, where N is a distinguished unary relation:*

1. *there is a polynomial reduction of the run fitting problem for M to the complement of evaluating the OMQ $(\mathcal{O}, q \leftarrow N(x))$;*
2. *for every UCQ q, evaluating the OMQ $(\mathcal{O}, q)$ is polynomially reducible to the complement of the run fitting problem for M.*

To establish Lemma 4, we re-use the ontology $\mathcal{O}_\mathfrak{P}$ from the proof of Theorem 10, using a trivial rectangle tiling problem. When the existence of the grid has been verified, instead of triggering a disjunction as before, we now start a simulation of M on the grid. For both $\mathcal{ALCIF}_\ell$ and uGF$_2^-(2,f)$, we represent states q and tape symbols G using the same formulas as in the CSP encoding of homomorphisms. Thus, for $\mathcal{ALCIF}_\ell$ we use formulas $\exists^{\geq 2} y q(x,y)$ and $\exists^{\geq 2} y G(x,y)$, respectively, using q and G as binary relations. Note that here the encoding $\exists^{=1} y q(x,y)$ from the tiling problem does not work because states and tape symbols can be positively preset in the input instance rather than negatively, which is in correspondence with the run fitting problem.

8. DECISION PROBLEMS

We study the decidability and complexity of the problem to decide whether a given ontology admits PTIME query evaluation. Realistically, we can only hope for positive results in cases where there is a dichotomy between PTIME and coNP: first, we have shown in Section 7 that for cases with provably no such dichotomy, meta problems are typically undecidable; and second, it does not seem very likely that in the CSP-hard cases, one can decide whether an ontology admits PTIME query evaluation without resolving the dichotomy question and thus solving the Feder-Vardi conjecture. Our main results are EXPTIME-completeness of deciding PTIME-query evalutation of $\mathcal{ALCHIQ}$ ontologies of depth one (the same complexity as for satisfiability) and a NEXPTIME upper bound for uGC$_2^-(1,=)$ ontologies. Note that, in both of the considered languages, PTIME-query evalutation coincides with rewritability into Datalog$^{\neq}$. We remind the reader that according to our experiments, a large majority of real world ontologies are $\mathcal{ALCHIQ}$ ontologies of depth 1. We also show that for $\mathcal{ALC}$ ontologies of depth 2, the mentioned problem is NEXPTIME-hard.

Since the ontology languages relevant here admit at most binary relations, an interpretation $\mathfrak{B}$ is cg-tree decomposable if and only if the undirected graph $G_\mathfrak{B} = \{\{a,b\} \mid R(a,b) \in \mathfrak{B}, a \neq b\}$ is a tree. For simplicity, we speak of *tree interpretations* and of *tree instances*, defined likewise. The *outdegree of* $\mathfrak{B}$ is the outdegree of $G_\mathfrak{B}$.

Theorem 13 *For uGC$_2^-(1,=)$ ontologies, deciding whether query evaluation w.r.t. a given ontology is in* PTIME *(equivalently: rewritable into Datalog$^{\neq}$) is in* NEXPTIME. *For $\mathcal{ALCHIQ}$ ontologies of depth 1, this problem is in* EXPTIME*-complete.*

The main insight underlying the proof of Theorem 13 is that for ontologies formulated in the mentioned languages, materializability (which by Theorem 7 coincides with PTIME query evaluation) already follows from the existence of materializations for tree instances of depth 1. We make this precise in the following lemma. Given a tree interpretation $\mathfrak{B}$ and $a \in \text{dom}(\mathfrak{B})$, define the *1-neighbourhood* $\mathfrak{B}_a^{\leq 1}$ of a in $\mathfrak{B}$ as $\mathfrak{B}_{|X}$, where X is the union of all guarded sets in $\mathfrak{B}$ that contain a. $\mathfrak{B}$ is a *bouquet with root* a if $\mathfrak{B}_a^{\leq 1} = \mathfrak{B}$ and it is *irreflexive* if there exists no atom of the form $R(b, b)$ in $\mathfrak{B}$.

Lemma 5 *Let $\mathcal{O}$ be a uGC$_2^-(1,=)$ ontology (resp. an $\mathcal{ALCHIQ}$ ontology of depth 1). Then $\mathcal{O}$ is materializable iff $\mathcal{O}$ is materializable for the class of all (respectively, all irreflexive) bouquets $\mathfrak{D}$ of outdegree $\leq |\mathcal{O}|$ with sig$(\mathfrak{D}) \subseteq$ sig$(\mathcal{O})$.*

PROOF. We require some notation. An instance $\mathfrak{D}$ is called *$\mathcal{O}$-saturated* for an ontology $\mathcal{O}$ if for all facts $R(\vec{a})$ with $\vec{a} \subseteq \text{dom}(\mathfrak{D})$ such that $\mathcal{O}, \mathfrak{D} \models R(\vec{a})$ it follows that $R(\vec{a}) \in \mathfrak{D}$. For every $\mathcal{O}$ and instance $\mathfrak{D}$ there exists a unique minimal (w.r.t. set-inclusion) $\mathcal{O}$-saturated instance $\mathfrak{D}_\mathcal{O} \supseteq \mathfrak{D}$. We call $\mathfrak{D}_\mathcal{O}$ the *$\mathcal{O}$-saturation of* $\mathfrak{D}$. It is easy to see that there is a materialization of $\mathcal{O}$ and $\mathfrak{D}$ if and only if there is a materialization of $\mathcal{O}$ and the $\mathcal{O}$-saturation of $\mathfrak{D}$.

We first prove Lemma 5 for uGC$_2^-(1,=)$ ontologies $\mathcal{O}$ and without the condition on the outdegree. Let $\Sigma_0 = \text{sig}(\mathcal{O})$ and assume that $\mathcal{O}$ is materializable for the class of all Σ_0-bouquets. By Theorem 7 it suffices to prove that $\mathcal{O}$ is materializable for the class of Σ_0-tree instances. Fix a Σ_0-tree instance $\mathfrak{D}$ that is consistent w.r.t. $\mathcal{O}$. We may assume that $\mathfrak{D}$ is $\mathcal{O}$-saturated. Note that a forest model materialization $\mathfrak{B}$ of an ontology $\mathcal{O}$ and an $\mathcal{O}$-saturated instance $\mathfrak{F}$ consists of $\mathfrak{F}$ and tree interpretations $\mathfrak{B}_a$, $a \in \text{dom}(\mathfrak{F})$, that are hooked to $\mathfrak{F}$ at a. Take for any $a \in \text{dom}(\mathfrak{D})$ the bouquet $\mathfrak{D}_a^{\leq 1}$ with root a and hook to $\mathfrak{D}$ at a the interpretation $\mathfrak{B}_a$ that is hooked to $\mathfrak{D}_a^{\leq 1}$ at a in a forest model materialization $\mathfrak{B}$ of $\mathfrak{D}_a^{\leq 1}$ and $\mathcal{O}$ (such a forest model materialization exists since $\mathfrak{D}_a^{\leq 1}$ is materializable). Denote by $\mathfrak{A}$ the resulting interpretation. Using the condition that $\mathcal{O}$ is a uGC$_2^-(1,=)$ ontology it is not difficult to prove that $\mathfrak{A}$ is a materialization of $\mathcal{O}$ and $\mathfrak{D}$.

We now prove the restriction on the outdegree. Assume $\mathcal{O}$ is given. Let $\mathfrak{D}$ be a bouquet with root a of minimal outdegree such that there is no materialization of $\mathcal{O}$ and $\mathfrak{D}$. We show that the outdegree of $\mathfrak{D}$ does not exceed $|\mathcal{O}|$. Assume the outdegree of $\mathfrak{D}$ is at least three (otherwise we are done). We may assume that $\mathfrak{D}$ is $\mathcal{O}$-saturated. Take for any formula $\chi = \exists^{\geq n} z_1 \alpha(z_1, z_2) \wedge \varphi(z_1, z_2)$ that occurs as a subformula in $\mathcal{O}$ the set Z_χ of all $b \neq a$ such that $\mathfrak{D} \models \alpha(b, a) \wedge \varphi(b, a)$. Let $Z'_\chi = Z_\chi$ if $|Z_\chi| \leq n + 1$; otherwise let Z'_χ be a subset of Z_χ of cardinality $n + 1$. Let $\mathfrak{D}'$ be the restriction $\mathfrak{D}_{|Z}$ of $\mathfrak{D}$ to the union Z of all Z'_χ and $\{a\}$. We show that there exists no materialization of $\mathfrak{D}'$ and $\mathcal{O}$. Assume for a proof by contradiction that there is a materialization $\mathfrak{B}$ of $\mathfrak{D}'$. Let $\mathfrak{B}'$ be the union of $\mathfrak{D} \cup \mathfrak{B}$ and the interpretations $\mathfrak{B}_b$, $b \in \text{dom}(\mathfrak{D}) \setminus (Z \cup \{a\})$, that are hooked to $\mathfrak{D}_{|\{a,b\}}$ at b in a forest model materialization of $\mathfrak{D}_{|\{a,b\}}$. We show that $\mathfrak{B}'$ is a materialization of $\mathfrak{D}$ and $\mathcal{O}$ (and thus derive a contradiction). Using the condition that $\mathfrak{D}$ is $\mathcal{O}$-saturated one can show that the restriction $\mathfrak{B}'_{|\text{dom}(\mathfrak{D})}$ of $\mathfrak{B}'$ to dom$(\mathfrak{D})$ coincides with $\mathfrak{D}$. Using the condition that $\mathcal{O}$ has depth 1 it is now easy to show that $\mathfrak{B}'$ is a model of $\mathcal{O}$. It is a materialization of $\mathfrak{D}$ and $\mathcal{O}$ since it is composed of materializations of subinstances of $\mathfrak{D}$ and $\mathcal{O}$.

The proof that irreflexive bouquets are sufficient for ontologies of depth 1 in $\mathcal{ALCHIQ}$ is similar to the proof above and uses the fact that one can always unravel models of $\mathcal{ALCHIQ}$ ontologies into irreflexive tree models. □

We now develop algorithms that decide PTIME query evaluation by checking the conditions given in Lemma 5, starting with the (easier) case of $\mathcal{ALCHIQ}$. Let $\mathfrak{D}$ be a bouquet with root a. Call a bouquet $\mathfrak{B} \supseteq \mathfrak{D}$ a *1-materialization of $\mathcal{O}$ and $\mathfrak{D}$* if

- there exists a model $\mathfrak{A}$ of $\mathcal{O}$ and $\mathfrak{D}$ such that $\mathfrak{B} = \mathfrak{A}_a^{\leq 1}$;
- for any model $\mathfrak{A}$ of $\mathfrak{D}$ and $\mathcal{O}$ there exists a homomorphism from $\mathfrak{B}$ to $\mathfrak{A}$ that preserves dom$(\mathfrak{D})$.

It turns out that, when checking materializability, not only is it sufficient to consider bouquets instead of unrestricted instances, but additionally one can concentrate on 1-materializations of bouquets.

Lemma 6 *Let $\mathcal{O}$ be an $\mathcal{ALCHIQ}$ ontology of depth 1. If for all irreflexive bouquets $\mathfrak{D}$ that are consistent w.r.t. $\mathcal{O}$, of outdegree $\leq |\mathcal{O}|$, and satisfy sig$(\mathfrak{D}) \subseteq$ sig$(\mathcal{O})$ there is a 1-materialization of $\mathcal{O}$ and $\mathfrak{D}$, then $\mathcal{O}$ is materializable for the class of all such bouquets.*

PROOF. For brevity, we call an irreflexive bouquet $\mathfrak{F}$ *relevant* if it is consistent w.r.t. $\mathcal{O}$, of outdegree $\leq |\mathcal{O}|$ and satisfies sig$(\mathfrak{F}) \subseteq$ sig$(\mathcal{O})$. An *irreflexive 1-materializability witness* $(\mathfrak{F}, a, \mathfrak{B})$ consists of a relevant irreflexive bouquet $\mathfrak{F}$ with root a and a 1-materialization $\mathfrak{B}$ of $\mathfrak{F}$ w.r.t. $\mathcal{O}$. One can show that $\mathfrak{B}$ is an irreflexive tree interpretation.

Now let $\mathfrak{D}$ be a relevant irreflexive bouquet with root a and assume that $\mathfrak{D}$ is 1-materializable w.r.t. $\mathcal{O}$. We have to show that there exists a materialization of $\mathcal{O}$ and $\mathfrak{D}$. Note that for every relevant irreflexive bouquet $\mathfrak{F}$, there is a 1-materializability witness $(\mathfrak{F}, a, \mathfrak{B})$. We construct the desired materialization step-by-step using these pairs also memorizing sets of frontier elements that have to be expanded in the next step. We start with the irreflexive 1-materializability witness $(\mathfrak{D}, a, \mathfrak{B})$ and set $\mathfrak{B}^0 = \mathfrak{B}$ and $F_0 = \text{dom}(\mathfrak{B}) \setminus \{a\}$. Then we construct a sequence of irreflexive tree interpretations $\mathfrak{B}^0 \subseteq \mathfrak{B}^1 \subseteq \ldots$ and frontier sets $F_{i+1} \subseteq \text{dom}(\mathfrak{B}^{i+1}) \setminus \text{dom}(\mathfrak{B}^i)$ inductively as follows: given $\mathfrak{B}^i$ and F_i, take for any $b \in F_i$ its predecessor a in $\mathfrak{B}^i$ and an irreflexive 1-materializability witness $(\mathfrak{B}^i_{|\{a,b\}}, b, \mathfrak{B}_b)$ and set

$$\mathfrak{B}^{i+1} := \mathfrak{B}^i \cup \bigcup_{b \in F_i} \mathfrak{B}_b \qquad F_{i+1} := \bigcup_{b \in F_i} \text{dom}(\mathfrak{B}_b) \setminus \{b\}$$

Let $\mathfrak{B}^*$ be the union of all $\mathfrak{B}_i$. We show that $\mathfrak{B}$ is a materialization of $\mathcal{O}$ and $\mathfrak{D}$. $\mathfrak{B}$ is a model of $\mathcal{O}$ by construction since $\mathcal{O}$ is an $\mathcal{ALCHIQ}$ ontology of depth 1. Consider a model $\mathfrak{A}$ of $\mathcal{O}$ and $\mathfrak{D}$. It suffices to construct a homomorphism h from $\mathfrak{B}^*$ to $\mathfrak{A}$ that preserves dom$(\mathfrak{D})$. We may assume that $\mathfrak{A}$ is an irreflexive tree interpretation. We construct h as the limit of a sequence $h_0, \ldots$ of homomorphisms from $\mathfrak{B}^i$ to $\mathfrak{A}$. By definition, there exists a homomorphism h_0 from $\mathfrak{B}^0$ to $\mathfrak{A}_a^{\leq 1}$ preserving dom$(\mathfrak{D})$. Now, inductively, assume that h_i is a homomorphism from $\mathfrak{B}^i$ to $\mathfrak{A}$. Assume c has been added to $\mathfrak{B}^i$ in the construction of $\mathfrak{B}^{i+1}$. Then there exists $b \in F_i$ and its predecessor a in $\mathfrak{B}^i$ such that $c \in \text{dom}(\mathfrak{B}_b) \setminus \{b\}$, where $\mathfrak{B}_b$ is the irreflexive tree interpretation that has been added to $\mathfrak{B}^i$ as the last component of the irreflexive model pair $(\mathfrak{B}^i_{|\{a,b\}}, b, \mathfrak{B}_b)$. But then, as $\mathfrak{B}_b$ is a 1-materialization of $\mathfrak{B}^i_{|\{a,b\}}$ and h_i is injective on $\mathfrak{B}^i_{|\{a,b\}}$ (since $\mathfrak{A}$ is irreflexive), we can expand the homomorphism h_i to a homomorphism to $\mathfrak{A}$ with domain dom$(\mathfrak{B}^i) \cup \{c\}$. Thus, we can expand h_i to a homomorphism from $\mathfrak{B}^{i+1}$ to $\mathfrak{A}$. □

Lemma 5 and Lemma 6 imply that an $\mathcal{ALCHIQ}$ ontology $\mathcal{O}$ of depth 1 enjoys PTIME query evaluation if and only if all irreflexive bouquets $\mathfrak{D}$ that are consistent w.r.t. $\mathcal{O}$, of outdegree $\leq |\mathcal{O}|$, and satisfy sig$(\mathfrak{D}) \subseteq$ sig$(\mathcal{O})$ have a 1-materialization w.r.t. $\mathcal{O}$.

The latter condition can be checked in deterministic exponential time since the satisfiability problem for $\mathcal{ALCHIQ}$ ontologies is in EXPTIME. Moreover, there are only exponentially many relevant bouquets. We have thus proved the EXPTIME upper bound in Theorem 13. A matching lower bound can be proved by a straightforward reduction from satisfiability.

The following example shows that, in contrast to $\mathcal{ALCHIQ}$ depth 1, for $\text{uGC}_2^-(1,=)$ the existence of 1-materializations does not guarantee materializability of bouquets.

Example 7 *We use $\exists^{\neq} yW(x,y)$ to abbreviate $\exists y(W(x,y) \wedge (x \neq y))$ and likewise for $\exists^{\neq} yW(y,x)$. Let S, S', R, R' be binary relation symbols and $\mathcal{O}$ the $\text{uGF}_2^-(1,=)$ ontology $\mathcal{O}$ that contains*

$$\forall x(S(x,x) \rightarrow (R(x,x) \rightarrow (\exists^{\neq} yR(x,y) \vee \exists^{\neq} yS(x,y))))$$
$$\forall x(\exists^{\neq} yW(y,x) \rightarrow \exists yW'(x,y))$$

where (W,W') range over $\{(R,R'),(S,S')\}$. Observe that for the instance $\mathfrak{D} = \{(S(a,a), R(a,a)\}$ and the Boolean UCQ

$$q \leftarrow R'(x,y) \vee S'(x,y),$$

we have $\mathcal{O}, \mathfrak{D} \models q$. Also, for $q_R \leftarrow R'(x,y)$ and $q_S \leftarrow S'(x,y)$ we have $\mathcal{O}, \mathfrak{D} \not\models q_R$ and $\mathcal{O}, \mathfrak{D} \not\models q_S$. Thus, $\mathcal{O}$ is not materializable. It is, however, easy to show that for every bouquet $\mathfrak{D}$ there exists a 1-materialization of $\mathfrak{D}$ w.r.t. $\mathcal{O}$.

In $\text{uGC}_2^-(1,=)$, we thus have to check unrestricted materializability of bouquets, instead of 1-materializability. In fact, it suffices to consider materializations that are tree interpretations. To decide the existence of such materialization, we use a mosaic approach. In each mosaic piece, we essentially record a 1-neighborhood of the materialization, a 1-neighborhood of a model of the bouquet and ontology, and a homomorphism from the former to the latter. We then identify certain conditions that characterize when a set of mosaics can be assembled into a materialization in a way that is similar to the model construction in the proof of Lemma 6. There are actually two different kinds of mosaic pieces that we use, with one kind of piece explicitly addressing reflexive loops which, as illustrated by Example 7, are the reason why we cannot work with 1-materializations. The decision procedure then consists of guessing a set of mosaics and verifying that the required conditions are satisfied. Details are in the long version.

Theorem 13 only covers ontology languages of depth 1. It would be desirable to establish decidability also for ontology languages of depth 2 that enjoy a dichotomy between PTIME and CONP, such as $\text{uGF}_2^-(2)$. The following example shows that this requires more sophisticated techniques than those used above. In particular, materializability of bouquets does not imply materializability.

Example 8 *We give a family of $\mathcal{ALC}$-ontologies $(\mathcal{O}_n)_{n\geq 0}$ of depth 2 such that each $\mathcal{O}_n$ is materializable for the class of tree interpretations of depth at most $2^n - 1$ while it is not materializable. The idea is that any instance $\mathfrak{D}$ that witnesses non-materializability of $\mathcal{O}_n$ must contain an R-chain of length 2^n, R a binary relation. The presence of this chain is verified by propagating a marker upwards along the chain. To avoid that $\mathcal{O}$ is 1-materializable, we represent this marker by a universally quantified formula and also hide some other unary predicates in the same way. For each unary predicate P, let $H_P(x)$ denote the formula $\forall y(S(x,y) \rightarrow P(y))$ and include in $\mathcal{O}_n$ the sentence $\forall x \exists y(S(x,y) \wedge P(y))$. The remaining sentences in $\mathcal{O}_n$ are:*

$$\overline{X}_1(x) \wedge \cdots \wedge \overline{X}_n(x) \rightarrow H_V(x)$$
$$X_i(x) \wedge \exists R.(X_i(y) \wedge X_j(y)) \rightarrow H_{\mathsf{ok}_i}(x)$$
$$\overline{X}_i(x) \wedge \exists R.(\overline{X}_i(y) \wedge X_j(y)) \rightarrow H_{\mathsf{ok}_i}(x)$$
$$X_i(x) \wedge \exists R.(\overline{X}_i(y) \wedge X_1(y) \wedge \cdots \wedge X_{i-1}(y)) \rightarrow H_{\mathsf{ok}_i}(x)$$
$$\overline{X}_i(x) \wedge \exists R.(X_i(y) \wedge X_1(y) \wedge \cdots \wedge \overline{X}_{i-1}(y)) \rightarrow H_{\mathsf{ok}_i}(x)$$
$$H_{\mathsf{ok}_1}(x) \wedge \cdots \wedge H_{\mathsf{ok}_n}(x) \wedge \exists R.H_V(y) \rightarrow H_V(x)$$
$$\exists R.X_i(y) \wedge \exists R.\overline{X}_i(y) \rightarrow \bot$$
$$X_1(x) \wedge \cdots \wedge X_n(x) \wedge H_V(x) \rightarrow B_1(x) \vee B_2(x)$$

where x is universally quantified, $\exists R.\varphi(y)$ is an abbreviation for $\exists y(R(x,y) \wedge \varphi(y))$, and i ranges over 1..n. Note that $X_1, \ldots, X_n$ and $\overline{X}_1, \ldots, \overline{X}_n$ represent a binary counter and that lines two to five implement incrementation of this counter. The second last formula is necessary to avoid that multiple successors of a node interact in undesired ways. On instances that contain no R-chain of length 2^n, a materialization can be constructed by a straightforward chase procedure.

We also observe that the ideas from Example 8 gives rise to a NEXPTIME lower bound.

Theorem 14 *For $\mathcal{ALC}$ ontologies of depth 2, deciding whether query-evaluation is in* PTIME *is* NEXPTIME*-hard (unless* PTIME = CONP*).*

We remark that the decidability of PTIME query evaluation of $\mathcal{ALC}$ ontologies of depth 2 remains open.

9. CONCLUSION

Perhaps the most surprizing result of our analysis is that it is possible to escape Ladner's Theorem and prove a PTIME/CONP dichotomy for query evaluation for rather large subsets of the guarded fragment that cover almost all practically relevant DL ontologies. This result comes with a characterization of PTIME query evaluation in terms of materializability and unravelling tolerance, with the guarantee that PTIME query evaluation coincides with Datalog$^{\neq}$-rewritability, and with decidability of (and complexity results for) meta problems such as deciding whether a given ontology enjoys PTIME query evaluation. Our study also shows that when we increase the expressive power in seemingly harmless ways, then often there is provably no PTIME/CONP dichotomy or one obtains CSP-hardness. The proof of the non-dichotomy results comes with a variation of Ladner's Theorem that could prove useful in other contexts where some form of precoloring of the input is unavoidable, such as in consistent query answering [43].

There are a number of interesting future research questions. The main open questions regarding dichotomies are whether the PTIME/CONP dichotomy can be generalized from $\text{uGF}_2^-(2)$ to $\text{uGF}^-(2)$ and whether the CSP-hardness results can be sharpened to either CSP-equivalence results (this is known for $\mathcal{ALC}$ ontologies of depth 3 [42]) or to non-dichotomy results. Also of interest is the complexity of deciding PTIME query evaluation for $\text{uGF}(1)$, where the characterization of PTIME query evaluation via hom-universal models fails. Improving our current complexity results to tight complexity bounds for PTIME query evaluation for $\mathcal{ALCHIF}$ ontologies of depth 2 and $\text{uGF}_2^-(2)$ ontologies appears to be challenging as well. It would also be interesting to study the case where invariance under disjoint union is not guaranteed (as we have observed, the complexities of CQ and UCQ evaluation might then diverge), and to add the ability to declare in an ontology that a binary relation is transitive.

10. ACKNOWLEDGMENTS

André Hernich, Fabio Papacchini, and Frank Wolter were supported by EPSRC UK grant EP/M012646/1. Carsten Lutz was supported by ERC CoG 647289 CODA.

11. REFERENCES

[1] H. Andréka, I. Németi, and J. van Benthem. Modal languages and bounded fragments of predicate logic. *J. Philosophical Logic*, 27(3):217–274, 1998.

[2] S. Arora and B. Barak. *Computational Complexity - A Modern Approach*. Cambridge University Press, 2009.

[3] A. Artale, D. Calvanese, R. Kontchakov, and M. Zakharyaschev. The DL-Lite family and relations. *J. of Artifical Intelligence Research*, 36:1–69, 2009.

[4] F. Baader, Deborah, D. Calvanese, D. L. McGuiness, D. Nardi, and P. F. Patel-Schneider, editors. *The Description Logic Handbook*. Cambridge University Press, 2003.

[5] V. Bárány, G. Gottlob, and M. Otto. Querying the guarded fragment. *Logical Methods in Computer Science*, 10(2), 2014.

[6] V. Bárány, B. ten Cate, and L. Segoufin. Guarded negation. *J. ACM*, 62(3):22:1–22:26, 2015.

[7] L. Barto. Constraint satisfaction problem and universal algebra. *SIGLOG News*, 1(2):14–24, 2014.

[8] C. Beeri and P. A. Bernstein. Computational problems related to the design of normal form relational schemas. *ACM Trans. Database Syst.*, 4(1):30–59, 1979.

[9] C. Beeri and M. Y. Vardi. A proof procedure for data dependencies. *J. ACM*, 31(4):718–741, 1984.

[10] M. Bienvenu and M. Ortiz. Ontology-mediated query answering with data-tractable description logics. In *Proc. of Reasoning Web*, pages 218–307, 2015.

[11] M. Bienvenu, B. ten Cate, C. Lutz, and F. Wolter. Ontology-based data access: A study through disjunctive datalog, csp, and MMSNP. *ACM Trans. Database Syst.*, 39(4):33:1–33:44, 2014.

[12] A. Calì, G. Gottlob, and M. Kifer. Taming the infinite chase: Query answering under expressive relational constraints. *J. Artif. Intell. Res. (JAIR)*, 48:115–174, 2013.

[13] A. Calì, G. Gottlob, and A. Pieris. Towards more expressive ontology languages: The query answering problem. *Artif. Intell.*, 193:87–128, 2012.

[14] D. Calvanese, G. De Giacomo, D. Lembo, M. Lenzerini, and R. Rosati. Data complexity of query answering in description logics. *Artificial Intelligence*, 195:335–360, 2013.

[15] D. Calvanese, G. De Giacomo, and M. Lenzerini. On the decidability of query containment under constraints. In *Proc. of PODS*, pages 149–158, 1998.

[16] D. Calvanese, G. D. Giacomo, D. Lembo, M. Lenzerini, and R. Rosati. Tractable reasoning and efficient query answering in description logics: The DL-Lite family. *J. Autom. Reasoning*, 39(3):385–429, 2007.

[17] D. Calvanese, G. D. Giacomo, M. Lenzerini, and M. Y. Vardi. View-based query processing and constraint satisfaction. In *LICS*, pages 361–371, 2000.

[18] D. Calvanese, G. D. Giacomo, M. Lenzerini, and M. Y. Vardi. View-based query containment. In *PODS*, pages 56–67, 2003.

[19] D. Cohen and P. Jeavons. *The complexity of constraint languages*, chapter 8. Elsevier, 2006.

[20] A. Deutsch, A. Nash, and J. B. Remmel. The chase revisited. In M. Lenzerini and D. Lembo, editors, *Proc. of PODS*, pages 149–158. ACM, 2008.

[21] R. Fagin, B. Kimelfeld, and P. G. Kolaitis. Dichotomies in the complexity of preferred repairs. In *Proc. of PODS*, pages 3–15, 2015.

[22] R. Fagin, P. G. Kolaitis, R. J. Miller, and L. Popa. Data exchange: semantics and query answering. *Theor. Comput. Sci.*, 336(1):89–124, 2005.

[23] T. Feder and M. Y. Vardi. The computational structure of monotone monadic SNP and constraint satisfaction: A study through datalog and group theory. *SIAM J. Comput.*, 28(1):57–104, 1998.

[24] G. Fontaine. Why is it hard to obtain a dichotomy for consistent query answering? *ACM Trans. Comput. Log.*, 16(1):7:1–7:24, 2015.

[25] C. Freire, W. Gatterbauer, N. Immerman, and A. Meliou. The complexity of resilience and responsibility for self-join-free conjunctive queries. *PVLDB*, 9(3):180–191, 2015.

[26] G. Gottlob, S. Kikot, R. Kontchakov, V. V. Podolskii, T. Schwentick, and M. Zakharyaschev. The price of query rewriting in ontology-based data access. *Artif. Intell.*, 213:42–59, 2014.

[27] G. Gottlob, M. Manna, and A. Pieris. Polynomial rewritings for linear existential rules. In *Proc. of IJCAI*, pages 2992–2998, 2015.

[28] G. Gottlob, G. Orsi, and A. Pieris. Query rewriting and optimization for ontological databases. *ACM Trans. Database Syst.*, 39(3):25:1–25:46, 2014.

[29] E. Grädel. On the restraining power of guards. *J. Symb. Log.*, 64(4):1719–1742, 1999.

[30] E. Grädel and M. Otto. The freedoms of (guarded) bisimulation. In *Johan van Benthem on Logic and Information Dynamics*, pages 3–31. 2014.

[31] M. Kaminski, Y. Nenov, and B. C. Grau. Datalog rewritability of disjunctive datalog programs and non-horn ontologies. *Artif. Intell.*, 236:90–118, 2016.

[32] Y. Kazakov. A polynomial translation from the two-variable guarded fragment with number restrictions to the guarded fragment. In *Proc. of JELIA*, pages 372–384, 2004.

[33] B. Kimelfeld. A dichotomy in the complexity of deletion propagation with functional dependencies. In M. Benedikt, M. Krötzsch, and M. Lenzerini, editors, *Proc. of PODS*, pages 191–202. ACM, 2012.

[34] R. Kontchakov and M. Zakharyaschev. An introduction to description logics and query rewriting. In *Proc. of Reasoning Web*, pages 195–244, 2014.

[35] P. Koutris and D. Suciu. A dichotomy on the complexity of consistent query answering for atoms with simple keys. In *Proc. of ICDT*, pages 165–176. OpenProceedings.org, 2014.

[36] P. Koutris and J. Wijsen. The data complexity of consistent query answering for self-join-free conjunctive queries under primary key constraints. In *Proc. of PODS*, pages 17–29, 2015.

[37] M. Krötzsch. OWL 2 profiles: An introduction to lightweight ontology languages. In *Proc. of Reasoning Web*, pages 112–183, 2012.

[38] R. E. Ladner. On the structure of polynomial time reducibility. *J. ACM*, 22(1):155–171, 1975.

[39] B. Larose and P. Tesson. Universal algebra and hardness results for constraint satisfaction problems. *Theor. Comput. Sci.*, 410(18):1629–1647, 2009.

[40] A. Y. Levy and M. Rousset. Combining horn rules and description logics in CARIN. *Artif. Intell.*, 104(1-2):165–209, 1998.

[41] C. Lutz, I. Seylan, and F. Wolter. Ontology-based data access with closed predicates is inherently intractable(sometimes). In *Proc. of IJCAI*, pages 1024–1030, 2013.

[42] C. Lutz and F. Wolter. Non-uniform data complexity of query answering in description logics. In *Proc. of KR*, 2012.

[43] C. Lutz and F. Wolter. On the relationship between consistent query answering and constraint satisfaction problems. In *Proc. of ICDT*, pages 363–379, 2015.

[44] J. Minker, editor. *Foundations of Deductive Databases and Logic Programming*. Elsevier, 1988.

[45] M. Mugnier and M. Thomazo. An introduction to ontology-based query answering with existential rules. In *Proc. of Reasoning Web*, pages 245–278, 2014.

[46] M. Ortiz, D. Calvanese, and T. Eiter. Data complexity of query answering in expressive description logics via tableaux. *Journal of Automated Reasoning*, 41(1):61–98, 2008.

[47] A. Poggi, D. Lembo, D. Calvanese, G. D. Giacomo, M. Lenzerini, and R. Rosati. Linking data to ontologies. *J. Data Semantics*, 10:133–173, 2008.

[48] I. Pratt-Hartmann. Complexity of the guarded two-variable fragment with counting quantifiers. *J. Log. Comput.*, 17(1):133–155, 2007.

[49] A. Rafiey, J. Kinne, and T. Feder. Dichotomy for digraph homomorphism problems. *CoRR*, abs/1701.02409, 2017.

[50] A. Schaerf. On the complexity of the instance checking problem in concept languages with existential quantification. *J. of Intel. Inf. Systems*, 2:265–278, 1993.

[51] D. Suciu, D. Olteanu, C. Ré, and C. Koch. *Probabilistic Databases*. Synthesis Lectures on Data Management. Morgan & Claypool Publishers, 2011.

[52] P. L. Whetzel, N. F. Noy, N. H. Shah, P. R. Alexander, C. Nyulas, T. Tudorache, and M. A. Musen. BioPortal: enhanced functionality via new web services from the national center for biomedical ontology to access and use ontologies in software applications. *Nucleic acids research*, 39(suppl 2):W541–W545, 2011.

APPENDIX

A. INTRODUCTION TO DESCRIPTION LOGIC

We give a brief introduction to the syntax and semantics of DLs and establish their relationship to the guarded fragment of FO. We consider the DL $\mathcal{ALC}$ and its extensions by inverse roles, role inclusions, qualified number restrictions, functional roles, and local functionality. Recall that $\mathcal{ALC}$*-concepts* are constructed according to the rule

$$C, D := \top \mid \bot \mid A \mid C \sqcap D \mid C \sqcup D \mid \neg C \mid \exists R.C \mid \forall R.C$$

where A ranges over unary relations and R ranges over binary relations. DLs extended by *inverse roles* (denoted in the name of a DL by the letter $\mathcal{I}$) admit, in addition, *inverse relations* denoted by R^-, with R a relation. Thus, in $\mathcal{ALCI}$ inverse relations can be used in place of relations in any $\mathcal{ALC}$ concept. DLs extended by *qualified number restrictions* (denoted by $\mathcal{Q}$) admit concepts of the form $(\geq n\ R\ C)$, $(= n\ R\ C)$, and $(\leq n\ R\ C)$, where $n \geq 1$ is a natural number, R is a relation or an inverse relation (if inverse relations are in the original DL), and C is a concept. When extending a DL with *local functionality* (denoted by $\mathcal{F}_\ell$) one can use only number restrictions of the form $(\leq 1\ R\ \top)$ in which R is a relation or an inverse relation (if inverse relations are in the original DL). We abbreviate $(\leq 1\ R\ \top)$ with $(\leq 1R)$ and use $(= 1R)$ as an abbreviation for $(\exists R.\top) \sqcap (\leq 1R)$ and $(\geq 2R)$ as an abbreviation for $(\exists R.\top) \sqcap \neg(\leq 1R)$.

In DLs, ontologies are formalized as finite sets of *concept inclusions* $C \sqsubseteq D$, where C, D are concepts in the respective language. We use $C \equiv D$ as an abbreviation for $C \sqsubseteq D$ and $D \sqsubseteq C$. In the DLs extended with *functionality* (denoted by $\mathcal{F}$) one can use *functionality assertions* $\mathsf{func}(R)$, where R is a relation or an inverse relation (if present in the original DL). Such an R is interpreted as a partial function. Extending a DL with *role inclusions* (denoted by $\mathcal{H}$) allows one to use expressions of the form $R \sqsubseteq S$, where R and S are relations or inverse relations (if present in the original DL), and which state that R is a subset of S.

The semantics of DLs is given by interpretations $\mathfrak{A}$. The interpretation $C^{\mathfrak{A}}$ of a concept C in an interpretation $\mathfrak{A}$ is defined inductively as follows:

$$\begin{aligned}
\top^{\mathfrak{A}} &= \mathrm{dom}(\mathfrak{A}) & \bot^{\mathfrak{A}} &= \emptyset\\
A^{\mathfrak{A}} &= \{a \in \mathrm{dom}(\mathfrak{A}) \mid A(a) \in \mathfrak{A}\} & (\neg C)^{\mathfrak{A}} &= \mathrm{dom}(\mathfrak{A}) \setminus C^{\mathfrak{A}}\\
(C \sqcap D)^{\mathfrak{A}} &= C^{\mathfrak{A}} \cap D^{\mathfrak{A}} & (C \sqcup D)^{\mathfrak{A}} &= C^{\mathfrak{A}} \cup D^{\mathfrak{A}}
\end{aligned}$$

$$\begin{aligned}
(\exists R.C)^{\mathfrak{A}} &= \{a \in \mathrm{dom}(\mathfrak{A}) \mid \exists a' : \ R(a, a') \in \mathfrak{A} \text{ and } a' \in C^{\mathfrak{A}}\}\\
(\forall R.C)^{\mathfrak{A}} &= \{a \in \mathrm{dom}(\mathfrak{A}) \mid \forall a' : \ R(a, a') \in \mathfrak{A} \text{ implies } a' \in A^{\mathfrak{A}}\}\\
(\geq n\ R\ C)^{\mathfrak{A}} &= \{a \in \mathrm{dom}(\mathfrak{A}) \mid |\{b \mid R(a, b) \in \mathfrak{A} \text{ and } b \in C^{\mathfrak{A}}\}| \geq n\}\\
(\leq n\ R\ C)^{\mathfrak{A}} &= \{a \in \mathrm{dom}(\mathfrak{A}) \mid |\{b \mid R(a, b) \in \mathfrak{A} \text{ and } b \in C^{\mathfrak{A}}\}| \leq n\}\\
(= n\ R\ C)^{\mathfrak{A}} &= \{a \in \mathrm{dom}(\mathfrak{A}) \mid |\{b \mid R(a, b) \in \mathfrak{A} \text{ and } b \in C^{\mathfrak{A}}\}| = n\}
\end{aligned}$$

Then $\mathfrak{A}$ *satisfies* a concept inclusion $C \sqsubseteq D$ if $C^{\mathfrak{A}} \subseteq D^{\mathfrak{A}}$. Alternatively, one can define the semantics of DLs by translating them into FO; the following table gives such a translation:

$$\begin{aligned}
\top^*(x) &= \top & \bot^*(x) &= \bot\\
A^*(x) &= A(x) & (\neg C)^*(x) &= \neg(C^*(x))\\
(C \sqcap D)^*(x) &= C^*(x) \wedge D^*(x) & (C \sqcup D)^*(x) &= C^*(x) \vee D^*(x)
\end{aligned}$$

$$\begin{aligned}
(\exists R.C)^*(x) &= \ \exists y\, (R(x, y) \wedge C^*(y))\\
(\forall R.C)^*(x) &= \ \forall y\, (R(x, y) \rightarrow C^*(y))\\
(\geq n\ R\ C)^*(x) &= \ \exists^{\geq n} y (R(x, y) \wedge C^*(y))
\end{aligned}$$

We observe the following relationships between DLs and fragments of the guarded fragment. For a DL $\mathcal{L}$ and fragment $\mathcal{L}'$ of the guarded fragment we say that an $\mathcal{L}$ *ontology* $\mathcal{O}$ *can be written as an* $\mathcal{L}'$ *ontology* if the translation given above translates $\mathcal{O}$ into an $\mathcal{L}'$ ontology.

Lemma 7 *The following inclusions hold:*

1. *Every $\mathcal{ALCHI}$ ontology can be written as a uGF$_2$ ontology. If the ontology has depth 2, then it can be written as a uGF$_2^-(2)$ ontology.*
2. *Every $\mathcal{ALCHIF}$ ontology can be written as a uGF$_2^-(f)$ ontology.*
3. *Every $\mathcal{ALCHIQ}$ ontology can be written as a uGC$_2$ ontology. If the ontology has depth 1, then it can be written as a uGC$_2^-(1)$ ontology.*

B. INTRODUCTION TO DATALOG

We give a brief introduction to the notation used for Datalog. A *datalog$^{\neq}$ rule* ρ takes the form

$$S(\vec{x}) \leftarrow R_1(\vec{x}_1) \wedge \cdots \wedge R_m(\vec{x}_m)$$

where S is a relation symbol, $m \geq 1$, and $R_1, \ldots, R_m$ are either relation symbols or the symbol $\neq$ for inequality. We call $S(\vec{x})$ the *head* of ρ and $R_1(\vec{x}_1) \wedge \cdots \wedge R_m(\vec{x}_m)$ its *body*. Every variable in the head of ρ is required to occur in its body. We call a datalog$^{\neq}$ rule that does not use inequality a *datalog rule*. A *Datalog$^{\neq}$ program* is a finite set Π of datalog$^{\neq}$ rules with a selected *goal relation symbol* goal that does not occur in rule bodies in Π and only in *goal rules* of the form $\mathrm{goal}(\vec{x}) \leftarrow R_1(\vec{x}_1) \wedge \cdots \wedge R_m(\vec{x}_m)$. The *arity* of Π is the arity of its goal relation. A *Datalog program* is a Datalog$^{\neq}$ program not using inequality.

For every instance $\mathfrak{D}$ and Datalog$^{\neq}$ program Π, we call a model $\mathfrak{A}$ of $\mathfrak{D}$ a *model of* Π if $\mathfrak{A}$ is a model of all FO sentences $\forall \vec{x} \forall \vec{x}_1 \cdots \forall \vec{x}_m (R_1(\vec{x}_1) \wedge \cdots \wedge R_m(\vec{x}_m) \rightarrow S(\vec{x}))$ with $S(\vec{x}) \leftarrow R_1(\vec{x}_1) \wedge \cdots \wedge R_m(\vec{x}_m) \in \Pi$. We set $\mathfrak{D} \models \Pi(\vec{a})$ if $\mathrm{goal}(\vec{a}) \in \mathfrak{A}$ for all models $\mathfrak{A}$ of $\mathfrak{D}$ and Π.

The Complexity of Ontology-Based Data Access with OWL 2 QL and Bounded Treewidth Queries

Meghyn Bienvenu
CNRS & University of Montpellier, France
meghyn@lirmm.fr

Stanislav Kikot
Birkbeck
University of London, UK
staskikotx@gmail.com

Roman Kontchakov
Birkbeck
University of London, UK
roman@dcs.bbk.ac.uk

Vladimir V. Podolskii
Steklov Mathematical Institute & National Research University Higher School of Economics, Moscow, Russia
podolskii@mi.ras.ru

Vladislav Ryzhikov
Free University of Bozen-Bolzano, Italy
ryzhikov@inf.unibz.it

Michael Zakharyaschev
Birkbeck
University of London, UK
michael@dcs.bbk.ac.uk

ABSTRACT

Our concern is the overhead of answering *OWL 2 QL* ontology-mediated queries (OMQs) in ontology-based data access compared to evaluating their underlying tree-shaped and, more generally, bounded treewidth conjunctive queries (CQs). We show that OMQs with bounded depth ontologies have nonrecursive datalog (NDL) rewritings that can be constructed and evaluated in LOGCFL for combined complexity, and even in NL if their CQs are tree-shaped with a bounded number of leaves. Thus, such OMQs incur no overhead in complexity-theoretic terms. For OMQs with arbitrary ontologies and bounded-leaf tree-shaped CQs, NDL-rewritings are constructed and evaluated in LOGCFL. We experimentally demonstrate feasibility and scalability of our rewritings compared to previously proposed NDL-rewritings. On the negative side, we prove that answering OMQs with tree-shaped CQs is not fixed-parameter tractable if the ontology depth or the number of leaves in the CQs is regarded as the parameter, and that answering OMQs with a fixed ontology (of infinite depth) is NP-complete for tree-shaped CQs and LOGCFL-complete for bounded-leaf CQs.

Keywords

Ontology-based data access; ontology-mediated query; query rewriting; combined complexity; parameterised complexity.

1. INTRODUCTION

The main aim of ontology-based data access (OBDA, for short) [50, 43] is to facilitate access to complex data for non-expert end-users. The ontology, given by a logical theory $\mathcal{T}$, provides a unified conceptual view of one or more data sources, so the users do not have to know the actual structure of the data and can formulate their queries in the vocabulary of the ontology, which is connected to the schemas of data sources by a mapping $\mathcal{M}$. The instance $\mathcal{M}(\mathcal{D})$ that can be obtained by applying $\mathcal{M}$ to a given dataset $\mathcal{D}$ is interpreted under the open-world assumption, and additional facts can be *inferred* using the domain knowledge provided by the ontology. A certain answer to a query $\boldsymbol{q}(\boldsymbol{x})$ over $\mathcal{D}$ is any tuple of constants $\boldsymbol{a}$ such that $\mathcal{T}, \mathcal{M}(\mathcal{D}) \models \boldsymbol{q}(\boldsymbol{a})$. OBDA is closely related to querying incomplete databases under (ontological) constraints [9], data integration [20], and data exchange [2].

In the classical approach to OBDA [13, 50], the computation of certain answers is reduced to standard database query evaluation: given an ontology-mediated query (OMQ) $\boldsymbol{Q} = (\mathcal{T}, \boldsymbol{q}(\boldsymbol{x}))$, one constructs a first-order (FO) query $\boldsymbol{q}'(\boldsymbol{x})$, called a rewriting of $\boldsymbol{Q}$, such that, for every dataset $\mathcal{D}$ and mapping $\mathcal{M}$,

$$\mathcal{T}, \mathcal{M}(\mathcal{D}) \models \boldsymbol{q}(\boldsymbol{a}) \quad \text{iff} \quad \mathcal{I}_{\mathcal{M}(\mathcal{D})} \models \boldsymbol{q}'(\boldsymbol{a}), \qquad (1)$$

where $\mathcal{I}_{\mathcal{M}(\mathcal{D})}$ is the FO-structure comprised of the atoms in $\mathcal{M}(\mathcal{D})$; note that the rewriting is interpreted in $\mathcal{I}_{\mathcal{M}(\mathcal{D})}$ under the closed-world semantics. When the form of $\mathcal{M}$ is appropriately restricted, e.g., to GAV mappings, in which case the ontology predicates are defined as views over the data sources, one can further unfold $\boldsymbol{q}'(\boldsymbol{x})$ using $\mathcal{M}$ to obtain an FO-query that can be evaluated directly over the original dataset $\mathcal{D}$ (so there is no need to materialise $\mathcal{M}(\mathcal{D})$).

For reduction (1) to hold for all OMQs, it is necessary to restrict the expressivity of $\mathcal{T}$ and $\boldsymbol{q}$. The *DL-Lite* family of description logics [13] was specifically designed to ensure (1) for OMQs with conjunctive queries (CQs) $\boldsymbol{q}$. Other ontology languages with this property include linear and sticky tuple-generating dependencies (tgds) [10, 11], and the *OWL 2 QL* profile [45] of the W3C-standardised Web Ontology Language *OWL 2*, which extends *DL-Lite* and is the focus of this work. Like many other ontology languages originating from description logics, *OWL 2 QL* admits only unary and binary predicates, but arbitrary relational instances can be queried due to the mapping. Various types of FO-rewritings $\boldsymbol{q}'(\boldsymbol{x})$ have been developed and implemented for the aforementioned ontology languages [50, 47, 41, 54, 15, 21, 53, 38, 28, 44, 40], and a few mature OBDA systems have emerged, including pioneering MASTRO [12], commercial Stardog [48]

PODS'17, May 14-19, 2017, Chicago, IL, USA.

DOI: http://dx.doi.org/10.1145/3034786.3034791

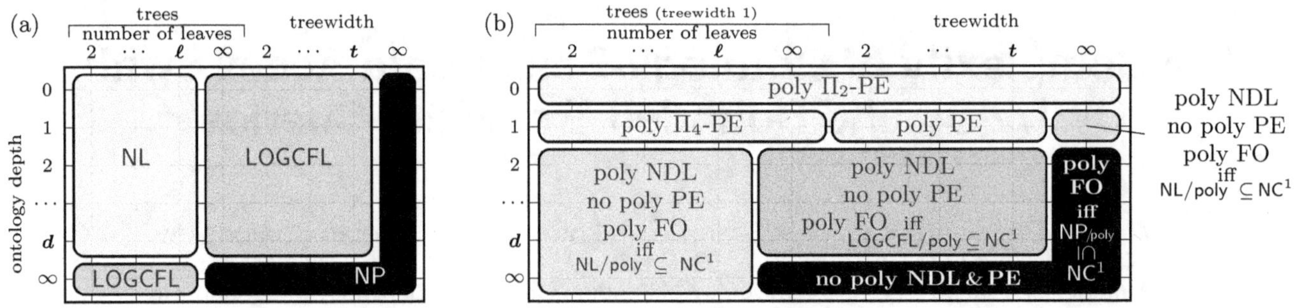

Figure 1: OMQ answering in *OWL 2 QL* (a) combined complexity and (b) the size of rewritings.

and Ultrawrap [55], and the Optique platform [24] with the query answering engine Ontop [51, 42].

Our concern in this paper is the overhead of OMQ answering—that is, checking whether the left-hand side of (1) holds—compared to evaluating the underlying CQs. At first sight, there is no apparent difference between the two problems when viewed through the lens of computational complexity: OMQ answering is in AC^0 for data complexity by (1) and is NP-complete for combined complexity [13], which for both measures corresponds to the complexity of evaluating CQs in the relational setting. Further analysis revealed, however, that answering OMQs is already NP-hard for combined complexity when the underlying CQs are tree-shaped (acyclic) [37], in sharp contrast to the well-known LOGCFL-completeness of evaluating bounded treewidth CQs [62, 14, 27]. This surprising difference motivated a systematic investigation of the combined complexity of OMQ answering along two dimensions: (*i*) the query topology (treewidth $\boldsymbol{t}$ of CQs, and the number $\boldsymbol{\ell}$ of leaves in tree-shaped CQs), and (*ii*) the 'existential' depth $\boldsymbol{d}$ of ontologies (i.e., the length of the longest chain of labelled nulls in the chase on any data). The resulting landscape, displayed in Fig. 1 (a) (under the assumption that datasets are given as RDF graphs—that is, sets of unary and binary ground atoms—and $\mathcal{M}$ is the identity) [13, 37, 35, 5], indicates three tractable cases:

$\mathsf{OMQ}(\boldsymbol{d}, \boldsymbol{t}, \infty)$: ontologies of depth $\leq \boldsymbol{d}$ coupled with CQs of treewidth $\leq \boldsymbol{t}$ (for fixed $\boldsymbol{d}, \boldsymbol{t}$);

$\mathsf{OMQ}(\boldsymbol{d}, 1, \boldsymbol{\ell})$: ontologies of depth $\leq \boldsymbol{d}$ with tree-shaped CQs with $\leq \boldsymbol{\ell}$ leaves (for fixed $\boldsymbol{d}, \boldsymbol{\ell}$);

$\mathsf{OMQ}(\infty, 1, \boldsymbol{\ell})$: ontologies of arbitrary depth coupled with tree-shaped CQs with $\leq \boldsymbol{\ell}$ leaves (for fixed $\boldsymbol{\ell}$).

Observe, in particular, that when the depth of ontologies is bounded by a fixed constant, the complexity of OMQ answering is precisely the same as of evaluating the underlying CQs. If we place no restriction on the ontology, then tractability for tree-shaped queries can be recovered by bounding the number of leaves, but we have LOGCFL rather than the expected NL.

While the results in Fig. 1 (a) appear to answer the question of the additional cost incurred by adding an *OWL 2 QL* ontology, they only tell part of the story. Indeed, in the context of classical rewriting-based OBDA [50], it is not the abstract complexity of OMQ answering that matters, but the cost of computing and evaluating OMQ rewritings. Fig. 1 (b) summarises what is known about the size of positive existential (PE), nonrecursive datalog (NDL) and FO-rewritings [36, 26, 35, 5]. Thus, we see, for example, that PE-rewritings for OMQs from $\mathsf{OMQ}(\boldsymbol{d}, \boldsymbol{t}, \infty)$ can be of superpolynomial size, and so are not computable and evaluable in polynomial time, even though Fig. 1 (a) shows that such OMQs can be answered in LOGCFL. The same concerns $\mathsf{OMQ}(\boldsymbol{d}, 1, \boldsymbol{\ell})$ and $\mathsf{OMQ}(\infty, 1, \boldsymbol{\ell})$, which can be answered in NL and LOGCFL, respectively, but do not enjoy polynomial-size PE-rewritings. Moreover, our experiments show that standard rewriting engines exhibit exponential behaviour on OMQs drawn from $\mathsf{OMQ}(1, 1, 2)$ lying in the intersection of the three tractable classes.

Our first aim is to show that the positive complexity results in Fig. 1 (a) can in fact be achieved using query rewriting. To this end, we develop NDL-rewritings for the three tractable cases that can be computed and evaluated by algorithms of optimal combined complexity. In theory, such algorithms are known to be space efficient and highly parallelisable. We demonstrate practical efficiency of our optimal NDL-rewritings by comparing them with the NDL-rewritings produced by Clipper [21], Presto [54] and Rapid [15], using a sequence of OMQs from the class $\mathsf{OMQ}(1,1,2)$.

Our second aim is to understand the contribution of the ontology depth and the number of leaves in tree-shaped CQs to the complexity of OMQ answering. (As follows from Fig. 1 (a), if these parameters are unbounded, this problem is harder than evaluating the underlying CQs unless, of course, LOGCFL = NP.) Unfortunately, it turns out that answering OMQs with ontologies of finite depth and tree-shaped CQs is not fixed-parameter tractable if either the ontology depth or the number of leaves in CQs is regarded as a parameter. More precisely, we prove that the problem is $W[2]$-hard in the former case and $W[1]$-hard in the latter. These results suggest that the ontology depth and the number of leaves are inherently in the exponent of the size of the input in any OMQ answering algorithm.

Finally, we revisit the NP- and LOGCFL-hardness results for OMQs with tree-shaped CQs. The known lower bounds were established using sequences $(\mathcal{T}_n, \boldsymbol{q}_n)$ of OMQs, where the depth of $\mathcal{T}_n$ grows with n [37, 5]. One might thus hope to make answering OMQs with tree-shaped CQs easier by restricting the ontology signature, size, or even by fixing the whole ontology, which is very relevant for applications because a typical OBDA scenario has users posing different queries over the same ontology. Our third main result is that this is surprisingly not the case: we present ontologies $\mathcal{T}_\dagger$ and $\mathcal{T}_\ddagger$ of infinite depth such that answering OMQs $(\mathcal{T}_\dagger, \boldsymbol{q})$ with tree-shaped CQs $\boldsymbol{q}$ and $(\mathcal{T}_\ddagger, \boldsymbol{q})$ with linear CQs $\boldsymbol{q}$ is NP- and LOGCFL-hard for query complexity, respectively. We also show that, unless P = NP, no polynomial-time algorithm can construct FO-rewritings of the OMQs $(\mathcal{T}_\dagger, \boldsymbol{q})$, even though polynomial-size FO-rewritings of these OMQs do exist.

The paper is organised as follows. We begin in Section 2 by introducing the *OWL 2 QL* ontology language and key notions like OMQ answering and query rewriting. In Section 3, we first identify fragments of NDL that can be evaluated in LOGCFL or NL, and then we use these results to develop NDL-rewritings of optimal combined complexity for the three tractable cases. Section 4 concerns the parameterised complexity of OMQ answering with tree-shaped CQs. For ontologies of finite depth, we show $W[2]$-hardness ($W[1]$-hardness) when the ontology depth (respectively, number of leaves) is taken as the parameter. For the infinite depth case, we show in Section 5 that NP-hardness holds even for a fixed ontology. The final section of the paper presents preliminary experiments that compare our new NDL-rewritings to those produced by existing rewriting engines and also discusses possible directions for future work. Concrete examples of our three types of NDL-rewriting are provided in the appendix. All omitted proofs and details of the experiments can be found in the long version of this paper [4].

2. PRELIMINARIES

An *OWL 2 QL ontology* (*TBox* in description logic), $\mathcal{T}$, is a finite set of sentences (*axioms*) of the form

$$\forall x\,(\tau(x) \to \tau'(x)), \qquad \forall x\,(\tau(x) \land \tau'(x) \to \bot),$$
$$\forall xy\,(\varrho(x,y) \to \varrho'(x,y)), \quad \forall xy\,(\varrho(x,y) \land \varrho'(x,y) \to \bot),$$
$$\forall x\,\varrho(x,x), \qquad \forall x\,(\varrho(x,x) \to \bot),$$

where $\tau(x)$ and $\varrho(x,y)$ are defined, using unary predicates A and binary predicates P, by the grammars

$$\tau(x) ::= \top \mid A(x) \mid \exists y\,\varrho(x,y),$$
$$\varrho(x,y) ::= \top \mid P(x,y) \mid P(y,x).$$

When writing ontology axioms, we omit the universal quantifiers and denote by $\boldsymbol{R}_\mathcal{T}$ the set of binary predicates P occurring in $\mathcal{T}$ and their inverses P^-, assuming that $P^{--} = P$. For every $\varrho \in \boldsymbol{R}_\mathcal{T}$, we take a fresh unary predicate A_ϱ and add $A_\varrho(x) \leftrightarrow \exists y\,\varrho(x,y)$ to $\mathcal{T}$ (where, as usual, $\varphi \leftrightarrow \psi$ is an abbreviation for $\varphi \to \psi$ and $\psi \to \varphi$). The resulting ontology is said to be in *normal form*, and we assume, without loss of generality, that all our ontologies are in normal form.

A *data instance*, $\mathcal{A}$, is a finite set of unary or binary ground atoms (called an *ABox* in description logic). We denote by $\mathsf{ind}(\mathcal{A})$ the set of individual constants in $\mathcal{A}$ and write $\varrho(a,b) \in \mathcal{A}$ if $P(a,b) \in \mathcal{A}$ and $\varrho = P$, or $P(b,a) \in \mathcal{A}$ and $\varrho = P^-$. We say that $\mathcal{A}$ is *complete* for an ontology $\mathcal{T}$ if $\mathcal{T}, \mathcal{A} \models S(\boldsymbol{a})$ implies $S(\boldsymbol{a}) \in \mathcal{A}$, for any ground atom $S(\boldsymbol{a})$ with $\boldsymbol{a} \subseteq \mathsf{ind}(\mathcal{A})$.[1]

A *conjunctive query* (CQ) $\boldsymbol{q}(\boldsymbol{x})$ is a formula of the form $\exists \boldsymbol{y}\,\varphi(\boldsymbol{x},\boldsymbol{y})$, where φ is a conjunction of atoms $S(\boldsymbol{z})$ all of whose variables are among $\boldsymbol{x} \cup \boldsymbol{y}$. We assume, without loss of generality, that CQs contain no constants. We often regard a CQ as the set of its atoms; in particular, $|\boldsymbol{q}|$ is the number of atoms in $\boldsymbol{q}$. With every CQ $\boldsymbol{q}$, we associate its *Gaifman graph* $\mathcal{G}$ whose vertices are the variables of $\boldsymbol{q}$ and whose edges are the pairs $\{u,v\}$ such that $P(u,v) \in \boldsymbol{q}$, for some P. We call $\boldsymbol{q}$ *connected* if $\mathcal{G}$ is connected; $\boldsymbol{q}$ is *tree-shaped* if $\mathcal{G}$ is a tree, and *linear* if $\mathcal{G}$ is a tree with two leaves.

[1] If the meaning is clear from the context, we use set-theoretic notation for lists.

By an *ontology-mediated query* (OMQ) we understand a pair $\boldsymbol{Q}(\boldsymbol{x}) = (\mathcal{T}, \boldsymbol{q}(\boldsymbol{x}))$, where $\mathcal{T}$ is an ontology and $\boldsymbol{q}(\boldsymbol{x})$ a CQ. A tuple $\boldsymbol{a} \subseteq \mathsf{ind}(\mathcal{A})$ is a *certain answer* to $\boldsymbol{Q}(\boldsymbol{x})$ over a data instance $\mathcal{A}$ if $\mathcal{I} \models \boldsymbol{q}(\boldsymbol{a})$ for all models $\mathcal{I}$ of $\mathcal{T}$ and $\mathcal{A}$; in this case we write $\mathcal{T}, \mathcal{A} \models \boldsymbol{q}(\boldsymbol{a})$. If $\boldsymbol{x} = \emptyset$, then a certain answer to $\boldsymbol{Q}$ over $\mathcal{A}$ is 'yes' if $\mathcal{T}, \mathcal{A} \models \boldsymbol{q}$ and 'no' otherwise. The *OMQ answering problem* (for a class of OMQs) is to decide whether $\mathcal{T}, \mathcal{A} \models \boldsymbol{q}(\boldsymbol{a})$ holds, given an OMQ $\boldsymbol{Q}(\boldsymbol{x})$ (in the class), $\mathcal{A}$ and $\boldsymbol{a} \subseteq \mathsf{ind}(\mathcal{A})$. If $\mathcal{T}$, $\boldsymbol{q}(\boldsymbol{x})$, and $\mathcal{A}$ are regarded as input, we speak about *combined complexity* of OMQ answering; if $\mathcal{A}$ and $\mathcal{T}$ are regarded as fixed, we speak about *query complexity*. The *size* of $\boldsymbol{Q}$ is $|\boldsymbol{Q}| = |\mathcal{T}| + |\boldsymbol{q}|$, where $|\mathcal{T}|$ is the number of symbols in $\mathcal{T}$.

Every consistent *knowledge base* (KB) $(\mathcal{T}, \mathcal{A})$ has a *canonical model* (or *chase* in database theory) [1] $\mathcal{C}_{\mathcal{T},\mathcal{A}}$ with the property that $\mathcal{T}, \mathcal{A} \models \boldsymbol{q}(\boldsymbol{a})$ iff $\mathcal{C}_{\mathcal{T},\mathcal{A}} \models \boldsymbol{q}(\boldsymbol{a})$, for all CQs $\boldsymbol{q}(\boldsymbol{x})$ and $\boldsymbol{a} \subseteq \mathsf{ind}(\mathcal{A})$. In our constructions, we use the following definition of $\mathcal{C}_{\mathcal{T},\mathcal{A}}$, where without loss of generality we assume that $\mathcal{T}$ contains no binary predicates P such that $\mathcal{T} \models \forall xy\,P(x,y)$. The domain, $\Delta^{\mathcal{C}_{\mathcal{T},\mathcal{A}}}$, consists of $\mathsf{ind}(\mathcal{A})$ and the *witnesses* (or *labelled nulls*) of the form $w = a\varrho_1 \dots \varrho_n$, for $n \geq 1$, such that

- $a \in \mathsf{ind}(\mathcal{A})$ and $\mathcal{T}, \mathcal{A} \models \exists y\,\varrho_1(a,y)$;
- $\mathcal{T} \not\models \varrho_i(x,x)$, for $1 \leq i \leq n$;
- $\mathcal{T} \models \exists x\,\varrho_i(x,y) \to \exists z\,\varrho_{i+1}(y,z)$ but $\mathcal{T} \not\models \varrho_i(x,y) \to \varrho_{i+1}(y,x)$, for $1 \leq i < n$.

We denote by $\boldsymbol{W}_\mathcal{T}$ the set consisting of the empty word ε and all words $\varrho_1 \dots \varrho_n \in \boldsymbol{R}_\mathcal{T}^+$ satisfying the last two conditions. Every $a \in \mathsf{ind}(\mathcal{A})$ is interpreted in $\mathcal{C}_{\mathcal{T},\mathcal{A}}$ by itself, and unary and binary predicates are interpreted as follows:

- $\mathcal{C}_{\mathcal{T},\mathcal{A}} \models A(u)$ iff either $u \in \mathsf{ind}(\mathcal{A})$ and $\mathcal{T}, \mathcal{A} \models A(u)$, or $u = w\varrho$ with $\mathcal{T} \models \exists y\,\varrho(y,x) \to A(x)$;
- $\mathcal{C}_{\mathcal{T},\mathcal{A}} \models P(u,v)$ iff one of the three conditions holds: (*i*) $u, v \in \mathsf{ind}(\mathcal{A})$ and $\mathcal{T}, \mathcal{A} \models P(u,v)$; (*ii*) $u = v$ and $\mathcal{T} \models P(x,x)$; (*iii*) $\mathcal{T} \models \varrho(x,y) \to P(x,y)$ and either $v = u\varrho$ or $u = v\varrho^-$.

We say that $\mathcal{T}$ is *of depth* 0 if it does not contain any axioms with $\exists$ on the right-hand side, excepting the normalisation axioms[2]. Otherwise, we say that $\mathcal{T}$ is *of depth* $0 < \boldsymbol{d} < \infty$ if $\boldsymbol{d}$ is the maximum length of the words in $\boldsymbol{W}_\mathcal{T}$, and it is *of depth* ∞ if $\boldsymbol{W}_\mathcal{T}$ is infinite. (Note that the depth of $\mathcal{T}$ is computable in NL; cf. [25, 8] for related results on chase termination for tgds.)

An FO-formula $\boldsymbol{q}'(\boldsymbol{x})$, possibly with equality, is an *FO-rewriting of an OMQ* $\boldsymbol{Q}(\boldsymbol{x}) = (\mathcal{T}, \boldsymbol{q}(\boldsymbol{x}))$ if, for *any* data instance $\mathcal{A}$ and any tuple $\boldsymbol{a} \subseteq \mathsf{ind}(\mathcal{A})$,

$$\mathcal{T}, \mathcal{A} \models \boldsymbol{q}(\boldsymbol{a}) \quad \text{iff} \quad \mathcal{I}_\mathcal{A} \models \boldsymbol{q}'(\boldsymbol{a}), \tag{2}$$

where $\mathcal{I}_\mathcal{A}$ is the FO-structure over the domain $\mathsf{ind}(\mathcal{A})$ such that $\mathcal{I}_\mathcal{A} \models S(\boldsymbol{a})$ iff $S(\boldsymbol{a}) \in \mathcal{A}$, for any ground atom $S(\boldsymbol{a})$. If $\boldsymbol{q}'(\boldsymbol{x})$ is a positive existential formula (that is, an FO-formula with $\exists$, $\lor$ and $\land$ only), we call it a *PE-rewriting of* $\boldsymbol{Q}(\boldsymbol{x})$. A PE-rewriting whose matrix is a Π_k-formula (with respect to $\land$ and $\lor$) is called a Π_k*-rewriting*. The size $|\boldsymbol{q}'|$ of a rewriting $\boldsymbol{q}'$ is the number of symbols in it.

[2] This somewhat awkward definition of depth 0 ontologies is due to the use of normalisation axioms, which may introduce unnecessary words on length 1 in $\boldsymbol{W}_\mathcal{T}$.

We also consider rewritings in the form of nonrecursive datalog queries. A *datalog program*, Π, is a finite set of Horn clauses $\forall \boldsymbol{z}\,(\gamma_0 \leftarrow \gamma_1 \land \dots \land \gamma_m)$, where each γ_i is an atom $Q(\boldsymbol{y})$ with $\boldsymbol{y} \subseteq \boldsymbol{z}$ or an equality $(z = z')$ with $z, z' \in \boldsymbol{z}$. (As usual, we omit $\forall \boldsymbol{z}$ from clauses.) The atom γ_0 is the *head* of the clause, and $\gamma_1, \dots, \gamma_m$ its *body*. All variables in the head must occur in the body, and $=$ can only occur in the body. The predicates in the heads of clauses in Π are *IDB predicates*, the rest (including $=$) *EDB predicates*. A predicate Q *depends* on P in Π if Π has a clause with Q in the head and P in the body. Π is a *nonrecursive datalog* (NDL) *program* if the (directed) *dependence graph* of the dependence relation is acyclic. The size $|\Pi|$ of Π is the number of symbols in it.

An *NDL query* is a pair $(\Pi, G(\boldsymbol{x}))$, where Π is an NDL program and $G(\boldsymbol{x})$ a predicate. A tuple $\boldsymbol{a} \subseteq \mathsf{ind}(\mathcal{A})$ is an *answer to* $(\Pi, G(\boldsymbol{x}))$ *over* a data instance $\mathcal{A}$ if $G(\boldsymbol{a})$ holds in the first-order structure with domain $\mathsf{ind}(\mathcal{A})$ obtained by closing $\mathcal{A}$ under the clauses in Π; in this case we write $\Pi, \mathcal{A} \models G(\boldsymbol{a})$. The problem of checking whether $\boldsymbol{a}$ is an answer to $(\Pi, G(\boldsymbol{x}))$ over $\mathcal{A}$ is called the *query evaluation problem*. The *depth* of $(\Pi, G(\boldsymbol{x}))$ is the length, $\mathsf{d}(\Pi, G)$, of the longest directed path in the dependence graph for Π starting from G. NDL queries are *equivalent* if they have exactly the same answers over any data instance.

An NDL query $(\Pi, G(\boldsymbol{x}))$ is called an *NDL-rewriting of an OMQ* $\boldsymbol{Q}(\boldsymbol{x}) = (\mathcal{T}, \boldsymbol{q}(\boldsymbol{x}))$ *over complete data instances* in case $\mathcal{T}, \mathcal{A} \models \boldsymbol{q}(\boldsymbol{a})$ iff $\Pi, \mathcal{A} \models G(\boldsymbol{a})$, for any complete $\mathcal{A}$ and any $\boldsymbol{a} \subseteq \mathsf{ind}(\mathcal{A})$. Rewritings *over arbitrary data instances* are defined by dropping the completeness condition. Given an NDL-rewriting $(\Pi, G(\boldsymbol{x}))$ of $\boldsymbol{Q}(\boldsymbol{x})$ over complete data instances, we denote by Π^* the result of replacing each predicate S in Π with a fresh IDB predicate S^* of the same arity and adding the clauses

$$\begin{aligned}
&A^*(x) \leftarrow \tau(x), && \text{if } \mathcal{T} \models \tau(x) \to A(x),\\
&P^*(x,y) \leftarrow \varrho(x,y), && \text{if } \mathcal{T} \models \varrho(x,y) \to P(x,y),\\
&P^*(x,x) \leftarrow \top(x), && \text{if } \mathcal{T} \models P(x,x),
\end{aligned}$$

where $\top(x)$ is an EDB predicate for the active domain [33]. Clearly, $(\Pi^*, G(\boldsymbol{x}))$ is an NDL-rewriting of $\boldsymbol{Q}(\boldsymbol{x})$ over arbitrary data instances and $|\Pi^*| \leq |\Pi| + |\mathcal{T}|^2$.

Finally, we remark that, without loss of generality, we can (and will) assume that our ontologies $\mathcal{T}$ do not contain $\bot$. Indeed, we can always incorporate into rewritings subqueries that check whether the left-hand side of an axiom with $\bot$ holds and output all tuples of constants if this is the case [10].

3. OPTIMAL NDL-REWRITINGS

In order to construct theoretically optimal NDL-rewritings for OMQs from the three tractable classes, we first identify two types of NDL queries whose evaluation problems are in NL and LOGCFL for combined complexity.

3.1 NL and LOGCFL Fragments of NDL

To simplify the analysis of non-Boolean NDL queries, it is convenient to regard certain variables as parameters to be instantiated with constants from the candidate answer. Formally, an NDL query $(\Pi, G(\boldsymbol{x}))$ is called *ordered* if each of its IDB predicates Q comes with a fixed list of variables $\boldsymbol{x}_Q \subseteq \boldsymbol{x}$, called the *parameters of* Q, such that

(i) in each occurrence of Q in Π, the parameters occupy the last $|\boldsymbol{x}_Q|$ positions: that is, $Q(\boldsymbol{z}, \boldsymbol{x}_Q)$; parameters can, however, occur in other positions too;

(ii) the parameters of G are $\boldsymbol{x}$; and

(iii) in every clause, the parameters of the head include all the parameters of the predicates in the body.

Observe that Boolean NDL queries are trivially ordered (the lists of parameters are empty for all IDBs).

The *width* $\mathsf{w}(\Pi, G)$ of an ordered $(\Pi, G(\boldsymbol{x}))$ is the maximal number of non-parameter variables in a clause of Π.

EXAMPLE 1. The NDL query $(\Pi, G(x))$, where

$$\Pi = \{\, G(x) \leftarrow R(x,y) \land Q(x),\ \ Q(x) \leftarrow R(y,x) \,\},$$

is ordered with parameter x and has width 1 (the conditions do not restrict the EDB predicate R). Replacing $Q(x)$ by $Q(y)$ in the first clause yields an NDL query that is not ordered in view of (i). A further change of $Q(x)$ in the second clause to $Q(y)$ would satisfy (i) but not (iii).

As all the NDL-rewritings we construct are ordered, with their parameters being the answer variables, from now on we only consider ordered NDL queries.

Given an NDL query $(\Pi, G(\boldsymbol{x}))$, a data instance $\mathcal{A}$ and a tuple $\boldsymbol{a}$ with $|\boldsymbol{x}| = |\boldsymbol{a}|$, the $\boldsymbol{a}$*-grounding* $\Pi^{\boldsymbol{a}}_{\mathcal{A}}$ *of* Π *on* $\mathcal{A}$ is the set of ground clauses obtained by first replacing each parameter in Π by the corresponding constant from $\boldsymbol{a}$, and then performing the standard grounding [18] of Π using the constants from $\mathcal{A}$. The size of $\Pi^{\boldsymbol{a}}_{\mathcal{A}}$ is bounded by $|\Pi| \cdot |\mathcal{A}|^{\mathsf{w}(\Pi,G)}$, and so checking whether $\Pi, \mathcal{A} \models G(\boldsymbol{a})$ can be done in time $poly(|\Pi| \cdot |\mathcal{A}|^{\mathsf{w}(\Pi,G)})$.

3.1.1 Linear NDL in NL

An NDL program is *linear* [1] if the body of its every clause contains at most one IDB predicate.

THEOREM 2. *For every* $\mathsf{w} > 0$, *evaluation of linear NDL queries of width at most* w *is* NL*-complete for combined complexity.*

PROOF. Let $(\Pi, G(\boldsymbol{x}))$ be a linear NDL query. Deciding whether $\Pi, \mathcal{A} \models G(\boldsymbol{a})$ is reducible to finding a path to $G(\boldsymbol{a})$ from a vertex in a certain set X in the grounding graph $\mathfrak{G}$, which is constructed as follows. The vertices of $\mathfrak{G}$ are the IDB atoms of $\Pi^{\boldsymbol{a}}_{\mathcal{A}}$, and $\mathfrak{G}$ has an edge from $Q(\boldsymbol{c})$ to $Q'(\boldsymbol{c}')$ iff $\Pi^{\boldsymbol{a}}_{\mathcal{A}}$ contains $Q'(\boldsymbol{c}') \leftarrow Q(\boldsymbol{c}) \land S_1(\boldsymbol{c}_1) \land \dots \land S_k(\boldsymbol{c}_k)$ with $S_i(\boldsymbol{c}_i) \in \mathcal{A}$, for $1 \leq i \leq k$ (we assume that $\mathcal{A}$ contains all $c = c$, for $c \in \mathsf{ind}(\mathcal{A})$). The set X consists of all vertices $Q(\boldsymbol{c})$ with IDB predicates Q being of in-degree 0 in the dependency graph of Π for which there is a clause $Q(\boldsymbol{c}) \leftarrow S_1(\boldsymbol{c}_1) \land \dots \land S_k(\boldsymbol{c}_k)$ in $\Pi^{\boldsymbol{a}}_{\mathcal{A}}$ such that $S_i(\boldsymbol{c}_i) \in \mathcal{A}$, for $1 \leq i \leq k$. Bounding the width of (Π, G) ensures that $\mathfrak{G}$ is of polynomial size and can be constructed by a deterministic Turing machine with read-only input, write-once output and logarithmic-size work tapes. ❑

The transformation * of NDL-rewritings over complete data instances into NDL-rewritings over arbitrary data instances does not preserve linearity. A more involved construction is given in the proof of the following:

LEMMA 3. *Fix any* $\mathsf{w} > 0$. *There is an* L^{NL}*-transducer that, for any linear NDL-rewriting* $(\Pi, G(\boldsymbol{x}))$ *of an OMQ* $\boldsymbol{Q}(\boldsymbol{x})$ *over complete data instances with* $\mathsf{w}(\Pi, G) \leq \mathsf{w}$, *computes a linear NDL-rewriting* $(\Pi', G(\boldsymbol{x}))$ *of* $\boldsymbol{Q}(\boldsymbol{x})$ *over arbitrary data instances such that* $\mathsf{w}(\Pi', G) \leq \mathsf{w} + 1$.

We note that a possible increase of the width by 1 is due to the 'replacement' of unary atoms $A(z)$ by binary atoms $\varrho(y, z)$ whenever $\mathcal{T} \models \exists y\, \varrho(y, z) \to A(z)$.

3.1.2 Skinny NDL in LOGCFL

The complexity class LOGCFL can be defined using *nondeterministic auxiliary pushdown automata* (NAuxPDAs) [16], which are nondeterministic Turing machines with an additional work tape constrained to operate as a pushdown store. Sudborough [58] proved that LOGCFL coincides with the class of problems that are solved by NAuxPDAs in logarithmic space and polynomial time (the space on the pushdown tape is not subject to the logarithmic bound). It is known that LOGCFL can equivalently be defined in terms of logspace-uniform families of semi-unbounded fan-in circuits (where OR-gates have arbitrarily many inputs, and AND-gates two inputs) of polynomial size and logarithmic depth. Moreover, there is an algorithm that, given such a circuit $\boldsymbol{C}$, computes the output using an NAuxPDA in logarithmic space in the size of $\boldsymbol{C}$ and exponential time in the depth of $\boldsymbol{C}$ [61, pp. 392–397].

We call an NDL query (Π, G) *skinny* if the body of any clause in Π has at most two atoms (cf. LOGCFL circuits).

LEMMA 4. *For any skinny $(\Pi, G(\boldsymbol{x}))$ and any data instance $\mathcal{A}$, query evaluation can be done by an NAuxPDA in space $\log|\Pi| + \mathsf{w}(\Pi, G)\cdot\log|\mathcal{A}|$ and time $2^{O(\mathsf{d}(\Pi,G))}$.*

PROOF. Using the atoms of the grounding $\Pi^{\boldsymbol{a}}_{\mathcal{A}}$ as gates and inputs, we define a monotone Boolean circuit $\boldsymbol{C}$ as follows: its output is $G(\boldsymbol{a})$; for every atom γ in the head of a clause in $\Pi^{\boldsymbol{a}}_{\mathcal{A}}$, we take an OR-gate whose output is γ and inputs are the bodies of the clauses with head γ; for every such body, we take an AND-gate whose inputs are the atoms in the body. We set input γ to 1 iff $\gamma \in \mathcal{A}$. Clearly, $\boldsymbol{C}$ is a semi-unbounded fan-in circuit of depth $O(\mathsf{d}(\Pi, G))$ with $O(|\Pi|\cdot|\mathcal{A}|^{\mathsf{w}(\Pi,G)})$ gates. Having observed that our $\boldsymbol{C}$ can be computed by a deterministic logspace Turing machine, we conclude that the query evaluation problem can be solved by an NAuxPDA in the required space and time. ❑

Observe that Lemma 4 holds for NDL queries with any *bounded* number of atoms, not only two. In the rewritings we propose in Sections 3.2 and 3.4, however, the number of atoms in the clauses is not bounded by a constant. We require the following notion to generalise skinny programs. A function ν from the predicate names in Π to $\mathbb{N}$ is called a *weight function* for an NDL query $(\Pi, G(\boldsymbol{x}))$ if

$$\nu(Q) > 0 \quad\text{and}\quad \nu(Q) \geq \nu(P_1) + \cdots + \nu(P_k),$$

for any clause $Q(\boldsymbol{z}) \leftarrow P_1(\boldsymbol{z}_1) \wedge \cdots \wedge P_k(\boldsymbol{z}_k)$ in Π. Note that $\nu(P)$ can be 0 for an EDB predicate P. To illustrate, we consider NDL queries with the following dependency graphs:

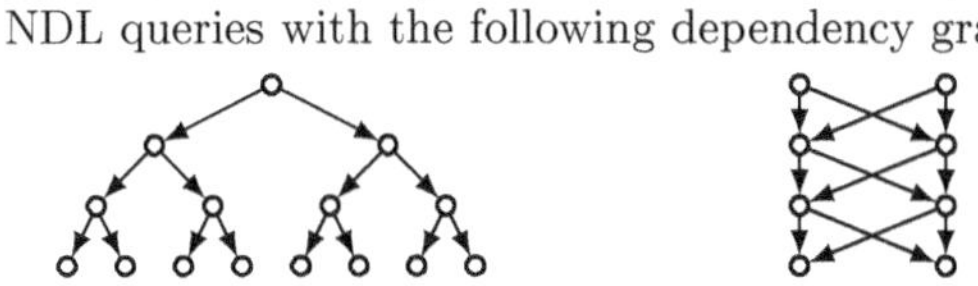

The one on the left has a weight function bounded by the number of predicates (i.e., linear in the size of the query); intuitively, this function corresponds to the number of directed paths from a vertex to the leaves. In contrast, any NDL query with the dependency graph on the right can only have a weight function whose values (numbers of paths) are exponential. Note that linear NDL queries have weight functions bounded by 1.

Let e_Π be the maximum number of EDB predicates in a clause of Π. The *skinny depth* $\mathsf{sd}(\Pi, G)$ of $(\Pi, G(\boldsymbol{x}))$ is the minimum value of $2\mathsf{d}(\Pi, G) + \log\nu(G) + \log\mathsf{e}_\Pi$ over possible weight functions ν. We show, using Huffman coding, that any NDL query $(\Pi, G(\boldsymbol{x}))$ can be transformed into an equivalent skinny NDL query of depth not exceeding $\mathsf{sd}(\Pi, G)$.

LEMMA 5. *Any NDL query $(\Pi, G(\boldsymbol{x}))$ is equivalent to a skinny NDL query $(\Pi', G(\boldsymbol{x}))$ such that $|\Pi'| = O(|\Pi|^2)$, $\mathsf{d}(\Pi', G) \leq \mathsf{sd}(\Pi, G)$, and $\mathsf{w}(\Pi', G) \leq \mathsf{w}(\Pi, G)$.*

PROOF. Suppose $\mathsf{sd}(\Pi, G) = 2\mathsf{d}(\Pi, G) + \log\nu(G) + \log\mathsf{e}_\Pi$. Without loss of generality, we assume that $\nu(E) = 0$ for EDB predicates E. First, we split clauses into EDB and IDB components by replacing each clause ψ of the form $Q(\boldsymbol{z}) \leftarrow \varphi(\boldsymbol{z}')$ with clauses $Q(\boldsymbol{z}) \leftarrow Q^\psi_E(\boldsymbol{z}_E) \wedge Q^\psi_I(\boldsymbol{z}_I)$ and $Q^\psi_\alpha(\boldsymbol{z}_\alpha) \leftarrow \varphi_\alpha(\boldsymbol{z}'_\alpha)$, where $\alpha \in \{E, I\}$, Q^ψ_E and Q^ψ_I are fresh predicates, and $\varphi_E(\boldsymbol{z}'_E)$ and $\varphi_I(\boldsymbol{z}'_I)$ are conjunctions of the EDB and IDB atoms in φ, respectively. The depth of the resulting NDL query $(\Pi_*, G(\boldsymbol{x}))$ is $2\mathsf{d}(\Pi, G)$. Now, each $Q^\psi_E(\boldsymbol{z}_E) \leftarrow \varphi_E(\boldsymbol{z}'_E)$ in Π_* is replaced by $\leq \mathsf{e}_\Pi - 1$ clauses with ≤ 2 atoms in the body, resulting in an NDL query of depth $\leq 2\mathsf{d}(\Pi, G) + \log\mathsf{e}_\Pi$. In the rest of the proof, we focus on the part $\Pi_\dagger$ of Π_* comprising clauses that have predicates Q and Q^ψ_I in their head (thus making the Q^ψ_E EDB predicates). The weight function for $(\Pi_\dagger, G(\boldsymbol{x}))$ is obtained by extending ν with $\nu(Q^\psi_I) = \nu(Q)$ and $\nu(Q^\psi_E) = 0$, for each clause ψ having Q as its head predicate.

Next, by induction on $\mathsf{d}(\Pi_\dagger, G)$, we show that there is an equivalent skinny NDL query $(\Pi'_\dagger, G(\boldsymbol{x}))$ of the required size and width such that $\mathsf{d}(\Pi'_\dagger, G) \leq \mathsf{d}(\Pi_\dagger, G) + \log\nu(G)$. We take $\Pi'_\dagger = \Pi_\dagger$ if $\mathsf{d}(\Pi_\dagger, G) = 0$. Otherwise, let ψ be a clause of the form $G(\boldsymbol{z}) \leftarrow P_1(\boldsymbol{z}_1) \wedge \cdots \wedge P_k(\boldsymbol{z}_k)$ in $\Pi_\dagger$, for $k > 2$. By construction, all clauses in $\Pi_\dagger$ with EDB predicates are of the form $Q(\boldsymbol{z}) \leftarrow Q^\psi_E(\boldsymbol{z}_E) \wedge Q^\psi_I(\boldsymbol{z}'_I)$, with two atoms in the body. So, the P_i in ψ are IDB predicates and $\nu(G) \geq \nu(P_i) > 0$. Suppose that, for each i $(1 \leq i \leq k)$, we have an NDL query (Π'_i, P_i) equivalent to $(\Pi_\dagger, P_i)$ with

$$\begin{aligned}\mathsf{d}(\Pi'_i, P_i) \;&\leq\; \mathsf{d}(\Pi_\dagger, P_i) + \log\nu(P_i)\\ &\leq\; \mathsf{d}(\Pi_\dagger, G) - 1 + \log\nu(P_i). \qquad (3)\end{aligned}$$

Construct the Huffman tree [31] for the alphabet $\{1, \ldots, k\}$, where the frequency of i is $\nu(P_i)/\nu(G)$. For example, for $\nu(G) = 39$, $\nu(P_1) = 15$, $\nu(P_2) = 7$, $\nu(P_3) = 6$, $\nu(P_4) = 6$ and $\nu(P_5) = 5$, we obtain the following tree:

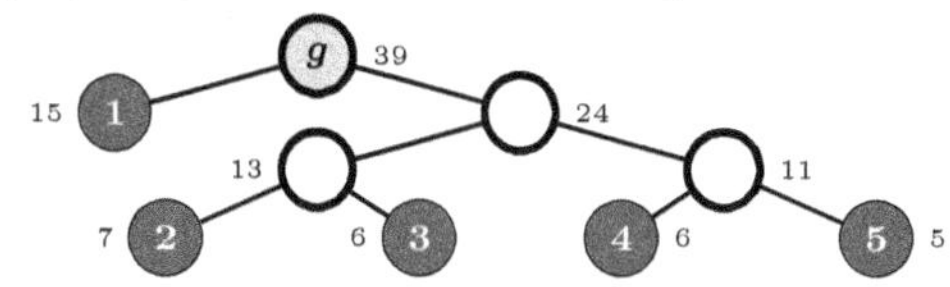

In general, the Huffman tree is a binary tree with k leaves $1, \ldots, k$, root g, and $k-2$ internal nodes such that the length of the path from g to any leaf i is $\leq \lceil\log(\nu(G)/\nu(P_i))\rceil$. For each internal node v, we take a predicate $P_v(\boldsymbol{z}_v)$, where $\boldsymbol{z}_v$ is the union of $\boldsymbol{z}_u$ for all descendants u of v; for root g, we take $P_g(\boldsymbol{z}_g) = G(\boldsymbol{z})$. Let Π'_ψ be the extension of the union of the Π'_i $(1 \leq i \leq k)$ with clauses $P_v(\boldsymbol{z}_v) \leftarrow P_{u_1}(\boldsymbol{z}_{u_1}) \wedge P_{u_2}(\boldsymbol{z}_{u_2})$, for each v with immediate successors u_1 and u_2. The number of the new clauses is $k - 1$. By (3), we have:

$$\begin{aligned}\mathsf{d}(\Pi'_\psi, G) &\leq \max_i\{\lceil\log(\nu(G)/\nu(P_i))\rceil + \mathsf{d}(\Pi'_i, P_i)\}\\ &\leq \max_i\{\log(\nu(G)/\nu(P_i)) + \mathsf{d}(\Pi_\dagger, G) + \log\nu(P_i)\}\\ &= \mathsf{d}(\Pi_\dagger, G) + \log\nu(G).\end{aligned}$$

Let $\Pi'_\dagger$ be the result of applying this transformation to each clause in $\Pi_\dagger$ with head $G(\boldsymbol{z})$ and > 2 atoms in the body.

Finally, we add to $\Pi'_{\dagger}$ the clauses with the Q_E predicates and denote the result by Π'. It is readily seen that (Π', G) is as required; in particular, $|\Pi'| = O(|\Pi|^2)$. ❑

We now use Lemmas 4 and 5 to obtain the following:

THEOREM 6. *For every $c > 0$ and $\mathsf{w} > 0$, evaluation of NDL queries $(\Pi, G(\boldsymbol{x}))$ of width at most w and such that $\mathsf{sd}(\Pi, G) \le c \log |\Pi|$ is in* LOGCFL *for combined complexity.*

We say that a class of OMQs is *skinny-reducible* if, for some fixed $c > 0$ and $\mathsf{w} > 0$, there is an $\mathsf{L}^{\mathsf{LOGCFL}}$-transducer that, given any OMQ $\boldsymbol{Q}(\boldsymbol{x})$ in the class, computes its NDL-rewriting $(\Pi, G(\boldsymbol{x}))$ over complete data instances such that $\mathsf{sd}(\Pi, G) \le c \log |\Pi|$ and $\mathsf{w}(\Pi, G) \le \mathsf{w}$. Theorem 6 and the transformation * give the following:

COROLLARY 7. *For any skinny-reducible class, the OMQ answering problem is in* LOGCFL *for combined complexity.*

In the following subsections, we will exploit the results obtained above to construct optimal NDL-rewritings for the three classes of tractable OMQs. Concrete examples of our rewritings are provided in the appendix of the present paper.

3.2 LOGCFL Rewritings for OMQ(d, t, ∞)

We begin by considering the case of bounded treewidth queries coupled with bounded depth ontologies. Recall (see, e.g., [23]) that a *tree decomposition* of an undirected graph $\mathcal{G} = (V, E)$ is a pair (T, λ), where T is an (undirected) tree and λ a function from the nodes of T to 2^V such that

- for every $v \in V$, there exists a node t with $v \in \lambda(t)$;
- for every $e \in E$, there exists a node t with $e \subseteq \lambda(t)$;
- for every $v \in V$, the nodes $\{t \mid v \in \lambda(t)\}$ induce a connected subgraph of T (called a *subtree* of T).

We call the set $\lambda(t) \subseteq V$ a *bag for* t. The *width* of (T, λ) is $\max_{t \in T} |\lambda(t)| - 1$. The *treewidth of a graph* $\mathcal{G}$ is the minimum width over all tree decompositions of $\mathcal{G}$. The *treewidth of a CQ* is the treewidth of its Gaifman graph.

EXAMPLE 8. Consider the CQ $\boldsymbol{q}(x_0, x_7)$ depicted below (black nodes represent answer variables):

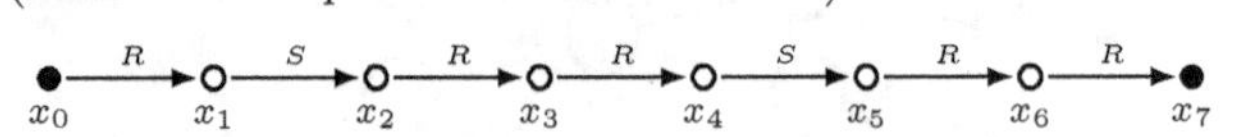

Its natural tree decomposition of treewidth 1 is based on the chain T of 7 vertices shown as bags below:

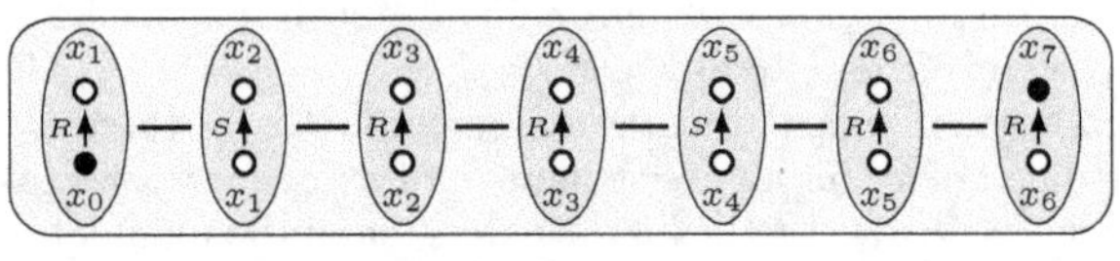

We now establish the following theorem, which, by the results of the preceding subsection, yields an NDL-rewriting with the desired LOGCFL complexity.

THEOREM 9. *For any fixed $\boldsymbol{d} \ge 0$ and $\boldsymbol{t} \ge 1$, the class* $\mathsf{OMQ}(\boldsymbol{d}, \boldsymbol{t}, \infty)$ *is skinny-reducible.*

In a nutshell, we split recursively a given CQ $\boldsymbol{q}$ into sub-CQs $\boldsymbol{q}_D$ based on subtrees D of the tree decomposition of $\boldsymbol{q}$, and combine their rewritings into a rewriting of $\boldsymbol{q}$. To guarantee compatibility of these rewritings, we use 'boundary conditions' $\boldsymbol{w}$ that describe the types of points on the boundaries of the $\boldsymbol{q}_D$ and, for each possible boundary condition $\boldsymbol{w}$, we define recursively a fresh IDB predicate $G^{\boldsymbol{w}}_D$. We now formalise the construction and illustrate it using the CQ from Example 8.

Fix a connected CQ $\boldsymbol{q}(\boldsymbol{x})$ and a tree decomposition (T, λ) of its Gaifman graph $\mathcal{G} = (V, E)$. Let D be a subtree of T. The *size* of D is the number of nodes in it. A node t of D is called *boundary* if T has an edge $\{t, t'\}$ with $t' \notin D$. The *degree* $\mathsf{deg}(D)$ of D is the number of its boundary nodes (T itself is the only subtree of T of degree 0). We say that a node t *splits* D into subtrees $D_1, \dots, D_k$ if the D_i partition D without t: each node of D different from t belongs to exactly one the D_i.

LEMMA 10 ([5]). *Let D be a subtree of T of size $n > 1$. If $\mathsf{deg}(D) = 2$, then there is a node t splitting D into subtrees of size $\le n/2$ and degree ≤ 2 and, possibly, one subtree of size $< n - 1$ and degree 1. If $\mathsf{deg}(D) \le 1$, then there is t splitting D into subtrees of size $\le n/2$ and degree ≤ 2.*

In Example 8, t splits T into D_1 and D_2 as follows:

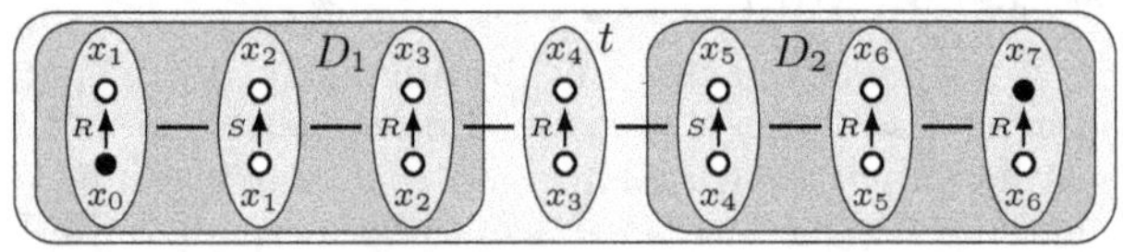

We define recursively a set $\mathfrak{D}$ of subtrees of T, a binary 'predecessor' relation $\prec$ on $\mathfrak{D}$, and a function σ on $\mathfrak{D}$ indicating the splitting node. We begin by adding T to $\mathfrak{D}$. Take any $D \in \mathfrak{D}$ that has not been split yet. If D is of size 1, then $\sigma(D)$ is the only node of D. Otherwise, by Lemma 10, we find a node t in D that splits it into $D_1, \dots, D_k$. We set $\sigma(D) = t$ and, for $1 \le i \le k$, add D_i to $\mathfrak{D}$ and set $D_i \prec D$; then, we apply the procedure recursively to each of $D_1, \dots, D_k$. In Example 8 with t splitting T, we have $\sigma(T) = t$, $D_1 \prec T$ and $D_2 \prec T$.

For each $D \in \mathfrak{D}$, we recursively define a set of atoms

$$\boldsymbol{q}_D \quad = \quad \{S(\boldsymbol{z}) \in \boldsymbol{q} \mid \boldsymbol{z} \subseteq \lambda(\sigma(D))\} \ \cup \ \bigcup\nolimits_{D' \prec D} \boldsymbol{q}_{D'}.$$

By the definition of tree decomposition, $\boldsymbol{q}_T = \boldsymbol{q}$. Denote by $\boldsymbol{x}_D$ the subset of $\boldsymbol{x}$ that occurs in $\boldsymbol{q}_D$. In Example 8, $\boldsymbol{x}_T = \{x_0, x_7\}$, $\boldsymbol{x}_{D_1} = \{x_0\}$ and $\boldsymbol{x}_{D_2} = \{x_7\}$. Let ∂D be the union of all $\lambda(t) \cap \lambda(t')$ for boundary nodes t of D and its neighbours t' in T *outside* D. In our example, $\partial T = \emptyset$, $\partial D_1 = \{x_3\}$ and $\partial D_2 = \{x_4\}$.

Let $\mathcal{T}$ be an ontology of depth $\le \boldsymbol{d}$. A *type* is a partial map $\boldsymbol{w}$ from V to $\boldsymbol{W}_{\mathcal{T}}$; its domain is denoted by $\mathsf{dom}(\boldsymbol{w})$. The unique partial type with $\mathsf{dom}(\boldsymbol{\varepsilon}) = \emptyset$ is denoted by $\boldsymbol{\varepsilon}$. We use types to represent how variables are mapped into $\mathcal{C}_{\mathcal{T},\mathcal{A}}$, with $\boldsymbol{w}(z) = w$ indicating that z is mapped to an element of the form aw (for some $a \in \mathsf{ind}(\mathcal{A})$), and with $\boldsymbol{w}(z) = \varepsilon$ that z is mapped to an individual constant. We say that a type $\boldsymbol{w}$ is *compatible* with a bag t if, for all $y, z \in \lambda(t) \cap \mathsf{dom}(\boldsymbol{w})$:

- if $z \in \boldsymbol{x}$, then $\boldsymbol{w}(z) = \varepsilon$;
- if $A(z) \in \boldsymbol{q}$, then either $\boldsymbol{w}(z) = \varepsilon$ or $\boldsymbol{w}(z) = w\varrho$ with $\mathcal{T} \models \exists y\, \varrho(y, x) \to A(x)$;
- if $P(y, z) \in \boldsymbol{q}$, then one of the three conditions holds: (*i*) $\boldsymbol{w}(y) = \boldsymbol{w}(z) = \varepsilon$; (*ii*) $\boldsymbol{w}(y) = \boldsymbol{w}(z)$, $\mathcal{T} \models P(x, x)$; (*iii*) $\mathcal{T} \models \varrho(x, y) \to P(x, y)$ and either $\boldsymbol{w}(z) = \boldsymbol{w}(y)\varrho$ or $\boldsymbol{w}(y) = \boldsymbol{w}(z)\varrho^-$.

In the sequel, we abuse notation and use sets of variables in place of sequences assuming that they are ordered in some (fixed) way. For example, we use $\boldsymbol{x}_D$ for a tuple of variables in the set $\boldsymbol{x}_D$ (ordered in some way). Also, given a tuple $\boldsymbol{a} \in \mathsf{ind}(\mathcal{A})^{|\boldsymbol{x}_D|}$ and $x \in \boldsymbol{x}_D$, we write $\boldsymbol{a}(x)$ to refer to the component of $\boldsymbol{a}$ that corresponds to x (that is, the component with the same index).

We now define an NDL-rewriting of $\boldsymbol{Q}(\boldsymbol{x}) = (\mathcal{T}, \boldsymbol{q}(\boldsymbol{x}))$. For every $D \in \mathfrak{D}$ and type $\boldsymbol{w}$ with $\mathsf{dom}(\boldsymbol{w}) = \partial D$, let $G_D^{\boldsymbol{w}}(\partial D, \boldsymbol{x}_D)$ be a fresh IDB predicate with parameters $\boldsymbol{x}_D$ (note that ∂D and $\boldsymbol{x}_D$ may not be disjoint). For each type $\boldsymbol{s}$ with $\mathsf{dom}(\boldsymbol{s}) = \lambda(\sigma(D))$ that is compatible with $\sigma(D)$ and agrees with $\boldsymbol{w}$ on their common domain, the NDL program $\Pi_{\boldsymbol{Q}}^{\mathrm{LOG}}$ contains

$$G_D^{\boldsymbol{w}}(\partial D, \boldsymbol{x}_D) \leftarrow \mathsf{At}^{\boldsymbol{s}} \land \bigwedge\nolimits_{D' \prec D} G_{D'}^{(\boldsymbol{s} \cup \boldsymbol{w}) \restriction \partial D'}(\partial D', \boldsymbol{x}_{D'}),$$

where $(\boldsymbol{s} \cup \boldsymbol{w}) \restriction \partial D'$ is the restriction of the union $\boldsymbol{s} \cup \boldsymbol{w}$ to $\partial D'$ (since $\mathsf{dom}(\boldsymbol{s} \cup \boldsymbol{w})$ covers $\partial D'$, the domain of the restriction is $\partial D'$), and $\mathsf{At}^{\boldsymbol{s}}$ is the conjunction of

(a) $A(z)$, for $A(z) \in \boldsymbol{q}$ with $\boldsymbol{s}(z) = \varepsilon$, and $P(y, z)$, for $P(y, z) \in \boldsymbol{q}$ with $\boldsymbol{s}(y) = \boldsymbol{s}(z) = \varepsilon$;

(b) $y = z$, for $P(y, z) \in \boldsymbol{q}$ with $\boldsymbol{s}(y) \neq \varepsilon$ or $\boldsymbol{s}(z) \neq \varepsilon$;

(c) $A_\varrho(z)$, for z with $\boldsymbol{s}(z) = \varrho w$, for some w.

The conjuncts in (a) ensure that atoms all of whose variables are assigned ε hold in the data instance. The conjuncts in (b) ensure that if one variable in a binary atom is not mapped to ε, then the images of both its variables share the same initial individual. Finally, the conjuncts in (c) ensure that if a variable is to be mapped to $a\varrho w$, then $a\varrho w$ is indeed in the domain of $\mathcal{C}_{\mathcal{T},\mathcal{A}}$.

EXAMPLE 11. With the query in Example 8, consider now the following ontology $\mathcal{T}$:

$$P(x,y) \to S(x,y), \qquad A_P(x) \leftrightarrow \exists y\, P(x,y),$$
$$P(x,y) \to R(y,x), \qquad A_{P^-}(x) \leftrightarrow \exists y\, P(y,x)$$

(the remaining normalisation axioms are omitted). Since $\lambda(t) = \{x_3, x_4\}$, there are two types compatible with t that can contribute to the rewriting: $\boldsymbol{s}_1 = \{x_3 \mapsto \varepsilon,\ x_4 \mapsto \varepsilon\}$ and $\boldsymbol{s}_2 = \{x_3 \mapsto \varepsilon,\ x_4 \mapsto P^-\}$. So we have $\mathsf{At}^{\boldsymbol{s}_1} = R(x_3, x_4)$ and $\mathsf{At}^{\boldsymbol{s}_2} = A_{P^-}(x_4) \land (x_3 = x_4)$. Thus, the predicate $G_T^{\boldsymbol{\varepsilon}}$ is defined by two clauses with the head $G_T^{\boldsymbol{\varepsilon}}(x_0, x_7)$ and the following bodies:

$$G_{D_1}^{x_3 \mapsto \varepsilon}(x_3, x_0) \land R(x_3, x_4) \land G_{D_2}^{x_4 \mapsto \varepsilon}(x_4, x_7),$$
$$G_{D_1}^{x_3 \mapsto \varepsilon}(x_3, x_0) \land A_{P^-}(x_4) \land (x_3 = x_4) \land G_{D_2}^{x_4 \mapsto P^-}(x_4, x_7),$$

for $\boldsymbol{s}_1$ and $\boldsymbol{s}_2$, respectively. Although $\{x_3 \mapsto P,\ x_4 \mapsto \varepsilon\}$ is also compatible with t, its predicate $G_{D_1}^{x_3 \mapsto P}$ will have no definition in the rewriting, and hence can be omitted. The same is true of the other compatible types $\{x_3 \mapsto \varepsilon,\ x_4 \mapsto R\}$ and $\{x_3 \mapsto R^-,\ x_4 \mapsto \varepsilon\}$.

By induction on $\prec$, one can now show that $(\Pi_{\boldsymbol{Q}}^{\mathrm{LOG}}, G_T^{\boldsymbol{\varepsilon}})$ is a rewriting of $\boldsymbol{Q}(\boldsymbol{x})$.

LEMMA 12. *For any complete data instance $\mathcal{A}$, subtree $D \in \mathfrak{D}$, type $\boldsymbol{w}$ with $\mathsf{dom}(\boldsymbol{w}) = \partial D$, and any $\boldsymbol{a} \in \mathsf{ind}(\mathcal{A})^{|\boldsymbol{x}_D|}$ and $\boldsymbol{b} \in \mathsf{ind}(\mathcal{A})^{|\partial D|}$, we have $\Pi_{\boldsymbol{Q}}^{\mathrm{LOG}}, \mathcal{A} \models G_D^{\boldsymbol{w}}(\boldsymbol{b}, \boldsymbol{a})$ iff there is a homomorphism $h\colon \boldsymbol{q}_D \to \mathcal{C}_{\mathcal{T},\mathcal{A}}$ such that $h(x) = \boldsymbol{a}(x)$, for $x \in \boldsymbol{x}_D$, and $h(z) = \boldsymbol{b}(z)\boldsymbol{w}(z)$, for $z \in \partial D$.*

Now fix $\boldsymbol{d}$ and $\boldsymbol{t}$, and consider $\boldsymbol{Q}(\boldsymbol{x}) = (\mathcal{T}, \boldsymbol{q}(\boldsymbol{x}))$ from $\mathsf{OMQ}(\boldsymbol{d}, \boldsymbol{t}, \infty)$. Let T be a tree decomposition of $\boldsymbol{q}$ of treewidth $\leq \boldsymbol{t}$; we may assume without loss of generality that T has at most $|\boldsymbol{q}|$ nodes. We take the following weight function: $\nu(G_D^{\boldsymbol{w}}) = |D|$, where $|D|$ is the number of nodes in D. Clearly, $\nu(G_T^{\boldsymbol{\varepsilon}}) \leq |\boldsymbol{q}|$. By Lemma 10, we have

$$\mathsf{w}(\Pi_{\boldsymbol{Q}}^{\mathrm{LOG}}, G_T^{\boldsymbol{\varepsilon}}) \leq \max_D |\partial D \cup \lambda(\sigma(D))| \leq 3(\boldsymbol{t}+1),$$
$$\mathsf{sd}(\Pi_{\boldsymbol{Q}}^{\mathrm{LOG}}, G_T^{\boldsymbol{\varepsilon}}) \leq 4 \log |T| + 2 \log |\boldsymbol{q}| \leq 6 \log |\boldsymbol{q}| \leq 6 \log |\Pi_{\boldsymbol{Q}}^{\mathrm{LOG}}|;$$

the last inequality is due to $\Pi_{\boldsymbol{Q}}^{\mathrm{LOG}}$ containing every atom of $\boldsymbol{q}$ (with variables renamed). Since $|\mathfrak{D}| \leq |T|^2$ and there are at most $|\mathcal{T}|^{2\boldsymbol{d}(\boldsymbol{t}+1)}$ options for $\boldsymbol{w}$, there are polynomially many predicates $G_D^{\boldsymbol{w}}$, so $\Pi_{\boldsymbol{Q}}^{\mathrm{LOG}}$ is of polynomial size. Finally, we note that a tree decomposition of treewidth $\leq \boldsymbol{t}$ can be computed using an $\mathsf{L}^{\mathsf{LOGCFL}}$-transducer [27], and so the NDL-rewriting can also be constructed by an $\mathsf{L}^{\mathsf{LOGCFL}}$-transducer. We have thus shown that the class $\mathsf{OMQ}(\boldsymbol{d}, \boldsymbol{t}, \infty)$ is skinny-reducible, establishing Theorem 9.

The obtained NDL-rewriting shows that answering OMQs $(\mathcal{T}, \boldsymbol{q}(\boldsymbol{x}))$ with $\mathcal{T}$ of finite depth $\boldsymbol{d}$ and $\boldsymbol{q}$ of treewidth $\boldsymbol{t}$ over any data instance $\mathcal{A}$ can be done in time

$$poly(|\mathcal{T}|^{\boldsymbol{dt}}, |\boldsymbol{q}|, |\mathcal{A}|^{\boldsymbol{t}}). \tag{4}$$

Indeed, we can evaluate $(\Pi_{\boldsymbol{Q}}^{\mathrm{LOG}}, G_T^{\boldsymbol{\varepsilon}}(\boldsymbol{x}))$ in time polynomial in $|\Pi_{\boldsymbol{Q}}^{\mathrm{LOG}}|$ and $|\mathcal{A}|^{\mathsf{w}(\Pi_{\boldsymbol{Q}}^{\mathrm{LOG}}, G_T^{\boldsymbol{\varepsilon}})}$, which are bounded by a polynomial in $|\mathcal{T}|^{3\boldsymbol{d}(\boldsymbol{t}+1)}$, $|\boldsymbol{q}|$ and $|\mathcal{A}|^{3(\boldsymbol{t}+1)}$.

3.3 NL Rewritings for OMQ($\boldsymbol{d}$, 1, $\boldsymbol{\ell}$)

For OMQs based upon bounded leaf queries and bounded depth ontologies, we establish the following theorem:

THEOREM 13. *Let $\boldsymbol{d} \geq 0$ and $\boldsymbol{\ell} \geq 2$ be fixed. There is an L^{NL}-transducer that, given an OMQ $\boldsymbol{Q} = (\mathcal{T}, \boldsymbol{q}(\boldsymbol{x}))$ in $\mathsf{OMQ}(\boldsymbol{d}, 1, \boldsymbol{\ell})$, constructs its polynomial-size linear NDL-rewriting of width $\leq 2\boldsymbol{\ell}$.*

Let $\mathcal{T}$ be an ontology of finite depth $\boldsymbol{d}$, and let $\boldsymbol{q}(\boldsymbol{x})$ be a tree-shaped CQ with at most $\boldsymbol{\ell}$ leaves. Fix one of the variables of $\boldsymbol{q}$ as root, and let M be the maximal distance to a leaf from the root. For $0 \leq n \leq M$, let $\boldsymbol{z}^n$ denote the set of all variables of $\boldsymbol{q}$ at distance n from the root; clearly, $|\boldsymbol{z}^n| \leq \boldsymbol{\ell}$. We call the $\boldsymbol{z}^n$ *slices* of $\boldsymbol{q}$ and observe that they satisfy the following: for every $P(z, z') \in \boldsymbol{q}$ with $z \neq z'$, there exists $n < M$ such that

$$\text{either } z \in \boldsymbol{z}^n \text{ and } z' \in \boldsymbol{z}^{n+1} \quad \text{or} \quad z' \in \boldsymbol{z}^n \text{ and } z \in \boldsymbol{z}^{n+1}.$$

For $0 \leq n \leq M$, let $\boldsymbol{q}_n(\boldsymbol{z}_\exists^n, \boldsymbol{x}^n)$ be the query consisting of all atoms $S(\boldsymbol{z})$ of $\boldsymbol{q}$ such that $\boldsymbol{z} \subseteq \bigcup_{n \leq k \leq M} \boldsymbol{z}^k$, where $\boldsymbol{x}^n$ is the subset of $\boldsymbol{x}$ that occurs in $\boldsymbol{q}_n$ and $\boldsymbol{z}_\exists^n = \boldsymbol{z}^n \setminus \boldsymbol{x}$.

By a *type for slice* $\boldsymbol{z}^n$, we mean a total map $\boldsymbol{w}$ from $\boldsymbol{z}^n$ to $\boldsymbol{W}_{\mathcal{T}}$. Analogously to Section 3.2, we define the notions of types compatible with slices. Specifically, we call $\boldsymbol{w}$ *locally compatible* with $\boldsymbol{z}^n$ if for every $z \in \boldsymbol{z}^n$:

- if $z \in \boldsymbol{x}$, then $\boldsymbol{w}(z) = \varepsilon$;
- if $A(z) \in \boldsymbol{q}$, then either $\boldsymbol{w}(z) = \varepsilon$ or $\boldsymbol{w}(z) = w\varrho$ with $\mathcal{T} \models \exists y\, \varrho(y, x) \to A(x)$;
- if $P(z, z) \in \boldsymbol{q}$, then either $\boldsymbol{w}(z) = \varepsilon$ or $\mathcal{T} \models P(x, x)$.

If $\boldsymbol{w}, \boldsymbol{s}$ are types for $\boldsymbol{z}^n$ and $\boldsymbol{z}^{n+1}$, respectively, then we say $(\boldsymbol{w}, \boldsymbol{s})$ *is compatible* with $(\boldsymbol{z}^n, \boldsymbol{z}^{n+1})$ if $\boldsymbol{w}$ is locally compatible with $\boldsymbol{z}^n$, $\boldsymbol{s}$ is locally compatible with $\boldsymbol{z}^{n+1}$,

- for every $P(z,z') \in \boldsymbol{q}$ with $z \in \boldsymbol{z}^n$ and $z' \in \boldsymbol{z}^{n+1}$, one of the three condition holds: $\boldsymbol{w}(z) = \boldsymbol{s}(z') = \varepsilon$, or $\boldsymbol{w}(z) = \boldsymbol{s}(z')$, $\mathcal{T} \models P(x,x)$, or $\mathcal{T} \models \varrho(x,y) \to P(x,y)$ and either $\boldsymbol{s}(z') = \boldsymbol{w}(z)\varrho$ or $\boldsymbol{w}(z) = \boldsymbol{s}(z')\varrho^-$.

Consider the NDL program $\Pi^{\text{LIN}}_{\boldsymbol{Q}}$ defined as follows. For every $0 \leq n < M$ and every pair of types $(\boldsymbol{w}, \boldsymbol{s})$ that is compatible with $(\boldsymbol{z}^n, \boldsymbol{z}^{n+1})$, we include the clause

$$G^{\boldsymbol{w}}_n(\boldsymbol{z}^n_\exists, \boldsymbol{x}^n) \leftarrow \mathsf{At}^{\boldsymbol{w}\cup\boldsymbol{s}}(\boldsymbol{z}^n, \boldsymbol{z}^{n+1}) \wedge G^{\boldsymbol{s}}_{n+1}(\boldsymbol{z}^{n+1}_\exists, \boldsymbol{x}^{n+1}),$$

where $\boldsymbol{x}^n$ are the parameters of $G^{\boldsymbol{w}}_n$ and $\mathsf{At}^{\boldsymbol{w}\cup\boldsymbol{s}}(\boldsymbol{z}^n, \boldsymbol{z}^{n+1})$ is the conjunction of atoms (a)–(c) as defined in Section 3.2, for the union $\boldsymbol{w} \cup \boldsymbol{s}$. For every type $\boldsymbol{w}$ locally compatible with $\boldsymbol{z}^M$, we include the clause

$$G^{\boldsymbol{w}}_M(\boldsymbol{z}^M_\exists, \boldsymbol{x}^M) \leftarrow \mathsf{At}^{\boldsymbol{w}}(\boldsymbol{z}^M).$$

(Recall that $\boldsymbol{z}^M$ is a disjoint union of $\boldsymbol{z}^M_\exists$ and $\boldsymbol{x}^M$.) We use G with parameters $\boldsymbol{x}$ as the goal predicate and include $G(\boldsymbol{x}) \leftarrow G^{\boldsymbol{w}}_0(\boldsymbol{z}^0_\exists, \boldsymbol{x})$ for every predicate $G^{\boldsymbol{w}}_0$ occurring in the head of one of the preceding clauses.

By induction on n, we show that $(\Pi^{\text{LIN}}_{\boldsymbol{Q}}, G(\boldsymbol{x}))$ is a rewriting of $(\mathcal{T}, \boldsymbol{q}(\boldsymbol{x}))$ over complete data instances.

Lemma 14. *For any complete data instance $\mathcal{A}$, any predicate $G^{\boldsymbol{w}}_n$, and any $\boldsymbol{a} \in \mathsf{ind}(\mathcal{A})^{|\boldsymbol{x}^n|}$ and $\boldsymbol{b} \in \mathsf{ind}(\mathcal{A})^{|\boldsymbol{z}^n_\exists|}$, we have $\Pi^{\text{LIN}}_{\boldsymbol{Q}}, \mathcal{A} \models G^{\boldsymbol{w}}_n(\boldsymbol{b}, \boldsymbol{a})$ iff there is a homomorphism $h\colon \boldsymbol{q}_n \to \mathcal{C}_{\mathcal{T},\mathcal{A}}$ such that $h(x) = \boldsymbol{a}(x)$, for $x \in \boldsymbol{x}^n$, and $h(z) = \boldsymbol{b}(z)\boldsymbol{w}(z)$, for $z \in \boldsymbol{z}^n_\exists$.*

It should be clear that $\Pi^{\text{LIN}}_{\boldsymbol{Q}}$ is a linear NDL program of width $\leq 2\boldsymbol{\ell}$ and containing $\leq |\boldsymbol{q}| \cdot |\mathcal{T}|^{2\boldsymbol{d}\boldsymbol{\ell}}$ predicates. Moreover, it takes only logarithmic space to store a type $\boldsymbol{w}$, which allows us to show that $\Pi^{\text{LIN}}_{\boldsymbol{Q}}$ can be computed by an L^{NL}-transducer. We apply Lemma 3 to obtain an NDL-rewriting for arbitrary data instances, and then use Theorem 2 to conclude that the resulting program can be evaluated in NL.

The obtained NDL-rewriting shows that answering OMQs $(\mathcal{T}, \boldsymbol{q}(\boldsymbol{x}))$ with $\mathcal{T}$ of finite depth $\boldsymbol{d}$ and tree-shaped $\boldsymbol{q}$ with $\boldsymbol{\ell}$ leaves over any data $\mathcal{A}$ can be done in time

$$poly(|\mathcal{T}|^{\boldsymbol{d}\boldsymbol{\ell}}, |\boldsymbol{q}|, |\mathcal{A}|^{\boldsymbol{\ell}}). \tag{5}$$

Indeed, $(\Pi^{\text{LIN}}_{\boldsymbol{Q}}, G(\boldsymbol{x}))$ can be evaluated in time polynomial in $|\Pi^{\text{LIN}}_{\boldsymbol{Q}}|$ and $|\mathcal{A}|^{\mathsf{w}(\Pi^{\text{LIN}}_{\boldsymbol{Q}}, G)}$, which are bounded by a polynomial in $|\mathcal{T}|^{2\boldsymbol{d}\boldsymbol{\ell}}$, $|\boldsymbol{q}|$ and $|\mathcal{A}|^{2\boldsymbol{\ell}}$.

3.4 LOGCFL Rewritings for OMQ(∞, 1, $\boldsymbol{\ell}$)

Unlike the previous two classes, answering OMQs from the class $\mathsf{OMQ}(\infty, 1, \boldsymbol{\ell})$ can be harder—LOGCFL-complete—than evaluating their CQs, which can be done in NL.

Theorem 15. *For any fixed number of leaves $\boldsymbol{\ell} \geq 2$, the class $\mathsf{OMQ}(\infty, 1, \boldsymbol{\ell})$ is skinny-reducible.*

For OMQs with bounded-leaf CQs and ontologies of unbounded depth, our rewriting uses the notion of tree witness [38]. Consider an OMQ $\boldsymbol{Q}(\boldsymbol{x}) = (\mathcal{T}, \boldsymbol{q}(\boldsymbol{x}))$. Suppose $\mathfrak{t} = (\mathfrak{t}_\mathsf{r}, \mathfrak{t}_\mathsf{i})$ is a pair of disjoint sets of variables in $\boldsymbol{q}$ such that $\mathfrak{t}_\mathsf{i} \neq \emptyset$ but $\mathfrak{t}_\mathsf{i} \cap \boldsymbol{x} = \emptyset$. Set

$$\boldsymbol{q}_\mathfrak{t} \;=\; \big\{\, S(\boldsymbol{z}) \in \boldsymbol{q} \mid \boldsymbol{z} \subseteq \mathfrak{t}_\mathsf{r} \cup \mathfrak{t}_\mathsf{i} \text{ and } \boldsymbol{z} \not\subseteq \mathfrak{t}_\mathsf{r} \,\big\}.$$

If $\boldsymbol{q}_\mathfrak{t}$ is a minimal subset of $\boldsymbol{q}$ containing every atom of $\boldsymbol{q}$ with a variable from $\mathfrak{t}_\mathsf{i}$ and such that there is a homomorphism $h\colon \boldsymbol{q}_\mathfrak{t} \to \mathcal{C}_{\mathcal{T},\{A_\varrho(a)\}}$ with $h^{-1}(a) = \mathfrak{t}_\mathsf{r}$, we call $\mathfrak{t}$ a *tree witness for $\boldsymbol{Q}(\boldsymbol{x})$ generated by ϱ*. Intuitively, $\mathfrak{t}$ identifies a minimal subset of $\boldsymbol{q}$ that can be mapped to the tree-shaped part of the canonical model consisting of labelled nulls: the variables in $\mathfrak{t}_\mathsf{r}$ are mapped to an individual constant, say, a, at the root of a tree and the $\mathfrak{t}_\mathsf{i}$ are mapped to the labelled nulls of the form aw, for some $w \in \boldsymbol{W}_\mathcal{T}$ that begins with ϱ. Note that the same tree witness can be generated by different ϱ.

The logarithmic-depth NDL-rewriting for OMQs drawn from $\mathsf{OMQ}(\infty, 1, \boldsymbol{\ell})$ is based on the following observation:

Lemma 16 ([35]). *Every tree T of size n has a node splitting it into subtrees of size $\leq \lceil n/2 \rceil$.*

Let $\boldsymbol{Q}(\boldsymbol{x}_0) = (\mathcal{T}, \boldsymbol{q}_0(\boldsymbol{x}_0))$ be an OMQ with a tree-shaped CQ. We will repeatedly apply Lemma 16 to decompose the CQ into smaller and smaller subqueries. Formally, for a tree-shaped CQ $\boldsymbol{q}$, we denote by $z_{\boldsymbol{q}}$ a vertex in the Gaifman graph $\mathcal{G}$ of $\boldsymbol{q}$ that satisfies the condition of Lemma 16; if $\boldsymbol{q}$ has two variables and at least one of them is existentially quantified, then we assume that $z_{\boldsymbol{q}}$ is such. Let $\mathfrak{Q}$ be the smallest set that contains $\boldsymbol{q}_0(\boldsymbol{x}_0)$ and the following CQs, for every $\boldsymbol{q}(\boldsymbol{x}) \in \mathfrak{Q}$ with existentially quantified variables:

- for each z_i adjacent to $z_{\boldsymbol{q}}$ in $\mathcal{G}$, the CQ $\boldsymbol{q}_i(\boldsymbol{x}_i)$ comprising all binary atoms with both z_i and $z_{\boldsymbol{q}}$, and all atoms whose variables cannot reach $z_{\boldsymbol{q}}$ in $\mathcal{G}$ without passing by z_i, where $\boldsymbol{x}_i$ is the set of variables in $\boldsymbol{x} \cup \{z_{\boldsymbol{q}}\}$ that occur in $\boldsymbol{q}_i$;
- for each tree witness $\mathfrak{t}$ for $(\mathcal{T}, \boldsymbol{q}(\boldsymbol{x}))$ with $\mathfrak{t}_\mathsf{r} \neq \emptyset$ and $z_{\boldsymbol{q}} \in \mathfrak{t}_\mathsf{i}$, the CQs $\boldsymbol{q}^\mathfrak{t}_1(\boldsymbol{x}^\mathfrak{t}_1), \dots, \boldsymbol{q}^\mathfrak{t}_k(\boldsymbol{x}^\mathfrak{t}_k)$ that correspond to the connected components of the set of atoms of $\boldsymbol{q}$ that are not in $\boldsymbol{q}_\mathfrak{t}$, where each $\boldsymbol{x}^\mathfrak{t}_i$ is the set of variables in $\boldsymbol{x} \cup \mathfrak{t}_\mathsf{r}$ that occur in $\boldsymbol{q}^\mathfrak{t}_i$.

The two cases are depicted below:

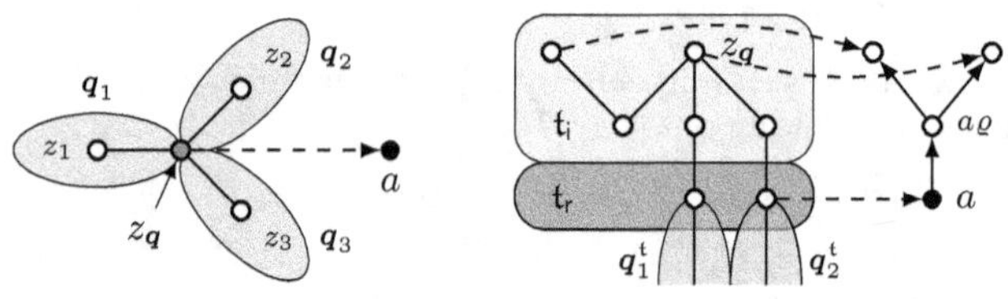

Note that $\mathfrak{t}_\mathsf{r} \neq \emptyset$ ensures that part of the query without $\boldsymbol{q}_\mathfrak{t}$ is mapped onto individual constants.

The NDL program $\Pi^{\text{TW}}_{\boldsymbol{Q}}$ uses IDB predicates $G_{\boldsymbol{q}}(\boldsymbol{x})$, for $\boldsymbol{q}(\boldsymbol{x}) \in \mathfrak{Q}$, whose parameters are the variables in $\boldsymbol{x}_0$ that occur in $\boldsymbol{q}(\boldsymbol{x})$. For each $\boldsymbol{q}(\boldsymbol{x}) \in \mathfrak{Q}$ that has no existentially quantified variables, we include the clause $G_{\boldsymbol{q}}(\boldsymbol{x}) \leftarrow \boldsymbol{q}(\boldsymbol{x})$. For any $\boldsymbol{q}(\boldsymbol{x}) \in \mathfrak{Q}$ with existential variables, we include

$$G_{\boldsymbol{q}}(\boldsymbol{x}) \quad\leftarrow\quad \bigwedge_{S(\boldsymbol{z}) \in \boldsymbol{q},\ \boldsymbol{z} \subseteq \{z_{\boldsymbol{q}}\}} S(\boldsymbol{z}) \;\;\wedge\;\; \bigwedge_{1 \leq i \leq n} G_{\boldsymbol{q}_i}(\boldsymbol{x}_i),$$

where $\boldsymbol{q}_1(\boldsymbol{x}_1), \dots, \boldsymbol{q}_n(\boldsymbol{x}_n)$ are the subqueries induced by the neighbours of $z_{\boldsymbol{q}}$ in $\mathcal{G}$, and, for any tree witness $\mathfrak{t}$ of $(\mathcal{T}, \boldsymbol{q}(\boldsymbol{x}))$ with $\mathfrak{t}_\mathsf{r} \neq \emptyset$ and $z_{\boldsymbol{q}} \in \mathfrak{t}_\mathsf{i}$ and any ϱ generating $\mathfrak{t}$, the clause

$$G_{\boldsymbol{q}}(\boldsymbol{x}) \quad \leftarrow A_\varrho(z_0) \;\wedge\; \bigwedge_{z \in \mathfrak{t}_\mathsf{r} \setminus \{z_0\}} (z = z_0) \;\;\wedge\;\; \bigwedge_{1 \leq i \leq k} G_{\boldsymbol{q}^\mathfrak{t}_i}(\boldsymbol{x}^\mathfrak{t}_i),$$

where z_0 is any variable in $\mathfrak{t}_\mathsf{r}$ and $\boldsymbol{q}^\mathfrak{t}_1, \dots, \boldsymbol{q}^\mathfrak{t}_k$ are the connected components of $\boldsymbol{q}$ without $\boldsymbol{q}_\mathfrak{t}$. Finally, if $\boldsymbol{q}_0$ is Boolean, then we include clauses $G_{\boldsymbol{q}_0} \leftarrow A(x)$ for all unary predicates A such that $\mathcal{T}, \{A(a)\} \models \boldsymbol{q}_0$.

The program $\Pi^{\text{TW}}_{\boldsymbol{Q}}$ is inspired by a similar construction from [35]. By adapting the proof, we can show that the NDL query $(\Pi^{\text{TW}}_{\boldsymbol{Q}}, G_{\boldsymbol{q}_0}(\boldsymbol{x}_0))$ is indeed a rewriting.

LEMMA 17. *For any OMQ $\boldsymbol{Q}(\boldsymbol{x}_0) = (\mathcal{T}, \boldsymbol{q}_0(\boldsymbol{x}_0))$ with a tree-shaped CQ, any complete data instance $\mathcal{A}$, any query $\boldsymbol{q}(\boldsymbol{x}) \in \mathfrak{Q}$ and any $\boldsymbol{a} \in \mathsf{ind}(\mathcal{A})^{|\boldsymbol{x}|}$, we have $\Pi_{\boldsymbol{Q}}^{\mathrm{Tw}}, \mathcal{A} \models G_{\boldsymbol{q}}(\boldsymbol{a})$ iff there is a homomorphism $h\colon \boldsymbol{q} \to \mathcal{C}_{\mathcal{T},\mathcal{A}}$ with $h(\boldsymbol{x}) = \boldsymbol{a}$.*

Now fix $\boldsymbol{\ell} > 1$ and consider $\boldsymbol{Q}(\boldsymbol{x}) = (\mathcal{T}, \boldsymbol{q}_0(\boldsymbol{x}))$ from the class $\mathsf{OMQ}(\infty, 1, \boldsymbol{\ell})$. The size of the program $\Pi_{\boldsymbol{Q}}^{\mathrm{Tw}}$ is polynomially bounded in $|\boldsymbol{Q}|$ since $\boldsymbol{q}_0$ has $O(|\boldsymbol{q}_0|^{\boldsymbol{\ell}})$ tree witnesses and tree-shaped subqueries. It is readily seen that the function ν defined by setting $\nu(G_{\boldsymbol{q}}) = |\boldsymbol{q}|$, for each $\boldsymbol{q} \in \mathfrak{Q}$, is a weight function for $(\Pi_{\boldsymbol{Q}}^{\mathrm{Tw}}, G_{\boldsymbol{q}_0}(\boldsymbol{x}))$ with $\nu(G_{\boldsymbol{q}_0}) \leq |\boldsymbol{Q}|$. Moreover, by Lemma 16, $\mathsf{d}(\Pi_{\boldsymbol{Q}}^{\mathrm{Tw}}, G_{\boldsymbol{q}_0}) \leq \log \nu(G_{\boldsymbol{q}_0}) + 1$; and clearly, $\mathsf{w}(\Pi_{\boldsymbol{Q}}^{\mathrm{Tw}}, G_{\boldsymbol{q}_0}) \leq \boldsymbol{\ell}+1$. Finally, we note that, since the number of leaves is bounded, it is in NL to decide whether a vertex satisfies the conditions of Lemma 16, and in LOGCFL to decide whether $\mathcal{T}, \{A(a)\} \models \boldsymbol{q}(a)$, for bounded-leaf tree-shaped CQs $\boldsymbol{q}(x)$ [5], or whether a (logspace) representation of a possible tree witness is indeed a tree witness. This allows us to show that $(\Pi_{\boldsymbol{Q}}^{\mathrm{Tw}}, G_{\boldsymbol{q}_0}(\boldsymbol{x}))$ can be generated by an $\mathsf{L}^{\mathsf{LOGCFL}}$-transducer. By Corollary 7, the obtained NDL-rewritings can be evaluated in LOGCFL.

It also follows that answering OMQs $(\mathcal{T}, \boldsymbol{q}(\boldsymbol{x}))$ with a tree-shaped CQ with $\boldsymbol{\ell}$ leaves over any $\mathcal{A}$ can be done in time

$$poly(|\mathcal{T}|, |\boldsymbol{q}|^{\boldsymbol{\ell}}, |\mathcal{A}|^{\boldsymbol{\ell}}). \tag{6}$$

Indeed, $(\Pi_{\boldsymbol{Q}}^{\mathrm{Tw}}, G(\boldsymbol{x}))$ can be evaluated in time polynomial in $|\Pi_{\boldsymbol{Q}}^{\mathrm{Tw}}|$ and $|\mathcal{A}|^{\mathsf{w}(\Pi_{\boldsymbol{Q}}^{\mathrm{Tw}}, G)}$, which are bounded by polynomials in $|\mathcal{T}|$, $|\boldsymbol{q}|^{\boldsymbol{\ell}}$ and $|\mathcal{A}|^{\boldsymbol{\ell}+1}$, respectively.

4. PARAMETERISED COMPLEXITY

The upper bounds (4) and (6) for the time required to evaluate NDL-rewritings of OMQs from $\mathsf{OMQ}(\boldsymbol{d}, 1, \infty)$ and $\mathsf{OMQ}(\infty, 1, \boldsymbol{\ell})$ contain $\boldsymbol{d}$ and $\boldsymbol{\ell}$ in the exponent of $|\mathcal{T}|$ and $|\boldsymbol{q}|$. Moreover, if we allow $\boldsymbol{d}$ and $\boldsymbol{\ell}$ to grow while keeping CQs tree-shaped, the combined complexity of OMQ answering will jump to NP; see Fig. 1 (a). In this section, we regard $\boldsymbol{d}$ and $\boldsymbol{\ell}$ as parameters and show that answering tree-shaped OMQs is not fixed-parameter tractable.

4.1 Ontology Depth

Consider the following problem *pDepth*-TREEOMQ:

Instance: an OMQ $\boldsymbol{Q} = (\mathcal{T}, \boldsymbol{q})$ with $\mathcal{T}$ of finite depth and tree-shaped Boolean CQ $\boldsymbol{q}$.
Parameter: the depth of $\mathcal{T}$.
Problem: decide whether $\mathcal{T}, \{A(a)\} \models \boldsymbol{q}$.

THEOREM 18. *pDepth-TREEOMQ is $W[2]$-hard.*

PROOF. The proof is by reduction of the parameterised problem p-HITTINGSET, known to be $W[2]$-complete [23]:

Instance: a hypergraph $H = (V, E)$ and $k \in \mathbb{N}$.
Parameter: k.
Problem: decide whether there is $A \subseteq V$ such that $|A| = k$ and $e \cap A \neq \emptyset$, for every $e \in E$.

(Such a set A of vertices is called a *hitting set of size k*.) Suppose that $H = (V, E)$ is a hypergraph with vertices $V = \{v_1, \dots, v_n\}$ and hyperedges $E = \{e_1, \dots, e_m\}$. Let $\mathcal{T}_H^k$ be the (normal form of an) ontology with the following axioms, for $1 \leq l \leq k$:

$$V_i^{l-1}(x) \to \exists z\,(P(z,x) \land V_{i'}^{l}(z)), \quad \text{for } 0 \leq i < i' \leq n,$$
$$V_i^{l}(x) \to E_j^{l}(x), \quad \text{for } v_i \in e_j,\ e_j \in E,$$
$$E_j^{l}(x) \to \exists z\,(P(x,z) \land E_j^{l-1}(z)), \quad \text{for } 1 \leq j \leq m.$$

Let $\boldsymbol{q}_H^k$ be a tree-shaped Boolean CQ with the following atoms, for $1 \leq j \leq m$:

$$P(y, z_j^{k-1}), \quad P(z_j^l, z_j^{l-1}) \text{ for } 1 \leq l < k, \quad \text{and } E_j^0(z_j^0).$$

The first axiom of $\mathcal{T}_H^k$ generates a tree of depth k, with branching ranging from n to 1, such that the points w of level k are labelled with subsets $X \subseteq V$ of size k that are read off the path from the root to w. The CQ $\boldsymbol{q}_H^k$ is a star with rays corresponding to the hyperedges of H. The second and third axioms generate 'pendants' ensuring that, for any hyperedge e, the central point of the CQ can be mapped to a point with a label X iff X and e have a common vertex. The canonical model of $(\mathcal{T}_H^2, \{V_0^0(a)\})$ and the CQ $\boldsymbol{q}_H^2$, for $H = (V, \{e_1, e_2, e_3\})$ with $V = \{1,2,3\}$, $e_1 = \{1,3\}$, $e_2 = \{2,3\}$ and $e_3 = \{1,2\}$, are shown below:

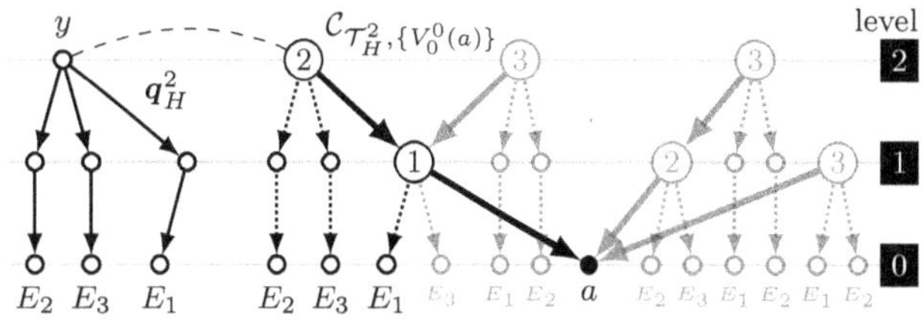

Points ⓘ at level l belong to V_i^l. In the long version [4], we prove that $\mathcal{T}_H^k, \{V_0^0(a)\} \models \boldsymbol{q}_H^k$ iff H has a hitting set of size k. In the example above, $\{1,2\}$ is a hitting set of size 2, which corresponds to the homomorphism from $\boldsymbol{q}_H^2$ into the part of $\mathcal{C}_{\mathcal{T}_H^2,\{V_0^0(a)\}}$ shown in black. ❑

By Theorem 9, OMQs $(\mathcal{T}, \boldsymbol{q})$ from $\mathsf{OMQ}(\boldsymbol{d}, 1, \infty)$ can be answered (via NDL-rewriting) over a data instance $\mathcal{A}$ in time $poly(|\mathcal{T}|^{\boldsymbol{d}}, |\boldsymbol{q}|, |\mathcal{A}|)$. Theorem 18 shows that no algorithm can do this in time $f(\boldsymbol{d}) \cdot poly(|\mathcal{T}|, |\boldsymbol{q}|, |\mathcal{A}|)$, for any computable function f, unless $W[2] = \mathrm{FPT}$.

4.2 Number of Leaves

Next we consider the problem *pLeaves*-TREEOMQ:

Instance: an OMQ $\boldsymbol{Q} = (\mathcal{T}, \boldsymbol{q})$ with $\mathcal{T}$ of finite depth and tree-shaped Boolean CQ $\boldsymbol{q}$.
Parameter: the number of leaves in $\boldsymbol{q}$.
Problem: decide whether $\mathcal{T}, \{A(a)\} \models \boldsymbol{q}$.

THEOREM 19. *pLeaves-TREEOMQ is $W[1]$-hard.*

PROOF. The proof is by reduction of the following $W[1]$-complete PARTITIONEDCLIQUE problem [22]:

Instance: a graph $G = (V, E)$ whose vertices are partitioned into p sets $V_1, \dots, V_p$.
Parameter: p, the number of partitions.
Problem: decide whether G has a clique of size p containing one vertex from each V_i.

Consider a graph $G = (V, E)$ with $V = \{v_1, \dots, v_M\}$ partitioned into $V_1, \dots, V_p$. The ontology $\mathcal{T}_G$ will create a tree rooted at $A(a)$ whose every branch corresponds to selecting one vertex from each V_i. Each branch has length $(p \cdot 2M)+1$ and consists of p 'blocks' of length $2M$, plus an extra edge at the end (used for padding). Each block corresponds to an enumeration of V, with positions $2j$ and $2j+1$ being associated with v_j. In the ith block of a branch, we will select a vertex v_{j_i} from V_i by marking the positions $2j_i$ and $2j_i+1$ with the binary predicate S; we also mark the positions of the neighbours of v_{j_i} in G with the predicate Y. We use the unary predicate B to mark the end of the pth block (square nodes in the picture below). The left side of the picture illustrates the construction for $p = 3$, where $V_1 = \{v_1, v_2\}$, $V_2 = \{v_3\}$, $V_3 = \{v_4, v_5\}$, and $E = \{\{v_1, v_3\}, \{v_3, v_5\}\}$.

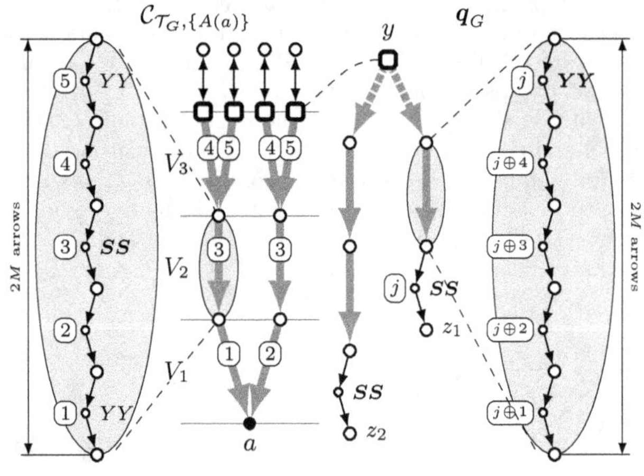

Since vertices are enumerated in the same order in every block, to check whether the selected vertex v_{j_i} for V_i is a neighbour of the vertices selected from $V_{i+1}, \dots, V_p$, it suffices to check that positions $2j_i$ and $2j_i + 1$ in blocks $i+1, \dots, p$ are marked YY. Moreover, the distance between the positions of a vertex in consecutive blocks is always $2M - 2$. The idea is thus to construct a CQ $\boldsymbol{q}_G$ (right side of the picture) which, starting from a variable labelled B (mapped to the end of a pth block), splits into $p - 1$ branches, with the ith branch checking for a sequence of i evenly-spaced YY markers leading to an SS marker. The distance from the end of the pth block (marked B) to the positions $2j_i$ and $2j_i + 1$ in the pth block (where the first YY should occur) depends on the choice of v_{j_i}. We thus add an outgoing edge at the end of the pth block, which can be navigated in both directions, to be able to 'consume' any *even number* of query atoms preceding the first YY.

The Boolean CQ $\boldsymbol{q}_G$ looks as follows (for readability, we use atoms with star-free regular expressions):

$$B(y) \wedge \bigwedge_{1 \le i < p} (U^{2M-2} \cdot (YY \cdot U^{2M-2})^i \cdot SS)(y, z_i),$$

and the ontology $\mathcal{T}_G$ contains the following axioms:

$$\begin{array}{ll}
A(x) \to \exists y\, L_j^1(x,y), & \text{for } v_j \in V_1,\\
\exists z\, L_j^k(z,x) \to \exists y\, L_j^{k+1}(x,y), & \text{for } 1 \le k < 2M,\ v_j \in V,\\
\exists z\, L_j^{2M}(z,x) \to \exists y\, L_{j'}^1(x,y), & \text{for } v_j \in V_i,\ v_{j'} \in V_{i+1},\\
L_j^k(x,y) \to S(y,x), & \text{for } k \in \{2j, 2j+1\},\\
L_j^k(x,y) \to Y(y,x), & \text{for } \{v_j, v_{j'}\} \in E\\
 & \quad \text{and } k \in \{2j', 2j'+1\},\\
L_j^k(x,y) \to U(y,x), & \text{for } 1 \le k \le 2M,\ v_j \in V,\\
\exists z\, L_j^{2M}(z,x) \to B(x), & \text{for } v_j \in V_p,\\
B(x) \to \exists y\, \big(U(x,y) \wedge U(y,x)\big). &
\end{array}$$

It can be shown that $\mathcal{T}_G, \{A(a)\} \models \boldsymbol{q}_G$ iff G has a clique containing one vertex from each set V_i. ❑

By (6), OMQs $(\mathcal{T}, \boldsymbol{q})$ from the class $\mathsf{OMQ}(\infty, 1, \boldsymbol{\ell})$ can be answered (via NDL-rewriting) over a data instance $\mathcal{A}$ in time $\mathit{poly}(|\mathcal{T}|, |\boldsymbol{q}|^{\boldsymbol{\ell}}, |\mathcal{A}|^{\boldsymbol{\ell}})$. Theorem 19 shows that no algorithm can do this in time $f(\boldsymbol{\ell}) \cdot \mathit{poly}(|\mathcal{T}|, |\boldsymbol{q}|, |\mathcal{A}|)$, for any computable function f, unless $W[1] = \text{FPT}$.

One may consider various other types of parameters that can hopefully reduce the complexity of OMQ answering. Obvious candidates are the size of ontology, the size of ontology signature or the number of role inclusions in ontologies. (Indeed, it was shown [6] that in the absence of role inclusions, tree-shaped OMQ answering is tractable.) Unfortunately, bounding any of these parameters does not make OMQ answering easier, as we establish in Section 5 that already one *fixed* ontology makes the problem NP-hard for tree-shaped CQs and LOGCFL-hard for linear ones.

5. OMQS WITH A FIXED ONTOLOGY

In a typical OBDA scenario [34], users are provided with an ontology in a familiar signature (developed by a domain expert) with which they formulate their queries. Thus, it is of interest to identify the complexity of answering tree-shaped OMQs $(\mathcal{T}, \boldsymbol{q})$ with a fixed ontology $\mathcal{T}$ of infinite depth (see Fig. 1). Surprisingly, we show that the problem is NP-hard even when both $\mathcal{T}$ and $\mathcal{A}$ are fixed (in the database setting, answering tree-shaped CQs is in LOGCFL for combined complexity).

THEOREM 20. *There is an ontology $\mathcal{T}_\dagger$ such that answering OMQs of the form $(\mathcal{T}_\dagger, \boldsymbol{q})$ with Boolean tree-shaped CQs $\boldsymbol{q}$ is NP-hard for query complexity.*

PROOF. The proof is by reduction of SAT. Given a CNF φ with variables $p_1, \dots, p_k$ and clauses $\chi_1, \dots, \chi_m$, take a Boolean CQ $\boldsymbol{q}_\varphi$ with $A(y)$ and, for $1 \le j \le m$, the following atoms with $z_j^k = y$:

$$\begin{array}{ll}
P_+(z_j^l, z_j^{l-1}), & \text{if } p_l \text{ occurs in } \chi_j \text{ positively},\\
P_-(z_j^l, z_j^{l-1}), & \text{if } p_l \text{ occurs in } \chi_j \text{ negatively},\\
P_0(z_j^l, z_j^{l-1}), & \text{if } p_l \text{ does not occur in } \chi_j,\\
B_0(z_j^0). &
\end{array}$$

Thus, $\boldsymbol{q}_\varphi$ is a star with centre $A(y)$ and m rays encoding the χ_j by the binary predicates P_+, P_- and P_0. Let $\mathcal{T}_\dagger$ be an ontology with the axioms

$$\begin{array}{l}
A(x) \to \exists y\, \big(P_+(y,x) \wedge P_0(y,x) \wedge B_-(y) \wedge A(y)\big),\\
\quad B_-(y) \to \exists x'\, \big(P_-(y,x') \wedge B_0(x')\big),\\
A(x) \to \exists y\, \big(P_-(y,x) \wedge P_0(y,x) \wedge B_+(y) \wedge A(y)\big),\\
\quad B_+(y) \to \exists x'\, \big(P_+(y,x') \wedge B_0(x')\big),\\
B_0(x) \to \exists y\, \big(P_+(x,y) \wedge P_-(x,y) \wedge P_0(x,y) \wedge B_0(y)\big).
\end{array}$$

Intuitively, $(\mathcal{T}_\dagger, \{A(a)\})$ generates an infinite binary tree, where nodes of depth n represent all 2^n truth assignments to n propositional variables. The CQ $\boldsymbol{q}_\varphi$ can only be mapped along a branch of this tree towards its root a, with the image of y, the centre of the star, giving a satisfying assignment for φ. Each non-root node of the tree also starts an infinite 'sink' branch of B_0-nodes, where the remainder of the ray for χ_j can be mapped as soon as one of its literals is satisfied. We can show that $\mathcal{T}_\dagger, \{A(a)\} \models \boldsymbol{q}_\varphi$ iff φ is satisfiable. To illustrate, the CQ $\boldsymbol{q}_\varphi$ for $\varphi = (p_1 \vee p_2) \wedge \neg p_1$ and a fragment of the canonical model $\mathcal{C}_{\mathcal{T}_\dagger,\{A(a)\}}$ are shown below:

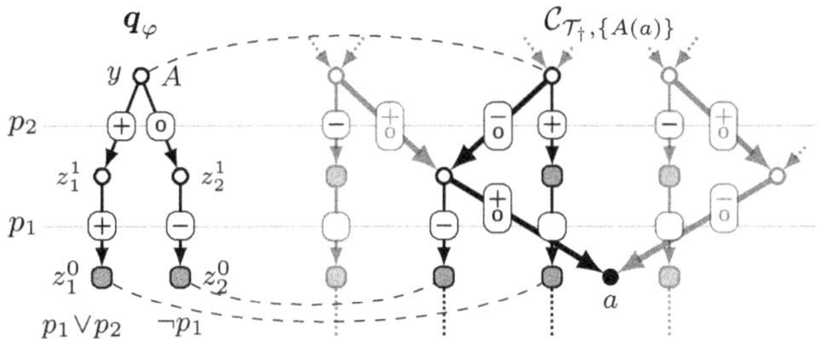

Here, ● are the points in B_0 and the labels on arrows indicate the subscripts of the binary predicates P (the empty label means all three: $+$, $-$ and 0); predicates A, B_+, B_- are not shown in $\mathcal{C}_{\mathcal{T}_\dagger,\{A(a)\}}$. ❑

The proof above uses OMQs $\boldsymbol{Q}_\varphi = (\mathcal{T}_\dagger, \boldsymbol{q}_\varphi)$ over a data instance with a single individual constant. Thus:

COROLLARY 21. *No polynomial-time algorithm can construct FO- or NDL-rewritings of $\boldsymbol{Q}_\varphi$ unless* P = NP.

PROOF. Indeed, if a polynomial-time algorithm could find a rewriting $\boldsymbol{q}'_\varphi$ of $\boldsymbol{Q}_\varphi$, then we would be able to check whether φ is satisfiable in polytime by evaluating $\boldsymbol{q}'_\varphi$ over $\{A(a)\}$. ❑

Curiously enough, Corollary 21 can be complemented with

THEOREM 22. *The $\boldsymbol{Q}_\varphi$ have polynomial FO-rewritings.*

PROOF. Define $\boldsymbol{q}'_\varphi$ as the FO-sentence

$$\forall xy\,\big((x = y) \land A(x) \land \varphi^*\big) \;\lor\; \exists xy\,\big((x \neq y) \land \boldsymbol{q}^*_\varphi(x, y)\big),$$

where φ^* is $\top$ if φ is satisfiable and $\bot$ otherwise, and $\boldsymbol{q}^*_\varphi(x, y)$ is the polynomial-size FO-rewriting of $\boldsymbol{Q}_\varphi$ over data with *at least 2* constants [26, Corollary 14]. Recall that the proof of Theorem 20 shows that, if $\mathcal{A}$ has a single constant, a, and there is a homomorphism from $\boldsymbol{q}_\varphi$ to $\mathcal{C}_{\mathcal{T}_\dagger,\mathcal{A}}$, then $A(a) \in \mathcal{A}$ and φ is satisfiable. Thus, the first disjunct of $\boldsymbol{q}'_\varphi$ is an FO-rewriting of $\boldsymbol{Q}_\varphi$ over data instances with a single constant; the case of at least 2 constants follows from [26]. ❑

Whether the OMQs $\boldsymbol{Q}_\varphi$ have a polynomial-size PE- or NDL-rewritings remains open. We have only managed to construct a modification $\bar{\boldsymbol{q}}_\varphi(x)$ of $\boldsymbol{q}_\varphi$ with the following interesting properties (details can be found in [4]). Let $\mathfrak{T}$ be the class of data instances representing finite binary trees with root a whose edges are labelled with P_+ and P_-, and some of whose leaves are labelled with B_0. Let $\mathcal{QL}$ be any query language such that, for every $\mathcal{QL}$-query $\Phi(x)$ and every $\mathcal{A} \in \mathfrak{T}$, the answer to $\Phi(a)$ over $\mathcal{A}$ can be computed in time polynomial in $|\Phi|$ and $|\mathcal{A}|$. Typical examples of $\mathcal{QL}$ are modal-like languages such as certain fragments of XPath [39] or description logic instance queries [3].

THEOREM 23. *The OMQs $(\mathcal{T}_\dagger, \bar{\boldsymbol{q}}_\varphi(x))$ do not have polynomial-size rewritings in $\mathcal{QL}$ unless* NP $\subseteq$ P/poly.

To our surprise, Theorem 23 is not applicable to PE.[3]

THEOREM 24. *Evaluating PE-queries over trees in $\mathfrak{T}$ is* NP*-hard.*

Finally, we consider bounded-leaf CQs (whose evaluation is NL-complete in the database setting) with fixed ontology and data.

THEOREM 25. *There is an ontology $\mathcal{T}_\ddagger$ such that answering OMQs of the form $(\mathcal{T}_\ddagger, \boldsymbol{q})$ with Boolean linear CQs $\boldsymbol{q}$ is* LOGCFL*-hard for query complexity.*

The proof is by reduction of the recognition problem for the hardest LOGCFL language $\mathcal{L}$ [30, 57]. We construct an ontology $\mathcal{T}_\ddagger$ and a logspace transducer that converts the words w over the alphabet of $\mathcal{L}$ to linear CQs $\boldsymbol{q}_w$ such that $w \in \mathcal{L}$ iff $\mathcal{T}_\ddagger, \{A(a)\} \models \boldsymbol{q}_w$. To illustrate, take the context-free language $\mathcal{B}$ over the alphabet $\Sigma = \{a_1, b_1, a_2, b_2\}$ generated by the grammar $S \to SS$, $S \to \varepsilon$, $S \to a_1 S b_1$, $S \to a_2 S b_2$. Let $\mathcal{T}_\mathcal{B}$ be an ontology such that the canonical model of $(\mathcal{T}_\mathcal{B}, \{A(a)\})$ looks like in the picture below:

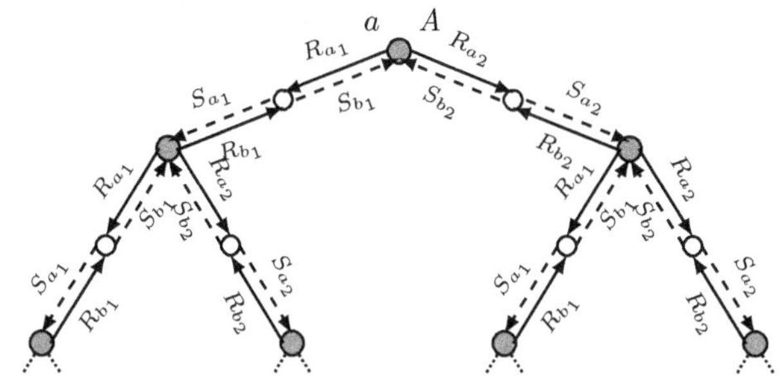

Then, for every word $w = c_0 \dots c_n$ over Σ, we have $w \in \mathcal{B}$ just in case $\mathcal{T}_\mathcal{B}, \{A(a)\} \models A(u_0) \land \gamma_w \land A(u_{n+1})$, where

$$\gamma_w = \bigwedge_{0 \le i \le n} \big(R_{c_i}(u_i, v_i), S_{c_i}(v_i, u_{i+1})\big).$$

Although $\mathcal{B}$ is not LOGCFL-hard, by adding axioms to $\mathcal{T}_\mathcal{B}$ that generate additional branches from the points ●, we can construct an ontology $\mathcal{T}_\ddagger$ recognising $\mathcal{L}$ (see [4] for details).

6. EXPERIMENTS & CONCLUSIONS

The main positive result of this paper is the development of theoretically optimal NDL-rewritings for OMQs belonging to one of the classes OMQ$(\boldsymbol{d}, \boldsymbol{t}, \infty)$, OMQ$(\boldsymbol{d}, 1, \boldsymbol{\ell})$, and OMQ$(\infty, 1, \boldsymbol{\ell})$. It was known that answering such OMQs is tractable, but the proofs employed elaborate algorithms tailored for each of the three cases. We have shown that the optimal complexity can be achieved *via NDL-rewriting*, thus reducing OMQ answering to standard query evaluation. This result is practically relevant as many user queries are tree-shaped (see, e.g., [49] for evidence in the RDF setting), and indeed, recent tools for query formulation over ontologies (like [56]) produce tree-shaped CQs. Moreover, the majority of important real-world *OWL 2* ontologies are of finite depth; see [17] for statistics. In the context of OBDA, *OWL 2 QL* ontologies are often built starting from the database schemas (bootstrapping [32]), which typically do not contain cycles such as 'every manager is managed by a manager.' For example, the NPD FactPages ontology,[4] designed to facilitate querying the datasets of the Norwegian Petroleum Directorate, is of depth 5.

The starting point of our research was the observation that standard query rewriting systems tend to produce suboptimal rewritings of the OMQs in these three classes. This is obviously so for UCQ-rewriters [50, 47, 15, 28, 44, 40], but is also true of more elaborate PE-rewriters (which use disjunctions inside conjunctions) [51, 59] whose rewritings in theory can be of superpolynomial size; see Fig. 1 (b). Surprisingly, even NDL-rewriters like Clipper [21], Presto [54],

[3]This result might be known but we could not find it in the literature, and so provide a proof in [4].

[4]http://sws.ifi.uio.no/project/npd-v2/

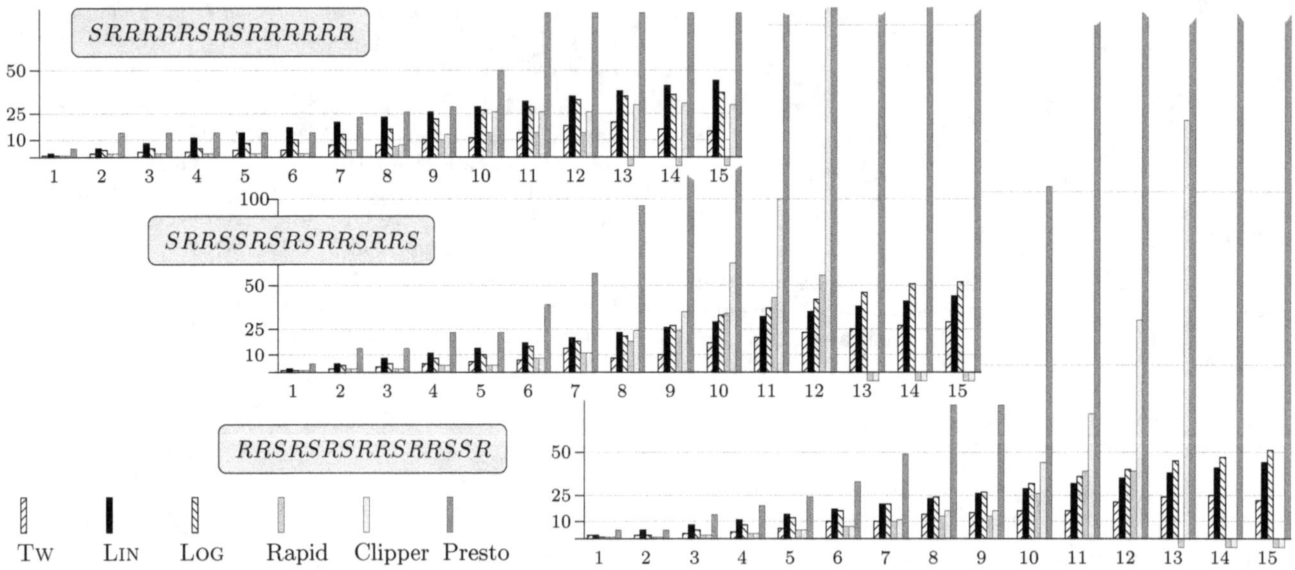

Figure 2: The size of NDL-rewritings produced by different algorithms.

and Rapid [15] do not fare much better in practice. To illustrate, we generated three sequences of OMQs in the class $\mathsf{OMQ}(1,1,2)$ (lying in the intersection of the classes $\mathsf{OMQ}(\boldsymbol{d},\boldsymbol{t},\infty)$, $\mathsf{OMQ}(\boldsymbol{d},1,\boldsymbol{\ell})$ and $\mathsf{OMQ}(\infty,1,\boldsymbol{\ell})$) with the ontology from Example 11 and linear CQs of up to 15 atoms as in Example 8 (which are associated with words from $\{R,S\}^*$). By Fig. 1 (a), answering these OMQs can be done in NL. The barcharts in Fig. 2 show the number of clauses in their NDL-rewritings produced by Clipper, Presto and Rapid, as well as by our algorithms Lin, Log and Tw from Sections 3.2–3.4, respectively. The first three NDL-rewritings display a clear exponential growth, with Clipper and Rapid failing to produce rewritings for longer CQs. In contrast, our rewritings grow linearly in accord with theory.

We evaluated the rewritings over a few randomly generated data instances using off-the-shelf datalog engine RDFox [46]. The experiments (detailed in [4]) show that our rewritings are usually executed faster than those produced by Clipper, Presto and Rapid.

The version of RDFox we used did not seem to take advantage of the structure of the $\mathsf{NL}/\mathsf{LOGCFL}$ rewritings, as it simply materialises all of the predicates without using magic sets or optimising programs before execution. It would be interesting to see whether the nonrecursiveness and parallelisability of our rewritings can be utilised to produce efficient execution plans. One could also investigate whether our rewritings can be efficiently implemented using views in standard DBMSs.

Our rewriting algorithms are based on the same idea: pick a point splitting the given CQ into sub-CQs, rewrite the sub-CQs recursively, and then formulate rules that combine the resulting rewritings. The difference between the algorithms is in the choice of the splitting points, which determines the execution plans for OMQs and has a big impact on their performance. The experiments show that none of the three splitting strategies systematically outperforms the others. This suggests that execution times may be dramatically improved by employing an 'adaptable' splitting strategy that would work similarly to query execution planners in DBMSs and use statistical information about the relational tables to generate efficient NDL programs. For example, one could first define a 'cost function' on some set of alternative rewritings that roughly estimates their evaluation time and then construct a rewriting minimising this function. Such a performance-oriented approach was introduced and exploited in [7], where the target language for OMQ rewritings was joins of UCQs (unions of CQs). Other optimisation techniques for removing redundant rules or sub-queries from rewritings [54, 51, 29, 40] or exploiting the emptiness of certain predicates [60] are also relevant here. In the context of OBDA with relational databases and mappings, integrity constraints [53, 52] and the structure of mappings [19] are particularly important for optimisation.

Having observed that (i) the ontology depth and (ii) the number of leaves in tree-shaped CQs occur in the exponent of our upper bounds for the complexity of OMQ answering algorithms, we regarded (i) and (ii) as parameters and investigated the parameterised complexity of the OMQ answering problem. We proved that the problem is $W[2]$-hard in the former case and $W[1]$-hard in the latter (it remains open whether these lower bounds are tight). Furthermore, we established that answering OMQs with a fixed ontology (of infinite depth) is NP-complete for tree-shaped CQs and LOGCFL-complete for linear CQs, which dashed hopes of taming intractability by restricting the ontology size, signature, etc. One remaining open problem is whether answering OMQs with a fixed ontology and tree-shaped CQs is fixed-parameter tractable if the number of leaves is regarded as the parameter.

A more general avenue for future research is to extend the study of succinctness and optimality of rewritings to suitable ontology languages with predicates of higher-arity, such as linear and sticky tgds.

Acknowledgments

This work was supported by the French ANR grant 12-JS02-007-01 'PAGODA: Practical Algorithms for Ontology-Based Data Access', the UK EPSRC grant EP/M012670 'iTract: Islands of Tractability in Ontology-Based Data Access', the Russian Foundation for Basic Research grant MK-7312.2016.1, and the Russian Academic Excellence Project 5-100. We thank the developers of Clipper and Rapid for making their systems freely available, and Riccardo Rosati for the opportunity to conduct experiments with Presto.

7. REFERENCES

[1] S. Abiteboul, R. Hull, and V. Vianu. *Foundations of Databases*. Addison-Wesley, 1995.

[2] M. Arenas, P. Barceló, L. Libkin, and F. Murlak. *Foundations of Data Exchange*. Cambridge University Press, 2014.

[3] F. Baader, D. Calvanese, D. McGuinness, D. Nardi, and P. Patel-Schneider, editors. *The Description Logic Handbook: Theory, Implementation and Applications*. Cambridge University Press, 2003.

[4] M. Bienvenu, S. Kikot, R. Kontchakov, V. Podolskii, V. Ryzhikov, and M. Zakharyaschev. The complexity of ontology-based data access with OWL 2 QL and bounded treewidth queries. *CoRR*, 2017.

[5] M. Bienvenu, S. Kikot, and V. V. Podolskii. Tree-like queries in OWL 2 QL: succinctness and complexity results. In *Proc. of the 30th Annual ACM/IEEE Symposium on Logic in Computer Science, LICS 2015*, pages 317–328. IEEE Computer Society, 2015.

[6] M. Bienvenu, M. Ortiz, M. Simkus, and G. Xiao. Tractable queries for lightweight description logics. In *Proc. of the 23nd Int. Joint Conf. on Artificial Intelligence, IJCAI 2013*, pages 768–774. IJCAI/AAAI, 2013.

[7] D. Bursztyn, F. Goasdoué, and I. Manolescu. Teaching an RDBMS about ontological constraints. *PVLDB*, 9(12):1161–1172, 2016.

[8] M. Calautti, G. Gottlob, and A. Pieris. Chase termination for guarded existential rules. In *Proc. of the 34th ACM Symposium on Principles of Database Systems, PODS 2015*, pages 91–103, 2015.

[9] A. Calì, G. Gottlob, and M. Kifer. Taming the infinite chase: Query answering under expressive relational constraints. *Journal of Artificial Intelligence Research (JAIR)*, 48:115–174, 2013.

[10] A. Calì, G. Gottlob, and T. Lukasiewicz. A general datalog-based framework for tractable query answering over ontologies. *Journal of Web Semantics*, 14:57–83, 2012.

[11] A. Calì, G. Gottlob, and A. Pieris. Towards more expressive ontology languages: The query answering problem. *Artificial Intelligence*, 193:87–128, 2012.

[12] D. Calvanese, G. De Giacomo, D. Lembo, M. Lenzerini, A. Poggi, M. Rodriguez-Muro, R. Rosati, M. Ruzzi, and D. F. Savo. The MASTRO system for ontology-based data access. *Semantic Web*, 2(1):43–53, 2011.

[13] D. Calvanese, G. De Giacomo, D. Lembo, M. Lenzerini, and R. Rosati. Tractable reasoning and efficient query answering in description logics: the *DL-Lite* family. *Journal of Automated Reasoning*, 39(3):385–429, 2007.

[14] C. Chekuri and A. Rajaraman. Conjunctive query containment revisited. *Theoretical Computer Science*, 239(2):211–229, 2000.

[15] A. Chortaras, D. Trivela, and G. Stamou. Optimized query rewriting for OWL 2 QL. In *Proc. of CADE-23*, volume 6803 of *LNCS*, pages 192–206. Springer, 2011.

[16] S. A. Cook. Characterizations of pushdown machines in terms of time-bounded computers. *Journal of the ACM*, 18(1):4–18, 1971.

[17] B. Cuenca Grau, I. Horrocks, M. Krötzsch, C. Kupke, D. Magka, B. Motik, and Z. Wang. Acyclicity notions for existential rules and their application to query answering in ontologies. *Journal of Artificial Intelligence Research (JAIR)*, 47:741–808, 2013.

[18] E. Dantsin, T. Eiter, G. Gottlob, and A. Voronkov. Complexity and expressive power of logic programming. *ACM Computing Surveys*, 33(3):374–425, 2001.

[19] F. Di Pinto, D. Lembo, M. Lenzerini, R. Mancini, A. Poggi, R. Rosati, M. Ruzzi, and D. F. Savo. Optimizing query rewriting in ontology-based data access. In *Proc. of the 16th Int. Conf. on Extending Database Technology, EDBT 2013*, pages 561–572. ACM, 2013.

[20] A. Doan, A. Y. Halevy, and Z. G. Ives. *Principles of Data Integration*. Morgan Kaufmann, 2012.

[21] T. Eiter, M. Ortiz, M. Šimkus, T.-K. Tran, and G. Xiao. Query rewriting for Horn-SHIQ plus rules. In *Proc. of the 26th AAAI Conf. on Artificial Intelligence, AAAI 2012*, pages 726–733. AAAI, 2012.

[22] M. R. Fellows, D. Hermelin, F. A. Rosamond, and S. Vialette. On the parameterized complexity of multiple-interval graph problems. *Theoretical Computer Science*, 410(1):53–61, 2009.

[23] J. Flum and M. Grohe. *Parameterized Complexity Theory*. Texts in Theoretical Computer Science. An EATCS Series. Springer, 2006.

[24] M. Giese, A. Soylu, G. Vega-Gorgojo, A. Waaler, P. Haase, E. Jiménez-Ruiz, D. Lanti, M. Rezk, G. Xiao, Ö. Özçep, and R. Rosati. Optique: Zooming in on big data. *IEEE Computer*, 48(3):60–67, 2015.

[25] T. Gogacz and J. Marcinkowski. All-instances termination of chase is undecidable. In *Proc. of the 41st Int. Colloquium on Automata, Languages, and Programming, ICALP 2014, Part II*, volume 8573 of *Lecture Notes in Computer Science*, pages 293–304. Springer, 2014.

[26] G. Gottlob, S. Kikot, R. Kontchakov, V. V. Podolskii, T. Schwentick, and M. Zakharyaschev. The price of query rewriting in ontology-based data access. *Artificial Intelligence*, 213:42–59, 2014.

[27] G. Gottlob, N. Leone, and F. Scarcello. Computing LOGCFL certificates. In *Proc. of the 26th Int. Colloquium on Automata, Languages and Programming, ICALP-99*, volume 1644 of *Lecture Notes in Computer Science*, pages 361–371. Springer, 1999.

[28] G. Gottlob, G. Orsi, and A. Pieris. Ontological queries: Rewriting and optimization. In *Proc. of ICDE 2011*, pages 2–13. IEEE Computer Society, 2011.

[29] G. Gottlob, G. Orsi, and A. Pieris. Query rewriting and optimization for ontological databases. *ACM Transactions on Database Systems (TODS)*, 39(3):25, 2014.

[30] S. A. Greibach. The hardest context-free language. *SIAM J. Comput.*, 2(4):304–310, 1973.

[31] D. A. Huffman. A method for the construction of minimum-redundancy codes. *Proceedings of the Institute of Radio Engineers*, 40(9):1098–1101, 1952.

[32] E. Jiménez-Ruiz, E. Kharlamov, D. Zheleznyakov, I. Horrocks, C. Pinkel, M. G. Skjæveland, E. Thorstensen, and J. Mora. BootOX: Bootstrapping OWL 2 ontologies and R2RML mappings from relational databases. In *Proc. of the ISWC 2015 Posters & Demonstrations Track at the 14th Int. Semantic Web Conf.*, volume 1486 of *CEUR Workshop Proceedings*. CEUR-WS, 2015.

[33] M. Kaminski, Y. Nenov, and B. Cuenca Grau. Datalog rewritability of Disjunctive Datalog programs and non-Horn ontologies. *Artificial Intelligence*, 236:90–118, 2016.

[34] E. Kharlamov, D. Hovland, E. Jiménez-Ruiz, D. Lanti, H. Lie, C. Pinkel, M. Rezk, M. G. Skjæveland, E. Thorstensen, G. Xiao, D. Zheleznyakov, and I. Horrocks. Ontology based access to exploration data at Statoil. In *Proc. of the 14th Int. Semantic Web Conf., ISWC 2015, Part II*, volume 9367 of *Lecture Notes in Computer Science*, pages 93–112. Springer, 2015.

[35] S. Kikot, R. Kontchakov, V. Podolskii, and M. Zakharyaschev. On the succinctness of query rewriting over shallow ontologies. In *Proc. of the Joint Meeting of the 23rd EACSL Annual Conf. on Computer Science Logic (CSL 2014) and the 29th Annual ACM/IEEE Symposium on Logic in Computer Science (LICS 2014)*, pages 57:1–57:10. ACM, 2014.

[36] S. Kikot, R. Kontchakov, V. V. Podolskii, and M. Zakharyaschev. Exponential lower bounds and separation for query rewriting. In *Proc. of the 39th Int. Colloquium on Automata, Languages and Programming, ICALP 2012*, volume 7392 of *Lecture Notes in Computer Science*, pages 263–274. Springer, 2012.

[37] S. Kikot, R. Kontchakov, and M. Zakharyaschev. On (in)tractability of OBDA with OWL 2 QL. In *Proc. of the 24th Int. Workshop on Description Logics, DL 2011*, volume 745, pages 224–234. CEUR-WS, 2011.

[38] S. Kikot, R. Kontchakov, and M. Zakharyaschev. Conjunctive query answering with OWL 2 QL. In *Proc. of the 13th Int. Conf. on Principles of Knowledge Representation and Reasoning, KR 2012*, pages 275–285. AAAI, 2012.

[39] C. Koch. Processing queries on tree-structured data efficiently. In *Proc. of the 25th ACM SIGMOD-SIGACT-SIGART Symposium on Principles of Database Systems, PODS 2006*, pages 213–224. ACM, 2006.

[40] M. König, M. Leclère, M.-L. Mugnier, and M. Thomazo. Sound, complete and minimal UCQ-rewriting for existential rules. *Semantic Web*, 6(5):451–475, 2015.

[41] R. Kontchakov, C. Lutz, D. Toman, F. Wolter, and M. Zakharyaschev. The combined approach to query answering in DL-Lite. In *Proc. of the 12th Int. Conf. on Principles of Knowledge Representation and Reasoning, KR 2010*, pages 247–257. AAAI Press, 2010.

[42] R. Kontchakov, M. Rezk, M. Rodriguez-Muro, G. Xiao, and M. Zakharyaschev. Answering SPARQL queries over databases under OWL 2 QL entailment regime. In *Proc. of the 13th Int. Semantic Web Conf., ISWC 2014, Part I*, volume 8796 of *Lecture Notes in Computer Science*, pages 552–567. Springer, 2014.

[43] M. Lenzerini. Ontology-based data management. *ACM SIGMOD Blog*, May 2013.

[44] J. Mora, R. Rosati, and Ó. Corcho. Kyrie2: query rewriting under extensional constraints in ELHIO. In *Proc. of the 13th Int. Semantic Web Conf., ISWC 2014*, volume 8796 of *Lecture Notes in Computer Science*, pages 568–583. Springer, 2014.

[45] B. Motik, B. Cuenca Grau, I. Horrocks, Z. Wu, A. Fokoue, and C. Lutz. *OWL 2 Web Ontology Language Profiles.* W3C Recommendation, 2012. Available at http://www.w3.org/TR/owl2-profiles.

[46] Y. Nenov, R. Piro, B. Motik, I. Horrocks, Z. Wu, and J. Banerjee. RDFox: A highly-scalable RDF store. In *Proc. of the 14th Int. Semantic Web Conf., ISWC 2015, Part II*, volume 9367 of *Lecture Notes in Computer Science*, pages 3–20. Springer, 2015.

[47] H. Pérez-Urbina, B. Motik, and I. Horrocks. A comparison of query rewriting techniques for DL-Lite. In *Proc. of the 22nd Int. Workshop on Description Logics, DL 2009*, volume 477 of *CEUR Workshop Proceedings*. CEUR-WS, 2009.

[48] H. Pérez-Urbina, E. Rodríguez-Díaz, M. Grove, G. Konstantinidis, and E. Sirin. Evaluation of query rewriting approaches for OWL 2. In *Proc. of SSWS+HPCSW 2012*, volume 943 of *CEUR Workshop Proceedings*. CEUR-WS, 2012.

[49] F. Picalausa and S. Vansummeren. What are real SPARQL queries like? In *Proc. of the Int. Workshop on Semantic Web Information Management (SWIM)*. ACM, 2011.

[50] A. Poggi, D. Lembo, D. Calvanese, G. De Giacomo, M. Lenzerini, and R. Rosati. Linking data to ontologies. *Journal on Data Semantics*, X:133–173, 2008.

[51] M. Rodriguez-Muro, R. Kontchakov, and M. Zakharyaschev. Ontology-based data access: Ontop of databases. In *Proc. of the 12th Int. Semantic Web Conf., ISWC 2013, Part I*, volume 8218 of *Lecture Notes in Computer Science*, pages 558–573. Springer, 2013.

[52] M. Rodriguez-Muro, R. Kontchakov, and M. Zakharyaschev. Query rewriting and optimisation with database dependencies in Ontop. In *Informal Proc. of the 26th Int. Workshop on Description Logics, DL 2013*, volume 1014 of *CEUR Workshop Proceedings*, pages 917–929. CEUR-WS, 2013.

[53] R. Rosati. Prexto: Query rewriting under extensional constraints in DL-Lite. In *Proc. of the 9th Extended Semantic Web Conf., ESWC 2012*, volume 7295 of

Lecture Notes in Computer Science, pages 360–374. Springer, 2012.

[54] R. Rosati and A. Almatelli. Improving query answering over DL-Lite ontologies. In *Proc. of the 12th Int. Conf. on Principles of Knowledge Representation and Reasoning, KR 2010*, pages 290–300. AAAI Press, 2010.

[55] J. F. Sequeda, M. Arenas, and D. P. Miranker. OBDA: query rewriting or materialization? In practice, both! In *Proc. of the 13th Int. Semantic Web Conf., ISWC 2014, Part I*, volume 8796 of *Lecture Notes in Computer Science*, pages 535–551. Springer, 2014.

[56] A. Soylu, M. Giese, E. Jimenez-Ruiz, G. Vega-Gorgojo, and I. Horrocks. Experiencing optiquevqs: A multi-paradigm and ontology-based visual query system for end users. *Universal Access in the Information Society*, 15(1):129–152, 2016.

[57] I. H. Sudborough. A note on tape-bounded complexity classes and linear context-free languages. *Journal of the ACM*, 22(4):499–500, Oct. 1975.

[58] I. H. Sudborough. On the tape complexity of deterministic context-free languages. *Journal of the ACM*, 25(3):405–414, 1978.

[59] M. Thomazo. Compact rewritings for existential rules. In *Proc. of the 23rd Int. Joint Conf. on Artificial Intelligence, IJCAI 2013*, pages 1125–1131. IJCAI/AAAI, 2013.

[60] T. Venetis, G. Stoilos, and V. Vassalos. Rewriting minimisations for efficient ontology-based query answering. In *Proc. of the 28th Int. Conf. on Tools with Artificial Intelligence, ICTAI 2016*, pages 1095–1102. IEEE, 2016.

[61] H. Venkateswaran. Properties that characterize LOGCFL. *Journal of Computer and System Sciences*, 43(2):380–404, 1991.

[62] M. Yannakakis. Algorithms for acyclic database schemes. In *Proc. of the 7th Int. Conf. on Very Large Data Bases, VLDB'81*, pages 82–94. IEEE Computer Society, 1981.

APPENDIX

We illustrate both standard UCQ-rewritings and the NDL-rewritings from Sections 3.2–3.4 for the OMQ given in Examples 8 and 11.

Consider the CQ $\boldsymbol{q}(x_0, x_7)$ depicted below (black nodes represent answer variables)

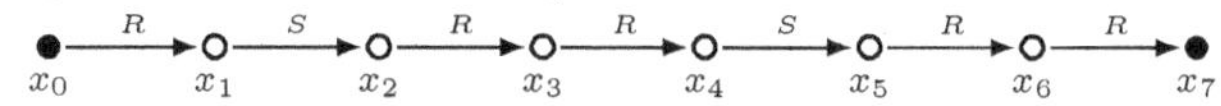

and the following ontology $\mathcal{T}$ in normal form:

$$
\begin{array}{ll}
P(x,y) \to S(x,y), & P(x,y) \to R(y,x), \\
A_P(x) \leftrightarrow \exists y\, P(x,y), & A_{P^-}(x) \leftrightarrow \exists y\, P(y,x), \\
A_R(x) \leftrightarrow \exists y\, R(x,y), & A_{R^-}(x) \leftrightarrow \exists y\, R(y,x), \\
A_S(x) \leftrightarrow \exists y\, S(x,y) & A_{S^-}(x) \leftrightarrow \exists y\, S(y,x).
\end{array}
$$

UCQ rewriting

The nine CQs below form a UCQ-rewriting of the OMQ $\boldsymbol{Q}(x_0, x_7) = (\mathcal{T}, \boldsymbol{q}(x_0, x_7))$ over complete data instances, which we give as an NDL program with goal predicate G:

$$
\begin{aligned}
G(x_0,x_7) \leftarrow & [R(x_0,x_1) \land S(x_1,x_2) \land R(x_2,x_3)] \land \\
& [R(x_3,x_4) \land S(x_4,x_5) \land R(x_5,x_6)] \land R(x_6,x_7), \\
G(x_0,x_7) \leftarrow & [A_{P^-}(x_0) \land R(x_0,x_3)] \land \\
& [R(x_3,x_4) \land S(x_4,x_5) \land R(x_5,x_6)] \land R(x_6,x_7), \\
G(x_0,x_7) \leftarrow & [R(x_0,x_3) \land A_P(x_3)] \land \\
& [R(x_3,x_4) \land S(x_4,x_5) \land R(x_5,x_6)] \land R(x_6,x_7), \\
G(x_0,x_7) \leftarrow & [R(x_0,x_1) \land S(x_1,x_2) \land R(x_2,x_3)] \land \\
& [A_{P^-}(x_3) \land R(x_3,x_6)] \land R(x_6,x_7), \\
G(x_0,x_7) \leftarrow & [R(x_0,x_1) \land S(x_1,x_2) \land R(x_2,x_3)] \land \\
& [R(x_3,x_6) \land A_P(x_6)] \land R(x_6,x_7), \\
G(x_0,x_7) \leftarrow & [A_{P^-}(x_0) \land R(x_0,x_3)] \land \\
& [A_{P^-}(x_3) \land R(x_3,x_6)] \land R(x_6,x_7), \\
G(x_0,x_7) \leftarrow & [A_{P^-}(x_0) \land R(x_0,x_3)] \land \\
& [R(x_3,x_6) \land A_P(x_6)] \land R(x_6,x_7), \\
G(x_0,x_7) \leftarrow & [R(x_0,x_3) \land A_P(x_3)] \land \\
& [A_{P^-}(x_3) \land R(x_3,x_6)] \land R(x_6,x_7), \\
G(x_0,x_7) \leftarrow & [R(x_0,x_3) \land A_P(x_3)] \land \\
& [R(x_3,x_6) \land A_P(x_6)] \land R(x_6,x_7).
\end{aligned}
$$

We note that a UCQ-rewriting over all data instances would in addition contain variants of the CQs above with each of the predicates R and S replaced by P (with arguments swapped appropriately).

The UCQ-rewriting above can be obtained by transforming the following PE-formula into UCQ form:

$$
\begin{aligned}
& \big[\big(R(x_0,x_1) \land S(x_1,x_2) \land R(x_2,x_3)\big) \\
& \quad \lor \big(A_{P^-}(x_0) \land R(x_0,x_3)\big) \lor \big(R(x_0,x_3) \land A_P(x_3)\big)\big] \\
\land \; & \big[\big(R(x_3,x_4) \land S(x_4,x_5) \land R(x_5,x_6)\big) \\
& \quad \lor \big(A_{P^-}(x_3) \land R(x_5,x_6)\big) \lor \big(R(x_3,x_6) \land A_P(x_6)\big)\big] \\
\land \; & R(x_6,x_7).
\end{aligned}
$$

(Intuitively, each of the two sequences RSR in the query can be derived in three possible ways: from RSR, from $A_{P^-}R$ and from RA_P).

Log-*rewriting*

As explained in Example 11, we split T into D_1 and D_2 and obtain the following two clauses:

$$G_T^{\boldsymbol{\varepsilon}}(x_0, x_7) \leftarrow G_{D_1}^{x_3 \mapsto \varepsilon}(x_3, x_0) \land R(x_3, x_4) \land G_{D_2}^{x_4 \mapsto \varepsilon}(x_4, x_7),$$
$$G_T^{\boldsymbol{\varepsilon}}(x_0, x_7) \leftarrow G_{D_1}^{x_3 \mapsto \varepsilon}(x_3, x_0) \land A_{P^-}(x_4) \land (x_3 = x_4) \land G_{D_2}^{x_4 \mapsto P^-}(x_4, x_7).$$

Next, we split each of D_1 and D_2 into single-atom subqueries, which yields the following clauses:

$$G_{D_1}^{x_3 \mapsto \varepsilon}(x_3, x_0) \leftarrow (x_0 = x_1) \land A_{P^-}(x_1) \land (x_1 = x_2) \land R(x_2, x_3),$$
$$G_{D_1}^{x_3 \mapsto \varepsilon}(x_3, x_0) \leftarrow R(x_0, x_1) \land (x_1 = x_2) \land A_P(x_2) \land (x_2 = x_3),$$
$$G_{D_1}^{x_3 \mapsto \varepsilon}(x_3, x_0) \leftarrow R(x_0, x_1) \land S(x_1, x_2) \land R(x_2, x_3),$$

$$G_{D_2}^{x_4 \mapsto \varepsilon}(x_4, x_7) \leftarrow (x_4 = x_5) \land A_P(x_5) \land (x_5 = x_6) \land R(x_6, x_7),$$
$$G_{D_2}^{x_4 \mapsto \varepsilon}(x_4, x_7) \leftarrow S(x_4, x_5) \land R(x_5, x_6) \land R(x_6, x_7),$$

$$G_{D_2}^{x_4 \mapsto P^-}(x_4, x_7) \leftarrow A_{P^-}(x_4) \land (x_4 = x_5) \land R(x_5, x_6) \land R(x_6, x_7).$$

Note that in each case we consider only those types that give rise to predicates that have definitions in the rewriting. The resulting NDL-rewriting with goal $G_T^{\boldsymbol{\varepsilon}}$ consists of 8 clauses. Note, however, that the rewriting illustrated above is a slight simplification of the definition given in Section 3.2: here, for the leaves of the tree decomposition, we directly use the atoms $\mathsf{At}^{\boldsymbol{s}}$ instead of including a clause $G_D^{\boldsymbol{w}}(\partial D, \boldsymbol{x}_D) \leftarrow \mathsf{At}^{\boldsymbol{s}}$ in the rewriting. This simplification clearly does not affect the width of the NDL query or the choice of weight function.

Lin-*rewriting*

We assume that x_0 is the root, which makes x_7 the only leaf of the query. (Note that we could have chosen another variable, say x_3, as the root, with x_0 and x_7 the two leaves.) So, the top-level clause is

$$G(x_0, x_7) \leftarrow G_0^{x_0 \mapsto \varepsilon}(x_0, x_7).$$

We then move along the query and consider the variables x_1, x_2 and x_3. The possible ways of mapping these variables to the canonical model give rise to the following 7 clauses:

$$G_0^{x_0 \mapsto \varepsilon}(x_0, x_7) \leftarrow R(x_0, x_1) \land P_1^{x_1 \mapsto \varepsilon}(x_1, x_7),$$
$$G_0^{x_0 \mapsto \varepsilon}(x_0, x_7) \leftarrow (x_0 = x_1) \land A_{P^-}(x_1) \land G_1^{x_1 \mapsto P^-}(x_1, x_7),$$

$$G_1^{x_1 \mapsto \varepsilon}(x_1, x_7) \leftarrow S(x_1, x_2) \land G_2^{x_2 \mapsto \varepsilon}(x_2, x_7),$$
$$G_1^{x_1 \mapsto \varepsilon}(x_1, x_7) \leftarrow (x_1 = x_2) \land A_P(x_2) \land G_2^{x_2 \mapsto P}(x_2, x_7),$$
$$G_1^{x_1 \mapsto P^-}(x_1, x_7) \leftarrow A_{P^-}(x_1) \land (x_1 = x_2) \land G_2^{x_2 \mapsto \varepsilon}(x_2, x_7),$$

$$G_2^{x_2 \mapsto \varepsilon}(x_2, x_7) \leftarrow R(x_2, x_3) \land G_3^{x_3 \mapsto \varepsilon}(x_3, x_7),$$
$$G_2^{x_2 \mapsto P}(x_2, x_7) \leftarrow A_P(x_2) \land (x_2 = x_3) \land G_3^{x_3 \mapsto \varepsilon}(x_3, x_7).$$

Next, we move to the variables x_4, x_5 and x_6, which give similar 7 clauses:

$$G_3^{x_3 \mapsto \varepsilon}(x_3, x_7) \leftarrow R(x_3, x_4) \land P_4^{x_4 \mapsto \varepsilon}(x_4, x_7),$$
$$G_3^{x_3 \mapsto \varepsilon}(x_3, x_7) \leftarrow (x_3 = x_4) \land A_{P^-}(x_4) \land G_4^{x_4 \mapsto P^-}(x_4, x_7),$$

$$G_4^{x_4 \mapsto \varepsilon}(x_4, x_7) \leftarrow S(x_4, x_5) \land G_5^{x_5 \mapsto \varepsilon}(x_5, x_7),$$
$$G_4^{x_4 \mapsto \varepsilon}(x_4, x_7) \leftarrow (x_4 = x_5) \land A_P(x_5) \land G_5^{x_5 \mapsto P}(x_5, x_7),$$
$$G_4^{x_4 \mapsto P^-}(x_4, x_7) \leftarrow A_{P^-}(x_4) \land (x_4 = x_5) \land G_5^{x_5 \mapsto \varepsilon}(x_5, x_7),$$

$$G_5^{x_5 \mapsto \varepsilon}(x_5, x_7) \leftarrow R(x_5, x_6) \land G_6^{x_6 \mapsto \varepsilon}(x_6, x_7),$$
$$G_5^{x_5 \mapsto P}(x_5, x_7) \leftarrow A_P(x_5) \land (x_5 = x_6) \land G_6^{x_6 \mapsto \varepsilon}(x_6, x_7).$$

Finally, the last variable can only be mapped to a constant in the data instance, which yields a single clause:

$$G_6^{x_6 \mapsto \varepsilon}(x_6, x_7) \leftarrow R(x_6, x_7).$$

Note that, like in the previous case, we consider only those types that give rise to predicates with definitions (and ignore the dead-ends in the construction).

Tw-*rewriting*

We begin by splitting the query roughly in the middle, that is, we choose x_3 and consider two subqueries:

$$\boldsymbol{q}_{03}(x_0, x_3) = \exists x_1 x_2 \big(R(x_0, x_1) \land S(x_1, x_2) \land R(x_2, x_3)\big),$$
$$\boldsymbol{q}_{37}(x_3, x_7) = \exists x_4 x_5 x_6 \big(R(x_3, x_4) \land S(x_4, x_5) \land R(x_5, x_6) \land R(x_6, x_7)\big).$$

Since there is no tree witness $\mathfrak{t}$ for $(\mathcal{T}, \boldsymbol{q}(x_0, x_7))$ that contains x_3 in $\mathfrak{t}_\mathsf{i}$, we have only one top-level clause:

$$G_{07}(x_0, x_7) \leftarrow G_{03}(x_0, x_3) \land G_{37}(x_3, x_7).$$

Next, we focus on $\boldsymbol{q}_{03}$ and choose x_1 as the splitting variable. In this case, there is a tree witness $\mathfrak{t}^1$ with $\mathfrak{t}^1_\mathsf{i} = \{x_1\}$ and $\mathfrak{t}^1_\mathsf{r} = \{x_0, x_2\}$, and so we obtain two clauses for G_{03}:

$$G_{03}(x_0, x_3) \leftarrow R(x_0, x_1) \land G_{13}(x_1, x_3),$$
$$G_{03}(x_0, x_3) \leftarrow A_{P^-}(x_0) \land (x_0 = x_2) \land R(x_2, x_3)$$

(although we should write $G_{03}(x_3, x_0)$, placing parameter x_0 last, we keep the natural ordering to improve readability).

The subquery $\boldsymbol{q}_{13}(x_1, x_3) = \exists x_2 \big(S(x_1, x_2) \land R(x_2, x_3)\big)$ contains two atoms and is split at x_2. Since there is a tree witness $\mathfrak{t}^2$ for $(\mathcal{T}, \boldsymbol{q}_{13}(x_1, x_3))$ with $\mathfrak{t}^2_\mathsf{i} = \{x_2\}$ and $\mathfrak{t}^2_\mathsf{r} = \{x_1, x_3\}$, we obtain two clauses:

$$G_{13}(x_1, x_3) \leftarrow S(x_1, x_2) \land R(x_2, x_3),$$
$$G_{13}(x_1, x_3) \leftarrow A_P(x_1) \land (x_1 = x_3).$$

By applying the same procedure to $\boldsymbol{q}_{37}(x_3, x_7)$, we obtain the following five clauses:

$$G_{37}(x_3, x_7) \leftarrow G_{35}(x_3, x_5) \land G_{57}(x_5, x_7),$$
$$G_{37}(x_5, x_7) \leftarrow R(x_3, x_4) \land A_P(x_4) \land (x_4 = x_6) \land R(x_6, x_7),$$
$$G_{35}(x_3, x_5) \leftarrow R(x_3, x_4) \land S(x_4, x_5),$$
$$G_{35}(x_3, x_5) \leftarrow A_{P^-}(x_3) \land (x_3 = x_5),$$
$$G_{57}(x_5, x_7) \leftarrow R(x_5, x_6) \land R(x_6, x_7).$$

Note that the rewriting illustrated above is slightly simpler than the definition in Section 3.4: here, we directly use the atoms of $\boldsymbol{q}(\boldsymbol{x})$ instead of including a clause $G_{\boldsymbol{q}}(\boldsymbol{x}) \leftarrow \boldsymbol{q}(\boldsymbol{x})$, for each $\boldsymbol{q}(\boldsymbol{x})$ without existentially quantified variables. This simplification does not affect the width of the NDL query and the choice of weight function.

Conjunctive Queries on Probabilistic Graphs: Combined Complexity

Antoine Amarilli
LTCI, Télécom ParisTech,
Université Paris-Saclay
Paris, France

Mikaël Monet
LTCI, Télécom ParisTech,
Université Paris-Saclay
& Inria Paris, France

Pierre Senellart
DI, École normale supérieure
PSL Research University
& Inria Paris, France

ABSTRACT

Query evaluation over probabilistic databases is known to be intractable in many cases, even in data complexity, i.e., when the query is fixed. Although some restrictions of the queries [20] and instances [4] have been proposed to lower the complexity, these known tractable cases usually do not apply to combined complexity, i.e., when the query is not fixed. This leaves open the question of which query and instance languages ensure the tractability of probabilistic query evaluation in combined complexity.

This paper proposes the first general study of the combined complexity of conjunctive query evaluation on probabilistic instances over binary signatures, which we can alternatively phrase as a probabilistic version of the graph homomorphism problem, or of a constraint satisfaction problem (CSP) variant. We study the complexity of this problem depending on whether instances and queries can use features such as edge labels, disconnectedness, branching, and edges in both directions. We show that the complexity landscape is surprisingly rich, using a variety of technical tools: automata-based compilation to d-DNNF lineages as in [4], β-acyclic lineages using [11], the $\underline{X}$-property for tractable CSP from [25], graded DAGs [28] and various coding techniques for hardness proofs.

1. INTRODUCTION

Uncertainty naturally arises in many data management applications, when integrating data that may be untrustworthy, erroneous, or outdated; or when generating or annotating data using information extraction or machine learning approaches. The framework of *probabilistic databases* [32] has been introduced to answer such needs: it provides a natural semantics for concise representations of probability distributions on data, and allows the user to evaluate queries directly on the representations. The simplest probabilistic framework is that of *tuple-independent databases* (TID), where each tuple in the relational database is annotated with a probability of actually being present, assuming independence across all tuples. Evaluating a Boolean query Q over a TID instance I means computing the probability that Q is true according to the distribution of I, or in other words, the total probability mass of the possible worlds of I that satisfy Q.

As is usual in database theory, the complexity of this probabilistic query evaluation problem (PQE) can be measured as a function of both I and Q, namely, *combined complexity* [34], or as a function of I when the query Q is fixed, called *data complexity*. Almost all works on PQE so far have focused on data complexity, where they have explored the general intractability of PQE in this sense. Indeed, while non-probabilistic query evaluation of fixed queries in first-order logic has polynomial-time data complexity (specifically, AC^0), the PQE problem is #P-hard[1] already for some fixed conjunctive queries [19]. Specifically, the celebrated PQE result by Dalvi and Suciu [20], has shown a dichotomy on unions of conjunctive queries: some are *safe queries*, enjoying PTIME data complexity (specifically, linear [15]), and all other queries are #P-hard. Earlier work by some of the present authors has shown also a dichotomy on instance families for fixed monadic second-order queries, with tractable data complexity for bounded-treewidth families [4], and intractability otherwise under some assumptions [7].

However, even when PQE is tractable in data complexity, the task may still be infeasible because of unrealistically large constants that depend on the query. For instance, our approach in [4] is nonelementary in the query, and the algorithm for safe queries in [20] is generally super-exponential in the query [32]. For this reason, we believe that it is also important to achieve a good understanding of the *combined* complexity of PQE, and to isolate cases where PQE is tractable in combined complexity; similarly to how, e.g., Yannakakis' algorithm can evaluate α-acyclic queries on non-probabilistic instances with tractable combined complexity [36]. This motivates the question studied in this paper: *for which classes of queries and instances does PQE enjoy tractable combined complexity?*

Related work. Surprisingly, the question of achieving combined tractability for PQE does not seem to have been studied before. To our knowledge, the only exception is in the setting of probabilistic XML [27], where deterministic tree automata queries were shown to enjoy tractable combined complexity [16]. In the context of relational databases, our recent work [2] shows the combined tractability of *provenance*

[1]#P is the class of counting problems that can be expressed as the number of accepting paths of a nondeterministic polynomial-time Turing machine.

PODS'17, May 14 - 19, 2017, Chicago, IL, USA

ISBN 978-1-4503-4198-1/17/05...$15.00

DOI: http://dx.doi.org/10.1145/3034786.3056121

computation for a specific Datalog fragment on bounded-treewidth instances, but observes that these results do not seem to give tractability of PQE, which is already intractable in much more restricted settings. These results, however (Propositions 36 and 38 of [3]), do not give a complete picture of the combined complexity of PQE; in particular, they do not even give any non-trivial setting where it is tractable.

Questions of combined tractability have also been studied in the setting of *constraint satisfaction problems* (CSP), following a well-known connection between CSP and the conjunctive query evaluation problem in database theory, or the study of the graph homomorphism problem (see, e.g., [24]). We can then see the restriction of PQE to conjunctive queries as a probabilistic, or weighted, variant of these problems, but we are not aware of any existing study of this variant. In the graph homomorphism setting, a related but different problem is that of *counting* graph homomorphisms [12]: but this amounts to counting the number of matches of a query in a database instance, which is different from counting the possible worlds of an instance where the query has some match, as we do. A more related problem is **#SUB** [18], which asks, given a query graph G and an instance graph H, for the *number of subgraphs* of H which are *isomorphic* to G. When all facts are labeled with $1/2$, our problem asks instead for the number of subgraphs of H to which G admits a *homomorphism*. A further difference is that we allow arbitrary probability annotations, amounting to a form of weighted counting; in particular, facts can be given probability 1.

Problem statement. Inspired by the connection to graph homomorphism and CSP, in this paper we investigate the probabilistic query evaluation problem for conjunctive queries on tuple-independent instances, over arity-two signatures. To our knowledge, our paper is the first to focus on the combined complexity of conjunctive query evaluation on probabilistic relational data. For simplicity of exposition, we will phrase our problem in terms of graphs: given a *query graph* and a probabilistic *instance graph*, where each edge is annotated by a probability, we must determine the probability that the query graph has a homomorphism to the instance graph, i.e., the total probability mass of the subgraphs which ensure this, assuming independence between edges. We always assume the query and instance graphs to be directed.

As we will see, the problem is generally intractable, so we will have to study restricted settings. We accordingly study this problem under assumptions on the query and input graphs. Inspired by our prior intractability results [7], one general assumption that we will make is to impose *tree-likeness* of the instance. In fact, we will generally restrict it to be a *polytree*, i.e., a directed graph whose underlying undirected graph is a tree. As we will see, however, even this restriction does not suffice to ensure tractability, so we study the impact of several other features:

- *Labels*, i.e., whether edges of the query and instance can be labeled by a finite alphabet, as would be the case on a relational signature with more than one binary predicate.
- *Disconnectedness*, i.e., allowing disconnected queries and instances.
- *Branching*, i.e., allowing graphs to branch out, instead of requiring them to be a path.
- *Two-wayness*, i.e., allowing edges with arbitrary orientation, instead of requiring all edges to have the same orientation (as in a one-way path, or downward tree).

We accordingly study our problem for *labeled graphs* and *unlabeled graphs*, and when query and instance graphs are in the following classes, that cover the possible combinations of the above characteristics: one-way and two-way paths, downward trees and polytrees, and disjoint unions thereof.

Results. This paper presents our combined complexity results for the probabilistic query evaluation problem in all these settings. After introducing the preliminaries and defining the problem in Section 2, we first study the impact of disconnectedness in instances and queries in Section 3. While we can easily show that disconnectedness does not matter for instances (Lemma 3.7), we show that disconnectedness of queries has an unexpected impact on complexity: in the labeled case, even the simplest disconnected queries on the simplest kinds of instances are intractable (Proposition 3.3): this result is shown via the hardness of counting edge covers in bipartite graphs. The picture for disconnected queries is more complex in the unlabeled case (see Table 1): indeed, the problem is still hard when allowing two-wayness in the query and instance (as it can be used to simulate labels, see Proposition 3.4), but disallowing two-wayness in the instance ensure tractability of all queries. This latter result (Proposition 3.6) is established by showing that all queries then essentially collapse to a one-way path: we do so by assigning a *level* to all vertices of the query using a notion of *graded DAGs* [28, 30].

We then focus on connected queries, and first study the labeled setting in Section 4; see Table 2 for a summary of results. We show that disallowing instance branching ensures the tractability of all connected queries (Proposition 4.11), and that disallowing branching in the query *and* two-wayness in the instance and query also does (Proposition 4.10). These two results are shown by computing a *Boolean lineage* of the query [32], and proving that we can tractably evaluate its probability because it is β-acyclic [11], thanks to the restricted instance structure. For the first result, this process further relies on a CSP tool to show the tractability of homomorphism testing in labeled two-way paths, a condition dubbed the $\underline{X}$-property [25, 23]. We show the intractability of all other cases (Propositions 4.1, 4.4, and 4.5), by coding #SAT-reduction, reusing in part a coding from [3].

We last study the unlabeled setting for connected queries in Section 5. We show that disallowing query branching and two-wayness suffices to obtain tractability, provided that the instance is a polytree (Proposition 5.4): this result is proven by building in PTIME a deterministic tree automaton to test the length of the longest path, and compiling a d-DNNF lineage as in [4]. This result immediately extends to branching queries, as they are equivalent to paths in this case (Proposition 5.5). We complete the picture by showing that, by contrast, allowing two-wayness in the query leads to intractability on polytrees, by a variant of our coding technique (Proposition 5.6). We then conclude in Section 6.

Our results completely classify the complexity of probabilistic conjunctive query evaluation for all combinations of instance and query restrictions, in the labeled and unlabeled setting. Full proofs are given in appendix.

2. PRELIMINARIES

We first provide some formal definitions of the concepts we use in this paper, and introduce the *probabilistic graph homomorphism* problem and the different classes of graphs that we consider.

Graphs and homomorphisms. Let σ be a finite non-empty set of labels. When $|\sigma| > 1$, we say that we are in the *labeled setting*; when $|\sigma| = 1$, in the *unlabeled setting*.

We consider *directed graphs* with edge labels from σ, i.e., triples $H = (V, E, \lambda)$ with V a non-empty finite set of vertices, $E \subseteq V^2$ a set of edges, and $\lambda : E \to \sigma$ a labeling function. We write $a \xrightarrow{R} b$ for an edge $e = (a, b)$ with label $\lambda(e) = R$. Note that we do not allow multi-edges: an edge e has a unique label $\lambda(e)$. When $|\sigma| = 1$, i.e., in the unlabeled setting, we simply write (V, E) for the graph and $a \to b$ for an edge. Unless otherwise specified, all graphs that we consider in this paper are directed.

A graph $H' = (V', E', \lambda')$ is a *subgraph* of the graph $H = (V, E, \lambda)$, written $H' \subseteq H$, when we have $V' = V$, $E' \subseteq E$, and when λ' is $\lambda_{|E'}$, i.e., the restriction of λ to E'. (Note that, in a slightly non-standard way, we impose that subgraphs have the same set of vertices than the original graph; this will simplify some notation.)

A *graph homomorphism* h from some graph $G = (V_G, E_G, \lambda_G)$ to some graph $H = (V_H, E_H, \lambda_H)$ is a function $h : V_G \to V_H$ such that, for all $(u, v) \in E_G$, we have $(h(u), h(v)) \in E_H$ and further $\lambda_H((h(u), h(v))) = \lambda_G((u, v))$. A *match* of G in H is the image in H of such a homomorphism h, i.e., the graph with vertices $h(u)$ for $u \in V_G$ and edges $(h(u), h(v))$ for $(u, v) \in E_G$. Note that two different homomorphisms may define the same match. Also note that two distinct nodes of G could have the same image by h, so a match of G in H is not necessarily homomorphic to G. We write $G \rightsquigarrow H$ when there exists a homomorphism from G to H. We call two graphs G and G' *equivalent* if, for any graph H, we have $G \rightsquigarrow H$ iff $G' \rightsquigarrow H$. It is easily seen that G and G' are equivalent if and only if $G \rightsquigarrow G'$ and $G' \rightsquigarrow G$.

Probabilistic graphs. A *probability distribution on graphs* is a function Pr from a finite set $\mathcal{W}$ of graphs (called the *possible worlds* of Pr) to values in $[0; 1]$ represented as rational numbers, such that the probabilities of all possible worlds sum to 1, namely, $\sum_{H \in \mathcal{W}} \Pr(H) = 1$.

A *probabilistic graph* is intuitively a concise representation of a probability distribution. Formally, it is a pair (H, π) where H is a graph with edge labels from σ and where π is a probability function $\pi : E \to [0; 1]$ that maps every edge e of H to a probability $\pi(e)$, represented as a rational number. Note that each edge (u, v) in a probabilistic graph (H, π) is annotated both with a label $\lambda((u, v)) \in \sigma$, and a probability $\pi((u, v))$.

The *probability distribution* Pr defined by the probabilistic graph (H, π) is obtained intuitively by considering that edges are kept or deleted independently according to the indicated probability. Formally, the possible worlds $\mathcal{W}$ of Pr are the subgraphs of $H = (V, E, \lambda)$, and for $H' = (V, E', \lambda_{|E'}) \subseteq H$ we define $\Pr(H') := \prod_{e \in E'} \pi(e) \times \prod_{e \in E \setminus E'} (1 - \pi(e))$. Note that, when H has edges labeled with 0 or 1, some possible worlds are given probability 0 by π.

EXAMPLE 2.1. *Figure 1 represents a probabilistic graph (H, π) on signature $\sigma = \{R, S\}$, where each edge is annotated with its label and probability value. There are 2^6 possible worlds, 2^5 of which have non-zero probability.*

The possible world where all R-edges are kept and all S-edges are removed has probability $0.1 \times 1 \times 0.8 \times 0.1 \times 0.05 \times (1 - 0.7)$.

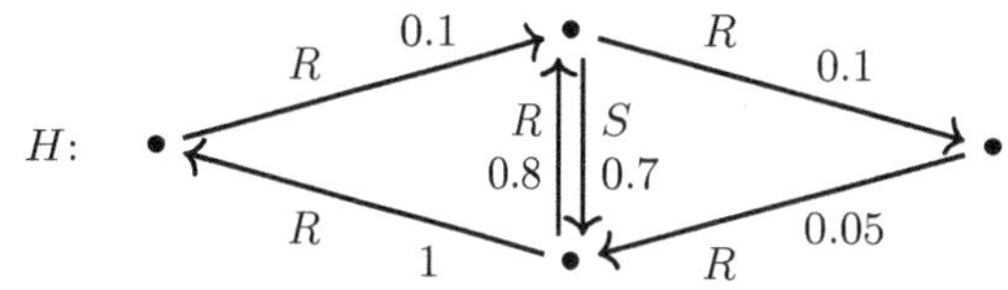

Figure 1: Example probabilistic graph H

Probabilistic graph homomorphism. The goal of this paper is to study the *probabilistic homomorphism problem* PHom, for the set of labels σ that we fixed: given a graph G on σ and a probabilistic graph (H, π) on σ, compute the probability that there exists a homomorphism from G to H under Pr, i.e., the sum of the probabilities of all subgraphs of H' to which G has a homomorphism:

$$\Pr(G \rightsquigarrow H) := \sum_{\substack{H' \subseteq H \\ G \rightsquigarrow H'}} \Pr(H').$$

EXAMPLE 2.2. *Continuing the example, consider the* PHom *problem for the graph $G : \xrightarrow{R}\xrightarrow{S}\xleftarrow{S}$ and the example probabilistic graph (H, π) in Figure 1. The graph G intuitively corresponds to the relational calculus query $\exists xyzt\ R(x, y) \wedge S(y, z) \wedge S(t, z)$. Of course, we can compute $\Pr(G \rightsquigarrow H)$ by summing over the possible worlds of H, but this process is generally intractable. Here, by considering the possible matches of G in H, we can see that $\Pr(G \rightsquigarrow H) = 0.7 \times (1 - (1 - 0.1) \times (1 - 0.8))$.*

Following database terminology, we call G the *query graph* and (H, π) the *(probabilistic) instance graph*. Indeed, the PHom problem is easily seen to be equivalent to conjunctive query evaluation on probabilistic tuple-independent relational databases [20], over binary relational signatures.

Note that, in this paper, we measure the complexity of PHom as a function of *both* the query graph G and of the instance graph (H, π), i.e., in database terminology, we measure the *combined complexity* [34] of probabilistic query evaluation. The PHom problem is known to be #P-hard in general [19] (even for some fixed query graphs): by this, we mean that it is hard (under polynomial-time reductions) for the class #P of counting problems that can be expressed as the number of accepting paths of a nondeterministic polynomial-time Turing machine. To achieve tractable complexity for PHom, we will classify the complexity of PHom under various restrictions. We say that the complexity of some variant of the problem is *tractable* if the probability can be computed by a deterministic polynomial-time Turing machine: by a slight abuse of terminology, we then say that it is *in PTIME*. All PHom variants that we study will be shown either to be PTIME in this sense, or to be #P-hard.

We will study restrictions of PHom first by distinguishing the *labeled* and *unlabeled* settings. We write $\mathsf{PHom}_{\mathsf{L}}$ for the problem when the fixed label set σ is such that $|\sigma| > 1$, and $\mathsf{PHom}_{\not\mathsf{L}}$ when the fixed σ is such that $|\sigma| = 1$.

Figure 2: Inclusions between classes of graphs

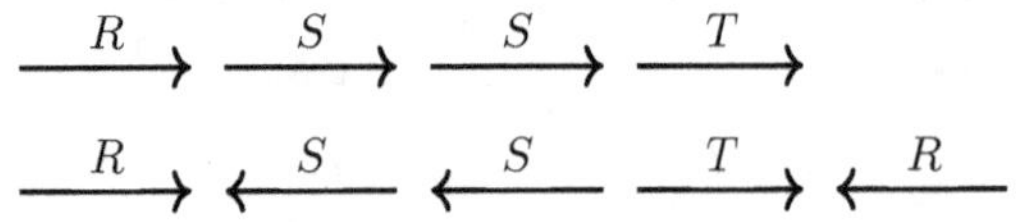

Figure 3: Example of labeled 1WP (top) and 2WP (bottom) for $\sigma = \{R, S, T\}$.

The second restriction concerns the input query graphs and instance graphs. We will model restrictions on these graphs by requiring them to be taken from specific graph classes, where by *graph class* we simply mean an infinite set of graphs. Inspired by the notation used in CSP, for two classes $\mathcal{G}$ and $\mathcal{H}$ of graphs in the labeled setting, we denote $\mathsf{PHom}_{\mathsf{L}}(\mathcal{G}, \mathcal{H})$ the problem that takes as input a graph G in class $\mathcal{G}$ and a probabilistic graph (H, π) with H in class $\mathcal{H}$, and computes the probability $\Pr(G \rightsquigarrow H)$. We denote the same problem in the unlabeled setting by $\mathsf{PHom}_{\not{\mathsf{L}}}(\mathcal{G}, \mathcal{H})$.

Graph classes. The graph classes which we study in this paper are defined as follows, on a graph G with edge labels from σ:

- G is a *one-way path* (1WP) if it is of the form $a_1 \xrightarrow{R_1} \cdots \xrightarrow{R_{m-1}} a_m$ for some m, with all $a_1, \ldots, a_m$ being pairwise distinct, and with $R_i \in \sigma$ for $1 \leqslant i < m$.
- G is a *two-way path* (2WP) if it is of the form $a_1 - \cdots - a_m$, with all $a_1, \ldots, a_m$ being pairwise distinct, and each $-$ being $\xrightarrow{R_i}$ or $\xleftarrow{R_i}$ (but not both) for some label $R_i \in \sigma$.
- G is a *downwards tree* (DWT) if it is a rooted unranked tree (each node can have an arbitrary number of children), with all edges going from parent to child in the tree.
- G is a *polytree* (PT) if its underlying undirected graph is an unranked tree, without restriction on edge directions.

We also consider the class Connected of connected graphs, and write All the class of all graphs. The inclusion diagram between our graph classes is shown in Figure 2. See Figure 3 for an example of a labeled one-way path and two-way path, and Figure 4 for an unlabeled downwards tree and polytree.

We also introduce the classes $\bigsqcup$1WP (resp., $\bigsqcup$2WP, $\bigsqcup$DWT, $\bigsqcup$PT) of graphs that are *disjoint unions of* 1WP (resp., 2WP, DWT, PT), that is, of possibly disconnected graphs whose connected components are 1WP (resp., 2WP, DWT, PT).

Our graph classes were chosen to be representative of different features of graphs that will have an impact in the complexity of the PHom problem, namely, *labeling, two-wayness, branching,* and *disconnectedness.* Indeed, 2WP (resp., PT) adds two-wayness to 1WP (resp., DWT); DWT (resp., PT) adds branching to 1WP (resp., 2WP); and $\bigsqcup$1WP (resp., $\bigsqcup$2WP, $\bigsqcup$DWT, $\bigsqcup$PT) adds disconnectedness to 1WP (resp., 2WP, DWT, PT).

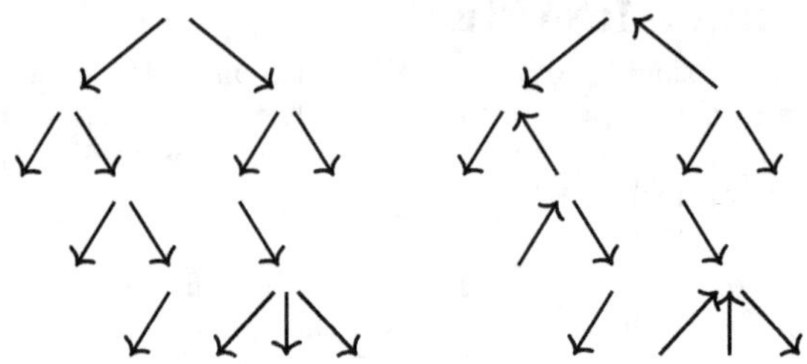

Figure 4: Examples of unlabeled DWT (left) and PT (right)

In the following sections, we investigate the complexity of probabilistic graph homomorphism for these various classes of conjunctive queries and instances.

3. DISCONNECTED CASE

We first consider the case where either the query or probabilistic instance graph is *disconnected*, i.e., not in the Connected class. When the query is disconnected, we show in this section that the probabilistic homomorphism problem is #P-hard in all but the most restricted of cases (in particular in the labeled setting), which justifies that we restrict to connected queries in the rest of the paper. On the other hand, we will show that disconnectedness in the probabilistic instance graph has essentially no impact on combined complexity.

3.1 Labeled Disconnected Queries

We establish our main intractability result on disconnected queries by reduction from the `#Bipartite-Edge-Cover` problem on *undirected* graphs:

Definition 3.1. *An undirected graph is* bipartite *if its vertices can be partitioned into two classes such that no edge connects two vertices of the same class. An* edge cover *of an undirected graph is a subset of its edges such that every vertex is incident to at least one edge of the subset.* `#Bipartite-Edge-Cover` *is the problem, given a bipartite undirected graph, of counting its number of edge covers.*

This problem was shown in [26] to be intractable. The result can also be proven using Valiant's holographic reductions [33] and the results of Cai, Lu, and Xia [14], as explained in [35]: see Appendix D.

Theorem 3.2. *[26, 14, 35] The* `#Bipartite-Edge-Cover` *problem is #P-complete.*

We can then use this result to show intractability for the simplest forms of disconnected query graphs ($\bigsqcup$1WP) on the simplest forms of probabilistic instance graphs (1WP), in the *labeled* case:

Proposition 3.3. $\mathsf{PHom}_{\mathsf{L}}(\bigsqcup \mathsf{1WP}, \mathsf{1WP})$ *is #P-hard.*

Proof. We reduce from `#Bipartite-Edge-Cover`. Let $\Gamma = (X \sqcup Y, E)$ be an input to `#Bipartite-Edge-Cover`, i.e., a bipartite undirected graph with parts X and Y; we write $X = (x_1, \ldots, x_{n_1})$, $Y = (y_1, \ldots, y_{n_r})$, $E = (e_1, \ldots, e_m)$, and for all $1 \leqslant i \leqslant m$ we write $e_i = (x_{l_i}, y_{r_i})$, with $1 \leqslant l_i \leqslant n_1$ and $1 \leqslant r_i \leqslant n_r$.

We first construct in PTIME the 1WP probabilistic graph (H, π): see Figure 5 for an illustration of the construction.

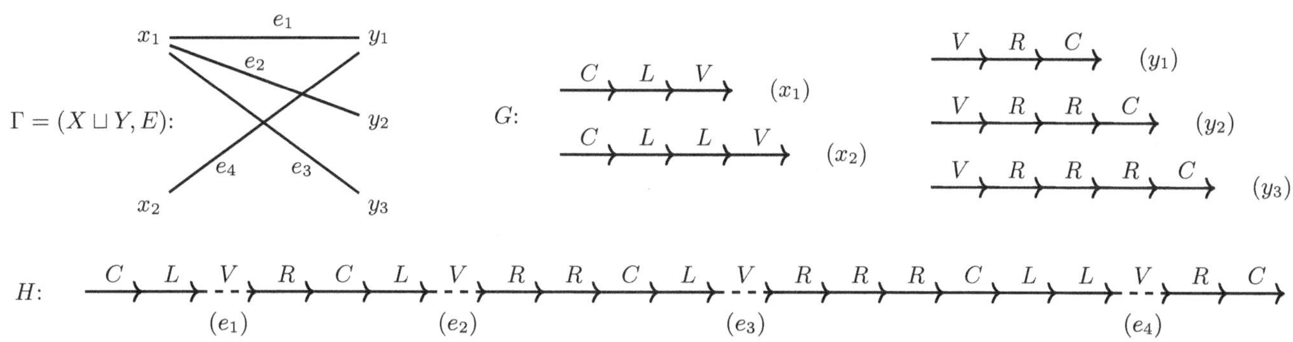

Figure 5: Illustration of the proof of Proposition 3.3, for the bipartite graph Γ. Dashed edges have probability $\frac{1}{2}$. We show (in parentheses) the edge of Γ coded by each V-labeled edge in the instance graph H, and the vertex of Γ coded by each 1WP component of the query graph G.

Specifically, for $1 \leqslant j \leqslant m$, we construct the following 1WP:

$$H_{e_j} := (\xrightarrow{L})^{l_j} \xrightarrow{V} (\xrightarrow{R})^{r_j}.$$

The graph H is then defined as:

$$\xrightarrow{C} H_{e_1} \xrightarrow{C} H_{e_2} \xrightarrow{C} \cdots \xrightarrow{C} H_{e_m} \xrightarrow{C}.$$

We define π as follows: edges labeled by V have probability $\frac{1}{2}$ (intuitively coding whether an edge is part of the candidate cover), all others have probability 1.

We then construct the query graph $G \in \bigsqcup$1WP, coding the edge covering constraints. For every $1 \leqslant i \leqslant n_l$, the graph G contains the 1WP component $\xrightarrow{C} (\xrightarrow{L})^i \xrightarrow{V}$, and for every $1 \leqslant i \leqslant n_r$, the graph G contains the 1WP component $\xrightarrow{V} (\xrightarrow{R})^i \xrightarrow{C}$.

It is clear that H is in 1WP, G is in $\bigsqcup$1WP and that both can be constructed in PTIME from Γ. We now show that $\Pr(G \rightsquigarrow H)$ is exactly the number of edge covers of Γ divided by 2^m, so that the computation of the latter reduces in PTIME to the computation of the former, concluding the proof.

To see why, we define a bijection between the subsets of edges of Γ, seen as valuations $\nu : E \to \{0, 1\}$, to the possible worlds H' of H of non-zero probability. We do so in the expected way: keep the one V-edge $\xrightarrow{V}$ of H_{e_i} iff $\nu(e_i) = 1$. We now show that there is a homomorphism from G to H' if and only if ν is an edge cover of Γ. As the number of H''s such that there is a homomorphism from G to H' is exactly $\Pr(G \rightsquigarrow H) \times 2^m$, this will allow us to conclude.

Indeed, if there is a homomorphism h from G to H', then, considering the 1WP component in G that codes the constraint on x_i (resp., on y_i), its image must be of the form $\xrightarrow{C} (\xrightarrow{L})^i \xrightarrow{V}$ (resp., $\xrightarrow{V} (\xrightarrow{R})^i \xrightarrow{C}$), but then by construction of H the V-fact must correspond to an edge e such that x_i (resp., y_i) is adjacent to e, so that we have $\nu(e) = 1$ and so x_i (resp., y_i) is covered. As this is true for each 1WP component, all the vertices are covered and ν is indeed an edge cover of Γ.

Conversely, suppose that ν is an edge cover of Γ, then for every vertex x_i (resp., y_i) we know that there exists $1 \leqslant j \leqslant m$ such that $\nu(e_j) = 1$ and $l_j = i$ (resp., $r_j = i$), and we can use the V-fact corresponding to e_j and the surrounding facts to build the homomorphism as above from each component of G to H'. □

Table 1: Tractability of PHom$_{\not L}$ for disconnected queries (Section 3.2). Results also hold when instances are unions of the indicated classes.

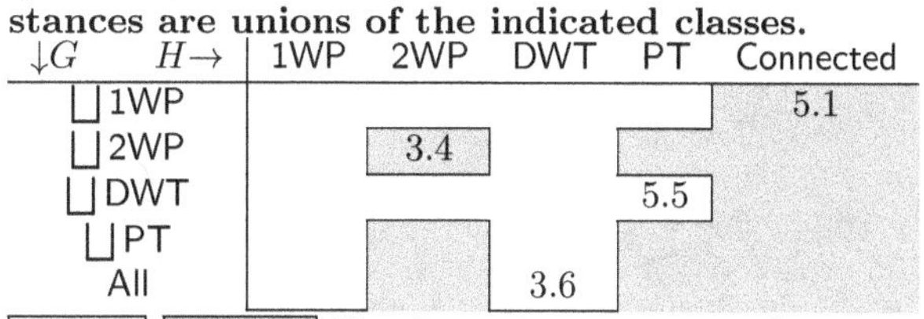

PTIME #P-hard Numbers given correspond to propositions for border cases, remaining cells can be filled using the inclusions from Figure 2.

The proof of Proposition 3.3 crucially requires multiple labels in the signature. Indeed, it is easy to see that, in the unlabeled setting, a query graph in $\bigsqcup$1WP (or even in $\bigsqcup$DWT) is equivalent to the longest path within the graph, and we will show further (Proposition 5.5) that PHom$_{\not L}$(1WP, 1WP) (indeed, even PHom$_{\not L}$($\bigsqcup$DWT, PT)) is PTIME.

3.2 Unlabeled Disconnected Queries

In light of this intractability result, let us now consider the unlabeled setting. We show in Table 1 where the tractability frontier lies. First, introducing two-wayness in both query and instance graphs is enough to obtain an analogue of the intractability of Proposition 3.3:

PROPOSITION 3.4. *PHom$_{\not L}$($\bigsqcup$2WP, 2WP) is #P-hard.*

PROOF. We reduce, again, from the #P-hard problem `#Bipartite-Edge-Cover`. The idea of the reduction is similar to that used in the proof of Proposition 3.3, but we face the additional difficulty of not being allowed to use labels. Fortunately, we can use two-wayness to simulate them.

Let $\Gamma = (X \sqcup Y, E)$ be an input of `#Bipartite-Edge-Cover`. Consider the reduction from Γ used in the proof of Proposition 3.3 and the 1WP probabilistic graph (H, π) and the $\bigsqcup$1WP query graph G that were constructed. We construct from H and G the unlabeled probabilistic graph H' and unlabeled $\bigsqcup$2WP query graph G' as follows:

- replace each L- or R-labeled edge $a \xrightarrow{L} b$ or $a \xrightarrow{R} b$ in H and G by 3 edges $a \to\to\leftarrow b$;
- replace each C-labeled edge $a \xrightarrow{C} b$ of H and G by 3 edges $a \leftarrow\leftarrow\leftarrow b$;

- replace each V-labeled edge $a \xrightarrow{V} b$ of H and G by 6 edges $a \to\to\to\to\to\leftarrow b$.

All edges of H' have probability 1, except the first edge of each sequence of 6 edges that replaced a V-labeled edge, which has probability $\frac{1}{2}$.

Consider a 1WP component of G that codes the constraint on a vertex from Y, e.g $\xrightarrow{V} (\xrightarrow{R})^i \xrightarrow{C}$, which was rewritten in G' into $\to\to\to\to\to\leftarrow (\to\to\leftarrow)^i \leftarrow\leftarrow\leftarrow$. A homomorphism from this component into a possible world J' of H' must actually map to a rewriting of a $\xrightarrow{V} (\xrightarrow{R})^i \xrightarrow{C}$ sequence in H': indeed, the key observation is that the first 5 $\to$ edges can only be matched to 5 consecutive $\to$ in J', which only exist as the first 5 edges of a sequence of 6 edges that replaced a V-labeled fact in H. There is no choice left to match the subsequent edges without failing. A similar observation holds for components coding the constraints on vertices from X ($\xrightarrow{C} (\xrightarrow{L})^i \xrightarrow{V}$). Hence, we can show correctness of the reduction using the same argument as before. □

Allowing two-wayness in both the query and the instance graphs thus allows us to simulate labels, so that $\mathsf{PHom}_{\not L}$ is intractable. We will study in Section 5 what happens for query graph classes without two-wayness (i.e., 1WP, DWT, and unions thereof); so let us now consider the case of instance graph classes where two-wayness is forbidden, i.e., is in $\bigsqcup$DWT. As we will show, $\mathsf{PHom}_{\not L}$ of *arbitrary* query graphs on such $\bigsqcup$DWT instance graphs is tractable. To this end, we need to introduce *level mappings* of acyclic directed graphs (DAGs):

DEFINITION 3.5. *A* level mapping *of a DAG G is a mapping μ from the vertices of G to $\mathbb{Z}$ such that for each directed edge $u \to v$ of G we have $\mu(v) = \mu(u) - 1$. We call G a* graded DAG *if it has a level mapping.*

An example of graded DAG together with a level mapping is given in Figure 6. It is easy to see (and shown in Proposition 1 of [28]) that a DAG G is graded iff there are no two vertices u, v and two directed paths χ, χ' in G from u to v such that χ and χ' have different lengths (in the terminology of [28], G does not have a *jumping edge*). Graded DAGs are related to the classical notion of graded ordered set [30], and the level mapping function has been called in the literature a *depth function* [28], a *grading function* [30], a *set of levels* [30], or a *rank function* [31].

To obtain such a level mapping, we can proceed by picking one vertex in each connected component of G, mapping each of these vertices to level 0, and then exploring G by a breadth-first traversal and assigning the level of each vertex according to the level of the vertex used to reach it, visiting all edges and defining the image of each vertex. It is clear that this process yields a level mapping of G unless it tries to assign two different levels to the same vertex v, which cannot happen if there is no jumping edge [28, Proposition 1].

We will now use the notion of graded DAG to show:

PROPOSITION 3.6. $\mathsf{PHom}_{\not L}(\mathsf{All}, \bigsqcup\mathsf{DWT})$ *is PTIME.*

PROOF SKETCH. We only give the idea when the query graph is connected and the graph instance H is a DWT (see Appendix for full proof). As we pointed out already, if the query graph G is not a graded DAG, then it has a cycle or a pair of vertices joined by two directed paths of different

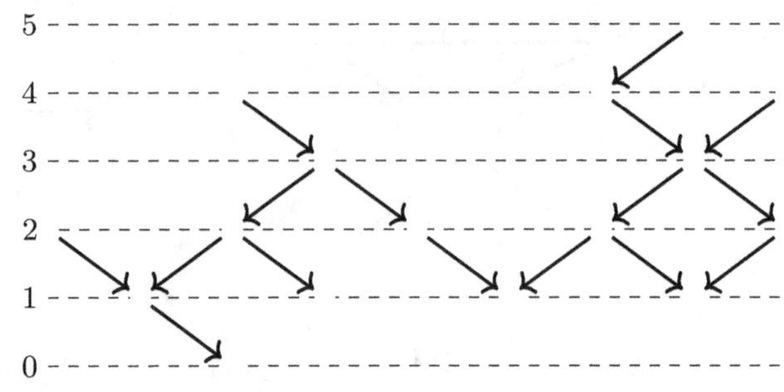

Figure 6: A DAG with a level mapping (dashed lines), see Definition 3.5.

lengths: then, from the structure of the DWT instance graph, this clearly implies that $\Pr(G \rightsquigarrow H) = 0$. So it suffices to study the case when G is a graded DAG.

As we explained earlier, we can then compute in PTIME a level mapping μ of G. It is clear that, as G is connected, the level mapping μ is uniquely defined up to an additive constant. Hence, we shift μ so that the smallest value of its image is 0, and we then call the *difference of levels* of G the largest value m in the image of μ. Note that m is *not* the maximal length from a root of G to a leaf of G (see, e.g., Figure 6). We then claim that, on any possible world H' of the DWT instance graph H, the query graph G is in fact equivalent to the 1WP query graph $\to^m$ of length m. This allows us to conclude using Proposition 5.5.

One direction is easy to observe, because μ directly gives a homomorphism from G to $\to^m$. For the converse, suppose that a homomorphism h from G to H' exists. Because G is connected and H' is in $\bigsqcup$DWT, the image of h is actually a DWT, call it T. Now it is easy to see that the image of a node that has level $m - i$ in G has depth i in T, so that T (and so H') contains the 1WP $\to^m$. □

3.3 Disconnected Instances

We conclude our study of the disconnected case with the case of disconnected *instance graphs*, which we show to be less interesting than the disconnected *query graphs* that we studied so far. Specifically, when the query is *connected*, PHom on arbitrary instances can reduce in PTIME to PHom of the same queries on a corresponding class of connected instances:

LEMMA 3.7. *For any class of graphs $\mathcal{H}$, let $\mathcal{H}'$ be the class of connected components of graphs in $\mathcal{H}$. Then for any class of* connected *graphs $\mathcal{G}$, $\mathsf{PHom_L}(\mathcal{G}, \mathcal{H})$ reduces in PTIME to $\mathsf{PHom_L}(\mathcal{G}, \mathcal{H}')$, and $\mathsf{PHom}_{\not L}(\mathcal{G}, \mathcal{H})$ reduces in PTIME to $\mathsf{PHom}_{\not L}(\mathcal{G}, \mathcal{H}')$.*

PROOF. Let $G \in \mathcal{G}$, $H \in \mathcal{H}$, and write $H = H'_1 \sqcup \ldots \sqcup H'_n$: we have $H'_i \in \mathcal{H}'$ for all $1 \leqslant i \leqslant n$. Let π be a probability distribution over H: the independence assumption ensures that the edges of any H'_i are pairwise independent from those of any H'_j for $i \neq j$. Now, as G is connected, any image of a homomorphism from G to H must actually be included in some H'_i. Thus, the computation of $\Pr(G \rightsquigarrow H)$ reduces to that of the $\Pr(G \rightsquigarrow H'_i)$ for $1 \leqslant i \leqslant n$, as follows:

$$\Pr(G \rightsquigarrow H) = 1 - \prod_{1 \leqslant i \leqslant n} (1 - \Pr(G \rightsquigarrow H'_i)). \quad \square$$

Table 2: Tractability of $\mathsf{PHom_L}$ in the connected case (Section 4)

$\downarrow G \quad H \rightarrow$	1WP	2WP	DWT	PT	Connected
1WP			4.10	4.1	
2WP			4.5		
DWT			4.4		
PT					
Connected		4.11			

PTIME #P-hard Numbers given correspond to propositions for border cases, remaining cells can be filled using the inclusions from Figure 2.

We last discuss the case when both the query and instance graphs are disconnected. Let us consider the results of Table 1 for connected instance graphs. Clearly, any hardness results of a connected class carries over to the corresponding disconnected class. Conversely, we have shown in Proposition 3.6 that $\mathsf{PHom}_{\not L}(\mathsf{All}, \bigsqcup \mathsf{DWT})$ is PTIME; this implies that all tractable cases in Table 1 also hold for unions of the indicated instance classes, except $\mathsf{PHom}_{\not L}(\bigsqcup \mathsf{1WP}, \bigsqcup \mathsf{PT})$ and $\mathsf{PHom}_{\not L}(\bigsqcup \mathsf{DWT}, \bigsqcup \mathsf{PT})$. But we have noted at the end of Section 3.1 that, in the unlabeled setting, $\bigsqcup \mathsf{1WP}$ or $\bigsqcup \mathsf{DWT}$ query graphs are equivalent to 1WP query graphs: thus, Lemma 3.7, together with tractability of $\mathsf{PHom}_{\not L}(\mathsf{1WP}, \mathsf{PT})$, implies $\mathsf{PHom}_{\not L}(\bigsqcup \mathsf{1WP}, \bigsqcup \mathsf{PT})$ and $\mathsf{PHom}_{\not L}(\bigsqcup \mathsf{DWT}, \bigsqcup \mathsf{PT})$ are both in PTIME. Hence, the results of Table 1 also hold when instances are unions of the indicated classes.

We have thus completed our study of $\mathsf{PHom_L}$ and $\mathsf{PHom}_{\not L}$ for disconnected instances and/or disconnected queries, We accordingly focus on connected queries and instances in the next two sections.

4. LABELED CONNECTED QUERIES

In this section, we focus on the *labeled* setting, i.e., the $\mathsf{PHom_L}$ problem, for classes of connected queries and instances. Table 2 shows the entire classification of the labeled setting for the classes that we consider.

Intuitively, we show intractability for polytree instance graphs, and for downward trees instance graphs when the query graphs allow either two-wayness or branching. Conversely, we show tractability of one-way path query graphs on downward trees, and of arbitrary connected queries on two-way path instances. We first present the hardness results, and then the tractability results.

4.1 Hardness Results

We recall that, if we allow *arbitrary* connected unlabeled probabilistic instance graphs (or even just 4-partite graphs), then computing the probability that there exists a path of length 2 is already #P-hard: this is shown in [32], and we will state this result in our context as Proposition 5.1 in the next section. Hence, if we want to obtain PTIME complexity for PHom, we need to restrict the class of instances. We can start by restricting the instances to be polytrees, but as we show, this does not suffice to ensure tractability:

PROPOSITION 4.1. $\mathsf{PHom_L}(\mathsf{1WP}, \mathsf{PT})$ *is #P-hard.*

To show this result, we will reduce from the problem of computing the probability of a Boolean formula, which we now define:

DEFINITION 4.2. *Given a set of variables $\mathcal{X}$ and a* probability assignment *π mapping each variable X in $\mathcal{X}$ to a rational probability $\pi(X) \in [0,1]$, we define the* probability *$\pi(\nu)$ of a valuation $\nu : \mathcal{X} \rightarrow \{0,1\}$ as*

$$\pi(\nu) := \Big(\prod_{X \in \mathcal{X},\ \nu(X)=1} \pi(X)\Big)\Big(\prod_{X \in \mathcal{X},\ \nu(X)=0} (1-\pi(X))\Big).$$

The Boolean probability computation problem *is defined as follows: given a Boolean formula φ on variables $\mathcal{X}$ and a probability assignment π on $\mathcal{X}$, compute the total probability of the valuations that satisfy φ, i.e., $\Pr(\varphi, \pi) = \sum_{\nu \text{ satisfies } \varphi} \pi(\nu)$.*

This problem is known to be #P-hard, even under severe restrictions on the formula φ. We will use the **#PP2DNF** formulation of the above problem, which is #P-hard [29, 32]:

DEFINITION 4.3. *A* positive DNF *is a Boolean formula φ of the form $\varphi = \bigvee_{1 \leqslant i \leqslant m} \left(\bigwedge_{1 \leqslant j \leqslant n_i} X_{i,j}\right)$, i.e., it is a disjunction of (conjunctive)* clauses *that are conjunctions of variables of $\mathcal{X}$. We assume that each variable of $\mathcal{X}$ occurs in φ, as we can eliminate the others without loss of generality.*

A positive partitioned 2-DNF *(PP2DNF) is intuitively a positive DNF φ on a partitioned set of variables where each clause contains one variable from each partition. Formally, the variables of φ are $\mathcal{X} \sqcup \mathcal{Y}$, where we write $\mathcal{X} = \{X_1, \ldots, X_{n_1}\}$ and $\mathcal{Y} = \{Y_1, \ldots, Y_{n_2}\}$, and φ is of the form $\bigvee_{j=1\ldots m}(X_{x_j} \wedge Y_{y_j})$ with $1 \leqslant x_j \leqslant n_1$ and $1 \leqslant y_j \leqslant n_2$ for $1 \leqslant j \leqslant m$.*

The **#PP2DNF** *problem is the Boolean probability computation problem when we impose that π maps every variable to $1/2$, and that φ is a PP2DNF.*

We show Proposition 4.1 by reducing from **#PP2DNF**:

PROOF SKETCH. The full proof is in appendix; see Figure 7 for an illustration. From the PP2DNF formula φ, we construct a PT probabilistic instance where each branch starting at the root describes a variable of the formula. The first edge is probabilistic and represents the choice of valuation. The edges are oriented upwards or downwards depending on whether the variable belongs to $\mathcal{X}$ or to $\mathcal{Y}$. We add a special gadget at different depths of the branch to code the index of each of the clauses where the variable occurs.

We code satisfaction of the formula by a query that tests for a path of a specific length that starts and ends with the gadget. The query has a match exactly on possible worlds where we have set two variables to true such that the sum of the depths of the gadgets corresponds to the query length: this happens iff the two variables occur in the same clause. □

Hence, restricting instances to polytrees is not sufficient to ensure tractability, even for 1WP query graphs. We must thus restrict the instance further, by disallowing one of the two remaining features, namely branching and two-wayness. The first option of disallowing branching, i.e., requiring the instance to be a 2WP, is studied in Section 4.2 below, where we show that the problem is tractable for arbitrary query graphs.

The second option is to forbid two-wayness on the instance, i.e., restrict it to be a DWT. In this case, we first show that intractability holds even when we also forbid two-wayness in the query graph, i.e., we also restrict it to be a DWT. The result follows from our earlier work on the combined complexity of query evaluation [2, 3]:

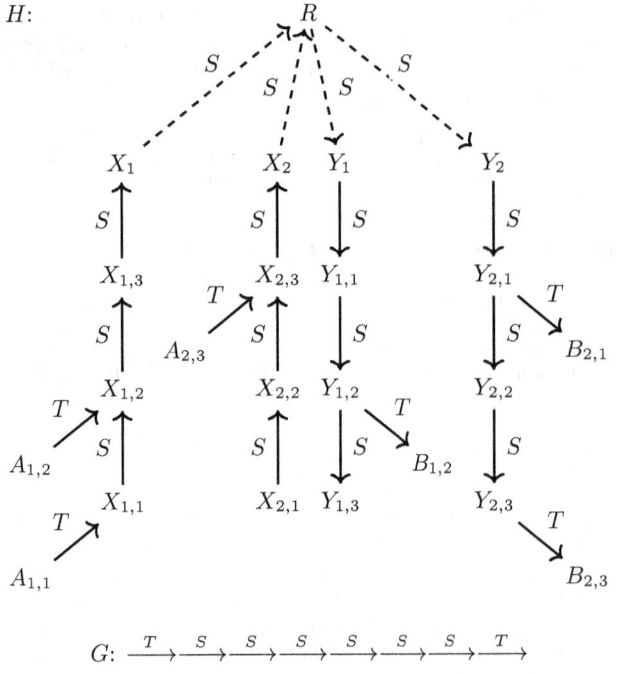

Figure 7: Illustration of the proof of Proposition 4.3 for the PP2DNF formula $X_1Y_2 \vee X_1Y_1 \vee X_2Y_2$. Dashed edges have probability $\frac{1}{2}$, all others have probability 1.

PROPOSITION 4.4 [3]. $\mathsf{PHom}_{\mathsf{L}}(\mathsf{DWT}, \mathsf{DWT})$ *is #P-hard.*

If we forbid branching in the query graph instead of two-wayness, requiring it to be a 2WP, then intractability still holds, which also follows from our earlier results:

PROPOSITION 4.5 [3]. $\mathsf{PHom}_{\mathsf{L}}(\mathsf{2WP}, \mathsf{DWT})$ *is #P-hard.*

Thus, on DWT instances, the only remaining case is when the query is a one-way path. We will now show in the section below that this case is tractable, in addition to the case of arbitrary queries on 2WP instances that we left open above.

4.2 Tractability Results

The general proof technique to obtain PTIME combined complexity in this section is inspired by the probabilistic database literature [32]: compute the *lineage* of G on H as a Boolean formula in positive disjunctive normal form (DNF), then compute its probability. Let us first define *lineages*:

DEFINITION 4.6. *Let G be a query graph and (H, π) be a probabilistic graph with edge set E. For any valuation $\nu : E \to \{0, 1\}$, we denote by $\nu(H)$ the possible world of H where each edge $e \in E$ is kept iff $\nu(e) = 1$. Letting φ be a Boolean function whose variables are the edges of E, we say that φ* captures the lineage of G on H *if, for any valuation $\nu : E \to \{0, 1\}$, the function φ evaluates to 1 under ν iff we have $G \leadsto \nu(H)$.*

Lineage representations allow us to reduce the PHom problem to the Boolean probability computation problem on the lineage function (recall Definition 4.2). Formally, for any query graph G and probabilistic graph (H, π), given a Boolean function φ that captures the lineage of G on H, we compute the answer to PHom on G and (H, π) as the probability $\Pr(\varphi, \pi)$ of φ under π: it is immediate by definition that these two quantities are equal.

Of course, computing a lineage representation does not generally suffice to show tractability, because, as we explained earlier, the Boolean probability computation problem is generally intractable. However, computing a Boolean lineage allows us to leverage the known tractable classes of Boolean formulas. Specifically, we will show how to use the class of *β-acyclic positive DNF formulas*, which are known to be tractable [11]. We define this notion, by first recalling the notion of a *β-acyclic hypergraph*, and then defining a *β-acyclic positive DNF*:

DEFINITION 4.7. *A* hypergraph $\mathcal{H} = (V, E)$ *is a finite set V of vertices and a set E of non-empty subsets of V, called* hyperedges. *For $v \in V$, we write $\mathcal{H} \setminus v$ for the hypergraph $(V \setminus \{v\}, E')$ where E' is $\{e \setminus \{v\} \mid e \in E\} \setminus \{\emptyset\}$.*

A vertex $v \in V$ of $\mathcal{H}$ is called a β-leaf *[10] if the set of hyperedges that contain it, i.e., $\{e \in E \mid v \in e\}$, is totally ordered by inclusion. In other words, we can write $\{e \in E \mid v \in e\}$ as $(e_1, \ldots, e_k)$ in a way that ensures that $e_i \subseteq e_{i+1}$ for all $1 \leqslant i < k$.*

A β-elimination order for a hypergraph $\mathcal{H} = (V, E)$ is defined inductively as follows:

- *if $E = \emptyset$, then the empty tuple is a β-elimination order for $\mathcal{H}$;*
- *otherwise, a tuple $(v_1, \ldots, v_n)$ of vertices of $\mathcal{H}$ is a β-elimination order for $\mathcal{H}$ if v_1 is a β-leaf in $\mathcal{H}$ and $(v_2, \ldots, v_n)$ is a β-elimination order for $\mathcal{H} \setminus v_1$.*

The hypergraph $\mathcal{H}$ is β-acyclic *if there is a β-elimination order for $\mathcal{H}$.*

We can see a positive DNF (recall Definition 4.3) as a hypergraph of clauses on the variables, and introduce the notion of *β-acyclic positive DNFs* accordingly:

DEFINITION 4.8. *The* hypergraph $\mathcal{H}(\varphi)$ *of a positive DNF on variables $\mathcal{X}$ has $\mathcal{X}$ as vertex set and has one hyperedge per clause, i.e., we have $\mathcal{H}(\varphi) := (\mathcal{X}, E)$ with $E := \{\{X_{i,j} \mid 1 \leqslant j \leqslant n_i\} \mid 1 \leqslant i \leqslant m\}$. We say that the positive DNF φ is* β-acyclic *if $\mathcal{H}(\varphi)$ is β-acyclic.*

It follows directly from results by Brault-Baron, Capelli, and Mengel about the β-acyclic **#CSP**$_\mathsf{d}$ problem [11] that we can tractably compute the probability of β-acyclic positive DNFs:

THEOREM 4.9. *The Boolean probability computation problem is in PTIME when restricted to β-acyclic positive DNF formulas.*

PROOF SKETCH. The **#CSP**$_\mathsf{d}$ problem studied in [11] is about computing a partition function over the hypergraph, under weighted constraints on hyperedges: it generalizes the problem of counting the number of valuations of β-acyclic formulae in conjunctive normal form (CNF) by [11, Lemma 3]. We show how the result extends to β-acyclic positive DNF, using de Morgan's law, and to probability computation for weighted variables, using additional constraints on singleton variable sets. □

We will then use the tractability of β-acyclic formulas to show PTIME combined complexity results for our $\mathsf{PHom}_{\mathsf{L}}$ problem. The first result that we show is tractability for labeled 1WP query graphs on DWT probabilistic instance graphs:[2]

PROPOSITION 4.10. $\mathsf{PHom_L}(\mathsf{1WP}, \mathsf{DWT})$ *is PTIME.*

PROOF SKETCH. Intuitively, the proof proceeds in three steps. The first step is to enumerate all candidate minimal matches of the query graph in the instance graph, i.e., subgraphs of the instance graph to which the query graph could have a homomorphism, and which are minimal for inclusion. As the query graph is a path, we know that the minimal matches are downward paths in the DWT instance: hence, as each vertex of the DWT instance can be the lowest vertex of at most one match, there are polynomially many matches to consider.

The second step is to decide which ones of these matches are actually a match of the query, by considering the labels: as both the query graph and the match are a 1WP, this is straightforward. These first two steps produce a positive DNF that captures the lineage of the query graph on the instance in the standard sense.

The third step is to notice that this lineage expression is β-acyclic: this is because its variables can be eliminated by considering the nodes of the instance DWT in a bottom-up fashion. □

Interestingly, we were not able to prove this result using tree automata-based dynamic programming approach (like we will do later for Proposition 5.4).

The second result that we show is tractability when restricting the instance to be a 2WP, and allowing arbitrary *connected* queries (remember from Proposition 3.3 that the problem is hard even on 1WP instances if we allow *disconnected* queries):

PROPOSITION 4.11. $\mathsf{PHom_L}(\mathsf{Connected}, \mathsf{2WP})$ *is PTIME.*

To show this result, we follow the same scheme as in the proof of Proposition 4.10 above: (i) enumerate all candidate matches; (ii) check whether they are indeed matches; and (iii) argue that the resulting lineage is β-acyclic. For the first step, there are polynomially many candidate matches to consider, because matches are necessarily connected subgraphs of the instance graph H, that are uniquely defined by their endpoints: this is where we use connectedness of the query. For the third step, the resulting lineage is β-acyclic for the same reason as in Proposition 4.10, as we can eliminate variables following the order of the path H: all connected subpaths containing an endpoint of the path are ordered by inclusion. What changes, however, is the second step: from the quadratically many possible matches, to compute the lineage expression, we must decide which ones are actually matches.

Deciding this for each subpath amounts to testing, given the connected query graph G and a candidate match H', whether $G \rightsquigarrow H'$, in the non-probabilistic sense. This graph homomorphism problem is generally intractable, but here the minimal match H' is a 2WP (as it is a subpath of H), so it turns out to enjoy combined tractability. The corresponding result was first shown by Gutjahr [25] for *unlabeled* graphs, when the instance graph is a path, or for more general instances satisfying a condition called the $\underline{X}$-property; this was generalized to labeled graphs by Gottlob, Koch, and Schulz in [23]. We recall here the definition of this property:

DEFINITION 4.12 (DEFINITION 3.2 OF [23]). *Let $H = (V, E, \lambda)$ be a directed graph with labels on σ, let $R \in \sigma$, and let $<$ be a total order on V. Then R is said to have the* $\underline{X}$-property *w.r.t. $<$ if for all $n_0, n_1, n_2, n_3 \in V$ such that $n_0 < n_1$ and $n_2 < n_3$, if we have $n_0 \xrightarrow{R} n_3$ and $n_1 \xrightarrow{R} n_2$ then we also have $n_0 \xrightarrow{R} n_2$. H is said to have the* $\underline{X}$-property *w.r.t. $<$ if it is the case of each label R.*

THEOREM 4.13. *(Theorem 3.5 of [23], extending Theorem 3.1 of [25]) Given a labeled query graph G, and given a labeled directed graph H with the $\underline{X}$-property w.r.t. some order $<$, we can determine in time $O(|H| \times |G|)$ whether $G \rightsquigarrow H$.*

We can use this result to check, for all connected subpaths of the 2WP instance graph, whether the query graph has a homomorphism to the subpath. This leads to the following sketch for the proof of Proposition 4.11 (the full proof is in Appendix):

PROOF SKETCH. We proceed following the three-step process outlined above. We first enumerate the possible query matches in the instance, i.e., the quadratic number of connected subpaths. Second, we test for each subpath $a_i - \cdots - a_{i+k}$ whether it satisfies the query. We can do so tractably because the subpath clearly has the $\underline{X}$-property w.r.t. the order $a_i < \cdots < a_{i+k}$: using the notation of Definition 4.12, there are in fact no n_0, n_1, n_2, n_3 that satisfy the conditions. Third, having computed the resulting DNF, we compute its probability using β-acyclicity, eliminating variables in the order of the path as we explained above. □

5. UNLABELED CONNECTED QUERIES

We now turn to the unlabeled setting, whose classification is presented in Table 3. We start with an intractability result which follows directly from the well-known intractability of query evaluation in probabilistic databases [32]:

PROPOSITION 5.1 [32]. *The* $\mathsf{PHom}_{\not L}(\mathsf{1WP}, \mathsf{Connected})$ *problem is #P-hard.*

PROOF. Example 3.3 of [32] states that the conjunctive query $\exists x \exists y \exists z\, U(x, y) \wedge U(y, z)$ is #P-hard on TID instances. In other words, $\mathsf{PHom}_{\not L}(\{\rightarrow\rightarrow\}, \mathsf{All})$ is #P-hard, which implies the #P-hardness of $\mathsf{PHom}_{\not L}(\mathsf{1WP}, \mathsf{All})$. We conclude using Lemma 3.7, which provides a PTIME (Turing) reduction[3] from the $\mathsf{PHom}_{\not L}(\mathsf{1WP}, \mathsf{Connected})$ problem to the $\mathsf{PHom}_{\not L}(\mathsf{1WP}, \mathsf{All})$ problem. □

Note that this $\mathsf{PHom}_{\not L}(\mathsf{1WP}, \mathsf{Connected})$ problem can be phrased in a very simple way: given an unlabeled connected probabilistic graph (H, π) and a length m as input (namely, that of the 1WP graph query), compute the probability that H contains a directed path of length m.

This result suggests that, to obtain tractability, we need to restrict the instance graphs. In fact, such tractability results were already obtained in the previous sections. In Section 3, we proved (Proposition 3.6) that $\mathsf{PHom}_{\not L}(\mathsf{All}, \mathsf{DWT})$ has PTIME combined complexity. Similarly, in the previous

[2]The connection to β-acyclicity in this context is due to Florent Capelli.

[3]Note that it is usual to define #P-hardness under Turing reductions rather than under Karp reductions, as #P is a counting complexity class.

Table 3: Tractability of $\mathsf{PHom}_{\not L}$ in the connected case (Section 5)

↓G H→	1WP	2WP	DWT	PT	Connected
1WP					5.1
2WP				5.6	
DWT				5.5	
PT					
Connected		4.11	3.6		

PTIME #P-hard Numbers given correspond to propositions for border cases, remaining cells can be filled using the inclusions from Figure 2.

section, we proved that $\mathsf{PHom}_{\mathsf{L}}(\mathsf{Connected}, \mathsf{2WP})$ is PTIME (Proposition 4.11), which means $\mathsf{PHom}_{\not L}(\mathsf{Connected}, \mathsf{2WP})$ is also PTIME. This completes the analysis of the unlabeled case for 1WP, 2WP and DWT instances (see Table 3), so the only remaining case is that of PT instances.

We start our study of $\mathsf{PHom}_{\not L}$ for PT instances with the simplest queries, namely, 1WP, for which we will show tractability. We will proceed by translating the 1WP query to a *bottom-up deterministic tree automata* [17]:

Definition 5.2. *Given an alphabet* Γ, *a* bottom-up deterministic tree automaton *on full binary (every node has either* 0 *or* 2 *children) rooted trees whose nodes are labeled by* Γ *is a tuple* $A = (Q, F, \iota, \Delta)$, *where:*

(i) Q *is a finite set of* states*;*
(ii) $F \in Q$ *is a subset of* accepting states*;*
(iii) $\iota : \Gamma \to Q$ *is an* initialization function *determining the state of a leaf from its label;*
(iv) $\Delta : \Gamma \times Q^2 \to Q$ *is a* transition function *determining the state of an internal node from its label and the states of its two children.*

Given a Γ*-tree* $\langle T, \lambda\rangle$ *(where* $\lambda : T \to \Gamma$ *is the* labeling function*), we define the* run *of* A *on* $\langle T, \lambda\rangle$ *as the function* $\varphi : T \to Q$ *such that (1)* $\varphi(l) = \iota(\lambda(l))$ *for every leaf* l *of* T*; and (2)* $\varphi(n) = \Delta(\lambda(n), \varphi(n_1), \varphi(n_2))$ *for every internal node* n *of* T *with children* n_1 *and* n_2*. The automaton* A accepts $\langle T, \lambda\rangle$ *if its run on* T *maps the root of* T *to a state of* F.

We will evaluate 1WP queries by translating them to a tree automaton and running it on an uncertain tree. This will use again the notion of *lineage* (recall Definition 4.6), which was extended in [4] to tree automata running on trees with uncertain Boolean labels: the *lineage* of an automaton on such a tree describes the set of annotations of the tree that makes the automaton accept. In this context, the lineage of *deterministic* tree automata was shown in [7] to be compilable to a *deterministic decomposable negation normal form* circuit [21]:

Definition 5.3. *A* deterministic decomposable negation normal form *(d-DNNF) is a Boolean circuit* C *with the following properties:*

(i) negations are only applied to input gates;
(ii) the inputs of any AND-gate depend on disjoint sets of input gates;
(iii) the inputs of any OR-gate are mutually exclusive, i.e., for any two input gates $g_1 \neq g_2$ *of* g*, there is no valuation of the inputs of* C *under which* g_1 *and* g_2 *both evaluate to true.*

We can then straightforwardly extend the Boolean probability computation problem (Definition 4.2) to take circuits as inputs, and the properties of d-DNNF circuits are designed to ensure that the Boolean probability computation problem restricted to d-DNNF has PTIME complexity [21]. Combining these tools, we can show that $\mathsf{PHom}_{\not L}$ on one-way path queries and polytree instances is tractable:

Proposition 5.4. $\mathsf{PHom}_{\not L}(\mathsf{1WP}, \mathsf{PT})$ *is PTIME.*

Proof sketch. The idea of the proof is to construct in polynomial time in the query graph G a bottom-up deterministic automaton A_G, which runs on binary trees T representing possible worlds of the polytree instance H, and accepts such a tree T iff the corresponding possible world satisfies G. We can then construct a d-DNNF representation of the lineage of G on H by [6, Theorem 6.11], which allows us to efficiently compute $\Pr(G \rightsquigarrow H)$: the complexity of this process is in $O(|A_G| \cdot |H|)$, hence polynomial in $|H| \cdot |G|$. (An alternative way to see this is to use the results of [16].)

Intuitively, the design of the bottom-up automaton ensures that, when it reaches a node n after having processed the subtree T_n rooted at n, its state reflects three linear-sized quantities about T_n:

1. the length of the longest path leading out of n;
2. the length of the longest path leading to n;
3. the length of the longest path overall in T_n (not necessarily via n).

The final states are those where the third quantity is greater than the length of G. The transitions compute each triple from the child triples by considering how the longest leading paths are extended, and how longer overall paths can be formed by joining an incoming and outgoing path. □

Hence, PT instances enjoy tractability for the simplest query graphs. We now study whether this result can be extended to more general queries. We first notice that this result immediately extends to branching (i.e., to DWT queries), and even to unions of DWT queries. Indeed, in the unlabeled setting, as we already observed at the end of Section 3.1, such queries are equivalent to 1WP queries:

Proposition 5.5. *The problems* $\mathsf{PHom}_{\not L}(\mathsf{DWT}, \mathsf{PT})$ *and* $\mathsf{PHom}_{\not L}(\bigsqcup \mathsf{DWT}, \mathsf{PT})$ *are PTIME.*

Proof. We first show the result for a DWT query graph G. Let m be its height, i.e., the length of the longest directed path it contains, and let G' be the 1WP of length m, which can be computed in PTIME from G. It is easy to observe that G and G' are equivalent. Indeed, we can find G' as a subgraph of G by taking any directed path of maximal length, and conversely there is a homomorphism from G to G': map the root of G to the first vertex of G' and each element of G' at distance i from the root to the i-th element of G'. Hence, $\mathsf{PHom}_{\not L}$ on G and an input probabilistic PT instance reduces to $\mathsf{PHom}_{\not L}$ on G' and the same instance, so that the result follows from Proposition 5.4.

The same argument extends to $\bigsqcup \mathsf{DWT}$ by considering the greatest height of a connected component of G. □

Thus, we have successfully extended from 1WP to $\bigsqcup \mathsf{DWT}$ queries while preserving tractability on PT instances. However, as we now show, tractability is not preserved if we extend queries to allow two-wayness. Indeed:

Proposition 5.6. $\mathsf{PHom}_{\not L}(\mathsf{2WP}, \mathsf{PT})$ *is #P-hard.*

PROOF. We adapt the proof of Proposition 4.1, but we face the additional difficulty of not being allowed to use labels. Fortunately, we can use the two-wayness in the query graph to simulate labels.

We reduce from #PP2DNF (recall Definition 4.3): the input consists of two disjoint sets $\mathcal{X} = \{X_1, \ldots, X_{n_1}\}$, $\mathcal{Y} = \{Y_1, \ldots, Y_{n_2}\}$ of Boolean variables, and a PP2DNF formula φ. We construct a 2WP query graph G' and PT instance H' with the same construction as the one that yielded H and G in that proof, except that we perform the following replacements (see Figure 8):

- replace every edge $a \xrightarrow{S} b$ of H and G by 3 edges $a \rightarrow\rightarrow\leftarrow b$;
- replace every edge $a \xrightarrow{T} b$ of H and G by 3 edges $a \rightarrow\rightarrow\rightarrow b$.

In particular, the query graph is then defined as follows: $G' := \rightarrow\rightarrow\rightarrow (\rightarrow\rightarrow\leftarrow)^{m+3} \rightarrow\rightarrow\rightarrow$. All the edges of H' have probability 1, except the middle edge of the edges that replaced the S-labeled edges used to code the valuation of the variables (e.g., for X_i, the middle edge of the 3 edges $X_i \rightarrow\rightarrow\leftarrow R$), which have probability $\frac{1}{2}$.

One can check that any image of G' must again go from the vertex $A_{x_j,j}$ to the vertex $B_{y_j,j}$ for some $1 \leqslant j \leqslant m$. The key insight is that the first $\rightarrow^5$ of G must be matched to a $\rightarrow^5$-path in H', which only exist as the concatenation of a $\rightarrow^3$ obtained by rewriting a T-edge for some variable X_j, and of the first $\rightarrow^2$ of the (undirected) path from $X_{x_j,j}$ to R. Then there is no choice left to match the next edges without failing.

From this we deduce that, from any possible world H'_{W} of the modified instance H', considering the corresponding possible world H_{W} of the unmodified instance H following the natural bijection, the modified query graph G' has a homomorphism to H'_{W} iff the unmodified query graph G has a homomorphism to H_{W}. We thus conclude that the probabilistic homomorphism problem on G' and H' has the same answer as the one on G and H, which finishes the proof. □

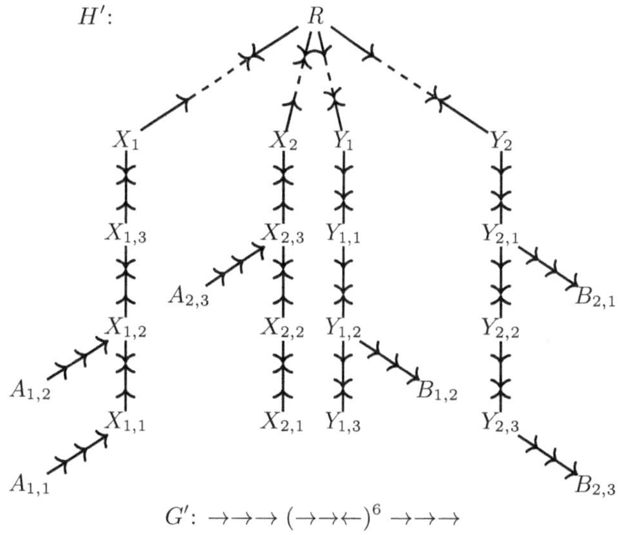

Figure 8: Illustration of the proof of Proposition 5.6 for the PP2DNF formula $X_1Y_2 \vee X_1Y_1 \vee X_2Y_2$. Dashed edges have probability $\frac{1}{2}$, all the others have probability 1.

6. CONCLUSION

We have introduced the probabilistic homomorphism problem, also known in the database community as probabilistic evaluation of conjunctive queries on TID instances, and studied its combined complexity for various restricted classes of query and instance graphs. Our classes illustrate the impact on PHom of various features: acyclicity, two-wayness, branching, connectedness, and labeling. As we show, the landscape is already quite enigmatic, even for those seemingly restricted classes! In particular, we have identified four incomparable maximal tractable cases, reflecting various tradeoffs between the expressiveness that we can allow in the queries and in the instances:

- arbitrary queries on unlabeled downward trees (Proposition 3.6);
- one-way path queries on labeled downward trees (Proposition 4.10);
- connected queries on two-way labeled path instances (Proposition 4.11);
- downward tree queries on unlabeled polytrees (Proposition 5.5);

These results all extend to disconnected instances, as shown in Section 3.3. The (somewhat sinuous) tractability border is described in Tables 1, 2, and 3.

It is debatable whether the tractable classes we have identified yield interesting tractable cases for practical applications. The settings of Propositions 3.6, 5.5, and 4.11 may look restrictive, as both labels and branching are important features of real-world instances, though some situations may involve unlabeled tree-like instances, or labeled words. The setting of Propositions 4.10 may be richer, and is reminiscent of probabilistic XML [27]: the instance is a labeled (downward) tree, while the query is a path evaluate on that tree.

Future work. The query and instance features studied in this paper could be completed by other dimensions: e.g., studying an *unweighted* case inspired by counting CSP where all probabilities are 1/2 (as our hardness proofs seem to heavily rely on some edges being certain); imposing *symmetry* in the sense of [8]; or alternatively restricting the *degree* of graphs (though all our hardness proofs on polytrees and lower classes can seemingly be modified to work on bounded-degree). Another option would be to modify some of the existing dimensions: first, polytrees could be generalized to *bounded-treewidth instances*, as we believe that the relevant tractability result (Proposition 5.5) adapts to this setting; second, non-branching instances could be generalized to *bounded-pathwidth instances*, or maybe general instances with the $\underline{X}$-property (recall Definition 4.12).

Of course, another natural direction would be to lift the arity-two restriction, although it is not immediate to generalize the definition of our classes to work in higher arity signatures. We could also extend the query language: in particular, allow *unions* of conjunctive queries as in [20]; allow a *descendant* axis in the spirit of XML query languages [9]; or more generally allow fixpoint constructs as done in [2] in the non-probabilistic case. An interesting question is whether an extended query language could capture the tractability results obtained in the context of probabilistic XML by [16] (remembering, however, that such results crucially depend on having an order relation on node children [1]). Another possibility would be to search for extensions of the β-acyclicity approach, and investigate which restrictions on the queries and instances ensure that the lineages are β-acyclic.

Last, the connection to CSP would seem to warrant further investigation. In particular, we do not know whether one could show a general dichotomy result on the combined complexity of query evaluation on TID instances, to provide a probabilistic analogue to the Feder–Vardi conjecture [22].

Acknowledgements. We are grateful to Florent Capelli for pointing out to us the connection to β-acyclic instances and suggesting the idea used in the proof of Proposition 4.10, and to Tyson Williams for explaining the connection to holographic algorithms, in a very informative CSTheory post [35]. We also thank anonymous referees for their valuable feedback. This work was partly funded by the Télécom ParisTech Research Chair on Big Data and Market Insights.

7. REFERENCES

[1] A. Amarilli. The possibility problem for probabilistic XML. In *AMW*, 2014.

[2] A. Amarilli, P. Bourhis, M. Monet, and P. Senellart. Combined tractability of query evaluation via tree automata and cycluits. In *ICDT*, 2017.

[3] A. Amarilli, P. Bourhis, M. Monet, and P. Senellart. Combined tractability of query evaluation via tree automata and cycluits (extended version). *ArXiv e-prints*, 2017. https://arxiv.org/abs/1612.04203v1. Extended version of [2].

[4] A. Amarilli, P. Bourhis, and P. Senellart. Provenance circuits for trees and treelike instances. In *ICALP*, volume 9135 of *LNCS*, 2015.

[5] A. Amarilli, P. Bourhis, and P. Senellart. Provenance circuits for trees and treelike instances (extended version). *CoRR*, abs/1511.08723, 2015. http://arxiv.org/abs/1511.08723. Extended version of [4].

[6] A. Amarilli, P. Bourhis, and P. Senellart. Tractable lineages on treelike instances: limits and extensions. *CoRR*, abs/1604.02761, 2016.

[7] A. Amarilli, P. Bourhis, and P. Senellart. Tractable lineages on treelike instances: Limits and extensions. In *PODS*, 2016.

[8] P. Beame, G. Van den Broeck, E. Gribkoff, and D. Suciu. Symmetric weighted first-order model counting. In *PODS*, 2015.

[9] M. Benedikt and C. Koch. XPath leashed. *CSUR*, 2009.

[10] J. Brault-Baron. Hypergraph acyclicity revisited. *ArXiv e-prints*, 2014.

[11] J. Brault-Baron, F. Capelli, and S. Mengel. Understanding model counting for β-acyclic CNF-formulas. In *STACS*, 2015.

[12] A. A. Bulatov. The complexity of the counting constraint satisfaction problem. *J. ACM*, 60(5), 2013.

[13] J. Cai, P. Lu, and M. Xia. Holographic reduction, interpolation and hardness. *Computational Complexity*, 21(4), 2008. Preprint of [14].

[14] J. Cai, P. Lu, and M. Xia. Holographic reduction, interpolation and hardness. *Computational Complexity*, 21(4), 2012.

[15] I. I. Ceylan, A. Darwiche, and G. Van den Broeck. Open-world probabilistic databases. In *KR*, 2016.

[16] S. Cohen, B. Kimelfeld, and Y. Sagiv. Running tree automata on probabilistic XML. In *PODS*, 2009.

[17] H. Comon, M. Dauchet, R. Gilleron, C. Löding, F. Jacquemard, D. Lugiez, S. Tison, and M. Tommasi. Tree automata: Techniques and applications, 2007. Available from http://www.grappa.univ-lille3.fr/tata.

[18] R. Curticapean and D. Marx. Complexity of counting subgraphs: Only the boundedness of the vertex-cover number counts. In *FOCS*, 2014.

[19] N. Dalvi and D. Suciu. Efficient query evaluation on probabilistic databases. *VLDBJ*, 16(4), 2007.

[20] N. Dalvi and D. Suciu. The dichotomy of probabilistic inference for unions of conjunctive queries. *JACM*, 59(6), 2012.

[21] A. Darwiche. On the tractable counting of theory models and its application to truth maintenance and belief revision. *J. Applied Non-Classical Logics*, 11(1-2), 2001.

[22] T. Feder and M. Y. Vardi. The computational structure of monotone monadic SNP and constraint satisfaction: A study through Datalog and group theory. *SIAM Journal on Computing*, 1998.

[23] G. Gottlob, C. Koch, and K. U. Schulz. Conjunctive queries over trees. *JACM*, 53(2), 2006.

[24] M. Grohe. The complexity of homomorphism and constraint satisfaction problems seen from the other side. *JACM*, 2007.

[25] W. Gutjahr, E. Welzl, and G. Woeginger. Polynomial graph-colorings. *Discrete Applied Mathematics*, 35(1), 1992.

[26] S. Khanna, S. Roy, and V. Tannen. Queries with difference on probabilistic databases. *PVLDB*, 2011.

[27] B. Kimelfeld and P. Senellart. Probabilistic XML: models and complexity. In Z. Ma and L. Yan, editors, *Advances in Probabilistic Databases for Uncertain Information Management*. Springer, 2013.

[28] S. Odagiri and H. Goto. On the greatest number of paths and maximal paths for a class of directed acyclic graphs. *IEICE Trans. Fundamentals*, E97-A(6), 2014.

[29] J. S. Provan and M. O. Ball. The complexity of counting cuts and of computing the probability that a graph is connected. *SIAM J. Computing*, 12(4), 1983.

[30] B. Schröder. *Ordered Sets*. Birkhäuser, second edition, 2016.

[31] R. Stanley. *Enumerative Combinatorics*, volume 1. Cambridge University Press, 1997.

[32] D. Suciu, D. Olteanu, C. Ré, and C. Koch. *Probabilistic Databases*. Morgan & Claypool, 2011.

[33] L. G. Valiant. Holographic algorithms. *SIAM J. Comput.*, 37(5), 2008.

[34] M. Y. Vardi. On the complexity of bounded-variable queries. In *PODS*, 1995.

[35] T. Williams. Complexity of counting the number of edge covers of a graph. http://cstheory.stackexchange.com/q/21309, 2014.

[36] M. Yannakakis. Algorithms for acyclic database schemes. In *VLDB*, 1981.

APPENDIX

A. Proofs for Section 3 (DISCONNECTED CASE)

PROPOSITION 3.6. $\mathsf{PHom}_{\not L}(\mathsf{All}, \bigsqcup \mathsf{DWT})$ *is PTIME.*

PROOF. Let G be an arbitrary unlabeled graph and (H, π) a probabilistic graph with $H \in \bigsqcup \mathsf{DWT}$. We observe that if G contains a directed cycle, then it cannot have a homomorphism to a subgraph of H (which is necessarily acyclic), so $\Pr(G \rightsquigarrow H) = 0$. Hence, it suffices to study the case where the query graph G is a DAG.

Likewise, if there are two vertices u, v of G and directed paths χ, χ' in G from u to v such that χ and χ' have different lengths, then again G cannot have a homomorphism to a subgraph of H: indeed, any subgraph of H is a directed forest and there is at most one directed path between each pair of nodes. So we can assume without loss of generality that there is no such pattern in G, and G is therefore graded.

Letting μ be a level mapping of G, we call the *difference of levels* of μ the difference between the largest and smallest value of its image; the *difference of levels* of G itself is the minimum difference of levels of a level mapping of G. As the level mappings of G only differ in the constant value that they add to all vertices of each connected component, the difference of levels can clearly be computed in PTIME by shifting each connected component so that its minimal level is zero, and computing the difference; we call the result of the shifting the *minimal level mapping* of G.

Letting m be the difference of levels of G, we now make the following claim: *in any subgraph H' of H, there is a homomorphism from G to H' if and only if H' has a directed path of length m.*

This claim implies the result. Indeed, we can first check in PTIME if G has no cycles and has no pairs of paths of different lengths between two endpoints, and return 0 if the conditions are violated. We can then compute in PTIME the difference of levels m of G using the observations above. Now, on any subgraph of H, the query G is equivalent to the 1WP graph $\to^m$, so our result follows from Proposition 5.5.

All that remains is to prove the claim. We first note that it suffices to show the claim under the assumption that G is connected. Indeed, if the claim is true for all connected G, then the claim is implied for arbitrary G by considering each of its connected components, applying the claim, and observing that G has a suitable homomorphism to H' iff each one of its connected components does, i.e., iff H' has a directed path whose length is the maximal difference of levels of a connected component of G, and this is precisely the difference of levels m of G. Hence, we now prove the claim for connected G.

We start with the backwards direction of the claim. It is easily seen that there is a homomorphism h' from G to the 1WP graph $\to^m$. Indeed, we define h' according to the minimal level mapping μ of G: we set h' to map all the vertices whose level is i to the i-th vertex of $\to^m$. From the existence of h', we know that, whenever there is a homomorphism h from $\to^m$ to H', then $h \circ h'$ is a homomorphism from G to H', which shows the backwards implication.

For the forward direction of the claim, suppose that there exists a homomorphism h from G to H', and let m be the difference of levels of G. Because G is connected and H' is in $\bigsqcup \mathsf{DWT}$, the image of h is actually a DWT, call it T. Now it is easy to see that the image of a node that has level $m - i$ in G has depth i in T, so that T (and so H') contains the 1WP $\to^m$. This finishes the proof of the converse and thus the proof of Proposition 3.6. □

B. Proofs for Section 4 (LABELED CONNECTED QUERIES)

PROPOSITION 4.1. $\mathsf{PHom}_{\mathsf{L}}(\mathsf{1WP}, \mathsf{PT})$ *is #P-hard.*

PROOF. We reduce from the #P-hard problem **#PP2DNF**. From the formula φ, we construct the following $\{S, T\}$-labeled probabilistic graph H (an example of this construction is presented in Figure 7):

- The vertices of H are $\{R\} \sqcup \{X_1, \ldots X_{n_1}\} \sqcup \{Y_1, \ldots, Y_{n_2}\} \sqcup \{X_{i,j} \mid 1 \leqslant i \leqslant n_1,\ 1 \leqslant j \leqslant m\} \sqcup \{Y_{i,j} \mid 1 \leqslant i \leqslant n_2,\ 1 \leqslant j \leqslant m\} \sqcup \{A_{x_j,j} \mid 1 \leqslant j \leqslant m\} \sqcup \{B_{y_j,j} \mid 1 \leqslant j \leqslant m\}$.
- The edges of H, all of which have probability 1 except when specified, are:
  - $X_i \xrightarrow{S} R$ for all $1 \leqslant i \leqslant n_1$ and $R \xrightarrow{S} Y_i$ for all $1 \leqslant i \leqslant n_2$, all having probability $\frac{1}{2}$ and intuitively coding the valuation of each variable;
  - For all $1 \leqslant i \leqslant n_1$, the edge $X_{i,m} \xrightarrow{S} X_i$ and the edges $X_{i,j} \xrightarrow{S} X_{i,j+1}$ for all $1 \leqslant j \leqslant m-1$;
  - For all $1 \leqslant i \leqslant n_2$, the edge $Y_i \xrightarrow{S} Y_{i,1}$ and the edges $Y_{i,j} \xrightarrow{S} Y_{i,j+1}$ for all $1 \leqslant j \leqslant m-1$;
  - For all $1 \leqslant j \leqslant m$, the edges $A_{x_j,j} \xrightarrow{T} X_{x_j,j}$ and $Y_{y_j,j} \xrightarrow{T} B_{y_j,j}$, intuitively indicating that variables X_{x_j} and Y_{y_j} belong to clause j.

The $\{S, T\}$-labeled graph G is then $\xrightarrow{T} (\xrightarrow{S})^{m+3} \xrightarrow{T}$. It is clear that G is a 1WP query graph, H is a polytree and that both can be constructed in PTIME from φ. We now show that $\Pr(G \rightsquigarrow H)$ is exactly the number of satisfying assignments of φ divided by 2^n, so that the computation of one reduces in PTIME to the computation of the other, concluding the proof. To see why, we define a bijection between the valuations ν of $\{X_1, \ldots, X_{n_1}\} \sqcup \{Y_1, \ldots, Y_{n_2}\}$ to the possible worlds H' of H that have non-zero probability, in the expected way: keep the edge $X_i \xrightarrow{S} R$ (resp., $R \xrightarrow{S} Y_i$) iff X_i (resp., Y_i) is assigned to true in the valuation. We then show that there is a homomorphism from G to H' if and only if φ evaluates to true under ν.

Indeed, if there is a homomorphism from G to H', then by considering the only possible matches of the T-edges, one can check easily that the image of the match in H' must be of the following form for some $1 \leqslant j \leqslant m$: $A_{x_j,j} \xrightarrow{T} X_{x_j,j} \xrightarrow{S} X_{x_j,j+1} \xrightarrow{S} \cdots \xrightarrow{S} X_{x_j,m} \xrightarrow{S} X_{x_j} \xrightarrow{S} R \xrightarrow{S} Y_{y_{j'}} \xrightarrow{S} Y_{y_{j'},1} \xrightarrow{S} Y_{y_{j'},2} \xrightarrow{S} \cdots \xrightarrow{S} Y_{y_{j'},j'} \xrightarrow{T} B_{y_{j'},j'}$; further, from the length of the S-path we must have $(m - j) + 4 + (j' - 1) = m + 3$, so that we must have $j = j'$. Then, by construction, X_{x_j} and Y_{y_j} belong to clause j, so the valuation satisfies φ. Conversely, suppose that the valuation satisfies φ, then for some $1 \leqslant j \leqslant m$ we know that X_{x_j} and Y_{y_j} are assigned to true by the valuation, and so we can build the homomorphism as above from G to H'. □

PROPOSITION 4.4 [3]. $\mathsf{PHom_L}(\mathsf{DWT}, \mathsf{DWT})$ *is #P-hard.*

PROOF. The proof is almost the same as that of Proposition 36 of [3], straightforwardly adapted to our setting of probabilistic graphs (in particular replacing the unary relation R by a binary relation), by observing that the probabilistic instance defined in this proof is actually a DWT (beyond having treewidth 1), and that the query actually corresponds to a DWT graph (beyond being α-acyclic). □

PROPOSITION 4.5 [3]. $\mathsf{PHom_L}(\mathsf{2WP}, \mathsf{DWT})$ *is #P-hard.*

PROOF. The proof is almost the same as that of Proposition 38 of [3], again adapted to our setting of probabilistic graphs, with one small modification: we do not materialize edges $b \xrightarrow{S_-} a$ in the instance graph for each edge $a \xrightarrow{S} b$ in the instance, and instead modify the query to replace all edges $x \xrightarrow{S_-} y$ by edges $x \xleftarrow{S} y$. This ensures that the query is a 2WP and the instance is a DWT, and hardness is shown similarly to the original proof. □

THEOREM 4.9. *The Boolean probability computation problem is in PTIME when restricted to β-acyclic positive DNF formulas.*

PROOF. We reduce our Boolean probability computation problem to the problem of β-acyclic **#CSP**$_\mathrm{d}$ of [11], which they show to be in PTIME (Theorem 26 of [11]). We will explain how probability computation in the sense of Definition 4.2 can be encoded in their setting, by a variant of their own encoding (in Lemma 3 of [11]): we give a full proof for completeness.

First, we recall their definition of **#CSP**$_\mathrm{d}$ (Definitions 1 and 2 in [11]) in the case of a Boolean domain. We denote by $\mathbb{Q}_+$ the nonnegative rational numbers. Denote by $\{0,1\}^{\mathcal{X}}$ the set of functions from $\mathcal{X}$ to $\{0,1\}$, i.e., the Boolean valuations of $\mathcal{X}$. For $\nu \in \{0,1\}^{\mathcal{X}}$ and $\mathcal{Y} \subseteq \mathcal{X}$, we denote by $\nu_{|\mathcal{Y}}$ the restriction of ν to $\mathcal{Y}$. A *weighted constraint (with default value)* on variables $\mathcal{X}$ is a pair $c = (f, \mu)$ that consists of a function $f : S \to \mathbb{Q}_+$ for some subset S of $\{0,1\}^{\mathcal{X}}$, called the *support* of c, and a *default value* $\mu \in \mathbb{Q}_+$; we write $\mathrm{var}(c) := \mathcal{X}$. The constraint c induces a total function on $\{0,1\}^{\mathcal{X}}$, also denoted c, that maps $\nu \in \{0,1\}^{\mathcal{X}}$ to $f(\nu)$ if $\nu \in S$, and to μ otherwise. The *size* of c is $|c| = |S| \times |\mathcal{X}|$. Intuitively, a constraint with default value assigns a weight in $\mathbb{Q}_+$ to all valuations of $\mathcal{X}$, but the default value mechanism allows us to avoid writing explicitly the complete table of this mapping.

An instance of the **#CSP**$_\mathrm{d}$ problem then consists of a finite set I of weighted constraints. The size of I is $|I| := \sum_{c \in I} |c|$, and we write $\mathrm{var}(I) := \bigcup_{c \in I} \mathrm{var}(c)$. The output of the problem is the *partition function*

$$w(I) = \sum_{\nu \in \{0,1\}^{\mathrm{var}(I)}} \prod_{c \in I} c(\nu_{|\mathrm{var}(c)}).$$

The *hypergraph* $\mathcal{H}(I)$ of the **#CSP**$_\mathrm{d}$ instance I (defined in Section 2.2 of [11]) is the hypergraph $(\mathrm{var}(I), E_I)$ where $E_I = \{\mathrm{var}(c) \mid c \in I\}$. We say that I is *β-acyclic* if $\mathcal{H}(I)$ is a β-acyclic hypergraph (recall Definition 4.7), and we call β-acyclic **#CSP**$_\mathrm{d}$ the problem #CSP$_d$ restricted to β-acyclic instances. By Theorem 26 of [11], the problem β-acyclic **#CSP**$_\mathrm{d}$ is in PTIME.

We now explain how to reduce the probability computation problem to the β-acyclic **#CSP**$_\mathrm{d}$ problem. Let $\varphi = \bigvee_{1 \leqslant i \leqslant m} \left(\bigwedge_{1 \leqslant j \leqslant n_i} X_{i,j} \right)$ be a Boolean β-acyclic DNF on variables $\mathcal{X}$, with probabilities $\pi(X) \in [0,1]$ for each $X \in \mathcal{X}$. We construct in linear time from φ and π the variable set $\mathcal{X}' := \{X' \mid X \in \mathcal{X}\}$, the CNF formula $\varphi' := \bigwedge_{1 \leqslant i \leqslant m} \left(\bigvee_{1 \leqslant j \leqslant n_i} X'_{i,j} \right)$, and the probability valuation π' on $\mathcal{X}'$ defined by $\pi'(X'_{i,j}) = 1 - \pi(X_{i,j})$. By De Morgan's duality law, φ' is equivalent to the negation of φ, so that we have $\Pr(\varphi, \pi) = 1 - \Pr(\varphi', \pi')$; hence, the probability computation problem for φ and π reduces in PTIME to the same problem for φ' and π'.

We then construct in linear time a β-acyclic **#CSP**$_\mathrm{d}$ instance I such that $\Pr(\varphi', \pi') = w(I)$, which concludes the proof. For each variable $X' \in \mathcal{X}'$, we define a weighted constraint $c_{X'}$ on variables $\{X'\}$ by $c_{X'}(X' \mapsto 1) = \pi'(X')$ and $c_{X'}(X' \mapsto 0) = 1 - \pi'(X')$, which codes the probability of the variables. Now, for each clause $1 \leqslant i \leqslant m$, just like in Lemma 3 of [11], we define a weighted constraint $c_i = (f_i, 1)$ with default value 1 whose variables are $\{X'_{i,j} \mid 1 \leqslant j \leqslant n_i\}$, i.e., those that occur in the clause: $f_i(\nu)$ is 0 for the (unique) valuation that sets all variables of the clause to 0, intuitively coding the constraint of the clause. From the fact that φ was β-acyclic, it is clear that I is also β-acyclic. Now, the result $w(I)$ of the partition function sums over all valuations of the variables of I, namely the variables $\mathcal{X}'$ of φ'. Whenever a valuation does not satisfy some clause $1 \leqslant i \leqslant m$, the weighted constraint c_i will give it weight 0, hence ensuring that the product evaluates to 0, so we can restrict the sum to valuations that satisfy φ': such valuations are given weight 1 by all weighted constraints c_i. Now, it is easy to see that the weight of valuations ν that satisfy φ is their probability $\pi'(\nu)$, as each $c_{X'}$ gives them weight $\pi'(X')$ or $1 - (\pi'(X'))$ depending on whether $\nu(X')$ is 1 or 0. Hence, we have reduced the probability computation problem for β-acyclic DNF formulas to β-acyclic **#CSP**$_\mathrm{d}$ in PTIME, which concludes the proof. □

PROPOSITION 4.10. $\mathsf{PHom_L}(\mathsf{1WP}, \mathsf{DWT})$ *is PTIME.*

PROOF. Let $G := u_1 \xrightarrow{R_1} \cdots \xrightarrow{R_{m-1}} u_m$ be the 1WP query (where all R_i are not necessarily distinct), and H be the downwards tree instance. The idea is to construct the lineage of G on H as a β-acyclic DNF φ, so that we can conclude with Theorem 4.9. It is clear that any match of G can only be a downwards path of H, hence we construct φ as follows: for every downwards path $a_1 \xrightarrow{R'_1} \cdots \xrightarrow{R'_{m-1}} a_m$ of length m of H (their number is linear in $|H|$ because each path is uniquely defined by the choice of a_m) check if the path is a match of G (i.e, check that $R_i = R'_i$ for $1 \leqslant i \leqslant m-1$), and if it is the case then create a new clause of φ whose variables are all the facts $a_i \xrightarrow{R_i} a_{i+1}$ for $1 \leqslant i \leqslant m-1$.

The formula φ thus obtained is then a DNF representation of the lineage of H on G, and has been built in time $O(|H| \cdot |G|)$, i.e., in PTIME. We now justify that φ is β-acyclic by giving a β-elimination order for φ: while H still has edges, repeatedly pick a leaf b of H and, letting a be the parent of b, eliminate the variable $a \xrightarrow{R} b$ from φ. Such a variable will always be a β-leaf, as any set of downwards paths of a downwards tree all ending at a leaf is necessarily ordered by inclusion. From the above, the fact that φ is β-acyclic suffices to conclude the proof. □

PROPOSITION 4.11. $\mathsf{PHom_L}(\mathsf{Connected}, \mathsf{2WP})$ *is PTIME.*

PROOF. First of all, notice that, as the query graph G is connected, the image of a homomorphism from the query G to the 2WP instance H is necessarily a connected component of H. Moreover, each connected component of H is also a 2WP and there are $O(|H|^2)$ of them. We then proceed as follows. For every connected subpath $C = a_1 - \cdots - a_n$ (with each $-$ being either $\xrightarrow{R}$ or $\xleftarrow{R}$ for some binary relation R in H) of H, we check if there is a homomorphism from G to C. This can be done in PTIME by Theorem 4.13, because C trivially has the $\underline{X}$-property w.r.t. the total order $a_1 < a_2 < \cdots < a_n$: the only possibility for (n_0, n_3) and (n_1, n_2) to be edges of C when n_0 comes before n_1 and n_2 comes before n_3 is if $n_0 = n_2$ and $n_1 = n_3$, in which case it cannot hold that $n_0 \xrightarrow{R} n_3$ and $n_1 \xrightarrow{R} n_2$ at the same time, because we disallow multi-edges. If there is such a homomorphism, then we create a new clause of φ whose variables are all the facts that belong to C.

From this, we obtain in PTIME a positive DNF φ that captures the lineage of G on H. We now justify that φ is β-acyclic by giving a β-elimination order for φ, by an argument similar to the proof of Proposition 4.10: repeatedly eliminate a variable $a - b$ from φ and this fact from H, where b is an endpoint of H. Indeed such a variable will always be a β-leaf, as any set of connected component of H including $a - b$ is necessarily ordered by inclusion. Hence, φ is β-acyclic, which allows us to conclude. □

C. Proofs for Section 5 (UNLABELED CONNECTED QUERIES)

PROPOSITION 5.4. $\mathsf{PHom}_{\not L}(\mathsf{1WP}, \mathsf{PT})$ *is PTIME.*

PROOF. Let G, (H, π) be the 1WP query graph and the probabilistic PT instance, and m be the length of G. Then $\Pr(G \rightsquigarrow H)$ is the probability that H contains a directed path of length at least m.

Because we will use automata that run on full binary trees, we will have to represent possible worlds of H as full binary trees. The first step is to transform in linear time H into a full binary polytree H' by applying a variant of the left-child-right-sibling encoding: in so doing, in addition to unlabeled edges of both orientations that exist in the polytree, we will also introduce some edges called *ε-edges* that are labeled by ε and whose orientation does not matter (so we see them as undirected edges and write them $a - b$); intuitively, the ε-edge $a - b$ means that a and b are in fact the same. For a node $a \in H$ and a child b of a, we say that b is an *up-child* of a if we have $b \to a$ and a *down-child* of a if we have $a \to b$. We do this transformation by processing H bottom-up as follows:

- If n is a leaf node of H, then create a node n' in H'.
- If n is an internal node of H with up-children $u_1, \ldots, u_k$ and down-children $d_1, \ldots, d_l$ then, letting $u'_1, \ldots, u'_k$ and $d'_1, \ldots, d'_l$ be the corresponding nodes in H': create a node n' in H' and nodes $n'_1, \ldots, n'_{k+l-2}$ with the following ε-edges: $n' - n'_1 - \ldots - n'_{k+l-2}$, all having probability 1. Create an edge $u'_1 \to n'$ whose probability is that of $u_1 \to n$. For $2 \leqslant i \leqslant k$ create an edge $u'_i \to n'_{i-1}$ annotated with the same probability as $u_i \to n$. For $1 \leqslant i \leqslant l-1$ create an edge $n'_{k-1+i} \to d'_i$ annotated with the same probability as $n \to d'_i$, and finally create an edge $n'_{k-2+l} \to d'_l$ annotated with the same probability as $n \to d'_l$. Last, if any node has exactly one children (specifically, n', in case $k + l = 1$), then create a node n'' in H' and connect it with an ε-edge to the node.

One can check that H' is indeed a full binary polytree (with some edges being labeled by ε and being undirected) and that $\Pr(G \rightsquigarrow H)$ equals the probability that H' contains a path of the form $(\to -^*)^m$, that is, m occurrences of a directed edge $\to$ followed by some sequence of ε-edges $-$.

The second step is to transform in linear time H' into a probabilistic tree T to which we can apply the construction of [5]. Specifically, T must be an ordered full binary rooted tree whose edges do not have a label or an orientation, but whose nodes n carry a label in some finite alphabet Γ (written $\lambda(n)$, where λ is the labeling function) and with a probability value written $\pi(n)$. Writing $\overline{\Gamma} := \Gamma \times \{0, 1\}$ as in [5], the semantics of T is that it stands for a probability distribution on $\overline{\Gamma}$-trees, i.e., trees T' labeled with $\Gamma \times \{0, 1\}$, which have same skeleton as T: for each node n of T, the corresponding node n' in a possible world T' has label $(\lambda(n), 1)$ with probability $\pi(n)$ and label $(\lambda(n), 0)$ otherwise. We do this transformation by first adding a new root vertex to H' with an ε-edge with probability 1 to the original root (this clearly does not change the probability that H' has a path of the prescribed form), and then simply create T from H' by assigning the label and probability of each node that is not the new root as the direction of its parent edge (in $\Gamma := \{\uparrow, \downarrow, -\}$) and its probability (so the root of T' has label $-$ and probability 1).

Our last step is to construct a bDTA A_G running on $\overline{\Gamma}$-trees such that for every possible world W of H', letting T_W be its representation as a $\overline{\Gamma}$-tree, A_G accepts T_W if and only if W contains a path of the form $(\to -^*)^m$. The states of A_G are of the form $\langle \uparrow\colon i, \downarrow\colon j, \mathrm{Max} : k \rangle$ for $0 \leqslant i, j \leqslant k \leqslant m$, which ensures that A_G is of size polynomial in $|G|$ (and we will construct it in PTIME from G). The idea is that when a node n of T_W will be in such a state, it will mean that:

- Letting W_n be the subinstance of W which is represented by the subtree of T_W rooted at n, and letting r_n be the root of W_n, the longest directed upwards path in W_n finishing at r_n has length i (the path is the longest of the form $(\uparrow -^*)^*$ that ends at r_n).
- The longest directed downwards path in W_n beginning at r_n has length j (the path is the longest of the form $(\downarrow -^*)^*$ that begins at r_n).
- The longest directed path in W_n has length k (the path is of the form $(\to -^*)^k$ and is the longest in W_n).

We now describe the initialization function ι of A_G:

- $\iota((s, 0)) := \langle \uparrow\colon 0, \downarrow\colon 0, \mathrm{Max} : 0 \rangle$ for any $s \in \Gamma$.
- $\iota((-, 1)) := \langle \uparrow\colon 0, \downarrow\colon 0, \mathrm{Max} : 0 \rangle$.
- $\iota((\uparrow, 1)) := \langle \uparrow\colon 1, \downarrow\colon 0, \mathrm{Max} : 1 \rangle$.
- $\iota((\downarrow, 1)) := \langle \uparrow\colon 0, \downarrow\colon 1, \mathrm{Max} : 1 \rangle$.
- $\Delta((\uparrow, 1), \langle \uparrow\colon i, \downarrow\colon j, \mathrm{Max} : k \rangle, \langle \uparrow\colon i', \downarrow\colon j', \mathrm{Max} : k' \rangle) := \langle \uparrow\colon i'', \downarrow\colon 0, \mathrm{Max} : k'' \rangle$ where $i'' := \min(m, \max(i + 1, i' + 1))$ and $k'' := \min(m, \max(i'', i + j', i' + j, k, k'))$.
- $\Delta((\downarrow, 1), \langle \uparrow\colon i, \downarrow\colon j, \mathrm{Max} : k \rangle, \langle \uparrow\colon i', \downarrow\colon j', \mathrm{Max} : k' \rangle) := \langle \uparrow\colon 0, \downarrow\colon j'', \mathrm{Max} : k'' \rangle$ where $j'' := \min(m, \max(j + 1, j' + 1))$ and $k'' := \min(m, \max(j'', i + j', i' + j, k, k'))$.
- $\Delta((-, 1), \langle \uparrow\colon i, \downarrow\colon j, \mathrm{Max} : k \rangle, \langle \uparrow\colon i', \downarrow\colon j', \mathrm{Max} : k' \rangle) := \langle \uparrow\colon i'', \downarrow\colon j'', \mathrm{Max} : k'' \rangle$ where $i'' := \max(i, i')$ and $j'' := \max(j, j')$ and $k'' := \min(m, \max(k, k', i + j', i' + j))$.

- $\Delta((s, 0), \langle\uparrow\!: i, \downarrow\!: j, \mathrm{Max} : k\rangle, \langle\uparrow\!: i', \downarrow\!: j', \mathrm{Max} : k'\rangle) := \langle\uparrow\!: 0, \downarrow\!: 0, \mathrm{Max} : k''\rangle$ where $k'' := \min(m, \max(k, k', i + j', i' + j))$ for every $s \in \{-, \uparrow, \downarrow\}$.

The final state of A_G are all the states $\langle\uparrow\!: i, \downarrow\!: j, \mathrm{Max} : k\rangle$ such that $k = m$. One can check by a straightforward induction that the semantics of each state is respected, so that indeed the automaton tests the query G.

We conclude thanks to Proposition 3.1 of [5] by computing in linear time in $|A_G|$ and $|H'|$ a representation of the lineage on H' of the query that checks whether the input contains a directed path of the form $(\rightarrow -^*)^m$, and observe by Theorem 6.11 of [6] that it is a d-DNNF. We then compute the probability of this d-DNNF [21], yielding $\Pr(G \rightsquigarrow H)$ in PTIME: this concludes the proof. □

D. PROOF OF HARDNESS OF COUNTING EDGE COVERS

In this appendix, following the connection pointed out in [35], we give a proof of the following strengthening of Theorem 3.2, which is independent from the proof of [26].

THEOREM D.1. *The* **#Bipartite-Edge-Cover** *problem is #P-complete. Hardness holds even for 2–3 regular bipartite undirected graphs that are planar.*

PROOF. Membership in #P is straightforward: the machine guesses a subset of edges and accepts in PTIME iff the subset is a matching. Hence, we focus on hardness.

Recall that 2–3 *regular bipartite undirected graphs* are bipartite undirected graphs $\Gamma = (U \sqcup V, E)$ where the degree of each vertex in U is 2 and that of each vertex in V is 3. We will show how the result derives from the holographic reduction results of [14].

For $t \in U \sqcup V$, we denote by $E(t)$ the set of edges to which t is adjacent. For a valuation of the edges $\nu : E \rightarrow \{0, 1\}$ and a vertex t, we write $\nu(E(t))$ the multiset $\{\!\{\nu(e) \mid e \in E(t)\}\!\}$. Given a multiset of bits B, the *Hamming weight* of B is the number of 1 bits in B. For each $x_0, \ldots, x_n \in \{0, 1\}$, let $[x_0, \ldots, x_n]$ denote the function that takes a multiset of n bits as input and outputs x_i if the Hamming weight of those n bits is i.

For every $x_0, x_1, x_2, y_0, y_1, y_2, y_3 \in \{0, 1\}$, the problem $\#[x_0, x_1, x_2]|[y_0, y_1, y_2, y_3]$ is the following [14]: given a 2–3 regular bipartite undirected graph $\Gamma = (U \sqcup V, E)$, compute the quantity

$$\sum_{\nu: E \rightarrow \{0,1\}} \prod_{u \in U} [x_0, x_1, x_2](\nu(E(u)) \times \prod_{v \in V} [y_0, y_1, y_2, y_3](\nu(E(v))).$$

Then, restricted to 2–3 regular bipartite undirected graphs, our problem **#Bipartite-Edge-Cover** can be seen to be the same as $\#[0, 1, 1]|[0, 1, 1, 1]$. Indeed, seeing a valuation ν of the edges as a set of edges, the value under the sum for a valuation ν will be 1 if and only if, for every vertex, there exists an adjacent edge such that $\nu(e) = 1$, which exactly means that ν is an edge cover of Γ.

Now, let us consider the problem $\#[1, 1, 0]|[1, 1, 1, 0]$. As observed at the end of Section 8 of [13], it is the *reversal* of the problem $\#[0, 1, 1]|[0, 1, 1, 1]$. Indeed, the problem $\#[1, 1, 0]|[1, 1, 1, 0]$ amounts to counting the number of subsets S of edges such that, for every vertex v, there exists at least one edge adjacent to v that is not in S, i.e., that is in $E \setminus S$. But this means that $\#[1, 1, 0]|[1, 1, 1, 0]$ counts the number of sets S such that $E \setminus S$ is an edge cover of Γ. As there is a trivial bijection between the sets S that are edge covers and the sets S' such that $E \setminus S'$ is an edge cover, **#Bipartite-Edge-Cover** is PTIME-equivalent to $\#[1, 1, 0]|[1, 1, 1, 0]$ on 2–3 regular bipartite undirected graphs. The problem $\#[1, 1, 0]|[1, 1, 1, 0]$ is shown in [13, 14] to be #P-hard on 2-3 regular bipartite graphs (even when the graphs are additionally required to be planar), which concludes the proof. □

Circuit Treewidth, Sentential Decision, and Query Compilation

Simone Bova
TU Wien (Austria)
bova@ac.tuwien.ac.at

Stefan Szeider
TU Wien (Austria)
sz@ac.tuwien.ac.at

ABSTRACT

The evaluation of a query over a probabilistic database boils down to computing the probability of a suitable Boolean function, the lineage of the query over the database. The method of query compilation approaches the task in two stages: first, the query lineage is implemented (compiled) in a circuit form where probability computation is tractable; and second, the desired probability is computed over the compiled circuit. A basic theoretical quest in query compilation is that of identifying pertinent classes of queries whose lineages admit compact representations over increasingly succinct, tractable circuit classes.

Fostering previous work by Jha and Suciu (ICDT 2012) and Petke and Razgon (SAT 2013), we focus on queries whose lineages admit circuit implementations with small treewidth, and investigate their compilability within tame classes of decision diagrams. In perfect analogy with the characterization of bounded circuit pathwidth by bounded OBDD width, we show that a class of Boolean functions has bounded circuit treewidth if and only if it has bounded SDD width. Sentential decision diagrams (SDDs) are central in knowledge compilation, being essentially as tractable as OBDDs but exponentially more succinct. By incorporating constant width (linear size) SDDs and polynomial size SDDs in the picture, we refine the panorama of query compilation for unions of conjunctive queries with and without inequalities.

1. INTRODUCTION

A basic problem in database theory is *query evaluation in probabilistic databases*: Given a (Boolean) query Q and a probabilistic database D, where each tuple has a given probability, compute the probability of the lineage of Q over D. The problem is computationally hard, even for fixed queries in simple syntactic forms [11, 18].

The *lineage of a (Boolean) query Q over a database D* is a monotone Boolean function $L(Q, D)$ over the tuples in D that accepts a subset D' of tuples of D if and only if Q is true in D'. A standard approach to probabilistic query evaluation is *query compilation* [34, Chapter 5]. Here, the lineage $L(Q, D)$, given as a Boolean circuit, which is computable in polynomial time if Q is fixed, is implemented within a succinct circuit class where its probability is efficiently computable. In other words, to avoid computing the probability of a circuit, which is hard, the circuit is first *compiled* to a tamer form.

Circuit classes supporting tractable probability computation, and model counting in particular, are central in *knowledge compilation* [15]; particular emphasis is posed on the hierarchy of deterministic decomposable circuits. A circuit is *decomposable* if its AND gates represent independent probabilistic events [12], and *deterministic* if its OR gates represent exclusive probabilistic events [13]: probability computation is then feasible in linear time on deterministic decomposable circuits.

Aimed at a detailed syntactic classification of tractable cases of probabilistic query evaluation, Jha and Suciu amply explored the compilability of various classes of queries into various classes of deterministic decomposable circuits, fruitfully bridging database theory and knowledge compilation [20, 22]. In this context, they studied the compilability of queries whose lineages have small circuit treewidth into decision diagrams, OBDDs in particular [21]; a study we continue in this article.

An *ordered binary decision diagram* (OBDD) is a deterministic read-once branching program where every path from the root to a leaf visits the Boolean variables in the same order [8].[1] The OBDD size of a Boolean function is the size (number of nodes) of its smallest OBDD implementation. The width of an OBDD is the largest number of nodes labeled by the same variable, and the OBDD width of a Boolean function is the smallest width attained by its OBDD implementations.

Unifying several known tractable cases of the probability computation problem, Jha and Suciu introduce a structural parameter for Boolean functions, called *expression width* [21] or *circuit treewidth* [32], that measures, for any Boolean function, the smallest treewidth of a circuit computing the function. They show that a Boolean function of n variables and circuit treewidth k has OBDD size

$$n^{O(f(k))} \tag{1}$$

where f is a fast growing (double exponential) function [21]. The bound is tight in the sense that there are Boolean func-

[1]OBDDs are special deterministic decomposable circuits.

PODS'17, May 14-19, 2017, Chicago, Illinois, USA

DOI: http://dx.doi.org/10.1145/3034786.3034787

tions of n variables and circuit treewidth k whose OBDD size is $n^{\Omega(k)}$ [30].[2]

The bound (1) gives polynomial size OBDD implementations for circuits of bounded treewidth, but the degree of the polynomial depends (badly) on the treewidth. However, as Jha and Suciu show [21], restricting to functions of small *circuit pathwidth* resolves this issue. Indeed, a Boolean function of n variables and circuit pathwidth k has OBDD width $f(k)$, hence OBDD size

$$O(f(k)n); \tag{2}$$

and conversely, every Boolean function of OBDD width k has circuit pathwidth $O(k)$. Therefore, *a class of Boolean functions has bounded circuit pathwidth if and only if it has bounded OBDD width.*

As Jha and Suciu conclude, the quest naturally arises for a similar characterization of bounded circuit treewidth. The quest involves, for starters, identifying a circuit class ideally as tractable as OBDDs but more succinct, and therefore capable of matching the bound (2). Natural candidates, like FBDDs or even nondeterministic read-once branching programs fail [31].

The question is natural and nontrivial. Compared to the substantial understanding of the compilability of CNF circuits parameterized by treewidth, or even cliquewidth [5, 25], the parameterized compilability of general circuits is relatively unexplored and poorly understood; which is unsatisfactory because, in theory, the circuit treewidth of a class of Boolean functions can be bounded on general circuits and unbounded on CNFs [21, Example 2.9]; and in practice, query lineages are often presented by circuits rather than by CNFs [19].

The only bound on the size of a compilation for a circuit that avoids a dependence on its treewidth in the exponent,[3] like in (2) as opposed to (1), is a compilation of *size m* circuits into *decomposable* forms of size

$$O(g(k)m) \tag{3}$$

by Petke and Razgon [32], where g is an exponential function. This compilation, however, lacks two features that are either needed by or desirable in its intended application to query compilation. The crucial missing feature is that decomposable circuits, in the absence of determinism, do not support model counting (nor, then, probability computation). Besides, in the upper bound (3), the size of the compilation depends on the size of the circuit, m, not just on the number of its variables, n, and the former can be much larger than the latter. Indeed, Petke and Razgon ask whether decomposable forms of size linear in n are attainable for circuits of bounded treewidth [32, Section 5].

Contribution

In the first part of the article (Section 3), we show that *a class of Boolean functions has bounded circuit treewidth if and only if it has bounded SDD width,* which perfectly complements the aforementioned characterization of circuit pathwidth via OBDD width by Jha and Suciu.

[2]The lower bound holds even for primal treewidth, which is (unboundedly) larger than circuit treewidth.

[3]A special case where such a compilation is available is that of lineages of an MSO query over databases of bounded treewidth, which have linear size deterministic decomposable forms [1, 2].

More precisely, we prove the following (Theorem 4 and surrounding discussion).

Result 1. *A Boolean circuit of n variables and treewidth k has SDD width $f(k)$, thus SDD size*

$$O(f(k)n), \tag{4}$$

where f is a triple exponential function. Conversely, every Boolean function of SDD width k has circuit treewidth $O(k)$.

Introduced by Darwiche [14], *sentential decision diagrams* (SDDs) are a relaxation of OBDDs based on a generalized form of Shannon decomposition. An OBDD respecting the variable ordering $x_1 < x_2 < \cdots < x_n$ takes a *binary decision* of the form

$$(x_1 \wedge S_1(x_2, \ldots, x_n)) \vee (\neg x_1 \wedge S_2(x_2, \ldots, x_n)),$$

where S_1 and S_2 are OBDDs respecting the variable ordering $x_2 < \cdots < x_n$. Intuitively, based on a binary case distinction on x_1, the OBDD executes subOBDDs respecting the subordering $x_2 < \cdots < x_n$. An SDD respecting the variable tree T, whose left and right subtrees split the variables in two disjoint blocks X and Y, takes a *sentential decision* of the form

$$\bigvee_{i=1}^{m} (P_i(X) \wedge S_i(Y)).$$

Here, based on an m-ary (exhaustive and disjoint) case distinction on X, implemented by the m SDDs $P_i(X)$ respecting the left subtree of T, the m SDDs $S_i(Y)$ respecting the right subtree of T are executed.

SDDs are theoretically very robust, being essentially as tractable as OBDDs [14, 16] but exponentially more succinct [4]. They are also appealing in practice since an SDD compiler is reasonable to design and implement (as opposed to an FBDD compiler for instance, whose design is already fairly elusive). Indeed, available SDDs compilers already yield more succinct SDDs than OBDDs, leveraging the additional flexibility offered by variable trees compared to variable orders [9, 27]. Moreover, SDDs have canonical forms, and hence carry a natural notion of width which in particular implies, if bounded, linear size implementations, exactly as OBDD width does for OBDDs [14]. Thus, quite remarkably, our study unveils that circuit treewidth is characterized by an independently introduced, theoretically solid, and practically useful notion of circuit width, namely, SDD width.[4]

Figure 1 depicts the compilability panorama for Boolean functions with respect to bounded circuit pathwidth/OBDD width, bounded circuit treewidth/SDD width, and polynomial OBDD and SDD size. The class OBDD($f(n)$) contains all Boolean functions of OBDD width $f(n)$, and similarly for SDDs; the class CTW($f(n)$) contains all Boolean functions of circuit treewidth $f(n)$, and similarly for CPW and circuit

[4]SDDs were not even a natural candidate as, until recently [4], they were conjectured to be quasipolynomially simulated by OBDDs (personal communication with Vincent Liew).

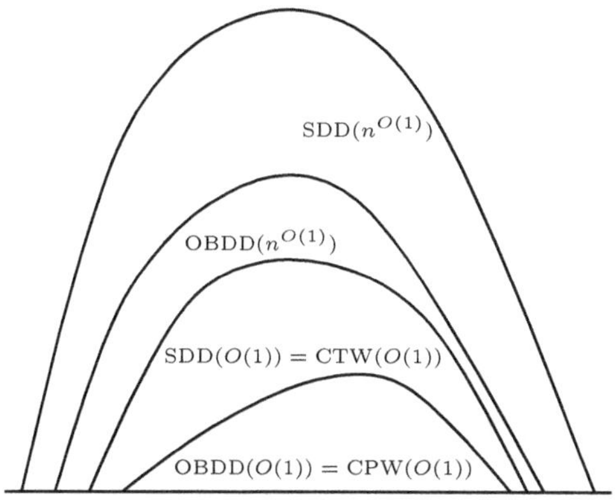

Figure 1: Boolean functions.

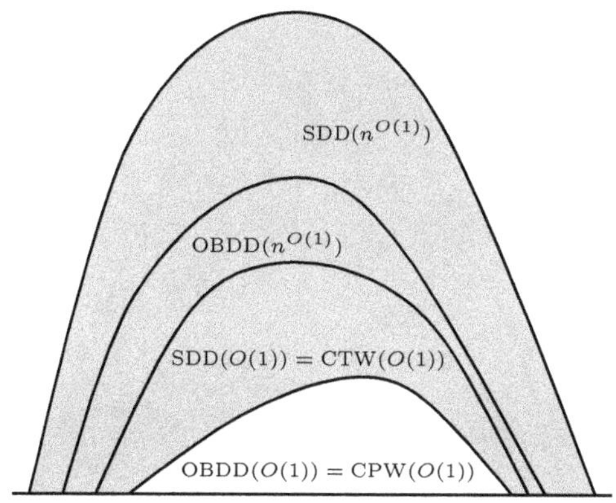

Figure 2: Lineages of UCQs. The gray region is empty.

pathwidth. We have

$$\begin{aligned}
\mathrm{CPW}(O(1)) &= \mathrm{OBDD}(O(1)) && [21]\\
&\subsetneq \mathrm{CTW}(O(1)) && [21]\\
&= \mathrm{SDD}(O(1)) && \text{Result 1}\\
&\subsetneq \mathrm{OBDD}(n^{O(1)}) && [21]\\
&\subsetneq \mathrm{SDD}(n^{O(1)}) && [4]
\end{aligned}$$

Jha and Suciu leave open the question of whether the circuit treewidth of a Boolean function is computable [21, Section 6]. Using the fact that satisfiability of MSO-sentences is decidable on graphs of bounded treewidth [33], we answer the question positively (Proposition 1).

Result 2. *The circuit treewidth of a Boolean function is computable.*

In the second part of the article (Section 4), we study the implications of our compilability results in query compilation, refining the picture drawn by Jha and Suciu for unions of conjunctive queries (UCQs) with and without inequalities [20, 21].

We prove the following statement (Theorem 5).

Result 3. *A union of conjunctive queries with or without inequalities containing inversions has lineages of exponential deterministic structured size.*

Introduced by Dalvi and Suciu [10], *inversion freeness* is a syntactic property of UCQs and UCQs with inequalities that implies compilability of their lineages in constant width (linear size) OBDDs and polynomial size OBDDs [20, 21]. On the other hand, if a query contains inversions, then it has lineages with large OBDD [20, 21], and even SDD [3], implementations.

Structuredness is a strong form of decomposability where not only for every AND gate the circuits leading into the gate are defined on disjoint sets of variables [12], but their variables are partitioned accordingly to an underlying variable tree [28].

As alluded in their informal description above, SDDs as well as OBDDs are special deterministic structured forms. Therefore Result 3 formally generalizes analogous previous incompilability results for SDDs and OBDDs [3, 20]. The proof has the main and sole merit to combine proof ideas of Jha and Suciu together with lower bound techniques for deterministic structured circuits based on single partition communication complexity [3, 6].

A careful inspection of the proof shows that Result 3 also exponentially separates disjunctive normal forms (DNFs), and even prime implicant forms (IPs), from structured deterministic negation normal forms (NNFs). In this interpretation Result 3 settles a special case of the much harder problem of separating DNFs (and IPs) and deterministic decomposable NNFs (d-DNNFs); which, thanks to the recently established separation of decomposable NNFs (DNNFs) and d-DNNFs [6], is the last open question about the relative succinctness of the compilation languages considered in the classic article by Darwiche and Marquis [15].

Figure 2 and Figure 3 give an overview of query compilability for lineages of UCQs with and without inequalities. For lineages of UCQs we have that

$$\begin{aligned}
\mathrm{OBDD}(O(1)) &= \mathrm{SDD}(O(1))\\
&= \mathrm{OBDD}(n^{O(1)}) = \mathrm{SDD}(n^{O(1)})
\end{aligned}$$

because by Result 3 inversions imply large structured deterministic forms, hence large SDDs; on the other hand, inversion freeness implies constant width OBDDs [20], so that $\mathrm{SDD}(n^{O(1)}) \setminus \mathrm{OBDD}(O(1)) = \emptyset$.

The picture for lineages of UCQs with inequalities is

$$\begin{aligned}
\mathrm{OBDD}(O(1)) &\subseteq \mathrm{SDD}(O(1))\\
&\subsetneq \mathrm{OBDD}(n^{O(1)}) = \mathrm{SDD}(n^{O(1)})
\end{aligned}$$

because again Result 3 implies large SDDs in the presence of inversions, and inversion freeness implies polynomial size OBDDs [21]. It follows that $\mathrm{SDD}(n^{O(1)}) \setminus \mathrm{OBDD}(n^{O(1)}) = \emptyset$. In a symmetric fashion, Jha and Suciu conjecture that, for lineages of UCQs with inequalities, it also holds that $\mathrm{SDD}(O(1)) \setminus \mathrm{OBDD}(O(1)) = \emptyset$.

Discussion

Our bound (4) amounts to a vast improvement of the available bounds. Compared to (1), it attains linear size versus (large degree) polynomial size compilation on bounded circuit treewidth classes. Compared to (3), it answers abundantly and positively the quest for linear size decomposable

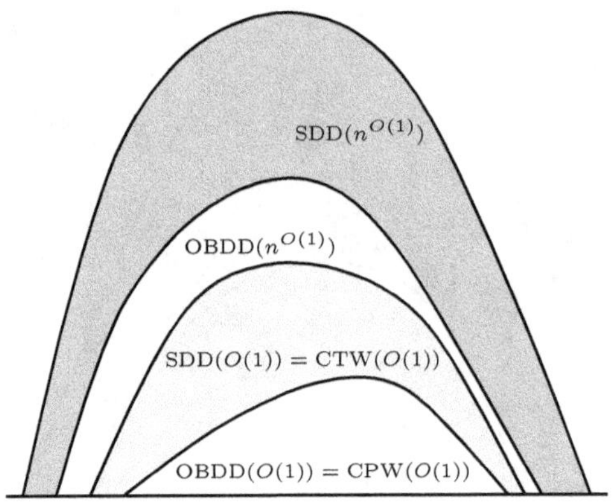

Figure 3: Lineages of UCQs with inequalities. The gray region is empty, and the light gray region is conjectured empty.

forms for Boolean functions of bounded treewidth: our forms are not just linear size and decomposable, but even deterministic and structured.

Pushing the dependency of the compilation size down from m (the size of the given circuit, as in (3)) to n (the number of its inputs, as in (4)) required an entirely new compilation idea.[5]

The idea used by Petke and Razgon [32] to obtain (3) was the following. Given a circuit $C(X)$ of $n = |X|$ variables and $m = |Z|$ gates, first compute its Tseitin CNF $T(X, Z)$; the circuit treewidth of the latter is roughly that of the former. To obtain a decomposable form for $C(X)$, existentially quantify the (gate) variables Z in a decomposable form $D_T(X, Z)$ for $T(X, Z)$:

$$C(X) \equiv (\exists Z) D_T(X, Z)$$

This indirect approach via Tseitin forms, however, introduces two critical issues. On the one hand, the size of $D_T(X, Z)$ depends on $|Z| = m$, so that the size of the compiled form will depend on m (as opposed to depending on n only). On the other hand, for $(\exists Z) D_T(X, Z)$ to have size polynomial in that of $D_T(X, Z)$, the latter cannot be deterministic [15]; hence the resulting compiled form will not be deterministic either.

Our compilation approach avoids Tseitin forms and compiles the circuit directly; it relies on a new insight on Boolean functions, and more specifically on the combinatorics of their *subfunctions* or *cofactors* [35].

Dually to the notion of cofactor, we introduce (Definition 1) the notion of *factor* of a Boolean function $F(Y, Y')$, that is, a function $G(Y)$ whose models correspond exactly to the assignments of Y generating some cofactor of F. We then show (Lemma 2) that first, the rectangle R formed by multiplying any two factors $G(Y)$ and $G'(Y')$ of $F(Y, Y')$ is either disjoint from F, that is $F \wedge R \equiv \bot$, or contained in F, that is $R \models F$.[6] And second (Lemma 3), the pairs of factors $G(Y)$ and $G'(Y')$ of $F(Y, Y')$ satisfying the latter condition, call them implicants, form a disjoint rectangle cover of F, that is,

$$F \equiv \bigvee_{(G, G') \text{ implicant}} (G(Y) \wedge G'(Y')),$$

where the disjunction is deterministic and the conjunctions are decomposable (structured, indeed).

We then elaborate on the main technical lemma of Jha and Suciu [21, Lemma 2.12] to turn the above structural insight into a compilation of small size. We show that a circuit of small treewidth computing a function F naturally delivers a variable tree where the number of cofactors of F generated by assigning the variables below every node in the tree is small (Lemma 1). It follows that the disjoint rectangle covers described above are small for every factor of F; we then obtain the desired compilation by an inductive construction up the variable tree (Lemma 4 and Theorem 3).

Indeed Result 1 is proved for a more basic canonical deterministic structured class of circuits (Theorem 3 and Proposition 2), which is equivalent to SDDs as far as the boundedness of their widths, and reduces to OBDDs in the special case of linear variable trees; the class is of independent interest and gives a fresh structural insight into SDDs (see also the conclusion).

Our construction, significantly shorter to describe and easier to analyze than its precursors, effectively encompasses the construction by Jha and Suciu in that, if carried out in the special case of circuit pathwidth, it compiles a circuit of n variables and pathwidth k into an OBDD (not just an SDD) of width $f(k)$ and size $O(f(k)n)$.

Organization

The article is organized as follows. The required notions from knowledge compilation and communication complexity are given in Section 2. The part of the article devoted to circuit treewidth and sentential decision (Section 3) deals first with the introduction and the development of the notion of factor and factor width for a Boolean function, and the relation of the latter with circuit treewidth (Section 3.1); next, it presents the actual compilations in canonical deterministic structured NNFs and SDDs (Section 3.2). Section 4 is devoted to query compilation. We present questions and directions for future research in Section 5.

2. PRELIMINARIES

For every integer $n \geq 1$, we let $[n] = \{1, \ldots, n\}$. We refer the reader to a standard source for the notions of treewidth, tree decomposition, and nice tree decomposition [24].

2.1 Circuits, Determinism, Structuredness

We consider (Boolean) circuits over the standard basis, namely DAGs whose non-source nodes, called internal gates, are unbounded fanin conjunction ($\wedge$) and disjunction ($\vee$) gates and fanin 1 negation ($\neg$) gates, and whose source nodes, called input gates, are pairwise distinct variables or constants ($\bot$ and $\top$). A designated sink node is called the

[5]This aspect of the bound, at first sight pedantic, is indeed relevant in query compilation, where the number n of Boolean variables of the query lineage $L(Q, D)$ is the (large) number of tuples in the database D, and m is the size of the circuit implementation of $L(Q, D)$. Roughly $m = O(n^q)$, where q is the size of the query Q. Hence, avoiding a dependence on m means obtaining a bound where the degree of the polynomial is a universal constant, not just independent of the circuit treewidth of $L(Q, D)$, but also independent of Q.

[6]The product of $G(Y)$ and $G'(Y')$ is a Boolean function over $Y \cup Y'$ whose models are exactly those assignments of $Y \cup Y'$ whose restriction to Y (Y') models G (G').

output gate. A circuit is in *negation normal form*, in short an *NNF*, if its negation gates are only wired by input gates. The size $|C|$ of a circuit C is the number of its gates.

Let X be a finite set of variables. A circuit C over X is a circuit whose input gates are labelled by variables in X or by constants. A circuit C on X computes a Boolean function $F_C = F_C(X)$ over the Boolean variables X,

$$F_C : \{0,1\}^X \to \{0,1\},$$

in the usual way. We let

$$\mathsf{sat}(C) = \mathsf{sat}(F_C) = F_C^{-1}(1) \subseteq \{0,1\}^X$$

denote the models of C and F_C. Two circuits C and C' over X are equivalent, in symbols $C \equiv C'$, if $\mathsf{sat}(C) = \mathsf{sat}(C')$; we also write $C \equiv F$ or say that C computes F if $F_C = F$.

For a gate g in a circuit C over X, we let C_g denote the subcircuit of C rooted at g. In particular, $C_g = C$ if g is the output gate of C. For a circuit C over variables X and a gate $g \in C$, we let $\mathsf{var}(C_g) \subseteq X$ denote the variables appearing at input gates of C_g.

Let g be an $\vee$-gate in a circuit C, and let h and h' be two distinct gates wiring g in C. Then g is called *deterministic* if $\mathsf{sat}(C_h) \cap \mathsf{sat}(C_{h'}) = \emptyset$, viewing each circuit involved in the equation as a circuit over $\mathsf{var}(C)$. The determinism of g in C implies that the two subcircuits C_h and $C_{h'}$ are "independent" in the sense that

$$|\mathsf{sat}(C_h \vee C_{h'})| = |\mathsf{sat}(C_h)| + |\mathsf{sat}(C_{h'})|,$$

where each circuit involved in the equation is viewed as a circuit over $\mathsf{var}(C)$. A circuit where all $\vee$-gates are deterministic is called *deterministic*.

Let Y be a finite nonempty set of variables. A *variable tree* (in short, a *vtree*) for the variable set Y is a rooted, ordered, binary tree T whose leaves correspond bijectively to Y; for simplicity, we identify each leaf in T with the variable in Y it corresponds to. For technical convenience, we slightly relax the standard definition not requiring for a vtree to be a full binary tree.

For every internal node v of the vtree T with two children, we let v_l and v_r denote resp. the left and right child of v. Moreover, we denote by T_v the subtree of T rooted at node v, and by $Y_v \subseteq Y$ (the variables corresponding to) the leaves of T_v.

Let C be a circuit over the variable set X, and let T be a vtree for the variable set Y. Let g be a fanin 2 $\wedge$-gate in C, having wires from gates h and h', and let $v \in T$ have two children v_l and v_r. We say that g is *structured by* v if $\mathsf{var}(C_h) \subseteq Y_{v_l}$ and $\mathsf{var}(C_{h'}) \subseteq Y_{v_r}$. We say that C *structured by* T if each $\wedge$-gate in C (has fanin 2 and) is structured by some node in T. A circuit is called *structured* if it is structured by some vtree.

A class of structured NNFs is *canonical* if, for every Boolean function $F(X)$ and vtree $T(Y)$ with $X \subseteq Y$, if two circuits C and C' in the class both compute F and are structured by T, then they are syntactically equal (not just semantically equivalent).

Note that if a gate $g \in C$ is structured, then it is also *decomposable*, i.e., every two distinct gates h and h' wiring g satisfy $\mathsf{var}(C_h) \cap \mathsf{var}(C_{h'}) = \emptyset$. The decomposability of g in C implies that the two subcircuits C_h and $C_{h'}$ are "independent" in the sense that

$$|\mathsf{sat}(C_h \wedge C_{h'})| = |\mathsf{sat}(C_h)| \cdot |\mathsf{sat}(C_{h'})|,$$

when viewing each circuit involved in the equation as a circuit over its own variables.

A *sentential decision diagram*, in short *SDD*, is a deterministic structured NNF C over X of the form

$$\bigvee_{i \in [m]} (P_i \wedge S_i), \tag{5}$$

structured by a vtree $T(Y)$, $X \subseteq Y$, such that the following holds. There exists a node $v \in T$ with two children w and w' structuring each $\wedge$-gate appearing in (5), the P_i's are SDDs over Y_w structured by T_w, the S_i's are SDDs over $Y_{w'}$ structured by $T_{w'}$, and moreover:

(1) $\bigvee_{i \in [m]} P_i \equiv \top$;

(2) $P_i \wedge P_j \equiv \bot$ for all $i \neq j$ in $[m]$.

Constants ($\bot$ and $\top$) are SDDs (over any variable set) structured by any vtree, and a literal (x or $\neg x$) is an SDD (over any variable set containing x) structured by any vtree containing x. SDDs become canonical forms if, in addition to the above, the following holds [14]:

(3) $S_i \not\equiv S_j$ for all $i \neq j$ in $[m]$.

2.2 Rectangles, Covers, Complexity

Let X be a finite set of variables. A partition of X is a sequence of pairwise disjoint subsets (blocks) of X whose union is X. Let (X_1, X_2) be a partition of X. For $b_1 : X_1 \to \{0,1\}$ and $b_2 : X_2 \to \{0,1\}$, we let $b_1 \cup b_2 : X_1 \cup X_2 \to \{0,1\}$ denote the assignment of X whose restriction to X_i equals b_i for $i = 1, 2$. Also, for $B_1 \subseteq \{0,1\}^{X_1}$ and $B_2 \subseteq \{0,1\}^{X_2}$, we let $B_1 \times B_2 = \{b_1 \cup b_2 : b_1 \in B_1, b_2 \in B_2\}$. A *(combinatorial) rectangle* over X is a Boolean function $R = R(X) : \{0,1\}^X \to \{0,1\}$ over the Boolean variables X such that there exist a partition (X_1, X_2) of X and Boolean functions $R_i : \{0,1\}^{X_i} \to \{0,1\}$ for $i = 1, 2$ such that $\mathsf{sat}(R) = \mathsf{sat}(R_1) \times \mathsf{sat}(R_2)$. We also call a subset S of $\{0,1\}^X$ a rectangle over X, with underlying partition (X_1, X_2), if there exists a rectangle $R : \{0,1\}^X \to \{0,1\}$, with underlying partition (X_1, X_2), such that $S = \mathsf{sat}(R)$.

Let $F = F(X)$ be a Boolean function over the Boolean variables X. A finite set $\{R_i : i \in [m]\}$ of rectangles over X is called a *rectangle cover* of F if

$$\mathsf{sat}(F) = \bigcup_{i \in [m]} \mathsf{sat}(R_i); \tag{6}$$

the rectangle cover is called *disjoint* if the union in (6) is disjoint. Disjoint rectangle covers and deterministic structured NNFs are tightly related.

THEOREM 1. [29, 6] *Let C be a (deterministic) structured NNF computing a function $F = F(X)$ and respecting a vtree T for X. For every node $v \in T$, F has a (disjoint) rectangle cover of size at most $|C|$ where each rectangle has underlying partition $(X_v, X \setminus X_v)$.*

Let $F(X)$ be a Boolean function, and let (X_1, X_2) be a partition of X where $|X_1| = |X_2| = n$. The *communication matrix* of F relative to (X_1, X_2), denoted by $\mathsf{cm}(F, X_1, X_2)$ is a Boolean matrix whose rows and columns are indexed by Boolean assignments of X_1 and X_2, resp., and whose (b_1, b_2)th entry equals $F(b_1 \cup b_2)$. We regard communication matrices as matrices over the reals.

A basic fact in communication complexity is that the rank of the communication matrix is a lower bound on the size of disjoint rectangle covers of a function.

THEOREM 2. [23, Section 4.1] *Let (X_1, X_2) be a partition of the variables of a function F, where $|X_1| = |X_2| = n$. Every disjoint rectangle cover of F into rectangles with underlying partition (X_1, X_2) contains at least* $\mathsf{rank}(\mathsf{cm}(F, X_1, X_2))$ *rectangles.*

A typical application is the *disjointness function*,

$$D_n(X_n, Y_n) = (\neg x_1 \vee \neg y_1) \wedge \cdots \wedge (\neg x_n \vee \neg y_n), \quad (7)$$

where $X_n = \{x_1, \ldots, x_n\}$ and $Y_n = \{y_1, \ldots, y_n\}$. It is folklore that

$$\mathsf{rank}(\mathsf{cm}(D_n, X_n, Y_n)) = 2^n, \quad (8)$$

i.e., the communication matrix of D_n relative to (X_n, Y_n) has full rank [23, Exercise 7.1]. Thus every disjoint rectangle cover of D_n into rectangles with underlying partition (X_n, Y_n) has at least 2^n rectangles.

3. CIRCUIT TREEWIDTH

In this section, we introduce the notion of factor width of a Boolean function, relate it with its circuit treewidth, and show that, when parameterized by its factor width, a Boolean function admits a linear size compilation into some natural classes of canonical deterministic structured NNFs (including SDDs).

3.1 Factor Width and Circuit Treewidth

We introduce the notion of *factor width*, and recall from the literature the notion of circuit treewidth [21].

Let $F(X) = F\colon \{0,1\}^X \to \{0,1\}$ be a Boolean function over a finite set of variables X. For a set of variables Y we use the notation

$$F(X) = F(Y \cap X, X \setminus Y)$$

to display a partition of the variables of F into the two blocks $Y \cap X$ and $X \setminus Y$. It is intended that if $b\colon Y \cap X \to \{0,1\}$ and $b'\colon X \setminus Y \to \{0,1\}$, then $F(b, b') = F(b \cup b')$.

The *cofactor* (or *subfunction*) of F induced by $b\colon Y \cap X \to \{0,1\}$ is the Boolean function $F' = F'(X \setminus Y) = F'\colon \{0,1\}^{X \setminus Y} \to \{0,1\}$ such that

$$F'(b') = F(b, b'),$$

for all $b'\colon X \setminus Y \to \{0,1\}$. A function $F''(X \setminus Y)$ is called a *cofactor of $F(X)$ relative to $X \setminus Y$* if it is equal to the cofactor of F induced by some $b\colon Y \cap X \to \{0,1\}$.

EXAMPLE 1. *Let $F(x, y) = x \to y$ be Boolean implication, i.e. $F(b, b') = 1$ iff $b \leq b'$, for all $b, b' \in \{0,1\}$. The cofactors of F relative to y, induced by Boolean assignments of x, are $F(0, y) \equiv \top(y)$ and $F(1, y) \equiv y$. The cofactors of F relative to x, induced by Boolean assignments of y, are $F(x, 0) \equiv \neg x$ and $F(x, 1) \equiv \top(x)$. The cofactors of F induced by Boolean assignments of both x and y are $F(1, 0) \equiv \bot$ and $F(0,0) = F(0,1) = F(1,1) \equiv \top$. The only cofactor of F induced by Boolean assignments of no variables is $F(x, y)$ itself.*

We introduce notation to denote the cofactor of a Boolean function $F(X)$ generated by replacing, in a partition of X, the variables in certain blocks by constants. Let $\{Y_1, \ldots, Y_l\}$ be a partition of X, let $L \subseteq [l]$, and let $b_i\colon Y_i \to \{0,1\}$ for all $i \in L$. We write $F(B_1, \ldots, B_l)$ where $B_i = b_i$ if $i \in L$ and $B_i = Y_i$ otherwise, for all $i \in [l]$, to denote the cofactor of F induced by $\bigcup_{i \in L} b_i$, i.e. the Boolean function over the variables $\bigcup_{i \in [l] \setminus L} Y_i$ defined, for every $\bigcup_{i \in [l] \setminus L}(b_i\colon Y_i \to \{0,1\})$, by

$$\bigcup_{i \in [l] \setminus L} b_i \mapsto F(b_1, \ldots, b_l).$$

EXAMPLE 2. *Let F be as in Example 1, so that $F = F(X)$ for $X = \{x, y\}$. Let $Y = \{x\}$. We write $F = F(X) = F(Y, X \setminus Y)$. Let $b\colon Y \to \{0,1\}$. We write $F(b, X \setminus Y)$ to denote the cofactor of F relative to $X \setminus Y$ induced by b. If $b(x) = 0$, then $F(b, X \setminus Y) \equiv \top(y)$.*

Let $Y \subseteq X$. Intuitively, a factor of $F(Y, X \setminus Y)$ is a function $G(Y)$ whose models correspond exactly to the assignments of Y that induce some fixed cofactor $F'(X \setminus Y)$ of F.

Definition 1. Let Y and X be finite sets of variables and let $F(X) = F(Y \cap X, X \setminus Y)$ be a Boolean function. A Boolean function $G = G(Y \cap X) = G\colon \{0,1\}^{Y \cap X} \to \{0,1\}$ is called a *factor of $F(X)$ relative to Y* if there exists a cofactor $F' = F'(X \setminus Y)$ of F such that

$$b \in \mathsf{sat}(G) \iff F(b, X \setminus Y) = F'.$$

The factors of F relative to Y are denoted by $\mathsf{factors}(F, Y)$.

EXAMPLE 3. *Let $F(x, y) = x \to y$ be Boolean implication as in Example 1. The function $G(x) \equiv x$ is a factor of F relative to x, because there exists a cofactor of F relative to y, namely $F'(y) \equiv y$, such that $b \models G(x)$ iff $F(b, y) = F'(y)$. The function $G(x) \equiv \neg x$ is a factor of F relative to x, because there exists a cofactor of F relative to y, namely $F'(y) \equiv \top(y)$, such that $b \models G(x)$ iff $F(b, y) = F'(y)$.*

Note that cofactors and factors of a Boolean function relative to a variable set are, in general, distinct.[7]

EXAMPLE 4. *Let $F(x, y) = x \to y$ be Boolean implication as in Example 1. Then $G(x) \equiv x$ is a factor of F relative to x (Example 3), but it is not a cofactor of F relative to x, since the only cofactors of F relative to x are equivalent to $\neg x$ and $\top(x)$ (Example 1).*

Note that, by Definition 1,

$$\mathsf{factors}(F, Y) = \mathsf{factors}(F, Y \cap X), \quad (9)$$

but we insist on Y being an arbitrary set of variables for technical convenience. Moreover, again by Definition 1,

$$\{0,1\}^{Y \cap X} = \bigcup_{G \in \mathsf{factors}(F, Y)} \mathsf{sat}(G) \quad (10)$$

and the union is disjoint. In words, $\mathsf{factors}(F, Y)$ naturally determines a partition of $\{0,1\}^{Y \cap X}$ whose blocks, of the form $\mathsf{sat}(G)$ for $G \in \mathsf{factors}(F, Y)$, correspond to the cofactors of F relative to $X \setminus Y$.

Finally, we introduce the notion of factor width of a Boolean function.

[7]Exceptions include the parity function.

Definition 2. Let $F = F(X)$ be a Boolean function and let T be a vtree for $Z \supseteq X$. The *factor width of F relative to T*, in symbols $\mathsf{fw}(F,T)$, is defined by

$$\mathsf{fw}(F,T) = \max_{v \in T} |\mathsf{factors}(F, Z_v)|.$$

The *factor width* of F is defined by

$$\mathsf{fw}(F) = \min\{\mathsf{fw}(F,T) \colon T \text{ vtree for } Z \supseteq X\}.$$

The *treewidth of a circuit* C, in symbols $\mathsf{tw}(C)$, is the treewidth of the undirected graph underlying (the directed acyclic graph underlying) C. The *circuit treewidth* $\mathsf{ctw}(F)$ of a Boolean function F is the minimum treewidth of a circuit computing F.

A crucial fact in our development is that the factor width of a Boolean function is bounded above by a function of its circuit treewidth. The proof, located in Appendix 6, is a revisitation of [21, Lemma 2.12].

LEMMA 1. *For all Boolean functions F,*

$$\mathsf{fw}(F) \leq 2^{(\mathsf{ctw}(F)+2)2^{\mathsf{ctw}(F)+1}}.$$

We conclude the section observing that circuit treewidth is computable, thus answering a question posed by Jha and Suciu [21, Section 6].

PROPOSITION 1. *The circuit treewidth of a Boolean function is computable.*

PROOF. Let $X = \{x_1, \ldots, x_n\}$ be a variable set. Say that a graph (with loops) G *implements* a circuit over X iff there exists a circuit C over X such that G is (isomorphic to) the graph whose edge set E is defined relative to C as follows:

- For every wire $g \to g'$ in C, add to E a path $\{g,h\}$, $\{h,h'\}$, $\{h',g'\}$ from g to g' with a loop on h', where h and h' are fresh vertices.
- Add to E a loop on the output gate g of C.
- Let
$$(\circ, j) \in \{(x_1,1),\ldots,(x_n,n),(\bot,n+1),(\top,n+2)\} \cup \{(\neg,n+3),(\wedge,n+4),(\vee,n+5)\}.$$
For every $\circ$-gate g in C, add to E a j-star $\{g,h_1\}$, …, $\{g,h_j\}$ centered at g, where $h_1,\ldots,h_j$ are fresh vertices.

Intuitively a graph (with loops) G implementing a circuit C is a faithful representation of C in the vocabulary of graphs, where the arcs and labels used to represent C in the vocabulary of circuits are suitably expressed by edges (and loops). Let F be a Boolean function over X. It is a tedious but straightforward exercise to write an MSO sentence ϕ_F that is true on a graph (with loops) G iff G implements a circuit C on X computing $F(X)$ [17, Examples 4.10, 4.13, and 4.18].[8]

Also note that, if the graph (with loops) G implements a circuit C, then the treewidth of G is equal to the treewidth of C. Now, let k be an upper bound on the circuit treewidth of F (for instance, the treewidth of the DNF whose terms are exactly the models of F). Seese proves that, given an MSO sentence on the vocabulary of graphs, it is decidable whether it is satisfied by a graph (with loops) of treewidth k [33]. We therefore cycle for $i = 1,2,\ldots$ until we find $i \leq k$ such that ϕ_F is modeled by a graph of treewidth i. □

[8]Recall that a (finite) digraph is acyclic iff every induced subgraph has a source and a sink.

3.2 Few Factors Imply Small Disjoint Rectangle Covers

We show that Boolean functions of small factor width have implementations of small width within natural canonical subclasses of deterministic structured NNFs (including canonical SDDs); conversely, small width implementations within such circuit classes imply small circuit treewidth. Thus a class of Boolean functions has bounded circuit treewidth iff it has bounded width implementations in some natural, canonical classes of deterministic structured NNFs, including SDDs.

3.2.1 *Factorized Implicant Width and Deterministic Structured Forms*

We introduce the notion of *factorized implicant* of a Boolean function $F(Y,Y')$, roughly

$$F'(Y) \wedge F''(Y') \models F(Y,Y'),$$

where Y and Y' are disjoint sets of variables, F' (resp., F'') is a factor of F relative to Y (resp., Y').

The first key insight is that the rectangle formed by multiplying any two factors $F'(Y)$ and $F''(Y')$ of $F(Y,Y')$ is either disjoint from F or contained in F.

LEMMA 2. *Let $F = F(X)$ be a Boolean function. Let Y and Y' be disjoint subsets of X. Let H, G, and G' be factors of F relative to $Y \cup Y'$, Y, and Y', respectively. Then either*

$$(\mathsf{sat}(G) \times \mathsf{sat}(G')) \subseteq \mathsf{sat}(H) \qquad (11)$$

or

$$(\mathsf{sat}(G) \times \mathsf{sat}(G')) \cap \mathsf{sat}(H) = \emptyset. \qquad (12)$$

PROOF. If $(\mathsf{sat}(G) \times \mathsf{sat}(G')) \cap \mathsf{sat}(H) \neq \emptyset$, then let $b \in \mathsf{sat}(G)$ and $b' \in \mathsf{sat}(G')$ be such that $b \cup b' \in \mathsf{sat}(H)$. Let $c \in \mathsf{sat}(G)$ and $c' \in \mathsf{sat}(G')$. It suffices to show that $c \cup c' \in \mathsf{sat}(H)$. Below, $X' = X \setminus (Y \cup Y')$.

Assume for a contradiction that $c \cup c' \notin \mathsf{sat}(H)$. Therefore, by definition, the cofactors of F induced by $b \cup b'$ and $c \cup c'$ are distinct, i.e.,

$$F(b,b',X') \neq F(c,c',X').$$

On the other hand, by definition, $\{b,c\} \subseteq \mathsf{sat}(G)$ implies that $F(b,Y',X') = F(c,Y',X')$, and similarly $\{b',c'\} \subseteq \mathsf{sat}(G')$ implies that $F(Y,b',X') = F(Y,c',X')$. In particular, $F(b,b',X') = F(c,b',X')$ and $F(c,b',X') = F(c,c',X')$. Then

$$F(b,b',X') = F(c,c',X'),$$

a contradiction. □

Intuitively, a factorized implicant of a function $F(Y,Y')$ is a pair of factors $F'(Y)$ and $F''(Y')$ entirely contained in F, as in (11). Formally,

Definition 3. Let $F = F(X)$ be a Boolean function. Let H, G, and G' be factors of F relative to $Y \cup Y'$, Y, and Y', resp., where Y and Y' are disjoint subsets of X. Then (G,G') is a *factorized implicant of H relative to* (F,Y,Y') if G and G' satisfy (11) relative to H. We let $\mathsf{impl}(F,H,Y,Y')$ be the set of factorized implicants of H relative to (F,Y,Y').

The second key insight is that the factorized implicants of $F(Y,Y')$ naturally induce a disjoint rectangle cover for $F(Y,Y')$.

LEMMA 3. *Let $F = F(X)$ be a Boolean function and let H be a factor of F relative to $Y \cup Y'$, where Y and Y' are disjoint subsets of X. Then*

$$\{\mathsf{sat}(G) \times \mathsf{sat}(G') \colon (G,G') \in \mathsf{impl}(F,H,Y,Y')\}$$

forms a disjoint rectangle cover of H, i.e.,

$$\mathsf{sat}(H) = \bigcup_{(G,G')\in\mathsf{impl}(F,H,Y,Y')} (\mathsf{sat}(G) \times \mathsf{sat}(G')), \tag{13}$$

and the union is disjoint.

A circuit interpretation of Lemma 3 is that

$$C_H \equiv \bigvee_{(G,G')\in\mathsf{impl}(F,H,Y,Y')} (C_G \wedge C_{G'}) \tag{14}$$

where C_H, C_G, and $C_{G'}$ are circuits using variables in $Y \cup Y'$, Y, and Y' computing H, G, and G', respectively. The $\wedge$-gates are decomposable as Y and Y' are disjoint, and by Lemma 3 the $\vee$-gate is deterministic.

PROOF OF LEMMA 3. We claim that the union on the right of (13) is disjoint. Indeed if (G_1, G'_1) and (G_2, G'_2) are distinct implicants in $\mathsf{impl}(F,H,Y,Y')$, then $G_1 \neq G_2$ or $G'_1 \neq G'_2$. If $G_1 \neq G_2$, then $\mathsf{sat}(G_1) \cap \mathsf{sat}(G_2) = \emptyset$ because distinct factors of F relative to Y have disjoint models by (10). Similarly, if $G'_1 \neq G'_2$, then $\mathsf{sat}(G'_1) \cap \mathsf{sat}(G'_2) = \emptyset$. Therefore, $(\mathsf{sat}(G_1) \times \mathsf{sat}(G'_1)) \cap (\mathsf{sat}(G_2) \times \mathsf{sat}(G'_2)) = \emptyset$, and we are done.

We prove the equality in (13). For the nontrivial inclusion ($\subseteq$), let $b \colon Y \cup Y' \to \{0,1\}$ be in $\mathsf{sat}(H)$. By (10), there exist $G \in \mathsf{factors}(F,Y)$ such that $b|_Y \in \mathsf{sat}(G)$ and $G' \in \mathsf{factors}(F,Y')$ such that $b|_{Y'} \in \mathsf{sat}(G')$. Then $b|_Y \cup b|_{Y'} = b \in (\mathsf{sat}(G) \times \mathsf{sat}(G')) \cap \mathsf{sat}(H)$. It follows by Lemma 2 that $\mathsf{sat}(G) \times \mathsf{sat}(G') \subseteq \mathsf{sat}(H)$. Then $(G,G') \in \mathsf{impl}(F,H,Y,Y')$ and b is contained in the union on the right. □

The above insight can be exploited recursively to implement Boolean functions within a natural, canonical class of deterministic structured forms.

Let F be a function and let T be a vtree, both over the variables X. For every node $v \in T$ and every factor H of F relative to X_v, we construct a circuit $C_{v,H}$ as follows.

If v is a leaf of T, then $X_v = \{x\}$ for some variable $x \in X$. There are two cases. Either $F(0, X \setminus \{x\}) = F(1, X \setminus \{x\})$, or $F(0, X \setminus \{x\}) \neq F(1, X \setminus \{x\})$. In the former case, $\mathsf{factors}(F, \{x\}) = \{H\}$ and

$$C_{v,H} = \top. \tag{15}$$

In the latter case, $\mathsf{factors}(F, \{x\}) = \{H_0, H_1\}$ and

$$C_{v,H_0} = \neg x, \tag{16}$$
$$C_{v,H_1} = x. \tag{17}$$

If v is a node of T with children w and w', we put

$$C_{v,H} = \bigvee_{(G,G')\in\mathsf{impl}(F,H,X_w,X_{w'})} (C_{w,G} \wedge C_{w',G'}). \tag{18}$$

Finally we put

$$C_{F,T} = C_{r,F}, \tag{19}$$

where r is the root of T; note that F itself is a factor of F relative to X; its models induce the cofactor $1 \colon \{0,1\}^\emptyset \to \{0,1\}$ of F.

LEMMA 4. *Let F be a Boolean function and let T be a vtree, both over the variables X. Let $v \in T$ and let $H \in \mathsf{factors}(F, X_v)$. The following holds.*

- *$C_{v,H}$ is a deterministic structured NNF respecting the vtree T_v.*
- *$C_{v,H}$ computes H.*

PROOF. The proof is a routine induction on the depth of v in T. The base case holds by inspection of (15)–(17). The inductive case holds by inspection of (18), using (13) in Lemma 3 and the induction hypothesis; indeed, note that the disjunction arising in (18) is deterministic because the union in (13) is disjoint, and the conjunctions arising in (18) are structured by T_v (namely the left and right conjuncts are over variables X_w and $X_{w'}$ resp., where w and w' are the children of v in T) by the induction hypothesis. □

Note that, by Lemma 4, it follows that $C_{F,T}$ is a deterministic structured NNF computing F, canonical in that it is uniquely determined by the vtree T and F; the notion of *factorized implicant width* of F relative to T arises naturally.

Definition 4. Let F be a Boolean function and let T be a vtree, both over the variables X. The *factorized implicant width of F relative to T*, in symbols $\mathsf{fiw}(F,T)$, is defined by[9]

$$\mathsf{fiw}(F,T) = \max_{v\in T} |\{g \in C_{F,T} \colon g \text{ is structured by } v\}|.$$

The *factorized implicant width* of F, in symbols $\mathsf{fiw}(F)$, is defined by

$$\mathsf{fiw}(F) = \min\{\mathsf{fiw}(F,T) \colon T \text{ vtree for } X\}.$$

Relative to its factorized implicant width, a Boolean function (of n variables) has linear (in n) size compilations into canonical deterministic structured forms.

THEOREM 3. *A Boolean function F of n variables and factorized implicant width k has canonical deterministic structured NNFs of size $O(kn)$.*

PROOF. Let X be the variables of F, so that $|X| = n$, and let T be a vtree for X witnessing factorized implicant width k for F. The circuit $C_{F,T}$ in (19) is a canonical deterministic structured NNF computing F by Lemma 4.

Moreover, we claim that $C_{F,T}$ has size $O(kn)$. The n leaves of T contribute at most $n+1$ input gates and n $\neg$-gates in $C_{F,T}$. The $n-1$ internal nodes of T contribute each at most k $\wedge$-gates (by the definition of factorized implicant width), and each such gate is linked with at most 3 $\vee$-gates. Hence $C_{F,T}$ contains at most $2n + 1 + 3k(n-1) = O(kn)$ gates. □

We conclude the section showing that a class of Boolean functions has bounded circuit treewidth iff it has bounded factorized implicant width. It is sufficient to prove that the factorized implicant width of a Boolean function is bounded below and above by computable functions of its circuit treewidth.

[9]Recall that, if $g \in C_{F,T}$ is an $\wedge$-gate arising from (18), we say that g is *structured* by $v \in T$.

For the upper bound, we have

$$\mathsf{fiw}(F) \leq \mathsf{fw}(F)^2 \leq 2^{(\mathsf{ctw}(F)+2)2^{\mathsf{ctw}(F)+2}}, \tag{20}$$

where the first inequality is justified by the observation that every $\wedge$-gate g in $C_{F,T}$, structured by a node $v \in T$, corresponds to a pair of factors of F, and the second inequality follows by Lemma 1.

For the lower bound, we verify that small factorized implicant width implies small circuit treewidth.

PROPOSITION 2. *For all Boolean functions F,*

$$\mathsf{ctw}(F)/3 \leq \mathsf{fiw}(F). \tag{21}$$

PROOF. Let T be a vtree for X such that

$$\mathsf{fiw}(F, T) = \mathsf{fiw}(F) = k.$$

We claim that $\mathsf{tw}(C_{F,T}) \leq 3k$, so that $\mathsf{ctw}(F) \leq 3k$ by Lemma 4.

For every gate $g \in C_{F,T}$, let $\mathsf{neigh}(g)$ denote the closed neighborhood of g in the undirected graph underlying $C_{F,T}$. We define a tree decomposition for the undirected graph underlying $C_{F,T}$, as follows. The bags of the tree decomposition have the form

$$B_v = \{\mathsf{neigh}(g) \colon g \text{ structured by } v\},$$

for all $v \in T$. The root of the tree decomposition is B_r. The bag B_w has an arc to the bag $B_{w'}$ iff w has an arc to w' in T. By definition, B_v contains all the $\wedge$-gates structured by the node $v \in T$; there are at most k such gates in $C_{F,T}$ by definition, and each such gate has indegree 2 and outdegree 1 by construction (therefore degree 3 in the undirected graph underlying $C_{F,T}$). Hence $|B_v| \leq 3k$.

Since every wire of $C_{F,T}$ enters or leaves an $\wedge$-gate and every $\wedge$-gate is structured by some $v \in T$, the edges of the undirected graph underlying $C_{F,T}$ are covered by the tree decomposition. Moreover let g be a gate of $C_{F,T}$ occurring in two distinct bags B_w and $B_{w'}$. Then $g \in \mathsf{neigh}(h) \cap \mathsf{neigh}(h')$ where h is a $\wedge$-gate structured by w and h' is a $\wedge$-gate structured by w'. By construction of $C_{F,T}$, either w has an arc to w' in T or w' has an arc to w in T. Hence B_w and $B_{w'}$ are adjacent. □

3.2.2 *Sentential Decision Width and Sentential Decision Diagrams*

We show that the notion of factorized implicant lies at the core of (and provides fresh insight on) the canonical construction of SDDs for Boolean functions.

We prepare the actual description of the construction in two steps. The first step yields, by a straightforward generalization of Lemma 3, a factorized implicant decomposition reminiscent of (14) for unions of factors.

LEMMA 5. *Let $F = F(X)$ be a Boolean function, let Y and Y' be disjoint subsets of X, and let $\mathcal{H} \subseteq \mathsf{factors}(F, Y \cup Y')$. Then*

$$\{\mathsf{sat}(G) \times \mathsf{sat}(G') \colon (G, G') \in \mathsf{impl}(F, H, Y, Y'), H \in \mathcal{H}\}$$

forms a disjoint rectangle cover of $\bigvee_{H \in \mathcal{H}} H$.

In terms of circuits, the statement means that

$$\bigvee_{H \in \mathcal{H}} C_H \equiv \bigvee_{\substack{H \in \mathcal{H} \\ (G,G') \in \mathsf{impl}(F,H,Y,Y')}} (C_G \wedge C_{G'}), \tag{22}$$

where C_H, C_G, and $C_{G'}$ are as in (14), the $\vee$-gate is deterministic, and the $\wedge$-gates are decomposable.

PROOF OF LEMMA 5. We have

$$\begin{aligned} \mathsf{sat}\left(\bigvee_{H \in \mathcal{H}} H\right) &= \bigcup_{H \in \mathcal{H}} \mathsf{sat}(H) \\ &= \bigcup_{\substack{H \in \mathcal{H} \\ (G,G') \in \mathsf{impl}(F,H,Y,Y')}} (\mathsf{sat}(G) \times \mathsf{sat}(G')), \end{aligned}$$

where the second equality follows by applying Lemma 3 to H. We claim that the union is disjoint. Indeed, by (10), distinct factors of F relative to $Y \cup Y'$, in particular those in $\mathcal{H}$, have disjoint models; moreover, by Lemma 3, distinct implicants of a factor have disjoint models. □

The second step enforces the properties of a proper sentential decision over the factorized implicant form (22) given by Lemma 5, as follows. For each $G \in \mathsf{factors}(F, Y)$, let

$$\begin{aligned} \mathcal{S}_G &= \{G' \colon (G, G') \in \mathsf{impl}(F, H, Y, Y'), H \in \mathcal{H}\} \\ &\subseteq \mathsf{factors}(F, Y') \end{aligned}$$

and observe that

$$\bigvee_{G \in \mathsf{factors}(F,Y)} \left(C_G \wedge \left(\bigvee_{G' \in \mathcal{S}_G} C_{G'}\right)\right), \tag{23}$$

where empty disjunctions are implemented by $\bot$, is equivalent to $\bigvee_{H \in \mathcal{H}} C_H$ and is a sentential decision form as the factors of F relative to Y partition $\{0,1\}^Y$.

However, (23) is not a canonical form because distinct G_1 and G_2 in $\mathsf{factors}(F, Y)$ can give $\mathcal{S}_{G_1} = \mathcal{S}_{G_2}$. Let

$$\begin{aligned} \{\mathcal{S}_1, \ldots, \mathcal{S}_m\} &= \{\mathcal{S}_G \colon G \in \mathsf{factors}(F, Y)\}, \\ \mathcal{P}_i &= \{G \in \mathsf{factors}(F, Y) \colon \mathcal{S}_G = \mathcal{S}_i\}, \end{aligned}$$

for all $i \in [m]$, and

$$\begin{aligned} \mathsf{sd}(F, \mathcal{H}, Y, Y') &= \{(\mathcal{P}_1, \mathcal{S}_1), \ldots, (\mathcal{P}_m, \mathcal{S}_m)\} \\ &\subseteq 2^{\mathsf{factors}(F,Y)} \times 2^{\mathsf{factors}(F,Y') \cup \{\bot\}}. \end{aligned}$$

It is readily observed that

$$\bigvee_{(\mathcal{P},\mathcal{S}) \in \mathsf{sd}(F,\mathcal{H},Y,Y')} \left(\left(\bigvee_{P \in \mathcal{P}} C_P\right) \wedge \left(\bigvee_{S \in \mathcal{S}} C_S\right)\right) \tag{24}$$

is equivalent to $\bigvee_{H \in \mathcal{H}} C_H$ and moreover:

(SD1) $\top \equiv \bigvee_{i \in [m]} \bigvee_{P \in \mathcal{P}_i} C_P$;

(SD2) $\bot \equiv \left(\bigvee_{P \in \mathcal{P}_i} C_P\right) \wedge \left(\bigvee_{P \in \mathcal{P}_j} C_P\right)$ for $i \neq j$ in $[m]$;

(SD3) $\left(\bigvee_{S \in \mathcal{S}_i} C_S\right) \not\equiv \left(\bigvee_{S \in \mathcal{S}_j} C_S\right)$ for $i \neq j$ in $[m]$.

We now use the above development to describe a recursive construction of a canonical SDD for a given Boolean function. Let F be a Boolean function and let T be a vtree, both over X. For every node $v \in T$ and every subset $\mathcal{H}$ of factors of F relative to X_v, we construct a circuit $C_{v,\mathcal{H}}$, as follows.

If v is a leaf of T, then $X_v = \{x\}$ for some variable $x \in X$. There are two cases. Either $F(0, X \setminus \{x\}) = F(1, X \setminus \{x\})$, or $F(0, X \setminus \{x\}) \neq F(1, X \setminus \{x\})$. In the former case, $\mathsf{factors}(F, \{x\}) = \{H\}$ and: $C_{v,\emptyset} = \bot$; $C_{v,\{H\}} = \top$. In the latter case, $\mathsf{factors}(F, \{x\}) = \{H_0, H_1\}$ and: $C_{v,\emptyset} = \bot$; $C_{v,\{H_0\}} = \neg x$; $C_{v,\{H_1\}} = x$; $C_{v,\{H_0,H_1\}} = \top$.

If v is a node of T with children w and w', we put

$$C_{v,\mathcal{H}} = \bigvee_{(\mathcal{P},\mathcal{S})\in\mathsf{sd}(F,\mathcal{H},Y,Y')} (C_{w,\mathcal{P}} \wedge C_{w',\mathcal{S}}). \tag{25}$$

Finally we put, where r is the root of T,

$$S_{F,T} = C_{r,\{F\}}. \tag{26}$$

LEMMA 6. *Let F be a Boolean function and let T be a vtree, both over the variables X. Let $v \in T$ and let $\mathcal{H} \subseteq \mathsf{factors}(F, X_v)$.*

- *$C_{v,\mathcal{H}}$ is a canonical SDD respecting the vtree T_v.*
- *$C_{v,\mathcal{H}}$ computes $\bigvee_{H\in\mathcal{H}} H$.*

PROOF. By induction on the depth of v in T. The base case holds by construction. The inductive case holds inspection of (25), using (24) together with (SD1)–(SD3), (23), Lemma 5, and the induction hypothesis. □

Therefore $S_{F,T}$ is the canonical SDD computing F, uniquely determined by the vtree T. We recall the notion of *sentential decision width* of F relative to T.

Definition 5. Let F be a Boolean function and let T be a vtree, both over X. The *sentential decision width of F relative to T*, in symbols $\mathsf{sdw}(F, T)$, is defined by

$$\mathsf{sdw}(F, T) = \max_{v\in T} |\{g \in S_{F,T} : g \text{ is structured by } v\}|.$$

The *SDD width* of F, in symbols $\mathsf{sdw}(F)$, is defined by

$$\mathsf{sdw}(F) = \min\{\mathsf{sdw}(F, T) : T \text{ vtree for } X\}.$$

It is well known that OBDDs are canonical SDDs respecting linear vtrees, i.e. vtrees where every left child is a leaf [14]; in this case, the notion of SDD width in Definition 5 reduces to the usual notion of OBDD width [35]. Moreover, as a Boolean function (of n variables) has linear (in n) OBDD size parameterized by its OBDD width, likewise it has linear SDD size parameterized by its SDD width.

THEOREM 4. *A Boolean function F of n variables and SDD width k has canonical SDD size $O(kn)$.*

PROOF OF THEOREM 4. Let X be the variables of F, so that $|X| = n$, and let T be a vtree for X witnessing SDD width k for F. The circuit $S_{F,T}$ in (26) is a canonical SDD by Lemma 6.

Moreover, we claim that $S_{F,T}$ has size $O(kn)$. The n leaves of T contribute at most $2(n + 1)$ input or negation gates in $C_{F,T}$. The $n-1$ internal nodes of T contribute each at most k $\wedge$-gates (by the definition of SDD width), and each such gate is linked with at most 3 $\vee$-gates. Hence $C_{F,T}$ contains at most $2(n + 1) + 3k(n - 1) = O(kn)$ gates. □

We conclude observing that, for classes of Boolean functions, bounded circuit treewidth and bounded SDD width collapse. Indeed, on the one hand, the SDD width of a Boolean function F is bounded above by a computable function of its circuit treewidth, namely,

$$\mathsf{sdw}(F) \leq 2^{2\cdot\mathsf{fw}(F)+1} \leq 2^{2^{(\mathsf{ctw}(F)+2)2^{\mathsf{ctw}(F)+1}+1}+1}, \tag{27}$$

since in the canonical SDD $S_{F,T}$ for T every $\wedge$-gate g structured by a node $v \in T$ corresponds to a pair of sets of factors of F (plus $\bot$), and $\mathsf{fw}(F)$ is bounded above by $\mathsf{ctw}(F)$ as in Lemma 1. On the other hand, for all Boolean functions F, along the lines of Proposition 2,

$$\mathsf{ctw}(F)/3 \leq \mathsf{sdw}(F). \tag{28}$$

By combining (20)–(21) and (27)–(28), the factorized implicant width (resp., SDD width) of a Boolean function is squeezed between computable functions of its SDD width (resp., factorized implicant width).

4. QUERY COMPILATION

In this section, we show that inversions in unions of conjunctive queries, with or without inequalities, imply large deterministic structured circuits for their lineages.

Let σ be a relational vocabulary. A *union of conjunctive queries (UCQs) with inequalities* Q is a disjunction of existentially closed conjunctions of atoms $Rx_1 \cdots x_m$ and inequalities $x \neq y$, where $R \in \sigma$ and x, y, x_i are variables, $i \in [m]$. We call Q a UCQs if it does not contain inequalities. The *lineage of a Boolean query Q over a database D* is a Boolean function $L(Q, D)$ whose Boolean variables are the tuples in D such that, for every subdatabase $D' \subseteq D$, it holds that $D' \models Q$ iff $b_{D'} \models L(Q, D)$, where $b_{D'} : D \to \{0, 1\}$ is defined by $b_{D'}(t) = 1$ iff $t \in D'$. A *lineage of a Boolean query* is a lineage of the query over some database.

4.1 Inversions Imply Large Deterministic Structured Forms

We prove the main result. For all $k, n \geq 1$, let $X = \{x_l : l \in [n]\}$, $Y = \{y_m : m \in [n]\}$, $Z^i = \{z^i_{l,m} : l, m \in [n]\}$ for $i \in [k]$, and $Z = \bigcup_{i\in[k]} Z^i$. For $i \in [k - 1]$, let:

$$H^0_{k,n}(X, Z^1) = \bigvee_{l,m\in[n]} (x_l \wedge z^1_{l,m}),$$

$$H^i_{k,n}(Z^i, Z^{i+1}) = \bigvee_{l,m\in[n]} (z^i_{l,m} \wedge z^{i+1}_{l,m}),$$

$$H^k_{k,n}(Z^k, Y) = \bigvee_{l,m\in[n]} (z^k_{l,m} \wedge y_m).$$

In [22, Proposition 7] and [21, Theorem 3.9] Jha and Suciu show the following, resp. for UCQs and UCQs with inequalities.

LEMMA 7. *Let Q be a UCQs with or without inequalities.*[10] *If Q "contains an inversion of length $k \geq 1$", then for every $n \geq 1$ there exist a lineage $F(X)$ of Q on $O(n^2)$ variables and assignments $b_i : X_i \to \{0, 1\}$ for $X_i \subseteq X$ and $i = 0, 1, \ldots, k$ such that*

$$F(b_i, X \setminus X_i) \equiv H^i_{k,n}.$$

As we only need the implication stated in Lemma 7, we omit the technical definition of the notion of inversion [10]. The following statement unifies and generalizes analogous results by Jha and Suciu for UCQs with inequalities vs. OBDDs [21, Theorem 3.9] and by Beame and Liew for UCQs vs. SDDs [3, Theorem 4.6].

[10] As a technical assumption, we assume that all queries and databases are ranked [34].

THEOREM 5. *Let Q be a UCQs with or without inequalities. If Q "contains an inversion of length $k \geq 1$", then for every $n \geq 1$ there exists a lineage F of Q on $O(n^2)$ variables whose deterministic structured NNF size is $2^{\Omega(n/k)}$.*

The proof idea is that, if a query Q "contains inversions", then it has a lineage $L(Q, D)$ of which each $H^i_{k,n}$ is a cofactor ($i = 0, 1, \ldots, k$). If C is a small deterministic form for $L(Q, D)$ respecting a vtree T, then small deterministic structured forms for each $H^i_{k,n}$, *all* respecting the vtree T, can be mined from C by suitably assigning its inputs. But this is impossible for communication complexity reasons (Lemma 8).

PROOF OF THEOREM 5. Let Q be a query with inequalities. If Q "contains an inversion of length $k \geq 1$", then by Lemma 7 for every $n \geq 1$ there exist a lineage $F(X)$ of Q on $O(n^2)$ variables and assignments $b_i \colon X_i \to \{0,1\}$ for $X_i \subseteq X$ and $i = 0, 1, \ldots, k$ such that $F(b_i, X \setminus X_i) \equiv H^i_{k,n}$.
Let C be a deterministic NNF of size s computing F, structured by the vtree T. Then by the properties of deterministic structured NNFs [28], it holds that $C_i(X \setminus X_i) = C(b_i, X \setminus X_i)$ is a deterministic NNF of size $s_i \leq s$ that computes $H^i_{k,n}$ and is structured by T, for all $i = 0, 1, \ldots, k$. By Lemma 8, there exists $i \in \{0, 1, \ldots, k\}$ such that C_i has size $s_i = 2^{\Omega(n/k)}$. Therefore C has size $2^{\Omega(n/k)}$. □

We conclude the section establishing the crucial fact.

LEMMA 8. *For every vtree T for $X \cup Y \cup Z$ and every family $\{C_0, \ldots, C_k\}$ of deterministic structured NNFs, where C_i is structured by T and computes $H^i_{k,n}$ ($i = 0, 1, \ldots, k$), there exists $i \in \{0, 1, \ldots, k\}$ such that C_i has size $2^{\Omega(n/k)}$.*

PROOF OF LEMMA 8. We let X_v denote the variables in $T_v \cap X$, Y_v denote the variables in $T_v \cap Y$, and Z_v denote the variables in $T_v \cap Z$.

CLAIM 1. *There exists $v \in T$ such that $2n/5 \leq |X_v \cup Y_v| \leq 4n/5$.*

PROOF OF CLAIM 1. Let $n_v = |X_v \cup Y_v|$, for all $v \in T$. Let $v_1, \ldots, v_l$ be a root-leaf path in T such that, letting $n_i = |X_{v_i} \cup Y_{v_i}|$,

$$n_{i+1} \geq n_i/2$$

for all $i = 1, \ldots, l-1$. Let $i \in [l]$ be minimum such that

$$n_i \leq |X \cup Y|/5,$$

so that

$$|X \cup Y|/5 < n_{i-1}.$$

By construction,

$$n_{i-1} \leq 2n_i \leq 2|X \cup Y|/5.$$

Hence, letting $v = v_{i-1}$, we have

$$2n/5 = |X \cup Y|/5 < |X_v \cup Y_v| \leq 2|X \cup Y|/5 = 4n/5,$$

and we are done. □

By Claim 1, let $v \in T$ be such that $2n/5 \leq |X_v \cup Y_v| \leq 4n/5$. Let $n_x = |X_v|$ and $n_y = |Y_v|$. Assume without loss of generality that $n_x \geq n_y$; otherwise the argument is similar. It follows by the choice of v that

$$n_x \geq n/5 \tag{29}$$

and that

$$n - n_y \geq n - n_x \geq n - 4n/5 = n/5. \tag{30}$$

We enter a case distinction. The first case is covered by the following claim.

CLAIM 2. *If there exists $j \in [n]$ such that for all $i \in [n]$ it holds that $x_i \in X_v$ implies $z^1_{i,j} \in T \setminus T_v$, then C_0 has size $2^{\Omega(n)}$.*

PROOF OF CLAIM 2. For $j \in [n]$, let $Z^1_j = \{z^1_{i,j} \colon x_i \in X_v\} \setminus T_v$. By hypothesis, there exists $j \in [n]$ such that $|Z^1_j| = n_x$. Write

$$C_0(X, Z^1) = C_0(X_v, X \setminus X_v, Z^1_j, Z^1 \setminus Z^1_j).$$

Then

$$C'_0(X_v, Z^1_j) = C_0(X_v, \{0\}^{X \setminus X_v}, Z^1_j, \{0\}^{Z^1 \setminus Z^1_j})$$

is a deterministic NNF structured by T of size $|C'_0| \leq |C_0|$ [28]. It follows from Theorem 1 that C'_0 has a disjoint rectangle cover of size at most $|C'_0|$ where each rectangle has underlying partition (X_v, Z^1_j).
By the choice of v, it holds that X_v contains n_x variables in X. For the sake of notation, say that $X_v = \{x_1, \ldots, x_{n_x}\}$, so that $Z^1_j = \{z^1_{1,j}, \ldots, z^1_{n_x,j}\}$. Then, since $C_0 \equiv H^0_{k,n}$, we have that

$$C'_0 \equiv (x_1 \wedge z^1_{1,j}) \vee \cdots \vee (x_{n_x} \wedge z^1_{n_x,j}).$$

Note that $C'_0(X_v, Z^1_j)$ is the complement of the disjointness function $D_{n_x}(X_v, Z^1_j)$ in (7). Therefore the complement of the communication matrix of C'_0 relative to (X_v, Z^1_j) is equal (up to a permutation of rows and columns) to the communication matrix of D_{n_x}, i.e.,

$$\mathsf{cm}(D_{n_x}, X_v, Z^1_j) = 1 - \mathsf{cm}(C'_0, X_v, Z^1_j),$$

where 1 denotes the $2^{n_x} \times 2^{n_x}$ all-1 matrix. Therefore, by (8) and basic linear algebra,

$$\begin{aligned} 2^{n_x} &= \mathsf{rank}(\mathsf{cm}(D_{n_x}, X_v, Z^1_j)) \\ &= \mathsf{rank}(1 - \mathsf{cm}(C'_0, X_v, Z^1_j)) \\ &\leq \mathsf{rank}(1) + \mathsf{rank}(\mathsf{cm}(C'_0, X_v, Z^1_j)) \\ &= 1 + \mathsf{rank}(\mathsf{cm}(C'_0, X_v, Z^1_j)), \end{aligned}$$

hence

$$\mathsf{rank}(\mathsf{cm}(C'_0, X_v, Z^1_j)) \geq 2^{n_x} - 1. \tag{31}$$

Therefore, by Theorem 2 and (31), every disjoint rectangle cover of C'_0 into rectangles with underlying partition (X_v, Z^1_j) contains at least $2^{n_x} - 1$ rectangles.
Summarizing, C'_0 has a disjoint rectangle cover of size at most $|C'_0|$ where each rectangle has underlying partition (X_v, Z^1_j), but every such rectangle cover contains at least $2^{n_x} - 1$ rectangles. Hence

$$|C_0| \geq |C'_0| \geq 2^{n_x} - 1 \geq 2^{n/5} - 1 = 2^{\Omega(n)},$$

and we are done (recall (29)). □

The second (and complementary) case is covered by the following claim.

CLAIM 3. *If for all $j \in [n]$ there exists $i \in [n]$ such that $x_i \in X_v$ and $z^1_{i,j} \in T_v$, then there exists $p \in [k]$ such that C_p has size $2^{\Omega(n/k)}$.*

PROOF OF CLAIM 3. Define a set S of pairs (i,j) as follows. For each $j \in [n]$ such that $y_j \in T \setminus T_v$, choose $i \in [n]$ such that $z^1_{i,j} \in T_v$, and add (i,j) to S. Note that

$$|S| = n - n_y. \tag{32}$$

For each $p = 1, \dots, k-1$, let $R_p \subseteq S$ be such that $(i,j) \in R_p$ iff $z^1_{i,j}, \dots, z^p_{i,j} \in T_v$ and $z^{p+1}_{i,j} \in T \setminus T_v$. Also, let

$$R_k = S \setminus \bigcup_{i=1}^{k-1} R_i.$$

Note that $R_1, \dots, R_k$ form a partition of S, so that

$$|R_1| + \cdots + |R_k| = |S|. \tag{33}$$

We show that

$$\sum_{p=1}^{k} |C_p| \geq k(2^{n/5k} - 1),$$

which implies that there exists $p \in [k]$ such that $|C_p| \geq 2^{n/5k} - 1$, and we are done.

Let $p \in [k-1]$. For all $(i,j) \in R_p$, it holds that $z^p_{i,j} \in T_v$ and $z^{p+1}_{i,j} \in T \setminus T_v$. Let $V^p = \{z^p_{i,j} : (i,j) \in R_p\}$ and $V^{p+1} = \{z^{p+1}_{i,j} : (i,j) \in R_p\}$. Write

$$C_p(Z^p, Z^{p+1}) = C_p(V^p, Z^p \setminus V^p, V^{p+1}, Z^{p+1} \setminus V^{p+1})$$

and let

$$C'_p(V^p, V^{p+1}) = C_p(V^p, \{0\}^{Z^p \setminus V^p}, V^{p+1}, \{0\}^{Z^{p+1} \setminus V^{p+1}}),$$

so that C'_p is a deterministic NNF structured by T of size $|C'_p| \leq |C_p|$ [28]. It follows from Theorem 1 that C'_p has a disjoint rectangle cover of size at most $|C'_p|$ where each rectangle has underlying partition (V^p, V^{p+1}).

Since $C_p \equiv H^p_{k,n}$, we have that

$$C'_p \equiv \bigvee_{(i,j) \in R_p} (z^p_{i,j} \wedge z^{p+1}_{i,j}),$$

and along the lines of Claim 2 we obtain

$$|C_p| \geq |C'_p| \geq 2^{|R_p|} - 1. \tag{34}$$

Similarly, we obtain

$$|C_k| \geq 2^{|R_k|} - 1. \tag{35}$$

Thus

$$\begin{aligned}
\sum_{p=1}^{k} |C_p| &\geq \sum_{p=1}^{k} (2^{|R_p|} - 1) && (34), (35)\\
&\geq \sum_{p=1}^{k} 2^{|R_p|} - k\\
&\geq k 2^{\sum_{p=1}^{k} |R_p|/k} - k\\
&= k 2^{|S|/k} - k && (33)\\
&\geq k 2^{n/5k} - k && (30), (32)
\end{aligned}$$

where the third inequality holds by plugging the convex function $f(r) = 2^r$ in Jensen's inequality $\sum_{p=1}^{k} f(r_p)/k \geq f(\sum_{p=1}^{k} r_p/k)$, which completes the proof. □

Claim 2 and Claim 3 imply the statement. □

5. CONCLUSION

We have related the circuit treewidth of a Boolean function with the width of its SDD implementation (and more generally its width in natural canonical classes of deterministic structured forms), and we have incorporated constant width SDDs and polynomial size SDDs in the panorama of query compilation for union of conjunctive queries with and without negations.

The comparison of Theorem 5 and [3, Theorem 4.6] reiterates the question about the relative succinctness of deterministic structured forms and SDDs [3, 4]. As Beame and Liew observe, a natural candidate function for an exponential separation is the *indirect access storage* (*ISA*) function, which is known to have large OBDDs but whose small deterministic structured forms deviate substantially from the SDD syntax [3, Section 6]. However, ISA has small SDD size,

PROPOSITION 3. [7] ISA *has SDD size* $O(n^{13/5})$*;*

which unfortunately leaves us with no candidates for a separation.

The canonical structured deterministic forms induced by factorized implicants, introduced in Section 3.2.1, deserve in our opinion both a direct investigation in the framework of the knowledge compilation map [15], and a thorough comparison with the data structures used in *factorized databases*, which are more than just reminiscent of structured deterministic forms [26].

The question remains whether bounded circuit treewidth lineages imply bounded OBDD width for UCQs with inequalities, as conjectured by Jha and Suciu [21].

Another intriguing conjecture is that SDDs with OR gates of bounded fanin are quasipolynomially simulated by OBDDs.[11] The containment of bounded width SDDs in polynomial size OBDDs, discussed in the introduction and obtained in Section 3, imply a polynomial simulation of bounded width SDDs, which have indeed bounded fanin ORs, by OBDDs.

6. ACKNOWLEDGMENTS

This research was supported by the FWF Austrian Science Fund (Parameterized Compilation, P26200).

7. REFERENCES

[1] A. Amarilli, P. Bourhis, and P. Senellart. Provenance Circuits for Trees and Treelike Instances. In *Proc. of ICALP 2015*, pp. 56–68. Springer, 2015.

[2] A. Amarilli, P. Bourhis, and P. Senellart. Tractable Lineages on Treelike Instances: Limits and Extensions. In *Proc. of PODS 2016*, pp. 355–370. ACM, 2016.

[3] P. Beame and V. Liew. New Limits for Knowledge Compilation and Applications to Exact Model Counting. In *Proc. of UAI 2015*, pp. 131–140. AUAI, 2015.

[4] S. Bova. SDDs are Exponentially More Succinct than OBDDs. In *Proc. of AAAI 2016*, pp. 929–935. AAAI, 2016.

[5] S. Bova, F. Capelli, S. Mengel, and F. Slivovsky. On Compiling CNFs into Structured Deterministic DNNFs. In *Proc. of SAT 2015*, pp. 199–214. Springer, 2015.

[11] Personal communication with Igor Razgon.

[6] S. Bova, F. Capelli, S. Mengel, and F. Slivovsky. Knowledge Compilation Meets Communication Complexity. In *Proc. of IJCAI 2016*, pp. 1008–1014. IJCAI/AAAI, 2016.

[7] S. Bova and S. Szeider. Circuit Treewidth, Sentential Decision, and Query Compilation. *CoRR*, abs/1701.04626, 2017.

[8] R. E. Bryant. Graph-Based Algorithms for Boolean Function Manipulation. *IEEE Trans. Computers*, 35(8):677–691, 1986.

[9] A. Choi and A. Darwiche. Dynamic Minimization of Sentential Decision Diagrams. In *Proc. of AAAI 2013*. AAAI, 2013.

[10] N. N. Dalvi and D. Suciu. The Dichotomy of Conjunctive Queries on Probabilistic Structures. In *Proc. of PODS 2007*, pp. 293–302. ACM, 2007.

[11] N. N. Dalvi and D. Suciu. Efficient Query Evaluation on Probabilistic Databases. *VLDB J.*, 16(4):523–544, 2007.

[12] A. Darwiche. Decomposable Negation Normal Form. *J. ACM*, 48(4):608–647, 2001.

[13] A. Darwiche. On the Tractable Counting of Theory Models and its Application to Truth Maintenance and Belief Revision. *Journal of Applied Non-Classical Logics*, 11(1-2):11–34, 2001.

[14] A. Darwiche. SDD: A New Canonical Representation of Propositional Knowledge Bases. In *Proc. of IJCAI 2011*, pp. 819–826. IJCAI/AAAI, 2011.

[15] A. Darwiche and P. Marquis. A Knowledge Compilation Map. *J. Artif. Intell. Res.*, 17:229–264, 2002.

[16] G. V. den Broeck and A. Darwiche. On the Role of Canonicity in Knowledge Compilation. In *Proc. of AAAI 2015*, pp. 1641–1648. AAAI, 2015.

[17] J. Flum and M. Grohe. *Parameterized Complexity Theory*. Springer, 2010.

[18] E. Grädel, Y. Gurevich, and C. Hirsch. The Complexity of Query Reliability. In *Proc. of PODS 1998*, pp. 227–234. ACM, 1998.

[19] T. J. Green, G. Karvounarakis, and V. Tannen. Provenance Semirings. In *Proc. of PODS 2007*, pp. 31–40. ACM, 2007.

[20] A. K. Jha and D. Suciu. Knowledge Compilation Meets Database Theory: Compiling Queries to Decision Diagrams. In *Proc. of ICDT 2011*, pp. 162–173. ACM, 2011.

[21] A. K. Jha and D. Suciu. On the Tractability of Query Compilation and Bounded Treewidth. In *Proc. of ICDT 2012*, pp. 249–261. ACM, 2012.

[22] A. K. Jha and D. Suciu. Knowledge Compilation Meets Database Theory: Compiling Queries to Decision Diagrams. *Theory Comput. Syst.*, 52(3):403–440, 2013.

[23] S. Jukna. *Boolean Function Complexity. Advances and Frontiers*. Springer, 2012.

[24] T. Kloks. *Treewidth: Computations and Approximations*. Springer, 1994.

[25] S. Mengel. Parameterized Compilation Lower Bounds for Restricted CNF-Formulas. In *Proc. of SAT 2016*, pp. 3–12. Springer, 2016.

[26] D. Olteanu. Factorized Databases: A Knowledge Compilation Perspective. *Proceedings of BeyondNP, AAAI 16 Workshop*, 2016.

[27] U. Oztok and A. Darwiche. A Top-Down Compiler for Sentential Decision Diagrams. In *Proc. of IJCAI 2015*, pp. 3141–3148. AAAI, 2015.

[28] K. Pipatsrisawat and A. Darwiche. New Compilation Languages Based on Structured Decomposability. In *Proc. of AAAI 2008*, pp. 517–522. AAAI, 2008.

[29] T. Pipatsrisawat and A. Darwiche. A Lower Bound on the Size of Decomposable Negation Normal Form. In *Proc. of AAAI 2010*. AAAI, 2010.

[30] I. Razgon. On OBDDs for CNFs of Bounded Treewidth. In *Proc. of KR 2014*. AAAI, 2014.

[31] I. Razgon. On the Read-Once Property of Branching Programs and CNFs of Bounded Treewidth. *Algorithmica*, 75(2):277–294, 2016.

[32] I. Razgon and J. Petke. Cliquewidth and Knowledge Compilation. In *Proc. of SAT 2013*, pp. 335–350. Springer, 2013.

[33] D. Seese. The Structure of Models of Decidable Monadic Theories of Graphs. *Ann. Pure Appl. Logic*, 53(2):169–195, 1991.

[34] D. Suciu, D. Olteanu, R. Christopher, and C. Koch. *Probabilistic Databases*. Morgan & Claypool Publishers, 2011.

[35] I. Wegener. *Branching Programs and Binary Decision Diagrams: Theory and Applications*. SIAM, 2000.

APPENDIX

Proof of the Jha-Suciu Lemma

PROOF OF LEMMA 1. Let C be a treewidth $k-1$ circuit computing the Boolean function $F(X)$. Let S be a *nice* tree decomposition of the gates of C, witnessing treewidth $k-1$; without loss of generality, the root of S is the empty bag, therefore each input gate of C (i.e., each variable in X) is forgotten exactly once in S.

We associate to S a vtree T for X as follows. Let W be a set of fresh variables in a bijective correspondence with the leaves of S. Label the leaves of S by pairwise distinct (dummy) variables in W. For every variable $x \in X$, append a fresh leaf labelled x to the node forgetting x in S. The resulting tree T is a vtree for $X \cup W \supseteq X$.

For every $v \in T$, let X_v denote the variables in X appearing in T_v (or equivalently, the variables in T_v that are not dummy variables). In light of (9), to show that

$$\mathsf{fw}(F, T) \leq 2^{(k+1)2^k}$$

it is sufficient to prove that $|\mathsf{factors}(F, X_v)|$ matches the bound for all $v \in T$.

If v is a leaf in T, then $X_v = \{x\}$ for some $x \in X$ and $|\mathsf{factors}(F, X_v)| \leq 2$, or v is labelled by some dummy variable in W, so that $X_v = \emptyset$ and $|\mathsf{factors}(F, X_v)| = 1$. Otherwise v is a bag B in S and in this case X_v contains the variables in X forgotten by nodes in the subtree of S rooted at v.

For a gate g in C, let $K(g) \subseteq B$ be the gates in B with a directed path to g in (the DAG underlying) C whose intermediate gates are not in B. Namely, $h \in K(g)$ iff $h \in B$ and there exists a directed path

$$h \stackrel{C}{\to} h_1 \stackrel{C}{\to} \cdots \stackrel{C}{\to} h_m \stackrel{C}{\to} g$$

in the DAG underlying C such that $\{h_1, \ldots, h_m\} \cap B = \emptyset$.

Let g be a gate in C. We freely identify C_g, the subcircuit of C rooted at g, with the Boolean function on X it computes.

CLAIM 4. *For every $g \in C$, it holds that*

$$|\mathsf{factors}(C_g, X_v)| \leq 2^{2^{|K(g)|}} \prod_{h \in K(g)} |\mathsf{factors}(C_h, X_v)|. \quad (36)$$

PROOF OF CLAIM 4. Let $Z = \{z_h : h \in K(g)\}$ be a set of fresh variables. Let C'_g denote the circuit obtained from C_g by transforming each gate $h \in K(g)$ into an input gate labelled by the variable $z_h \in Z$. We distinguish two cases depending on whether or not g is in B.

If $g \notin B$, then observe that $\mathsf{var}(C'_g) \subseteq X_v \cup Z$, or $\mathsf{var}(C'_g) \subseteq (X \setminus X_v) \cup Z$; otherwise, if C'_g uses variables in both X_v and $X \setminus X_v$ then, in the graph underlying C, there exists a path from X_v to $X \setminus X_v$ not intersecting B, contradicting the properties of S.

If $\mathsf{var}(C'_g) \subseteq X_v \cup Z$ then, for every $b : X_v \to \{0,1\}$, $C'_g(b)$ is a function of Z among at most

$$2^{2^{|Z|}} = 2^{2^{|K(g)|}}$$

possibilities. Otherwise, if $\mathsf{var}(C'_g) \subseteq (X \setminus X_v) \cup Z$, then every $b : X_v \to \{0,1\}$ yields the same function $C'_g(b) = C'_g$ of $(X \setminus X_v) \cup Z$. Since each variable $z_h \in Z$ in C'_g represents the subcircuit C_h of C for $h \in K(g)$, it follows that

$$|\mathsf{factors}(C_g, X_v)| \leq 2^{2^{|K(g)|}} \prod_{h \in K(g)} |\mathsf{factors}(C_h, X_v)|.$$

If $g \in B$, then each proper subcircuit of C'_g uses only variables in $X_v \cup Z$ or only variables in $(X \setminus X_v) \cup Z$; otherwise we obtain a contradiction as above. Let $G_1, \ldots, G_m$ and $H_1, \ldots, H_l$ be a bipartition of the immediate subcircuits of C'_g such that the G_i's only use variables in $X_v \cup Z$ and the H_i's only use variables in $(X \setminus X_v) \cup Z$.

If g is an $\wedge$-gate, then

$$C'_g \equiv (G_1 \wedge \cdots \wedge G_m) \wedge (H_1 \wedge \cdots \wedge H_l).$$

For every $b : X_v \to \{0,1\}$, $(G_1 \wedge \cdots \wedge G_m)(b)$ is a function G_b over Z; on the other hand, every $b : X_v \to \{0,1\}$ yields the same function H over $(X \setminus X_v) \cup Z$, namely $H_1 \wedge \cdots \wedge H_l$. Therefore, for all $b : X_v \to \{0,1\}$, $C'_g(b)$ is a function over $(X \setminus X_v) \cup Z$ of the form

$$G_b \wedge H,$$

where G_b is a function over Z, so that

$$|\{C'_g(b) : b \in \{0,1\}^{X_v}\}| \leq 2^{2^{|Z|}}.$$

Recalling that each variable $z_h \in Z$ in C'_g represents the subcircuit C_h of C for $h \in K(g)$, we have

$$|\mathsf{factors}(C_g, X_v)| \leq 2^{2^{|K(g)|}} \prod_{h \in K(g)} |\mathsf{factors}(C_h, X_v)|.$$

The cases where g is a $\vee$-gate or a $\neg$-gate are similar, and the claim is proved. □

For all $g \in C$, let $L(g) = (C_g \setminus \{g\}) \cap B$. By induction on $|L(g)| \geq 0$ we prove that for all $g \in B$ it holds that

$$|\mathsf{factors}(C_g, X_v)| \leq 2^{2^{|L(g)|}}. \quad (37)$$

For the base case, let $g \in B$ be such that $|L(g)| = 0$. Then

$$|\mathsf{factors}(C_g, X_v)| \leq 2^{2^0} \cdot 1 = 2^{2^{|L(g)|}},$$

where the first inequality holds by (36) as $K(g) = \emptyset$ in this case.

For the inductive case, let $g \in B$ be such that $|L(g)| \geq 1$. Then, resp. by (36) and the induction hypothesis as $|L(h)| < |L(g)|$ for all $h \in K(g)$,

$$\begin{aligned} |\mathsf{factors}(C_g, X_v)| &\leq 2^{2^{|K(g)|}} \prod_{h \in K(g)} |\mathsf{factors}(C_h, X_v)| \\ &\leq 2^{2^{|K(g)|}} \prod_{h \in K(g)} 2^{2^{|L(h)|}}. \end{aligned}$$

But

$$2^{2^{|K(g)|}} \prod_{h \in K(g)} 2^{2^{|L(h)|}} \leq 2^{2^{|K(g)| + \sum_{h \in K(g)} |L(h)|}} \leq 2^{2^{|L(g)|}}$$

where $|K(g)| + \sum_{h \in K(g)} |L(h)| \leq |L(g)|$ justifies the last inequality.

We now conclude the proof. Let g be the output gate of C, i.e., $C = C_g$. Then, justifying the first and second inequalities resp. by (36) and by (37), $K(g) \subseteq B$ and $|B| \leq k$,

$$\begin{aligned} |\mathsf{factors}(F, X_v)| &= |\mathsf{factors}(C_g, X_v)| \\ &\leq 2^{2^{|K(g)|}} \prod_{h \in K(g)} |\mathsf{factors}(C_h, X_v)| \\ &\leq 2^{2^k} \left(2^{2^k}\right)^k \\ &= 2^{(k+1)2^k}, \end{aligned}$$

and we are done. □

2-3 Cuckoo Filters for Faster Triangle Listing and Set Intersection

David Eppstein
Department of Computer Science
Univ. of California, Irvine
eppstein@uci.edu

Michael T. Goodrich
Department of Computer Science
Univ. of California, Irvine
goodrich@uci.edu

Michael Mitzenmacher
Department of Computer Science
Harvard Univ.
michaelm@eecs.harvard.edu

Manuel R. Torres
Department of Computer Science
Univ. of California, Irvine
mrtorres@uci.edu

ABSTRACT

We introduce new dynamic set intersection data structures, which we call ***2-3 cuckoo*** filters and hash tables. These structures differ from the standard cuckoo hash tables and cuckoo filters in that they choose two out of three locations to store each item, instead of one out of two, ensuring that any item in an intersection of two structures will have at least one common location in both structures. We demonstrate the utility of these structures by using them in improved algorithms for listing triangles and answering set intersection queries in internal or external memory. For a graph G of n vertices and m edges, our internal-memory triangle listing algorithm runs in $O(m\lceil(\alpha(G)\log w)/w\rceil + k)$ expected time, where $\alpha(G)$ is the arboricity of G, w is the number of bits in a machine word, and k is the number of output triangles. Our external-memory algorithm uses $O(\mathrm{sort}(n\,\alpha(G)) + \mathrm{sort}(m\lceil(\alpha(G)\log w)/w\rceil) + \mathrm{sort}(k))$ expected number of I/Os.

1. INTRODUCTION

Set intersection queries have a multitude of database applications. They are the "inner loop" computation for performing inner joins, and can be used to answer ***triangle listing*** queries for databases of graphs and networks, where we must report every triple of mutually-adjacent vertices [13, 46]. In this paper, we provide asymptotic improvements to set intersection and triangle listing queries, by taking advantage of the bit-level parallelism available in the ***practical RAM*** model [41] (which is also known as the ***word-RAM*** model [33]) or in the ***external-memory (EM)*** model [1,52]. We present a dynamic set representation that outperforms previous representations: it allows for updates in $O(1)$ expected time, and supports the output-sensitive intersection of two sets of size $O(n)$ in expected time $o(n) + O(k)$ in the practical RAM model, where k is the number of elements in the intersection, and with related efficiency in the EM model. Further, we apply this data structure to the triangle listing problem.

Our solutions exploit a novel combination of two powerful algorithmic techniques. The first of these two techniques is an interesting variant of an algorithmic paradigm known as the ***power of two choices***, which has previously been used for load balancing and data structures [6, 39, 43, 44]. In a nutshell, the main idea of the power of two choices paradigm is to place items in one of two randomly chosen places so as to improve space or time performance. This paradigm is used, for example, in ***cuckoo***[1] hashing [20, 31, 47]. The second technique we exploit is ***filtering***, which involves storing data in compressed form using hash functions to support fast set-query operations. A well-known, classic example of this paradigm is the Bloom filter [10, 18, 22]. Instead of Bloom filters, however, we modify a more recent filtering structure known as the ***cuckoo filter***, which improves on Bloom filters in its space usage, locality of reference, and ease of updating [17, 20].

In this paper, we generalize the power-of-two-choices paradigm to a ***two-out-of-three*** paradigm. We explore how this idea leads to useful variations of cuckoo filters and hash tables, which we call ***2-3 cuckoo*** filters and hash tables. We use these structures to design improved algorithms for dynamic set intersection, which can in turn be used for answering triangle listing queries faster than with previous approaches, in the practical RAM and EM models. As with previous works, we characterize our algorithms in terms of multiple parameters, including the following:

- n: the size of a set or the number of vertices in a graph (depending on the context).
- m: the number of edges in a given graph, G.
- k: the number of elements to be output, e.g., the number of elements in the intersection of two sets or the number of triangles (i.e., cycles of length three) in an undirected graph.

[1]This name comes from the reproductive behavior of the female common cuckoo, which lays an egg in the nest of another bird after pushing out the other bird's egg.

PODS '17, May 14-19, 2017, Chicago, IL, USA

ISBN 978-1-4503-4198-1/17/05...$15.00

DOI: http://dx.doi.org/10.1145/3034786.3056115

- $\alpha(G)$: the ***arboricity*** [12] of a graph G, i.e., the minimum number of forests that cover all its edges. This parameter is within a factor of 2 of a related parameter, the ***degeneracy*** $d(G)$ [37], which is the maximum over subgraphs of G of the minimum degree of the subgraph.
- w: the number of bits in a word of memory.
- M: the number of words in internal memory.
- B: the number of words in a block of memory that can be transferred in one I/O between internal and external memory.

For more on the external-memory model, see the seminal work of Aggarwal and Vitter [1] and survey of Vitter [52].

1.1 Related Work

Miltersen [41] introduced the ***practical RAM*** model in 1996. This model is like the standard RAM model in that it has a single processor that can access any memory word in constant time. It also allows constant-time bit-parallel operations [4, 50], such as shifts, bitwise Boolean operations, and most-significant-bit finding, that are included in modern programming languages such as C, C++, Java, Python, and T-SQL. Exploiting such operations can speed up algorithms for large-scale problems on conventional hardware and software, including solutions for sorting and searching [4, 21, 50, 53].

Bille *et al.* [8] present a data structure that can compute the intersection of t sets of total size n in expected time $O(\lceil n(\log^2 w)/w \rceil + kt + \log w)$, where k is the size of the output. Kopelowitz *et al.* [33] introduce a dynamic set intersection data structure and use it to list the triangles in a graph G in $O(m\lceil (\alpha(G) \log^2 w)/w + \log w \rceil + k)$ expected time. Both of these papers work in the practical RAM model. The lower-order $O(\log w)$ terms in their analysis come from their reliance on a sophisticated bit-parallel list-merging algorithm of Albers and Hagerup [2]. The data structure of Kopelowitz *et al.* supports item insertion and deletion in $O(\log w)$ expected time and supports pairwise set intersection queries of sets of size $O(n)$ in expected time $O(\lceil n(\log^2 w)/w \rceil + k + \log w)$. The triangle listing algorithm of Kopelowitz *et al.* improves an $O(m\,\alpha(G))$ time algorithm by Chiba and Nishizeki [13] for triangle listing. Ortmann and Brandes [46] show that almost every previous internal-memory triangle listing algorithm can be implemented to run in $O(m\,\alpha(G))$ worst-case optimal time for any non-output-sensitive algorithm, or slightly worse (see their paper for an extensive survey). Hence, although it does not appear to be very practical, the method of Kopelowitz *et al.* [33] has the best asymptotic expected running time of any triangle listing algorithm prior to our work. Alternatively, Björklund *et al.* [9] study triangle listing from an asymptotic worst-case perspective, but do not characterize their running times in terms of graph parameters such as arboricity or degeneracy.

Amossen and Pagh [3] introduce a data structure, the "batmap," using the same two-out-of-three placement strategy that we do. However, they do not combine it with the filtering techniques that are essential for our improved dynamic set intersection and triangle listing algorithms. Moreover, they do not combine 2-3 cuckoo hashing with a stash, as we do, which allows us to significantly boost success probabilities.

Hu *et al.* [27, 28] study the I/O complexity of triangle listing in the EM model. They present an algorithm using $O(m^2/(MB) + \text{scan}(k))$ I/Os to list all k triangles in a graph of m edges, where $\text{scan}(n)$ is the I/O complexity for scanning an array of n elements.[2] In PODS 2014, Pagh and Silvestri [48] study the I/O complexity of the related ***triangle enumeration*** problem, where, rather than outputting all triangles in a graph, one is interested instead in calling an internal emit function for each triangle, which could, for example, be used to compute an aggregation function on all triangles in a graph.[3] Their method uses $O(m^{3/2}/(M^{1/2}B))$ expected I/Os. In PODS 2015, Hu *et al.* [26] present a triangle enumeration algorithm that uses $O(m^{3/2}/(M^{1/2}B))$ I/Os in the worst case. They also survey other previous work on the I/O complexity of triangle listing (please see their paper for additional references) and they show that the triangle listing algorithm of Dementiev [16] can be implemented to use $O(\text{sort}(m) \cdot \alpha(G))$ I/Os, where $\text{sort}(n)$ is the I/O complexity for sorting n elements.[4] Our approach is complementary to this prior work in PODS focusing on the I/O complexity of the triangle enumeration problem, in that we focus on the triangle listing problem.

1.2 Our Results

We present new dynamic set intersection data structures based on cuckoo filtering and two-out-of-three hashing. Our structure uses both cuckoo hash tables, which store full items, and ***cuckoo filters*** [17,20], which instead store smaller fingerprints of the items. We use a "stash" to improve the success likelihood, and use parallel pairs of 2-3 cuckoo filters and hash tables to guide the rearrangement of fingerprints within the filter. Our data structures can maintain sets of size $O(n)$, support element insertions and deletions in $O(1)$ expected time, and perform set-intersection queries in $O(\lceil (n \log w)/w \rceil + k)$ expected time, where k is the number of output elements. This speeds up the set-intersection times for the data structure of Kopelowitz *et al.* [33] by a logarithmic factor. Our solution is also simpler.

As an application of our data structures, we solve the triangle listing problem for a graph G of n vertices and m edges in $O(m\lceil (\alpha(G) \log w)/w \rceil + k)$ expected time, where k is the number of triangles in G. This also improves upon the previous solution of Kopelowitz *et al.* [33] by a logarithmic factor. All of our algorithms are for the practical RAM model [41] and can be easily implemented using standard instructions used in modern programming languages, as we discuss in a section on experimental results.

Further, we show how to implement external-memory versions of cuckoo-filters and hash tables. We use these to solve triangle listing in external memory with an expected $O(\text{sort}(n\,\alpha(G)) + \text{sort}(m\lceil (\alpha(G) \log w)/w \rceil) + \text{sort}(k))$ number of I/Os. This improves previous external-memory solutions for triangle listing in sparse graphs with small internal memory in scenarios where the output is asymptotically less than its worst case. Our external-memory solution, therefore, is well suited for large naturally sparse graphs that typically arise in practice (e.g., see [19, 24]).

[2] $\text{scan}(n) = O(n/B)$.

[3] Note that the I/O complexity of triangle listing is always at least that for triangle enumeration.

[4] $\text{sort}(n) = \Theta((n/B) \log_{M/B}(n/B))$ [1].

2. 2-3 CUCKOO HASH-FILTERS

In this section, we describe our 2-3 cuckoo hashing data structures, explaining how they can be used to maintain sets of size $O(n)$ to support insertions, deletions, and set intersection queries in internal memory. In subsequent sections, we describe how to use these for set intersection and triangle listing queries and how to adapt them for external memory.

Suppose, then, we wish to maintain a collection of sets, $\mathcal{S} = \{S_1, S_2, \ldots, S_l\}$, such that each set is of size at most $O(n)$, taken from a universe such that each element can be stored in a single memory word (which itself could be a unique pointer to a larger data file). For each S_i, we construct the following (see Figure 1):

- A hash table T_i of size $O(n)$, using three random hash functions h_1, h_2, and h_3, which map elements of S_i to triples of distinct integers in the range $[0, n-1]$. (We assume that our hash functions are perfectly random for our theoretical results, although our experiments show realistic hash functions perform similarly. See [5, 15] for more on this issue.) Each element x in S_i is stored, if possible, in two of the three possible locations for x based on these hash functions. We refer to each T_i as a ***2-3 cuckoo hash table***. Each table, T_i, also has a stash cache [31], C_i, of size λ_i, where λ_i is constant w.h.p. C_i stores elements for which it was not possible to store properly in two distinct locations in T_i (e.g., due to collisions with other elements). We maintain each C_i as a sorted linked list or growable hash table of size $O(\lambda_i)$, so that it is possible to insert and delete elements into/from any C_i in $O(1)$ amortized time and to list the elements in any C_i in $O(\lambda_i)$ time.

- A table, F_i, having $O(n)$ cells, that parallels T_i, so that $F_i[j]$ stores a non-zero fingerprint digest, $f(x)$, for an element x, if and only if $T_i[j]$ stores a copy of x. The digest $f(x)$ is a non-zero random hash function comprising δ bits, where $\delta = \Theta(\log w)$ is a parameter whose value is set to achieve a good false positive rate (e.g., $\delta = 2 \log w$). The table F_i is called a ***2-3 cuckoo filter***, and it is stored in a packed format, so that we store $O(w/\log w)$ cells of F_i per memory word. In addition to the vector F_i, we store a bit-mask, M_i, that is the same size as F_i and has all 1s in the corresponding cell of each cell of F_i that is occupied. The total space (in words) needed for F_i and M_i is $O(\lceil n(\log w)/w \rceil)$.

We assume we can read and write individual cells of F_i and M_i in $O(1)$ time. These cells amount to subfields of words of $O(\log w)$ size, which can be read from or written to using standard bit-level operations, such as AND, OR, XOR, and shift, built into modern programming languages, like C, C++, Java, Python, and T-SQL. We omit the details. Any read and write operation takes $O(1)$ such operations; hence, we assume that reading and writing individual cells of F_i takes $O(1)$ time in the practical RAM model [41].

Let us next describe how to perform insertions and deletions in pairs of parallel cuckoo filters and hash tables. We begin with deletion, because it is the easiest.

2.1 Deletion

Suppose we are given an element x, to be deleted from a 2-3 cuckoo hash-filter structure for a set S_i. To perform

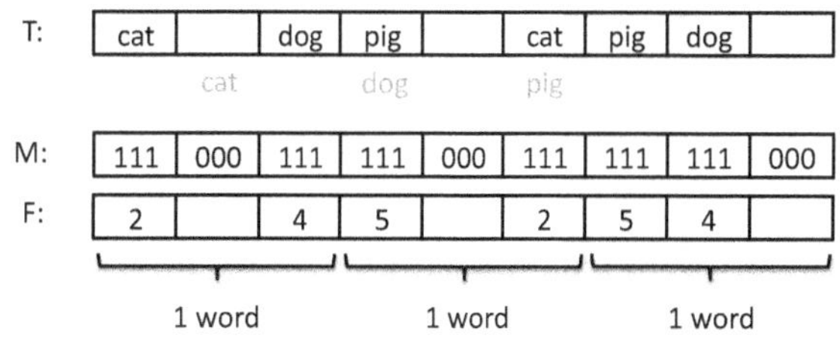

Figure 1: A simplified example of a parallel 2-3 cuckoo hash table, T, and filter, F, including the bit-mask, M. In this example, we are representing the set, $S = \{\text{cat}, \text{dog}, \text{pig}\}$, in an instance of the practical RAM model that can store three fingerprint values per word. In this case, the filters are defined so $f(\text{cat}) = 2$, $f(\text{dog}) = 4$, and $f(\text{pig}) = 5$. Note: every element is stored in two out of three locations; we are showing the third potential location for each element below its third location in grey. In this figure, we are not showing the stash cache, C, which in this simplified example would be empty. © Michael Goodrich.

this operation, we first search for x in the stash, C_i. This takes $O(\lambda_i)$ time, which is constant w.h.p. If $x \in C_i$, then we remove it from C_i and we are done, since in this case, x is not stored in the cells of T_i or F_i. Otherwise, if $x \notin C_i$, then we search for x in $T_i[h_1(x)]$, $T_i[h_2(x)]$, and $T_i[h_3(x)]$. We remove x from each of these cells in which it is stored. For each such index, a_x, because F_i is parallel to T_i, we then zero-out the cell $F_i[a_x]$, and we zero-out the corresponding bit-mask cell, $M_i[a_x]$, to show this cell as empty. This step takes $O(\lambda_i + 1)$ time in the practical RAM model [41].

2.2 Insertion

Suppose we are given an element, x, to be inserted into some set S_i. We first attempt to insert x into the 2-3 cuckoo table, T_i, performing a 2-3 cuckoo (two-out-of-three) insertion for x. Following [3], let us consider this as our inserting two instances of x into T_i via a one-out-of-three cuckoo insertion. Each element x has three possible locations, $T_i[h_1(x)]$, $T_i[h_2(x)]$, and $T_i[h_3(x)]$, where it may be stored. If one of these is empty, then we add x to it, completing that instance of inserting x. (If this is the second insertion for x, then we are completely done). If none of these three cells is empty, we choose one of them at random and add x to it, evicting its previous occupant y. We add y to a temporary buffer queue, Q. When we add x to cell $T_i[j]$ we zero out cell $F_i[j]$ and insert $f(x)$ into that cell, and we also perform an OR operation that sets the corresponding mask cell, $M_i[j]$, to all 1s, to show this cell as occupied.

We then process the buffer, Q, while it is non-empty. We take the next element, y, from Q. We then read the cells, $T_i[h_1(y)]$, $T_i[h_2(y)]$, and $T_i[h_3(y)]$. One of these cells may already store y; in this case, we consider the other two. If one of these two is empty, we add y to it, and we are done with y. If both of these cells are occupied, however, we choose one of them at random, evict its previous occupant z, and insert y into that cell. Then we add z to Q. Each time we add x to a cell $T_i[j]$ we zero-out the cell $F_i[j]$ and insert $f(x)$ into that cell (the mask cell $M_i[j]$ is already all 1s in this case). We repeat this processing of Q until we either succeed in emptying all the elements in Q or we reach a ***stopping condition***, which is defined to be the condition that we have spent more than L iterations processing Q during this insertion, where L is a threshold parameter set in the analysis. We then perform a deletion operation in T_i and F_i for each element in Q, and we add each such element to the stash, C_i. This step takes $O(L+1)$ steps in the practical RAM model (possibly amortized, if we are implementing C_i as a standard growable hash table).

As we show in Section 3, we can set L to be logarithmic in n and set a constant threshold $s > 0$ such that, with high probability throughout the process, $\lambda_i \leq s$. Thus, with high probability, our 2-3 cuckoo hash filters has stashes of constant size. This property provides a "safety net" for our data structures: with low probability, they could always fall back to a standard hash table or sorted linked list to store their sets, but with high probability, our structures will be much faster than this.

3. ANALYSIS

In this section, we give an analysis of 2-3 cuckoo hashing with a stash, which forms the theoretical foundation for our set intersection and triangle listing algorithms.

3.1 A Review of Standard Cuckoo Hashing

We now review useful characterizations and results for standard cuckoo hashing, which are good to know for when we generalize them to 2-3 cuckoo hashing.

We begin by recalling that in (standard) cuckoo hashing, as proposed by Pagh and Rodler [48], one inserts n items into a table T with $2(1+\epsilon)n$ buckets (for a fixed constant $\epsilon > 0$), via hash functions h_1 and h_2 whose values are always distinct. (Cuckoo hashing is often instead described using two separate tables for h_1 and h_2, avoiding the need for distinctness, but this makes little difference to its analysis.) Each bucket can store at most one item. To insert an item x, we place it in $T[h_1(x)]$ if that bucket is empty. Otherwise, we ***evict*** the item y in $T[h_1(x)]$, replace it with x, and attempt to insert y into its other cell $T[h_1(y)+h_2(y)-h_1(x)]$. If that location is free, then we are done. If not, we evict the item z in that location, attempt to insert z into its other cell, and so on. We can view the hash functions as defining a random multigraph with m vertices corresponding to the buckets in T, with each of the n items x yielding an edge $(h_1(x), h_2(x))$. The insertion procedure successfully places all n items if and only if each connected component in this ***cuckoo graph*** has at most one cycle. With high probability all connected components have at most cycle and no component is of size larger than $O(\log n)$. In what follows we allow the eviction process to occur up to $C \log n$ times for some constant C before declaring a failure in the placement.

There is, however, a small probability that an insertion cannot be done or takes longer time than expected. In such cases, rather than failing, unplaced items can be placed in a small additional memory, called a *stash* cache (e.g., similar to how we describe above for 2-3 cuckoo hash tables). The main previous result for stashing in standard cuckoo hash tables is the following theorem by Kirsch *et al.* [31].

THEOREM 1. *For any constant integer $s \geq 1$, for a sufficiently large constant C, the size S of the stash in a standard cuckoo hash table after all items have been inserted satisfies* $\Pr(S \geq s) = O(n^{-s})$.

In fact, the result of Theorem 1 can be extended somewhat beyond constant s with some care; for $s = O(\log \log n)$, for example, we have $\Pr(S \geq s) = \tilde{O}(n^{-s+1})$ [31]. Our main goal here is to extend such results on stashes to the setting of 2-3 cuckoo hashing.

3.2 Modeling 2-3 Cuckoo Hashing

We start our analysis of 2-3 cuckoo hashing by reviewing known results. In 2-3 cuckoo hashing, we insert n items into a table T via three hash functions h_1, h_2, and h_3 with distinct values. Each item is stored at two of the three locations given by its hash values, except that an item that cannot be stored successfully may be placed into a stash. In this setting, we require the table to have $6(1+\epsilon)n$ total bucket spaces, so that the final "load" of the hash table is less than $1/6$. (This contrasts with the standard cuckoo hash table, where it suffices that the final load is less than $1/2$.) It is known that a load strictly less than $1/6$ allows all items to be placed with high probability, but a load strictly greater than $1/6$ will fail to place all items with high probability. These results are discussed and proven by Amossen and Pagh [3] and Loh and Pagh [38] (see also the related combinatorial results in [30]). Indeed, they also show the following results for 2-3 cuckoo hashing, which are similar to the known results for standard cuckoo hashing:

- A natural insertion procedure succeeds in placing all items with high probability.
- This insertion procedure has constant expected time.
- With high probability the maximum insertion time is $O(\log n)$.

These results are derived by considering the corresponding *cuckoo hypergraph*, where each bucket is represented by a vertex and each item is represented by a hyperedge attached to the three vertices (buckets) that are the chosen locations for that item. The following subsection defines these hypergraphs more formally, including what it means for them to be acyclic or unicyclic (corresponding to trees or pseudotrees in ordinary graphs), and what their connected components are. The previous results show that the insertion procedure succeeds exactly when every component of this hypergraph is acyclic or unicyclic, and the time to insert an item is proportional to the size of its component. When n hyperedges are randomly selected for $6(1+\epsilon)n$ vertices, all hypergraph components are acyclic or unicyclic with high probability; all components are of size $O(\log n/\epsilon^2)$ with high probability; and the average size of the component containing any given vertex is constant.

Our result shows how to improve these results by using a stash, similar to how stashes improve the success probabilities for standard cuckoo hashing. For convenience, we prove a slightly easier and weaker version of the result that is sufficient for our purposes. Specifically, we prove the following:

THEOREM 2. *For any constant integer $s \geq 1$, for a sufficiently large constant C, the size S of the stash in a 2-3 cuckoo hash table after all items have been inserted satisfies* $\Pr(S \geq s) = \tilde{O}(n^{-s})$.

The $\tilde{O}$ notation allows for extra polylogarithmic factors. These do not appear to actually be necessary; we believe

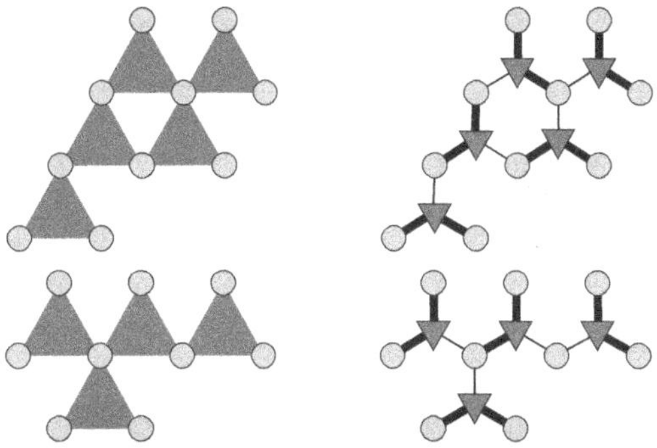

Figure 2: A 3-uniform hypergraph (left) with a unicyclic component (top) and an acyclic component (bottom), and a 2-assignment in its incidence graph (right, with the edges of the assignment shown using thick edges). © David Eppstein.

with more work the bound of Theorem 1 applies here as well. The proof, however, is simpler by allowing these factors, and the resulting bound is sufficient for our purposes.

Our proof follows the approach of Kirsch *et al.* [31], suitably modified for this situation, including a number of interesting changes that come from translating the previous results for cuckoo graphs to cuckoo hypergraphs.

3.3 Formalization of Acyclic Hypergraphs and Related Concepts

Before proving our result on stashes, this subsection provides a basis for thinking about acyclic hypergraphs and unicyclic hypergraphs more formally in this context, as there are various ways they can be defined.

A 3-uniform hypergraph $H = (V, T)$ consists of a set V of vertices and a set or multiset T of triples of vertices, the hyperedges of the hypergraph. It can be represented by a bipartite ***incidence graph*** (V, T, I), a graph that has $V \cup T$ as its vertices and the set of vertex-hyperedge incidences $I = \{(v, t) \mid v \in V, t \in T, v \in t\}$ as its edges. Even if the hypergraph has repeated pairs or triples among its vertices, the incidence graph is a simple graph. Following Berge [7], we call a hypergraph ***acyclic*** if its incidence graph is acyclic as an undirected graph. The ***connected components*** of a hypergraph are the subsets of vertices and hyperedges corresponding to connected components of the incidence graph. A hypergraph is ***connected*** if it has exactly one connected component. We define acyclicity of components in the same way as acyclicity of the whole hypergraph. We say that a connected component of the hypergraph is ***unicyclic*** if the corresponding connected component of the incidence graph is unicyclic: that is, that it has exactly one undirected cycle. For examples of these concepts, see Figure 2.

If a 3-uniform hypergraph is connected and acyclic, then its incidence graph must be a tree. Each hyperedge forms an interior vertex of degree three, so all leaves of the tree must be vertices of the hypergraph. We define a ***twig*** of this tree to be a hyperedge that is incident to exactly two leaves. If we remove the hyperedge and its two leaves, we are left with a smaller hypergraph that remains connected and acyclic.

LEMMA 1. *Every connected acyclic 3-uniform hypergraph with more than one hyperedge has at least two twigs.*

PROOF. Apply the standard result that every nontrivial tree has at least two leaves to the subtree of the incidence graph formed by removing all its leaves. □

It follows by induction (repeatedly removing one twig, with a one-edge hypergraph as base case) that a connected acyclic 3-uniform hypergraph with $n > 1$ vertices must have n odd and exactly $(n-1)/2$ hyperedges. Similarly, a connected unicyclic 3-uniform hypergraph must have an incidence graph in the form of a ***pseudotree***, a graph formed by adding one edge to a tree. We can modify this pseudotree into a tree by replacing this edge of the incidence graph by a different edge from the same hyperedge to a new vertex. It follows that, in a connected unicyclic 3-uniform hypergraph with n vertices, n must be even and there must be exactly $n/2$ hyperedges. If a connected 3-uniform hypergraph with n vertices is neither acyclic nor unicyclic, then any spanning tree of its incidence graph omits more than one edge, and it must have more than $n/2$ hyperedges.

We define a ***2-assignment*** of a 3-uniform hypergraph (V, T) to be a subset A of incidence graph edges such that each vertex of V is incident to at most one edge in A and each hyperedge in T is incident to exactly two edges in A. An example is shown by the thick edges on the right of Figure 2. We say that a 2-assignment A ***omits*** a vertex v if there is no edge in A incident to v.

LEMMA 2. *For any connected acyclic 3-uniform hypergraph (V, T), and any vertex $v \in V$, there is a 2-assignment of (V, T) that omits v.*

PROOF. By induction on the number n of vertices in (V, T). As a base case, the result is true when there is one vertex and no hyperedge, or when there are three vertices and one hyperedge. Otherwise, by Lemma 1 there exists a twig t neither of whose incident leaves is v. By induction, the hypergraph formed by removing this twig and its leaves has a 2-assignment A omitting v. This can be augmented to a 2-assignment of (V, T) by adding to A the two edges of the incidence graph that connect t to its two leaves. □

LEMMA 3. *Every connected unicyclic 3-uniform hypergraph (V, T) has a 2-assignment.*

PROOF. Decompose the incidence graph of (V, T) into a tree and an added edge (v, t) with $v \in V$ and $t \in T$. Let w be a new vertex, not in V, and consider the 3-uniform hypergraph (V', T') where $V = V \cup \{w\}$ and T' is formed by replacing t by a new triple with w in the place of v. Then (V', T') is a connected acyclic hypergraph and by the previous lemma it has a 2-assignment A that omits w. Then A also forms a valid 2-assignment for (V, T). □

LEMMA 4. *Any 3-uniform hypergraph has a 2-assignment if and only if each of its connected components is acyclic or unicyclic.*

PROOF. A 2-assignment can be found separately within each of the connected components, if it exists at all. By the previous two lemmas, it does exist within components that are acyclic or unicyclic. However, if a component with k vertices is neither acyclic nor unicyclic, then it has more than $k/2$ hyperedges, and any 2-assignment would necessarily include more than k edges of the incidence graph. This is incompatible with the requirement that a 2-assignment can only have one edge incident to each vertex. □

3.4 Stashes for 2-3 Cuckoo Hashing

We now prove Theorem 2 through a sequence of lemmas.

In analyzing the stash for standard cuckoo hashing, the approach of Kirsch *et al.* [31] begins by noting that the cyclomatic number of a graph G, denoted by $\gamma(G)$, is defined to be the smallest number of graph edges which should be removed from G so that there are no cycles. It is well known that if G is connected and has $v+k$ edges, then $\gamma(G)=k+1$. As explained by Kirsch *et al.* [31], if $c(G)$ is the number of cyclic components in G, the size of the stash equals $\gamma(G)-c(G)$.

For 2-3 cuckoo hashing, our corresponding "random graph" H consists not of random edges, but instead random triangles in a 3-uniform hypergraph. A placement in the 2-3 cuckoo hash table corresponds to a 2-assignment, or equivalently to a matching in a graph with a triangle for each hyperedge such that each triangle has a matched edge. As shown above, a 2-assignment can be found in a 3-uniform hypergraph if and only if each of its connected components is acyclic or unicyclic. Following the analysis for standard cuckoo hashing, we now let the cyclomatic number $\alpha(H)$ be the smallest number of triangles which should be removed from a 3-uniform hypergraph H in order to make H become acyclic. We have $\alpha(H)=\sum_h \alpha(h)$ where the sum is understood to be over components h of H, and the size of the stash required for 2-3 cuckoo hashing is $\alpha(H)-c(H)$, where $c(H)$ is the number of cyclic components in H. (Subtracting $c(H)$ accounts for the fact that we can tolerate components that are unicyclic instead of acyclic.)

To characterize the use of stashes in 2-3 cuckoo hashing, we follow the argument of Kirsch *et al.* [31] for stashes in standard cuckoo hashing, simplified somewhat so that we can extend the analysis to deal with random hypergraphs (albeit accordingly achieve slightly worse bounds, with additional polylogarithmic terms, due to this simplification). Also, following Kirsch *et al.*, we work in the setting where our table is split, so there are three subtables each with m edges, and the hash functions choose one vertex from each subtable. Again, this setting is essentially equivalent to requiring distinct hash values—as long as the load is less than 1/6, the 2-3 cuckoo table will function suitably. We begin with some useful lemmas, well known for the graph case, but that apply here as well.

LEMMA 5. *Consider a random triangle graph (3-uniform hypergraph) where the number of triangles (hyperedges) included is a Poisson random variable with mean λ. Conditioned on the number of triangles being at least n, the cyclomatic number of of the Poisson hypergraph stochastically dominates the cyclomatic number of a random hypergraph chosen with exactly n triangles.*

This follows readily from the fact that the cyclomatic number is stochastically increasing in the number of triangles, and after condtioning on the number of triangles in a random triangle graph with a Poisson distributed number of triangles, the resulting graph is a random triangle graph with that number of triangles. The lemma as stated is meant to hold for the case where triangles may be chosen more than once, but it also holds as well for the case where the random triangles chosen are required to be distinct.

LEMMA 6. *Let $\lambda=(1+\epsilon')n$ for some constant $\epsilon'>0$. Then with probability $e^{-\Omega(n)}$, the value of a Poisson random variable with mean λ is at least n.*

This is a simple application of Chernoff bounds.

We choose $\lambda=(1+\epsilon')n$ so that if the total number of cells in our 2-3 table is $3m=6(1+\epsilon)n$, we have $m(1-\epsilon')>2\lambda$. This ensures that with all but exponentially small probability the number of triangles is at least n but still less than $\lambda(1+\epsilon')<m/2$.

We now bound the probability that the required size of the stash, which we denote by S, is at least s as follows. Let H be a random triangle hypergraph chosen with a Poisson number of triangles as above. later. Let C_v be the component containing v in the randomly chosen hypergraph, and let E_v represent the set of edges in C_v. Let C be a constant to be determined Then

$$\begin{aligned}\Pr(S\geq s) \quad &\leq \quad \Pr(\max_v |E_v|>C\log n)+\\ &\qquad \Pr(\alpha(H)\geq s \mid \max_v |E_v|\leq C\log n)+e^{-\Omega(n)}.\end{aligned}$$

Here the first term corresponds to the probability that some component is too large, and the last term corresponds to the case where the random triangle hypergraph has fewer than n triangles or more than $\lambda(1+\epsilon)$ triangles.

We first bound the probability of a large component.

LEMMA 7. *There exists a constant $\beta\in(0,1)$ such that for any fixed vertex v and integer $k>0$,*

$$\Pr(|E_v|\geq k)\leq \beta^k.$$

PROOF. We picture doing a breadth first search starting from v. We overcount by assuming each additional edge we explore in the breadth first search provides two new vertices. Let $X_1, X_2, \ldots$ be independent binomial random variables $\mathrm{Bin}(m^2,(1+\epsilon')n/m^3)$. Then the number of new edges added to the component as we explore the ith vertex in the breadth first search is stochastically dominated by X_i (as there are at most m^2 possible choices for another pair of vertices, and each of the m^3 edges appears independently with probability at most $(1+\epsilon')n/m^3$), and the number of new vertices is stochastically dominated by $2X_i$. For there to be more than k edges in the component, as we explore the first $2k+1$ vertices, we must generate more than $k+1$ edges, or the breadth first search process will terminate. Hence,

$$\Pr(|E_v|\geq 2k+1)\leq \Pr\left(\sum_{i=1}^{2k+1} X_i\geq k+1\right),$$

which is equal to

$$\Pr\left(\mathrm{Bin}\left((2k+1)m^2,(1+\epsilon')n/m^3\right)\geq k+1\right).$$

We have $(2k+1)(1+\epsilon')n/m\leq (k+1)/(1+\gamma)$ for a constant γ; if $\gamma\leq 1$, then applying a standard Chernoff bounds the above probability by

$$e^{-(1+\gamma)^2(k+1)/3}\leq \beta^k,$$

for $\beta=e^{-(1+\gamma)^2/3}$. (For $\gamma>1$, we note that the bound for when $\gamma=1$ would hold as well.) □

Lemma 7 already implies that for any constant ζ, for a sufficiently large constant C, all components are at most $C\log n$ with probability at most $n^{-\zeta-1}$.

We next bound the probability of a single component having a large cyclomatic number.

LEMMA 8. *For every vertex v and $t, k \geq 1$, $k \leq m^{1/3}$,*

$$\Pr(\alpha(C_v) \geq a \mid |E_v| \leq k) \leq 2\left(\frac{126e^5k^3}{m}\right)^a,$$

PROOF. In what follows we begin by ignoring duplicate edges; we return to them at the end of the proof.

We reveal the edges in C_v following a breadth-first search starting at v. Let us assume that the number of edges in our breadth first search stays below k; otherwise, it will not matter how the process continues. Note that we may therefore assume at any point of our breadth first search there are at most $3k$ vertices in the component.

Equivalently, we can consider the process up through the first k edges. We let $K(u)$ be the number edges that, when we first connect to u, add to cyclomatic number of C_v. This can occur because u is involved with an edge that contains two vertices already found in the breadth first search, or because two (or more) distinct edges from vertices already in the component connect to u. We therefore see that $K(u)$ is stochastically dominated by the sum of two random variables. The first is a Poisson random variable $X_u = \mathrm{Po}(\lambda\binom{3k}{2}/m^3)$ for the first case. For the second case, consider a distribution $Y_u = \max \mathrm{Po}(3\lambda k/m^2) - 1, 0$; then the contribution to the cyclomatic number due to two (or more) distinct edges from vertices already in the component connecting to u is stochastically dominated by the distribution L_u.

As we go through at most $3k$ steps of our breadth first search, each step has $2m$ possible vertices that can be added. Let $X_1, X_2, \ldots, X_{6mk}$ and $Y_1, Y_2, \ldots, Y_{6mk}$ be independent copies of the random variables X_u and Y_u described above. Thus the contribution to the cyclomatic number of C_v is stochastically dominated by $\sum_{i=1}^{6mk} X_i + \sum_{i=1}^{6mk} Y_i$. The first summation corresponds to a Poisson random variable of mean less than $27k^3\lambda/m^2$. To bound $\sum_{i=1}^{6mk} Y_i$, note that the probability that any individual Y_i is greater than 0 is at most the mean squared, $9\lambda^2k^2/m^4$. Let Z be the number of non-zero Y_i in $\sum_{i=1}^{k} Y_i$. Then the probability,

$$\Pr(\sum_{i=1}^{6mk} Y_i \geq a)$$

is at most

$$\Pr(Z > a) + \sum_{\ell=1}^{a} \Pr(Z \geq \ell) \cdot \Pr(\sum_{i=1}^{6mk} Y_i \geq a \mid Z = \ell).$$

We note

$$\begin{aligned}\Pr(Z \geq \ell) &\leq \binom{mk}{\ell}\left(\frac{9\lambda^2k^2}{m^4}\right)^\ell \\ &\leq \left(\frac{mke}{\ell}\right)^\ell \left(\frac{9\lambda^2k^2}{m^4}\right)^\ell \\ &= \left(\frac{9e\lambda^2k^3}{m^3\ell}\right)^\ell.\end{aligned}$$

Also, let Y_i' be a (the) Poisson random variable $\mathrm{Po}(3\lambda k/m^2)$ associated with Y_i. Then a straightforward calculation gives:

$$\Pr(Y_i = j+1 \mid Y_i > 0) \leq \frac{2m^4}{\lambda^2k^2}\Pr(Y_i' = j+2).$$

We then have that

$$\Pr\left(\sum_{i=1}^{6mk} Y_i \geq a \mid Z = \ell\right)$$

is equal to

$$\begin{aligned}&\sum_{j_1,\ldots,j_\ell;\sum_{i=1}^{\ell} j_i \geq a-\ell} \prod_{i=1} \ell \Pr(Y_i = j_i + 1 \mid Y_i > 0) \\ \leq& \left(\frac{2m^4}{\lambda^2k^2}\right)^\ell \sum_{j_1,\ldots,j_\ell;\sum_{i=1}^{\ell} j_i \geq a-\ell} \prod_{i=1} \ell \Pr(Y_i' = j_i + 2) \\ \leq& \left(\frac{2m^4}{\lambda^2k^2}\right)^\ell \Pr\left(\sum_{i=1}^{\ell} Y_i' \geq a+\ell\right) \\ =& \left(\frac{2m^4}{\lambda^2k^2}\right)^\ell \Pr\left(\mathrm{Po}(3\lambda k\ell/m^2) \geq a+\ell\right) \\ \leq& \left(\frac{2m^4}{\lambda^2k^2}\right)^\ell \left(\frac{3ek\ell\lambda}{m^2(a+\ell)}\right)^{a+\ell} \\ =& \left(\frac{\lambda}{m^2}\right)^{a-\ell}\left(\frac{6e^3\ell}{k(a+\ell)}\right)^\ell \left(\frac{3ek\ell}{a+\ell}\right)^a.\end{aligned}$$

Here we use a standard tail bound on a Poisson random variable (Theorem 5.4 of [45]).

It follows from the above bounds that the probability

$$\Pr\left(\sum_{i=1}^{6mk} Y_i \geq a\right)$$

is at most

$$\begin{aligned}&\left(\tfrac{9e\lambda^2k^3}{m^3a}\right)^a + \textstyle\sum_{\ell=1}^{a}\left(\tfrac{9e\lambda^2k^3}{m^3\ell}\right)^\ell\left(\tfrac{\lambda}{m^2}\right)^{a-\ell}\left(\tfrac{6e^3\ell}{k(a+\ell)}\right)^\ell\left(\tfrac{3ek\ell}{a+\ell}\right)^a \\ \leq& \left(\tfrac{9e\lambda^2k^2}{m^3a}\right)^a + \left(\tfrac{3e\lambda k}{m^2}\right)^a \textstyle\sum_{\ell=1}^{a}\left(\tfrac{54e^4\lambda k^2}{m(a+\ell)}\right)^\ell\left(\tfrac{\ell}{(a+\ell)}\right)^\ell \\ \leq& \left(\tfrac{9e\lambda^2k^2}{m^3a}\right)^a + \left(\tfrac{3e\lambda k}{m^2}\right)^a\left(54e^4k^2\right)^a \\ \leq& \left(\tfrac{63e^5k^3}{m}\right)^a.\end{aligned}$$

Finally, we require $\Pr(\sum_{i=1}^{6mk} X_i + \sum_{i=1}^{6mk} Y_i \geq a)$. The first summation is a Poisson random variable wth mean less than $63e^5k^3/m$. Some additional calculations give

$$\Pr\left(\sum_{i=1}^{6mk} X_i + \sum_{i=1}^{6mk} Y_i \geq a\right) \leq \left(\frac{126e^5k^3}{m}\right)^a.$$

The above assumed no duplicate edges. The number of duplicate edges in total, however, is stochastically dominated by a binomial random variable $\mathrm{Bin}(n, (1+\epsilon')n/m^3)$. The probability of j duplicate edges is easily seen to be $O(n^{-j})$ and our additional factor of two in the lemma statement can account for the possiblity of duplicate edges. □

We note that in our analysis above, we are conditioning on the largest component size being at most logarithmic in n. The above shows that for any single vertex, the probability that it is in a component that requires putting an element in a stash, which corresponds to $\Pr(\sum_{i=1}^{6mk} X_i + \sum_{i=1}^{6mk} Y_i \geq 2)$, is $\tilde{O}(1/n^2)$. As there are $3m$ vertices total, we have shown the probability a stash is used at all is $\tilde{O}(1/n)$, and intuitively the path to show that the probability a stash of size s overflows is $\tilde{O}(n^{-s+1})$ follows readily.

We can formalize this by next bounding the probability of all components together having a large assignment number. We first note that the sum of the assignment numbers is bounded above by the sum of $3m$ independent copies of the random variable which gives the number of excess edges given to the assignment number for a component of a single vertex. (See, e.g., Lemma 2.10 of [31]; intuitively this follows from the fact that we need only count the excess once for each component, and as each component's vertices can be handled separately, the distinction of components reduces the possible excess for other vertices.) Let $V_i = \alpha(C_{v_i})$, the cyclomatic number of the ith vertes. Then for any constant s and for sufficiently large n, we have for some constants $c_1, c_2 > 0$,

$$
\begin{aligned}
& \Pr(\alpha(H) - c(H) \geq s) \\
\leq\ & \Pr\left(\sum_{i=1}^{6m} V_i \geq s + |\{i\ :\ V_i \geq 1\}|\right) \\
\leq\ & \sum_{\{j_1,\ldots,j_{6m}\ :\ \sum_{i=1}^{6m} j_i = s\}} \prod_{\{i\ :\ j_i \geq 1\}} \Pr(V_i \geq j_i + 1) \\
\leq\ & \sum_{\{j_1,\ldots,j_{6m}\ :\ \sum_{i=1}^{6m} j_i = s\}} \prod_{\{i\ :\ j_i \geq 1\}} c_1 n^{-j_i} (\log n)^{c_2} \\
\leq\ & \sum_{\{j_1,\ldots,j_{6m}\ :\ \sum_{i=1}^{6m} j_i = s\}} c_1^s n^{-s-|\{i\ :\ j_i \geq 1\}|} (\log n)^{sc_2} \\
\leq\ & \sum_{k=1}^{s} \binom{6m}{k} s^k c_1^s n^{-s-k} (\log n)^{sc_2} \\
=\ & \tilde{O}(n^{-s}).
\end{aligned}
$$

This gives the desired result on the stash size for a 2-3 cuckoo table, thereby proving Theorem 2.

4. SET INTERSECTION ALGORITHM

In this section, we describe our algorithm for performing set intersection queries.

Let S_i and S_j be two sets represented using our 2-3 cuckoo hash-filter pairs, as described above, and suppose we wish to answer a set-intersection query for S_i and S_j, to list out the elements in $S_i \cap S_j$.

We begin our set-intersection algorithm by computing a vector that identifies the matching non-empty cells in F_i and F_j. For example, we could compute the vector defined by the following bit-wise vector expression:

$$A = (M_i \text{ AND NOT } (F_i \text{ XOR } F_j)).$$

We view A as being a parallel vector to F_i and F_j. Note that a cell, $A[r]$, consists of δ bits and this cell is all 1s if and only if $F_i[r]$ stores a fingerprint digest for some element and $F_i[r] = F_j[r]$, since fingerprint digests are non-zero. Thus, we can create the list, L, of members of the common intersection of S_i and S_j, by visiting each word of A and storing to L the element in $T_i[r]$ corresponding to each cell, $A[r]$, that is all 1s, but doing so only after confirming that $T_i[r] = T_j[r]$. Doing the listing can be done in time $O(1 + k + t)$, where k is the number of elements in the intersection and t is the number of false positives, by using bit-level operations in the practical RAM model (e.g., see [17]). Then, the check to weed out false positives is a constant-time operation per element in the list, involving a lookup in the two cuckoo hash tables, to remove elements that map to the same locations and have the same fingerprint digests but are nevertheless different elements. That is, we remove from this list any elements, x and y, that happen to map to the same cell, r, in their respective 2-3 cuckoo hash tables and they also have the same fingerprint digest, that is, $f(x) = f(y)$. Note that by requiring $\delta > \log w$, we can guarantee that the probability of such false positives is at most $1/w$. Figure 3 illustrates a simplified example of this algorithm.

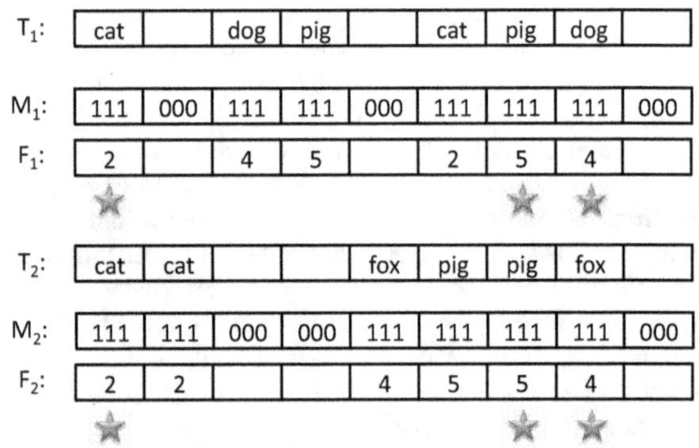

Figure 3: An example of parallel 2-3 cuckoo hash tables and filters for two sets. In this example, we are representing the set, S_1 = {cat, dog, pig}, and the set, S_2 = {cat, pig, fox}. The intersection algorithm does bit-parallel operations to find the matching non-zero cells in F_1 and F_2, and then checks the matches found using T_1 and T_2, to identify the set of intersecting items, {cat, pig}. In this case the filters are defined so $f(\text{cat}) = 2$, $f(\text{dog}) = 4$, $f(\text{pig}) = 5$, and $f(\text{fox}) = 4$. We show the matching filter locations with stars, including the false positive match for dog and fox, which would be culled when we check the potential matches against T_1 and T_2. In this figure, we are not showing the stash caches, C_1 and C_2, which in this simplified example would be empty. © Michael Goodrich.

Because we only include in L elements that are confirmed to belong to both S_i and S_j, we can guarantee that every member of L is a member of $S_i \cap S_j$. Nevertheless, we might still be missing some elements in this intersection. In particular, some elements might be stored in the stashes C_i and C_j, so we have additional work to do. For each x in C_i, we search for x at locations $T_j[h_1(x)]$ and $T_j[h_2(x)]$, and add x to L if it is found. Likewise, for each x in C_j, we perform a search for x at the locations $T_i[h_1(x)]$ and $T_i[h_2(x)]$, and add x to L if it is found. Finally, for each x in C_i, we do a search for x in C_j, adding it to L if found. If we let λ_i denote the size of C_i and if we let λ_j denote the size of C_j, then the time needed for this extra work to complete our algorithm is $O(\lambda_i + \lambda_j)$.

The running time of our entire algorithm for computing the intersection of S_i and S_j, therefore, is

$$O(n(\log w)/w + k + t + \lambda_i + \lambda_j),$$

where k is the size of the intersection (i.e., the output) and t is the number of false positives. As we have shown in the previous section, λ_i and λ_j are $O(1)$ with high probability. Thus, the expected running time for our set intersection algorithm is at most

$$O(\lceil n(\log w)/w \rceil + k + t).$$

In addition, by choosing $\delta > \log w$, we can bound the probability that two different elements have the same fingerprint value as being at most $1/2w$. Thus, $\mathbf{E}[t] \leq n/w$, since each element is stored in at most two places in a 2-3 cuckoo hash table. Therefore, we have the following.

THEOREM 3. *Let S_i and S_j be two sets of size $O(n)$, represented by using parallel 2-3 cuckoo filters and hash tables. Then we can compute the intersection $S_i \cap S_j$ in $O(\lceil n(\log w)/w \rceil + k)$ expected time, where k is the size of the intersection.*

5. TRIANGLE LISTING

In this section, we describe how to use 2-3 cuckoo filters to list the triangles in an undirected graph G.

We begin by computing a ***degeneracy ordering*** of G, an order of the vertices as $(v_1, \ldots, v_n)$ such that each vertex v_i has at most d edges to vertices v_j with $i < j$, for a suitable value d. The smallest possible d for such an ordering is the ***degeneracy*** [37] of G, which satisfies $d \leq 2\alpha(G)$. Such a degeneracy ordering can be found in time $O(n + m)$ by a simple greedy algorithm (e.g., see [40]) that repeatedly chooses the next vertex in the ordering to be the one with the fewest edges to other not-yet-selected vertices. Given this ordering, note that any triangle in G can be written as (v_i, v_j, v_l) with $i < j < l$.

For each node v_i in G, we construct a 2-3 cuckoo hash filter (including stash caches, as needed) for the set S_i of adjacent vertices v_j with $i < j$, by inserting these vertices into an initially-empty cuckoo hash-filter structure. Note that the size of each S_i is at most d. Because of this fact, in order for our algorithm to work in the desired expected time bounds, we need to be a little more careful in how we choose the sizes of our 2-3 cuckoo hash filters.

By Theorem 2, the probability that a set, S_i, stored in a two-three cuckoo hash table of size $n_i = \Omega(|S_i|)$, can be represented using a stash of size at most s, is $\tilde{O}(n_i^{-s})$. Thus, we can choose a stash threshold size, λ, depending on s, so that this probability is at most $1/n_i^2$. In order to obtain the time bounds we desire, however, we need this failure probability to be at most $1/2w$ (even if $|S_i|$ is small). For this reason, our algorithm depends on the value of d as follows:

- If $d \geq w/\log w$, then we use our 2-3 cuckoo hash-tables (with sorted or growable hash-table stash caches) to have size $\Theta(d)$ and we choose λ to be a sufficiently large constant so that the failure probability for any stash growing past λ size in our representation of any given set is at most $1/2w$.

- If $d < w/\log w$, then we use our 2-3 cuckoo hash-tables (with sorted or growable hash-table stash caches), with parameters chosen for tables of size $\Theta(w/\log w)$, even though the actual sets to be intersected will be at most d. This oversizing of our hash tables improves their success probability, and the choice of table size allows intersections to be performed in expected time $O(1 + k_{i,j})$, where $k_{i,j}$ is the number of elements in the intersection, when no failure occurs. To keep the failure probability less than $1/2w$, we again set $\lambda = O(1)$.

If the stash for any set grows to be over size λ, then we say that the 2-3 cuckoo hash filter for the set is in an ***overflow*** state. Nevertheless, we still use our cuckoo hash-filter representation to compute intersections with such sets in the overflow state—we just have to be careful to account for the time needed for such intersection computations.

Our triangle listing algorithm, then, considers each edge (v_i, v_j) in G and performs a set-intersection query for S_i and S_j, using the algorithm given in Section 4. The output of all these $O(m)$ queries will give us a listing of all the triangles in G. We characterize the performance for this algorithm in the following theorem, including the time needed to process sets in an overflow state.

THEOREM 4. *Given a connected graph G with n vertices, m edges, arboricity $\alpha(G)$, and k triangles, we can list all triangles in G in $O(m\lceil(\alpha(G)\log w)/w\rceil + k)$ expected time in the practical RAM model.*

PROOF. If $d < w/\log w$, our desired expected time bound is itself bounded by $O(m + k)$, since d is $\Theta(\alpha(G))$. Furthermore, we would get this same desired expected time bound even if $d = w/\log w$. Note that when $d < w/\log w$ we expand our 2-3 cuckoo hash filters to be of size $\Theta(w/\log w)$; hence, without loss of generality, let us assume for the remainder of the proof that $d \geq w/\log w$.

By the algorithm and analysis in Section 4, for any edge (i, j), representing two sets, S_i and S_j, we can report the intersection, $S_i \cap S_j$, in time

$$O(\lceil(\alpha(G)\log w)/w\rceil + k_{i,j} + t_{i,j} + \lambda_i + \lambda_j)$$

where $k_{i,j}$ is the number of elements in their common intersection, $t_{i,j}$ is the number of false positives found in the computation of their common intersection, and λ_i and λ_j are the respective sizes of the stashes for S_i and S_j. Summing these time bounds across all the edges of G, then, gives us a running time that is $O(m\lceil(\alpha(G)\log w)/w\rceil + k)$ plus time proportional to

$$\sum_{(i,j)\in G} t_{i,j} + \lambda_i + \lambda_j.$$

By a similar analysis as in Section 4, and the facts that, for each i, $|S_i| \leq 2\alpha(G)$, and we chose δ so that fingerprint collisions occur with probability at most $1/2w$,

$$\mathbf{E}[t_{i,j}] \leq \alpha(G)/w,$$

for any edge (i, j) in G. Thus, by the linearity of expectation, the expected value of $\sum_{(i,j)\in G} t_{i,j}$ is $O(m\lceil\alpha(G)/w\rceil)$. For any i, clearly we have that $\lambda_i \leq |S_i| \leq 2\alpha(G)$. In addition, by Theorem 2 and how we built our 2-3 cuckoo hash tables to have capacity at least $w/\log w$, so that the probability λ_i is more than a constant (i.e., the 2-3 cuckoo hash-filter for S_i is in an overflow state) is at most $1/2w$, $\mathbf{E}[\lambda_i]$ is $O(1+\alpha(G)/w)$. Thus, by the linearity of expectation, the expected value of $\sum_{(i,j)\in G} \lambda_i + \lambda_j$ is $O(m\lceil\alpha(G)/w\rceil)$. Therefore, by another application of the linearity of expectation, the expected time to list all the triangles in G is $O(m\lceil(\alpha(G)\log w)/w\rceil + k)$. □

6. EXPERIMENTS

Even though the contributions of this paper are primarily theoretical explorations of topics central to data management, we present some preliminary experimental results in this section. Our main goal in this preliminary empirical work is to test whether our algorithms are easy to implement and are competitive with the state of the art. Although we believe there are further optimizations available to improve the performance of our code, as we describe elsewhere in this section, our experiments provide evidence that 2-3 cuckoo hash filters are indeed simple and fast in practice.

For our experiments, we first present some simple empirical results that provide evidence of the practicality of 2-3 cuckoo hash filters and provide insight into the parameters involved in the definitions of 2-3 cuckoo hash filters. We then turn to empirical results for triangle listing, first considering performance on a collection of random graphs, and then on real-world networks. We compare our algorithm with the algorithm of Chiba and Nishizeki [13], using an implementation we constructed based on their description. This simple algorithm is known to have both good theoretical guarantees and good performance in practice, with asymptotic running times matching other existing triangle-listing algorithms (e.g., see Ortmann and Brandes [46]). We did not empirically compare our algorithm with the triangle-listing algorithm of Kopelowitz *et al.* [33], however, because, even though it provides an asymptotic improvement in theory, it appears too complicated for practice.

We ran our experiments on a machine with a 3.1 GHz Intel Core i7 CPU and 16 GB of RAM. Throughout the experiments, we set $w = 64$, as that is the native word-length on the machine used for the experiments. For our hash functions, we use random polynomial hash functions (e.g., see [25]) modulo an appropriate value to get values within the desired range. We set the number of bits used in the fingerprint digest, δ, to be 8 unless otherwise specified.

We begin by describing empirical results considering the average insertion time for a 2-3 cuckoo hash filter as we vary the size of the table. Recall the 2-3 cuckoo hash filter includes both the 2-3 cuckoo filter and the associated 2-3 cuckoo hash table. For our experiments we tested size values n = 1,000, 10,000, and 100,000. Recall that table sizes should be at least $6n$; hence, we vary the size of the table as cn for $c = 6.2, 6, 5, 6.8, 7.1, 7.4, 7.7, 8.0$. We chose to bound the number of iterations L that we perform during an insertion before putting an item in the stash at 200. Our experiment involved the insertion of a random permutation of the integers from 1 to n into a 2-3 cuckoo hash table. The average insertion time per element, averaging the results over 1,000 experiments, is presented in Figure 4. As might be expected, the insertion time decreases slightly as we increase the memory used, as then there are fewer collisions, but the decrease from larger table sizes is relatively small.

We also plot the average number of elements in the stashes at the end of the process against c in Figure 5, using the same setup as for the average insertion time. As can be seen, the average stash sizes are very small, as predicted by the theory in Section 3. Similarly in Figure 6, we plot the maximum number of elements in the stash over the 1,000 trials. The stash sizes are sufficiently small that it suggests that they will not be a performance issue for our triangle-listing algorithm. We have found that the stash sizes decrease significantly if we allow a larger maximum number of iterations, $L = 500$.

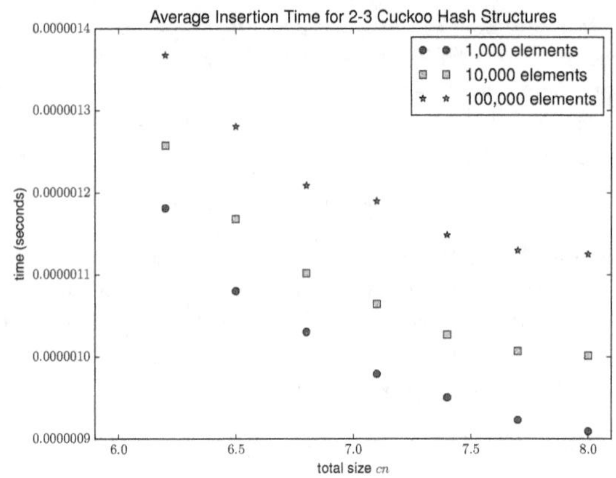

Figure 4: Wall-clock times for the average insertion time into a 2-3 cuckoo hash structure as a function of the size of the 2-3 cuckoo hash tables.

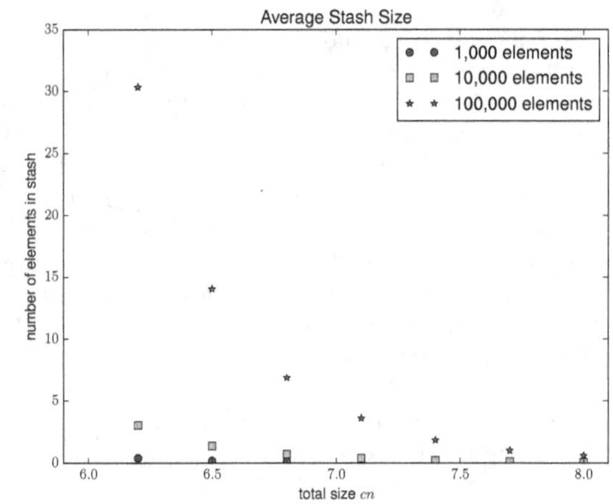

Figure 5: Average size of the stash cache as a function of the size of the 2-3 cuckoo hash tables.

The need for so many iterations to find an empty location suggests that the "random walk" approach is inefficient in this setting. A more efficient alternative approach may be to either use breadth first search on an insertion as in [36], or assign elements to locations in the hash tables in an offline rather than online fashion, using methods such as peeling [29] to quickly place many elements. We plan to explore these options in future implementations.

We now turn to examining our triangle-listing algorithm. To begin, we consider an artificial data set, namely, Erdős-Rényi random graphs with n vertices and edge probability $p = 1/\sqrt{n}$. The choice of p yields sparse enough graphs to make both our algorithm and Chiba and Nishizeki's algorithm significantly faster asymptotically than an algorithm using, say, a direct bitmap structure for its sets (which would be a natural alternative representation in the practical RAM model for sets that are dense relative to the universe size). In Figure 7, we present results for our algorithm for n = 100,000, which shows a typical behavior we see at other sizes. Each data point is the average of three runs. Recall that in this setting, our table size depends on the degeneracy, as

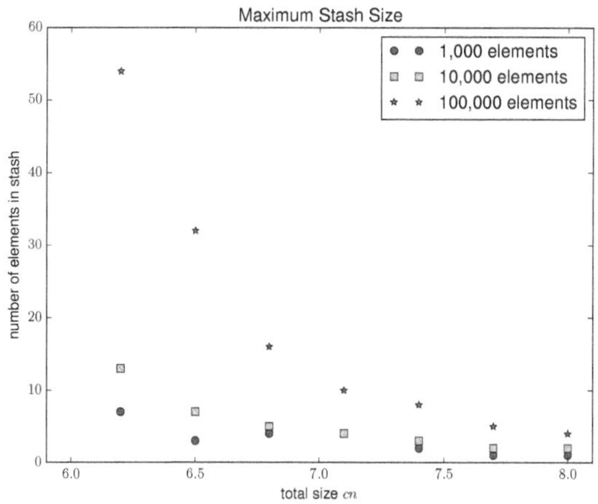

Figure 6: Maximum size of the stash cache as a function of the size of the 2-3 cuckoo hash tables T_i. The elements inserted are a random permutation of the integers starting from 1.

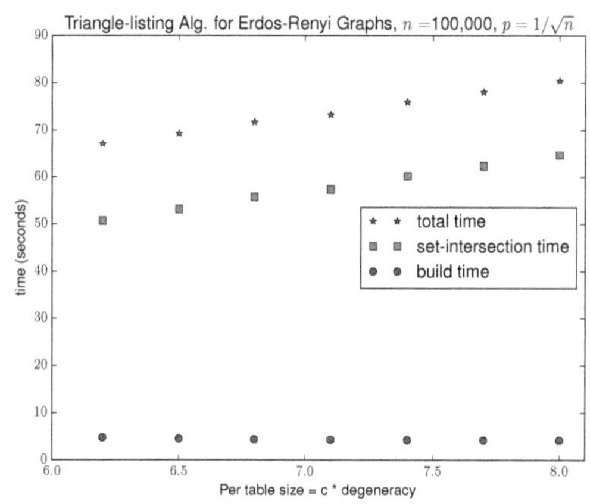

Figure 7: Wall-clock times for our triangle-listing algorithm as a function of the size of the 2-3 cuckoo hash tables for 100,000 node Erdős-Rényi random graphs with $p = 1/\sqrt{n}$.

that determines the maximum sized set of neighbors we must consider for each vertex. We vary the table size as c times the calculated degeneracy. We find that increasing the table size decreases the build time (as expected), but increases the set-intersection time at a faster rate. Thus we find that choosing a c close to 6 is best for our performance.

The time to find the set intersection appears significant, and we believe here our implementation can be improved. Indeed, we note that the set intersection algorithm we provide can naturally be parallelized, which would immediately improve performance.

In Figure 8, we compare the result of our algorithm against the algorithm of Chiba and Nishizeki [13], for Erdős-Rényi random graphs with $p = 1/\sqrt{n}$. The purpose of this exercise is not to claim that one algorithm is necessarily better than the other, but to show that there are families of graphs where our algorithm competes successfully against the state of the art. We use $c = 6.2$, $L = 200$, and $\delta = 8$ in this experiment. As can be seen, our algorithm outperforms the algorithm of Chiba and Nishizeki handily for this graph density, with the improvement increasing with the size of the graph.

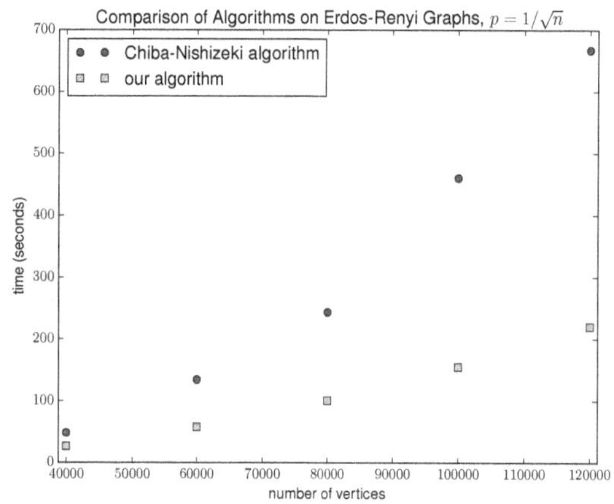

Figure 8: Comparing Chiba and Nishizeki's triangle-listing algorithm with our algorithm on Erdős-Rényi graphs.

We further compare Chiba and Nishizeki's algorithm with our algorithm by running both on a collection of real-world graphs, with the results in Table 1. The graphs used in the comparison are from various domains. We give a name to each graph in Table 1 and we describe each one of them here. "Amazon" is a snapshot of a co-purchasing network of Amazon [54]. "YouTube" is a snapshot of a subgraph of the social network of users on YouTube [42]. "Enron" represents the email communication network of the former Enron corporation [32]. "Astrophysics," "Condensed," and "High Energy" are the collaboration networks from the preprint server arXiv submitted to the astrophysics, condensed matter, and high energy physics categories, respectively [34]. "DBLP" is a collaboration network of the DBLP computer science bibliography [54]. "Skitter," "Oregon 1," and "Oregon 2" are all Internet autonomous systems networks [11, 51]. "Gowalla" and "Brightkite" are location-based online social networks [14]. "California," "Pennsylvania," and "Texas" are road networks [35]. The data for the graphs was gathered from the Stanford Network Analysis Project [49].

For each of the graphs in Table 1, we average the running times in seconds over 10 trials, as reported in the last two columns of the table. The constant c determines the size of the 2-3 cuckoo hash tables: each table is of size c times the calculated degeneracy. For each of the graphs in Table 1, we set $c = 6.2$, $\delta = 7$ and $L = 200$; we found $\delta = 7$ worked slightly better in these experiments. On the real-world graphs tested, our algorithm outperforms Chiba and Nishizeki's algorithm on 5 out of the 15 graphs. We believe that these real-world graphs are generally sparse and have heavy-tailed degree distributions, and these features may generally favor Chiba and Nishizeki's algorithm. In particular, since our tables are based on the graph degeneracy, a large maximum-to-average degree ratio appears less favorable to our algorithm; this explains in part why we outperform Chiba and Nishizeki's algorithm on Erdős-Rényi random graphs, where the vertex degrees are tightly concentrated around their expectation. We believe that additional optimizations may reduce the impact of this issue.

graph	# nodes	# edges	# triangles	degeneracy	our time (sec)	Chiba-Nishizeki time (sec)
Amazon	334,863	925,872	667,129	6	1.315	1.302
Astrophysics	18,772	198,080	1,351,441	56	0.555	0.463
Brightkite	58,228	214,078	494,728	52	0.610	0.413
California	1,965,206	2,766,607	120,676	3	4.165	4.571
Condensed	23,133	93,468	173,361	25	0.173	0.106
DBLP	317,080	1,049,866	2,224,385	113	5.484	1.697
Enron	36,692	183,831	727,044	43	0.452	0.444
Gowalla	196,591	950,327	2,273,138	51	2.735	2.948
High Energy	12,008	118,505	3,358,499	238	0.992	0.388
Oregon1	11,174	23,409	19,894	17	0.041	0.021
Oregon2	11,461	32,730	89,541	31	0.075	0.034
Pennsylvania	1,088,092	1,541,898	67,150	3	2.260	2.491
Skitter	1,696,415	11,095,298	28,769,868	111	51.048	43.282
Texas	1,379,917	1,921,660	82,869	3	2.857	3.154
YouTube	1,134,890	2,987,624	3,056,386	51	9.839	11.230

Table 1: Wall-clock times for our triangle-listing algorithm and Chiba and Nishizeki's algorithm for real-world graphs.

7. EXTERNAL-MEMORY ALGORITHM

In this section, we describe our external-memory algorithm for listing triangles in a large graph, G. Our method follows the general framework described above, but it batches constructions and searches so as to be more I/O efficient. Specifically, our external-memory algorithm is as follows:

1. Compute an approximate degeracy ordering for G, so that each vertex, v, has its edges oriented so that every vertex has $O(\alpha(G))$ outgoing edges. This can be done using $O(\text{sort}(n\,\alpha(G)))$ I/Os, by an algorithm due to Goodrich and Pszona [24].
2. Construct a data structure, $(H(v), F(v))$, of parallel 2-3 cuckoo hash tables and filters for the outgoing adjacencies for each vertex, v. This step amounts to doing two cuckoo insertions for each element (so as to implement the two-three cuckoo hashing paradigm). Goodrich and Mitzenmacher [23] show how to construct a cuckoo table of size N in external memory using $O(\text{sort}(N))$ I/Os. Thus, we can use this algorithm by making two copies of each element and repeating this construction in a batched fashion for all the nodes of G, which requires $O(\text{sort}(n\,\alpha(G)))$ I/Os.
3. For each edge, (u, v), perform an intersection operation for the sets represented by $F(u)$ and $F(v)$, without any culling of false positives. That is, we produce a list, P, of potential triangles, each of which is represented as triple, $(u, v, i_{u,v})$, where $i_{u,v}$ is the index in $F(u)$ and $F(v)$ for a matching fingerprint digest in these two cuckoo filters. We can do this by creating degree(v) copies of each $F(v)$ and sorting this list to bring together the filters that need to be merged and intersected. (Note that the EM model doesn't limit the kinds of operations that are performed in internal memory; hence, we can do these internal-memory computations using the practical-RAM algorithm described above.) Thus, this step takes $O(\text{sort}(m(\alpha(G)\log w)/w))$ I/Os.
4. Remove the false positives from P, depending on the size of $\alpha(G)$, as follows.
   (a) Sort the triples in P lexicographically by first and third coordinates.
   (b) Do a mergesort-type scan of P and the $H(u)$ tables, replacing each triple, $(u, v, i_{u,v})$, with $(u, v, z, i_{u,v})$, where z is the vertex listed at index $i_{u,v}$ of $H(u)$, i.e., at $H(u)[i_{u,v}]$.
   (c) Sort this new list, P, lexicographically by second and fourth coordinates.
   (d) Do a mergesort-type scan of P and the $H(u)$ tables, replacing each tuple, $(u, v, z, i_{u,v})$, with (u, v, z), if z is the vertex listed at index $i_{u,v}$ of $H(v)$, i.e., at $H(v)[i_{u,v}]$. Otherwise, discard this tuple.

   The total number of I/Os for performing this last step is $O(\text{sort}(n\,\alpha(G)) + \text{sort}(k+t))$, where t is the number of false positives. Recall that in our use of cuckoo filters, false positives occur with probability at most $1/w$; hence, the expected value of t is $O(m\,\alpha(G)/w)$. Thus, the expected number of I/Os for this last step is $O(\text{sort}(n\,\alpha(G)) + \text{sort}(m\,\lceil\alpha(G)/w\rceil) + \text{sort}(k))$.

Therefore, the expected number of I/Os for our entire algorithm is $O(\text{sort}(n\,\alpha(G)) + \text{sort}(m\lceil(\alpha(G)\log w)/w\rceil) + \text{sort}(k))$.

THEOREM 5. *Given a graph, G, with n vertices and m edges, one can list all the triangles in G using an expected number of I/Os in the external-memory (EM) model that is* $O(\text{sort}(n\,\alpha(G)) + \text{sort}(m\lceil(\alpha(G)\log w)/w\rceil) + \text{sort}(k))$.

8. CONCLUSION

We have studied new data structures based on 2-3 cuckoo hashing, and we showed how to use these data structures to derive improved algorithms for answering set intersection and triangle listing queries. Open problems include whether our techniques can be extended so as not to require each cuckoo hash-filter be of the same size and whether it is possible to intersect as many as t sets of total size n in expected time $O(\lceil n(\log w)/w\rceil + kt)$, where k is the output size.

Acknowledgments

This article reports on work supported by the DARPA under agreement no. AFRL FA8750-15-2-0092. The views expressed are those of the authors and do not reflect the official policy or position of the Department of Defense or the U.S. Government. This work was also supported in part from NSF grants CCF-1228639, CCF-1526631, CCF-1618301, CCF-1616248, CNS-1228598, CCF-1320231, CCF-1535795, and CCF-1563710.

9. REFERENCES

[1] A. Aggarwal and J. S. Vitter. The input/output complexity of sorting and related problems. *C. ACM* 31(9):1116–1127, 1988, doi:10.1145/48529.48535.

[2] S. Albers and T. Hagerup. Improved parallel integer sorting without concurrent writing. *Inf. & Comput.* 136(1):25–51, 1997, doi:10.1006/inco.1997.2632.

[3] R. R. Amossen and R. Pagh. A new data layout for set intersection on GPUs. *IEEE Int. Parallel Distributed Processing Symp. (IPDPS)*, pp. 698-708, 2011, doi:10.1109/IPDPS.2011.71.

[4] A. Andersson, P. B. Miltersen, and M. Thorup. Fusion trees can be implemented with AC^0 instructions only. *Theor. Comput. Sci.* 215(1-2):337–344, 1999, doi:10.1016/S0304-3975(98)00172-8.

[5] M. Aumüller, M. Dietzfelbinger, and P. Woelfel. Explicit and efficient hash families suffice for cuckoo hashing with a stash. *Algorithmica* 70(3):428–456, 2014.

[6] Y. Azar, A. Z. Broder, A. R. Karlin, and E. Upfal. Balanced allocations. *SIAM J. Comput.* 29(1):180–200, 1999, doi:10.1137/S0097539795288490.

[7] C. Berge. *Graphs and Hypergraphs.* North-Holland Mathematical Library 6. North-Holland, 2nd edition, 1976.

[8] P. Bille, A. Pagh, and R. Pagh. Fast evaluation of union-intersection expressions. *Int. Symp. Algorithms and Computation (ISAAC)*, pp. 739–750. Springer, LNCS 4835, 2007, doi:10.1007/978-3-540-77120-3_64.

[9] A. Björklund, R. Pagh, V. V. Williams, and U. Zwick. Listing triangles. *Int. Coll. Automata, Languages, and Programming (ICALP)*, pp. 223–234. Springer, LNCS 8572, 2014, doi:10.1007/978-3-662-43948-7_19.

[10] A. Broder and M. Mitzenmacher. Network applications of Bloom filters: A survey. *Internet Mathematics* 1(4):485–509, 2004, doi:10.1080/15427951.2004.10129096.

[11] Center for Applied Internet Data Analysis. Skitter. http://www.caida.org/tools/measurement/skitter/.

[12] G. Chartrand, H. V. Kronk, and C. E. Wall. The point-arboricity of a graph. *Israel J. Math.* 6(2):169–175, 1968, doi:10.1007/BF02760181.

[13] N. Chiba and T. Nishizeki. Arboricity and subgraph listing algorithms. *SIAM J. Comput.* 14(1):210–223, 1985, doi:10.1137/0214017.

[14] E. Cho, S. A. Myers, and J. Leskovec. Friendship and mobility: user movement in location-based social networks. *17th ACM SIGKDD Int. Conf. Knowledge Discovery and Data Mining*, pp. 1082–1090, 2011, doi:10.1145/2020408.2020579.

[15] K.-M. Chung, M. Mitzenmacher, and S. P. Vadhan. Why simple hash functions work: Exploiting the entropy in a data stream. *Theory OF Computing* 9:897–945, 2013.

[16] R. Dementiev. *Algorithm Engineering for Large Data Sets.* Ph.D. thesis, Saarland Univ., 2006.

[17] D. Eppstein. Cuckoo filter: Simplification and analysis. *15th Scand. Symp. and Worksh. Algorithm Theory (SWAT)*, pp. 8:1–8:12. Leibniz-Zentrum für Informatik, LIPIcs 53, 2016, doi:10.4230/LIPIcs.SWAT.2016.8.

[18] D. Eppstein and M. T. Goodrich. Straggler identification in round-trip data streams via Newton's identities and invertible Bloom filters. *IEEE Trans. Knowledge and Data Engineering* 23(2):297–306, 2011, doi:10.1109/TKDE.2010.132.

[19] D. Eppstein, M. Löffler, and D. Strash. Listing all maximal cliques in large sparse real-world graphs. *J. Exp. Algorithmics* 18:3.1–3.21, 2013, doi:10.1145/2543629.

[20] B. Fan, D. G. Andersen, M. Kaminsky, and M. D. Mitzenmacher. Cuckoo filter: Practically better than Bloom. *10th ACM Int. Conf. on Emerging Networking Experiments and Technologies (CoNEXT)*, pp. 75–88, 2014, doi:10.1145/2674005.2674994.

[21] M. L. Fredman and D. E. Willard. Surpassing the information theoretic bound with fusion trees. *J. Comput. Syst. Sci.* 47(3):424–436, 1993, doi:10.1016/0022-0000(93)90040-4.

[22] M. T. Goodrich and M. Mitzenmacher. Invertible Bloom lookup tables. *2011 49th Allerton Conference on Communication, Control, and Computing (Allerton)*, pp. 792–799, 2011, doi:10.1109/Allerton.2011.6120248.

[23] M. T. Goodrich and M. Mitzenmacher. Privacy-preserving access of outsourced data via oblivious RAM simulation. *38th Int. Colloq. Automata, Languages and Programming (ICALP)*, pp. 576–587, 2011, doi:10.1007/978-3-642-22012-8_46, http://dx.doi.org/10.1007/978-3-642-22012-8_46.

[24] M. T. Goodrich and P. Pszona. External-memory network analysis algorithms for naturally sparse graphs. *19th European Symp. on Algorithms (ESA)*, pp. 664–676. Springer, LNCS 6942, 2011, doi:10.1007/978-3-642-23719-5_56.

[25] M. T. Goodrich and R. Tamassia. *Algorithm design and applications.* Wiley Publishing, 2015.

[26] X. Hu, M. Qiao, and Y. Tao. Join dependency testing, Loomis-Whitney join, and triangle enumeration. *34th ACM Symp. on Principles of Database Systems (PODS)*, pp. 291–301, 2015, doi:10.1145/2745754.2745768.

[27] X. Hu, Y. Tao, and C.-W. Chung. Massive graph triangulation. *ACM SIGMOD Int. Conf. on Management of Data*, pp. 325–336, 2013, doi:10.1145/2463676.2463704.

[28] X. Hu, Y. Tao, and C.-W. Chung. I/O-efficient algorithms on triangle listing and counting. *ACM Trans. Database Syst.* 39(4):27:1–27:30, 2014, doi:10.1145/2691190.2691193.

[29] J. Jiang, M. Mitzenmacher, and J. Thaler. Parallel peeling algorithms. *Proceedings of the 26th ACM Symposium on Parallelism in Algorithms and Architectures*, pp. 319–330, 2014.

[30] M. Karoński and T. Łuczak. The phase transition in a random hypergraph. *J. Computational and Applied Mathematics* 142(1):125–135, 2002.

[31] A. Kirsch, M. Mitzenmacher, and U. Wieder. More robust hashing: Cuckoo hashing with a stash. *SIAM J. Comput.* 39(4):1543–1561, 2010, doi:10.1137/080728743, MR2580539.

[32] B. Klimt and Y. Yang. Introducing the enron corpus. *1st Conf. Email and Anti-Spam (CEAS)*, 2004, http://www.ceas.cc/papers-2004/168.pdf.

[33] T. Kopelowitz, S. Pettie, and E. Porat. Dynamic set intersection. *14th Symp. on Algorithms and Data Structures (SODA)*, pp. 470–481, 2015,

doi:10.1007/978-3-319-21840-3_39.

[34] J. Leskovec, J. Kleinberg, and C. Faloutsos. Graph evolution: Densification and shrinking diameters. *ACM Trans. Knowledge Discovery from Data* 1(1):2, 2007, doi:10.1145/1217299.1217301.

[35] J. Leskovec, K. J. Lang, A. Dasgupta, and M. W. Mahoney. Community structure in large networks: Natural cluster sizes and the absence of large well-defined clusters. *Internet Mathematics* 6(1):29–123, 2009, doi:10.1080/15427951.2009.10129177.

[36] X. Li, D. G. Andersen, M. Kaminsky, and M. J. Freedman. Algorithmic improvements for fast concurrent cuckoo hashing. *Proceedings of the Ninth European Conference on Computer Systems*, p. 27, 2014.

[37] D. R. Lick and A. T. White. k-degenerate graphs. *Canad. J. Math.* 22:1082–1096, 1970, doi:10.4153/CJM-1970-125-1, MR0266812.

[38] P.-S. Loh and R. Pagh. Thresholds for extreme orientability. *Algorithmica* 69(3):522–539, 2014, doi:10.1007/s00453-013-9749-4, MR3201231.

[39] S. Lumetta and M. Mitzenmacher. Using the power of two choices to improve Bloom filters. *Internet Mathematics* 4(1):17–33, 2007, doi:10.1080/15427951.2007.10129136.

[40] D. W. Matula and L. L. Beck. Smallest-last ordering and clustering and graph coloring algorithms. *J. ACM* 30(3):417–427, 1983, doi:10.1145/2402.322385, MR0709826.

[41] P. B. Miltersen. Lower bounds for static dictionaries on RAMs with bit operations but no multiplication. *23rd Int. Colloq. on Automata, Languages and Programming (ICALP)*, pp. 442–453. Springer, LNCS 1099, 1996, doi:10.1007/3-540-61440-0_149.

[42] A. Mislove, M. Marcon, K. P. Gummadi, P. Druschel, and B. Bhattacharjee. Measurement and analysis of online social networks. *5th ACM/Usenix Internet Measurement Conference (IMC'07)*, pp. 29–42, 2007, doi:10.1145/1298306.1298311.

[43] M. Mitzenmacher. The power of two choices in randomized load balancing. *IEEE Trans. Parallel and Distributed Systems* 12(10):1094–1104, 2001, doi:10.1109/71.963420.

[44] M. Mitzenmacher, A. W. Richa, and R. Sitaraman. The power of two random choices: A survey of techniques and results. *Handbook of Randomized Computing*, vol. 1, pp. 255–312, 2001.

[45] M. Mitzenmacher and E. Upfal. *Probability and computing: Randomized algorithms and probabilistic analysis*. Cambridge University Press, 2005.

[46] M. Ortmann and U. Brandes. Triangle listing algorithms: Back from the diversion. *ACM-SIAM Works. Algorithm Engineering & Experiments (ALENEX)*, pp. 1–8, 2014.

[47] R. Pagh and F. F. Rodler. Cuckoo hashing. *J. Algorithms* 51(2):122–144, 2004, doi:10.1016/j.jalgor.2003.12.002, MR2050140.

[48] R. Pagh and F. Silvestri. The input/output complexity of triangle enumeration. *33rd ACM Symp. on Principles of Database Systems (PODS)*, pp. 224–233, 2014, doi:10.1145/2594538.2594552.

[49] Stanford University. Stanford network analysis project. https://snap.stanford.edu/data/index.html.

[50] M. Thorup. On AC^0 implementations of fusion trees and atomic heaps. *14th ACM-SIAM Symp. on Discrete Algorithms (SODA)*, pp. 699–707, 2003, http://dl.acm.org/citation.cfm?id=644108.644221.

[51] University of Oregon. University of Oregon route views project. http://www.routeviews.org/.

[52] J. S. Vitter. Algorithms and data structures for external memory. *Found. Trends Theor. Comput. Sci.* 2(4):305–474, 2008, doi:10.1561/0400000014.

[53] D. E. Willard. Examining computational geometry, Van Emde Boas trees, and hashing from the perspective of the fusion tree. *SIAM J. Comput.* 29(3):1030–1049, 2000, doi:10.1137/S0097539797322425.

[54] J. Yang and J. Leskovec. Defining and evaluating network communities based on ground-truth. *Knowledge and Information Systems* 42(1):181–213, 2015, doi:10.1007/s10115-013-0693-z, arXiv:1205.6233.

On Asymptotic Cost of Triangle Listing in Random Graphs

Di Xiao, Yi Cui, Daren B.H. Cline, and Dmitri Loguinov
Texas A&M University, College Station, TX 77843 USA
{di, yicui, dmitri}@cse.tamu.edu, dcline@stat.tamu.edu

ABSTRACT

Triangle listing has been a long-standing problem, with many heuristics, bounds, and experimental results, but not much asymptotically accurate complexity analysis. To address this issue, we introduce a novel stochastic framework, based on Glivenko-Cantelli results for functions of order statistics, that allows modeling cost of in-memory triangle enumeration in families of random graphs. Unlike prior work that usually studies the $O(.)$ notation, we derive the exact limits of CPU complexity of all vertex/edge iterators under arbitrary acyclic orientations as graph size $n \to \infty$. These results are obtained in simple closed form as functions of the degree distribution. This allows us to establish optimal orientations for all studied algorithms, compare them to each other, and discover the best technique within each class.

1. INTRODUCTION

With an ever increasing flood of data, it is no longer sufficient just to process input correctly; instead, the underlying algorithms must exhibit scalability and high performance when operating on enormous datasets. This becomes quite evident in *graph mining*, which aims to discover interesting patterns within the connectivity network of participating agents. One specific problem that has recently gained attention [3], [14], [18], [22], [25] is enumeration of small subgraphs whose occurrence in nature is much more frequent than in classical random graphs [5], [19].

The most widely considered subgraphs are triangles, which have applications in numerous areas – databases, computer graphics, information retrieval, graph theory, algorithm complexity, and bioinformatics [4], [6], [7], [10], [16], [20], [24], [31], [37], [38], [40], [43]. Triangle listing has a four-decade history [23]; however, even for in-memory operation, this problem remains poorly understood, both mathematically and computationally. Open issues include how to accurately model the overhead, optimally arrange the nodes, select the best neighbor-traversal pattern, and minimize the runtime. Our goal in this paper is to shed light on these questions.

PODS'17, May 14-19, 2017, Chicago, IL, USA

DOI: http://dx.doi.org/10.1145/3034786.3034790

1.1 Deterministic Graphs

Assume $G = (V, E)$ is a simple undirected graph with n nodes and m edges. Triangle listing involves a large number of comparisons during verification of edge existence. Expressing this complexity as a function of n and/or m has captivated the community for a long time [13], [28].

Exhaustively checking all 3-node subsets is the most obvious solution, but its $\approx n^3/6$ overhead is far from optimal unless G is complete. The first widely known algorithm with $O(m^{1.5})$ cost is [23]; however, it requires n^2 RAM to store the adjacency matrix, certainly an impossibility for large graphs. An improvement to $O(m)$ space is [13], which visits its nodes in descending order of degree and removes them from the graph. The best result about its CPU complexity is $O(\delta m)$, where δ is the *arboricity* of G, i.e., minimum number of edge-disjoint spanning forests into which G can be decomposed. Unfortunately, δ is an elusive quantity, only known to be $O(1)$ for trees and $O(\sqrt{m})$ otherwise.

In subsequent literature, two competing algorithms emerged – *vertex iterator* and *edge iterator* – which we review in the next section. Without enforcing order among the nodes in each triangle, these methods examine $\Theta(\sum_{i=1}^{n} d_i^2)$ candidate edges, where d_i is the degree of node i. Following [2], the majority of subsequent implementations run node/edge iterators after performing some type of acyclic orientation on G, which is a technique that assigns direction to each edge and ensures that no cycles are present in the resulting structure. Experimentally, it was observed that certain orientations reduced the runtime; however, their usage did not lead to any improvement to the asymptotic bound $O(\delta m) = O(m^{1.5})$ [2], [28].

Each acyclic orientation on G can be viewed as some permutation θ_n on V, where an undirected edge (i, j) becomes $i \to j$ if and only if $\theta_n(i) > \theta_n(j)$. After the shuffle, let the out-degree of the node in position i be $X_i(\theta_n)$ and its total degree be $d_i(\theta_n)$. Intuitively, orientations reduce overhead because they replace second moments of d_i with those of $X_i(\theta_n)$, $d_i(\theta_n) - X_i(\theta_n)$, or some combination thereof. Since the directed degree can be made significantly smaller, the resulting cost is orders of magnitude better.

In general, per-node complexity of triangle enumeration can be expressed using

$$c_n(\mathcal{M}, \theta_n) = \frac{1}{n} \sum_{i=1}^{n} f(X_i(\theta_n), d_i(\theta_n)), \qquad (1)$$

where f is some non-linear function that depends on the listing method $\mathcal{M}$. The main challenge with directly minimizing (1) is the likelihood that building such permutations is NP-hard. This intuition comes from the relationship between acyclic orientations and graph-coloring problems [26]. While optimization of (1) has not been considered before, there exist so-called *degenerate* orientations that minimize the largest out-degree, i.e., $\min_{\theta_n} \max_i X_i(\theta_n)$. This can be done in $O(m)$ time [2], [29]; however, compared to simpler strategies, the negligible improvement in cost often fails to justify the extra computation [32], [33].

As a result, attaining the lowest sum in (1) for a given deterministic graph may be a moot objective. Instead, more insight can be gleaned from the analysis of random graphs, which is our next topic.

1.2 Stochastic Graphs

Assume $F(x)$ is a CDF on integers in $[1, \infty)$, function $t_n \to \infty$ is monotonically increasing, and $F_n(x) = F(x)/F(t_n)$ is the original distribution truncated to the range $[1, t_n]$. Now suppose $\mathbf{D}_n = (D_{n1}, \ldots, D_{nn})$ is an iid (independent and identically distributed) sequence drawn from $F_n(x)$, which we assume is graphic with probability $1 - o(1)$, or can be made such by removal of one edge. This allows construction of a random graph $G_n = (V_n, E_n)$ that realizes $\mathbf{D}_n$. Since (1) is now a random variable, performance analysis focuses on its expectation over all G_n, which we write as $E[c_n(\mathcal{M}, \theta_n)|\mathbf{D}_n]$.

Let $D_n \sim F_n(x)$ be a random variable with the same distribution as the degree in G_n. Early results [28] with Pareto $F(x) = 1 - (1 + \lfloor x \rfloor/\beta)^{-\alpha}$ typically bound the expected cost using a growing function of n. Recent work [9] obtains tighter bounds by focusing on a particular version of vertex iterator, which we call T_1, and using the descending-degree orientation θ_D. Assuming $t_n = \sqrt{n}$, they derive that $E[c_n(T_1, \theta_D)|\mathbf{D}_n]$ converges as $n \to \infty$ to

$$\frac{E[(Z_1^2 - Z_1)Z_2Z_3\mathbf{1}_{\min(Z_2,Z_3)>Z_1}]}{2E^2[D]}, \tag{2}$$

where $D, Z_1, Z_2, Z_3 \sim F(x)$ are iid variables and $\mathbf{1}_A$ is an indicator variable of event A. While useful in general, these results are limited to a single method T_1 and one specific permutation θ_D. Due to the complexity of derivation in [9], it is unclear if the same theoretical techniques can be extended into more general scenarios.

As the field stands today, it remains unknown which orientations are fundamentally better than others, under what conditions these advantages hold, whether orientations change the asymptotics of complexity or just the constants inside $O(.)$, and how the degree distribution impacts the overhead of alternative methods. We address these questions next.

1.3 Technical Results

To understand the overhead of triangle listing, our first contribution is to dissect the various ways that vertex and edge iterators can be executed in an acyclic digraph. We find that there are a total of 18 different neighbor-search patterns, but only four of them – which we call T_1, T_2, E_1, and E_4 – are non-isomorphic when considering CPU complexity. The former two are vertex iterators, while the latter are scanning edge iterators. We discuss how to efficiently implement them and outline a three-step algorithmic framework that does exactly that.

Conditioning on the degree sequence $\mathbf{D}_n$, our second contribution is to model $E[X_i(\theta_n)|\mathbf{D}_n]$ and introduce a family of asymptotically accurate approximations that admit simple analysis of cost. We show that under certain constraints on the maximum degree and for sufficiently large n all methods have expected overhead in the form of

$$E[c_n(\mathcal{M}, \theta_n)|\mathbf{D}_n] \approx \frac{1}{n}\sum_{i=1}^{n} g(d_i(\theta_n))h(q_i(\theta_n)), \tag{3}$$

where $g(x) = x^2 - x$, $q_i(\theta_n) = \sum_{j=1}^{i-1} d_j(\theta_n)/\sum_{k=1}^{n} d_k$ and h is a function that depends on $\mathcal{M}$.

Our third contribution is to analyze convergence of (3) using Glivenko-Cantelli results for functions of order statistics [39], [44] and obtain closed-form limits for all four methods under both ascending/descending-degree permutations. For example, vertex iterator T_1 under θ_D converges to

$$\lim_{n\to\infty} E[c_n(T_1, \theta_D)|\mathbf{D}_n] = \frac{E[g(D)(1 - J(D))^2]}{2}, \tag{4}$$

where $D \sim F(x)$ and $J(x) = 1/E[D]\int_0^x ydF(y)$ is the spread distribution from renewal theory. The result in (4) is finite iff $\alpha > 4/3$, which agrees with the conclusion of [9], [12]. While (2) captures the same limit, our derivation and result are both much simpler.

To understand the effect of θ_n, our fourth contribution is to develop a novel framework for modeling the limit of permutations. To this end, suppose $u, v \in [0, 1]$ are constants. We define sequence $\{\theta_n\}_{n=1}^{\infty}$ to be *admissible* if $P(\theta_n(\lceil un \rceil) < vn)$ converges to a continuous, measure-preserving probability kernel $K(v; u)$. Letting $\xi(u)$ be a (possibly degenerate) random variable with distribution $K(v; u)$, we show that (3) converges for any admissible sequence of permutations to

$$\lim_{n\to\infty} E[c_n(\mathcal{M}, \theta_n)|\mathbf{D}_n] = E[g(D)h(\xi(J(D)))]. \tag{5}$$

Armed with (5), our fifth contribution is to analyze optimality of θ_n for the algorithms under consideration. We establish that the expected cost of both T_1 and E_1 is minimized using the descending-degree permutation. Their optimal complexity is respectively (4) and

$$\lim_{n\to\infty} E[c_n(E_1, \theta_D)|\mathbf{D}_n] = \frac{E[g(D)(1 - J^2(D))]}{2}. \tag{6}$$

Method T_2 requires a new ordering we call *Round-Robin* (RR), which spreads large degree towards the outside of the range $[1, n]$. Its best cost is half of E_1's in (6). On the other hand, E_4 is optimized by the *Complementary Round-Robin* (CRR) permutation, which positions large degree towards the middle. If θ_n is optimal for a given $\mathcal{M}$, we also explain how to construct its opposite that achieves the worst cost.

Comparison across the four methods is our final contribution. We first prove that T_1 is faster than T_2 and E_1 is better than E_4 for all $F(x)$. However, the choice between T_1 and E_1 must take into account additional factors beyond cost – the speed of elementary comparison instructions on target hardware and in a specific graph G_n. This tradeoff arises because scanning edge iterators perform as many operations as both vertex iterators combined, i.e., $c_n(E_1, \theta_n) = c_n(T_1, \theta_n) + c_n(T_2, \theta_n)$, but at significantly higher speed [17]. The decision is simple only for $\alpha \in (4/3, 1.5]$ and $n \to \infty$, where T_1 *always* beats E_1 in the limit (i.e., the former has finite cost, while the latter has infinite). Although it is commonly believed that vertex and edge iterators have the same asymptotic complexity [28], [33], we prove that this is not true for $\alpha \in (4/3, 1.5]$ and scanning edge iterators.

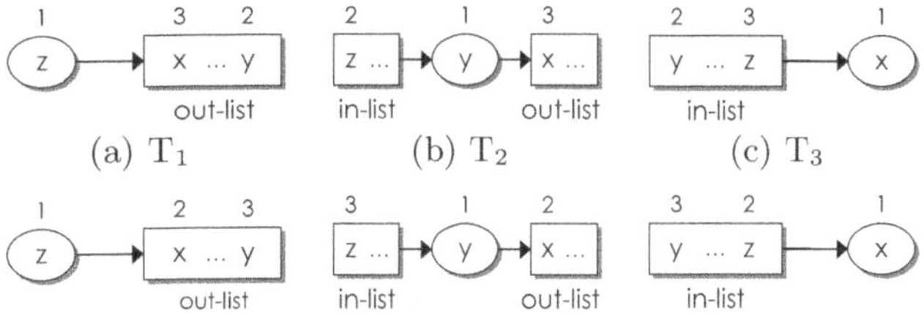

(a) T_1 (b) T_2 (c) T_3

(d) T_4 (e) T_5 (f) T_6

Figure 1: Search order in vertex iterator.

We conclude with developing an algorithm for efficient computation of our models, examining their accuracy under finite n, and highlighting the impact of Pareto α on the scaling behavior of cost.

2. UNIFYING FRAMEWORK

In this section, we condition on G and treat it as deterministic. We start by generalizing all previous work under a novel umbrella of 18 baseline algorithms and discussing how to extract the highest performance out of them.

Throughout the paper, we assume that adjacency lists in graphs are sorted ascending by node ID, which corresponds to left-to-right orientation in the figures. The omitted proofs can be found in [42].

2.1 Preprocessing

Each triangle $\triangle_{xyz}$ can be listed in $3! = 6$ equivalent ways by permuting its node sequence (x, y, z). To avoid this redundancy and improve efficiency, it is common [3], [22], [25], [34] to consider only triangles that satisfy some global transitive order $\mathcal{O}$, which results in exactly one listing per actual triangle. Three most-commonly used orders are random (e.g., hash-based) [14], [23], descending-degree [3], [22], [28], [33], and ascending-degree [34]. We propose that such techniques be implemented by a three-step process – 1) sort the nodes by $\mathcal{O}$ and sequentially assign IDs from sequence $(1, 2, \ldots, n)$; 2) create a directed graph in which the out-neighbors of each y have smaller labels and in-neighbors have larger, which is denoted by $y \to x$ and $y \leftarrow z$, respectively; and 3) in the directed graph, list triangles in ascending order of node ID, i.e., $x < y < z$.

The first step, called *relabeling* [28], [34], requires sorting n items using $\mathcal{O}$ and rewriting the labels of all edges in G. The second step, known as *orientation* [22], [33], splits each list of undirected neighbors $N(y)$ into in/out sets $N^-(y)$ and $N^+(y)$, respectively. These two steps can be modeled by a permutation $\theta_n : V \to V$ that always starts with ascending-degree order and maps each node in position i to a label $\theta_n(i)$. After re-writing the IDs, i's out-list consists of original neighbors j whose permuted label precedes that of i, i.e., $\theta_n(j) < \theta_n(i)$. In the directed graph $G(\theta_n) = (V, E(\theta_n))$, suppose i has out-degree $X_i(\theta_n)$, in-degree $Y_i(\theta_n)$, and total degree $d_i(\theta_n) = X_i(\theta_n) + Y_i(\theta_n)$.

While prior work is mostly concerned with the third step, i.e., triangle listing, we begin by noting that deciding on θ_n is an important factor for runtime, despite not having been studied in much detail before. With $n!$ possible permutations, it is unclear which of them produces the smallest overhead, how to approach modeling complexity of triangle listing in a relabeled/oriented graph, and which of the methods are better under various circumstances. The rest of the section lays a foundation for addressing these issues.

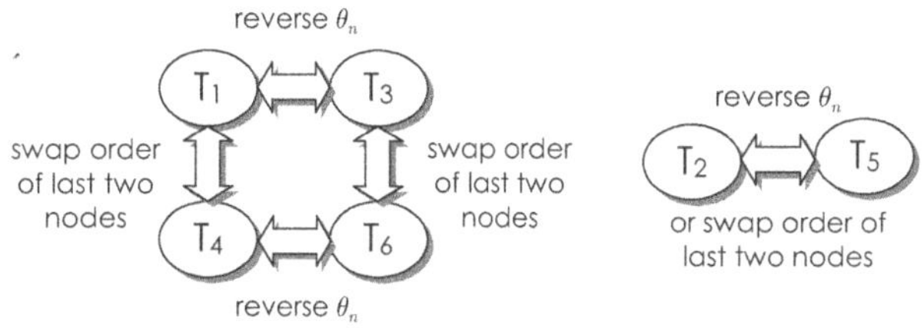

Figure 2: Vertex-iterator equivalence classes.

2.2 Vertex Iterator

Vertex iterator is a classical algorithm [18], [22], [33], [36] that visits each node and verifies edge existence between all pairs of non-redundant neighbors. For an oriented graph $G(\theta_n)$, vertex iterator admits six distinct search patterns, each specifying a different order in which the nodes (x, y, z) are traversed.

In the first pattern, which we call T_1, the algorithm considers the first node to be the largest in the triangle. This is illustrated in Figure 1(a), where the search starts from z, continues to $y < z$, and finishes with $x < y$. This method generates candidate edges $y \to x$, which are checked against $E(\theta_n)$ using a hash table. Each match indicates a unique triangle $\triangle_{xyz}$. Assuming the overhead is measured in the volume of tuples (y, x), the per-node cost of T_1 is

$$c_n(T_1, \theta_n) = \frac{1}{n} \sum_{i=1}^{n} \frac{X_i(\theta_n)(X_i(\theta_n) - 1)}{2}. \tag{7}$$

The second search order, which we call T_2, treats the initial node as being neither the smallest, nor the largest in the triangle. The corresponding technique, shown in Figure 1(b), verifies existence of edges $z \to x$, where pairs (z, x) sweep all possible combinations of y's in and out neighbors. The number of such tuples is given by

$$c_n(T_2, \theta_n) = \frac{1}{n} \sum_{i=1}^{n} X_i(\theta_n) Y_i(\theta_n). \tag{8}$$

As sketched in Figure 1(c), method T_3 starts from the smallest node x and examines presence of edges $z \to y$ between all pairs of in-neighbors such that $y < z$. Its overhead is similar to that of T_1, but with $X_i(\theta_n)$ and $Y_i(\theta_n)$ trading places, i.e.,

$$c_n(T_3, \theta_n) = \frac{1}{n} \sum_{i=1}^{n} \frac{Y_i(\theta_n)(Y_i(\theta_n) - 1)}{2}. \tag{9}$$

The remaining three methods in the figure (i.e., T_4-T_6) change the order in which the last two neighbors are visited; however, their cost formulas are identical to those of the counter-parts above them. Symmetry of T_1 and T_3 suggests even wider *equivalence classes*, which are groups of methods that have the same complexity and speed of elementary operations. Let the *reverse permutation* $\theta'_n : V \to V$ be such that $\theta'_n(i) = n + 1 - \theta_n(i)$ and consider the following.

PROPOSITION 1. *Reversing the permutation results in the overhead function swapping $X_i(\theta_n)$ with $Y_i(\theta_n)$.*

Since $c_n(T_1, \theta_n) = c_n(T_3, \theta'_n)$, we conclude that T_1 and T_3 are indeed equivalent. In addition, T_2 and T_5 reverse

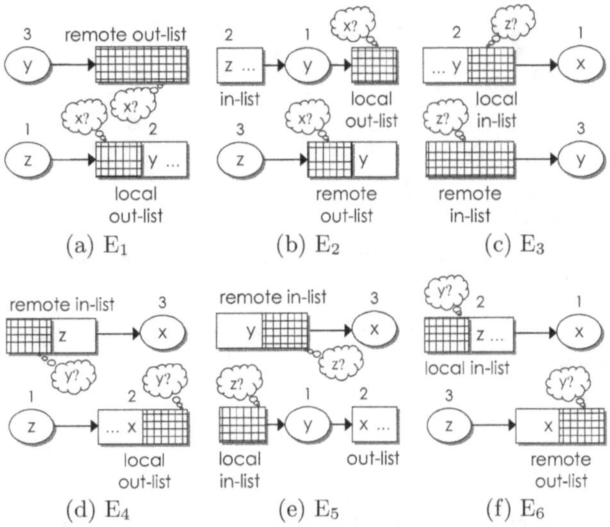

Figure 3: Search order in SEI.

	E_1	E_2	E_3	E_4	E_5	E_6
Local cost	T_1	T_2	T_3	T_1	T_2	T_3
Remote cost	T_2	T_1	T_2	T_3	T_3	T_1

Table 1: Intersection complexity of SEI.

into each other and thus form a standalone equivalence class. This is schematically shown in Figure 2. From this point on, we dismiss T_3-T_6 and keep only T_1-T_2 under consideration.

2.3 Edge Iterator

Instead of generating candidate pairs and checking them later, it is possible to traverse each directed edge and intersect the sets of neighbors at both incident vertices [14], [28], [33]. A *scanning edge iterator* (SEI) sequentially rolls through both neighbor lists, performing comparison using two pointers. An alternative, which we call *lookup-based edge iterator* (LEI), intersects using hash tables.

We start analysis with SEI, which also admits six search orders in the oriented graph. Using Figure 3(a), algorithm E_1 visits node z, examines each out-neighbor y, and intersects $N^+(y)$ with $N^+(z)$ to discover nodes x that complete triangle $\triangle_{xyz}$. Note that intersection at z does not involve all of its out-neighbors; only those smaller than y (shown with a grid pattern). This is a consequence of the $x < y < z$ relationship and transitivity of $\mathcal{O}$.

The cost of SEI is based on the number of comparisons in list intersection. We split this overhead into *local*, which takes into account scans over z's out-neighbor list $N^+(z)$, and *remote*, which does the same for y.

PROPOSITION 2. *The CPU cost of E_1 is given by $c_n(E_1, \theta_n) = c_n(T_1, \theta_n) + c_n(T_2, \theta_n)$, where the former term is local overhead and the latter is remote.*

The remaining SEI methods E_2-E_6 in Figure 3 are self-explanatory. Their complexity is shown in Table 1, which covers all ordered ways to choose local and remote overhead from the first three vertex-iterator options. It should be noted that LEI has the same six algorithms, which we call L_1-L_6, except that it hashes the local neighbor list of the first visited node and performs lookups against it for all remote nodes [17]. Complexity of populating the hash tables is $\sum_{i=1}^{n} X_i(\theta_n) = \sum_{i=1}^{n} Y_i(\theta_n) = m$, while the lookup overhead is given by Table 2 (which is also the second row of Table 1). Since LEI can be reduced to vertex iterator (in terms of both operation speed and cost), there is no need to consider it separately in the remainder of the paper.

	L_1	L_2	L_3	L_4	L_5	L_6
Cost	T_2	T_1	T_2	T_3	T_3	T_1

Table 2: Lookup complexity of LEI.

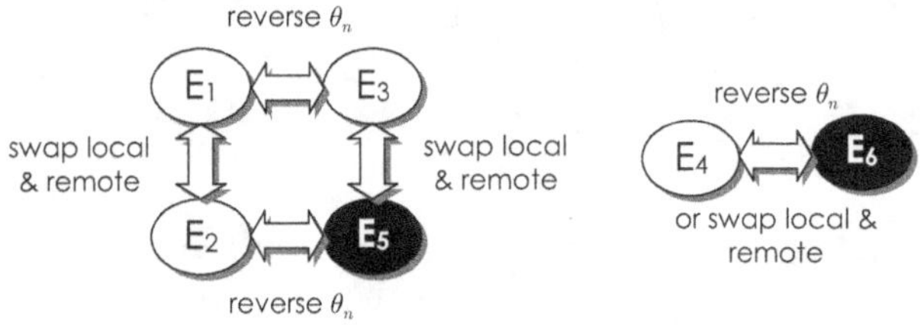

Figure 4: SEI equivalence classes.

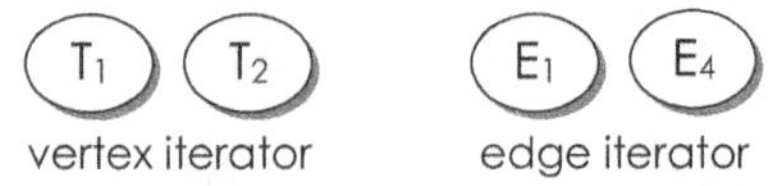

Figure 5: Competing algorithms.

Complexity of scanning edge iterator combines two terms, where the equivalence classes are built either by reversing the permutation or swapping local/remote overhead. The result is shown in Figure 4, where we again find just two distinct families of algorithms. However, SEI requires more careful pruning than vertex iterator since additional factors must be taken into account, which we discuss next.

For E_5, notice that the starting location of the intersection (i.e., y) is buried in the middle of x's in-neighbor list. Therefore, compared to E_1-E_3, this method requires either an extra binary search through $N^-(x)$ or intersection backwards (on the Intel i7-2600K, a backwards search is 26% slower than forward, which may be explained by poor CPU prefetch and/or less efficient auto-vectorization in the compiler). For similar reasons, E_6 is not competitive against E_4. Next, reversal of θ_n has no impact on runtime, which means that E_1 and E_3 are identical in all aspects. However, deciding between E_1 and E_2 requires modeling I/O complexity under a specific graph-partitioning scheme, which is a topic for another paper [17]. For now, we drop E_2-E_3 and obtain the four fundamental techniques in Figure 5.

2.4 Discussion

We now translate prior techniques into our notation. The oldest method for which this mapping is possible is [13], which proposes a variation of L_3 where acyclic orientation holds only for two of the three edges in each triangle. As a result, its complexity is $c_n(E_1, \theta_n)$ rather than $c_n(T_2, \theta_n)$. Incomplete orientation is remedied in [33] using a dynamically growing set of vectors to implement E_2 under the name *Forward*. This is extended to *Compact Forward* in [28] by removing the vector constraint. In more recent studies, T_1 appears in [22], [25], [36], E_1 in [3], [21], [35], E_3 in [14], and E_5 in [34]. At least six methods, i.e., T_1-T_3, E_1, E_3, E_4 are identified in [32].

Family of algorithms	Operations	Speed
Vertex iterator	Hash table	19
Lookup edge iterator (LEI)	Hash table	19
Scanning edge iterator (SEI)	SIMD intersection	1,801

Table 3: Single-core speed (million nodes/sec) using an Intel i7-3930K @ 4.4 GHz.

The majority of literature [3], [21], [22], [25], [33], [35], [36] omits relabeling and performs only orientation. Consequently, nodes in each of the directed neighbor lists are not ordered in any particular way *against each other*, which doubles the cost of all terms that depends on T_1 or T_3. For example, T_1 must check all pairs $x, y \in N^+(z)$ instead of only those with $x < y$. Similarly, scanning of the local list in E_1 cannot stop at y and must traverse the entire $N^+(z)$. On the other hand, T_2 takes advantage of preprocessing that separates in/out-neighbors into different sets, which allows it to keep complexity unchanged.

A limited number of studies [28], [33], [34] utilize relabeling; however, they omit orientation. In this setting, some of the methods require a binary search in remote neighbor lists to locate the boundary between the candidates larger and smaller than the current node. Vertex iterators T_1 and T_3 are not impacted, but T_2 must perform an additional $\zeta = \sum_{i=1}^{n} \log_2 d_i$ random memory accesses. Scanning edge iterators E_1/E_2 use the same ζ extra jumps, while E_3/E_5 and E_4/E_6 take a larger performance hit – one binary search per edge. This adds up to $\sum_{i=1}^{n} X_i \log_2 d_i$ or $\sum_{i=1}^{n} Y_i \log_2 d_i$ unnecessary memory lookups depending on the method. Using backwards-sorted lists, this overhead can be reduced to ζ for E_3/E_5, but not for E_4/E_6. Besides slowing down the computation, binary search may be impossible altogether in certain graphs (e.g., with compressed neighbor lists).

Our three-step framework ensures the smallest cost within each class of techniques, while imposing no restrictions on adjacency lists. The 18 introduced algorithms are converted to pseudocode and benchmarked in [17]. Table 3 summarizes these results using neighbor lists of sufficiently large size (i.e., best-case scenario for intersection). Even though SEI executes up to 95 times faster *per node*, Table 1 show that it requires more operations. To understand this tradeoff, define w_n to be the ratio of the lowest cost in SEI to that in the other two families of algorithms. It then follows that SEI, assuming it can match the speed in Table 3 over the adjacency lists of $G_n(\theta_n)$, has a better runtime on modern Intel CPUs iff $w_n < 95$. Since both instruction speed and w_n are functions of $G_n(\theta_n)$, this decision cannot be made unless the specific graph (or at least its degree distribution) is known. The only exception is $n \to \infty$ and graphs with $w_n \to \infty$, where SEI is always slower in the limit. We identify and discuss these cases later in the paper.

3. MODELING OUT-DEGREE

We now examine how to model the out-degree $X_i(\theta_n)$ in a family of random graphs $G_n(\theta_n)$.

3.1 Degree Growth

Recall that $F(x)$ is some fixed CDF, $t_n \to \infty$ is a monotonic function, and $F_n(x) = F(x)/F(t_n)$ is a truncated distribution. Suppose $D \sim F(x)$ represents the limiting degree and let $\mathbf{D}_n = (D_{n1}, \ldots, D_{nn})$ be an iid degree sequence drawn from $F_n(x)$. Note that $t_n \le n-1$ is required for $\mathbf{D}_n$ to be graphic (i.e., realizable by a graph). For the results that follow, it is convenient to sort $\mathbf{D}_n$ in ascending order, produce a new sequence $\mathbf{A}_n = (A_{n1}, \ldots, A_{nn})$, where $A_{ni} \le A_{n,i+1}$, and apply permutation to the result. Then, our earlier notation $d_i(\theta_n)$ refers to A_{nj} such that $\theta_n(j) = i$.

As we show below, the cost of triangle listing depends on one crucial parameter – the probability of edge existence between each pair of nodes (i, j) in G_n. We assume a traditional random-graph model that realizes a given degree sequence [8], [30], in which this metric is proportional to the product of corresponding degrees [1], [15]

$$p_{ij}(\theta_n) \approx \frac{d_i(\theta_n) d_j(\theta_n)}{2m}. \tag{10}$$

For this to be a probability, the numerator must not exceed the denominator, which we formalize next.

Definition 1. *Suppose $L_n = \max_i\{D_{ni}\}$ is the largest degree in G_n. A sequence of distributions $\{F_n(x)\}$ is called* asymptotically max-root-constrained (AMRC) *if $P(L_n > \sqrt{n}) \to 0$ as $n \to \infty$.*

AMRC sequences ensure that (10) is accurate for sufficiently large n. One option for satisfying this condition is to use distributions $F(x)$ with finite variance (i.e., $E[D^2] < \infty$), which is a consequence of the following result.

Proposition 3. *For $n \to \infty$ and some constant $c > 0$, $P(L_n > n^c) \to 0$ if $E[D^{1/c}] < \infty$.*

The second option is to scale t_n slowly enough, but without placing any restrictions on $F(x)$. To this end, define truncation to be *linear* if $t_n = n - 1$ and *root* if $t_n = \sqrt{n}$. Now observe that the latter case deterministically yields $L_n \le \sqrt{n}$, which keeps $p_{ij}(\theta_n) \le 1$ for all n.

If Definition 1 fails to hold, we call sequence $\{F_n(x)\}$ *unconstrained*. Unfortunately, the probability of edge existence in G_n built by such degree distributions is extremely difficult (if not impossible) to obtain in closed-form due to the high levels of dependency in the edge-construction process. At this point, it is even unclear if useful approximations to $p_{ij}(\theta_n)$ can be made for such cases. However, depending on the objectives, this may not be required.

Assume $\mathcal{M}$ is a particular triangle-listing method. Throughout the paper, we develop two sets of results – those that rely on $F_n(x)$ to establish $E[c_n(\mathcal{M}, \theta_n)|\mathbf{D}_n]$ and those that use $F(x)$ to arrive at the corresponding limit as $n \to \infty$. The former models are accurate for finite (but sufficiently large) n if the degree sequence is AMRC. In contrast, the asymptotic limits hold *unconditionally* because the rate at which $F_n(x)$ approaches $F(x)$ has no impact on the convergence point, i.e., linear and root truncation yield the same result. Therefore, all models in the form of (4)-(6) are exact even in unconstrained graphs.

3.2 Expected Degree and Cost

Notice that the expected out-degree at node i is the summation of $p_{ij}(\theta_n)$ for all nodes j smaller than i. Excluding self-loops in the denominator, this leads to

$$E[X_i(\theta_n)|\mathbf{D}_n] \approx d_i(\theta_n) \frac{\sum_{j=1}^{i-1} d_j(\theta_n)}{2m - d_i(\theta_n)}. \tag{11}$$

While (11) is asymptotically precise, it may exhibit large errors for finite n in unconstrained graphs. This occurs

T1	T2	E1	E4
$\frac{x^2}{2}$	$x(1-x)$	$\frac{x(2-x)}{2}$	$\frac{x^2+(1-x)^2}{2}$

Table 4: Function $h(x)$.

because it over-estimates the number of edges delivered to high-degree nodes, in essence treating G_n as allowing duplicate links. To curb this tendency, we propose to extend (11) by applying some positive and monotonically non-decreasing function $w(x)$ to the degree of potential neighbors, i.e.,

$$E[X_i(\theta_n)|\mathbf{D}_n] \approx d_i(\theta_n)\frac{\sum_{j=1}^{i-1} w(d_j(\theta_n))}{\sum_{k=1}^{n} w(d_k) - w(d_i(\theta_n))}. \quad (12)$$

For example, $w(x) = \min(x, a)$, where a is a constant, is one such option we consider below. By tuning $w(x)$ to suit $F(x)$, it may be possible to make (12) accurate in unconstrained graphs under finite n; however, discovery of this relationship is not necessary for proving optimality of different permutations/methods since our results below cover a wide range of $w(x)$.

Define the fraction of i's neighbors with smaller ID as

$$q_i(\theta_n) = \frac{E[X_i(\theta_n)|\mathbf{D}_n]}{d_i(\theta_n)} \quad (13)$$

and consider the next result.

PROPOSITION 4. *In asymptotically large AMRC graphs, all four triangle-listing techniques in Figure 5 are covered by one formula*

$$E[c_n(\mathcal{M}, \theta_n)|\mathbf{D}_n] \approx \frac{1}{n}\sum_{i=1}^{n} g(d_i(\theta_n))h(q_i(\theta_n)), \quad (14)$$

where $g(x) = x^2 - x$ and $h(x)$ is given by Table 4.

4. CONVERGENCE OF COST

We next examine the limit of (14) as $n \to \infty$. Note that we use Lebesgue-Stieltjes integrals and treat CDFs as measures, i.e., $dF(x)$ applies to both discrete and continuous distributions.

4.1 Functions of Order Statistics

For now, assume $\theta_n(i) = i$ is the ascending-degree permutation, which means that $d_i(\theta_n) = A_{ni}$. Let $\{\phi_n(t)\}_{n=1}^{\infty}$ be a sequence of functions that for all $t \in [0, 1]$ satisfies

$$\lim_{n\to\infty} \int_0^t \phi_n(u)du = \int_0^t \phi(u)du, \quad (15)$$

where $\phi(u)$ is some integrable function. Then, given a sufficiently smooth $g(x)$, results in the field of L-estimators [39], [44] show that

$$\lim_{n\to\infty} \frac{1}{n}\sum_{i=1}^{n} g(A_{ni})\phi_n(i/n) = \int_0^1 g(F^{-1}(u))\phi(u)du. \quad (16)$$

Limits in the form of (16) are known as Glivenko-Cantelli results for functions of order statistics. Letting U be uniform in $[0, 1]$, the integral in (16) can be written shorter as $E[g(F^{-1}(U))\phi(U)]$. When $F(x)$ is continuous, it is often convenient to represent the expectation as $E[g(D)\phi(F(D))]$, where $D \sim F(x)$.

Our first result extends (16) to cover partial sums.

LEMMA 1. *For a fixed $u \in [0, 1]$,*

$$\lim_{n\to\infty} \frac{1}{n}\sum_{i=1}^{\lceil nu \rceil} g(A_{ni}) = \int_0^u g(F^{-1}(x))dx. \quad (17)$$

To allow (16) to handle summations in the form of (14), it is important to understand the asymptotic properties of $q_i(\theta_n)$. The following result sheds light on this issue.

LEMMA 2. *For the ascending permutation θ_A and fixed $u \in [0, 1]$, random variable $q_{\lceil nu \rceil}(\theta_A)$ converges to $J(F^{-1}(u))$ as $n \to \infty$, where*

$$J(x) := \frac{1}{E[w(D)]}\int_0^x w(y)dF(y). \quad (18)$$

For $E[w(D)] < \infty$, (18) defines a CDF. We study its properties next.

PROPOSITION 5. *Assume a process that picks node i in G_n in proportion to $w(D_{ni})$ and let S_n be the random degree of the chosen nodes. Then, $P(S_n \le x) \to J(x)$ as $n \to \infty$.*

Variable $S \sim J(x)$ is known as *spread* in renewal process theory. Given n intervals of size $w(d_1), \dots, w(d_n)$, suppose a random point is thrown into $[0, \sum_{k=1}^{n} w(d_k)]$. Then, the length of the interval that the point hits follows the spread distribution as $n \to \infty$. The selected intervals are biased towards larger $w(d_i)$, which is known as the *inspection paradox* [41]. In graphs $G_n(\theta_n)$, the bias reflects the probability to select neighbors in proportion to their weight $w(d_i)$. For $w(x) = x$, variable S represents the degree of nodes adjacent to a random link, or that seen by a random walk on the graph. In such cases, spread $J(x)$ is well-studied, e.g., exponential D produces $S \sim$ Erlang(2) and Pareto(α, β) yields

$$J(x) = 1 - \frac{\beta + \alpha x}{\beta}\left(1 + \frac{x}{\beta}\right)^{-\alpha}, \quad (19)$$

which has Pareto-like tails with a heavier shape $\alpha - 1$.

4.2 Monotonic Permutations

We are now ready to derive the expected cost of triangle listing for the ascending/descending permutations.

THEOREM 1. *The ascending permutation produces*

$$\lim_{n\to\infty} E[c_n(\mathcal{M}, \theta_A)|\mathbf{D}_n] = E[g(D)h(J(D))]. \quad (20)$$

This means that random variable (14) becomes independent of $\mathbf{D}_n$ as $n \to \infty$, which allows us to treat it as a constant for sufficiently large n. The descending case is handled similarly since $q_i(\theta_D) = 1 - q_i(\theta_A)$. This implies $q_{\lceil nu \rceil}(\theta_D)$ converges to $1 - J(F^{-1}(u))$ and consequently

$$\lim_{n\to\infty} E[c_n(\mathcal{M}, \theta_D)|\mathbf{D}_n] = E[g(D)h(1 - J(D))]. \quad (21)$$

Applying these observations and recalling Table 4,

$$\lim_{n\to\infty} E[c_n(T_1, \theta_A)|\mathbf{D}_n] = \frac{E[g(D)J^2(D)]}{2}, \quad (22)$$

$$\lim_{n\to\infty} E[c_n(T_1, \theta_D)|\mathbf{D}_n] = \frac{E[g(D)(1 - J(D))^2]}{2}. \quad (23)$$

For T2, symmetry $h(1 - x) = h(x)$ shows that both permutations have the same limiting cost. It is thus sufficient to consider only the descending case

$$\lim_{n\to\infty} E[c_n(T_2, \theta_D)|\mathbf{D}_n] = E[g(D)J(D)(1 - J(D))]. \quad (24)$$

Interestingly, T_1 under θ_A is finite iff $\alpha > 2$, which is shown by expanding the integral in (22) using $1 - J(x) \sim x^{1-\alpha}$. Thus, θ_A offers no finiteness benefits over omitting orientation, where the cost is $E[D^2 - D]/2$. Next, T_2 in (24) is finite iff $\alpha > 1.5$, which is a noticeable improvement over (22). But this is eclipsed by T_1 under θ_D, where the finiteness condition is $\alpha > 4/3$. Therefore, as $n \to \infty$, vertex iterator exhibits at least four regimes of operation, i.e., $\alpha \leq 4/3$, $\alpha \in (4/3, 1.5]$, $\alpha \in (1.5, 2]$, and $\alpha > 2$.

Note that (20) and (21) require no constraints on $\{F_n(x)\}$. For finite n, however, accurate results are guaranteed only for AMRC sequences. In these cases, Theorem 1 yields the following approximation to the expected cost across all degree sequences drawn from $F_n(x)$

$$E[c_n(\mathcal{M}, \theta_A)] \approx E[g(D_n)h(J_n(D_n))], \tag{25}$$

where spread $J_n(x)$ is computed from the truncated distribution $F_n(x) = F(x)/F(t_n)$ and $D_n \sim F_n(x)$.

5. CONVERGENCE OF PERMUTATIONS

Our initial investigation into cost of triangle listing handles only the simplest permutations. The next goal is to understand what makes sequences $\{\theta_n\}_{n=1}^{\infty}$ convergent and propose a framework for modeling their limits.

5.1 Admissibility

We start with a background on measures.

Definition 2. *For a set S and its σ-algebra Σ, function $\mu : \Sigma \to \mathbb{R}$ is called a* measure *if a) $\mu(C) \geq 0$ for all elements $C \in \Sigma$; b) $\mu(\emptyset) = 0$; c) $\mu(\cup_{i=1}^{\infty} C_i) = \sum_{i=1}^{\infty} \mu(C_i)$ for pairwise disjoint $C_i \in \Sigma$.*

It is sufficient for us to consider just two cases of S. For finite sets, the σ-algebra consists of all subsets of S, in which case $\mu(C) = |C|$. For continuum S, we use the Lebesgue measure $\mu([a, b]) = b - a$.

Definition 3. *For a set S, function $K(v; u) : \mathbb{R} \times S \to \mathbb{R}$ is called a* probability kernel *if for each $u \in S$ it is a CDF in variable v, i.e., non-decreasing, defined for all $v \in \mathbb{R}$, and compliant with $K(-\infty; u) = 0$, and $K(\infty; u) = 1$.*

Kernels are useful mechanisms for capturing the distribution of non-iid collections of random variables; however, only some of them will be suitable for our purposes.

Definition 4. *Let S be a set with measure μ and U be a uniformly random variable in S. Kernel $K(v; u)$ is called* measure-preserving *if it satisfies for all $v \in \mathbb{R}$*

$$E[K(v; U)] = \frac{\mu(\{s \in S : s \leq v\})}{\mu(S)}, \tag{26}$$

in which case the corresponding variable $\xi(u) \sim K(v; u)$ is a random map, *i.e., $P(\xi(u) \leq v) = K(v; u)$.*

Note that $\xi(u)$ can be viewed as a random bijection on S. As before, sequence of functions $\theta_n : [1, n] \to [1, n]$ specifies a relationship between the position in the ascending-order vector $\mathbf{A}_n$ and that in the permuted sequence. If these functions are deterministic, $i = \theta_n(j)$ means that $d_i(\theta_n) = A_{nj}$. Since each θ_n is a bijection, its inverse exists and satisfies $\theta_n^{-1}(\theta_n(j)) = j$. For more general cases, where specifying a deterministic relationship is inconvenient, θ_n may be random. Either way, there must exist a measure-preserving kernel $M_n(j; i)$ such that $P(\theta_n(i) \leq j) = M_n(j; i)$. However, to have a reasonable mapping as $n \to \infty$, we need to impose certain asymptotic constraints.

Definition 5. *Suppose sequence $k(n) \to \infty$ is such that $k(n)/n \to 0$ as $n \to \infty$. If for all $u, v \in [0, 1]$ the fraction of values in the $k(n)$-neighborhood of u that are mapped to the interval $[0, v]$, i.e.,*

$$K_n(v; u) := \frac{1}{2k(n) + 1} \sum_{i=-k(n)}^{k(n)} M_n(nv; \lceil nu \rceil + i), \tag{27}$$

converges weakly to some limit $K(v; u)$, sequence $\{\theta_n\}$ is called admissible.

Outside of specially crafted counter-examples (e.g., $\theta_n = \theta_A$ for odd n and θ_D for even), most reasonable permutation sequences are admissible. For such cases, the limiting behavior of θ_n is a random process $\{\xi(u)\}$ with distribution $K(v; u) = P(\xi(u) \leq v)$. Note that if (27) converges, the limit must be measure-preserving. The opposite is true as well – any such kernel has some sequence of permutations $\{\theta_n\}$ that converges to it.

5.2 Cost Under General Permutations

We start by generalizing (16) beyond monotonic θ_n.

Lemma 3. *For an admissible sequence $\{\theta_n\}$,*

$$\lim_{n\to\infty} \frac{1}{n} \sum_{i=1}^{n} g(d_i(\theta_n))h(i/n) = E[g(F^{-1}(U))h(\xi(U))]. \tag{28}$$

Re-writing (28) as $E[g(D)h(\xi(F(D)))]$ and using the same logic as in Theorem 1, we get the following.

Theorem 2. *For an admissible sequence $\{\theta_n\}$,*

$$\begin{aligned} c(\mathcal{M}, \xi) &:= \lim_{n\to\infty} E[c_n(\mathcal{M}, \theta_n)|\mathbf{D}_n] \\ &= E[g(D)h(\xi(J(D)))]. \end{aligned} \tag{29}$$

For AMRC graphs, we can use the limiting map $\xi(u)$ to achieve accurate cost analysis even under finite n

$$E[c_n(\mathcal{M}, \theta_n)] \approx E[g(D_n)h(\xi(J_n(D_n)))]. \tag{30}$$

Not surprisingly, the ascending map $\xi(u) = u$ and descending $\xi(u) = 1 - u$ produce in (29) the already-established (22)-(24). Additional cases are covered next.

5.3 Non-Monotonic Permutations

Besides θ_A and θ_D, another previously used option is *uniform* [14], where the direction of edges in the acyclic orientation is based on original (e.g., hashed) node IDs. In this case, $\xi_U(u)$ is a uniform variable in $[0, 1]$, independent of the starting position u. This yields

$$c(\mathcal{M}, \xi_U) = E[g(D)]E[h(U)] = E[D^2 - D]E[h(U)], \tag{31}$$

where U is uniform in $[0, 1]$. Simple calculations show that $E[h(U)] = 1/6$ for both vertex iterators and $1/3$ for both edge iterators. Compared to not performing orientation at all, where the corresponding cost is $E[D^2 - D]/2$ and $E[D^2 - D]$, both families of algorithms reduce complexity by a factor of 3. This agrees with common sense since orientation avoids counting each triangle three times.

Analysis of T_2's function $h(x) = x(1-x)$ suggests that larger values of degree should be scattered towards the outside of the range $[1,n]$ in an effort to pair them with smaller products $q_i(\theta_n)(1-q_i(\theta_n))$ in (14). This leads to a new permutation we call *Round-Robin* (RR)

$$\theta_n(i) = \begin{cases} \lceil \frac{n+i}{2} \rceil & i \text{ is odd} \\ \lfloor \frac{n-i}{2} \rfloor + 1 & i \text{ is even} \end{cases}, \tag{32}$$

whose map is derived next.

PROPOSITION 6. *Permutation* (32) *converges to a random map* $\xi_{RR}(u)$ *that equals* $(1-u)/2$ *or* $(1+u)/2$, *each with probability 1/2.*

Re-writing (29), we have a general result

$$c(\mathcal{M}, \xi_{RR}) = \frac{E\Big[g(D)\Big(h\big(\frac{1-J(D)}{2}\big) + h\big(\frac{1+J(D)}{2}\big)\Big)\Big]}{2}. \tag{33}$$

Applying this to T_2 yields

$$c(T_2, \xi_{RR}) = \frac{E[g(D)(1-J^2(D))]}{4}, \tag{34}$$

which is finite iff $\alpha > 1.5$. Since the complexity of E_1 combines that of T_1 and T_2, it is interesting whether it performs better under the descending or RR permutation. Full comparison is delayed until the next section, but Proposition 6 can be used to reveal the likely outcome. Combining (23) and (24) leads to

$$c(E_1, \xi_D) = \frac{E[g(D)(1-J^2(D))]}{2} \tag{35}$$

and expanding (33) using $h(x) = x(2-x)/2$ produces

$$c(E_1, \xi_{RR}) = \frac{E[g(D)(3-J^2(D))]}{8}. \tag{36}$$

While (35) is finite iff $\alpha > 1.5$, this cannot be said about (36), where the condition shifts to $\alpha > 2$. This can be explained by the fact that T_1 suffers a significant cost increase under RR, which more than offsets the benefits that T_2 may be gaining.

For E_4, function $h(x)$ behaves the opposite of that for T_2, i.e., smaller values are found towards the center. To handle such cases, suppose the *complementary permutation* $\theta''_n(i) = \theta_n(n-i+1)$ applies the same mapping as θ_n, but starting from the descending order of degree rather than ascending. With this in mind, it might be interesting to examine E_4 under the *Complementary Round-Robin* (CRR) permutation. To determine the corresponding map, consider the following.

PROPOSITION 7. *Suppose sequence* $\{\theta_n\}$ *converges to some map* $\xi(u)$ *as* $n \to \infty$. *Then, its reverse* $\{\theta'_n\}$ *converges to* $\xi'(u) = 1-\xi(u)$ *and its complement* $\{\theta''_n\}$ *to* $\xi''(u) = \xi(1-u)$.

This leads to $\xi_{CRR}(u) = \xi''_{RR}(u) = \xi_{RR}(1-u)$, which equals $u/2$ or $1-u/2$ with probability 1/2 each. Expanding (29), it can be shown that CRR coupled with any of the considered methods has finite cost iff $\alpha > 2$.

In summary, we have five different permutations (i.e., ascending, descending, RR, CRR, and uniform) that cover cases where $\theta_n(i)$ and $\xi(u)$ are both deterministic, both random, and one is deterministic but the other is random. Our next task is create a framework for minimizing (29) over all measure-preserving maps $\{\xi(u)\}$.

Algorithm 1: Construction of optimal permutations

```
Function OPT (h)
    for (i = 1; i ≤ n; i++) do
        z[i].key = h(i/n)
        z[i].index = i
    if r(x) is an increasing function then
        sort array z descending by key
    else
        sort array z ascending by key
    for (i = 1; i ≤ n; i++) do
        theta[i] = z[i].index
    return theta
```

6. COMPARISON AND OPTIMALITY

This section obtains the optimal permutation and cost under various monotonic relationships among $g(x)$, $h(x)$, and $w(x)$. It also compares the best methods within each triangle-listing class.

6.1 Minimizing Cost

Assume that $J(x)$ is a continuous spread distribution from (18). This implies that $J(S)$, where $S \sim J(x)$, is a uniform variable in $[0,1]$. For heavy-tailed $F(x)$, such as Pareto, this assumption holds iff $E[w(D)] < \infty$. For the results below, it is convenient to define $r(x) = g(J^{-1}(x))/w(J^{-1}(x))$. We will be mostly concerned with its monotonicity, which is the same as that of $g(x)/w(x)$ since $J(x)$ is a CDF.

LEMMA 4. *Model* (29) *can be written as*

$$c(\mathcal{M}, \xi) = E[w(D)]E[r(U)h(\xi(U))], \tag{37}$$

where U *is uniform in [0,1].*

Note that (37) is better-suited for our purposes in this section because it replaces a combination of D and $J(D)$ with a simpler variable U. The next result shows that there exists a percolation point in the behavior of $r(x)$ at which all permutations are equal.

PROPOSITION 8. *For a constant function* $r(x) = b$ *and a fixed method* $\mathcal{M}$, *all permutations yield the same complexity*

$$c(\mathcal{M}, \xi) = E[g(D)]E[h(U)]. \tag{38}$$

Interestingly, this is exactly the same overhead as under the random permutation in (31). When $r(x)$ deviates from being a constant in either direction (i.e., becomes increasing or decreasing in x), there exists a simple technique for deciding the optimal order. Assume $r(x)$ is monotonic and consider Algorithm 1, which creates a sequence

$$\mathbf{z} := (h(1/n), h(2/n), \dots, h(1)) \tag{39}$$

and sorts it in the opposite order of monotonicity of $r(x)$. If $\mathbf{z}$ transforms into $h(i_1/n), h(i_2/n), \dots, h(i_n/n)$, the algorithm assigns $\theta_n(j) = i_j$, where ties are broken arbitrarily.

THEOREM 3. *When* $r(x)$ *is monotonic, Algorithm 1 builds permutations that minimize* (37).

This result leads to several useful conclusions.

COROLLARY 1. *If* $h(x)$ *has the same monotonicity in* $[0,1]$ *as* $g(x)/w(x)$ *in* $[0,\infty)$, *descending order is optimal. If monotonicity of these functions is opposite of each other, ascending order is optimal.*

For triangle listing with $w(x) = \min(x, a)$, where $a > 0$ is a constant, ratio $g(x)/w(x) = (x^2 - x)/\min(x, a)$ is monotonically increasing. Recalling Table 4, as well as the various relationships in Figures 2 and 4, we get that θ_D is optimal for $T_1/E_1/E_2$ and [13], while θ_A is for $T_3/E_3/E_5$.

COROLLARY 2. *Suppose $h(1/2 + x) = h(1/2 - x)$ for all $x \in [0, 1/2]$. Then, if $h(x)$ has the same monotonicity in $[0, 1/2)$ as $g(x)/w(x)$ in $[0, \infty)$, RR is optimal. If these functions have opposing monotonicity, CRR is optimal.*

This implies that the cost of T_2 is indeed minimized by RR and that of E_4/E_6 by CRR. Theorem 3 also provides a means for creating permutations with the highest cost.

COROLLARY 3. *Map $\xi(u)$ is the best for a given method iff its complement $\xi''(u)$ is the worst.*

6.2 Comparison

We now decide which vertex iterator is better under their respective optimal permutations. Re-write (23) and (34) as

$$c(T_1, \xi_D) = \frac{E[r(U)(1-U)^2]}{2}, \quad (40)$$

$$c(T_2, \xi_{RR}) = \frac{E[r(U)(1-U^2)]}{4} \quad (41)$$

and consider the next result.

THEOREM 4. *If $r(x)$ is increasing, (40) is smaller than (41). If $r(x)$ is decreasing, the inequality is reversed. If $r(x)$ is a constant, they produce the same cost.*

For $w(x) = \min(x, a)$, we already know that $r(x)$ is increasing, which implies that T_1 is faster than T_2. For edge iterator, we have

$$c(E_1, \xi_D) = \frac{E[r(U)(1-U^2)]}{2}, \quad (42)$$

$$c(E_4, \xi_{CRR}) = \frac{E[r(U)(U^2 - 2U + 2)]}{4}, \quad (43)$$

with the corresponding comparison next.

THEOREM 5. *If $r(x)$ is increasing, (42) is smaller than (43). If $r(x)$ is decreasing, the opposite holds. If $r(x)$ is a constant, they are identical.*

6.3 Asymptotics

Our study revealed that the best vertex iterator is T_1 and the fastest scanning edge iterator is E_1, with the corresponding optimal cost

$$c(T_1, \xi_D) = \frac{E[(D^2 - D)(1 - J(D))^2]}{2}, \quad (44)$$

$$c(E_1, \xi_D) = \frac{E[(D^2 - D)(1 - J^2(D))]}{2}. \quad (45)$$

Using Pareto $F(x)$, we established earlier that the finiteness condition was $\alpha > 4/3$ for (44) and $\alpha > 1.5$ for (45). This means that as $n \to \infty$, T_1 is provably faster than E_1 in all graphs with $\alpha \in (4/3, 1.5]$, *no matter how these algorithms are implemented.* For $\alpha \in (1.5, \infty)$, both methods produce finite cost and the winner must be decided by taking into account the speed of their elementary operations, i.e., hash-table lookups vs scanning intersection similar to Table 3, but customized to a particular graph $G_n(\theta_n)$.

When α drops below the finiteness thresholds of each method, the scaling rate of cost is determined by the tail of the spread distribution

$$1 - J_n(x) \sim \begin{cases} x^{1-\alpha} & \alpha > 1 \\ 1 - \log(x)/\log(t_n) & \alpha = 1 \\ 1 - x^{1-\alpha}/t_n^{1-\alpha} & 0 < \alpha < 1 \end{cases}, \quad (46)$$

where the last two cases arise due to $E[D_n] \to \infty$. For root truncation, we get that $E[c_n(T_1, \theta_D)|\mathbf{D}_n]/a_n \to 1$, where

$$a_n = \begin{cases} \log n & \alpha = 4/3 \\ n^{2-1.5\alpha} & 1 < \alpha < 4/3 \\ \sqrt{n}/\log^2 n & \alpha = 1 \\ n^{1-\alpha/2} & 0 < \alpha < 1 \end{cases}, \quad (47)$$

and $E[c_n(E_1, \theta_D)|\mathbf{D}_n]/b_n \to 1$, where

$$b_n = \begin{cases} \log n & \alpha = 1.5 \\ n^{1.5-\alpha} & 1 < \alpha < 1.5 \\ \sqrt{n}/\log n & \alpha = 1 \\ n^{1-\alpha/2} & 0 < \alpha < 1 \end{cases}. \quad (48)$$

These results show that T_1 grows slower than E_1 for all $\alpha \in [1, 1.5)$; however, interestingly enough, they have the same scaling behavior when $\alpha \in (0, 1)$. Determining the corresponding rates under *linear* truncation requires modeling families of unconstrained graphs under finite n, which is beyond the scope of our investigation here.

7. EVALUATION

We now use finite n, where the models are only approximate, to examine the impact of α, truncation, and graph size on the distance between the model and actual cost.

7.1 Model Computation

Recall that we start with a continuous Pareto distribution $F^*(x) = 1 - (1 + x/\beta)^{-\alpha}$ defined on $[0, \infty)$ and discretize it by rounding up each generated value. This produces $F(x) = 1 - (1 + \lfloor x \rfloor/\beta)^{-\alpha}$ defined on natural numbers, which we employ in the construction of random graphs and comparison against the model. In general, (30) expands into a double Lebesgue-Stieltjes integral

$$\int_0^{t_n} g(x) h\Big(\xi\Big(\frac{\int_0^x w(y) dF_n(y)}{\int_0^{t_n} w(z) dF_n(z)}\Big)\Big) dF_n(x), \quad (49)$$

which can be easily computed in Matlab if $F_n(x)$ is continuous, e.g., using $F_n(x) = F^*(x)/F^*(t_n)$. However, this is only a crude approximation to the outcome observed in simulations. Therefore, a more prudent approach is to write these integrals as summations

$$\sum_{i=1}^{t_n} g(i) h\Big(\xi\Big(\frac{\sum_{j=1}^{i} w(j) p_j}{\sum_{k=1}^{t_n} w(k) p_k}\Big)\Big) p_i, \quad (50)$$

where $p_i := F_n(i) - F_n(i-1)$ is the PMF (probability mass function) of truncated degree.

Even though (50) contains two nested sums and appears to exhibit quadratic complexity, it can be computed in linear time and $O(1)$ space. This works well for many scenarios, except when a good estimate of the limiting cost is needed under linear truncation and a slowly-decaying tail $1 - F(x)$. For such cases, the runtime can be improved to

Algorithm 2: Quick computation of (50)

```
Function DiscreteModel (Fn, g, w, h, xi; tn, eps)
    EDn = J = cost = 0
    for (i=1; i ≤ tn; i += jump) do                         ▷ E[D_n]
        jump = ceil(eps * i)
        EDn += w(i)*(Fn(i + jump − 1) − Fn(i − 1))
    for (i=1; i ≤ tn; i += jump) do                         ▷ E[c_n(M, θ_n)]
        jump = ceil(eps * i)
        p = Fn(i + jump − 1) − Fn(i − 1)
        J += w(i) * p / EDn
        cost += w(i) * h(xi(J)) * p
    return cost
```

n	$F^*(x)$ in (49)		$F(x)$ in (50)		Algorithm 2	
	value	time	value	time	value	time
10^3	144.86	7.4	142.85	<0.01	142.85	<0.01
10^4	245.29	7.6	241.15	<0.01	241.15	<0.01
10^7	353.92	7.8	346.92	1.2	346.92	0.04
10^8	359.85	7.9	352.73	12	352.73	0.05
10^9	362.18	7.9	354.94	117	354.94	0.07
10^{10}	363.06	8.0	355.79	1170	355.79	0.08
10^{12}	363.51	8.2			356.22	0.10
10^{13}	363.56	8.2	too slow		356.26	0.11
10^{14}	363.57	8.2			356.28	0.12
10^{17}	363.57	8.3			356.28	0.13

Table 5: Model results and computation time (in seconds) for T_1 under descending order ($\alpha = 1.5$, $\epsilon = 10^{-5}$, linear truncation).

$O((1+\log(\epsilon t_n))/\epsilon)$ by compressing all summands from large intervals $[i, (1+\epsilon)i]$ into a single term, where $1/t_n \le \epsilon < 1$ is a chosen parameter. This is demonstrated in Algorithm 2, in which $\epsilon = 1/t_n$ yields the exact result and larger values offer varying degrees of approximation.

Table 3 compares the continuous result, the exact discrete model, and Algorithm 2. Using two decimal digits of precision, notice that the continuous model does not converge until $n = 10^{14}$. Based on the result in columns 4-5 of the table, this value of n would require an extrapolated four months in the exact model (50). On the other hand, Algorithm 2 computes this case in a fraction of a second due to its $\log n$ complexity. Additionally, the table shows that the continuous model indeed deviates from the discrete version by non-negligible amounts (i.e., 1.5 – 2%).

7.2 Random Graph Generation

Traditional methods [8], [30] that aim to realize a random graph with a given degree sequence $(d_1, \ldots, d_n)$ place d_i copies (i.e., stubs) of each node i into an array and uniformly draw pairs of available nodes at each step. The two selected stubs are removed and the process is repeated. This, however, leads to self-loops and duplicate edges. Since we are interested in simple graphs, these extraneous edges must be removed, which has a noticeable impact on the realized degree, especially when Pareto α drops below 2 and truncation function $t_n = n - 1$. Specifically, if the desired degree of node i is d_i but the constructed graphs G_n are allowed to implement smaller values in the range $[1, d_i]$, simulations may not match theoretical predictions of $E[X_i(\theta_n)|\mathbf{D}_n]$.

To overcome this problem, we employ a variation of the method from [11] that picks neighbors in proportion to their residual degree and excludes the already-attached neighbors when performing selection. If implemented naively, this requires quadratic complexity; however, this can also be done in $n \log n$ time using interval trees that record the residual probability mass of degree on both sides of each node. As a result, graphs with 10M nodes to be generated in several seconds, which is sufficient for our analysis below. With the exception of possibly one last edge (i.e., if $\sum_{i=1}^{n} d_i$ is odd), G_n in our simulations implements $\mathbf{D}_n$ exactly.

n	$T_1 + \theta_A$			$T_1 + \theta_D$		
	sim	(50)	error	sim	(50)	error
10^4	159.1	155.6	−2.2%	40.2	39.3	−2.2%
10^5	518.0	516.6	−0.3%	87.8	87.0	−0.9%
10^6	1,355.6	1,354.5	−0.1%	143.7	142.9	−0.6%
10^7	3,089.1	3,089.2	0.003%	196.9	196.2	−0.4%
∞		∞			356.3	

Table 6: Cost with $\alpha = 1.5$ and root truncation.

n	$T_2 + \theta_D$			$T_2 + \theta_{RR}$		
	sim	(50)	error	sim	(50)	error
10^4	102.3	103.7	1.4%	79.5	75.8	−4.6%
10^5	260.0	261.4	0.5%	186.4	181.8	−2.5%
10^6	467.0	467.4	0.1%	315.4	310.4	−1.6%
10^7	674.6	675.4	0.1%	436.1	432.4	−0.8%
∞		1,307.6			770.4	

Table 7: Cost with $\alpha = 1.7$ and root truncation.

n	$T_1 + \theta_D$			$T_2 + \theta_{RR}$		
	sim	(50)	error	sim	(50)	error
10^4	178.6	179.3	0.4%	318.9	371.9	16.6%
10^5	182.2	181.3	−0.5%	363.7	383.0	5.3%
10^6	182.6	181.5	−0.6%	382.0	384.2	0.6%
10^7	182.6	181.5	−0.6%	383.5	384.3	0.2%
∞		181.5			384.3	

Table 8: Cost with $\alpha = 2.1$ and linear truncation.

7.3 Constrained Degree

We start with AMRC graphs, where the obtained results should be accurate even for finite n. All simulations in the rest of the paper are averaged over 100 random degree sequences $\mathbf{D}_n$, each with 100 random graphs G_n (i.e., 10K graph instances total). We keep Pareto $\beta = 30(\alpha - 1)$, which yields $E[D] \approx 30.5$ after discretization. We use (50) for small n, while the corresponding limits as $n \to \infty$ are provided by Algorithm 2. Unless mentioned otherwise, $w(x) = x$. Note that simulation results averaged over 10K iterations are still pretty noisy, which explains non-monotonicity of error in certain cases as n increases.

Tables 6-7 examine $\alpha < 2$ under root truncation. Since these graphs deterministically limit the maximum degree to $\sqrt{n}$, (50) is accurate even for n as small as 10K. Table 8 shows another AMRC scenario, where $\alpha = 2.1$ and truncation is linear. Because these graphs are only asymptotically constrained, larger discrepancy for small n was expected. However, even the slowest-converging method studied here (i.e., $T_2 + \theta_{RR}$) exhibits less than 1% error for $n \ge$ 1M nodes.

7.4 Unconstrained Degree

We now transition to more challenging cases. Table 9 revisits the data in Table 6 under linear truncation. Both permutations now produce larger cost and quicker convergence

n	$T_1 + \theta_A$			$T_1 + \theta_D$		
	sim	(50)	error	sim	(50)	error
10^4	7,158	6,452	−9.9%	209.5	241.1	15.1%
10^5	25,770	24,303	−5.7%	261.0	302.1	15.8%
10^6	84,441	82,815	−1.9%	294.1	333.0	13.3%
10^7	274,876	270,125	−1.7%	317.0	346.9	9.4%
∞		∞			356.3	

Table 9: Cost with $\alpha = 1.5$ and linear truncation.

n	$T_2 + \theta_D$			$T_2 + \theta_{RR}$		
	sim	(50)	error	sim	(50)	error
10^4	499.4	854.4	71.1%	354.5	532.6	50.3%
10^5	725.4	1,096.6	51.2%	476.5	662.3	39.0%
10^6	907.7	1,216.7	34.0%	570.2	724.4	27.0%
10^7	1,041.5	1,270.0	21.9%	631.2	751.5	19.1%
∞		1,307.6			770.4	

Table 10: Cost with $\alpha = 1.7$ and linear truncation.

n	$T_1 + \theta_D$		$T_2 + \theta_D$		$T_2 + \theta_{RR}$	
	$w_1(x)$	$w_2(x)$	$w_1(x)$	$w_2(x)$	$w_1(x)$	$w_2(x)$
10^4	38%	−54.1%	304%	21.6%	216%	−3.1%
10^5	107%	−52.3%	619%	17.9%	458%	−2.2%
10^6	214%	−50.4%	1,207%	12.9%	856%	−2.3%
10^7	386%	−48.7%	2,353%	9.1%	4,105%	−0.5%

Table 11: Relative error of (50) under $\alpha = 1.2$ and linear truncation (asymptotically infinite cost).

towards their respective limits, which is especially noticeable under θ_A. A similar scenario for T_2 is shown in Table 10. Compared to Table 7, the error is much larger; however, it still monotonically decays towards zero as n increases. This is a consequence of the limiting cost being finite.

A drastically different result can be observed when the asymptotic complexity is infinite, i.e., $c(\mathcal{M}, \xi) = \infty$. This arises from the difference in the rates at which simulations and (50) scale as $n \to \infty$, which yields an error that grows with n. We use this opportunity to investigate how $w(x)$ can be used to create a more accurate result for such scenarios. Specifically, define $w_1(x) = x$ and $w_2(x) = \min(x, \sqrt{m})$. Table 11 examines $\alpha = 1.2$ under linear truncation. While $w_1(x)$ builds a hefty error against T_1 by the time n reaches 10M, its alternative $w_2(x)$ settles into a growth rate that is essentially the same as that of simulations. Furthermore, it eliminates most of the error in the other two cases.

Both functions w_1, w_2 have the same limit as $n \to \infty$, which can be shown using root-truncated $F_n(x)$, but the convergence speed is clearly different. As discussed earlier, finding $w(x)$ that keeps (50) provably accurate in unconstrained graphs of finite size is a topic for future work. However, if such functions exist and $(x^2 - x)/w(x)$ is monotonic, optimality and comparison results of the previous section apply to them just the same.

7.5 Real Graphs

We now examine our conclusions and model applicability to Twitter [27], which is a standard graph in this field with n = 41M nodes and m = 1.2B edges (9.3 GB). In addition to the five main permutations, i.e., ascending θ_A, descending θ_D, round-robin θ_{RR}, complementary round-robin θ_{CRR}, and uniform θ_U, we also consider the degenerate orientation, built using the algorithm from [29]. Because this orientation requires 5 hours to compute, which is two orders of magnitude longer than it takes E_1 to list all triangles [17], we do not consider it competitive. Instead, we provide the corresponding cost to shed light on how much theoretical improvement it may offer to $c_n(\mathcal{M}, \theta_n)$.

	Permutation					
	θ_D	θ_A	θ_{RR}	θ_{CRR}	θ_U	θ_{degen}
T_1	150B	123T	63T	31T	45T	136B
T_2	360B	360B	255B	62T	41T	815B
E_1	511B	123T	63T	93T	86T	951B
E_4	123T	123T	123T	62T	82T	123T

Table 12: CPU operations on Twitter.

Table 12 displays the total number of CPU instructions $nc_n(\mathcal{M}, \theta_n)$ on Twitter, highlighting in gray the optimal permutation for each row. These results agree with our analysis, in both the choice of best/worst orientation and comparison between the methods. For example, θ_{RR} is best for T_2, θ_A is worst for E_1, and the cost of E_1 under θ_D is double that of T_2 under θ_{RR}. The degenerate orientation reduces the best cost of T_1 by 10%, but increases that of the other methods by $2-3\times$. Note that our results minimize the expected cost over all graphs with a given degree distribution. This does not prevent existence of algorithms that can take a particular instance of G_n and customize θ_n to its edge structure, which explains how the degenerate permutation manages to beat θ_D for T_1.

The overhead ratio between the worst and best permutations is 817 for T_1, 241 for T_2 and E_1, and only 2 for E_4. The last case can be explained by the fact that E_4 is almost equally expensive under all permutations, exhibiting *at least* 62T/511B = 121 times more overhead than the best orientation for E_1. Also notice that T_1 and T_2 are only within a factor of 255B/150B = 1.7 of each other, which shows that keeping the graph non-relabeled would have doubled the cost of T_1 and made it worse than T_2. This also would have caused a 29% increase for E_1 and 100% for E_4. Our final observation is that lack of relabeling in prior work [36] explains reports of 300B tuples for T_1 on Twitter.

8. CONCLUSION

Our efforts produced the first accurate result on the asymptotics of triangle listing under arbitrary permutations. We proved that expected cost could be optimized using four different orientations and derived the corresponding complexity models. Our results showed that only two methods were generally worth considering – one from the vertex-iterator family and the other from the scanning edge-iterator. In many cases the winner will be determined by the edge-existence verification speed of these algorithms; however, we discovered degree sequences for which the former would always outperform the latter as $n \to \infty$.

Our results answered many open questions in the area of triangle listing; however, additional challenges remain. Among them is analysis of unconstrained graphs, design of better external-memory partitioning schemes, and modeling of I/O complexity in scenarios such as [17].

9. REFERENCES

[1] W. Aiello, F. R. K. Chung, and L. Lu, "A Random Graph

Model for Massive Graphs," in *Proc. ACM STOC*, May 2000, pp. 171–180.

[2] N. Alon, R. Yuster, and U. Zwick, "Finding and Counting Given Length Cycles," *Algorithmica*, vol. 17, no. 3, pp. 209–223, Mar. 1997.

[3] S. Arifuzzaman, M. Khan, and M. Marathe, "PATRIC: A Parallel Algorithm for Counting Triangles in Massive Networks," in *Proc. ACM CIKM*, Oct. 2013, pp. 529–538.

[4] Z. Bar-Yossef, R. Kumar, and D. Sivakumar, "Reductions in Streaming Algorithms, With an Application to Counting Triangles in Graphs," in *Proc. ACM-SIAM SODA*, Jan. 2002, pp. 623–632.

[5] A.-L. Barabasi and R. Albert, "Emergence of Scaling in Random Networks," *Science*, vol. 286, no. 5439, pp. 509–512, Oct. 1999.

[6] V. Batagelj and M. Zaversnik, "Short Cycle Connectivity," *Discrete Math.*, vol. 307, no. 3–5, pp. 310–318, Feb. 2007.

[7] L. Becchetti, P. Boldi, C. Castillo, and A. Gionis, "Efficient Semi-streaming Algorithms for Local Triangle Counting in Massive Graphs," in *Proc. ACM SIGKDD*, Aug. 2008, pp. 16–24.

[8] E. A. Bender and E. R. Canfield, "The Asymptotic Number of Labeled Graphs with Given Degree Sequences," *J. Combin. Theory Ser. A*, vol. 24, pp. 296–307, May 1978.

[9] J. W. Berry, L. A. Fostvedt, D. J. Nordman, C. A. Phillips, C. Seshadhri, and A. G. Wilsone, "Why Do Simple Algorithms for Triangle Enumeration Work in the Real World?" *Internet Mathematics*, vol. 11, no. 6, pp. 555–571, May 2015.

[10] J. W. Berry, B. Hendrickson, R. A. LaViolette, and C. A. Phillips, "Tolerating the Community Detection Resolution Limit With Edge Weighting," *Physical Review E*, vol. 83, no. 5, p. 056119, 2011.

[11] J. Blitzstein and P. Diaconis, "A Sequential Importance Sampling Algorithm for Generating Random Graphs With Prescribed Degrees," *Internet Mathematics*, vol. 6, no. 4, pp. 489–522, 2011.

[12] P. Brach, M. Cygan, J. Łącki, and P. Sankowski, "Algorithmic Complexity of Power Law Networks," in *Proc. ACM-SIAM SODA*, Jan. 2016, pp. 1306–1325.

[13] N. Chiba and T. Nishizeki, "Arboricity and Subgraph Listing Algorithms," *SIAM J. Comput.*, vol. 14, no. 1, pp. 210–223, Feb. 1985.

[14] S. Chu and J. Cheng, "Triangle Listing in Massive Networks and Its Applications," in *Proc. ACM SIGKDD*, Aug. 2011, pp. 672–680.

[15] F. R. K. Chung and L. Lu, "Connected Components in Random Graphs with Given Expected Degree Sequences," *Annals of Combinatorics*, vol. 6, no. 2, pp. 125–145, Nov. 2002.

[16] J. Cohen, "Graph Twiddling in a MapReduce World," *Computing in Science & Engineering*, vol. 11, no. 4, pp. 29–41, Jul. 2009.

[17] Y. Cui, D. Xiao, and D. Loguinov, "On Efficient External-Memory Triangle Listing," in *Proc. IEEE ICDM*, Dec. 2016, pp. 101–110.

[18] R. Dementiev, "Algorithm Engineering for Large Data Sets," Ph.D. dissertation, Universität des Saarlandes, 2006.

[19] P. Erdös and A. Rényi, "On Random Graphs I," *Publication Math. Debrecen*, vol. 6, pp. 290–297, 1959.

[20] I. Fudos and C. M. Hoffmann, "A Graph-Constructive Approach to Solving Systems of Geometric Constraints," *ACM Transactions on Graphics*, vol. 16, no. 2, pp. 179–216, Apr. 1997.

[21] I. Giechaskiel, G. Panagopoulos, and E. Yoneki, "PDTL: Parallel and Distributed Triangle Listing for Massive Graphs," in *Proc. IEEE ICPP*, Sep. 2015, pp. 370–379.

[22] X. Hu, Y. Tao, and C. Chung, "Massive Graph Triangulation," in *Proc. ACM SIGMOD*, Jun. 2013, pp. 325–336.

[23] A. Itai and M. Rodeh, "Finding a Minimum Circuit in a Graph," *SIAM Journal on Computing*, vol. 7, no. 4, pp. 413–423, Nov. 1978.

[24] Z. R. Kashani, H. Ahrabian, E. Elahi, A. Nowzari-Dalini, E. S. Ansari, S. Asadi, S. Mohammadi, F. Schreiber, and A. Masoudi-Nejad, "Kavosh: A New Algorithm for Finding Network Motifs," *Bioinformatics*, vol. 10, no. 1, p. 318, Oct. 2009.

[25] J. Kim, W. Han, S. Lee, K. Park, and H. Yu, "OPT: A New Framework for Overlapped and Parallel Triangulation in Large-scale Graphs," in *Proc. ACM SIGMOD*, 2014, pp. 637–648.

[26] A. Kostochka, E. Sopena, and X. Zhu, "Acyclic and Oriented Chromatic Numbers of Graphs," *Journal of Graph Theory*, vol. 24, no. 4, pp. 331–340, Apr. 1997.

[27] H. Kwak, C. Lee, H. Park, and S. Moon, "What is Twitter, A Social Network or a News Media?" in *Proc. WWW*, Apr. 2010, pp. 591–600.

[28] M. Latapy, "Main-memory Triangle Computations for Very Large (Sparse (Power-law)) Graphs," *Theor. Comput. Sci.*, vol. 407, no. 1-3, pp. 458–473, Nov. 2008.

[29] D. W. Matula and L. L. Beck, "Smallest-Last Ordering and Clustering and Graph Coloring Algorithms," *Journal of the ACM*, vol. 30, no. 3, pp. 417–427, Jul. 1983.

[30] M. Molloy and B. Reed, "A Critical Point for Random Graphs with a Given Degree Sequence," *Random Structures and Algorithms*, vol. 6, no. 2/3, pp. 161–180, Mar./May 1995.

[31] M. E. Newman, D. J. Watts, and S. H. Strogatz, "Random Graph Models of Social Networks," *Proceedings of the National Academy of Sciences*, vol. 99, no. 1, pp. 2566–2572, Feb. 2002.

[32] M. Ortmann and U. Brandes, "Triangle Listing Algorithms: Back from the Diversion," in *Proc. ALENEX*, Jan. 2014, pp. 1–8.

[33] T. Schank and D. Wagner, "Finding, Counting and Listing All Triangles in Large Graphs, an Experimental Study," in *Proc. WEA*, May 2005, pp. 606–609.

[34] M. Sevenich, S. Hong, A. Welc, and H. Chafi, "Fast In-Memory Triangle Listing for Large Real-World Graphs," in *Proc. ACM SNA-KDD*, Aug. 2014, pp. 1–9.

[35] J. Shun and K. Tangwongsan, "Multicore Triangle Computations Without Tuning," in *Proc. IEEE ICDE*, Apr. 2015, pp. 149–160.

[36] S. Suri and S. Vassilvitskii, "Counting Triangles and the Curse of the Last Reducer," in *Proc. WWW*, Mar. 2011, pp. 607–614.

[37] N. Wang, J. Zhang, K.-L. Tan, and A. K. Tung, "On Triangulation-Based Dense Neighborhood Graph Discovery," *PVLDB*, vol. 4, no. 2, pp. 58–68, 2010.

[38] D. J. Watts and S. Strogatz, "Collective Dynamics of 'Small World' Networks," *Nature*, vol. 393, pp. 440–442, Jun. 1998.

[39] J. A. Wellner, "A Glivenko-Cantelli Theorem and Strong Laws of Large Numbers for Functions of Order Statistics," *The Annals of Statistics*, vol. 5, no. 3, pp. 473–480, May 1977.

[40] V. Willians and R. Williams, "Subcubic Equivalences Between Path, Matrix, and Triangle Problems," in *Proc. IEEE FOCS*, Oct. 2010, pp. 645–654.

[41] R. W. Wolff, *Stochastic Modeling and the Theory of Queues.* Prentice Hall, 1989.

[42] D. Xiao, Y. Cui, D. B. Cline, and D. Loguinov, "On Asymptotic Cost of Triangle Listing in Random Graphs," Texas A&M University, Tech. Rep. 2016-9-2, Sep. 2016. [Online]. Available: http://irl.cs.tamu.edu/publications/.

[43] Z. Yang, C. Wilson, X. Wang, T. Gao, B. Zhao, and Y. Dai, "Uncovering Social Network Sybils in the Wild," in *Proc. ACM IMC*, Nov. 2011, pp. 259–268.

[44] W. van Zwet, "A Strong Law for Linear Functions of Order Statistics," *Annals of Probability*, vol. 8, no. 5, pp. 986–990, 1980.

Efficiently Enumerating Minimal Triangulations

Nofar Carmeli
Technion
Haifa, Israel
snofca@cs.technion.ac.il

Batya Kenig
Technion
Haifa, Israel
batyak@cs.technion.ac.il

Benny Kimelfeld
Technion
Haifa, Israel
bennyk@cs.technion.ac.il

ABSTRACT

We present an algorithm that enumerates all the minimal triangulations of a graph in incremental polynomial time. Consequently, we get an algorithm for enumerating all the proper tree decompositions, in incremental polynomial time, where "proper" means that the tree decomposition cannot be improved by removing or splitting a bag. The algorithm can incorporate any method for (ordinary, single result) triangulation or tree decomposition, and can serve as an anytime algorithm to improve such a method. We describe an extensive experimental study of an implementation on real data from different fields. Our experiments show that the algorithm improves upon central quality measures over the underlying tree decompositions, and is able to produce a large number of high-quality decompositions.

Keywords

Minimal triangulation; Tree decomposition; Enumeration algorithm; Minimal separators; Maximal independent sets; Maximal cliques

1. INTRODUCTION

Many intractable computational problems on graphs admit tractable algorithms when applied to trees or forests. A *tree decomposition* extracts a tree structure from a graph by grouping nodes into *bags* (each treated as a single node). The corresponding operation on hypergraphs is that of a *generalized hypertree decomposition* [16] that consists of a tree decomposition of the *primal* graph (which has the same set of nodes, and an edge between every two hyperedge neighbors), and an assignment of hyperedge labels (edge covers) to the tree nodes [17]. Tree decompositions and generalized hypertree decompositions have a plethora of applications, including optimization of (multi)join queries in databases [16, 24, 37], containment of database queries, constraint satisfaction problems [27], prediction of RNA secondary structure [40], computation of Nash equilibria in games [16], inference in probabilistic graphical models [29], and weighted model counting [25].

Past research has focused on obtaining a "good" tree decompositions, where goodness is typically by means of the *width* [34]—the maximal cardinality of a bag (minus one). Nevertheless, finding a tree decomposition of the minimal width is NP-hard [2], as is the case for other common measures of goodness for tree decompositions such as *fill* [39], and in the case of hypergraphs *hypertree width* [18], *generalized hypertree width* [19], and *fractional hypertree width* [30]. Therefore, heuristic algorithms are often applied [3, 5]. The different measures of goodness are motivated by the fact that the needs of different applications are often different from (though related to) the width. Additional examples are the complexity of weighted model counting, induced by a parameter associated with the "CNF-tree" of the formula [17, 25], and the effectiveness of *adhesions* (parent-child intersection) for caching in terms of dimension and skew [24]. In fact, Kalinsky et al. [24] have illustrated how, in real-life scenarios, isomorphic tree decompositions of a minimal width may result in orders-of-magnitude difference in (join) performance.

The common approach is to devise a decomposition algorithm (exact, approximate or heuristic) to capture the desired measure of goodness per application. However, this is a nontrivial challenge that (to the least) requires high expertise in algorithms and tree decompositions. We propose an alternative approach—produce a large number of different tree decompositions, using a baseline decomposition method, and allow the application at hand to choose the best according to its internal measure function. Our approach brings together results and techniques from two seemingly unrelated areas, *chordal graphs* and *enumeration theory*, in order to establish a practical tool for enhancing decomposition algorithms and, by implication, the performance of various inference and optimization algorithms. Specifically, we explore the task of *enumerating* all (or a subset of) the tree decompositions. Such algorithms have been proposed in the past for small graphs (representing database queries), without complexity guarantees [37]. Our main result is an enumeration algorithm that runs in *incremental polynomial time* [22], that is, the time between producing the Nth result and the $(N+1)$st result is polynomial in N and in the size of the input.

We first need to define which tree decompositions should be enumerated, as many of them are effectively useless. For example, if we take a graph that is already a tree, we do not wish to enumerate the tree decompositions that group nodes

PODS'17, May 14-19, 2017, Chicago, IL, USA

DOI: http://dx.doi.org/10.1145/3034786.3056109

with no reason; in fact, the tree itself is the only reasonable decomposition in this case. Therefore, we consider only tree decompositions that cannot be "improved" by removing or splitting a bag, and we call such tree decompositions *proper*. We prove that the proper tree decompositions are in a bijective (and efficiently computable) correspondence to the *minimal triangulations* of the graph at hand, defined a follows. A *triangulation* of a graph g is a graph g' that is obtained from g by adding edges so that g' is *chordal*, that is, g' does not have any induced simple cycle of more than three nodes. A triangulation is *minimal* if no triangulation can be obtained using only a strict subset of the added edges.

So, the problem is reduced to the task of enumerating all of the minimal triangulations of a graph. In this paper we devise an algorithm for performing this task in incremental polynomial time. Our approach is as follows. Parra and Scheffler [32] have shown that there is a one-to-one correspondence between the minimal triangulations of a graph g and the maximal independent sets of a special graph $\mathcal{G}$. The nodes of $\mathcal{G}$ are the so called *minimal separators of* g, and the edges are between *crossing* minimal separators. (Precise definitions are in Section 2.) So, enumerating the minimal triangulations of a graph boils down to enumerating these maximal sets. It is well known that all the maximal independent sets of a graph can be enumerated with polynomial delay [10, 22]. However, this is insufficient for us, since the graph $\mathcal{G}$ is not given as input, and in fact, its number of nodes can be exponential in the size of the original graph g. Therefore, we cannot construct this graph ahead of time, and cannot directly use existing algorithms to establish incremental polynomial time.

We address this problem by defining an abstraction of the graph $\mathcal{G}$ of minimal separators by means of a *Succinct Graph Representation* (SGR), which is represented compactly by two algorithms: one for enumerating the nodes and one for testing whether a given pair of nodes forms an edge. In particular, we can access the nodes of $\mathcal{G}$ through a polynomial-delay iterator, due to a result by Berry et al. [4] (who show how to enumerate the minimal separators of a graph). Applying previous results, we prove that the SGR for the minimal separator graph (i.e., $\mathcal{G}$) meets certain tractability conditions termed *tractable expansion*, which enable the enumeration of its maximal independent sets (i.e., g's minimal triangulations) in incremental polynomial time in the size of the representation (which can be logarithmic in the size of the graph itself).

In summary, we reduce the problem of enumerating the proper tree decompositions to that of enumerating the minimal triangulations, which we reduce to the problem of enumerating the maximal independent sets of an SGR with tractability properties, and we devise an algorithm for the latter task. An important feature of the algorithm is that it can incorporate any black-box procedure for expanding a given independent set into a maximal one. When applied to enumerating the proper tree decompositions, such a procedure can be any off-the-shelf algorithm for minimal triangulation or tree decomposition (e.g., Maximum Cardinality Search [3] and LB-Triang [5]). However, our algorithm executes this procedure on different versions of the original graph, each time with some new edges added. Hence, our algorithm has the potential of using a high-quality decomposition algorithm for producing *many* high-quality decompositions, enabling the user to choose the best one generated according to the specific measures of her use case (may it be width or anything else).

After establishing our algorithm, we describe an experimental study where we have tested the ability of the algorithm to utilize the aforementioned triangulation algorithms. The experimental study covers graphs of a wide range of domains (where tree decomposition is needed for efficient analysis): join queries (from the TPC-H collection), Bayesian networks, Markov Random Fields, grids, and random graphs. We tested the execution time (delay) of the algorithm, its ability to reduce the width or fill (number of edges added to establish chordality), and the number of decompositions of quality (width/fill) the same or better than that of the original off-the-shelf algorithm. The results show that, indeed, our algorithm can effectively enhance the quality of the corresponding decomposition algorithm.

The rest of the paper is organized as follows. In Section 2 we give preliminary definitions and notation, and recall basic results from the literature. The SGR framework is presented in Section 3, along with the enumeration algorithm for maximal independent sets. In Section 4 we prove that the graph of minimal separating sets satisfies the tractability requirements needed for the SGR enumeration algorithm, and thereby establish an algorithm for enumerating the minimal triangulations. We show how this algorithm can enumerate the proper tree decompositions in Section 5. We present our experimental study in Section 6, and conclude in Section 7. Some of the proofs are in the appendix.

2. PRELIMINARIES

In this section we give some basic notation and terminology that we use throughout the paper. In addition, we recall some basic theory that we need in this paper.

2.1 Graphs

The graphs in this work are undirected. For a graph g, the set of nodes is denoted by $\mathsf{V}(g)$, and the set of edges (pairs $\{u, v\}$ of distinct nodes) is denoted by $\mathsf{E}(g)$. Let U be a set of nodes of a graph g. We denote by $g_{|U}$ the subgraph of g *induced* by U; that is, $\mathsf{V}(g_{|U}) = U$ and $\mathsf{E}(g_{|U}) = \{\{u, v\} \in \mathsf{E}(g) \mid \{u, v\} \subseteq U\}$. We denote by $g \setminus U$ the graph obtained from g by removing all the nodes in U (along with their incident edges), that is, the graph $g_{|\mathsf{V}(g)\setminus U}$.

Let g be a graph and U a set of nodes of g. We say that U is an *independent set* if it does not contain both endpoints of any edge, and it is a *maximal independent set* if it is an independent set and it is not strictly contained in any other independent set. We denote by $\mathit{MaxInd}(g)$ the set of all the maximal independent sets of g. We say that U is a *clique* (*of* g) if every two nodes of U are connected by an edge, and it is a *maximal clique* (*of* g) if it is a clique that is not strictly contained in any other clique. We denote by $\mathit{MaxClq}(g)$ the set of all the maximal cliques of g. The operation of *saturating* U (*in* g) is that of connecting every non-adjacent pair of nodes in U by a new edge. Hence, if h is obtained from g by saturating U, then U is a clique of h.

2.2 Minimal Separators

Let g be a graph, and let S be a subset of $\mathsf{V}(g)$. Let u and v be two nodes of g. We say that S is a (u, v)*-separator* if u and v belong to distinct connected components of $g \setminus S$. We say that S is a *minimal* (u, v)-separator if no strict subset of S is a (u, v)-separator. We say that S is a *minimal separator* if there are two nodes u and v such that S is a minimal (u,v)-separator. We denote by $\mathit{MinSep}(g)$ the set of all the minimal separators of g. We mention that the number of minimal separators (i.e., $|\mathit{MinSep}(g)|$) may be exponential in the number of nodes (i.e., $|\mathsf{V}(g)|$).

Let g be a graph, and let S and T be two minimal separators of g. We say that S *crosses* T, in notation $S\natural_g T$, if there are nodes u and v in T such that S is a (u,v)-separator. If g is clear from the context, we may omit it and write simply $S \natural T$. It is known that $\natural$ is a symmetric relation: if S crosses T then T crosses S [26,32]. Hence, if $S \natural T$ then we may also say that S and T are *crossing*. When S and T are non-crossing, then we also say that S and T are *parallel*.

2.3 Chordality and Triangulation

Let g be a graph. A *cycle* of g is a path that starts and ends with the same node. A *chord* of a cycle c of g is an edge $e \in \mathsf{E}(g)$ that connects two nodes that are non-adjacent in c. We say that g is *chordal* if every cycle of length greater than three has a chord. Whether a given graph is chordal can be decided in linear time [36]. Dirac [12] has shown a characterization of chordal graphs by means of their minimal separators.

THEOREM 2.1. (Dirac [12]) *A graph g is chordal if and only if every minimal separator of g is a clique.*

Rose [35] has shown that a chordal graph g has fewer minimal separators than nodes (that is, if g is chordal then $|\mathit{MinSep}(g)| < |\mathsf{V}(g)|$), and Kumar and Madhavan [28] have shown that we can find all of these minimal separators in linear time.

THEOREM 2.2. (Kumar and Madhavan [28]) *Let g be a chordal graph. The set $\mathit{MinSep}(g)$ can be computed in linear time.*

A *triangulation* of a graph g is a graph h such that $\mathsf{V}(g) = \mathsf{V}(h)$, $\mathsf{E}(g) \subseteq \mathsf{E}(h)$, and h is chordal. A *minimal triangulation* of g is a triangulation h of g with the following property: for every graph h' with $\mathsf{V}(g) = \mathsf{V}(h')$, if $\mathsf{E}(g) \subseteq \mathsf{E}(h') \subsetneq \mathsf{E}(h)$ then h' is non-chordal (or in other words, h' is not a triangulation of g). In particular, if g is already chordal then g is the only minimal triangulation of itself. We denote by $\mathit{MinTri}(g)$ the set of all the minimal triangulations of g.

2.4 Tree Decomposition

Let g be a graph. A *tree decomposition* d of g is a pair (t, β), where t is a tree and $\beta : \mathsf{V}(t) \to 2^{\mathsf{V}(g)}$ is a function that maps every node of t into a set of nodes of g, so that all of the following hold.

- Nodes are covered: for every node $u \in \mathsf{V}(g)$ there is a node $v \in \mathsf{V}(t)$ such that $u \in \beta(v)$.
- Edges are covered: for every edge $e \in \mathsf{E}(g)$ there is a node $v \in \mathsf{V}(t)$ such that $e \subseteq \beta(v)$.
- *Junction-tree* (or *running-intersection*) property: for all nodes $u, v, w \in \mathsf{V}(t)$, if v is on the path between u and w, then $\beta(v)$ contains $\beta(u) \cap \beta(w)$.

Let g be a graph, and let $d = (t, \beta)$ be a tree decomposition of g. For a node v of t, the set $\beta(v)$ is called a *bag* of d. We denote by bags(d) the set $\{\beta(v) \mid v \in \mathsf{V}(t)\}$, and we denote by $\mathsf{saturate}(g, d)$ the graph obtained from g by saturating (i.e., adding an edge between every pair of nodes in) every bag of d.

Jordan [23] shows the following characterization of chordal graphs by means of tree decompositions.

THEOREM 2.3. (Jordan [23]) *A graph g is chordal if and only if it has a tree decomposition d such that every bag of d is a clique of g.*

2.5 Enumeration

An *enumeration problem* P is a collection of pairs (x, Y) where x is an *input* and Y is a finite set of *answers* for x, denoted by $\mathsf{P}(x)$. A *solver* for an enumeration problem P is an algorithm that, when given an input x, produces (or *prints*) a sequence of answers such that every answer in $\mathsf{P}(x)$ is printed precisely once. A solver for an enumeration problem is also referred to as an *enumeration algorithm*.

Johnson, Papadimitriou and Yannakakis [22] introduced several different notions of *efficiency* for enumeration algorithms, and we recall these now. Let P be an enumeration problem, and let A be solver for P. We say that A runs in:

- *polynomial total time* if the total execution time of A is polynomial in $(|x| + |\mathsf{P}(x)|)$;
- *polynomial delay* if the time between printing every two consecutive answers is polynomial in $|x|$;
- *incremental polynomial time* if, after printing N answers, the time to print the next $(N+1)$st answer is polynomial in $(|x| + N)$. [1]

Observe that a solver that enumerates with polynomial delay also enumerates with incremental polynomial time, which, in turn, implies polynomial total time.

3. ENUMERATING MAXIMAL INDEPENDENT SETS ON SUCCINCT GRAPHS

The main result of this paper is an algorithm for enumerating the minimal triangulations of a graph g. As we explain in the next section, this problem amounts to enumerating the maximal independent sets of a graph h. It is known that the maximal independent sets of a graph can be enumerated with polynomial delay [22]. However, we cannot instantiate h, since the number of nodes of h can be exponential in the size of g. Hence, known algorithms for enumerating maximal independent sets cannot be applied to solve our problem. Nevertheless, h possesses some tractability properties that, in fact, allow us to efficiently enumerate the maximal independent sets of h. In this section we identify these properties within an abstract framework of *succinct graph representations*, where a graph may be exponentially larger than its representation, and we have access to the nodes and edges through efficient algorithms. Mainly, we devise an algorithm for enumerating the maximal independent sets for such graphs.

[1]The definition of Johnson et al. [22] requires the delay to be polynomial in the size of the input and the *size* of the previously produced results (not just their *number* N as we define here). However, the definitions are equivalent when the size of each answer is polynomial in that of the input, as in our case.

3.1 Succinct Graph Representations

We begin with the formal definition of a succinct graph representation.

Definition 1 (SGR). *A Succinct Graph Representation (SGR) is a triple $(\mathcal{G}, A_{\mathsf{V}}, A_{\mathsf{E}})$, where:*

- *$\mathcal{G}$ is a function that maps every input x, referred to as an* instance*, to a graph $\mathcal{G}(x)$;*
- *A_{V} is an enumeration algorithm that, given an instance x, enumerates the nodes of $\mathcal{G}(x)$;*
- *A_{E} is a decision algorithm that, given an instance x and nodes v and u of $\mathcal{G}(x)$, determines whether v and u are connected by an edge in $\mathcal{G}(x)$.* □

An SGR $(\mathcal{G}, A_{\mathsf{V}}, A_{\mathsf{E}})$ is said to be *tractably accessible* if both the following hold.

1. A_{V} enumerates with polynomial delay.
2. A_{E} terminates in polynomial time.

Here, both polynomials are with respect to $|x|$ (the length of x). Observe that in a tractably accessible SGR, the (representation) size of every node v of $\mathcal{G}(x)$ is polynomial in that of x (since writing v is within the polynomial delay).

For efficient enumeration of $\mathit{MaxInd}(\mathcal{G}(x))$, we need some more tractability conditions.

Definition 2 (Tractable Expansion). *A tractably accessible SGR $(\mathcal{G}, A_{\mathsf{V}}, A_{\mathsf{E}})$ is said to have a* tractable expansion *if both of the following conditions hold.*

1. *There is a polynomial p such that $|I| \le p(|x|)$ for all instances x and independent sets I of $\mathcal{G}(x)$.*
2. *There is a polynomial-time algorithm that, given x and an independent set I of $\mathcal{G}(x)$, either determines that I is maximal or returns a node $v \notin I$ such that $I \cup \{v\}$ is independent.*

Following is an example of an SGR that is central to this paper.

3.1.1 The Separator Graph as an SGR

The *separator graph* of a graph g is the graph that has the set $\mathit{MinSep}(g)$ of minimal separators as its node set, and an edge between every two minimal separators that are crossing (i.e., $S, T \in \mathit{MinSep}(g)$ such that $S \natural T$). Throughout this paper we denote by MSGraph the SGR $(\mathcal{G}^{\mathsf{ms}}, A_{\mathsf{V}}^{\mathsf{ms}}, A_{\mathsf{E}}^{\mathsf{ms}})$, where:

- $\mathcal{G}^{\mathsf{ms}}$ is a function that maps the representation of a graph g to its separator graph $\mathcal{G}^{\mathsf{ms}}(g)$.
- A_{V} is an enumeration algorithm that, given a graph g, enumerates its set $\mathit{MinSep}(g)$ of minimal separators. We can use here a variation of the algorithm of Berry et al. [4] that enumerates $\mathit{MinSep}(g)$ with polynomial delay, as we describe later in Section 4.2.
- A_{E} is an algorithm that, given a graph g and two minimal separators S and T, determines whether $S \natural T$ efficiently (e.g., by removing S and testing whether T is split along multiple connected components).

In particular, MSGraph is a tractably accessible SGR.

Algorithm EnumMIS(x)

```
J := Extend(x, ∅)
print J
Q := {J}
P := ∅
V := ∅
iterator := A_V(x)
while Q ≠ ∅ do
   J := Q.pop()
   P.push(J)
   for all v ∈ V do
      J_v := {v} ∪ {u ∈ J | ¬A_E(x, v, u)}
      K := Extend(x, J_v)
      if K ∉ Q ∪ P then
         print K
         Q := Q ∪ {K}
   while Q = ∅ and iterator.hasNext() do
      v := iterator.next()
      V := V ∪ {v}
      for all J' ∈ P do
         J'_v := {v} ∪ {u ∈ J' | ¬A_E(x, v, u)}
         K := Extend(x, J'_v)
         if K ∉ Q ∪ P then
            print K
            Q := Q ∪ {K}
```

Figure 1: Enumerating maximal independent sets of an input x for an SGR $(\mathcal{G}, A_{\mathsf{V}}, A_{\mathsf{E}})$

3.2 Enumerating Maximal Independent Sets in SGRs

Our main result for this section is the following.

Theorem 3.1. *Let $(\mathcal{G}, A_{\mathsf{V}}, A_{\mathsf{E}})$ be a tractably accessible SGR with a tractable expansion. There is an algorithm that, given an instance x, enumerates $\mathit{MaxInd}(\mathcal{G}(x))$ in incremental polynomial time.*

The proof is via the algorithm EnumMIS that is depicted in Figure 1. This algorithm is a nontrivial adaptation of the algorithm for computing full disjunctions in databases [9,10]. In this section, we describe the algorithm and prove its correctness and efficiency. In the remainder of this section, we fix a tractably accessible SGR $(\mathcal{G}, A_{\mathsf{V}}, A_{\mathsf{E}})$ with tractable expansion, and an input instance x. Our goal is to enumerate $\mathit{MaxInd}(\mathcal{G}(x))$.

3.2.1 Algorithm Description

The underlying idea is as follows. The algorithm extends every maximal independent set J that it generates in the direction of every node v that it generates. By *extending J in the direction of v* we mean producing an arbitrary maximal independent set K that contains v and all nodes in J that are non-neighbors of v. As long as there are unprocessed sets, they are extended in the direction of all previously generated nodes. When no unprocessed sets are left, additional nodes are generated, and the previously processed sets are extended in the direction of the new nodes.

The algorithm maintains two collections, $\mathcal{Q}$ and $\mathcal{P}$, for storing answers (which are maximal independent sets of the graph $\mathcal{G}(x)$). The algorithm inserts answers into $\mathcal{Q}$, and repeatedly *removes* (or *pops*) an answer from $\mathcal{Q}$ and *processes* that answer (while possibly inserting new answers into $\mathcal{Q}$), until $\mathcal{Q}$ is empty. The set $\mathcal{P}$ stores the answers that have already been removed from $\mathcal{Q}$ and processed. Importantly, both collections feature membership testing, element removal and element insertion with a number of comparisons logarithmic in their cardinality (i.e., the number of answers they hold at the time of the operation). In addition, the algorithm maintains a collection $\mathcal{V}$ of the nodes of $\mathcal{G}(x)$ generated thus far. The collection $\mathcal{Q}$ is initialized with a single result (which is printed after generated), which is an arbitrary maximal independent set. This result is obtained through the procedure $\mathsf{Extend}(x, I)$ that extends a given independent set I into a maximal one. Note that this procedure can be implemented in polynomial time, since $(\mathcal{G}, A_{\mathsf{V}}, A_{\mathsf{E}})$ has a tractable expansion. The sets $\mathcal{P}$ and $\mathcal{V}$ are initialized empty.

The algorithm accesses the nodes of $\mathcal{G}(x)$ through an iterator object that is obtained by executing $A_{\mathsf{V}}(x)$, and features two polynomial-time operations:

- Boolean hasNext() determines whether there are additional nodes of $\mathcal{G}(x)$ to enumerate.
- next() returns the next node in the iteration.

The algorithm applies the iteration of line 7 until $\mathcal{Q}$ becomes empty, and then terminates. In every iteration, the algorithm pops an element from $\mathcal{Q}$, stores it in $\mathcal{P}$ (lines 8–9), and then processes it. The algorithm iterates through the nodes in $\mathcal{V}$, and for each node v it applies (in lines 11–15) what we call *extension of J in the direction of v*:

1. Generate the set J_v that consists of v and all the nodes in J that are non-neighbors of v, using the algorithm A_{E} for testing adjacency;
2. Extend J_v into an arbitrary maximal independent set K, again using $\mathsf{Extend}(x, J_v)$;
3. If K is in neither $\mathcal{Q}$ nor $\mathcal{P}$ (meaning it was not printed before), then print K and add it to $\mathcal{Q}$.

Observe that J_v is an independent set, and hence, it is valid to invoke $\mathsf{Extend}(x, J_v)$ with J_v.

Up to this point, the algorithm is very similar to the algorithm of Cohen et al. [9] for computing full disjunctions, except that $\mathcal{V}$ does not hold all nodes but only the nodes generated so far. The twist (and the source of extra challenge in proving correctness and efficiency) is in lines 16–24, where we generate additional nodes and compensate for them being missing in the previous iterations. In these lines, the algorithm tests whether it is the case that $\mathcal{Q}$ is empty and the node iterator has additional nodes to process (line 16). While this is the case, the algorithm repeats the following procedure (lines 17–24): generate the next node using the iterator of $A_{\mathsf{V}}(x)$, add it to $\mathcal{V}$, and extend *every* previously processed result (i.e., the results in $\mathcal{P}$) in the direction of the newly generated node v (as previously described).

3.2.2 Correctness and Efficiency

The following lemma states the correctness of the algorithm. That is, the algorithm enumerates *every* element in $\mathit{MaxInd}(\mathcal{G}(x))$, *only* elements in $\mathit{MaxInd}(\mathcal{G}(x))$, and every element is printed exactly once.

LEMMA 3.2. $\mathsf{EnumMIS}(x)$ *enumerates $\mathit{MaxInd}(\mathcal{G}(x))$.*

PROOF. The algorithm prints only elements that are created by invoking the procedure Extend. Therefore, the algorithm prints only elements in $\mathit{MaxInd}(\mathcal{G}(x))$. The tests of lines 13 and 22 ensure that whenever an element is printed, this element has not been seen before. Hence, no element is printed more than once. It is left to prove that every maximal independent set of $\mathcal{G}(x)$ is printed by the algorithm.

Observe the following. When the algorithm terminates we have $\mathcal{Q} = \emptyset$. Therefore, in the previous iteration the loop of line 16 could only have terminated due to iterator.hasNext() returning false. Therefore, upon termination $\mathcal{V} = \mathsf{V}(\mathcal{G}(g))$.

Suppose, by way of contradiction, that there is some maximal independent set H that is not printed by the algorithm. Let J be a maximal independent set of $\mathcal{G}(x)$, among all the printed ones, that contains a maximal number of elements from H. The set J must exist, since the algorithm prints at least one maximal independent set. Let H_m be the intersection $H \cap J$. Since $H \neq H_m$ (or else H is not maximal), there is at least one node in $H \setminus J$; let v be such a node.

At this point we have established that before the algorithm terminated, *(a)* the node v has been generated, *and (b)* J has been printed. We now branch into two cases, as follows.

1. The set J was inserted into $\mathcal{P}$ before the node v was generated. Immediately after v is generated (in line 17), the set $J_v = \{v\} \cup \{u \in J \mid \neg A_{\mathsf{E}}(x, v, u)\}$ will be constructed (in line 20) and expanded to a maximal independent set K that contains J_v.
2. The node v was generated before J was inserted into $\mathcal{P}$. At the iteration when J is inserted into $\mathcal{P}$, we have $v \in \mathcal{V}$, and so the set $J_v = \{v\} \cup \{u \in J \mid \neg A_{\mathsf{E}}(x, v, u)\}$ will be constructed (in line 11) and expanded to a maximal independent set K that contains J_v.

So, we have established that before the algorithm terminates, the set J_v is generated and expanded to a maximal independent set K that contains J_v. Furthermore, $H_m \cup \{v\} \subseteq J_v$ (since $H_m \subseteq J$, and does not contain any neighbor of v), and therefore $H_m \cup \{v\} \subseteq K$. According to the algorithm, one of the following options must hold: (1) K is inserted into $\mathcal{Q}$, (2) K is already in $\mathcal{Q}$ (3) K was in $\mathcal{Q}$ in the past and is now in $\mathcal{P}$. Since the algorithm prints every maximal independent set that is inserted into $\mathcal{Q}$, we get a contradiction to the maximality of H_m. □

We now prove that the algorithm EnumMIS enumerates with incremental polynomial time. We do so in two steps. We first define an algorithm that is similar to EnumMIS, but with a small twist that makes it easier to prove incremental polynomial time. Then, we prove a general result that will imply that, if the new algorithm enumerates in incremental polynomial time then so does EnumMIS.

The new algorithm is similar to EnumMIS, except that each of the print commands (lines 2, 14 and 23) is replaced with an operation that takes the time of the printing, but is actually void (e.g., printing to `/dev/null` in Unix). Instead, each maximal independent set is printed immediately after being removed from $\mathcal{Q}$ (line 8). Hence, answers are *held* until removed from $\mathcal{Q}$. Next, we prove that EnumMISHold enumerates in incremental polynomial time. Observe that to bound the delay EnumMISHold, we only need to bound the time between two executions of line 8 of EnumMIS.

LEMMA 3.3. EnumMISHold(x) *enumerates with incremental polynomial time.*

PROOF. We begin by showing that the size of the node set $\mathcal{V}$ is polynomial in the size of the printed result set $\mathcal{P}$. Whenever a new node v is inserted into $\mathcal{V}$ (line 18), the set $\mathcal{Q}$ is empty. The following calls to Extend (line 21) will generate maximal independent sets containing v. Each of these maximal independent sets is either already in $\mathcal{P}$, or it is inserted into $\mathcal{Q}$ (line 24). Therefore, at the end of the iteration of the main loop in which v was inserted into $\mathcal{V}$, all maximal independent sets in $\mathcal{Q}$ contain v. In the next iteration of the main loop, if such an iteration exists, one of these newly generated independent sets will be printed and inserted into $\mathcal{P}$ (line 9). That is, at the beginning of every iteration of the algorithm (specifically, line 10), every node $v \in \mathcal{V}$ belongs to some maximal independent set that has already been printed (and thus part of $\mathcal{P}$). Since we assume tractable expansion, each independent set in $\mathcal{P}$ contains at most $p(|x|)$ nodes, and we can conclude that $|\mathcal{V}| \leq p(|x|) \cdot |\mathcal{P}|$.

We now bound the time between two executions of line 8 of EnumMIS. Line 9 takes polynomial time in $|x|$ (since there are at most exponentially many independent sets, $(\mathcal{G}, A_{\mathsf{V}}, A_{\mathsf{E}})$ has a tractable expansion, and operations on $\mathcal{P}$ require a logarithmic number of comparisons in the cardinality). The number of iterations of line 10 is at most the size of $\mathcal{V}$, which is polynomial in the number of answers printed so far (due to the above observation). Each operation in that iteration takes time polynomial in $|x|$.

The loop of line 16 repeats (at most) until a node that belongs to none of the printed answers is generated. Hence, the observation that this number is polynomial in the size of the output, along with the tractable expansion, again implies that we iterate a number of times that is polynomial in the number of answers printed so far. The loop of line 19 repeats at most as many times as the number of answers in $\mathcal{P}$, and all of these have been printed before. Besides the loops, each of lines 17–24 takes polynomial time in $|x|$. □

Lemma 3.3 shows that EnumMISHold enumerates with incremental polynomial time. Next, we show the same for EnumMIS. The key point is that every answer is printed in EnumMIS *earlier* than it is printed in EnumMISHold. We will prove that this suffices to conclude that if EnumMISHold enumerates in incremental polynomial time, then so does EnumMIS. We prove here a general result. Let P be an enumeration problem, and let A be a solver for P. For input x and answer $y \in \mathsf{P}(x)$, we denote by $\mathrm{time}_{A,x}(y)$ the time in which y is printed. We prove the following theorem.

THEOREM 3.4. *Let* P *be an enumeration problem, and let A and B be two solvers for* P. *Suppose that for all instances x and for all answers $y \in \mathsf{P}(x)$ we have $\mathrm{time}_{A,x}(y) \leq \mathrm{time}_{B,x}(y)$. If B enumerates in incremental polynomial time, then so does A.*

Theorem 3.4 is not a vacuous statement, since the order of results may differ between A and B. Furthermore, the corollary no longer holds when substituting "incremental polynomial time" with "polynomial delay."

Using the algorithms EnumMIS and EnumMISHold as A and B in Theorem 3.4, respectively, the combination with Lemma 3.3 implies that EnumMIS enumerates in incremental polynomial time, as claimed.

4. ENUMERATING MINIMAL TRIANGULATIONS

In Section 3.1.1 we introduced MSGraph and claimed that it is an SGR. In this section, we will use known results to reduce the problem of enumerating the minimal triangulations of a graph to the problem of enumerating the maximal independent sets for MSGraph. We will describe how to enumerate the nodes of MSGraph with polynomial delay, concluding that it is in fact an SGR. We will further show that MSGraph has a tractable expansion (Definition 2), and therefore Theorem 3.1 can be applied to conclude that the minimal triangulations can be enumerated in incremental polynomial time.

4.1 Reduction

We use the following notation. Let g be a graph. We denote by *ClqMinSep*(g) the set of minimal separators S of g, such that S is a clique of g. Let φ be a subset of *MinSep*(g). We denote by $g_{[\varphi]}$ the graph that results from saturating the minimal separators in φ.

Parra and Scheffler [32] have shown the following connection between minimal triangulations and maximal sets of *pairwise-parallel minimal separators* (that is, every two minimal separators in the set are non-crossing).

THEOREM 4.1. (Parra and Scheffler [32]) *Let g be a graph.*

1. *If φ is a maximal set of pairwise-parallel minimal separators of g, then $g_{[\varphi]}$ is a minimal triangulation of g, and MinSep($g_{[\varphi]}$) $= \varphi$.*
2. *If h is a minimal triangulation of g, then the set $\varphi =$ MinSep(h) is a maximal set of pairwise-parallel minimal separators in g, and $h = g_{[\varphi]}$.*

Theorem 4.1, combined with Theorem 2.2, gives the desired reduction in the following corollary. Recall that the graph $\mathcal{G}^{\mathsf{ms}}(g)$ is defined in Section 3.1.1, as part of the SGR MSGraph $= (\mathcal{G}^{\mathsf{ms}}, A^{\mathsf{ms}}_{\mathsf{V}}, A^{\mathsf{ms}}_{\mathsf{E}})$.

COROLLARY 4.2. *For a graph g, there is a polynomial-time-computable bijection between the following two sets:*

- *MaxInd($\mathcal{G}^{\mathsf{ms}}(g)$), that is, the set of all maximal sets of pairwise-parallel minimal separators of g.*
- *MinTri(g), that is, the set of all minimal triangulations of g.*

Hence, it suffices to prove that MSGraph has a tractable expansion, which we do next.

4.2 Enumerating Minimal Separators

We now describe a variation of the algorithm of Berry et al. [4] that, given a graph g, enumerates its set *MinSep*(g) of minimal separators. Their algorithm enumerates with polynomial total time, and with a simple change (that we explain next) can enumerate with polynomial delay. Our variation is depicted in Figure 2. There, for $v \in \mathsf{V}(g)$ we denote by $N(v)$ the set of neighbors of v. For $U \subseteq \mathsf{V}(g)$ we denote by $N(U)$ the set of neighbors of nodes in U, excluding the nodes of U themselves; that is,

$$N(U) \stackrel{\text{def}}{=} \Big(\bigcup_{v \in U} N(v)\Big) \setminus U .$$

Algorithm PDelayAllMinSep(g)

```
1: Q := ∅
2: P := ∅
3: for all v ∈ V(g) do
4:   for all C ∈ 𝒞({v} ∪ N(v)) do
5:     Q := Q ∪ {N(C)}
6: while Q ≠ ∅ do
7:   S := Q.pop()
8:   for all x ∈ S do
9:     S' := {N(C) | C ∈ 𝒞(S ∪ N(x))}
10:    if S' ∉ P then
11:      Q := Q ∪ {S'}
12:  P := P ∪ {S}
13:  print S
```

Figure 2: Enumerating *MinSep*(g) with polynomial delay (a variation of the algorithm by Berry et al. [4])

We also denote by $\mathscr{C}(U)$ the set of connected components of the graph $g \setminus U$ (the graph obtained from g by removing all the nodes of U).

The algorithm remains intrinsically the same as that of Berry et al. [4]. Minimal separators are considered as neighborhoods of connected components. The algorithm finds minimal separators contained in a set $U \subseteq \mathsf{V}(g)$ by taking the neighborhoods of the connected components of $g \setminus U$, that is, $N(C)$ for all $C \in \mathscr{C}(U)$. Initially, the minimal separators that are contained in the neighborhoods of single nodes are generated (lines 3–5). Then, every previously generated minimal separator S is processed to produce more minimal separators that are *close* to S (lines 7–12). For every node v in the minimal separator S, it produces minimal separators that are contained in $S \cup N(v)$.

Our modification is in the data structures and the time of printing answers. In Figure 2, $\mathcal{Q}$ and $\mathcal{P}$ play the role of $\mathscr{S} \setminus \mathscr{T}$ and $\mathscr{T}$ of the original algorithm [4], respectively. There, $\mathscr{S}$ holds all minimal separators generated, and $\mathscr{T}$ is a subset that holds the separators that were processed. The easy access to the separators yet to be processed (i.e. $\mathscr{S} \setminus \mathscr{T}$), along with printing answers when processed (in line 13, rather then when revealed in line 11), provides the polynomial delay. Correctness is derived directly by the correctness of the original algorithm, and the polynomial delay can be easily verified. In particular, the time between two consecutive results is $O(|\mathsf{V}(g)|^3)$.

4.3 Tractable Expansion

Recall that Rose [35] proved that a chordal graph has fewer minimal separators than nodes. Combined with this result, Theorem 4.1 gives the first of the two conditions of Definition 2.

COROLLARY 4.3. *Let g be a graph. If I is a (maximal) independent set of $\mathcal{G}^{\mathsf{ms}}(g)$, then $|I| < \mathsf{V}(g)$.*

PROOF. Suppose that I is a maximal set of pairwise-parallel minimal separators of g. Then by Theorem 4.1, $h = g_{[I]}$ is a minimal triangulation of g, and $MinSep(h) = I$. The graph h is chordal, hence from Rose [35] we get that $|MinSep(h)| < |V(h)| = |V(g)|$. □

Algorithm Extend(g,φ)

```
g_t := Triangulate(g_[φ])
h := MinTriSandwich(g_[φ], g_t)
return ExtractMinSeps(h)
```

Figure 3: An algorithm for extending a set φ of pairwise-parallel minimal separators

We now turn to proving the second condition of Definition 2. We do so by describing a general procedure for extending a set of pairwise-parallel minimal separators of a graph g to a maximal such set. Algorithm Extend of Figure 3 can apply any known polynomial time triangulation heuristic, referred to as Triangulate, as a black box. It uses the following procedures as subroutines.

- Saturate(g, S) receives a graph g and a set $S \subseteq V(g)$ of vertices, and saturates S (i.e., modifies g such that S becomes a clique).
- Triangulate(g) receives a graph g and returns a (not necessarily minimal) triangulation g' of g. We assume that this procedure runs in polynomial time. (For example, a näive implementation would be to add every possible edge; later we discuss smarter alternatives.)
- MinTriSandwich(g, g') receives a graph g and a triangulation g' of g, and returns a *minimal* triangulation of g. We note that, using one of the known algorithms [6, 11, 33], this procedure runs in time that is polynomial in the size of the graph.
- ExtractMinSeps(h) receives a chordal graph h and returns its set of minimal separators. Using the algorithm of Kumar [28], the execution time of this procedure is linear in h.

Extend takes as input a graph g and a set φ of pairwise-parallel minimal separators. It then proceeds by saturating the separators in φ, resulting in $g_{[\varphi]}$. At this stage it passes $g_{[\varphi]}$ to the triangulation heuristic Triangulate. We note that Triangulate does not have to produce a minimal triangulation. This is important since it allows us to incorporate *any* method for triangulation or tree decomposition. (We discuss in detail the translation between triangulations and tree decompositions in Section 5.)

The problem of transforming a non-minimal triangulation into a minimal one is called the *minimal triangulation sandwich problem* [20]. Various polynomial-time algorithms for this problem exist [11, 33], and these were reported to perform well in practice [6].

So, at this stage we have a minimal triangulation h of $g_{[\varphi]}$. Theorem 4.4 (that we give in the next section) shows that h is also a minimal triangulation of g. Lemma 4.5 (also in the next section) shows that the set of minimal separators of h contains φ, which is essential as we need to *extend* φ. Finally, we can apply the algorithm of Kumar [28] to extract the minimal separators of the (chordal) graph h in linear time.

4.3.1 Correctness.

To prove correctness of the algorithm Extend of Figure 3, we need the following result by Heggernes [20].

THEOREM 4.4. (Heggernes [20]) *Given a graph g, let φ be an arbitrary set of pairwise-parallel minimal separators of g. Obtain a graph $g_{[\varphi]}$ by saturating each separator in φ.*

1. *$\varphi \subseteq ClqMinSep(g_{[\varphi]})$, that is, φ consists of clique minimal separators of $g_{[\varphi]}$.*
2. *$ClqMinSep(g) \subseteq MinSep(g_{[\varphi]})$; that is, every clique minimal separator of g is a (clique) minimal separator of $g_{[\varphi]}$.*
3. *Every minimal triangulation of $g_{[\varphi]}$ is a minimal triangulation of g.*

The next lemma builds on Theorems 4.1 and 4.4.

LEMMA 4.5. *Let g be a graph, and φ a set of pairwise-parallel minimal separators of g. Let h be a minimal triangulation of $g_{[\varphi]}$. Then $\varphi \subseteq MinSep(h)$.*

PROOF. By Part 1 of Theorem 4.4 we have that $\varphi \subseteq ClqMinSep(g_{[\varphi]})$. Since h is a minimal triangulation of $g_{[\varphi]}$ then by Part 2 of Theorem 4.1, h is the result of saturating a maximal set, say φ', of pairwise-parallel minimal separators of $g_{[\varphi]}$. Therefore, by Part 2 of Theorem 4.4 we have $ClqMinSep(g_{[\varphi]}) \subseteq MinSep(h)$. This implies that $\varphi \subseteq MinSep(h)$, as claimed. □

We then conclude the correctness of the algorithm.

LEMMA 4.6. *Let φ be a set of pairwise-parallel minimal separators of a graph g.* Extend(g, φ) *returns a maximal set I of pairwise-parallel minimal separators of g such that $\varphi \subseteq I$. Furthermore, the algorithm terminates in polynomial time.*

PROOF. Assuming correctness of procedures Triangulate, and MinTriSandwich, the graph h is a minimal triangulation of $g_{[\varphi]}$. By Part 3 of Theorem 4.4, we have that h is a minimal triangulation of g. Consequently, from Part 2 of Theorem 4.1 we get that $MinSep(h) = I$ is a maximal set of pairwise-parallel minimal separators of g. By Lemma 4.5 it holds that $\varphi \subseteq MinSep(h)$, making I an extension of φ. All of the procedures in Figure 3 run in time that is polynomial in the size of the graph making it polynomial as well. □

From Corollary 4.3 and Lemma 4.6 we get the main result of this part.

THEOREM 4.7. *The SGR* MSGraph *has a tractable expansion of independent sets.*

This theorem allows us to establish the main result of this paper.

4.4 Main Result

From Theorems 4.7 and 3.1 we conclude that it is possible to enumerate the maximal independent sets of MSGraph in incremental polynomial time. Applying the bijection of Corollary 4.2, we get the main result of this paper.

COROLLARY 4.8. *Given a graph, the minimal triangulations can be enumerated in incremental polynomial time.*

In the next section we will use this result for enumerating tree decompositions.

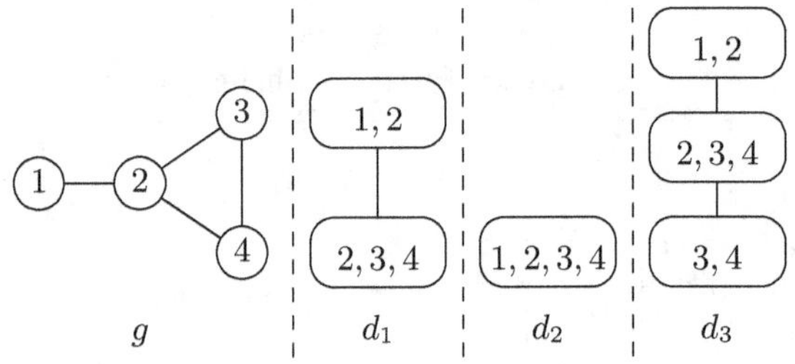

Figure 4: A graph g and tree decompositions d_1, d_2 and d_3 of g. The decomposition d_1 is proper, but d_2 and d_3 are subsumed by d_1, and hence, improper.

5. ENUMERATING THE PROPER TREE DECOMPOSITIONS

In this section we define the notion of a *proper* tree decomposition, which is essentially a tree decomposition that is, intuitively, not deemed redundant due to another tree decomposition. Our ultimate goal is to enumerate *only* the proper tree decompositions, and we will show that this translates to enumerating the minimal triangulations.

5.1 Proper Tree Decompositions

Let d_1 and d_2 be two tree decompositions of a graph g. We say that d_1 and d_2 are *bag equivalent*, denoted $d_1 \equiv_b d_2$, if $\text{bags}(d_1) = \text{bags}(d_2)$. We denote by $d_1 \sqsubseteq d_2$ the fact that for every bag $b_1 \in \text{bags}(d_1)$ there exists a bag $b_2 \in \text{bags}(d_2)$ such that $b_1 \subseteq b_2$.

Let g be a graph, and let d and d' be tree decompositions of g. We say that d' *strictly subsumes* d if $d' \sqsubseteq d$ and $\text{bags}(d) \not\subseteq \text{bags}(d')$. A tree decomposition is *proper* if it is not strictly subsumed by any tree decomposition, and it is *improper* otherwise.

Figure 4 shows examples of proper and improper tree decompositions. It can be shown that d_1 is proper (e.g., since every clique of g is contained in some bag of d, as we prove in Proposition A.2 in the appendix). But d_2 is not proper, since it is subsumed by d_1; that is, every bag of d_1 is contained in some bag of d_2, but the bag $\{1, 2, 3, 4\}$ is not a bag of d_1. For the same reason, d_2 is subsumed also by d_3. Finally, d_3 is subsumed by d_1 since every bag of d_1 is a bag of d_3, but the bag $\{3, 4\}$ is not a bag of d_1.

5.2 Enumeration

The main result of this section is the following, showing that enumerating the proper tree decompositions reduces to enumerating the minimal triangulations.

THEOREM 5.1. *Let g be a graph. There is a bijection M between $MinTri(g)$ and the equivalence classes of $\equiv_b$ over the proper tree decompositions of g. Moreover, given a minimal triangulation h of g, the proper tree decompositions in the class $M(h)$ can be enumerated with polynomial delay.*

Combined with Corollary 4.8, we get the following.

COROLLARY 5.2. *The set of proper tree decompositions of a given graph can be enumerated in incremental polynomial time.*

Next, we discuss the proof of Theorem 5.1, and in particular show how M is defined. The definition of M is based on the following lemma.

LEMMA 5.3. *If g is a chordal graph and d is a proper tree decomposition g, then* $\text{bags}(d) = \mathit{MaxClq}(g)$.

Based on Lemma 5.3, we define M to be the function that maps every $h \in \mathit{MinTri}(g)$ to the equivalence class of the proper tree decomposition of h. The following lemma states the M has the required properties.

LEMMA 5.4. *Let g be a graph. The mapping M is a bijection between $\mathit{MinTri}(g)$ and the equivalence classes of $\equiv_{\mathsf{b}}$ over the proper tree decompositions of g.*

To complete the proof of Theorem 5.1, we explain how the proper tree decompositions in the class $M(h)$ can be enumerated with polynomial delay for $h \in \mathit{MinTri}(g)$. Jordan [23] shows that, given a chordal graph h, a tree over the bags that represent the maximal cliques of h is a tree decomposition if and only if it is a maximal spanning tree, where the weight of an edge between two bags is the size of their intersection. Hence, this enumeration problem is reduced to enumerating all maximal spanning trees, which can be solved in polynomial delay [38]. Since Gavril [14] has shown that in chordal graphs the number of maximal cliques of h is at most the number of nodes of h, we have a polynomial delay algorithm for enumerating the tree decompositions. This concludes the proof.

6. EXPERIMENTAL EVALUATION

We now describe an experimental study over an implementation of our enumeration algorithm for minimal triangulations, namely the algorithm EnumMIS of Figure 1 for the SGR $(\mathcal{G}^{\mathsf{ms}}, A^{\mathsf{ms}}_{\mathsf{V}}, A^{\mathsf{ms}}_{\mathsf{E}})$, calling the procedure Extend of Figure 3. The goal of the experimental study is twofold. First, we wish to understand how practical the execution cost of the algorithm is for enumerating many minimal triangulations (and tree decompositions). Second, we wish to study the ability of the algorithm to produce many *high-quality* triangulations, given an underlying triangulation algorithm (for Extend), and even to improve upon standard quality measures of the underlying algorithm itself. In Section 6.1 we describe the experimental setup, in Section 6.2 we report on the efficiency of the algorithm in terms of its delay, and in Sections 6.3 and 6.4 we study the quality of the results.

6.1 Experimental Setup

We first describe the general setup for our study.

Implementation and Hardware. We implemented all algorithms in C++, with STL data structures.[2] All experiments were carried out on a 2.6GHz dual-core laptop with 8GB of RAM running Windows 10 professional.

Triangulation Algorithms. We implemented two well known triangulation algorithms as the procedure Triangulate in line 1 of the procedure Extend (Figure 3). Both algorithms apply the general technique of *node-elimination ordering* [31], where nodes are eliminated from the graph in turn, by adding a subset of edges (called *fill* edges) between the eliminated node and its neighbors in the (leftover) graph. Both algorithms guarantee a minimal triangulation (hence there was no need to call MinTriSandwich$(g_{[\varphi]}, g_t)$ in line 2 of Extend).

- MCS_M [3]. This is an extension of the *Maximum Cardinality Search* (MCS) algorithm for recognizing chordal graphs [36], which finds a minimal elimination ordering along with its corresponding minimal triangulation.
- LB_TRIANG [5]. This algorithms guarantees minimality of the triangulation by adding only a subset of the fill edges at each of the elimination steps, and allows for complete flexibility in determining the elimination order. We applied the *min fill* heuristic that selects, at each iteration, the node whose elimination results in the smallest number of edges to add.

Datasets. We used three types of datasets: probabilistic graphical models, database queries, and random (synthetic) graphs. For the first type, we used the following benchmark networks from the UAI probabilistic inference challenge.[3] The datasets Alchemy and DBN from the challange are not described here as each of their graphs had only one or two minimal triangulations, and the enumeration ended instantaneously.

- **Promedas**: "PRObabilistic MEdical Diagnostic Advisory System." The Promedas Markov networks represent medical diagnosis cases, and consist of binary variables that were converted from layered noisy-or Bayesian networks. The dataset includes 33 graphs with 26-1039 nodes and 36-1696 edges, and many of them are considered too difficult for exact inference.[4]
- **Object detection**: Markov Random Fields for object-detection tasks in computer vision. It includes 79 instances of connected networks, each containing 60 nodes and between 135 to 180 edges.
- **Image segmentation**: Bayesian networks generated from image-segmentation tasks. It includes 6 graphs with 226-235 nodes and 617-647 edges.
- **Grids**: An $N \times N$ grid network. Such networks that are common in image processing [7], and networks that model problems such as medical diagnosis and object detection. This dataset includes 8 grids with $N = 10$ and $N = 20$, resulting in graphs with 100 or 400 nodes, and 180-760 edges.
- **Pedigree**: Bayesian networks used to model genetic information [13]. The data set includes 3 graphs, each has 385 nodes and 930 edges.
- **CSP**: Constraint-satisfaction problems. There are 3 instances in the dataset, with 67-100 nodes and 226-619 edges.

The datasets of second and third types are as follows.

- **TPC-H**: Graphs induced from TPC-H. These are the Gaifman (primal) graphs of joins for implementing the TPC-H benchmark queries in LogiQL, the Datalog variant of LogicBlox [1].[5] The queries include up to 22 nodes, and up to 46 edges, and their treewidth is up to 7.

[2]The code is available online: https://github.com/NofarCarmeli/MinTriangulationsEnumeration

[3]http://www.cs.huji.ac.il/project/PASCAL/showNet.php

[4]http://graphmod.ics.uci.edu/uai08/Evaluation/Report/Benchmarks

[5]The queries, provided to us by LogicBlox, are used for benchmarking the engine.

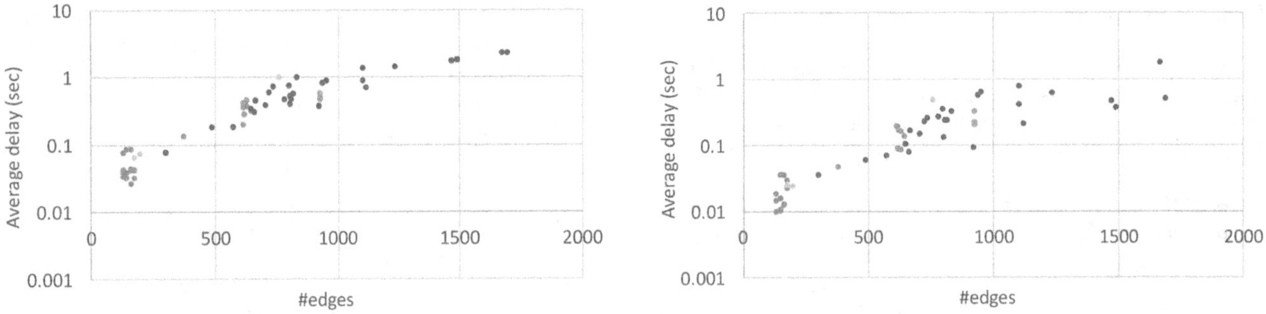

(a) LB_TRIANG (b) MCS_M

Figure 5: Average delay (in seconds) for the two triangulation algorithms over the probabilistic-graphical-model benchmarks: Object Detection (•), Segmentation (•), Pedigree (•), Grids (•), Promedas (•), CSP (•)

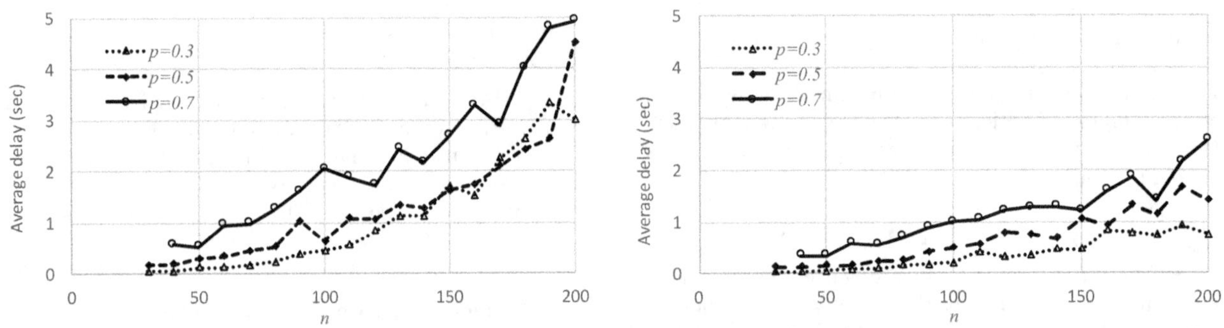

(a) LB_TRIANG (b) MCS_M

Figure 6: Average delay over 54 graphs randomly generated from the Erdős-Rényi $G(n, p)$ for varying n and p

- **Random**: Random $G(n, p)$ graphs in the Erdős-Rényi model. The number of nodes is n and every pair of nodes is connected by an edge with probability p (independently). We generated 54 random graphs for varying n between 30 and 200, and three values of p: 0.3 (sparsest), 0.5 and 0.7 (densest).

As a baseline approach, we implemented the algorithm of DunceCap [37] for generating all of the generalized hypertree decompositions (each involving an underlying tree decomposition). However, this algorithm is designed to handle small join queries and to span a much greater space of objects (namely, the generalized hypertree decompositions). In particular, on the TPC-H dataset we observed that on the smaller queries our algorithm is faster by 3 to 4 orders of magnitude, and on some of the larger queries (Q7 and Q9) we could not get their algorithm to terminate in less than two hours (while our algorithms terminated in a few seconds, as we later discuss). Therefore, we decided to exclude comparisons to this implementation. As of today, we are not aware of any other published algorithms for enumerating (minimal) triangulations or tree decompositions with guarantees of correctness (completeness).

6.2 Execution Cost

In what follows we report on the delay of the two variants of the implementation, corresponding to the two triangulation algorithms LB_TRIANG and MCS_M.

Probabilistic graphical models. We measured the average delay between minimal triangulation printouts for the network datasets from the UAI challenge. The measurements were conducted during 30 minutes executions. 5 of the graphs in Promedas, and one graph of CSP completed the enumeration within this time. We plotted the delay of the other graphs against the number of their edges. The plots, corresponding to the two minimal triangulation algorithms LB_TRIANG and MCS_M, are presented in Figures 5a and 5b, respectively. Overall, we see an exponential relationship between the number of edges and the average delay. However, this trend widely varies between the different benchmarks. While this dependency is apparent for the Promedas data set, the average delay for object detection has little correlation with the number of edges in the graph.

Random graphs. We measured the average delay (in seconds) between the printout of consecutive minimal triangulations during a 30 minute execution. The plots in Figures 6a and 6b show the average delay vs. the size of the graph for the two variants. We can see that the delay increases with the size of the graph, and that the general trend is that the delay is larger for denser graphs. We also see that for LB_TRIANG the delay is generally longer than for MCS_M.

Database queries. We evaluated our enumeration algorithm over a set of 22 queries from the TPC-H dataset. The graphs of these queries are quite small when compared to

Dataset	#trng	min-w	#≤$\mathbf{w}_1$ (%)	%w↓ (max)	min-f	#≤$\mathbf{f}_1$ (%)	%f↓ (max)
MCS_M							
Promedas (28)	11064.5	25.8	3713.6 (33.6%)	2.2 (15.2)	3353.4	8136.0 (73.5%)	18.1 (49.9)
Grids (8)	40319.8	18.4	93.6 (0.2%)	0.0 (0.0)	2752.6	15771.4 (39.1%)	4.2 (28.1)
Obj. Detection (79)	100349.9	6.1	42743.9 (42.6%)	0.4 (12.5)	30.0	27614.1 (27.5%)	19.9 (47.1)
Segmentation (5)	12836.5	23.0	20.5 (0.2%)	0.0 (0.0)	2555.2	5269.7 (41.1%)	5.9 (12.5)
Pedigree (3)	7789.0	31.7	3087.3 (39.6%)	0.0 (0.0)	3525.7	743.0 (9.5%)	2.8 (3.5)
CSP (2)	29450.5	16.5	26741.5 (90.8%)	13.2 (26.3)	46.0	18815.5 (63.9%)	35.2 (55.8)
LB_TRIANG							
Promedas (28)	4220.7	18.6	2352.0 (55.7%)	1.9 (16.7)	1239.4	175.0 (4.1%)	0.2 (11.1)
Grids (8)	13881.3	24.5	1273.0 (9.2%)	3.0 (8.7)	1600.3	1.0 (0.0%)	0.0 (0.0)
Obj. Detection (79)	33295.4	5.8	15709.3 (47.2%)	0.0 (0.0)	27.6	5110.7 (15.3%)	10.4 (27.6)
Segmentation (5)	5174.2	21.8	2141.8 (41.4%)	10.3 (20.7)	1402.0	130.2 (2.5%)	1.2 (4.2)
Pedigree (3)	3646.0	23.7	3227.7 (88.5%)	5.3 (14.8)	1491.0	1.0 (0.0%)	0.0 (0.0)
CSP (2)	11772.0	16.5	3760.5 (31.9%)	0.0 (0.0)	34.5	664.0 (5.6%)	1.4 (3.0)

Table 1: Statistics on generated triangulations following 30 minutes execution

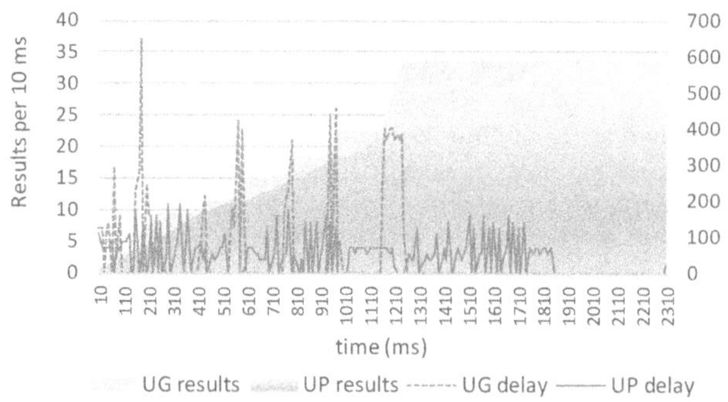

Figure 7: Delay behavior in two printing modes: UG (Upon Generation, as in EnumMIS), and UP (Upon Pop, as in EnumMISHold)

the UAI datasets (< 23 nodes). Moreover, half of these graphs are chordal to begin with (i.e., have only one minimal triangulation—the graph itself), and hence, irrelevant for us. Except for two queries, all of the rest had at most 5 minimal triangulations. The remaining two queries are Q7 (Volume shipping Query) and Q9 (Product Type Profit Measure Query), and they have a considerable number of minimal triangulations: 700 and 588, respectively. When considering the minimum-width tree decomposition for each of the queries, the largest bag was of size 8; this is due to a relation of arity 8 in the query. In fact the largest bag in each of the queries had at most two variables more than the size of the largest relation. The execution for all 22 queries completed within 5 seconds.

In one of the queries we compared the delays for two modes of printing: the one of EnumMIS and the one of EnumMISHold that prints upon extraction from the queue, as described in Section 3.2.2. We refer to the former as UG (Upon Generation) and to the latter as UP (Upon Pop). Recall that both modes guarantee incremental polynomial time (Theorem 3.4). The results are in Figure 7. While the dotted line (of UG) has bursts of high-frequency prints followed by periods where no new triangulation is created, the solid line (UP) has a more steady pace as can be seen by the constant slope in Figure 7. As expected, despite the fact that the last result of UG is printed earlier that of UP, termination is at the same time in both modes, as the algorithm still needs to check that there are no additional minimal triangulations.

6.3 Quality

In what follows we report on the quality of the generated minimal triangulations in terms of two standard measures of quality for triangulations and tree decompositions: *fill* and *width*. *Fill* refers to the total number of edges added in order to make the resulting graph chordal, while *width* refers to the size of the largest clique in the generated triangulation (minus one).[6] The natural benchmark for the quality of the triangulations is the first result our enumeration returns, as it is the result we would get by running the minimal triangulation algorithm we used, on the original input graph.

For each graph of the probabilistic inference dataset, we executed the enumeration algorithm for 30 minutes. The results in Table 1 include only the experiments where the enumeration did not complete. For each graph we measured the following: the number of generated triangulations (**#trng**), the minimum observed width over all printed triangulations (**min-w**), the number of printed triangulations of width at most that of the first (#≤$\mathbf{w}_1$), the average reduction in width (over the dataset) and the maximum improvement in parentheses (**w**↓ (%)), and the same results for fill instead of width (**min-f**, #≤$\mathbf{f}_1$ and **f**↓ (%)).

We can see that the algorithm, in both variants, is able to generate a significant number of triangulations of high quality, in terms of both width and fill. Moreover, it amplifies the quality of the underlying triangulation, by means of width, and much more by means of fill. According to the number of triangulations printed, MCS_M enables generating twice as many triangulations as LB_TRIANG. However, with the exception of only a handful of the graphs tested,

[6] Recall that is NP-hard to find a triangulation that minimizes the fill [39] or the width [2].

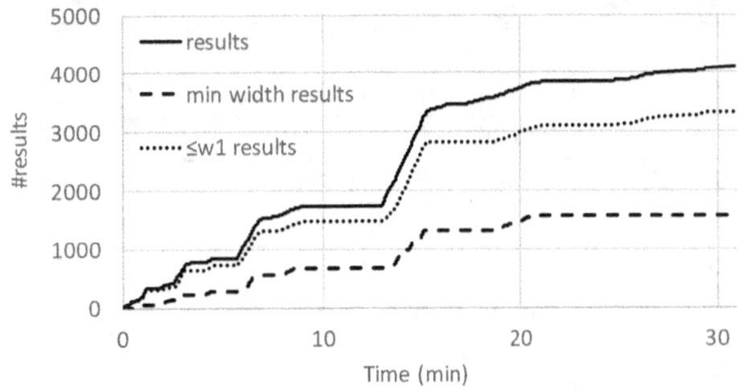

Figure 8: Cumulative number of triangulations

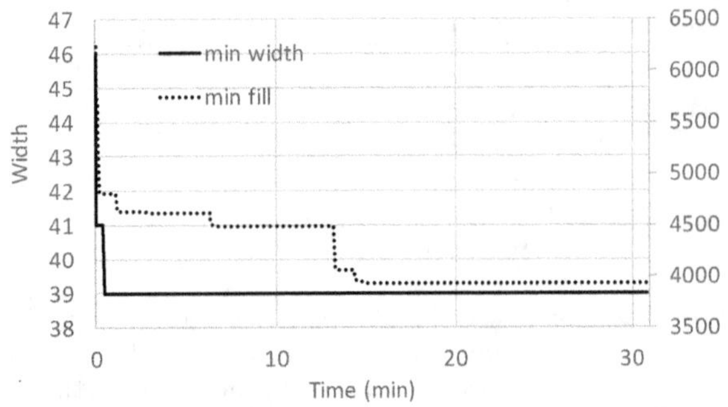

Figure 9: Minimum width and fill over time

the triangulations generated by LB_TRIANG are superior in both the width and fill metrics (this is especially apparent for the Promedas and Pedigree datasets). Furthermore, this set of superior triangulations accounts for a larger portion of the total number of triangulations that generated.

6.4 Case Study

In this section we take a closer look at the behaviour of the enumeration during a single execution. We use a graph from the Promedas dataset. In Figure 8 we show the cumulative number of results generated over time. We consider three types of results: *(a)* all minimal triangulations, *(b)* minimal triangulations of the minimum width (where the minimum is taken over the printed triangulations), *and (c)* those with a width at most that of the first triangulation ($\leq$w1), which is the one that we would obtain by using only the triangulation algorithm at hand. The reduction in the number of new triangulations over time is consistent with the increase in the delay entailed in the guarantee of incremental polynomial time, rather than polynomial delay.

Figure 9 presents the reduction in the minimum width and minimum fill obtained during the execution of the algorithm. Each time slice records the minimum width (solid curve) and minimum fill (dotted curve) observed up to that time. We can see that both the width and the fill reduce over time, but the minimum observed width is reached very quickly, while attaining the minimum observed fill takes longer.

7. CONCLUDING REMARKS

We introduced the concept of a succinct graph representation (SGR), and presented an enumeration algorithm for its maximal independent sets. The algorithm enumerates in incremental polynomial time under complexity assumptions: the SGR is tractably accessible, and it has a tractable expansion. Consequently, we established an algorithm for enumerating the minimal triangulations of a graph by reducing the problem to the enumeration of the maximal independent sets of an SGR, and showing that the complexity assumptions hold. We also proved that enumerating the minimal triangulations enables the enumeration of the proper tree decompositions. Our experimental study showed that the algorithm is effective on graphs of various domains, and is able to enhance off-the-shelf algorithms for triangulation (or tree decomposition) by generating many (rather than just one) high-quality different triangulations, and even improve standard quality measures such as width and fill.

This work opens up quite a few directions for future work. On the theoretical side, it is left open whether the enumeration of the minimal triangulations can be carried out with polynomial delay. It is clearly possible when the number of minimal separators is polynomial in the size of the input graph, using known polynomial-delay enumerations of maximal independent sets [10, 22]. Bouchitté and Todinca [8] have shown that, in this case, we can find in polynomial time a tree decomposition of a minimal width. A question we wish to explore is whether we can extend that result to enumerating the proper tree decomposition by *increasing width* (or finding the top-k decompositions of a restricted version of the problem). From the practical aspect, we believe that there are many interesting opportunities for optimizing the implementation, both in its execution cost (e.g., applying techniques for enumeration parallelization [15]) and the quality of results (e.g., heuristics for queue selections).

Acknowledgements

This work was supported in part by the US-Israel Binational Science Foundation (BSF) Grant No. 2014391, and by the Israel Science Foundation (ISF) Grant No. 1295/15. Benny Kimelfeld is a Taub Fellow, supported by the Taub Foundation. The authors are greatly thankful to LogicBlox, and in particular Hung Ngo, for insightful discussions and for providing test data.

8. REFERENCES

[1] M. Aref, B. ten Cate, T. J. Green, B. Kimelfeld, D. Olteanu, E. Pasalic, T. L. Veldhuizen, and G. Washburn. Design and implementation of the logicblox system. In *SIGMOD*, pages 1371–1382. ACM, 2015.

[2] S. Arnborg, D. G. Corneil, and A. Proskurowski. Complexity of finding embeddings in ak-tree. *SIAM Journal on Algebraic Discrete Methods*, 8(2):277–284, 1987.

[3] A. Berry, J. R. S. Blair, and P. Heggernes. Maximum cardinality search for computing minimal triangulations. In *WG*, WG '02, pages 1–12, London, UK, UK, 2002. Springer-Verlag.

[4] A. Berry, J. P. Bordat, and O. Cogis. Generating all the minimal separators of a graph. In P. Widmayer, G. Neyer, and S. Eidenbenz, editors, *WG*, volume 1665 of *Lecture Notes in Computer Science*, pages 167–172. Springer, 1999.

[5] A. Berry, J.-P. Bordat, P. Heggernes, G. Simonet, and Y. Villanger. A wide-range algorithm for minimal

triangulation from an arbitrary ordering. *Journal of Algorithms*, 58(1):33 – 66, 2006.

[6] J. R. Blair, P. Heggernes, and J. A. Telle. A practical algorithm for making filled graphs minimal. *Theoretical Computer Science*, 250(1–2):125 – 141, 2001.

[7] A. Blake, P. Kohli, and C. Rother. *Markov Random Fields for Vision and Image Processing.* The MIT Press, 2011.

[8] V. Bouchitté and I. Todinca. Treewidth and minimum fill-in: Grouping the minimal separators. *SIAM J. Comput.*, 31(1):212–232, 2001.

[9] S. Cohen, I. Fadida, Y. Kanza, B. Kimelfeld, and Y. Sagiv. Full disjunctions: Polynomial-delay iterators in action. In *VLDB*, pages 739–750. ACM, 2006.

[10] S. Cohen, B. Kimelfeld, and Y. Sagiv. Generating all maximal induced subgraphs for hereditary and connected-hereditary graph properties. *J. Comput. Syst. Sci.*, 74(7):1147–1159, 2008.

[11] D. Dahlhaus. *WG*, chapter Minimal elimination ordering inside a given chordal graph, pages 132–143. Springer Berlin Heidelberg, Berlin, Heidelberg, 1997.

[12] G. A. Dirac. On rigid circuit graphs. Abhandlungen aus dem Mathematischen Seminar der Universität Hamburg 25, Universität Hamburg, 1961.

[13] M. Fishelson and D. Geiger. Exact genetic linkage computations for general pedigrees. In *ISMB/ECCB*, pages 189–198, 2002.

[14] F. Gavril. The intersection graphs of subtrees in trees are exactly the chordal graphs. *J. Combinatorial Theory*, 16:47–56, 1974.

[15] K. Golenberg, B. Kimelfeld, and Y. Sagiv. Optimizing and parallelizing ranked enumeration. *PVLDB*, 4(11):1028–1039, 2011.

[16] G. Gottlob, G. Greco, and F. Scarcello. Pure nash equilibria: Hard and easy games. *J. Artif. Intell. Res. (JAIR)*, 24:357–406, 2005.

[17] G. Gottlob, M. Grohe, N. Musliu, M. Samer, and F. Scarcello. Hypertree decompositions: Structure, algorithms, and applications. In *WG*, volume 3787 of *Lecture Notes in Computer Science*, pages 1–15. Springer, 2005.

[18] G. Gottlob, N. Leone, and F. Scarcello. Hypertree decompositions and tractable queries. *Journal of Computer and System Sciences*, 64(3):579 – 627, 2002.

[19] G. Gottlob, Z. Miklós, and T. Schwentick. Generalized hypertree decompositions: NP-hardness and tractable variants. *J. ACM*, 56(6), 2009.

[20] P. Heggernes. Minimal triangulations of graphs: A survey. *Discrete Mathematics*, 306(3):297 – 317, 2006. Minimal Separation and Minimal Triangulation.

[21] P. Heggernes. Treewidth, partial k-trees, and chordal graphs. *unpublished*, 2006.

[22] D. S. Johnson, C. H. Papadimitriou, and M. Yannakakis. On generating all maximal independent sets. *Inf. Process. Lett.*, 27(3):119–123, 1988.

[23] M. Jordan. *An Introduction to Probabilistic Graphical Models*, chapter 17. University of California, Berkeley, 2002.

[24] O. Kalinsky, Y. Etsion, and B. Kimelfeld. Flexible caching in trie joins. *CoRR*, abs/1602.08721, 2016.

[25] B. Kenig and A. Gal. On the impact of junction-tree topology on weighted model counting. In *SUM*, volume 9310 of *Lecture Notes in Computer Science*, pages 83–98. Springer, 2015.

[26] T. Kloks, D. Kratsch, and J. P. Spinrad. On treewidth and minimum fill-in of asteroidal triple-free graphs. *Theor. Comput. Sci.*, 175(2):309–335, 1997.

[27] P. G. Kolaitis and M. Y. Vardi. Conjunctive-query containment and constraint satisfaction. *J. Comput. Syst. Sci.*, 61(2):302–332, 2000.

[28] P. Kumar and C. Madhavan. Minimal vertex separators of chordal graphs. *Discrete Applied Mathematics*, 89(1–3):155 – 168, 1998.

[29] S. Lauritzen and D. J. Spiegelhalter. Local computations with probabilities on graphical structures and their application to expert systems. *Journal of the Royal Statistical Society*, B, 50(2):157–224, 1988.

[30] D. Marx. Approximating fractional hypertree width. *ACM Trans. Algorithms*, 6(2), 2010.

[31] T. Ohtsuki, L. K. Cheung, and T. Fujisawa. Minimal triangulation of a graph and optimal pivoting order in a sparse matrix. *Journal of Mathematical Analysis and Applications*, 54(3):622 – 633, 1976.

[32] A. Parra and P. Scheffler. Characterizations and algorithmic applications of chordal graph embeddings. *Discrete Applied Mathematics*, 79(1-3):171–188, 1997.

[33] B. W. Peyton. Minimal orderings revisited. *SIAM J. Matrix Analysis Applications*, 23(1):271–294, 2001.

[34] N. Robertson and P. Seymour. Graph minors. iii. planar tree-width. *Journal of Combinatorial Theory, Series B*, 36(1):49 – 64, 1984.

[35] D. J. Rose. Triangulated graphs and the elimination process. *Journal of Mathematical Analysis and Applications*, 32(3):597 – 609, 1970.

[36] R. E. Tarjan and M. Yannakakis. Simple linear-time algorithms to test chordality of graphs, test acyclicity of hypergraphs, and selectively reduce acyclic hypergraphs. *SIAM J. Comput.*, 13(3):566–579, July 1984.

[37] S. Tu and C. Ré. DunceCap: Query plans using generalized hypertree decompositions. In *SIGMOD*, pages 2077–2078. ACM, 2015.

[38] T. Yamada, S. Kataoka, and K. Watanabe. Listing all the minimum spanning trees in an undirected graph. *Int. J. Comput. Math.*, 87(14):3175–3185, 2010.

[39] M. Yannakakis. Computing the minimum fill-in is np-complete. *SIAM Journal on Algebraic Discrete Methods*, 2(1):77–79, 1981.

[40] J. Zhao, R. L. Malmberg, and L. Cai. Rapid *ab initio* RNA folding including pseudoknots via graph tree decomposition. In *WABI*, pages 262–273, 2006.

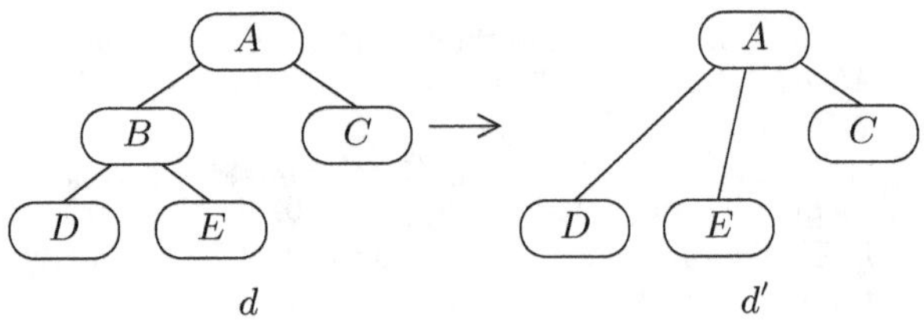

Figure 10: Obtaining a strictly subsuming tree decomposition d' given a tree decomposition d with $B \subseteq C$.

APPENDIX

A. ADDITIONAL PROOFS

In this section we give proofs that are missing from the body of the paper.

A.1 Proof of Theorem 3.4

Let P be an enumeration problem, let A be a solver for P, and let x be input for A. If τ is a time tick during the execution of $A(x)$, then we denote by $\text{out}_{A,x}(\tau)$ the answers $y \in \mathsf{P}(x)$ that have been printed before time τ is reached. We have the following lemma.

LEMMA A.1. *Let* P *be an enumeration problem, and A a solver for* P*. The following are equivalent.*

1. *A enumerates in incremental polynomial time.*
2. *There is a polynomial p such that for all x and τ we have $p(|x| + |\text{out}_{A,x}(\tau)|) > \tau$.*

PROOF. Denote the time of the Nth result by t_N.

1 ⇒ 2. If A enumerates in incremental polynomial time, there exists a polynomial p_1 such that $t_{N+1} - t_N \leq p_1(|x| + N)$. Without loss of generality, we assume that p_1 is monotone (as every polynomial is upper bounded by some monotone polynomial, and we can replace p_1 with such polynomial). We get the following on the printing time of the Nth result.

$$t_N = \sum_{i=1}^{N} t_i - t_{i-1} \leq \sum_{i=1}^{N} p_1(|x| + i - 1) \leq N \cdot p_1(|x| + N - 1)$$

In this case we get that for any time τ there exists a polynomial p_2 such that the following holds.

$$\begin{aligned}\tau &< t_{|\text{out}_{A,x}(\tau)|+1} \\ &\leq (|\text{out}_{A,x}(\tau)| + 1) \cdot p_1(|x| + |\text{out}_{A,x}(\tau)|) \\ &\leq p_2(|x| + |\text{out}_{A,x}(\tau)|)\end{aligned}$$

2 ⇒ 1. Assume now that $p_3(|x| + |\text{out}_{A,x}(\tau)|) > \tau$ for any time τ. Consider the delay after the Nth answer.

$$t_{N+1} - t_N \leq t_{N+1} < p_3(|x| + N + 1)$$

This shows that there exists a polynomial p_4 such that $t_{N+1} - t_N < p_4(|x| + N)$, meaning that A enumerates in incremental polynomial time. □

We can now prove the theorem.

THEOREM 3.4. *Let* P *be an enumeration problem, and let A and B be two solvers for* P*. Suppose that for all instances x and for all answers $y \in \mathsf{P}(x)$ we have $\text{time}_{A,x}(y) \leq \text{time}_{B,x}(y)$. If B enumerates in incremental polynomial time, then so does A.*

PROOF. Using the characterization of Lemma A.1, let p be a polynomial such that for all x and τ we have $p(|x| + |\text{out}_{B,x}(\tau)|) > \tau$. The condition of the theorem implies that at every time tick τ, the set of answers printed by B is a subset of the set of answers printed by A, and therefore, $|\text{out}_{A,x}(\tau)| \geq |\text{out}_{B,x}(\tau)|$. Again since we can assume monotonicity, we conclude that $p(|x| + |\text{out}_{A,x}(\tau)|) > \tau$ as well. We use Lemma A.1 to conclude that A enumerates in incremental polynomial time. □

A.2 Proof of Lemma 5.3

LEMMA 5.3. *If g is a chordal graph and d is a proper tree decomposition g, then* $\text{bags}(d) = \mathit{MaxClq}(g)$.

PROOF. According to Proposition A.2, every clique of g is contained in some bag of d, and according to Theorem 2.3, g has some tree decomposition, say d', where all the bags are cliques of g. So we have that $d' \sqsubseteq d$. If $\text{bags}(d) \not\subseteq \text{bags}(d')$, then d' strictly subsumes d, in contradiction to the fact that d is proper. Hence $\text{bags}(d) \subseteq \text{bags}(d')$, meaning that the bags of d are cliques of g. It thus follows that every maximal clique is a bag of d, or in notation, $\mathit{MaxClq}(g) \subseteq \text{bags}(d)$. Finally, Proposition A.3 states that the bags of d are an antichain w.r.t. set inclusion, and hence, $\text{bags}(d) \subseteq \mathit{MaxClq}(g)$. We conclude that $\text{bags}(d) = \mathit{MaxClq}(g)$, as claimed. □

A.3 Proof of Lemma 5.4

In this section we prove Lemma 5.4. We first need some propositions. The following proposition is a folklore, and it is using a result by Heggernes [21], showing that every collection of subtrees of a tree satisfies the *Helly property*.

PROPOSITION A.2. *If d is a tree decomposition of a graph g, then every clique of g is contained in some bag of d.*

PROOF. We use the fact that the junction-tree property of a tree decomposition is equivalent to the property that for every node v of the graph, the bags of the tree decomposition that contain v form a (connected) subtree. Denote $d = (t, \beta)$ and let C be a clique of g. Every node v in C defines a subtree of t that is induced by the bags that contain v. Since d covers the edges of g, every two nodes in C must share some bag in d, and hence, their subtrees must share a vertex. Heggernes [21] shows that every collection of subtrees of a tree satisfies the *Helly property*: if every two subtrees share a vertex, then there exists a vertex that is shared by all the subtrees. In particular, there exists a vertex in d common to all of these subtrees; this shared node corresponds to a bag that contains C. □

The following proposition states that in a proper tree decomposition, there is no containment among bags.

PROPOSITION A.3. *If d is a proper tree decomposition of a graph g, then* $\text{bags}(d)$ *is an antichain w.r.t. set inclusion (that is, no bag contains another)*

PROOF. We need to show that a proper tree decomposition cannot have two bags with one contained in the other. Assume, by way of contradiction, that d is a proper tree decomposition of g with two bags $B, C \in \text{bags}(d)$ where $B \subseteq C$. Let A be the second bag in the path from B to C.

Since d is a tree decomposition and A is on the path from B to C, we get that $B = B \cap C \subseteq A$.

Define d' to be the graph obtained from d by removing B and connecting A to all other neighbors of B, as illustrated in Figure 10. We will show that d' is a tree decomposition for g. The first two properties of the tree decomposition still hold because A contains B. Consider the path between two bags α and β of d'. If the path between them is the same as in d, the third property still holds. If it changed, then the path used to go through B, and the only new bag that may appear in this path is A. In this case, $\alpha \cap \beta \subseteq B \subseteq A$, and the third property holds as well. We have found a tree decomposition d' for g that strictly subsumes d, hence d is improper, and this is a contradiction. □

From Theorem 2.3, the following easily follows.

PROPOSITION A.4. *If d is a tree decomposition of a graph g, then* $\mathsf{saturate}(g, d)$ *is a triangulation of g.*

PROOF. From Proposition A.2 is easily follows that d is a tree decomposition of $\mathsf{saturate}(g, d)$. Hence, since every bag of d is a clique of $\mathsf{saturate}(g, d)$, it follows from Theorem 2.3 that $\mathsf{saturate}(g, d)$ is chordal. □

The next proposition states that a chordal graph g has a single proper tree decomposition, up to the equivalence $\equiv_{\mathsf{b}}$, with the set of bags being precisely the set of maximal cliques. We can now prove Lemma 5.4.

LEMMA 5.4. *Let g be a graph. The mapping M is a bijection between $MinTri(g)$ and the equivalence classes of $\equiv_{\mathsf{b}}$ over the proper tree decompositions of g.*

PROOF. We will show that M has the correct range, that it is surjective, and that it is bijective.

M has a proper range. Let h be a minimal triangulation of g, and let d be a proper tree decomposition of h in $M(h)$. Then d is also a tree decomposition of g, as the three properties of a tree decomposition still hold. We need to show that d is a *proper* tree decomposition of g. According to Lemma 5.3, we have $\mathrm{bags}(d) = MaxClq(h)$, and therefore, $\mathsf{saturate}(g, d) = h$. Assume, by way of contradiction, that d is improper. Then d is strictly subsumed by some tree decomposition d' of g, meaning that $d' \sqsubseteq d$ and $\mathrm{bags}(d) \nsubseteq \mathrm{bags}(d')$. Let h' be the graph $\mathsf{saturate}(g, d')$. From Proposition A.4 it follows that h' is a triangulation of g. From $d' \sqsubseteq d$ and the fact that every bag of d is a clique of h, we conclude that $\mathsf{E}(h') \subseteq \mathsf{E}(h)$. And since h is a minimal triangulation, we get that $h = h'$. We can now conclude that d' is also a tree decomposition of g: the junction-tree property holds and the nodes are covered since it is a tree decomposition of g, and the edges are covered since those are the edges of h' that are covered by its definition. We get that both d and d' are tree decompositions of h, and d is strictly subsumed by d', which contradicts the fact that d is a proper tree decomposition of h.

M is injective. Let h_1 and h_2 be two minimal triangulations such that $h_1 \neq h_2$. Without loss of generality, assume that the edge $\{u, v\}$ is in h_1 but not in h_2. The nodes u and v are part of some maximal clique of h_1, so they share a bag in $M(h_1)$. But they are not part of any clique of h_2, so they do not share any bag in $M(h_2)$. Therefore, $M(h_1) \neq M(h_2)$.

M is surjective. Given a proper tree decomposition d of g, we need to show that there exists a minimal triangulation h of g such that $d \in M(h)$. Consider the graph $h = \mathsf{saturate}(g, d)$. We will show that h is a minimal triangulation, and that d belongs to $M(h)$.

We first show that h is a minimal triangulation of g. According to Proposition A.4, h is a triangulation of g. Assume, by way of contradiction, that h is not minimal. Then there exists a minimal triangulation h' of g that is obtained from h by removing some edges; denote one of these edges by e. Consider a tree decomposition $d' \in M(h')$. The clique containing e in h is not a clique in h', and therefore $\mathrm{bags}(d) \nsubseteq \mathrm{bags}(d')$. Also note that since $h' \subseteq h$, every maximal clique of h' is contained in some maximal clique of h, and therefore $d' \sqsubseteq d$. Then d' strictly subsumes d, in contradiction to the fact that d is proper.

Finally, we need to show that d is a proper tree decomposition of h. The nodes of h are covered in d, and the junction-tree property holds, since d is a tree decomposition of g. The new edges of h are covered in d since they are all a result of saturation of the bags of d. So d is a tree decomposition of h, and we claim that it is proper. Assume, by way of contradiction, that d is not a proper tree decomposition of h, then the tree decomposition d' that strictly subsumes it is also a tree decomposition for g, contradicting the fact that d is a proper tree decomposition of g. □

Counting and Enumerating (Preferred) Database Repairs

Ester Livshits
Technion - Israel Institute of Technology
Haifa 32000, Israel
esterliv@cs.technion.ac.il

Benny Kimelfeld
Technion - Israel Institute of Technology
Haifa 32000, Israel
bennyk@cs.technion.ac.il

ABSTRACT

In the traditional sense, a subset repair of an inconsistent database refers to a consistent subset of facts (tuples) that is maximal under set containment. Preferences between pairs of facts allow to distinguish a set of preferred repairs based on relative reliability (source credibility, extraction quality, recency, etc.) of data items. Previous studies explored the problem of categoricity, where one aims to determine whether preferences suffice to repair the database unambiguously, or in other words, whether there is precisely one preferred repair. In this paper we study the ability to quantify ambiguity, by investigating two classes of problems. The first is that of counting the number of subset repairs, both preferred (under various common semantics) and traditional. We establish dichotomies in data complexity for the entire space of (sets of) functional dependencies. The second class of problems is that of enumerating (i.e., generating) the preferred repairs. We devise enumeration algorithms with efficiency guarantees on the delay between generated repairs, even for constraints represented as general conflict graphs or hypergraphs.

Keywords

Inconsistent Databases; Repairs; Preferred Repairs; Repair Counting; Enumeration; Functional Dependencies; Conflict Hypergraph

1. INTRODUCTION

Database inconsistency arises for different reasons and in different applications. For example, in common applications of Big Data, information is obtained from imprecise sources (e.g., social encyclopedias, social networks, and sensors attached to appliances) via imprecise procedures (e.g., natural-language and signal processing). It may also arise when integrating conflicting data from different (possibly consistent) sources. Arenas, Bertossi and Chomicki [3] introduced a principled approach to managing inconsistency, via the notions of *repairs* and *consistent query answering*.

PODS'17, May 14-19, 2017, Chicago, IL, USA

DOI: http://dx.doi.org/10.1145/3034786.3056107

Informally, a *repair* of an inconsistent database I is a consistent database J that differs from I in a "minimal" way, where *minimality* refers to the *symmetric difference.* In the case of anti-symmetric integrity constraints (e.g., functional dependencies), a repair is a maximal consistent subinstance (not properly contained in any consistent subinstance), and is referred to as a *subset repair* [1].

Various computational problems around database repairs have been extensively investigated [4]. Most studied is the problem of computing the *consistent answers* of a query on an inconsistent database; these are the tuples that are obtained in every possible repair [3,26]. Another well studied question is that of *repair checking* [1]: given instances I and J, determine whether J is a repair of I. Depending on the type of repairs and the type of integrity constraints, these problems may vary from tractable to highly intractable complexity classes.

In the traditional framework, all repairs are treated on a par with each other. There are situations, however, in which it is natural to prefer one repair over another [8,16,33,34]. For example, this is the case if one source is regarded more reliable than another (e.g., enterprise data vs. Internet harvesting, precise vs. imprecise sensing equipment, etc.) or if available timestamp information implies that a more recent fact should be preferred over an earlier fact. Recency may be implied not only by timestamps, but also by evolution semantics; for example, "divorced" is likely to be more updated than "single," and similarly is "Sergeant" compared to "Private". Various models for incorporating preferences in database repairing have been studied. They focus on three main classes of preferences: attribute level preferences [8, 16, 20], tuple level prefereneces [7, 31, 34] and repair level preferences [18].

In this work, we follow the framework of tuple-level *preferred repairs* [33,34], where a *priority relation* between conflicting facts distinguishes a set of *preferred* (or *optimal*) repairs. There are actually three types of preferred repairs: *greedy* (or *completion optimal*), *Pareto optimal*, and *globally optimal* (used previously by Van Nieuwenborgh and Vermeir [31]). A *greedy repair* is a repair that can be obtained by scanning the facts by descending priority, and adding each visited fact to the repair as long as consistency is preserved. (There may be many greedy repairs, since there can be many possible scan orders.) In the other two notions, a preferred repair is one that cannot be *improved* by replacing a subset of the facts with a "preferred" set of facts; they differ in the way "preferred" is interpreted. (See Section 2 for the exact definitions.)

Fagin et al. [15] have shown that preferred repairs capture ad-hoc cleaning operations and strategies of some prominent existing systems for text analytics [2,9]. Staworko et al. [34] showed several results on preferred repairs, for example, that repair checking can be solved in polynomial time for the greedy and Pareto semantics, but there is a set of FDs for which repair checking is coNP-hard in the global semantics. Later, Fagin et al. [14] extended that hardness result to a full dichotomy in complexity over all sets of FDs within the global semantics: repair checking is solvable in polynomial time whenever the set of FDs is equivalent to a single FD or two key constraints per relation; in every other case, the problem is coNP-complete. Moreover, the presence of priorities gives rise to the *ambiguity* problem, which Staworko et al. [34] refer to as *categoricity* (and is called *determinism* by Fan et al. [17]): Determine whether the provided priority relation contains enough information to clean the database unambiguously, or in other words, decide whether there is exactly one preferred repair.

In a recent work [24], we investigated the complexity of the ambiguity problem. We have shown that in the Pareto semantics, every set of FDs features intractability unless it is equivalent to a single FD for every relation. We showed results of a similar nature for the global semantics. For the greedy semantics, though, we devised a polynomial-time algorithm that solves the categoricity problem in the general case where dependencies are provided in the form of a *conflict hypergraph* (that can represent, e.g., FDs, the more general *conditional FDs* [5] and *denial constraints* [19]).

A natural next step is to *quantify* the ambiguity in the repair declaration. In particular, instead of just determining whether there is a single optimal repair, we would like to be able to *count* the optimal repairs. Clearly, in cases where categoricity is intractable, the counting task is hopeless. But do the tractable cases of categoricity generalize to counting? In order to answer this question, we first need to understand the simpler, traditional case, where there are no preferences: what is the complexity of counting subset repairs? Yet, here we encounter the first challenge: not much is known about this problem. Maslowski and Wijsen [29, 30] have studied the problem of counting repairs that satisfy a Boolean conjunctive query, in the case of key constraints. They established dichotomy results, classifying CQs into those where counting can be done in polynomial time, and those where counting is #P-complete.[1] The challenge in their work is due to the query. If we ignore the query and simply count the repairs, then we get the straightforward case of counting subset repairs under key constraints. What about a general FD? (still straightforward). What about more than a single FD? It is not at all clear whether their results on CQs can be used to count the subset repairs (i.e., maximal consistent subsets) for arbitrary sets of FDs.

So, we begin by exploring the problem of counting subset repairs (in the traditional sense, without preferences), or equivalently, the maximal independent sets of the *conflict graph*, which is the graph that has the facts of the database as nodes and an edge between every inconsistent pair of facts. We focus on FDs and study the *data complexity* of counting repairs (where each schema with FDs is a separate computational problem). Counting the maximal independent sets of a graph is #P-complete [32]. Special tractable cases include the class of *P_4-free* graphs [12] (also known as *complement reducible graphs* or *cographs*), that is, the graphs that do not have any induced subgraph that forms a simple path of length 4 (with no edges crossing the path). We establish a dichotomy result, showing that P_4-free graphs capture *precisely* the tractable cases of counting subset repairs: for a given schema, either the conflict graph of every instance over the schema is P_4-free, or the problem is #P-complete. We also present a polynomial-time algorithm to determine the side to which a given schema belongs.

When bringing preferences into the picture, complexity increases. We prove the following dichotomy for each one of the three semantics of optimal repairs. If the restriction of the set of FDs to each relation is equivalent to a single FD (or no FDs), then the optimal repairs can be counted in polynomial time. In *any* other case, the problem is #P-complete. The proofs build on the above dichotomy for subset repairs, past reductions (called *fact-wise reductions* [24]) by Fagin et al. [14] and Kimelfeld et al. [23], and new hardness results that we prove in this work. The most challenging new hardness result applies to greedy repairs (where, as said above, categoricity is solvable in polynomial time).

The above #P-completeness is due to the fact that there could be exponentially many optimal repairs. But this does not preclude the existence of an efficient procedure to determine whether there are *at least a thousand* repairs, or at least any manageable (e.g., polynomial) number of repairs. We could efficiently determine that *if* we had an algorithm for efficiently *enumerating* (producing) the optimal repairs. Such an algorithm is desirable for another fundamental reason. One could expect that, in certain occasions, preferences could reduce the space of repairs (compared to the subset repairs) so much that we would be able to store all of them explicitly, and thereby solve related problems (e.g., consistent query answering) efficiently. In fact, this has been one of the motivations of Staworko et al. [33] to embark on the investigation of repairs with priorities.[2] Nevertheless, the fact that there are only a few optimal repairs does not necessarily imply that we can efficiently *find* them. An efficient enumeration algorithm for optimal repairs would resolve this problem in a positive way, as the time it would take to generate all optimal repairs is polynomial in the number of such repairs (in addition to the size of the input).

We adopt the classic yardsticks of Johnson et al. [21], who view an *efficient* enumeration algorithm as one that produces a set of (possibly exponentially many) answers in *polynomial total time* (that is, polynomial in the combined size of the input and the output). Stronger notions are *incremental polynomial time* and *polynomial delay*, which bound the time between producing every two consecutive answers. In the traditional case of subset repairs (i.e., without preferences), the task is that of enumerating the maximal independent sets of a given hypergraph h (the conflict hypergraph). This task is also known (or more precisely can be phrased) as enumerating the *minimal transversals* of a hypergraph, a problem well studied in past decades [13], wherein the existence of a polynomial-total-time solver is still an open question. Yet, efficient algorithms are known for the case where h is a graph [11, 21], or more generally, a hypergraph of bounded dimension [6].

[1]To be precise, for general key constraints they classified the CQs without self joins, and for key constraits where the key consists of a single attribute they classified all CQs.

[2]Private communication with Jan Chomicki.

Our contribution incorporates priorities in the problem of enumerating maximal independent sets. For the Pareto and global semantics, past results on categoricity imply that the problem of deciding whether there is precisely one Pareto or globally optimal repair is intractable in common cases (e.g., more than a single FD per relation) [23]. Clearly, in cases where categoricity is intractable, enumeration is intractable as well. Yet, in the case of a single functional dependency, enumeration can be done with polynomial delay for all three semantics. Furthermore, we establish two new algorithms.

The first algorithm enumerates the greedy repairs, with polynomial delay, for general conflict graphs (e.g., arbitrary FDs). The algorithm builds upon an algorithm for enumerating the maximal independent sets of a graph [11], and applies a nontrivial adjustment to greedy repairs. The second applies to the case where priorities behave as if determined by a *confidence score*, where a fact is preferred to a conflicting one if and only if the score of the former is higher than that of the latter. Our algorithm enumerates the optimal repairs *under each of the three semantics* in incremental polynomial time, for arbitrary conflict hypergraphs of bounded dimension. This algorithm deploys as a subroutine an existing algorithm for enumerating the maximal independent sets of a hypergraph of bounded dimension [6].

The rest of the paper is organized as follows. In the next section we introduce some basic terminology that will be used throughout the paper. In Section 3 we present the problems that we study in this paper. We investigate the problem of counting repairs (both subset and preferred repairs) in Section 4, and the problem of enumerating preferred repairs in Section 5. We summarize our results and discuss directions for future work in Section 6. Proofs are omitted, and will be given in the full version of the paper.

2. PRELIMINARIES

We first present some basic terminology and notation that we use throughout the paper.

2.1 Relational Signatures and Instances

We assume three infinite collections: *attributes* (column names), *relation symbols* (table names), and *constants* (cell values). A *heading* is a sequence $(A_1, \dots, A_k)$ of distinct attributes, where k is the *arity* of the heading. A *signature* $\mathcal{S}$ is a mapping from a finite set of relation symbols R to headings $\mathcal{S}(R)$. We use the conventional notation $R(A_1, \dots, A_k)$ to denote that R is a relation symbol that is assigned the heading $(A_1, \dots, A_k)$. An *instance* I of a signature $\mathcal{S}$ maps every relation symbol $R(A_1, \dots, A_k)$ to a finite set, denoted R^I, of tuples $(c_1, \dots, c_k)$ where each c_i is a constant. We may omit stating the signature $\mathcal{S}$ of an instance I when $\mathcal{S}$ is clear from the context or irrelevant.

Let $\mathcal{S}$ be a signature, R a relation symbol of $\mathcal{S}$, I an instance of $\mathcal{S}$, and t be a tuple in R^I. We refer to the expression $R(t)$ as a *fact of* I. By a slight abuse of notation, we identify an instance I with the set of its facts. For example, $R(t) \in I$ denotes that t is a tuple in R^I. As another example, $J \subseteq I$ means that $R^J \subseteq R^I$ for every relation symbol R of $\mathcal{S}$; in this case, we say that J is *subinstance* of I.

2.2 Functional Dependencies

A *Functional Dependency* (*FD* for short) over a signature $\mathcal{S}$ is an expression of the form $R : X \to Y$, where R is a relation symbol and X and Y are sets of attributes of R.

Table 1: Specific FD schemas.

FD Schema	Signature	FDs
$(\mathcal{S}_{2k}, \Delta_{2k})$	$R(A, B)$	$A \to B$,$B \to A$
$(\mathcal{S}_{ch}, \Delta_{ch})$	$R(A, B, C)$	$\emptyset \to A$, $B \to C$
$(\mathcal{S}_{2fd}, \Delta_{2fd})$	$R(A, B, C, D)$	$A \to B$, $C \to D$

When R is clear from the context, we simply write $X \to Y$. We may also write X and Y by simply concatenating the attribute symbols; for example, we may write $AB \to C$ instead of $\{A, B\} \to \{C\}$ for the relation symbol $R(A, B, C)$. An FD $X \to Y$ is *trivial* if $Y \subseteq X$, and otherwise it is *nontrivial.*

An instance I *satisfies* an FD $R : X \to Y$ if for every two facts f and g over R, if f and g agree on (i.e., have the same constants in the position of) the attributes of X, then they also agree on the attributes of Y. We say that I satisfies a set Δ of FDs if I satisfies every FD in Δ; otherwise, we say that I *violates* Δ. Two sets of FDs over the same signature are *equivalent* if every instance that satisfies one also satisfies the other. For example, $\Delta = \{R : A \to BC, R : C \to A\}$ and $\{R : A \to C, R : C \to AB\}$ are equivalent. An FD $X \to Y$ is *entailed* by Δ (denoted by $\Delta \models X \to Y$) if for every instance I over the schema, if I satisfies Δ, then it also satisfies $X \to Y$. We denote by $\Delta_{|R}$ the restriction of Δ to the FDs over R (i.e., those of the form $R : X \to Y$).

Let Δ be a set of FDs. A *minimal cover* [28] of Δ is a set Δ_m of FDs that satisfies the following properties: *(a)* Δ and Δ_m are equivalent, *(b)* FDs in Δ_m contain a single attribute on their right hand side, that is, they have the form $X \to A$, *(c)* no FD in Δ_m is redundant, that is, no $X \to A$ in Δ_m satisfies $(\Delta \setminus \{X \to A\}) \models X \to A$, *and (d)* there is no redundant attribute in Δ_m, that is, no FD $XB \to A$ in Δ_m satisfies $\Delta \models X \to A$.

An *FD schema* is a pair $(\mathcal{S}, \Delta)$, where $\mathcal{S}$ is a signature and Δ is a set of FDs over $\mathcal{S}$. Two FD schemas $(\mathcal{S}, \Delta)$ and $(\mathcal{S}', \Delta')$ are *equivalent* if $\mathcal{S} = \mathcal{S}'$ and Δ is equivalent to Δ'. For example, Table 1 depicts specific schemas that we refer to throughout the paper. In $(\mathcal{S}_{2k}, \Delta_{2k})$ the subscript "2k" stands for "two keys" as it includes two key constraints (one where A is the key and one where B is the key). In $(\mathcal{S}_{ch}, \Delta_{ch})$ the subscript "ch" stands for "chain" and we introduce this term later in Section 4. In $(\mathcal{S}_{2fd}, \Delta_{2fd})$ the subscript "2fd" refers to simply "two FDs," and its two FDs are disjoint in the attributes they involve.

EXAMPLE 2.1. Figure 1 depicts a (hypothetical) inconsistent single-relation instance that stores information about traffic camera records, as established by integrating several data sources. The names of the facts have the form x_b, where x denotes the brand of the recorded car 1(e.g., a for `Acura`), and b denotes a *reliability* that we later discuss. For instance, the fact a_3 states that an Acura car with a California plate number AA11 has been recorded by the Huston Police Department at time 1500.

In the corresponding FD schema $(\mathcal{S}, \Delta)$, the signature $\mathcal{S}$ consists of a single relation schema

$$\mathit{Image}(\mathsf{dept}, \mathsf{time}, \mathsf{plate}, \mathsf{state}, \mathsf{make})$$

and Δ consists of the two FDs: $\mathsf{plate}\ \mathsf{state} \to \mathsf{make}$ (the brand of the car is determined by the state and plate num-

fact	dept	time	plate	state	make
a_3	HPD	1500	AA11	CA	Acura
a_{iii}	NYPD	1800	AA11	CA	Acura
h_2	PPD	1900	AA11	CA	Honda
h_3	LAPD	2000	AA11	CA	Honda
h_{ii}	LAPD	1000	AA11	CA	Honda
m_1	LAPD	1600	AA11	CA	Mazda
m_2	HPD	1600	AA11	CA	Mazda
m_{i}	HPD	1100	AA11	CA	Mazda
n_4	NYPD	1500	AA11	CA	Nissan

Figure 1: Inconsistent prioritizing instance over the schema $(\mathcal{S}, \Delta)$ of Example 2.1.

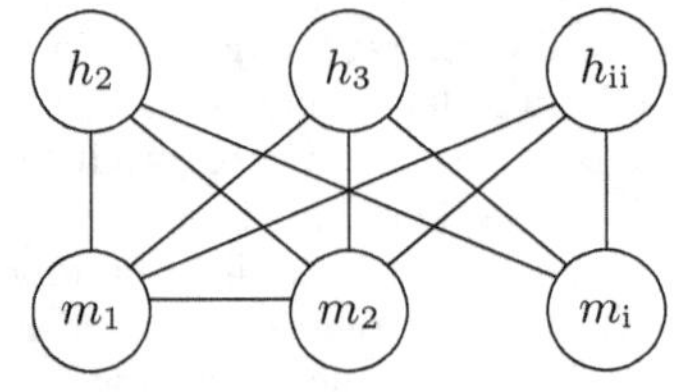

Figure 2: The conflict graph of the subinstance $\{h_2, h_3, h_{\text{ii}}, m_1, m_2\}$ of Figure 1.

ber), and time plate state $\rightarrow$ dept (a car cannot be recorded by two police departments at the same time). Note, however, that the instance of Figure 1 violates the FDs. In particular, all records mention the same plate and state, but there is no agreement on the brand. Moreover, m_1 and m_2 mention recordings of the same car at the same time in Los Angeles and Huston, respectively. ☐

2.3 Conflict Hypergraphs

All hypergraphs (and graphs) used in this paper are finite and undirected. The set of nodes of a hypergraph h is denoted by $\mathsf{N}(h)$, and its set of hyperedges is denoted by $\mathsf{E}(h)$; here, every hyperedge $e \in \mathsf{E}(h)$ is a subset of $\mathsf{N}(h)$. In the special case where every hyperedge is a pair $\{u, v\}$ of distinct nodes, the hypergraph is simply a *graph* and a hyperedge is simply an *edge*. Two nodes of a hypergraph h are *neighbors* if at least one hyperedge of h contains both. An *independent set* of a hypergraph h is a set U of nodes that does not contain any hyperedge; that is, $U \subseteq \mathsf{N}(h)$ and $e \not\subseteq U$ for all $e \in \mathsf{E}(h)$. (Observe that an independent set may include neighboring nodes.) An independent set U of a hypergraph h is *maximal* if U is not strictly contained in any other independent set of h.

Conventionally, inconsistent databases are instances that violate integrity constraints [3]. Here, we use the abstraction of a *conflict hypergraph* that can represent inconsistencies for various types of integrity constraints, including FDs, the more general *conditional FDs* [5], and the more general *denial constraints* [19]. In fact, every constraint that is anti-monotonic (i.e., where subsets of consistent sets are always consistent) can be represented as a conflict hypergraph. In the case of the above constraints, the translation from the logical constraints to the conflict hypergraph can be done in polynomial time under *data complexity* (i.e., when the signature and constraints are assumed to be fixed).

Formally, a *conflict hypergraph* over an instance I is simply a hypergraph h over the facts of I (that is, $\mathsf{N}(h) = I$) [10]. A special case of a conflict hypergraph is defined by an FD schema $(\mathcal{S}, \Delta)$ and an instance I over $\mathcal{S}$. In that case, the conflict hypergraph, called a *conflict graph* and denoted $\mathcal{G}^I_\Delta$, is the graph over the facts of I that has an edge between every two facts that violate one or more FDs in Δ. Note, however, that a conflict graph could express constraints that are defined over pairs of facts that are not FDs,[3] such as (in the context of our running example) there cannot be recordings of the same car in different departments if the time difference is smaller than 200 (hence, h_2 and h_3 of Figure 1 become inconsistent with each other).

Let h be a conflict hypergraph over an instance I. An independent set of h is also called a *consistent subinstance* (of I w.r.t. h), and a *maximal* independent set of h is also called a *subset repair* (of I w.r.t. h) [1, 3], or *s-repair* for short. We denote by SRep(h) the set of all s-repairs of I w.r.t. h.

EXAMPLE 2.2. Figure 2 depicts the graph $\mathcal{G}^K_\Delta$, where Δ is given in Figure 1, and K consists of a subset of the facts of Figure 1. (We do not include all the facts to avoid clutter.) Observe that there is an edge between h_2 and m_1 since the pair $\{h_2, m_1\}$ violates the FD plate state $\rightarrow$ make, and there is an edge between m_1 and m_2 since they violate the FD time plate state $\rightarrow$ dept. Table 2 shows the subset repairs of the instance. (We explain the columns of the table later in this section.) The reader can verify that, indeed, each subset repair corresponds to a maximal consistent subset, and that no other subset repairs exist. ☐

2.4 Priorities and Preferred Repairs

We now recall the framework of preferred repairs by Staworko et al. [34]. A *priority* relation $\succ$ over an instance I is an acyclic[4] binary relation over the facts of I. If $\succ$ is a priority relation over I and K is a subinstance of I, then $\max_\succ(K)$ denotes the set of facts $f \in K$ such that no $g \in K$ satisfies $g \succ f$.

An *inconsistent prioritizing instance* over a signature $\mathcal{S}$ is a triple $(I, h, \succ)$, where I is an instance over $\mathcal{S}$, h is a conflict hypergraph over I, and $\succ$ is a priority relation over I with the following property: for every two facts f and g of I, if $f \succ g$ then f and g are neighbors in h.[5] For example, if $h = \mathcal{G}^I_\Delta$ for a set Δ of FDs, then $f \succ g$ implies that $\{f, g\}$ violates at least one FD. An inconsistent prioritizing instance over an FD schema $(\mathcal{S}, \Delta)$ is just a pair $(I, \succ)$, and it stands for the triple $(I, \mathcal{G}^I_\Delta, \succ)$.

EXAMPLE 2.3. We continue with our running example around the instance of Figure 1. The preference $\succ$ among

[3]This observation is relevant to Section 5 where we give an algorithm for general conflict graphs (but not hypergraphs).
[4]By *acyclic* we mean that I does not contain any sequence $f_1, \dots, f_k$ of facts such that $f_i \succ f_{i+1}$ for all $i = 1, \dots, k-1$ and $f_k \succ f_1$.
[5]This requirement has been made with the introduction of the framework [34]. Since the instances we consider here remain valid in the general setting as well, the hardness complexity results we present hold even without this requirement.

Table 2: Repairs of the inconsistent prioritizing instance of Figure 1.

subset repair	p-repair?	g-repair?	c-repair?
$\{a_3, a_{\text{iii}}\}$	✓	✓	✓
$\{h_2, h_3, h_{\text{ii}}\}$	✓	✓	
$\{m_1, m_{\text{i}}\}$			
$\{m_2, m_{\text{i}}\}$	✓		
$\{n_4\}$	✓	✓	✓

the facts is encoded by the subscripts of the fact denotations, and is defined as follows: $x_a \succ y_b$ whenever $x \neq y$, a and b are numbers of the same type (Arabic/Roman), and $a > b$. For example, we have $a_3 \succ h_2$ since the two disagree on the car brand, and $3 > 2$. But $a_{\text{iii}} \not\succ h_2$ since "iii" and "3" are of different number languages. In addition, m_1 and m_2 are in conflict since they disagree on the department, and it holds that $m_2 \succ m_1$. □

Staworko et al. [34] define three different notions of *preferred* repairs that take the priority relation into account. The first notion is that of *globally-optimal* repairs (also used previously by Van Nieuwenborgh and Vermeir [31]). This notion is based on checking whether a repair J of I can be improved by replacing a set of facts in J with a "better preferred" set of facts from I. The high computational cost of using global optimality (e.g., for the problem of repair checking) led them to seek different notions of optimality with a lower computational complexity. Inspired by the work of Koltun et al. [25], they defined the notion of *Pareto-optimal* repairs. The difference between the two notions is in the way "better preferred" is interpreted. Next, we give the formal definitions.

Definition 2.4 (Improvement). *Let $(I, h, \succ)$ be an inconsistent prioritizing instance, and let J and J' be two distinct consistent subinstances of I w.r.t. h.*

- *J is a* global improvement *of J' if for every $f' \in J' \setminus J$ there exists $f \in J \setminus J'$ such that $f \succ f'$.*
- *J is a* Pareto improvement *of J' if there exists $f \in J \setminus J'$ such that $f \succ f'$ for all $f' \in J' \setminus J$.*

That is, J is a global improvement of J' if, to obtain J from J', we insert and delete facts, such that every deleted fact is preferred to by some inserted one. The subinstance J is a Pareto improvement of J' if we similarly obtain J from J', but now one of the inserted facts is preferred to all deleted ones. Then, we get the following.

Definition 2.5 (Global/Pareto optimality). *Let $(I, h, \succ)$ be an inconsistent prioritizing instance, and let J be a consistent subinstance of I w.r.t. h.*

- *J is a* globally-optimal *repair of $(I, h, \succ)$ if there is no global improvement of J.*
- *J is a* globally-optimal *repair of $(I, h, \succ)$ if there is no Pareto improvement of J*

The last notion of preferred repairs defined by Staworko et al. [34] is that of a *greedy repair*, also called *completion optimal*. A greedy repair is a repair J that can be obtained by scanning the facts by descending $\succ$ (i.e., if $f \succ g$ then f is visited before g) and adding to J each visited fact as long as consistency is preserved, as depicted in Figure 3.

Algorithm GreedyRepair$(I, h, \succ)$

```
1: J := ∅
2: while max≻(I) ≠ ∅ do
3:    choose a fact f in max≻(I)
4:    I := I \ {f}
5:    if J ∪ {f} is consistent w.r.t. h then
6:       J := J ∪ {f}
7: return J
```

Figure 3: Finding a greedy repair J [34].

The algorithm of Figure 3 takes as input an inconsistent prioritizing instance $(I, h, \succ)$ and returns a greedy repair J. It begins with an empty J, and incrementally inserts tuples to J, as follows. In each iteration of lines 3–6, the algorithm selects a fact f from $\max_{\succ}(I)$ and removes it from I. Then, f is added to J if it does not violate consistency, that is, if h does not contain any hyperedge e such that $e \subseteq J \cup \{f\}$. The specific way of choosing the fact f among all those in $\max_{\succ}(I)$ is (deliberately) left unspecified, and hence, different executions may result in different greedy repairs. In that sense, the algorithm is nondeterministic.

Let $(I, h, \succ)$ be an inconsistent prioritizing instance. A *completion* of $\succ$ is a priority relation $\succ'$ over I such that $\succ$ is a subset of $\succ'$ and $\succ'$ is total on the neighbors of h (i.e., every pair of neighbors is comparable). Staworko et al. [34] proved that the possible results of the different executions of the algorithm of Figure 3 (that is, the greedy repairs) are all the consistent subinstances J of I that are globally-optimal repairs of $(I, h, \succ')$ for some completion $\succ'$ of $\succ$. Thus, we get the following alternative definition for greedy repairs.

Definition 2.6 (Completion-optimal repair). *Let $(I, h, \succ)$ be an inconsistent prioritizing instance, and let J be a consistent subinstance of I w.r.t. h. Then, J is a* completion-optimal *repair of I if there exists a completion $\succ'$ of $\succ$, such that J is a globally-optimal repair of $(I, h, \succ')$.*

We remark that in the definition of a completion-optimal repair, we could replace "globally-optimal" with "Pareto-optimal" and obtain an equivalent definition [34]. We use *g-repair*, *p-repair* and *c-repair*[6] as abbreviations of "globally-optimal repair," "Pareto-optimal repair," and "completion-optimal repair," respectively. For an inconsistent prioritizing instance $(I, h, \succ)$, we denote the set of all g-repairs, p-repairs and c-repairs by $\text{GRep}_{\succ}(h)$, $\text{PRep}_{\succ}(h)$ and $\text{CRep}_{\succ}(h)$, respectively.

Example 2.7. Consider Table 2 again. For each subset repair J the table states whether J is a p-repair, a g-repair, or a c-repair. We discuss several examples.

- $\{m_1, m_{\text{i}}\}$ is not a p-repair, since $\{m_2, m_{\text{i}}\}$ is a Pareto improvement of $\{m_1, m_{\text{i}}\}$ (as $m_2 \succ m_1$).

[6]Do not confuse our c-repairs with C-repairs that were used to denote *cardinality repairs* [27].

- $\{m_2, m_{\rm i}\}$ is a p-repair, but not a g-repair, since $\{h_3, h_{\rm ii}\}$ is a global improvement of $\{m_2, m_{\rm i}\}$ (as both $h_3 \succ m_2$ and $h_{\rm ii} \succ m_{\rm i}$ hold).
- $\{h_2, h_3, h_{\rm ii}\}$ is a g-repair, since it cannot be globally improved.
- $\{h_2, h_3, h_{\rm ii}\}$ is not a c-repair, since every c-repair must include either $a_{\rm iii}$ or n_4 (which are the only maximal facts under $\succ$).
- $\{a_3, a_{\rm iii}\}$ is a c-repair. The following is one of the executions of GreedyRepair that realize it, where $+f$ means that f is added to J (line 4) and $-f$ that f is ignored: $+a_{\rm iii}$, $-h_{\rm ii}$, $-m_{\rm i}$, $-n_4$, $+a_3$, $-h_3$, $-h_2$, $-m_2$, $-m_1$.

The table consists of all of the preferred repairs since, as we explain next, every preferred repair is a subset repair (and we already stated in Example 2.2 that all subset repairs are in the table). Observe that in this example, every c-repair is a g-repair, and every g-repair is a p-repair, and as we also explain next, this is not a coincidence. □

The following theorem states the relationship between the different types of repairs defined in this section.

THEOREM 2.8. [34] *Let $(I, h, \succ)$ be an inconsistent prioritizing instance. It holds that* $\text{CRep}_{\succ}(h) \subseteq \text{GRep}_{\succ}(h) \subseteq \text{PRep}_{\succ}(h) \subseteq \text{SRep}(h)$.

Importantly, the theorem states that the most restricted class of repairs is that of the greedy repairs, and moreover, every preferred repair is also a subset repair.

3. PROBLEMS AND COMPLEXITY

We investigate the problems of *counting* and *enumerating* ordinary and preferred repairs. In this section we present the problems and the relevant measures of computational complexity.

3.1 Counting Repairs

We first define the counting problems. Specifically, we study the problems of counting subset repairs and preferred repairs (for all three types of preferred repairs) for fixed FD schemas $(\mathcal{S}, \Delta)$. In the problem $\#\text{SREP}\langle\mathcal{S}, \Delta\rangle$ the goal is to compute the cardinality $|\text{SRep}(\mathcal{G}^I_\Delta)|$ for a given instance I over $\mathcal{S}$. In $\#X\text{REP}\langle\mathcal{S}, \Delta\rangle$, where X is one of G, P and C, the goal is to compute $|X\text{Rep}_{\succ}(\mathcal{G}^I_\Delta)|$ for a given inconsistent prioritizing instance $(I, \succ)$. For ease of reference, the different problems are given in Table 3.

For counting problems, a basic tractable class is FP (functions computable in polynomial time), and a common measure of intractability is #P-hardness (or #P-completeness). #P is the class of functions that count the number of witnesses for an NP problem (e.g., the number of satisfying assignments for a given formula in propositional logic). Hardness for #P is defined by means of a Turing reduction. Using an oracle to a #P-hard function, one can solve in polynomial time every problem in the polynomial hierarchy [35].

3.2 Enumerating Repairs

We now consider the task of enumerating (i.e., generating) the g-repairs, p-repairs, and c-repairs. Enumerating the s-repairs is the well known problem of enumerating the maximal independent sets of a graph or a hypergraph, a problem that has been well studied [6, 11, 13, 21]. In Table 3 we specify two variants of the problem of enumerating x-repairs (where x is one of g, c and p). In the problem XREPENUM the input is an inconsistent prioritizing instance $(I, h, \succ)$, and in the problem $X\text{REPENUM}\langle\mathcal{S}, \Delta\rangle$ we fix the FD-schema $(\mathcal{S}, \Delta)$, and the input consists of only a prioritizing instance $(I, \succ)$ over $(\mathcal{S}, \Delta)$. We first investigate the problems $\text{GREPENUM}\langle\mathcal{S}, \Delta\rangle$ and $\text{PREPENUM}\langle\mathcal{S}, \Delta\rangle$, where we have mainly negative results (that is, the problems are hard even when considering only FDs). Our positive results (e.g., for CREPENUM), on the other hand, apply not only to FDs, but rather to general constraints that can be represented as a conflict graph or hypergraph.

Table 3: Studied problems. The letter X stands for each of P, G and C.

Problem	Input	Compute
$\#\text{SREP}\langle\mathcal{S}, \Delta\rangle$	I	$\lvert\text{SRep}(\mathcal{G}^I_\Delta)\rvert$
$\#X\text{REP}\langle\mathcal{S}, \Delta\rangle$	$(I, \succ)$	$\lvert X\text{Rep}_{\succ}(\mathcal{G}^I_\Delta)\rvert$
XREPENUM	$(I, h, \succ)$	$X\text{Rep}_{\succ}(h)$
$X\text{REPENUM}\langle\mathcal{S}, \Delta\rangle$	$(I, \succ)$	$X\text{Rep}_{\succ}(\mathcal{G}^I_\Delta)$

The task of enumerating repairs requires the solver algorithm to produce all repairs (unless execution is terminated before completion). In the worst case there could be exponentially many repairs, and so *polynomial time* is not a proper yardstick of efficiency. For such problems, Johnson, Papadimitriou and Yannakakis [21] introduced several complexity guarantees, which we recall here. An *enumeration problem* $\mathcal{P}$ is a collection of pairs (x, Y) where x is an *input* and Y is a finite set of *answers* for x, denoted by $\mathcal{P}(x)$. A *solver* for an enumeration problem $\mathcal{P}$ is an algorithm that, when given an input x, produces a sequence of answers such that every answer in $\mathcal{P}(x)$ is printed precisely once. We say that a solver A for an enumeration problem $\mathcal{P}$ runs in:

- *polynomial total time* if the total execution time of A is polynomial in $(|x| + |\mathcal{P}(x)|)$;
- *polynomial delay* if the time between every two consecutive answers produced is polynomial in $|x|$;
- *incremental polynomial time* if, after generating N answers, the time to generate the next $(N+1)$st answer is polynomial in $(|x| + N)$.

In Section 5 we present algorithms that run with polynomial delay and with incremental polynomial time.

4. COUNTING REPAIRS

In this section we study the problems of counting subset repairs and preferred repairs, when conflicts are induced by FDs.

4.1 Counting Subset Repairs

A class of graphs where we can count the maximal independent sets in polynomial time is that of P_4-free graphs (i.e., the graphs in which no induced subgraph is a path of length 4). A P_4-free graph is also called *cograph*, and the class of P_4-free graphs is characterized as the one generated from single nodes by repeatedly applying disjoint unions and complementation [12].

PROPOSITION 4.1. [12] $|\mathrm{SRep}(g)|$ *can be computed in polynomial time for P_4-free graphs g.*

Interestingly, it turns out that P_4-free graphs capture precisely the class of FD sets for which subset repairs can be computed in polynomial time.

THEOREM 4.2. *Let $(\mathcal{S}, \Delta)$ be an FD schema. Assuming* FP $\neq$ #P *(or* P $\neq$ NP*), the following are equivalent.*

- $\#\mathrm{SREP}\langle \mathcal{S}, \Delta \rangle$ *is solvable in polynomial time.*
- $\mathcal{G}_\Delta^I$ *is P_4-free for every instance I of $\mathcal{S}$.*

Moreover, whether these conditions hold can be decided in polynomial time in the size of $(\mathcal{S}, \Delta)$.

Next, we illustrate the application of Theorem 4.2 for classifying FD schemas into tractable and intractable ones (w.r.t. counting repairs).

EXAMPLE 4.3. Consider again the conflict graph of Figure 2. The reader can verify that this graph is P_4-free, by inspecting every four nodes (though there are more efficient ways of verifying P_4-freeness [12]). For example, the nodes along the path m_1—m_2—h_{ii}—m_i do not induce a P_4, since there is an edge between m_1 and h_{ii}. Later we will show that every conflict graph of the FDs of our running example (Figure 1) is P_4-free. Consequently, from Theorem 4.2 we conclude that $\#\mathrm{SREP}\langle \mathcal{S}, \Delta \rangle$ can be solved in polynomial time for the FD schema of our running example. On the other hand, consider the FD schema $(\mathcal{S}_{2k}, \Delta_{2k})$ of Table 1, and the instance $I = \{R(0,1), R(0,2), R(1,2), R(1,3)\}$. Then $\mathcal{G}_\Delta^I$ is a P_4 graph, and hence, Theorem 4.2 implies that $\#\mathrm{SREP}\langle \mathcal{S}_{2k}, \Delta_{2k} \rangle$ cannot be solved in polynomial time (under standard complexity assumptions). We get a similar lower bound for $(\mathcal{S}_{2fd}, \Delta_{2fd})$, as evidenced by the instance $\{R(0,0,0,0), R(0,1,1,1), R(1,1,1,2), R(1,2,2,2)\}$ that has a P_4 conflict graph as well. □

In the remainder of this section we sketch the proof of the theorem.

4.1.1 Proof Sketch for Theorem 4.2

The proof of Theorem 4.2 is based on the concept of a *chain* FD schema.

DEFINITION 4.4. [Chain FD Schema] An FD schema is a *chain* if for every two FDs $X_1 \to Y_1$ and $X_2 \to Y_2$ over the same relation symbol, either $X_1 \subseteq X_2$ or $X_2 \subseteq X_1$. □

As an example, every FD schema with at most one FD per relation is a chain. As another example, the FD schema $(\mathcal{S}_{ch}, \Delta_{ch})$ of Table 1 is a chain. However, the FD schema $(\mathcal{S}_{2k}, \Delta_{2k})$ in that table is not a chain, since there is no containment among $\{A\}$ and $\{B\}$. Interestingly, being a chain captures precisely the guarantee of P_4-freeness of conflict graphs, as stated in the following lemma.

LEMMA 4.5. *Let $(\mathcal{S}, \Delta)$ be an FD schema. The following are equivalent.*

1. *$\mathcal{G}_\Delta^I$ is P_4-free for every instance I of $\mathcal{S}$.*
2. *$(\mathcal{S}, \Delta)$ is equivalent to some chain FD schema.*

To prove the first direction of the lemma, $1 \to 2$, we use a *minimal cover* Δ_m of Δ, and prove the contrapositive by induction on the number of FDs in Δ_m: if Δ_m is not equivalent to any chain FD schema, then we can construct an instance I over $\mathbf{S}$ such that $\mathcal{G}_\Delta^I$ is a path of length four. For the other direction, $2 \to 1$, we look at an equivalent chain FD schema, an instance I of four facts, and do a case analysis to show that $\mathcal{G}_\Delta^I$ cannot be a path of length four. Next, we illustrate the lemma in an example.

EXAMPLE 4.6. Lemma 4.5 establishes the claim that we made in Example 4.3, that the schema of our running example satisfies the tractability condition of Theorem 4.2. Indeed, the FD set Δ, shown in Figure 1 is a chain schema. Observe that we could equivalently write Δ with redundancy, as consisting of the following FDs.

$$\mathsf{plate\ state} \to \mathsf{make}$$
$$\mathsf{time\ plate\ state} \to \mathsf{dept}$$
$$\mathsf{dept\ plate\ state} \to \mathsf{make}$$

In this case, $(\mathcal{S}, \Delta)$ would not be a chain schema, but rather *equivalent* to a chain schema. □

Recall that the tractability condition claimed by Theorem 4.2 on the FD schema $(\mathcal{S}, \Delta)$ is that $\mathcal{G}_\Delta^I$ is P_4-free for every instance I of $\mathcal{S}$. Hence, the tractability side is due to Proposition 4.1. Lemma 4.5 states that the condition is equivalent to $(\mathcal{S}, \Delta)$ being a chain FD schema. So, to prove the hardness side of Theorem 4.2, we begin with the simplest FD schema that is not a chain: $(\mathcal{S}_{2k}, \Delta_{2k})$ of Table 1. Consider an instance I of $\mathcal{S}_{2k}$. If I is viewed as the set of edges of a bipartite graph g (where the constants of I correspond to the nodes of g, assuming, without the loss of generality, that the sets of constants of each attribute are disjoint), then counting the subset repairs of I is the problem of finding the *maximal matchings* of g, which is #*P*-complete [36]. Hence, we get the following result.

PROPOSITION 4.7. *The problem $\#\mathrm{SREP}\langle \mathcal{S}_{2k}, \Delta_{2k} \rangle$ is #P-complete.*

Next, we use the concept of a *fact-wise reduction* [22]. Let $(\mathcal{S}, \Delta)$ and $(\mathcal{S}', \Delta')$ be two FD schemas. A *mapping* from $\mathcal{S}$ to $\mathcal{S}'$ is a function μ that maps facts over $\mathcal{S}$ to facts over $\mathcal{S}'$. (We say that f is a fact *over* $\mathcal{S}$ if f is a fact of some instance I over $\mathcal{S}$.) We extend a mapping μ to map instances I over $\mathcal{S}$ to instances over $\mathcal{S}'$ by defining $\mu(I)$ to be $\{\mu(f) \mid f \in I\}$. A *fact-wise reduction* from $(\mathcal{S}, \Delta)$ to $(\mathcal{S}', \Delta')$ is a mapping Π from $\mathcal{S}$ to $\mathcal{S}'$ with the following properties.

1. Π is injective; that is, for all facts f and g over $\mathcal{S}$, if $\Pi(f) = \Pi(g)$ then $f = g$.
2. Π preserves consistency and inconsistency; that is, for every instance I over $\mathcal{S}$, the instance $\Pi(I)$ satisfies Δ' if and only if I satisfies Δ.
3. Π is computable in polynomial time.

The following lemma is straightforward.

LEMMA 4.8. *Let $(\mathcal{S}, \Delta)$ and $(\mathcal{S}', \Delta')$ be FD schemas, and suppose that there is a fact-wise reduction from $(\mathcal{S}, \Delta)$ to $(\mathcal{S}', \Delta')$. If $\#\mathrm{SREP}\langle \mathcal{S}, \Delta \rangle$ is #P-hard, then $\#\mathrm{SREP}\langle \mathcal{S}', \Delta' \rangle$ is #P-hard as well.*

Hence, we complete the proof by proving the following lemma, which is a nontrivial part of the proof of Theorem 4.2.

LEMMA 4.9. *Let $(\mathcal{S}, \Delta)$ be an FD schema that is not equivalent to any chain FD schema. There is a fact-wise reduction from $(\mathcal{S}_{2k}, \Delta_{2k})$ to $(\mathcal{S}, \Delta)$.*

To prove the lemma, we again look at a minimal cover Δ_m of Δ. We prove, by induction on the number of FDs in Δ_m, that there is a fact-wise reduction from $(\mathcal{S}_{2k}, \Delta_{2k})$ to $(\mathcal{S}, \Delta_m)$. This fact-wise reduction is actually an application of two fact-wise reductions: one from $(\mathcal{S}_{2k}, \Delta_{2k})$ to $(\mathcal{S}, \Delta'_m)$ for some subset Δ'_m of Δ_m, and another one from $(\mathcal{S}, \Delta'_m)$ to $(\mathcal{S}, \Delta_m)$.

Finally, we discuss the tractability of testing whether the condition of Theorem 4.2 holds for a given $(\mathcal{S}, \Delta)$. This condition is that of testing whether $(\mathcal{S}, \Delta)$ is equivalent to some chain FD set. We have the following.

LEMMA 4.10. *Suppose that $(\mathcal{S}, \Delta)$ is an FD schema and Δ_m a minimal cover of Δ. Then, $(\mathcal{S}, \Delta)$ is equivalent to a chain FD schema if and only if $(\mathcal{S}, \Delta_m)$ is a chain FD schema.*

The "if" direction is straightforward. For the "only if" direction, we look at a chain FD schema $(\mathcal{S}, \Delta')$ that is equivalent to Δ. Clearly, Δ_m is also a minimal cover of Δ'. We then prove, by induction on the number of FDs in Δ', that Δ_m is a chain. Hence, to test whether $(\mathcal{S}, \Delta)$ is equivalent to a chain FD schema, we first remove redundancy from Δ to obtain a minimal cover, and then test whether the result is a chain.

4.2 Counting Preferred Repairs

A simple algorithm for counting preferred repairs can be devised for the case of a single FD per relation. Are there algorithms for other sets of FDs? Counting preferred repairs is at least as hard as counting subset repairs, since the semantics converge when the priority relation is empty. In particular, the hard cases of Theorem 4.2 remain hard for preferred repairs. Unfortunately, the class of FDs for which preferred repairs can be efficiently counted is much more restricted.

THEOREM 4.11. *Let $(\mathcal{S}, \Delta)$ be an FD schema. Assuming* FP $\neq$ #P *(or* P $\neq$ NP*), the following are equivalent.*

- *#XREP$\langle \mathcal{S}, \Delta \rangle$ is solvable in polynomial time for each $X \in \{\mathsf{P}, \mathsf{G}, \mathsf{C}\}$.*
- *$\Delta_{|R}$ is equivalent to a single FD for every relation symbol R of $\mathcal{S}$.*

In the remainder of this section we sketch the proof of Theorem 4.11. The tractability side of the theorem (i.e., polynomial-time counting for a single FD per relation) is done by decomposing the input instance into *blocks* and *subblocks* as done by Kimelfeld et al. [23]. So, we focus on the hardness side. The proof uses known fact-wise reductions that were established by Kimelfeld et al. [23], who built on earlier results of Fagin et al. [14].

THEOREM 4.12. [14] *Let $(\mathcal{S}, \Delta)$ be an FD schema, and let R be a relation symbol of $\mathcal{S}$. If $\Delta_{|R}$ is not equivalent to any single FD, then there is a fact-wise reduction from either $(\mathcal{S}_{2k}, \Delta_{2k})$ or $(\mathcal{S}_{ch}, \Delta_{ch})$ to $(\mathcal{S}, \Delta)$.*

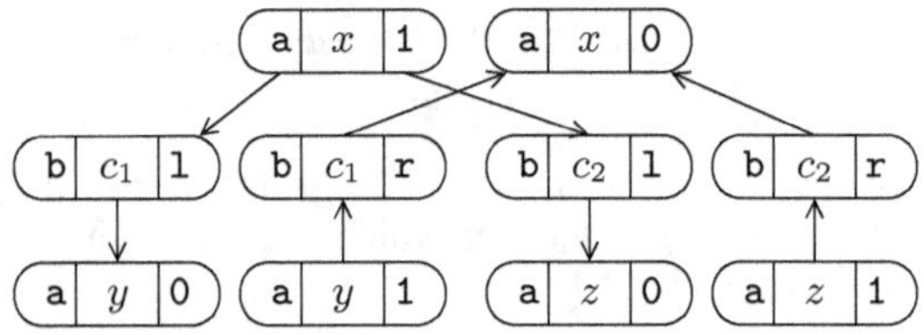

Figure 4: Reduction from #2SAT over monotone bipartite formulas in the proof of Lemma 4.13 for #CREP$\langle \mathcal{S}_{ch}, \Delta_{ch} \rangle$: constructed $(I, \prec)$ for the formula $c_1 \wedge c_2$ where $c_1 = (x \vee y)$ and $c_2 = (x \vee z)$. The priority $f_1 \succ f_2$ is depicted by an edge $f_1 \rightarrow f_2$.

In the case where there is a fact-wise reduction from the schema $(\mathcal{S}_{2k}, \Delta_{2k})$ to $(\mathcal{S}, \Delta)$, we combine Proposition 4.7 and Lemma 4.8 to establish hardness, and we are done. Therefore, it suffices to prove the following.

LEMMA 4.13. *#XREP$\langle \mathcal{S}_{ch}, \Delta_{ch} \rangle$ is #P-complete for each $X \in \{\mathsf{P}, \mathsf{G}, \mathsf{C}\}$.*

To prove Lemma 4.13 for p-repairs and g-repairs, we construct a reduction from #3SAT, which is the problem of counting the truth assignments that satisfy a given 3-CNF formula. The most intricate proof is the one for c-repairs. There, we construct a reduction from #2SAT over *monotone bipartite* formulas (which is similar to counting the vertex covers of a bipartite graph), a problem known to be #P-complete [32].

The reduction is illustrated in Figure 4. There, we construct an inconsistent prioritizing instance $(I, \succ)$ over the schema $(\mathcal{S}_{ch}, \Delta_{ch})$ from the formula $c_1 \wedge c_2$, where $c_1 = (x \vee y)$ and $c_2 = (x \vee z)$, by adding to I two facts for each c_i, namely $(\mathtt{b}, c_i, \mathtt{r})$ and $(\mathtt{b}, c_i, \mathtt{1})$, where the letters $\mathtt{r}$ and $\mathtt{1}$ stand for "right" and "left," respectively. In addition, we add to I two facts, $(\mathtt{a}, w, \mathtt{1})$ and $(\mathtt{a}, w, \mathtt{0})$, for each variable $w \in \{x, y, z\}$. Then, the priority relation is defined as follows. For each variable w that appears on the left-hand side of a clause c_i, it holds that $(\mathtt{a}, w, \mathtt{1}) > (\mathtt{b}, c_i, \mathtt{1})$ and $(\mathtt{b}, c_i, \mathtt{r}) > (\mathtt{a}, w, \mathtt{0})$. Similarly, for each variable w that appears on the right-hand side of a clause c_i, it holds that $(\mathtt{a}, w, \mathtt{1}) > (\mathtt{b}, c_i, \mathtt{r})$ and $(\mathtt{b}, c_i, \mathtt{1}) > (\mathtt{a}, w, \mathtt{0})$. For example, the variable x appears on the left-hand side of the clause c_1, thus $(\mathtt{a}, x, \mathtt{1}) > (\mathtt{b}, c_1, \mathtt{1})$ and $(\mathtt{b}, c_1, \mathtt{r}) > (\mathtt{a}, x, \mathtt{0})$. The assignment of $b \in \{0, 1\}$ to a variable x corresponds to including the fact $(\mathtt{a}, x, b)$ in the repair. Then, the reader can verify that, indeed, the satisfying assignments for the monotone 2-CNF formula φ correspond to c-repairs of the constructed instance $(I, \succ)$.

5. ENUMERATING REPAIRS

In this section we investigate the problem of enumerating repairs. We begin with s-repairs, where the problem is essentially solved by prior art, but the background on the solution is critical for the preferred repairs. We then provide (mainly negative) results for g-repairs and p-repairs, and a polynomial-delay algorithm for c-repairs (assuming constraints that are defined over pairs of facts). Finally, we look at a natural case where all three types of x-repairs coincide, and give an algorithm for enumerating the preferred repairs in incremental polynomial time for conflict hypergraphs of a bounded dimension.

5.1 Enumerating s-Repairs

The problem of enumerating subset repairs is the problem of enumerating the maximal independent sets of a given hypergraph h. This problem has been well studied in the past decades. An algorithm with polynomial delay is known for the case where h is a graph [21]. Note that the complement of maximal independent set of a hypergraph h is also a *minimal hitting set* of the set of hyperedges, also known as a *minimal transversal* of h [13]. The question of whether the maximal independent sets (or, equivalently, minimal transversals) of a given hypergraph can be enumerated with polynomial total time is still open (following decades of research). It is known, however, that for hypergraphs of bounded dimension (where the *dimension* is the maximal cardinality of a hyperedge), the maximal independent sets can be enumerated with incremental polynomial time [6, 13]. In particular, if h is the conflict hypergraph defined by a fixed set of denial constraints, then the subset repairs can be enumerated in incremental polynomial time.

As a reference for the next section, Figure 5 depicts a very simple algorithm, $\mathsf{EnumGraphMIS}(g)$, for enumerating the maximal independent sets of a graph g with polynomial delay. This algorithm has been originally introduced by Cohen et al. [11] in the context of computing *full disjunctions.*

Let us now understand why $\mathsf{EnumGraphMIS}(g)$ is correct and efficient, that is, why the following claims are true: *(a)* the time between every two consecutive prints is polynomial, *(b)* no answer is printed more than once, *(c)* every printed answer is a maximal independent set, *and (d)* every maximal independent set is eventually printed (completeness). The only claim that is not straightforward is the last one, completeness, and the proof is by means of contradiction, as follows. Let U be a maximal independent set, and assume by contradiction that U is not printed. Let U' be a maximal subset of U such that some printed independent set, say L, contains U. Let v be a node in $U \setminus U'$, and consider the iteration of line 8 where v is selected after L is printed (in line 6). In that iteration, the set K contains $U' \cup \{v\}$, and thus J contains $U' \cup \{v\}$. Since J is printed at some point, we get a contradiction to the maximality of U'.

Algorithm $\mathsf{EnumGraphMIS}(g)$

```
1: J := Expand(∅)
2: Q := {J}
3: O := ∅
4: while Q ≠ ∅ do
5:    L := Q.remove()
6:    print L
7:    O.insert(L)
8:    for all v ∈ N(g) \ L do
9:       K := {v} ∪ {u ∈ L | {u, v} ∉ E(g)}
10:      J := Expand(K)
11:      if J ∉ Q ∪ O then
12:         Q.insert(J)
```

Subroutine $\mathsf{Expand}(K)$

```
J := K
for all nodes v of g do
   if J ∪ {v} is independent then
      J := J ∪ {v}
return J
```

Figure 5: Enumerating the maximal independent sets [11].

5.2 Enumerating g-Repairs and p-Repairs

We first consider the task of enumerating (i.e., generating) the g-repairs and p-repairs; we handle c-repairs in the next section. In this section we focus on FD schemas and study the problems $\text{GRepEnum}\langle \mathcal{S}, \Delta \rangle$ and $\text{PRepEnum}\langle \mathcal{S}, \Delta \rangle$. In the case of a single functional dependency per relation, a preferred repair is the (disjoint) union of optimal repairs of *blocks*, where a block is a subset of a relation that consists of facts that agree on the left-hand side of the corresponding FD [23]. Moreover, the optimal repairs of every block can be generated in polynomial time. Therefore, enumerating the p-repairs and g-repairs amounts to enumerating the results of a Cartesian product, which can easily be done with polynomial delay. Therefore, we get the following.

PROPOSITION 5.1. *Let $(\mathcal{S}, \Delta)$ be an FD schema. If $\Delta_{|R}$ is equivalent to a single FD for every relation symbol R of $\mathcal{S}$, then $X\text{RepEnum}\langle \mathcal{S}, \Delta \rangle$ can be solved with polynomial delay for each $X \in \{\mathsf{P}, \mathsf{G}\}$.*

On the other hand, Kimelfeld et al. [23] have shown the following results on categoricity.

THEOREM 5.2. [23] *Let $(\mathcal{S}, \Delta)$ be an FD schema.*

1. *If $\Delta_{|R}$ is* not *equivalent to any single FD, for some relation symbol R, then it is coNP-complete to decide whether there is at most one p-repair.*
2. *If $(\mathcal{S}, \Delta)$ is one of $(\mathcal{S}_{\text{ch}}, \Delta_{\text{ch}})$ and $(\mathcal{S}_{\text{2fd}}, \Delta_{\text{2fd}})$, then it is Π^{p}_2-complete to decide whether there is at most one g-repair.*

Therefore, we conclude the following.

COROLLARY 5.3. *Let $(\mathcal{S}, \Delta)$ be an FD schema.*

1. *If $\Delta_{|R}$ is* not *equivalent to any single FD, for some relation symbol R, then $\text{PRepEnum}\langle \mathcal{S}, \Delta \rangle$ is not solvable in polynomial total time, unless $\text{P} = \text{NP}$.*
2. *If $(\mathcal{S}, \Delta)$ is one of $(\mathcal{S}_{\text{ch}}, \Delta_{\text{ch}})$ and $(\mathcal{S}_{\text{2fd}}, \Delta_{\text{2fd}})$, then $\text{GRepEnum}\langle \mathcal{S}, \Delta \rangle$ cannot be solved in polynomial total time, unless $\text{P} = \text{NP}$.*

The second result of Theorem 5.2, and consequently the second result of Corollary 5.3, can be extended to the larger class of FD sets discussed by Kimelfeld et al. [23, Theorem 7.3]. The argument for a single FD applies to c-repairs as well. However, the c-repairs can be enumerated with polynomial delay for *every* class of FDs, as we show in the next section.

5.3 Enumerating c-Repairs

We now turn to enumerating the c-repairs. In this section we study the problem CRepEnum and inrtoduce a polynomial delay algorithm for enumerating the c-repairs for every conflict graph. One might propose to invoke the algorithm $\mathsf{EnumGraphMIS}(g)$ of Figure 5, but have the subroutine $\mathsf{Expand}(K)$ return a c-repair (that contains K) and

Algorithm $\mathsf{EnumCRepairs}(I, g, \succ)$

1: $J := \mathsf{ExpandMaxPrefix}(\emptyset)$
2: $\mathcal{Q} := \{J\}$
3: $\mathcal{O} := \emptyset$
4: **while** $\mathcal{Q} \neq \emptyset$ **do**
5: $\quad L := \mathcal{Q}.\mathsf{remove}()$
6: $\quad$ **print** L
7: $\quad \mathcal{O}.\mathsf{insert}(L)$
8: $\quad$ **for all** $f \in I \setminus L$ **do**
9: $\quad\quad K := \{f\} \cup \{u \in L \mid \{u, f\} \notin \mathsf{E}(g)\}$
10: $\quad\quad J := \mathsf{ExpandMaxPrefix}(K)$
11: $\quad\quad$ **if** $J \notin \mathcal{Q} \cup \mathcal{O}$ **then**
12: $\quad\quad\quad \mathcal{Q}.\mathsf{insert}(J)$

Subroutine $\mathsf{ExpandMaxPrefix}(K)$

1: $J := \emptyset$
2: $I' := I$
3: **while** $I' \neq \emptyset$ **do**
4: $\quad M := \{f \in I' \mid J \cup \{f\}$ is inconsistent$\}$
5: $\quad$ **if** $\max_{\succ}(I') \cap K \neq \emptyset$ **then**
6: $\quad\quad f :=$ arbitrary fact in $\max_{\succ}(I') \cap K$
7: $\quad$ **else**
8: $\quad\quad$ **if** $\max_{\succ}(I') \cap M \neq \emptyset$ **then**
9: $\quad\quad\quad f :=$ arbitrary fact in $\max_{\succ}(I') \cap M$
10: $\quad\quad$ **else**
11: $\quad\quad\quad f :=$ arbitrary fact in $\max_{\succ}(I')$
12: $\quad I' := I' \setminus \{f\}$
13: $\quad$ **if** $J \cup \{f\}$ is consistent **then**
14: $\quad\quad J := J \cup \{f\}$
15: **return** J

Figure 6: Enumerating c-repairs.

not just an s-repair (maximal independent set). There are, though, some major problems with this proposal. First, a set K of line 9 may be such that cannot be extended to *any* c-repair. For example, the reader can verify that the set of facts $\{e_1, e_3, e_6\}$ from the instance of Figure 7 is a consistent set of facts that is not contained in any c-repair. If we allowed the subroutine $\mathsf{Expand}(K)$ to fail and return nothing, then we would lose completeness (and the above proof of completeness would fail). Finally, it is not even tractable to decide whether a given K can be extended to *any* c-repair, even if K is a singleton, as stated in the following theorem.

THEOREM 5.4. *The following problem is NP-complete for the FD schema* $(\mathcal{S}_{2\mathrm{fd}}, \Delta_{2\mathrm{fd}})$ *of Table 1: Given a prioritizing instance* $(I, \succ)$ *and a fact* $f \in I$*, determine whether* f *belongs to at least one c-repair.*

We prove Theorem 5.4 by giving a polynomial-time reduction from CNF satisfiability. Nevertheless, we can show that, in the case of conflict graphs (i.e., conflict hypergraphs of dimension two), the c-repairs can be enumerated (i.e., CREPENUM can be solved) with polynomial delay. The enumeration algorithm, which we call $\mathsf{EnumCRepairs}$, is depicted in Figure 6. The algorithm takes as input an inconsistent prioritizing instance $(I, g, \succ)$, and prints all c-repairs. In the reminder of this section, we describe the algorithm, and we fix an input $(I, g, \succ)$ for it.

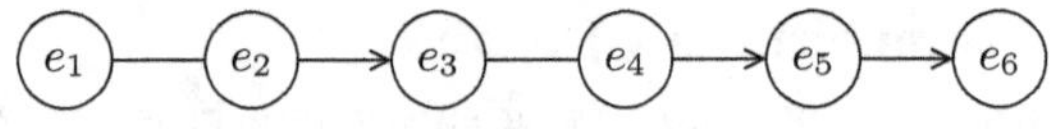

Figure 7: An example of a conflict graph with priorities depicted as edge directions.

5.3.1 The Algorithm

The algorithm $\mathsf{EnumCRepairs}$ is *exactly* the same as the algorithm $\mathsf{EnumGraphMIS}$ of Figure 5 (under some variable renaming), with the only difference being the use of the subroutine $\mathsf{ExpandMaxPrefix}$ instead of Expand (that maximizes a given independent set). Next, we explain what this subroutine does.

Let L be a c-repair. Recall that L is, by definition, a subinstance of I that can be obtained by applying the algorithm $\mathsf{GreedyRepair}$ of Figure 3. An ordering $f_1, \dots, f_n$ of the facts of L in the order they are inserted into L in an execution of $\mathsf{GreedyRepair}$ (i.e., f_1 is inserted first, then f_2, and so on), is called a *greedy ordering of* L. Note that there can be many greedy orderings of a c-repair L. If $f_1, \dots, f_n$ is a greedy ordering of a c-repair L, then for $i = 0, \dots, n$ the set $\{f_1, \dots, f_i\}$ is called a *greedy prefix*. Let K be a consistent subinstance of I (not necessarily a c-repair). A *greedy prefix of* K is a set K' of facts such that $K' \subseteq K$ and K' is a greedy prefix. A *maximal greedy prefix* of K is a greedy prefix of K that is maximal w.r.t. set containment (i.e., not properly contained in any greedy prefix of K). We can prove the following.

LEMMA 5.5. *If* K *is a consistent subinstance of* I*, then* K *has precisely one maximal greedy prefix.*

Hence, we refer to *the* maximal greedy prefix of a consistent subinstance. The subroutine $\mathsf{ExpandMaxPrefix}$ takes as input a consistent subinstance K, and returns a c-repair J such that J contains the maximal greedy prefix of K. Note that J does not necessarily contain K. Next, we explain how this subroutine works.

$\mathsf{ExpandMaxPrefix}$ is a variation of $\mathsf{GreedyRepair}$ of Figure 3, with the following critical difference. Recall that $\mathsf{GreedyRepair}$ selects, in each iteration, a maximal fact f among those not considered yet, and inserts it to the intermediate subinstance J if and only if its insertion does not cause inconsistency of J. In contrast, the subroutine $\mathsf{ExpandMaxPrefix}$ looks for a fact f according to the following sequence of rules.

1. First, it looks for an f that is both maximal and in K (lines 5–6).
2. If no f is found in by the first rule, then it looks for an f that is both maximal and inconsistent with the intermediate J (lines 8–9).
3. Only if no f is found by the above two rules, then f is taken arbitrarily from the maximal remaining elements (line 11).

This concludes the description of the algorithm. Next, we illustrate it on an example.

EXAMPLE 5.6. We illustrate a part of the execution of the algorithm on the conflict graph of Figure 7. Priorities are shown as directed edges. For example, e_2 and

e_3 are in conflict, and $e_2 \succ e_3$. On the call of line 1 to ExpandMaxPrefix($\emptyset$), this subroutine behaves just like the algorithm GreedyRepair. Suppose that the c-repair that it constructs is $\{e_1, e_4, e_6\}$. Now consider the first iteration of lines 5–12 of EnumCRepairs. In that iteration we have $L = \{e_1, e_4, e_6\}$, and we jump to the iteration of lines 8–12 where $f = e_3$. Then $K = \{e_1, e_3, e_6\}$. Observe that the maximal prefix of K is $\{e_1, e_3\}$. Next, we consider the execution of ExpandMaxPrefix(K).

We begin with an empty J. In lines 5–6 we look for a maximal item in K, and we find $f = e_1$. We then insert e_1 into J, remove it from I' and continue. On the next iteration of lines 4–14, no fact in K is maximal in I', since $I' \cap K$ contains only e_3 and e_6, which are both non-maximal. Then, we look for a maximal fact in I' that is also in M. Note that $M = \{e_2\}$ since $J = \{e_1\}$. Since e_2 is both maximal in I' and in M, we select $f = e_2$. Then the condition of line 13 is false, and we continue (after removing e_2 from I'). On the next iteration, $I' \cap K$ is again $\{e_3, e_6\}$, but now e_3 is maximal in I' (since e_2 has been removed). Then, in the end of that iteration we have $J = \{e_1, e_3\}$. On the next iteration we select $f = e_4$ (which is maximal and inconsistent with J). On the next iteration, we have only e_6 in $I' \cap K$, and e_6 is not maximal. Moreover, $M = \emptyset$. Therefore, we reach line 11 and select e_5, which is added to J. Finally, e_6 (which belongs to K) is selected, but not added to J as the condition of line 13 is false. The returned value is then $\{e_1, e_3, e_5\}$.

Interestingly, if we did not apply the case of lines 8–9, then we could have selected e_4 to be inserted into $J = \{e_1\}$, and then we would not be able to insert e_3 into J (and the algorithm would fail to return a c-repair that contains the maximal greedy prefix). □

5.3.2 Correctness of the Algorithm

We now discuss the proof of correctness of EnumCRepairs. The first step in the proof is the correctness of the subroutine ExpandMaxPrefix. Recall from Lemma 5.5 that the maximal greedy prefix of a consistent subinstance is unique. As claimed earlier, we have the following.

LEMMA 5.7. *Let K be a consistent subinstance of I. Then,* ExpandMaxPrefix(K) *returns a c-repair J such that J contains the maximal greedy prefix of K.*

It is easy to show that ExpandMaxPrefix(K) returns a c-repair. To prove that it contains the maximal greedy prefix of K, we show that ExpandMaxPrefix(K) selects the facts of the maximal greedy prefix before selecting any fact that is not in K, but consistent with the intermediate J. As in the case of maximal independent sets, it is quite easy to prove that EnumCRepairs prints only c-repairs (given Lemma 5.7), does not print the same c-repair more than once, and has a polynomial delay. It remains to prove completeness.

LEMMA 5.8. EnumCRepairs *is complete; that is, every c-repair is printed by* EnumCRepairs($I, g, \succ$).

To prove Lemma 5.8 we assume, by way of contradiction, that there is a c-repair J that is not printed. We then look at a printed c-repair J' that has a maximal intersection $\{f_1, \dots, f_i\}$ with a prefix of some greedy ordering $f_1, \dots, f_n$ of J. Finally, we consider the iteration of line 8 where f_{i+1} is selected after J' is printed (in line 6). We show that ExpandMaxPrefix(K) returns a c-repair J'' that contains the facts $\{f_1, \dots, f_{i+1}\}$ and get a contradiction to the maximality of J'. Consequently, we conclude the correctness and efficiency of the algorithm EnumCRepairs.

THEOREM 5.9. *The algorithm* EnumCRepairs *enumerates the c-repairs with polynomial delay.*

5.3.3 Complexity Result

To summarize this section, we establish the following result due to Theorem 5.9.

COROLLARY 5.10. *For conflict graphs (i.e., conflict hypergraphs of dimension two),* CREPENUM *can be solved with polynomial delay.*

In particular, contrasting with Corollary 5.3, the problem CREPENUM$\langle \mathcal{S}, \Delta \rangle$ can be solved with polynomial delay for every set Δ of functional dependencies.

5.4 The Case of Score Priorities

We now discuss a case that is tractable for all types of preferred repairs. Here, we consider the problem XREPENUM (where X is one of $\{G, P, C\}$) for conflict hypergraphs of a bounded dimension. We recall that the dimension of a hypergraph is the maximal cardinality of its hyperedges. We assume that every fact is associated with a (not necessarily unique) *confidence score* that determines its priority. For instance, this score can represent a reliability level for the source of the tuple (e.g., the accuracy of the extraction program or the generating sensor), or the currency (timestamp) of the tuple.

Formally, an inconsistent prioritizing instance $(I, h, \succ)$ is *score structured* if there is a function $s : I \to \mathbb{R}$ such that for all pairs f_1 and f_2 of neighbors of h it is the case that $f_1 \succ f_2$ if and only if $s(f_1) > s(f_2)$. We say that s is a *score realization* of $(I, h, \succ)$. Note that f_1 and f_2 are incomparable by $\succ$ if $s(f_1) = s(f_2)$. For example, if $\succ$ is empty then $(I, h, \succ)$ is score structured. We have the following.

THEOREM 5.11. *Whether a given inconsistent prioritizing instance $(I, h, \succ)$ is score structured can be decided in polynomial time. Moreover, if $(I, h, \succ)$ is score structured, then* $\mathrm{CRep}_{\succ}(h) = \mathrm{GRep}_{\succ}(h) = \mathrm{PRep}_{\succ}(h)$.

In particular, for score structured inputs, the problems PREPENUM, GREPENUM and CREPENUM are the same. In order to prove the first part of Theorem 5.11, we build, given an instance $(I, h, \succ)$, a system of inequalities, such that for each pair of facts f and g that are neighbors in h, one of the following inequalities is added to the system: *(a)* $s_f > s_g$ if $f \succ g$, *(b)* $s_g > s_f$ if $g \succ f$, or *(c)* $s_g = s_f$ if neither $f \succ g$ nor $g \succ f$. Then, we show that if the system contains a cycle, the instance $(I, h, \succ)$ is not score structured. Otherwise, we can sort the variables that appear in the system by topological order and assign values to the variables according to this order, such that the result is a score realization of $(I, h, \succ)$. Theorem 2.8 implies that in order to prove the second part of Theorem 5.11, it suffices to prove that $\mathrm{PRep}_{\succ}(h) \subseteq \mathrm{CRep}_{\succ}(h)$. And indeed, we prove that for every p-repair there exists an execution of GreedyRepair that produces it, thus it also a greedy repair. We can show the following.

THEOREM 5.12. *For each $X \in \{\mathsf{P}, \mathsf{G}, \mathsf{C}\}$ and fixed $b > 0$, the problem XREPENUM is solvable in incremental polynomial time over score structured $(I, h, \succ)$ where the dimension of h is bounded by b.*

Algorithm $\mathsf{EnumXRep}(I, h, \succ)$

```
1: s := a score realization of (I, h, ≻)
2: M := {f ∈ I | s(f) is maximal}
3: h_M := (M, {e ∈ h | e ⊆ M})
4: for all J ∈ EnumMIS(h_M) do
5:   if M = I then
6:     print J
7:   else
8:     I' = I \ M
9:     h' := (I', {e \ J | e ⊆ J ∪ I'})
10:    ≻' := {(f_1, f_2) ∈ neighbors(h') | f_1 ≻ f_2}
11:    for all J' ∈ EnumXRep(I', h', ≻') do
12:      print J ∪ J'
```

Figure 8: Enumerating x-repairs for score structured $(I, h, \succ)$.

Observe that bounded dimension captures the general case of a fixed set of denial constraints. Hence, we can enumerate the preferred repairs (of all three kinds) in incremental polynomial time *if* the inconsistent prioritizing instance is score structured. In the remainder of this section, we describe the enumeration algorithm.

5.4.1 Enumeration Algorithm

The algorithm, depicted in Figure 8, begins by constructing a score realization s of $(I, h, \succ)$. The function s can be constructed by the same algorithm that decides whether $(I, h, \succ)$ is score structured (Theorem 5.11). The algorithm then constructs the set M of all the facts f with a maximal score $s(f)$. It then deploys an algorithm for enumerating the maximal independent sets of a hypergraph of a bounded dimension in incremental polynomial time [6, 13]. We refer to this algorithm as EnumMIS, and we assume that it operates in an iterator fashion in the "for" of line 4, where the time between two elements is the delay.[7] We begin by constructing the set M of all the maximal facts of I, and the hypergraph h_M that consists of all the hyperedges of h that are contained in M (and contains only the nodes of M). We then iterate over the maximal independent sets J of h_M. If M consists of all the facts of I, then we simply print each such J. Otherwise, we construct a new inconsistent prioritizing instance $(I', h', \succ')$, as follows.

- I' consists of all facts with a non-maximal score.
- h' has the node set I' and every hyperedge e that contains only facts from J and I', with all the facts of J removed.
- $\succ'$ consists of all the neighbors in h' that are comparable by $\succ$.

It can be shown that the resulting $(I', h', \succ')$ is also score structured. We execute the algorithm recursively on the input $(I', h', \succ')$, again assuming an iterator fashion, and for every result J' we print the union $J \cup J'$.

The following lemma states the correctness and efficiency of the algorithm.

[7]See the work of Cohen et al. [11] for a more formal construction of iterators from enumeration algorithms.

LEMMA 5.13. *Suppose that $(I, h, \succ)$ is an inconsistent prioritizing instance that is score structured. Then, executing* $\mathsf{EnumXRep}(I, h, \succ)$ *enumerates* $X\mathrm{Rep}_{\succ}(h)$ *for each* $X \in \{\mathsf{P}, \mathsf{G}, \mathsf{C}\}$*. Moreover, if* EnumMIS *enumerates in incremental polynomial time then so does* EnumXRep.

We prove by induction on the number of distinct scores in $(I, h, \succ)$ that EnumXRep prints only c-repairs. For each printed set of facts we show that there exists an execution of GreedyRepair that produces it. The proof that every c-repair of $(I, h, \succ)$ is printed is also by induction on the number of distinct scores in $(I, h, \succ)$. We start by proving that every c-repair contains an s-repair of M_{max} - the set of facts with the maximal score. Then, we show that every c-repair is a union of an s-repair of M_{max} and a c-repair of the rest of the facts.

6. CONCLUSIONS

We investigated the complexity of two classes of problems, counting and enumerating repairs, both for the traditional subset repairs and for preferred repairs. For counting, we focused on FD constraints and established dichotomies in data complexity for each type of repairs, partitioning FD schemas into polynomial-time counting and #P-complete counting. For preferred repairs, the tractable FD schemas are those where each relation is assigned (at most) one FD, and for subset repairs the tractable FD schemas are the chain ones, or equivalently, those guaranteeing P_4-free conflicts graphs. For enumeration, we gave lower bounds for enumerating p-repairs and g-repairs, except for the case of a single FD per relation, where enumeration can be carried out with polynomial delay. In constrast, we presented a polynomial-delay algorithm for enumerating c-repairs under general conflict graphs. Finally, for score-structured instances we presented an enumeration algorithm that works for all three types of preferred repairs, allowing arbitrary conflict hypergraphs, and guaranteeing incremental polynomial time when the dimension of the conflict hypergraph is bounded.

In this work we have continued the line of work [15,23,33] that explores the impact of the choice of one of the notions of x-repairs on the entailed computational complexity. Starowko et al. [33], followed by Fagin et al. [15], showed that as far as repair checking is concerned, the Pareto and the greedy semantics behave much better than the global one. Kimelfeld et al. [23] later showed that from the viewpoint of categoricity (deciding whether there is precisely one preferred repair), the greedy semantics is far more tractable than the other two. In this work we have shown that the three behave similarly when it comes to counting repairs. However, on enumeration the greedy semantics again behaves much better than the other two, and hence, continues to outstand as the most efficient alternative to adopt.

Finally, we highlight two directions for future fundamental research. The first one is *approximate* counting of repairs. The second is that of counting and enumerating repairs in more general repair frameworks that support additional types of integrity constraints and repairing operations (e.g., tuple addition and cell updates [20, 37]).

Acknowledgments

This work was supported in part by the Israeli Science Foundation, Grant 1295/15. Benny Kimelfeld is a Taub Fellow, supported by the Taub Foundation.

7. REFERENCES

[1] F. N. Afrati and P. G. Kolaitis. Repair checking in inconsistent databases: algorithms and complexity. In *ICDT*, pages 31–41. ACM, 2009.

[2] D. E. Appelt and B. Onyshkevych. The common pattern specification language. In *TIPSTER Text Program: Phase III*, pages 23–30. Association for Computational Linguistics, 1998.

[3] M. Arenas, L. E. Bertossi, and J. Chomicki. Consistent query answers in inconsistent databases. In *PODS*, pages 68–79. ACM, 1999.

[4] L. E. Bertossi. *Database Repairing and Consistent Query Answering*. Synthesis Lectures on Data Management. Morgan & Claypool Publishers, 2011.

[5] P. Bohannon, W. Fan, F. Geerts, X. Jia, and A. Kementsietsidis. Conditional functional dependencies for data cleaning. In *ICDE*, pages 746–755. IEEE, 2007.

[6] E. Boros, K. M. Elbassioni, V. Gurvich, and L. Khachiyan. An efficient incremental algorithm for generating all maximal independent sets in hypergraphs of bounded dimension. *Parallel Processing Letters*, 10(4):253–266, 2000.

[7] C. Bourgaux, M. Bienvenu, and F. Goasdoué. Querying inconsistent description logic knowledge bases under preferred repair semantics. In *DL*, pages 96–99, 2014.

[8] Y. Cao, W. Fan, and W. Yu. Determining the relative accuracy of attributes. In *SIGMOD*, pages 565–576. ACM, 2013.

[9] L. Chiticariu, R. Krishnamurthy, Y. Li, S. Raghavan, F. Reiss, and S. Vaithyanathan. SystemT: An algebraic approach to declarative information extraction. In *ACL*, pages 128–137, 2010.

[10] J. Chomicki and J. Marcinkowski. Minimal-change integrity maintenance using tuple deletions. *Inf. Comput.*, 197(1-2):90–121, 2005.

[11] S. Cohen, I. Fadida, Y. Kanza, B. Kimelfeld, and Y. Sagiv. Full disjunctions: Polynomial-delay iterators in action. In *VLDB*, pages 739–750. ACM, 2006.

[12] D. Corneil, H. Lerchs, and L. Burlingham. Complement reducible graphs. *Discrete Applied Mathematics*, 3(3):163 – 174, 1981.

[13] T. Eiter and G. Gottlob. Identifying the minimal transversals of a hypergraph and related problems. *SIAM J. Comput.*, 24(6):1278–1304, 1995.

[14] R. Fagin, B. Kimelfeld, and P. G. Kolaitis. Dichotomies in the complexity of preferred repairs. In *PODS*, pages 3–15. ACM, 2015.

[15] R. Fagin, B. Kimelfeld, F. Reiss, and S. Vansummeren. Cleaning inconsistencies in information extraction via prioritized repairs. In *PODS*, pages 164–175. ACM, 2014.

[16] W. Fan, F. Geerts, and J. Wijsen. Determining the currency of data. *ACM Trans. Database Syst.*, 37(4):25, 2012.

[17] W. Fan, S. Ma, N. Tang, and W. Yu. Interaction between record matching and data repairing. *J. Data and Information Quality*, 4(4):16:1–16:38, 2014.

[18] S. Flesca, F. Furfaro, and F. Parisi. Preferred database repairs under aggregate constraints. In *SUM*, pages 215–229, 2007.

[19] T. Gaasterland, P. Godfrey, and J. Minker. An overview of cooperative answering. *J. Intell. Inf. Syst.*, 1(2):123–157, 1992.

[20] F. Geerts, G. Mecca, P. Papotti, and D. Santoro. The LLUNATIC data-cleaning framework. *PVLDB*, 6(9):625–636, 2013.

[21] D. S. Johnson, C. H. Papadimitriou, and M. Yannakakis. On generating all maximal independent sets. *Inf. Process. Lett.*, 27(3):119–123, 1988.

[22] B. Kimelfeld. A dichotomy in the complexity of deletion propagation with functional dependencies. In *PODS*, pages 191–202, 2012.

[23] B. Kimelfeld, E. Livshits, and L. Peterfreund. Unambiguous prioritized repairing of databases. To appear in ICDT, 2017.

[24] B. Kimelfeld, J. Vondrák, and R. Williams. Maximizing conjunctive views in deletion propagation. *ACM Trans. Database Syst.*, 37(4):24, 2012.

[25] V. Koltun and C. H. Papadimitriou. Approximately dominating representatives. *Theor. Comput. Sci.*, 371(3):148–154, 2007.

[26] P. Koutris and J. Wijsen. The data complexity of consistent query answering for self-join-free conjunctive queries under primary key constraints. In *PODS*, pages 17–29. ACM, 2015.

[27] A. Lopatenko and L. E. Bertossi. Complexity of consistent query answering in databases under cardinality-based and incremental repair semantics. In *ICDT*, pages 179–193, 2007.

[28] D. Maier. Minimum covers in relational database model. *J. ACM*, 27(4):664–674, 1980.

[29] D. Maslowski and J. Wijsen. A dichotomy in the complexity of counting database repairs. *J. Comput. Syst. Sci.*, 79(6):958–983, 2013.

[30] D. Maslowski and J. Wijsen. Counting database repairs that satisfy conjunctive queries with self-joins. In *ICDT*, pages 155–164. OpenProceedings.org, 2014.

[31] D. V. Nieuwenborgh and D. Vermeir. Preferred answer sets for ordered logic programs. In *JELIA*, pages 432–443, 2002.

[32] J. S. Provan and M. O. Ball. The complexity of counting cuts and of computing the probability that a graph is connected. *SIAM J. Comput.*, 12(4):777–788, 1983.

[33] S. Staworko, J. Chomicki, and J. Marcinkowski. Preference-driven querying of inconsistent relational databases. In *EDBT Workshops*, volume 4254 of *LNCS*, pages 318–335. Springer, 2006.

[34] S. Staworko, J. Chomicki, and J. Marcinkowski. Prioritized repairing and consistent query answering in relational databases. *Ann. Math. Artif. Intell.*, 64(2-3):209–246, 2012.

[35] S. Toda and M. Ogiwara. Counting classes are at least as hard as the polynomial-time hierarchy. *SIAM Journal on Computing*, 21(2), 1992.

[36] S. P. Vadhan. The complexity of counting in sparse, regular, and planar graphs. *SIAM J. Comput.*, 31(2):398–427, 2001.

[37] J. Wijsen. Database repairing using updates. *ACM Trans. Database Syst.*, 30(3):722–768, 2005.

Answering Conjunctive Queries under Updates

Christoph Berkholz
Humboldt-Universität zu Berlin
Unter den Linden 6
10099 Berlin, Germany
berkholz@informatik.hu-berlin.de

Jens Keppeler
Humboldt-Universität zu Berlin
Unter den Linden 6
10099 Berlin, Germany
keppelej@informatik.hu-berlin.de

Nicole Schweikardt
Humboldt-Universität zu Berlin
Unter den Linden 6
10099 Berlin, Germany
schweika@informatik.hu-berlin.de

ABSTRACT

We consider the task of enumerating and counting answers to k-ary conjunctive queries against relational databases that may be updated by inserting or deleting tuples.

We exhibit a new notion of *q-hierarchical* conjunctive queries and show that these can be maintained efficiently in the following sense. During a linear time preprocessing phase, we can build a data structure that enables constant delay enumeration of the query results; and when the database is updated, we can update the data structure and restart the enumeration phase within constant time. For the special case of self-join free conjunctive queries we obtain a dichotomy: if a query is not q-hierarchical, then query enumeration with sublinear* delay and sublinear update time (and arbitrary preprocessing time) is impossible.

For answering Boolean conjunctive queries and for the more general problem of counting the number of solutions of k-ary queries we obtain complete dichotomies: if the query's homomorphic core is q-hierarchical, then size of the the query result can be computed in linear time and maintained with constant update time. Otherwise, the size of the query result cannot be maintained with sublinear update time.

All our lower bounds rely on the OMv-conjecture, a conjecture on the hardness of online matrix-vector multiplication that has recently emerged in the field of fine-grained complexity to characterise the hardness of dynamic problems. The lower bound for the counting problem additionally relies on the orthogonal vectors conjecture, which in turn is implied by the strong exponential time hypothesis.

*) By *sublinear* we mean $O(n^{1-\varepsilon})$ for some $\varepsilon > 0$, where n is the size of the active domain of the current database.

CCS Concepts

•Theory of computation → Complexity theory and logic; Data structures and algorithms for data management; Database query processing and optimization (theory); *Problems, reductions and completeness; Data structures design and analysis; Logic and databases;*

PODS'17, May 14 - 19, 2017, Chicago, Illinois, USA

ISBN 978-1-4503-4198-1/17/05...$15.00

DOI: http://dx.doi.org/10.1145/3034786.3034789

Keywords

query evaluation, constant delay enumeration, counting complexity, dichotomy, dynamic algorithms, online matrix-vector multiplication

1. INTRODUCTION

We study the algorithmic problem of answering a conjunctive query φ against a dynamically changing relational database D. Depending on the problem setting, we want to answer a Boolean query, count the number of output tuples of a non-Boolean query, or enumerate the query result with constant delay. We consider finite relational databases over a possibly infinite domain in the fully dynamic setting where new tuples can be inserted or deleted.

At the beginning, a dynamic query evaluation algorithm gets a query φ together with an initial database D_0. It starts with a preprocessing phase where a suitable data structure is built to represent the result of evaluating φ against D_0. Afterwards, when the database is updated by inserting or deleting a tuple, the data structure is updated, too, and the result of evaluating φ on the updated database is reported.

The *update time* is the time needed to compute the representation of the new query result. In order to be efficient, we require that the update time is way smaller than the time needed to recompute the entire query result. In particular, we consider *constant* update time that only depends on the query but not on the database, as feasible. One can even argue that update time that scales polylogarithmically ($\log^{O(1)} \|D\|$) with the size $\|D\|$ of the database is feasible. On the other hand, we regard update time that scales polynomially ($\|D\|^{\Omega(1)}$) with the database as infeasible.

This paper's aim is to classify those conjunctive queries (CQs, for short) that can be efficiently maintained under updates, and to distinguish them from queries that are hard in this sense.

1.1 Our Contribution

We identify a subclass of conjunctive queries that can be efficiently maintained by a dynamic evaluation algorithm. We call these queries *q-hierarchical*, and this notion is strongly related to the *hierarchical* property that was introduced by Dalvi and Suciu in [12] and has already played a central role for efficient query evaluation in various contexts (see Section 3 for a definition and discussion of related concepts). We show that after a linear time preprocessing phase the result of any q-hierarchical conjunctive query can be maintained with constant update time. This means that after every update we can answer a Boolean q-hierarchical query and compute the number of result tuples of a non-Boolean query in constant time. Moreover, we can enumerate the query result with constant delay.

We are also able to prove matching lower bounds. These bounds are conditioned on the *OMv-conjecture*, a conjecture on the hardness of online matrix-vector multiplication that was introduced by Henzinger, Krinninger, Nanongkai, and Saranurak in [22] to characterise the hardness of many dynamic problems. The lower bound for the counting problem additionally relies on the *OV-conjecture*, a conjecture on the hardness of the orthogonal vectors problem which in turn is implied by the well-known strong exponential time hypothesis [?]. We obtain the following dichotomies, which are stated from the perspective of data complexity (i.e., the query is regarded to be fixed) and hold for any fixed $\varepsilon > 0$. By n we always denote the size of the active domain of the current database D. For the enumeration problem we restrict our attention to *self-join free* CQs, where every relation symbol occurs only once in the query.

Theorem 1.1. *Let φ be a self-join free CQ.*
If φ is q-hierarchical, then after a linear time preprocessing phase the query result $\varphi(D)$ can be enumerated with constant delay and constant update time.
Otherwise, unless the OMv-conjecture fails, there is no dynamic algorithm that enumerates φ with arbitrary preprocessing time, and $O(n^{1-\varepsilon})$ delay and update time.

Theorem 1.2. *Let φ be a Boolean CQ.*
If the homomorphic core of φ is q-hierarchical, then the query can be answered with linear preprocessing time and constant update time.
Otherwise, unless the OMv-conjecture fails, there is no algorithm that answers φ with arbitrary preprocessing time and $O(n^{1-\varepsilon})$ update time.

Theorem 1.3. *Let φ be a CQ.*
If φ is q-hierarchical, then the number $|\varphi(D)|$ of tuples in the query result can be computed with linear preprocessing time and constant update time.
Otherwise, assuming the OMv-conjecture and the OV-conjecture, there is no algorithm that computes $|\varphi(D)|$ with arbitrary preprocessing time and $O(n^{1-\varepsilon})$ update time.

For the databases we construct in our lower bound proofs it holds that $n \approx \sqrt{\|D\|}$. Therefore all our lower bounds of the form $n^{1-\varepsilon}$ translate to $\|D\|^{\frac{1}{2}-\varepsilon}$ in terms of the size of the database.

1.2 Related Work

In more practically motivated papers the task of answering a fixed query against a dynamic database has been studied under the name *incremental view maintenance* (see e. g. [21]). Given the huge amount of theoretical results on the complexity of query evaluation in the static setting, surprisingly little is known about the computational complexity of query evaluation under updates.

The *dynamic descriptive complexity* framework introduced by Patnaik and Immerman [32] focuses on the expressive power of (fragments or extensions of) first-order logic on dynamic databases and has led to a rich body of literature (see [33] for a survey). This approach, however, is quite different from the algorithmic setting considered in the present paper, as in every update step the internal data structure is updated by evaluating a first-order query. As this may take polynomial time even for the special case of conjunctive queries (as considered e.g. by Zeume and Schwentick in [39]), this is too expensive in the area of dynamic algorithms.

We are aware of only a few papers dealing with the computational complexity of query evaluation under updates, namely the study of XPath evaluation of Björklund, Gelade, and Martens [7] and the studies of MSO queries on trees by Balmin, Papakonstantinou, and Vianu [5] and by Losemann and Martens [26], the latter of which is to the best of our knowledge the only work that deals with efficient query enumeration under updates.[1]

In the static setting, a lot of research has been devoted to classify those conjunctive queries that can be answered efficiently. Below we give an overview of known results.

Complexity of Boolean Queries. The complexity of answering Boolean conjunctive queries on a static database is fairly well understood. For every fixed database schema σ, extending a result of [20], Grohe [19] gave a tight characterisation of the *tractable* CQs under the complexity theoretic assumption FPT $\neq$ W[1]: If we are given a Boolean CQ φ of size $\|\varphi\|$ and a σ-database D of size m, then φ can be answered against D in time $f(\|\varphi\|)\cdot m^{O(1)}$ for some computable function f if, and only if, the homomorphic core of φ has bounded treewidth. Marx [27] extended this classification to the case where the schema is part of the input.

Counting Complexity. For computing the number of output tuples of a given join query (i.e., a quantifier-free CQ) over a fixed schema σ, a characterisation was proven by Dalmau and Jonsson [11]: Assuming FPT $\neq$ #W[1], the output size $|\varphi(D)|$ of a join query φ evaluated on a σ-database D of size m can be computed in time $f(\|\varphi\|) \cdot m^{O(1)}$ if, and only if, φ has bounded treewidth. The result has recently been extended to all conjunctive queries over a fixed schema by Chen and Mengel [10]. Structural properties that make the counting problem for CQs tractable in the case where the schema is part of the input have been identified in [15, 18].

Join Evaluation. When the entire result of a non-Boolean query has to be computed, the evaluation problem cannot be modelled as a decision or counting problem and one has to come up with different measures to characterise the hardness of query evaluation. One approach that has been fruitfully applied to join evaluation is to study the worst-case output size as a measure of the hardness of a query. Atserias, Grohe, and Marx [3] identified the fractional edge cover number of the join query as a crucial measure for lower bounding its worst-case output size. This bound was also shown to be optimal and is matched by so called "worst-case optimal" join evaluation algorithms, see [30, 37, 29, 23].

Query Enumeration. Another way of studying non-Boolean queries that is independent of the actual or worst-case output size is *query enumeration*. A query enumeration algorithm evaluates a non-Boolean query by reporting, one by one without repetition, the tuples in the query result. The crucial measure to characterise queries that are tractable w.r.t. enumeration is the delay between two output tuples. In the context of constraint satisfaction, the

[1]Let us mention that in a follow-up of the present paper, we characterise the dynamic complexity of counting and enumerating the results of first-order queries (and their extensions by modulo-counting quantifiers) on bounded degree databases [6].

combined complexity, where the query as well as the database are given as input, has been considered. As the size of the query result might be exponential in the input size in this setting, queries that can be enumerated with *polynomial delay* and polynomial preprocessing are regarded as "tractable." Classes of conjunctive queries that can be enumerated with polynomial delay have been identified in [9, 17]. However, a complete characterisation of conjunctive queries that are tractable in this sense is not in sight.

More relevant to the database setting, where one evaluates a small query against a large database, is the notion of *constant delay enumeration* introduced by Durand and Grandjean in [14]. The preprocessing time is supposed to be much smaller than the time needed to evaluate the query (usually, linear in the size of the database), and the delay between two output tuples may depend on the query, but not on the database. A lot of research has been devoted to this subject, where one usually tries to understand which structural restrictions on the query or on the database allow constant delay enumeration. For an introduction to this topic and an overview of the state-of-the-art we refer the reader to the surveys [36, 35, 34].

Bagan, Durand, and Grandjean [4] showed that acyclic conjunctive queries that are *free-connex* can be enumerated with constant delay after a linear time preprocessing phase (cf. [8] for a simplified proof of their result). They also showed that for self-join free acyclic conjunctive queries the free-connex property is essential by proving the following lower bound. Assume that multiplying two $n \times n$ matrices cannot be done in time $O(n^2)$. Then the result of a self-join free acyclic conjunctive query that is not free-connex cannot be enumerated with constant delay after a linear time preprocessing phase.

It turns out that our notion of q-hierarchical conjunctive queries is a proper subclass of the free-connex conjunctive queries. Thus, there are queries that can be efficiently enumerated in the static setting but are hard to maintain under database updates.

Organisation. The remainder of the paper is structured as follows. In Section 2 we fix the basic notation along with the concept of dynamic algorithms for query evaluation. Section 3 introduces *q-hierarchical* queries and formally states our main theorems. We then present an alternative characterisation of q-hierarchical queries in Section 4 and prove our lower and upper bound theorems in Sections 5 and 6, respectively. We conclude in Section 7. Due to space restrictions, some proof details had to be omitted; they will appear in the paper's full version (preprint available at https://arxiv.org/abs/1702.06370).

2. PRELIMINARIES

We write $\mathbb{N}$ for the set of non-negative integers and let $\mathbb{N}_{\geqslant 1} := \mathbb{N} \setminus \{0\}$ and $[n] := \{1, \ldots, n\}$ for all $n \in \mathbb{N}_{\geqslant 1}$. By 2^M we denote the power set of a set M.

Databases. We fix a countably infinite set **dom**, the *domain* of potential database entries. Elements in **dom** are called *constants*. A *schema* is a finite set σ of relation symbols, where each $R \in \sigma$ is equipped with a fixed *arity* $\operatorname{ar}(R) \in \mathbb{N}_{\geqslant 1}$. Let us fix a schema $\sigma = \{R_1, \ldots, R_s\}$, and let $r_i := \operatorname{ar}(R_i)$ for $i \in [s]$. A *database* D of schema σ (σ-db, for short), is of the form $D = (R_1^D, \ldots, R_s^D)$, where R_i^D is a finite subset of $\mathbf{dom}^{r_i}$. The *active domain* $\operatorname{adom}(D)$ of D is the smallest subset A of **dom** such that $R_i^D \subseteq A^{r_i}$ for all $i \in [s]$.

Updates. We allow to update a given database of schema σ by inserting or deleting tuples as follows. An *insertion* command is of the form insert $R(a_1, \ldots, a_r)$ for $R \in \sigma$, $r = \operatorname{ar}(R)$, and $a_1, \ldots, a_r \in \mathbf{dom}$. When applied to a σ-db D, it results in the updated σ-db D' with $R^{D'} := R^D \cup \{(a_1, \ldots, a_r)\}$ and $S^{D'} := S^D$ for all $S \in \sigma \setminus \{R\}$. A *deletion* command is of the form delete $R(a_1, \ldots, a_r)$ for $R \in \sigma$, $r = \operatorname{ar}(R)$, and $a_1, \ldots, a_r \in \mathbf{dom}$. When applied to a σ-db D, it results in the updated σ-db D' with $R^{D'} := R^D \setminus \{(a_1, \ldots, a_r)\}$ and $S^{D'} := S^D$ for all $S \in \sigma \setminus \{R\}$. Note that both types of commands may change the database's active domain.

Queries. We fix a countably infinite set **var** of *variables*. An *atomic query* (for short: *atom*) ψ of schema σ is of the form $Ru_1 \cdots u_r$ with $R \in \sigma$, $r = \operatorname{ar}(R)$, and $u_1, \ldots, u_r \in \mathbf{var}$. The set of variables occurring in ψ is denoted by $\operatorname{vars}(\psi) := \{u_1, \ldots, u_r\}$. A *conjunctive query* (CQ, for short) of schema σ is of the form

$$\exists y_1 \cdots \exists y_\ell \, (\psi_1 \wedge \cdots \wedge \psi_d) \tag{1}$$

where $\ell \in \mathbb{N}$, $d \in \mathbb{N}_{\geqslant 1}$, ψ_j is an atomic query of schema σ for every $j \in [d]$, and $y_1, \ldots, y_\ell$ are pairwise distinct elements in **var**. *Join queries* are quantifier-free CQs, i.e., CQs of the form $(\psi_1 \wedge \cdots \wedge \psi_d)$. A CQ is called *self-join free* (or *non-repeating* or *simple*) if no relation symbol occurs more than once in the query.

For a CQ φ of the form (1) we let $\operatorname{vars}(\varphi)$ be the set of all variables occurring in φ, and we let $\operatorname{free}(\varphi) := \operatorname{vars}(\varphi) \setminus \{y_1, \ldots, y_\ell\}$ be the set of *free* variables.

For $k \in \mathbb{N}$, a *k-ary conjunctive query* (k-ary CQ, for short) is of the form $\varphi(x_1, \ldots, x_k)$, where φ is a CQ of schema σ, $k = |\operatorname{free}(\varphi)|$, and $x_1, \ldots, x_k$ is a list of the free variables of φ. We will often assume that the tuple $(x_1, \ldots, x_k)$ is clear from the context and simply write φ instead of $\varphi(x_1, \ldots, x_k)$. The semantics of CQs are defined as usual: A *valuation* is a mapping $\beta : \mathbf{var} \to \mathbf{dom}$. For a σ-db D and an atomic query $\psi = Ru_1 \cdots u_r$ we write $(D, \beta) \models \psi$ to indicate that $(\beta(u_1), \ldots, \beta(u_r)) \in R^D$. For a k-ary CQ $\varphi(x_1, \ldots, x_k)$ where φ is of the form (1), and for a tuple $\overline{a} = (a_1, \ldots, a_k) \in \mathbf{dom}^k$, a valuation β is said to be *compatible* with $\overline{a}$ iff $\beta(x_i) = a_i$ for all $i \in [k]$. We write $D \models \varphi[\overline{a}]$ to indicate that there is a valuation β that is compatible with $\overline{a}$ such that $(D, \beta) \models \psi_j$ for all $j \in [d]$. The *query result* $\varphi(D)$ is defined as the set of all tuples $\overline{a} \in \mathbf{dom}^k$ with $D \models \varphi[\overline{a}]$. Clearly, $\varphi(D) \subseteq \operatorname{adom}(D)^k$.

A *Boolean* CQ is a CQ φ with $\operatorname{free}(\varphi) = \emptyset$. As usual, for Boolean CQs φ we will write $\varphi(D) = \texttt{yes}$ instead of $\varphi(D) \neq \emptyset$, and $\varphi(D) = \texttt{no}$ instead of $\varphi(D) = \emptyset$.

Sizes and Cardinalities. The *size* $\|\varphi\|$ of a CQ φ is defined as the length of φ when viewed as a word over the alphabet $\sigma \cup \mathbf{var} \cup \{\exists, \wedge, (,)\}$. For a k-ary CQ $\varphi(x_1, \ldots, x_k)$ and a σ-DB D, the *cardinality of the query result* is the number $|\varphi(D)|$ of tuples in $\varphi(D)$.

The *cardinality* $|D|$ of a σ-db D is defined as the number of tuples stored in D, i.e., $|D| := \sum_{R \in \sigma} |R^D|$. The *size* $\|D\|$ of D is defined as $|\sigma| + |\operatorname{adom}(D)| + \sum_{R \in \sigma} \operatorname{ar}(R) \cdot |R^D|$ and corresponds to the size of a reasonable encoding of D. We will often write n to denote the cardinality $|\operatorname{adom}(D)|$ of D's active domain.

Dynamic Algorithms for Query Evaluation. We use Random Access Machines (RAMs) with $O(\log n)$ word-size and a uniform cost measure as a model of computation. In particular, adding and multiplying integers that are polynomial in the input size can be done in constant time.

For our purposes it will be convenient to assume that **dom** $= \mathbb{N}_{\geqslant 1}$. We will assume that the RAM's memory is initialised to 0. In particular, if an algorithm uses an array, we will assume that all array entries are initialised to 0, and this initialisation comes at no cost (in real-world computers this can be achieved by using the *lazy array initialisation technique*, cf. e.g. the textbook [28]). A further assumption that is unproblematic within the RAM-model, but unrealistic for real-world computers, is that for every fixed dimension $d \in \mathbb{N}_{\geqslant 1}$ we have available an unbounded number of d-ary arrays $\mathtt{A}$ such that for given $(n_1, \ldots, n_d) \in \mathbb{N}^d$ the entry $\mathtt{A}[n_1, \ldots, n_d]$ at position $(n_1, \ldots, n_d)$ can be accessed in constant time.[2]

Our algorithms will take as input a k-ary CQ $\varphi(x_1, \ldots, x_k)$ and a σ-db D_0. For all query evaluation problems considered in this paper, we aim at routines **preprocess** and **update** which achieve the following:

- upon input of $\varphi(x_1, \ldots, x_k)$ and D_0, **preprocess** builds a data structure $\mathtt{D}$ which represents D_0 (and which is designed in such a way that it supports efficient evaluation of φ on D_0)
- upon input of a command $\mathtt{update}\ R(a_1, \ldots, a_r)$ (with $\mathtt{update} \in \{\mathtt{insert}, \mathtt{delete}\}$), calling **update** modifies the data structure $\mathtt{D}$ such that it represents the updated database D.

The *preprocessing time* t_p is the time used for performing **preprocess**; the *update time* t_u is the time used for performing an **update**.

In the following, D will always denote the database that is currently represented by the data structure $\mathtt{D}$. To solve the *enumeration problem under updates*, apart from the routines **preprocess** and **update** we aim at a routine **enumerate** such that calling **enumerate** invokes an enumeration of all tuples (without repetition) that belong to $\varphi(D)$. The *delay* t_d is the maximum time used during a call of **enumerate**

- until the output of the first tuple (or the end-of-enumeration message $\mathtt{EOE}$, if $\varphi(D) = \emptyset$),
- between the output of two consecutive tuples, and
- between the output of the last tuple and the end-of-enumeration message $\mathtt{EOE}$.

To solve the *counting problem under updates*, instead of **enumerate** we aim at a routine **count** which outputs the cardinality $|\varphi(D)|$ of the query result. The *counting time* t_c is the time used for performing a **count**. To *answer* a *Boolean* conjunctive query under updates, instead of **enumerate** or **count** we aim at a routine **answer** that produces the answer $\mathtt{yes}$ or $\mathtt{no}$ of φ on D. The *answer time* t_a is the time used for performing **answer**.

Whenever speaking of a *dynamic algorithm*, we mean an algorithm that has routines **preprocess** and **update** and, depending on the problem at hand, at least one of the routines **enumerate**, **count**, and **answer**.

Throughout the paper, we often adopt the view of *data complexity* and use the O-notation to suppress factors that may depend on the query but not on the database. For example, "linear preprocessing time" means $t_p = f(\varphi) \cdot \|D_0\|$ and "constant update time" means $t_u = f(\varphi)$, for a function f with codomain $\mathbb{N}$. By *poly*(φ) we mean $\|\varphi\|^{O(1)}$.

[2]While this can be accomplished easily in the RAM-model, for an implementation on real-world computers one would probably have to resort to replacing our use of arrays by using suitably designed hash functions.

3. MAIN RESULTS

Our notion of *q-hierarchical* conjunctive queries is related to the *hierarchical* property that has already played a central role for efficient query evaluation in various contexts. It has been introduced by Dalvi and Suciu in [12] to characterise the Boolean CQs that can be answered in polynomial time on probabilistic databases. They obtained a dichotomy stating for self-join free queries that the complexity of query evaluation on probabilistic databases is in PTIME for hierarchical queries and #P-complete for non-hierarchical queries. Fink and Olteanu [16] generalised the notion and the dichotomy result to non-Boolean queries and to queries using negation. In the different context of query evaluation on massively parallel architectures, Koutris and Suciu [24] considered hierarchical join queries and singled out a subclass of so-called tall-flat queries as exactly those queries that can be computed with only one broadcast step in their *Massively Parallel* model of query evaluation. For further information on the various uses of the hierarchical property we refer the reader to [16].

The definition of hierarchical queries relies on the following notion. Consider a CQ φ of the form (1). For every variable $x \in \text{vars}(\varphi)$ we let atoms(x) be the set of all atoms ψ_j of φ such that $x \in \text{vars}(\psi_j)$. Dalvi and Suciu [12] call a Boolean CQ φ *hierarchical* iff the condition

$(*)$: $\text{atoms}(x) \subseteq \text{atoms}(y)$ or $\text{atoms}(x) \supseteq \text{atoms}(y)$ or $\text{atoms}(x) \cap \text{atoms}(y) = \emptyset$

is satisfied by all variables $x, y \in \text{vars}(\varphi)$. An example for a hierarchical Boolean CQ is $\exists x \exists y \exists z \exists y' \exists z' \big(Rxyz \wedge Rxyz' \wedge Exy \wedge Exy'\big)$.

In [24], Koutris and Suciu transferred the notion to join queries φ, which they call hierarchical iff condition $(*)$ is satisfied by all variables $x, y \in \text{vars}(\varphi)$. In [16], Fink and Olteanu introduced a slightly different notion for a more general class of queries. Translated into the setting of CQs, their notion (only) requires that condition $(*)$ is satisfied by all *quantified* variables, i.e., variables $x, y \in \text{vars}(\varphi) \setminus \text{free}(\varphi)$. Obviously, both notions coincide on *Boolean* CQs, but on *join queries* Koutris and Suciu's notion is more restrictive than Fink and Olteanu's notion (according to which *all* quantifier-free CQs are hierarchical). For example, the join query

$$\varphi_{S\text{-}E\text{-}T} \quad := \quad \big(\, Sx \wedge Exy \wedge Ty \,\big) \qquad (2)$$

is hierarchical w.r.t. Fink and Olteanu's notion, and non-hierarchical w.r.t. Koutris and Suciu's notion.

In the context of answering queries under updates, our lower bound results show that the join query $\varphi_{S\text{-}E\text{-}T}$, as well as its Boolean version

$$\varphi'_{S\text{-}E\text{-}T} \quad := \quad \exists x\, \exists y\, \big(\, Sx \wedge Exy \wedge Ty \,\big) \qquad (3)$$

are intractable. A further query that is hierarchical, but intractable in our setting is

$$\varphi_{E\text{-}T} \quad := \quad \exists y\, \big(\,Exy \wedge Ty\,\big). \qquad (4)$$

To ensure tractability of a CQ in our setting, we will require that its quantifer-free part is hierarchical in Koutris and Suciu's notion and, additionally, the quantifiers respect the query's hierarchical form. We call such queries *q-hierarchical.*

Definition 3.1. A CQ φ is *q-hierarchical* if for any two variables $x, y \in \text{vars}(\varphi)$ the following is satisfied:

(i) $\text{atoms}(x) \subseteq \text{atoms}(y)$ or $\text{atoms}(x) \supseteq \text{atoms}(y)$ or $\text{atoms}(x) \cap \text{atoms}(y) = \emptyset$, and

(ii) if $\text{atoms}(x) \subsetneq \text{atoms}(y)$ and $x \in \text{free}(\varphi)$, then $y \in \text{free}(\varphi)$.

Note that a *Boolean* CQ is q-hierarchical iff it is hierarchical, and a join query is q-hierarchical iff it is hierarchical w.r.t. Koutris and Suciu's notion. The queries $\varphi_{S\text{-}E\text{-}T}$ and $\varphi_{E\text{-}T}$ are minimal examples for queries that are not q-hierarchical because they do not satisfy condition (i) and (ii), respectively. Regarding the query $\varphi_{E\text{-}T}$, note that all other versions such as the query $\exists x\,\big(Exy \wedge Ty\big)$, the join query $\big(Exy \wedge Ty\big)$, and the Boolean query $\exists x \exists y\,\big(Exy \wedge Ty\big)$, are q-hierarchical.

It is not hard to see that we can decide in polynomial time whether a given CQ is q-hierarchical (see Lemma 4.2). Our first main result shows that all q-hierarchical CQs can be efficiently maintained under database updates:

Theorem 3.2. *There is a dynamic algorithm that receives a q-hierarchical CQ φ and a σ-db D_0, and computes within $t_p = poly(\varphi) {\cdot} O(\|D_0\|)$ preprocessing time a data structure that can be updated in time $t_u = poly(\varphi)$ and allows to*

(a) enumerate $\varphi(D)$ with delay $t_d = poly(\varphi)$, and

(b) compute the cardinality $|\varphi(D)|$ in time $t_c = O(1)$,

where D is the current database.

Note that this implies that q-hierarchical *Boolean* conjunctive queries can be answered in constant time. Our algorithm crucially relies on the tree-like structure of hierarchical queries, which has already been used for efficient query evaluation in [13, 12, 24, 16, 31]. In Section 4 we present the notion of a *q-tree* and show that it precisely characterises the *q-hierarchical* conjunctive queries. These q-trees serve as a basis for the data structure used in our dynamic algorithm for query answering. Details on this algorithm along with a proof of Theorem 3.2 can be found in Section 6. Let us mention that every q-tree is an *f-tree* in the sense of [31], but there exist f-trees that are no q-trees. The dynamic data structure that is computed by our algorithm can be viewed as an *f-representation* of the query result [31], but not every f-representation can be efficiently maintained under database updates.

We now discuss our further main results, which show that the *q-hierarchical* property is necessary for designing efficient dynamic algorithms, and that the results from Theorem 3.2 cannot be extended to queries that are not q-hierarchical. As discussed in the introduction, our lower bounds rely on the OMv-conjecture and the OV-conjecture. For more details on these conjectures, as well as proofs of our lower bound theorems, we refer the reader to Section 5. In the following, D_0 denotes the initial database that serves as input for the **preprocess** routine, and $n = |\text{adom}(D)|$ denotes the size of the active domain of a dynamically changing database D. Our first lower bound theorem states that non-q-hierarchical *self-join free* conjunctive queries cannot be enumerated efficiently under updates.

Theorem 3.3. *Fix a number $\varepsilon > 0$ and a self-join free conjunctive query φ. If φ is not q-hierarchical, then there is no algorithm with arbitrary preprocessing time and $O(n^{1-\varepsilon})$ update time that enumerates $\varphi(D)$ with $O(n^{1-\varepsilon})$ delay, unless the OMv-conjecture fails.*

For *Boolean* CQs we obtain a lower bound for *all* queries, i.e., also for queries that are not self-join free. To state the result, we need the standard notion of a homomorphic core. A *homomorphism* from a CQ $\varphi(x_1, \ldots, x_k)$ to a CQ $\varphi'(y_1, \ldots, y_k)$ is a mapping h from $\text{vars}(\varphi)$ to $\text{vars}(\varphi')$ such that $h(x_i) = y_i$ for all $i \in [k]$, and if $Ru_1 \cdots u_r$ is an atom of φ, then $R\,h(u_1) \cdots h(u_r)$ is an atom of φ'. The *homomorphic core* (for short, *core*) of a conjunctive query φ is a minimal subquery φ' of φ such that there is a homomorphism from φ to φ', but no homomorphism from φ' to a proper subquery of φ'. By Chandra and Merlin's homomorphism theorem, every CQ φ has a unique (up to isomorphism) core φ', and $\varphi'(D) = \varphi(D)$ for all databases D (cf., e.g., [2]). While self-join free queries are their own cores, the situation is different for general CQs. Consider, for example, the queries

$$\varphi \;:=\; \exists x\, \exists y\, \big(\,Exx \wedge Exy \wedge Eyy\,\big) \quad \text{and}$$
$$\varphi' \;:=\; \exists x\, \big(\,Exx\,\big).$$

Here, φ' is a core of φ and thus $\varphi(D) = \varphi'(D)$ for every database D. However, φ' is q-hierarchical, whereas φ is not. The next lower bound theorem states that the result of a Boolean conjunctive query cannot be maintained efficiently if the query's core is not q-hierarchical.

Theorem 3.4. *Fix a number $\varepsilon > 0$ and a Boolean conjunctive query φ. If the homomorphic core of φ is not q-hierarchical, then there is no algorithm with arbitrary preprocessing time and $t_u = O(n^{1-\varepsilon})$ update time that answers $\varphi(D)$ in time $t_a = O(n^{2-\varepsilon})$, unless the OMv-conjecture fails.*

Let us now turn to the problem of computing the cardinality $|\varphi(D)|$ of the result of a query $\varphi(x_1, \ldots, x_k)$. From the Theorems 3.2 and 3.4 we know that we can efficiently decide whether $|\varphi(D)| > 0$ if, and only if, the homomorphic core of $\exists x_1 \cdots \exists x_k\, \varphi$ is q-hierarchical. The complexity of actually counting the number of tuples in $\varphi(D)$, however, depends on whether the core of the query $\varphi(x_1, \ldots, x_k)$ itself (rather than the core of its Boolean version $\exists x_1 \cdots \exists x_k\, \varphi$) is q-hierarchical. As in the Boolean case, the next theorem (together with Theorem 3.2) implies a dichotomy for all conjunctive queries. One difference is that we have to additionally rely on the OV-conjecture.

Theorem 3.5. *Fix a number $\varepsilon > 0$ and a conjunctive query φ. If the homomorphic core of φ is not q-hierarchical, then there is no algorithm with arbitrary preprocessing time and $t_u = O(n^{1-\varepsilon})$ update time that computes $|\varphi(D)|$ in time $t_c = O(n^{1-\varepsilon})$, assuming the OMv-conjecture and the OV-conjecture.*

Combining Theorem 3.2 with the Theorems 3.3, 3.4, and 3.5 immediately leads to the dichotomies (Theorems 1.1, 1.2, and 1.3) stated in the introduction.

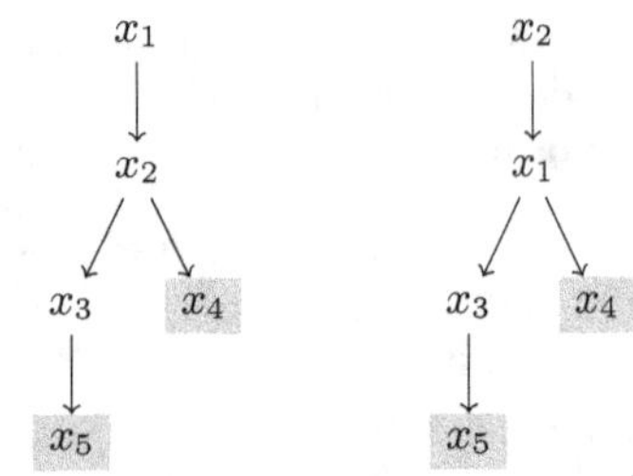

Figure 1: Two q-trees for $\varphi(x_1, x_2, x_3) = \exists x_4 \exists x_5 \left(Ex_1x_2 \wedge Rx_4x_1x_2x_1 \wedge Rx_5x_3x_2x_1\right)$

4. THE TREE-LIKE STRUCTURE OF Q-HIERARCHICAL QUERIES

We now give an alternative characterisation of q-hierarchical queries that sheds more light on their "tree-like" structure and will be useful for designing efficient query evaluation algorithms. We say that a CQ φ is *connected* if for any two variables $x, y \in \text{vars}(\varphi)$ there is a path $x = z_0, \ldots, z_\ell = y$ such that for each $j < \ell$ there is an atom ψ of φ such that $\{z_j, z_{j+1}\} \subseteq \text{vars}(\psi)$. Note that every CQ can be written as a conjunction $\bigwedge_i \varphi_i$ of connected CQs φ_i over pairwise disjoint variable sets. We call these φ_i the *connected components* of the query. Note that a query is q-hierarchical if, and only if, all its connected components are q-hierarchical. Next, we define the notion of a *q-tree* for a connected query φ and show that φ is q-hierarchical iff it has a q-tree.

Definition 4.1. Let φ be a connected CQ. A *q-tree* for φ is a rooted directed tree $T_\varphi = (V, E)$ with $V = \text{vars}(\varphi)$ where

(1) for all atoms ψ in φ the set $\text{vars}(\psi)$ forms a directed path in T_φ that starts from the root, and

(2) if $\text{free}(\varphi) \neq \emptyset$, then $\text{free}(\varphi)$ is a connected subset in T_φ that contains the root.

See Figure 1 for examples of q-trees. The following lemma characterises the *q-hierarchical* CQs via q-trees.

Lemma 4.2. *A CQ φ is q-hierarchical if, and only if, every connected component of φ has a q-tree. Moreover, there is a polynomial time algorithm which decides whether an input CQ φ is q-hierarchical, and if so, outputs a q-tree for each connected component of φ.*

To prove the lemma we inductively apply the following.

Claim 4.3. For every connected q-hierarchical CQ φ there is a variable $x \in \text{vars}(\varphi)$ that is contained in every atom of φ. Moreover, if $\text{free}(\varphi) \neq \emptyset$, then $x \in \text{free}(\varphi)$.

Proof. For simplicity, we associate with every conjunctive query φ the hypergraph $\mathcal{H}_\varphi$ with vertex set $\text{vars}(\varphi)$ and hyperedges $e_\psi := \text{vars}(\psi)$ for every atom ψ in φ. For a variable x we let $\text{E}(x) := \{e_\psi : x \in \text{vars}(\psi)\}$ be the set of hyperedges that contain x. Let us recall some basic notation concerning hypergraphs. A *path* of length ℓ in $\mathcal{H}_\varphi$ is a sequence of variables $x_0, \ldots, x_\ell$ such that for every $i < \ell$ there is a hyperedge containing x_i and x_{i+1}. Two variables have *distance* ℓ if they are connected by a path of length ℓ, but not by a path of length $\ell - 1$. We first show that $(*)$ every pair of hyperedges in $\mathcal{H}_\varphi$ has a non-empty intersection. Suppose for contradiction that there are two hyperedges e_1 and e_2 with $e_1 \cap e_2 = \emptyset$, let $x_0 \in e_1$ and $x_\ell \in e_2$ be two variables of distance $\ell \geqslant 2$, and $x_0, \ldots, x_\ell$ be a shortest path connecting both variables. Hence, for every $i < \ell$ there is a hyperedge containing x_i and x_{i+1} but no other variable from the path. Therefore it holds that $\text{E}(x_0) \cap \text{E}(x_1) \neq \emptyset$. Furthermore, we have $e_1 \notin \text{E}(x_1)$ and hence $\text{E}(x_0) \not\subseteq \text{E}(x_1)$. On the other hand, the hyperedge containing x_1 and x_2 does not contain x_0 and therefore $\text{E}(x_1) \not\subseteq \text{E}(x_0)$, which contradicts the assumption that φ is q-hierarchical.

We now prove that there is a variable that is contained in every hyperedge (and hence in every atom of φ). We consider two cases. First suppose that for every pair of hyperedges e_i, e_j it holds that either $e_i \subseteq e_j$ or $e_j \subseteq e_i$. Then there is a minimal hyperedge e that is contained in every other hyperedge, and thus all of the variables in this hyperedge are contained in all other hyperedges as well.

Now suppose that there are two hyperedges e_i, e_j such that $e_i \not\subseteq e_j$ and $e_j \not\subseteq e_i$. By $(*)$, both hyperedges have a non-empty intersection. Thus, we can choose some $x \in e_i \cap e_j$. We want to argue that x is contained in every hyperedge of $\mathcal{H}_\varphi$ and assume for contradiction that there is a hyperedge e_k that does *not* contain x. By $(*)$ we can choose some $y \neq x$ that is contained in the non-empty intersection of e_j and e_k. But now we have $e_j \in \text{E}(x) \cap \text{E}(y)$, $e_i \in \text{E}(x) \setminus \text{E}(y)$, and $e_k \in \text{E}(y) \setminus \text{E}(x)$, contradicting that φ is q-hierarchical.

Let S be the set of all variables that are contained in every hyperedge. We have already shown that $S \neq \emptyset$. To ensure that there is a free variable in S, note that (by the definition of *q-hierarchical* CQs) if $x \in \text{free}(\varphi)$ and $x \notin S$, then $S \subset \text{free}(\varphi)$. Hence, $\text{free}(\varphi) \neq \emptyset$ implies that we can choose a variable from $\text{free}(\varphi) \cap S$ that satisfies the conditions of the claim. ☐

Proof of Lemma 4.2. The proof of the "if" direction is easy, as every connected component that has a q-tree T must be q-hierarchical, because if y is a descendant of x in T, then $\text{atoms}(y) \subseteq \text{atoms}(x)$.

For proving the "only if" direction of Lemma 4.2 we inductively apply Claim 4.3 to construct a q-tree T_φ for all *connected* conjunctive queries φ with at most ℓ variables. The induction start for empty queries is trivial. For the induction step, assume that there is a q-tree for every connected q-hierarchical query with at most ℓ variables, and let φ be a connected q-hierarchical query with $\ell + 1$ variables. By Claim 4.3 there is at least one variable that is contained in every atom, and if $\text{free}(\varphi) \neq \emptyset$ there is a free variable with this property. We choose such a variable x (preferring free over quantified variables) and let x be the root of T_φ.

Now we consider the query φ' that is obtained from φ by "removing" x from every atom. As this query is still q-hierarchical, we can find by induction a tree T_i for every connected component φ'_i of φ'. We let T_φ be the disjoint union of the T_i together with the root x and conclude the construction by adding an edge from x to the root of each T_i. It is easy to see that this construction can be computed in polynomial time. ☐

5. LOWER BOUNDS

5.1 The OMv-conjecture

We write $\vec{w}_i$ to denote the i-th component of an n-dimensional vector $\vec{w}$, and we write $M_{i,j}$ for the entry in row i and column j of an $n \times n$ matrix M.

We consider matrices and vectors over $\{0,1\}$. All the arithmetic is done over the Boolean semiring, where multiplication means conjunction and addition means disjunction. For example, for n-dimensional vectors $\vec{u}$ and $\vec{v}$ we have $\vec{u}^{\mathsf{T}}\vec{v} = 1$ if and only if there is an $i \in [n]$ such the $\vec{u}_i = \vec{v}_i = 1$. Let M be an $n \times n$ matrix and let $\vec{v}^{\,1}, \dots, \vec{v}^{\,n}$ be a sequence of n vectors, each of which has dimension n. The *online matrix-vector multiplication problem* is the following algorithmic task. At first, the algorithm gets an $n \times n$ matrix M and is allowed to do some preprocessing. Afterwards, the algorithm receives the vectors $\vec{v}^{\,1}, \dots, \vec{v}^{\,n}$ one by one and has to output $M\vec{v}^{\,t}$ before it has access to $\vec{v}^{\,t+1}$ (for each $t < n$). The running time is the overall time the algorithm needs to produce the output $M\vec{v}^{\,1}, \dots, M\vec{v}^{\,n}$.

It is easy to see that this problem can be solved in $O(n^3)$ time; the best known algorithm runs in time $n^3/f(n)$ for some $f(n) \in n^{o(1)}$ [25]. The *OMv-conjecture* was introduced by Henzinger, Krinninger, Nanongkai, and Saranurak in [22] and states that the online matrix-vector multiplication problem cannot be solved in "truly subcubic" time $O(n^{3-\varepsilon})$ for any $\varepsilon > 0$. Note that the hardness of online matrix-vector multiplication crucially depends on the requirement that the algorithm does not receive all vectors $\vec{v}^{\,1}, \dots, \vec{v}^{\,n}$ at once. In fact, without this requirement the output could be computed in time $O(n^{3-\varepsilon})$ by using any fast matrix multiplication algorithm. The OMv-conjecture has been used to prove conditional lower bounds for various dynamic problems and is a common barrier for improving these algorithms, see [22]. Contrary to classical complexity theoretic assumptions such as $P \neq NP$, this conjecture shares with other recently proposed algorithmic conjectures the less desirable fact that it can hardly be called "well-established". However, at least we know that improving dynamic query evaluation algorithms for queries that are hard under the OMv-conjecture is a very difficult task and (even if not completely inconceivable) would lead to major breakthroughs in algorithms for e.g. matrix multiplication (see [22] for a discussion).

A variant of OMv that is useful as an intermediate step in our reductions is the following OuMv problem. Again, we are given an $n \times n$ matrix M and are allowed to do some preprocessing. Afterwards, a sequence of pairs of vectors $\vec{u}^{\,t}, \vec{v}^{\,t}$ arrives for each $t \in [n]$, and the task is to compute $(\vec{u}^{\,t})^{\mathsf{T}} M \vec{v}^{\,t}$. As before, the algorithm has to output $(\vec{u}^{\,t})^{\mathsf{T}} M \vec{v}^{\,t}$ before it gets $\vec{u}^{\,t+1}, \vec{v}^{\,t+1}$ as input. It is known that OuMv is at least as difficult as OMv.

Theorem 5.1 (Theorem 2.4 in [22]). *If there is some $\varepsilon > 0$ such that OuMv can be solved in $n^{3-\varepsilon}$ time, then the OMv-conjecture fails.*

5.2 The OV-conjecture

While OuMv and OMv turn out to be suitable for Boolean CQs and the enumeration of k-ary CQs, our lower bound for the counting complexity additionally relies on the *orthogonal vectors conjecture* (also known as the *Boolean orthogonal detection problem*, see [1, ?]). It is not known whether this conjecture implies or is implied by the OMv-conjecture. However, it is implied by the strong exponential time hypothesis (SETH) [?] and typically serves as a basis for SETH-based lower bounds of polynomial time algorithms.

The *orthogonal vectors problem* (OV) is the following static decision problem. Given two sets U and V of n Boolean vectors of dimension d, decide whether there are $\vec{u} \in U$ and $\vec{v} \in V$ such that $\vec{u}^{\mathsf{T}}\vec{v} = 0$. This problem can clearly be solved in time $O(n^2 d)$ by checking all pairs of vectors, and also slightly better algorithms are known [1]. The *OV-conjecture* states that this problem cannot be solved in truly subquadratic time if $d = \omega(\log n)$. The exact formulation of this conjecture in terms of the parameters varies in the literature, but all of them imply the following simple variant which is sufficient for our purposes.

Conjecture 5.2 (OV-conjecture). For every $\varepsilon > 0$ there is no algorithm that solves OV for $d = \lceil \log^2 n \rceil$ in time $O(n^{2-\varepsilon})$.

5.3 Proof Ideas

Before we establish the lower bounds in full generality, we illustrate the main ideas along the two representative examples $\varphi'_{S\text{-}E\text{-}T}$ and $\varphi_{E\text{-}T}$ defined in (3) and (4). Note that if a CQ is not q-hierarchical, then according to Definition 3.1 there are two distinct variables x and y that do not satisfy one of the two conditions. The Boolean query $\varphi'_{S\text{-}E\text{-}T}$ is an example of a query where x and y do not satisfy the first condition (i.e., the condition of being hierarchical), and $\varphi_{E\text{-}T}$ is a query where the quantifier-free part is hierarchical, but where x and y do not satisfy the second condition on the free variables. Intuitively, every non-q-hierarchical query has a subquery whose shape is similar to either $\varphi'_{S\text{-}E\text{-}T}$ or $\varphi_{E\text{-}T}$ (we will make this precise in Section 5.4).

Let us show how the OMv-conjecture can be applied to obtain a lower bound for answering the Boolean query $\varphi'_{S\text{-}E\text{-}T}$ under updates.

Lemma 5.3. *Suppose there is an $\varepsilon > 0$ and a dynamic algorithm with arbitrary preprocessing time and $t_u = n^{1-\varepsilon}$ update time that answers $\varphi'_{S\text{-}E\text{-}T}$ in time $t_a = n^{2-\varepsilon}$ on databases whose active domain has size n, then OuMv can be solved in time $O(n^{3-\varepsilon})$.*

Proof. We show how a query evaluation algorithm for $\varphi'_{S\text{-}E\text{-}T}$ can be used to solve OuMv. We get the $n \times n$ matrix M and start the preprocessing phase of our evaluation algorithm for $\varphi'_{S\text{-}E\text{-}T}$ with the empty database $D = (E^D, S^D, T^D)$ where $E^D = S^D = T^D = \emptyset$. As this database has constant size, the preprocessing phase finishes in constant time. We apply at most n^2 update steps to ensure that $E^D = \{(i,j) : M_{i,j} = 1\}$. This preprocessing takes time $n^2 t_u = O(n^{3-\varepsilon})$. If we get two vectors $\vec{u}^{\,t}$ and $\vec{v}^{\,t}$ in the dynamic phase of the OuMv problem, we update S^D and T^D so that their characteristic vectors agree with $\vec{u}^{\,t}$ and $\vec{v}^{\,t}$, respectively. Now we answer $\varphi'_{S\text{-}E\text{-}T}$ on D within time t_a and output 1 if $\varphi'_{S\text{-}E\text{-}T}(D) = \texttt{yes}$ and 0 otherwise. Note that by construction this answer agrees with $(\vec{u}^{\,t})^{\mathsf{T}} M \vec{v}^{\,t}$. The time of each step of the dynamic phase of OuMv is bounded by $2nt_u + t_a = O(n^{2-\varepsilon})$, and the overall running time for OMv accumulates to $O(n^{3-\varepsilon})$. □

Note that a lower bound on the answer time t_a of a Boolean query directly implies the same lower bounds for the time t_c needed to count the number of tuples and for the delay t_d of an enumeration algorithm. Furthermore, this also holds true for any query that is obtained from the Boolean query by removing quantifiers.

Now we turn to our second example $\varphi_{E\text{-}T}$. Note that the Boolean version $\exists x\, \varphi_{E\text{-}T}(x)$ is q-hierarchical and hence can be answered in constant time under updates by Theorem 3.2. Thus, a lower bound on the delay t_d does not follow from a corresponding lower bound on the Boolean version. Instead we obtain the lower bound by a direct reduction from OMv.

Lemma 5.4. *Suppose there is an $\varepsilon > 0$ and a dynamic algorithm with arbitrary preprocessing time and $t_u = n^{1-\varepsilon}$ update time that enumerates $\varphi_{E\text{-}T}$ with $t_d = n^{1-\varepsilon}$ delay on databases whose active domain has size n, then OMv can be solved in time $O(n^{3-\varepsilon})$.*

Proof. We show that an enumeration algorithm with $n^{1-\varepsilon}$ update time and $n^{1-\varepsilon}$ delay helps to solve OMv in time $O(n^{3-\varepsilon})$. As in the proof of Lemma 5.3, we are given an $n\times n$ matrix M, start with the empty database $D = (E^D, T^D)$ where $E^D = T^D = \emptyset$ and perform at most n^2 update steps to ensure that $E^D = \{(i,j) : M_{i,j} = 1\}$. In the dynamic phase of OMv, when a vector $\vec{v}^{\,t}$ arrives, we perform at most n insertions or deletions to the relation T^D such that $\vec{v}^{\,t}$ is the characteristic vector of T^D. Afterwards, we wait until the enumeration algorithm outputs the set $\varphi_{E\text{-}T}(D)$ and output the characteristic vector $\vec{u}^{\,t}$ of this set. By construction we have $\vec{u}^{\,t} = M\vec{v}^{\,t}$. If the enumeration algorithm has update time t_u and delay t_d, then the overall running time of this step is bounded by $nt_u + nt_d$ which by the assumptions of our lemma is bounded by $O(n^{2-\varepsilon})$. Hence, the overall running time for solving the OMv is bounded by $O(n^{3-\varepsilon})$. □

Finally, we consider the counting problem for $\varphi_{E\text{-}T}$. Again, we cannot reduce from its tractable Boolean version. Moreover, we were not able to use OMv directly, in a similar way as in the proof of the previous lemma, because computing the output vector $\vec{u}^{\,t}$ by (possibly iterated) reference to the size $|\varphi_{E\text{-}T}(D)|$ seems to take $\Omega(n)$ time. Instead, we reduce from the orthogonal vectors problem.

Lemma 5.5. *Suppose there is an $\varepsilon > 0$ and a dynamic algorithm with arbitrary preprocessing time and $t_u = n^{1-\varepsilon}$ update time that computes $|\varphi_{E\text{-}T}(D)|$ in time $t_c = n^{1-\varepsilon}$ on databases whose active domain has size n, then the OV-conjecture fails.*

Proof. As in the previous proof we assume that there is a dynamic counting algorithm for $\varphi_{E\text{-}T}$ and start its preprocessing with the empty database over the schema $\{E, T\}$. Afterwards, we use at most nd updates (where $d = \lceil \log^2(n) \rceil$) to encode all d-dimensional vectors $\vec{u}^{\,1}, \ldots, \vec{u}^{\,n}$ in U into the binary relation $E^D \subseteq [n]\times[d]$ such that $(i,j) \in E^D$ if and only if the j-th component of $\vec{u}^{\,i}$ is 1. Then we make at most d updates to T^D to ensure that the first vector $\vec{v}^{\,1} \in V$ is the characteristic vector of T^D. Now we compute $|\varphi_{E\text{-}T}(D)|$. Note that $|\varphi_{E\text{-}T}(D)| < n$ if and only if $(\vec{u}^{\,i})^{\mathsf{T}}\vec{v}^{\,1} = 0$ for some $i \in [n]$. If this is the case, we output that there is a pair of orthogonal vectors. Otherwise, we know that $\vec{v}^{\,1}$ is not orthogonal to any $\vec{u}^{\,i}$ and apply the same procedure for $\vec{v}^{\,2}$, which requires again at most d updates to T^D and one call of the **count** routine. Repeating this procedure for all n vectors in V takes time $O\big(ndt_u + n(dt_u + t_c)\big) \leqslant O(n^{2-\varepsilon/2})$ and solves OV in subquadratic time. □

5.4 Proofs of the Main Theorems

We now prove our lower bound Theorems 3.3, 3.4, and 3.5. We will use standard notation concerning homomorphisms (cf., e.g. [2]). In particular, for CQs φ and φ' we will write $h : \varphi \to \varphi'$ to indicate that h is a homomorphism from φ to φ' (as defined in Section 3). A homomorphism $g : D \to \varphi$ from a database D to a CQ φ is a mapping from adom(D) to vars(φ) such that whenever $(a_1, \ldots, a_r)$ is a tuple in some relation R^D of D, then $Rg(a_1)\cdots g(a_r)$ is an atom of φ. A homomorphism $h : \varphi \to D$ from a CQ φ to a database D is a mapping from vars(φ) to adom(D) such that whenever $Ru_1 \cdots u_r$ is an atom of φ, then $\big(h(u_1), \ldots, h(u_r)\big) \in R^D$. Obviously, for a k-ary CQ $\varphi(x_1, \ldots, x_k)$ and a database D, we have $\varphi(D) = \{(h(x_1), \ldots, h(x_k)) : h : \varphi \to D\}$.

We first generalise the proof idea of Lemma 5.3 to all Boolean CQs φ that do not satisfy the requirement (i) of Definition 3.1. Thus assume that there are two variables $x, y \in$ vars(φ) and three atoms $\psi^x, \psi^{x,y}, \psi^y$ of φ with vars(ψ^x) $\cap \{x,y\} = \{x\}$, vars($\psi^{x,y}$) $\cap \{x,y\} = \{x,y\}$, and vars(ψ^y) $\cap \{x,y\} = \{y\}$. Without loss of generality we assume that vars(φ) $= \{x, y, z_1, \ldots, z_\ell\}$. For a given $n \times n$ matrix M we fix a domain dom$_n$ that consists of $2n + \ell$ elements $\{a_i, b_i : i \in [n]\} \cup \{c_s : s \in [\ell]\}$. For $i, j \in [n]$ we let $\iota_{i,j}$ be the injective mapping from vars(φ) to dom$_n$ with $\iota_{i,j}(x) = a_i$, $\iota_{i,j}(y) = b_j$, and $\iota_{i,j}(z_s) = c_s$ for all $s \in [\ell]$.

For the matrix M and for n-dimensional vectors $\vec{u}$ and $\vec{v}$, we define a σ-db $D = D(\varphi, M, \vec{u}, \vec{v})$ with adom(D) $\subseteq$ dom$_n$ as follows (recall our notational convention that $\vec{u}_i$ denotes the i-th entry of a vector $\vec{u}$). For every atom $\psi = Rw_1 \cdots w_r$ in φ we include in R^D the tuple $\big(\iota_{i,j}(w_1), \ldots, \iota_{i,j}(w_r)\big)$

- for all $i, j \in [n]$ such that $\vec{u}_i = 1$, if $\psi = \psi^x$,
- for all $i, j \in [n]$ such that $\vec{v}_j = 1$, if $\psi = \psi^y$,
- for all $i, j \in [n]$ such that $M_{i,j} = 1$, if $\psi = \psi^{x,y}$, and
- for all $i, j \in [n]$, if $\psi \notin \{\psi^x, \psi^{x,y}, \psi^y\}$.

Note that the relations in the atoms ψ^x, ψ^y, and $\psi^{x,y}$ are used to encode $\vec{u}$, $\vec{v}$, and M, respectively. Moreover, since ψ^x (ψ^y) does not contain the variable y (x), two databases $D = D(\varphi, M, \vec{u}, \vec{v})$ and $D' = D(\varphi, M, \vec{u}\,', \vec{v}\,')$ differ only in at most $2n$ tuples. Therefore, D' can be obtained from D by $2n$ update steps.

It follows from the definitions that $\iota_{i,j}$ is a homomorphism from φ to D if and only if $\vec{u}_i = 1$, $\vec{v}_j = 1$, and $M_{i,j} = 1$. Therefore, $\vec{u}^{\mathsf{T}} M \vec{v} = 1$ if and only if there are $i, j \in [n]$ such that $\iota_{i,j}$ is a homomorphism from φ to D.

We let $g_{\varphi,n}$ be the (surjective) mapping from dom$_n$ to vars(φ) defined by $g_{\varphi,n}(c_s) := z_s$, $g_{\varphi,n}(a_i) := x$, and $g_{\varphi,n}(b_j) := y$ for all $i, j \in [n]$ and $s \in [\ell]$. Clearly, $g_{\varphi,n}$ is a homomorphism from D to φ.

Obviously, the following is true for every mapping h from vars(φ) to adom(D) and for all $w \in$ vars(φ): if $h(w) = c_s$ for some $s \in [\ell]$, then $(g_{\varphi,n} \circ h)(w) = z_s$; if $h(w) = a_i$ for some $i \in [n]$, then $(g_{\varphi,n} \circ h)(w) = x$; if $h(w) = b_j$ for some $j \in [n]$, then $(g_{\varphi,n} \circ h)(w) = y$.

We define the partition $\mathcal{P}_{\varphi,n} = \big\{\{c_1\}, \ldots, \{c_\ell\}, \{a_i : i \in [n]\}, \{b_j : j \in [n]\}\big\}$ of dom$_n$ and say that a mapping h from vars(φ) to adom(D) *respects* $\mathcal{P}_{\varphi,n}$, if for each set from the partition there is exactly one element in the image of h. The next two claims are straightforward.

Claim 5.6. $\vec{u}^{\mathsf{T}} M \vec{v} = 1 \iff$ There exists a homomorphism $h\colon \varphi \to D$ that respects $\mathcal{P}_{\varphi,n}$.

Claim 5.7. If φ is a core, then every homomorphism $h\colon \varphi \to D$ respects $\mathcal{P}_{\varphi,n}$.

Proof of Theorem 3.4. Assume for contradiction that the query answering problem for φ and hence for its non-q-hierarchical core φ_{core} can be solved with update time $t_u =$

$O(n^{1-\varepsilon})$ and answer time $t_a = O(n^{2-\varepsilon})$. We can use this algorithm to solve OuMv in time $O(n^{3-\varepsilon})$ as follows.

In the preprocessing phase, we are given the $n \times n$ matrix M and let $\vec{u}^0$, $\vec{v}^0$ be the all-zero vectors of dimension n. We start the preprocessing phase of our evaluation algorithm for φ_{core} with the empty database. As this database has constant size, the preprocessing phase finishes in constant time. Afterwards, we use at most n^2 insert operations to build the database $D(\varphi_{\text{core}}, M, \vec{u}^0, \vec{v}^0)$. All this is done within time $O(n^2 t_u) = O(n^{3-\varepsilon})$.

When a pair of vectors $\vec{u}^t$, $\vec{v}^t$ (for $t \in [n]$) arrives, we change the current database $D(\varphi_{\text{core}}, M, \vec{u}^{t-1}, \vec{v}^{t-1})$ into $D(\varphi_{\text{core}}, M, \vec{u}^t, \vec{v}^t)$ by using at most $2n$ update steps. By the Claims 5.6 and 5.7 we know that $(\vec{u}^t)^\mathsf{T} M \vec{v}^t = 1$ if, and only if, there is a homomorphism from φ_{core} to $D := D(\varphi_{\text{core}}, M, \vec{u}^t, \vec{v}^t)$. Hence, after answering the Boolean query φ_{core} on D in time $t_a = |\text{adom}(D)|^{2-\varepsilon} = O(n^{2-\varepsilon})$ we can output the value of $(\vec{u}^t)^\mathsf{T} M \vec{v}^t$. The time of each step of the dynamic phase of OuMv is bounded by $2nt_u + t_a = O(n^{2-\varepsilon})$. The overall running time sums up to $O(n^{3-\varepsilon})$, contradicting the OMv-conjecture by Theorem 5.1. □

The same reduction from OuMv to the query evaluation problem for CQs is also useful for the lower bound on the counting problem, provided that the query is not hierarchical. If the query is hierarchical, but the quantifiers are not in the correct form (such that the query is not q-hierarchical), then OuMv does not provide us with the desired lower bound proof and we have to stick to the OV-conjecture instead. Another crucial difference between the Boolean and the non-Boolean case is the following: the dynamic counting problem for the Boolean query $\varphi = \exists x\, \exists y\, \big(Exx \wedge Exy \wedge Eyy\big)$ is easy (because its core is $\exists x\, Exx$), whereas the dynamic counting problem for its non-Boolean version $\varphi(x, y) = \big(Exx \wedge Exy \wedge Eyy\big)$ is hard (because the query is a non-q-hierarchical core). To take care of this phenomenon, we utilise the following lemma.

Lemma 5.8. *Let $\varphi(x_1, \ldots, x_k)$ be a conjunctive query and $X_{x_1}, \ldots, X_{x_k}$ be pairwise disjoint subsets of* **dom**. *Suppose that for every database D under consideration there is a homomorphism $g\colon D \to \varphi$ such that $g(X_{x_i}) = \{x_i\}$ for all $i \in [k]$. If $|\varphi(D)|$ can be computed with t_p preprocessing time, t_u update time, and t_c counting time, then the number $\big|\varphi(D) \cap \big(X_{x_1} \times \cdots \times X_{x_k}\big)\big|$ can be computed with $2^{O(k)}(t_u + t_c)$ update time and $O(1)$ counting time after $2^{O(\|\varphi\|)} + 2^{O(k)}(t_p + t_c)$ preprocessing.*

In the static setting, a similar result on the simulation of unary relations was shown by Chen and Mengel (see Section 7.1 in [10]) and it turns out that our dynamic version can be proven using the same techniques. We remark that the lemma holds even if we drop the additional requirement on the existence of the homomorphism g. However, as the databases we construct in our proof of Theorem 3.5 have the desired structure, this additional requirement helps to simplify the proof. Due to space limitations, the proof is omitted here; it will be included in the paper's full version.

Details concerning the proofs of Theorem 3.5 and 3.3 can be found in Appendix A.

6. UPPER BOUND

This section is devoted to the proof of Theorem 3.2. First of all, note that if we can prove the theorem for *connected* q-hierarchical queries, then the result easily follows also for non-connected q-hierarchical queries: If $\varphi_1(\overline{x}_1), \ldots, \varphi_j(\overline{x}_j)$ are the connected components of a q-hierarchical query $\varphi(\overline{x}_1, \ldots, \overline{x}_j)$ for (possibly empty) tuples $\overline{x}_1, \ldots, \overline{x}_j$ of variables, then during the preprocessing phase we build the data structures for all the φ_i, and when the database is updated, we update all these data structures. Note that $\varphi(D) = \varphi_1(D) \times \cdots \times \varphi_j(D)$. Thus, the **count** routine for φ can perform a **count** for each φ_i and output the number $|\varphi(D)| = \prod_{i=1}^{j} |\varphi_i(D)|$. Accordingly, the **enumerate** routine can easily be obtained by a nested loop through the **enumerate** routines for all the φ_i's

For the remainder of this section we assume w.l.o.g. that $\varphi(x_1, \ldots, x_k)$ is a *connected* q-hierarchical conjunctive query, $\text{vars}(\varphi) = \{x_1, \ldots, x_m\}$ with $0 \leqslant k \leqslant m$, and φ is of the form

$$\varphi \quad = \quad \exists x_{k+1} \cdots \exists x_m \, \big(\psi_1 \wedge \cdots \wedge \psi_\ell\big) \,. \qquad (5)$$

From Lemma 4.2 we know that φ has a q-tree. We use the lemma's algorithm to construct in time $\textit{poly}(\varphi)$ a q-tree T_φ of φ. For the remainder of this section, we simply write T to denote T_φ. Recall that the vertex set V of T is the set of variables in φ, i.e., $V = \{x_1, \ldots, x_m\}$. We will write v_{root} to denote the root node of T.

6.1 Further notation

The following notation will be convenient for describing and analysing our algorithm. For a node v of T, we write $\text{path}[v]$ to denote the set of all nodes of T that occur in the path from v_{root} to v in T (including v), and we let $\text{path}[v) := \text{path}[v] \setminus \{v\}$. $N(v) := \{u \,:\, (v, u) \in E(T)\}$ is the set of children of v in T. A node v of T *represents* an atomic query ψ iff $\text{path}[v] = \text{vars}(\psi)$, i.e., the variables in $\text{path}[v]$ are exactly the variables in ψ. For each $v \in V$, we write $\text{rep}(v)$ for the set of all atoms ψ_j of φ that are represented by v. Note that $\text{rep}(v) \subseteq \text{atoms}(v)$.

An *assignment* is a partial mapping from **var** to **dom**. As usual, we write $\text{dom}(\alpha)$ for the domain of α. For a set $S \subseteq$ **var**, by $\alpha_{|S}$ we denote the restriction of α to $\text{dom}(\alpha) \cap S$. For $x \in$ **var** and $a \in$ **dom** we write $\alpha\frac{a}{x}$ for the assignment α' with domain $\text{dom}(\alpha) \cup \{x\}$, where $\alpha'(x) = a$ and $\alpha'(y) = \alpha(y)$ for all $y \notin \text{dom}(\alpha) \setminus \{x\}$. An assignment β is called an *expansion* of α (for short: $\beta \supseteq \alpha$) if $\text{dom}(\beta) \supseteq \text{dom}(\alpha)$ and $\beta_{|\text{dom}(\alpha)} = \alpha$. The *empty assignment* $\emptyset$ is the assignment with empty domain. For pairwise distinct variables $v_1, \ldots, v_d$ and constants $a_1, \ldots, a_d \in$ **dom** we write $\frac{a_1, \ldots, a_d}{v_1, \ldots, v_d}$ to denote the assignment α with $\text{dom}(\alpha) = \{v_1, \ldots, v_d\}$ and $\alpha(v_i) = a_i$ for all $i \in [d]$.

6.2 The data structure

We now describe the data structure $\mathtt{D}$ that will be built by the **preprocess** routine and maintained while executing the **update** routine. Our data structure for a given database D represents so-called *items*. Each item is determined by a variable $v \in V$, an assignment $\alpha : \text{path}[v) \to$ **dom**, and a constant $a \in$ **dom**; we will write $[v, \alpha, a]$ to denote this item. For an item $i = [v, \alpha, a]$ we write v^i, α^i, and a^i to denote the item's variable v, assignment α, and constant a. Moreover, for every item $i = [v, \alpha, a]$ and every child u of v in T there is a doubly linked list $\mathcal{L}^i_u$ (the *u-list* of i) which contains items of the form $[u, \alpha\frac{a}{v}, b]$ and we have one pointer $\textit{child}^i_u$ that points from i to the first element in $\mathcal{L}^i_u$. It is important to note that not every item of the form $[u, \alpha\frac{a}{v}, b]$ that is present in our data structure will be contained in the corresponding list $\mathcal{L}_u^i$, but for those items that are contained we store two pointers *next-listitem*^{i} and *prev-listitem*^{i} to navigate in $\mathcal{L}_u^i$. The *parent item* of an item of the form $[u, \alpha\frac{a}{v}, b]$, where u is a child of v in T, is defined to be the item $[v, \alpha, a]$.

Let us now state which items are actually contained in our data structure.

An item $[v, \alpha, a]$ is present in our data structure if and only if there is an atom $\psi \in \text{atoms}(v)$ such that there is an expansion $\beta \supseteq \alpha\frac{a}{v}$ with $\text{dom}(\beta) = \text{vars}(\psi)$ and $(D, \beta) \models \psi$. It follows that every fact $R(a_1, \ldots, a_r)$ in the database gives rise to a constant number of items and that the overall number of items in our data structure is therefore linear in the size of the database. The definition also ensures that whenever an item is present in our data structure, then so is its parent item.

Let us now specify which of the present items are actually contained in the corresponding list $\mathcal{L}_u^i$. We will need the following definition.

An item $[v, \alpha, a]$ is *fit* if and only if there is a expansion $\beta \supseteq \alpha\frac{a}{v}$ such that $(D, \beta) \models \bigwedge_{\psi \in \text{atoms}(v)} \psi$. The doubly linked list $\mathcal{L}_u^i$ contains precisely those items that are fit. Being fit is a necessary requirement for participating in the query result and this is why we exclude unfit items from the lists. Note that whenever a tuple is inserted into or deleted from the database, this affects the "fit"-status of only a constant number of items. Furthermore, provided we have constant-time access to the items, we can update their status and include or exclude them from the corresponding lists in constant time. In addition to the items, our data structure also has a designated *start* pointer that points to (the first element of) a doubly linked list *start*-list $\mathcal{L}_{\text{start}}$, which consists of all fit items of the form $[v_{root}, \emptyset, b]$.

In order to count the number of output tuples, we store for every item i its *weight* C^i. The weight is used to measure the number of tuples in the query result that extend the item's partial assignment and is defined as follows. For an item $i = [v, \alpha, a]$ we let

$$\mathcal{E}^i := \left\{ \beta \supseteq \alpha\tfrac{a}{v} : \begin{array}{c} \text{dom}(\beta) = \bigcup_{\psi \in \text{atoms}(v)} \text{vars}(\psi); \\ (D, \beta) \models \bigwedge_{\psi \in \text{atoms}(v)} \psi \end{array} \right\},$$

$$C^i := |\mathcal{E}^i|.$$

By definition we have that i is fit if and only if $C^i > 0$, and we will use the weights to quickly determine whether an item becomes fit after an insertion of a tuple (or unfit after a deletion). In order to efficiently update these numbers, we store for every list $\mathcal{L}_u^i$ in our data structure as well for the *start*-list the sum of the weights of their elements

$$C_u^i := \textstyle\sum_{i' \in \mathcal{L}_u^i} C^{i'} \quad \text{and} \quad C_{\text{start}} := \sum_{i \in \mathcal{L}_{\text{start}}} C^i.$$

The weights will also be used to determine the size of the query result. For example, suppose that φ is quantifier-free. Then it follows from the definition of that $\varphi(D)$ is the disjoint union of the sets $\mathcal{E}^i$ for all $i \in \mathcal{L}_{\text{start}}$ (where every tuple in $\varphi(D)$ is viewed as an assignment $\beta : \text{free}(\varphi) \to \textbf{dom}$). Therefore, $|\varphi(D)| = C_{\text{start}}$ and we can immediately answer a **count** request by reporting the stored value C_{start}. Now suppose that φ is Boolean. Then we respond to an **answer** request by reporting whether $C_{\text{start}} > 0$. The remaining case, when φ contains quantified and free variables, is similar and will be handled in Section 6.5. To illustrate the overall shape of our data structure, let us consider the following example.

Example 6.1. Consider the query $\varphi(x, y, z, y', z') :=$

$$(\, Rxyz \wedge Rxyz' \wedge Exy \wedge Exy' \wedge Sxyz \,)$$

and the database D_0 with $E^{D_0} = \{(a,e), (a,f), (b,d), (b,g), (b,h)\}$, $S^{D_0} = \{(a,e,a), (a,e,b), (a,f,c), (b,g,b), (b,p,a)\}$, $R^{D_0} = S^{D_0} \cup \{(a,e,c), (b,g,a), (b,g,c), (b,p,b), (b,p,c)\}$. Figure 2 (on the paper's last page) depicts a q-tree T for φ. The data structure $\texttt{D}_0$ that represents the database D_0 is shown in Figure 3(a) (on the paper's last page). Every box represents an item $i = [v, \alpha, a]$ and contains the item's constant a. The number below each box is the weight C^i of the item. The arrows labelled with u represent the pointer from an item i to the first element of its u-list $\mathcal{L}_u^i$. Horizontal lines between the items indicate pointers in the doubly linked lists $\mathcal{L}_u^i$ and $\mathcal{L}_{\text{start}}$. There are seven further unfit items (omitted in the figure) that do not have connections to any other items: $[y, \frac{b}{x}, d]$, $[y, \frac{b}{x}, h]$, $[z, \frac{a,e}{x,y}, c]$, $[z, \frac{b,g}{x,y}, a]$, $[z, \frac{b,g}{x,y}, c]$, $[z, \frac{b,p}{x,y}, b]$, and $[z, \frac{b,p}{x,y}, c]$.

To enable quick access to the existing items, we store a number of arrays, where the elements of **dom** are used to index the positions in an array. For every $v \in V$ we store a d-ary array $\texttt{A}_v$, where $d := |\text{path}[v]|$. We let $v_1, \ldots, v_d$ be the list of variables in path$[v]$ in the order in which they are encountered in the path from T's root to the node v (in particular, $v_1 = v_{root}$ and $v_d = v$). For constants $a_1, \ldots, a_d \in \textbf{dom}$, the entry $\texttt{A}_v[a_1, \ldots, a_d]$ represents the item $[v, \frac{a_1,\ldots,a_{d-1}}{v_1,\ldots,v_{d-1}}, a_d]$, if such an item exists. Otherwise, the entry $\texttt{A}_v[a_1, \ldots, a_d]$ is initialised to 0. This will enable us to check in constant time whether a particular item exists, and if so, to also access this item within constant time. In the following, whenever an item $i = [v, \frac{a_1,\ldots,a_{d-1}}{v_1,\ldots,v_{d-1}}, a_d]$ is newly created, we tacitly let $\texttt{A}_v[a_1, \ldots, a_d] := i$, and we set $\texttt{A}_v[a_1, \ldots, a_d] := 0$ if i is deleted.

Note that while the support of all arrays (i.e., the non-0 entries) is linear in the size of the current database D, a huge amount of storage has to be reserved for these arrays. In more practical settings one has to replace these arrays by more space-efficient data structures, such as suitable hash tables, that allow quick access to the items.

6.3 Enumeration

We now discuss how the data structure can be used to enumerate the query result with constant delay. For our Example 6.1, the 23 result tuples of the enumeration process are shown in Table 1 (on the paper's last page). To enumerate the result of a non-Boolean conjunctive query $\varphi(x_1, \ldots, x_k)$, let T' be the subtree of T induced on $V' := \text{free}(\varphi) = \{x_1, \ldots, x_k\}$. Note that by the definition of a q-tree, we know that T' is connected and contains v_{root}. For each node v of T', let us fix an (arbitrary) linear order on the children of v in T'. In our example query we have $T' = T$ and we let $y < y'$ and $z < z'$.

If the *start*-list is empty, the **enumerate** routine stops immediately with output $\texttt{EOE}$. Otherwise, we proceed as follows to determine the first tuple in the query result. Let $i_{v_{root}}$ be the first item in the *start*-list. Inductively, for every $v \in V'$ for which i_v has been chosen already, we choose i_u for every child u of v in T' by letting i_u be the first item in the u-list of i_v. From the resulting items $\mathcal{I} := (i_v)_{v \in V'}$

we obtain the first tuple $(a_1, \ldots, a_k)$ in the query result by letting a_ℓ be the constant of item i_{x_ℓ} for each $\ell \in [k]$. Thus, within time $O(k)$ we can output the first tuple that belongs to the query result.

To jump from one output tuple to the next, we proceed as follows. Assume that $\mathcal{I} = (i_v)_{v \in V'}$ are the items which determined the result tuple $(a_1, \ldots, a_k)$ that has just been output. Let $y_1, \ldots, y_k$ be the list of all nodes V' of T' in *document order*, i.e., obtained by a pre-order depth-first left-to-right traversal of T' (in particular, $y_1 = v_{\text{root}}$). In Example 6.1, the vertices thus are ordered x, y, z, z', y'.

Determine the maximum index $j \in [k]$ such that the item i_{y_j} is *not* the last item of its doubly linked list. If no such j exists, stop with output EOE. Otherwise, let i'_{y_j} be the item indicated by *next-listitem*$^{i_{y_j}}$. For every $\mu < j$ we let $i'_{y_\mu} := i_{y_\mu}$. For $\mu = j{+}1, \ldots, k$ the item i'_{y_μ} is determined inductively (along the document order) to be the first element of the μ-list of its parent.

From the resulting items $i'_{y_1}, \ldots, i'_{y_k}$ we obtain the next tuple $(a'_1, \ldots, a'_k)$ in the query result by letting a'_ℓ be the constant of item i'_{x_ℓ} for each $\ell \in [k]$. Note that the delay between outputting two consecutive result tuples is $O(k)$. The result of the enumeration process for Example 6.1 is given in Table 1 (on the paper's last page), where the change of an item for a variable y_ℓ (i. e. $i'_{y_\ell} \neq i_{y_\ell}$) for two consecutive tuples is indicated by a separating line.

The pseudo-code for the described **enumerate** routine is given in Algorithm 1 (in Appendix C); a correctness proof for the algorithm will be included in the paper's full version.

6.4 Preprocessing and update

In the preprocessing phase we compute the q-tree (by Lemma 4.2 this can be done in time *poly*(φ)), and we initialise the data structure for the empty database. Afterwards, we perform $|D_0|$ update steps to ensure that the data structure represents the initial database D_0. By ensuring that the update time is constant, it follows that the preprocessing time is linear in the size of the initial database.

To illustrate the result of an update step, consider again our database D_0 from Example 6.1 and suppose that the tuple (b, p) is inserted into relation E. The data structure $\mathtt{D}_1$ for the resulting database D_1 is shown in Figure 3(b) (on the paper's last page).

When an update command arrives, we have to modify our data structure accordingly so that it meets the requirements described in Section 6.2. For convenience, we summarise the conditions below.

(a) An item $[v, \alpha, a]$ is present in our data structure if and only if there is an atom $\psi \in \text{atoms}(v)$ such that there is an expansion $\beta \supseteq \alpha\frac{a}{v}$ with $\text{dom}(\beta) = \text{vars}(\psi)$ and $(D, \beta) \models \psi$.

(b) For every item $i = [v, \alpha, a]$ and every $u \in N(v)$ the list $\mathcal{L}^i_u$ consists of all fit items of the form $[u, \alpha\frac{a}{v}, b]$ that are present in the data structure.

(c) The *start*-list $\mathcal{L}_{\text{start}}$ contains all fit items of the form $[v_{root}, \emptyset, b]$ that are present in the data structure.

(d) All values of C^i, C^i_u, and C_{start} are correct.

To be able to quickly decide whether an item meets the requirement (a), we store for every $i = [v, \alpha, a]$ and every $\psi \in \text{atoms}(v)$ the number C^i_ψ of expansions $\beta \supseteq \alpha\frac{a}{v}$ with $\text{dom}(\beta) = \text{vars}(\psi)$ and $(D, \beta) \models \psi$. Whenever a tuple is inserted into or deleted from a relation, we increment or decrement these numbers accordingly. The number of values C^i_ψ that change after an insertion or deletion of a tuple into an r-ary relation R is r times the number of occurrences of R in φ. Hence these numbers can be updated in time *poly*(φ). An item $i = [v, \alpha, a]$ satisfies condition (a) if, and only if, there is a $\psi \in \text{atoms}(v)$ such that $C^i_\psi > 0$. By using the arrays $\mathtt{A}_v$ and maintaining these numbers we can therefore create or remove items in constant time in order to preserve invariant (a).

Now we show how to update the weights C^i and the variables C^i_u, C_{start} which store sums of weights of list elements. The key lemma is the following (where we let products ranging over the empty set be 1).

Lemma 6.2. *For every item $i = [v, \alpha, a]$ in the data structure it holds that*

$$C^i \quad = \quad \textstyle\prod_{\psi \in \text{rep}(v)} C^i_\psi \cdot \prod_{u \in N(v)} C^i_u. \tag{6}$$

Proof. Note that for $\psi \in \text{rep}(v)$ we have $C^i_\psi \in \{0, 1\}$. Furthermore, $\prod_{\psi \in \text{rep}(v)} C^i_\psi = 1$ if and only if $(D, \alpha\frac{a}{v}) \models \psi$ for all $\psi \in \text{rep}(v)$. Now we have two cases.

First suppose that v is a leaf in T. In this situation we know that $\text{rep}(v) = \text{atoms}(v)$ and therefore we have to show that $C^i = \prod_{\psi \in \text{atoms}(v)} C^i_\psi$, which follows immediately from the definition of $\mathcal{E}^i$.

For the second case suppose that $N(v) = \{u_1, \ldots, u_\ell\}$ for $\ell \geqslant 1$. Note that atoms(v) can be decomposed into pairwise disjoint sets rep(v), atoms(u_1), ..., atoms(u_ℓ) and that the pairwise intersection of sets $U_j := \bigcup_{\psi \in \text{atoms}(u_j)} \text{vars}(\psi)$ is $\text{dom}(\alpha) \cup \{v\}$. If there is some $\psi \in \text{rep}(v)$ such that $(D, \alpha\frac{a}{v}) \not\models \psi$, then $C^i_\psi = 0$, and hence $\mathcal{E}^i = \emptyset$ and $C^i = 0$. Otherwise, $C^i_\psi = 1$ for all $\psi \in \text{rep}(v)$ and we have to show that $C^i = \prod_{u \in N(v)} C^i_u$. Note that for every $\beta \in \mathcal{E}^i$ and every $u_j \in N(v)$ there is a unique $i' \in \mathcal{L}^i_{u_j}$ such that $\beta_{|U_j} \in \mathcal{E}^{i'}$. Furthermore, for every choice of ℓ assignments $\beta_j \in \mathcal{E}^{i'_j}$ with $i'_j \in \mathcal{L}^i_{u_j}$ for $j \in [\ell]$, there is a unique $\beta = \beta_1 \cup \cdots \cup \beta_\ell$ such that $\beta \in \mathcal{E}^i$. It follows that $C^i = \prod_{j \in [\ell]} \big(\sum_{i' \in \mathcal{L}^i_{u_j}} |\mathcal{E}^{i'}|\big) = \prod_{u \in N(v)} C^i_u$, which concludes the proof. □

We have already argued that upon insertion and deletion of a fact only a constant number of values C^i_ψ change. It follows from Lemma 6.2 that the same holds true for the values of C^i, C^i_u, and C_{start}. Moreover, the lemma enables us to compute the new values bottom up in time *poly*(φ).

Now we argue how to ensure condition (b) and (c). While recomputing the new weights C^i we check for every considered item i whether C^i becomes zero or non-zero (recall that i is fit if and only if $C^i > 0$) and add or remove i from the corresponding list. For every item this takes constant time, as we have random access to the items and the lists are doubly linked.

To summarise, the update procedure is as follows. Upon receiving update $R(b_1, \ldots, b_r)$ we repeat the following for all atoms $\psi = Rz_1 \cdots z_r$ of φ that satisfy $(z_s = z_t \Rightarrow b_s = b_t)$ for all $s, t \in [r]$. Let $d = |\{z_1, \ldots, z_r\}|$, let $v_{root} = v_1, \ldots, v_d$ be the path in T from v_{root} to the vertex v_d that represents ψ, and denote by $\alpha = \frac{a_1, \ldots, a_d}{v_1, \ldots, v_d}$ the assignment with $\alpha(z_j) = b_j$ for all $j \in [r]$. Then for $j = d, \ldots, 1$ and $i_j := [v_j, \frac{a_1, \ldots, a_{j-1}}{v_1, \ldots, v_{j-1}}, a_j]$ we repeat the following steps.

1. If $\mathsf{update} = \mathsf{insert}$, then create i_j (if it not already exists) and increment $C^{i_j}_{\psi}$.
   Otherwise, decrement $C^{i_j}_{\psi}$.

2. Let $C^{i_j}_{\text{old}} := C^{i_j}$ and compute C^{i_j} using Lemma 6.2 as a product of $poly(\varphi)$ numbers.

3. If $C^{i_j} > 0$, then add i_j to $\mathcal{L}^{i_{j-1}}_{v_j}$ (if $j > 1$) or $\mathcal{L}_{\text{start}}$ (if $j = 1$) (unless it is already present in the according list).
   Otherwise, remove i_j from the corresponding list.

4. Compute the new value of $C^{i_{j-1}}_{v_j}$ (if $j > 1$) or C_{start} (if $j = 1$) by subtracting $C^{i_j}_{\text{old}}$ and adding C^{i_j}.

5. If $\mathsf{update} = \mathsf{delete}$ and $C^{i_j}_{\psi} = 0$ for all $\psi \in \text{atoms}(v_j)$, then delete i_j from the data structure.

6.5 Counting in the presence of quantifiers

We have already shown that in order to count the number of output tuples in the case where φ is quantifier-free, it suffices to report the value of C_{start}. If φ is non-Boolean and contains quantified variables $\overline{x} = (x_{k+1}, \ldots, x_m)$, we maintain the same numbers C^i, C^i_u, C_{start} as before and additionally store numbers $\widetilde{C}^i$, $\widetilde{C}^i_u$, $\widetilde{C}_{\text{start}}$ for all present items $i = [v, \alpha, a]$ with $v \in \text{free}(\varphi)$. Let $\widetilde{\mathcal{E}}^i := \{\beta_{|\text{free}(\varphi)} : \beta \in \mathcal{E}^i\}$. For an item $i = [v, \alpha, a]$ with $v \in \text{free}(\varphi)$ we let

$$\begin{aligned} \widetilde{C}^i &:= |\widetilde{\mathcal{E}}^i| \\ \widetilde{C}^i_u &:= \textstyle\sum_{i' \in \mathcal{L}^i_u} \widetilde{C}^{i'} \qquad \text{for all } u \in N(v) \cap \text{free}(\varphi) \\ \widetilde{C}_{\text{start}} &:= \textstyle\sum_{i' \in \mathcal{L}_{\text{start}}} \widetilde{C}^{i'}. \end{aligned}$$

By definition we have $|\varphi(D)| = \widetilde{C}_{\text{start}}$, and we use this stored value to answer a **count** request in time $O(1)$. To efficiently update the values, we utilise the following technical lemma, whose proof is similar to the proof of Lemma 6.2 (for details see Appendix C).

Lemma 6.3. *For every item $i = [v, \alpha, a]$ with $v \in \text{free}(\varphi)$ it holds that*

$$\widetilde{C}^i \;=\; \begin{cases} 0 & \textit{if } C^i = 0 \\ \prod_{u \in N(v) \cap \text{free}(\varphi)} \widetilde{C}^i_u & \textit{otherwise.} \end{cases} \tag{7}$$

Now we can update the numbers $\widetilde{C}^i$, $\widetilde{C}^i_u$, $\widetilde{C}_{\text{start}}$ in the same way as we have done for C^i, C^i_u, C_{start}. In particular, we enrich the update procedure described in Section 6.4 by the following two steps 2a and 4a and execute them after 2 and 4, respectively.

2a. If $v_j \in \text{free}(\varphi)$, let $\widetilde{C}^{i_j}_{\text{old}} := \widetilde{C}^{i_j}$ and compute $\widetilde{C}^{i_j}$ using Lemma 6.3.

4a. If $v_j \in \text{free}(\varphi)$, compute the new value of $\widetilde{C}^{i_{j-1}}_{v_j}$ (if $j > 1$) or $\widetilde{C}_{\text{start}}$ (if $j = 1$) by subtracting $\widetilde{C}^{i_j}_{\text{old}}$ and adding $\widetilde{C}^{i_j}$.

7. DISCUSSION

We studied the complexity of answering conjunctive queries under database updates and showed that they can be evaluated efficiently if they are q-hierarchical. For *Boolean* conjunctive queries and the task of computing the result size of non-Boolean queries we proved corresponding lower bounds based on algorithmic conjectures and obtained a complete picture of the queries that can be answered efficiently under updates. Moreover, the q-hierarchical property also precisely characterises those *self-join free* conjunctive queries that can be enumerated efficiently under updates.

A natural open problem is the missing classification of the enumeration problem for conjunctive queries that contain self-joins. As an intriguing example consider the two CQs

$$\begin{aligned} \varphi_1(x,y) &:= \big(Exx \wedge Exy \wedge Eyy\big) && (8) \\ \varphi_2(x,y,z_1,z_2) &:= \big(Exx \wedge Exy \wedge Eyy \wedge Ez_1z_2\big). && (9) \end{aligned}$$

It is easy to see that in the static setting, the results of both queries can be enumerated with constant delay after linear time preprocessing (this also immediately follows from [4], since the queries are free-connex acyclic). But both queries are non-q-hierarchical. By similar arguments as in our lower bound proofs in Section 5, one can show that the results of φ_1 cannot be enumerated with $O(n^{1-\varepsilon})$ update time and $O(n^{1-\varepsilon})$ delay, unless the OMv-conjecture fails (see Appendix B). However, φ_2 *can* be enumerated with constant delay and constant update time after a linear time preprocessing phase, as the following argument shows. If the $\{E\}$-database D is a digraph without loops, then the query result is empty. Otherwise, there is a loop $(c,c) \in E^D$ and we can immediately report the output tuples $(c,c) \times E^D$ with constant delay. During this enumeration process, which takes time $\Theta(\|D\|)$, we have enough time to preprocess, from scratch, the query φ_1 on the database D' obtained from D by deleting the tuple (c,c). Afterwards, we can enumerate with constant delay the remaining tuples, i.e., the tuples in $\varphi_1(D') \times E^D$ (see Appendix B for details).

Note that even in the static setting, a complexity classification for enumerating the results of join queries with self-joins is not in sight and it seems likely that there is no structural characterisation of tractable queries (see [9] for a discussion on that matter).

On a more conceptual level, the main contribution of this paper is to initiate a systematic theoretical investigation of the computational complexity of query evaluation under database updates. We are excited by the fruitful connections between database theory and the theory of dynamic algorithms — in particular, that a known concept from the database literature that classifies hard queries in various settings ("being non-hierarchical") is tightly connected to the underlying combinatorial hardness shared by many dynamic algorithms (as captured by the OMv-conjecture). We suspect that there are further settings in which the theory of dynamic algorithms helps to advance our understanding of query evaluation under a dynamically changing database. Currently, we are working towards characterising the complexity of more expressive queries such conjunctive queries with negation and unions of conjunctive queries.

Acknowledgements

Funded by the Deutsche Forschungsgemeinschaft (DFG, German Research Foundation) – SCHW 837/5-1. The first author wants to thank Thatchaphol Saranurak and Ryan Williams for helpful discussions on algorithmic conjectures.

8. REFERENCES

[1] A. Abboud, R. R. Williams, and H. Yu. More applications of the polynomial method to algorithm design. In *Proc. SODA'15*, pages 218–230, 2015.

[2] S. Abiteboul, R. Hull, and V. Vianu. *Foundations of Databases*. Addison-Wesley, 1995.

[3] A. Atserias, M. Grohe, and D. Marx. Size bounds and query plans for relational joins. *SIAM J. Comput.*, 42(4):1737–1767, 2013.

[4] G. Bagan, A. Durand, and E. Grandjean. On acyclic conjunctive queries and constant delay enumeration. In *Proc. CSL'07*, pages 208–222, 2007.

[5] A. Balmin, Y. Papakonstantinou, and V. Vianu. Incremental validation of XML documents. *ACM Trans. Database Syst.*, 29(4):710–751, 2004.

[6] C. Berkholz, J. Keppeler, and N. Schweikardt. Answering FO+MOD queries under updates on bounded degree databases. In *Proc. ICDT'17*, LIPIcs, 2017. To appear. Preprint available at https://arxiv.org/abs/1702.08764

[7] H. Björklund, W. Gelade, and W. Martens. Incremental XPath evaluation. *ACM Trans. Database Syst.*, 35(4):29, 2010.

[8] J. Brault-Baron. *De la pertinence de l'énumération : complexité en logiques propositionnelle et du premier ordre. (The relevance of the list: propositional logic and complexity of the first order)*. PhD thesis, University of Caen Normandy, France, 2013.

[9] A. A. Bulatov, V. Dalmau, M. Grohe, and D. Marx. Enumerating homomorphisms. *J. Comput. Syst. Sci.*, 78(2):638–650, 2012.

[10] H. Chen and S. Mengel. A trichotomy in the complexity of counting answers to conjunctive queries. In *Proc. ICDT'15*, pages 110–126, 2015.

[11] V. Dalmau and P. Jonsson. The complexity of counting homomorphisms seen from the other side. *Theor. Comput. Sci.*, 329(1-3):315–323, 2004.

[12] N. Dalvi and D. Suciu. The dichotomy of conjunctive queries on probabilistic structures. In *Proc. PODS'07*, pages 293–302. ACM, 2007.

[13] N. N. Dalvi and D. Suciu. Efficient query evaluation on probabilistic databases. *VLDB J.*, 16(4):523–544, 2007.

[14] A. Durand and E. Grandjean. First-order queries on structures of bounded degree are computable with constant delay. *ACM Trans. Comput. Log.*, 8(4), 2007.

[15] A. Durand and S. Mengel. Structural tractability of counting of solutions to conjunctive queries. *Theory Comput. Syst.*, 57(4):1202–1249, 2015.

[16] R. Fink and D. Olteanu. Dichotomies for queries with negation in probabilistic databases. *ACM Trans. Database Syst.*, 41(1):4, 2016.

[17] G. Greco and F. Scarcello. Structural tractability of enumerating CSP solutions. *Constraints*, 18(1):38–74, 2013.

[18] G. Greco and F. Scarcello. Counting solutions to conjunctive queries: structural and hybrid tractability. In *Proc. PODS'14*, pages 132–143, 2014.

[19] M. Grohe. The complexity of homomorphism and constraint satisfaction problems seen from the other side. *J. ACM*, 54(1), 2007.

[20] M. Grohe, T. Schwentick, and L. Segoufin. When is the evaluation of conjunctive queries tractable? In *Proc. STOC'01*, pages 657–666, 2001.

[21] A. Gupta, I. S. Mumick, and V. S. Subrahmanian. Maintaining views incrementally. *SIGMOD Rec.*, 22(2):157–166, June 1993.

[22] M. Henzinger, S. Krinninger, D. Nanongkai, and T. Saranurak. Unifying and strengthening hardness for dynamic problems via the online matrix-vector multiplication conjecture. In *Proc. STOC'15*, pages 21–30, 2015.

[23] M. A. Khamis, H. Q. Ngo, C. Ré, and A. Rudra. Joins via geometric resolutions: Worst-case and beyond. In *Proc. PODS'15*, pages 213–228, 2015.

[24] P. Koutris and D. Suciu. Parallel evaluation of conjunctive queries. In *Proc. PODS'11*, pages 223–234, 2011.

[25] K. G. Larsen and R. R. Williams. Faster online matrix-vector multiplication. In *Proc. SODA'17*, pages 2182–2189, 2017.

[26] K. Losemann and W. Martens. MSO queries on trees: enumerating answers under updates. In *Proc. CSL-LICS'14*, pages 67:1–67:10, 2014.

[27] D. Marx. Tractable hypergraph properties for constraint satisfaction and conjunctive queries. *J. ACM*, 60(6):42, 2013.

[28] B. M. E. Moret and H. D. Shapiro. *Algorithms from P to NP: Volume 1: Design & Efficiency*. Benjamin-Cummings, 1991.

[29] H. Q. Ngo, D. T. Nguyen, C. Re, and A. Rudra. Beyond worst-case analysis for joins with minesweeper. In *Proc. PODS'14*, pages 234–245, 2014.

[30] H. Q. Ngo, E. Porat, C. Ré, and A. Rudra. Worst-case optimal join algorithms: [extended abstract]. In *Proc. PODS'12*, pages 37–48, 2012.

[31] D. Olteanu and J. Závodný. Size bounds for factorised representations of query results. *ACM Trans. Database Syst.*, 40(1):2, 2015.

[32] S. Patnaik and N. Immerman. Dyn-fo: A parallel, dynamic complexity class. *J. Comput. Syst. Sci.*, 55(2):199–209, 1997.

[33] T. Schwentick and T. Zeume. Dynamic complexity: recent updates. *SIGLOG News*, 3(2):30–52, 2016.

[34] L. Segoufin. Enumerating with constant delay the answers to a query. In *Proc. ICDT'13*, pages 10–20, 2013.

[35] L. Segoufin. A glimpse on constant delay enumeration (invited talk). In *Proc. STACS'14*, pages 13–27, 2014.

[36] L. Segoufin. Constant delay enumeration for conjunctive queries. *SIGMOD Record*, 44(1):10–17, 2015.

[37] T. L. Veldhuizen. Triejoin: A simple, worst-case optimal join algorithm. In *Proc. ICDT'14*, pages 96–106, 2014.

[38] R. Williams. Matrix-vector multiplication in sub-quadratic time: (some preprocessing required). In *Proc. SODA'07*, pages 995–1001, 2007.

[39] T. Zeume and T. Schwentick. Dynamic conjunctive queries. In *Proc. ICDT'14*, pages 38–49, 2014.

APPENDIX

This appendix contains details that were omitted from the main body of the paper.

A. DETAILS OMITTED IN THE LOWER BOUNDS SECTION

Proof idea for Theorem 3.5. Let φ be the non-q-hierarchical homomorphic core of the given CQ.

In case that φ does not satisfy condition (i) of Definition 3.1, we proceed similarly as in the proof of Theorem 3.4 and reduce from OuMv. To overcome the difficulties caused by the fact that it might be the case that the core of the Boolean version $\exists x\, \exists y\, \exists z_1 \cdots \exists z_\ell\, \varphi$ of φ actually *is* q-hierarchical (consider $\varphi = (Exx \wedge Exy \wedge Eyy)$ for example), we use Lemma 5.8.

For the case where φ satisfies condition (i), but not condition (ii) of Definition 3.1, we reduce from OV in a similar way as in the proof of Lemma 5.5, and again we use Lemma 5.8.

Details will be given in the paper's full version. □

After having obtained the lower bounds for answering Boolean queries and for solving the counting problem for non-Boolean queries, we now prove the hardness result for enumerating the results of self-join free conjunctive queries.

Proof of Theorem 3.3. If φ does not satisfy condition (i) of Definition 3.1, the lower bound follows immediately from Theorem 3.4. We can therefore assume that φ satisfies condition (i), but not (ii). Hence there are a free variable x, a quantified variable y, and two atoms $\psi^{x,y}$, ψ^y such that $\text{vars}(\psi^{x,y}) \cap \{x, y\} = \{x, y\}$ and $\text{vars}(\psi^y) \cap \{x, y\} = \{y\}$. W.l.o.g. we let $\text{vars}(\varphi) = \{x, y, z_1, \ldots, z_\ell\}$ and $\text{free}(\varphi) = \{x, z_1, \ldots, z_{\ell'}\}$ and consider the query $\varphi(x, z_1, \ldots, z_{\ell'})$.

For contradiction, assume that there is a dynamic algorithm that enumerates φ with $O(n^{1-\varepsilon})$ delay and $O(n^{1-\varepsilon})$ update time. We want to use this algorithm to solve OMv in time $O(n^{3-\varepsilon})$. For this we encode an $n \times n$ matrix M and an n-dimensional vector $\vec{v}$ into a database, in a similar way as we have done for OuMv in the proof of Theorem 3.4: We define the σ-db $D = D(\varphi, M, \vec{v})$ over the domain $\text{dom}_n = \{a_i, b_i : i \in [n]\} \cup \{c_s : s \in [\ell]\}$ consisting of $2n+\ell$ elements. For $i, j \in [n]$ we let $\iota_{i,j} : \text{vars}(\varphi) \to \text{dom}_n$ be the injective mapping that sets $\iota_{i,j}(x) = a_i$, $\iota_{i,j}(y) = b_j$, and $\iota_{i,j}(z_s) = c_s$ for all $s \in [\ell]$. For every atom $\psi = Rw_1 \cdots w_r$ in φ we include in R^D the tuple $(\iota_{i,j}(w_1), \ldots, \iota_{i,j}(w_r))$

- for all $i, j \in [n]$ such that $\vec{v}_j = 1$, if $\psi = \psi^y$,
- for all $i, j \in [n]$ such that $M_{i,j} = 1$, if $\psi = \psi^{x,y}$, and
- for all $i, j \in [n]$, if $\psi \notin \{\psi^{x,y}, \psi^y\}$.

Note that $\iota_{i,j}$ is a homomorphism from φ to D iff $M_{i,j} = 1$ and $\vec{v}_j = 1$. Since φ is self-join free, every homomorphism from φ to D agrees with some $\iota_{i,j}$. Thus, $\varphi(D)$ is the set of all tuples $(a_i, c_1, \ldots, c_{\ell'})$ for which there exists an index j such that $\iota_{i,j}$ is a homomorphism from φ to D. Hence, $(a_i, c_1, \ldots, c_{\ell'}) \in \varphi(D)$ iff $(M\vec{v})_i = 1$. As $|\varphi(D)| \leqslant n$, we can compute the vector $M\vec{v}$ in time $O(nt_d) = O(n^{2-\varepsilon})$ from the query's result.

When a vector $\vec{v}^{\,t}$ arrives in the dynamic phase of OMv, we update $D(\varphi, M, \vec{v}^{\,t-1})$ to $D(\varphi, M, \vec{v}^{\,t})$ using $\leqslant n$ insertions or deletions of tuples in the relation of the atom ψ^y. As this can be done in time $nt_u = O(n^{2-\varepsilon})$, we compute $M\vec{v}^{\,t}$ in overall time $O(n^{2-\varepsilon})$ and hence solve OMv in time $O(n^{3-\varepsilon})$. □

B. DETAILS OMITTED IN THE DISCUSSION SECTION

We prove the statements about the dynamic enumeration complexity of the queries φ_1 and φ_2 as discussed in Section 7.

Lemma B.1. *Suppose there is an $\epsilon > 0$ and a dynamic algorithm with arbitrary preprocessing time and $t_u = n^{1-\varepsilon}$ update time that enumerates $\varphi_1(x, y) := (Exx \wedge Exy \wedge Eyy)$ with $t_d = n^{1-\varepsilon}$ delay on databases whose active domain has size n, then the OMv-conjecture fails.*

Proof. We show that a dynamic enumeration algorithm for $\varphi_1(x, y)$ helps to solve OuMv in time $O(n^{3-\varepsilon})$. We start the preprocessing phase of our evaluation algorithm for φ_1 with the empty database $D = (E^D)$ where $E^D = \emptyset$. As this empty database has constant size, the preprocessing phase finishes in constant time.

Given an $n \times n$ matrix M, we fix $2n$ distinct elements $\{a_i, b_i : i \in [n]\}$ of **dom**, and perform at most n^2 update steps to insert the tuple (a_i, b_j) into E^D, for all (i, j) with $M_{i,j} = 1$. All this is done within time $n^2 t_u = O(n^{3-\varepsilon})$, and afterwards $E^D = \{(a_i, b_j) : M_{i,j} = 1\}$.

When receiving two vectors $\vec{u}^{\,t}$ and $\vec{v}^{\,t}$ in the dynamic phase of OuMv, we insert and delete loops in D such that the following is true:

- $(a_i, a_i) \in E^D \iff$ the i-th entry of $\vec{u}^{\,t}$ is 1,
- $(b_i, b_i) \in E^D \iff$ the i-th entry of $\vec{v}^{\,t}$ is 1.

Now we enumerate the result of $\varphi_1(x, y) = (Exx \wedge Exy \wedge Eyy)$ evaluated on D for $2n+1$ steps, and we output 1 if there was some pair (a_i, b_j) in the output, and otherwise we output 0. Note that such a pair occurs among the first $2n+1$ output pairs as there are at most $2n$ loops (a_i, a_i) and (b_j, b_j). From the definition of D it follows that the output agrees with $(\vec{u}^{\,t})^{\mathsf{T}} M \vec{v}^{\,t}$. For each $t \in [n]$, all this is done within time $2nt_u + (2n+1)t_d = O(n^{2-\epsilon})$. The overall running time is $O(n^{3-\varepsilon})$. This contradicts the OMv-conjecture by Theorem 5.1. □

Lemma B.2. *The results of the query $\varphi_2(x, y, z_1, z_2) := (Exx \wedge Exy \wedge Eyy \wedge Ez_1z_2)$ can be enumerated with constant delay and constant update time after a linear time preprocessing phase.*

Proof. We first observe that in the static setting, the results of the query $\varphi_1(x, y) := (Exx \wedge Exy \wedge Eyy)$ can be enumerated with constant delay after $O(\|D\|)$ preprocessing (this is easy to see and also follows from [4], since the query is free-connex acyclic).

Our dynamic algorithm for enumerating the results of φ_2 stores a doubly linked list of all elements c such that $(c, c) \in E^D$. Furthermore, we store an adjacency matrix of E^D as well as a doubly linked list of all tuples in E^D.

To achieve constant update time, we implement the latter by three 2-dimensional arrays $\mathtt{A}$, $\mathtt{B}_{next}$, $\mathtt{B}_{prev}$ and two tuples $\mathtt{first_B}$ and $\mathtt{last_B}$, all of which are initialised by 0.

Upon an update command of the form insert $E(i, j)$, we proceed as follows. If $\mathtt{A}[i, j] = 1$, we are done. Otherwise, we set $\mathtt{A}[i, j] := 1$. If $\mathtt{last_B} = 0$, then we set $\mathtt{first_B} := \mathtt{last_B} := [i, j]$. Otherwise, we set $[i', j'] := \mathtt{last_B}$, $\mathtt{B}_{prev}[i, j] := [i', j']$, $\mathtt{B}_{next}[i', j'] := [i, j]$, and $\mathtt{last_B} := [i, j]$.

Upon an update command of the form delete $E(i, j)$, we proceed as follows. If $\mathtt{A}[i, j] = 0$, we are done. Otherwise, we set $\mathtt{A}[i,j] := 0$. If $[i,j] = \mathtt{first_B} = \mathtt{last_B}$, then we set $\mathtt{first_B} := \mathtt{last_B} := 0$ and $\mathtt{B}_{next}[i,j] := \mathtt{B}_{prev}[i,j] := 0$. Otherwise, if $\mathtt{first_B} = [i,j]$, then we set $\mathtt{first_B} := \mathtt{B}_{next}[i,j]$ and $\mathtt{B}_{prev}\mathtt{first_B} := \mathtt{B}_{next}[i,j] := 0$. Otherwise, if $\mathtt{last_B} = [i,j]$, then we set $\mathtt{last_B} := \mathtt{B}_{prev}[i,j]$ and $\mathtt{B}_{next}\mathtt{last_B} := \mathtt{B}_{prev}[i,j] := 0$. Otherwise, we set $\mathtt{B}_{next}\mathtt{B}_{prev}[i,j] := \mathtt{B}_{next}[i,j]$, $\mathtt{B}_{prev}\mathtt{B}_{next}[i,j] := \mathtt{B}_{prev}[i,j]$, and $\mathtt{B}_{prev}[i,j] := \mathtt{B}_{next}[i,j] := 0$.

Of course, we can use a similar data structure to store, and update within constant time, the doubly linked list of all elements c such that $(c,c) \in E^D$.

Upon a call of the **enumerate** routine, we let c_0 be the first element in the list of all elements c such that $(c,c) \in E^D$. If no such element exists, we know that the query result is empty, and we can immediately output the end-of-enumeration message EOE. Otherwise, we immediately start to output all tuples $(c_0, c_0) \times E^D$ with constant delay t_d (where we choose the constant t_d to be large enough). As this takes time $t_d|E^D| = \Omega(t_d\|D\|)$, there is enough time to perform, in the meantime, the full linear time preprocessing phase of the static enumeration algorithm for the query $\varphi_1(x,y)$ on the database D' that is obtained from D by deleting the tuple (c_0, c_0). This allows to afterwards enumerate with constant delay all remaining tuples in $\varphi_2(D)$, i.e., all tuples in $\varphi_1(D') \times E^D$. □

C. DETAILS OMITTED IN THE UPPER BOUND SECTION

Proof of Lemma 6.3.
First note that, in general, we have $\widetilde{\mathcal{E}}^i = \emptyset \iff \mathcal{E}^i = \emptyset$, and hence $\widetilde{C}^i = 0 \iff C^i = 0$. If $N(v) \cap \text{free}(\varphi) = \emptyset$, then the lemma holds as $\widetilde{\mathcal{E}}^i$ is either empty or consists (only) of the assignment $\alpha_{|\text{free}(\varphi)}$, and hence $\widetilde{C}^i \in \{0,1\}$. Now suppose that $N(v) \cap \text{free}(\varphi) \neq \emptyset$ and $C^i > 0$. Because i is fit and because all descendants of quantified variables are quantified, it follows that for every $u \in N(v) \setminus \text{free}(\varphi)$ we have $(D, \alpha\frac{a}{v}) \models \exists\overline{x} \bigwedge_{\psi \in \text{atoms}(u)} \psi$. Therefore, by the same argument as in the proof of Lemma 6.2 we obtain that $|\widetilde{\mathcal{E}}^i| = \prod_{u \in N(v)\cap\text{free}(\varphi)} \big(\sum_{i' \in \mathcal{L}^i_u} |\widetilde{\mathcal{E}}^{i'}|\big) = \prod_{u \in N(v)\cap\text{free}(\varphi)} \widetilde{C}^i_u$. □

Algorithm 1 Enumeration algorithm

Input: Data structure D, tree T' with vertices $V' = \{y_1, \ldots, y_k\}$ (in document order) for query $\varphi(x_1, \ldots, x_k)$ (with $\{x_1, \ldots, x_k\} = V'$)
Variables: Item variables $i_{y_\ell} = [y_\ell, \alpha, a_\ell]$ for $\ell \in [k]$.

if $\mathcal{L}_{\text{start}} = \emptyset$ **then**
  Halt and output the end-of-enum. message EOE.
Let i_{y_1} be the first element of the start-list $\mathcal{L}_{\text{start}}$.
for $\mu = 2$ **to** k **do**
  $i_{y_\mu} \leftarrow \text{SET}((i_{y_1}, \ldots, i_{y_{\mu-1}}), \mu)$
VISIT$(i_{y_1}, \ldots, i_{y_k})$

function SET$(\mathcal{I}, \mu)$
  Input: $\mu \in \{2, \ldots, k\}$ and a list of items $\mathcal{I} = (i_{y_1}, \ldots, i_{y_{\mu-1}})$.
  Let $i_{y_\ell} \in \mathcal{I}$ with $\ell \in [\mu-1]$ be the item such that y_ℓ is the parent of y_μ in T'.
    ▷ Note that $\ell < \mu$ since $y_1, \ldots, y_\mu$ are sorted in document order.
  return the first element of the y_μ-list of i_{y_ℓ}

procedure VISIT$(\mathcal{I})$
  Input: A list of items $\mathcal{I} = (i_{y_1}, \ldots, i_{y_k})$.
  Output the tuple $(a_1, \ldots, a_k)$, where a_ℓ is the constant of item i_{x_ℓ}, for all $\ell \in [k]$.
  if every item in $\mathcal{I}$ is the last of its list **then**
    Halt and output the end-of-enum. message EOE.
  Let $j \in [k]$ be maximal such that i_{y_j} is not the last item of its list.
  for $\mu = 1$ **to** $j-1$ **do**
    $i'_{y_\mu} \leftarrow i_{y_\mu}$
  $i'_{y_j} \leftarrow$ *next-listitem*$^{i_{y_j}}$
  for $\mu = j+1$ **to** k **do**
    $i'_{y_\mu} \leftarrow \text{SET}((i'_{y_1}, \ldots, i'_{y_{\mu-1}}), \mu)$
  VISIT$(i'_{y_1}, \ldots, i'_{y_k})$.

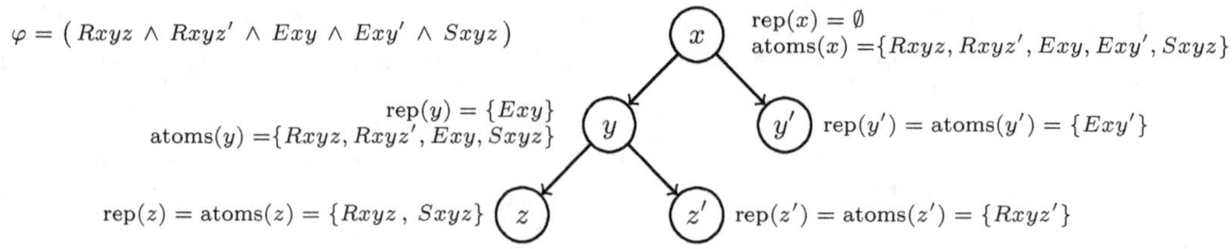

Figure 2: A q-tree T for the query in Example 6.1 along with the atoms represented by the tree's nodes.

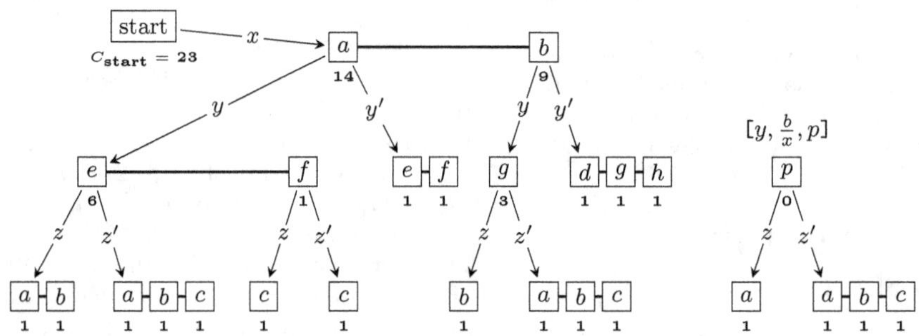

(a) Data structure $\mathtt{D}_0$ for the database D_0.

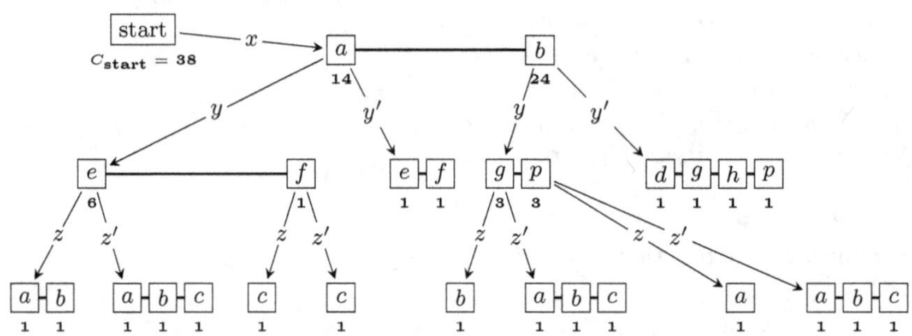

(b) Data structure $\mathtt{D}_1$ after inserting $E(b, p)$ into D_0.

Figure 3: Data structure for the database in Example 6.1. Some unfit items are omitted.

x	a	a	a	a	a	a	a	a	a	a	a	a	a	a	b	b	b	b	b	b	b	b	b
y	e	e	e	e	e	e	e	e	e	e	e	e	f	f	g	g	g	g	g	g	g	g	g
z	a	a	a	a	a	a	b	b	b	b	b	b	c	c	b	b	b	b	b	b	b	b	b
z'	a	a	b	b	c	c	a	a	b	b	c	c	c	c	a	a	a	b	b	b	c	c	c
y'	e	f	e	f	e	f	e	f	e	f	e	f	e	f	d	g	h	d	g	h	d	g	h

Table 1: Enumeration of $\varphi(D_0)$ using data structure $\mathtt{D}_0$ depicted in Figure 3(a).

Communication Cost in Parallel Query Evaluation
A Tutorial

Dan Suciu
University of Washington

We consider the following problem: what is the amount of communication required to compute a query in parallel on p servers, over a large input database? To study this problem we define a variant of Valiant's BSP model [10], called the Massively Parallel Communication (MPC) model, where servers are infinitely powerful and where the cost is measured in terms of the maximum communication per server, and the number of rounds. Query evaluation in this model has been studied for full conjunctive queries in [6, 7, 9]. The model is similar to the MapReduce model of computation, where full conjunctive queries were studied in [1–4].

This tutorial presents parallel algorithms for conjunctive queries and proves lower bounds, under various settings. Using Atserias, Grohe, and Marx' (AGM) upper bound on the query size [5] one can derive a lower bound for the MPC model expressed in terms of the fractional edge covering number of the query's hypergraph, however, no matching algorithm is known for this bound. All algorithms are based on Afrati and Ullman's *Shares* algorithm for the MapReduce model [4], called the *HyperCube* algorithm for the MPC model [6]. The algorithm is based on partitioning the input data using randomized hash functions, and requires the data to be skew-free to ensure uniform partitioning.

We will start by discussing the case when the computation is limited to a single round of communication. In this case, if the data is skew-fee, then a tight bound is given in terms of the fractional vertex (not edge!) covering number of the query's hypergraph, and this result can be extended to skewed input data. Next, we consider the multi-round case. Here, the key algorithmic ingredient is a technique that uses additional rounds in order to handle skewed values in the data. Using this technique it has been shown recently [8] that the tight bound for evaluating a query where all relations have arity at most two is given by the general bound derived from the AGM inequality. The case when the input relations have arbitrary arities remains open; it is not known whether this bound is given in terms of fractional edge cover, or the fractional vertex cover.

Supported by NSF AITF-1535565 and IIS-1247469.

PODS'17, May 14-19, 2017, Chicago, IL, USA
ACM 978-1-4503-4198-1/17/05.
http://dx.doi.org/10.1145/3034786.3056449

1. REFERENCES

[1] F. N. Afrati, M. Joglekar, C. Ré, S. Salihoglu, and J. D. Ullman. GYM: A multiround join algorithm in mapreduce. *CoRR*, abs/1410.4156, 2014.

[2] F. N. Afrati, A. D. Sarma, S. Salihoglu, and J. D. Ullman. Upper and lower bounds on the cost of a map-reduce computation. *PVLDB*, 6(4):277–288, 2013.

[3] F. N. Afrati, N. Stasinopoulos, J. D. Ullman, and A. Vasilakopoulos. Sharesskew: An algorithm to handle skew for joins in mapreduce. *CoRR*, abs/1512.03921, 2015.

[4] F. N. Afrati and J. D. Ullman. Optimizing joins in a map-reduce environment. In *EDBT 2010, 13th International Conference on Extending Database Technology, Lausanne, Switzerland, March 22-26, 2010, Proceedings*, pages 99–110, 2010.

[5] A. Atserias, M. Grohe, and D. Marx. Size bounds and query plans for relational joins. *SIAM J. Comput.*, 42(4):1737–1767, 2013.

[6] P. Beame, P. Koutris, and D. Suciu. Communication steps for parallel query processing. In *Proceedings of the 32nd ACM SIGMOD-SIGACT-SIGART Symposium on Principles of Database Systems, PODS 2013, New York, NY, USA - June 22 - 27, 2013*, pages 273–284, 2013.

[7] P. Beame, P. Koutris, and D. Suciu. Skew in parallel query processing. In *Proceedings of the 33rd ACM SIGMOD-SIGACT-SIGART Symposium on Principles of Database Systems, PODS'14, Snowbird, UT, USA, June 22-27, 2014*, pages 212–223, 2014.

[8] B. Ketsman and D. Suciu. A worst-case optimal multi-round algorithm for parallel computation of conjunctive queries. In *PODS*, 2017.

[9] P. Koutris, P. Beame, and D. Suciu. Worst-case optimal algorithms for parallel query processing. In *19th International Conference on Database Theory, ICDT 2016, Bordeaux, France, March 15-18, 2016*, pages 8:1–8:18, 2016.

[10] L. G. Valiant. A bridging model for parallel computation. *Commun. ACM*, 33(8):103–111, 1990.

Tight Space-Approximation Tradeoff for the Multi-Pass Streaming Set Cover Problem*

Sepehr Assadi†
University of Pennsylvania
sassadi@cis.upenn.edu

ABSTRACT

We study the classic set cover problem in the streaming model: the sets that comprise the instance are revealed one by one in a stream and the goal is to solve the problem by making one or few passes over the stream while maintaining a sublinear space $o(mn)$ in the input size; here m denotes the number of the sets and n is the universe size. Notice that in this model, we are mainly concerned with the space requirement of the algorithms and hence do not restrict their computation time.

Our main result is a resolution of the space-approximation tradeoff for the streaming set cover problem: we show that any α-approximation algorithm for the set cover problem requires $\widetilde{\Omega}(mn^{1/\alpha})$ space, even if it is allowed polylog(n) passes over the stream, and even if the sets are arriving in a random order in the stream. This space-approximation tradeoff matches the best known bounds achieved by the recent algorithm of Har-Peled et al. (PODS 2016) that requires only $O(\alpha)$ passes over the stream in an adversarial order, hence settling the space complexity of approximating the set cover problem in data streams in a quite robust manner. Additionally, our approach yields tight lower bounds for the space complexity of $(1-\varepsilon)$-approximating the streaming maximum coverage problem studied in several recent works.

1. INTRODUCTION

The *set cover* problem is one of the most fundamental optimization problems in computer science, with a wide range of applications in various domains including data mining and information retrieval [2, 46], web host analysis [21], operation research [31], and many others. In this problem, we are given a collection of m sets from a universe $[n]$ and the goal is to output a smallest number of sets whose union is $[n]$, or in other words, *cover* the universe. The set cover problem is one of Karp's original 21 NP-hard problems [38]. A simple greedy algorithm that iteratively picks the set that covers the most number of uncovered elements achieves a $(\ln n)$-approximation [36, 47] and this is best possible unless P = NP [25, 29, 41, 43].

The aforementioned results focus on the tradeoff between approximation guarantee and time complexity of the set cover problem. Nevertheless, in many settings, *space complexity* of the algorithms is crucial to optimize. A canonical example is in applications in big data analysis: in such settings, one would like to design algorithms capable of processing massive datasets using only few passes over the input and limited space. The well-established *streaming model* of computation [1, 44] precisely captures this setting.

In the *streaming set cover* problem, originally introduced by Saha and Getoor [46], the input sets are provided one by one in a stream and the algorithms are allowed to make a small number of passes over the stream while maintaining a sublinear space $o(mn)$ for processing the stream. The streaming set cover problem and the closely related maximum coverage problem have received quite a lot of attention in recent years [4, 6, 10, 19, 22, 24, 27, 33, 34, 42, 46]; we refer the reader to [4, 42] for a comprehensive summary of these results.

Particularly relevant to our work, Demaine et al. [24], have shown an α-approximation algorithm that uses $O(\alpha)$ passes over the stream and needs $\widetilde{O}(mn^{\Theta(1/\log\alpha)})$ space. Recently, Har-Peled et al. [33] provide a significant improvement over this algorithm: they developed an α-approximation, $O(\alpha)$-pass streaming algorithm that requires $\widetilde{O}(mn^{\Theta(1/\alpha)})$ space. They further conjectured that the tradeoff between the number of passes and the space in their algorithm is tight: this is supported by a lower bound of $\widetilde{\Omega}(mn^{1/2p})$ space for p-pass streaming algorithms that compute an *exact* set cover [33].

Notice however that the algorithm of [33] (and [24]) exhibits a somewhat unusual behavior: allowing a larger number of passes over the stream results in a weaker approximation guarantee obtained by the algorithm. This highlights the following natural question: can we achieve a (fixed) *constant* approximation in p-passes and $\widetilde{O}(mn^{\Theta(1/p)})$ space? (a recent algorithm of Bateni et al. [10] achieves a $\log n$-approximation within these bounds.) In general, what is the *space-approximation tradeoff* for streaming set cover if we consider algorithms that are allowed a relatively small number of passes, say up to polylog(n), over the stream? This is precisely the question addressed in this work.

†Supported in part by National Science Foundation grants CCF-1552909, CCF-1617851, and IIS-1447470.

*A full version of this paper is available as an online preprint at [3].

PODS'17, May 14-19, 2017, Chicago, IL, USA

DOI: http://dx.doi.org/10.1145/3034786.3056116

1.1 Our Contributions

Our main result is a tight resolution of the space approximation tradeoff for the streaming set cover problem:

RESULT 1 (MAIN RESULT). *Any α-approximation* polylog(n)*-pass streaming algorithm for the set cover problem requires $\widetilde{\Omega}(mn^{1/\alpha})$ space even on random arrival streams. This lower bound applies even for the weaker goal of estimating the optimal value of the set cover instance (as opposed to finding the actual sets that cover the universe).*

Result 1 is formalized as Theorem 1.

Prior to our work, the best known lower bounds for *randomized multi-pass* streaming algorithms ruled out the possibility of $(\log n/2)$-approximation in p passes and $o(m/p)$ space [45], and exact solution in p passes and $o(mn^{1/2p})$ space [33] (the later holds only if $m = O(n)$). These results left open the possibility of obtaining, say, a 2-approximation in two passes or even an exact answer in $O(\log n)$ passes and $\widetilde{O}(m)$ space. On the other hand, Result 1 smoothly extends the bounds in [45] to the whole range of approximation factors $\alpha = o(\log n)$, proving the first *super-linear* in m lower bound for approximating set cover in *multi-pass* streams. It also significantly improves the bounds in [33] to $\widetilde{\Omega}(mn/p)$ (and all range of m = poly(n)) for p pass streaming algorithms that recover an exact answer[1].

As mentioned earlier, Har-Peled et al. [33] designed an α-approximation algorithm for the set cover problem that requires $\widetilde{O}(mn^{\Theta(1/\alpha)})$ space (for some unspecified constant larger than 2 in the Θ-notation in the exponent). We can show that with proper modifications, this algorithm in fact only requires $\widetilde{O}(mn^{1/\alpha})$ space (see Theorem 2), hence proving a *tight* upper bound for Result 1 (up to logarithmic factors). These results together resolve the space-approximation tradeoff for streaming set cover problem in multi-pass streams. It is worth mentioning that the space-approximation tradeoff for *single-pass* streaming algorithms of set cover has been previously resolved in [4].

Finally, we point out that the lower bound in Result 1 is quite *robust* in the sense that it holds even when the sets are arriving in a random order. This is particularly relevant to the streaming set cover problem as most known techniques for this problem are based on element and set sampling and a-priori one may expect that random arrival streams can facilitate the use of such techniques, resulting in better bounds than the ones achievable in adversarial streams. We point that in general, many streaming problems are known to be distinctly easier in random arrival streams in compare to adversarial streams (see, e.g., [32,37,39]).

We further show an application of our techniques in establishing Result 1 to the *streaming maximum coverage* problem that has been studied in several recent works [5,6,10,20,28,42,46]. In this problem, we are given a collection of m sets from a universe $[n]$ and an integer $k \geq 1$, and the goal is to find k sets that cover the most number of elements in $[n]$. We prove that,

RESULT 2. *Any $(1-\varepsilon)$-approximation* polylog(n)*-pass streaming algorithm for the maximum coverage problem requires $\widetilde{\Omega}(m/\varepsilon^2)$ space even on random arrival streams. This lower bound applies even for the case $k = O(1)$.*

Result 2 is formalized as Theorem 4.

Single-pass $(1-\varepsilon)$-approximation algorithms for this problem that use, respectively, $\widetilde{O}(mk/\varepsilon^2)$ space and $\widetilde{O}(m/\varepsilon^3)$ have been proposed recently in [10,42], and [10]. Our Result 2 is hence *tight* for any $k = O(1)$ (up to logarithmic factors) and within an $O(1/\varepsilon)$ factor of the best upper bound for the larger values of k.

McGregor and Vu [42] have very recently proved an $\widetilde{\Omega}(m)$ lower bound for polylog(n)-pass streaming algorithms that approximate the maximum coverage problem to within a factor better than $(1-1/e)$ (a single-pass $(1-1/e)$-approximation algorithm in $\widetilde{O}(m)$ space is also developed in [10,42]). The importance of Result 2 is thus in establishing the tight dependence on the parameter ε for this problem. This is important as $(1-\varepsilon)$-approximation algorithms for this problem for very small values of ε, i.e., $\varepsilon = 1/n^{\Omega(1)}$, are typically used as a sub-routine in approximating the streaming set cover problem in multiple passes [10,24,33] (see Section 3.4).

En route, we also obtain the following result which may be of independent interest: the communication complexity of computing an exact solution to the set cover problem or the maximum coverage problem in the two-player communication model is $\widetilde{\Omega}(mn)$ bits (see Theorems 3 and 5). This improves upon the previous $\Omega(m)$ lower bounds of Nisan [45] (for set cover) and McGregor and Vu [42] (for maximum coverage). The two-player communication model for set cover has also been studied in [4,19,24,33].

We conclude this section by highlighting the following important aspect of our lower bounds.

REMARK 1.1. *In the hard instances we consider in proving Results 1 and 2, the minimum set cover size and the parameter k in maximum coverage are* small constants *and hence these instances admit a trivial poly-time algorithm in the classical (offline) setting. Our results hence establish the "hardness" of these instances under the space restrictions of the streaming model, independent of the* NP*-hardness of approximating these problems.*

1.2 Technical Overview

We focus here on providing a technical overview of the proof of Result 1 - Result 2 is also proven along similar lines. The starting point of our work is [4], which proved a tight space lower bound for single-pass streaming algorithms of set cover by analyzing the *one-way communication complexity* of this problem (see Section 2 for details on communication complexity).

The overall approach of [4] can be summarized as follows. Consider a communication problem whereby Alice is given a collection of sets $S_1, \ldots, S_m$, Bob is given a set T, and they need to compute an α-approximation of the set cover instance $(S_1, \ldots, S_m, T)$ in the one-way communication model. The input to the players are correlated in that there exists a set $S_{i^\star}$ in Alice's collection which together with Bob's set T cover the whole universe except for a single element. However, if the content of the set $S_{i^\star}$ is unknown to Bob, i.e., Alice's message does not reveal almost all $S_{i^\star}$, Bob needs to

[1]This result also implies that the "right" tradeoff between space and number of passes for obtaining an exact solution to the streaming set cover is in fact linear as opposed to exponential, i.e., n/p as opposed to $n^{1/p}$, as was previously shown in [33].

cover $[n]\setminus T$ (which is a subset of $S_{i^\star}$ except for one element) with sets other than $S_{i^\star}$ to ensure that the single element outside $S_{i^\star}$ is covered. The collection $S_1,\ldots,S_m$ is designed to satisfy the so-called *r-covering* property [41] that states that no small collection of S_i's set can cover another set S_j entirely[2], hence forcing Bob to use many sets to cover the universe. The authors then use the *information complexity* paradigm to reduce the set cover problem on this distribution to multiple instances of a simpler problem (called the *Trap* problem) and prove a lower bound for this problem.

In this paper, we extend this approach to lower bound the two-way communication complexity of the set cover problem and ultimately obtain the desired lower bound in Result 1 for multi-pass streaming algorithms. To do this, we need to address the following issues:

First, the type of distribution used in [4] is clearly not suitable for proving lower bounds in the two-way model. In particular, we need a distribution with both Alice and Bob having $\Omega(m)$ sets and additionally, no clear "signal" to either party as which of the sets are more important, i.e., correspond to the sets $S_{i^\star}$ and T in the above distribution. To achieve this, we employ the r-covering property in a novel way: we first design a collection of sets $Z_1,\ldots,Z_m$ such that no collection of α sets Z_i's can cover the universe $[n]$ unless they contain a single set $Z_{i^\star}$ which is in fact equal to $[n]$ already (for remaining sets Z_i, we have $|Z_i| \approx n - n^{1-1/\alpha}$). Next, we decompose each Z_i into two sets S_i and T_i and provide Alice with S_i, and Bob with T_i. This way, the sets $S_{i^\star}$ and $T_{i^\star}$ form a set cover of size two, and the r-covering property ensures that no other collection of α pairs (S_i,T_i) can cover the universe; we further prove that "mix and matching" the sets (i.e., picking S_i but not T_i or vice versa) in the solution is not helpful either, hence implying that any α-approximation algorithm for set cover needs to find the sets $S_{i^\star}$ and $T_{i^\star}$.

The next step is to prove the lower bound for the above distribution. Unlike the lower bound in the one-way model that was based on hiding the content of the set $S_{i^\star}$, here we need to argue that in fact the index $i^\star$ itself is hidden from the players (as otherwise, one more round of communication can reveal the content of the sets $S_{i^\star}$ and $T_{i^\star}$ as well). Similar to [4], we also use the information complexity paradigm to prove the communication lower bound for this distribution. We embed different instances of the well-known *set disjointness* problem in each pair (S_i,T_i) such that all embedded instances are *intersecting* except for the instance for $S_{i^\star}$ and $T_{i^\star}$ which is *disjoint*. As we seek a direct-sum style argument for two-way protocols, we need a more careful argument than the one in [4] that was tailored for one-way protocols. In particular, we now use the notion of *internal* information complexity (as opposed to *external* information complexity used in [4]) that allows us to use the powerful techniques developed in [9, 11, 14] to obtain the direct-sum result.

Finally, we need to lower bound the information complexity of the set disjointness problem on the specific distribution induced by the set cover instances. The set cover distribution is designed in a way to ensure that the distribution of underlying set disjointness instances matches the known hard input distributions for this problem. However, there is a subtlety here; known information complexity lower bounds for set disjointness (that we are aware of) are all over distributions that are supported only on disjoint sets, i.e., Yes-instances of the problem (see, e.g., [7, 12, 48])[3]. However, for our purpose, we need to lower bound the information cost of set disjointness protocols on distributions that are intersecting. We achieve this using an application of the "information odometer" of [15] (and subsequent work in [30]) to relate the information cost of the protocols on Yes and No instances of the problem together and obtain the result.

We are not done though, as we seek a lower bound for random arrival streams and for this, we extend the previous communication complexity lower bound to the case when the input sets are partitioned randomly across the players, in a similar way as done in previous work [4] (itself based on [16]). There are however some technical differences needed to execute this approach in our two-way communication model in compare to the one-way model in [4] (see Lemma 3.7 for details).

2. PRELIMINARIES

Notation. For any integer $a \geq 1$, we let $[a] := \{1,\ldots,a\}$. We say that a set $S \subseteq [n]$ with $|S| = s$ is a *s-subset* of $[n]$. For a k-dimensional tuple $X = (X_1,\ldots,X_k)$ and index $i \in [k]$, we define $X^{<i} := (X_1,\ldots,X_{i-1})$ and $X^{-i} := (X_1,\ldots,X_{i-1},X_{i+1},\ldots,X_k)$.

We use capital letters to denote random variables. For a random variable A, $\textsc{supp}(A)$ denotes the support of A and $|A| := \log|\textsc{supp}(A)|$. We use $A \perp B$ to denote that the random variables A and B are independent. The notation "$A \in_R U$" indicates that A is chosen uniformly at random from the set U.

We denote the *Shannon Entropy* of a random variable A by $\mathbb{H}(A)$ and the *mutual information* of two random variables A and B by $\mathbb{I}(A:B) = \mathbb{H}(A) - \mathbb{H}(A \mid B) = \mathbb{H}(B) - \mathbb{H}(B \mid A)$. If the distribution $\mathcal{D}$ of the random variables is not clear from the context, we use $\mathbb{H}_{\mathcal{D}}(A)$ (resp. $\mathbb{I}_{\mathcal{D}}(A:B)$). Appendix A summarizes the relevant information theory tools that we use in this paper.

Concentration bounds. We use the following standard version of Chernoff bound (see, e.g., [26]).

PROPOSITION 2.1. *Let $X_1,\ldots,X_n$ be n independent random variables taking values in $[0,1]$ and let $X := \sum_{i=1}^{n} X_i$. Then, for any $0 \leq \varepsilon \leq 1$,*

$$\mathbb{P}\left(|X - \mathbb{E}[X]| > \varepsilon \cdot \mathbb{E}[X]\right) \leq 2 \cdot \exp\left(-\frac{\varepsilon^2 \cdot \mathbb{E}[X]}{2}\right)$$

We also prove the following useful auxiliary lemma that upper bounds the number of elements that a collection of large random sets can cover. The proof is deferred to the full version of the paper [3].

LEMMA 2.2. *Let $\mathcal{S} = \{S_1,\ldots,S_k\}$ be a collection of $(n-s)$-subsets of $[n]$ that are chosen independently and uniformly*

[2]It is worth mentioning that essentially all known lower bounds for the streaming set cover problem, on their core, are based on some variant of this r-covering property; see [19] for more details.

[3]We remark that this is not just a coincidence and in fact is crucial for performing the typical reduction to the AND problem used in proving the lower bound for set disjointness, see, e.g., [48] for more details.

at random. Suppose $U \subseteq [n]$ is another set chosen independent of $\mathcal{S}$; if $k = o(e^s)$, then,

$$\mathbb{P}\left(|U \setminus (S_1 \cup \ldots \cup S_k)| < \frac{|U|}{2} \cdot \left(\frac{s}{2n}\right)^k\right)$$
$$< 2 \cdot \exp\left(-\frac{|U|}{8} \cdot \left(\frac{s}{2n}\right)^k\right).$$

2.1 Communication Complexity and Information Complexity

Communication complexity and information complexity play an important role in our lower bound proofs. We now provide necessary definitions for completeness.

Communication complexity. Our lowers bounds for streaming algorithms are established via communication complexity lower bounds. We use standard definitions of the *two-party communication* model introduced by Yao [49]; see [40] for an extensive overview of communication complexity.

Let P be a relation with domain $\mathcal{X} \times \mathcal{Y} \times \mathcal{Z}$. Alice receives an input $X \in \mathcal{X}$ and Bob receives $Y \in \mathcal{Y}$, where (X, Y) are chosen from a joint distribution $\mathcal{D}$ over $\mathcal{X} \times \mathcal{Y}$. They communicate with each other by exchanging messages such that each message depends only on the private input of the player sending the message and the already communicated messages. The last message communicated is the answer Z such that $(X, Y, Z) \in P$. We allow players to have access to both public and private randomness.

We use π to denote a protocol used by the players. We always assume that the protocol π can be randomized (using both public and private randomness), *even against a prior distribution $\mathcal{D}$ of inputs*. For any $0 < \delta < 1$, we say π is a δ-error protocol for P over a distribution $\mathcal{D}$, if the probability that for an input (X, Y), π outputs some Z where $(X, Y, Z) \notin P$ is at most δ (the probability is taken over the randomness of both the distribution and the protocol).

Definition 1. *The* communication cost *of a protocol π for a problem P on an input distribution $\mathcal{D}$, denoted by $\|\pi\|$, is the worst-case bit-length of the transcript communicated between Alice and Bob in the protocol π, when the inputs are chosen from $\mathcal{D}$.*
The communication complexity *$\mathsf{CC}^{\delta}_{\mathcal{D}}(P)$ of a problem P with respect to a distribution $\mathcal{D}$ is the minimum communication cost of a δ-error protocol π over $\mathcal{D}$.*

Information complexity. There are several possible definitions of information complexity of a communication problem that have been considered depending on the application (see, e.g., [7–9, 14, 18]). We use the notion of *internal information complexity* [9] that measures the average amount of (Shannon) information each player learns about the input of the other player by observing the transcript of the protocol. Formally,

Definition 2. *Consider an input distribution $\mathcal{D}$ and a protocol π (for some problem P). Let $(X, Y) \sim \mathcal{D}$ be the input of Alice and Bob and assume $\Pi := \Pi(X, Y)$ denotes the transcript of the protocol* concatenated *with the public randomness R used by π. The* (internal) information cost *$\mathsf{ICost}_{\mathcal{D}}(\pi)$ of a protocol π with respect to $\mathcal{D}$ is then $\mathbb{I}_{\mathcal{D}}(\Pi : X \mid Y) + \mathbb{I}_{\mathcal{D}}(\Pi : Y \mid X)$.*
The information complexity *$\mathsf{IC}^{\delta}_{\mathcal{D}}(P)$ of P with respect to a distribution $\mathcal{D}$ is the minimum $\mathsf{ICost}_{\mathcal{D}}(\pi)$ taken over all δ-error protocols π for P over $\mathcal{D}$.*

Note that any public coin protocol is a distribution over private coins protocols, run by first using public randomness to sample a random string $R = r$ and then running the corresponding private coin protocol π^r. We also use Π^r to denote the transcript of the protocol π^r. We have the following well-known claim (see full version of the paper [3] for a proof).

Claim 2.3. *For any distribution $\mathcal{D}$ and any protocol π, let R be the public randomness used in π; then, $\mathsf{ICost}_{\mathcal{D}}(\pi) = \mathbb{I}_{\mathcal{D}}(\Pi : X \mid Y, R) + \mathbb{I}_{\mathcal{D}}(\Pi : Y \mid X, R)$.*

The following well-known proposition relates communication complexity and internal information complexity (see, e.g., [14] for a proof).

Proposition 2.4. *For any distribution $\mathcal{D}$ and any protocol π: $\mathsf{ICost}_{\mathcal{D}}(\pi) \leq \|\pi\|$. Moreover, for any parameter $0 < \delta < 1$: $\mathsf{IC}^{\delta}_{\mathcal{D}}(P) \leq \mathsf{CC}^{\delta}_{\mathcal{D}}(P)$.*

2.2 The Set Disjointness Problem

We shall use the well-known *set-disjointness* communication problem (denoted by Disj) in proving Result 1. Fix an integer $t \geq 1$; in Disj_t, Alice and Bob are given two sets $A \subseteq [t]$ and $B \subseteq [t]$, and their goal is to return Yes if $A \cap B = \emptyset$ and No otherwise.

The following is a known hard distribution for Disj_t.

Distribution $\mathcal{D}_{\mathsf{Disj}}$. A hard input distribution for Disj_t.

- Start with $A = B = [t]$.
- For each element $e \in [t]$ independently: w.p. 1/3 drop e from both A and B, w.p. 1/3 drop e from A, and w.p. 1/3 drop e from B.
- Pick $Z \in_R \{0, 1\}$ uniformly at random. If $Z = 1$, pick a uniformly at random element $e^\star \in [t]$ and let A and B both contain $e^\star$ (if $Z = 0$, keep the sets as before).

We further use $\mathcal{D}^{\mathsf{Y}}_{\mathsf{Disj}}$ and $\mathcal{D}^{\mathsf{N}}_{\mathsf{Disj}}$ to denote, respectively, the distribution of Yes and No instances of Disj on $\mathcal{D}_{\mathsf{Disj}}$; in other words, $\mathcal{D}^{\mathsf{Y}}_{\mathsf{Disj}} := (\mathcal{D}_{\mathsf{Disj}} \mid Z = 0)$ and $\mathcal{D}^{\mathsf{N}}_{\mathsf{Disj}} := (\mathcal{D}_{\mathsf{Disj}} \mid Z = 1)$.

The following proposition on the information complexity of Disj is well-known (see, e.g., [7, 12]).

Proposition 2.5. *For any $\delta < 1/2$ and any δ-error protocol π_{Disj} of Disj_t on the distribution $\mathcal{D}_{\mathsf{Disj}}$,*

$$\mathsf{ICost}_{\mathcal{D}^{\mathsf{Y}}_{\mathsf{Disj}}}(\pi_{\mathsf{Disj}}) = \Omega(t).$$

3. THE SPACE-APPROXIMATION TRADE-OFF FOR SET COVER

We prove our main result on the space-approximation tradeoff for the streaming set cover problem in this section. Formally,

Theorem 1. *For any $\alpha = o(\log n / \log\log n)$, $m = poly(n)$, and $p \geq 1$, any* randomized *algorithm that can make p passes over any collection of m subsets of $[n]$ presented one by one in a random order stream and outputs an α-approximation to the optimal value of the set cover problem w.p. larger than 3/4 (over the randomness of both the stream order and the algorithm) must use $\widetilde{\Omega}(mn^{\frac{1}{\alpha}}/p)$ space.*

Theorem 1 formalizes Result 1 in the introduction. We further prove that the tradeoff achieved in Theorem 1 is in fact tight up to logarithmic factors; this is achieved by performing some proper modifications to the algorithm of [33]. Formally,

THEOREM 2. *There exists a streaming algorithm that for any integer $\alpha \geq 1$, and any parameter $\varepsilon > 0$, with high probability, computes an $(\alpha+\varepsilon)$-approximation to the streaming set cover problem using $(2\alpha+1)$ passes over the stream in adversarial order and $\widetilde{O}(mn^{1/\alpha}/\varepsilon^2 + n/\varepsilon)$ space.*

We emphasize that the main contribution of the paper is in proving Theorem 1; we mainly present Theorem 2 to prove a matching upper bound on the bounds in Theorem 1, hence establishing a tight space-approximation tradeoff for the streaming set cover problem.

The rest of this section is mainly devoted to the proof of Theorem 1. We start by introducing some notation. In Section 3.1, we introduce a hard input distribution for the set cover problem in adversarial streams. We prove a lower bound for this distribution in Section 3.2. We extend this lower bound to random arrival streams in Section 3.3 and finish the proof of Theorem 1. Section 3.4 contains the proof of Theorem 2.

Notation. To prove Theorem 1, we prove a lower bound on the communication complexity of the set cover problem: Fix a (sufficiently large) value for n, $m = \text{poly}(n)$, and $\alpha = o(\log n/\log\log n)$; in this section, SetCover refers to the problem of α-approximating the optimal value of the set cover problem with $2m$ sets[4] defined over the universe $[n]$ in the two-player communication model, whereby the sets are partitioned between Alice and Bob.

3.1 A Hard Input Distribution for SetCover

Let t be an integer to be determined later; we use the distribution $\mathcal{D}_{\mathsf{Disj}}$ for Disj_t (introduced in Section 2.2) to design a hard input distribution for SetCover. Before that, we need a simple definition.

DEFINITION 3 (MAPPING-EXTENSION). *For the two sets $[t]$ and $[n]$, we define a* mapping-extension *of $[t]$ to $[n]$ as a function $f : [t] \mapsto 2^{[n]}$, whereby for each $i \in [t]$, $f(i) \subseteq [n]$ is mapped to n/t* unique *elements in $[n]$. Similarly, for any set $A \subseteq [t]$, we abuse the notation and define $f(A) := \bigcup_{i\in A} f(i)$.*

We are now ready to define our hard input distribution for SetCover.

Distribution $\mathcal{D}_{\mathsf{SC}}$. A hard input distribution for SetCover.

Notation. Let $t := 2^{-15} \cdot \left(\frac{n}{\log m}\right)^{\frac{1}{\alpha}}$ and $\mathcal{F}$ be the set of all mapping-extensions of $[t]$ to $[n]$.

- For each $i \in [m]$:
  - Let $(A_i, B_i) \sim \mathcal{D}^{\mathsf{N}}_{\mathsf{Disj}}$ for Disj_t and pick $f_i \in_R \mathcal{F}$ uniformly at random.
  - Let $S_i = [n] \setminus f_i(A_i)$ and $T_i := [n] \setminus f_i(B_i)$.
- Pick $\theta \in_R \{0,1\}$ uniformly at random. If $\theta = 0$, do nothing, otherwise:
  - Sample $i^\star \in_R [m]$ uniformly at random.
  - Resample $(A_{i^\star}, B_{i^\star}) \sim \mathcal{D}^{\mathsf{Y}}_{\mathsf{Disj}}$ for Disj_t and redefine $S_{i^\star}$ and $T_{i^\star}$ as before using the new pair $(A_{i^\star}, B_{i^\star})$.
- Let the input to Alice and Bob be $\mathcal{S} := \{S_i\}_{i\in[m]}$ and $\mathcal{T} := \{T_i\}_{i\in[m]}$, respectively.

[4]To simplify the exposition, we use $2m$ instead of m as the number of sets.

In the following, we use Z to denote any set in $\mathcal{S} \cup \mathcal{T}$, i.e., when it is not relevant whether it belongs to $\mathcal{S}$ or $\mathcal{T}$. For a collection of sets $\mathcal{Z} = \{Z_1, \ldots, Z_\ell\}$, we use $C(\mathcal{Z})$ to denote the set of elements that $\mathcal{Z}$ covers, i.e., $C(\mathcal{Z}) := \bigcup_{i=1}^{\ell} Z_i$. We say that $\mathcal{Z}$ is a *singleton-collection*, if for any $i \in [m]$, at least one of S_i or T_i is *not* present in $\mathcal{Z}$. In contrast, we say that $\mathcal{Z}$ is a *pair-collection*, if for all $i \in [m]$, $S_i \in \mathcal{Z}$ iff $T_i \in \mathcal{Z}$ as well.

REMARK 3.1. *A few remarks are in order:*

(i) W.h.p., for any $i \in [m]$, $|S_i| = 2n/3 \pm o(n)$ and $|T_i| = 2n/3 \pm o(n)$.
(Proof. follows from the definition of the distribution $\mathcal{D}_{\mathsf{Disj}}$ and Chernoff bound).

(ii) For any $i \in [m]$, conditioned on $|S_i| = \ell$, the set S_i is chosen uniformly at random from all ℓ-subsets of $[n]$; similarly for T_i

(iii) For any $i \in [m]$, $S_i \cup T_i = [n] \setminus f_i(A_i \cap B_i)$. Moreover, whenever $(A_i, B_i) \sim \mathcal{D}^{\mathsf{N}}_{\mathsf{Disj}}$, the set $f_i(A_i \cap B_i)$ is a (n/t)-subset of $[n]$ chosen uniformly at random.
(Proof. the first part follows from the fact that f_i maps each $j \in [t]$ to unique elements; the second part is by the random choice of $f_i \in_R \mathcal{F}$ and the fact that $|A_i \cap B_i| = 1$ in this case).

(iv) Whenever $\theta = 0$, for any $i \neq j$, the sets $Z_i \in \{S_i, T_i\}$ and $Z_j \in \{S_j, T_j\}$ are chosen independent of each other ($Z_i \perp Z_j$).

Let $\text{opt}(\mathcal{S}, \mathcal{T})$ denote the size of an optimal set cover in the instance $(\mathcal{S}, \mathcal{T})$. It follows from Remark 3.1-(iii) that whenever $\theta = 1$ in the distribution $\mathcal{D}_{\mathsf{SC}}$, $\text{opt}(\mathcal{S}, \mathcal{T}) = 2$; simply take $S_{i^\star}$ and $T_{i^\star}$ and since $A_{i^\star} \cap B_{i^\star} = \emptyset$, they cover the whole universe. In the following, we prove that when $\theta = 0$, $\text{opt}(\mathcal{S}, \mathcal{T})$ is relatively large. This implies that any α-approximation protocol for SetCover has to essentially determine the value of θ. In the next section, we prove that this task requires a large communication by the players.

LEMMA 3.2. *For $(\mathcal{S}, \mathcal{T}) \sim \mathcal{D}_{\mathsf{SC}}$:*

$$\mathbb{P}\left(\text{opt}(\mathcal{S}, \mathcal{T}) > 2\alpha \mid \theta = 0\right) = 1 - o(1).$$

PROOF. Let $\mathcal{C}$ be any collection of 2α sets from $(\mathcal{S}, \mathcal{T})$. We bound the probability that $\mathcal{C}$ covers the universe $[n]$ entirely, i.e., is a feasible set cover, and then use a union bound on all possible choices for $\mathcal{C}$ to finalize the proof. In the following, we condition on the event $\mathcal{E}_1$ that states that $|S_i| \leq 3n/4$ and $|T_i| \leq 3n/4$ for all $i \in [m]$ (which happens with probability $1 - o(1)$ by Remark 3.1-(i)).

Partition the collection $\mathcal{C}$ into a pair-collection $\mathcal{C}_P$, and a singleton-collection $\mathcal{C}_S$ (this partitioning is always possible and unique by definition). We first lower bound the number of elements that are not covered by the singleton-collection:

CLAIM 3.3. $\mathbb{P}\left(\left|\overline{C(\mathcal{C}_S)}\right| \leq \frac{n}{2^{6\alpha+1}} \mid \mathcal{E}_1\right) \leq 1 - \frac{1}{m^{\omega(\alpha)}}$.

PROOF. Let $\mathcal{C}_S := \{Z_1, \ldots, Z_k\}$; clearly $k = |\mathcal{C}_S| \leq |\mathcal{C}| = 2\alpha$. Without loss of generality, we assume that $k = 2\alpha$. By conditioning on the event $\mathcal{E}_1$ and Remark 3.1-(ii), we know that each Z_i is an ℓ_i-subset of $[n]$, for some $\ell_i \leq 3n/4$, chosen uniformly at random from all ℓ_i-subsets of $[n]$. Again without loss of generality, we simply increase the size of each Z_i so that they all have size exactly $3n/4$. Moreover, since no two sets S_i and T_i are both simultaneously present in $\mathcal{C}_S$, by Remark 3.1-(iv), all sets in $\mathcal{C}_S$ are chosen independent of each other.

Consequently, by Lemma 2.2, for $U = [n]$, $s = n/4$, and collection $\mathcal{C}_S$, we have,

$$\mathbb{P}\left(\left|\overline{C(\mathcal{C}_S)}\right| < \frac{n}{2}\cdot\left(\frac{1}{8}\right)^{2\alpha} \mid \mathcal{E}_1\right) < 2\cdot\exp\left(-\frac{n}{8}\cdot\left(\frac{1}{8}\right)^{2\alpha}\right)$$

A simplification of the above equation, plus using the fact that $\alpha = o(\log n/\log\log n)$, and hence $n/2^{\Theta(\alpha)} = \omega(\alpha\log m)$, proves the final result. ∎

Let $\mathcal{E}_2$ be the event that $\left|\overline{C(\mathcal{C}_S)}\right| \geq \frac{n}{2^{6\alpha+1}}$; in the following, we condition on this event. Now consider the sets in the pair-collection $\mathcal{C}_P$. For any pair $(S_i, T_i) \in \mathcal{C}_P$, we define $C_i := S_i \cup T_i$. Note that there are at most α different possible sets C_i. By Remark 3.1-(iii), the sets C_i's are random sets of size $(n - n/t)$, and by Remark 3.1-(iv), they are chosen independent of each other. By Lemma 2.2, for $U = \overline{C(\mathcal{C}_S)}$, $s = n/t$, and collection of sets C_i's, we have,

$$\begin{aligned}&\mathbb{P}\left(U \setminus (C(\mathcal{C}_P)) = \emptyset \mid \mathcal{E}_1, \mathcal{E}_2\right)\\ &\leq 2\cdot\exp\left(-\frac{n}{2^{6\alpha+4}}\cdot\left(\frac{1}{2t}\right)^{\alpha}\right) \leq \frac{1}{m^{3\alpha}}\end{aligned}$$

We can now conclude,

$$\begin{aligned}&\mathbb{P}\left(\text{opt}(\mathcal{S},\mathcal{T}) \leq 2\alpha\right)\\ &\leq \mathbb{P}\left(\overline{\mathcal{E}_1}\right) + \mathbb{P}\left(\exists\, \mathcal{C} \text{ that covers } [n] \mid \mathcal{E}_1\right)\\ &\leq \mathbb{P}\left(\overline{\mathcal{E}_1}\right) + \sum_{\mathcal{C}}\left(\mathbb{P}\left(\overline{\mathcal{E}_2} \mid \mathcal{E}_1\right) + \mathbb{P}\left(C(\mathcal{C}) = [n] \mid \mathcal{E}_1, \mathcal{E}_2\right)\right)\\ &\leq o(1) + \binom{m}{2\alpha}\cdot\left(\frac{1}{m^{\omega(\alpha)}} + \frac{1}{m^{3\alpha}}\right) = o(1)\end{aligned}$$

proving the lemma. ∎

3.2 The Lower Bound for the Distribution $\mathcal{D}_{\mathsf{SC}}$

Throughout this section, fix π_{SC} as a δ-error protocol for SetCover on the distribution $\mathcal{D}_{\mathsf{SC}}$. We first show that protocol π_{SC} is essentially solving m copies of the Disj_t problem on the distribution $\mathcal{D}_{\mathsf{Disj}}$ (for the parameter t in the distribution $\mathcal{D}_{\mathsf{SC}}$) and then use a direct-sum style argument (similar in spirit to the ones in [9, 11, 14]) to argue that the information cost of π_{SC} shall be m times larger than the information complexity of solving Disj_t. However, to make the direct-sum argument work, we can only consider π_{SC} on the distribution $\mathcal{D}_{\mathsf{SC}} \mid \theta = 0$, i.e., when *all* underlying Disj_t instances are sampled from $\mathcal{D}^{\mathsf{N}}_{\mathsf{Disj}}$. Consequently, we can only lower bound the information cost of π_{SC} based on the information complexity of Disj_t on the distribution $\mathcal{D}^{\mathsf{N}}_{\mathsf{Disj}}$.

LEMMA 3.4. *There exists a $(\delta + o(1))$-protocol π_{Disj} for Disj_t on the distribution $\mathcal{D}_{\mathsf{Disj}}$ such that:*

1. $\mathsf{ICost}_{\mathcal{D}^N_{\mathsf{Disj}}}(\pi_{\mathsf{Disj}}) = \frac{O(1)}{m}\cdot\mathsf{ICost}_{\mathcal{D}_{\mathsf{SC}}}(\pi_{SC})$.

2. $\|\pi_{\mathsf{Disj}}\| = \|\pi_{SC}\|$.

PROOF. We design the protocol π_{Disj} as follows:

Protocol π_{Disj}**.** The protocol for solving Disj_t using a protocol π_{SC} for SetCover.

Input: An instance $(A, B) \sim \mathcal{D}_{\mathsf{Disj}}$. **Output:** Yes if $A \cap B = \emptyset$ and No otherwise.

1. Using public randomness, the players sample an index $i^\star \in_R [m]$ and m mapping-extensions $f_1, \ldots, f_m$ independently and uniformly at random from $\mathcal{F}$.
2. Using public randomness, the players sample the sets $A^{<i^\star}$ and $B^{>i^\star}$ each from $\mathcal{D}^{\mathsf{N}}_{\mathsf{Disj}}$ independently.
3. Using private randomness, Alice samples the sets $A^{>i^\star}$ such that $(A_j, B_j) \sim \mathcal{D}^{\mathsf{N}}_{\mathsf{Disj}}$ (for all $j > i^\star$); similarly Bob samples the sets $B^{<i^\star}$.
4. The players construct the collections $\mathcal{S} := \{S_1, \ldots, S_m\}$ and $\mathcal{T} := \{T_1, \ldots, T_m\}$ by setting $S_i := [n] \setminus f_i(A_i)$ and $T_i := [n] \setminus f_i(B_i)$ (exactly as in distribution $\mathcal{D}_{\mathsf{SC}}$).
5. The players solve the SetCover instance using π_{SC} and output No iff π_{SC} estimates $\text{opt}(\mathcal{S},\mathcal{T}) \leq 2\alpha$ and Yes otherwise.

It is easy to see that the distribution of instances $(\mathcal{S},\mathcal{T})$ created in the protocol π_{Disj} matches the distribution $\mathcal{D}_{\mathsf{SC}}$ for SetCover exactly. Moreover, by Lemma 3.2, $\text{opt}(\mathcal{S},\mathcal{T}) > 2\alpha$ w.p. $1 - o(1)$, whenever $(A, B) \sim \mathcal{D}^{\mathsf{N}}_{\mathsf{Disj}}$ and $\text{opt}(\mathcal{S},\mathcal{T}) = 2$ whenever $(A, B) \sim \mathcal{D}^{\mathsf{Y}}_{\mathsf{Disj}}$. Consequently, since π_{SC} is an α-approximation protocol,

$$\mathbb{P}_{\mathcal{D}_{\mathsf{Disj}}}(\pi_{\mathsf{Disj}}\text{ errs}) \leq \mathbb{P}_{\mathcal{D}_{\mathsf{SC}}}(\pi_{\mathsf{SC}}\text{ errs}) + o(1) \leq \delta + o(1)$$

and hence π_{Disj} is indeed a $(\delta + o(1))$-error protocol for Disj on the distribution $\mathcal{D}_{\mathsf{Disj}}$. Moreover, it is clear that the communication cost of π_{Disj} is at most the communication cost of π_{SC}. We now prove the bound on the information cost of this protocol.

Our goal is to bound the information cost of π_{Disj} whenever the instance (A, B) is sampled from $\mathcal{D}^{\mathsf{N}}_{\mathsf{Disj}}$. Let F be a random variable denoting the tuple $(f_1, \ldots, f_m)$, I be a random variable for $i^\star$ and R be the set of public randomness used by the players. By Claim 2.3,

$$\begin{aligned}\mathsf{ICost}_{\mathcal{D}^{\mathsf{N}}_{\mathsf{Disj}}}(\pi_{\mathsf{Disj}}) &= \mathbb{I}_{\mathcal{D}^{\mathsf{N}}_{\mathsf{Disj}}}(\Pi_{\mathsf{Disj}} : A \mid B, R)\\ &+ \mathbb{I}_{\mathcal{D}^{\mathsf{N}}_{\mathsf{Disj}}}(\Pi_{\mathsf{Disj}} : B \mid A, R)\end{aligned}$$

We now bound the first term in the RHS above (the second term can be bounded exactly the same).

$\mathbb{I}_{\mathcal{D}^{\mathsf{N}}_{\mathsf{Disj}}}(\Pi_{\mathsf{Disj}} : A \mid B, R)$

$$= \mathbb{I}_{\mathcal{D}^{\mathsf{N}}_{\mathsf{Disj}}}(\Pi_{\mathsf{Disj}} : A \mid B, R, I)$$

(I is chosen using public randomness)

$$= \sum_{i=1}^{m} \mathbb{P}(I = i) \cdot \mathbb{I}_{\mathcal{D}^{\mathsf{N}}_{\mathsf{Disj}}}\left(\Pi_{\mathsf{Disj}} : A_i \mid B_i, A^{<i}, B^{>i}, F, I = i\right)$$

($R = (A^{<i}, B^{>i}, F, I)$)

$$= \sum_{i=1}^{m} \frac{1}{m} \cdot \mathbb{I}_{\mathcal{D}^{\mathsf{N}}_{\mathsf{Disj}}}\left(\Pi_{\mathsf{Disj}} : A_i \mid B_i, A^{<i}, B^{>i}, F\right)$$

where the last equality is true since conditioned on $(A, B) \sim \mathcal{D}^{\mathsf{N}}_{\mathsf{Disj}}$, all sets A_j, B_j (for $j \in [m]$) are chosen from $\mathcal{D}^{\mathsf{N}}_{\mathsf{Disj}}$ and hence are independent of the "$I = i$" event[5]. Define $\boldsymbol{A} := (A_1, \ldots, A_m)$ and $\boldsymbol{B} := (B_1, \ldots, B_m)$; we can further derive,

$$\mathbb{I}_{\mathcal{D}^{\mathsf{N}}_{\mathsf{Disj}}}(\Pi_{\mathsf{Disj}} : A \mid B, R)$$

$$= \sum_{i=1}^{m} \frac{1}{m} \cdot \mathbb{I}_{\mathcal{D}^{\mathsf{N}}_{\mathsf{Disj}}}\left(\Pi_{\mathsf{Disj}} : A_i \mid B_i, A^{<i}, B^{>i}, F\right)$$

$$\leq \frac{1}{m} \cdot \sum_{i=1}^{m} \mathbb{I}_{\mathcal{D}^{\mathsf{N}}_{\mathsf{Disj}}}\left(\Pi_{\mathsf{Disj}} : A_i \mid A^{<i}, \boldsymbol{B}, F\right)$$

($A_i \perp B^{<i}$ and hence we can apply Fact A.2)

$$= \frac{1}{m} \cdot \mathbb{I}_{\mathcal{D}^{\mathsf{N}}_{\mathsf{Disj}}}(\Pi_{\mathsf{Disj}} : \boldsymbol{A} \mid \boldsymbol{B}, F)$$

(chain rule of mutual information, Fact A.1-(4))

$$= \frac{1}{m} \cdot \mathbb{I}_{\mathcal{D}^{\mathsf{N}}_{\mathsf{Disj}}}(\Pi_{\mathsf{Disj}} : \mathcal{S} \mid \mathcal{T}, F)$$

$$= \frac{1}{m} \cdot \mathbb{I}_{\mathcal{D}_{\mathsf{SC}}}(\Pi_{\mathsf{SC}} : \mathcal{S} \mid \mathcal{T}, F, \theta = 0)$$

where the second last equality is because $\boldsymbol{A}$ (resp. $\boldsymbol{B}$) and $\mathcal{S}$ (resp. $\mathcal{T}$) determine each other conditioned on F, and last equality is because the distribution of set cover instances and the messages communicated by the players under $\mathcal{D}^{\mathsf{N}}_{\mathsf{Disj}}$ and under $\mathcal{D}_{\mathsf{SC}} \mid \theta = 0$ exactly matches.

Moreover,

$$\mathbb{I}_{\mathcal{D}^{\mathsf{N}}_{\mathsf{Disj}}}(\Pi_{\mathsf{Disj}} : A \mid B, R)$$

$$\leq \frac{1}{m} \cdot \mathbb{I}_{\mathcal{D}_{\mathsf{SC}}}(\Pi_{\mathsf{SC}} : \mathcal{S} \mid \mathcal{T}, F, \theta = 0)$$

$$\leq \frac{2}{m} \cdot \mathbb{I}_{\mathcal{D}_{\mathsf{SC}}}(\Pi_{\mathsf{SC}} : \mathcal{S} \mid \mathcal{T}, F, \theta)$$

(by definition of $\mathbb{I}(\cdot)$ as $\mathbb{P}(\theta = 0) = 1/2$)

$$\leq \frac{2}{m} \cdot (\mathbb{I}_{\mathcal{D}_{\mathsf{SC}}}(\Pi_{\mathsf{SC}} : \mathcal{S} \mid \mathcal{T}, F) + H(\theta)) \qquad \text{(by Fact A.4)}$$

$$= \frac{2}{m} \cdot \mathbb{I}_{\mathcal{D}_{\mathsf{SC}}}(\Pi_{\mathsf{SC}} : \mathcal{S} \mid \mathcal{T}, F) + \frac{2}{m}$$

($H(\theta) = 1$ by Fact A.1-(1))

$$\leq \frac{2}{m} \cdot \mathbb{I}_{\mathcal{D}_{\mathsf{SC}}}(\Pi_{\mathsf{SC}} : \mathcal{S} \mid \mathcal{T}) + \frac{2}{m}$$

($\Pi_{\mathsf{SC}} \perp F \mid \mathcal{S}, \mathcal{T}$ and hence we can apply Fact A.3)

By performing the same exact calculation for $\mathbb{I}_{\mathcal{D}^{\mathsf{N}}_{\mathsf{Disj}}}(\Pi_{\mathsf{Disj}} : B \mid A, R)$, we obtain that,

$$\mathsf{ICost}_{\mathcal{D}^{\mathsf{N}}_{\mathsf{Disj}}}(\pi_{\mathsf{Disj}})$$

$$\leq \frac{2}{m} \cdot (\mathbb{I}_{\mathcal{D}_{\mathsf{SC}}}(\Pi_{\mathsf{SC}} : \mathcal{S} \mid \mathcal{T}) + \mathbb{I}_{\mathcal{D}_{\mathsf{SC}}}(\Pi_{\mathsf{SC}} : \mathcal{T} \mid \mathcal{S})) + \frac{4}{m}$$

$$= \frac{2}{m} \cdot \mathsf{ICost}_{\mathcal{D}_{\mathsf{SC}}}(\pi_{\mathsf{SC}}) + \frac{4}{m} = \frac{O(1)}{m} \cdot \mathsf{ICost}_{\mathcal{D}_{\mathsf{SC}}}(\pi_{\mathsf{SC}})$$

where in the last inequality we used the fact that information cost of π_{SC} is at least 1. ∎

Recall that in Lemma 3.4, we bound the information cost of π_{Disj} on the distribution $\mathcal{D}^{\mathsf{N}}_{\mathsf{Disj}}$ (as opposed to $\mathcal{D}_{\mathsf{Disj}}$); in the following we prove that this weaker bound is still sufficient for our purpose.

LEMMA 3.5. *For any $\delta < 1/2$, any δ-error protocol π_{Disj} for Disj_t on $\mathcal{D}_{\mathsf{Disj}}$ with $\|\pi_{\mathsf{Disj}}\| = 2^{o(t)}$ has*

$$\mathsf{ICost}_{\mathcal{D}^{\mathsf{N}}_{\mathsf{Disj}}}(\pi_{\mathsf{Disj}}) = \Omega(t).$$

By Proposition 2.5, any δ-error protocol for Disj_t (with $\delta < 1/2$) on $\mathcal{D}_{\mathsf{Disj}}$ has $\mathsf{ICost}_{\mathcal{D}^{\mathsf{Y}}_{\mathsf{Disj}}}(\pi_{\mathsf{Disj}}) = \Omega(t)$ (notice again that the information cost is measured on the distribution $\mathcal{D}^{\mathsf{Y}}_{\mathsf{Disj}}$). From this, it is also easy to obtain that $\mathsf{ICost}_{\mathcal{D}_{\mathsf{Disj}}}(\pi_{\mathsf{Disj}}) = \Omega(t)$. However, to prove Lemma 3.5, we need to lower bound the information cost of π_{Disj} under the distribution $\mathcal{D}^{\mathsf{N}}_{\mathsf{Disj}}$.

To achieve this, we can relate the costs $\mathsf{ICost}_{\mathcal{D}^{\mathsf{Y}}_{\mathsf{Disj}}}(\pi_{\mathsf{Disj}})$ and $\mathsf{ICost}_{\mathcal{D}^{\mathsf{N}}_{\mathsf{Disj}}}(\pi_{\mathsf{Disj}})$ to each other. The goal is to argue that if there is a large discrepancy in the information cost of π_{Disj} on $\mathcal{D}^{\mathsf{Y}}_{\mathsf{Disj}}$ and $\mathcal{D}^{\mathsf{N}}_{\mathsf{Disj}}$, then the information cost of the protocol itself can be used to distinguish between these two cases. We can achieve this goal using an elegant construction of an "information odometer" by [15]; informally speaking, the odometer allows the players to "keep track" of the amount of information revealed in a protocol (i.e., the information cost of the protocol), while incurring a relatively small additional information cost overhead.

Intuitively, we can use the odometer to argue that the costs $\mathsf{ICost}_{\mathcal{D}^{\mathsf{N}}_{\mathsf{Disj}}}(\pi_{\mathsf{Disj}}) = \Theta(\mathsf{ICost}_{\mathcal{D}^{\mathsf{Y}}_{\mathsf{Disj}}}(\pi_{\mathsf{Disj}}))$ as follows: suppose towards a contradiction that $\mathsf{ICost}_{\mathcal{D}^{\mathsf{N}}_{\mathsf{Disj}}}(\pi_{\mathsf{Disj}}) = \tau$ for some $\tau = o(\mathsf{ICost}_{\mathcal{D}^{\mathsf{Y}}_{\mathsf{Disj}}}(\pi_{\mathsf{Disj}}))$ and consider a new protocol π'_{Disj} for Disj on $\mathcal{D}_{\mathsf{Disj}}$ which runs π_{Disj} and the information odometer for π_{Disj} in parallel. Whenever the odometer estimates the information cost of π_{Disj} to be larger than $c \cdot \tau$ (for some sufficiently large constant c), the players terminate the protocol and declare that the answer for Disj is No (as information cost of π_{Disj} on $\mathcal{D}^{\mathsf{N}}_{\mathsf{Disj}}$ is typically not much more than τ, while its information cost on $\mathcal{D}^{\mathsf{Y}}_{\mathsf{Disj}}$ is $\omega(\tau)$). If the cost is not estimated more than $c \cdot \tau$ by the end of the protocol, the players output the same answer as in π_{Disj}. As the information cost of the information odometer itself is bounded by $O(\tau)$, this results in protocol π'_{Disj} to have $\mathsf{ICost}_{\mathcal{D}_{\mathsf{Disj}}}(\pi'_{\mathsf{Disj}}) = o(t)$, a contradiction. This argument was first made explicit in [30].

LEMMA 3.6 (LEMMA 15 IN [30]). *Fix any function F, constants $0 < \varepsilon_1 < \varepsilon_2 < 1/2$, input distribution $\mathcal{D}$, and define $\mathcal{D}^N := \mathcal{D} \mid F^{-1}(\mathsf{No})$. For every ε_1-error protocol π for F on $\mathcal{D}$, there exists an ε_2-error protocol π' for F on $\mathcal{D}$ such that:*

$$\mathsf{ICost}_{\mathcal{D}}(\pi') = O\left(\mathsf{ICost}_{\mathcal{D}^N}(\pi) + \log\|\pi\|\right).$$

PROOF OF LEMMA 3.5. Let π'_{Disj} be any δ'-error protocol for Disj on $\mathcal{D}_{\mathsf{Disj}}$ for $\delta' < 1/2$. We first prove that

[5]We point out that this is the exact reason we need to consider information cost of π_{Disj} on $\mathcal{D}^{\mathsf{N}}_{\mathsf{Disj}}$ (instead of $\mathcal{D}_{\mathsf{Disj}}$) as otherwise (A_j, B_j)'s are *not* independent of $I = i$ and hence this equality would not hold.

$\mathsf{ICost}_{\mathcal{D}_{\mathsf{Disj}}}(\pi'_{\mathsf{Disj}}) = \Omega(t)$ using the fact that $\mathsf{ICost}_{\mathcal{D}^{\mathsf{Y}}_{\mathsf{Disj}}}(\pi'_{\mathsf{Disj}}) = \Omega(t)$ as follows:

$$\begin{aligned}
&\mathsf{ICost}_{\mathcal{D}_{\mathsf{Disj}}}(\pi'_{\mathsf{Disj}}) \\
&= \mathbb{I}_{\mathcal{D}_{\mathsf{Disj}}}(\Pi'_{\mathsf{Disj}} : A \mid B) + \mathbb{I}_{\mathcal{D}_{\mathsf{Disj}}}(\Pi'_{\mathsf{Disj}} : B \mid A) \\
&\geq \mathbb{I}_{\mathcal{D}_{\mathsf{Disj}}}(\Pi'_{\mathsf{Disj}} : A \mid B, \theta) + \mathbb{I}_{\mathcal{D}_{\mathsf{Disj}}}(\Pi'_{\mathsf{Disj}} : B \mid A, \theta) - 2\mathbb{H}(\theta) \\
&\qquad\qquad\qquad\qquad\qquad\qquad\qquad\qquad\text{(by Fact A.4)} \\
&\geq \frac{1}{2} \cdot \mathbb{I}_{\mathcal{D}_{\mathsf{Disj}}}(\Pi'_{\mathsf{Disj}} : A \mid B, \theta = 0) \\
&\quad + \frac{1}{2} \cdot \mathbb{I}_{\mathcal{D}_{\mathsf{Disj}}}(\Pi'_{\mathsf{Disj}} : B \mid A, \theta = 0) - 2 \\
&\qquad\qquad\text{(by definition of } \mathbb{I}(\cdot) \text{ and since } \mathbb{H}(\theta) = 1) \\
&= \frac{1}{2} \cdot \left(\mathbb{I}_{\mathcal{D}^{\mathsf{Y}}_{\mathsf{Disj}}}(\Pi'_{\mathsf{Disj}} : A \mid B) + \mathbb{I}_{\mathcal{D}^{\mathsf{Y}}_{\mathsf{Disj}}}(\Pi'_{\mathsf{Disj}} : B \mid A)\right) - 2 \\
&\qquad\qquad\qquad\qquad\qquad\qquad(\mathcal{D}^{\mathsf{Y}}_{\mathsf{Disj}} = \mathcal{D}_{\mathsf{Disj}} \mid \theta = 0) \\
&= \frac{1}{2} \cdot \mathsf{ICost}_{\mathcal{D}^{\mathsf{Y}}_{\mathsf{Disj}}}(\pi'_{\mathsf{Disj}}) - 2 = \Omega(t) \qquad \text{(by Proposition 2.5)}
\end{aligned}$$

Now suppose towards a contradiction that $\mathsf{ICost}_{\mathcal{D}^{\mathsf{N}}_{\mathsf{Disj}}}(\pi_{\mathsf{Disj}})$ is $o(t)$. We can then apply Lemma 3.6 for the function $F = \mathsf{Disj}$, $\varepsilon_1 = \delta$ and $\varepsilon_2 = \delta' < 1/2$ to obtain a protocol π'_{Disj} with $\mathsf{ICost}_{\mathcal{D}_{\mathsf{Disj}}}(\pi'_{\mathsf{Disj}}) = O\left(\mathsf{ICost}_{\mathcal{D}^{\mathsf{N}}}(\pi_{\mathsf{Disj}}) + \log \|\pi_{\mathsf{Disj}}\|\right)$ which is $o(t)$; a contradiction. ∎

THEOREM 3. *For any constant* $\delta < 1/2$, $\alpha = o(\frac{\log n}{\log\log n})$, *and* $m = poly(n)$,

$$\mathsf{CC}^{\delta}_{\mathcal{D}_{\mathsf{SC}}}(\mathsf{SetCover}) = \widetilde{\Omega}(mn^{\frac{1}{\alpha}})$$

PROOF. Let $t = \Theta\left((\frac{n}{\log m})^{\frac{1}{\alpha}}\right)$ and suppose towards a contradiction that there exists a δ-error protocol π_{SC} for $\mathsf{SetCover}$ on the distribution $\mathcal{D}_{\mathsf{SC}}$ with $\|\pi_{\mathsf{SC}}\| = o(mt)$; by Proposition 2.4, $\mathsf{ICost}_{\mathcal{D}_{\mathsf{SC}}}(\pi_{\mathsf{SC}}) = o(mt)$ also. By Lemma 3.4, this implies that there exists a $(\delta + o(1))$-error protocol π_{Disj} for Disj on the distribution $\mathcal{D}_{\mathsf{Disj}}$ such that $\mathsf{ICost}_{\mathcal{D}^{\mathsf{N}}_{\mathsf{Disj}}}(\pi_{\mathsf{Disj}}) = o(t)$, and $\|\pi_{\mathsf{Disj}}\| = o(mt) \leq 2^{o(t)}$ (since $m = \text{poly}(n)$ and $\alpha = o(\frac{\log n}{\log\log n})$). However, this is in contradiction with Lemma 3.5, implying that $\|\pi_{\mathsf{SC}}\| = \Omega(mt)$, hence proving the theorem. ∎

As a corollary of Theorem 3, we have that the space complexity of any α-approximation streaming algorithm for set cover that uses polylog(n) passes on *adversarial streams* is $\widetilde{\Omega}(mn^{\frac{1}{\alpha}})$. In the next section, we extend this result to random arrival streams and complete the proof of Theorem 1.

3.3 Proof of Theorem 1

In order to prove the lower bound in Theorem 1 for random arrival streams, we need to relax the "adversarial partitioning" of the sets in the distribution $\mathcal{D}_{\mathsf{SC}}$, to a randomized partition.

> **Distribution $\mathcal{D}^{\mathsf{rnd}}_{\mathsf{SC}}$.** A random partitioning of the distribution $\mathcal{D}_{\mathsf{SC}}$
>
> - Sample the collections $(\mathcal{S}, \mathcal{T}) \sim \mathcal{D}_{\mathsf{SC}}$.
> - Assign each set in $\mathcal{S} \cup \mathcal{T}$ to Alice w.p. 1/2 and the remainings to Bob.

We show that even this seemingly easier distribution still captures the "hardness" of distribution $\mathcal{D}_{\mathsf{SC}}$. Formally,

LEMMA 3.7. *For any constant* $\delta < 1/4$, $\alpha = o(\frac{\log n}{\log\log n})$, *and* $m = poly(n)$,

$$\mathsf{CC}^{\delta}_{\mathcal{D}^{\mathsf{rnd}}_{\mathsf{SC}}}(\mathsf{SetCover}) = \widetilde{\Omega}(mn^{\frac{1}{\alpha}}).$$

PROOF. Let $\mathcal{S} = \{S_1, \ldots, S_m\}$ and $\mathcal{T} = \{T_1, \ldots, T_m\}$ be the collections of sets sampled from $\mathcal{D}_{\mathsf{SC}}$ in the distribution $\mathcal{D}^{\mathsf{rnd}}_{\mathsf{SC}}$. For a sampled instance in $\mathcal{D}^{\mathsf{rnd}}_{\mathsf{SC}}$, we say that the index $i \in [m]$ is *good* iff S_i is given to one player and T_i to another. Let $G \subseteq [m]$ be the collection of all good indices. The index $i^\star$ is chosen independent of the random partitioning in $\mathcal{D}^{\mathsf{rnd}}_{\mathsf{SC}}$, and hence the probability that $i^\star \in G$ is exactly $|G|/m$. Let $\mathcal{E}$ denote the event that $|G| \geq m/2 - o(m)$ and $i \in G$. We have,

$$\begin{aligned}
\mathbb{P}(\mathcal{E}) &= \mathbb{P}(|G| \geq m/2 - o(m)) \\
&\quad\cdot \mathbb{P}(i^\star \in G \mid |G| \geq m/2 - o(m)) \\
&\geq \mathbb{P}(|G| \geq (1 - o(1)) \cdot \mathbb{E}[G]) \cdot \frac{1 - o(1)}{2} \\
&\geq (1 - o(1)) \cdot \frac{1}{2}
\end{aligned}$$

where the last inequality is by Chernoff bound. Now fix a δ-error protocol π_{SC} for $\mathsf{SetCover}$ on the distribution $\mathcal{D}^{\mathsf{rnd}}_{\mathsf{SC}}$. Then,

$$\mathbb{P}(\pi_{\mathsf{SC}} \text{ errs} \mid \mathcal{E}) \leq \frac{\mathbb{P}(\pi_{\mathsf{SC}} \text{ errs})}{\mathbb{P}(\mathcal{E})} \leq 2\delta + o(1) \qquad (1)$$

This in particular implies that there exists a set $G^\star \subseteq [n]$ with $|G^\star| \geq m/2 - o(m)$, such that conditioned on the set of good indices being $G^\star$ and conditioned on $i^\star \in G^\star$, the probability that π_{SC} errs is at most $2\delta + o(1)$. Note that conditioned on the aforementioned events, the index $i^\star$ is chosen from $G^\star$ uniformly at random. This implies that the distribution of the input given to Alice and Bob limited to the sets in $G^\star$ matches the distribution $\mathcal{D}_{\mathsf{SC}}$ (with the number of the sets being $2 \cdot |G^\star|$ instead of $2m$). We can then use this to embed an instance of $\mathsf{SetCover}$ over the distribution $\mathcal{D}_{\mathsf{SC}}$ into the sets $G^\star$ and obtain a protocol π'_{SC} for $\mathcal{D}_{\mathsf{SC}}$.

More formally, the protocol π'_{SC} works as follows: Given an instance $(\mathcal{S}', \mathcal{T}')$ sampled from $\mathcal{D}_{\mathsf{SC}}$ (with $|\mathcal{S}'| = |\mathcal{T}'| = |G^\star|$), Alice and Bob use public coins to complete their input (i.e., increase the number of the sets to $2m$) by sampling from the distribution $\mathcal{D}^{\mathsf{rnd}}_{\mathsf{SC}}$ conditioned on $G^\star$ (this is possible without any communication as the sets outside $G^\star$ are sampled independent of the sets in $G^\star$). The players then run the protocol π_{SC} on this new instance and return the same answer as this protocol. As the distribution of the $\mathsf{SetCover}$ instances sampled in the protocol π'_{SC} matches the distribution $\mathcal{D}^{\mathsf{rnd}}_{\mathsf{SC}}$ conditioned on $G^\star$ and $i^\star \in G^\star$, by Eq (1), the probability that π'_{SC} errs is at most $2\delta + o(1)$. Since $\delta < 1/4$, we obtain a δ'-error protocol for $\mathsf{SetCover}$ on the distribution $\mathcal{D}_{\mathsf{SC}}$ with $2|G^\star| = \Theta(m)$ sets and universe of size n, for a constant $\delta' < 1/2$. Consequently, by Theorem 3, $\|\pi_{\mathsf{SC}}\| = \|\pi'_{\mathsf{SC}}\| = \widetilde{\Omega}(|G^\star| \cdot n^{\frac{1}{\alpha}}) = \widetilde{\Omega}(mn^{\frac{1}{\alpha}})$, proving the lemma. ∎

We are now ready to prove Theorem 1.

PROOF OF THEOREM 1. Fix a p-pass s-space streaming algorithm $\mathcal{A}$ for the set cover problem over random arrival streams that outputs an α-approximation w.p. at least $1 - \delta$ for $\delta < 1/4$. One can easily turn $\mathcal{A}$ into a δ-error protocol for SetCover on the distribution $\mathcal{D}_{SC}^{rnd}$: Alice and Bob take a random permutation of their inputs and then treat their combined input as a set stream and run $\mathcal{A}$ on that. The random partitioning of the input plus the random permutation taken by the players ensure that the constructed stream is a random permutation of the input sets. Consequently, this protocol is a δ-error protocol for SetCover on $\mathcal{D}_{SC}^{rnd}$ that uses $O(p \cdot s)$ bits of communication. Since $\delta < 1/4$, by Lemma 3.7, $p \cdot s = \widetilde{\Omega}(mn^{\frac{1}{\alpha}})$, proving the theorem. ∎

3.4 An α-Approximation Algorithm for the Set Cover Problem

In this section, we prove the optimality of the lower bound in Theorem 1 by proving a matching upper bound (i.e. Theorem 2). As stated earlier, our algorithm is a simple modification of the algorithm of [33]. In particular, we obtain our improved algorithm by using a one-shot pruning step as opposed to the iterative pruning of [33], and employing a more careful element sampling (compare the bounds in Lemma 3.12 in this paper with Lemma 2.5 in [33]).

In the following, we assume that we are given a value $\widetilde{\text{opt}}$ which is a $(1+\varepsilon)$-approximation of opt, i.e., the optimal solution size of the given instance. This is without loss of generality as we can run the algorithm in parallel for $O(\log n/\varepsilon)$ guesses for $\widetilde{\text{opt}} \in [1, n]$ and return the smallest computed set cover among all parallel runs.

The general idea behind the algorithm is as follows: we know that $\widetilde{\text{opt}}$ sets are enough to cover the whole universe $[n]$; hence, if we find a $(1-\rho)$-approximate k-cover of the input sets for the parameter $k = \widetilde{\text{opt}}$ and $\rho = 1/n^{1/\alpha}$, we can reduce the number of uncovered elements by a factor of $n^{1/\alpha}$. Repeating this process α times then results in a collection of at most $\alpha \cdot \widetilde{\text{opt}}$ sets that covers the whole universe, i.e., an α-approximate set cover. It is worth mentioning that this is the general principle behind most (but not all) streaming algorithms for set cover, see, e.g. [10, 24, 33, 46].

Notice that we can readily use the maximum coverage streaming algorithms of [10, 42] as a sub-routine to find the approximate k-cover above; however, doing so would result in a sub-optimal algorithm for set cover as these algorithms have space dependence of (at least) $\Omega(m/\rho^2) = \Omega(mn^{2/\alpha})$ (even ignoring the dependence on k, i.e., $\widetilde{\text{opt}}$). In fact, as we prove in the next section (see Result 2), any $(1-\rho)$-approximate k-cover algorithm needs $\Omega(m/\rho^2)$ space in general. To bypass this, we crucially use the fact that the aforementioned maximum coverage instances have the additional property that the optimal answer is the whole universe and hence the element sampling technique of [33] (and similar ones in [10, 42]) can be improved for this special case. We now provide the formal description of the algorithm.

Algorithm 1. An α-approximation algorithm for the streaming set cover problem.

Input. A stream $\mathcal{S} = (S_1, \ldots, S_m)$ of subsets of $[n]$, and a $(1+\varepsilon)$-approximation $\widetilde{\text{opt}}$ of $\text{opt}(\mathcal{S})$.
Output. A collection of $(1+\varepsilon) \cdot \alpha \cdot \widetilde{\text{opt}}$ sets that cover the universe.

1. Let $U \leftarrow [n]$ and $\mathsf{SOL} \leftarrow \emptyset$.
2. Make a single pass over the stream and if $|S_i \cap U| \geq n/(\varepsilon \cdot \widetilde{\text{opt}})$, then:
   (a) $\mathsf{SOL} \leftarrow \mathsf{SOL} \cup \{i\}$ and $U \leftarrow U \setminus S_i$.
3. For $j = 1$ to α iterations:
   (a) Let U_{smpl} be a subset of U chosen by picking each element independently and w.p. $p = 16 \cdot \widetilde{\text{opt}} \cdot \log m/n^{1-1/\alpha}$.
   (b) Make a single pass over the stream and for all $i \in [m]$, store $S'_i = S_i \cap U_{\mathsf{smpl}}$ in the memory.
   (c) Find an optimal set cover OPT' of the instance $(S'_1, \ldots, S'_m)$ and let $\mathsf{SOL} \leftarrow \mathsf{SOL} \cup \mathsf{OPT}'$.
   (d) Make another pass over the stream and let $U_{\mathsf{smpl}} \leftarrow U_{\mathsf{smpl}} \setminus \bigcup_{i \in \mathsf{OPT}'} S_i$.
4. Return SOL as a set cover of the input instance.

We start by bounding the space requirement of Algorithm 1 .

LEMMA 3.8. *Algorithm 1 requires $\widetilde{O}(mn^{1/\alpha}/\varepsilon + n)$ space w.p. at least $1 - 1/m^2$.*

PROOF. It is easy to see that maintaining SOL and U requires, respectively, $O(m)$ and $O(n)$ space. In the following, we analyze the space required for storing the sets $(S'_1, \ldots, S'_m)$. After the first pass of the algorithm, no set contains more than $n/(\varepsilon \cdot \widetilde{\text{opt}})$ elements in U. Fix a set $S_i \in \mathcal{S}$; we have,

$$\begin{aligned}\mathbb{E}\,|S_i \cap U_{\mathsf{smpl}}| &= |S_i| \cdot p \\ &\leq n/(\varepsilon \cdot \widetilde{\text{opt}}) \cdot \left(16 \cdot \widetilde{\text{opt}} \cdot \log m/n^{1-1/\alpha}\right) \\ &= 16 \cdot n^{1/\alpha} \cdot \log m/\varepsilon\end{aligned}$$

Hence, by Chernoff bound, w.p. $1 - 1/m^3$, $|S_i \cap U_{\mathsf{smpl}}| = \widetilde{O}(n^{1/\alpha}/\varepsilon)$. The final bound now follows from this and a union bound on all m sets in $\mathcal{S}$. ∎

REMARK 3.9. *One can make the space requirement of Algorithm 1 deterministic by terminating the algorithm whenever it attempts to use a memory more than the bounds in Lemma 3.8. As this event happens with negligible probability, the correctness of the algorithm can be argued exactly the same.*

The following two lemmas establish the correctness of the algorithm.

LEMMA 3.10. *Algorithm 1 picks at most $(\alpha + \varepsilon) \cdot \widetilde{\text{opt}}$ sets in SOL.*

PROOF. It is immediate to see that in the first pass, the algorithm picks at most $\varepsilon \cdot \widetilde{\text{opt}}$ sets as otherwise U would be empty. Moreover, in each subsequent α iterations, the algorithm picks at most $\widetilde{\text{opt}}$ sets since $(S'_1, \ldots, S'_m)$ has a set cover of size at most $\widetilde{\text{opt}}$ (as the original instance had a set cover of size $\leq \widetilde{\text{opt}}$). ∎

LEMMA 3.11. *The set SOL computed by Algorithm 1 is a feasible set cover of $[n]$ w.p. $1 - 1/m$.*

To prove Lemma 3.11, we use the following property of element sampling that first appeared in [24] (similar ideas also appear in [33, 42]); for completeness we provide a self-contained proof of this lemma here.

LEMMA 3.12. *Let $0 < \rho < 1$ be a parameter and $\mathcal{S} = (S_1, \ldots, S_m)$ be a collection of m subsets of $[n]$ with* $\text{opt}(\mathcal{S}) \leq k$. *Suppose U_{smpl} is a subset of $[n]$ obtained by picking each element independently and w.p. $p \geq 16 \cdot k \cdot \log m/(\rho \cdot n)$; then, w.p. $1 - 1/m^2$, any collection of k sets in $\mathcal{S}$ that covers U_{smpl} entirely also covers at least $(1-\rho) \cdot n$ elements in $[n]$.*

PROOF. Fix a collection $\mathcal{C}$ of k subsets in $\mathcal{S}$ that covers less than $(1-\rho) \cdot n$ elements in $[n]$. The probability that this collection covers U_{smpl} entirely is equal to the probability that none of the $\rho \cdot n$ elements in $[n]$ that are not appearing in $\mathcal{C}$ are sampled in U_{smpl}. Hence,

$$\begin{aligned}\mathbb{P}\left(\mathcal{C} \text{ covers } U_{\mathsf{smpl}}\right) &\leq (1-p)^{\rho \cdot n} \\ &\leq \exp\left(-\left(16 \cdot k \cdot \log m/(\rho \cdot n)\right) \cdot (\rho \cdot n)\right) \\ &\leq 1/m^{8k}\end{aligned}$$

Taking a union bound over all $\binom{m}{k} \leq m^k$ possible choices for $\mathcal{C}$ finalizes the result. ∎

PROOF OF LEMMA 3.11. In each of the α iterations, Algorithm 1 implements the sampling in Lemma 3.12 with the parameters $k = \widetilde{\text{opt}}$, and $\rho = n^{-1/\alpha}$. Hence, after each iteration, the number of uncovered elements in U reduces to $|U|/n^{1/\alpha}$ w.p. $1 - 1/m^2$. Consequently, by taking a union bound over the $\alpha \leq m$ iterations, after the α iterations, number of uncovered elements reduces to less than 1, hence proving the lemma. ∎

Theorem 2 now follows from Lemmas 3.8, 3.10, and 3.11 (see the full version [3] for a complete proof).

4. THE SPACE-APPROXIMATION TRADE-OFF FOR MAXIMUM COVERAGE

In this section, we prove a space-approximation tradeoff for the maximum coverage problem (i.e., Result 2),

THEOREM 4. *For any $\varepsilon = \omega(1/\sqrt{n})$, $m = poly(n)$, and $p \geq 1$, any* randomized *algorithm that can make p passes over any collection of m subsets of $[n]$ presented one by one in a random order stream and outputs a $(1-\varepsilon)$-approximation to the optimal value of the maximum coverage problem for $k = 2$ with a sufficiently large constant probability (over the randomness of both the stream order and the algorithm) must use $\widetilde{\Omega}(m/(\varepsilon^2 \cdot p))$ space.*

Similar to previous section, we prove Theorem 4 by considering the communication complexity of the maximum coverage problem: Fix a (sufficiently large) n, $\varepsilon = \omega(1/\sqrt{n})$ and $m = \text{poly}(n)$; $\mathsf{MaxCover}$ refers to the communication problem of $(1-\varepsilon)$-approximating the optimal value of the maximum coverage problem with $2m$ sets defined over the universe $[n]$ and parameter $k = 2$, in the two-player communication model.

Our lower bound for $\mathsf{MaxCover}$ is obtained by reducing this problem to multiple instances of the well-known *gap-hamming-distance* problem via a similar distribution as $\mathcal{D}_{\mathsf{SC}}$ (using an additional simple gadget). In the following, we first introduce the gap-hamming-distance problem and then describe a hard distribution for $\mathsf{MaxCover}$ based on this problem and finalize the proof of Theorem 4.

4.1 The Gap-Hamming-Distance Problem

The *gap-hamming-distance* (GHD) problem is defined as follows. Fix an integer $t \geq 1$; in GHD_t, Alice is given a set $A \subseteq [t]$, Bob is given a set $B \subseteq [t]$ and the goal is to output:

$$\mathsf{GHD}(A,B) = \begin{cases} \mathsf{Yes} & \Delta(A,B) \geq t/2 + \sqrt{t} \\ \mathsf{No} & \Delta(A,B) \leq t/2 - \sqrt{t} \\ \star & \text{otherwise} \end{cases}$$

where $\star$ means that the answer can be arbitrary; here $\Delta(A,B)$ denotes the hamming distance between A and B, i.e., the size of the symmetric difference of A and B.

This problem was originally introduced by [35] and has been studied extensively in the literature (see [17] and references therein). We use the following result on the information complexity of this problem proven in [13][6].

LEMMA 4.1 ([13]). *Let $\mathcal{U}$ be the uniform distribution on pairs of subsets of $[t]$ (chosen independently); there exists an absolute constant $\delta > 0$ such that*

$$\mathsf{IC}^{\delta}_{\mathcal{U}}(\mathsf{GHD}) = \Omega(t).$$

For our purpose, we need to consider the following distribution $\mathcal{D}_{\mathsf{GHD}}$ for GHD instead. Let $a, b \in [t]$ be two parameters to be determined later[7]. Define:

- $\mathcal{D}^{\mathsf{Y}}_{\mathsf{GHD}}$ as the distribution of instances $(A,B) \sim \mathcal{U} \mid \Delta(A,B) \geq t/2 + \sqrt{t}, |A| = a, |B| = b$.
- $\mathcal{D}^{\mathsf{N}}_{\mathsf{GHD}}$ as the distribution of instances $(A,B) \sim \mathcal{U} \mid \Delta(A,B) \leq t/2 - \sqrt{t}, |A| = a, |B| = b$.
- $\mathcal{D}_{\mathsf{GHD}} := \frac{1}{2} \cdot \mathcal{D}^{\mathsf{Y}}_{\mathsf{GHD}} + \frac{1}{2} \cdot \mathcal{D}^{\mathsf{N}}_{\mathsf{GHD}}$.

We use Lemma 4.1 to prove the following result on the information cost of δ-error protocols on the distribution $\mathcal{D}_{\mathsf{GHD}}$, which could be independently useful also. The proof is deferred to the full version of the paper [3].

LEMMA 4.2. *Let $\delta > 0$ be a sufficiently small constant and π_{GHD} be a δ-error protocol for GHD_t on $\mathcal{D}_{\mathsf{GHD}}$ with $\|\pi_{\mathsf{GHD}}\| = 2^{o(t)}$; then, $\mathsf{ICost}_{\mathcal{D}^{\mathsf{N}}_{\mathsf{GHD}}}(\pi_{\mathsf{GHD}}) = \Omega(t)$.*

4.2 Communication Complexity of MaxCover

We propose the following distribution for proving a lower bound on the communication complexity of $\mathsf{MaxCover}$.

Distribution $\mathcal{D}_{\mathsf{MC}}$. A hard input distribution for $\mathsf{MaxCover}$.

Notation. Let $t_1 := 1/\varepsilon^2$, $t_2 := 10 \cdot t_1$, $U_1 := [t_1]$ and $U_2 := [t_1 + 1, t_1 + t_2]$.

- For each $i \in [m]$:
  - Let $(A_i, B_i) \sim \mathcal{D}^{\mathsf{N}}_{\mathsf{GHD}}$ for GHD_{t_1} on the universe U_1.

[6]Technically speaking, [13] bounds the *external* information complexity of GHD as opposed to its *internal* information complexity used in our paper. However, since the distribution in Lemma 4.1 is a product distribution, these two quantities are equal and hence we simply state the bound for the internal information complexity.

[7]The values of a and b are not important for our purpose and are hence only determined in the proof of Lemma 4.2.

- Create $C_i, D_i \subseteq U_2$, by assigning each element in U_2 w.p. 1/2 to C_i and o.w. to D_i.
- Let $S_i := A_i \cup C_i$ and $T_i := B_i \cup D_i$.

- Pick $\theta \in_R \{0,1\}$ uniformly at random. If $\theta = 0$, do nothing, otherwise:
  - Sample $i^\star \in_R [m]$ uniformly at random.
  - Resample $(A_{i^\star}, B_{i^\star}) \sim \mathcal{D}^{\mathsf{Y}}_{\mathsf{GHD}}$ for GHD_{t_1} and redefine $S_{i^\star}$ and $T_{i^\star}$ as before using the new pair $(A_{i^\star}, B_{i^\star})$ (do not change C_i and D_i).
- Let the input to Alice and Bob be $\mathcal{S} := \{S_i\}_{i\in[m]}$ and $\mathcal{T} := \{T_i\}_{i\in[m]}$, respectively.

Define $\text{opt}(\mathcal{S},\mathcal{T})$ as the value of the optimal solution of the maximum coverage problem (for the parameter $k=2$) for the instance $(\mathcal{S},\mathcal{T})$. We wish to argue that $\text{opt}(\mathcal{S},\mathcal{T})$ differs by a $(1\pm\varepsilon)$ factor depending on the choice of θ in the distribution and hence any $(1-\varepsilon)$ approximation algorithm for maximum coverage on this distribution needs to determine the value of θ.

LEMMA 4.3. *Assuming $\varepsilon = o(1/\log n)$, there exists a fixed $\tau \in [n]$ such that for any instance $(\mathcal{S},\mathcal{T}) \sim \mathcal{D}_{\mathsf{MC}}$:*

$$\mathbb{P}\left(\text{opt}(\mathcal{S},\mathcal{T}) \geq (1+\Theta(\varepsilon))\cdot\tau \mid \theta = 1\right) = 1 - o(1)$$
$$\mathbb{P}\left(\text{opt}(\mathcal{S},\mathcal{T}) \leq (1-\Theta(\varepsilon))\cdot\tau \mid \theta = 0\right) = 1 - o(1)$$

PROOF. We first prove that, any $(1-\varepsilon)$-approximate 2-cover in this distribution always has to pick a pair of (S_i, T_i) sets (for some $i \in [m]$). This is achieved by considering the projection of the sets on the universe U_2.

CLAIM 4.4. *W.p. $1-o(1)$:*

(a) For any $i \in [m]$, $|S_i \cup T_i| \geq t_2$.

(b) For any $i \neq j \in [m]$, for any $Z_i \in \{S_i, T_i\}$, and $Z_j \in \{S_j, T_j\}$, $|Z_i \cup Z_j| \leq (3/4 + 0.2)\cdot t_2$.

PROOF. Part (*a*) follows immediately from the fact that U_2 is partitioned between S_i and T_i, and that $|U_2| = t_2$. We now prove Part (*b*). To do so, we prove that $Z_i \cup Z_j$ can only cover (essentially) 3/4 fraction of U_2 w.h.p and since the rest of $Z_i \cup Z_j$ is a subset of U_1 with $|U_1| \leq 0.1 \cdot t_2$, we get the final result.

For any element $e \in U_2$, define an indicator random variable $X_e \in \{0,1\}$ whereby $X_e = 1$ iff $e \in Z_i \cup Z_j$. Since $i \neq j$, the elements in Z_i and Z_j that are in U_2 are chosen independent of each other, and hence $\mathbb{P}(X_e = 1) = 1 - (1/2)^2 = 3/4$. Define $X := \sum_{e\in U_2} X_e$; we have $\mathbb{E}[X] = 3/4 \cdot t_2$ and since X_e variables are independent, by Chernoff bound, $\mathbb{P}(X \geq \mathbb{E}[X] + 0.1\cdot t_2) \leq \exp(-c\cdot t_2) = o(1/m^2)$ (as $t_2 = \omega(\log n)$ and $m = \text{poly}(n)$). The final result now follows from a union bound on all possible ($\leq (2m)^2$) pairs. ∎

Now consider a pair (S_i, T_i) for some $i \in [m]$ and note that $|S_i \cup T_i| = |U_2| + |A_i \cup B_i| = t_2 + |A_i \cup B_i|$; hence we can simply focus on $A_i \cup B_i \subseteq U_1$ part of $S_i \cup T_i$. Moreover, we have that,

$$|A_i \cup B_i| = \frac{1}{2}\cdot(|A_i| + |B_i| + \Delta(A_i, B_i))$$
$$= \frac{1}{2}\cdot(a + b + \Delta(A_i, B_i))$$

where we used the fact that in the distribution $\mathcal{D}_{\mathsf{GHD}}$, $|A_i| = a$ and $|B_i| = b$ always.

Consequently, whenever $(A_i, B_i) \sim \mathcal{D}^{\mathsf{N}}_{\mathsf{GHD}}$, we have,

$$|S_i \cup T_i| = t_2 + |A_i \cup B_i|$$
$$\leq t_2 + (a+b)/2 + t_1/4 - \sqrt{t_1}/2 = (1-\Theta(\varepsilon))\cdot\tau$$

for $\tau = t_2 + (a+b)/2 + t_1/4$. Similarly, whenever $(A_i, B_i) \sim \mathcal{D}^{\mathsf{Y}}_{\mathsf{GHD}}$,

$$|S_i \cup T_i| \geq t_2 + |A_i \cup B_i|$$
$$\geq t_2 + (a+b)/2 + t_1/4 + \sqrt{t_1}/2 = (1+\Theta(\varepsilon))\cdot\tau$$

Combining this with Claim 4.4 finalizes the proof. ∎

By Lemma 4.3, we can use any $(1-\varepsilon)$-approximation protocol for $\mathsf{MaxCover}$ to determine the parameter θ in the distribution $\mathcal{D}_{\mathsf{MC}}$ (by a simple re-parametrizing of the ε by a constant factor). The proof is essentially identical to that of Lemma 3.4 in Section 3.2 and is provided only for the sake of completeness.

LEMMA 4.5. *Let π_{MC} be a δ-error protocol for $\mathsf{MaxCover}$ on $\mathcal{D}_{\mathsf{MC}}$. There exists a $(\delta + o(1))$-protocol π_{GHD} for GHD_{t_1} on the distribution $\mathcal{D}_{\mathsf{GHD}}$ such that:*

1. $\mathsf{ICost}_{\mathcal{D}^{\mathsf{N}}_{\mathsf{GHD}}}(\pi_{\mathsf{GHD}}) = \frac{O(1)}{m}\cdot \mathsf{ICost}_{\mathcal{D}_{\mathsf{MC}}}(\pi_{\mathsf{MC}})$.
2. $\|\pi_{\mathsf{GHD}}\| = \|\pi_{\mathsf{MC}}\|$.

PROOF. We design the protocol π_{GHD} as follows:

Protocol π_{GHD}**.** The protocol for solving GHD_{t_1} using a protocol π_{MC} for $\mathsf{MaxCover}$.

Input: An instance $(A,B) \sim \mathcal{D}_{\mathsf{GHD}}$. **Output:** $\mathsf{GHD}(A,B)$.

1. Using public randomness, the players sample an index $i^\star \in_R [m]$.
2. Using public randomness, the players sample the sets $A^{<i^\star}$ and $B^{>i^\star}$ each from $\mathcal{D}^{\mathsf{N}}_{\mathsf{GHD}}$ independently.
3. Using private randomness, Alice samples the sets $A^{>i^\star}$ such that $(A_j, B_j) \sim \mathcal{D}^{\mathsf{N}}_{\mathsf{GHD}}$ (for all $j > i^\star$); similarly Bob samples the sets $B^{<i^\star}$.
4. Using public randomness the players sample the sets (C_i, D_i) for all $i \in [m]$ from a (distinct) universe U_2 the same as distribution $\mathcal{D}_{\mathsf{MC}}$.
5. The players construct the collections $\mathcal{S} := \{S_1,\ldots,S_m\}$ and $\mathcal{T} := \{T_1,\ldots,T_m\}$ by setting $S_i := A_i \cup C_i$ and $T_i := B_i \cup D_i$ (exactly as in distribution $\mathcal{D}_{\mathsf{MC}}$).
6. The players solve the $\mathsf{MaxCover}$ instance using π_{MC} and output No iff π_{MC} estimates $\text{opt}(\mathcal{S},\mathcal{T}) \leq \tau$ (for the parameter τ in Lemma 4.3) and Yes otherwise.

It is easy to see that the distribution of instances $(\mathcal{S},\mathcal{T})$ created in the protocol π_{MC} matches the distribution $\mathcal{D}_{\mathsf{MC}}$ for

MaxCover exactly, and hence by Lemma 4.3, π_{GHD} is a $(\delta + o(1))$-error protocol for GHD in the distribution $\mathcal{D}_{\mathsf{MC}}$. The bound on the communication cost of π_{MC} is also immediate; in the following we bound the information cost of π_{MC} for (A, B) sampled from $\mathcal{D}^{\mathsf{N}}_{\mathsf{GHD}}$.

Let I be a random variable for $i^\star$ and R be the set of public randomness used by the players. By Claim 2.3,

$$\mathsf{ICost}_{\mathcal{D}^{\mathsf{N}}_{\mathsf{GHD}}}(\pi_{\mathsf{GHD}}) = \mathbb{I}_{\mathcal{D}^{\mathsf{N}}_{\mathsf{GHD}}}(\Pi_{\mathsf{GHD}} : A \mid B, R) + \mathbb{I}_{\mathcal{D}^{\mathsf{N}}_{\mathsf{GHD}}}(\Pi_{\mathsf{GHD}} : B \mid A, R)$$

We now bound the first term in the RHS above (the second term can be bounded exactly the same). In the following, let $\boldsymbol{C}$ and $\boldsymbol{D}$ denote the vector of random variables for C_i's and D_i's, respectively.

$$\begin{aligned}
&\mathbb{I}_{\mathcal{D}^{\mathsf{N}}_{\mathsf{GHD}}}(\Pi_{\mathsf{GHD}} : A \mid B, R) \\
&= \mathbb{I}_{\mathcal{D}^{\mathsf{N}}_{\mathsf{GHD}}}(\Pi_{\mathsf{GHD}} : A \mid B, R, I) && (I \text{ is chosen using public randomness}) \\
&= \mathop{\mathbb{E}}_{i}\left[\mathbb{I}_{\mathcal{D}^{\mathsf{N}}_{\mathsf{GHD}}}\left(\Pi_{\mathsf{GHD}} : A_i \mid B_i, A^{<i}, B^{>i}, \boldsymbol{C}, \boldsymbol{D}, I = i\right)\right] && (R = (A^{<i}, B^{>i}, \boldsymbol{C}, \boldsymbol{D})) \\
&= \sum_{i=1}^{m} \frac{1}{m} \cdot \mathbb{I}_{\mathcal{D}^{\mathsf{N}}_{\mathsf{GHD}}}\left(\Pi_{\mathsf{GHD}} : A_i \mid B_i, A^{<i}, B^{>i}, \boldsymbol{C}, \boldsymbol{D}\right)
\end{aligned}$$

where the last equality is because conditioned on $(A, B) \sim \mathcal{D}^{\mathsf{N}}_{\mathsf{GHD}}$, all sets A_j, B_j (for $j \in [m]$) are chosen from $\mathcal{D}^{\mathsf{N}}_{\mathsf{GHD}}$ and hence are independent of the "$I = i$" event. We can further derive,

$$\begin{aligned}
&\mathbb{I}_{\mathcal{D}^{\mathsf{N}}_{\mathsf{GHD}}}(\Pi_{\mathsf{GHD}} : A \mid B, R) \\
&= \sum_{i=1}^{m} \frac{1}{m} \cdot \mathbb{I}_{\mathcal{D}^{\mathsf{N}}_{\mathsf{GHD}}}\left(\Pi_{\mathsf{GHD}} : A_i \mid B_i, A^{<i}, B^{>i}, \boldsymbol{C}, \boldsymbol{D}\right) \\
&\leq \frac{1}{m} \cdot \sum_{i=1}^{m} \mathbb{I}_{\mathcal{D}^{\mathsf{N}}_{\mathsf{GHD}}}\left(\Pi_{\mathsf{GHD}} : A_i \mid A^{<i}, \boldsymbol{B}, \boldsymbol{C}, \boldsymbol{D}\right) && (A_i \perp B^{<i} \text{ and hence we can apply Fact A.2}) \\
&= \frac{1}{m} \cdot \mathbb{I}_{\mathcal{D}^{\mathsf{N}}_{\mathsf{GHD}}}(\Pi_{\mathsf{GHD}} : \boldsymbol{A} \mid \boldsymbol{B}, \boldsymbol{C}, \boldsymbol{D}) && (\text{chain rule of mutual information, Fact A.1-(4)}) \\
&= \frac{1}{m} \cdot \mathbb{I}_{\mathcal{D}^{\mathsf{N}}_{\mathsf{GHD}}}(\Pi_{\mathsf{GHD}} : \mathcal{S} \mid \mathcal{T}, \boldsymbol{C}, \boldsymbol{D}) \\
&= \frac{1}{m} \cdot \mathbb{I}_{\mathcal{D}_{\mathsf{MC}}}(\Pi_{\mathsf{MC}} : \mathcal{S} \mid \mathcal{T}, \boldsymbol{C}, \boldsymbol{D}, \theta = 0)
\end{aligned}$$

where the second last equality is because $\boldsymbol{A}$ (resp. $\boldsymbol{B}$) and $\mathcal{S}$ (resp. $\mathcal{T}$) determine each other conditioned on $\boldsymbol{C}$ and $\boldsymbol{D}$, and last equality is because the distribution of maximum coverage instances and the messages communicated by the players under $\mathcal{D}^{\mathsf{N}}_{\mathsf{GHD}}$ and under $\mathcal{D}_{\mathsf{MC}} \mid \theta = 0$ exactly matches. Moreover,

$$\begin{aligned}
&\mathbb{I}_{\mathcal{D}^{\mathsf{N}}_{\mathsf{GHD}}}(\Pi_{\mathsf{GHD}} : A \mid B, R) \\
&\leq \frac{1}{m} \cdot \mathbb{I}_{\mathcal{D}_{\mathsf{MC}}}(\Pi_{\mathsf{MC}} : \mathcal{S} \mid \mathcal{T}, \boldsymbol{C}, \boldsymbol{D}, \theta = 0) \\
&\leq \frac{2}{m} \cdot \mathbb{I}_{\mathcal{D}_{\mathsf{MC}}}(\Pi_{\mathsf{MC}} : \mathcal{S} \mid \mathcal{T}, \boldsymbol{C}, \boldsymbol{D}, \theta) && (\text{by definition of } \mathbb{I}(\cdot) \text{ as } \mathbb{P}(\theta = 0) = 1/2) \\
&\leq \frac{2}{m} \cdot (\mathbb{I}_{\mathcal{D}_{\mathsf{MC}}}(\Pi_{\mathsf{MC}} : \mathcal{S} \mid \mathcal{T}, \boldsymbol{C}, \boldsymbol{D}) + H(\theta)) && (\text{by Fact A.4}) \\
&= \frac{2}{m} \cdot \mathbb{I}_{\mathcal{D}_{\mathsf{MC}}}(\Pi_{\mathsf{MC}} : \mathcal{S} \mid \mathcal{T}, \boldsymbol{C}, \boldsymbol{D}) + \frac{2}{m} && (H(\theta) = 1 \text{ by Fact A.1-(1)}) \\
&\leq \frac{2}{m} \cdot \mathbb{I}_{\mathcal{D}_{\mathsf{MC}}}(\Pi_{\mathsf{MC}} : \mathcal{S} \mid \mathcal{T}) + \frac{2}{m} && (\Pi_{\mathsf{MC}} \perp \boldsymbol{C}, \boldsymbol{D} \mid \mathcal{S}, \mathcal{T} \text{ and hence we can apply Fact A.3})
\end{aligned}$$

By performing the same exact calculation for $\mathbb{I}_{\mathcal{D}^{\mathsf{N}}_{\mathsf{GHD}}}(\Pi_{\mathsf{GHD}} : B \mid A, R)$, we obtain that,

$$\begin{aligned}
&\mathsf{ICost}_{\mathcal{D}^{\mathsf{N}}_{\mathsf{GHD}}}(\pi_{\mathsf{GHD}}) \\
&\leq \frac{2}{m} \cdot (\mathbb{I}_{\mathcal{D}_{\mathsf{MC}}}(\Pi_{\mathsf{MC}} : \mathcal{S} \mid \mathcal{T}) + \mathbb{I}_{\mathcal{D}_{\mathsf{MC}}}(\Pi_{\mathsf{SC}} : \mathcal{T} \mid \mathcal{S})) + \frac{4}{m} \\
&= \frac{2}{m} \cdot \mathsf{ICost}_{\mathcal{D}_{\mathsf{MC}}}(\pi_{\mathsf{MC}}) + \frac{4}{m} = \frac{O(1)}{m} \cdot \mathsf{ICost}_{\mathcal{D}_{\mathsf{MC}}}(\pi_{\mathsf{MC}})
\end{aligned}$$

where in the last inequality we used the fact that information cost of π_{MC} is at least 1. ∎

THEOREM 5. *There exists a sufficiently small constant $\delta > 0$, such that for any $\omega(1/\sqrt{n}) \leq \varepsilon \leq o(1/\log n)$, and $m = poly(n)$,*

$$\mathsf{CC}^{\delta}_{\mathcal{D}_{\mathsf{MC}}}(\mathsf{MaxCover}) = \Omega(m/\varepsilon^2).$$

PROOF. Suppose there exists a δ-error protocol π_{MC} for MaxCover on $\mathcal{D}_{\mathsf{MC}}$ for a sufficiently small constant δ (to be determined later), with $\|\pi_{\mathsf{GHD}}\| = o(m/\varepsilon^2)$; by Proposition 2.4, $\mathsf{ICost}_{\mathcal{D}_{\mathsf{MC}}}(\pi_{\mathsf{MC}}) = o(m/\varepsilon^2)$ as well. Hence, by Lemma 4.5, we obtain a $(\delta + o(1))$-error protocol π_{GHD} for GHD_{t_1} on $\mathcal{D}_{\mathsf{GHD}}$ with $\|\pi_{\mathsf{GHD}}\| = o(m/\varepsilon^2)$ and information cost $\mathsf{ICost}_{\mathcal{D}^{\mathsf{N}}_{\mathsf{GHD}}}(\pi_{\mathsf{GHD}}) = o(1/\varepsilon^2) = o(t_1)$. However, since $\|\pi_{\mathsf{GHD}}\| = o(m/\varepsilon^2) = 2^{o(t_1)}$ as $m = \text{poly}(n)$ and $t_1 = \omega(\log n)$, we can apply Lemma 4.2 and have $\mathsf{ICost}_{\mathcal{D}^{\mathsf{N}}_{\mathsf{GHD}}}(\pi_{\mathsf{GHD}})$ is $\Omega(t_1)$ (by taking δ smaller than the bounds in Lemma 4.2); a contradiction with the information cost of π_{GHD} obtained by Lemma 4.5. ∎

We point out that to extend the results in Theorem 5 to $\varepsilon > 1/\log n$ case (i.e., the case not handled by Theorem 5), we can simply use an existing $\widetilde{\Omega}(m)$ lower bound of [42] (Theorem 21) for this range of the parameter ε. We can now prove Theorem 4 by using Theorem 5, the same exact way as we proved Theorem 1; we briefly sketch the proof.

PROOF SKETCH OF THEOREM 4. Define the distribution $\mathcal{D}'_{\mathsf{MC}}$ similar to $\mathcal{D}_{\mathsf{MC}}$ with the difference that after creating the sets $\mathcal{S}$ and $\mathcal{T}$, we randomly partition the sets between the players (i.e., assign each set to Alice w.p. 1/2 and o.w. to Bob). The same argument in Lemma 3.7, combined with Theorem 5 (instead of Theorem 3) proves that for small enough constant δ, $\mathsf{CC}^{\delta}_{\mathcal{D}'_{\mathsf{MC}}}(\mathsf{MaxCover}) = \Omega(m/\varepsilon^2)$.

Furthermore, any p-pass s-space streaming algorithm for maximum coverage on random arrival streams can be turned into an $O(s \cdot p)$-bit communication protocol for MaxCover on $\mathcal{D}'_{\mathsf{MC}}$ (with the same error probability); see the proof of Theorem 1 for more details. This, together with the lower bound on the distribution $\mathcal{D}'_{\mathsf{MC}}$ implies that $s = \Omega(m/(\varepsilon^2 \cdot p))$ as desired. ∎

Acknowledgements

I am grateful to my advisor Sanjeev Khanna for valuable discussions, and to Ehsan Emamjomeh-Zadeh and Sanjeev Khanna for carefully reading the paper and many helpful comments. I also thank the anonymous reviewers of PODS 2017 for many insightful comments and suggestions.

5. REFERENCES

[1] N. Alon, Y. Matias, and M. Szegedy. The space complexity of approximating the frequency moments. In *STOC*, pages 20–29. ACM, 1996.

[2] A. Anagnostopoulos, L. Becchetti, I. Bordino, S. Leonardi, I. Mele, and P. Sankowski. Stochastic query covering for fast approximate document retrieval. *ACM Trans. Inf. Syst.*, 33(3):11:1–11:35, 2015.

[3] S. Assadi. Tight space-approximation tradeoff for the multi-pass streaming set cover problem. *CoRR*, abs/1703.01847, 2017.

[4] S. Assadi, S. Khanna, and Y. Li. Tight bounds for single-pass streaming complexity of the set cover problem. In *Proceedings of the 48th Annual ACM SIGACT Symposium on Theory of Computing, STOC 2016, Cambridge, MA, USA, June 18-21, 2016*, pages 698–711, 2016.

[5] G. Ausiello, N. Boria, A. Giannakos, G. Lucarelli, and V. T. Paschos. Online maximum k-coverage. *Discrete Applied Mathematics*, 160(13-14):1901–1913, 2012.

[6] A. Badanidiyuru, B. Mirzasoleiman, A. Karbasi, and A. Krause. Streaming submodular maximization: massive data summarization on the fly. In *The 20th ACM SIGKDD International Conference on Knowledge Discovery and Data Mining, KDD '14, New York, NY, USA - August 24 - 27, 2014*, pages 671–680, 2014.

[7] Z. Bar-Yossef, T. S. Jayram, R. Kumar, and D. Sivakumar. An information statistics approach to data stream and communication complexity. In *43rd Symposium on Foundations of Computer Science (FOCS 2002), 16-19 November 2002, Vancouver, BC, Canada, Proceedings*, pages 209–218, 2002.

[8] Z. Bar-Yossef, T. S. Jayram, R. Kumar, and D. Sivakumar. Information theory methods in communication complexity. In *Proceedings of the 17th Annual IEEE Conference on Computational Complexity, Montréal, Québec, Canada, May 21-24, 2002*, pages 93–102, 2002.

[9] B. Barak, M. Braverman, X. Chen, and A. Rao. How to compress interactive communication. In *Proceedings of the 42nd ACM Symposium on Theory of Computing, STOC 2010, Cambridge, Massachusetts, USA, 5-8 June 2010*, pages 67–76, 2010.

[10] M. Bateni, H. Esfandiari, and V. S. Mirrokni. Almost optimal streaming algorithms for coverage problems. *CoRR*, abs/1610.08096, 2016.

[11] M. Braverman. Interactive information complexity. In *Proceedings of the 44th Symposium on Theory of Computing Conference, STOC 2012, New York, NY, USA, May 19 - 22, 2012*, pages 505–524, 2012.

[12] M. Braverman, A. Garg, D. Pankratov, and O. Weinstein. From information to exact communication. In *Symposium on Theory of Computing Conference, STOC'13, Palo Alto, CA, USA, June 1-4, 2013*, pages 151–160, 2013.

[13] M. Braverman, A. Garg, D. Pankratov, and O. Weinstein. Information lower bounds via self-reducibility. In *Computer Science - Theory and Applications - 8th International Computer Science Symposium in Russia, CSR 2013, Ekaterinburg, Russia, June 25-29, 2013. Proceedings*, pages 183–194, 2013.

[14] M. Braverman and A. Rao. Information equals amortized communication. In *IEEE 52nd Annual Symposium on Foundations of Computer Science, FOCS 2011, Palm Springs, CA, USA, October 22-25, 2011*, pages 748–757, 2011.

[15] M. Braverman and O. Weinstein. An interactive information odometer and applications. In *Proceedings of the Forty-Seventh Annual ACM on Symposium on Theory of Computing, STOC 2015, Portland, OR, USA, June 14-17, 2015*, pages 341–350, 2015.

[16] A. Chakrabarti, G. Cormode, and A. McGregor. Robust lower bounds for communication and stream computation. In *Proceedings of the 40th Annual ACM Symposium on Theory of Computing, Victoria, British Columbia, Canada, May 17-20, 2008*, pages 641–650, 2008.

[17] A. Chakrabarti and O. Regev. An optimal lower bound on the communication complexity of gap-hamming-distance. In *Proceedings of the 43rd ACM Symposium on Theory of Computing, STOC 2011, San Jose, CA, USA, 6-8 June 2011*, pages 51–60, 2011.

[18] A. Chakrabarti, Y. Shi, A. Wirth, and A. C. Yao. Informational complexity and the direct sum problem for simultaneous message complexity. In *42nd Annual Symposium on Foundations of Computer Science, FOCS 2001, 14-17 October 2001, Las Vegas, Nevada, USA*, pages 270–278, 2001.

[19] A. Chakrabarti and A. Wirth. Incidence geometries and the pass complexity of semi-streaming set cover. In *Proceedings of the Twenty-Seventh Annual ACM-SIAM Symposium on Discrete Algorithms, SODA 2016, Arlington, VA, USA, January 10-12, 2016*, pages 1365–1373, 2016.

[20] J. Chen, H. L. Nguyen, and Q. Zhang. Submodular maximization over sliding windows. *CoRR*, abs/1611.00129, 2016.

[21] F. Chierichetti, R. Kumar, and A. Tomkins. Max-cover in map-reduce. In *Proceedings of the 19th International Conference on World Wide Web, WWW 2010, Raleigh, North Carolina, USA, April 26-30, 2010*, pages 231–240, 2010.

[22] G. Cormode, H. J. Karloff, and A. Wirth. Set cover algorithms for very large datasets. In *Proceedings of the 19th ACM Conference on Information and Knowledge Management, CIKM 2010, Toronto, Ontario, Canada, October 26-30, 2010*, pages 479–488, 2010.

[23] T. M. Cover and J. A. Thomas. *Elements of information theory (2. ed.)*. Wiley, 2006.

[24] E. D. Demaine, P. Indyk, S. Mahabadi, and A. Vakilian. On streaming and communication complexity of the set cover problem. In *Distributed Computing - 28th International Symposium, DISC 2014, Austin, TX, USA, October 12-15, 2014. Proceedings*, pages 484–498, 2014.

[25] I. Dinur and D. Steurer. Analytical approach to parallel repetition. In *Symposium on Theory of Computing, STOC 2014, New York, NY, USA, May 31 - June 03, 2014*, pages 624–633, 2014.

[26] D. P. Dubhashi and A. Panconesi. *Concentration of Measure for the Analysis of Randomized Algorithms.* Cambridge University Press, 2009.

[27] Y. Emek and A. Rosén. Semi-streaming set cover - (extended abstract). In *Automata, Languages, and Programming - 41st International Colloquium, ICALP 2014, Copenhagen, Denmark, July 8-11, 2014, Proceedings, Part I*, pages 453–464, 2014.

[28] A. Epasto, S. Lattanzi, S. Vassilvitskii, and M. Zadimoghaddam. Submodular optimization over sliding windows. *CoRR*, abs/1610.09984, To appear in WWW (2017), 2016.

[29] U. Feige. A threshold of ln n for approximating set cover. *J. ACM*, 45(4):634–652, 1998.

[30] M. Göös, T. S. Jayram, T. Pitassi, and T. Watson. Randomized communication vs. partition number. *Electronic Colloquium on Computational Complexity (ECCC)*, 22:169, 2015.

[31] T. Grossman and A. Wool. Computational experience with approximation algorithms for the set covering problem. *European Journal of Operational Research*, 101(1):81–92, 1997.

[32] S. Guha and A. McGregor. Stream order and order statistics: Quantile estimation in random-order streams. *SIAM J. Comput.*, 38(5):2044–2059, 2009.

[33] S. Har-Peled, P. Indyk, S. Mahabadi, and A. Vakilian. Towards tight bounds for the streaming set cover problem. In *Proceedings of the 35th ACM SIGMOD-SIGACT-SIGAI Symposium on Principles of Database Systems, PODS 2016, San Francisco, CA, USA, June 26 - July 01, 2016*, pages 371–383, 2016.

[34] P. Indyk, S. Mahabadi, and A. Vakilian. Towards tight bounds for the streaming set cover problem. *CoRR*, abs/1509.00118, 2015.

[35] P. Indyk and D. P. Woodruff. Tight lower bounds for the distinct elements problem. In *44th Symposium on Foundations of Computer Science (FOCS 2003), 11-14 October 2003, Cambridge, MA, USA, Proceedings*, pages 283–288, 2003.

[36] D. S. Johnson. Approximation algorithms for combinatorial problems. *J. Comput. Syst. Sci.*, 9(3):256–278, 1974.

[37] M. Kapralov, S. Khanna, and M. Sudan. Approximating matching size from random streams. In *Proceedings of the Twenty-Fifth Annual ACM-SIAM Symposium on Discrete Algorithms, SODA 2014, Portland, Oregon, USA, January 5-7, 2014*, pages 734–751, 2014.

[38] R. M. Karp. Reducibility among combinatorial problems. In *Proceedings of a symposium on the Complexity of Computer Computations, held March 20-22, 1972, at the IBM Thomas J. Watson Research Center, Yorktown Heights, New York.*, pages 85–103, 1972.

[39] C. Konrad, F. Magniez, and C. Mathieu. Maximum matching in semi-streaming with few passes. In *Approximation, Randomization, and Combinatorial Optimization. Algorithms and Techniques - 15th International Workshop, APPROX 2012, and 16th International Workshop, RANDOM 2012, Cambridge, MA, USA, August 15-17, 2012. Proceedings*, pages 231–242, 2012.

[40] E. Kushilevitz and N. Nisan. *Communication complexity.* Cambridge University Press, 1997.

[41] C. Lund and M. Yannakakis. On the hardness of approximating minimization problems. *J. ACM*, 41(5):960–981, 1994.

[42] A. McGregor and H. T. Vu. Better streaming algorithms for the maximum coverage problem. *CoRR*, abs/1610.06199. To appear in ICDT (2017), 2016.

[43] D. Moshkovitz. The projection games conjecture and the np-hardness of ln n-approximating set-cover. *Theory of Computing*, 11:221–235, 2015.

[44] S. Muthukrishnan. Data streams: Algorithms and applications. *Foundations and Trends in Theoretical Computer Science*, 1(2), 2005.

[45] N. Nisan. The communication complexity of approximate set packing and covering. In *Automata, Languages and Programming, 29th International Colloquium, ICALP 2002, Malaga, Spain, July 8-13, 2002, Proceedings*, pages 868–875, 2002.

[46] B. Saha and L. Getoor. On maximum coverage in the streaming model & application to multi-topic blog-watch. In *Proceedings of the SIAM International Conference on Data Mining, SDM 2009, April 30 - May 2, 2009, Sparks, Nevada, USA*, pages 697–708, 2009.

[47] P. Slavík. A tight analysis of the greedy algorithm for set cover. *J. Algorithms*, 25(2):237–254, 1997.

[48] O. Weinstein and D. P. Woodruff. The simultaneous communication of disjointness with applications to data streams. In *Automata, Languages, and Programming - 42nd International Colloquium, ICALP 2015, Kyoto, Japan, July 6-10, 2015, Proceedings, Part I*, pages 1082–1093, 2015.

[49] A. C. Yao. Some complexity questions related to distributive computing (preliminary report). In *Proceedings of the 11h Annual ACM Symposium on Theory of Computing, April 30 - May 2, 1979, Atlanta, Georgia, USA*, pages 209–213, 1979.

APPENDIX

A. TOOLS FROM INFORMATION THEORY

Here, we briefly introduce some basic facts from information theory that are needed in this paper. We refer the interested reader to the textbook by Cover and Thomas [23] for an excellent introduction to this field.

We use the following basic properties of entropy and mutual information (proofs can be found in [23], Chapter 2).

FACT A.1. *Let A, B, and C be three (possibly correlated) random variables.*

1. $0 \leq \mathbb{H}(A) \leq |A|$. $\mathbb{H}(A) = |A|$ *iff A is uniformly distributed over its support.*
2. $\mathbb{I}(A : B) \geq 0$. *The equality holds iff A and B are* independent.
3. Conditioning on a random variable reduces entropy*:* $\mathbb{H}(A \mid B, C) \leq \mathbb{H}(A \mid B)$. *The equality holds iff $A \perp C \mid B$.*
4. The chain rule for mutual information*:* $\mathbb{I}(A, B : C) = \mathbb{I}(A : C) + \mathbb{I}(B : C \mid A)$.

We also use the following two simple facts, which assert conditions in which conditioning can provably increase (resp. decrease) the mutual information.

FACT A.2. *For random variables A, B, C, D, if $A \perp D \mid C$, then $\mathbb{I}(A : B \mid C) \leq \mathbb{I}(A : B \mid C, D)$.*

PROOF. Since A and D are independent conditioned on C, by Fact A.1-(3), $\mathbb{H}(A \mid C) = \mathbb{H}(A \mid C, D)$ and $\mathbb{H}(A \mid C, B) \geq \mathbb{H}(A \mid C, B, D)$. We have,

$$\begin{aligned}\mathbb{I}(A : B \mid C) &= \mathbb{H}(A \mid C) - \mathbb{H}(A \mid C, B) \\ &= \mathbb{H}(A \mid C, D) - \mathbb{H}(A \mid C, B) \\ &\leq \mathbb{H}(A \mid C, D) - \mathbb{H}(A \mid C, B, D) \\ &= \mathbb{I}(A : B \mid C, D)\end{aligned}$$

∎

FACT A.3. *For random variables A, B, C, D, if $A \perp D \mid B, C$, then, $\mathbb{I}(A : B \mid C) \geq \mathbb{I}(A : B \mid C, D)$.*

PROOF. Since $A \perp D \mid B, C$, by Fact A.1-(3), $\mathbb{H}(A \mid B, C) = \mathbb{H}(A \mid B, C, D)$. Moreover, since conditioning can only reduce the entropy (again by Fact A.1-(3)),

$$\begin{aligned}\mathbb{I}(A : B \mid C) &= \mathbb{H}(A \mid C) - \mathbb{H}(A \mid B, C) \\ &\geq \mathbb{H}(A \mid D, C) - \mathbb{H}(A \mid B, C) \\ &= \mathbb{H}(A \mid D, C) - \mathbb{H}(A \mid B, C, D) \\ &= \mathbb{I}(A : B \mid C, B)\end{aligned}$$

∎

Finally, we use the following simple inequality that states that conditioning on a random variable can only increase the mutual information by the entropy of the conditioned variable.

FACT A.4. *For any random variables A, B and C, $\mathbb{I}(A : B \mid C) \leq \mathbb{I}(A : B) + \mathbb{H}(C)$.*

PROOF.

$$\begin{aligned}\mathbb{I}(A : B \mid C) &= \mathbb{I}(A : B, C) - \mathbb{I}(A : C) \\ &= \mathbb{I}(A : B) + \mathbb{I}(A : C \mid B) - \mathbb{I}(A : C) \\ &\leq \mathbb{I}(A : B) + \mathbb{H}(C \mid B) \leq \mathbb{I}(A : B) + \mathbb{H}(C)\end{aligned}$$

where the first two equalities are by chain rule (Fact A.1-(4)), the second inequality is by definition of mutual information and its positivity (Fact A.1-(2)), and the last one is because conditioning can only reduce the entropy (Fact A.1-(3)). ∎

Streaming Algorithms for Measuring H-Impact

Priya Govindan
Rutgers University
Piscataway, NJ, USA
priyagn@cs.rutgers.edu

Morteza Monemizadeh
Rutgers University
Piscataway, NJ, USA
mortezam@cs.rutgers.edu

S. Muthukrishnan
Rutgers University
Piscataway, NJ, USA
muthu@cs.rutgers.edu

ABSTRACT

We consider publication settings with positive user feedback, such as, users publishing tweets and other users retweeting them, friends posting photos and others liking them or even authors publishing research papers and others citing these publications. A well-accepted notion of "impact" for users in these settings is the *H-Index*, which is the largest k such that at least k publications have k or more (positive) feedback.

We study how to calculate H-index on large streams of user publications and feedback. If all the items can be stored, H-index of a user can be computed by sorting. We focus on the streaming setting where as is typical, we do not have space to store all the items.

We present the first known streaming algorithm for computing the H-index of a user in the cash register streaming model using space $\text{poly}(1/\epsilon, \log(1/\delta), \log n)$; this algorithm provides an additive ϵ approximation. For the aggregated model where feedback for a publication is collated, we present streaming algorithms that use much less space, either only dependent on ϵ and even a small constant. We also address the problem of finding "heavy hitters" users in H-index without estimating everyones' H-index. We present randomized streaming algorithms for finding $1+\epsilon$ approximation to heavy hitters that uses space $\text{poly}(1/\epsilon, \log(1/\delta), \log n)$ and succeeds with probability at least $1-\delta$. Again, this is the first sublinear space algorithm for this problem, despite extensive research on heavy hitters in general. Our work initiates study of streaming algorithms for problems that estimate impact or identify impactful users.

1. INTRODUCTION

Consider a system that lets users u_i publish items $p(i, j)$ and have other users respond to the items. These could be for example users in Twitter. Users publish their tweets or embed hashtags, and the others may respond by retweeting the publication or posting with the same hashtag handle and so on. Likewise, a user in Facebook may post a story or picture, and their friends can "like" it. In a more familiar setting, researchers publish their results and others cite the publications. In any publication setting, these responses may be positive or negative to varying extents or even just neutral or mix of these responses. Our research is on the positive impact of users, and hence, for the purposes of our research here, we will only focus on the positive responses. [1]

PODS'17, May 14-19, 2017, Chicago, IL, USA
© 2017 ACM. ISBN 978-1-4503-4198-1/17/05...$15.00
DOI: http://dx.doi.org/10.1145/3034786.3056118

Our focus is on how to measure users' impact. There is a vast theory of studying influence of individual user actions on webpages, posts, etc and also the cumulative impact of all of a users' publications [14, 13, 12]. We adopt a very simple and fundamental notion of impact, well-known in academic world, called the H-index [7]. For each item $p(i, j)$ published by user i, say the *number* of positive responses is $R(i, j)$. Then, the H-index of user i is the largest k such that at least k publications $j_1, j_2, \ldots, j_k$ have k or more (positive) feedback, that is, $R(i, j_\ell) \geq k$, for $1 \leq \ell \leq k$. This is one of the most popular measures of impact in academia, it arose to popularity in the Physics community and is now widespread, with Google Scholar cited frequently by researchers. One of its attractions is that it is parameter-free, for example, it does not focus on the total responses for top 10 cited publications or the total number of publications with at least 10 citations each etc., where 10 is a parameter. It combines the number of publications and the number of responses (citations) for each in a nifty way, to eke out an impact measure. There is vast literature on extensions of H-index, for example, normalizing for areas, years of publication, different transformations like at least k publications have total of k^2 or more (positive) feedback , or applying it to groups of users, and so on [2, 4, 3]. See [1] for a discussion of the research on H-index.

We veer from prior research on H-index, in not studying its applicability or in extending its definition, but in computing it. If we have memory to store every response $r(k, i, j)$ for each publication $p(i, j)$, then it is easy to compute the H-index of user i. For example, one can calculate $R(i, j)$ by aggregating over k for each (i, j), sorting based on $R(i, j)$'s, and determining H-index by considering them in say the decreasing order. However, in applications, the publications and responses arrive *online* over time as they are composed and released. Further, the number of publications and responses maybe very large, and certainly they are prohibitive if we have a large number of users like the popular publication forums. Motivated by this, we study the *streaming versions* of the problem of computing the H-index.

1.1 Our Contribution

Our main results are very small space streaming algorithms for computing the H-index. We consider both aggregated and unaggregated models of streaming, and not only study computing H–index

[1] Our discussion can be extended to the setting when the responses are positive to different extent or when responses are negative only or when responses can be a mix of positive and negative, etc. This will lead to notions of impact of users different from the one we study here.

per user, but also computing the heavy-hitter users, that is, users who have a large H-index without explicitly computing each users' H-index. In more detail, our results are as follows.

- *(Aggregate Streaming Model)* We consider a stream of numbers $R(i,j)$ in arbitrary order of i's and j's, and we design an algorithm for computing H-index of each user i. We present a streaming algorithm that uses only $O(\epsilon^{-1}\log\epsilon^{-1})$ space and returns an $1-\epsilon$ approximation to the H-index of a user. Further if there is a mild lower bound $\Omega(\epsilon^{-3}\log\log n)$ on the ultimate H-index and the publications are considered in a random order, we present an improved algorithm that uses only $O(1)$ storage[2], independent of the number of publications j', number of feedbacks $R(i,j)$'s or the approximation factor ϵ. These are some of the most efficient streaming algorithms one could hope for, not even using $O(\log n)$ words that is standard for a lot of streaming analysis over signals of size n.
- *(Cash Register Streaming Model)* In the so called "cash register" streaming model, we get a stream of responses $r(k,i,j)$, that is, the responses arrive unaggregated. We present randomized streaming algorithms for estimating the H-index to ϵ additive error using space $\text{poly}(1/\epsilon, \log(1/\delta), \log n)$ and with success probability at least $1-\delta$. This is the first sublinear space algorithm for this problem.
- *(Heavy Hitters in H-index)* We address a data mining problem, given a cash register stream of publications and responses, identify the users whose H-index is large. For user i, let their H-index be denoted $h(i)$. We formulate this as a "heavy hitters" problems, that is output set S of users such that for each user $i\in S$, $h(i)\geq \epsilon R$, where R is the total number of responses. In the cash-register streaming model, we present randomized streaming algorithms for finding $1+\epsilon$ approximation to heavy hitters using space $\text{poly}(1/\epsilon, \log(1/\delta), \log n)$ that succeeds with probability at least $1-\delta$. Again, this is the first sublinear space algorithm for this problem, despite extensive research on heavy hitters in general.

We use many of the tools that have been developed in streaming research over the past few years. This includes exponential bucketing methods, distinct or L_0 sampling, group testing with a subset of items to find the heavy hitting ones, etc. We adopt them to calculate H-index, but in the process we significantly improve the results one can get. For example, while using exponential bucketing, we prove that the bucket counters can be reused for our problem and as a result get streaming algorithms that use very little space, sublogarithmic or constant space even, while typical use of these techniques for other streaming problems use logarithmic space or more. In application of group testing to find heavy hitters, there are no decoding methods for finding the one heavy hitter in H-index among a set of users: we design a new algorithm for this problem using the properties of H-index. Our work initiates study of streaming algorithms for problems that estimate impact or identify impactful users. There are many variations of H-index and other impact measures for users, and streaming algorithms for calculating them per user, or mining anomalous users on such impact measures is a rich area for further study.

2. PRELIMINARIES

In this section, we present the definition of H-index and the different data stream models.

[2]The constant is just 6 as our proof shows.

2.1 H-Index

The H-index was suggested in 2005 by Jorge E. Hirsch as a tool for determining theoretical physicists' relative quality and is sometimes called the *Hirsch index* or *Hirsch number*.

DEFINITION 1 (H-INDEX [7]). *Let $V\in\mathbb{N}^n$ be a vector of natural numbers of dimension n. We denote by $h^*(V)$ the maximum number $i\in[n]$ such that the number of elements of V that are greater than or equal to i is at least i, i.e.,*

$$h^*(V) = \arg\max_{i\in[n]} |\{j\in[n] : V[j]\geq i\}| ,$$

where we denote $[n]=\{1,2,\cdots,n\}$. In other words, for the sorted vector V' of V in descending order, h-index of V' (and V) is defined as $h^*(V)=h^*(V')=\max_{i\in[n]}(\min(V'[i]),i)$.

We let $H(V)=\{V[i] : V[i]\geq h^*(V)\}$ be the *support* of the H-index of the vector V which is defined as the set of numbers $V[i]$ that are greater than or equal to the H-index $h^*(V)$. We drop V and V' from $h^*(V)$ and $h^*(V')$ when it is clear from the context.

EXAMPLE 2. *Let $V'=[5,5,6,5,5,5,6,5,5,6]$ be a vector of 10 numbers. Let $V'=[6,6,6,5,5,5,5,5,5,5]$ be the sorted variant of V. Then, for the H-index $h^*(V)$ of V which is the same as $h^*(V')$ we have $h^*(V)=h^*(V')=5=\max_{i\in[10]}\min(V'[i],i))$, but $H(V)=H(V')=V'$.*

2.2 Author, Paper and Citation Model

In this work, we consider publication settings that allows users to give positive feedback on other users's activities. Examples of such a setting include tweets and re-tweeting, Facebook posts and likes and academic papers and citations. We define this setting in the general terms of authors, papers and citations.

Let $\mathcal{A}$ be a set of authors and $\mathcal{P}$ be a set of papers. Each paper $p\in\mathcal{P}$ has a *citation number* c_p which is the number of papers in $\mathcal{P}$ that cite the paper p. As is common in science we assume a paper p cannot cite itself.

We denote the set of papers of an $a\in\mathcal{A}$ by $P_a\subseteq\mathcal{P}$. Similarly, we denote the set of authors of a $p\in\mathcal{P}$ by $A_p\subseteq\mathcal{A}$. For the sake of simplicity, we assume that there is a natural number x for the maximum number of authors that a paper p can have, that is, $|A_p|\leq x$. We represent a paper $p\in\mathcal{P}$ by a tuple $(p,a_1^p,\cdots,a_y^p,c_p)$ for $y\leq x$, where $a_1^p,\cdots,a_y^p$ and c_p are the authors and the citation number of the paper p, respectively. Thus, from now on, we consider a paper $p\in\mathcal{P}$ or $(p,a_1^p,\cdots,a_y^p,c_p)\in\mathcal{P}$, interchangeably.

2.3 Aggregate and Cash-Register Streams

Let $V\in\mathbb{N}^n$ be a vector of natural numbers of dimension n. Let $h^*(V)$ be the H-index of V. We say $\mathcal{S}$ is an *aggregate* stream of the vector V if $\mathcal{S}$ is a (possibly adversarially ordered) stream of the elements of the underlying vector V. We say $\mathcal{S}$ is a *randomly ordered* aggregate stream if $\mathcal{S}$ is a random order chosen uniformly at random from the set of all permutations (or orders) of the elements of the underlying vector V. We say $\mathcal{S}$ is a *cash register* stream if $\mathcal{S}$ is a stream of updates to the underlying vector V, where an update at time t is a pair (i_t,z) for a natural number z that replaces the entity $V[i_t]$ by $V[i_t]+z$.

For the data model described in Section 2.2, the aggregate streaming model would consist of one tuple $(p,a_1^p,\cdots,a_y^p,c_p)$ for each paper p in the dataset, where c_p is the number of citations of the paper. In the cash register model for the above data model, each tuple $(p,a_1^p,\cdots,a_y^p,c_p^i)$ corresponds to the ith update to the number of citations of paper p, such that $c_p=\sum_i c_p^i$. Note that in Section 3, for the sake of simplicity we assume the case when there is only one author in the stream. This can easily be extended to papers with multiple authors and computing H-index for each author.

We say a streaming algorithm $\mathcal{A}$ is a multiplicative (ϵ, δ, s)-approximation algorithm for a stream $\mathcal{S}$ (either aggregate or cash register) if over one pass over $\mathcal{S}$, $\mathcal{A}$ uses a space s to report an estimator $h(V)$ such that

$$\mathbf{Pr}\left[|h^*(V) - h(V)| \le \epsilon h^*(V)\right] \ge 1 - \delta \ .$$

Similarly, we say a streaming algorithm $\mathcal{A}$ is an additive (ϵ, δ, s)-approximation algorithm for a stream $\mathcal{S}$ (either aggregate or cash register) if one pass over $\mathcal{S}$, $\mathcal{A}$ uses a space s reports an estimator $h(V)$ such that

$$\mathbf{Pr}\left[|h^*(V) - h(V)| \le \epsilon n\right] \ge 1 - \delta \ .$$

2.4 ℓ_0 -Sampler

We define an ℓ_0-Sampler as follows.

DEFINITION 3. *(ℓ_0-SAMPLER [5, 11]) Let $0 < \delta < 1$ be a parameter. Let $S = (a_1, t_1), \cdots, (a_i, t_i), \cdots$ be a stream of updates of an underlying vector $x \in \mathbb{R}^n$ where $a_i \in [n]$ and $t_i \in \mathbb{R}$. The i-th update (a_i, t_i) updates the a_i-th element of x using $x[a_i] = x[a_i] + t_i$. An ℓ_0-sampler algorithm for $x \neq 0$ returns FAIL with probability at most δ. Else, with probability $1 - \delta$, it returns an element $j \in [n]$ such that the probability that j-th element is returned is $\Pr[j] = \frac{|x[i]|^0}{\ell_0(x)}$.*

Here, $\ell_0(x) = (\sum_{i \in [n]} |x[i]|^0)$ is the (so-called) "0-norm" of x that counts the number of non-zero entries.

LEMMA 4 ([9]). *Let $0 < \delta < 1$ be a parameter. Then, there exists a linear sketch-based algorithm for ℓ_0-sampling using $O(\log^2 n \log \delta^{-1})$ bits of space.*

3. H-INDEX IN STREAMS

In this section we present our algorithms to compute H-index of a single user in different streaming settings, namely aggregate, random order and cash-register models. In Section 3.1, we consider the aggregate streaming model, where the input stream is the *number* of likes or retweets of different posts of a user. In Section 3.2, we assume that the stream of number of positive feedback is given in a random order. In a cash-register streaming model the input is not the total number of likes or retweets per post, but a sequence of updates when a new like or retweet occurs. In Section 3.3, we present our algorithm to compute H-index of a user when the input is a cash-register model.

3.1 Aggregate Streaming Model

In this section, we first develop a streaming algorithm that using a space $2\epsilon^{-1} \log n$ words reports an $(1 \pm \epsilon)$-estimator of the H-index of a stream. A similar approach was used by Govindan et. al. [6] to compute H-index of core number of nodes in an effort to compute k-cores in graphs. Later we improve the space of this algorithm down to $6\epsilon^{-1} \log 3\epsilon^{-1}$ words. Formally, we first prove the following theorem. The pseudocode of the algorithm and the correctness proof of the algorithm are given after it.

THEOREM 5 (EXPONENTIAL HISTOGRAM). *Let $0 < \epsilon < 1$ be a parameter. Let $V \in \mathbb{N}^n$ be a vector of natural numbers of dimension n whose H-index is $h^*(V)$. Let $\mathcal{S}$ be an arbitrarily (possibly adversarially ordered) stream of the elements of the underlying vector V. Then, there exists a one-pass deterministic streaming algorithm (Algorithm 1) that using space $2\epsilon^{-1} \log n$ words (where each word consists of $\log n$ bits) reports an estimator $h(V)$ such that*

$$(1 - \epsilon)h^*(V) \le h(V) \le h^*(V) \ .$$

Here for the simplicity of the exposition, we assume $n = (1 + \epsilon)^k$ is a power of $(1 + \epsilon)$ and we observe that n is a trivial upper bound for the H-index $h^*(V)$ of an underlying vector V. We consider $\log_{1+\epsilon} n$ guesses of $(1 + \epsilon)^i$ for $h^*(V)$. For each guess $(1+\epsilon)^i$, we design a counter c_i that counts the number of elements of the stream $\mathcal{S}$ that are greater than or equal to $(1+\epsilon)^i$. At the end of the stream, we find the greatest guess $(1 + \epsilon)^i$ whose counter is at least $(1+\epsilon)^i$, but the counter of the subsequent guess $(1+\epsilon)^{i+1}$ is less than $(1 + \epsilon)^{i+1}$.

Algorithm 1: Exponential Histogram

Input: Stream $\mathcal{S}$ of elements of V.
(1) Initialize counters $c_i = 0$ to zero for $i \in [\log_{1+\epsilon} n]$.
(2) For step t that the element $\mathcal{S}_t$ arrives
(3) For $i = 1$ to $\log_{1+\epsilon} n$
(4) If $\mathcal{S}_t \ge (1 + \epsilon)^i$, then $c_i = c_i + 1$
(5) Let $h(V)$=$(1 + \epsilon)^i$ be the greatest threshold such that

$$c_i \ge (1 + \epsilon)^i \text{ and } c_{i+1} < (1 + \epsilon)^{i+1} \ .$$

(6) Output $h(V)$.

PROOF. Observe that there exists an index $i \in [\log_{1+\epsilon} n]$ such that $(1 + \epsilon)^i \le h^*(V) < (1 + \epsilon)^{i+1}$. Let us consider two counters c_i and c_{i+1}. The counter c_i corresponds to the number of elements of the stream $\mathcal{S}$ that are greater than or equal to $(1 + \epsilon)^i$. Similarly, the counter c_{i+1} corresponds to the number of elements of the stream $\mathcal{S}$ that are greater than or equal to $(1 + \epsilon)^{i+1}$. Observe that since $(1+\epsilon)^i \le h^*(V) < (1+\epsilon)^{i+1}$, we have $c_{i+1} < (1+\epsilon)^{i+1}$ and $c_i \ge h^*(V) \ge (1 + \epsilon)^i = h(V)$. Therefore,

$$(1 - \epsilon)h^*(V) \le \frac{h^*(V)}{(1 + \epsilon)} \le h(V) = (1 + \epsilon)^i \le h^*(V) \ .$$

The space of the algorithm is $\log_{1+\epsilon} n \le 2\epsilon^{-1} \log n$ words, where each word consists of $\log n$ bits. □

Next we improve the space of this algorithm to $6\epsilon^{-1} \log 3\epsilon^{-1}$ words by observing that we do not need to keep the counters for all the guesses at each step of the stream, but only a shifting window of $x = O(1/\epsilon)$ consecutive counters.

THEOREM 6 (SHIFTING WINDOW). *Let $0 < \epsilon < 1$ be a parameter. Let $V \in \mathbb{N}^n$ be a vector of natural numbers of dimension n whose H-index is $h^*(V)$. Let $\mathcal{S}$ be an arbitrarily (possibly adversarially ordered) stream of the elements of the underlying vector V. Then, there exists a one-pass deterministic streaming algorithm (Algorithm 2) that using space $6\epsilon^{-1} \log 3\epsilon^{-1}$ words (where each word consists of $\log n$ bits) reports an estimator $h(V)$ such that*

$$(1 - \epsilon)h^*(V) \le h(V) \le h^*(V) \ .$$

We maintain a window of $x = O(1/\epsilon)$ consecutive counters $c_i, c_{i+1}, \cdots, c_{i+\log x}$ where the counter c_{i+j} corresponds to the revealed elements of the stream that are greater than or equal to $(1 + \epsilon)^{i+j}$. At every step t of the stream if the number of elements that are greater than or equal to $(1 + \epsilon)^{i+1}$ becomes at least $(1 + \epsilon)^{i+1}$, we shift the window of counters by one, i.e., we delete the counter c_i, create a new counter c_{i+x+1}, and set $i = i + 1$.

We prove that the number of elements of the stream that are greater than or equal to $(1+\epsilon)^{i+j}$, but not counted by the counter c_{i+j} (mainly because they have been revealed before the counter c_{i+j} is created) is at most $\epsilon(1+\epsilon)^{i+j}$ which is an ϵ-fraction of the H-index of the stream if the H-index of the stream is at least $(1+\epsilon)^{i+j}$.

Algorithm 2: Shifting Window

Input: Stream $\mathcal{S}$ of elements of V.
(1) Let $X = \{0, 1, 2, \cdots, r = \lceil \log_{1+\epsilon} \epsilon^{-1} \rceil\}$ and $i = 1$.
(2) Initialize counters $c_{i+j} = 0$ for $j \in X$.
(3) For step t that the element $\mathcal{S}_t$ arrives
(4) For each $j \in X$
(5) If $\mathcal{S}_t \geq (1+\epsilon)^{i+j}$, then $c_{i+j} = c_{i+j} + 1$
(6) If $c_{i+1} \geq (1+\epsilon)^{i+1}$, then
(7) Delete the counter c_i.
(8) Let $i = i + 1$.
(9) Initialize new counter $c_{i+r} = 0$.
(10) If $\mathcal{S}_t \geq (1+\epsilon)^{i+r}$, then $c_{i+r} = c_{i+r} + 1$.
(11) Let $h(V)=(1+\epsilon)^{i+j}$ be the greatest threshold for $j \in X$ such that

$$c_{i+j} \geq (1+\epsilon)^{i+j} \text{ and } c_{i+j+1} < (1+\epsilon)^{i+j+1} .$$

(12) Output $h(V)$.

PROOF. For the sake of simplicity we assume $\epsilon^{-1} = (1+\epsilon)^{\ell}$ is a power of $(1+\epsilon)$. Thus, $r = \log_{1+\epsilon} \epsilon^{-1} = \ell$. Observe that for the H-index $h^*(V)$ of the vector $V \in \mathbb{N}^n$, there exists a natural number k for which we have $(1+\epsilon)^k \leq h^*(V) < (1+\epsilon)^{k+1}$. Let us set $i = k+1-\ell$, $x = (1+\epsilon)^i$ and so, $\frac{x}{\epsilon} = (1+\epsilon)^{i+\ell}$. Observe that

$$\frac{x}{\epsilon} \cdot (1+\epsilon)^{-1} = (1+\epsilon)^{i+\ell-1} \leq h^*(V) < (1+\epsilon)^{i+\ell} = \frac{x}{\epsilon} .$$

Let us consider the set $Y = \{0, i-s\ell, \cdots, i-2\ell, i-\ell, i, i+\ell\}$ of the powers of $(1+\epsilon)$ where $s = \lfloor i/\ell \rfloor$. The powers in Y correspond to the guesses $Z = \{1, \epsilon^s x, \cdots, \epsilon^2 x, \epsilon x, x, \frac{x}{\epsilon}\}$ for $h^*(V)$. Indeed, for each number $j \in Y$, there exists a counter c_j that

- is initialized when the counter $c_{j-\ell}$ is deleted. That in turn, occurs when $c_{j-\ell+1} \geq (1+\epsilon)^{j-\ell+1}$. Note that the case $j = 1$ is an exception which starts by seeing the first element of the stream $\mathcal{S}$.
- is deleted when for the subsequent counter c_{j+1}, we have $c_{j+1} \geq (1+\epsilon)^{j+1}$. Observe that at the same time the new counter $c_{j+\ell}$ is created and set to zero.

Observe that since $j \in Y$, we must have $j+\ell, j-\ell \in Y$. We decompose the stream $\mathcal{S}$ into $s+2$ substreams recursively as follows. Corresponding to each number $j \in Y$, we define the substream $\mathcal{S}_j$ which starts when the counter c_j is created and set to zero and ends when the counter c_j is deleted. The substream $\mathcal{S}_j$ corresponds to the sub-vector V_j of the vector V including those entries of the vector V that are revealed in the substream $\mathcal{S}_j$. In the remainder of the proof, we assume that the H-index of the sub-vector V_j is $h^*(V_j) = h^*(\mathcal{S}_j)$.

CLAIM 7. *Let $j \in Y$ be an index in Y. Let c_j be the counter corresponding to the index j. At the time when c_j is deleted, there are at least $(1+\epsilon)^{j+1}$ and at most $(1+\epsilon)^{j+2}$ numbers in the union of the substreams $\cup_{k \leq j \text{ and } j \in Y} \mathcal{S}_k$ that are greater than or equal to $(1+\epsilon)^{j+1}$. Moreover,*

$$(1+\epsilon)^{j+1} \leq c_{j+1} \leq (1+\epsilon)^{j+2} .$$

PROOF. For a fix number $j \in Y$, let us consider three subsequent substreams $\mathcal{S}_{j-\ell}, \mathcal{S}_j, \mathcal{S}_{j+\ell}$ that start when the counters $c_{j-\ell}, c_j, c_{j+\ell}$ are created and end when these counters are deleted, respectively.

Recall that the counters c_j and c_{j+1} (observe that $j+1 \notin Y$) are created when the counters $c_{j-\ell}$ and $c_{j-\ell+1}$ are deleted what in turn, happen when $c_{j-\ell+1} \geq (1+\epsilon)^{j-\ell+1}$ and $c_{j-\ell+2} \geq (1+\epsilon)^{j-\ell+2}$, respectively. The substream $\mathcal{S}_j$ starts when the counter c_j is created and the counter $c_{j-\ell}$ is deleted. Therefore, the counter c_{j+1} may not count all the elements of sub-vector V_j that are greater than or equal to $(1+\epsilon)^{j+1}$. Moreover, the substreams $\mathcal{S}_k$ for $k < j$ and $j \in Y$ were ended before the counter c_{j+1} was created. Thus, the counter c_{j+1} does not count the elements of the sub-vectors V_k for $k \leq j$ and $j \in Y$ that are greater than or equal to $(1+\epsilon)^{j+1}$. We will bound the number of such elements in the union of the sub-vectors $\cup_{k \leq j \text{ and } j \in Y} V_k$ that are not counted in c_{j+1}.

Let us first consider the elements of the sub-vector V_j that are greater than or equal to $(1+\epsilon)^{j+1}$ but are not counted in c_{j+1}. Let us consider the counter $c_{j-\ell+1}$. This counter is deleted when the counter c_{j+1} is created and is created when the counter $c_{j-2\ell+1}$ is deleted. Therefore the counter $c_{j-\ell+1}$ exists before the substream $\mathcal{S}_j$ starts. That is, the number of elements of the sub-vector V_j that are greater than or equal to $(1+\epsilon)^{j+1}$ but are not counted in the counter c_{j+1} have already been counted by the counter $c_{j-\ell+1}$. Observe that those elements of the substream $\mathcal{S}_j$ that are counted by the counter $c_{j-\ell+1}$ must be greater than or equal to $(1+\epsilon)^{j-\ell+1}$ not necessarily greater than or equal to $(1+\epsilon)^{j+1}$, but that gives an upper bound for those elements that are greater than or equal to $(1+\epsilon)^{j+1}$ which is enough for the analysis. Thus, at most $(1+\epsilon)^{j-\ell+2}$ such elements are not counted by the counter c_{j+1}. Indeed, when $c_{j-\ell+2} \geq (1+\epsilon)^{j-\ell+2}$, the counter $c_{j-\ell+1}$ is deleted and the counter c_{j+1} is created and start counting the elements of the the substream $\mathcal{S}_j$ (interchangeably, the sub-vector V_j) that are greater than or equal to $(1+\epsilon)^{j+1}$.

On the other hand, the counter c_j is deleted when $c_{j+1} \geq (1+\epsilon)^{j+1}$. Therefore, the substream $\mathcal{S}_j$ (interchangeably, the sub-vector V_j) contains at least $(1+\epsilon)^{j+1}$ elements greater than or equal to $(1+\epsilon)^{j+1}$.

Overall, the substream $\mathcal{S}_j$ (and respectively, in the sub-vector V_j) contains at least $(1+\epsilon)^{j+1}$ and at most $(1+\epsilon)^{j+1} + (1+\epsilon)^{j-\ell+2} = (1+\epsilon)^{j+1}(1+\epsilon(1+\epsilon))$ elements that are greater than or equal to $(1+\epsilon)^{j+1}$. Let T_j be the exact number of such elements in the the substream $\mathcal{S}_j$. Then,

$$(1+\epsilon)^{j+1} \leq T_j \leq (1+\epsilon)^{j+1}(1+\epsilon(1+\epsilon)) .$$

Thus,

$$c_{j+1} \leq T_j \leq c_{j+1} \cdot (1+\epsilon(1+\epsilon)) .$$

Similarly, for every substream $\mathcal{S}_{j-x\ell}$ for $1 \leq x \leq s = \lfloor i/\ell \rfloor$ (observe that $j - x\ell \in Y$) we can prove that the number of elements of $\mathcal{S}_{j-x\ell}$ that are greater than or equal to $(1+\epsilon)^{j-x\ell}$ (what could be greater than or equal to $(1+\epsilon)^{j+1}$) are at most $(1+\epsilon)^{j-x\ell}$. Let $T_{j-x\ell}$ be the exact number of such elements in the the substream $\mathcal{S}_{j-x\ell}$. Thus, for $\epsilon \leq 1/2$ we have

$$(1+\epsilon)^{j+1} \leq \sum_{j-x\ell \text{ and } 1 \leq x \leq s} T_{j-\ell} \leq \sum_{j-x\ell \text{ and } 0 \leq x \leq s} (1+\epsilon)^{j-x\ell+1} .$$

That is,

$$\begin{aligned}
c_{j+1} &\leq \sum_{j-x\ell \text{ and } 1\leq x\leq s} T_{j-\ell} \leq c_{j+1}\cdot(1+\sum_{1\leq x\leq s}\epsilon^{x}(1+\epsilon)) \\
&\leq c_{j+1}\cdot(1+\epsilon(1+\epsilon)\sum_{0\leq x\leq s}\epsilon^{x}) \\
&\leq c_{j+1}\cdot(1+2\epsilon(1+\epsilon)) \\
&\leq c_{j+1}\cdot(1+3\epsilon)\ .
\end{aligned}$$

By replacing ϵ with $\epsilon/3$ we finish the proof of this claim. □

Similar to the proof of Claim 7 we can prove the general case.

CLAIM 8. *Let $j \in Y$ be an index in Y. Let c_j be the counter corresponding to the index j. At the time t_{j+r} of the stream $\mathcal{S}$ when the counter c_{j+r} for $0 \leq r \leq \ell$ is deleted, there are at least $(1+\epsilon)^{j+r}$ and at most $(1+\epsilon)^{j+r+1}$ numbers from the beginning of the stream $\mathcal{S}$ till that time that are greater than or equal to $(1+\epsilon)^{j+r}$. Moreover, $(1+\epsilon)^{j+r} \leq c_{j+r} \leq (1+\epsilon)^{j+r+1}$.*

Having the above claims, we observe that at the time when every counter c_i is deleted, the next counter c_{i+1} is a $(1\pm\epsilon)$-approximation of the H-index of the stream seen so far.

The space of the algorithm is $\log_{1+\epsilon}\epsilon^{-1} \leq 2\epsilon^{-1}\log\epsilon^{-1}$ words. Since in the proofs of Claims 7 and 8 we need to replace ϵ by $\epsilon/3$, the space of the algorithm will be $6\epsilon^{-1}\log 3\epsilon^{-1}$ words where each word consists of $\log n$ bits.

3.2 Random Order Stream

In this section we show that if a stream $\mathcal{S}$ of items is uniformly randomly ordered, we can develop an $(1\pm\epsilon)$-estimator for the H-index of the stream $\mathcal{S}$ using much smaller space. In particular, if we know a mild lower bound $O(\epsilon^{-3}\log\log(n))$ for the H-index of the stream, we only need six words (where each word consists of $\log n$ bits) to $(1\pm\epsilon)$-estimate the H-index of the stream. Without having such a mild lower bound, the space of our new streaming algorithm is $O(\epsilon^{-1}\log\epsilon^{-1})$ words where each word consists of $O(\log\log\log n)$ bits. On the other hand, the streaming algorithm in Theorem 6 uses $O(\epsilon^{-1}\log\epsilon^{-1})$ words where each word in that algorithm consists of $\log n$ bits. Formally, we state this main result in theorem below.

THEOREM 9 (RANDOM ORDER STREAM). *Let $\mathcal{S}$ be a randomly ordered stream of elements of an underlying vector $V \in \mathbb{N}^n$ whose H-index is $h^*(V)$. Let $0<\epsilon,\delta<1$ and $\beta = 150\epsilon^{-2}\log\log n$. Then, there exists a one-pass streaming algorithm that reports an estimator $h(V)$ such that $\Pr[|h^*(V)-h(V)| \leq \epsilon h^*(V)] \geq 1-\delta$.*

- *Let $\beta/\epsilon \leq h^*(V)$ be a lower bound for $h^*(V)$. Then, the space usage of this algorithm is six words, where a word is a binary vector of length $\log n$ bits.*
- *If $h^*(V)$ is upper bounded by $h^*(V) \leq \beta/\epsilon$, then the space usage of this algorithm is $6\epsilon^{-1}\log 3\epsilon^{-1}$ words each one consists of $\log(\beta/\epsilon)$ bits.*

We first give an overview of the algorithm. We runs two subroutines corresponding two different cases for $h^*(V)$ in parallel. The first case is when we have a lower bound β/ϵ for $h^*(V)$. The second case is when $h^*(V)$ is upper bounded by β/ϵ. For the latter case we simply run the streaming algorithm of Theorem 5 that needs a space of $O(\epsilon^{-1}\log\epsilon^{-1})$ words where each word consists of $\log(\beta/\epsilon)$ bits. Note that in the latter case the H-index is upper bounded by β/ϵ and hence each word requires $\log(\beta/\epsilon)$ bits.

For the former case, we consider $\log_{1+\epsilon}(n/\beta)$ guesses for $h^*(V)$ such that the i-th guess corresponds to $n/(1+\epsilon)^i \leq h^*(V) \leq n/(1+\epsilon)^{i-1}$. For the i-th guess, we look at a window W_i of the stream $\mathcal{S}$ of size $\beta(1+\epsilon)^{i-1}(2+\epsilon)$ and count the number of elements of this window that are greater than or equal to $n/(1+\epsilon)^i$. We should mention that every two windows W_{i-1} and W_i corresponding to two consecutive guesses $i-1$ and i overlap. Indeed, let $Z = \{r_0 = 1, r_1, \cdots, r_i, \cdots, r_{\lceil\log_{1+\epsilon}(n/\beta)\rceil}\}$, where $r_i = r_{i-1} + \beta(1+\epsilon)^i$. The window W_i contains all the elements in the interval $(r_{i-1}, r_{i+1}]$ of the stream $\mathcal{S}$. Observe that W_i contains $\beta(1+\epsilon)^{i-1} + \beta(1+\epsilon)^i = \beta(1+\epsilon)^{i-1}(2+\epsilon)$ elements of the stream $\mathcal{S}$. Let $x = \beta(2+\epsilon)/(1+\epsilon)$. We then accept the i-th guess and report $n/(1+\epsilon)^i$ as an $(1\pm\epsilon)$-approximation of $h^*(V)$ if $(1\pm\epsilon)x$ elements of this window are greater than or equal to $n/(1+\epsilon)^i$.

We analyze the algorithm in three steps. Suppose that the i-th guess is correct, that is, $n/(1+\epsilon)^i \leq h^*(V) \leq n/(1+\epsilon)^{i-1}$. First, we show that if we ignore the elements in the interval $[1, r_{i-1}]$ of the stream $\mathcal{S}$ then we lose only ϵ-fraction of $h^*(V)$. Second, we observe that in expectation x elements of the window W_i are greater than or equal to $n/(1+\epsilon)^i$. Finally, we use a Chernoff concentration bound for the hypergeometric distribution (i.e., sampling without replacement) to prove that with high probability (i.e., with probability at least $1-\delta$ for $0<\delta<1$), $(1\pm\epsilon)x$ elements of the window W_i are greater than or equal to $n/(1+\epsilon)^i$.

The Pseudocode of the algorithm is given in below.

Algorithm 3: Random Order Stream

Input: Stream $\mathcal{S}$ of elements of V.
(1) Let $\beta = 150\epsilon^{-2}\log\log n$.
(2) Let h_1 be the output of Algorithm 2 with input $(\mathcal{S}, \beta)$.
  (We stop Algorithm 2 if the reported H-index of this algorithm is greater than β.)
(4) Let h_2 be the output of Algorithm 4 with input $(\mathcal{S})$.
(5) $h(V) = \max(h_1, h_2)$.

Algorithm 4: Sampling Without Replacement

Input: Stream $\mathcal{S}$ of elements of V.
(1) Let $\beta = 150\epsilon^{-2}\log\log n$, $x = \beta(2+\epsilon)/(1+\epsilon)$, $k = 1$ and $c, c', r = 0$.
(2) For $i = 0, 1, 2, \cdots, \lceil\log_{1+\epsilon}(n/\beta)\rceil$
(3)   Let $r' = r$ and $r = r + \beta(1+\epsilon)^i$.
(4)   While $r' < k \leq r$
(5)   If $\mathcal{S}_k > n/(1+\epsilon)^i$, then $c = c+1$.
(6)   If $\mathcal{S}_k > n/(1+\epsilon)^{i+1}$, then $c' = c'+1$.
(7)   Let $k = k+1$.
(8)   If $(1-\epsilon/3)x \leq c \leq (1+\epsilon)x$, then
(9)   Output $n/(1+\epsilon)^i$ and quit.
(10) Else
(11) $c = c'$ and $c' = 0$.
(12) Output $c = 0$.

Next we prove Theorem 9. First we consider the case that the H-index $h^*(V)$ is upper bounded by β/ϵ. In this case we invoke Algorithm 2 that returns $(1\pm\epsilon)$-approximation of $h^*(V)$ using $6\epsilon^{-1}\log 3\epsilon^{-1}$ words where each word consists of $\log h^*(V) \leq \log(\beta/\epsilon) = 9\log(\epsilon^{-1}\log\log n)$ bits.

Next we consider the case that the H-index $h^*(V)$ is lower bounded by β/ϵ. We prove the following lemma.

LEMMA 10 (H-INDEX IS NOT VERY SMALL). *Let us assume that $h^*(V) \geq \beta/\epsilon$. Then, Algorithm 4 approximates the H-index $h^*(V)$ within $(1 \pm \epsilon)$-approximation.*

We prove this lemma using a series of lemmas that we prove first. Let $i \in [\log_{1+\epsilon} n]$ be the guess for $h^*(V)$ such that $\frac{n}{(1+\epsilon)^i} \leq h^*(V) \leq \frac{n}{(1+\epsilon)^{i-1}}$. The first lemma shows that if we take a random sample subset of size $t_i = \beta(1+\epsilon)^{i-1}(2+\epsilon)$, the number of elements in this set that are greater than or equal to $\frac{n}{(1+\epsilon)^i}$ is sharply concentrated its expectation.

LEMMA 11 (SAMPLING CONCENTRATION BOUND). *Let $i \in [\log_{1+\epsilon} n]$ be a guess for $h^*(V)$ such that $\frac{n}{(1+\epsilon)^i} \leq h^*(V) \leq \frac{n}{(1+\epsilon)^{i-1}}$. Let T_i be a random sample subset of size $t_i = \beta(1+\epsilon)^{i-1}(2+\epsilon)$ from the indices of the vector V taken uniformly at random without replacement. Let $T'_i = \{j \in T_i : V[j] \geq \frac{n}{(1+\epsilon)^i}\}$ and $c = |T'_i|$.*

- *Then, for $t_i = \beta(1+\epsilon)^{i-1}(2+\epsilon)$ we have*

$$\Pr[(1-\epsilon/3)x \leq c \leq (1+\epsilon)x] \geq 1-\delta \ .$$

- ***Noisy Sampling:** Suppose that due to a noise (E.g., previously incorrect guesses of $h^*(V)$) up to $\epsilon h^*(V)$ elements of V that are at least $\frac{n}{(1+\epsilon)^i}$ have been deleted. Then, for $t_i = \beta(1+\epsilon)^{i-1}(2+\epsilon)$ and the same definition for T'_i and c we have*

$$\Pr[(1-\epsilon/3)x \leq c \leq (1+\epsilon)x] \geq 1-\delta \ .$$

PROOF. We first prove the first claim. We define a random variable X_i which corresponds to the number of indices $j \in T_i$ for which $V[j] \geq \frac{n}{(1+\epsilon)^i}$. Observe that X_i has the hypergeometric distribution $X_i \sim H(n, h^*(V), t_i)$ with the probability mass function (pmf)

$$\Pr[X_i = k] = \frac{\binom{h^*(V)}{k}\binom{n-h^*(V)}{t_i-k}}{\binom{n}{t_i}} ,$$

and the expectation $\mathbf{E}[X_i] = p_i t_i$ where $p_i = h^*(V)/n$.

Then, for $0 < \epsilon < 1$ and $t_i = \frac{4\ln(2/\delta)}{\epsilon^2 p_i}$ we have the following tail bound for X_i,

$$\Pr[|X_i - \mathbf{E}[X_i]| \geq \epsilon \mathbf{E}[X_i]] \leq 2\exp(-\epsilon^2 \mathbf{E}[X_i]/4) = \delta \ .$$

Recall that $\frac{1}{(1+\epsilon)^i} \leq p_i = h^*(V)/n \leq \frac{1}{(1+\epsilon)^{i-1}}$ which means that $\frac{t_i}{(1+\epsilon)^i} \leq \mathbf{E}[X_i] \leq \frac{t_i}{(1+\epsilon)^{i-1}}$. Thus, $x \leq \mathbf{E}[X_i] \leq (1+\epsilon)x$.

From the above tail bound for X_i, with probability at least $1-\delta$, we have $(1-\epsilon)\mathbf{E}[X_i] \leq X_i \leq (1+\epsilon)\mathbf{E}[X_i]$. Now we replace ϵ by $\epsilon/3$ to obtain

$$(1-\epsilon/3)x \leq X_i \leq (1+\epsilon)^2 x \leq (1+\epsilon)x \ .$$

Next, we prove the second claim. Let V' be the new vector after removing up to $\epsilon h^*(V)$ elements that are at least $\frac{n}{(1+\epsilon)^i}$. Then, since $(1-\epsilon)h^*(V) \leq h^*(V') \leq h^*(V)$, we have

$$\frac{n}{(1+\epsilon)^{i+1}} \leq (1-\epsilon) \cdot \frac{n}{(1+\epsilon)^i} \leq h^*(V') \leq \frac{n}{(1+\epsilon)^{i-1}} \ .$$

Similar to the first claim, since $\frac{1}{(1+\epsilon)^{i+1}} \leq p_i = h^*(V)/n \leq \frac{1}{(1+\epsilon)^{i-1}}$, we obtain $x \leq \mathbf{E}[X_i] \leq (1+\epsilon)^2 x$.

Recall that with probability at least $1-\delta$, we have $(1-\epsilon)\mathbf{E}[X_i] \leq X_i \leq (1+\epsilon)\mathbf{E}[X_i]$. Now we replace ϵ by $\epsilon/3$ to obtain

$$(1-\epsilon/3)x \leq X_i \leq (1+\epsilon)^3 x \leq (1+\epsilon)x \ .$$

□

Next we show that if we ignore the first r_{i-1} elements of the randomly ordered stream $\mathcal{S}$, the H-index of the remaining part of the stream is at least $(1-\epsilon)h^*(V)$.

LEMMA 12 (FIRST SAMPLE IS A TINY NOISE). *Suppose that $h^*(V) \geq \frac{n}{(1+\epsilon)^i} \geq \frac{(1+\epsilon)^2\beta}{\epsilon^2}$. Let V' be the vector after sampling and removing r_{i-1} elements from V uniformly at random without replacement. Then, for H-index of V' we have $h^*(V') \geq (1-\epsilon)h^*(V)$.*

PROOF. We first compute an upper bound on r_{i-1}. Recall that $Z = \{r_0 = 1, r_1, \cdots, r_i, \cdots, r_{\lceil \log_{1+\epsilon}(n/\beta)\rceil}\}$, where $r_i = r_{i-1} + \beta(1+\epsilon)^i$. The window W_i contains all the elements in the interval $(r_{i-1}, r_{i+1}]$ of the stream $\mathcal{S}$. Recall that W_i contains $\beta(1+\epsilon)^{i-1} + \beta(1+\epsilon)^i = \beta(1+\epsilon)^{i-1}(2+\epsilon)$ elements of the stream $\mathcal{S}$. Also we have $x = \beta(2+\epsilon)/(1+\epsilon)$. Thus,

$$r_{i-1} = \beta \sum_{j=0}^{i-1} (1+\epsilon)^j$$
$$= \beta(1+\epsilon)^{i-1}(1 + \frac{1}{(1+\epsilon)} + \frac{1}{(1+\epsilon)^2} + \cdots + \frac{1}{(1+\epsilon)^{i-1}})$$
$$\leq \beta(1+\epsilon)^{i-1} \cdot (\frac{1}{1-\frac{1}{(1+\epsilon)}}) = \frac{\beta(1+\epsilon)^i}{\epsilon} ,$$

elements of the stream, by the Taylor series $\frac{1}{1-x} = \sum_{j=0}^{\infty} x^j$ for $x \in (-1, 1)$.

Let us define a random variable Y_i which corresponds to the number of indices $j \in [r_{i-1}] = \{1, 2, \cdots, r_{i-1}\}$ for which $V[j] \geq \frac{n}{(1+\epsilon)^i}$. Once again, Y_i has the hypergeometric distribution $Y_i \sim H(n, h^*(V), r_{i-1})$. Therefore, similar to the random variable X_i in Lemma 11, we can prove that with probability $1-\delta$, the random variable Y_i is sharply concentrated around its expectation

$$\mathbf{E}[Y_i] = r_{i-1} \cdot h^*(V)/n \leq \frac{\beta(1+\epsilon)^i}{\epsilon} \cdot \frac{h^*(V)}{n} ,$$

that is, $(1-\epsilon)\mathbf{E}[Y_i] \leq Y_i \leq (1+\epsilon)\mathbf{E}[Y_i]$.

Thus, if $\frac{n}{(1+\epsilon)^i} \leq h^*(V) \leq \frac{n}{(1+\epsilon)^{i-1}}$, we then have

$$Y_i \leq (1+\epsilon) \cdot \frac{\beta(1+\epsilon)^i}{\epsilon} \cdot \frac{h^*(V)}{n}$$
$$\leq \frac{\beta(1+\epsilon)^{i+1}}{\epsilon}(\frac{n}{n(1+\epsilon)^{i-1}}) \frac{(1+\epsilon)^2\beta}{\epsilon} ,$$

Therefore, if we ignore the first r_{i-1} elements of the uniformly randomly ordered stream $\mathcal{S}$, in the rest of the stream $\mathcal{S}$ we have at least $\frac{n}{(1+\epsilon)^i} - \frac{(1+\epsilon)^2 t}{\epsilon}$ elements that are at least $n/(1+\epsilon)^i$.

Recall that $h^*(V) \geq \frac{n}{(1+\epsilon)^i} \geq \frac{(1+\epsilon)^2\beta}{\epsilon^2}$. Let V' be the vector after seeing at most $\frac{t(1+\epsilon)^i}{\epsilon}$ elements of the stream $\mathcal{S}$ that are at least $n/(1+\epsilon)^i$. We then have

$$h^*(V') \geq h^*(V) - \frac{(1+\epsilon)^2\beta}{\epsilon} \geq (1-\epsilon) \cdot \frac{n}{(1+\epsilon)^i} \geq (1-\epsilon)h^*(V) \ .$$

□

Now we apply the union bound to show that all the guesses that are far from $h^*(V)$ fail and a guess which is close to $h^*(V)$ will be well-approximated.

LEMMA 13 (UNION BOUND). *Let $\beta = 36\epsilon^{-2}\ln(\frac{2\log_{1+\epsilon} n}{\delta})$. Then, with probability at least $1-\delta$ we have*

- *for each guess* $i \in [\log_{1+\epsilon} n]$ *such that* $h^*(V) < \frac{n}{(1+\epsilon)^{i+5}}$, *we have* $X_i < (1-\epsilon/3)x$;
- *for the guess* i *such that* $\frac{n}{(1+\epsilon)^i} \le h^*(V) \le \frac{n}{(1+\epsilon)^{i-1}}$, *we have* $(1-\epsilon/3)x \le X_i \le (1+\epsilon)x$.

PROOF. The second part of this lemma was proved in Lemma 11. Next, we prove the first part. Let $i \in [\log_{1+\epsilon} n]$ be a guess for which $h^*(V) < \frac{n}{(1+\epsilon)^{i+5}}$. We define the random variable X_i corresponding to the number of elements in the window W_i (i.e, which is the interval $(r_{i-1}, r_{i+1}]$) of the stream $\mathcal{S}$ that are greater than or equal to $\frac{n}{(1+\epsilon)^i}$. Recall that $p_i = \frac{h^*(V)}{n} < \frac{1}{(1+\epsilon)^{i+5}}$, $t_i = \beta(1+\epsilon)^{i-1}(2+\epsilon)$, and $x = \beta(2+\epsilon)/(1+\epsilon)$. Similar to Lemma 11, the expectation of X_i is upper-bounded by

$$\begin{aligned}\mathbf{E}[X_i] = p_i t_i &< \frac{t_i}{(1+\epsilon)^{i+5}} \\ &= \frac{\beta(2+\epsilon)}{(1+\epsilon)^6} \le \frac{x}{(1+\epsilon)^5} \le x(1-\epsilon+\epsilon^2)^5 \\ &\le x(1-3\epsilon/4)^5 \le x(1-4\epsilon/3) ,\end{aligned}$$

where $t_i = (1+\epsilon)^{i+1}\beta$, $\epsilon \le 1/4$ and the Taylor series $\frac{1}{1-x} = \sum_{j=0}^{\infty} x^j$ for $x \in (-1,1)$. Since with probability at least $1-\delta$, $(1-\epsilon)\mathbf{E}[X_i] \le X_i \le (1+\epsilon)\mathbf{E}[X_i]$, we then have

$$\begin{aligned}X_i &\le (1+\epsilon)(1-4\epsilon/3)x \\ &= (1+\epsilon-4\epsilon/3-4\epsilon^2/3)x < (1-\epsilon/3)x ,\end{aligned}$$

We have $\log_{1+\epsilon} n$ guesses $i \in [\log_{1+\epsilon} n]$ for $h^*(V)$ such that for one of them, say $j \in [\log_{1+\epsilon} n]$ we have $\frac{n}{(1+\epsilon)^j} \le h^*(V) \le \frac{n}{(1+\epsilon)^{j-1}}$. We replace δ by $\delta/\log_{1+\epsilon} n$ and apply the union bound to show that with probability at least $1-\delta$ for the guess j, we have $(1-\epsilon/3)x \le X_j \le (1+\epsilon)x$ and for the other guesses $i \in [\log_{1+\epsilon} n]$ such that $h^*(V) < \frac{n}{(1+\epsilon)^{i+5}}$, we have $X_i < (1-\epsilon/3)x$ what finishes the proof of this lemma. As for the sample size t_i we have

$$\begin{aligned}t_i = \frac{4\ln(2/\delta)}{\epsilon^2 p_i}\cdot(1+\epsilon) &\le \frac{4(1+\epsilon)^{i+1}\ln(2/(\delta/\log_{1+\epsilon} n))}{(\epsilon/4)^2} \\ &= \beta(1+\epsilon)^{i+1} ,\end{aligned}$$

for $\beta = 36\epsilon^{-2}\ln(\frac{2\log_{1+\epsilon} n}{\delta}) \le 150\epsilon^{-2}\log\log n$. □

Now we have enough tools to prove Lemma 10.

Finishing the Proof of Lemma 10.

Observe that we take the elements in the window W_i (i.e, which is the interval $(r_{i-1}, r_{i+1}]$) of the stream $\mathcal{S}$ when the tests for the guesses $j < i$ in Step 8 of Algorithm 4 fail. Since $r_{i-1} \le \beta(1+\epsilon)^i/\epsilon$, the last guess that we can make is for $i = \log_{1+\epsilon}(\epsilon n/\beta)$ where we test if

$$\frac{n}{(1+\epsilon)^{\log_{1+\epsilon}(\epsilon n/\beta)}} \le h^*(V) \le \frac{n}{(1+\epsilon)^{\log_{1+\epsilon}(\epsilon n/\beta)-1}} ,$$

that is, $\beta/\epsilon \le h^*(V) \le (1+\epsilon)\beta/\epsilon$ since that guess r_{i-1} is the last guess such that $r_{i-1} \le n$.

Now we put all the things together. Let $i \in [\log_{1+\epsilon} n]$ be a guess for $h^*(V)$ such that $\frac{n}{(1+\epsilon)^i} \le h^*(V) \le \frac{n}{(1+\epsilon)^{i-1}}$. First, we use Lemma 12 for the uniformly randomly ordered stream $\mathcal{S}$ to prove that if we ignore the first set of $r_{i-1} \le \frac{\beta(1+\epsilon)^i}{\epsilon}$ elements of the stream $\mathcal{S}$, then the H-index of the rest of the stream $\mathcal{S}$ is at least $(1-\epsilon)h^*(V)$. Let $\mathcal{S}'$ be the remaining set of elements of the stream $\mathcal{S}$ after ignoring the first $\frac{\beta(1+\epsilon)^i}{\epsilon}$ elements of $\mathcal{S}$. Second, we use Lemma 11 that shows if we take a random set T_i of size $t_i = \beta(1+\epsilon)^{i-1}(2+\epsilon)$ from $\mathcal{S}'$ and let $T_i' = \{j \in T_i : V[j] \ge \frac{n}{(1+\epsilon)^i}\}$ and $c = |T_i'|$, then, $\Pr[(1-\epsilon/3)x \le c \le (1+\epsilon)x] \ge 1-\delta$. Finally, we use Lemma 13 that shows that for the big guesses $j \in [\log_{1+\epsilon} n]$ such that $h^*(V) < \frac{n}{(1+\epsilon)^{j+5}}$, we have $X_j < (1-\epsilon/3)x$. Therefore, such big guesses fail. This finishes the proof of Lemma 10.

3.3 Cash Register Streaming Model

In this section we prove our result for the cash register model.

THEOREM 14 (UNBIASED SAMPLING). *Let* $0 < \epsilon < 1$ *be a parameter. Let* $V \in \mathbb{N}^n$ *be a vector of natural numbers of dimension* $n = (1+\epsilon)^k$ *whose* H*-index is* $h^*(V)$ *where* $k \in \mathbb{N}$. *Let* $\mathcal{S}$ *be a stream of updates* (i_t, z) *of the underlying vector* V. *Then, there exists a one-pass randomized streaming algorithm (Algorithm 6) that reports an estimator* $h(V)$.

- ***Multiplicative Error:*** *Let* $h^*(V) \ge \beta$ *be a lower bound for* $h^*(V)$. *If this algorithm uses* x *instances of* ℓ_0*-Sampler, where* $x = \frac{n}{\beta}\cdot\frac{3}{\epsilon^2}\cdot\ln(2/\delta)$, *then* $(1-\epsilon)h^*(V) \le h(V) \le h^*(V)$.
- ***Additive Error:*** *Suppose we do not have a lower bound for* $h^*(V)$. *If this algorithm uses* x *instances of* ℓ_0*-Sampler where* $x = \frac{3}{\epsilon^2}\cdot\ln(2/\delta)$, *then* $h^*(V) - \epsilon\cdot n \le h(V) \le h^*(V) + \epsilon\cdot n$.

The success probability of this algorithm is $1-\delta$.

The outline of the algorithm is as follows. We sample entries of the vector V (almost) uniformly at random. Given a stream $\mathcal{S}$ of updates to the vector V, we keep track of changes to these samples to find an unbiased estimator for the H-index $h^*(V)$ whose expectation is $h^*(V)$. We show that with high probability the estimator is sharply concentrated around its expectation $h^*(V)$.

Algorithm 5: Unbiased Sampling

Input: Stream $\mathcal{S}$ of updates (i_t, z) to an underlying n-dimensional vector V and a lower bound β for $h^*(V) \ge \beta$.
(1) Let X be the output set of x instances of ℓ_0-Sampler.
(X is a uniformly sample set of non-zero indices of V.)
(2) Let y be an $(1 \pm \epsilon)$-approximation of the number of non-zero indices of V using algorithm of [10].
(3) For $i = 0$ to $\lceil \log_{1+\epsilon} n \rceil$
(4) Let $R_i = \{j \in X : V[j] \ge (1+\epsilon)^i\}$.
(5) Let $r_i = |R_i| \cdot y/x$.
(6) Let z be the greatest $(1+\epsilon)^i$ s.t. $r_i \ge (1+\epsilon)^i(1-\epsilon)$.
(7) Output z.

PROOF. We first prove the multiplicative error bound. Suppose that $(1+\epsilon)^i \le h^*(V) \le (1+\epsilon)^{i+1}$. Observe that z is a random variable which depends on random variable $|R_i|$. In the following we prove that $\mathbf{E}[|R_i|] \ge x\cdot\frac{\beta}{n}$ what yields $\mathbf{E}[z] = (1+\epsilon)^i$.

Let $X = \{a_1, \cdots, a_j, \cdots, a_x\}$ be the set of indices that x instances of ℓ_0-Sampler return. Here we assume that none of x instances of ℓ_0-Sampler and the algorithm of [10] fail which can be easily guaranteed by a simple union bound argument. Recall that $R_i = \{j \in X : V[j] \ge (1+\epsilon)^i\}$ and $r_i = |R_i|\cdot y/x$. Let us define an indicator random variable I_j corresponding to the j-th instance of the ℓ_0-Sampler which is one if $V[a_j] \ge h^*(V) \ge (1+\epsilon)^i$ and zero otherwise. Let $I = \sum_{j=1}^{x} I_j$. Recall that ℓ_0-Sampler takes samples with replacement. Observe that $\mathbf{E}[I_j] = \Pr[I_j = 1] \ge \frac{h^*(V)}{y} \ge$

$\frac{(1+\epsilon)^i}{y}$. Thus, $\mathbf{E}[|R_i|] \geq \mathbf{E}[I] \geq x \cdot \frac{h^*(V)}{y} \geq x \cdot \frac{(1+\epsilon)^i}{y} \geq x \cdot \frac{\beta}{n}$ which means that $\mathbf{E}[r_i] \geq (1+\epsilon)^i$.

We use the Chernoff bound which is stated in below.

LEMMA 15 (CHERNOFF INEQUALITY). *[8] Let $Z_1, \cdots, Z_m$ denote m independent random variables such that $0 \leq Z_i \leq 1$ for $1 \leq i \leq m$. For $Z = \sum_{i=1}^{m} Z_i$ we get*

$$\Pr[|Z - \mathbf{E}[Z]| \geq \epsilon \mathbf{E}[Z] \leq 2\exp\left(-\frac{\epsilon^2 \mathbf{E}[Z]}{3}\right).$$

Using the Chernoff bound for $x = 3\epsilon^{-2}\log(2/\delta) \cdot \frac{\beta}{n}$ we have

$$\Pr[|z - \mathbf{E}[z]| \geq \epsilon \mathbf{E}[z]] = \Pr[|r_i - \mathbf{E}[r_i]| \geq \epsilon(1+\epsilon)^i]$$

$$= \Pr[||R_i| - \mathbf{E}[|R_i|]| \geq \epsilon \mathbf{E}[|R_i|]] \leq 2\exp(-\frac{\epsilon^2 \mathbf{E}[|R_i|]}{3}) \leq \delta \ .$$

Now we proof the second claim of this theorem. To this end, we use the additive Hoeffding inequality which is given below.

LEMMA 16 (ADDITIVE HOEFFDING INEQUALITY). *[8] Let $Y_1, \cdots, Y_m$ denote m independent random variables such that $0 \leq Y_i \leq M$ for $1 \leq i \leq n$. For $Y = \sum_{i=1}^{m} Y_i$ we get*

$$\Pr[|Y - \mathbf{E}[Y]| \geq t] \leq 2\exp\left(-\frac{mt^2}{3M^2}\right).$$

Using the additive Hoeffding inequality for $x = 3\epsilon^{-2}\log(2/\delta)$ and $M = 1$ we have

$$\Pr[|z - \mathbf{E}[z]| \geq \epsilon n] = \Pr[|r_i - \mathbf{E}[r_i]| \geq \epsilon n]$$

$$= \Pr[||R_i| - \mathbf{E}[|R_i|]| \geq \epsilon n \frac{y}{x}] \leq \Pr[||R_i| - \mathbf{E}[|R_i|]| \geq \epsilon n]$$

$$\leq 2\exp(-\frac{x\epsilon^2 n^2}{3M^2}) = 2\exp(-\frac{x\epsilon^2 n^2}{3}) \leq \delta^n \leq \delta \ ,$$

for $x \leq y \leq n$ and $0 < \delta < 1$. □

4. HEAVY HITTERS H-INDICES

Let $\mathcal{A}$ and $\mathcal{P}$ be sets of authors and papers, where we assume every author and paper is a number from domains $|\mathcal{A}|$ and $|\mathcal{P}|$, respectively. Let $a \in \mathcal{A}$ be an author for which we show the set of its papers as $P_a \subseteq \mathcal{P}$. Let $p \in \mathcal{P}$ be a paper for which we show the set of its authors as $A_p \subseteq \mathcal{A}$. We represent a paper $p \in \mathcal{P}$ by a tuple $(p, a_1^p, \cdots, a_y^p, c_p)$ for $y \leq x$, where $a_1^p, \cdots, a_y^p$ and c_p are the authors and the citation number of the paper p, respectively.

Let $\mathcal{S}$ be a stream of papers/tuples $(p, a_1^p, \cdots, a_y^p, c_p)$. Suppose that $h^*(\mathcal{S}) = \sum_{a \in \mathcal{S}} h^*(a)$ is the sum of H-indices of authors whose papers are given in $\mathcal{S}$. Here we first develop a streaming algorithm that distinguishes the following two cases:

1. **1-Heavy Hitter:** The case when $\mathcal{S}$ has only one heavy hitter. That is, there exists an author a_j in the stream $\mathcal{S}$ whose H-index $h(a_j) \geq (1-\epsilon) \cdot h^*(\mathcal{S})$.
2. **Noisy Stream/Heavy Hitters:** There is no author a_j whose H-index $h(a_j) \geq (1-\epsilon) \cdot h^*(\mathcal{S})$. That includes the cases when either $\mathcal{S}$ does not have any heavy hitter or it has more than one heavy hitter. We call the former case *noisy stream* $\mathcal{S}$ and the latter case *noisy heavy hitters.*

We develop Algorithm 7 to distinguish between these two cases. Later, we use this algorithm as a primitive to develop a streaming algorithm that detects up to $1/\epsilon$ heavy hitters of a stream $\mathcal{S}$.

4.1 1-Heavy Hitter of H-indices

THEOREM 17 (1-HEAVY HITTER OF H-INDICES). *Let $\mathcal{S}$ be a stream of papers $(p, a_1^p, \cdots, a_y^p, c_p)$, where $\{a_1^p, \cdots, a_y^p\} \subseteq \mathcal{A}$ and c_p are the authors and the citation number of the paper $p \in \mathcal{P}$, respectively. Let $0 < \epsilon, \delta < 1$. Let $h^*(\mathcal{S}) = \sum_{a \in \mathcal{S}} h^*(a)$ be the sum of H-indices of authors whose papers are given in $\mathcal{S}$. Then, Algorithm 7 uses space $2\epsilon^{-2}\log(\log(n)/\delta)$ words and with probability at least $1-\delta$ distinguish the following cases.*

1. *There exists an author a_j in the stream $\mathcal{S}$ whose H-index $h(a_j) \geq (1-\epsilon) \cdot h^*(\mathcal{S})$.*
2. *There is no author a_j whose H-index $h(a_j) \geq (1-\epsilon) \cdot h^*(\mathcal{S})$.*

Algorithm 7: 1-Heavy Hitter

Input: Stream $\mathcal{S}$ of tuples/papers $(p, a_1^p, \cdots, a_y^p, c_p)$, where $a_1^p, \cdots, a_y^p$ and c_p are the authors and the citation number of the paper p, respectively.

(1) Let $s = \frac{2\log(\log(n)/\delta)}{\epsilon^2}$.
(2) Initialize counters $c_i = 0$ to zero for $i \in [\log_{1+\epsilon} n]$.
(3) For each paper $p \in \mathcal{S}$ and each $i \in [\log_{1+\epsilon} n]$
(4) If $c_p \geq (1+\epsilon)^i$, then
(5) Let $c_i = c_i + 1$.
(6) Let T_i be a sample of s papers ps.t. $c_p \geq (1+\epsilon)^i$.
(7) Let $h(\mathcal{S})$=$(1+\epsilon)^i$ be the greatest threshold s.t.

$$c_i \geq (1+\epsilon)^i \text{ and } c_{i+1} < (1+\epsilon)^{i+1} \ .$$

(8) Let i^* be the i for which $h(\mathcal{S})$=$(1+\epsilon)^i$.
(9) If $(1-\epsilon)$ fraction of papers in T_{i^*} has author a_j
(10) Return a_j with $h(\mathcal{S})$; otherwise return FAIL.

The algorithm is similar to Algorithm 1. The only difference here is that for every threshold $(1+\epsilon)^i$ in Step 4 we sample a set T_i of $s = \frac{2\log(\log(n)/\delta)}{\epsilon^2}$ papers. At the end of the stream once we found the greatest threshold for which $c_i \geq (1+\epsilon)^i$ and $c_{i+1} < (1+\epsilon)^{i+1}$, we look at its corresponding sample set T_i of papers and check if there is an author a_j who is the author of at least $(1-\epsilon)$-fraction of the papers in T_i. If that is the case, we return that author and whose H-index which is $(1-\epsilon)$-approximated by the H-index $h(\mathcal{S})$; otherwise we return the FAIL symbol.

Theorem 17 is proved using Theorem 5 and a simple application of Chernoff bound and the union bound argument for counters c_i where $i \in [\log_{1+\epsilon} n]$.

4.2 Multiple Heavy Hitters of H-indices

THEOREM 18 (HEAVY HITTERS OF H-INDICES). *Let $\mathcal{S}$ be a stream of papers $(p, a_1^p, \cdots, a_y^p, c_p)$, where $\{a_1^p, \cdots, a_y^p\} \subseteq \mathcal{A}$ and c_p are the authors and the citation number of the paper $p \in \mathcal{P}$, respectively. Let $0 < \epsilon, \delta < 1$. Let $h^*(\mathcal{S}) = \sum_{a \in \mathcal{S}} h^*(a)$ be the sum of H-indices of authors whose papers are given in $\mathcal{S}$. Then, Algorithm 8 with probability at least $1-\delta$ outputs a set $\mathcal{A}' = \{(a_1, h(a_1)), \cdots, (a_r, h(a_r))\}$ of authors for $0 \leq r \leq 1/\epsilon$ such that for each author $a_i \in \mathcal{A}'$ and his/her reported H-index $h(a_i)$ we have $h^*(a_i) \geq \epsilon \cdot h^*(\mathcal{S})$ and $(1-\epsilon)h^*(a_i) \leq h(a_i) \leq (1+\epsilon)h^*(a_i)$. The space usage of this algorithm is $O(\epsilon^{-4}\log(\log(n)\delta^{-1})) \cdot \log(\epsilon^{-1}\delta^{-1})$.*

The algorithm is an extension of a known heavy hitter algorithm. Indeed, suppose the distribution of H-indices of authors whose papers are given in a streaming fashion is heavy-tail. We hash the authors using a pair-wise independent hash function into $O(\epsilon^{-1})$ buckets and treat the sub-stream of papers of those authors that are hashed into every bucket i as a substream $\mathcal{S}_i$ of papers of one author for which we run the streaming algorithm of Theorem 5 to find the H-index of the substream $\mathcal{S}_i$. We prove that with high probability the authors that have heavy hitter H-indices are hashed into different buckets and the sum of H-indices of non-heavy hitter authors are evenly distributed among the buckets such that each bucket that corresponds to a heavy hitter author receives a noise of at most ϵ-fraction of the H-index of that author. A simple sampling test from each bucket then finds those buckets that correspond to heavy hitter authors. The Pseudocode of the algorithm is given in below and the proof of the correctness of the algorithm is given after it.

Algorithm 8: Heavy Hitters

Input: Stream $\mathcal{S}$ of tuples/papers $(p, a_1^p, \cdots, a_y^p, c_p)$, where $a_1^p, \cdots, a_y^p$ and c_p are the authors and the citation number of the paper p, respectively.
(1) Let $\mathcal{H}_j : [\mathcal{A}] \to [t = 2\epsilon^{-2}]$ for $j \in [x = \log(\epsilon^{-1}\delta^{-1})]$ be an independently sample function from a set of pair-wise independent hash functions.
(2) Let $B[x, t]$ be a $x \times t$ array buckets.
(3) For every paper $(p, a_1^p, \cdots, a_y^p, c_p) \in \mathcal{S}$
(4) For each author a_i^p in the paper p and each $j \in [x]$
(5) Hash $(p, a_1^p, \cdots, a_y^p, c_p)$ into the $B[j, \mathcal{H}_j(a_i^p)]$.
(6) For $j \in [x]$ and $k \in [t]$
(7) Let $\mathcal{S}_{j,k}$ be papers hashed into bucket $B[j, k]$.
(8) Invoke Algorithm 1-Heavy Hitter with input $\mathcal{S}_{j,k}$.
(9) If the output of Step 7 is author a_j with $h(a_j)$
(10) Output a_j and H-index $h(a_j)$ as a heavy hitter.

PROOF. Recall that $\mathcal{A} = \{a_1, \cdots, a_{|\mathcal{A}|}\}$ is the set of authors. We say an author $a_i \in \mathcal{A}$ is a heavy hitter author if for the H-index of each author $a_i \in \mathcal{A}$ we have

$$h^*(a_i) \geq \epsilon \cdot h^*(\mathcal{A}) = \epsilon \cdot \sum_{a_j \in \mathcal{A}} h^*(a_j) \ .$$

Without lost of generality suppose that the first r authors in $\mathcal{A}$ for $r \leq 1/\epsilon$ are the heady hitter authors, that is, $X = \{a_1, \cdots, a_r\} \subseteq \mathcal{A}$ is the set of heavy hitter authors. Let us fix a heavy hitter author $a_i \in X$.

Let $I_{i,j,k}$ be an indicator random variable which corresponds to the event that another author $a_k \in \mathcal{A}$ for $a_k \neq a_i$ (including other heavy hitter authors) is hashed into the same bucket as $B[j, \mathcal{H}_j[a_i]]$. Observe that since $\mathcal{H}_j$ is a pairwise independent hash function we have $\mathbf{E}[I_{i,j,k}] = \Pr(\mathcal{H}_j[a_k] = \mathcal{H}[a_i]) \leq \frac{1}{t}$.

We define a random variable $J_{i,j} = \sum_{k=1 \wedge k \neq i}^{|\mathcal{A}|} I_{i,j,k} h^*(a_k)$ for the H-index noise of the bucket $B[j, \mathcal{H}_j[a_i]]$. Observe that by linearity of expectation we obtain

$$\mathbf{E}[J_{i,j}] = \sum_{k=1 \wedge k \neq i}^{|\mathcal{A}|} h^*(a_k) \cdot \mathbf{E}[I_{i,j,k}] \leq \frac{1}{t} \cdot (h^*(\mathcal{A}) - h^*(a_i)) \ .$$

Now we use the Markov inequality

$$\begin{aligned}\Pr(h^*(B[\mathcal{H}_j[a_i]]) \geq (1+\epsilon)h^*(a_i)) &\leq \Pr(J_{i,j} \geq \epsilon^2 h^*(\mathcal{A})) \\ &= \Pr(J_{i,j} \geq e\mathbf{E}[J_{i,j}]) \leq e \ ,\end{aligned}$$

for $t = \frac{e}{\epsilon^2}$. We say an event BAD_i occurs if for each hash function $\mathcal{H}_j$ for $j \in [x]$, the H-index of the bucket $B[\mathcal{H}_j[a_i]]$ is more than $(1+\epsilon)h^*(a_i)$, that is, $h^*(B[\mathcal{H}_j[a_i]]) \geq (1+\epsilon)h^*(a_i)$. Therefore, for $x = \log(\frac{1}{\epsilon\delta})$ hash functions $\mathcal{H}_1, \cdots, \mathcal{H}_x$,

$$\Pr[BAD_i] \leq e^x = \epsilon\delta \ .$$

Observe that there can be at most $1/\epsilon$ heavy hitter authors (i.e., $|X| \leq 1/\epsilon$). We define an event BAD if one of bad events BAD_i for $i \in [r]$ occurs. Thus, using the union bound we obtain

$$\Pr[BAD] \leq \sum_{i \in [r]} \Pr[BAD_i] \leq r \cdot \epsilon\delta \leq \delta \ ,$$

□

5. EXTENSIONS AND CONCLUDING REMARKS

We have initiated the study of streaming algorithms for problems that estimate impact or identify impactful users, and focused on the H-index of users. There are many variations of the H-index, including those that take publication dates, response timestamps, responder's H-index, and so on into account; there are also variations based on different functions of the number of responses with respect to the number of publications like k publications with a total of k^2 responses each; heavy hitters that are users with H-index that are large in the count or in square of the counts (so called L_2 heavy hitters); etc. While our techniques will extend naturally to some of these problems, there is much that remains to be done in obtaining the best bounds for these streaming problems.

Acknowledgments

This work was supported by the NSF IIS 1247696, NSF CCF 1535878, NSF IIS 1447793 and NSF CCF 1161151.

6. REFERENCES

[1] L. Bornmann. h-index research in scientometrics: A summary. *Journal of Informetrics*, 8(3):749 – 750, 2014.

[2] L. Bornmann, W. Marx, A. Y. Gasparyan, and G. D. Kitas. Diversity, value and limitations of the journal impact factor and alternative metrics. *Rheumatology International*, 32(7):1861–1867, 2012.

[3] G. Cormode, Q. Ma, S. Muthukrishnan, and B. Thompson. Socializing the h-index. *J. Informetrics*, 7(3):718–721, 2013.

[4] L. Egghe. Theory and practise of the g-index. *Scientometrics*, 69(1):131–152, 2006.

[5] G. Frahling, P. Indyk, and C. Sohler. Sampling in dynamic data streams and applications. In *Proceedings of the 21st Annual Symposium on Computational Geometry (SoCG)*, pages 142–149, 2005.

[6] P. Govindan, S. Soundarajan, T. Eliassi-Rad, and C. Faloutsos. Nimblecore: A space-efficient external memory algorithm for estimating core numbers. In *2016 IEEE/ACM International Conference on Advances in Social Networks Analysis and Mining (ASONAM)*, pages 207–214, Aug 2016.

[7] J. E. Hirsch. An index to quantify an individual's scientific research output. *Proceedings of the National Academy of Sciences of the United States of America*, 102(46):16569–16572, 2005.

[8] W. Hoeffding. Probability inequalities for sums of bounded random variables. *Journal of the American Statistical Association*, 58(301):13–30, 1963.

[9] H. Jowhari, M. Saglam, and G. Tardos. Tight bounds for L_p samplers, finding duplicates in streams, and related problems. In *Proceedings of the 17th ACM SIGMOD Symposium on Principles of Database Systems (PODS)*, pages 49–58, 2011.

[10] D. M. Kane, J. Nelson, and D. P. Woodruff. An optimal algorithm for the distinct elements problem. In *Proceedings of the Twenty-Ninth ACM SIGMOD-SIGACT-SIGART Symposium on Principles of Database Systems, PODS 2010, June 6-11, 2010, Indianapolis, Indiana, USA*, pages 41–52, 2010.

[11] M. Monemizadeh and D. Woodruff. 1-Pass Relative-Error L_p-Sampling with Applications. In *Proceedings of the 21st Annual ACM-SIAM Symposium on Discrete Algorithms (SODA)*, pages 1143–1160, 2010.

[12] F. Riquelme. Measuring user influence on twitter: A survey. *CoRR*, abs/1508.07951, 2015.

[13] J. Sun and J. Tang. *A Survey of Models and Algorithms for Social Influence Analysis*, pages 177–214. Springer US, Boston, MA, 2011.

[14] S. Wasserman and K. Faust. *Social network analysis : methods and applications*. Structural analysis in the social sciences. Cambridge University Press, 1997, Cambridge, New York, Melbourne, 1994. Autres tirages : 1998, 1999, 2007, 2008.

Efficient Matrix Sketching over Distributed Data

Zengfeng Huang
UNSW
Sydney, Australia
z3515594@unsw.edu.au

Xuemin Lin
UNSW
Sydney, Australia
lxue@cse.unsw.edu.au

Wenjie Zhang
UNSW
Sydney, Australia
zhangw@cse.unsw.edu.au

Ying Zhang
UTS
Sydney, Australia
Ying.Zhang@uts.edu.au

ABSTRACT

A sketch or synopsis of a large dataset captures vital properties of the original data while typically occupying much less space. In this paper, we consider the problem of computing a sketch of a massive data matrix $A \in \mathbb{R}^{n\times d}$, which is distributed across a large number of s servers. Our goal is to output a matrix $B \in \mathbb{R}^{\ell\times d}$ which is significantly smaller than but still approximates A well in terms of *covariance error*, i.e., $\|A^TA - B^TB\|_2$. Here, for a matrix A, $\|A\|_2$ is the spectral norm of A, which is defined as the largest singular value of A. Following previous works, we call B a covariance sketch of A. We are mainly focused on minimizing the communication cost, which is arguably the most valuable resource in distributed computations. We show a gap between deterministic and randomized communication complexity for computing a covariance sketch. More specifically, we first prove a tight deterministic lower bound, then show how to bypass this lower bound using randomization. In *Principle Component Analysis* (PCA), the goal is to find a low-dimensional subspace that captures as much of the variance of a dataset as possible. Based on a well-known connection between covariance sketch and PCA, we give a new algorithm for distributed PCA with improved communication cost. Moreover, in our algorithms, each server only needs to make one pass over the data with limited working space.

CCS Concepts

•**Theory of computation** → **Massively parallel algorithms;** *Sketching and sampling;*

Keywords

Matrix sketching; communication complexity; distributed data

1. INTRODUCTION

Computing a compact sketch or synopsis of the data, then executing queries against the sketch rather than the entire dataset is a classical technique in big data processing. Traditionally, a sketch is computed through a streaming algorithm which makes one pass over the data using limited working space. However, modern massive data is often distributed across a shared-nothing cluster with a large number of servers. In these systems, the communication cost and the number of rounds become the most critical complexity parameters.

PODS'17, May 14-19, 2017, Chicago, IL, USA

DOI: http://dx.doi.org/10.1145/3034786.3056119

In many applications such as textual analysis, machine learning, and image processing, the underlying data sets are represented as large-scale matrices and stored in massively distributed databases. To analyze such large data matrices, exact computations are often infeasible and unnecessary, and thus randomized and approximate methods are widely used. Computing a sketch matrix first, and then doing expensive computations such as Singular Value Decomposition (SVD) on the sketch matrix is also a common approach (e.g. [31, 7, 29]). Therefore, the task is reduced to designing communication- and round-efficient algorithms to compute sketches with required accuracy.

Covariance sketch. Given a matrix $A \in \mathbb{R}^{n\times d}$, a *covariance sketch* of A is another much smaller matrix $B \in \mathbb{R}^{\ell\times d}$ such that the *covariance error* $\|A^TA - B^TB\|_2$ is small, where $\|A\|_2$ denotes the spectral norm of A. Equivalently, the Euclidean norm $\|Ax\|_2$ for any $x \in \mathbb{R}^d$ is approximately preserved by $\|Bx\|_2$. Covariance sketch has a wide range of applications including low-rank approximation, PCA, clustering, anomaly detection, etc. [11, 16, 8, 23, 20, 36]. Due to its importance, computing a covariance sketch has been extensively studied in various computational models e.g., [10, 27, 17, 15, 34, 9]. In this paper, we study the problem of computing a covariance sketch in the distributed model, and its application to PCA and low-rank approximation.

Distributed models. We assume that the rows of the input matrix are initially partitioned into s parts, each of which is held by a distributed server (with no replication of data). The partition can be arbitrary; we do not make any assumption on how the data is partitioned. The s servers can communicate with each other through an inter-connected communication network. The communication is point-to-point, and we call this the *message passing model* in comparison to the *broadcast model* (aka. the *blackboard model* in complexity community), where each message can be seen by all servers. All of the algorithms in this paper only needs a small constant number of rounds (mostly one or two rounds), so the focus of this paper is to characterize the communication complexity, i.e., the amount of data exchanged. While our algorithms work in the message passing model, our communication lower bound holds for the *blackboard model*, and also holds for protocols with any number of rounds. In our model, there is one special server which acts as the central *coordinator*.

We exhibit new algorithms that improve on the communication cost of the best previous algorithms. For instance, assume $s = d$ and we want to compute a covariance sketch with error $\|A\|_F^2/d$, where $\|A\|_F^2$ is the Frobenius norm of A (the sum of squares of the entries of A). The deterministic algorithm of [27] has cost $O(d^3)$, and the cost of using random sampling is also $O(d^3)$ [10], which is the same as the cost of the trivial algorithm. However, our new randomized algorithm can achieve this with communication cost $\tilde{O}(d^{2.5})$. On the other hand, we show that $\Omega(d^3)$ is the lower bound for any deterministic algorithms, and thus separate the randomized and deterministic communication complexity.

Moreover, in our algorithms, each server only needs to make one pass over the data with limited working space. The algorithms follows the same framework: each server first independently computes a local sketch using a streaming algorithm, then all servers run a distributed algorithm on top the local sketches without further access of the original data. Therefore, they are still efficient even when the local input does not fit into the main memory or is received in a streaming fashion. This is similar to the *distributed streaming model* of [18, 19]. In this model, each server processes a stream of items with bounded memory, and when a query is requested, a special player called *coordinator*, who can communicate with the servers, needs to output the answer for the union of the streams. We call these *distributed streaming* algorithms, in comparison to *distributed batch* algorithms if servers needs to access local data multiple times.

1.1 Matrix preliminaries and notations

We always use s for the number of machines, n for the number rows, and d for the dimension of each row. For a d-dimensional vector x, $\|x\|$ is the ℓ_2 norm of x. We use x_i to denote the ith entry of x, and $\mathsf{Diag}(x) \in \mathbb{R}^{d\times d}$ is a diagonal matrix such that the i-th diagonal entry is x_i. Let $A \in \mathbb{R}^{n\times d}$ be a matrix of dimension $n \times d$ with $d \le n$. We use A_i to denote the i-th row of A, and $a_{i,j}$ for the (i, j)-th entry of A. $\mathsf{rows}(A)$ is the number of rows in A.

We write the (reduced) singular value decomposition of A as $(U, \Sigma, V) = \mathsf{SVD}(A)$, where $A = U\Sigma V^T$, $U \in \mathbb{R}^{n\times d}$ and $V \in \mathbb{R}^{d\times d}$ are orthonormal matrices, and $\Sigma \in \mathbb{R}^{d\times d}$ is a diagonal matrix with nonnegative diagonal values. The diagonal entries of Σ are singular values of A sorted in non-decreasing order; the columns of U and V are called left and right singular vectors respectively. The computation time of standard SVD algorithms is $O(nd^2)$. We use $\|A\|_2$ or $\|A\|$ to denote the Spectral Norm of A, which is the largest singular value of A, and $\|A\|_F$ for the *Frobenius Norm*, which is $\sqrt{\sum_{i,j} a_{i,j}^2}$. For a real symmetric matrix $X \in \mathbb{R}^{d\times d}$, let $\lambda_i(X)$ be the i-th largest eigenvalue of X. We can also characterize the spectral norm of X as

$$\|X\|_2 = \max(|\lambda_1|, |\lambda_d|) = \max_{y:\|y\|=1} |y^T X y|.$$

Hence,

$$\begin{aligned}\|A^T A - B^T B\|_2 &= \max_{x:\|x\|=1} |x^T(A^T A - B^T B)x| \\ &= \max_{x:\|x\|=1} \left|\|Ax\|_2^2 - \|Bx\|_2^2\right|.\end{aligned}$$

Let $\sigma_i(A)$ be the i-th singular values of A in non-decreasing order. We have $\sigma_i^2(A) = \lambda_i(A^T A)$. It is well-known that

$$\|A\|_F^2 = \mathsf{trace}(A^T A) = \sum_i \lambda_i(A^T A) = \sum_i \sigma_i^2(A).$$

For $k \le \mathsf{rank}(A)$, we will use $[A]_k$ to denote the best rank k approximation of A, i.e.,

$$[A]_k = \arg\min_{C:\mathsf{rank}(C)\le k} \|A - C\|_F.$$

We define $[A]_0 = \mathbf{0}$. Given another matrix B with the same number of columns as A, we will use $\pi_B^k(A)$ to denote the right projection of A on the top-k right singular vectors of B, i.e. $\pi_B^k(A) = AVV^T$, where the columns of V are the top-k right singular vectors of B. We use $[A; B]$ to denote the matrix formed by concatenating the rows of A and B.

1.2 Definitions

Given a matrix $A \in \mathbb{R}^{n\times d}$, we want to compute a much smaller matrix $B \in \mathbb{R}^{\ell\times d}$, which approximates A well. We are interested in *covariance sketch* and its application to PCA.

DEFINITION 1. *The covariance error of B with respect to A is defined as $\|A^T A - B^T B\|_2$. For notational convenience, we will also use $\mathsf{coverr}(A, B)$ to denote this.*

A different but related error measure is so called *projection error* or *low rank approximation error* [16].

DEFINITION 2. *The k-projection error of B with respect to A is defined as $\|A - \pi_B^k(A)\|_F^2$, where $\pi_B^k(A)$ is the rank-k matrix resulting from project each row of A onto the subspace spanned by the top-k right singular vectors of B.*

These two error measures are related by the following lemma from [16]. For completeness, we provide a proof in Appendix A.

LEMMA 1 ([16] (MODIFIED)).

$$\|A - \pi_B^k(A)\|_F^2 \le \|A - [A]_k\|_F^2 + 2k \cdot \|A^T A - B^T B\|_2.$$

It is well-known that if we randomly sample $O(1/\varepsilon^2)$ rows from A with replacement according to probability proportional to the squared norm of each row, and rescale sampled rows appropriately, the resulting matrix has covariance error at most $\varepsilon\|A\|_F^2$ with constant probability [11]. Since many matrices of interest in practice can be well approximated by a matrix with relatively lower rank, i.e., $\|A - [A]_k\|_F^2$ is much smaller than $\|A\|_F^2$, where $[A]_k$ is the best rank-k approximation of A. Hence an error bound in terms of $\|A - [A]_k\|_F^2$ can potentially be much stronger. In addition, a covariance error of $\varepsilon\|A - [A]_k\|_F^2/2k$ directly implies a relative error low rank approximation by Lemma 1.

DEFINITION 3. *We call B an (ε, k)-sketch of A if*

$$\|A^T A - B^T B\|_2 \le \varepsilon\|A - [A]_k\|_F^2/k.$$

By abusing notation slightly, we say B is an $(\varepsilon, 0)$-sketch if

$$\mathsf{coverr}(A, B) \le \varepsilon\|A\|_F^2.$$

In *Principle Component Analysis* (PCA), the goal is to find a low-dimensional subspace that captures as much of the variance of a dataset as possible. The following approximate version of PCA with Frobenius norm error is widely studied (see e.g. [25, 5]).

DEFINITION 4. *In the (approximate) PCA problem, given $A \in \mathbb{R}^{n\times d}$, an integer $k \le \mathsf{rank}(A)$, and $0 < \varepsilon < 1$, the goal is to output a $d \times k$ orthonormal matrix such that*

$$\|A - AVV^T\|_F^2 \le (1 + \varepsilon)\|A - [A]_k\|_F^2. \tag{1}$$

The columns of V are also known as $(1 + \varepsilon)$-approximate top-k principle components (PCs).

Here V can also be viewed as a type of matrix sketch. By Lemma 1, the top k right singular vectors of any $(\varepsilon/2, k)$-sketch of A satisfy (1). However, a set of approximate PCs does not directly give good covariance error, although it has low projection error by definition. The distributed version studied in [5] requires all servers to output the same answer, while we only require one server (the coordinator) to know the answer. However, the coordinator can broadcast the answer to all servers using $O(skd)$ communication cost, which is dominated by the cost of computing the answer.

Note that, without further restrictions, an (ε, k)-sketch B may have Frobenius norm much larger than the original matrix. For technical reasons, we will always want the Frobenius norm of the sketch matrix B to be bounded: $\|B\|_F^2 \leq \|A\|_F^2 + O(\|A - [A]_k\|_F^2)$.

We study the word/bit complexity of communication costs, and assume each machine word has $O(\log(nd/\varepsilon))$ bits and each entry of the input matrix can be represented by a single machine word. W.l.o.g. we assume the entries are integers of magnitude at most $\mathrm{poly}(nd/\varepsilon)$.

1.3 Previous results

Liberty [27] adapts a well-known algorithm for finding frequent items, the MG algorithm [28], to sketching a matrix, which is called *Frequent Directions* (FD). It computes an (ε, k)-sketch containing only $O(k/\varepsilon)$ rows in one pass, which is deterministic and directly applicable to the distributed setting: each server computes a local (ε, k)-sketch independently using FD and sends it to the coordinator; the coordinator combines these local sketches and compute an (ε, k)-sketch of the combined sketch matrix. It is shown that the result is a (ε, k)-sketch of the input matrix. The communication cost is thus $O(skd/\varepsilon)$ real numbers.[1]

An alternative approach is to use random sampling. The matrix formed by a random sample of $O(1/\varepsilon^2)$ rescaled rows from A has covariance error at most $\varepsilon\|A\|_F^2$ with constant probability [10]. Random sampling can be implemented in the distributed model with communication cost $O(s + d/\varepsilon^2)$. However, it has a quadratic dependent on ε and only gives a weak error bound.

For the PCA problem, the current best algorithm is by Boutsidis et al. [5]. See section 1.4 for more details on the communication bounds.

1.4 Our contributions

In this paper, we obtain distributed streaming algorithms for computing covariance sketch with improved communication cost, and prove a tight deterministic lower bound in the blackboard model. We also improve the communication cost for the distributed PCA problem.

As there is no bound on maximum wordsize required by the original FD of Liberty [27], the communication cost is only in terms of real numbers. We show how to modify it so that the communication cost is $O(skd/\varepsilon)$ words.[2] Note this communication cost is simply s times the size of a single sketch, where s is the number of servers. Since the sketch size $O(kd/\varepsilon)$ was shown to be optimal [35] (up to a log factor) for an (ε, k)-sketch, it seems difficult to reduce this communication cost. Indeed, we show that this is optimal for deterministic algorithms by proving a deterministic communication lower bound of $O(skd/\varepsilon)$ bits.

On the other hand, we propose a new algorithms with communication cost $o(s) \times$ sketch size, which is the first improvement over [27]. In particular, for (ε, k)-sketch, our communication cost is $O(sdk +$

[1]Currently there is no word complexity analysis on FD.

[2]Our technique only works for communication cost, and the space usage of each server is still in real numbers.

	$\varepsilon\|A\|_F^2$	$\varepsilon\|A - [A]_k\|_F^2/k$
[27, 16]	$O(sd/\varepsilon)$	$O(skd/\varepsilon)$
Sampling [10]	$O(s + d/\varepsilon^2)$	
New	$O(\frac{\sqrt{s}d}{\varepsilon} \cdot \sqrt{\log d})$	$O(sdk + \frac{\sqrt{s}kd}{\varepsilon} \cdot \sqrt{\log d})$
Deterministic LB	$\tilde{\Omega}(sd/\varepsilon)$	$\Omega(skd/\varepsilon)$

Table 1: Communication costs for covariance sketch. The communication costs our algorithms are in words. The lower bounds are in terms of bits

	Communication
[5]	$O(skd + \frac{sk}{\varepsilon^2} \cdot \min\{d, k/\varepsilon^2\})$
New	$O(skd + \frac{\sqrt{s \log d} \cdot k}{\varepsilon} \cdot \min\{d, k/\varepsilon^2\})$

Table 2: Communication costs for distributed PCA. The communication costs are in words.

$\frac{\sqrt{s}dk}{\varepsilon} \cdot \sqrt{\log d})$ words, while the optimal sketch size is $\Theta(dk/\varepsilon)$ [35]. We achieve this by designing a new algorithm which further compresses the local (ε, k)-sketches computed by FD. Since this new algorithm is applied on sketches, the servers do not need to access the original data in this step. The results are summarized in Table 1.

Directly applying our (ε, k)-sketch algorithm to the PCA problem (by Lemma 1), the cost is also $O(sdk) + \tilde{O}(\sqrt{s}dk/\varepsilon)$ words. Boutsidis et al. [5] recently gave an algorithm with communication cost $O(sdk + \frac{sk}{\varepsilon^2} \cdot \min\{d, k/\varepsilon^2\})$ words in the distributed batch model, which is the first algorithm that beats the $O(sdk/\varepsilon)$ bound of [22] when d is larger than k/ε^3. Our result is $o(sdk/\varepsilon)$ as long as $d = 2^{o(s)}$. They also showed an $\Omega(sdk)$ low bound if all servers are required to know the answer. When $s \geq \tilde{\Omega}(\frac{1}{\varepsilon^2})$, our cost is $O(skd)$ which is optimal in this setting[3]. But for smaller s, the cost is dominated by the $\tilde{O}(\sqrt{s}dk/\varepsilon)$ term. We then show how to improve this to $\tilde{O}(\sqrt{s}k/\varepsilon \cdot \min\{d, k/\varepsilon^2\})$ by utilizing the algorithm of [5].

In our algorithm, each server can independently computes a matrix $B^{(i)}$ (with little communication), such that $B = [B^{(1)}; \cdots; B^{(s)}]$ is a (ε, k)-sketch of A and the number of rows in B is $O(sk + \frac{\sqrt{s}k}{\varepsilon} \cdot \sqrt{\log d})$. We call B a *distributed covariance sketch*. To solve PCA, we do not need to send B; we could compute the top k singular vectors of B using any distributed algorithm. We show that only approximate singular vectors of B are needed. More precisely, if B is an (ε, k)-sketch of A, then any $(1 + \varepsilon)$-approximate top-k PCs of B is a $(1 + O(\varepsilon))$-approximate answer for A. Therefore, we can run the algorithm of [5] on B to compute the approximate PCs of B, which then solves the PCA problem for A. The communication cost of this combined algorithm is $O(skd) + \tilde{O}(\sqrt{s}k/\varepsilon \cdot \min\{d, k/\varepsilon^2\})$. While the algorithm of [5] needs to access the input multiple times, our combined algorithm is a distributed streaming algorithm (since the algorithm of [5] is only applied on top of a distributed sketch).

We emphasize that the PCA algorithm of [5] works for *arbitrary partition* model, where each server gets a matrix $A^{(i)} \in \mathbb{R}^{n \times d}$ and $A = \sum_{i=1}^{s} A^{(i)}$, while our algorithm only works for row-partition models.

1.5 Other related works

The problem of computing covariance matrix sketch was widely studied in the row-wise update streaming model [27, 16, 15, 34]. Optimal space lower bounds was proved in [35]. In the distributed setting, there was no improvement in communication cost since [27].

[3]Broadcasting the answer only needs $O(skd)$ communication.

Ghashami et al [17] studied the problem in the distributed monitoring model. This model is similar to the distributed streaming model but the coordinator needs to track the answer continuously, which is a stronger requirement. It is an interesting question whether our techniques can be used to improve the communication costs of their algorithms. The approximate distributed PCA problem was studied in [14, 22, 25, 26, 4, 5]. Zhang et al. [37] studied the distributed generalized matrix rank problem. Streaming numerical linear algebra problems were studied in [6]. The communication complexity of boolean matrix multiplication in the two-party model was studied in [33]. Li et al. proved multi-party communication lower bounds for several linear algebraic problems, but only hold in the message passing model. Our distributed computation model is similar to the Massively Parallel Communication model (MPC) [2, 3], which is motivated by MapReduce.

2. DETERMINISTIC MATRIX SKETCHING

In this section, we investigate the deterministic communication complexity of computing a covariance sketch in the distributed model. Recall that each server S_i gets a local input matrix $A^{(i)} \in \mathbb{R}^{n_i \times d}$; and the entire input matrix is $A = [A^{(1)}; \cdots ; A^{(s)}]$ with $n = \sum_i n_i$ rows.

Frequent Directions. We will use the *Frequent Directions* (FD) algorithm by Liberty [27], denoted as FD. Ghashami and Phillips [16] gave an improved analysis, which is summarized in the following theorem.

THEOREM 1 ([27, 16]). *Given $A \in \mathbb{R}^{n\times d}$, $\mathsf{FD}(A, \varepsilon, k)$ processes A in one pass using $O(dk/\varepsilon)$ working space. It maintains a sketch matrix $B \in \mathbb{R}^{O(k/\varepsilon)\times d}$ such that*

$$\|A^T A - B^T B\|_2 \leq \varepsilon \|A - [A]_k\|_F^2/k.$$

The original FD algorithm of [27] is deterministic and has running time $O(ndk/\varepsilon)$ to process an $n \times d$ matrix. More recently, the running time was improved to $\tilde{O}(\mathsf{nnz}(A)k/\varepsilon)$ by [15] based on fast randomized (approximate) singular value decomposition (thus the algorithm of [15] is randomized), where $\mathsf{nnz}(A)$ denotes the number of non-zero entries in A. We remark that the working space of FD is in terms of real numbers rather than words.

One nice property of FD is that it is mergeable [1]. Formally, let $B = \mathsf{FD}(A, \varepsilon, k)$ and $B' = \mathsf{FD}(A', \varepsilon, k)$ for any A and A' with the same number of columns, then it was shown that $C' = \mathsf{FD}([B; B'], \varepsilon, k)$ has the same covariance error as $C = \mathsf{FD}([A; A'], \varepsilon, k)$. By induction, the number of sketches to merge can be arbitrary. This mergeable property makes FD directly applicable to the distributed model, i.e., each server sketches its local matrix independently, and sends the covariance sketch to the coordinator; the coordinator simply combines the sketches using another FD. Therefore, the algorithm is deterministic and works in the distributed streaming model. Note that the total communication cost is $O(skd/\varepsilon)$ real numbers. A real number may take a large number of bits to represent. We will show how to resolve this issue in section 3.3.

THEOREM 2. *There is a deterministic algorithm in the distributed streaming model which computes a sketch matrix with covariance error at most $\varepsilon\|A-[A]_k\|_F^2/k$. The communication cost is $O(sdk/\varepsilon)$ words ,and the space usage of each server is $O(kd/\varepsilon)$ real numbers.*

2.1 Deterministic Lower Bound

In this section we will prove communication lower bound in the s-party number-in-hand model with a shared blackboard. We first provide some preliminaries on multi-party communication complexity.

2.1.1 *Rectangle property of communication complexity in the blackboard model*

Let Π be any deterministic protocol in this model for some problem f, and let π be a particular transcript of Π (concatenation of all messages). Define ρ to be the subset of all possible inputs for f, which generate the same transcript π under protocol Π. It is well-known [24] that ρ is a combinatorial rectangle. Formally, ρ is a Cartesian product $\rho = B_1 \times B_2 \times \cdots \times B_s$, where B_i is a subset of all possible inputs for player i. For a deterministic protocol, each input always generates the same transcript, therefore Π partitions the set of all possible inputs into a set of combinatorial rectangles $P = \{\rho_1, \rho_2, \cdots, \rho_h\}$, each of which corresponds to a unique transcript. In particular, the protocol cannot distinguish those inputs in each ρ_j—in other words any correct protocol Π should produce a rectangle partition such that all inputs in any rectangle share a common correct output. Since the transcript corresponds to each rectangle is unique, the maximum length among all transcripts (i.e. the communication cost) is at least $\log|P|$.

2.1.2 *Proof of the lower bound*

In this section, we show a deterministic lower bound of $\Omega(sd/\varepsilon)$ bits for $(\varepsilon, 0)$-sketch, i.e. with covariance error $\varepsilon\|A\|_F^2$. Note that this directly implies a lower bound of $\Omega(skd/\varepsilon)$ bits for (ε, k)-sketch. Put $t = \frac{\sigma}{\varepsilon}$ for constant $\sigma \leq 1$ to be determined later. In our lower bound proof, each server S_i gets a $t \times d$ matrix $A^{(i)} \in \{-1, +1\}^{t\times d}$, and thus the total number of possible inputs is 2^{std} and all input matrices have Frobenius norm exactly std. Our goal is to show that if the size of a combinatorial rectangle ρ is larger than $2^{(1-\beta)std}$ for some absolute constant β, then there must be two input matrices A, A' in ρ such that $\|A^T A - A'^T A'\|_2$ is too large, which means they cannot share the same answer. Therefore, the rectangle partition produced by any correct determnisitic protocol cannot contain a rectangle of size above $2^{(1-\beta)std}$, which implies the communication cost is at least $\Omega(\beta std) = \Omega(sd/\varepsilon)$.

LEMMA 2. *There exists a constant $\beta < 1/2$, such that, for any rectangle ρ of size larger than $2^{(1-\beta)std}$, we can find $A, A' \in \rho$ satisfying*

$$\|A^T A - A'^T A'\|_2 \geq \Omega(sd) - st.$$

PROOF. We write $\rho = B_1 \times B_2 \cdots \times B_s$, where $B_i \subseteq \{-1, +1\}^{t\times d}$ for each i, and define $U = \{i \mid |B_i| \geq 2^{(1-2\beta)td}\}$. We have the following simple property.

CLAIM 1. *If $|\rho| \geq 2^{(1-\beta)td}$, then $|U| \geq s/2$.*

PROOF. U is the same as $\{i \mid \log|B_i| \geq (1-2\beta)td\}$. By our assumption, we have

$$\sum_{i=1}^{s} \log|B_i| = \log|\rho| \geq (1-\beta)std.$$

Using the fact that $\log|B_i| \leq td$ for all i and an averaging argument, we conclude that $|U| \geq s/2$. □

Note that each B_i is a subset of $\{-1, +1\}^{t\times d}$; we define $B_{i,j}$ be the projection of B_i onto the jth row, i.e.,

$$B_{i,j} = \{b \mid b \text{ is the } j\text{th row of some matrix in } B_i\}.$$

It is not hard to verify that

$$|B_i| \leq \prod_{j=1}^{t} |B_{i,j}|,$$

and thus there exists j with $|B_{i,j}| \geq 2^{(1-2\beta)d}$, provided that $|B_i| \geq 2^{(1-2\beta)td}$. For each $i \in U$, we fix such a j_i, and for simplicity we write $Q_i = B_{i,j_i}$. The following lemma is proved in [21], where x is distributed uniformly in $\{-1,+1\}^d$.

LEMMA 3 ([21]). *Assume $L \subseteq \{-1,+1\}^d$ and $|L| \geq 2^{(1-\alpha)d}$ for a sufficient small constant α, then we have*

$$\mathsf{Pr}_x[\max_{y \in L} x^T y \geq 0.2d] \geq 3/4.$$

Applying the above lemma we prove the follow result.

CLAIM 2. *Let $\ell = |U|$. We have*

$$\mathsf{E}_x\left[\sum_{i \in U} \max_{y^{(i)} \in Q_i} (x^T y^{(i)})^2\right] = \Omega(\ell d^2).$$

PROOF. We have $|Q_i| \geq 2^{(1-2\beta)d}$ for each $i \in U$, therefore, by setting β small enough, we can apply Lemma 3 on each Q_i and get

$$\mathsf{Pr}_x\left[\max_{y^{(i)} \in Q_i} x^T y^{(i)} \geq 0.2d\right] \geq 3/4.$$

It follows that

$$\begin{aligned}\mathsf{E}_x[\max_{y \in Q_i}(x^T y^{(i)})^2] &\geq \mathsf{Pr}_x\left[\max_{y^{(i)} \in Q_i} x^T y^{(i)} \geq 0.2d\right] \cdot \Omega(d^2) \\ &= \Omega(d^2).\end{aligned}$$

Hence,

$$\begin{aligned}\mathsf{E}_x\left[\sum_{i \in U} \max_{y^{(i)} \in Q_i} (x^T y^{(i)})^2\right] &= \sum_{i \in U} \mathsf{E}_x\left[\max_{y^{(i)} \in Q_i} (x^T y^{(i)})^2\right] \\ &= \ell \cdot \Omega(d^2).\end{aligned}$$

□

Obviously, for any x

$$\max_{M^{(i)} \in B_i} \|M^{(i)} x\|^2 \geq \max_{y^{(i)} \in Q_i} (x^T y^{(i)})^2.$$

By Claim 2 and the fact $|U| \geq s/2$, it holds

$$\mathsf{E}_x\left[\sum_{i=1}^{s} \max_{M^{(i)} \in B_i} \|M^{(i)} x\|^2\right] = \Omega(sd^2). \quad (2)$$

Let $W^{(i)}$ be any matrix in $B^{(i)}$ for $i = 1, \cdots, s$. According to standard calculation, it can be shown that

$$\mathsf{E}_x\left[\|W^{(i)} x\|^2\right] = td.$$

Therefore, we have

$$\mathsf{E}_x\left[\sum_{i=1}^{s} \|W^{(i)} x\|^2\right] = std.$$

Combined with (2), we get

$$\mathsf{E}_x\left[\sum_{i=1}^{s}\left(\max_{M^{(i)} \in B_i} \|M^{(i)} x\|^2 - \|W^{(i)} x\|^2\right)\right] = \Omega(sd^2) - std.$$

Then there exist a vector $x^* \in \{-1,+1\}^d$ and matrices $M^{(i)} \in B_i$, for $i = 1, \cdots, s$, such that

$$\sum_{i=1}^{s} \|M^{(i)} x^*\|^2 - \sum_{i=1}^{s} \|W^{(i)} x^*\|^2 = \Omega(sd^2) - std. \quad (3)$$

We set $A = [M^{(1)}; \cdots; M^{(s)}]$ and $A' = [W^{(1)}; \cdots; W^{(i)}]$, and obviously $A, A' \in \rho$. From (3), we have

$$\begin{aligned}\|A^T A - A'^T A'\|_2 &= \max_{x \in \mathbb{R}^d} \frac{\left|\|Ax\|^2 - \|A'x\|^2\right|}{\|x\|^2} \\ &\geq \frac{\left|\sum_{i=1}^{s} \|M^{(i)} x^*\|^2 - \sum_{i=1}^{s} \|W^{(i)} x^*\|^2\right|}{\|x^*\|_2^2} \\ &= \Omega(sd) - st,\end{aligned}$$

which proves the lemma. □

Now we are ready to prove our main theorem for deterministic complexity.

THEOREM 3. *Let $A \in \{-1,+1\}^{n \times d}$ be the input matrix which is row-partitioned across s servers. If $1/\varepsilon \leq d$, then the deterministic communication complexity of computing a $(\varepsilon, 0)$-sketch matrix X is $\Omega(sd/\varepsilon)$ bits.*

PROOF. In our hard instance, each server gets a matrix $A^{(i)} \in \{-1,+1\}^{t \times d}$ where $t = \sigma/\varepsilon$ for a sufficiently small constant σ, and thus $n = st$.[4] As a result, $\varepsilon\|A\|_F^2 = \sigma sd$, which is the maximum covariance error of X allowed. Let us consider any correct deterministic protocol Π, which partitions the set of all possible inputs into combinatorial rectangles $P = \{\rho_1, \rho_2, \cdots, \rho_h\}$.

Assume, for some i, $|\rho_i| \geq 2^{(1-\beta)td}$, then by Lemma 2, there exist A and A' in ρ_i such that $\|A^T A - A'^T A'\|_2 = \Omega(sd) - st$. By our assumption, $t \leq \sigma d$, and thus $\|A^T A - A'^T A'\|_2 > 2\varepsilon\|A\|_F^2$ for sufficiently small σ. Let X be the output corresponding to ρ_i. We have

$$\begin{aligned}\|A^T A - X^T X\|_2 + \|A'^T A' - X^T X\|_2 \geq& \|A^T A - A'^T A'\|_2 \\ >& 2\varepsilon\|A\|_F^2.\end{aligned}$$

It implies that the error of X is too large for either A or A', which contradicts the correctness, so $|\rho_i| < 2^{(1-\beta)std}$ for all i. Since the number of all possible inputs is 2^{std}, we have $|P| \geq 2^{\beta std}$, thus the communication cost of Π is at least $\log|P| = \Omega(std) = \Omega(sd/\varepsilon)$ bits. □

Since the problem can be trivially solved with $O(sd^2)$ words of communication, our bound is also tight for the case when $1/\varepsilon \geq d$. The error allowed for an (ε, k)-sketch is $\varepsilon\|A - [A]_k\|_F^2/k \leq \varepsilon\|A\|_F^2/k$, so the above theorem implies a lower bound of $\Omega(skd/\varepsilon)$ bits for (ε, k)-sketch.

3. RANDOMIZED ALGORITHMS

The key step that enables us to bypass the deterministic lower bound is a better randomized algorithm which computes a sketch with covariance error $\varepsilon\|A\|_F^2/k$ for any input matrix A. For this problem, the deterministic lower bound is $\Omega(skd/\varepsilon)$, however, we give a new randomized algorithm with communication cost $O(\frac{\sqrt{s}kd}{\varepsilon} \cdot \sqrt{\log d})$.

We first present our communication-efficient algorithm in distributed model with covariance error $\alpha\|A\|_F^2$. Then show how to use this algorithm as a subroutine to get an efficient algorithm with stronger error bound.

[4]Note that, for general n, we can append 0 rows at the end of each $A^{(i)}$, which will not affect the proof.

3.1 Covariance error $\alpha\|A\|_F^2$

As we have shown, this problem can be solve deterministically with $O(sd/\alpha)$ communication. An alternative approach is to use random sampling [10, 30, 12]. Sampling can be adapted to the distributed setting, however the communication cost is $O(d/\alpha^2)$, which has an undesirable quadratic dependence on $1/\alpha$.

Our new approach has $\tilde{O}(\sqrt{s}d/\alpha)$ communication cost, which is $o(s)$ times the optimal sketch size for $(\alpha, 0)$-sketch (which is $\Theta(d/\alpha)$ [35]). In this section, we give an algorithm with cost in terms of real numbers, then will discuss how to improve this to word complexity in section 3.3. Our approach also performs random sampling, but we sample the rows of an "aggregated" form of the input matrix.

3.1.1 Our algorithm

The core procedure is the *singular-value-sampling* algorithm (SVS), which is presented in Algorithm 1. In this algorithm, given an input matrix A, we first compute its SVD $A = U\Sigma V^T$, and then sample each right singular vector v_j with probability depending on the corresponding (squared) singular value σ_j^2. We use a function $g()$ to characterize the sampling distribution, i.e., $g(\sigma_j^2)$ is the probability to sample jth singular vector. If it is sampled, we rescale v_j by $\frac{\sigma_j}{\sqrt{g(\sigma_j^2)}}$. In our distributed algorithm, each server S_i runs SVS on the input matrix $A^{(i)}$, and then sends the output to the coordinator (Algorithm 2).

Note that, in our algorithm, each server also performs row sampling. The differences between our algorithms and the row sampling algorithms from [10, 30, 12] for covariance sketch are as follows. (1) We sample the rows of the "aggregated" form of the input matrix instead of the original. Let $U\Sigma V^T$ be the singular value decomposition of A. We view $\mathsf{agg}(A) := \Sigma V^T$ as the "aggregated" form of A. (2) Our sampling scheme is different—in previous works, each row of the sketch matrix is an i.i.d. sample from the original matrix (with replacement) and rescaled, but we use independent Bernoulli sampling. Although this seems insignificant, it is actually crucial to our analysis. It is not clear whether a similar bound holds if we use i.i.d. sampling instead.

Algorithm 1: $\mathsf{SVS}(A, g)$: $A \in \mathbb{R}^{n\times d}$; g is the sampling function.

Set B empty
Compute $(U, \Sigma, V) = \mathsf{SVD}(A)$
for $j = 0$ **to** d **do**
    Set $x_j = 1$ with probability $g(\sigma_j^2)$, and $x_j = 0$ with probability $1 - g(\sigma_j^2)$
    Let $w_j = \sigma_j / \sqrt{g(\sigma_j^2)}$
    Append v_j^T rescaled by $x_j w_j$ (i.e., $x_j \cdot w_j \cdot V_j^T$) to B, where v_j is the j-th right singular vector
Remove zero rows in B
Output B

Algorithm 2: Algorithm for S_i. Input: $A^{(i)} \in \mathbb{R}^{n_i\times d}$ and sampling function g.

$B^{(i)} = \mathsf{SVS}(A^{(i)}, g)$
Send $B^{(i)}$ to the coordinator

Let $B = [B^{(1)}, \cdots, B^{(s)}]$. For technical reasons, we also want the Frobenius norm of the sketch matrix B to be bounded: $\|B\|_F^2 \le O(1) \cdot \|A\|_F^2$. It is quite standard to bound the norm of B for our algorithm (see Appendix B), so we will focus on bounding the covariance error $\|A^TA - B^TB\|_2$. We first prove a theorem for a general sampling function g, then discuss how to pick a good sampling function in the next section.

THEOREM 4. *Let $A^{(i)}$ be the input of the i-th server, and $B^{(i)}$ be matrix sent by S_i. Let A and B be the concatenation of $A^{(i)}$'s and $B^{(i)}$'s respectively. We define*

$$M = \max_{i,j} \frac{\sigma_{i,j}^2}{g(\sigma_{i,j}^2)}, \text{ and } \kappa^2 = \sum_{i=1}^{s} \max_j \frac{\sigma_{i,j}^4 \cdot (1 - g(\sigma_{i,j}^2))}{g(\sigma_{i,j}^2)},$$

where $\sigma_{i,j}$ is the jth largest singular value of $A^{(i)}$, then the following inequality holds:

$$\mathsf{Pr}[\|B^TB - A^TA\|_2 \ge t] \le 2d \cdot \exp\left(\frac{-t^2/2}{\kappa^2 + Mt/3}\right).$$

Before giving the proof, we first briefly summarize the main idea behind the proof.

Main idea. Previous row sampling approaches sample t rows from A using i.i.d. sampling, so, in the analysis, B^TB can be treated as the sum of t i.i.d. random matrices of rank 1. To bound the covariance error, [30, 12] used a matrix concentration inequality, while [10] used a variance argument. On the other hand, in our analysis, we will view B^TB as the sum of s random matrices with potentially high rank, i.e., $\sum_{i=1}^{s} B^{(i)T}B^{(i)}$. Since we sample the rows of the "aggregated" matrix (with orthogonal rows) using Bernoulli sampling, each resulting random matrix $B^{(i)}$ has orthogonal rows, which is important to our analysis. However, the random matrices have high rank and are not i.i.d. now, so we cannot apply the same inequality used in [30, 12]. Instead, we use *Matrix Bernstein Inequality* (see [32]).

The main theorem follows from the following three claims, which are about the output matrix of the SVS sampling algorithm. Let $x = [x_1, \cdots, x_d]$ be a random vector, where x_j is defined in Algorithm 1. More precisely, x_j's are Bernoulli random variables:

$$x_j = \begin{cases} 1 & \text{the } j\text{th singular vector is sampled} \\ 0 & \text{otherwise.} \end{cases}$$

Clearly, the distribution of x_j^2 is the same as x_j, which take value 1 with probability $g(\sigma_j^2)$, where σ_j is the jth largest singular value of A. Let $w \in \mathbb{R}^d$ be a vector, with w_j defined in Algorithm 1, i.e. $w_j = \frac{\sigma_j}{\sqrt{g(\sigma_j^2)}}$.

CLAIM 3. *If A and B be the input and output of Algorithm 1 respectively, then $\mathsf{E}[B^TB] = A^TA$.*

PROOF. Let v_j be the jth column of V. We have

$$A^TA = \sum_{j=1}^{d} \sigma_j^2 v_j v_j^T.$$

By definition, $B = \mathsf{Diag}(x)\mathsf{Diag}(w)V^T$, then we have

$$\begin{aligned} B^TB &= V \cdot \mathsf{Diag}(x)^2\mathsf{Diag}(w)^2 \cdot V^T \\ &= \sum_{j=1}^{d} x_j^2 w_j^2 v_j v_j^T \end{aligned} \tag{4}$$

So we have

$$\begin{aligned}\mathsf{E}[B^TB] &= \mathsf{E}[\sum_{j=1}^{d} x_j^2 w_j^2 v_j v_j^T] \\ &= \sum_{j=1}^{d} \mathsf{E}[x_j^2] w_j^2 v_j v_j^T \\ &= \sum_{j=1}^{d} \sigma_j^2 v_j v_j^T = A^T A.\end{aligned}$$

□

CLAIM 4. *If A and B are the input and output of Algorithm 1 respectively, then we have*

$$\lambda_{\max}(B^TB - A^TA) \le \max_j \frac{\sigma_j^2}{g(\sigma_j^2)}.$$

PROOF. Using Eq (4), we have

$$B^TB - A^TA = \sum_{j=1}^{d} (x_j^2 w_j^2 - \sigma_j^2) v_j v_j^T = VDV^T, \quad (5)$$

where D is a diagonal matrix with $D_{j,j} = x_j^2 w_j^2 - \sigma_j^2$. Since V is orthonormal, VDV^T is the eigen-decomposition of $B^TB - A^TA$, and thus

$$\begin{aligned}\lambda_{\max}(B^TB - A^TA) &= \max_j (x_j^2 w_j^2 - \sigma_j^2) \\ &\le \max w_j^2 = \max_j \frac{\sigma_j^2}{g(\sigma_j^2)}.\end{aligned}$$

□

CLAIM 5. *If A and B are the input and output of Algorithm 1 respectively, then we have*

$$\|\mathsf{E}[(B^TB - A^TA)^2]\|_2 = \max_j \frac{\sigma_j^4 \cdot (1 - g(\sigma_j^2))}{g(\sigma_j^2)}.$$

PROOF. From Eq (5), we have

$$(B^TB - A^TA)^2 = VD^2V^T = \sum_{j=1}^{d} (x_j^2 w_j^2 - \sigma_j^2)^2 \cdot v_j v_j^T.$$

By definition, we have $\mathsf{E}[x_j^2 w_j^2] = \sigma_j^2$, and thus

$$\begin{aligned}\mathsf{E}[(x_j^2 w_j^2 - \sigma_j^2)^2] &= \mathsf{E}[(x_j^2 w_j^2 - \mathsf{E}[x_j^2 w_j^2])^2] \\ &= \mathsf{Var}[x_j^2 w_j^2] = w_j^4 \cdot \mathsf{Var}[x_j^2] \\ &= \frac{\sigma_j^4}{g^2(\sigma_j^2)} \cdot g(\sigma_j^2)(1 - g(\sigma_j^2)) \\ &= \sigma_j^4 \cdot \frac{1 - g(\sigma_j^2)}{g(\sigma_j^2)}.\end{aligned}$$

Here we use the fact that the variance of a Bernoulli random variable with parameter p is $p(1-p)$. So we have

$$\begin{aligned}\mathsf{E}[(B^TB - A^TA)^2] &= \sum_{j=1}^{d} \mathsf{E}[(x_j^2 w_j^2 - \sigma_j^2)^2] \cdot v_j v_j^T \\ &= \sum_{j=1}^{d} \sigma_j^4 \cdot \frac{1 - g(\sigma_j^2)}{g(\sigma^2)} \cdot v_j v_j^T \\ &= VD'V^T,\end{aligned}$$

where D' is a diagonal matrix with $D'_{j,j} = \sigma_j^4 \cdot \frac{1-g(\sigma_j^2)}{g(\sigma_j^2)}$ for all j. Therefore, $VD'V^T$ is the eigen-decomposition of $\mathsf{E}[(B^TB - A^TA)^2]$, and the diagonals of D' are the eigenvalues. Since $g(\sigma_j^2) \le 1$, the eigenvalues are all non-negative. It follows that

$$\begin{aligned}\|\mathsf{E}[(B^TB - A^TA)^2]\|_2 &= \max_j |D'_{j,j}| \\ &= \max_j \frac{\sigma_j^4 \cdot (1 - g(\sigma_j^2))}{g(\sigma^2)}.\end{aligned}$$

□

Now we are ready to prove the main theorem.

PROOF OF THEOREM 4. To prove this theorem, we will use the following *Matrix Bernstein Inequality*, which can be found in [32] (Theorem 6.1).

LEMMA 4 (MATRIX BERNSTEIN). *Consider a finite sequence $\{X_k\}$ of independent, random, self-adjoint (or Hermitian) matrices with dimension d. Assume that*

$$\mathsf{E}[X_k] = 0 \text{ and } \lambda_{\max}(X_k) \le R$$

almost surely for all k. Define $\sigma^2 := \|\sum_k \mathsf{E}[X_k^2]\|_2$. Then the following inequality holds for all $t \ge 0$.

$$\Pr[\lambda_{\max}(\sum_k X_k) \ge t] \le d \cdot \exp\left(\frac{-t^2/2}{\sigma^2 + Rt/3}\right).$$

To use the Matrix Bernstein Inequality, we define

$$X_i = B^{(i)T} B^{(i)} - A^{(i)^T} A^{(i)}.$$

By Claim 3, $\mathsf{E}[X_i] = 0$ for all i. By Claim 4, $\lambda_{\max}(X_i) = \max_j \frac{\sigma_{i,j}^2}{g(\sigma_{i,j}^2)}$ for all i, which will always be bounded in our case, and thus we just set $R = \max_i \lambda_{\max}(X_i)$, that is

$$R = \max_i \lambda_{\max}(X_i) = \max_{i,j} \frac{\sigma_{i,j}^2}{g(\sigma_{i,j}^2)} = M.$$

The last equality is by definition of M in the statement of Theorem 4. Using Claim 5, we can bound σ^2:

$$\begin{aligned}\sigma^2 &= \|\sum_i \mathsf{E}[X_i^2]\| \le \sum_i \|\mathsf{E}[X_i^2]\| && \text{Triangle inequality} \\ &= \sum_i \max_j \frac{\sigma_{i,j}^4 \cdot (1 - g(\sigma_{i,j}^2))}{g(\sigma_{i,j}^2)} && \text{Claim 5.} \\ &= \kappa^2 && \text{By definition of } \kappa^2\end{aligned}$$

Now we can directly use Lemma 4 and prove that

$$\Pr[\lambda_{\max}(B^TB - A^TA) \ge t] \le d \cdot \exp\left(\frac{-t^2/2}{\kappa^2 + Mt/3}\right).$$

To establish the theorem, we still need to show

$$\Pr[\lambda_{\max}(A^TA - B^TB) \ge t] \le d \cdot \exp\left(\frac{-t^2/2}{\kappa^2 + Mt/3}\right),$$

but this inequality can be proved in exactly the same way, which we omit. □

3.1.2 Sampling functions

Next we discuss which sampling functions to use. For our application, we need to set $t = \alpha\|A\|_F^2$ in Theorem 4. Observe that, given any g, the total communication cost is $d \cdot \sum_{i,j} g(\sigma_{i,j}^2)$ in expectation. The most natural choice is a linear function, i.e., $g(x) = ax$ for some a. We present the analysis of linear functions in Appendix C.

THEOREM 5 (LINEAR). *If we set*

$$g(x) = \min\{\frac{\sqrt{s}}{\alpha\|A\|_F^2}\log(d/\delta)\cdot x, 1\},$$

then with probability $1-\delta$

$$\|B^TB - A^TA\|_2 \le 3\alpha\|A\|_F^2, \text{ and } \|B\|_F \le 2\|A\|_F.$$

The communication cost is $O(\frac{\sqrt{s}d}{\alpha}\cdot\log\frac{d}{\delta})$.

However, due to technical reasons, the above linear function is sub-optimal. We show that a less intuitive quadratic function gives a better bound on the communication cost.

THEOREM 6 (QUADRATIC). *If we set*

$$g(x) = \begin{cases}\min\{\frac{s}{\alpha^2\|A\|_F^4}\log(d/\delta)\cdot x^2, 1\} & \text{if } x \ge \frac{\alpha\|A\|_F^2}{s}\\ 0 & \text{otherwise}\end{cases},$$

then with probability $1-\delta$,

$$\|B^TB - A^TA\| \le 4\alpha\|A\|, \text{ and } \|B\|_F \le 2\|A\|_F.$$

The communication cost is $O(\frac{\sqrt{s}d}{\alpha}\cdot\sqrt{\log\frac{d}{\delta}})$.

PROOF. We observe that $\frac{\sigma^4\cdot(1-g(\sigma^2))}{g(\sigma^2)} \le \frac{\sigma^4}{g(\sigma^2)}$. If we use a quadratic function, i.e., $g(x) = bx^2$, the above inequality is bounded by $1/b$. So we have

$$\kappa^2 \le \sum_i \frac{1}{b} = \frac{s}{b}. \tag{6}$$

Since we set $b = \tilde{O}\left(\frac{s}{\alpha^2\|A\|_F^4}\right)$, it holds that $\kappa^2 \le \tilde{O}\left(\alpha^2\|A\|_F^4\right)$. However, now

$$M = \max_{i,j}\frac{\sigma_{i,j}^2}{g(\sigma_{i,j}^2)} = \tilde{O}\left(\max_{i,j}\frac{\alpha^2\|A\|_F^4}{s\cdot\sigma_{i,j}^2}\right),$$

which could be infinitely small when $\sigma_{i,j}$ is very close to zero. Therefore, in order to make this sampling function work, we need to drop all the small singular values. This is the reason why we set $g(x) = 0$ for $x \le \frac{\alpha\|A\|_F^2}{s}$.

For the i-th server, given $A^{(i)}$, we define a new matrix $\bar{A}^{(i)}$ as follows. We write its SVD as $A^{(i)} = (U,\Sigma,V)$, and define a diagonal matrix $\bar{\Sigma}$:

$$\bar{\Sigma}_{j,j} = \begin{cases}\sigma_j & \text{if } \sigma_j \ge \frac{\sqrt{\alpha}\|A\|_F}{\sqrt{s}}\\ 0 & \text{otherwise.}\end{cases}$$

Let $\bar{A}^{(i)} = \bar{\Sigma}V^T$. It holds that

$$\|A^{(i)T}A^{(i)} - \bar{A}^{(i)T}\bar{A}^{(i)}\|_2 = \|V(\Sigma^2 - \bar{\Sigma}^2)V^T\|_2 \le \frac{\alpha\|A\|_F^2}{s}.$$

Let $\bar{A}$ be the concatenation of $\bar{A}^{(i)}$'s, we have

$$\begin{aligned}\|A^TA - \bar{A}^T\bar{A}\|_2 &\le \sum_{i=1}^s \|A^{(i)T}A^{(i)} - \bar{A}^{(i)T}\bar{A}^{(i)}\|_2\\ &\le \sum_{i=1}^s \frac{\alpha\|A\|_F^2}{s} = \alpha\|A\|_F^2.\end{aligned} \tag{7}$$

This is the error resulting from dropping all the small singular values. By triangle inequality, it is now sufficient to bound $\|\bar{A}^T\bar{A} - B^TB\|_2 \le \alpha\|A\|_F^2$. Here B is the output for A, but B essentially has the same distribution as the output of the algorithm being applied on $\bar{A}$. So, to bound $\|\bar{A}^T\bar{A} - B^TB\|_2$, we can use Theorem 4 on $\bar{A}$ which has the property that all the squared singular values are larger than $\frac{\alpha\|A\|_F^2}{s}$. We set $t = \alpha\|A\|_F^2$, and it is easy to verify that

$$\begin{aligned}Mt/3 &\le \frac{t}{3}\cdot\max_{i,j}\frac{\sigma_{i,j}^2}{g(\sigma_{i,j}^2)} = \frac{t}{3}\cdot\max_{i,j}\frac{\alpha^2\|A\|_F^4}{s\cdot\sigma_{i,j}^2\cdot\log\frac{d}{\delta}}\\ &\le \frac{t}{3}\cdot\alpha\|A\|_F^2/\log\frac{d}{\delta} = \frac{\alpha^2\|A\|_F^4}{3\log\frac{d}{\delta}}.\end{aligned} \tag{8}$$

Since $\kappa^2 \le s/b = \alpha^2\|A\|_F^4/\log\frac{d}{\delta}$ (Eq (6)). By Theorem 4 with $t = \alpha\|A\|_F^2$, we get

$$\Pr\left[\|B^TB - \bar{A}^T\bar{A}\| \ge \alpha\|A\|_F^2\right] \le \delta.$$

By triangle inequality and Eq. (7), we have

$$\begin{aligned}\|B^TB - A^TA\| &\le \|B^TB - \bar{A}^T\bar{A}\| + \|A^TA - \bar{A}^T\bar{A}\|\\ &\le 2\alpha\|A\|_F^2\end{aligned}$$

with probability at least $1-\delta$.

Since $x \le \sqrt{x}$ for all $0 \le x \le 1$, we have

$$\begin{aligned}g(\sigma_{i,j}^2) &\le \min\{\frac{s\sigma_{i,j}^4}{\alpha^2\|A\|_F^4}\cdot\log\frac{d}{\delta}, 1\}\\ &\le \min\{\frac{\sqrt{s}\sigma_{i,j}^2}{\alpha\|A\|_F^2}\cdot\sqrt{\log\frac{d}{\delta}}, 1\}\end{aligned}$$

Then the communication cost is

$$\begin{aligned}d\cdot\sum_{i,j} g(\sigma_{i,j}^2) &\le d\cdot\sum_{i,j}\frac{\sqrt{s}\sigma_{i,j}^2}{\alpha\|A\|_F^2}\cdot\sqrt{\log\frac{d}{\delta}}\\ &= \frac{\sqrt{s}d}{\alpha}\cdot\sqrt{\log\frac{d}{\delta}}.\end{aligned}$$

□

3.2 Covariance error $\varepsilon\|A - [A]_k\|_F^2/k$ via adaptive sampling

We will first present a randomized algorithm with communication cost $O(skd + \frac{\sqrt{s}kd}{\varepsilon}\cdot\sqrt{\log d})$ in terms of real numbers, then discuss how to obtain bit/word complexity.

In the deterministic algorithm, each server S_i invokes FD to compute a local sketch $B^{(i)}$ in one pass, i.e. $B^{(i)} = \mathsf{FD}(A^{(i)},\varepsilon,k)$ (Theorem 1), then sends $B^{(i)}$ to the coordinator. To save communication, we will further compress each $B^{(i)}$ computed by FD. It was shown that not only $B^{(i)}$ has small covariance error, the Frobenius norm of $B^{(i)}$ is also smaller than the Frobenius norm of $A^{(i)}$ [27]. From this property, it is not difficult prove the following lemma.

LEMMA 5. *Assume* $B = \mathsf{FD}(A,\varepsilon,k)$, *then*

$$\|B - [B]_k\|_F^2 \le (1+\varepsilon)\|A - [A]_k\|_F^2.$$

PROOF. Let v_i be i-th right singular vector of B. We have

$$\begin{aligned}\|B - [B]_k\|_F^2 &= \|B\|_F^2 - \sum_{i=1}^k\|Bv_i\|^2\\ &\le \|B\|_F^2 - \sum_{i=1}^k\|Av_i\|^2 + k\|A^TA - B^TB\|_2\\ &\le \|A\|_F^2 - \sum_{i=1}^k\|Av_i\|^2 + \varepsilon\|A - [A]_k\|_F^2\\ &\le \|A - [A]_k\|_F^2 + \varepsilon\|A - [A]_k\|_F^2.\end{aligned}$$

The last inequality holds because

$$\sum_{i=1}^{k}\|Av_i\|^2 \le \sum_{i=1}^{k}\|Au_i\|^2,$$

where u_i is the i-th right singular vector of A, and $\|A-[A]_k\|_F^2 = \|A\|_F^2 - \sum_{i=1}^{k}\|Au_i\|^2$. □

The following lemma directly follows from singular value decomposition.

LEMMA 6. *For any matrix $B \in \mathbb{R}^{n\times d}$, there exist two matrices $T \in \mathbb{R}^{k\times d}$ and $R \in \mathbb{R}^{(d-k)\times d}$ such that*

$$B^TB = T^TT + R^TR,$$

and $\|R\|_F^2 = \|B-[B]_k\|_F^2$.

PROOF. Let $B = U\Sigma V^T$ be the singular value decomposition of B. Clearly,

$$B^TB = V\Sigma^2V^T = \sum_{i=1}^{d}\sigma_i^2 v_i v_i^T.$$

Let T be the matrix consists of the top-k rows of the matrix ΣV^T and let R contain the rest $d-k$ rows. It is well-known that $\|B-[B]_k\|_F^2 = \sum_{i=k+1}^{d}\sigma_i^2 = \|R\|_F^2$. Hence, T and R satisfy the requirements of the lemma. □

For convenience, we use $(T,R) = \mathsf{Decomp}(B,k)$ to denote this decomposition.

In our algorithm, each server S_i computes

$$(T^{(i)},R^{(i)}) = \mathsf{Decomp}(B^{(i)},k).$$

Let $B = [B^{(1)};\cdots;B^{(s)}]$, and we define T and R similarly. By the mergeability of FD, it holds that $\|A^TA - B^TB\|_2 \le \varepsilon\|A-[A]_k\|_F^2/k$. From Lemma 6, we have

$$\|A^TA - T^TT - R^TR\|_2 \le \varepsilon\|A-[A]_k\|_F^2/k, \text{ and}$$

$$\|R\|_F^2 = \sum_{i=1}^{s}\|R^{(i)}\|_F^2 = \sum_{i=1}^{s}\|B^{(i)}-[B^{(i)}]_k\|_F^2.$$

Then by Lemma 5, we get

$$\|R\|_F^2 \le (1+\varepsilon)\sum_{i=1}^{s}\|A^{(i)}-[A^{(i)}]_k\|_F^2. \quad (9)$$

Let $[A]_k^{(i)}$ be the ith block of $[A]_k$ corresponding to the rows in $A^{(i)}$. We observe

$$\sum_i\|A^{(i)}-[A^{(i)}]_k\|_F^2 \le \sum_i\|A^{(i)}-[A]_k^{(i)}\|_F^2 = \|A-[A]_k\|_F^2, \quad (10)$$

since $[A]_k^{(i)}$ has rank at most k, and $[A^{(i)}]_k$ is the best rank k approximation for $A^{(i)}$. Combine (9) and (10), we get

$$\|R\|_F^2 \le (1+\varepsilon)\|A-[A]_k\|_F^2. \quad (11)$$

Now, each server S_i applies the SVS algorithm on $R^{(i)}$, and outputs $W^{(i)} = \mathsf{SVS}(R^{(i)})$. Let $W = [W^{(1)};\cdots;W^{(s)}]$. From Theorem 6, we have

$$\|W^TW - R^TR\|_2 \le \varepsilon\|R\|_F^2/k \le (\varepsilon+\varepsilon^2)\|A-[A]_k\|_F^2/k,$$

and the number of rows in W is $O(\frac{\sqrt{sk}d}{\varepsilon}\cdot\sqrt{\log d})$. Then each server S_i sends $Q^{(i)} = [T^{(i)};W^{(i)}]$ to the coordinator. Define Q similarly, and we have

$$\begin{aligned}\|A^TA - Q^TQ\|_2 &= \|A^TA - T^TT - W^TW\| \\ &= \|A^TA - T^TT - R^TR + R^TR - W^TW\| \\ &\le \|A^TA - B^TB\|_2 + \|W^TW - R^TR\|_2 \\ &\le \varepsilon\|A-[A]_k\|_F^2/k + 2\varepsilon\|A-[A]_k\|_F^2/k \\ &\le 3\varepsilon\cdot\|A-[A]_k\|_F^2/k\end{aligned}$$

which means Q is an $(3\varepsilon,k)$-sketch of A. The total communication cost of this algorithm is $O(sdk + \frac{\sqrt{sk}d}{\varepsilon}\cdot\sqrt{\log d})$. Since $\|W\|_F^2 = O(1)\cdot\|R\|_F^2 = O(1)\cdot\|A-[A]_k\|_F^2$ from Theorem 6, we also have $\|Q\|_F^2 = \|A\|_F^2 + O(\|A-[A]_k\|_F^2)$.

THEOREM 7. *There is a distributed streaming algorithm which computes an (ε,k)-sketch Q. The communication cost is $O(sdk + \frac{\sqrt{sk}d}{\varepsilon}\cdot\sqrt{\log d})$, and space used by each server is $O(kd/\varepsilon)$. Moreover, $\|Q\|_F^2 = \|A\|_F^2 + O(\|A-[A]_k\|_F^2)$.*

Note that the size of Q is not optimal, but we can apply another FD on Q. Assume $Q' = \mathsf{FD}(Q,\varepsilon,k)$, we have $\|Q^TQ - Q'^TQ'\|_2 \le \varepsilon\|Q-[Q]_k\|_F^2/k$, and thus the covariance error of Q' (w.r.t. A) depends on $\|Q-[Q]_k\|_F^2$. However, since $\|Q\|_F^2 = \|A\|_F^2 + O(\|A-[A]_k\|_F^2)$, using the same argument as in the proof of Lemma 5, it can be shown that $\|Q-[Q]_k\|_F^2 = O(\|A-[A]_k\|_F^2)$. As a result, it holds that

$$\|A^TA - Q'^TQ'\|_2 \le O(\varepsilon)\cdot\|A-[A]_k\|_F^2/k.$$

After adjusting ε by a constant factor in the beginning, Q' is an (ε,k)-sketch of A with optimal sketch size.

3.3 Bit complexity for communication cost

Similar to [5], our main idea is to conduct a case analysis based on the rank of A.

Case 1: $\mathsf{rank}(A) \le 2k$. In this case, each $A^{(i)}$ also has rank at most $2k$. Then we can find at most $2k$ rows of $A^{(i)}$ which span the row space of $A^{(i)}$. Let Q be the matrix consists of such a set of rows. We use the standard notation Q^+ to denote the Moore-Penrose pseudoinverse of Q. It is known that the $d\times d$ matrix Q^+Q is the orthogonal projector which projects any d-dimensional vector x onto the row space of Q, and thus onto the row space of $A^{(i)}$. Hence, if x belongs to the row space of $A^{(i)}$, $Q^+Qx = x$. In particular, we have $Q^+QA^{(i)T} = A^{(i)T}$.

Based on the above observation, each server S_i runs the following algorithm. S_i first deterministically selects any maximal set of linearly independent rows from $A^{(i)}$, denoted as Q, then sends both Q and $QA^{(i)T}A^{(i)}Q^T$ to the coordinator. Given Q, the coordinator can compute Q^+, and then computes $Q^+QA^{(i)T}A^{(i)}Q^TQ^{T+}$, which is exactly $A^{(i)T}A^{(i)}$. In other words, the coordinator can compute A^TA exactly. For the communication cost, Q takes at most $2kd$ words, since Q consists rows chosen from A. On the other hand, it is easy to verify that each entry of $QA^{(i)T}A^{(i)}Q^T$ needs at most $O(\log(nd/\varepsilon))$ bits, and thus takes $O(k^2)$ words to represent. Since $k \le d$, the total communication cost is $O(skd)$ words.

Naively, it requires two passes for each server: one pass for computing Q and one pass for $QA^{(i)T}A^{(i)}Q^T$. With a little more effort, the algorithm can be implemented in only one pass using $O(kd)$ space. We maintain a maximal set of linearly independent rows Q along the way, and also maintain an orthonormal basis of Q, denoted as V, on the side. The matrix $Z = VA^{(i)T}A^{(i)}V^T$ can be maintained in the streaming model using $O(k^2)$ space (in real numbers): when a new row u is added to V, compute $U = V[V; u]^T$ (with $O(k^2)$ space) and then update Z as $Z = U^T ZU$. In the end, we compute $QV^T ZVQ^T$, which is $QA^{(i)T}A^{(i)}Q^T$. Here we have used the fact that $V^T Vx = x$ if x is in the row space of V.

Case 2: $\mathsf{rank}(A) > 2k$. In this case, each server S_i first computes a matrix $Q^{(i)}$ as in the above section such that $Q = [Q^{(1)}; \cdots; Q^{(s)}]$ is an (ε, k)-sketch of A. Note that Q may contain entries exponentially small in k/ε [5], which leads to an extra k/ε factor in communication cost. We use the following result which gives a lower bound on the singular values of a matrix with integer entries of bounded magnitude.

LEMMA 7 (LEMMA 4.1 OF [6]). *If an $n \times d$ matrix A has integer entries bounded in magnitude by γ, and has rank ρ, then the k-th largest singular value of A satisfies*

$$\sigma_k^2 \geq (nd\gamma^2)^{-k/(\rho-k)}.$$

Since we assume each entry of the input matrix A is an integer with magnitude bounded by $\text{poly}(nd/\varepsilon)$ and $\mathsf{rank}(A) > 2k$, we get from the above lemma

$$\|A - [A]_k\|_F^2 \geq \sigma_{k+1}^2 \geq \text{poly}^{-1}(nd/\varepsilon).$$

Observe that each entry of Q is upper bounded by $\text{poly}(nd/\varepsilon)$, since otherwise the covariance error of Q must be too large. Therefore, it suffice to round each entry of Q to an additive $\text{poly}^{-1}(nd/\varepsilon)$ precision. In other words, after rounding, each entry of Q is representable with $O(\log(nd/\varepsilon))$ bits, and thus the communication cost is $O(skd) + \tilde{O}(\sqrt{s}kd/\varepsilon)$ words. The deterministic case is the same; just replace each $Q^{(i)}$ in the above argument with an (ε, k)-sketch computed by the deterministic FD.

4. DISTRIBUTED PCA

To solve the distributed PCA problem, we can use Theorem 7 to obtain an (ε, k)-sketch Q, and then the coordinator computes the top k right singular vectors of Q. The communication cost is thus $O(sdk + \frac{\sqrt{s}dk}{\varepsilon} \cdot \sqrt{\log d})$ words. When $s \geq \frac{\log d}{\varepsilon^2}$, this cost is $O(skd)$. In the model where all servers need to output the same answer, a lower bound of $\Omega(skd)$ bits was proved in [5]. Since it takes $O(skd)$ communication for the coordinator to broadcast the answer to all servers, our algorithm is optimal in this setting (up to a log factor).

On the other hand, when s is small, the term $O(\frac{\sqrt{s}dk}{\varepsilon} \cdot \sqrt{\log d})$ dominates the cost. In this case, we can further improve the communication cost when d is large using the distributed algorithm of [5].

THEOREM 8 (DISTRIBUTED PCA OF [5]). *Given any $A \in \mathbb{R}^{n\times d}$ which is distributed across s servers, there is a batch algorithm for PCA with communication cost*

$$O(sdk + \min\{d, k\varepsilon^{-2}\} \cdot \min\{n, sk\varepsilon^{-2}\}).$$

The key is the following lemma, the proof of which can be found in section 4.1.[5]

LEMMA 8. *Let Q be a strong $(\varepsilon/2, k)$-sketch of A, and we assume $\|Q\|_F^2 = \|A\|_F^2 + O(\|A - [A]_k\|_F^2)$. Let $V \in \mathbb{R}^{d\times k}$ be any orthonormal matrix satisfying $\|Q - QVV^T\|_F^2 \leq (1+\varepsilon)\|Q - [Q]_k\|_F^2$, then*

$$\|A - AVV^T\|_F^2 \leq (1 + O(\varepsilon)) \cdot \|A - [A]_k\|_F^2.$$

This lemma can be viewed as a robust version of Lemma 1. With this result, we can apply the standard "sketch-and-solve" approach to solve the distributed PCA problem. More formally, in the "sketch" step, all servers compute a distributed (ε, k)-sketch, i.e., each server S_i output matrix $Q^{(i)}$, such that $Q = [Q^{(1)}; \cdots; Q(s)]$ is an (ε, k)-sketch of A. Note that, in our algorithm for (ε, k)-sketch, if we do not require servers to send their local sketches to the coordinator, the communication cost is negligible[6], and the number of rows in Q is $\tilde{O}(\sqrt{s}kd/\varepsilon)$. In the "solve" step, we can apply any communication-efficient distributed PCA algorithm with input Q, which then solve the PCA problem for A due to Lemma 8 (where we also use the property that $\|Q\|_F^2 = \|A\|_F^2 + O(\|A - [A]_k\|_F^2)$). The communication cost of the combined algorithm is dominated by the "solve" step, while local computation cost is dominated by the "sketch" step. Since each server only makes one pass over its local data with small working space for computing an (ε, k)-sketch, the above approach can convert any batch distributed PCA algorithm to a distributed streaming algorithm.

If we use the distributed PCA algorithm of [5] to compute the approximate PCs for Q, we solve the PCA problem for A with communication cost $O(skd + \frac{\sqrt{s}k\sqrt{\log d}}{\varepsilon} \cdot \min\{d, k/\varepsilon^2\})$. The cost in Theorem 8 is in terms of words as long as the entries of the input matrix are representable by $O(\log(nd/\varepsilon))$ bits. As discussed in section 3.3, each entry of Q takes $O(\log(nd/\varepsilon))$ bits, and thus the cost of the combined algorithm is also in words. Using (ε, k)-sketch as a sketch for solving distributed PCA, our algorithm is faster and more space-efficient than the algorithm of [5].

THEOREM 9. *Given $A \in \mathbb{R}^{n\times d}$, there is a distributed streaming algorithm which solves PCA for A. The communication cost is $O(sdk + \frac{\sqrt{s}k\sqrt{\log d}}{\varepsilon} \cdot \min\{d, k/\varepsilon^2\})$ words, and space used by each server is $O(dk/\varepsilon)$ real numbers.*

4.1 Proof of Lemma 8

PROOF. By definition of $(\varepsilon/2, k)$-sketch, we have

$$\|A^T A - B^T B\|_2 \leq \frac{\varepsilon}{2k}\|A - [A]_k\|_F^2,$$

which is equivalent to

$$\max_{x:\|x\|=1} \left|\|Ax\|^2 - \|Bx\|^2\right| \leq \frac{\varepsilon}{2k}\|A - [A]_k\|_F^2 \tag{12}$$

[5]We remark that a similar result has been proved in [8] under a slightly different setting. However, their proof is quite complicated, so we present a direct proof for our application here.

[6]In fact, all the computations are local and parallel; the only communication needed is to set the same sampling function g.

Let u_i and w_i be the ith right singular vector of B and A respectively. We have

$$\begin{aligned}\|B-[B]_k\|_F^2 &= \|B\|_F^2 - \sum_{i=1}^k \|Bu_i\|^2 \\ &\le \|A\|_F^2 + O(\|A-[A]_k\|_F^2) - \sum_{i=1}^k \|Bu_i\|^2 \\ &\le \|A\|_F^2 + O(\|A-[A]_k\|_F^2) - \sum_{i=1}^k \|Bw_i\|^2 \\ &\le \|A\|_F^2 + O(\|A-[A]_k\|_F^2) - \sum_{i=1}^k \|Aw_i\|^2 \\ &\quad + k\frac{\varepsilon}{2k}\|A-[A]_k\|_F^2 \quad \text{by (12)} \\ &\le O(\|A-[A]_k\|_F^2). \end{aligned} \tag{13}$$

The first equality is from Pythagorean theorem. Let v_i be the ith column of V. Again by Pythagorean theorem, we have

$$\begin{aligned}\|B-BVV^T\|_F^2 &= \|B\|_F^2 - \|BVV^T\|_F^2 \\ &= \|B\|_F^2 - \sum_{i=1}^k \|Bv_i\|^2,\end{aligned}$$

and

$$(1+\varepsilon)\|B-[B]_k\|_F^2 = \|B\|_F^2 - \sum_{i=1}^k \|Bu_i\|^2 + \varepsilon\|B-[B]_k\|_F^2.$$

Since $\|B-BVV^T\|_F^2 \le (1+\varepsilon)\|B-[B]_k\|_F^2$ from our assumption, we have

$$\begin{aligned}\sum_{i=1}^k \|Bv_i\|^2 &\ge \sum_{i=1}^k \|Bu_i\|^2 - \varepsilon\|B-[B]_k\|_F^2 \\ &\ge \sum_{i=1}^k \|Bu_i\|^2 - O(\varepsilon)\|A-[A]_k\|_F^2.\end{aligned} \tag{14}$$

The last inequality is from (13). We have

$$\begin{aligned}\|A-AVV^T\|_F^2 =& \|A\|_F^2 - \|AVV^T\|_F^2 \\ =& \|A\|_F^2 - \sum_{i=1}^k \|Av_i\|^2 \\ \le& \|A\|_F^2 - \sum_{i=1}^k \|Bv_i\|^2 + k\cdot\frac{\varepsilon}{2k}\|A-[A]_k\|_F^2 \\ \le& \|A\|_F^2 - \sum_{i=1}^k \|Bu_i\|^2 + O(\varepsilon)\|A-[A]_k\|_F^2 \\ \le& \|A\|_F^2 - \sum_{i=1}^k \|Bw_i\|^2 + O(\varepsilon)\|A-[A]_k\|_F^2 \\ \le& \|A\|_F^2 - \sum_{i=1}^k \|Aw_i\|^2 + k\frac{\varepsilon}{2k}\|A-[A]_k\|_F^2 \\ &+ O(\varepsilon)\|A-[A]_k\|_F^2 \\ =& \|A-[A]_k\|_F^2 + O(\varepsilon)\|A-[A]_k\|_F^2,\end{aligned}$$

where the second inequality is by (14) □

5. CONCLUSION

In this paper, we study the covariance sketch and its application to PCA in the distributed model. We provide efficient one pass algorithms with improved communication costs, and also prove a tight deterministic lower bound in the blackboard model. There are lots of interesting open questions left. For instance, is our randomized algorithm for covariance sketch optimal? For PCA, whether the $\Omega(skd)$ lower bound of [5] still holds in the case when only one server needs to know the answer; it is also interesting to determine the right order of the poly$(s, k, 1/\varepsilon)$ term in the cost. Another question is what the communication complexity of covariance sketch is in the arbitrary partition model

6. REFERENCES

[1] P. K. Agarwal, G. Cormode, Z. Huang, J. M. Phillips, Z. Wei, and K. Yi. Mergeable summaries. *ACM Transactions on Database Systems (TODS)*, 38(4):26, 2013.

[2] P. Beame, P. Koutris, and D. Suciu. Communication steps for parallel query processing. In *PODS*. ACM, 2013.

[3] P. Beame, P. Koutris, and D. Suciu. Skew in parallel query processing. In *PODS*. ACM, 2014.

[4] S. Bhojanapalli, P. Jain, and S. Sanghavi. Tighter low-rank approximation via sampling the leveraged element. In *SODA*. SIAM, 2015.

[5] C. Boutsidis, D. Woodruff, and P. Zhong. Optimal principal component analysis in distributed and streaming models. *STOC*, 2016.

[6] K. L. Clarkson and D. P. Woodruff. Numerical linear algebra in the streaming model. In *STOC*. ACM, 2009.

[7] K. L. Clarkson and D. P. Woodruff. Low rank approximation and regression in input sparsity time. In *STOC*, 2013.

[8] M. B. Cohen, C. Musco, and C. Musco. Input sparsity time low-rank approximation via ridge leverage score sampling. *arXiv preprint arXiv:1511.07263*, 2015.

[9] A. Desai, M. Ghashami, and J. M. Phillips. Improved practical matrix sketching with guarantees. *IEEE Transactions on Knowledge and Data Engineering*, 28(7):1678–1690, 2016.

[10] P. Drineas, R. Kannan, and M. W. Mahoney. Fast monte carlo algorithms for matrices i: Approximating matrix multiplication. *SIAM Journal on Computing*, 36(1):132–157, 2006.

[11] P. Drineas, R. Kannan, and M. W. Mahoney. Fast monte carlo algorithms for matrices ii: Computing a low-rank approximation to a matrix. *SIAM Journal on Computing*, 36(1):158–183, 2006.

[12] P. Drineas, M. W. Mahoney, S. Muthukrishnan, and T. Sarlós. Faster least squares approximation. *Numerische Mathematik*, 117(2):219–249, 2011.

[13] D. P. Dubhashi and A. Panconesi. *Concentration of measure for the analysis of randomized algorithms*. Cambridge University Press, 2009.

[14] D. Feldman, M. Schmidt, and C. Sohler. Turning big data into tiny data: Constant-size coresets for k-means, pca and projective clustering. In *SODA*. SIAM, 2013.

[15] M. Ghashami, E. Liberty, and J. M. Phillips. Efficient frequent directions algorithm for sparse matrices. *KDD*, 2016.

[16] M. Ghashami and J. M. Phillips. Relative errors for deterministic low-rank matrix approximations. In *SODA*, pages 707–717. SIAM, 2014.

[17] M. Ghashami, J. M. Phillips, and F. Li. Continuous matrix approximation on distributed data. *Proceedings of the VLDB Endowment*, 7(10):809–820, 2014.

[18] P. B. Gibbons and S. Tirthapura. Estimating simple functions on the union of data streams. In *SPAA*. ACM, 2001.

[19] P. B. Gibbons and S. Tirthapura. Distributed streams algorithms for sliding windows. In *SPAA*. ACM, 2002.

[20] H. Huang and S. P. Kasiviswanathan. Streaming anomaly detection using randomized matrix sketching. *Proceedings of the VLDB Endowment*, 2015.

[21] Z. Huang and K. Yi. The communication complexity of distributed epsilon-approximations. In *FOCS*, 2014.

[22] R. Kannan, S. Vempala, and D. P. Woodruff. Principal component analysis and higher correlations for distributed data. In *COLT*, 2014.

[23] Z. Karnin and E. Liberty. Online pca with spectral bounds. In *Proceedings of the 28th Annual Conference on Computational Learning Theory (COLT)*, 2015.

[24] E. Kushilevitz and N. Nisan. *Communication Complexity*. Cambridge University Press, 1997.

[25] Y. Liang, M.-F. F. Balcan, V. Kanchanapally, and D. Woodruff. Improved distributed principal component analysis. In *NIPS*, 2014.

[26] Y. Liang, B. Xie, D. Woodruff, L. Song, and M.-F. Balcan. Communication efficient distributed kernel principal component analysis.

[27] E. Liberty. Simple and deterministic matrix sketching. In *KDD*, pages 581–588. ACM, 2013.

[28] J. Misra and D. Gries. Finding repeated elements. *Science of computer programming*, 2(2):143–152, 1982.

[29] J. Nelson and H. L. Nguyên. Osnap: Faster numerical linear algebra algorithms via sparser subspace embeddings. In *FOCS*. IEEE, 2013.

[30] R. I. Oliveira. Sums of random hermitian matrices and an inequality by rudelson. *Electron. Commun. Probab*, 15(203-212):26, 2010.

[31] T. Sarlos. Improved approximation algorithms for large matrices via random projections. In *FOCS*, 2006.

[32] J. A. Tropp. User-friendly tail bounds for sums of random matrices. *Foundations of Computational Mathematics*, 12(4):389–434, 2012.

[33] D. Van Gucht, R. Williams, D. P. Woodruff, and Q. Zhang. The communication complexity of distributed set-joins with applications to matrix multiplication. In *PODS*. ACM, 2015.

[34] Z. Wei, X. Liu, F. Li, S. Shang, X. Du, and J.-R. Wen. Matrix sketching over sliding windows. *SIGMOD*, 2016.

[35] D. Woodruff. Low rank approximation lower bounds in row-update streams. In *NIPS*, 2014.

[36] S. Yoo, H. Huang, and S. P. Kasiviswanathan. Streaming spectral clustering. ICDE, 2016.

[37] Y. Zhang, M. Wainwright, and M. Jordan. Distributed estimation of generalized matrix rank: Efficient algorithms and lower bounds. In *ICML*, 2015.

APPENDIX

A. PROOF OF LEMMA 1

LEMMA 9 (RESTATEMENT OF LEMMA 1).

$$\|A - \pi_B^k(A)\|_F^2 \le \|A - [A]_k\|_F^2 + 2k \cdot \|A^T A - B^T B\|_2.$$

PROOF. For any x with $\|x\| = 1$, we have

$$\begin{aligned} \left| \, \|Ax\|^2 - \|Bx\|^2 \, \right| &= \left| x^T (A^T A - B^T B) x \right| \\ &\le \|A^T A - B^T B\|_2 \end{aligned} \tag{15}$$

Let u_i and w_i be the ith right singular vector of B and A respectively

$$\begin{aligned} &\|A - \pi_B^k(A)\|_F^2 = \|A\|_F^2 - \|\pi_B^k(A)\|_F^2 \\ &= \|A\|_F^2 - \sum_{i=1}^k \|Au_i\|^2 \\ &\le \|A\|_F^2 - \sum_{i=1}^k \|Bu_i\|^2 + k \cdot \|A^T A - B^T B\|_2 \\ &\le \|A\|_F^2 - \sum_{i=1}^k \|Bw_i\|^2 + k \cdot \|A^T A - B^T B\|_2 \\ &\le \|A\|_F^2 - \sum_{i=1}^k \|Aw_i\|^2 + 2k \cdot \|A^T A - B^T B\|_2 \\ &= \|A - [A]_k\|_F^2 + 2k \cdot \|A^T A - B^T B\|_2. \end{aligned}$$

□

B. BOUNDING $\|B\|_F$

We next provide a result on bounding $\|B\|_F^2$.

THEOREM 10. *Assume the same setting as in Theorem 4, and define*

$$M = \max_{i,j} \frac{\sigma_{i,j}^2}{g(\sigma_{i,j}^2)} \text{ and } \tau^2 = \sum_{i,j} \frac{\sigma_{i,j}^4 \cdot (1 - g(\sigma_{i,j}^2))}{g(\sigma_{i,j}^2)},$$

then the following inequality holds:

$$\Pr[\|B\|_F^2 \ge \|A\|_F^2 + t] \le \exp\left(\frac{-t^2/2}{\tau^2 + Mt/3} \right).$$

The proof of this theorem is actually a special case of the proof of Theorem 4; here we only need to bound the sum of squared singular values, so we apply the usual *Bernstein Inequality* [13] for scalar random variables. We omit the proof here.

C. LINEAR FUNCTION (PROOF OF THEOREM 5)

From Theorem 4 and 10, we want to bound M, κ^2 and τ^2. It is easy to bound M if we pick a linear function, i.e., $g(x) = \beta x$ for some β. Since $g(x)$ is a probability, it also must be bounded by 1, and thus we will set $g(x) = \min\{\beta x, 1\}$. Then the communication cost is

$$d \sum_{i,j} g(\sigma_{i,j}^2) \le \beta d \sum_{i,j} \sigma_{i,j}^2 = \beta d \sum_{i,j} \|A^{(i)}\|_F^2 = \beta d \|A\|_F^2.$$

For any σ, we have

$$\begin{aligned} \frac{\sigma^4 \cdot (1 - g(\sigma^2))}{g(\sigma^2)} &= \frac{\sigma^2}{\beta} - \sigma^4 \le \frac{\sigma^2}{\beta} - \sigma^4 - \frac{1}{4\beta^2} + \frac{1}{4\beta^2} \\ &= -\left(\frac{1}{2\beta} - \sigma^2 \right)^2 + \frac{1}{4\beta^2} \\ &\le \frac{1}{4\beta^2}. \end{aligned}$$

So it follows that

$$\kappa^2 \le \sum_i 1/4\beta^2 = s/4\beta^2.$$

We also have

$$\tau^2 \;=\; \sum_{i,j} \frac{\sigma_{i,j}^4 \cdot (1 - g(\sigma_{i,j}^2))}{g(\sigma_{i,j}^2)} \le \sum_{i,j} \frac{\sigma_{i,j}^2}{\beta} = \frac{\|A\|_F^2}{\beta}.$$

To achieve our error bound, we set $\beta = \frac{\sqrt{s}}{\alpha\|A\|_F^2} \cdot \log \frac{d}{\delta}$, and set $t = \alpha\|A\|_F^2$ in Theorem 4. We have $M \le 1/\beta$, and thus

$$\kappa^2 + Mt/3 \le \alpha^2\|A\|_F^4/(4 \cdot \log \frac{d}{\delta}) + \alpha^2\|A\|_F^4/(3\sqrt{s}\cdot \log \frac{d}{\delta}),$$

which is at most $\alpha^2\|A\|_F^4/(2\log(d/\delta))$. From Theorem 4 with $t = \alpha\|A\|_F^2$, the probability $\Pr[\|B^TB - A^TA\| \ge \alpha\|A\|_F^2]$ is smaller than

$$\begin{aligned} d \cdot \exp\left(\frac{-\alpha^2\|A\|_F^4/2}{\alpha^2\|A\|_F^4/(2\log(d/\delta))}\right) \;&\le\; d \cdot \exp\left(-\log \frac{d}{\delta}\right) \\ &=\; \delta. \end{aligned}$$

To bound $\|B\|_F$, we set $t = \|A\|_F^2$ in Theorem 10, and have

$$\begin{aligned} \tau^2 + Mt/3 \;&\le\; \frac{\alpha\|A\|_F^4}{(\sqrt{s} \cdot \log \frac{d}{\delta})} + \frac{\alpha\|A\|_F^4}{(3\sqrt{s} \cdot \log \frac{d}{\delta})} \\ &\le\; \|A\|_F^4/\log \frac{d}{\delta}. \end{aligned}$$

By Theorem 10 with $t = \|A\|_F^2$, we have

$$\Pr[\|B\|_F^2 \ge 2\|A\|_F^2] \le \delta/d.$$

The communication cost is at most $O(\frac{\sqrt{s}d}{\alpha} \cdot \log \frac{d}{\delta})$.

BPTree: an ℓ_2 Heavy Hitters Algorithm Using Constant Memory

Vladimir Braverman* Stephen R. Chestnut† Nikita Ivkin‡ Jelani Nelson§
Zhengyu Wang¶ David P. Woodruff||

ABSTRACT

The task of finding heavy hitters is one of the best known and well studied problems in the area of data streams. One is given a list $i_1, i_2, \ldots, i_m \in [n]$ and the goal is to identify the items among $[n]$ that appear frequently in the list. In sub-polynomial space, the strongest guarantee available is the ℓ_2 guarantee, which requires finding all items that occur at least $\varepsilon\|f\|_2$ times in the stream, where the vector $f \in \mathbb{R}^n$ is the count histogram of the stream with ith coordinate equal to the number of times i appears $f_i := \#\{j \in [m] : i_j = i\}$. The first algorithm to achieve the ℓ_2 guarantee was the CountSketch of [11], which requires $O(\varepsilon^{-2}\log n)$ words of memory and $O(\log n)$ update time and is known to be space-optimal if the stream allows for deletions. The recent work of [7] gave an improved algorithm for insertion-only streams, using only $O(\varepsilon^{-2}\log\varepsilon^{-1}\log\log n)$ words of memory. In this work, we give an algorithm BPTree for ℓ_2 heavy hitters in insertion-only streams that achieves $O(\varepsilon^{-2}\log\varepsilon^{-1})$ words of memory and $O(\log\varepsilon^{-1})$ update time, which is the optimal dependence on n and m. In addition, we describe an algorithm for tracking $\|f\|_2$ at all times with $O(\varepsilon^{-2})$ memory and update time. Our analyses rely on bounding the expected supremum of a Bernoulli process involving Rademachers with limited independence, which we accomplish via a Dudley-like chaining argument that may have applications elsewhere.

*vova@cs.jhu.edu. Johns Hopkins University. Supported in part by NSF grants IIS-1447639 and CCF-1650041 and by a Google Faculty Research Award.

†stephenc@ethz.ch. ETH Zurich

‡nivkin1@jhu.edu. Johns Hopkins University. Supported in part by NSF grants IIS-1447639 and CCF-1650041 and by DARPA grant N660001-1-2-4014.

§minilek@seas.harvard.edu. Harvard University. Supported by NSF grant IIS-1447471 and CAREER CCF-1350670, ONR Young Investigator award N00014-15-1-2388, and a Google Faculty Research Award.

¶zhengyuwang@g.harvard.edu. Harvard University. Supported in part by NSF grant CCF-1350670.

||dpwoodru@us.ibm.com. IBM Research.

PODS'17, May 14-19, 2017, Chicago, Illinois, USA

 ISBN 978-1-4503-4198-1/17/05...$15.00

DOI: http://dx.doi.org/10.1145/3034786.3034798

1. INTRODUCTION

The *streaming model* of computation is well-established as one important model for processing massive datasets. A sequence of data is seen which could be, for example, destination IP addresses of TCP/IP packets or query terms submitted to a search engine, and which is modeled as a list of integers $i_1, i_2, \ldots, i_m \in [n]$. Each item $i \in [n]$ has a *frequency* in the stream that is the number of times it appears and is denoted $f_i := \#\{j \in [m] : i_j = i\}$. The challenge is to define a system to answer some pre-defined types of queries about the data, such as distinct element counts, quantiles, frequent items, or other statistics of the vector f, to name a few. The system is allowed to read the stream only once, in the order it is given, and it is typically assumed that the stream being processed is so large that explicitly storing it is undesirable or even impossible. Ideally, streaming algorithms should use space sublinear, or even exponentially smaller than, the size of the data to allow the algorithm's memory footprint to fit in cache for fast stream processing. The reader is encouraged to read [2, 29] for further background on the streaming model of computation.

Within the study of streaming algorithms, the problem of finding frequent items is one of the most well-studied and core problems, with work on the problem beginning in 1981 [5, 6]. Aside from being an interesting problem in its own right, algorithms for finding frequent items are used as subroutines to solve many other streaming problems, such as moment estimation [21], entropy estimation [10, 18], ℓ_p-sampling [28], finding duplicates [15], and several others.

Stated simply, the goal is to report a list of items that appear least τ times, for a given threshold τ. Naturally, the threshold τ should be chosen to depend on some measure of the size of the stream. The point of a frequent items algorithm is to highlight a *small* set of items that are frequency outliers. A choice of τ that is independent of f misses the point; it might be that all frequencies are larger than τ.

With this in mind, previous work has parameterized τ in terms of different norms of f with MisraGries [27] and CountSketch [11] being two of the most influential examples. A value $\varepsilon > 0$ is chosen, typically ε is a small constant independent of n or m, and τ is set to be $\varepsilon\|f\|_1 = \varepsilon m$ or $\varepsilon\|f\|_2$. These are called the ℓ_1 and ℓ_2 guarantees, respectively. Choosing the threshold τ in this manner immediately limits the focus to outliers since no more than $1/\varepsilon$ items can have frequency larger than $\varepsilon\|f\|_1$ and no more than $1/\varepsilon^2$ can have frequency $\varepsilon\|f\|_2$ or larger.

A moments thought will lead one to conclude that the ℓ_2 guarantee is stronger, i.e. harder to achieve, than the ℓ_1 guarantee because $\|x\|_1 \geq \|x\|_2$, for all $x \in \mathbb{R}^n$. Indeed, the ℓ_2 guarantee is much stronger. Consider a stream with all frequencies equal to 1 except one which is equal j. With $\varepsilon = 1/3$, achieving the ℓ_1 guarantee only requires finding an item with frequency $j = n/2$, which means that it occupies more than one-third of the positions in the stream, whereas achieving the ℓ_2 guarantee would require finding an item with frequency $j = \sqrt{n}$, such an item is a negligible fraction of the stream!

As we discuss in Section 1.1, the algorithms achieving ℓ_2 guarantee, like CountSketch [11], achieve essentially the best space-to-τ trade-off. But, since the discovery of CountSketch, which uses $O(\varepsilon^{-2}\log n)$ words of memory[1], it has been an open problem to determine the smallest space possible for achieving the ℓ_2 guarantee. Since the output is a list of up to ε^{-2} integers in $[n]$, $\Omega(\varepsilon^{-2})$ words of memory are necessary. The recent algorithm CountSieve shrunk the storage to $O(\varepsilon^{-2}\log\varepsilon^{-1}\log\log n)$ words [7]. Our main contribution is to describe an algorithm BPTree that uses only $O(\varepsilon^{-2}\log\varepsilon^{-1})$ words—independent of n and m!—and obviously optimal in the important setting where ε is a constant.

1.1 Previous work

Work on the heavy hitters problem began in 1981 with the MJRTY algorithm of [5, 6], which is an algorithm using only two machine words of memory that could identify an item whose frequency was strictly more than half the stream. This result was generalized by the MisraGries algorithm in [27], which, for any $0 < \varepsilon \leq 1/2$, uses $2(\lceil 1/\varepsilon\rceil - 1)$ counters to identify every item that occurs strictly more than an εm times in the stream. This data structure was rediscovered at least two times afterward [13, 23] and became also known as the Frequent algorithm. It has implementations that use $O(1/\varepsilon)$ words of memory, $O(1)$ expected update time to process a stream item (using hashing), and $O(1/\varepsilon)$ query time to report all the frequent items. Similar space requirements and running times for finding ε-frequent items were later achieved by the SpaceSaving [26] and LossyCounting [25] algorithms.

A later analysis of these algorithms in [3] showed that they not only identify the heavy hitters, but they also provided estimates of the frequencies of the heavy hitters. Specifically, when using $O(k/\varepsilon)$ counters they provide, for each heavy hitter $i \in [n]$, an estimate $\tilde{f}_i$ of the frequency f_i such that $|\tilde{f}_i - f_i| \leq (\varepsilon/k)\cdot\|f_{tail(k)}\|_1 \leq (\varepsilon/k)\|f\|_1$. Here $f_{tail(k)}$ is the vector f but in which the largest k entries have been replaced by zeros (and thus the norm of $f_{tail(k)}$ can never be larger than that of f). We call this the $((\varepsilon/k), k)$-*tail guarantee.* A recent work of [4] shows that for $0 < \alpha < \varepsilon \leq 1/2$, all ε-heavy hitters can be found together with approximate for them $\tilde{f}_i$ such that $|\tilde{f}_i - f_i| \leq \alpha\|f\|_1$, and the space complexity is $O(\alpha^{-1}\log(1/\varepsilon) + \varepsilon^{-1}\log n + \log\log\|f\|_1)$ bits.

All of the algorithms in the previous paragraph work in one pass over the data in the *insertion-only* model, also known as the *cash-register* model [29], where deletions from the stream are not allowed. Subsequently, many algorithms have been discovered that work in more general models such as the strict turnstile and general turnstile models. In the turnstile model, the vector $f \in \mathbb{R}^n$ receives updates of the form (i, Δ), which triggers the change $f_i \leftarrow f_i + \Delta$; note that we recover the insertion-only model by setting $\Delta = 1$ for every update. The value Δ is assumed to be some bounded precision integer fitting in a machine word, which can be either positive or negative. In the *strict* turnstile model we are given the promise that $f_i \geq 0$ at all times in the stream. That is, items cannot be deleted if they were never inserted in the first place. In the general turnstile model no such restriction is promised (i.e. entries in f are allowed to be negative). This can be useful when tracking differences or changes across streams. For example, if f^1 is the query stream vector with f_i^1 being the number of times word i was queried to a search engine yesterday, and f^2 is the similar vector corresponding to today, then finding heavy coordinates in the vector $f = f^1 - f^2$, which corresponds to a sequence of updates with $\Delta = +1$ (from yesterday) followed by updates with $\Delta = -1$ (from today), can be used to track changes in the queries over the past day.

In the general turnstile model, an ε-heavy hitter in the ℓ_p norm is defined as an index $i \in [n]$ such that $|f_i| \geq \varepsilon\|f\|_p$. Recall $\|f\|_p$ is defined as $(\sum_{i=1}^n |f_i|^p)^{1/p}$. The CountMin sketch treats the case of $p = 1$ and uses $O(\varepsilon^{-1}\log n)$ memory to find all ε-heavy hitters and achieve the $(\varepsilon, 1/\varepsilon)$-tail guarantee [12]. The CountSketch treats the case of $p = 2$ and uses $O(\varepsilon^{-2}\log n)$ memory, achieving the $(\varepsilon, 1/\varepsilon^2)$-tail guarantee. It was later showed in [22] that the CountSketch actually solves ℓ_p-heavy hitters for all $0 < p \leq 2$ using $O(\varepsilon^{-p}\log n)$ memory and achieving the $(\varepsilon, 1/\varepsilon^p)$-tail guarantee. In fact they showed something stronger: that *any* ℓ_2 heavy hitters algorithm with error parameter $\varepsilon^{p/2}$ achieving the tail guarantee automatically solves the ℓ_p heavy hitters problem with error parameter ε for any $p \in (0, 2]$. In this sense, solving the heavy hitters for $p = 2$ with tail error, as CountSketch does, provides the strongest guarantee among all $p \in (0, 2]$.

Identifying ℓ_2 heavy hitters is optimal in another sense, too. When $p > 2$ by Hölder's Inequality $\varepsilon\|f\|_p \geq \frac{\varepsilon}{n^{1/2-1/p}}\|f\|_2$. Hence, one can use an ℓ_2 heavy hitters algorithm to identify items with frequency at least $\varepsilon\|f\|_p$, for $p > 2$, by setting the heaviness parameter of the ℓ_2 algorithm to $\varepsilon/n^{1/2-1/p}$. The space needed to find ℓ_p heavy hitters with a CountSketch is therefore $O(\varepsilon^{-2}n^{1-2/p}\log n)$ which is known to be optimal [24]. We conclude that the ℓ_2 guarantee leads to the best space-to-frequency-threshold ratio among all $p > 0$.

It is worth pointing out that both the CountMin sketch and CountSketch are randomized algorithms, and with small probability $1/n^c$ (for a user specified constant $c > 0$), they can fail to achieve their stated guarantees. The work [22] also showed that the CountSketch algorithm is optimal: they showed that *any* algorithm, even in the strict turnstile model, solving ℓ_p heavy hitters even with $1/3$ failure probability must use $\Omega(\varepsilon^{-p}\log n)$ memory.

The reader may also recall the Pick-and-Drop algorithm of [8] for finding ℓ_p heavy hitters, $p \geq 3$, in insertion-only streams. Pick-and-Drop uses $O(n^{1-2/p})$ words, so it's natural to wonder whether the same approach would work for ℓ_2 heavy hitters in $O(1)$ memory. However, Pick-and-Drop breaks down in multiple, fundamental ways that seem to prevent any attempt to repair it, as we describe in Appendix A.

[1]Unless explicitly stated otherwise, space is always measured in machine words. It is assumed a machine word has at least $\log_2\max\{n, m\}$ bits, to store any ID in the stream and the length of the stream.

In particular, for certain streams it has only polynomially small probability to correctly identify an ℓ_2 heavy hitter.

Of note is that the MisraGries and other algorithms in the insertion-only model solve ℓ_1 heavy hitters using (optimal) $O(1/\varepsilon)$ memory, whereas the CountMin and CountSketch algorithms use a larger $\Theta(\varepsilon^{-1} \log n)$ memory in the strict turnstile model, which is optimal in that model. Thus there is a gap of $\log n$ between the space complexities of ℓ_1 heavy hitters in the insertion-only and strict turnstile models. [7] recently showed that a gap also exists for ℓ_2 heavy hitters.

The paper [7] also introduced a $(1 \pm \varepsilon)$-relative error F_2 tracking scheme based on a linear sketch that uses only $O(\log m \log\log m)$ bits of memory, for constant ε. This is known to be optimal when $n = (\log m)^{O(1)}$ by a lower bound of [19].

1.2 Our contributions

We provide a new one-pass algorithm, BPTree, which in the insertion-only model solves ℓ_2 heavy hitters and achieves the $(\varepsilon, 1/\varepsilon^2)$-tail guarantee. For any constant ε our algorithm only uses a constant $O(1)$ words of memory, which is optimal. This is the first optimal-space algorithm for ℓ_2 heavy hitters in the insertion-only model for constant ε. The algorithm is described in Theorem 11.

En route to describing BPTree and proving its correctness we describe another result that may be of independent interest. Theorem 1 is a new limited randomness supremum bound for Bernoulli processes. Lemma 9 gives a more advanced analysis of the algorithm of Alon, Matias, and Szegedy (AMS) for approximating $\|f\|_2$ [1], showing that one can achieve the same (additive) error as the AMS algorithm *at all points in the stream*, at the cost of using 8-wise independent random signs rather than 4-wise independent signs. An alternative is described in Appendix B where we show that if one accepts an additional $\log 1/\varepsilon$ space then 4-wise independent signs suffice. Note that [7] describes an algorithm using $O(\log\log n)$ words that does F_2 tracking in an insertion only stream with a multiplicative error $(1 \pm \varepsilon)$. The multiplicative guarantee is stronger, albeit with more space for the algorithm, but the result can be recovered as a corollary to our additive F_2 tracking theorem, which has a much simplified algorithm and analysis compared to [7].

After some preliminaries, Section 3 presents both algorithms and their analyses. The description of BPTree is split into three parts. Section 3.2 states and proves the chaining inequality. Section 4 presents the results of some numerical experiments.

1.3 Overview of approach

Here we describe the intuition for our heavy hitters algorithm in the case of a single heavy hitter $H \in [n]$ such that $f_H^2 \geq \frac{9}{10}\|f\|_2^2$. The reduction from multiple heavy hitters to this case is standard. Suppose also for this discussion we knew a constant factor approximation to $F_2 := \|f\|_2^2$. Our algorithm and its analysis use several of the techniques developed in [7]. We briefly review that algorithm for comparison.

Both CountSieve and BPTree share the same basic building block, which is a subroutine that tries to identify one bit of information about the identity of H. The one-bit subroutine hashes the elements of the stream into two buckets, computes one *Bernoulli process* in each bucket, and then compares the two values. The Bernoulli process is just the inner product of the frequency vector with a vector of Rademacher (i.e., uniform ± 1) random variables. The hope is that the Bernoulli process in the bucket with H grows faster than the other one, so the larger of the two processes reveals which bucket contains H. In order to prove that the process with H grows faster, [7] introduce a chaining inequality for insertion-only streams that bounds the supremum of the Bernoulli processes over all times. The one-bit subroutine essentially gives us a test that H will pass with probability, say, at least 9/10 and that any other item passes with probability at most 6/10. The high-level strategy of both algorithms is to repeat this test sequentially over the stream.

CountSieve uses the one-bit subroutine in a two part strategy to identify ℓ_2 heavy hitters with $O(\log\log n)$ memory. The two parts are (1) amplify the heavy hitter so $f_H \geq (1 - \frac{1}{\operatorname{poly}(\log n)})\|f\|_2$ and (2) identify H with independent repetitions of the one-bit subroutine. Part (1) winnows the stream from, potentially, n distinct elements to at most $n/\operatorname{poly}(\log n)$ elements. The heavy hitter remains and, furthermore, we get $f_H \geq (1 - \frac{1}{\operatorname{poly}(\log n)})\|f\|_2$ because many of the other elements are removed. CountSieve accomplishes this by running $\Theta(\log\log n)$ independent copies of the one-bit subroutine in parallel, and discarding elements that do not pass a super-majority of the tests. A standard Chernoff bound implies that only $n/2^{O(\log\log n)} = n/\operatorname{poly}(\log n)$ items survive. Part (2) of the strategy identifies $\Theta(\log n)$ 'break-points' where $\|f\|_2$ of the winnowed stream increases by approximately a $(1+1/\log n)$ factor from one break-point to the next. Because H already accounts for nearly all of the value of $\|f\|_2$ it is still a heavy hitter within each of the $\Theta(\log n)$ intervals. CountSieve learns one bit of the identity of H on each interval by running the one-bit subroutine. After all $\Theta(\log n)$ intervals are completed the identity of H is known.

BPTree merges the two parts of the above strategy. As above, the algorithm runs a series of $\Theta(\log n)$ rounds where the goal of each round is to learn one bit of the identity of H. The difference from CountSieve is that BPTree discards more items after every round, then recurses on learning the remaining bits. As the algorithm proceeds, it discards more and more items and H becomes heavier and heavier in the stream. This is reminiscent of work on adaptive compressed sensing [20], but here we are able to do everything in a single pass given the insertion-only property of the stream. Given that the heavy hitter is even heavier, it allows us to weaken our requirement on the two counters at the next level in the recursion tree: we now allow their suprema to deviate even further from their expectation, and this is precisely what saves us from having to worry that one of the $O(\log n)$ Bernoulli processes that we encounter while walking down the tree will have a supremum which is too large and cause us to follow the wrong path. The fact that the heavy hitter is even heavier also allows us to "use up" even fewer updates to the heavy hitter in the next level of the tree, so that overall we have enough updates to the heavy hitter to walk to the bottom of the tree.

2. PRELIMINARIES

An insertion only stream is a list of items $p_1, \ldots, p_m \in [n]$. The frequency of j at time t is $f_j^{(t)} := \#\{i \leq t \mid p_i = j\}$, $f^{(t)} \in \mathbb{Z}_{\geq 0}^n$ is called the *frequency vector*, we denote $f :=$

$f^{(m)}$, $F_2^{(t)} = \sum_{i=1}^n (f_i^{(t)})^2$, $F_2 = \sum_{j=1}^n f_j^2$, and $F_0 = \#\{j \in [n] : f_j > 0\}$. An item $H \in [n]$ is a α-heavy hitter[2] if $f_H^2 \geq \alpha^2 \sum_{j \neq H} f_j^2 = \alpha^2(F_2 - f_H^2)$. For $W \subseteq [n]$, denote by $f^{(t)}(W) \in \mathbb{Z}^n_{\geq 0}$ the frequency vector at time t of the stream restricted to the items in W, that is, a copy of $f^{(t)}$ with the ith coordinate replaced by 0 for every $i \notin W$. We also define $f^{(s:t)}(W) := f^{(t)}(W) - f^{(s)}(W)$ and $F_2(W) = \sum_{j \in W} f_j^2$. In a case where the stream is semi-infinite (it has no defined end) m should be taken to refer to the time of a query of interest. When no time is specified, quantities like F_2 and f refer to the same query time m.

Our algorithms make use of 2-universal (pairwise independent), 4-wise independent, and 8-wise independent hash functions. We will commonly denote such a function $h : [n] \to [p]$ where p is a prime larger than n, or we may use $h : [n] \to \{0,1\}^R$, which may be taken to mean a function of the first type for some prime $p \in [2^{R-1}, 2^R)$. We use $h(x)_i$ to denote the ith bit, with the first bit most significant (big-endian). A crucial step in our algorithm involves comparing the bits of two values $a, b \in [p]$. Notice that, for any $0 \leq r \leq \lceil \log_2 p \rceil$, we have $a_i = b_i$, for all $1 \leq i \leq r$, if and only if $|a - b| < 2^{\lceil \log_2 p \rceil - r}$. Therefore, the test $a_i = b_i$, for all $1 \leq i \leq r$, can be performed with a constant number of operations.

We will use, as a subroutine, and also compare our algorithm against CountSketch [11]. To understand our results, one needs to know that CountSketch has two parameters, which determine the number of "buckets" and "repetitions" or "rows" in the table it stores. The authors of [11] denote these parameters b and r, respectively. The algorithm selects, independently, r functions $h_1, \ldots, h_r$ from a 2-universal family with domain $[n]$ and range $[b]$ and r functions $\sigma_1, \ldots, \sigma_r$ from a 2-universal family with domain $[n]$ and range $\{-1, 1\}$. CountSketch stores the value $\sum_{j : h_t(j) = i} \sigma(j) f_j$ in cell $(t, i) \in [r] \times [b]$ of the table.

In our algorithm we use the notation $\mathbf{1}(A)$ denote the indicator function of the event A. Namely, $\mathbf{1}(A) = 1$ if A is true and 0 otherwise. We sometimes use $x \lesssim y$ to denote $x = O(y)$.

3. ALGORITHM AND ANALYSIS

We will now describe and analyze the main algorithm, which is broken into several subroutines. The most important subroutine is HH1, Algorithm 1, which finds a single $O(1)$-heavy hitter assuming we have an estimate σ of $\sqrt{F_2}$ such that $\sqrt{F_2} \leq \sigma \leq 2\sqrt{F_2}$. Next is HH2, Algorithm 2, which removes the assumption entailing σ by repeatedly "guessing" values for σ and restarting HH1 as more items arrive. The guessing in HH2 is where we need F_2 tracking. Finally, a well known reduction from finding ε-heavy hitters to finding a single $O(1)$-heavy hitter leads us to the main heavy hitters algorithm BPTree, which is formally described in Theorem 11.

This section is organized as follows. The first subsection gives an overview of the algorithm and its analysis. Section 3.2 proves the bound on the expected supremum of the Bernoulli processes used by the algorithm. Section 3.3 uses the supremum bound to prove the correctness of the main subroutine HH1. Section 3.4 establishes the correctness of F_2 tracking. The subroutine HH2, which makes use of the F_2 tracker, and the complete algorithm BPTree are described and analyzed in Section 3.5.

[2]This definition is in a slightly different form from the one given in the introduction, but this form is more convenient when f_H^2 is very close to F_2.

Algorithm 1 Identify a heavy hitter.

```
procedure HH1(σ, p_1, p_2, ..., p_m)
    R ← 3⌊log_2(min{n, σ^2} + 1)⌋
    Initialize b = b_1 b_2 ··· b_R = 0 ∈ [2^R]
    Sample h : [n] → {0,1}^R ~ 2-wise indep. family
    Sample Z ∈ {−1,1}^n 4-wise indep.
    X_0, X_1 ← 0
    r ← 1, H ← −1
    β ← 3/4, c ← 1/32
    for t = 1, 2, ..., m and r < R do
        if h(p_t)_i = b_i, for all i ≤ r − 1 then
            H ← p_t
            X_{h(p_t)_r} ← X_{h(p_t)_r} + Z_{p_t}
            if |X_0 + X_1| ≥ cσβ^r then
                Record one bit b_r ← 1(|X_1| > |X_0|)
                Refresh (Z_i)_{i=1}^n, X_0, X_1 ← 0
                r ← r + 1
            end if
        end if
    end for
    return H
end procedure
```

3.1 Description of the algorithm

The crux of the problem is to identify one K-heavy hitter for some constant K. HH1, which we will soon describe in detail, accomplishes that task given a suitable approximation σ to $\sqrt{F_2}$. HH2, which removes the assumption of knowing an approximation $\sigma \in [\sqrt{F}_2, 2\sqrt{F}_2]$, is described in Algorithm 2. The reduction from finding all ε-heavy hitters to finding a single K-heavy hitter is standard from the techniques of CountSketch; it is described in Theorem 11.

HH1, Algorithm 1, begins with randomizing the item labels by replacing them with pairwise independent values on $R = \Theta(\log \min\{n, \sigma^2\})$ bits, via the hash function h. Since n and $\sigma^2 \geq F_2$ are both upper bounds for the number of distinct items in the stream, R can be chosen so that every item receives a distinct hash value.

Once the labels are randomized, HH1 proceeds in rounds wherein one bit of the randomized label of the heavy hitter is determined during each round. It completes all of the rounds and outputs the heavy hitter's identity within one pass over the stream. As the rounds proceed, items are discarded from the stream. The remaining items are called *active*. When the algorithm discards an item it will never reconsider it (unless the algorithm is restarted). In each round, it creates two Bernoulli processes X_0 and X_1. In the rth round, X_0 will be determined by the active items whose randomized labels have their rth bit equal to 0, and X_1 determined by those with rth bit 1. Let $f_0^{(t)}, f_1^{(t)} \in \mathbb{Z}^n_{\geq 0}$ be the frequency vectors of the active items in each category, respectively, initialized to 0 at the beginning of the round. Then the Bernoulli processes are $X_0^{(t)} = \langle Z, f_0^{(t)} \rangle$ and $X_1^{(t)} = \langle Z, f_1^{(t)} \rangle$, where Z is a vector of 4-wise independent Rademacher random variables (i.e. the Z_i are marginally uniformly random in $\{-1, 1\}$).

The rth round ends when $|X_0 + X_1| > c\sigma\beta^{r-1}$, for specified[3] constants c and β. At this point, the algorithm compares the values $|X_0|$ and $|X_1|$ and records the identity of the larger one as the rth bit of the candidate heavy hitter. All those items with rth bit corresponding to the smaller counter are discarded (made inactive), and the next round is started.

After R rounds are completed, if there is a heavy hitter then its randomized label will be known with good probability. The identity of the item can be determined by selecting an item in the stream that passes all of the R bit-wise tests, or by inverting the hash function used for the label. If it is a K-heavy hitter, for a sufficiently large $K = O(1)$, then the algorithm will find it with probability at least $2/3$. The algorithm is formally presented in Algorithm 1.

The most important technical component of the analysis is the following theorem, which is proved in Section 3.2. Theorem 1 gives us control of the evolution of $|X_0|$ and $|X_1|$ so we can be sure that the larger of the two identifies a bit of H.

THEOREM 1. *If $Z \in \{-1,1\}^n$ is drawn from a 4-wise independent family,* $\mathbb{E}\sup_t |\langle f^{(t)}, Z\rangle| < 23 \cdot \|f^{(m)}\|_2$.

We will use $C_* < 23$ to denote the optimal constant in Theorem 1.

The key idea behind the algorithm is that as we learn bits of the heavy hitter and discard other items, it becomes easier to learn additional bits of the heavy hitter's identity. With fewer items in the stream as the algorithm proceeds, the heavy hitter accounts for a larger and larger fraction of the remaining stream as time goes on. As the heavy hitter gets heavier the discovery of the bits of its identity can be sped up. When the stream does not contain a heavy hitter this acceleration of the rounds might not happen, though that is not a problem because when there is no heavy hitter the algorithm is not required to return any output. Early rounds will each use a constant fraction of the updates to the heavy hitter, but the algorithm will be able to finish all $R = \Theta(\log n)$ rounds because of the speed-up. The parameter β controls the speed-up of the rounds. Any value of $\beta \in (\frac{1}{2}, 1)$ can be made to work (possibly with an adjustment to c), but the precise value affects the heaviness requirement and the failure probability.

3.2 Proof of Theorem 1

Let $Z \in \{-1,1\}^n$ be random. We are interested in bounding $\mathbb{E}\sup_t |\langle f^{(t)}, Z\rangle|$. It was shown in [7] that if each entry in Z is drawn independently and uniformly from $\{-1,1\}$, then $\mathbb{E}\sup_t |\langle f^{(t)}, Z\rangle| \lesssim \|f^{(m)}\|_2$. We show that this inequality still holds if the entries of Z are drawn from a 4-wise independent family, which is used both in our analyses of HH1 and our F_2 tracking algorithm. The following lemma is implied by [16].

LEMMA 2 (KHINTCHINE'S INEQUALITY). *Let $Z \in \{-1,1\}^n$ be chosen uniformly at random, and $x \in \mathbb{R}^n$ a fixed vector. Then for any even integer p,* $\mathbb{E}\langle Z, x\rangle^p \le \sqrt{p}^p \cdot \|x\|_2^p$.

PROOF OF THEOREM 1. To simplify notation, we first normalize the vectors in $\{f^{(0)} = 0, f^{(1)}, \ldots, f^{(m)}\}$ (i.e., divide by $\|f^{(m)}\|_2$). Denote the set of these normalized vectors by $T = \{v_0, \ldots, v_m\}$, where $\|v_m\|_2 = 1$. Recall that an ε-net of some set of points T under some metric d is a set of point T' such that for each $t \in T$, there exists some $t' \in T'$ such that $d(t, t') \le \varepsilon$. For every $k \in \mathbb{N}$, we can find a $1/2^k$-net of T in ℓ_2 with size $|S_k| \le 2^{2k}$ by a greedy construction as follows.

To construct an ε-net for T, we first take v_0, then choose the smallest i such that $\|v_i - v_0\|_2 > \varepsilon$, and so on. To prove the number of elements selected is upper bounded by $1/\varepsilon^2$, let $u_0, u_1, u_2, \ldots, u_t$ denote the vectors we selected accordingly, and note that the second moments of $u_1 - u_0, u_2 - u_1, \ldots, u_t - u_{t-1}$ are greater than ε^2. Because the vectors $u_i - u_{i-1}$ have non-negative coordinates, $\|u_t\|_2^2$ is lower bounded by the summation of these moments, while on the other hand $\|u_t\|_2^2 \le 1$. Hence the net is of size at most $1/\varepsilon^2$.

Let S be a set of vectors. Let $Z \in \{-1,1\}^n$ be drawn from a p-wise independent family, where p is an even integer. By Markov and Khintchine's inequality,

$$\Pr(|\langle x, Z\rangle| > \lambda \cdot |S|^{1/p} \cdot \|x\|_2) < \frac{\mathbb{E}|\langle x, Z\rangle|^p}{\lambda^p \cdot |S| \cdot \|x\|_2^p} < \frac{1}{|S|} \cdot \left(\frac{\sqrt{p}}{\lambda}\right)^p.$$

Hence,

$$\begin{aligned}\mathbb{E}\sup_{x\in S}|\langle x, Z\rangle| &= \int_0^\infty \Pr(\sup_{x\in S}|\langle x, Z\rangle| > u)du \\ &= |S|^{1/p} \cdot \sup_{x\in S}\|x\|_2 \cdot \\ &\quad \int_0^\infty \Pr(\sup_{x\in S}|\langle x, Z\rangle| > \lambda \cdot |S|^{1/p} \cdot \sup_{x\in S}\|x\|_2)d\lambda \\ &< |S|^{1/p} \cdot \sup_{x\in S}\|x\|_2 \cdot \left(\sqrt{p} + \int_{\sqrt{p}}^\infty \left(\frac{\sqrt{p}}{\lambda}\right)^p d\lambda\right) \\ &\quad \text{(union bound)} \\ &= |S|^{1/p} \cdot \sup_{x\in S}\|x\|_2 \cdot \sqrt{p} \cdot \left(1 + \frac{1}{p-1}\right)\end{aligned}$$

Now we apply a similar chaining argument as in the proof of Dudley's inequality (cf. [14]). For $x \in T$, let x^k denote the closest point to x in S_k. Then $\|x^k - x^{k-1}\|_2 \le \|x^k - x\|_2 + \|x - x^{k-1}\|_2 \le (1/2^k) + (1/2^{k-1})$. Note that if for some $x \in T$ one has that $x_k = v_t$ is the closest vector to x in T_k (under ℓ_2), then the closest vector x_{k-1} to x in T_{k-1} must either be the frequency vector $v_{t'}$ in T_{k-1} such that t' is the smallest timestamp after t of a vector in T_{k-1}, or the largest timestamp before t in T_{k-1}. Thus the size of $\{x^k - x^{k-1} | x \in T\}$ is upper bounded by $2|S_k| \le 2^{2k+1}$, implying for $p = 4$

$$\begin{aligned}\mathbb{E}\sup_{x\in T}|\langle x, Z\rangle| &\le \sum_{k=1}^\infty \mathbb{E}\sup|\langle x^k - x^{k-1}, Z\rangle| \\ &< 3 \cdot 2^{1/p}\sqrt{p}\left(1 + \frac{1}{p-1}\right)\sum_{k=1}^\infty (2^{2k})^{1/p} \cdot (1/2^k) \\ &< 23.\end{aligned}$$

□

3.3 Identifying a single heavy hitter given an approximation to F_2

This section analyzes the subroutine HH1, which is formally presented in Algorithm 1. The goal of this section is

[3] $c = 1/32$ and $\beta = 3/4$ would suffice.

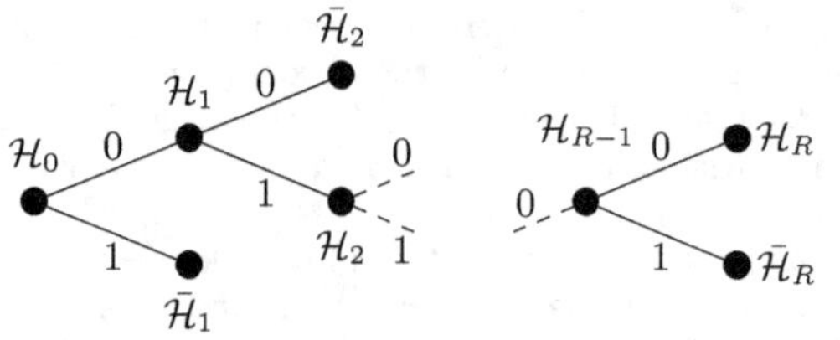

Figure 1: In this example of the execution of HH1, the randomized label $h(H)$ of the heavy hitter H begins with 01 and ends with 00. Each node in the tree corresponds to a round of HH1, which must follow the path from $\mathcal{H}_0$ to $\mathcal{H}_R$ for the output to be correct.

to prove Lemma 6, the correctness of HH1. We use $H \in [n]$ to stand for the identity of the most frequent item in the stream. It is not assumed to be a heavy hitter unless explicitly stated.

3.3.1 Randomizing the labels

The first step of HH1 is to choose a hash function $h : [n] \to \{0,1\}^R$, for $R = O(\log n)$, that relabels the universe of items $[n]$. For each $r \geq 0$, let

$$\mathcal{H}_r := \{i \in [n] \setminus \{H\} \mid h(i)_k = h(H)_k \text{ for all } 1 \leq k \leq r\},$$

and let $\bar{\mathcal{H}}_r := \mathcal{H}_{r-1} \setminus \mathcal{H}_r$, with $\bar{\mathcal{H}}_0 = \emptyset$ for convenience. By definition, $\mathcal{H}_R \subseteq \mathcal{H}_{R-1} \subseteq \cdots \subseteq \mathcal{H}_0 = [n] \setminus \{H\}$, and, in round $r \in [R]$, our hope is that the active items are those in $\mathcal{H}_{r-1}$.

The point of randomizing the labels is as a sort of "load balancing" among the item labels. The idea is that each bit of $h(H)$ partitions the active items into two roughly equal sized parts, i.e. $|\mathcal{H}_r| \approx |\bar{\mathcal{H}}_r|$ in every round r. This leads HH1 to discard roughly half of the active items after each round, allowing us to make progress on learning the (hashed) identity of a heavy hitter. We will make use of the randomized labels in the next section, within the proof of Lemma 3.

For h, we recommend choosing a prime $p \approx \min\{n, F_2\}^2$ and assigning the labels $h(i) = a_0 + a_1 i \bmod p$, for a_0 and a_1 randomly chosen in $\{0, 1, \ldots, p-1\}$ and $a_1 \neq 0$. We can always achieve this with $R = 3\log_2(\min\{n, F_2\} + 1)$, which is convenient for the upcoming analysis. This distribution on h is known to be a 2-wise independent family [9]. Note computing $h(i)$ for any i takes $O(1)$ time. It is also simple to invert: namely $x = a_1^{-1}(h(x) - a_0) \bmod p$, so x can be computed quickly from $h(x)$ when $p > n$. Inverting requires computing the inverse of a_1 modulo p, which takes $O(\log \min\{n, F_2\})$ time via repeated squaring, however this computation can be done once, for example during initialization of the algorithm, and the result stored for all subsequent queries. Thus, the time to compute $a_1^{-1} \bmod p$ is negligible in comparison to reading the stream.

3.3.2 Learning the bits of the randomized label

After randomizing the labels HH1 proceeds with the series of R rounds to identify the (randomized) label $h(H)$ of the heavy hitter H. The sequence of rounds is depicted in Figure 1. Each node in the tree corresponds to one round of HH1. The algorithm traverses the tree from left to right as the rounds progress. Correctness of HH1 means it traverses the path from $\mathcal{H}_0$ to $\mathcal{H}_R$. The 0/1 labels on the path leading to $\mathcal{H}_R$ are the bits of $h(H)$, and when $R = O(\log n)$ is sufficiently large we get $\mathcal{H}_R = \{H\}$ with high probability. Thus the algorithm correctly identifies $h(H)$, from which it can determine H with the method discussed in Section 3.3.1.

Now let us focus on one round and suppose that H is a K-heavy hitter, for some large constant K. Suppose the algorithm is in round $r \geq 1$, and recall that the goal of the round is to learn the rth bit of $h(H)$. Our hope is that the active items are those in $\mathcal{H}_{r-1}$ (otherwise the algorithm will fail), which means that the algorithm has correctly discovered the first $r-1$ bits of $h(H)$. The general idea is that HH1 partitions $\mathcal{H}_{r-1} \cup \{H\}$ into $\mathcal{H}_r \cup \{H\}$ and $\bar{\mathcal{H}}_r$, creates a Bernoulli process for each of those sets of items, and compares the values of the two Bernoulli processes to discern $h(H)_r$. Suppose that the active items are indeed $\mathcal{H}_{r-1}$ and, for the sake of discussion, that the rth bit of the heavy hitter's label is $h(H)_r = 0$. Then the Bernoulli processes X_0 and X_1, defined in Algorithm 1, have the following form

$$X_0(t) = Z_H f_H^{(s:t)} + \sum_{i \in \mathcal{H}_r} Z_i f_i^{(s:t)}, \quad X_1(t) = \sum_{i \in \bar{\mathcal{H}}_r} Z_i f_i^{(s:t)},$$

where $s \leq m$ is the time of the last update to round $r-1$ and t is the current time. To simplify things a little bit we adopt the notation $f(S)$ for the frequency vector restricted to only items in S. For example, in the equations above become $X_0 = Z_H f_H^{(s:t)} + \langle Z, f^{(s:t)}(\mathcal{H}_r)\rangle$ and $X_1 = \langle Z, f^{(s:t)}(\bar{\mathcal{H}}_r)\rangle$.

The round is a success if $|X_0| > |X_1|$ (because we assumed $h(H)_r = 0$) at the first time when $|X_0 + X_1| > c\sigma\beta^r$. When that threshold is crossed, we must have $|X_0| \geq c\sigma\beta^r/2$, $|X_1| \geq c\sigma\beta^r/2$, or both. The way we will ensure that the round is a success is by establishing the following bound on the Bernoulli process X_1: $|X_1| = |\langle Z, f^{(s:t)}(\bar{\mathcal{H}}_r)\rangle| < c\sigma\beta^r/2$, for all times $t \geq s$. Of course, the round does not end until the threshold is crossed, so we will also establish a bound on the complementary Bernoulli process $|X_0 - Z_H f_H^{(s:t)}| = |\langle Z, f^{(s:t)}(\bar{\mathcal{H}}_r)\rangle| < c\sigma\beta^r/2$, at all times $t \geq s$. When this holds we must have $|X_0 + X_1| > c\sigma\beta^r$ no later than the first time t where $f_H^{(s:t)} \geq 2c\sigma\beta^r$, so the round ends after at most $2c\sigma\beta^r$ updates to H. In total over all of the rounds this uses up no more than $\sum_{r\geq 0} 2c\sigma\beta^r < f_H$ updates to H, where we have used $\sigma < 2\sqrt{F_2} < 3f_H$ by our assumption that H is a heavy hitter. In truth, both of those inequalities fail to hold with some probability, but the failure probability is $O(1/\beta^r 2^{r/2})$ so the probability that the algorithm succeeds will turn out to be $1 - \sum_{r\geq 0} O(1/\beta^r 2^{r/2}) > 2/3$.

The next lemma establishes the control on the Bernoulli processes that we have just described (compare the events E_i with the previous paragraph). We will use it later with $K \approx \beta^r$ so that, while the rounds progress, the upper bounds on the process maxima and the failure probabilities both decrease geometrically as desired. This means that the lengths of the rounds decreases geometrically and the latter means that a union bound suffices to guarantee that all of the events E_i occur. In our notation $F_2 - f_H^2 = F_2(\mathcal{H}_0)$.

Lemma 3. *For any $r \in \{0, 1, \ldots, R\}$ and $K > 0$, the events*

$$E_{2r-1} := \left\{\max_{s,t\leq m} |\left\langle Z, f^{(s:t)}(\bar{\mathcal{H}}_r)\right\rangle| \leq K F_2(\mathcal{H}_0)^{1/2}\right\}$$

and

$$E_{2r} := \left\{\max_{s,t\leq m} |\left\langle Z, f^{(s:t)}(\mathcal{H}_r)\right\rangle| \leq K F_2(\mathcal{H}_0)^{1/2}\right\}$$

have respective probabilities at least $1 - \frac{4C_*}{K2^{r/2}}$ of occurring, where $C_* < 23$ is the constant from Theorem 1.

PROOF. By the Law of Total Probability and Theorem 1 with Markov's Inequality we have

$$\begin{aligned}\Pr\left(\max_{t\le m}|\langle Z, f^{(t)}(\mathcal{H}_r)\rangle| \ge \frac{1}{2}KF_2(\mathcal{H}_0)^{1/2}\right) \\ = \mathbb{E}\left\{\Pr\left(\max_{t\le m}|\langle Z, f^{(t)}(\mathcal{H}_r)\rangle| \ge \frac{1}{2}KF_2(\mathcal{H}_0)^{1/2}\middle|\mathcal{H}_r\right)\right\} \\ \le \mathbb{E}\left\{\frac{2C_*F_2(\mathcal{H}_r)^{1/2}}{KF_2(\mathcal{H}_0)^{1/2}}\right\} \le \frac{2C_*F_2(\mathcal{H}_0)^{1/2}}{KF_2(\mathcal{H}_0)^{1/2}2^{r/2}},\end{aligned}$$

where the last inequality is Jensen's. The same holds if $\mathcal{H}_r$ is replaced by $\bar{\mathcal{H}}_r$.

Applying the triangle inequality to get $|\langle Z, f^{(s:t)}(\mathcal{H}_r)\rangle| \le |\langle Z, f^{(s)}(\mathcal{H}_r)\rangle| + |\langle Z, f^{(t)}(\mathcal{H}_r)\rangle|$ we then find $P(E_{2r}) \ge 1 - \frac{4C_*}{K2^{r/2}}$. A similar argument proves $P(E_{2r-1}) \ge 1 - \frac{4C_*}{K2^{r/2}}$. □

From here the strategy to prove the correctness of HH1 is to inductively use Lemma 3 to bound the success of each round. The correctness of HH1, Lemma 6, follows directly from Lemma 4.

Let U be the event $\{h(j) \neq h(H)$ for all $j \neq H, f_j > 0\}$ which has, by pairwise independence, probability $\Pr(U) \ge 1 - F_0 2^{-R} \ge 1 - \frac{1}{\min\{n, F_2\}^2}$, recalling that $F_0 \le \min\{n, F_2\}$ is the number of distinct items appearing before time m. The next lemma is the main proof of correctness for our algorithm.

LEMMA 4. *Let $K' \ge 128$, $c = 1/32$, and $\beta = 3/4$. If $2K'C_*\sqrt{F_2(\mathcal{H}_0)} \le \sigma \le 2\sqrt{2}f_H$ and $f_H > 2K'C_*\sqrt{F_2(\mathcal{H}_0)}$ then, with probability at least $1 - \frac{1}{\min\{F_2, n\}^2} - \frac{8}{K'c(\sqrt{2}\beta - 1)}$ the algorithm HH1 returns H.*

PROOF. Recall that H is *active* during round r if it happens that $h(H)_i = b_i$, for all $1 \le i \le r-1$, which implies that updates from H are not discarded by the algorithm during round r. Let $K = K(r) = K'cC_*\beta^r$ in Lemma 3, and let E be the event that U and $\cap_{r=1}^{2R} E_r$ both occur. We prove by induction on r that if E occurs then either $b_r = h(H)_r$, for all $r \in [R]$ or H is the only item appearing in the stream. In either case, the algorithm correctly outputs H, where in the former case it follows because $E \subseteq U$.

Let $r \ge 1$ be such that H is still active in round r, i.e. $b_i = h(H)_i$ for all $1 \le i \le r-1$. Note that all items are active in round 1. Since H is active, the remaining active items are exactly $\mathcal{H}_{r-1} = \mathcal{H}_r \cup \bar{\mathcal{H}}_r$. Let t_r denote the time of the last update received during the rth round, and define $t_0 = 0$. At time $t_{r-1} \le t < t_r$ we have

$$\begin{aligned}c\sigma\beta^r &> |X_0 + X_1| \\ &= |\langle Z, f^{(t_{r-1}:t)}(\mathcal{H}_r \cup \bar{\mathcal{H}}_r)\rangle + Z_H f_H^{(t_{r-1}:t)}| \\ &\ge f_H^{(t_{r-1}:t)} - K(r-1)F_2(\mathcal{H}_0)^{1/2},\end{aligned}$$

where the last inequality follows from the definition of $E_{2(r-1)}$. Rearranging and using the assumed lower bound on σ, we get the bound

$$K(r-1)F_2(\mathcal{H}_0)^{1/2} \le \frac{K(r-1)}{2K'C_*}\sigma = \frac{1}{2}c\sigma\beta^{r-1}. \quad (1)$$

Therefore, by rearranging we see $f_H^{(t_{r-1}:t_r)} \le 1 + f_H^{(t_{r-1}:t)} < 1 + \frac{3}{2}c\sigma\beta^{r-1}$. That implies $f_H^{(t_r)} = \sum_{k=1}^{r} f_H^{(t_{k-1}:t_k)} < r + \frac{3}{2}c\sigma\sum_{k=1}^{r}\beta^{k-1} \le r + \frac{3\sqrt{2}c}{1-\beta}f_H$. Thus, if $f_H - \frac{3\sqrt{2}c}{1-\beta}f_H > R$ then round $r \le R$ is guaranteed to be completed and a further update to H appears after the round. Suppose, that is not the case, and rather $R \ge f_H - \frac{3\sqrt{2}c}{1-\beta}f_H \ge \frac{1}{2}f_H$, where the last inequality follows from our choices $\beta = 3/4$ and $c = 1/32$. Then, by the definition of R, $9(1 + \log_2 8f_H^2)^2 \ge R^2 \ge \frac{1}{4}f_H^2$. One can check that this inequality implies that $f_H \le 104$. Now $K' \ge 128$ and the heaviness requirement of H implies that $F_2(\mathcal{H}_0) = 0$. Therefore, H is the only item in the stream, and, in that case the algorithm will always correctly output H.

Furthermore, at the end of round r, $|X_0 + X_1| \ge c\sigma\beta^r$, so we have must have either $|X_0| \ge c\sigma\beta^r/2$ or $|X_1| \ge c\sigma\beta^r/2$. Both cannot occur for the following reason. The events E_{2r-1} and E_{2r} occur, recall these govern the non-heavy items contributions to X_0 and X_1, and these events, with the inequality (1), imply

$$|\langle Z, f^{(t_{r-1}:t_r)}(\mathcal{H}_r)\rangle| \le K(r)F_2(\mathcal{H}_0)^{1/2} < \frac{1}{2}c\sigma\beta^r$$

and the same holds for $\bar{\mathcal{H}}_r$. Therefore, the Bernoulli process not including H has its value smaller than $c\sigma\beta^r/2$, and the other, larger process identifies the bit $h(H)_r$. By induction, the algorithm completes every round $r = 1, 2, \ldots, R$ and there is at least one update to H after round R. This proves the correctness of the algorithm assuming the event E occurs.

It remains to compute the probability of E. Lemma 3 provides the bound

$$\begin{aligned}\Pr(U \text{ and } \cap_{i=1}^{2R} E_i) &\ge 1 - \frac{1}{\min\{n, F_2\}^2} - \sum_{r=0}^{R}\frac{8C_*}{K(r)2^{r/2}} \\ &= 1 - \frac{1}{\min\{n, F_2\}^2} - \sum_{r=0}^{R}\frac{8}{K'c\beta^r 2^{r/2}} \\ &> 1 - \frac{1}{\min\{n, F_2\}^2} - \frac{8}{K'c(\sqrt{2}\beta - 1)}.\end{aligned}$$

□

PROPOSITION 5. *Let $\alpha \ge 1$. If $F_2^{1/2} \le \sigma \le 2F_2^{1/2}$ and $f_H \ge \alpha\sqrt{F_2(\mathcal{H}_0)}$ then $\alpha\sqrt{F_2(\mathcal{H}_0)} \le \sigma \le 2\sqrt{2}f_H$.*

PROOF. $\sigma^2 \ge F_2 \ge f_H^2 = F_2 - F_2(\mathcal{H}_0) \ge (1 - \frac{1}{1+\alpha^2})F_2 \ge \frac{1}{8}\sigma^2$. □

LEMMA 6 (HH1 CORRECTNESS). *There is a constant K such that if H is a K-heavy hitter and $\sqrt{F_2} \le \sigma \le 2\sqrt{F_2}$, then with probability at least 2/3 algorithm HH1 returns H. HH1 uses $O(1)$ words of storage.*

PROOF. The Lemma follows immediately from Proposition 5 and Lemma 4 by setting $K' = 2^{13}$, which allows $K = 2^{14}C_* \le 380{,}000$. □

3.4 F_2 Tracking

This section proves that the AMS algorithm with 8-wise, rather than 4-wise, independent random signs has an additive εF_2 approximation guarantee at all points in the stream. We will use the tracking to "guess" a good value of σ for input to HH1, but, because the AMS algorithm is a fundamental streaming primitive, it is of independent interest from the BPTree algorithm. The following theorem is a direct consequence of Lemma 9 and [1].

THEOREM 7. *Let $0 < \varepsilon < 1$. There is a streaming algorithm that outputs at each time t a value $\hat{F}_2^{(t)}$ such that $\Pr(|\hat{F}_2^{(t)} - F_2^{(t)}| \le \varepsilon F_2$, for all $0 \le t \le m) \ge 1-\delta$. The algorithm use $O(\frac{1}{\varepsilon^2}\log\frac{1}{\delta})$ words of storage and has $O(\frac{1}{\varepsilon^2}\log\frac{1}{\delta})$ update time.*

Let us remark that it follows from Theorem 7 and a union bound that one can achieve a $(1\pm\varepsilon)$ *multiplicative* approximation to F_2 at all points in the stream using $O(\varepsilon^{-2}\log\log m)$ words. The proof that this works breaks the stream into $O(\log m)$ intervals of where the change in F_2 doubles.

In its original form [1], the AMS sketch is a product of the form Πf, where Π is a random $k \times n$ matrix chosen with each row independently composed of 4-wise independent ± 1 random variables. The sketch uses $k = \Theta(1/\varepsilon^2)$ rows to achieve a $(1 \pm \varepsilon)$-approximation with constant probability. We show that the AMS sketch with $k \simeq 1/\varepsilon^2$ rows and 8-wise independent entries provides ℓ_2-tracking with additive error $\varepsilon\|f\|_2$ at all times. We define $v_t = f^{(t)}/\|f^{(m)}\|_2$ so $\|v_t\|_2 \le 1$, for all $t \ge 0$, and $\|v_m\|_2 = 1$. Define $T = \{v_0, v_1, \ldots, v_m\}$. We use $\|A\|$ to denote the spectral norm of A, which is equal to its largest singular value, and $\|A\|_F$ for the Frobenious norm, which is the Euclidean length of A when viewed as a vector. Our proof makes use of the following moment bound for quadratic forms. Recall that given a metric space (X, d) and $\varepsilon > 0$, an *ε-net* of X is a subset $N \subseteq X$ such that $d(x, N) = \inf_{y\in N} d(x, y) \le \varepsilon$ for all $x \in X$.

THEOREM 8 (HANSON-WRIGHT [17]). *For $B \in \mathbb{R}^{n\times n}$ symmetric with (Z_i) uniformly random in $\{-1, 1\}^n$, for all $p \ge 1$, $\|Z^TBZ - \mathbb{E}Z^TBZ\|_p \lesssim \sqrt{p}\|B\|_F + p\|B\|$.*

Observe the sketch can be written $\Pi x = A_xZ$, where

$$A_x := \frac{1}{\sqrt{k}}\sum_{i=1}^{k}\sum_{j=1}^{n} x_j^i e_i \otimes e_{n(i-1)+j}$$

$$= \frac{1}{\sqrt{k}}\begin{bmatrix} -x- & 0 & \cdots & 0 \\ 0 & -x- & \cdots & 0 \\ \vdots & \vdots & & \vdots \\ 0 & 0 & \cdots & -x- \end{bmatrix}.$$

We are thus interested in bounding $\mathbb{E}_Z \sup_{x\in T}|Z^TB_xZ - \mathbb{E}Z^TB_xZ|$,for $B_x = A_x^TA_x$. Note for any $\|x\|_2, \|y\|_2 \le 1$,

$$\|xx^T - yy^T\|_F \le 4\|x - y\|_2. \tag{2}$$

LEMMA 9 (F_2 TRACKING). *If $k \gtrsim 1/\varepsilon^2$ and $Z \in \{-1, +1\}^{kn}$ are 8-wise independent then*

$$\mathbb{E}\sup_t \left|\|\Pi f^{(t)}\|_2^2 - \|f^{(t)}\|_2^2\right| \le \varepsilon\|f\|_2^2.$$

PROOF. Let $A_x, x \in T$, as defined above and $B_x = A_x^TA_x$. By (2), $\|B_x - B_y\|_F \le \frac{4}{\sqrt{k}}\|x - y\|_2$, for all $x, y \in T$. In particular, $\sup_{x\in T}\|B_x\| \le \sup_{x\in T}\|B_x\|_F \le 1/\sqrt{k}$. Let T_ℓ be a $(1/2^\ell)$-net of T under ℓ_2; we know we can take $|T_\ell| \le 4^\ell$. $\mathcal{B}_\ell = \{B_x : x \in T_\ell\}$ is a $1/\sqrt{k}2^\ell$-net under $\|\cdot\|$ and also under $\|\cdot\|_F$. For $x \in T$, let $x_\ell \in T_\ell$ denote the closest element in T_ℓ, under ℓ_2. Then we can write $B_x = B_{x_0} + \sum_{\ell=1}^{\infty}\Delta_{x_\ell}$, where $\Delta_{x_\ell} = B_{x_\ell} - B_{x_{\ell-1}}$. For brevity, we will also define $\gamma(A) := |Z^TAZ^T - \mathbb{E}Z^TAZ^T|$. Thus if the (Z_i) are $2p$-wise independent

$$\begin{aligned}\mathbb{E}\sup_{x\in T}\gamma(B_x) &\le \mathbb{E}\sup_{x\in T}\gamma(B_{x_0}) + \mathbb{E}\sup_{x\in T}\sum_{\ell=1}^{\infty}\gamma(\Delta_{x_\ell}) \\ &\lesssim \frac{p}{\sqrt{k}} + \sum_{\ell=1}^{\infty}\mathbb{E}\sup_{x\in T}\gamma(\Delta_{x_\ell}) \qquad (3)\end{aligned}$$

If $A \in \mathbb{R}^{n\times n}$ is symmetric, then by the Hanson-Wright Inequality

$$\Pr(\gamma(A) > \lambda \cdot S^{1/p}) < \frac{1}{S}\cdot\left[\left(\frac{C\sqrt{p}\|A\|_F}{\lambda}\right)^p + \left(\frac{Cp\|A\|}{\lambda}\right)^p\right]$$

for some constant $C > 0$. Thus if $\mathcal{A}$ is a collection of such matrices, $|\mathcal{A}| = S$, choosing $u^* = C(\sqrt{p}\cdot\sup_{A\in\mathcal{A}}\|A\|_F + p\cdot\sup_{A\in\mathcal{A}}\|A\|)$

$$\begin{aligned}\mathbb{E}\sup_{A\in\mathcal{A}}\gamma(A) &= \int_0^\infty \Pr(\sup_{A\in\mathcal{A}}\gamma(A) > u)du \\ &= S^{1/p}\cdot\int_0^\infty \Pr(\sup_{A\in\mathcal{A}}\gamma(A) > \lambda\cdot S^{1/p})d\lambda \\ &= S^{1/p}(u^* + \int_{u^*}^\infty \Pr(\sup_{A\in\mathcal{A}}\gamma(A) > \lambda\cdot S^{1/p})d\lambda) \\ &\lesssim S^{1/p}(\sqrt{p}\cdot\sup_{A\in\mathcal{A}}\|A\|_F + p\cdot\sup_{A\in\mathcal{A}}\|A\|) \qquad (4)\end{aligned}$$

Now by applying (4) to (3) repeatedly with $\mathcal{A} = \mathcal{A}_\ell = \{B_{x_\ell} - B_{x_{\ell-1}} : x \in T\}$, noting $\sup_{A\in\mathcal{A}_\ell}\|A\| \le \sup_{A\in\mathcal{A}_\ell}\|A\|_F \le 1/\sqrt{k}2^\ell$ and $|\mathcal{A}_\ell| \le 2|T_\ell| \le 2\cdot 2^{2\ell}$,

$$\mathbb{E}\sup_{x\in T}\gamma(B_x) \lesssim \frac{p}{\sqrt{k}} + \sum_{\ell=1}^{\infty}\frac{p2^{2\frac{\ell}{p}-\ell}}{\sqrt{k}} \lesssim \frac{p}{\sqrt{k}}$$

for $p \ge 4$. Thus it suffices for the entries of Z to be $2p$-wise independent, i.e. 8-wise independent. □

3.5 The complete heavy hitters algorithm

We will now describe HH2, formally Algorithm 2, which is an algorithm that removes the assumption on σ needed by HH1. It is followed by the complete algorithm BPTree. The step in HH2 that guesses an approximation σ for $\sqrt{F_2}$ works as follows. We construct the estimator $\hat{F}_2$ of the previous section to (approximately) track F_2. HH2 starts a new instance of HH1 each time the estimate $\hat{F}_2$ crosses a power of 2. Each new instance is initialized with the current estimate of $\sqrt{F_2}$ as the value for σ, but HH2 maintains only the two most recent copies of HH1. Thus, even though, overall, it may instantiate $\Omega(\log n)$ copies of HH1 at most two will running concurrently and the total storage remains $O(1)$ words. At least one of the thresholds will be the "right" one, in the sense that HH1 gets initialized with σ in the interval $[\sqrt{F_2}, 2\sqrt{F_2}]$, so we expect the corresponding instance of HH1 to identify the heavy hitter, if one exists.

The scheme could fail if $\hat{F}_2$ is wildly inaccurate at some points in the stream, for example if $\hat{F}_2$ ever grows too large then the algorithm could discard every instance of HH1 that was correctly initialized. But, Theorem 7 guarantees that it fails only with small probability.

We begin by proving the correctness of HH2 in Lemma 10 and then complete the description and correctness of BPTree in Theorem 11.

LEMMA 10. *There exists a constant $K > 0$ and a 1-pass streaming algorithm HH2, Algorithm 2, such that if the stream*

Algorithm 2 Identify a heavy hitter by guessing σ.

```
procedure HH2(p_1, p_2, ..., p_m)
    Run F̂_2 from Theorem 7 with ε = 1/100 and δ = 1/20
    Start HH1 (1, p_1, ..., p_m)
    Let t_0 = 1 and t_k = min{t | F̂_2^(t) ≥ 2^k}, for k ≥ 1.
    for each time t_k do
        Start HH1((F̂_2^(t_k))^(1/2), p_{t_k}, p_{t_k+1}, ... p_m)
        Let H_k denote its output if it completes
        Discard H_{k-2} and the copy of HH1 started at t_{k-2}
    end for
    return H_{k-1}
end procedure
```

contains a K-heavy hitter then with probability at least 0.6 HH2 returns the identity of the heavy hitter. The algorithm uses $O(1)$ words of memory and $O(1)$ update time.

PROOF. The space and update time bounds are immediate from the description of the algorithm. The success probability follows by a union bound over the failure probabilities in Lemma 6 and Theorem 7, which are 1/3 and $\delta = 0.05$ respectively. It remains to prove that there is a constant K such that conditionally given the success of the F_2 estimator, the hypotheses of Lemma 6 are satisfied by the penultimate instance of HH1 by HH2.

Let K' denote the constant from Lemma 6 and set $K = 12K'$, so if H is a K-heavy hitter then for any $\alpha > 2/K$ and in any interval $(t, t']$ where $(F_2^{(t')})^{1/2} - (F_2^{(t)})^{1/2} \geq \alpha\sqrt{F_2}$ we will have

$$f_H^{(t:t')} + F_2(\mathcal{H}_0)^{1/2} \geq \|f^{(t:t')}\|_2 \geq \|f^{(t')}\|_2 - \|f^{(t)}\|_2 \geq \alpha\sqrt{F_2}.$$

If follows with in the stream $p_t, p_{t+1}, \ldots, p_{t'}$ the heaviness of H is at least

$$\frac{f_H^{(t:t')}}{F_2^{(t:t')}(\mathcal{H}_0)^{1/2}} \geq \frac{\alpha\sqrt{F_2} - \sqrt{F_2(\mathcal{H}_0)}}{\sqrt{F_2(\mathcal{H}_0)}} \geq K\alpha - 1 \geq \frac{K\alpha}{2}. \quad (5)$$

Of course, if $F_2^{(t:t')}(\mathcal{H}_0) = 0$ the same heaviness holds.

Let k be the last iteration of HH2. By the definition of t_k, we have $(\hat{F}_2^{(t_{k-1})})^{1/2} \geq \frac{1}{4}(\hat{F}_2)^{1/2} \geq \frac{1}{4}\sqrt{(1-\varepsilon)F_2}$. Similar calculations show that there exists a time $t_* > t_{k-1}$ such that $(F_2^{(t_*)})^{1/2} - (F_2^{(t_{k-1})})^{1/2} \geq \frac{1}{6}F_2$ and $\|f^{t_{k-1}:t_*}\|_2 \leq (\hat{F}_2^{(t_{k-1})})^{1/2} \leq 2\|f^{t_{k-1}:t_*}\|_2$. In particular, the second pair of inequalities implies that $\hat{F}_2^{(t_k-1)}$ is a good "guess" for σ on the interval $(t_{k-1}, t^*]$. We claim H is a K' heavy hitter on that interval, too. Indeed, because of (5), with $\alpha = 1/6$, we get that H is a K'-heavy hitter on the interval $(t_{k-1}, t^*]$. This proves that the hypotheses of Lemma 6 are satisfied for the stream $p_{t_{k-1}+1}, \ldots, p_{t^*}$. It follows that from Lemma 6 that HH1 correctly identifies $H_{k-1} = H$ on that substream and the remaining updates in the interval $(t_*, t_m]$ do not affect the outcome. □

A now standard reduction from ε-heavy hitters to $O(1)$-heavy hitters gives the following theorem. The next section describes an implementation that is more efficient in practice.

THEOREM 11. *For any $\varepsilon > 0$ there is 1-pass streaming algorithm BPTree that, with probability at least $(1-\delta)$, returns a set of $\frac{\varepsilon}{2}$-heavy hitters containing every ε-heavy hitter and an approximate frequency for every item returned satisfying the $(\varepsilon, 1/\varepsilon^2)$-tail guarantee. The algorithm uses $O(\frac{1}{\varepsilon^2}\log\frac{1}{\varepsilon\delta})$ words of space and has $O(\log\frac{1}{\varepsilon\delta})$ update and $O(\varepsilon^{-2}\log\frac{1}{\varepsilon\delta})$ retrieval time.*

PROOF. The algorithm BPTree constructs a hash table in the same manner as CountSketch where the items are hashed into $b = O(1/\varepsilon^2)$ buckets for $r = O(\log 1/\varepsilon\delta)$ repetitions. On the stream fed into each bucket we run an independent copy of HH2. A standard $r \times b$ CountSketch is also constructed. The constants are chosen so that when an ε-heavy hitter in the stream is hashed into a bucket it becomes a K-heavy hitter with probability at least 0.95. Thus, in any bucket with a the ε-heavy hitter, the heavy hitter is identified with probability at least 0.55 by Lemma 10 and the aforementioned hashing success probability.

At the end of the stream, all of the items returned by instances of HH2 are collected and their frequencies checked using the CountSketch. Any items that cannot be ε-heavy hitters are discarded. The correctness of this algorithm, the bound on its success probability, and the $(\varepsilon, 1/\varepsilon^2)$-tail guarantee follow directly from the correctness of CountSketch and the fact that no more than $O(\varepsilon^{-2}\log(1/\delta\varepsilon))$ items are identified as potential heavy hitters. □

We can amplify the success probability of HH2 to any $1-\delta$ by running $O(\log(1/\delta))$ copies in parallel and taking a majority vote for the heavy hitter. This allows one to track $O(1)$-heavy hitters at all points in the stream with an additional $O(\log\log m)$ factor in space and update time. The reason is because there can be a succession of at most $O(\log m)$ 2-heavy hitters in the stream, since their frequencies must increase geometrically, so setting $\delta = \Theta(1/\log m)$ is sufficient. The same scheme works for BPTree tree, as well, and if one replaces each of the counters in the attached CountSketch with an F_2-at-all-times estimator of [7] then one can track the frequencies of all ε-heavy hitters at all times as well. The total storage becomes $O(\frac{1}{\varepsilon^2}(\log\log n + \log\frac{1}{\varepsilon}))$ words and the update time is $O(\log\log n + \log\frac{1}{\varepsilon})$.

4. EXPERIMENTAL RESULTS

We implemented HH2 in C to evaluate its performance and compare it against the CountSketch for finding one frequent item. The source code is available from the authors upon request. In practice, the hashing and repetitions perform predictably, so the most important aspect to understand the performance of BPTree is determine the heaviness constant K where HH2 reliably finds K-heavy hitters. Increasing the number of buckets that the algorithm hashes to effectively decreases n. Therefore, in order to maximize the "effective" n of the tests that we can perform within a reasonable time, we will just compare CountSketch against HH2.

The first two experiments help to determine some parameters for HH2 and the heaviness constant K. Afterwards, we compare the performance of HH2 and CountSketch for finding a single heavy hitter in the regime where the heavy hitter frequency is large enough so that both algorithms work reliably.

Streams. The experiments were performed using four types of streams (synthetic data). In all cases, one heavy hitter is present. For a given n and α there are n items with frequency 1 and one item, call it H, with frequency $\alpha\sqrt{n}$. If α is not specified then it is taken to be 1. The four types of streams are (1) all occurrences of H occur at the start of the stream, (2) all occurrences of H at the end of the stream, (3) occurrences of H placed randomly in the stream, and (4) occurrences of H placed randomly in blocks of $n^{1/4}$.

The experiments were run on a server with two 2.66GHz Intel Xenon X5650 processors, each with 12MB cache, and 48GB of memory. The server was running Scientific Linux 7.2.

4.1 F_2 tracking experiment

The first experiment tests the accuracy of the F_2 tracking for different parameter settings. We implemented the F_2 tracking in C using the speed-up of [30], which can be proved to correct for tracking using Appendix B. The algorithm uses the same $r \times b$ table as a CountSketch. To query F_2 one takes the median of r estimates, each of which is the sum of the squares of the b entries in a row of the table. The same group of ten type (3) streams with $n = 10^8$ and $\alpha = 1$ was used for each of the parameter settings.

The results are presented in Table 4.1. Given the tracker $\hat{F}_2(t)$ and true evolution of the second moment $F_2(t)$, we measure the maximum F_2 tracking error of one instance as $\max_t |\hat{F}_2(t) - F_2(t)|/F_2$, where F_2 is the value of the second moment at the end of the stream. We report the average maximum tracking error and the worst (maximum) maximum tracking over each of the ten streams for every choice of parameters.

The table indicates that, for every choice of parameter settings, the worst maximum tracking error is not much worse than the average maximum tracking error. We observe that the tracking error has relatively low variance, even when $r = 1$. It also shows that the smallest possible tracker, with $r = b = 1$, is highly unreliable.

4.2 Implementations of HH2 and CountSketch

HH2 implementation details. We have implemented the algorithm HH2 as described in Algorithm 2. The maximum number of rounds is $R = \min\{\lceil 3\log_2 n\rceil, 64\}$. We implemented the four-wise independent hashing using the "CW" trick using the C code from [31] Appendix A.14. We use the code from Appendix A.3 of [31] to generate 2-universal random variables for random relabeling of the item. The F_2 tracker from the previous section was used, we found experimentally that setting the tracker parameters as $r = 1$ and $b = 30$ is accurate enough for HH2. We also tried four-wise hashing with the tabulation-based hashing for 64-bit keys with 8 bit characters and compression as implemented in C in Appendix A.11 of [31]. This led to a 48% increase in speed (updates/millisecond), but at the cost of a 55 times increase in space.

CountSketch implementation details. We implemented CountSketch in C as described in the original paper [11] with parameters that lead to the smallest possible space. We use the CountSketch parameters as $b = 2$ (number of buckets/row) and $r = \lceil 3 + \log_2 n\rceil$ (number of rows). The choice of b is the smallest possible value. The choice of r is the minimum needed to guarantee that, with probability 7/8, there does not exist an item $i \in [n] \setminus \{H\}$ that collides the heavy hitter in every row of the data structure. In particular, if we use only $r' < r$ rows then we expect $2^{\log_2 N - r'}$ collisions with the heavy hitter, which would break the guarantee of the CountSketch. Indeed, suppose there is a collision with the heavy hitter and consider a stream where all occurrences of H appear at the beginning, then CountSketch will not correctly return H as the most frequent item because some item that collides with it and appears after it will replace H as the candidate heavy hitter in the heap. In our experiments, the CountSketch does not reliably find the α-heavy hitter with these parameters when $\alpha < 32$. This gives some speed and storage advantage to the CountSketch in the comparison against HH2, since b and/or r would need to increase to make CountSketch perform as reliably as HH2 during these tests.

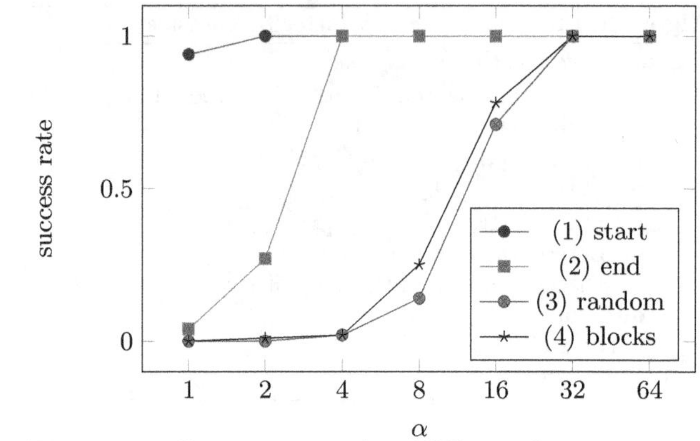

Figure 2: Success rate for HH2 on four types of streams with $n = 10^8$ and heavy hitter frequency $\alpha\sqrt{n}$.

We also tried implementing the four-wise hashing with the Thorup-Zhang tabulation. With the same choices of b and r this led to an 18% speed-up and a 192 times average increase in space. Since the hash functions are such a large part of the space and time needed by the data structure this could likely be improved by taking $b > 2$, e.g. $b = 100$, and $r \approx \lceil \log_b n\rceil$. No matter what parameters are chosen the storage will be larger than using the CW trick because each tabulation-based hash function occupies 38kB, which already ten times larger than the whole CountSketch table.

4.3 Heaviness

The goal of this experiment is to approximately determine the minimum value K where if $f_H \geq K\sqrt{n}$ then HH2 correctly identifies H. As shown in Lemma 10, $K \leq 12 \cdot 380{,}000$ but we hope this is a very pessimistic bound. For this experiment, we take $n = 10^8$ and consider $\alpha \in \{1, 2, 2^2, \ldots, 2^6\}$. For each value of α and all four types of streams we ran HH2 one hundred times independently. Figure 4.3 displays the success rate, which is the fraction of the one hundred trials where HH2 correctly returned the heavy hitter. The figure indicates that HH2 succeeds reliably when $\alpha \geq 32$.

4.4 HH2 versus CountSketch comparison

In the final experiment we compare HH2 against CountSketch. The goal is to understand space and time trade-off in a regime where both algorithms reliably find the heavy hitter.

For each choice of parameters we compute the update rate of the CountSketch and HH2 (in updates/millisecond) and the storage used (in kilobytes) for all of the variables in the associated program. The results are presented in Figure 3.

The figure shows that HH2 is much faster and about one third of the space. The dramatic difference in speed is to be expected because two bottlenecks in CountSketch are com-

	avg. maximum F_2 tracking error					worst maximum F_2 tracking error				
b \ r	**1**	**2**	**4**	**8**	**16**	**1**	**2**	**4**	**8**	**16**
1	1.2	0.71	0.82	0.66	0.59	4.3	1.2	2.7	0.85	0.86
10	0.35	0.30	0.33	0.19	0.16	1.1	0.68	0.91	0.28	0.20
100	0.12	0.095	0.080	0.074	0.052	0.24	0.17	0.13	0.13	0.10
1000	0.044	0.030	0.028	0.018	0.017	0.076	0.060	0.045	0.029	0.024

Table 1: Average and maximum F_2 tracking error over 10 streams for different choices of b and r.

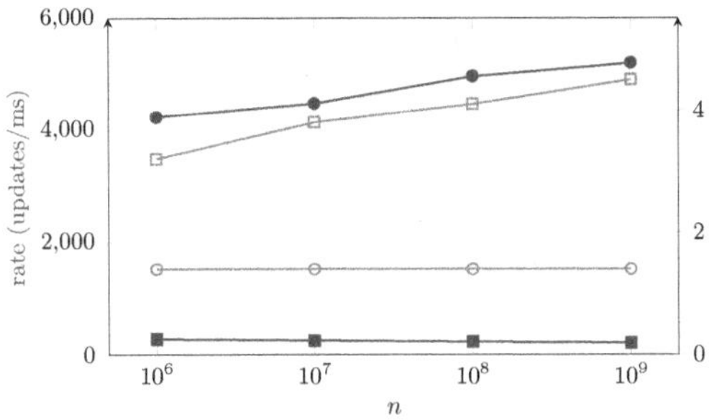

Figure 3: Update rate in updates/ms (•) and storage in kB (○) for HH2 and CountSketch (■ and □, respectively) with the CW trick hashing.

puting the median of the $\Theta(\log n)$ values and evaluating $\Theta(\log n)$ hash functions. HH2 removes both bottlenecks. Furthermore, as the subroutine HH1 progresses a greater number of items are rejected from the stream, which means the program avoids the associated hash function evaluations in HH2. This phenomena is responsible for the observed *increase* in the update rate of HH2 as n increases. An additional factor that contributes to the speedup is amortization of the start-up time for HH2 and of the restart time for each copy of HH1.

4.5 Experiments summary

We found HH2 to be faster and smaller than CountSketch. The number of rows strongly affects the running time of CountSketch because during each update r four-wise independent hash functions must be evaluated and of a median r values is computed. The discussion in Section 4.2 explains why the number of rows r cannot be reduced by much without abandoning the CountSketch guarantee or increasing the space. Thus, when there is a K-heavy hitter for sufficiently large K our algorithm significantly outperforms CountSketch. Experimentally we found $K = 32$ was large enough.

The full BPTree data structure is needed to find an item with smaller frequency, but for finding an item of smaller frequency CountSketch could outperform BPTree until n is very large. For example, to identify an α-heavy hitter in the stream our experiments suggest that one can use a BPTree structure with about $\lceil(32/\alpha)^2\rceil$ buckets per row. In comparison a CountSketch with roughly $\max\{2, 1/\alpha^2\}$ buckets per row should suffice. When α is a small constant, e.g. 0.1, what we find is that one can essentially reduce the number rows of the data structure from $\log(n)$ to just a few, e.g. one or two, at the cost of a factor $32^2 = 1024$ increase in space.[4] This brief calculation suggests that CountSketch will outperform BPTree when the heaviness is $\alpha < 1$ until $n \gtrsim 2^{1024}$—which is to say always in practice. On the other hand, our experiments demonstrate that HH2 clearly outperforms CountSketch with a sufficiently heavy heavy hitter. More experimental work is necessary to determine the heaviness threshold (as a function of n) where BPTree outperforms CountSketch. There are many parameters that affect the trade-offs among space, time, and accuracy, so such an investigation is beyond the scope of the preliminary results reported here.

[4]Recall, $\Omega(\log n/\log(1/\alpha))$ rows are necessary CountSketch whereas BPTree needs only $O(\log 1/\alpha)$ rows.

5. CONCLUSION

In this paper we studied the heavy hitters problem, which is arguably one of the most important problems for data streams. The problem is heavily inspired from practice and algorithms for it are used in commercial systems. We presented the first space and time optimal algorithm for finding ℓ_2-heavy hitters, which is the strongest notion of heavy hitters achievable in polylogarithmic space. By optimal, we mean the time is $O(1)$ to process each stream update, and the space is $O(\log n)$ bits of memory. These bounds match trivial lower bounds (for constant ε). We also provided new techniques which may be of independent interest: (1) a one-pass implementation of a multi-round adaptive compressed-sensing scheme where we use that after filtering a fraction of items, the heavy item is becoming even heavier (2) a derandomization of Bernoulli processes relevant in this setting using limited independence. Both are essential in obtaining an optimal heavy hitters algorithm with $O(1)$ memory. Technique (1) illustrates a new power of insertion-only streams and technique (2) can be stated as a general chaining result with limited independence in terms of the size of the nets used. Given the potential practical value of such an algorithm, we provided preliminary experiments showing our savings over previous algorithms.

Acknowledgments

We would like to thank Huy L. Nguyễn for pointing out that our original proof that 6-wise independence suffices for the conclusion of Theorem 1 could be slightly tweaked to in fact show that 4-wise independence suffices. We would also like to thank the anonymous referees for their suggestions to improve the readability of this paper.

6. REFERENCES

[1] N. Alon, Y. Matias, and M. Szegedy. The space complexity of approximating the frequency moments. *J. Comput. Syst. Sci.*, 58(1):137–147, 1999.

[2] B. Babcock, S. Babu, M. Datar, R. Motwani, and J. Widom. Models and issues in data stream systems. In *Proceedings of the Twenty-first ACM*

SIGACT-SIGMOD-SIGART Symposium on Principles of Database Systems (PODS), pages 1–16, 2002.

[3] R. Berinde, G. Cormode, P. Indyk, and M. J. Strauss. Space-optimal heavy hitters with strong error bounds. In *Proceedings of the Twenty-Eigth ACM SIGMOD-SIGACT-SIGART Symposium on Principles of Database Systems (PODS)*, pages 157–166, 2009.

[4] A. Bhattacharyya, P. Dey, and D. P. Woodruff. An optimal algorithm for ℓ_1-heavy hitters in insertion streams and related problems. *CoRR*, abs/1511.00661, 2016.

[5] R. S. Boyer and J. S. Moore. A fast majority vote algorithm. Technical Report Technical Report ICSCA-CMP-32, Institute for Computer Science, University of Texas, 1981.

[6] R. S. Boyer and J. S. Moore. MJRTY: A fast majority vote algorithm. In *Automated Reasoning: Essays in Honor of Woody Bledsoe*, pages 105–118, 1991.

[7] V. Braverman, S. R. Chestnut, N. Ivkin, and D. P. Woodruff. Beating CountSketch for Heavy Hitters in Insertion Streams. In *Proceedings of the 48th Annual ACM Symposium on Theory of Computing (STOC), to appear*, 2016. Full version at arXiv abs/1511.00661.

[8] V. Braverman and R. Ostrovsky. Approximating large frequency moments with pick-and-drop sampling. In *Approximation, Randomization, and Combinatorial Optimization. Algorithms and Techniques*, pages 42–57. Springer, 2013.

[9] L. Carter and M. N. Wegman. Universal classes of hash functions. *J. Comput. Syst. Sci.*, 18(2):143–154, 1979.

[10] A. Chakrabarti, G. Cormode, and A. McGregor. A near-optimal algorithm for estimating the entropy of a stream. *ACM Transactions on Algorithms*, 6(3), 2010.

[11] M. Charikar, K. C. Chen, and M. Farach-Colton. Finding frequent items in data streams. *Theor. Comput. Sci.*, 312(1):3–15, 2004.

[12] G. Cormode and S. Muthukrishnan. An improved data stream summary: the count-min sketch and its applications. *J. Algorithms*, 55(1):58–75, 2005.

[13] E. D. Demaine, A. López-Ortiz, and J. I. Munro. Frequency estimation of Internet packet streams with limited space. In *Proceedings of the 10th Annual European Symposium on Algorithms (ESA)*, pages 348–360, 2002.

[14] R. M. Dudley. The sizes of compact subsets of Hilbert space and continuity of Gaussian processes. *J. Functional Analysis*, 1:290–330, 1967.

[15] P. Gopalan and J. Radhakrishnan. Finding duplicates in a data stream. In *Proceedings of the Twentieth Annual ACM-SIAM Symposium on Discrete Algorithms (SODA)*, pages 402–411, 2009.

[16] U. Haagerup. The best constants in the Khintchine inequality. *Studia Math.*, 70(3):231–283, 1982.

[17] D. L. Hanson and F. T. Wright. A bound on tail probabilities for quadratic forms in independent random variables. *The Annals of Mathematical Statistics*, 42(3):1079–1083, 1971.

[18] N. J. A. Harvey, J. Nelson, and K. Onak. Sketching and streaming entropy via approximation theory. In *49th Annual IEEE Symposium on Foundations of Computer Science (FOCS)*, pages 489–498, 2008.

[19] Z. Huang, W. M. Tai, and K. Yi. Tracking the frequency moments at all times. *arXiv preprint arXiv:1412.1763*, 2014.

[20] P. Indyk, E. Price, and D. P. Woodruff. On the power of adaptivity in sparse recovery. In *IEEE 52nd Annual Symposium on Foundations of Computer Science (FOCS)*, pages 285–294, 2011.

[21] P. Indyk and D. P. Woodruff. Optimal approximations of the frequency moments of data streams. In *Proceedings of the 37th Annual ACM Symposium on Theory of Computing (STOC)*, pages 202–208, 2005.

[22] H. Jowhari, M. Sağlam, and G. Tardos. Tight bounds for Lp samplers, finding duplicates in streams, and related problems. In *Proceedings of the 30th ACM SIGMOD-SIGACT-SIGART Symposium on Principles of Database Systems (PODS)*, pages 49–58, 2011.

[23] R. M. Karp, S. Shenker, and C. H. Papadimitriou. A simple algorithm for finding frequent elements in streams and bags. *ACM Trans. Database Syst.*, 28:51–55, 2003.

[24] Y. Li and D. P. Woodruff. A tight lower bound for high frequency moment estimation with small error. In *Approximation, Randomization, and Combinatorial Optimization. Algorithms and Techniques*, pages 623–638. Springer, 2013.

[25] G. S. Manku and R. Motwani. Approximate frequency counts over data streams. *PVLDB*, 5(12):1699, 2012.

[26] A. Metwally, D. Agrawal, and A. El Abbadi. Efficient computation of frequent and top-k elements in data streams. In *Proceedings of the 10th International Conference on Database Theory (ICDT)*, pages 398–412, 2005.

[27] J. Misra and D. Gries. Finding repeated elements. *Sci. Comput. Program.*, 2(2):143–152, 1982.

[28] M. Monemizadeh and D. P. Woodruff. 1-pass relative-error L_p-sampling with applications. In *Proceedings of the Twenty-First Annual ACM-SIAM Symposium on Discrete Algorithms (SODA)*, pages 1143–1160, 2010.

[29] S. Muthukrishnan. Data streams: Algorithms and applications. *Foundations and Trends in Theoretical Computer Science*, 1(2), 2005.

[30] M. Thorup and Y. Zhang. Tabulation based 4-universal hashing with applications to second moment estimation. In *Proceedings of the Fifteenth Annual ACM-SIAM Symposium on Discrete Algorithms, SODA 2004, New Orleans, Louisiana, USA, January 11-14, 2004*, pages 615–624, 2004.

[31] M. Thorup and Y. Zhang. Tabulation-based 5-independent hashing with applications to linear probing and second moment estimation. *SIAM Journal on Computing*, 41(2):293–331, 2012.

APPENDIX

A. Pick-and-Drop COUNTER EXAMPLE

We begin with a brief description of the Pick-and-Drop algorithm and refer the reader to [8] for the full details. Afterwards we will describe a stream where the algorithm fails, with probability at least $1 - n^{-1/8}$, to find a ℓ_2 heavy hitter and give some intuition about why the algorithm has this behavior. That is, the probability the algorithm succeeds is inverse polynomially small.

There is a parameter to the algorithm t and the algorithm begins by partitioning the stream into m/t consecutive intervals of t updates each. The value of t is chosen such that m/t is roughly the smallest frequency of a heavy hitter that we wish to find. Hence, the average number of heavy hitter updates per interval is $\Omega(1)$. In each interval, independently, a position $T \in \{1, 2, \ldots, t\}$ is chosen at random and the item in the Tth position within the interval is sampled. We also count how many times the sampled item it appears within $\{T, T+1, \ldots, t\}$. Next, the following "competition" is performed. We traverse the intervals sequentially from the first to the last and maintain a global sample and counter. Initially, the global sample is the sample from the first interval and the global counter is the counter from the first interval. For each future interval i, two options are possible: (1) the global sample is replaced with the sample from i and the global counter is replaced with the counter from interval i, or (2) the global sample remains unchanged and the global counter is increased by the number of times the global sample item appears in interval i. Also, the algorithm maintains X which is the current number of intervals for which the current global counter has not been replaced. If the maximum between X and the counter from the ith interval is greater than the global counter then (1) is executed, otherwise (2) is executed.

Consider the following counter example that shows Pick-and-Drop cannot find ℓ_2 heavy hitters in $O(1)$ words. $f \in \mathbb{R}^{2n}$ is a frequency vector where one coordinate H has frequency $\sqrt{n}$, n elements have frequency 1, and $\sqrt{n}$ elements have frequency $n^{1/4}$, call the latter "pseudo-heavy". The remaining coordinates of f are 0. Consider the stream that is split into t intervals $B_1, \ldots, B_t$ where $t = \sqrt{n}$ and each interval has size $\Theta(t)$. The items are distributed as follows.

- Each interval w where $w = qn^{1/4}$ for $q = 1, 2, \ldots, n^{1/4}$, is filled with $n^{1/4}$ pseudo-heavy elements each appearing $n^{1/4}$ times and appearing in no other interval.
- Each interval $w+h$, for $h = 1, 2, \ldots, n^{1/8}$ contains $n^{1/8}$ appearances of H and remaining items that appear only once in the stream.
- Each interval $w+h$, for $h = n^{1/8}+1, \ldots, n^{1/4}-1$ contains items that appear only once in the stream.

Obviously, a pseudo-heavy element will be picked in every "w interval". In order for it to be beaten by H, its count must be smaller than $n^{1/8}$ and H must be picked from one of the $n^{1/8}$ intervals immediately following. The intersection of these events happens with probability no more than $n^{-1/8}\left(n^{1/8} \cdot \frac{n^{1/8}}{n^{1/2}}\right) = n^{-3/8}$. As there are only $n^{1/4}$ "w intervals", the probability that the algorithm outputs H is smaller than $n^{-1/8}$.

Note that the algorithm cannot be fixed by choosing other values of t in the above example. If $t \gg \sqrt{n}$ then H might be sampled with higher probability but the pseudo-heavy elements will also have higher probabilities and the above argument can be repeated with a different distribution in the intervals. If $t \ll \sqrt{n}$ then the probability to sample H in any of the rounds becomes too small.

This counterexample is not contrived—it shows why the whole Pick-and-Drop sampling algorithm fails to shed any light on the ℓ_2 heavy hitters problem. Let us explain why the algorithm will not work in polylogarithmic space for $k=2$. Consider the case when the global sample is $h \neq H$ and the global counter is f_h. In this case, the global sample can "kill" f_h appearances of H in the next f_h intervals, by the description of the algorithm. The probability to sample h is f_h/t, so the expected number of appearances of H that will be killed is upper bounded by $\sum_h f_h^3/t = F_3/t$. In the algorithm, we typically choose $t = \sqrt{F_1}$. Consider the case when $F_1 = \Theta(n)$, $F_2 = \Theta(n)$ but $F_2 = o(F_3)$. In this case the algorithm needs f_H to be at least $CF_3/\sqrt{F_2}$ for a constant C. This is impossible if $f_H^2 = \Theta(F_2)$. For $t = o(\sqrt{n})$ the probability that H is sampled becomes $o(1)$. For $t = \omega(\sqrt{n})$ we need a smaller decay for H to survive until the end in which case the above analysis can be repeated with the new decay factor for pseudo-heavy elements.

B. ALTERNATIVE F_2 TRACKING ANALYSIS

This section describes an alternative F_2 tracking analysis. It shows that 4-wise independence is enough, that is the original setting used by [1], but at the cost of an extra $\log 1/\varepsilon$ factor on the space complexity. Let $N \in \mathbb{N}$, Z^j be a vector of 4-wise independent Rademacher random variables for $j \in N$, and define $X_{j,t} = \langle Z^j, f^{(t)} \rangle$. Let $Y_t = \frac{1}{N}\sum_{j=1}^N X_{j,t}^2$, obviously Y_t can be computed by a streaming algorithm.

THEOREM 12. *Let $0 < \varepsilon < 1$. There is a streaming algorithm that outputs at each time t a value $\hat{F}_2^{(t)}$ such that*

$$\Pr(|\hat{F}_2^{(t)} - F_2^{(t)}| \leq \varepsilon F_2, \text{ for all } 0 \leq t \leq m) \geq 1 - \delta.$$

The algorithm use $O(\frac{1}{\varepsilon^2}\log\frac{1}{\delta\varepsilon})$ words of storage and has $O(\frac{1}{\varepsilon^2}\log\frac{1}{\delta\varepsilon})$ update time.

The proof of Theorem 7 uses the following technical lemma that bounds the divergence the estimate over an entire interval of updates. It follows along the lines of Lemma 22 from the full version of [7].

LEMMA 13. *Let $\varepsilon < 1$, $N \geq 12/\varepsilon^2$, and $\Delta > 0$. If $F_2^{(v)} - F_2^{(u)} \leq (\frac{\varepsilon}{20NC_*})^2 F_2$, then*

$$\Pr\left(Y_t - F_2^{(t)} \leq 2\varepsilon F_2, \forall t \in [u,v]\right) \geq \frac{2}{3}.$$

PROOF. We denote $\Delta = (F_2^{(v)} - F_2^{(u)})/F_2$ and split the expression above as follows

$$Y_t - F_2^{(t)} = (Y_t - Y_u) + (Y_u - F_2^{(u)}) + (F_2^{(t)} - F_2^{(u)}).$$

Let $b_1 > 0$. For the second term, and it is shown in [1] that

$$\Pr(Y_u - F_2^{(u)} \geq b_1) \leq \frac{2(F_2^{(u)})^2}{Nb_1^2}.$$

Let $X^{(t)} = \frac{1}{\sqrt{N}}(X_{1,t}, X_{2,t}, \ldots, X_{N,t})$ and $X^{(u:t)} = X_t - X_u$, in particular $Y_t = \|X^{(t)}\|_2^2$. For the first term, we have

$$Y_t = \|X^{(u)} + X^{(u:t)}\|_2^2 \leq \left(\|X^{(u)}\|_2 + \|X^{(u:t)}\|_2\right)^2,$$

so

$$Y_t - Y_u \leq 2\sqrt{Y_u}\|X^{(u:t)}\|_2 + \|X^{(u:t)}\|_2^2.$$

Now from Theorem 1 and a union bound it follows that for $b_2 > 0$

$$P\left(\sup_{j\in[N], u\leq t\leq v} |X_{j,t} - X_{j,u}| \geq b_2\right) \leq \frac{NC_*\|f^{(u:v)}\|_2}{b_2},$$

so $P(\sup_{t\geq u} \|X^{(u:t)}\|_2 \geq b_2) \leq NC_* \|f^{(u:v)}\|_2/b_2$.

With probability at least $1 - \frac{2(F_2^{(u)})^2}{Nb_1^2} - \frac{NC_*\|f^{(u:v)}\|_2}{b_2}$ we get, for all $t \geq u$

$$Y_t - F_2^{(t)} \leq 2(F_2^{(u)} + b_1)^{\frac{1}{2}} b_2 + b_2^2 + b_1 + \Delta F_2.$$

Now we set $b_1 = \varepsilon F_2$ and $b_2 = 6NC_*\sqrt{\Delta F_2}$ and the above expression is bounded by

$$\begin{aligned} Y_t - F_2^{(t)} &\leq 12\sqrt{2}NC_* F_2\sqrt{\Delta} + \varepsilon F_2 + 2\Delta \\ &\leq 20NC_* F_2\sqrt{\Delta} + \varepsilon F_2, \\ &\leq 2\varepsilon F_2 \end{aligned}$$

since $\Delta \leq F_2$. The probability of success is at least

$$1 - \frac{2(F_2^{(u)})^2}{N\varepsilon^2 F_2^2} - \frac{\|f^{(u:m)}\|_2}{6\sqrt{\Delta}} \leq 1 - \frac{1}{3}.$$

□

We now proceed to describe the F_2 estimation algorithm and prove Theorem 7.

Proof proof of Theorem 7. The algorithm returns at each time t the value

$$\hat{F}_2(t) = \max_{s\leq t} \text{median}(Y_{1,t}, Y_{2,t}, \ldots, Y_{M,t}),$$

which are $M = \Theta(\log \frac{1}{\delta\varepsilon})$ independent copies of Y_t with $N = 12(\frac{3}{\varepsilon})^2$. Let $\Delta = (\frac{\varepsilon/3}{20NC_*})^2$ and define $t_0 = 0$ and $t_k = \max\{t \leq m \mid F_2^{(t_k)} \leq F_2^{(t_{k-1})} + \Delta F_2\}$, for $k \geq 1$. These times separate the stream into no more than $2/\Delta$ intervals during which the second moment increases no more than ΔF_2. Lemma 13 and an application of Chernoff's Inequality imply that for each interval k

$$\Pr\left(\text{median}_{j\in[M]}(Y_{j,t}) - F_2^{(t)} \leq \frac{2}{3}\varepsilon F_2, \forall t \in [t_{k-1}, t_k)\right) \geq 1 - \text{poly}(\delta\varepsilon).$$

The original description of the AMS algorithm [1] implies that, for all k,

$$\Pr\left(\text{median}_{j\in[M]}(Y_{j,t_k}) \geq (1 - \varepsilon/3)F_2^{(t)}\right) \geq 1 - \text{poly}(\delta\varepsilon).$$

By choosing the constants appropriately and applying a union bound over all $O(\varepsilon^{-2})$ intervals and endpoints we achieve all of these events events occur with probability at least $1 - \delta$. One easily checks that this gives the desired guarantee. □

C. FASTER WITH LESS SPACE

Maintaining all of the $O(\varepsilon^{-2} \log \frac{1}{\varepsilon\delta})$ instances of the F_2 tracking algorithm is a significant speed and memory bottleneck for BPTree. For example, Section 4 uses a tracker with thirty counters, which is a lot of additional storage. Furthermore, evaluating the four-wise hash functions is one of the main bottlenecks limiting the speed, so it is much slower to have update one F_2 tracker for every row of the datastructure. This section addresses that bottleneck by reducing the number of instances of F_2 tracking to only one. This is the most efficient way we have found to implement the algorithm. It does not improve (nor degrade) the space complexity or update time for BPTree. In this section we will describe the intuition behind the following theorem. Its proof appears in the full version of this paper.

Theorem 14. *The algorithm BPTree can be implemented with a single F_2 tracker, which periodically restarts. The storage, update time, and retrieval times all retain the same asymptotic complexity.*

The single-tracker version will use the same data structure with $b \cdot r$ buctets, where $\frac{K^2}{\varepsilon^2} < b = O(1/\varepsilon^2)$ and $r = O(\log 1/\delta\varepsilon)$. However, the supressed constants may be larger. For convenience, we will take $b{\cdot}r$ to be the dimensions of the auxiliary CountSketch, too. However, it is not necessary that the same size table is used for the auxiliary CountSketch.

We will make two modifications to BPTree. The first is to change how we determine when to restart HH1. Instead of using one F_2 tracker in each of the $b{\cdot}r = O(\varepsilon^{-2}\log\frac{1}{\delta\varepsilon})$ buckets, we will use only one F_2 tracker overall, which periodically restarts. To be precise, replace all $b{\cdot}r = O(\varepsilon^{-2}\log 1/\delta\varepsilon)$ copies of the F_2 trackers used by the instances of HH2 in each bucket with a single tracker that is periodically restarted. At the beginning we start T_1, the first F_2 tracker, we label the first restart T_2, then T_3, and so on. The random bits used for each new tracker are independent of the previous ones. For $k \geq 1$, we recursively define $t_k = \min\{t \geq 0 \mid T_k^{(t)} \geq 2^k\}$ and $T_k^{(t)}$, $t \geq t_{k-1}$, is an F_2 estimate on the stream at times $t_{k-1}, t_{k-1}+1, \ldots t$. Let $\hat{\ell}$ be the index of the last tracker started, and we define $t_0 = 1$ and $t_{\hat{\ell}} = m$ for convenience even though $T_{\hat{\ell}}^{(t)} < 2^{\hat{\ell}}$ by definition. We will take the trackers to each have error probability $\delta' = O(\delta/\log\varepsilon^{-1})$, where the supressed constant will be taken sufficiently small, and accuracy $\varepsilon' = 1/100$. Upon each time t_k, for $k = 0, 1, 2, \ldots, \hat{\ell}$, the instance of HH1 in every bucket is restarted simultaneously with the value $\sigma = \frac{\varepsilon}{16}2^{k/2}$ given as the input "guess" of F_2. When a restart happens at time t_k, the old F_2 tracker T_k and the corresponding HH1 instance are discarded by the algorithm. Here is another difference from the implementation using HH2, this faster version does not stagger-start the instances of HH1, only a single copy of HH1 is operating in each bucket at one time.

The second modification is to guarantee that we do not discard a heavy hitter after it is identified. Let us focus on a singe bucket. In this bucket, HH1 is restarted repeatedly, and each time it could output a candidate heavy hitter. Rather than keep the last two candidates, as in BPTree, we maintain the identity of one candidate, call it H_0, and each time a new candidate is identified for this bucket, we compare its estimated frequency with an estimate of f_{H_0} and replace H_0 with the new candidate if only if the freqency estimate of H_0 is the smaller of the two. When comparing frequencies we use estimates from the auxiliary CountSketch.

The rest of this section contains the details of the proof of Theorem 14, but here is a rough outline. We define two favorable events, these are E_1:"the F_2 tracking is accurate" and E_2:"the auxiliary CountSketch is accurate" and show that they have high enough probability in Lemmas 15 and 16. Next, we show that the probability that some heavy hitter H is identified, conditionally given the random bits used by the F_2 trackers and $E := E_1 \cap E_2$, is $\Omega(1)$ per each of the r rows of the data structure (Lemmas 17 and 18). That is enough to guarantee that H is identified at least once among all $r = O(\log 1/\delta\varepsilon)$ rows with probability at least $1-\text{poly}(\delta\varepsilon)$ using a Chernoff Bound, so we can apply a union bound over all heavy hitters. A more detailed version of that argument completes the proof of Theorem 14 at the end of this section.

We need the conditioning because the rows of the BPTree data structure are no longer independent, since all of the restarts are timed from the same F_2 tracker, and that precludes a Chernoff Bound. However, the rows are conditionally independent. In order to show that H is indeed identified with probability $\Omega(1)$, we will define the event that a restart k is "good" in a particular bucket of the data structure. If k is good it means two things. First, the corresponding interval of updates, $t_k, t_k+1, \ldots, t_{k+1}-1$, in this bucket satisfies the hypotheses of Lemma 4, so H is identified with (conditional) probability at least 2/3, and second, H is never eclipsed as the heavy hitter in any of the subsequent rounds. The rationale behind the proof of the bound itself is that, on average, rounds that are not good use up few of the updates to H, because the correspond to intervals in the stream where H is not a heavy hitter.

Let $\mathcal{T}_k$ denote the random bits used for all trackers started at times $t_{k'}$, for $k' \leq k$, and let $\mathcal{T}$ denote the random bits for all of the trackers in total. Similarly, let $\mathcal{C}$ denote the collection of random bits used by the auxiliary CountSketch. In most of the events we need to consider we can as well condition on $\mathcal{C}$ without any extra legwork because $\mathcal{C}$ is independent of $\mathcal{T}$ and all instances of HH1. Let $t^* = \min\{t \geq 0 \mid F_2^{(t)} \geq \frac{\varepsilon^2}{100^2} F_2\}$ and let $\ell^* = \min\{k \mid t_k \geq t^*\}$. We define E_1 to be the event that, for all k where $t_k \geq t^*$ and all $t \in [t_{k-1}, t_k)$, $|\hat{T}_k^{(t)} - F_2^{(t_{k-1}:t)}| \leq \frac{1}{100} F_2^{(t_{k-1}:t_k)}$.

Lemma 15. $\Pr(E_1) \geq 1 - \delta/3$

Proof. Let D_k be the event that, for all $t \in [t_{k-1}, t_k)$, $|\hat{T}_k^{(t)} - F_2^{(t_{k-1}:t)}| \leq \frac{1}{100} F_2^{(t_{k-1}:t_k)}$. By Theorem 7 and our choice $\delta' = O(\delta/\log \varepsilon^{-1})$ for the error probability of the F_2 tracking, we have that, for all $k = 1, 2, \ldots, \hat{\ell}+1$, $\Pr(D_k \mid \mathcal{T}_{k-1}) \geq 1 - \delta'$. Starting from t^*, the value of $F_2^{(t)}$ doubles only $O(\log \varepsilon^{-1})$ times in the remainder of the stream. Therefore, $\hat{\ell} - \ell^* = O(\log \varepsilon^{-1})$ on the event E_1, and $E_1 \subseteq \bigcup_{k=\hat{\ell}-O(\log \frac{1}{\varepsilon})}^{\hat{\ell}+1} D_k$. The bound follows as

$$\begin{aligned}1 - \Pr(E_1) &\leq \sum_{k \in L} 1 - \Pr(D_k) \\ &= \sum_{k \in L} 1 - \mathbb{E} \Pr(D_k \mid \mathcal{T}_{k-1}) \\ &\leq O(\log \varepsilon^{-1}) \cdot \delta' \leq \frac{\delta}{3}.\end{aligned}$$

The last inequality follows by taking the supressed constant in the definition of δ' to be sufficiently small. □

An observation from the last proof that we will use again is E_1 implies $O(\log \varepsilon^{-1})$ restarts are enough to go from t^* to the start of the stream. Let $L = \{\ell^*, \ell^*+1, \ldots, \hat{\ell}\}$. Although L is random ($\hat{\ell}$ and ℓ^* depend on the F_2 trackers), $|L| = O(\log \varepsilon^{-1})$ over the event E_1, which is sufficient for our purposes.

Now we will define the event E_2 that the auxiliary CountSketch frequency estimates are accurate enough. Let $\mathcal{H}$ denote the (random) set of candidate heavy hitters returned from a given bucket by instances of HH1 started at times t_k, for $k \in L$, i.e. the final $O(\log \varepsilon^{-1})$ instances of HH1 run on the items in this bucket. Let $\mathcal{H}_{tot}$ denote the union over all of the buckets of the sets $\mathcal{H}$. E_2 is the event that at every time t_k, $k \in L$, and every $H' \in \mathcal{H}_{tot}$, the auxiliary CountSketch returns a $(1 \pm 1/2)$ approximation to $f_{H'}^{(t_k)}$ when it is queried at time t_k.

Lemma 16. $\Pr(E_2 | E_1) \geq 1 - \delta/3$.

Proof. The number of buckets is $br = O(\varepsilon^{-2} \log 1/\delta\varepsilon)$, in each bucket the number of candidate heavy hitters returned by the L instances of HH1 is $|\mathcal{H}| \leq |L| = O(\log \varepsilon^{-1})$, and we are requesting that the CountSketch gives an accurate estimate of each of those items on $|L| = O(\log \varepsilon^{-1})$ different queries. Thus we need a union bound over at most $|\mathcal{H}_{tot}| \cdot |L| \leq b \cdot r \cdot |L|^2 = \text{poly}(1/\varepsilon)$ queries to the CountSketch. The set $\mathcal{H}_{tot}$ and the times t_k, $k \in L$, are independent of the auxiliary CountSketch, and since the auxiliary CountSketch has $r = O(\log 1/\delta\varepsilon)$ rows we can guarantee that $P(E_2|E_1) \geq 1 - \delta/3$ by choosing the surpressed constant on r to be sufficiently large. □

Let us narrow our focus to a single bucket within the data structure and suppose it contains some ε-heavy hitter H. Let $B \subseteq [n] \setminus \{H\}$ be the (random) set of items in the bucket besides H. Let us say that index $k \in L$ is *good* in this bucket if the following three things happen, where $K = 2^{12} C_*$,

(i) $f_H^{(t_{k-1}:t_k)} \geq \frac{\varepsilon}{16} 2^{k/2}$,
(ii) for all indices $k' \geq k$ and items $i \in B$, we have $f_H^{(t_{k'})} \geq 4 f_i^{(t_{k'})}$, and
(iii) $F_2^{(t_{k-1}:t_k)}(B)^{1/2} \leq \frac{\varepsilon}{16K} 2^{k/2}$.

The next two lemmas prove that within any bucket holding a heavy hitter there is a good index with (conditional) probability at least 1/2. The first lemma establishes properties (i) and (ii). The second lemma establishes (iii).

Lemma 17. *If H is an item with frequency $f_H \geq \varepsilon\sqrt{F_2}$ and is B the set of items going into some bucket with H, then conditionally given $\mathcal{T}$ and E the probability that there exists an index $k^* \in L$ satisfying both* (i) *and* (ii) *it at least 3/4.*

Proof. Let $j \in L$ be the largest index such that exists an element $i \in B$ such that $4 f_i^{(t_j)} > f_H^{(t_j)}$, or $j = \ell^* - 1$ if no such index exists. Then $f_H^{(t_j)} \leq 4 f_i^{(t_j)} \leq 4\sqrt{F_2(B)}$. Let F be the event that there is no $k^* \in L$ satisfying both (i) and (ii). F implies $f_H^{(t_{k-1}:t_k)} < \frac{\varepsilon}{16} 2^{k/2}$, for all $k > j$. Therefore, on the event F we have

$$\begin{aligned}f_H = f_H^{(t_j)} + \sum_{k=j+1}^{\hat{\ell}} f_H^{(t_{k-1}:t_k)} &\leq 4\sqrt{F_2(B)} + \sum_{k=j+1}^{\hat{\ell}} \frac{\varepsilon}{16} 2^{k/2} \\ &\leq 4\sqrt{F_2(B)} + \frac{\varepsilon}{16} 2^{\hat{\ell}/2} \sum_{k=0}^{\infty} 2^{k/2} = 4\sqrt{F_2(B)} + \frac{\varepsilon}{4} 2^{\hat{\ell}}.\end{aligned}$$

The event E implies $4F_2 \geq 2^{\hat{\ell}}$, so $f_H - \frac{\varepsilon}{4} 2^{\hat{\ell}/2} \geq \frac{\varepsilon}{2}\sqrt{F_2}$. Thus, $F_2(B) \geq \frac{\varepsilon^2}{32} F_2$, and it implies $\Pr(F | \mathcal{T}, E) \leq \Pr(F_2(B) \geq \frac{\varepsilon^2}{32} F_2 | \mathcal{T}, E)$. However, $\mathbb{E}(F_2(B) | \mathcal{T}, E) = \mathbb{E}(F_2(B)) = \frac{1}{b}(F_2 - f_H^2)$. The conditional probability can be bounded with Markov's Inequality to find $\Pr(F_2(B) \geq \frac{\varepsilon^2}{32} F_2 | \mathcal{T}, E) \leq \frac{16}{\varepsilon^2 b}$, so $b = O(1/\varepsilon^2)$ can be chosen large enough to guarantee $\Pr(F | \mathcal{T}, E) \leq 1/4$, as desired. □

Lemma 18. *For every $k \in L$*

$$\Pr\left(F_2^{(t_{k-1}:t_k)}(B) \leq \frac{\varepsilon^2}{16K} 2^k \mid \mathcal{T}, E\right) \geq 3/4.$$

PROOF. We have

$$\mathbb{E}(F_2^{(t_{k-1}:t_k)}(B)|\mathcal{T},E) = \frac{1}{b}\mathbb{E}(F_2^{(t_{k-1}:t_k)} - (f_H^{(t_{k-1}:t_k)})^2|\mathcal{T},E)$$
$$\leq \frac{1}{b}\mathbb{E}(F_2^{(t_{k-1}:t_k)}|\mathcal{T},E)$$
$$\leq \frac{1}{b}2^k(1+1/100).$$

Upon choosing $b = O(1/\varepsilon^2)$ sufficiently large, Markov's Inequality shows that the desired inequality holds with conditional probability at least $3/4$. □

PROOF PROOF OF THEOREM 14. It is enough to show that if $H \in [n]$ has freqency $f_H \geq \varepsilon\sqrt{F_2}$ then in each repetition $r' \leq r$ the probability, conditionally given $\mathcal{T}$, $\mathcal{C}$, and $E := E_1 \cap E_2$, that H is identified by some instance of HH1 and is not discarded thereafter is $\Omega(1)$. The reason that this enough is that the $r = \Theta(\log 1/\delta\varepsilon)$ rows of the data structure are independent conditionally given $\mathcal{T}$, $\mathcal{C}$, and E, so a Chernoff's Bound guarantees that H is found with probability $1 - \delta\varepsilon^2/3$. Let A represent the event that all ε-heavy hitters are returned. By a union bound, what we have is $\Pr(A|\mathcal{T},\mathcal{C},E) \geq 1 - \delta/3$. Thus, by Lemmas 15 and 16, $\Pr(A) \geq \Pr(A|E) - \Pr(\bar{E}) \geq \mathbb{E}(\Pr(A|\mathcal{T},\mathcal{C},E)) - 2\delta/3 \geq 1-\delta$.

It remains to prove that within a given bucket containing a heavy hitter H the probability that H is reported from the bucket is $\Omega(1)$. Conditioning on $\mathcal{C}$, as well, doesn't change Lemmas 17 and 18. Thus, the probability that an index is good conditionally given $\mathcal{T}$, $\mathcal{C}$, and E is at least $1 - 2 \cdot 1/4 = 1/2$. If index k is good then $f_H \geq \sigma = \frac{\varepsilon}{16}2^{k/2} \geq K(F_2^{(t_{k-1}:t_k)}(B))^{1/2}$. Therefore, the hypotheses for Lemma 4 are met and H is returned by the modified algorithm with (conditional) probability at least $2/3$. Furthermore, after H is identified it is never discarded because the estimated frequencies from the auxiliary CountSketch are guaranteed by (ii) and E to satisfy $\hat{f}_H^{(t_{k'})} > \hat{f}_j^{(t_{k'})}$, for all $j \in B$ and $k' \geq k$. The probability that H is identified, conditionally given $\mathcal{C}$, $\mathcal{T}$, and E is at least $2/3 - 1/2 = 1/6$, which completes the proof. □

Stable Model Semantics for Tuple-Generating Dependencies Revisited

Mario Alviano
Dept. of Mathematics and CS
University of Calabria
alviano@mat.unical.it

Michael Morak
Inst. of Information Systems
TU Wien
morak@dbai.tuwien.ac.at

Andreas Pieris
School of Informatics
University of Edinburgh
apieris@inf.ed.ac.uk

ABSTRACT

Normal tuple-generating dependencies (NTGDs) are TGDs enriched with default negation, a.k.a. negation as failure. Query answering under NTGDs, where negation is interpreted according to the stable model semantics, is an intriguing new problem that gave rise to flourishing research activity in the database and KR communities. So far, all the existing works that investigate this problem, except for one recent paper that adopts an operational semantics based on the chase, follow the so-called logic programming (LP) approach. According to the LP approach, the existentially quantified variables are first eliminated via Skolemization, which leads to a normal logic program, and then the standard stable model semantics for normal logic programs is applied. However, as we discuss in the paper, Skolemization is not appropriate in the presence of default negation since it fails to capture the intended meaning of NTGDs, while the operational semantics mentioned above fails to overcome the limitations of the LP approach. This reveals the need to adopt an alternative approach to stable model semantics that is directly applicable to NTGDs with existentially quantified variables. We propose such an approach based on a recent characterization of stable models in terms of second-order logic, which indeed overcomes the limitations of the LP approach. We then perform an in-depth complexity analysis of query answering under prominent classes of NTGDs based on the main decidability paradigms for TGDs, namely weak-acyclicity, guardedness and stickiness. Interestingly, weakly-acyclic NTGDs give rise to robust and highly expressive query languages that allow us to solve in a declarative way problems in the second level of the polynomial hierarchy.

1. INTRODUCTION

Rule-based languages lie at the core of several areas of central importance to databases and artificial intelligence, such as data exchange and integration, deductive databases, and knowledge representation and reasoning, to name a few. The well-known *tuple-generating dependencies (TGDs)* [6] (a.k.a. *existential rules* [4] and *Datalog$^{\pm}$ rules* [9]) form a prominent rule-based formalism. TGDs are implications of the form $\forall \mathbf{X} \forall \mathbf{Y} (\varphi(\mathbf{X}, \mathbf{Y}) \rightarrow \exists \mathbf{Z}\, \psi(\mathbf{X}, \mathbf{Z}))$, where φ and ψ are conjunctions of (positive) atoms, and they essentially state that certain tuples in a database imply the presence of some other tuples in the database (hence the term "tuple-generating"). Notably, during the last decade, TGDs have found many uses and applications in different areas of database and AI research. For example, they have been used in formalizing and investigating inter-operability tasks such as data exchange [17]. TGDs have also been used for metadata management tasks, and in particular to formalize operations on schema mappings [16]. Finally, they have been employed for knowledge representation purposes, and in fact as an alternative way to model ontologies [4, 9].

The main algorithmic task that is relevant for the above applications is conjunctive query answering: given a database D, a set Σ of TGDs, a conjunctive query q, and a tuple $\mathbf{t}$ of constants, decide whether $(D, \Sigma) \models q(\mathbf{t})$, or, equivalently, whether each (possibly infinite) model of the logical theory $(D \wedge \Sigma)^1$ is also a model of $q(\mathbf{t})$. Unfortunately, query answering under TGDs is undecidable; see, e.g., [5], and [4, 7] for tight undecidable classes. This has led to a flurry of activity to identify syntactic restrictions on sets of TGDs that lead to decidable query answering; see, e.g., [4, 7, 8, 24]. In general, decidable classes of TGDs are based on the notions of weak-acyclicity [17], introduced in the context of data exchange, as well as guardedness [7] and stickiness [10], proposed in the context of ontological reasoning.

Although decidable classes of TGDs are well-suited for modeling positive information, none of them can express default negation, a.k.a. negation as failure, which is a key feature for deductive databases and knowledge representation.

Example 1. Consider the set Σ consisting of the rules

$$\forall X(\texttt{person}(X) \rightarrow \exists Y\, \texttt{hasFather}(X, Y))$$
$$\forall X \forall Y(\texttt{hasFather}(X, Y) \rightarrow \texttt{sameAs}(Y, Y))$$
$$\forall X \forall Y \forall Z(\texttt{hasFather}(X, Y) \wedge \texttt{hasFather}(X, Z) \wedge \neg \texttt{sameAs}(Y, Z) \rightarrow \texttt{abnormal}(X)),$$

which states that each person has at most one biological father; otherwise, (s)he is abnormal. The above rules cannot be equivalently expressed using (negation-free) TGDs. ■

One of the standard approaches to interpret negation is the stable model semantics [20], which is the main subject of this paper. Other approaches include perfect model [28] and well-founded semantics [19], which go beyond the scope of this work. Conjunctive query answering under TGDs extended with default negation, called *normal TGDs (NTGDs)*, w.r.t. the stable model semantics, is an intriguing new problem that gave rise to flourishing research

[1]By abuse of notation, D refers to the logical formula given by the conjunction of atoms occurring in D. This suffices since we adopt the open world assumption.

PODS'17, May 14-19, 2017, Chicago, Illinois, USA

DOI: http://dx.doi.org/10.1145/3034786.3034794

activity in the database and KR communities. In [2, 25], acyclicity and stratification conditions for NTGDs have been considered, which give rise to formalisms that admit finite and/or unique stable models. In [3], a notion of stable models that can be directly applied to NTGDs is proposed, and NTGDs that satisfy certain acyclicity conditions are investigated. The classes that are based on guardedness and stickiness have been recently studied in [22] and [1], respectively. A closely related work is [15], which focuses on disjunctive logic programs, where the so-called $\mathbb{FDNC}$ programs are proposed. $\mathbb{FDNC}$ programs combine default negation with function symbols, and decidability is obtained by restricting the rule syntax to one of seven predefined forms.

The Logic Programming approach. All the above works, except for [3] that we discuss below, follow what we call the logic programming (LP) approach to stable model semantics for NTGDs. This means that the existentially quantified variables are first eliminated via Skolemization, which leads to a normal logic program, and then the standard stable model semantics for normal logic programs with function symbols is applied. Consider the set Σ of NTGDs given in Example 1. The first NTGD is replaced by the rule

$$\mathtt{hasFather}(X, f(X)) \leftarrow \mathtt{person}(X),$$

where f is a Skolem function, while all the other NTGDs of Σ can be directly conceived as normal rules since they do not have existentially quantified variables. The database $\{\mathtt{person}(\mathit{Alice})\}$ together with the obtained normal logic program have exactly one stable model M consisting of

$$\mathtt{person}(\mathit{Alice}), \mathtt{hasFather}(\mathit{Alice}, f(\mathit{Alice})), \\ \mathtt{sameAs}(f(\mathit{Alice}), f(\mathit{Alice})).$$

It is easy to verify that the (Boolean) query

$$\exists X(\mathtt{person}(X) \wedge \neg\mathtt{abnormal}(X))$$

is entailed by M, while the query

$$\exists X(\mathtt{person}(X) \wedge \mathtt{abnormal}(X))$$

is refuted by M.

Is the LP Approach the Right One?

Although the LP approach has so far been considered as the standard approach to stable model semantics for NTGDs, we claim it is not the right way to reconcile existentially quantified variables with default negation. In fact, as we discuss below, we believe Skolemization is not appropriate in the presence of stable negation since it fails to capture the intuitive meaning of NTGDs. But let us first say a few words about Skolemization and (positive) TGDs.

Skolemization and $\neg$-free TGDs. In the absence of default negation, TGDs are essentially first-order theories, and conjunctive query answering can be reduced to a satisfiability check of a first-order formula. Given a database D, a set Σ of TGDs, a conjunctive query q, and a tuple of constants $\mathbf{t}$, $(D, \Sigma) \models q(\mathbf{t})$ iff $(D \wedge \Sigma \wedge \neg q(\mathbf{t}))$ is unsatisfiable. Furthermore, a classical result in first-order logic guarantees that the formula $(D \wedge \mathsf{sk}(\Sigma) \wedge \neg q(\mathbf{t}))$, where $\mathsf{sk}(\Sigma)$ is obtained after Skolemizing the TGDs of Σ, is equisatisfiable with $(D \wedge \Sigma \wedge \neg q(\mathbf{t}))$. Roughly, this is true since, for each tuple $\mathbf{u}$ of terms replacing the universally quantified variables occurring in a TGD σ, each existentially quantified variable Z occurring in σ can be satisfied by a different witness, which can be represented by $f_{\sigma,Z}(\mathbf{u})$, where $f_{\sigma,Z}$ is a Skolem function. Moreover, due to Herbrand's theorem, the satisfiability of a theory can be checked by considering only Herbrand interpretations, that is, interpretations associating constants and functions with themselves. Hence, whenever $\mathbf{u} \neq \mathbf{u}'$, it is safe to assume that $f(\mathbf{u})$ and $f(\mathbf{u}')$ are different objects. Similarly, we can assume that Skolem terms using different function symbols represent different objects, and also that they are different from any constant in the theory. Due to the above key results, it is easy to see that Skolemization can be safely applied in the absence of default negation.

Skolemization and normal TGDs. In contrast to $\neg$-free TGDs, Skolemization is not appropriate in the presence of default negation. In fact, a result which guarantees that Skolemization provides an equisatisfiable theory in the case of NTGDs is missing. This is illustrated by the following example.

Example 2. Let $D = \{\mathtt{person}(\mathit{Alice})\}$, and Σ be the set of NTGDs in Example 1. From D and Σ there is no evidence that Bob is not the father of Alice, and thus, it is intuitive to say that

$$q = \neg\mathtt{hasFather}(\mathit{Alice}, \mathit{Bob})$$

is not entailed by (D, Σ). In fact, it is natural to consider

$$\{\mathtt{person}(\mathit{Alice}), \mathtt{hasFather}(\mathit{Alice}, \mathit{Bob}), \\ \mathtt{sameAs}(\mathit{Bob}, \mathit{Bob})\},$$

as a stable model of $(D \wedge \Sigma)$, which does not satisfy q. However, $(D, \mathsf{sk}(\Sigma)) \models q$, where $\mathsf{sk}(\Sigma)$ is the set of normal rules obtained by Skolemizing Σ, since the unique stable model of $(D \wedge \mathsf{sk}(\Sigma))$, where $\mathit{Bob} \neq f(\mathit{Alice})$, satisfies q. ■

From the above discussion, it is apparent that the LP approach to stable model semantics for NTGDs does not capture the intended meaning of NTGDs. This reveals the need to adopt an alternative approach to stable model semantics for NTGDs, which is more general than the LP approach in the sense that is directly applicable to normal rules with existentially quantified variables. This has also been recognized by other researchers, and there are attempts in the literature to resolve this issue. Notably, Baget et al. [3] propose a notion of stable models, which relies on the well-known chase procedure, that can be directly applied to NTGDs without requiring Skolemization. Roughly, given a database D and a set Σ of NTGDs, a (possibly infinite) set of atoms M is a stable model of $(D \wedge \Sigma)$ if it can be obtained by the chase procedure starting from D and applying the TGDs of Σ^+, where Σ^+ is obtained from Σ by eliminating the negative literals, under the assumptions that (i) all TGD applications are sound, i.e., none of the negative literals of a TGD can be found in M (or, in other words, the TGD is not blocked), and (ii) the chase is complete, i.e., all the applicable TGDs that are not blocked are eventually being applied. Although this is an interesting approach, there are still simple cases in which we infer unexpected answers. For instance, if we consider again Example 2, and we apply the operational semantics of [3], then we unexpectedly conclude that $(D, \Sigma) \models q$. The reason for this is the fact that the chase procedure always invents a new null value, but never a constant, in order to satisfy an existentially quantified variable in the head of a TGD. This implies that there is no way to have the atom $\mathtt{hasFather}(\mathit{Alice}, \mathit{Bob})$ in a stable model of $(D \wedge \Sigma)$, which in turn implies that $(D, \Sigma) \models q$.

Another promising approach to default negation, which avoids Skolemization, is the so-called *equality-friendly well-founded semantics (EFWFS)* [21]. Although this approach deviates from the idea of stable models, we would like to include it in our discussion since in some cases it yields the intended query answer. The key idea is that, given a database D and a set Σ of NTGDs, the meaning of (D, Σ) may be captured by the set of all normal programs Π obtained by (i) unifying constants occurring in D (note that the unique name assumption is not adopted), and (ii) replacing each NTGD $\sigma \in \Sigma$ by arbitrary instances of σ, at least one for each possible variable assignment for its body; an instance of a normal TGD $\forall \mathbf{X} \forall \mathbf{Y}(\varphi(\mathbf{X}, \mathbf{Y}) \rightarrow \exists \mathbf{Z}\, \psi(\mathbf{X}, \mathbf{Z}))$ is simply a rule $\varphi(\mathbf{a}, \mathbf{b}) \rightarrow \psi(\mathbf{a}, \mathbf{c})$, where $\mathbf{a}, \mathbf{b}, \mathbf{c}$ are tuples of constants. Let $\mathcal{I}(D, \Sigma)$ be the set of all programs Π obtained from (D, Σ) as described above. The equality-friendly well-founded models of (D, Σ) are defined as $\{ \mathit{WFS}(\Pi) \mid \Pi \in \mathcal{I}(D, \Sigma)\}$, where $\mathit{WFS}(\Pi)$ are the well-founded models of Π. Interestingly, if we apply the EFWFS to Example 2, then we get the expected answer. Unfortunately, as we explain below, this is not always the case.

Example 3. Let $D = \{\mathtt{person}(\mathit{Alice})\}$, and Σ be the set of NTGDs given in Example 1. One expects that the query

$$q = \neg\mathtt{abnormal}(\mathit{Alice})$$

is entailed by (D, Σ) since there is no evidence that Alice has two biological fathers, and thus that she is abnormal. However, by following the EFWFS, q is not entailed. Observe that at least one normal program $\Pi \in \mathcal{I}(D, \Sigma)$ contains the rules

$$\mathtt{person}(\mathit{Alice}) \rightarrow \mathtt{hasFather}(\mathit{Alice}, \mathit{Bob})$$
$$\mathtt{person}(\mathit{Alice}) \rightarrow \mathtt{hasFather}(\mathit{Alice}, \mathit{John}),$$

where $\mathit{Bob} \neq \mathit{John}$. Therefore, there exists an equality-friendly well-founded model of (D, Σ) where Alice has two fathers, and thus the atom $\mathtt{abnormal}(\mathit{Alice})$ is entailed. ∎

Research Challenges. In order to overcome the limitations discussed previously, we focus on the following questions:

- How can we define a new approach to stable model semantics for NTGDs, such that it is directly applicable to rules with existentially quantified variables without requiring Skolemization?
- What is the data and combined complexity of conjunctive query answering under the main classes of NTGDs (based on weak-acyclicity, guardedness and stickiness) w.r.t. our new approach to stable models? Notice that the query may also contain negation.
- How is conjunctive query answering affected if, in addition, we allow disjunction to appear in rule-heads?
- How is the expressive power affected by allowing default negation and existentially quantified variables to coexist? Does disjunction in rule-heads increase the expressive power of the various formalisms?

Our Contributions

Our answers to the above questions, and the main contributions of the present paper, can be summarized as follows:

► We provide a precise definition of our new approach to stable models for normal TGDs, which in turn is based on a recent characterization of stable models via second-order logic [18]. The stable models of a database D and a set Σ of NTGDs are defined as the classical models of a second-order formula $\mathsf{SM}[D, \Sigma]$, which goes beyond MSO and encodes the vital properties of stable models. We formally show that our new approach is indeed a generalization of the LP approach (Theorem 1). We then establish a sufficient criterion for the decidability of query answering under stable models via the so-called *stable tree model property* (Theorem 2).

► We proceed to understand how conjunctive query answering behaves under NTGDs interpreted according to our new approach. We show that weak-acyclicity preserves the decidability of query answering (Theorem 3). However, if we focus on stickiness and guardedness, then query answering is undecidable (Theorems 4 and 5, respectively). Although for sticky NTGDs this was expected, for guarded NTGDs this is a rather surprising result. We show that the tree model property, the key property of guarded-based logics, is not preserved when stable negation and existentially quantified variables coexist. The reason for this can be found in the fact that we can "guess" an appropriate guard, whose domain can be restricted to an arbitrary set of values, and thus the property of guardedness that only atoms derived from a common guard ancestor can interact, is destroyed.

► Query answering under weakly-acyclic sets of NTGDs is Π_2^P-complete in data complexity, and $\text{coN2EXPTIME}^{\text{NP}}$-complete in combined complexity, even for predicates of bounded arity, and $\neg$-free atomic queries (Theorem 6).

► Interestingly, weak-acyclicity can be enriched with disjunction in the rule-heads without paying a price in terms of complexity (Theorem 12). The reason for this unexpected outcome is the fact that we can simulate disjunction using existentially quantified variables and stable negation.

► The class of weakly-acyclic NTGDs gives rise to powerful query languages that express exactly the queries with Π_2^P (resp., Σ_2^P) data complexity when the cautious (resp., brave) semantics is adopted (Theorem 17); this implies that disjunction in rule-heads does not add expressive power (Theorem 18). This expressivity result exposes an additional advantage of our approach compared to the LP approach, the operational semantics of [3], and the EFWFS of [21], that is, we obtain languages that can be used for declarative solving of problems that lie at the second level of the polynomial hierarchy. To justify this statement, we devise novel encodings for central problems in the second level of the polynomial hierarchy: (i) consistent query answering under weakly-acyclic TGDs relative to set-based repairs [30]; (ii) satisfiability for quantified Boolean formulas with two alternations of quantifiers (2-QBF); and (iii) an interesting variation of graph k-colorability, which generalizes the well-known problem CERT3COL [29].

2. PRELIMINARIES

General Definitions. We define the following pairwise disjoint countably infinite sets of symbols: a set $\mathbf{C}$ of *constants*, a set $\mathbf{N}$ of *labeled nulls* (used as placeholders for unknown values), and a set $\mathbf{V}$ of *variables* (used in queries and dependencies). Different constants represent different values (*unique name assumption*), while different nulls may represent the same value. We denote by $\mathbf{X}$ sequences (or sets, with a slight abuse of notation) of variables $X_1, \ldots, X_k$ with $k \geqslant 0$. Let $[n] = \{1, \ldots, n\}$, for any $n \geqslant 1$.

A (*relational*) *schema* $\mathcal{R}$ is a (finite) set of *relational symbols* (or *predicates*). We write p/n for the fact that p is an n-ary predicate. A *term* is a constant, null or variable. An *atomic formula* over $\mathcal{R}$ (or $\mathcal{R}$*-atom*) has the form $p(\mathbf{t})$, where $p \in \mathcal{R}$ and $\mathbf{t}$ is a tuple of terms. An $\mathcal{R}$*-literal* is either an $\mathcal{R}$-atom (i.e., a positive literal), or an $\mathcal{R}$-atom preceded by the negation symbol "$\neg$" (i.e., a negative literal). For a literal ℓ, we write $dom(\ell)$ for the set of its terms; this notation naturally extends to sets of literals. For brevity, conjunctions of literals are often identified with the sets of their literals. A (*total* or *two-valued*) $\mathcal{R}$*-interpretation* I is a set of $\mathcal{R}$-literals which contain only constants and nulls such that, for every $\mathcal{R}$-atom $p(t_1, \ldots, t_n)$, where $(t_1, \ldots, t_n) \in dom(I)^n$, either $p(t_1, \ldots, t_n) \in I$ or $\neg p(t_1, \ldots, t_n) \in I$. We write I^+ (I^-) for the set of positive (negative) literals of I.

A *homomorphism* from a set of literals L to a set of literals L' is a mapping $h : \mathbf{C} \cup \mathbf{N} \cup \mathbf{V} \rightarrow \mathbf{C} \cup \mathbf{N} \cup \mathbf{V}$ that is defined on

$dom(L)$ and is the identity on $\mathbf{C}$, and $p(t_1,\ldots,t_n) \in L$ (resp., $\neg p(t_1,\ldots,t_n) \in L$) implies $p(h(t_1),\ldots,h(t_n)) \in L'$ (resp., $\neg p(h(t_1),\ldots,h(t_n)) \in L'$).

A *database* D over a schema $\mathcal{R}$ is a finite set of $\mathcal{R}$-atoms such that $dom(D) \subset \mathbf{C}$. We sometimes treat a database D as a logical formula given by $\bigwedge_{p(\mathbf{t})\in D} p(\mathbf{t})$, that is, the conjunction of atoms occurring in D. An $\mathcal{R}$-interpretation I is a *model* of D, denoted $I \models D$, if there exists a homomorphism h such that $h(D) \subseteq I$. Since h is the identity on $dom(D)$, $I \models D$ iff $D \subseteq I$.

Normal TGDs. A *normal tuple-generating dependency (NTGD)* σ is a constant-free[2] first-order formula of the form

$$\forall \mathbf{X} \forall \mathbf{Y} (\varphi(\mathbf{X},\mathbf{Y}) \rightarrow \exists \mathbf{Z}\, \psi(\mathbf{X},\mathbf{Z})),$$

where φ (resp., ψ) is a conjunction of literals (resp., atoms), with variables from $\mathbf{X} \cup \mathbf{Y}$ (resp., $\mathbf{X} \cup \mathbf{Z}$). If there are no negative literals in φ, then σ is a TGD. We focus on *safe* NTGDs, i.e., every variable in a negative literal occurs also in a positive literal in φ. Formula φ is the *body* of σ, denoted $B(\sigma)$, while ψ is the *head* of σ, denoted $H(\sigma)$. The schema of a set Σ of NTGDs, denoted $sch(\Sigma)$, is the set of predicates occurring in Σ. We sometimes treat a set Σ of NTGDs as a logical formula given by $\bigwedge_{\sigma\in\Sigma} \sigma$, that is, the conjunction of NTGDs in Σ. A $sch(\Sigma)$-interpretation I is a model of an NTGD $\sigma \in \Sigma$, denoted $I \models \sigma$, if, whenever there exists a homomorphism h such that $h(B(\sigma)) \subseteq I$, then there exists $h' \supseteq h$, called *extension* of h, such that $h'(H(\sigma)) \subseteq I$. I is a *model* of Σ, denoted $I \models \Sigma$, if $I \models \sigma$ for each $\sigma \in \Sigma$. The class of all (finite) sets of NTGDs is denoted $\mathsf{TGD}^\neg$.

Normal (Boolean) Conjunctive Queries. An n-ary *normal conjunctive query (NCQ)* q over a schema $\mathcal{R}$, where $n \geqslant 0$, is a first-order formula of the form

$$\exists \mathbf{Y} \left(\bigwedge_{i=1}^{m} p_i(\mathbf{X},\mathbf{Y}) \wedge \bigwedge_{j=m+1}^{m+k} \neg p_j(\mathbf{X},\mathbf{Y}) \right),$$

where $m \geqslant 1$, $k \geqslant 0$, $\{p_i\}_{i\in[m+k]} \subseteq \mathcal{R}$, each atom contains variables from $(\mathbf{X} \cup \mathbf{Y}) \subset \mathbf{V}$ (and possibly constants of $\mathbf{C}$), and $|\mathbf{X}| = n$. A 0-ary NCQ is called *normal Boolean conjunctive query (NBCQ)*. We focus on *safe* queries, i.e., every variable in a negative literal occurs also in a positive literal. The *answer* to an n-ary NCQ q of the form $\exists \mathbf{Y}\, \varphi(\mathbf{X},\mathbf{Y})$ over an interpretation I, denoted $q(I)$, is the set of all tuples $\mathbf{t} \in \mathbf{C}^n$ for which there exists a homomorphism h such that $h(\varphi(\mathbf{X},\mathbf{Y})) \subseteq I$ and $h(\mathbf{X}) = \mathbf{t}$. A NBCQ q has only the empty tuple as possible answer, and it has a *positive* answer over I, denoted $I \models q$, if $q(I) \neq \varnothing$. The class of all (finite) normal (B)CQs is denoted $(\mathsf{B})\mathsf{CQ}^\neg$.

3. STABLE MODEL SEMANTICS: A NEW APPROACH

We proceed to introduce our new approach to stable model semantics for NTGDs that adopts a recent characterization of stable models in terms of second-order logic [18]. We first recall the logic programming (LP) approach considered so far (see, e.g., [1, 22, 25]). Since minimality is one of the key properties of stable models, we then recall, by means of a simple example, how the (subset) minimal models of a database D and a set Σ of NTGDs can be characterized via a second-order formula. We then proceed to explain why this formula fails to precisely capture the stable models of D and Σ, and how it can be modified in order to accurately encode the properties of stable models; this leads to our new approach to stable model semantics. Finally, we introduce the main problem tackled in this work, that is, query answering under NTGDs interpreted according to our new approach.

[2]Constants are excluded for technical clarity; however, our results can be extended to NTGDs with constants.

3.1 The Logic Programming Approach

Consider a database D, and a set $\Sigma \in \mathsf{TGD}^\neg$. Following the LP approach to stable model semantics for NTGDs, we first need to transform D and Σ into a normal logic program $\Pi_{D,\Sigma}$. If existentially quantified variables occur in the head of an NTGD of Σ, then they are eliminated via the standard process of *Skolemization*. The Skolemization of an NTGD σ of the form $\forall \mathbf{X} \forall \mathbf{Y} (\varphi(\mathbf{X},\mathbf{Y}) \rightarrow \exists \mathbf{Z}\, \psi(\mathbf{X},\mathbf{Z}))$ is the normal rule $\psi(\mathbf{X},\mathbf{f}_\sigma(\mathbf{X},\mathbf{Y})) \leftarrow \varphi(\mathbf{X},\mathbf{Y})$, where $\mathbf{f}_\sigma$ is a vector of function symbols $f_{\sigma,Z}$, one for each $Z \in \mathbf{Z}$. Then, the so-called grounding of $\Pi_{D,\Sigma}$, denoted $ground(\Pi_{D,\Sigma})$, is computed by constructing all the ground instances of a rule ρ in $\Pi_{D,\Sigma}$, i.e., all the rules that can be constructed by replacing each variable of ρ with a term from the Herbrand universe of $\Pi_{D,\Sigma}$, that is, all the terms that can be formed using constants and function symbols occurring in D and Σ.

Consider a $sch(\Sigma)$-interpretation I. I is a stable model of $\Pi_{D,\Sigma}$ if I is a (classical) model of $\Pi_{D,\Sigma}$, and a (subset) minimal model (w.r.t. positive literals) of the so-called reduct of $\Pi_{D,\Sigma}$ w.r.t. I, written $\Pi^I_{D,\Sigma}$, obtained from $ground(\Pi_{D,\Sigma})$ as follows: first, remove all the rules with a negative literal not in I, and then eliminate the remaining negative literals. Intuitively, I is a stable model of $\Pi_{D,\Sigma}$ if it can be obtained by "executing" $\Pi_{D,\Sigma}$ using I as an oracle for the negative literals. The stable models of D and Σ are defined as the stable models of the normal logic program $\Pi_{D,\Sigma}$.

3.2 Minimal Models

The minimality of a (classical) model of a database D and a set Σ of NTGDs can be captured via a second-order formula $\mathsf{MM}[D,\Sigma]$. Consider the database $D = \{p(0)\}$, and the set Σ of NTGDs consisting of

$$\forall X(p(X) \wedge \neg t(X) \rightarrow r(X)) \qquad \forall X(r(X) \rightarrow t(X)).$$

The second-order formula $\mathsf{MM}[D,\Sigma]$ is defined as follows:

$$\begin{aligned} & D \wedge \Sigma \wedge \\ & \neg\exists p^\star \exists t^\star \exists r^\star \Bigg(\bigwedge_{u\in\{p,t,r\}} (\forall X(u^\star(X) \rightarrow u(X))) \wedge \\ & \quad \neg\Bigg(\bigwedge_{u\in\{p,t,r\}} (\forall X(u(X) \rightarrow u^\star(X))) \Bigg) \wedge \\ & \quad p^\star(0) \wedge \forall X(p^\star(X) \wedge \neg t^\star(X) \rightarrow r^\star(X)) \wedge \\ & \qquad\qquad \forall X(r^\star(X) \rightarrow t^\star(X)) \Bigg), \end{aligned}$$

where $p^\star, t^\star, r^\star$ are predicate variables. An interpretation I is a model of the above formula if (i) I is a model of $(D \wedge \Sigma)$, and (ii) there is no way to obtain a model of $(D \wedge \Sigma)$ from I by eliminating a positive literal. In other words, the models of $\mathsf{MM}[D,\Sigma]$ are precisely the minimal models of $(D \wedge \Sigma)$.

The syntactic transformation from $(D \wedge \Sigma)$ into $\mathsf{MM}[D,\Sigma]$ is actually *circumscription*, a logical approach, introduced by McCarthy [26], suitable for modeling what normally holds. The idea is to define, using first-order logic, both domain knowledge and so-called abnormality predicates that identify instances of a class that violate the normal properties of that class; e.g., a bird that cannot fly is abnormal, stored in a unary predicate $\mathtt{ab_{bird}}$. To capture the intuition that abnormality is exceptional, inference is restricted to those models where the extension of the abnormality predicates is minimal w.r.t. set inclusion. So, to transform $(D \wedge \Sigma)$ into $\mathsf{MM}[D, \Sigma]$ we basically apply circumscription where all the predicates in D and Σ are conceived as abnormality predicates.

3.3 The New Approach

Our ultimate goal is to transform a database D and a set Σ of NTGDs into a second-order formula $\mathsf{SM}[D, \Sigma]$ that characterizes the stable models of D and Σ. Interestingly, $\mathsf{SM}[D, \Sigma]$ is obtained by slightly modifying $\mathsf{MM}[D, \Sigma]$. But let us first expose the key reason why $\mathsf{MM}[D, \Sigma]$ fails to recognize that an interpretation is not a stable model of $(D \wedge \Sigma)$.

Consider the database D and the set Σ of NTGDs given in Section 3.2. It can be verified that, according to the LP approach, D and Σ do not have a stable model. Furthermore, since Σ does not contain existentially quantified variables, the LP approach and our new approach should coincide, and thus, the formula $\mathsf{SM}[D, \Sigma]$ should not have a model. Consider now the interpretation $J = \{p(0), t(0), \neg r(0)\}$, which is clearly a model of $\mathsf{MM}[D, \Sigma]$. During the minimality check, the content of the predicate t that appears in a negative literal may change. Indeed, $J \models \mathsf{MM}[D, \Sigma]$ since the interpretation $K = \{p(0), \neg t(0), \neg r(0)\}$, which converts $t(0)$ into $\neg t(0)$, is not a model of D and Σ. But, this is in a conflict with the idea of stable models, where the reduct $\Pi^J_{D,\Sigma}$ is obtained by essentially fixing in J the content of the predicates that appear in negative literals of $\Pi_{D,\Sigma}$. This can be resolved by stating that $\neg t(X)$ holds instead of $\neg t^\star(X)$, i.e., $\mathsf{SM}[D, \Sigma]$ is obtained from $\mathsf{MM}[D, \Sigma]$ by replacing the atom $t^\star(X)$ in $\forall X(p^\star(X) \wedge \neg t^\star(X) \rightarrow r^\star(X))$ with $t(X)$; clearly, J is not a model of $\mathsf{SM}[D, \Sigma]$.

The syntactic transformation from $(D \wedge \Sigma)$ into $\mathsf{SM}[D, \Sigma]$ discussed above can be extended to arbitrary NTGDs. In what follows, we formalize this transformation, which will be at the basis of our new approach to stable model semantics for NTGDs. For convenience, we employ the following notation. For predicates p and s of the same arity $m \geqslant 0$, $(p \leqslant s)$ stands for the formula $\forall \mathbf{X}(p(\mathbf{X}) \rightarrow s(\mathbf{X}))$, where $\mathbf{X}$ is a tuple of m distinct variables. If $\mathbf{p} = (p_1, \ldots, p_n)$ and $\mathbf{s} = (s_1, \ldots, s_n)$ are tuples of predicates, where p_i and s_i have the same arity, then $(\mathbf{p} \leqslant \mathbf{s})$ stands for $\bigwedge_{i=1}^n (p_i \leqslant s_i)$, while $(\mathbf{p} < \mathbf{s})$ stands for $(\mathbf{p} \leqslant \mathbf{s}) \wedge \neg(\mathbf{s} \leqslant \mathbf{p})$. In second-order logic, we apply the same notation to tuples of predicate variables. Consider a set $\Sigma \in \mathsf{TGD}^\neg$, and a database D over $sch(\Sigma)$. Let $\mathbf{p} = (p_1, \ldots, p_n)$ be the list of predicates of $sch(\Sigma)$, and $\mathbf{s} = (s_1, \ldots, s_n)$ a list of n distinct predicate variables. For a literal ℓ occurring in D or Σ, we define

$$\tau_{\mathbf{p} \rhd \mathbf{s}}(\ell) \quad = \quad \begin{cases} s_i(\mathbf{t}), & \text{if } \ell = p_i(\mathbf{t}), \\ \neg p_i(\mathbf{t}), & \text{if } \ell = \neg p_i(\mathbf{t}). \end{cases}$$

We define $\tau_{\mathbf{p} \rhd \mathbf{s}}(D)$ and $\tau_{\mathbf{p} \rhd \mathbf{s}}(\Sigma)$ as the database and the set of NTGDs obtained by applying $\tau_{\mathbf{p} \rhd \mathbf{s}}$ to every literal in D and Σ, respectively. $\mathsf{UNA}[D]$ is the formula $\bigwedge_{c,d \in dom(D), c \neq d} \neg(c = d)$, which encodes the unique name assumption. $\mathsf{SM}[D, \Sigma]$ is defined as:

$$\mathsf{UNA}[D] \wedge D \wedge \Sigma \wedge \neg \exists \mathbf{s}((\mathbf{s} < \mathbf{p}) \wedge \tau_{\mathbf{p} \rhd \mathbf{s}}(D) \wedge \tau_{\mathbf{p} \rhd \mathbf{s}}(\Sigma)).$$

We are now ready to introduce our new approach to stable model semantics for NTGDs.

Definition 1. **(Stable Models)** Consider a set $\Sigma \in \mathsf{TGD}^\neg$, and a database D over $sch(\Sigma)$. A $sch(\Sigma)$-interpretation I is a *stable model* of D and Σ if I is a model of $\mathsf{SM}[D, \Sigma]$. We define $SMS(D, \Sigma)$ as the set of stable models of D and Σ. ∎

The conceptual advantage of our new approach over the classical LP approach is shown by the following example.

Example 4. Let $D = \{\mathtt{person}(Alice)\}$, and Σ be the set of NTGDs given in Example 1. As discussed in Example 2, it is natural to consider the interpretation I, where

$$I^+ \;=\; \{\mathtt{person}(Alice), \mathtt{hasFather}(Alice, Bob), \mathtt{sameAs}(Bob, Bob)\},$$

as a stable model of D and Σ, which in turn implies that

$$q = \neg\mathtt{hasFather}(Alice, Bob)$$

is not entailed by (D, Σ), which is what we expect since from D and Σ there is no evidence that *Bob* is not the father of *Alice*. Recall that, according to the LP approach, I is not a stable model of $(D \wedge \Sigma)$. However, $I \models \mathsf{SM}[D, \Sigma]$, and thus, according to our new approach, I is a stable model. ∎

Our new approach directly deals with existentially quantified variables without requiring Skolemization or grounding. The crucial question though that we need to answer, in order to safely conclude that the new approach is a generalization of the LP approach, is whether the two approaches coincide if we focus on dependencies that can be treated by both of them, that is, Skolemized NTGDs; note that Definition 1 can be directly applied to normal logic programs. The answer to this question is affirmative, and immediately follows from Corollary 1 in [18]. To avoid notational clutter, $SMS_{LP}(\cdot)$ and $SMS_{SO}(\cdot)$ is the set of stable models according to the LP and the new approach (which relies on second-order logic, hence the subscript "SO"), respectively.[3] Recall that $\Pi_{D,\Sigma}$ is the program obtained from D and Σ by applying Skolemization.

THEOREM 1. *Consider a database D, and $\Sigma \in \mathsf{TGD}^\neg$. It holds that, $SMS_{LP}(\Pi_{D,\Sigma}) = SMS_{SO}(\Pi_{D,\Sigma})$.*

3.4 Query Answering

The answer to an n-ary NCQ q over D and Σ under the stable model semantics is defined as the set of tuples

$$\bigcap_{M \in SMS(D,\Sigma)} \{\mathbf{t} \in \mathbf{C}^n \mid \mathbf{t} \in q(M)\}.$$

A NBCQ q has a *positive* answer over D and Σ under the stable model semantics, denoted $(D, \Sigma) \models_{SMS} q$, if $M \models q$, for each $M \in SMS(D, \Sigma)$. For clarity, we focus on NBCQs; however, our results can be extended to NCQs. The main decision problem tackled in this work is defined as follows; $\mathbb{C}$ is a class of sets of NTGDs (e.g., weakly-acyclic, sticky, etc., which are defined below):

PROBLEM:	$\mathsf{SMS\text{-}QAns}(\mathbb{C})$
INPUT:	Database D, $\Sigma \in \mathbb{C}$, and $q \in \mathsf{BCQ}^\neg$.
QUESTION:	Does $(D, \Sigma) \models_{SMS} q$?

We assume, w.l.o.g., that both the database and the query use only predicates that already occur in the set of NTGDs.

A Criterion for Decidability

It is possible to establish a sufficient (semantic) condition for the decidability of SMS-QAns via the so-called stable tree model property. To introduce this property, we first need to recall what is the treewidth of an interpretation. A *tree decomposition* of a (possibly infinite) interpretation I is a labeled tree $T = (V, E, \lambda)$, where λ is the labeling function $V \rightarrow 2^{dom(I)}$, such that: (i) for a (positive) literal $p(t_1, \ldots, t_n) \in I$, there exists $v \in V$ such that

[3] In the rest of the paper, $SMS(\cdot)$ without a subscript refers to the set of stable models according to our new approach.

$\lambda(v) \supseteq \{t_1, \ldots, t_n\}$; and (ii) for every term $t \in dom(I)$, the set of nodes $\{v \in V \mid t \in \lambda(v)\}$ induces a connected subtree of T. The *width* of T is $\max_{v \in V}\{|\lambda(v)| - 1\}$. The *treewidth* of I is the minimum width among all tree decompositions. Intuitively, the treewidth of an interpretation I, which can be represented as a graph via its Gaifman graph, measures how similar I is to a tree; the smaller the treewidth, the closer the interpretation is to a tree. We are now ready to introduce the stable tree model property:

Definition 2. We say that a class $\mathbb{C}$ of NTGDs enjoys the *stable tree model property* if the following holds: for every database D, $\Sigma \in \mathbb{C}$, and $q \in \mathsf{BCQ}^{\neg}$, if $(\mathsf{SM}[D, \Sigma] \wedge \neg q)$ has a model, then it has a model of finite treewidth. ∎

The next result establishes that the stable tree model property implies the decidability of query answering:

THEOREM 2. $\mathsf{SMS\text{-}QAns}(\mathbb{C})$ *is decidable if* $\mathbb{C}$ *is a class of NTGDs that enjoys the stable tree model property.*

Let us sketch the proof of the above result. Consider a database D, a set $\Sigma \in \mathbb{C}$, where $\mathbb{C}$ enjoys the stable tree model property, and $q \in \mathsf{BCQ}^{\neg}$. Since $(D, \Sigma) \models_{SMS} q$ iff $(\mathsf{SM}[D, \Sigma] \wedge \neg q)$ is unsatisfiable, it suffices to show that the problem whether $(\mathsf{SM}[D, \Sigma] \wedge \neg q)$ is satisfiable is decidable. We can construct an MSO formula $\mathsf{SM}[D, \Sigma]_1$ such that: (i) $(\mathsf{SM}[D, \Sigma] \wedge \neg q)$ and $(\mathsf{SM}[D, \Sigma]_1 \wedge \neg q)$ are equisatisfiable; and (ii) if $(\mathsf{SM}[D, \Sigma]_1 \wedge \neg q)$ is satisfiable, then it has a model of finite treewidth. Therefore, by Courcelle's classical result, which states that the satisfiability problem for fragments of MSO that enjoy the tree model property is decidable [11], we get that the problem whether $(\mathsf{SM}[D, \Sigma] \wedge \neg q)$ is satisfiable is decidable, as needed. The key idea underlying the construction of $\mathsf{SM}[D, \Sigma]_1$ can be described as follows: we attach, via a first-order formula, to every tuple of terms $\mathbf{t}$ occurring in a model of $(D \wedge \Sigma)$ a unique identifier; this allows us to access $\mathbf{t}$ via a unary predicate that stores all the valid identifiers. Then, we can rewrite $\mathsf{SM}[D, \Sigma]$ in such a way that only unary predicates are quantified.

4. QUERY ANSWERING UNDER STABLE MODELS: A CASE STUDY

The goal of this section is to investigate how the problem of query answering under stable models behaves. We consider classes of NTGDs that are based on the main decidability paradigms proposed for TGDs, namely weak-acyclicity [17], stickiness [10] and guardedness [7], and we study query answering.

4.1 Weak-Acyclicity

Weak-acyclicity is defined by posing an acyclicity condition on the position (dependency) graph, introduced in [17], which encodes how terms are propagated during the "execution" of the program. A position in a schema $\mathcal{R}$, written $p[i]$, is a pair of an n-ary predicate $p \in \mathcal{R}$ and an integer $i \in [n]$, which represents the i-th attribute of p. The set of positions of $\mathcal{R}$, denoted $pos(\mathcal{R})$, is defined as $\{p[i] \mid p/n \in \mathcal{R} \text{ and } i \in [n]\}$.

Definition 3. The *position graph* of a set $\Sigma \in \mathsf{TGD}$ is a directed graph $PoG(\Sigma) = (V, E)$, where $V = pos(sch(\Sigma))$, and E is defined as follows: for each $\sigma \in \Sigma$ of the form $\forall \mathbf{X}(\varphi(\mathbf{X}) \rightarrow \exists \mathbf{Y}\, \psi(\mathbf{X}, \mathbf{Y}))$, for each $X \in \mathbf{X}$ that occurs in ψ, and for each X in φ in position π: (1) for each occurrence of X in ψ in position π', there is a regular edge $(\pi, \pi') \in E$; (2) for each $Y \in \mathbf{Y}$, and for each occurrence of Y in ψ in position π', there is a special edge $(\pi, \pi') \in E$; and (3) no other edges occur in E. ∎

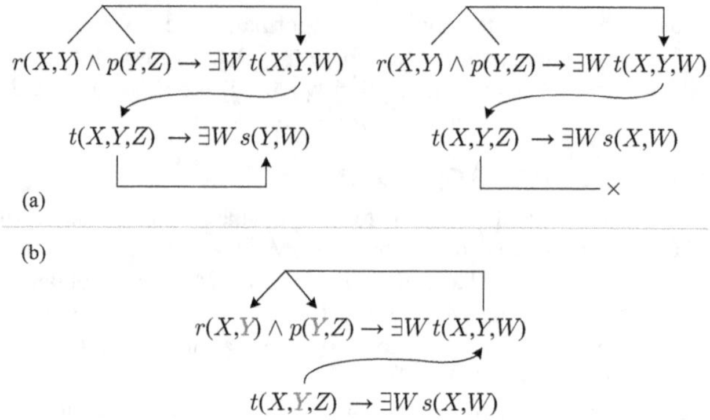

Figure 1: Stickiness and marking; for brevity, the universal quantifiers are omitted.

Roughly speaking, a regular edge (π, π') keeps track of the fact that a term may propagate from π to π' during the "execution" of Σ. A special edge (π, π'') keeps track of the fact that the propagation of a value from π to π' also creates a new value at position π''. We are now ready to define weakly-acyclic NTGDs. A set Σ of NTGDs is *weakly-acyclic* if no cycle in $PoG(\Sigma^+)$, where Σ^+ is obtained from Σ by eliminating the negative literals, containing a special edge exists. The corresponding class is denoted $\mathsf{WATGD}^{\neg}$.

As one may expect, if a database and a weakly-acyclic set of NTGDs admit a stable model, then they admit a stable model of finite size, and thus, $\mathsf{WATGD}^{\neg}$ enjoys the stable tree model property. Hence, by Theorem 2, we get that:

THEOREM 3. $\mathsf{SMS\text{-}QAns}(\mathsf{WATGD}^{\neg})$ *is decidable.*

The fact that $\mathsf{WATGD}^{\neg}$ enjoys the stable tree model property is shown in two steps: (i) we establish that a stable model M of a database D and a set Σ of NTGDs (not necessarily weakly-acyclic) is obtained by "executing" Σ, starting from D, using M as an oracle for its negative literals, and (ii) we show that whenever the input set Σ of NTGDs is weakly-acyclic, then its "execution" terminates. In fact, the same approach is followed in Section 5 to pinpoint the complexity of query answering under stable models for weakly-acyclic sets of NTGDs, which is one of the main contributions of this work; thus, all the details are deferred to Section 5.

4.2 Stickiness

Let us first recall the key property underlying the class of sticky sets of (positive) TGDs [10]. During the execution of the TGDs, or, in other words, during the chase procedure, terms that are associated (via a homomorphism) with variables that appear more than once in the body of a TGD (i.e., join variables) are always propagated (or "stick") to the inferred atoms. This is illustrated in Figure 1(a); the first set of TGDs is sticky, while the second is not. The formal definition is based on an inductive marking procedure that marks the variables that may violate the semantic property of the chase described above [10]. Roughly, during the base step of this procedure, a variable that appears in the body of a TGD σ but not in every head-atom of σ is marked. Then, the marking is inductively propagated from head to body as shown in Figure 1(b). Finally, a set of TGDs Σ is *sticky* if no TGD in Σ contains two occurrences of a marked variable. The notion of stickiness can be straightforwardly extended to NTGDs: a set Σ of NTGDs is sticky if the set of TGDs obtain by converting every literal $\neg p(\mathbf{t})$ occurring in Σ into the atom $p(\mathbf{t})$ is sticky [1]; the corresponding class is denoted $\mathsf{STGD}^{\neg}$. Although stickiness guarantees not only the decidability, but also the data tractability of CQ answering under TGDs [10], the situation changes for NTGDs under the stable model semantics:

THEOREM 4. SMS-QAns(STGD$^\neg$) *is undecidable, even if the query is* $\neg$*-free.*

The above negative result is not surprising since the problem is undecidable even if we follow the LP approach [1]. The reason for this undesirable behavior should be found in the fact that sticky sets of NTGDs are powerful enough for expressing cartesian products, that is, rules of the form $\forall \mathbf{X} \forall \mathbf{Y}(p(\mathbf{X}) \wedge s(\mathbf{Y}) \rightarrow t(\mathbf{X}, \mathbf{Y}))$, with $\mathbf{X} \cap \mathbf{Y} = \varnothing$. Using cartesian products we can build infinite grids, while the stable negation gives us the power of guessing. This combination allows us to simulate the behavior of a Turing machine.

4.3 Guardedness

An NTGD σ is guarded if there exists an atom, called guard, in $B^+(\sigma)$ that contains all the variables in $B(\sigma)$. A set Σ of NTGDs is called *guarded* if every NTGD of Σ is guarded, and the corresponding class is denoted GTGD$^\neg$. Guardedness is a well-accepted paradigm that gives rise to robust rule-based languages. As shown in [7], query answering under guarded TGDs is decidable, while this decidability result has been recently extended to guarded NTGDs interpreted according to the LP approach to stable model semantics [22]. Contrary to what one might expect, this is not the case for guarded NTGDs interpreted according to our new approach to stable model semantics. As for sticky NTGDs, we can build grids of unbounded size, while the stable negation gives us the power of guessing. This allows us to simulate the behavior of a Turing machine, and show that:

THEOREM 5. SMS-QAns(GTGD$^\neg$) *is undecidable, even if the query is* $\neg$*-free.*

The above result, together with Theorem 2, immediately implies that GTGD$^\neg$ does not enjoy the stable tree model property. This is a surprising negative outcome since guardedness usually gives rise to robust and decidable computational logics, such as the guarded fragment of first-order logic, while the model-theoretic reason for this desirable behavior is the tree model property; see, e.g., [23]. The reason for this negative outcome can be informally described as follows. In the classical setting, the guard atoms occurring in rule-bodies force the existence of a model that follows an inherent tree structure, where its branches cannot interact. This holds also for the LP approach to stable model semantics, which refers to Skolemization and grounding, since the obtained reduct can be seen as a set of (positive first-order) guarded TGDs [22]. However, by following our new approach to stable negation for NTGDs, it is possible to "guess" an appropriate guard, whose domain can be restricted to an arbitrary set, and thus the key property of guardedness, i.e., only atoms derived from a common guard ancestor can interact, is destroyed. In fact, by restricting the domain of an (existentially guessed) guard in an appropriate way, joins between any two atoms can be forced, destroying the inherent tree structure of the underlying models.

4.4 Our Conclusions

From the above analysis, we conclude that:

- The class that is based on weak-acyclicity can be reconciled with the new approach to stable model semantics, without sacrificing the decidability of query answering. This is because, whenever a database and a set of weakly-acyclic NTGDs have a model, then they admit a finite model, which implies that WATGD$^\neg$ enjoys the stable tree model property.
- It is not possible to reconcile stickiness and guardedness with our new approach to stable negation for NTGDs, since query answering becomes undecidable. Although for sticky sets of NTGDs this was expected, for guarded NTGDs this is a surprising outcome.

The former gives rise to the problem of closing the complexity of SMS-QAns(WATGD$^\neg$), which will be the subject of Section 5. The latter demonstrates the need to provide a more refined definition of stickiness and guardedness. This task goes beyond the scope of the present work.

5. WEAK-ACYCLICITY: ALGORITHMS AND COMPLEXITY

We proceed to pinpoint the complexity of NBCQ answering under stable models focussing on weakly-acyclic sets of NTGDs. We consider the standard complexity measures, i.e., *data complexity*, calculated by considering only the database as input, and *combined complexity*, which considers everything as input. We show that:

THEOREM 6. SMS-QAns(WATGD$^\neg$) *is*

- Π_2^P*-complete in data complexity, and*
- coN2EXPTIME^{NP}*-complete in combined complexity.*

The lower bounds hold for predicates of bounded arity, and CQs consisting of a single 0*-ary predicate.*

The above result shows that the complexity of query answering significantly increases in the presence of default negation; recall that for weakly-acyclic sets of TGDs the problem is PTIME-complete in data complexity [17], and 2EXPTIME-complete in combined complexity [10]. The rest of this section is devoted to establishing the above result. The desired upper bounds are obtained via a guess and check algorithm for the complement of the problem, which guesses a stable model, and checks that it does not entail the query. However, in order to apply such a simple procedure, we need to solve two non-trivial subtasks: (i) establish an upper bound on the size of stable models under WATGD$^\neg$, and (ii) check the stability of a model in an optimal way.

5.1 Bounding the Size of Stable Models

In this section, we establish an upper bound on the size of stable models under WATGD$^\neg$, which will then allow us to obtain optimal data and combined complexity upper bounds for query answering. Let us first introduce our technical tool.

Immediate Consequence Operator

Consider a set Σ of NTGDs, a set S of $sch(\Sigma)$-atoms, and a $sch(\Sigma)$-interpretation I. An atom $p(\mathbf{t}) \in I$ is an *immediate consequence* for S and Σ relative to I if there exists $\sigma \in \Sigma$, and a homomorphism h such that $h(B(\sigma)) \subseteq S \cup I^-$ and $p(\mathbf{t}) \in h(H(\sigma))$. The *immediate consequence operator* of Σ relative to I follows:

$$T_{\Sigma,I}(S) = \{p(\mathbf{t}) \in I^+ \mid p(\mathbf{t}) \text{ is an immediate consequence for } S \text{ and } \Sigma \text{ relative to } I\}.$$

We write $T^i_{\Sigma,I}(S)$ for the result obtained after i applications of the operator $T_{\Sigma,I}$ starting from S. Formally,

$$T^0_{\Sigma,I}(S) = S \qquad T^{i+1}_{\Sigma,I}(S) = T_{\Sigma,I}(T^i_{\Sigma,I}(S)) \cup T^i_{\Sigma,I}(S)$$

and

$$T^{\infty}_{\Sigma,I}(S) = \bigcup_{i=0}^{\infty} T^i_{\Sigma,I}(S).$$

Note that $T_{\Sigma,I}$ is monotone; thus, $T^{\infty}_{\Sigma,I}(S)$ is defined as its least fixpoint. The next result formalizes the idea that a stable model M of a database D and $\Sigma \in \mathsf{TGD}^{\neg}$ can be obtained by "executing" Σ, starting from D, using M as an oracle for its negative literals.

LEMMA 7. *Consider a database D, and* $\Sigma \in \mathsf{TGD}^{\neg}$. *For every* $M \in SMS(D,\Sigma)$, $M^+ = T^{\infty}_{\Sigma,M}(D)$.

It is important to clarify that the $T_{\Sigma,I}$ operator cannot be used to characterize the stable models of D and Σ. In particular, given a $sch(\Sigma)$-interpretation I, $I^+ = T^{\infty}_{\Sigma,I}(D)$ does not imply $I \in SMS(D,\Sigma)$. Consider, for example,

$$D = \{s(a)\} \quad \text{and} \quad \Sigma = \{\forall X(s(X) \rightarrow \exists Y\, p(X,Y))\}.$$

For the interpretation I with $I^+ = \{s(a), p(a,b), p(a,c)\}$ it is clear that $I^+ = T^{\infty}_{\Sigma,I}(D)$, but $I \notin SMS(D,\Sigma)$. However, as we shall see, the immediate consequence operator is a useful technical tool for bounding the size of stable models.

Establishing a Bound

Consider a model $M \in SMS(D,\Sigma)$, where $\Sigma \in \mathsf{WATGD}^{\neg}$. The least fixpoint of $T_{\Sigma,M}$, starting from D, can be reached after a finite number of applications.

LEMMA 8. *Consider a database D, a set* $\Sigma \in \mathsf{WATGD}^{\neg}$, *and let* $M \in SMS(D,\Sigma)$. *It holds that,*

$$|T^{\infty}_{\Sigma,M}(D)| \leqslant f(D,\Sigma),$$

where f is polynomial in D, and doubly exponential in Σ.

The above lemma relies on the fact that, given a database D and a weakly-acyclic set Σ of (positive) TGDs, the result of every chase sequence of D and Σ has size at most polynomial in D, and doubly exponential in Σ; implicit in [17].[4] In particular, given a database D and a set $\Sigma \in \mathsf{WATGD}^{\neg}$, we show that $T^{\infty}_{\Sigma,M}(D)$ induces a chase sequence C of D and Σ^+ such that $|T^{\infty}_{\Sigma,M}(D)|$ is bounded by the size of the result of C, which in turn implies that $|T^{\infty}_{\Sigma,M}(D)|$ is at most polynomial in D, and doubly exponential in Σ, as needed. The next key result follows from Lemma 7 and 8:

PROPOSITION 9. *Consider a database D, and a set* $\Sigma \in \mathsf{WATGD}^{\neg}$. *For every* $M \in SMS(D,\Sigma)$,

$$|M^+| \leqslant f(D,\Sigma),$$

where f is polynomial in D, and doubly exponential in Σ.

5.2 Checking Stability

We now investigate the stability problem, i.e., checking whether a model M of a database D and $\Sigma \in \mathsf{WATGD}^{\neg}$ satisfies the formula $\neg\exists\mathbf{s}((\mathbf{s} < \mathbf{p}) \wedge \tau_{\mathbf{p}\triangleright\mathbf{s}}(D) \wedge \tau_{\mathbf{p}\triangleright\mathbf{s}}(\Sigma))$. Unfortunately, if we perform this check blindly, without having available any additional information about the model M in question, then we cannot do better than Π^P_2, which in turn does not lead to the desired upper bounds stated in Theorem 6. This is because such a check involves model checking for NTGDs, that is, to decide whether an interpretation is a model of a set of NTGDs, and it is known that already for TGDs model checking is Π^P_2-hard, even if we focus on a single non-recursive TGD [27]. The crucial question that we should answer is the following: having available some additional information about the model M, which can be computed on-the-fly during the execution of our guess and check algorithm, is the above checking feasible in coNP? The answer to the above question is affirmative, which, as we shall see in the next section, will allows us to obtain the worst-case optimal upper bounds stated in Theorem 6. In particular, the additional information about the model M that we need is the set of homomorphisms that acts as a witness for the fact that M is a model of Σ. The notion of the witness is defined as follows:

Definition 4. Consider an NTGD σ, and an interpretation I. The *witness* for I w.r.t. σ, denoted $\mathcal{W}^{\sigma}_I$, is defined as

$$\left\{\left(h, E^{h,\sigma}_I\right) \mid h \text{ is a homomorphism s.t. } h(B(\sigma)) \subseteq I\right\},$$

where $E^{h,\sigma}_I = \{\mu \mid \mu \supseteq h \text{ and } \mu(H(\sigma)) \subseteq I\}$. The witness $\mathcal{W}^{\sigma}_I$ is called *negative* if there exists $(h,E) \in \mathcal{W}^{\sigma}_I$ such that $E = \varnothing$; otherwise, $\mathcal{W}^{\sigma}_I$ is called *positive*. ∎

It is clear that having the positive witness $\mathcal{W}^{\sigma}_I$ in place, we know precisely via which homomorphisms $B(\sigma)$ is satisfied by I (if there exists one), and how they are extended in order to satisfy $H(\sigma)$, and therefore σ itself. The next auxiliary lemma follows by definition:

LEMMA 10. *Consider a set* $\Sigma \in \mathsf{TGD}^{\neg}$, *and a* $sch(\Sigma)$-*interpretation I. The following are equivalent:*

1. $I \models \Sigma$.
2. $\mathcal{W}^{\sigma}_I$ *is positive, for every* $\sigma \in \Sigma$.

We now introduce a refined version of the stability problem, based on the notion of witness; let $\mathbb{C}$ be a class of NTGDs, and $\Phi_{D,\Sigma} = \neg\exists\mathbf{s}((\mathbf{s} < \mathbf{p}) \wedge \tau_{\mathbf{p}\triangleright\mathbf{s}}(D) \wedge \tau_{\mathbf{p}\triangleright\mathbf{s}}(\Sigma))$:

PROBLEM:	W-Stability($\mathbb{C}$)
INPUT:	Datab. D, $\Sigma \in \mathbb{C}$, model M of $(D \wedge \Sigma)$, and positive witnesses $\{\mathcal{W}^{\sigma}_M\}_{\sigma\in\Sigma}$.
QUESTION:	Does $M \models \Phi_{D,\Sigma}$?

We establish the following technical result, which is crucial for our later complexity analysis:

PROPOSITION 11. W-Stability($\mathsf{WATGD}^{\neg}$) *is in* coNP.

We can decide the complement of the problem in question via the following non-deterministic algorithm:

1. Guess $J \subset M^+$ such that $J \supseteq D$, and let I be the total interpretation with $dom(I) = dom(J)$ and $I^+ = J$.
2. If for each $\sigma \in \tau_{\mathbf{p}\triangleright\mathbf{s}}(\Sigma)$ the witness $\mathcal{W}^{\sigma}_{(M\cup\tau_{\mathbf{p}\triangleright\mathbf{s}}(J))}$ is positive, then *accept*; otherwise, *reject*.

It is easy to see that, by Lemma 10, the above algorithm accepts iff $M \models \exists\mathbf{s}((\mathbf{s} < \mathbf{p}) \wedge \tau_{\mathbf{p}\triangleright\mathbf{s}}(D) \wedge \tau_{\mathbf{p}\triangleright\mathbf{s}}(\Sigma))$. It is clear that both steps are feasible in polynomial time. In particular, the witness for $(M \cup \tau_{\mathbf{p}\triangleright\mathbf{s}}(I))$ w.r.t. some $\sigma \in \tau_{\mathbf{p}\triangleright\mathbf{s}}(\Sigma)$ can be obtained in polynomial time from $\mathcal{W}^{\hat{\sigma}}_M$, where $\hat{\sigma} \in \Sigma$ and $\sigma = \tau_{\mathbf{p}\triangleright\mathbf{s}}(\hat{\sigma})$. Thus, W-Stability($\mathsf{WATGD}^{\neg}$) is in coNP, as needed.

5.3 Finalizing the Complexity Analysis

We are now ready to close the complexity of SMS-QAns for $\mathsf{WATGD}^{\neg}$, and obtain Theorem 6.

Upper Bounds

The upper bounds stated in Theorem 6 are obtained in a uniform way via a guess and check algorithm, which exploits Propositions 9 and 11. Fix a database D, $\Sigma \in \mathsf{WATGD}^{\neg}$, and $q \in \mathsf{BCQ}^{\neg}$. Let $\mathbf{p} = (p_1,\ldots,p_n)$ be the list of predicates of $sch(\Sigma)$, and $\mathbf{s} = (s_1,\ldots,s_n)$ a list of n predicate variables. We write $\delta_{D,\Sigma}$ for the bound provided by Proposition 9. The following procedure decides if $(D,\Sigma) \not\models_{SMS} q$, i.e., the complement of our problem:

[4]Here, we refer to the standard (a.k.a. the restricted) version of the chase, where a TGD is being applied only if its necessary.

1. Guess a set of atoms J, where $|J| \leqslant \delta_{D,\Sigma}$, and let I be the total $sch(\Sigma)$-interpretation with $dom(I) = dom(J)$ and $I^+ = J$ such that $I \models (D \wedge \Sigma \wedge \neg q)$; if such a set of atoms does not exist, then *reject*.
2. If $I \models \neg \exists \mathbf{s}((\mathbf{s} < \mathbf{p}) \wedge \tau_{\mathbf{p} \triangleright \mathbf{s}}(D) \wedge \tau_{\mathbf{p} \triangleright \mathbf{s}}(\Sigma))$, then *accept*; otherwise, *reject*.

The above procedure runs in polynomial time in $\delta_{D,\Sigma}$ with an $\mathcal{S}$-oracle, where $\mathcal{S}$ is a complexity class powerful enough for solving W-Stability; $\{\mathcal{W}_I^{\sigma}\}_{\sigma \in \Sigma}$ is implicitly constructed during the first step of the algorithm. Consequently, the complement of SMS-QAns is in $\text{NP}^{\mathcal{S}}$ in data complexity, and in $\text{N2ExpTime}^{\mathcal{S}}$ in combined complexity. The desired upper bounds follow by Proposition 11 since $\mathcal{O}^{\text{coNP}} = \mathcal{O}^{\text{NP}}$, where $\mathcal{O} \in \{\text{NP}, \text{N2ExpTime}\}$.

Lower Bounds

We give the reduction for the Π_2^P-hardness in data complexity, while for the combined complexity we simply mention the problem from which we provide a reduction.

Π_2^P-hard Data Complexity

We reduce satisfiability of 2-QBF$_\exists$ formulas to the complement of SMS-QAns(WATGD$^\neg$). Let $\varphi = \exists \mathbf{X} \forall \mathbf{Y}\, \psi(\mathbf{X}, \mathbf{Y})$ be a 2-QBF$_\exists$ formula, and $\psi = \vee_{i=1}^{k} (\ell_i^1 \wedge \ell_i^2 \wedge \ell_i^3)$ be a 3DNF formula. We construct a database D_φ, and $\Sigma \in$ WATGD$^\neg$, which does not depend on φ, such that φ is satisfiable iff $(D_\varphi, \Sigma) \not\models_{SMS} \texttt{error}$, where $\texttt{error}$ is a 0-ary predicate.

Database. For a variable V, let $\pi(V) = \nu(\neg V) = V$ and $\pi(\neg V) = \nu(V) = \star$, where $\star$ is a special constant. The database D_φ is defined as follows:

$$\{\texttt{exists}(X) \mid X \in \mathbf{X}\} \cup \{\texttt{forall}(Y) \mid Y \in \mathbf{Y}\} \cup$$
$$\{\texttt{cl}(\pi(\ell_i^1), \pi(\ell_i^2), \pi(\ell_i^3), \nu(\ell_i^1), \nu(\ell_i^2), \nu(\ell_i^3))\}_{i \in [k]} \cup \{\texttt{nil}(\star)\}.$$

This completes the definition of D_φ.

NTGDs. The set $\Sigma \in$ WATGD$^\neg$ is defined as follows. First, we guess an assignment for the variables of φ:

$$\rightarrow \exists X\, \texttt{zero}(X) \quad \rightarrow \exists X\, \texttt{one}(X)$$
$$\forall X(\texttt{zero}(X) \wedge \texttt{one}(X) \rightarrow \texttt{error})$$
$$\forall X(\texttt{zero}(X) \rightarrow \texttt{truthVal}(X))$$
$$\forall X(\texttt{one}(X) \rightarrow \texttt{truthVal}(X))$$
$$\forall X(\texttt{exists}(X) \rightarrow \exists Y\, \texttt{assign}(X, Y))$$
$$\forall X(\texttt{forall}(X) \rightarrow \exists Y\, \texttt{assign}(X, Y))$$
$$\forall X \forall Y(\texttt{assign}(X, Y) \wedge \neg \texttt{truthVal}(Y) \rightarrow \texttt{error}).$$

By exploiting the well-known technique of saturation [13], we proceed to perform the universal check as follows:

$$\neg \texttt{saturate} \rightarrow \texttt{saturate}$$
$$\forall X \forall Y(\texttt{forall}(X) \wedge \texttt{truthVal}(Y) \wedge \texttt{saturate} \rightarrow \texttt{assign}(X, Y))$$
$$\forall X \forall Y(\texttt{nil}(X) \wedge \texttt{truthVal}(Y) \rightarrow \texttt{assign}(X, Y))$$
$$\forall \mathbf{P} \forall \mathbf{N} \forall O \forall Z(\texttt{cl}(P_1, P_2, P_3, N_1, N_2, N_3) \wedge \bigwedge_{i=1}^{3} \texttt{assign}(P_i, O) \wedge \texttt{one}(O) \wedge \bigwedge_{i=1}^{3} \texttt{assign}(N_i, Z) \wedge \texttt{zero}(Z) \rightarrow \texttt{saturate}).$$

This completes the definition of Σ.

We can show that φ is satisfiable iff $(D_\varphi, \Sigma) \not\models_{SMS} \texttt{error}$, and the claim follows.

coN2ExpTime^{NP}-hard Combined Complexity

By reduction from the complement of finite tiling extension: for a grid of double-exponential size, decide whether a top-row tiling exists that cannot be extended into a grid tiling.[5] We define a database D, and $\Sigma \in$ WATGD$^\neg$ such that the instance of finite tiling extension is negative iff $(D, \Sigma) \models_{SMS} q$, where q is 0-ary predicate.

6. ADDING DISJUNCTION

An interesting question that comes up is how SMS-QAns is affected if we extend WATGD$^\neg$ with disjunction in rule-heads. Disjunction is a crucial feature for KR and database query languages; thus, WATGD$^{\neg,\vee}$ deserves our attention. We consider *normal disjunctive tuple-generating dependencies (NDTGDs)* of the form

$$\forall \mathbf{X} \forall \mathbf{Y} \left(\varphi(\mathbf{X}, \mathbf{Y}) \rightarrow \bigvee_{i=1}^{n} \exists \mathbf{Z}_i\, \psi_i(\mathbf{X}, \mathbf{Z}_i) \right),$$

where φ is a conjunction of literals, and ψ_i is a conjunction of atoms; we write TGD$^{\neg,\vee}$ for the corresponding class. Extending weak-acyclicity with disjunction is done in the obvious way. A set $\Sigma \in$ TGD$^{\neg,\vee}$ is weakly-acyclic if no cycle in $PoG(\Sigma^{+,\wedge})$, where $\Sigma^{+,\wedge}$ is obtained from Σ by removing the negative literals and converting the disjunction into a conjunction, contains a special edge. The corresponding class is denoted WATGD$^{\neg,\vee}$. Similarly to NTGDs, we exploit the notion of homomorphism to define when an interpretation is a model of a set of NDTGDs. For a database D and a set $\Sigma \in$ TGD$^{\neg,\vee}$, $SMS(D, \Sigma)$ is defined, as for NTGDs, via the second-order formula SM$[D, \Sigma]$, which is obtained by simply applying the operator $\tau_{\mathbf{p} \triangleright \mathbf{s}}$ to every literal occurring in D and Σ.

6.1 Complexity of Query Answering

Weak-acyclicity can be enriched with disjunction in the rule-heads without paying a price in terms of complexity. As we shall see, the reason for this is the fact that we can simulate disjunction using existential quantification and stable negation. We show that:

THEOREM 12. *SMS-QAns(WATGD$^{\neg,\vee}$) is*

- *Π_2^P-complete in data complexity, and*
- *coN2ExpTime^{NP}-complete in combined complexity.*

The lower bounds hold for predicates of bounded arity, and CQs consisting of a single 0-ary predicate.

The lower bounds are immediately inherited from Theorem 6; thus, in the rest of this section, we concentrate on the upper bounds. We show that the problem in question can be reduced in polynomial time into query answering under (non-disjunctive) NTGDs. Fix a database D, a set $\Sigma \in$ WATGD$^{\neg,\vee}$, and a query $q \in$ BCQ$^\neg$:

LEMMA 13. *A database D' and a set $\Sigma' \in$ TGD$^\neg$, which does not depend on D, can be constructed in polynomial time such that $(D, \Sigma) \models_{SMS} q$ iff $(D', \Sigma') \models_{SMS} q$.*

Before we proceed with the construction of D' and Σ', let us clarify that Σ' is, in general, *not* weakly-acyclic. Once we define Σ'

[5]This problem is known to be Σ_2^P-hard for a grid of polynomial size; see, e.g., [12]. Interestingly, the same construction shows that for a grid of double-exponential size it is N2ExpTime^{NP}-hard.

below, we will explain, via an example, the reason why Σ' violates weak-acyclcity, and we will discuss why Lemma 13 is still useful for our purposes.

Database. The database D' is obtained from D by adding sufficiently many indices for the disjuncts in Σ. In particular, assuming that $k > 0$ is the maximum number of disjuncts occurring in the head of a NDTGD of Σ,

$$D' = D \cup \{\mathtt{nil}(\star), \mathtt{idx}_1(c_1), \ldots, \mathtt{idx}_k(c_k)\}.$$

This completes the construction of D'

NTGDs. Before defining Σ', let us explain how a NDTGD $\sigma \in \Sigma$, which has the general form given at the beginning of the section, can be simulated via a set Σ_σ of (non-disjunctive) NTGDs. Clearly, if σ is already non-disjunctive, then $\Sigma_\sigma = \{\sigma\}$. Assume now that σ is disjunctive. First, we need to guess a disjunct of σ, which can be done via the set Σ_σ^{guess} consisting of the NTGDs:

$$\forall \mathbf{X} \forall \mathbf{Y} (\varphi(\mathbf{X}, \mathbf{Y}) \rightarrow \exists I \exists \mathbf{Z}\, t_\sigma(I, \mathbf{X}, \mathbf{Z}))$$
$$\forall I \forall \mathbf{X} \forall \mathbf{Z} (t_\sigma(I, \mathbf{X}, \mathbf{Z}) \wedge \neg \mathtt{idx}_1(I) \wedge \ldots \wedge \neg \mathtt{idx}_n(I) \rightarrow \mathtt{false}),$$

where $\mathbf{Z} = \mathbf{Z}_1, \ldots, \mathbf{Z}_n$, and $\mathtt{false}$ is a 0-ary predicate that is forced to be false in every stable model via the rule

$$\mathtt{false} \wedge \neg \mathtt{aux} \rightarrow \mathtt{aux},$$

which also belongs to Σ_σ^{guess}. Depending on the previous guess, we should infer the right disjunct from the head of σ, which is done via the set Σ_σ^{infer} consisting of the NTGDs:

$$\forall I \forall \mathbf{X} \forall \mathbf{Z} (t_\sigma(I, \mathbf{X}, \mathbf{Z}) \wedge \mathtt{idx}_i(I) \rightarrow \psi_i(\mathbf{X}, \mathbf{Z}_i)), \text{ for each } i \in [n].$$

Finally, we should ensure stability, that is, the first NTGD will not support any new disjunct from the head of σ if one is already true. This is done via the set Σ_σ^{stab} consisting of the NTGDs:

$$\forall \mathbf{X} \forall \mathbf{Y} \forall \mathbf{Z}_i \forall I \forall N (\varphi(\mathbf{X}, \mathbf{Y}) \wedge \psi_i(\mathbf{X}, \mathbf{Z}_i) \wedge \mathtt{idx}_i(I) \wedge \mathtt{nil}(N) \rightarrow t_\sigma(I, \mathbf{X}, \mathbf{N}_1^{i-1}, \mathbf{Z}_i, \mathbf{N}_{i+1}^{n})), \text{ for each } i \in [n],$$

where $\mathbf{N}_x^y = N, \ldots, N$ consisting of $(|\mathbf{Z}_x| + \ldots + |\mathbf{Z}_y|)$ variables. The set Σ_σ is defined as $(\Sigma_\sigma^{guess} \cup \Sigma_\sigma^{infer} \cup \Sigma_\sigma^{stab})$, while Σ' is defined as $\bigcup_{\sigma \in \Sigma} \Sigma_\sigma$. It can be shown that $(D, \Sigma) \models_{SMS} q$ iff $(D', \Sigma') \models_{SMS} q$, and Lemma 13 follows.

Although we have Lemma 13 in place, we cannot inherit yet the desired upper bounds from our results on SMS-QAns(WATGD$^\neg$), since in general Σ' violates weak-acyclicity.

Example 5. Consider the set $\Sigma \in$ WATGD$^{\neg,\vee}$

$$\forall X (p(X) \rightarrow \exists Y\, s(X, Y))$$
$$\forall X (r(X) \rightarrow p(X) \vee s(X, X)).$$

According to our construction, Σ' contains (among others)

$$\forall X (p(X) \rightarrow \exists Y\, s(X, Y))$$
$$\forall I \forall X (t_\sigma(I, X) \wedge \mathtt{idx}_1(I) \rightarrow p(X))$$
$$\forall X \forall Y (r(X) \wedge s(X, X) \wedge \mathtt{idx}_2(I) \wedge \mathtt{nil}(N) \rightarrow t_\sigma(I, X)).$$

Due to the first rule, in the position graph we have the special edge $(p[1], s[2])$. In addition, due to the other rules, we have the regular edges $(t_\sigma[2], p[1])$ and $(s[2], t_\sigma[2])$. Therefore, we have a cycle in the position graph that contains a special edge, which implies that Σ' is not weakly-acyclic. ■

Even if Σ' is not weakly-acyclic, we can show that the new cycles in the position graph that destroy weak-acyclicity are harmless. As it can be verified in Example 5, these cycles do not encode the situation where the generation of a term in a certain position causes the generation of some other term in the same position, which eventually leads to an infinite generation of terms. By using this fact, we can show that Propositions 9 and 11, which were decisive for the analysis performed in the previous section, hold for Σ'. This, combined with Lemma 13, gives us the desired upper bounds.

7. EXPRESSIVE QUERY LANGUAGES

It turns out that the class of weakly-acyclic NTGDs, focussing on our new approach to stable negation, gives rise to expressive database query languages. Interestingly, the language based on WATGD$^\neg$ with cautious (resp., brave) stable model semantics captures precisely Π_2^P (resp., Σ_2^P). Cautious (resp., brave) reasoning refers to the approach where the answer to the query is computed by considering the intersection (resp., union) of the underlying stable models. In the sequel, we introduce the new query languages, analyze their complexity, and demonstrate their practical relevance by exhibiting prominent queries that can be naturally expressed in WATGD$^\neg$. We finally investigate their expressive power.

7.1 New Query Languages

A WATGD$^\neg$ query is a pair (Σ, q), where $\Sigma \in$ WATGD$^\neg$ is the query program, and q/n is a predicate not occurring in the body of an NTGD. The *extensional (database) schema* of Σ, denoted $edb(\Sigma)$, consists of all the extensional predicates of $sch(\Sigma)$, whose values are given via an input database, while the *intensional schema* of Σ, denoted $idb(\Sigma)$, consists of all the intensional predicates of $sch(\Sigma)$, whose values are computed by the program. Given a database D over $edb(\Sigma)$, the answer to $Q = (\Sigma, q)$ over D under the *cautious* stable model semantics is defined as

$$Q(D) = \{\mathbf{t} \in \mathbf{C}^n \mid (D, \Sigma) \models_{SMS} q(\mathbf{t})\}.$$

The answer to Q over D under the *brave* stable model semantics is

$$Q(D) = \{\mathbf{t} \in \mathbf{C}^n \mid \exists M \in SMS(D, \Sigma), M \models q(\mathbf{t})\}.$$

Let WATGD$_\text{c}^\neg$ and WATGD$_\text{b}^\neg$ be the query language WATGD$^\neg$ with cautious and brave stable model semantics, respectively. The query evaluation problem for a query language $\mathcal{Q}$ is as follows: given a database D, a query $Q \in \mathcal{Q}$, and a tuple $\mathbf{t}$, decide whether $\mathbf{t} \in Q(D)$; if it is $\mathcal{C}$-complete, then we say that $\mathcal{Q}$ is $\mathcal{C}$-complete.

Computational Complexity

By exploiting the complexity analysis performed in Section 5, it is not difficult to show that:

THEOREM 14. *$\mathcal{Q}$ is $\mathcal{D}$-complete in data complexity, and $\mathcal{C}$-complete in combined complexity, where*

$$\mathcal{D} = \begin{cases} \Pi_2^P, & \text{if } \mathcal{Q} = \text{WATGD}_\text{c}^\neg, \\ \Sigma_2^P, & \text{if } \mathcal{Q} = \text{WATGD}_\text{b}^\neg, \end{cases}$$

and

$$\mathcal{C} = \begin{cases} \text{coN2ExpTime}^{\text{NP}}, & \text{if } \mathcal{Q} = \text{WATGD}_\text{c}^\neg, \\ \text{N2ExpTime}^{\text{NP}}, & \text{if } \mathcal{Q} = \text{WATGD}_\text{b}^\neg. \end{cases}$$

The lower bounds hold even for predicates of bounded arity.

Applications

The obtained query languages can be employed to solve in a declarative way problems that lie at the second level of the polynomial hierarchy. For example, by using our languages, we can devise novel encodings for the following problems: (i) consistent query answering under weakly-acyclic TGDs relative to subset repairs [30]; (ii) satisfiability for 2-QBF; and (iii) an interesting variation of graph k-colorability, which generalizes the well-known problem CERT3COL [29]. Due to space reasons, we focus only on (ii).

Satisfiability of 2-QBF. As shown in Section 5.3, 2-QBF$_\exists$ can be reduced to $\mathsf{SMS\text{-}QAns}(\mathsf{WATGD}^\neg)$. The given formula φ is encoded in a database D_φ, and a fixed set $\Sigma \in \mathsf{WATGD}^\neg$ is constructed such that φ is satisfiable iff $(D_\varphi, \Sigma) \not\models_{SMS} \mathtt{error}$, where $\mathtt{error}$ is a propositional predicate. By using this construction, we can show that 2-QBF$_\exists$ can be decided using $\mathsf{WATGD}^\neg_\mathsf{b}$; notice that it cannot be decided using $\mathsf{WATGD}^\neg_\mathsf{c}$, unless the polynomial hierarchy collapses. We define the query

$$Q = (\Sigma \cup \{\neg\mathtt{error} \rightarrow \mathtt{ans}\}, \mathtt{ans}) \in \mathsf{WATGD}^\neg_\mathsf{b}.$$

For every 2-QBF$_\exists$ formula φ, φ is satisfiable iff the empty tuple belongs to $Q(D_\varphi)$, i.e., there exists $M \in SMS(D_\varphi, \Sigma)$ such that $M \models \mathtt{ans}$. Analogously, 2-QBF$_\forall$ can be decided using $\mathsf{WATGD}^\neg_\mathsf{c}$.

7.2 Expressive Power

We proceed to investigate the expressive power of our new query languages. For a query language $\mathcal{Q}$, we say that its *absolute expressive power* is $\mathcal{C}$, where $\mathcal{C}$ is a complexity class, written $\mathcal{Q} = \mathcal{C}$, if it expresses exactly the queries with $\mathcal{C}$ data complexity. For two languages $\mathcal{Q}$ and $\mathcal{Q}'$, we write $\mathcal{Q} \leq \mathcal{Q}'$, if for each query $Q \in \mathcal{Q}$, we can construct a query $Q' \in \mathcal{Q}'$ such that $Q(D) = Q'(D)$, for every database D. $\mathcal{Q}'$ is *more expressive* than $\mathcal{Q}$, written $\mathcal{Q} < \mathcal{Q}'$, if $\mathcal{Q} \leq \mathcal{Q}' \not\leq \mathcal{Q}$, while $\mathcal{Q}$ and $\mathcal{Q}'$ have the *same expressive power*, written $\mathcal{Q} = \mathcal{Q}'$, if $\mathcal{Q} \leq \mathcal{Q}' \leq \mathcal{Q}$.

Two query languages that are extremely important for our analysis are $\mathsf{DATALOG}^{\neg,\vee}_s$, where $s \in \{\mathsf{c}, \mathsf{b}\}$. These languages are defined in the same way as $\mathsf{WATGD}^\neg_s$ with the only difference that the query program is a set of NDTGDs of the form

$$\forall \mathbf{X} \forall \mathbf{Y} \left(\varphi(\mathbf{X}, \mathbf{Y}) \rightarrow \bigvee_{i=1}^{n} p_i(\mathbf{X}) \right),$$

where p_i is a single predicate, i.e., NDTGDs where the heads are existential-free disjunctions of atoms. Interestingly, $\mathsf{WATGD}^\neg_\mathsf{c}$ and $\mathsf{DATALOG}^{\neg,\vee}_\mathsf{c}$ have the same expressive power:

THEOREM 15. $\mathsf{WATGD}^\neg_\mathsf{c} = \mathsf{DATALOG}^{\neg,\vee}_\mathsf{c}$.

$\mathsf{DATALOG}^{\neg,\vee}_\mathsf{c}$ expresses exactly the queries with Π^P_2 data complexity [14]. By Theorem 14, $\mathsf{WATGD}^\neg_\mathsf{c}$ is in Π^P_2 in data complexity, and the "$\leq$" direction follows. Consider now a $\mathsf{DATALOG}^{\neg,\vee}_\mathsf{c}$ query $Q = (\Sigma, q)$. We construct the query $Q' = (\Sigma', q')$, where Σ' is defined as follows.

Simulate Predicates. We uniquely identify each predicate p in Σ via an atom $\mathtt{pred}_p(\cdot)$. This is done using the following set of rules: for each $p \in sch(\Sigma)$,

$$\rightarrow \exists X\, \mathtt{pred}_p(X),$$

and for each pair of distinct predicates $p, s \in sch(\Sigma)$,

$$\forall X (\mathtt{pred}_p(X) \wedge \mathtt{pred}_s(X) \rightarrow \mathtt{false}).$$

Notice that $\mathtt{false}$ is a special 0-ary predicate that is forced to be false in every stable model via the usual auxiliary rule $\mathtt{false} \wedge \neg\mathtt{aux} \rightarrow \mathtt{aux}$, where $\mathtt{aux} \notin sch(\Sigma)$.

Simulate Disjunction. We proceed to simulate disjunction. We could apply the construction given above for showing Lemma 13. However, since the query program Σ is existential-free, we can present a simplified version of it, which will allows us to easily verify that the obtained set Σ' of NTGDs is weakly-acyclic. Formally, for each rule ρ in Σ of the form

$$p_1(\mathbf{X}) \vee \ldots \vee p_m(\mathbf{X}) \leftarrow \varphi(\mathbf{X}, \mathbf{Y}),$$

we have in Σ' the following NTGDs:

$$\forall \mathbf{X} \forall \mathbf{Y} (\varphi(\mathbf{X}, \mathbf{Y}) \rightarrow \exists Z\, t_\rho(Z, \mathbf{X}))$$

$$\forall Z \forall \mathbf{X} (t_\rho(Z, \mathbf{X}) \wedge \neg\mathtt{pred}_{p_1}(Z) \wedge \ldots \wedge \neg\mathtt{pred}_{p_m}(Z) \rightarrow \mathtt{false})$$

$$\forall Z \forall \mathbf{X} (t_\rho(Z, \mathbf{X}) \wedge \mathtt{pred}_{p_i}(Z) \rightarrow p_i(\mathbf{X})), \text{ for each } i \in [m]$$

$$\forall \mathbf{X} \forall \mathbf{Y} \forall Z (\varphi(\mathbf{X}, \mathbf{Y}) \wedge p_i(\mathbf{X}) \wedge \mathtt{pred}_{p_i}(Z) \rightarrow t_\rho(Z, \mathbf{X})), \text{ for each } i \in [m]$$

$$\forall \mathbf{X} (q(\mathbf{X}) \rightarrow q'(\mathbf{X})).$$

We can show that $Q(D) = Q'(D)$, for every database D. Moreover, in the position graph G of $(\Sigma')^+$ the only special edges are edges of the form $(\cdot, t_\rho[1])$, due to the first NTGD above, while there are no edges of the form $(t_\rho[1], \cdot)$ since there is no NTGD in Σ' with a body-variable that appears at position $t_\rho[1]$ and is also propagated to the head. Therefore, in G there is no cycle that contains a special edge, which implies that $\Sigma' \in \mathsf{WATGD}^\neg$, and Theorem 15 follows. By employing a similar construction, we can show that Theorem 15 holds even for the brave semantics:

THEOREM 16. $\mathsf{WATGD}^\neg_\mathsf{b} = \mathsf{DATALOG}^{\neg,\vee}_\mathsf{b}$.

As already mentioned above, $\mathsf{DATALOG}^{\neg,\vee}_\mathsf{c}$ expresses exactly the database queries that can be decided in Π^P_2 in data complexity [14]. Moreover, $\mathsf{DATALOG}^{\neg,\vee}_\mathsf{b}$ expresses exactly the queries that can be decided in Σ^P_2 in data complexity [14]. Consequently, by Theorem 14, which establishes the desired data complexity upper bounds, and Theorems 15 and 16, we obtain the following:

THEOREM 17. *It holds that,*

$$\mathsf{WATGD}^\neg_s = \begin{cases} \Pi^P_2, & \text{if } s = \mathsf{c}, \\ \Sigma^P_2, & \text{if } s = \mathsf{b}. \end{cases}$$

By exploiting the complexity analysis in Section 6, we can show that: $\mathsf{WATGD}^{\neg,\vee}_s$ is Π^P_2-complete, if $s = \mathsf{c}$, and Σ^P_2-complete, if $s = \mathsf{b}$, both in data complexity. Thus, an immediate consequence of Theorem 17 is that disjunction does not add expressive power:

THEOREM 18. *It holds that,*

$$\mathsf{WATGD}^\neg_\mathsf{c} = \mathsf{WATGD}^{\neg,\vee}_\mathsf{c} \qquad \mathsf{WATGD}^\neg_\mathsf{b} = \mathsf{WATGD}^{\neg,\vee}_\mathsf{b}.$$

It remains to understand how the different approaches to stable model semantics affect expressiveness. We would like to compare, in terms of expressive power, our new approach with the LP approach. To this end, we consider the class of normal rules obtained after Skolemizing weakly-acyclic sets of N(D)TGDs. Formally,

$$\mathsf{SWATGD}^{\neg(,\vee)} = \{\mathsf{sk}(\Sigma) \mid \Sigma \in \mathsf{WATGD}^{\neg(,\vee)}\},$$

where $\mathsf{sk}(\Sigma)$ is the set of normal rules obtained after Skolemizing the N(D)TGDs of Σ. By Theorem 1, the LP approach coincides with our approach when we focus on Skolemized NDTGDs,[6] and

[6]In fact, Theorem 1 considers only NTGDs, but it can be easily extended to NDTGDs.

thus we simply need to compare $\mathsf{WATGD}^{\neg}_{s}$, where $s \in \{\mathsf{c}, \mathsf{b}\}$, with $\mathsf{SWATGD}^{\neg}_{s}$ and $\mathsf{SWATGD}^{\neg,\vee}_{s}$ relative to our new stable model semantics. By employing a simple complexity-theoretic argument, it can be shown that our new approach gives rise to more expressive query languages than the LP approach when disjunction is not allowed, assuming that the polynomial hierarchy does not collapse. In particular, it is possible to show that $\mathsf{SWATGD}^{\neg}_{\mathsf{c}}$ is in coNP and $\mathsf{SWATGD}^{\neg}_{\mathsf{b}}$ is in NP, which immediately implies that:

THEOREM 19. *If* NP $\subsetneq \Sigma^P_2$ *and* coNP $\subsetneq \Pi^P_2$, *then*

$$\mathsf{WATGD}^{\neg}_{\mathsf{c}} > \mathsf{SWATGD}^{\neg}_{\mathsf{c}} \qquad \mathsf{WATGD}^{\neg}_{\mathsf{b}} > \mathsf{SWATGD}^{\neg}_{\mathsf{b}}.$$

Now, if disjunction is allowed to appear in rule-heads, then the LP approach gives rise to equally expressive languages:

THEOREM 20. *It holds that,*

$$\mathsf{WATGD}^{\neg}_{\mathsf{c}} = \mathsf{SWATGD}^{\neg,\vee}_{\mathsf{c}} \quad \mathsf{WATGD}^{\neg}_{\mathsf{b}} = \mathsf{SWATGD}^{\neg,\vee}_{\mathsf{b}}.$$

8. CONCLUSIONS

We propose a new approach to stable model semantics for NTGDs, based on a recent characterization of stable models in terms of second-order logic [18], that can be directly applied to rules with existentially quantified variables without requiring Skolemization. We show that the class of NTGDs based on weak-acyclicity can be reconciled with our new approach to stable negation, and we obtain precise complexity results for query answering. However, once we focus on stickiness and guardedness query answering becomes undecidable. Although for sticky sets of NTGDs this was expected, for guarded NTGDs this is a surprising negative result. Our next step is to understand whether there is a way to reconcile stickiness and guardedness with our new approach to stable models.

Acknowledgements: We thank the anonymous referees for their helpful feedback. Alviano has been partially supported by project "Smarter Solutions in the Big Data World (S2BDW)" funded by the Italian Ministry for Economic development (MISE), PON "Imprese e competitività" 2014-2020. Morak was supported by the Austrian Science Fund (FWF), project Y698. Pieris was supported by the EPSRC Programme Grant EP/M025268/ "VADA: Value Added Data Systems – Principles and Architecture".

9. REFERENCES

[1] M. Alviano and A. Pieris. Default negation for non-guarded existential rules. In *PODS*, pages 79–90, 2015.
[2] J. Baget, F. Garreau, M. Mugnier, and S. Rocher. Extending acyclicity notions for existential rules. In *ECAI*, pages 39–44, 2014.
[3] J. Baget, F. Garreau, M. Mugnier, and S. Rocher. Revisiting chase termination for existential rules and their extension to nonmonotonic negation. In *NMR*, 2014.
[4] J. Baget, M. Leclère, M. Mugnier, and E. Salvat. On rules with existential variables: Walking the decidability line. *Artif. Intell.*, 175(9-10):1620–1654, 2011.
[5] C. Beeri and M. Y. Vardi. The implication problem for data dependencies. In *ICALP*, pages 73–85, 1981.
[6] C. Beeri and M. Y. Vardi. A proof procedure for data dependencies. *J. ACM*, 31(4):718–741, 1984.
[7] A. Calì, G. Gottlob, and M. Kifer. Taming the infinite chase: Query answering under expressive relational constraints. *J. Artif. Intell. Res.*, 48:115–174, 2013.
[8] A. Calì, G. Gottlob, and T. Lukasiewicz. A general Datalog-based framework for tractable query answering over ontologies. *J. Web Sem.*, 14:57–83, 2012.
[9] A. Calì, G. Gottlob, T. Lukasiewicz, B. Marnette, and A. Pieris. Datalog+/-: A family of logical knowledge representation and query languages for new applications. In *LICS*, pages 228–242, 2010.
[10] A. Calì, G. Gottlob, and A. Pieris. Towards more expressive ontology languages: The query answering problem. *Artif. Intell.*, 193:87–128, 2012.
[11] B. Courcelle. The monadic second-order logic of graphs, II: infinite graphs of bounded width. *Mathematical Systems Theory*, 21(4):187–221, 1989.
[12] B. Durand and A. Fabret. On the complexity of deadlock detection in families of planar nets. *Theor. Comput. Sci.*, 215(1-2):225–237, 1999.
[13] T. Eiter and G. Gottlob. On the computational cost of disjunctive logic programming: Propositional case. *Ann. Math. Artif. Intell.*, 15(3-4):289–323, 1995.
[14] T. Eiter, G. Gottlob, and H. Mannila. Disjunctive datalog. *ACM Trans. Database Syst.*, 22(3):364–418, 1997.
[15] T. Eiter and M. Simkus. FDNC: decidable nonmonotonic disjunctive logic programs with function symbols. *ACM Trans. Comput. Log.*, 11(2), 2010.
[16] R. Fagin. Inverting schema mappings. *ACM Trans. Database Syst.*, 32(4), 2007.
[17] R. Fagin, P. G. Kolaitis, R. J. Miller, and L. Popa. Data exchange: Semantics and query answering. *Theor. Comput. Sci.*, 336(1):89–124, 2005.
[18] P. Ferraris, J. Lee, and V. Lifschitz. Stable models and circumscription. *Artif. Intell.*, 175(1):236–263, 2011.
[19] A. V. Gelder, K. A. Ross, and J. S. Schlipf. The well-founded semantics for general logic programs. *J. ACM*, 38(3):620–650, 1991.
[20] M. Gelfond and V. Lifschitz. The stable model semantics for logic programming. In *ICLP/SLP*, pages 1070–1080, 1988.
[21] G. Gottlob, A. Hernich, C. Kupke, and T. Lukasiewicz. Equality-friendly well-founded semantics and applications to description logics. In *AAAI*, 2012.
[22] G. Gottlob, A. Hernich, C. Kupke, and T. Lukasiewicz. Stable model semantics for guarded existential rules and description logics. In *KR*, 2014.
[23] E. Grädel. On the restraining power of guards. *J. Symb. Log.*, 64(4):1719–1742, 1999.
[24] N. Leone, M. Manna, G. Terracina, and P. Veltri. Efficiently computable Datalog$^{\exists}$ programs. In *KR*, 2012.
[25] D. Magka, M. Krötzsch, and I. Horrocks. Computing stable models for nonmonotonic existential rules. In *IJCAI*, 2013.
[26] J. McCarthy. Circumscription - A form of non-monotonic reasoning. *Artif. Intell.*, 13(1-2):27–39, 1980.
[27] R. Pichler and S. Skritek. The complexity of evaluating tuple generating dependencies. In *ICDT*, pages 244–255, 2011.
[28] T. C. Przymusinski. On the declarative semantics of deductive databases and logic programs. In *Foundations of Deductive Databases and Logic Programming*, pages 193–216. Morgan Kaufmann, 1988.
[29] I. A. Stewart. Complete problems involving boolean labelled structures and projection transactions. *J. Log. Comput.*, 1(6):861–882, 1991.
[30] B. ten Cate, G. Fontaine, and P. G. Kolaitis. On the data complexity of consistent query answering. *Theory Comput. Syst.*, 57(4):843–891, 2015.

Schema Mappings for Data Graphs

Nadime Francis
School of Informatics
University of Edinburgh
nfranci2@inf.ed.ac.uk

Leonid Libkin
School of Informatics
University of Edinburgh
libkin@inf.ed.ac.uk

ABSTRACT

Schema mappings are a fundamental concept in data integration and exchange, and they have been thoroughly studied in different data models. For graph data, however, mappings have been studied in a restricted context that, unlike real-life graph databases, completely disregards the *data* they store. Our main goal is to understand query answering under graph schema mappings – in particular, in exchange and integration of graph data – for graph databases that mix graph structure with data. We show that adding data querying alters the picture in a significant way.

As the model, we use data graphs: a theoretical abstraction of property graphs employed by graph database implementations. We start by showing a very strong negative result: using the simplest form of nontrivial navigation in mappings makes answering even simple queries that mix navigation and data undecidable. This result suggests that for the purposes of integration and exchange, schema mappings ought to exclude recursively defined navigation over target data. For such mappings and analogs of regular path queries that take data into account, query answering becomes decidable, although intractable. To restore tractability without imposing further restrictions on queries, we propose a new approach based on the use of null values that resemble usual nulls of relational DBMSs, as opposed to marked nulls one typically uses in integration and exchange tasks. If one moves away from path queries and considers more complex patterns, query answering becomes undecidable again, even for the simplest possible mappings.

1. INTRODUCTION

Schema mappings are a fundamental notion in data interoperability tasks such as data integration and exchange. They prescribe a virtual or physical transformation of one database into another, and guide notions of query answering over integrated or exchanged data. They have been thoroughly investigated over relational data (see recent books [5, 9, 19] reporting on the developments of the last two decades). Schema mappings are specified by queries over source and target schemas and some relationship between them, typically containment. For relational mappings, we understand how to build database instances based on them, how to query such instances, and where tractability boundaries lie.

While relational data continues to dominate, there are many other models around, and it is thus natural that efforts have been made to understand schema mappings for other data formats. Notably there were both theoretical investigations and practical implementations of schema mappings for XML, see, e.g., [4,23,33]. While they addressed the same questions as in the relational world, the techniques involved were quite different, as one had to reconcile navigational queries and querying data stored in XML documents.

Another popular data model is graph data. It shows up in many modern applications such as social networks and the Semantic Web, that are naturally modeled as graphs, and where querying graph topology is important. Several industrial strength implementations of graph databases are available, such as Neo4j, Virtuoso, AllegroGraph and others. We refer to [2,3] for surveys of graph data models, languages for them, and implementations. Typical queries for graph data are based on paths or patterns in graphs. In database theory, the most commonly studied classes of queries are based on *regular path queries*, or (RPQs) [16].

When it comes to schema mappings on graph databases, we have much less knowledge compared to relational or XML mappings. Mappings based on containment of path queries were studied in [8, 12–14]. These papers looked into both static analysis questions and answering RPQs and their extensions under such mappings, but the setting as described there falls short of modeling graph databases that occur in practice.

Real-world graph databases mix graph structure with data that resides in nodes and edges. These are referred to as *property graphs* [36]; they form the basic data model of Neo4j and are now advocated by LDBC [27] as the standard model to be adopted by graph database implementations. A theoretical abstraction of property graphs is *data graphs* [30], an analog of data trees that have been actively studied as a similar abstraction of XML documents, cf. [10,37]. In property graphs, each node and each edge can carry a record of values, while in a data graph, just as in data trees, each node contains a single data value. From the point of view of theoretical investigation whose goal is to understand the complexity of the main computational tasks associated with a data model, this abstraction suffices, as property graphs

PODS'17, May 14 - 19, 2017, Chicago, IL, USA

ISBN 978-1-4503-4198-1/17/05...$15.00

DOI: http://dx.doi.org/10.1145/3034786.3056113

can be modeled by data graphs, by pushing data from edges to nodes and by creating additional nodes to store multiple data values.

Our main goal is to understand the behavior of schema mappings on data graphs where both navigation and data are taken into account, much as was done for relational and XML data in the past, and to go beyond [8, 12–14] where only navigational aspects have been considered. In doing so, we discover that adding data alters the picture dramatically: some basic tasks quickly become undecidable, and recovering decidability, and especially tractability, requires new techniques that do not mimic those for other data models.

As in [8,12–14], our schema mappings are based on RPQs, but RPQs are applied to data graphs. For such mappings and purely navigational queries based on RPQs and some extensions, query answering is decidable, with coNP data complexity [8,12]; to achieve tractability, regular expressions need to be severely restricted [8]. Answering queries refers to finding *certain answers* that are true in all instances satisfying the conditions of a schema mapping for given source data. This is the standard approach in data exchange and virtual data integration [5, 28].

If graphs contain data, the ability to query it makes a strong impact. For very simple mappings based on RPQs, and very simple queries that combine navigation and data querying, the query answering problem becomes *undecidable.* Even if RPQs used in mappings do not allow any recursion (in essence, we deal with the usual relational schema mappings), answering queries that combine navigation and data is intractable, although decidable.

The undecidability result is rather strong and leaves essentially no hope of having any kind of navigation in mappings except what can be expressed by standard relational schema mappings. It applies to schema mappings whose rules are very simple: they are both *local-as-view* (LAV) and *global-as-view* [28] at the same time, except just one rule which involves the simplest unconstrained reachability query. Moreover the query to be answered is given by a regular expression with equality, which is the simplest kind of regular expressions on paths with data [31].

Thus, either in graph data exchange, or in virtual integration of graph databases, answering queries that refer to data stored in graph nodes is impossible without a dramatic restriction on schema mappings. Such a restriction tells us to forget that we are dealing with a graph database (at least on the target side) and treat it as a relational database instead; then many queries can be answered, albeit with a high complexity.

Having shown these negative results, we need to see what can be recovered. It turns out that we can have efficient query answering for a large class of queries (e.g., all RPQs based on the strongest known class of regular expressions that use data [31]), and do it using the standard route: find a universal solution (cf. [5]) and evaluate the query on it. This works for relational mappings under the additional assumption that the domain of data values contains a special *null* value that behaves as in SQL [17]: no comparison involving a null can be true. This differs from the more common assumption of labeled or marked nulls [5, 19] but is actually more in line with storing graphs in a relational DBMS and uses it for querying.

For the last question addressed in the paper, we look at query languages for graphs that combine navigation and data querying, but are not path-based. In particular, we look at the adaptation of XML language XPath [38] to graphs, as was investigated in [15,30]. Here we show a strong negative result: even if mappings treat graph databases as relational, query answering for graph XPath queries under such mappings is undecidable.

To summarize, our results have the following implications.

1. For the model underlying real-life graph database applications, such as property graphs of Neo4j, schema mappings have to treat graphs as if they were relational databases, i.e., no recursively defined navigational properties are allowed in mappings.
2. Even under such mappings, to achieve tractability of answering path queries in exchange/integration scenarios, one has to populate target instances with null values interpreted as SQL nulls, when it comes to querying them.
3. Moving from RPQs that use data to more general patterns is problematic even for the simplest mappings, as query answering becomes undecidable already for simple fragments of Graph XPath.

Organization Section 2 defines data graph and navigational queries; in Section 3 we describe queries that combine navigation and data querying. Section 4 defines graph schema mappings and querying under them. In Section 5 we prove the main undecidability result for querying under graph schema mappings. Section 6 looks at the restriction of schema mappings that does not allow recursion over targets, and proves decidability and intractability of query answering. Section 7 shows how to restore tractability via null values. Section 8 looks at queries with restricted comparisons, and Section 9 shows undecidability of query answering for Graph XPath. Conclusions are in Section 10. Due to space limitations, we are only able to give sketches and ideas of the proofs.

2. PRELIMINARIES

Graph databases and data graphs For the purposes of navigational querying, graph databases are usually abstracted as labeled directed graphs, i.e., their edges are of the form (v, a, v'), where v, v' are two nodes and a is a label. For data graphs, we follow exactly the same approach except that a node now consists of a node id and a data value.

More precisely, let Σ be a finite set of edge labels, $\mathcal{N}$ a countably infinite set of node ids, and $\mathcal{D}$ be a countably infinite set of data values. A pair $v = (n, d)$ where $n \in \mathcal{N}$ and $d \in \mathcal{D}$ is a *node.* A *data graph* is $G = \langle V, E\rangle$ where V is a finite set of nodes (i.e., $V \subset \mathcal{N} \times \mathcal{D}$) such that no two nodes have the same node id, and $E \subseteq V \times \Sigma \times V$ is a set of labeled edges. For a node $v = (n, d)$, we let $\delta(v)$ refer to the data value d.

A data graph G can also be seen as a relational structure $\langle V, (E_a)_{a\in\Sigma}\rangle$ where each E_a is the binary relation $\{(v, v') \in V \mid (v, a, v') \in E\}$. We will freely move back and forth between these two representations of data graphs.

A *path* π in a data graph G from a node v_1 to a node v_{n+1} is a finite sequence $\pi = v_1 a_1 v_2 \ldots v_n a_n v_{n+1}$, where each v_i is a node of G, each a_i is a symbol of Σ, and (v_i, a_i, v_{i+1}) is an edge of G for each $i \leq n$. We use $\lambda(\pi)$ to refer to the word $a_1 \ldots a_n$, called the *label* of π. The *length* of π, denoted by

$|\pi|$, is the length of the word $\lambda(\pi) = a_1 \dots a_n$, in this case n. To denote the fact that π is a path from v_1 to v_{n+1}, we will write $v_1 \xrightarrow{\pi} v_{n+1}$. Similarly, for a word $w \in \Sigma^*$, we will write $v_1 \xrightarrow{w} v_{n+1}$ to say that there exists a path going from v_1 to v_{n+1} of label w.

A *data path* is a sequence $d_1 a_1 d_2 \dots d_n a_n d_{n+1}$ where all the d_is are elements of $\mathcal{D}$ and all the a_js are labels from Σ. Given a path $\pi = v_1 a_1 v_2 \dots v_n a_n v_{n+1}$ in a data graph $G = \langle V, E \rangle$, the corresponding *data path* is defined as $\delta(\pi) = \delta(v_1) a_1 \delta(v_2) \dots \delta(x_n) a_n \delta(v_{n+1})$. That is, each node in π is replaced by its data value. Note that data paths are very similar to data words [10, 37] which are words over $\Sigma \times \mathcal{D}$; data paths are data words with one extra data value.

Navigational queries A k-ary *query* q (over Σ) is a mapping that associates with each Σ-labeled data graph $G = \langle V, E \rangle$ a set of k-tuples of nodes $q(G) \subseteq V^k$. We refer to k as the arity of q. We mainly deal with binary queries, i.e., $k = 2$.

The basic queries we consider are *regular path queries (RPQs)*. An RPQ over Σ is just a regular expression e over Σ. Over a (data) graph G, it outputs pairs of nodes connected by a path whose label is in e:

$$e(G) = \{(v, v') \mid \exists \pi : \ v \xrightarrow{\pi} v' \text{ and } \lambda(\pi) \in e\}$$

A *word* RPQ is an RPQ where e is a word $w \in \Sigma^*$. A *reachability* RPQ is simply $e = \Sigma^*$.

A special case of a word RPQ is an *atomic* RPQ a, where $a \in \Sigma$. Such a query returns the binary relation $E_a = \{(v, v') \mid (v, a, v') \in E\}$.

3. DATA RPQs ON DATA GRAPHS

In this section we review queries on data graphs that combine navigation and data querying. In general, there are three main approaches to such queries. *Data RPQs* are extensions of RPQs with regular expressions that mix alphabet letters and data values [30, 31]; these are the queries we mainly concentrate on as they are natural analogs of navigational queries most commonly studied in graph databases. A different approach is that of *walk logic* [24], initially defined for a slightly different model and then extended to data graphs in [7]. The language is elegant and very expressive, but it was shown to have non-elementary complexity, ruling out its practical applications [7]. Finally, one can have pattern-based languages, like Cypher of Neo4j [36] or analogs of XPath for graphs [15, 30, 36]. We look at those in Section 9.

We now define data RPQs that mix navigation and data. They work on data paths, which are essentially data words; thus, data RPQs will be based on regular languages for data words/paths. The most common automata model that provides the notion of regularity for them is *register automata* [25]. Of course queries are not specified by automata but rather by more declarative regular expressions. While register automata have been around for a while, the study of regular expressions for them is more recent [31], and we shall look at two types of them: expressions with memory, that capture register automata, and weaker expressions with equality that have attractive computational properties. We now define those, specifically for data paths. In all definitions below, we assume a countably infinite set $\mathcal{X}$ of variables (registers).

Regular expressions with memory [30]. These expressions use *conditions* on variables from $\mathcal{X}$ defined by

$$c \ := \ x^= \mid x^{\neq} \mid c \wedge c \mid c \vee c$$

with x ranging over $\mathcal{X}$. Their satisfaction is defined with respect to a pair (σ, d), where σ is a partial map from $\mathcal{X}$ to $\mathcal{D}$ with finite support (i.e., $\sigma : \mathcal{X} \to \mathcal{D} \cup \{\perp\}$ where $\perp$ stands for undefined, and $\sigma(x) \neq \perp$ only for finitely many $x \in \mathcal{X}$), and $d \in \mathcal{D}$. The rules are:

- $\sigma, d \models x^=$ iff $\sigma(x) = d$;
- $\sigma, d \models x^{\neq}$ iff $\sigma(x) \neq d$.

and we use the standard rules for $\wedge$ and $\vee$. Note that conditions are closed under negation; in order to express $\neg c$, we can propagate $\neg$ through $\wedge$ and $\vee$ all the way to basic comparisons and then swap $x^=$ with $x^{\neq}$.

The class $\text{REM}(\Sigma, \mathcal{X})$ of *regular expressions with memory* over alphabet Σ and variables $\mathcal{X}$ is defined by the grammar:

$$e \ := \ \varepsilon \mid a \mid e + e \mid e \cdot e \mid e^+ \mid e[c] \mid \downarrow \bar{x}.e$$

where a ranges over Σ, c over conditions, and $\bar{x}$ over tuples of variables from $\mathcal{X}$. They extend the usual regular expressions with two features: $e[c]$ checks if condition c is satisfied after matching e, and $\downarrow \bar{x}.e$ assigns the current data value to variables in $\bar{x}$ before matching e. To give a couple of examples, the expression $\downarrow x.(a[x^{\neq}])^+$ defines data paths labeled a along which all data values are different from the first one, i.e., data paths of the form $d a d_1 a \cdots a d_{n-1} a d_n$ where $d_i \neq d$ for every $i \leq n$. It binds the first data value d, and then checks after reading each letter that the letter was a, and the following data value was different from d. As another example, the expression $\Sigma^* \cdot \downarrow x.\Sigma^+[x^=] \cdot \Sigma^*$ defines data paths in which the same data value occurs more than once: it skips up to that data value, binds it to x, moves one or more labels forward, and checks if the same data value occurs. As usual, Σ^* is $\varepsilon + \Sigma^+$.

The semantics is defined by means of a relation $(e, w, \sigma) \vdash \sigma'$, where $e \in \text{REM}(\Sigma, \mathcal{X})$, w is a data path, and σ, σ' are variable assignments. Intuitively, it says that if one starts with assignment σ and parses w according to e, then one ends up with σ'. The language of e is then defined as:

$$L(e) \ = \ \{w \mid \exists \sigma : \ (e, w, \perp) \vdash \sigma\}$$

where $\perp$ is the initial empty assignment (i.e., each variable is undefined). That is, $L(e)$ gives all the data paths that can be parsed according to e without any prior variable binding.

Relation $\vdash$ is defined inductively on the structure of expressions. It uses the notion of *concatenation* of two data paths $w = d_1 a_1 \dots a_{n-1} d_n$ and $w' = d_n a_n \dots a_{m-1} d_m$ that share the last and the first data value, defined as $w \cdot w' = d_1 a_1 \dots a_{n-1} d_n a_n \dots a_{m-1} d_m$.

- $(\varepsilon, w, \sigma) \vdash \sigma'$ iff $w = d$ for some $d \in \mathcal{D}$ and $\sigma' = \sigma$.
- $(a, w, \sigma) \vdash \sigma'$ iff $w = d_1 a d_2$ and $\sigma' = \sigma$.
- $(e_1 \cdot e_2, w, \sigma) \vdash \sigma'$ iff $w = w_1 \cdot w_2$ for some data paths and there exists σ'' such that $(e_1, w_1, \sigma) \vdash \sigma''$ and $(e_2, w_2, \sigma'') \vdash \sigma'$.
- $(e_1 + e_2, w, \sigma) \vdash \sigma'$ iff $(e_1, w, \sigma) \vdash \sigma'$ or $(e_2, w, \sigma) \vdash \sigma'$.
- $(e^+, w, \sigma) \vdash \sigma'$ iff $w = w_1 \cdots w_m$ for some $w_1, \dots, w_m$ and there exist $\sigma = \sigma_0, \sigma_1, \dots, \sigma_m = \sigma'$ such that $(w, w_i, \sigma_{i-1}) \vdash \sigma_i$ for all $i \leq m$.

- $(\downarrow \bar{x}.e, w, \sigma) \vdash \sigma'$ iff $(e, w, \sigma_{\bar{x}=d}) \vdash \sigma'$, where d is the first data value of w and $\sigma_{\bar{x}=d}$ modifies σ by assigning value d to all variables in $\bar{x}$.
- $(e[c], w, \sigma) \vdash \sigma'$ iff $(e, w, \sigma) \vdash \sigma'$ and $\sigma', d \models c$, where d is the last data value of w.

Regular expressions with memory have the same expressiveness as register automata and share many computational properties with them: for example, their nonemptiness problem is PSPACE-complete, and membership problem is NP-complete [18,31]. They are closed under union, intersection, concatenation, Kleene star, but not under complement.

Remark The definition of REM needs to exclude pathological cases $e[c]$ where either c uses a variable that has not been bound to a value, or e is equivalent to ε. This is a small technicality that does not affect us at all as we shall never encounter such expressions. We refer to [30] for details.

Regular expressions with equality This particularly simple class of expressions allows us to capture many useful properties expressed by register automata. The class REE(Σ) of *regular expressions with equality* is defined by:

$$e \ := \ \varepsilon \mid a \mid e+e \mid e \cdot e \mid e^+ \mid e_= \mid e_{\neq}$$

where a ranges over alphabet letters. The language $L(e)$ of data paths denoted e is given as follows:

- $L(\varepsilon) = \{d \mid d \in \mathcal{D}\}$.
- $L(a) = \{dad' \mid d, d' \in \mathcal{D}\}$.
- $L(e \cdot e') = L(e) \cdot L(e')$.
- $L(e + e') = L(e) \cup L(e')$.
- $L(e^+) = \{w_1 \cdots w_k \mid k \geq 1 \text{ and each } w_i \in L(e)\}$.
- $L(e_=) = \{d_1 a_1 \dots a_{n-1} d_n \in L(e) \mid d_1 = d_n\}$.
- $L(e_{\neq}) = \{d_1 a_1 \dots a_{n-1} d_n \in L(e) \mid d_1 \neq d_n\}$.

For example, the language of data paths on which the same data value occurs more than once is given by $\Sigma^* \cdot (\Sigma^+)_= \cdot \Sigma^*$.

While these expressions are strictly weaker than register automata, they have attractive computational properties: for example, both nonemptiness and membership are solvable in PTIME. They have the same closure properties as expressions with memory except they are not closed under intersection [30,31].

We shall also look at particularly simple expressions, called *path with tests*, defined by $e \ := \ a \mid e \cdot e \mid e_= \mid e_{\neq}$. These are just words, where some subwords carry an annotation indicating whether data values at the beginning and the end of the subword are the same. For example, $(a(bc)_=)_{\neq}$ matches data paths $d_1 a d_2 b d_3 c d_2$ with $d_1 \neq d_2$.

Queries. As queries, we consider RPQs given by regular expressions of one of the above classes. The output $e(G)$ is the set of pairs (v, v') of nodes such that there is a path π in G going from v to v' and with $\delta(\pi) \in L(e)$.

If it is not important which class the expression comes from (with memory or with equality), we use a generic term *data RPQs*. When we want to be more specific, for REMs we refer to *memory RPQs*, for REEs to *equality RPQ*, and for paths with tests, to *data path queries*.

4. SCHEMA MAPPINGS AND QUERY ANSWERING

We now define schema mappings for graph databases, query answering based on them, and explain how standard data exchange and virtual data integration scenarios for graph data are captured.

From now on, we adopt the convention that queries used in mappings will be denoted by lower case letters q, q' etc., and queries that one needs to answer will be denoted by upper case letters Q, Q' etc.

Schema mappings for data graphs As in [8, 12, 14, 21], we define mappings based on RPQs. Assume that we are given two sets of edge labels Σ_s and Σ_t, called *source* and *target* alphabets respectively.

DEFINITION 1. *A* graph schema mapping (GSM) $\mathcal{M}$ *is a set of pairs of RPQs* (q, q'), *where* q *is an RPQ over* Σ_s *and* q' *is an RPQ over* Σ_t.

If $G_s = \langle V_s, E_s \rangle$ *and* $G_t = \langle V_t, E_t \rangle$ *are data graphs over* Σ_s *and* Σ_t *respectively, we write* $(G_s, G_t) \models \mathcal{M}$ *if* $q(G_s) \subseteq q'(G_t)$ *for every* $(q, q') \in \mathcal{M}$, *and call* G_t *a* solution *for* G_s *under* $\mathcal{M}$.

This looks just like the standard definition of schema mappings for graph databases [8, 14]; the difference is that now we deal with *data* graphs, whose nodes are pairs $v = (n, d) \in \mathcal{N} \times \mathcal{D}$. Thus, if $\big((n, d), (n', d')\big) \in q(G_s)$, we require that $\big((n, d), (n', d')\big) \in q(G_t)$. Hence it is not just node ids that must appear in the target graph but also data values that they carry.

A GSM $\mathcal{M}$ is called LAV, or *local-as-view*, if for every pair $(q, q') \in \mathcal{M}$, query q is atomic, i.e., just a letter $a \in \Sigma_s$. These mappings are most commonly used in virtual data integration, and we shall see that most negative results are already true under the LAV restriction. When we say that a LAV mapping is defined using a certain query language, it means that it consists of pairs (a, q') where $a \in \Sigma_s$ and q' belongs to this language. Similarly, a GSM $\mathcal{M}$ is called GAV, or *global-as-view*, if for every pair $(q, q') \in \mathcal{M}$, query q' is atomic.

Query answering As is standard [5,28], we shall adopt the certain answers semantics for query answering under schema mappings.

DEFINITION 2. *Given a data graph* G_s *over* Σ_s, *a GSM* $\mathcal{M}$ *over* Σ_s, Σ_t, *and a query* Q *over* Σ_t, *the set of* certain answers *to* Q *on* G_s *under* $\mathcal{M}$ *is defined as:*

$$\square_{\mathcal{M}}(Q, G_s) = \bigcap \{Q(G_t) \mid (G_s, G_t) \models \mathcal{M}\}$$

In other words, we look at answers true in all Σ_t data graphs G_t that, together with the source G_s, satisfy conditions of mapping $\mathcal{M}$.

This gives us the main computational problem we study, *query answering under graph schema mappings.* We look primarily at data complexity of the problem when the mapping $\mathcal{M}$ and the query Q are fixed.

PROBLEM :	QUERYANSWERING_GSM($\mathcal{M}, Q$)
INPUT :	A data graph G_s over Σ_s a tuple $\bar{v}$ of nodes of G_s.
QUESTION :	Is $\bar{v}$ in $\square_{\mathcal{M}}(Q, G_s)$?

When $\mathcal{M}$ and Q are clear from the context or not important, we simply refer to *data complexity* of QUERYANSWERING_GSM. When we speak of *combined complexity*, we assume that Q and $\mathcal{M}$ are part of the input.

Data exchange and virtual data integration We now explain how the setting described earlier subsumes graph data exchange and virtual data integration.

In relational data exchange, one has source and target schemas σ and τ, and schema mappings $\mathcal{M}$ are typically specified by *source-to-target tgds (st-tgds)* $\forall \bar{x}\ (\varphi_\sigma(\bar{x}) \rightarrow \exists \bar{z}\ \psi_\tau(\bar{x}, \bar{z}))$, where $\varphi_\sigma(\bar{x})$ is a query over σ and $\psi_\tau(\bar{x}, \bar{z})$ is a query over τ (usually both are conjunctive). In this case if q is given by φ_σ and q' by $\exists \bar{z}\ \psi_\tau(\bar{x}, \bar{z})$, the above st-tgd just says that for source and target instances S and T satisfying the mapping we must have $q(S) \subseteq q'(T)$. For answering queries Q over the target for a given source database D_s, one defines certain answers as $\Box_{\mathcal{M}}(Q, D_s) = \bigcap\{Q(D_t) \mid (D_s, D_t) \models \mathcal{M}\}$, cf. [5]. Thus, for graph schema mappings, we mimic the relational case: graph databases are viewed as relational structures, but we use RPQs instead of conjunctive queries.

Under LAV, the setting also subsumes virtual data integration of graph databases [13, 14, 21]. In general, in data integration, we have sources $S_1, \ldots, S_n$, and a global schema γ; the mapping $\mathcal{M}$ is given by queries $q_1, \ldots, q_n$ over γ which is satisfied by an instance D of γ, written as $((S_1, \ldots, S_n), D) \models \mathcal{M}$, if $S_i \subseteq q_i(D)$ for all $i \leq n$. For a query Q posed against a database of schema γ, virtual data integration defines answers as $\Box_{\mathcal{M}}(Q, (S_1, \ldots, S_n)) = \bigcap\{Q(D) \mid ((S_1, \ldots, S_n), D) \models \mathcal{M}\}$, see [28].

Query answering over LAV GSMs corresponds precisely to virtual integration of several graph databases. Indeed, we can view these source graphs as relations E_a for a virtual graph database G. Then our setting – that is, the notions of LAV schema mappings and query answering – is precisely the same as the virtual data integration scenario described above.

5. UNDECIDABILITY OF DATA RPQs

The problem of query answering under graph schema mappings has been studied for purely navigational queries. For mappings given by RPQs, finding $\Box_{\mathcal{M}}(Q, G)$ can be done in CONP if Q is an RPQ, or belongs to one of several navigational languages that extend RPQs (conjunctive RPQs, nested regular expressions, or conjunctive nested regular expressions); the problem is CONP-hard even when Q is an RPQ [8, 12].

We show here that the situation is completely different for queries that combine data and navigation: query answering under schema mappings becomes *undecidable* for data RPQs. In fact we show that undecidability holds under three strong restrictions:

- queries are equality RPQs, i.e., are based on the simplest class of data RPQs;
- mappings are local-as-view; and
- queries in mappings are either atomic or the simplest reachability queries Σ_t^*.

We start by introducing a new concept that will help us describe the class of mappings for which the query answering problem is undecidable, and will also be will be important for restrictions that let us regain decidability.

DEFINITION 3. *We call a mapping $\mathcal{M}$* relational *if for each $(q, q') \in \mathcal{M}$, the query q' is a word RPQ, i.e., is given by a word $w_t \in \Sigma_t^*$.*

The reason for the name is that queries over Σ_t in these mappings are relational conjunctive queries. A LAV relational mapping consists of pairs (a, w_t) with $a \in \Sigma_s$ and $w_t \in \Sigma_t^*$.

LAV relational mappings eliminate all recursion in queries that define them, and for such mappings, based on what we know from relational data exchange [5], we would expect many query answering tasks to be decidable (more on that in the next section). So what is the smallest addition to such mappings that cannot be expressed with first-order relational queries? Such an addition is the simplest form of reachability, namely reachability by an arbitrary path, in which we do not impose any restriction at all on label use.

To capture this, we define *relational/reachability* mappings $\mathcal{M}$ as those where in all pairs $(q, q') \in \mathcal{M}$, either q' is a word RPQ, as in relational mappings, or the simplest reachability query Σ_t^*. In particular, in a LAV relational/reachability mapping, pairs of queries are of two kinds: either (a, w_t), with $a \in \Sigma_s$ and $w_t \in \Sigma_t^*$, or (a, Σ_t^*).

We can make it even simpler and impose the restriction that every rule in a mapping, except for reachability, be both LAV and GAV (global-as-view [28]). In such a *LAV/GAV relational/reachability mappings*, pairs of queries are of two kinds:

- (a, b) with $a \in \Sigma_s$ and $b \in \Sigma_t$, and
- (a, Σ_t^*) with $a \in \Sigma_s$.

Already for these very simple mappings, answering the simplest data RPQs is undecidable.

THEOREM 1. QUERYANSWERING_GSM *is undecidable in data complexity for data RPQs.*

In fact, there exists a LAV/GAV relational/reachability mapping $\mathcal{M}$, and an equality RPQ Q such that QUERYANSWERING_GSM$(\mathcal{M}, Q)$ *is undecidable.*

Proof idea. The proof is rather involved; we now explain the key idea of the encoding and illustrate the main gadgets used in the proof. We reduce from the Post Correspondence Problem (PCP), by building a GSM $\mathcal{M}$ and a query Q from the alphabet such that for each PCP instance, there exist a source database G_s and a pair of nodes $(start, end)$ of G_s such that $(start, end) \notin \Box_{\mathcal{M}}(Q, G_s)$ if and only if the PCP instance is satisfiable. We assume that PCP instances are sets of n pairs of nonempty words (referred to as tiles) $(u_r, v_r)_{1 \leq r \leq n}$ over $\Sigma = \{a, b\}$. Both alphabets Σ_s and Σ_t are $\{a, b, i, t, m, \bar{m}, id, s, v, \leftrightarrow, \#\}$. Symbols other than a and b are separators: i, s and v mark what we call the input, solution and verification parts of the encoding; t marks the start of the encoding of a tile and $\leftrightarrow$ marks the separation between words u_r and v_r of a given tile (u_r, v_r); m and $\bar{m}$ designate a specific tile in a list of tiles; id will be used to insert additional data values along paths; and $\#$ marks the end of the encoding.

The source database G_s built from the PCP instance is shown below.

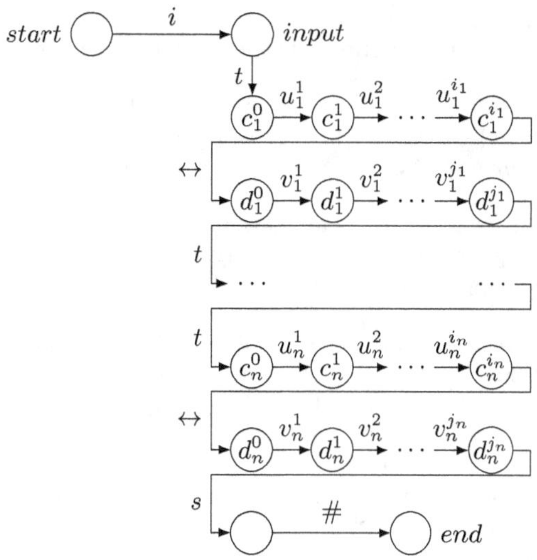

In the figure, the u_i^js and v_i^js are letters of u_i, v_i, and all data values c_i^j and d_i^j are distinct.

The mapping $\mathcal{M}$ has rules (ℓ, ℓ) for $\ell = a, b, t, i, s, \leftrightarrow$ and $(\#, \Sigma_t^*)$. Under this mapping, G_s will be copied into a target graph G_t, but some path can be inserted in place of the # edge of the input. Now our query will ensure that this path is of a special shape. It will start with an s-edge and then have an encoding of the paths $\pi_{r_1}, \ldots, \pi_{r_m}$ corresponding to the solution of the PCP instance, i.e., a sequence $r_1, \ldots, r_m$ of indexes from $\{1, \ldots, n\}$ (if a solution exists). Then, after a v separator, there is a verification section with labels forming the path $u_{r_1} \cdots u_{r_m}$ (which is the same as $v_{r_1} \cdots v_{r_m}$).

For each r among $r_1, \ldots, r_m$, the path π_r looks as follows.

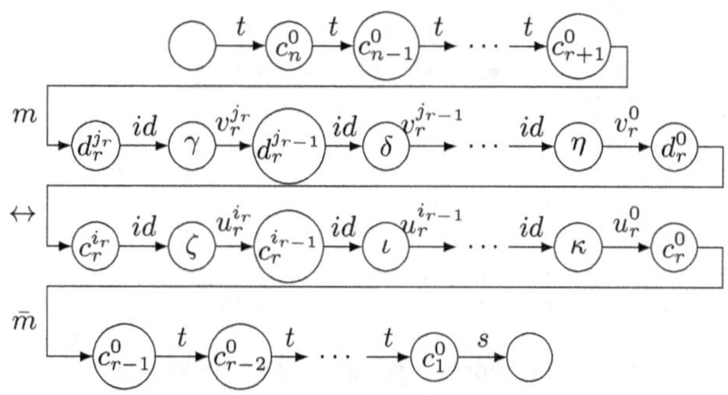

The path π_r starts and ends with the encoding of r split into paths of $n-r$ and r nodes carrying distinct data values, and connected with t-edges. In between, we have encodings of v_r and u_r in reverse order, with extra nodes inserted as additional ids for the purpose of verifying that the solution is correct. These are the nodes connected with id edges, and whose data values are shown as Greek letters in the picture. These four sections of the encoding of π_r are separated with m, $\leftrightarrow$, and $\bar{m}$ letters.

The intuition behind the query Q is that it works on a target instance described above and checks for *errors*, that is, properties that tell us that it is not a correct encoding of a PCP instance and its solution. Then having *(start, end)* $\notin \Box_{\mathcal{M}}(Q, G_s)$ implies that there exists a target instance in which none of the errors occur, and thus implies satisfiability of the PCP instance.

There are several kinds of errors, and to ensure that we do have an encoding of PCP, we need to eliminate all of them.

For this, the query Q will be a disjunction of several expressions. One of them, that does not have any references to data values (and thus is an ordinary regular expression) ensures that the path from *start* to *end* is shaped as explained above (rather, it needs to check for errors, i.e., that the path is not shaped as described above, but in this case we have a usual regular expression and can take complement).

Next one can show how to write REE expressions whose negation ensures the following. First, each subpath between two s labels is the encoding of some pair (u_i, v_i) from the input. Thus, the subpath between the first and last s labels is the encoding of a sequence of tiles of the PCP instance.

Next, we use REE expressions to deduce that the subpath that starts after label v only contains pairwise distinct data values, and that the sequence of data values that occur after each label id in the encoding of the solution on the left-hand (resp. right-hand) side of each tile is a copy, in the reverse order, of the sequence of data values in the verification path.

Finally, we use another REE expression whose negation ensures that these data values correspond to the same letter, i.e. it is satisfied if it can find a mismatch. Thus, the sequence of letters on the right-hand side of the tiles in the solution path is the same as the sequence of letters on the left-hand side of the tiles. Thus, the subpath between the first and last s labels is indeed the encoding of a solution to the PCP instance, from which we deduce that it is satisfiable if *(start, end)* $\notin \Box_{\mathcal{M}}(Q, G_s)$.

For the other direction, if there is a PCP solution, we build a single-path instance G_t as described above, and then it is a simple matter of checking that *(start, end)* $\notin Q(G_s)$. $\Box$

Since LAV/GAV relational/reachability mappings represent the simplest possible non-relational addition to the simplest imaginable mappings, this result strongly suggests that for data exchange and integration tasks, target graph databases ought to be viewed as relational databases, and mappings ought to exclude any form of recursive navigation over target data.

6. RELATIONAL MAPPINGS FOR DATA GRAPHS

Given the conclusion of the previous section, we now restrict our attention to relational graph schema mappings in which no recursion over the target schema is allowed. These are GSMs $\mathcal{M}$ (see Definition 3) in which for all $(q, q') \in \mathcal{M}$, the query q' is a word RPQ.

One might be tempted to think that these can be cast as the usual relational mappings over relational representations of graphs, and then results about them can be obtained from what we know in the relational case. While the premise is true, the conclusion is not: we cannot obtain results for such mappings simply by appealing to the relational case. We first explain why this is so, and then present our results about relational GSMs.

Do relational results suffice? Relational GSMs can be easily modeled by the usual relational mappings on graphs viewed as relational databases. A standard representation of a data graph G over Σ_s as a relational database D_G uses binary relations N^s and E_a^s for each $a \in \Sigma_s$ (and likewise N^t and E_a^t for Σ_t). Each node (n, d) is a tuple in N^s, and for each edge $((n, d), a, (n', d'))$, we have the pair (n, n') in E_a^s. Note that since such databases are over disjoint domains

$\mathcal{N}$ and $\mathcal{D}$, we assume that in addition predicates $\mathcal{N}(x)$ and $\mathcal{D}(x)$ are available to distinguish them.

A relational GSM $\mathcal{M}$ between Σ_s and Σ_t data graph can be expressed by means of the relational schema mapping $\mathcal{M}_{\text{rel}}$ defined as shown below.

- For each pair $(q, w) \in \mathcal{M}$ with $w \in \Sigma_t$, we have an st-tgds $\forall x, y\ q(x, y) \rightarrow q_w(x, y)$, where, for a word $w = a_1 \dots a_n$, the query $q_w(x, y)$ is the conjunctive query $\exists x_1 \dots x_{n-1}\ E^t_{a_1}(x, x_1) \wedge E^t_{a_2}(x_1, x_2) \cdots \wedge E^t_{a_n}(x_{n-1}, y)$. Note that query q itself need not be conjunctive or even first-order, as in relational st-tgds.

- For each $(q, q') \in \mathcal{M}$, add an st-tgd $\forall x, y\ N^s(x, y) \wedge \exists z\ q(x, z) \rightarrow N^t(x, y)$ and symmetrically with $\exists z\ q(z, x)$. They say that every node that occurs in the result of a source query must be moved to the target.

- Add a key constraint $\forall x, y, y'\ (N^t(x, y) \wedge N^t(x, y') \rightarrow y = y')$ (i.e., each node id has one data value), and target tgds $\forall x, y\ N^t(x, y) \rightarrow \mathcal{N}(x) \wedge \mathcal{D}(y)$ as well as $\forall x, y\ E^t_a(x, y) \rightarrow \exists z, z'\ (N^t(x, z) \wedge N^t(y, z'))$ for each $a \in \Sigma_t$, saying that every node in the target graph must have a data value.

Such a mapping $\mathcal{M}_{\text{rel}}$ precisely describes the action of $\mathcal{M}$ on relational representations of graphs, as the following straightforward result shows.

PROPOSITION 1. *If $\mathcal{M}$ is a relational GSM and G_s is a Σ_s data graph, then solutions for D_{G_s} under $\mathcal{M}_{rel}$ are exactly the structures of the form D_{G_t} where G_t is a solution for G_s under $\mathcal{M}$.*

Despite this close connection, we cannot directly derive the complexity of query answering from known relational results. To start with, relational mappings can contain pairs (q, w) where q is a complex reachability query, and thus relational results do not apply to it. Even when all such queries q are conjunctive, we still cannot easily apply known results to $\mathcal{M}_{\text{rel}}$. The reason is that answering first-order relational queries under mappings of relational databases, even without target constraints, is already undecidable, cf. [5]. Data RPQs, on the other hand, go beyond first-order queries. Trying to encode data RPQs in a language for which the complexity of query answering in data exchange is known is also problematic, given the scarcity of such languages. For example, [6] looked at a well behaved (in data exchange) fragment of datalog with negation, but the natural coding of equality RPQs in datalog with inequalities over databases D_G does not fall into that fragment. And for memory RPQs, it is not even clear what fragment of a natural relational language they correspond to (e.g., coding of regular expressions into datalog breaks for them).

When it comes to lower bounds, we cannot directly take advantage of existing techniques such as [20, 32] as they use queries that cannot be expressed with RPQs.

Upper and lower bounds for relational mappings Despite the difficulties with the naive approach to reducing to relational results, we can establish both upper and lower bounds on the complexity of query answering. We start with the upper bound.

THEOREM 2. *For relational GSMs, data complexity of* QUERYANSWERING_GSM *for data RPQs is in* CONP, *and its combined complexity is in* PSPACE.

In fact this follows from a more general result. A *homomorphism* between two data graphs $G = \langle V, E \rangle$ and $G' = \langle V', E' \rangle$ is a map $h : \mathcal{N} \rightarrow \mathcal{N}$ such that for each edge (v_1, a, v_2) in E, the edge $(h(v_1), a, h(v_2))$ is in E', where h is extended to nodes by $h\big((n, d)\big) = \big(h(n), d\big)$. A query Q is closed under homomorphisms if, whenever we have a homomorphism $h : G \rightarrow G'$ and $\bar{v} \in Q(G)$, then $h(\bar{v}) \in Q(G')$. It can be readily checked that under this definition, data RPQs are closed under homomorphisms (in fact, a more general result will be shown in Section 7, Proposition 6). The result then follows from the proposition below.

PROPOSITION 2. *Let $\mathcal{C}$ be a class of queries on data graphs that has* PTIME *data complexity and* PSPACE *combined complexity. Assume that every query $q \in \mathcal{C}$ is closed under homomorphisms. Then, for relational GSMs and queries in $\mathcal{C}$, the problem* QUERYANSWERING_GSM *is in* CONP *in data complexity and in* PSPACE *in combined complexity.*

Proof sketch. We first prove an auxiliary result. Assume that $\mathcal{M}$ is a GSM and G_s is a source graph database such that there exists a number $k > 0$ such that, for every rule $(q, q') \in \mathcal{M}$, the language $L(q')$ is contained in Σ_t^k. If G_t is a solution for G_s, we can show that there is another solution $G'_t \subseteq G_t$ whose size is bounded by $(2k + 1) \cdot |\mathcal{M}| \cdot |G_s|^2$.

With this, the proposition follows, since deciding whether $(x, y) \in \Box_{\mathcal{M}}(Q, G_s)$ can be done with the following nondeterministic algorithm: first nondeterministically guess a target database G'_t of size at most $(2|\mathcal{M}|^2 + |\mathcal{M}|) \cdot |G_s|^2$, then check whether $(G_s, G'_t) \models \mathcal{M}$ and $(x, y) \notin Q(G'_t)$. Correctness follows from the fact that the mapping is relational, and thus words in $L(q')$ for each $(q, q') \in \mathcal{M}$ have bounded length, which is $\leq |\mathcal{M}|$. It is easy to check that the algorithm has the required complexity under the assumptions. □

In fact, the proof shows a slightly stronger result: the right-hand side queries in mappings need not be single words but could also be regular expressions of the form $w_1 + \cdots + w_m$, where each $w_i \in \Sigma_t^*$ for $i \leq m$.

For query answering under mappings of relational databases, CONP-hardness is already known for unions of conjunctive queries with inequalities [20, 32]. However, as we noticed earlier, reductions used queries that do not correspond to data path queries (non-recursive data RPQs). Nonetheless, it is not hard to come up with a direct reduction to show the following.

PROPOSITION 3. *There exists a data path query Q and a LAV relational mapping $\mathcal{M}$ such that the problem* QUERYANSWERING_GSM($\mathcal{M}, Q$) *is* CONP*-complete.*

For the proof, we use a reduction from 3-colorability; there are some technicalities involved, compared to the relational case, due to a very restricted type of query Q.

The query in Proposition 3 uses three inequalities. A similar relational result in [20] uses three inequalities as well, although it also showed that for unions of conjunctive queries with at most one inequality per disjunct, query answering under mappings based on st-tgds is in PTIME. We can adapt the proof and further lower the complexity guarantee for data path queries.

PROPOSITION 4. *For relational GSMs $\mathcal{M}$ and data path queries that have at most one subexpression of the form $e_{\neq}$, data complexity of* QUERYANSWERING_GSM *is in* NLOGSPACE.

As a final remark, we note that for data path queries, query answering is decidable for arbitrary GSMs, not just relational mappings.

PROPOSITION 5. *If Q is a data path query and $\mathcal{M}$ is an arbitrary GSM, then the problem* QUERYANSWERING_GSM$(\mathcal{M}, Q)$ *is in* CONP.

The idea of the proof is that mapping rules that can produce words of length greater than the length of Q are of no use in detecting whether a tuple is a certain answer, and thus one can cut the mapping to a simpler one that essentially resembles the relational case.

7. TRACTABLE QUERY ANSWERING VIA SQL NULLS

Our next question is how to achieve tractability of query answering under graph schema mappings. A standard solution in the case of relations and XML documents is to find a *universal* solution such that running a query over it gives us certain answers, cf. [5]. The CONP-hardness result of the previous section shows that this approach cannot be used directly even with simple equality RPQs. Nonetheless, we show that under some assumptions on data values in target graphs, it can be recovered.

To explain this approach, we recall that when target instances are built in relational data exchange, they are populated either by constants or *marked nulls* [5]. For instance, if we have a relational st-tgd $\forall x, y\ S(x, y) \rightarrow \exists z\ T(x, z) \wedge T(z, y)$, and a source $\{S(a, b), S(c, d)\}$, then the common way is to construct a target instance with tuples $T(a, \mathbf{N}_1), T(\mathbf{N}_1, b), T(c, \mathbf{N}_2), T(\mathbf{N}_2, d)$, where $\mathbf{N}_1, \mathbf{N}_2$ are marked nulls. That is, for each tuple satisfying $S(x, y)$, a new marked null z is invented, and tuples $(x, z), (z, y)$ are put in T.

Such marked nulls are really nothing but constants that did not occur in the source instance: they are new values for which equality is purely syntactic, i.e., $\mathbf{N}_1 = \mathbf{N}_1$ but $\mathbf{N}_1 \neq \mathbf{N}_2$, $\mathbf{N}_1 \neq a$, etc. Thus we can simply view them as elements of the set $\mathcal{D}$ of data values.

In real-life implementations of SQL relational databases, nulls behave differently: there is just one null value $\mathbf{N}$, and no comparison involving $\mathbf{N}$ can evaluate to true. We now show that with nulls behaving like SQL nulls, tractability of query answering can be restored using universal solutions.

Formally, we expand the domain $\mathcal{D}$ of data values with a single null value $\mathbf{N}$, writing $\mathcal{D}_{\mathbf{N}}$ for $\mathcal{D} \cup \{\mathbf{N}\}$. A node $v = (n, \mathbf{N})$ is called a *null node.* Following SQL's rule for nulls, we do not let any comparisons involving nulls evaluate to true. That is, we modify the evaluation of conditions of memory RPQs over $\mathcal{D}_{\mathbf{N}}$ by:

- $\sigma, d \models x^{=}$ iff $\sigma(x) = d$ and $\sigma(x), d \neq \mathbf{N}$;
- $\sigma, d \models x^{\neq}$ iff $\sigma(x) \neq d$ and $\sigma(x), d \neq \mathbf{N}$,

and for equality RPQs, we allow equalities and inequalities to be true only when both arguments are different from $\mathbf{N}$. Note that we do not use SQL's three-valued logic; at the end of the section we explain why we can use the simpler approach without any loss of generality.

With this, for a GSM $\mathcal{M}$ and a Σ_s data graph G_s with data values in $\mathcal{D}$, we define certain answers over graphs with null nodes as:

$$\square^{\mathbf{N}}_{\mathcal{M}}(Q, G_s) = \bigcap \left\{ Q(G_t) \;\middle|\; \begin{array}{c} (G_s, G_t) \models \mathcal{M} \\ \text{and } G_t \text{ over } \mathcal{D}_{\mathbf{N}} \end{array} \right\}$$

This corresponds to the standard data exchange setting [5, 20]: source instances do not have nulls, while nulls can appear in the targets.

How does this notion relate to certain answers $\square_{\mathcal{M}}(Q, G_s)$? Since we increase the domain of values, it is immediate that

$$\square^{\mathbf{N}}_{\mathcal{M}}(Q, G_s) \subseteq \square_{\mathcal{M}}(Q, G_s).$$

Thus, our approach can be seen as providing an underapproximation of query answering in the general case. What makes it attractive is that such an underapproximation can be found efficiently for data RPQs.

THEOREM 3. *If the domain of data values contains the null value $\mathbf{N}$, then data complexity of answering data RPQs under relational graph schema mappings (i.e., checking if $\bar{v} \in \square^{\mathbf{N}}_{\mathcal{M}}(Q, G_s)$) is in* NLOGSPACE. *Its combined complexity is in* PSPACE *for memory RPQs and in* PTIME *for equality RPQs.*

One has matching NLOGSPACE and PSPACE lower bounds as well, as evaluation of data RPQs is NLOGSPACE-hard in data complexity and PSPACE-hard in combined complexity. This theorem will follow from a more general result that provides an algorithm for query answering, even for a larger class of queries.

Recall that a relational GSM $\mathcal{M}$ over Σ_s and Σ_t consists of pairs (q, w) where q is an RPQ over Σ_s and $w \in \Sigma_t^*$. Given such a mapping and a Σ_s data graph G_s, a Σ_t data graph G_t is a *universal solution* for G_s under $\mathcal{M}$ if it is constructed by the following procedure:

1. compute dom$(\mathcal{M}, G_s)$ which is the set of all nodes appearing in query results $q(G_s)$, for $(q, w) \in \mathcal{M}$, and add all nodes of dom$(\mathcal{M}, G_s)$ to G_t;
2. then, for each pair $(q, a_1 \ldots, a_k)$ in $\mathcal{M}$, and each pair of nodes $(v, v') \in q(G_s)$, create fresh null nodes $v_1, \ldots, v_k$ and add the path $v a_1 v_1 a_2 \ldots v_{k-1} a_k v$ to G_t.

Note that all universal solutions are actually unique up to a renaming of node ids. Indeed, the only source of nondeterminism in the procedure is the choice of node ids for the newly created null nodes.

Just like the usual universal solutions in relational or XML data exchange, these solutions have homomorphisms into all other solutions. To show this, we first need to extend homomorphisms to data graphs with null nodes. Recall that a homomorphism between data graphs G and G' without null nodes was defined as a map $h : \mathcal{N} \rightarrow \mathcal{N}$ such that for each edge $\big((n_1, d_1), a, (n_2, d_2)\big)$ of G, the edge $\big((h(n_1), d_1), a, (h(n_2), d_2)\big)$ is in G'. We now say that a map $h : \mathcal{N} \rightarrow \mathcal{N}$ is a *homomorphism between graphs with nulls nodes* if for each edge $\big((n_1, d_1), a, (n_2, d_2)\big)$ of G, there is an edge $\big((h(n_1), d_1'), a, (h(n_2), d_2')\big)$ in G' such that either $d_i = d_i'$ or $d_i = \mathbf{N}$, for $i = 1, 2$. That is, non-null data values are preserved, but a homomorphism has the freedom to replace $\mathbf{N}$ with another data value. The lemma below justifies the name *universal*.

LEMMA 1. *If $\mathcal{M}$ is a relational mapping, G_s is a Σ_s data graph, G_t is a universal solution for G_s under $\mathcal{M}$ and G'_t is an arbitrary solution over $\mathcal{D}_\mathbf{N}$ for G_s under $\mathcal{M}$, then there is a homomorphism from G_t to G'_t that is the identity on* $\text{dom}(\mathcal{M}, G_s)$.

Our goal is to compute certain answers $\Box^\mathbf{N}_\mathcal{M}(Q, G_s)$ by evaluating a query Q over a universal solution G_t. This strategy works for queries that are preserved under homomorphisms. As before, Q is preserved under homomorphisms if, whenever we have two data graphs G and G' with null nodes and a homomorphism h from G to G', then for a tuple $\big((n_1, d_1), \ldots, (n_k, d_k)\big) \in Q(G)$, there is a tuple $\big((h(n_1), d'_1), \ldots, (h(n_k), d'_k)\big) \in Q(G')$, where $d_i = d'_i$ whenever $d_i \neq \mathbf{N}$.

The following is a standard observation that is often made in data exchange scenarios to enable efficient computation of certain answers.

THEOREM 4. *Let $\mathcal{M}$ be a relational GSM, G_s a Σ_s data graph over $\mathcal{D}$, and let G_t be a universal solution for it under $\mathcal{M}$. If Q is a query preserved under homomorphisms, then $\Box^\mathbf{N}_\mathcal{M}(Q, G_s)$ is the restriction of $Q(G_t)$ to tuples that do not contain any null nodes.*

Proof. If (x, y) is a pair of constant nodes such that $(x, y) \in Q(G_t)$, then the definition of G_t implies that x and y are nodes of G_s. If G'_t is an arbitrary solution for G_s under $\mathcal{M}$, by Lemma 1, there is a homomorphism from G_t to G'_t such that $h(x) = x$ and $h(y) = y$. Since Q is closed under homomorphism, this implies that $(x, y) \in Q(G'_t)$. Thus, $(x, y) \in \Box^\mathbf{N}_\mathcal{M}(Q, G_s)$.

Conversely, if $(x, y) \in \Box^\mathbf{N}_\mathcal{M}(Q, G_s)$, then x and y are nodes of G_s, and thus are constant nodes. Furthermore, since G_t is a solution, we conclude that $(x, y) \in Q(G_t)$, by the definition of certain answers. ☐

Theorem 4 gives us an algorithm for finding answers to queries preserved under homomorphism. First we construct a universal solution; for relational mappings, this can be done in NLOGSPACE. Then we evaluate Q on it, and then again in NLOGSPACE eliminate null nodes from the result. Thus, it is the data complexity of Q (as long as it is above NLOGSPACE) that determines the complexity of finding certain answers; for instance, if data complexity of Q is NLOGSPACE (or PTIME), then so is the data complexity of QUERYANSWERING_GSM over data domains containing null value $\mathbf{N}$.

Since the data complexity of data RPQs is in NLOGSPACE [30], the last bit that we need to finish the proof of Theorem 3 is the proposition below.

PROPOSITION 6. *Data RPQs are closed under homomorphisms on data graphs with null nodes.*

Proof sketch. It suffices to show that for a REM e, if we have a data path π and its homomorphic image $\pi' = h(\pi)$, then if $\delta(\pi)$ is in $L(e)$, then so is $\delta(\pi')$. This is done by induction on the clauses of the definition of $L(e)$, using the following claim. For any two data paths $w = d_0 a_1 d_1 \ldots d_{n-1} a_n d_n$ and $w' = d'_0 a_1 d'_1 \ldots d'_{n-1} a_n d'_n$ such that $d_i = d'_i$ whenever $d_i \neq \mathbf{N}$, for all REMs e', and for all valuations $\sigma_0, \sigma'_0, \sigma$ such that $\sigma_0(x) = \sigma'_0(x)$ whenever $\sigma_0(x) \neq \mathbf{N}$ and $(e, w, \sigma_0) \vdash \sigma$, there exists a valuation σ' such that $(e, w', \sigma'_0) \vdash \sigma'$ and $\sigma(x) = \sigma'(x)$ whenever $\sigma(x) \neq \mathbf{N}$. ☐

REMARK 1. We know that $\Box^\mathbf{N}_\mathcal{M}(Q, G_s)$ provides an approximation to $\Box_\mathcal{M}(Q, G_s)$, i.e., $\Box^\mathbf{N}_\mathcal{M}(Q, G_s) \subseteq \Box_\mathcal{M}(Q, G_s)$. But how good is such an approximation? The question is akin to those asked about approximations of certain answers over incomplete databases [22, 29] and, just like in those cases, precise theoretical answers are hard to obtain. For example, in the case of Boolean queries, whenever $\Box^\mathbf{N}_\mathcal{M}(Q, G_s) \neq \Box_\mathcal{M}(Q, G_s)$ – which is bound to happen due to the complexity mismatch – the approximation misses all the correct answers (since *false* is represented as $\emptyset$ and *true* as the singleton empty tuple $\{()\}$). To see how well such schemes actually perform the best one can do is an experimental study, as for instance was done in [22]. For now we have only studied theoretical aspects of such mappings, but the hope is for good quality approximations, given the fact that we have a minimal extension of the domain of values, with just one element.

REMARK 2. SQL nulls use three-valued logic, with truth values *true*, *false*, and *unknown*, and conditions $d = \mathbf{N}$ and $d \neq \mathbf{N}$ evaluate to *unknown*. Here we did not use the three-valued logic and instead made them evaluate to *false*. While this modification could make difference for some queries, for the language of data RPQs there is no change; this is why we chose the simpler way of handling nulls.

Indeed, let $\mathsf{eval}(c, \sigma)$ be the evaluation of condition c as we defined it (i.e., with both $d = \mathbf{N}$ and $d \neq \mathbf{N}$ being *false*). Let $\mathsf{eval}_{\text{SQL}}(c, \sigma)$ be the three-valued SQL evaluation of conditions. Under this evaluation, both $d = \mathbf{N}$ and $d \neq \mathbf{N}$ are *unknown*, and then *unknown* is propagated through $\wedge$ and $\vee$ by *unknown* $\wedge$ *true* = *unknown* $\vee$ *false* = *unknown*; *unknown* $\vee$ *true* = *true*; *unknown* $\wedge$ *false* = *false*. Then it is straightforward to see that $\mathsf{eval}(c, \sigma) = \textit{true}$ iff $\mathsf{eval}_{\text{SQL}}(c, \sigma) = \textit{true}$.

8. QUERIES WITHOUT INEQUALITIES

We now look at the behavior of two different languages for data graphs. First, in this section we look at restriction of data RPQs that forbids inequalities, and show that for them, query answering behaves better, at least for relational GSMs. In the next section we show that in contrast, the language that permits non-path patterns behaves rather badly with respect to query answering.

By $\text{REM}_=$ and $\text{REE}_=$ we mean restrictions of data RPQs based on regular expressions with memory and equality that only use equality comparisons and disallow inequality comparisons. That is, $\text{REM}_=$ queries are the same as memory RPQs, but $x^{\neq}$ is not allowed in conditions, and $\text{REE}_=$ queries are the same as equality RPQs, but expressions $e_{\neq}$ are not allowed.

Results of Section 6 tell us that data complexity of answering $\text{REM}_=$ and $\text{REE}_=$ queries under relational GSMs is in coNP. A better NLOGSPACE bound was given for data path queries in $\text{REE}_=$ (see Proposition 4), but not for queries outside this narrow class. We now show that tractable bounds can be obtained for *all* queries in $\text{REM}_=$ and $\text{REE}_=$ under relational mappings.

The idea here follows along the lines of the ideas of Section 7. We define a new kind of canonical solutions, which bear close resemblance to the universal solutions of Section 7 and play a very similar role. Formally, given a relational GSM $\mathcal{M}$ over Σ_s and Σ_t and a Σ_s data graph G_s, a Σ_t data graph G_t is a *least informative solution* for G_s under $\mathcal{M}$ if it is constructed by the following procedure:

1. compute $\text{dom}(\mathcal{M}, G_s)$ and add all nodes of $\text{dom}(\mathcal{M}, G_s)$ to G_t;
2. then, for each pair $(q, a_1 \dots, a_k)$ in $\mathcal{M}$, and each pair of nodes $(v, v') \in q(G_s)$, create fresh nodes $v_1, \dots, v_k$, with respective fresh data values $d_1, \dots, d_k$ and add the path $va_1v_1a_2 \dots v_{k-1}a_kv$ to G_t.

The main point of this definition is that the new nodes that are created during the procedure are populated with fresh and distinct data values instead of nulls as in the case for the universal solutions. Then we can prove an analog of Theorem 4:

THEOREM 5. *Let $\mathcal{M}$ be a relational GSM, G_s a Σ_s data graph and let G_t be a least informative solution for G_s under $\mathcal{M}$. Let Q be an REM$_=$ or an REE$_=$ query. Then $\Box_{\mathcal{M}}(Q, G_s)$ is the restriction of $Q(G_t)$ to tuples with values in $\text{dom}(\mathcal{M}, G_s)$.*

As before, this leads to an algorithm for computing certain answers. We first construct a least informative solution, which can be done in NLOGSPACE for relational mappings. Then we run the query on it, and remove from the output the tuples that use values outside of $\text{dom}(\mathcal{M}, G_s)$. This yields the following corollary:

COROLLARY 1. *For relational GSMs, data complexity of* QUERYANSWERING_GSM *is in* NLOGSPACE *for both* REM$_=$ *and* REE$_=$ *queries, and its combined complexity is in* PSPACE *for* REM$_=$ *queries and in* PTIME *for* REE$_=$ *queries.*

For arbitrary mappings, query answering of RPQs could be coNP-hard even without data values [12], so eliminating inequality would not give us tractability as in Theorem 1. It is still a valid question whether such restriction gives us decidability, in contrast with Theorem 1. This question appears to be quite hard, and we only have a result for REE$_=$.

PROPOSITION 7. *For arbitrary graph schema mappings, the problem* QUERYANSWERING_GSM *for* REE$_=$ *queries is in* coNP *for data complexity, and has elementary combined complexity.*

This result already requires an involved proof which establishes a small model property based on Ramsey theorem. This in particular accounts for the high combined complexity bound (which is quadruple exponential, due to Ramsey bounds). Full details are omitted here due to space constraints.

9. GRAPH XPATH

We now look at a different language for expressing queries on data graphs, that is not restricted to path patterns such as data RPQs. In fact languages for graph data such as Cypher of Neo4j [36] or navigational SPARQL [35] do allow non-path patterns.

As a concrete language to work with, we take Graph XPath (GXPath), that adapts the standard XML path language XPath [38] to work on graphs. This language is rather natural for expressing navigational properties that go beyond path patterns, and we have a good understanding of the expressive power of its fragments [30] and their static analysis [26]. GXPath has also been implemented and tested in a distributed environment [34].

There are several variations of GXPath, and we use a minimalistic one, as we prove an undecidability result: a fragment of core GXPath with data value comparisons, denoted by $\text{GXPath}_{\sim}^{\text{core}}$ (following the convention in the literature on data trees, we use $\sim$ to denote data value comparisons).

In defining the language, we assume that for every label $a \in \Sigma$, the alphabet also contains a label a^- which defines the inverse: $E_{a^-} = \{(v, v') \mid (v', v) \in E_a\}$. That is, each edge can be traversed in either direction. As usual for XPath, expressions include node expressions (denoted by φ, ψ) that select nodes, and path expressions (denoted by α, β) that select pairs of nodes. These are given by mutually recursive definitions below:

$$\begin{array}{rcl} \alpha, \beta & := & \varepsilon \mid a \mid a^* \mid \alpha \cdot \beta \mid \alpha \cup \beta \mid \alpha_= \mid \alpha_{\neq} \mid [\varphi] \\ \varphi, \psi & := & \neg\varphi \mid \varphi \wedge \psi \mid \varphi \vee \psi \mid \langle \alpha \rangle \end{array}$$

Given a data graph $G = \langle V, E \rangle$, the semantics of a path expression is $[\![\alpha]\!]_G \subseteq V \times V$, and the semantics of a node expression expression is $[\![\varphi]\!]_G \subseteq V$. Precise definitions of those are in Figure 1. Intuitively, ε defines the set of pairs (v, v), while a defines E_a and a^* defines its transitive closure. Expressions $\alpha \cdot \beta$ and $\alpha \cup \beta$ define composition and union, and $\alpha_=$ (or $\alpha_{\neq}$) gives pairs of nodes defined by α that carry the same (or different) data value. Two types of expressions connect path and node expressions: $\langle \alpha \rangle$ is the first projection of the semantics of α (i.e., nodes from which a path satisfying α can start), and $[\varphi]$ gives pairs of nodes (v, v) satisfying φ. Node expressions are closed under Boolean operations.

Note that this fragment excludes many features of full GXPath, such as negation of path expressions $\neg\alpha$, arbitrary transitive closure α^*, and even simpler features such as checking for a constant data value and intersection of paths. But even for this simple fragment of GXPath, query answering is undecidable in data complexity for the simplest possible mappings.

THEOREM 6. *There is a relational GSM $\mathcal{M}$ that is both LAV and GAV and a $GXPath_{\sim}^{core}$ node expression φ so that the problem* QUERYANSWERING_GSM$(\mathcal{M}, \varphi)$ *is undecidable.*

The problem is undecidable for path expressions as well, since $v \in \Box_{\mathcal{M}}(\varphi, G)$ iff $(v, v) \in \Box_{\mathcal{M}}([\varphi], G)$. The proof of Theorem 6 is based on the following.

LEMMA 2. *There is a fixed labeling alphabet Σ and a $GXPath_{\sim}^{core}$ node expression φ such that the following problem is undecidable: given a data graph G over Σ and a node v, is there a data graph $G' \supseteq G$ such that $v \notin [\![\varphi]\!]_{G'}$.*

Theorem 6 is an immediate consequence of Lemma 2: take $\mathcal{M}$ to be $\{(a, a) \mid a \in \Sigma\}$ (i.e., the source and target alphabets are the same). Then $v \notin \Box_{\mathcal{M}}(\varphi, G)$ iff $v \notin [\![\varphi]\!]_{G'}$ for some $G' \supseteq G$.

Proof idea (Lemma 2). We prove a stronger statement. A labeled *tree* is said to have the *non-repeating property* if no

Path expressions	Node expression
$\llbracket \varepsilon \rrbracket_G = \{(v,v) \mid v \in V\}$	
$\llbracket a \rrbracket_G = \{(v,v') \mid (v,a,v') \in E\}$	$\llbracket \langle \alpha \rangle \rrbracket_G = \{v \mid \exists v' \, (v,v') \in \llbracket \alpha \rrbracket_G\}$
$\llbracket a^* \rrbracket_G = \{(v,v') \mid \exists\, v \xrightarrow{\pi} v' \text{ with } \lambda(\pi) \in a^*\}$	$\llbracket \neg\varphi \rrbracket_G = V - \llbracket \varphi \rrbracket_G$
$\llbracket \alpha \cdot \beta \rrbracket_G = \llbracket \alpha \rrbracket_G \circ \llbracket \beta \rrbracket_G$	$\llbracket \varphi \wedge \psi \rrbracket_G = \llbracket \varphi \rrbracket_G \cap \llbracket \psi \rrbracket_G$
$\llbracket \alpha \cup \beta \rrbracket_G = \llbracket \alpha \rrbracket_G \cup \llbracket \beta \rrbracket_G$	$\llbracket \varphi \vee \psi \rrbracket_G = \llbracket \varphi \rrbracket_G \cup \llbracket \psi \rrbracket_G$
$\llbracket [\varphi] \rrbracket_G = \{(v,v) \in G \mid v \in \llbracket \varphi \rrbracket_G\}$	
$\llbracket \alpha_{=} \rrbracket_G = \{(v,v') \in \llbracket \alpha \rrbracket_G \mid \delta(v) = \delta(v')\}$	
$\llbracket \alpha_{\neq} \rrbracket_G = \{(v,v') \in \llbracket \alpha \rrbracket_G \mid \delta(v) \neq \delta(v')\}$	

Figure 1: Semantics of $\text{GXPath}_{\sim}^{\text{core}}$ with respect to $G = \langle V, E \rangle$

alphabet letter can label two different children of the same node. Then Lemma 2 is true under the following assumptions: G is a tree with the non-repeating property, v is its root, all data values in G are distinct, and if there exists $G' \supseteq G$ satisfying $v \notin \llbracket \varphi \rrbracket_{G'}$, then such a G' can be chosen to be a tree with the non-repeating property and the same root v.

To show this, as in Theorem 1, we use reduction from PCP. We assume that PCP instances $\{(u_r, v_r) \mid 1 \leq r \leq n\}$ are over the alphabet $\{a, b\}$, and in the encoding we use additional separator labels t, $t_{\#}$, s, v, $\#$, $\leftarrow$, $\rightarrow$, $\leftarrow_{\#}$, $\rightarrow_{\#}$, m, id. Some of them have the same meaning as in the proof of Theorem 1, but new ones are needed to encode the instance in a tree structure: $t_{\#}$ marks the end of the encoding of a list of pairs from the instance; $\leftarrow$ and $\rightarrow$ mark tree branches that encode u_is and v_is, and $\leftarrow_{\#}$ and $\rightarrow_{\#}$ respectively terminate these branches. The PCP instance is encoded as a source tree:

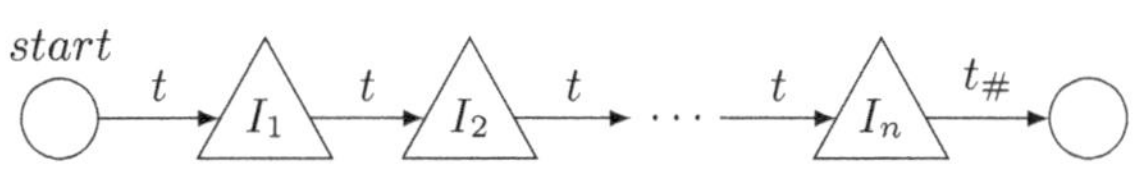

where each I_r encodes the pair (u_r, v_r) as follows:

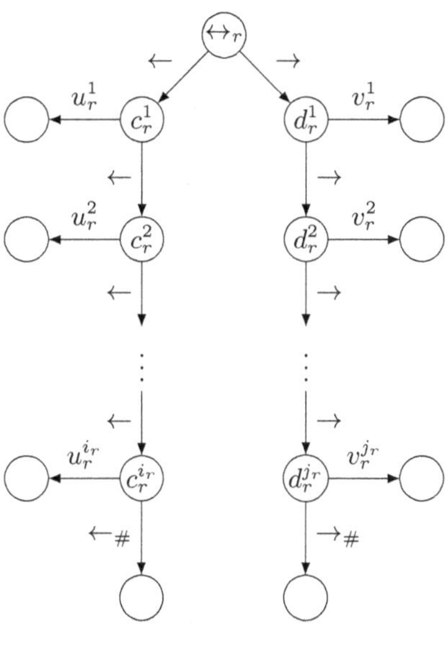

In the encoding of the entire PCP instance, the "horizontal" path from the *start* node goes via roots of trees I_r. Additionally, data values of all the nodes are pairwise distinct.

The idea is then to construct a node expression φ such that the PCP instance is satisfiable iff there exists a data tree $G' \supseteq G$ rooted at *start* with the non-repeating property satisfying $start \notin \llbracket \varphi \rrbracket_{G'}$. The construction uses the idea of attaching the solution and the verification sections to G: the solution section codes a possible solution to the PCP instance and the verification section verifies that it is a solution. The query φ essentially looks for "errors" in the construction of these additional sections. If $start \notin \llbracket \varphi \rrbracket_{G'}$, it means there are no errors, and thus a solution was found. The construction is somewhat lengthy and involved, and is given in the appendix. □

Static analysis of GXPath In addition to applications in query answering under GSMs, we can use Lemma 2 to answer some open questions on static analysis of GXPath expressions. Typical static analysis problems are:

- *satisfiability*: given an expression φ, is there a data graph G such that $\llbracket \varphi \rrbracket_G \neq \emptyset$?, and
- *containment*: given two expressions φ and ψ, is it true that $\llbracket \varphi \rrbracket_G \subseteq \llbracket \psi \rrbracket_G$ for every G?

These problems have been studied in depth for XPath on trees, and more recently they were looked at in the context of GXPath, with [26] showing several undecidability results for *regular* GXPath. This more expressive language allows path expressions α^*, i.e., transitive closure of arbitrary path expressions. In our case of *core* GXPath, transitive closure only applies to alphabet labels. For core GXPath, decidability of containment and satisfiability was not known.

We can now use techniques of Lemma 2 to strengthen results of [26] and prove undecidability of static analysis of core GXPath with data value comparisons.

THEOREM 7. *Both satisfiability and containment problems are undecidable for* $\text{GXPath}_{\sim}^{\text{core}}$.

Proof sketch. We give a proof for the satisfiability problem; undecidability of containment easily follows from it. We use the strong version of Lemma 2 described in the sketch of the proof of Theorem 6. Let Σ and φ be the schema and query fixed by the statement of the lemma. Let G be a data tree with the non-repeating property, all distinct data values, and root v such that if there exists a data graph $G' \supseteq G$ such that $v \notin \llbracket \varphi \rrbracket_{G'}$, then such a G' can be chosen to be a tree with the non-repeating property whose root is also v. To prove the theorem, we define a new $\text{GXPath}_{\sim}^{\text{core}}$ formula φ' that depends on φ and G such that φ' is satisfiable iff there exists a data graph $G' \supseteq G$ such that $v \notin \llbracket \varphi \rrbracket_{G'}$.

For this, we define two queries, φ_G and φ_δ, that will ensure that any witness for φ' is a data graph that contains G. The goal for φ_G is to ensure that any data graph satisfying it contains the topological structure of G. The formula φ_G is defined inductively: for a single-node tree it is $\langle\varepsilon\rangle$, and for a tree with children of the root labeled $a_1, \ldots, a_n$ and having subtrees $G_1, \ldots, G_n$, we define φ_G as $\langle a_1 \cdot [\varphi_{G_1}]\rangle \wedge \ldots \wedge \langle a_n \cdot [\varphi_{G_n}]\rangle$.

For φ_δ, let w_x, for a node x of G, be the label of the unique path from the root to x in G. We define $\varphi_\delta = \bigwedge\{\neg\langle w_y \cdot (w_y^- \cdot w_z)_=\rangle \mid y, z \text{ nodes of } G \text{ and } y \neq z\}$. Then one can show that G embeds homomorphically into any graph G' that satisfies φ_G and, if φ_δ in addition holds in G', then G is contained in G', up to a renaming of data values and nodes ids.

With this, we define φ' as $\varphi_G \wedge \varphi_\delta \wedge \neg\varphi$. It is then routine to verify that φ' is satisfiable iff there exists a data graph $G' \supseteq G$ such that $v \notin [\![\varphi]\!]_{G'}$. $\square$

10. CONCLUSIONS

Our main conclusion is that under graph schema mappings, answering queries that combine navigation and data is very different from answering purely navigational queries. Undecidability arises very easily; even under strong restrictions one has intractability of query answering; and achieving tractability requires new techniques that do not mirror those known for relational and XML data.

There are several directions in which we would like to extend this work. First of all, now that we understand what is needed to achieve tractability for the abstraction of data graph, we would like to see how these restrictions look in the case of property graphs of Neo4j [36] and language and constraint formalisms advocated by LDBC [27]. The eventual goal of such a project is to build an integration/exchange system on top of a commercial graph database.

Our results suggest viewing target databases as relational, at least from the point of view of mappings. An alternative of going from relations to graphs has been explored in [11], although mainly intractability results were shown. It would be interesting to see if useful restrictions on relational-to-graph mappings can be found, perhaps using techniques developed here.

We would also like to investigate the use of SQL nulls, as exploited here, in relational data exchange systems. Such systems normally use marked nulls, which need to be implemented on top of relational DBMSs. The advantage of using SQL nulls is that no additional implementation of relational database features is needed, and they appear to allow efficient answering of a rather large class of queries in integration and exchange scenarios.

Acknowledgments We thank referees for their comments. This work was supported by EPSRC grants M025268 and N023056.

11. REFERENCES

[1] S. Abiteboul, R. Hull, and V. Vianu. *Foundations of Databases.* Addison-Wesley, 1995.

[2] R. Angles, C. Gutiérrez. Survey of graph database models. *ACM Comput. Surv.* 40(1): (2008).

[3] R. Angles, M. Arenas, P. Barcelo, A. Hogan, J. Reutter, D. Vrgoč. Foundations of modern graph query languages. arXiv preprint 1610.06264, 2016.

[4] S. Amano, C. David, L. Libkin, F. Murlak. XML schema mappings: data exchange and metadata management. *J. ACM* 61(2): 12:1-12:48 (2014).

[5] M. Arenas, P. Barceló, L. Libkin, F. Murlak. *Foundations of Data Exchange.* Cambridge Univ. Press, 2014.

[6] M. Arenas, P. Barceló, J. Reutter. Query languages for data exchange: beyond unions of conjunctive queries. *Theory of Computing Systems* 49(2):489–564 (2011).

[7] P. Barceló, G. Fontaine, A. W. Lin. Expressive path queries on graphs with data. *LMCS*, 11(4:1) 2015.

[8] P. Barceló, J. Pérez, J. Reutter. Schema mappings and data exchange for graph databases. In *ICDT 2013*, pages 189-200.

[9] Z. Bellahsene, A. Bonifati, E. Rahm, eds. *Schema Matching and Mapping.* Springer, 2011.

[10] M. Bojanczyk. Automata for data words and data trees. In *RTA 2010*, pages 1-4.

[11] I. Boneva, A. Bonifati, R. Ciucanu. Graph data exchange with target constraints. In *EDBT/ICDT Workshop GraphQ*, 2015, pages 171–176.

[12] D. Calvanese, G. De Giacomo, M. Lenzerini, M. Vardi. View-based query processing and constraint satisfaction. *LICS 2000*, pages 361–371.

[13] D. Calvanese, G. De Giacomo, M. Lenzerini, M. Vardi. Rewriting of regular expressions and regular path queries. *J. Comput. Syst. Sci.* 64(3): 443-465 (2002).

[14] D. Calvanese, G. De Giacomo, M. Lenzerini, M. Vardi. On simplification of schema mappings. *J. Comput. Syst. Sci.* 79(6): 816-834 (2013).

[15] S. Cassidy. Generalizing XPath for directed graphs. In *Extreme Markup Languages*, 2003.

[16] I. Cruz, A. Mendelzon, P. Wood. A graphical query language supporting recursion. In *SIGMOD'87*, pages 323–330.

[17] C. J. Date and H. Darwen. *A Guide to the SQL Standard.* Addison-Wesley, 1996.

[18] S. Demri, R. Lazic. LTL with the freeze quantifier and register automata. *ACM TOCL* 10(3): (2009).

[19] A. Doan, A. Halevy, Z. Ives. *Principles of Data Integration.* Morgan Kaufmann, 2012.

[20] R. Fagin, P. Kolaitis, R. Miller, and L. Popa. Data exchange: semantics and query answering. *Theoretical Computer Science*, 336(1):89–124, 2005.

[21] N. Francis, L. Segoufin, C. Sirangelo. Datalog rewritings of regular path queries using views. In *ICDT 2014*, pages 107-118.

[22] P. Guagliardo and L. Libkin. Making SQL queries correct on incomplete databases: A feasibility study. In *PODS 2016*, pages 211–223.

[23] L. M. Haas, M. A. Hernández, H. Ho, L. Popa, and M. Roth. Clio grows up: from research prototype to industrial tool. In *SIGMOD*, pages 805–810, 2005.

[24] J. Hellings, B. Kuijpers, J. Van den Bussche, X. Zhang. Walk logic as a framework for path query languages on graph databases. In *ICDT 2013*, pages 117–128.

[25] M. Kaminski and N. Francez. Finite memory automata. *TCS*, 134(2):329-363, 1994.

[26] E. Kostylev, J. Reutter, D. Vrgoč. Containment of data graph queries. In *ICDT 2014*, pages 131–142.

[27] LDBC. Linked Data Benchmark Council. http://www.ldbcouncil.org.

[28] M. Lenzerini. Data integration: a theoretical perspective. In *PODS 2002*, pages 233–246.

[29] L. Libkin. SQL's three-valued logic and certain answers. *ACM TODS*, 41(1) (2016), 1–28.

[30] L. Libkin, W. Martens, and D. Vrgoč. Querying graphs with data. *Journal of the ACM* 63(2): 14 (2016).

[31] L. Libkin, T. Tan, D. Vrgoč. Regular expressions for data words. *JCSS* 81(7): 1278-1297 (2015).

[32] A. Mądry. Data exchange: On the complexity of answering queries with inequalities. *IPL*, 94 (2005), 253–257.

[33] B. Marnette, G. Mecca, P. Papotti, S. Raunich, and D. Santoro. ++Spicy: an opensource tool for second-generation schema mapping and data exchange. *PVLDB*, 4 (2011),1438–1441.

[34] M. Nolé, C. Sartiani. A distributed implementation of GXPath. In *EDBT/ICDT Workshops 2016*.

[35] J. Pérez, M. Arenas, C. Gutierrez. nSPARQL: A navigational language for RDF. In *J. Web Sem.* 8(4): 255–270 (2010).

[36] I. Robinson, J. Webber, E. Eifrem. *Graph Databases.* O'Reilly, 2013.

[37] L. Segoufin. Static analysis of XML processing with data values. *SIGMOD Record* 36(1): 31–38 (2007).

[38] XML Path Language (XPath). www.w3.org/TR/xpath.

Dependencies for Graphs

Wenfei Fan
University of Edinburgh and Beihang University
wenfei@inf.ed.ac.uk

Ping Lu
BDBC, Beihang University
luping@buaa.edu.cn

ABSTRACT

This paper proposes a class of dependencies for graphs, referred to as *graph entity dependencies* (GEDs). A GED is a combination of a graph pattern and an attribute dependency. In a uniform format, GEDs express graph functional dependencies with constant literals to catch inconsistencies, and keys carrying id literals to identify entities in a graph.

We revise the chase for GEDs and prove its Church-Rosser property. We characterize GED satisfiability and implication, and establish the complexity of these problems and the validation problem for GEDs, in the presence and absence of constant literals and id literals. We also develop a sound and complete axiom system for finite implication of GEDs. In addition, we extend GEDs with built-in predicates or disjunctions, to strike a balance between the expressive power and complexity. We settle the complexity of the satisfiability, implication and validation problems for the extensions.

Keywords

graph dependencies; conditional functional dependencies; keys; EGDs; TGDs; satisfiability, implication, validation; axiom system; built-in predicates; disjunction

1. INTRODUCTION

As primitive integrity constraints for relations, functional dependencies (FDs) are found in almost every database textbook. FDs specify a fundamental part of the semantics of data, and have proven important in conceptual design, query optimization, and prevention of update anomalies, among other things. Moreover, FDs and their extensions such as conditional functional dependencies (CFDs) [21] and denial constraints [3] have been widely used in practice to detect semantic inconsistencies and repair data.

Among our most familiar FDs are keys. As a special case of FDs, keys provide an invariant connection between tuples and the real-world entities they represent, and are crucial to data models and transformations.

PODS '17, May 14–19, 2017, Chicago, IL, USA.

DOI: http://dx.doi.org/10.1145/3034786.3056114

The need for FDs and keys is also evident in graphs. Unlike relational data, real-life graphs often do not come with a schema, and dependencies such as FDs and keys provide one of few means for us to specify the integrity and semantics of the data. They are useful in consistency checking, spam detection, entity resolution and knowledge base expansion.

Example 1: Consider the following from knowledge bases and social networks, which are modeled as graphs.

(1) Consistency checking. It is common to find inconsistencies in real-life knowledge bases, *e.g.,*

- psychologist Tony Gibson is credited for creating Ghetto Blaster, while the video game was actually created by programmer Tony 'Gibbo' Gibson (Yago3);
- both Saint Petersburg and Helsinki are labeled as the capital of Finland (Yago3);
- it is claimed that all birds can fly, and that moa are birds, although moa are "flightless" (DBPedia);
- Philip Sclater is marked as both a child and a parent of William Lutley Sclater (DBPedia).

As shown in [23], such inconsistencies can be captured by FDs defined on graphs, referred to as GFDs.

(2) Spam detection. Fake accounts are common in social networks [14]. A rule for identifying spam is as follows.

- If account x' is confirmed fake, both accounts x and x' like blogs $P_1, \ldots, P_k$, x posts blog y, x' posts y', and if both y and y' have a peculiar keyword c, then x can also be identified fake.

Such rules can also be expressed as GFDs [23].

(3) Knowledge base expansion [19]. We want to decide whether to add a newly extracted album to a knowledge base G. To avoid duplicates, we need keys to identify an album entity in G, defined in terms of

ψ_1: its title and the id of its primary artist, or
ψ_2: its title and the year of initial release.

These can be expressed as keys for graphs studied in [19]. Note that the title of an album and the name of its artist cannot uniquely identify an album. For instance, an American band and a British band are both called "Bleach", and both bands had an album "Bleach".

To cope with ψ_1, we also need a key to identify artists:

ψ_3: the name of the artist, and the id of an album recorded by the artist.

As opposed to our familiar keys for relations, these keys are "recursively defined": to identify an album, we may need to identify its primary artist, and vice versa. □

Dependencies	Satisfiability	Implication	Validation	Connection with GEDs
GEDs	coNP-complete (Th. 3)	NP-complete (Th. 5)	coNP-complete (Th. 6)	$Q[\bar{x}](X \to Y)$
GFDs	coNP-complete (Th. 3)	NP-complete (Th. 5)	coNP-complete (Th. 6)	GEDs without id literals
GKeys	coNP-complete (Th. 3)	NP-complete (Th. 5)	coNP-complete (Th. 6)	$Q[\bar{x}](X \to x.\mathsf{id} = y.\mathsf{id})$
$\mathsf{GED_xs}$	coNP-complete (Th. 3)	NP-complete (Th. 5)	coNP-complete (Th. 6)	GEDs without constant literals
$\mathsf{GFD_xs}$	$O(1)$ (Th. 3)	NP-complete (Th. 5)	coNP-complete (Th. 6)	GFDs without constant literals
GDCs	Σ_2^p-complete (Th. 8)	Π_2^p-complete (Th. 8)	coNP-complete (Th. 8)	adding built-in predicates
$\mathsf{GED^\vee s}$	Σ_2^p-complete (Th. 9)	Π_2^p-complete (Th. 9)	coNP-complete (Th. 9)	disjunctive Y in $Q[\bar{x}](X \to Y)$

Table 1: Complexity for reasoning about GEDs

Moreover, FDs and keys help us optimize queries that are costly on large graphs in the real world, *e.g.,* Facebook, which have billions of nodes and trillions of edges [27].

Keys and FDs on graphs are a departure from their relational counterparts. (1) A relational FD $R(X \to Y)$ is defined on a relation schema R with attributes X and Y, where R specifies the "scope" of the FD, *i.e.,* $X \to Y$ is to be applied to tuples in an instance of R. In contrast, graphs are semistructured and often schemaless. To cope with this, we need a combination of (a) a topological constraint to identify entities, *i.e.,* to specify its "scope", and (b) an "FD" on the attributes of the entities identified. (2) Relational FDs and keys are "value-based", while keys and FDs for graphs are often necessarily "id-based" as shown by ψ_1–ψ_3 of Example 1. That is, they are based on node identity. In particular, if two vertices are identified as the same entity, then they must have the same attributes and edges.

There has been work on FDs for RDF [2,13,16,28,30,32,42] in particular and for general property graphs [23] in general, and on keys for RDF [19]. However, many questions remain open. For example, as opposed to relational FDs and keys, none of these FD proposals can express keys for graphs [19].

The practical need calls for a full treatment of the topic, to answer the following questions. (1) Is there a simple class of graph dependencies for us to uniformly express FDs and keys? (2) Can we adapt the chase [39] to reason about the dependencies? (3) What is the complexity of fundamental problems associated with the dependencies? (4) Is there a finite axiom system for their implication analysis, like Armstrong's axioms for traditional FDs [5]? (5) How can we strike a balance between their expressivity and complexity?

Contributions. This paper tackles these questions.

(1) GEDs. We propose a class of dependencies, referred to as *graph entity dependencies* and denoted by GEDs (Section 3). A GED is a combination of (a) a graph pattern Q as a topological constraint, and (b) an "FD" $X \to Y$ with sets X and Y of equality literals. Pattern Q identifies a set of entities in a graph, and the FD is enforced on these entities. GEDs may specify conditions carrying literals with constants, like relational CFDs [21]. They may carry id literals to identify vertices in a graph, beyond equality on attribute values.

GEDs subsume GFDs of [23] and keys of [19] as special cases (subject to adaption of graph pattern matching with graph homomorphism instead of subgraph isomorphism, to uniformly express GFDs and keys; see Section 3). They can express traditional FDs, CFDs and equality-generating dependencies (EGDs [7]), when relations are represented as graphs. That is, GEDs can do the job of keys, FDs, CFDs and EGDs for graph-structured data, *e.g.,* to specify integrity, detect inconsistencies, identify entities and optimize queries.

(2) The chase revised. We extend the chase [39] to GEDs (Section 4). Chasing with GEDs is more involved than with traditional FDs: it may run into conflicts introduced by id literals or constant literals, and may "generate" new attributes when enforcing GEDs on a schemaless graph. Nonetheless, we show that the chase with GEDs is finite and has the Church-Rosser property. That is, all chasing sequences of a graph (pattern) by a set of GEDs are finite and yield the same result, regardless of the order of GEDs applied.

(3) Classical problems for GEDs. We investigate three fundamental problems associated with GEDs (Section 5).

(a) The *satisfiability* problem is to decide, given a set Σ of GEDs, whether there exists a nonempty finite model G of Σ that satisfies Σ, denoted by $G \models \Sigma$ as usual.

(b) The *implication* problem is to decide whether a set Σ of GEDs entails another GED φ, denoted by $\Sigma \models \varphi$, *i.e.,* for any finite graph G, if $G \models \Sigma$, then $G \models \varphi$.

(c) The *validation* problem is to decide, given a finite graph G and a set Σ of GEDs, whether $G \models \Sigma$.

These problems not only are of theoretical interest, but also find practical applications. The satisfiability analysis helps us check whether a set of GEDs makes sense before the GEDs are used as rules for data cleaning or query optimization. The implication analysis serves as an optimization strategy to get rid of redundant rules. The validation analysis can detect violations of GEDs, and catch "dirty" entities.

To understand where the complexity arises, we consider two dichotomies when studying these problems:

- the presence of id literals vs. their absence, and
- the presence of constant values vs. their absence.

For instance, keys of [19] are recursively defined in terms of id literals while GFDs of [23] are not. In these settings, we characterize GED satisfiability and implication, based on the chase. We also establish complexity bounds of these problems for GEDs, GFDs, keys and other sub-classes, all matching (see Table 1). As opposed to relational FDs, these problems are all intractable for GEDs, and the intractability is robust even for restricted special cases. The complexity is, however, comparable to, *e.g.,* (a) relational CFDs, for which the satisfiability and implication problems are NP-complete and coNP-complete, respectively [21], and (b) EGDs, for which the implication problem is NP-complete [8].

(4) Finite axiomatizability. We study the finite axiomatizability of GEDs (Section 6). One naturally wants a finite set $\mathcal{A}$ of inference rules that is sound and complete for the implication analysis of GEDs, along the same lines as Armstrong's axioms for relational FDs (see [1]). That is, for any set Σ of GEDs and another GED φ, $\Sigma \models \varphi$ if and only if φ is provable

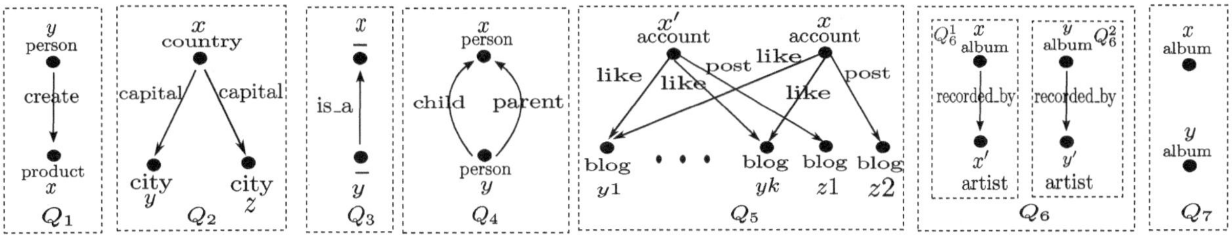

Figure 1: Graph patterns

from Σ using $\mathcal{A}$. Here we focus on finite graphs and study finite implication, rather than unrestricted implication.

We provide a set of six inference rules for GEDs, and show that it is sound and complete for GED implication analyses, based on the revised chase. We also show that the axiom system is independent (non-redundant and minimal), *i.e.*, removing any rule makes it no longer complete.

(5) Extensions. To strike a balance between the expressivity and complexity, we investigate extensions of GEDs (Section 7). We extend GEDs by supporting

- built-in predicates $=, \neq, <, >, \leq, \geq$ (GDCs); or
- limited disjunction of literals (GED$^\vee$s).

We can express, for instance, denial constraints [3] as GDCs, disjunctive EGDs [17] as GED$^\vee$s, and "domain constraints" for attributes of an entity to have a finite domain as both GDCs and GED$^\vee$s, among other things.

With the increased expressive power, the extensions increase the complexity of static analyses. We show that their satisfiability and implication problems become Σ_2^p-complete and Π_2^p-complete, as opposed to coNP-complete and NP-complete for GEDs, respectively. Their validation problems remain coNP-complete, the same as for GEDs (Table 1).

The dependency classes studied in the paper and their complexity results are summarized in Table 1, annotated with their corresponding theorems. This work is a preliminary step toward developing a dependency theory for graphs. The intractability results reveal the challenges inherent to entities with a graph structure. The revised chase, characterizations of satisfiability and implication, and axiom system provide insight into the analyses of graph dependencies.

The related work will be discussed in Section 8.

2. PRELIMINARIES

Before we define GEDs, we first review some basic notations. Assume three countably infinite sets Γ, Υ and U of labels, attributes and constants, respectively.

Graphs. A *graph* G is specified as (V, E, L, F_A), where (a) V is a finite set of nodes; (b) $E \subseteq V \times \Gamma \times V$ is a finite set of edges, in which (v, ι, v') denotes an edge from node v to v', and the edge is labeled with ι, referred to as its *label*; (c) each node $v \in V$ has label $L(v)$ from Γ; and (d) each node $v \in V$ carries a tuple $F_A(v) = (A_1 = a_1, \ldots, A_n = a_n)$ of *attributes* of a finite arity, where $A_i \in \Upsilon$ and $a_i \in U$, written as $v.A_i = a_i$, and $A_i \neq A_j$ if $i \neq j$. In particular, each v has a special attribute id denoting its *node identity*.

That is, we consider finite directed graphs in which nodes and edges are labeled. Nodes carry attributes for, *e.g.*, properties and keywords and rating, as in property graphs. Unlike relational databases, we assume no schema for graphs. Hence for an attribute $A \in \Upsilon$ and a node $v \in V$, $v.A$ may not exist, except that v has a unique v.id as found in practice.

Graph patterns. A *graph pattern* is a directed graph $Q[\bar{x}] = (V_Q, E_Q, L_Q)$, where (1) V_Q (resp. E_Q) is a finite set of pattern nodes (resp. edges) as before; (2) L_Q is a function that assigns a label $L_Q(u)$ to each node $u \in V_Q$; and (3) $\bar{x}$ denotes the nodes in V_Q as a list of variables.

Labels of pattern nodes and edges are drawn from Γ. Moreover, we allow wildcard '_' as a special label in Q.

A pattern $Q_2[\bar{y}]$ is a *copy* of $Q_1[\bar{x}]$ via a bijection f: $\bar{x} \mapsto \bar{y}$ if $Q_2[\bar{y}]$ is $Q_1[\bar{x}]$ with variables renamed by f. More specifically, let $Q_1[\bar{x}] = (V_{Q1}, E_{Q1}, L_{Q1})$ and $Q_2[\bar{y}] = (V_{Q2}, E_{Q2}, L_{Q2})$. Then (a) $\bar{x}$ and $\bar{y}$ are disjoint, and (b) f is an isomorphism from Q_1 to Q_2; *i.e.*, for each $x \in \bar{x}$, $L_{Q1}(x) = L_{Q2}(f(x))$; and (x_1, ι, x_2) is an edge in E_{Q_1} if and only if $(f(x_1), \iota, f(x_2))$ is in E_{Q_2}, with the same label ι.

Example 2: Figure 1 depicts seven graph patterns: (1) $Q_1[x, y]$ specifies a person entity and a product entity, which are connected by a create edge; similarly for $Q_2[x, y, z]$ and $Q_4[x, y]$; (2) $Q_3[x, y]$ depicts a generic is_a relationship between two entities labeled with wildcard '_'; (3) $Q_5[x, x', z_1, z_2, y_1, \ldots, y_k]$ specifies two accounts x and x', $k+2$ blogs $z_1, z_2, y_1, \ldots, y_k$ and their relationships; (4) $Q_6[x, x', y, y']$ consists of (a) a pattern $Q_6^1[x, x']$ with variables x and x', specifying a relationship between an album entity x and an artist entity x'; and (b) a copy $Q_6^2[y, y']$ of $Q_6^1[x, x']$ with variables renamed; similarly for $Q_7[x, y]$. □

Matches. We say that a label ι *matches* ι', denoted by $\iota \asymp \iota'$, if either (a) ι and ι' are in Γ and $\iota = \iota'$, or (b) $\iota' \in \Gamma$ and ι is '_', *i.e.*, wildcard matches any label in Γ.

A *match* of pattern $Q[\bar{x}]$ in graph G is a homomorphism h from Q to G such that (a) for each node $u \in V_Q$, $L_Q(u) \asymp L(h(u))$; and (b) for each edge $e = (u, \iota, u')$ in Q, there exists an edge $e' = (h(u), \iota', h(u'))$ in G such that $\iota \asymp \iota'$. Note that when ι is '_', there may exist multiple edges e' with $\iota \asymp \iota'$. The match picks one of them, and denotes it by $h(\iota_v^u)$.

Abusing the notations, we also denote the match as a vector $h(\bar{x})$ if it is clear from the context, where $h(\bar{x})$ consists of $h(x)$ for all variables $x \in \bar{x}$. Intuitively, $h(\bar{x})$ is a list of entities identified by pattern Q in graph G.

3. GRAPH ENTITY DEPENDENCIES

We now define *graph entity dependencies* (GEDs).

GEDs. A GED φ is defined as $Q[\bar{x}](X \to Y)$, where $Q[\bar{x}]$ is a graph pattern, and X and Y are two (possibly empty) sets of literals of $\bar{x}$; we refer to $Q[\bar{x}]$ and $X \to Y$ as the *pattern* and FD of φ, respectively.

A *literal* of $\bar{x}$ is one of the following: for $x, y \in \bar{x}$,

(a) *constant literal* $x.A = c$, where c is a constant in U, and A is an attribute in Υ that is not id;

(b) *variable literal* $x.A = y.B$, where A and B are attributes in Υ that are not id; or

(c) id *literal* $x.\mathsf{id} = y.\mathsf{id}$.

Intuitively, GED φ is a combination of (1) a *topological constraint* imposed by pattern Q, to identify entities in a graph, and (2) an FD $X \to Y$, to be applied to the entities identified by Q. Constant literals $x.A = c$ enforce bindings of semantically related constants, along the same lines as relational CFDs [21]. An id literal $x.\mathsf{id} = y.\mathsf{id}$ states that x and y denote the same vertex (entity).

Example 3: We can use GEDs to detect the inconsistencies, catch spam and identify entities observed in Example 1. These GEDs are defined with graph patterns of Fig. 1.

(1) GED $\varphi_1 = Q_1[x, y](X_1 \to Y_1)$. Here X_1 consists of a single constant literal $x.\mathsf{type}$ = "video game", Y_1 consists of a literal $y.\mathsf{type}$ = "programmer", and type is an attribute of person and product (not shown in Q_1). It states that a video game can only be created by programmers.

(2) GED $\varphi_2 = Q_2[x, y, z](\emptyset \to y.\mathsf{name} = z.\mathsf{name})$. It says that if a country x has two capitals y and z, then y and z must have the same name. Here name is an attribute, X is empty, and Y consists of a single variable literal.

(3) GED $\varphi_3 = Q_3[x, y](x.A = x.A \to y.A = x.A)$, where A is an attribute of x, *e.g.*, can_fly. It says that if y is_a x and if x has property A, then y inherits $x.A$, *i.e.*, y also has attribute A and $y.A = x.A$. Note that x and y are labeled '_', representing generic entities regardless of labels.

(4) GED $\varphi_4 = Q_4[x, y](\emptyset \to \mathsf{false})$, where false is a syntactic sugar for Boolean constant (see details shortly). It states that pattern Q_4 is "illegal", *i.e.*, no person can be both a child and a parent of another person.

GEDs φ_1–φ_4 catch the errors described in Example 1, *e.g.*, φ_3 can detect the inconsistency between birds and moa.

(5) GED $\varphi_5 = Q_5[x, x', z_1, z_2, y_1, \ldots, y_k](X_5 \to Y_5)$ specifies the rule of Example 1 for catching spam. Here X_5 consists of three constant literals $x'.\mathsf{is\_fake} = 1$, $z_1.\mathsf{keyword} = c$ and $z_2.\mathsf{keyword} = c$, Y_5 is $x.\mathsf{is\_fake} = 1$, and c is a constant. The GED says that for accounts and blogs that match Q_5, if account x' is confirmed fake and if blogs z_1 and z_2 both contain a peculiar keyword c, then x is also a fake account.

(6) The keys of Example 1 can be expressed as GEDs:

For album: $\psi_1 = Q_6[x, x', y, y'](X_6 \to x.\mathsf{id} = y.\mathsf{id})$,
$\psi_2 = Q_7[x, y](X_7 \to x.\mathsf{id} = y.\mathsf{id})$.
For artist: $\psi_3 = Q_6[x, x', y, y'](X_8 \to x'.\mathsf{id} = y'.\mathsf{id})$.

Here X_6 consists of $x.\mathsf{title} = y.\mathsf{title}$ and id literal $x'.\mathsf{id} = y'.\mathsf{id}$; X_7 includes $x.\mathsf{title} = y.\mathsf{title}$ and $x.\mathsf{release} = y.\mathsf{release}$; and X_8 consists of $x'.\mathsf{name} = y'.\mathsf{name}$ and id literal $x.\mathsf{id} = y.\mathsf{id}$, defined with attributes title, release, name and id.

To identify a pair of album entities x and y, we check either their title attributes and the ids of their artists (ψ_1), or their title and release attributes (ψ_2). Similarly, to identify artist entities x' and y' as required by ψ_1, we need to check the ids of a pair of albums they recorded (ψ_3) in turn. □

Semantics. To interpret GED $\varphi = Q[\bar{x}](X \to Y)$, we use the following notations. Consider a match $h(\bar{x})$ of Q in a graph G, and a literal l of $\bar{x}$. We say that $h(\bar{x})$ *satisfies* l, denoted by $h(\bar{x}) \models l$, if (a) when l is $x.A = c$, then attribute $v.A$ *exists* at node $v = h(x)$, and $v.A = c$; (b) when l is $x.A = y.B$, then attributes A and B *exist* at $v = h(x)$ and $v' = h(y)$, respectively, and $v.A = v'.B$; and (c) when l is $x.\mathsf{id} = y.\mathsf{id}$, then $h(x)$ and $h(y)$ refer to the same node; hence, they have the same set of attributes and edges.

We denote by $h(\bar{x}) \models X$ if the match $h(\bar{x})$ satisfies *all* the literals in X; in particular, if X is $\emptyset$, then $h(\bar{x}) \models X$ for any match $h(\bar{x})$ of Q in G; similarly for $h(\bar{x}) \models Y$. We write $h(\bar{x}) \models X \to Y$ if $h(\bar{x}) \models X$ implies $h(\bar{x}) \models Y$.

A graph G *satisfies* GED φ, denoted by $G \models \varphi$, if *for all* matches $h(\bar{x})$ of Q in G, $h(\bar{x}) \models X \to Y$.

We say that a graph G *satisfies* a set Σ of GEDs if for all $\varphi \in \Sigma$, $G \models \varphi$, *i.e.*, G satisfies every GED in Σ.

Given the semantics, we also write $Q[\bar{x}](X \to Y)$ as

$$Q[\bar{x}](\textstyle\bigwedge_{l \in X} l \to \bigwedge_{l' \in Y} l').$$

Existence of attributes. Note that attributes are not specified in pattern Q, and that we consider schemaless graphs. For a literal $x.A = c$, node $h(x)$ does not necessarily have attribute A, to accommodate the semistructured nature of graphs. Observe the following. (a) When $x.A = c$ is a literal in X, if $h(x)$ has *no* A-attribute, then $h(\bar{x})$ trivially satisfies $X \to Y$ by the definition of $h(\bar{x}) \models X$. (b) In contrast, if $x.A = c$ is in Y, then for $h(\bar{x}) \models Y$, node $h(x)$ must have A-attribute by the definition; similarly for $x.A = y.B$.

As a consequence, we can use, *e.g.*, $Q[x](\emptyset \to x.A = x.A)$ to enforce that all entities x of "type" τ must have an A attribute, where Q consists of a single vertex x labeled τ. This is in the flavor of tuple generating dependencies [7], limited to attributes. Such constraints cannot be expressed as EGDs [7] or FDs for relations and RDF [2,16,30,42].

However, GEDs *cannot* enforce attribute $x.A$ to have a finite domain, *e.g.*, Boolean, as opposed to database schema.

Special cases. We list some special cases of GEDs.

(1) GFDs. GFDs of [23] are syntactically defined as GEDs without id literals, *i.e.*, $Q[\bar{x}](X \to Y)$ in which neither X nor Y contains $x.\mathsf{id} = y.\mathsf{id}$. They adopt the semantics of subgraph isomorphism for graph pattern matching.

We refer to GEDs of this form also as GFDs, and interpret graph pattern matching in terms of homomorphism. For instance, φ_1–φ_5 in Example 3 are GFDs, but ψ_1–ψ_3 are not.

(2) Keys. A key ψ of [19] is defined as $Q[\bar{x}, x_o]$, where $Q[\bar{x}]$ is a graph pattern and x_o is a designated node in $\bar{x}$. A graph G satisfies ψ if for any two matches $h(\bar{x})$ and $h'(\bar{x})$ of $Q[\bar{x}]$ in G such that $h(\bar{x})$ and $h'(\bar{x})$ are isomorphic, $h(x_o)$ and $h'(x_o)$ denote the same node. Pattern Q is defined as a set of RDF triples, carrying variables and constants, and interpreted under the semantics of subgraph isomorphism.

We define a *key for graphs*, denoted by GKey, as a GED of the form $Q[\bar{z}](X \to x_0.\mathsf{id} = y_0.\mathsf{id})$, where (a) $Q[\bar{z}]$ is composed of patterns $Q_1[\bar{x}]$ and $Q_2[\bar{y}]$, and $Q_2[\bar{y}]$ is a copy of $Q_1[\bar{x}]$ via a bijection f: $\bar{x} \mapsto \bar{y}$ (see Example 2), (b) $\bar{z}$ consists of $\bar{x}$ followed by $\bar{y}$, (c) $x_0 \in \bar{x}$ and $y_0 = f(x_0)$ are designated nodes in Q, and (d) X is a set of literals as before.

For instance, ψ_1, ψ_2 and ψ_3 of Example 3 are GKeys. GKeys express recursive keys of [19] in terms of id literals.

The key $\psi = Q[\bar{x}, x_o]$ of [19] can be expressed as a GKey $Q'[\bar{z}](X \to x_0.\mathsf{id} = y_0.\mathsf{id})$, where X consists of literals to express constant and variable bindings embedded in pattern Q, and Q' is composed of Q and a copy of Q, interpreted in terms of homomorphism instead of subgraph isomorphism.

It is to uniformly express keys and GFDs that we adopt the homomorphism semantics for graph pattern matching.

To illustrate this, consider GKey ψ_3 given in Example 3. The GKey catches no violations if it is interpreted under subgraph isomorphism. Indeed, for any match $h[\bar{x}]$ of pattern Q_6 in a graph G, $h(x)$ and $h(y)$ have to be distinct nodes as required by isomorphism. As a result, $h[\bar{x}] \not\models X_8$ and hence, $h[\bar{x}]$ trivially satisfies ψ_3. As opposed to [19] that interprets a key with three isomorphic mappings, we interpret GEDs with a single match of pattern, and thus isomorphism is too strict to allow two variables to be mapped to the same node.

The issue becomes more subtle when it comes to the satisfiability of a set Σ of GEDs (see Section 5.1), where a model of Σ requires that every GED in Σ finds a match of its pattern, to assure that the GEDs in Σ do not conflict with each other. Consider a GKey $\varphi = Q[x, y](\emptyset \rightarrow x.\mathsf{id} = y.\mathsf{id})$, where Q consists of two isolated nodes, which are labeled with "UoE". This GKey states that all nodes representing "UoE" are essentially the same node. One can verify that under the semantics of subgraph isomorphism, GKeys like φ cannot find a model in any sensible graph.

<u>*(3)* GED$_\mathsf{x}$s</u>. We also study the class of GFDs that include no constant literals, referred to as *variable* GFDs and denoted by GFD$_\mathsf{x}$s. For instance, φ_2 and φ_3 are GFD$_\mathsf{x}$s, but φ_1, φ_4 and φ_5 are not. Intuitively, (a) GFDs are an extension of relational CFDs to graphs, (b) while GFD$_\mathsf{x}$s extend FDs, carrying neither constant literals nor id literals.

Similarly, we study GEDs without constant literals, referred to as *variable* GEDs and denoted by GED$_\mathsf{x}$s. Obviously GFD$_\mathsf{x}$s are a proper sub-class of GEDs; *e.g.*, ψ_1–ψ_3 of Example 3 are GED$_\mathsf{x}$s, but they are not GFD$_\mathsf{x}$s.

<u>*(4) Forbidding* GEDs</u>. GEDs can express limited negation, in the form of $Q[\bar{x}](X \rightarrow \mathsf{false})$, where false is an abbreviation for, *e.g.*, Y consisting of $y.A = c$ and $y.A = d$ for distinct constants c and d, where y is a variable in $\bar{x}$. Following [16], we refer to such GEDs as *forbidding constraints*.

<u>*(5) Relational dependencies*</u>. Following [23], one can show that FDs and CFDs can be expressed as GEDs if relation tuples are represented as nodes in a graph. In fact, equality-generating dependencies (EGDs) can be expressed as GFDs (GEDs) in the same setting. An EGD has the form $\forall \bar{z}(\phi(\bar{z}) \rightarrow y_1 = y_2)$, where ϕ is a conjunction of relation atoms $R(w_1, \ldots, w_l)$ and equality atoms $w_i = w_j$, w_i and w_j are variables in $\bar{z}$, and so are y_1 and y_2 (cf. [1]). Here each variable w corresponds to an attribute $R_w[A_w]$ in a relation atom of ϕ. The EGD can be expressed as a pair of GFDs:

(1) $\varphi_R = Q_E[\bar{x}](\emptyset \rightarrow Y_R)$, where (a) Q_E is a pattern such that for each relation atom R in ϕ, there exists a node $x_R \in \bar{x}$ in Q_E that is labeled with R; and Q_E has no edges; and (b) Y_R consists of $x_R.A_R = x_R.A_R$ for each variable $x \in \bar{z}$, which indicates attribute $R[A_R]$; intuitively, φ_R ensures that the relations in ϕ have the attributes required; and

(2) $\varphi_E = Q_E[\bar{x}](X_E \rightarrow Y_E)$, where (a) for each equality atom $w_i = w_j$ in ϕ, which corresponds to $R_i[A_{R_i}] = R_j[A_{R_j}]$ as remarked above, X_E includes a literal $x_{R_i}.A_{R_i} = x_{R_j}.A_{R_j}$; and (b) Y_E is $x_{R_{y1}}.A_{R_{y1}} = x_{R_{y2}}.A_{R_{y2}}$, which corresponds to $y_1 = y_2$. This enforces that ϕ entails $y_1 = y_2$.

One might be tempted to encode GEDs as relational dependencies. As will be discussed in Section 8, such encoding makes it awkward to express id literals, and the relational techniques do not simplify the analyses of GEDs.

4. THE CHASE REVISITED FOR GEDS

We next revise the chase [39] for GEDs over graphs (Section 4.1), and show that chasing with GEDs has the Church-Rosser property (Section 4.2). As will be seen in later sections, the chase helps us characterize the static analyses of GEDs and develop finite axiomatization for GEDs.

4.1 Chasing with GEDs

Consider a graph $G = (V, E, L, F_A)$ and a finite set Σ of GEDs. We study the chase of G by Σ, to (a) check the satisfiability of Σ (resp. implication of GED φ by Σ) when G encodes the patterns of Σ (resp. φ; see Section 5), (b) optimize graph pattern queries Q with Σ when G represents Q, and (c) identify entities and catch errors by using Σ in a knowledge base or a social graph G, among other things.

Equivalence relations. We define the chase as a sequence of equivalence relations Eq on nodes x and attributes $x.A$ in G. For each node x in V, its equivalence class, denoted by $[x]_{\mathsf{Eq}}$, is a set of nodes $y \in V$ that are identified as x. For each attribute $x.A$ of x, its equivalence class $[x.A]_{\mathsf{Eq}}$ is a set of attributes $y.B$ and constants c, if $x.A = y.B$ and $x.A = c$ are enforced by GEDs in Σ (see below), respectively. The relation is reflexive, symmetric and transitive, such that

(a) if node $y \in [x]_{\mathsf{Eq}}$, then $x \in [y]_{\mathsf{Eq}}$ and $[x]_{\mathsf{Eq}} = [y]_{\mathsf{Eq}}$; that is, we merge $[x]_{\mathsf{Eq}}$ and $[y]_{\mathsf{Eq}}$ into one; similarly, if attribute $y.B \in [x.A]_{\mathsf{Eq}}$, then $[y.B]_{\mathsf{Eq}} = [x.A]_{\mathsf{Eq}}$;
(b) if there is attribute $y.B$ such that $y.B \in [x.A]_{\mathsf{Eq}}$ and $y.B \in [z.C]_{\mathsf{Eq}}$, then $[x.A]_{\mathsf{Eq}} = [z.C]_{\mathsf{Eq}}$; similarly for constant c if $c \in [x.A]_{\mathsf{Eq}}$ and $c \in [z.C]_{\mathsf{Eq}}$;
(c) if there exists node y such that $y \in [x]_{\mathsf{Eq}}$ and $y \in [z]_{\mathsf{Eq}}$, then $[x]_{\mathsf{Eq}} = [z]_{\mathsf{Eq}}$ by transitivity; and
(d) if node $y \in [x]_{\mathsf{Eq}}$, then for each attribute $y.B$ of y, $[x.B]_{\mathsf{Eq}} = [y.B]_{\mathsf{Eq}}$; similarly for attribute $x.A$; that is, if x and y are the same node, then they have the same attributes and corresponding values.

<u>*Consistency*</u>. Inconsistencies may be introduced by id literals and constant literals when enforcing GEDs.

We say that Eq is *inconsistent* in G if

(a) there exists node $y \in [x]_{\mathsf{Eq}}$ such that $L(x) \not\asymp L(y)$ and $L(y) \not\asymp L(x)$ (label conflict), or
(b) there exists $y.B \in [x.A]_{\mathsf{Eq}}$ such that $x.A = c$ and $y.B = d$ for distinct c, d in U (attribute conflict).

Otherwise we say that Eq is *consistent.*

We use $\asymp$ to compare labels (recall $\asymp$ from Section 2). This is to cope with wildcard in a pattern Q when we chase Q as a graph (see Section 5 for such examples). In this case, we treat '_' in Q as a special label. Recall that $\asymp$ is asymmetric: $x \asymp y$ does not mean that $y \asymp x$.

<u>*Coercion*</u>. When an equivalence relation Eq is consistent in graph G, we can enforce Eq on G and revise G by merging nodes and their corresponding attributes and edges, and by equalizing and extending attributes, as follows.

We define the *coercion of a consistent* Eq *on* G as graph $G_{\mathsf{Eq}} = (V', E', L', F'_A)$ obtained from G as follows: for each node $x \in V$, (a) x_{Eq} is a node in V', denoting $[x]_{\mathsf{Eq}}$; (b) for each edge $(x, \iota, y) \in E$, $(x_{\mathsf{Eq}}, \iota, y_{\mathsf{Eq}})$ is an edge in E'; similarly for each edge $(y, \iota, x) \in E$; (c) $L'(x_{\mathsf{Eq}})$ is '_' if all nodes in $[x]_{\mathsf{Eq}}$ are labeled '_'; otherwise $L'(x_{\mathsf{Eq}}) = L(z)$, where $z \in [x]_{\mathsf{Eq}}$ with $L(z) \neq$ '_'; and (d) $F'_A(x_{\mathsf{Eq}}) = \bigcup_{y \in [x]_{\mathsf{Eq}}} F_A(y)$, the union of the attributes of all the nodes in $[x]_{\mathsf{Eq}}$.

When Eq is consistent, G_{Eq} is well defined. In particular, when x and y are identified as the same node, $F'_A([x]_{\mathsf{Eq}})$ merges the attributes of x and y; moreover, if A is an attribute of both x and y, then $x.A = y.A$, and hence $F'_A(\cdot)$ is well defined. In addition, for all nodes $z_1, z_2 \in [x]_{\mathsf{Eq}}$, if $L(z_1) \neq$ '_' and $L(z_2) \neq$ '_', then $L(z_1) = L(z_2)$.

When Eq is inconsistent, G_{Eq} is undefined.

Chasing. We start with Eq_0, an initial equivalence relation that includes $[x]_{\mathsf{Eq}_0} = \{x\}$ and $[x.A]_{\mathsf{Eq}_0} = \{x.A, c\}$, for each node $x \in V$ and attribute $x.A = c$ in $F_A(x)$. Each chase step i extends Eq_{i-1} to get Eq_i, by applying a GED.

We define *a chase step of* G *by* Σ *at* Eq as

$$\mathsf{Eq} \Rightarrow_{(\varphi,h)} \mathsf{Eq}',$$

where $\varphi = Q[\bar{x}](X \to Y)$ is a GED in Σ, and $h(\bar{x})$ is a match of pattern Q in the coercion G_{Eq} of Eq on graph G such that (a) $h(\bar{x}) \models X$, and (b) Eq' is the equivalence relation of the extension of Eq by adding one literal $l \in Y$; more specifically, l and Eq' satisfies one of the following conditions:

(1) if l is $x.A = c$ and $c \notin [h(x).A]_{\mathsf{Eq}}$, then Eq' extends Eq by (a) including a new equivalence class $[h(x).A]_{\mathsf{Eq}'}$ if $h(x).A$ is not in Eq, and (b) adding c to $[h(x).A]_{\mathsf{Eq}'}$;

(2) if l is $x.A = y.B$ and $h(y).B \notin [h(x).A]_{\mathsf{Eq}}$, then Eq' extends Eq by adding (a) $[h(x).A]_{\mathsf{Eq}'}$ if $h(x).A$ is not in Eq, and (b) $h(y).B$ to $[h(x).A]_{\mathsf{Eq}'}$; and

(3) if l is $x.\mathsf{id} = y.\mathsf{id}$ and $h(y) \notin [h(x)]_{\mathsf{Eq}}$, then Eq' extends Eq by adding $h(y)$ to $[h(x)]_{\mathsf{Eq}'}$.

The step is *valid* if Eq' is consistent in G_{Eq}.

Note that cases (1) and (2) above may expand the set of attributes of $h(x)$ when enforcing φ: attribute $h(x).A$ in Y is added if it is not already an attribute of $h(x)$, as required by $h(\bar{x}) \models Y$ (Section 3), since otherwise the chase will not lead to a graph that satisfies φ (see Theorem 1 below).

A *chasing sequence* ρ of G by Σ is a sequence

$$\mathsf{Eq}_0, \ \ldots, \ \mathsf{Eq}_k,$$

where for all $i \in [0, k-1]$, there exist a GED $\varphi = Q[\bar{x}](X \to Y)$ in Σ and a match h of pattern Q in coercion graph G_{Eq_i} such that $\mathsf{Eq}_i \Rightarrow_{(\varphi,h)} \mathsf{Eq}_{i+1}$ is a valid chase step.

The sequence is *terminal* if there exist no GED $\varphi \in \Sigma$, match h of pattern Q of φ in G_{Eq_k} and equivalence relation Eq_{k+1} such that $\mathsf{Eq}_k \Rightarrow_{(\varphi,h)} \mathsf{Eq}_{k+1}$ is a valid chase step. More specifically, it terminates in one of the following cases.

(a) No GEDs in Σ can be applied to expand the chasing sequence. If so, we say that the sequence is *valid*, and refer to $(\mathsf{Eq}_k, G_{\mathsf{Eq}_k})$ as *its result*. It is easy to verify that in a valid ρ, for all $i \in [0, k]$, Eq_i is consistent in G_{Eq_i}.

(b) Either Eq_0 is inconsistent to start with (see the case in Section 5.2), or there exist φ, h and Eq_{k+1} such that $\mathsf{Eq}_k \Rightarrow_{(\varphi,h)} \mathsf{Eq}_{k+1}$ but Eq_{k+1} is inconsistent in G_{Eq_k}. If so, we say that ρ is *invalid*, with result $\perp$ (undefined).

In particular, a forbidding constraint $Q[\bar{x}](X \to \mathsf{false})$ can be applied only when G is "inconsistent" or "dirty", and as a result, it makes the chasing sequence invalid.

Example 4: Consider graph G shown in Fig. 2, where v_1 and v_2 have attribute A with $v_1.A = 1$ and $v_2.A = 1$.

(1) Consider a set Σ_1 consisting of a single GED $\phi_1 = Q_1[x, y](x.A = y.A \to x.\mathsf{id} = y.\mathsf{id})$ with Q_1 in Fig. 2. Then $\mathsf{Eq}_0 \Rightarrow_{(\phi_1,h_1)} \mathsf{Eq}_1$ is a chase step, where (a) Eq_0 consists of

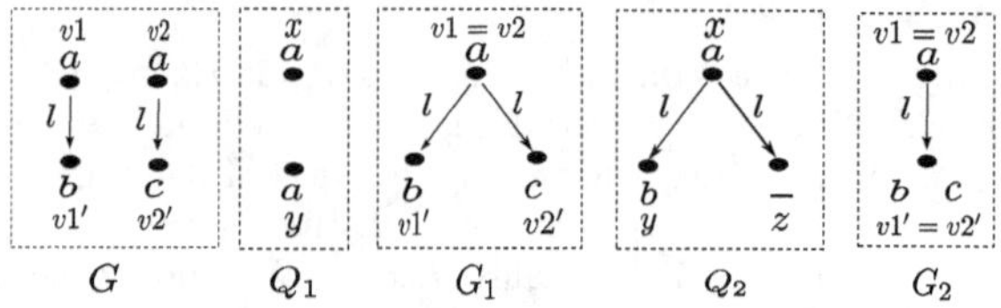

Figure 2: Graphs and patterns used in chasing

$[v]_{\mathsf{Eq}_0} = \{v\}$ for v ranging over v_1, v_2, v'_1, v'_2, and $[v_1.A]_{\mathsf{Eq}_0} = [v_2.A]_{\mathsf{Eq}_0} = \{v_1.A, v_2.A, 1\}$; (b) h_1: $x \mapsto v_1$ and $y \mapsto v_2$; and (c) Eq_1 extends Eq_0 by letting $[v_1]_{\mathsf{Eq}_1} = [v_2]_{\mathsf{Eq}_1} = \{v_1, v_2\}$. The coercion G_1 of Eq_1 on G is shown in Fig. 2, which merges v_1 and v_2. One can verify that $\mathsf{Eq}_0 \Rightarrow_{(\phi_1,h_1)} \mathsf{Eq}_1$ is a terminal chasing sequence of G by Σ_1 since no more GEDs can be applied. Moreover, it is valid, yielding result (Eq_1, G_1).

(2) Consider $\Sigma_2 = \{\phi_1, \phi_2\}$, where $\phi_2 = Q_2[x, y, z](\emptyset \to y.\mathsf{id} = z.\mathsf{id})$ (Q_2 in Fig. 2). Now $\mathsf{Eq}_1 \Rightarrow_{(\phi_2,h_2)} \mathsf{Eq}_2$ is a chase step, where h_2: $x \mapsto v_1$, $y \mapsto v'_1$, $z \mapsto v'_2$; and (b) Eq_2 extends Eq_1 by adding v'_2 to $[v'_1]_{\mathsf{Eq}_1}$. Then $\mathsf{Eq}_0 \Rightarrow_{(\phi_1,h_1)} \mathsf{Eq}_1$ is still terminal, but it is invalid as there exists a chase step $\mathsf{Eq}_1 \Rightarrow_{(\phi_2,h_2)} \mathsf{Eq}_2$, where Eq_2 is inconsistent in G_1. As shown in Fig. 2, the coercion G_2 of Eq_2 on G is to merge v'_1 and v'_2 with distinct labels. The result of this sequence is $\perp$. □

As opposed to chase of relations or RDF with EGDs or FDs [2, 7, 16, 30], a chasing sequence with GEDs operates on a graph (pattern), and may be invalid due to label or attribute conflicts. Moreover, it supports "attribute generation" (cases (1) and (2) of chase steps above) to cope with schemaless graphs. In addition, the relational and RDF chasing rules do not deal with id literals. When $x.\mathsf{id} = y.\mathsf{id}$ is enforced, all their attributes and edges have to be merged.

4.2 The Church Rosser Property

The chase with relational FDs has the Church-Rosser property (cf. [1]). We show that chasing with GEDs retains the property. To present this, we use the following notions. We consider finite sets Σ of GEDs as usual.

(a) Chasing with GEDs is *finite* if for all sets Σ of GEDs and graphs G, all chasing sequences of G by Σ are finite.

(b) Chasing with GEDs has the *Church-Rosser property* if for all Σ and G, all terminal chasing sequences of G by Σ have the same result, regardless of in what order the GEDs are applied. That is, terminal sequences are either (a) all valid with the same $(\mathsf{Eq}, G_{\mathsf{Eq}})$, or (b) all invalid with $\perp$.

While chasing with GEDs may get into conflicts, all terminal valid chasing sequences yield the same result.

Theorem 1: *Chasing with* GEDs *is finite and has the Church-Rosser property. Moreover, for any set* Σ *of* GEDs *and graph* G*, if there exists a valid terminal chasing sequences of* G *by* Σ*, then* $G_{\mathsf{Eq}} \models \Sigma$*, where* $(\mathsf{Eq}, G_{\mathsf{Eq}})$ *is the result of the terminal sequence.* □

By Theorem 1, we can define *the result of chasing* G *by* Σ as the result of any terminal chasing sequence of G by Σ, denoted by $\mathsf{chase}(G, \Sigma)$. We say that $\mathsf{chase}(G, \Sigma)$ is *consistent* if there exists such a valid terminal chasing sequence, with result $(\mathsf{Eq}, G_{\mathsf{Eq}})$. It is *inconsistent* otherwise, *i.e.*, when all terminal chasing sequences are invalid.

Proof: (a) We show that in any chasing sequence ρ of G by Σ, the equivalence relation Eq_i in any chase step has size at most $|\mathsf{Eq}_i| \leq 4 \cdot |G| \cdot |\Sigma|$. Based on the bound, one can readily verify that the length of ρ is at most $8 \cdot |G| \cdot |\Sigma|$.

(b) We show the Church-Rosser property by contradiction. Assume that there exist two terminal chasing sequences with different results. We show that one of the sequences must not be terminal, by distinguishing the case when both sequences are valid and the case when only one is valid.

(c) We show that $G_{\mathsf{Eq}} \models \Sigma$ by the definition of terminal chasing sequences and the Church-Rosser property. □

5. REASONING ABOUT GEDS

We next study three fundamental problems associated with GEDs and their sub-classes identified in Section 3. We characterize their static analyses and establish their complexity in various settings (Sections 5.1 and 5.2). We also investigate their validation problem (Section 5.3).

5.1 The Satisfiability Problem

We study a strong notion of satisfiability. Consider a set Σ of GEDs. A *model* of Σ is a graph G such that (a) $G \models \Sigma$, and (b) for each $Q[\bar{x}](X \rightarrow Y)$ in Σ, Q has a match in G.

Intuitively, if Σ has a model, then the GEDs in Σ are sensible and do not conflict with each other. Hence we can apply these GEDs without worrying about their conflicts.

The *satisfiability* problem for GEDs is as follows.

- Input: A finite set Σ of GEDs.
- Question: Does there exist a model of Σ?

We say that Σ is *satisfiable* if it has a model.

For relational FDs, the satisfiability problem is trivial: there always exists a nonempty relation that satisfies a given set of FDs (cf. [20]). When it comes to GEDs over graphs, however, the satisfiability analysis is more intriguing.

Example 5: (1) Consider a set Σ_1 consisting of

$$\phi_1 = Q_1[x, y, z](x.A = x.B \rightarrow y.\mathsf{id} = z.\mathsf{id}),$$
$$\phi_2 = Q_2[x_1, y_1, z_1, x_2, y_2, z_2](\emptyset \rightarrow x_1.A = x_1.B),$$

where Q_1 and Q_2 are depicted in Fig. 3. One can verify that each of ϕ_1 and ϕ_2 has a model when they are taken separately; however, Σ_1 does not have a model. To see this, consider a homomorphism f from Q_2 to Q_1, mapping x_1 and x_2 to x, y_1 and y_2 to y, and z_1 and z_2 to z. Hence for any match h of Q_1 in a graph G, the composition of h and f makes a match of Q_2 in G. When taken together, ϕ_1 and ϕ_2 require us to merge two nodes y and z with distinct labels.

(2) GEDs may interact with each other even when their patterns are not homomorphic. To see this, consider Σ_2 consisting of ϕ_1 and $\phi_2' = Q_2'[\bar{x}](\emptyset \rightarrow x_1.A = x_1.B)$, where Q_2' extends Q_2 by adding a connected component C_2, as shown in Fig. 3. Obviously, Q_1 is not homomorphic to Q_2' and vice versa. However, Σ_2 is not satisfiable. To see this, suppose by contradiction that Σ_2 has a model G, in which Q_2' has a match $h_2(\bar{x})$. Then for any match h_1 of Q_1 in G, we can construct a match h_2' of Q_2' such that (a) over C_2, h_2' is the same as h_2, and (b) over Q_2, h_2' is the composition of h_1 and f given above. Then the same conflict emerges as in (1). □

The example also illustrates complications introduced by the homomorphism semantics for pattern matching. Under the semantics of subgraph isomorphism [23], Q_2 and Q_2' cannot find a match in Q_1 and introduce no conflicts.

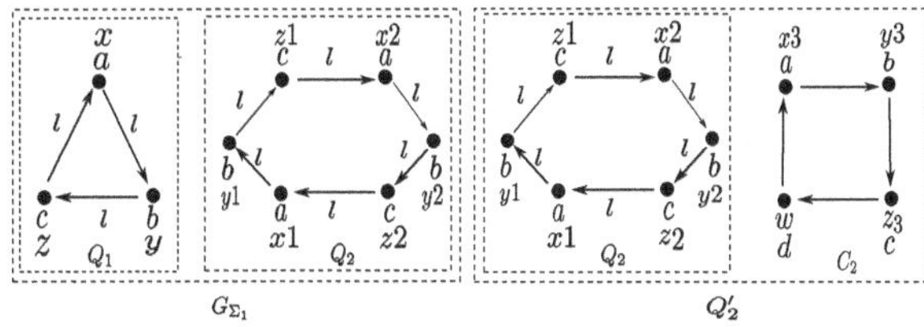

Figure 3: The satisfiability of GEDs

Characterization. We develop a sufficient and necessary condition to characterize the satisfiability of a set Σ of GEDs.

Consider a set Σ of GEDs $\varphi_i = Q_i[\bar{x}_i](X_i \rightarrow Y_i)$ for $i \in [1, n]$, where $Q_i = (V_i, E_i, L_i)$, and we assume *w.l.o.g.* that V_i and V_j are disjoint if $i \neq j$, after naming the nodes in Q_i.

The *canonical graph* G_Σ of Σ is defined to be a graph $(V_\Sigma, E_\Sigma, L_\Sigma, F_A^\Sigma)$, where V_Σ is the union of V_i's, and similarly for E_Σ and L_Σ; but F_A^Σ is empty.

Intuitively, G_Σ is the union of all graph patterns in Σ, in which patterns from different GEDs are disjoint.

We chase the pattern graph G_Σ with Σ, and characterize the satisfiability of Σ based on the chase (Section 4).

Theorem 2: *A set Σ of GEDs is satisfiable if and only if* $\mathsf{chase}(G_\Sigma, \Sigma)$ *is consistent.* □

Example 6: Recall the set Σ_1 of GEDs from Example 5. Its canonical graph is the union G_{Σ_1} of Q_1 and Q_2 shown in Fig. 3. One can verify that $\mathsf{chase}(G_{\Sigma_1}, \Sigma_1)$ is inconsistent, *i.e.*, there exists a terminal chasing sequence of G_{Σ_1} by Σ_1 with result $\perp$. This confirms the observation of Example 5 that Σ_1 is not satisfiable; similarly for Σ_2. □

Proof: (a) If $\mathsf{chase}(G_\Sigma, \Sigma)$ is consistent, *i.e.*, there exists a valid terminal chasing sequence ρ of G_Σ by Σ, we show that one can build a model of Σ from G_Σ based on ρ, using Theorem 1. We take special care to handle '_' in Σ.

(b) If Σ is satisfiable, *i.e.*, Σ has a model G, we show that each terminal chasing sequence ρ of G_Σ by Σ is valid. For a pattern Q, an equivalence relation Eq on the nodes and attributes of G and a match h of Q in G, we represent Eq as a set of equality literals, and write $h \models \mathsf{Eq}$ if $h \models l$ for all literals l in Eq. We construct a match h of G_Σ in G by treating G_Σ as a graph pattern, and show that $h \models \mathsf{Eq}_{i+1}$ for each chase step $\mathsf{Eq}_i \Rightarrow_{(\varphi,h)} \mathsf{Eq}_{i+1}$ of ρ. □

Complexity. Using Theorem 2, we give the complexity of the satisfiability analysis of GEDs and its sub-classes.

Theorem 3: *The satisfiability problem is*

- coNP*-complete for* GEDs, GFDs, GKeys, $\mathsf{GED_x}$s*;*
- *it is in $O(1)$ time for* $\mathsf{GFD_x}$s. □

Theorem 3 tells us the following. (1) The intractability of the satisfiability analysis is rather robust: it arises either from constant literals in GFDs, or from id literals in GKeys and $\mathsf{GED_x}$s. As will be seen in the proof, the problem is coNP-hard even when Σ consists of a fixed number of GEDs. (2) In the absence of constant and id literals, the problem is trivial: any set of $\mathsf{GFD_x}$s can find a model.

For relational EGDs, the satisfiability problem is not an issue. The satisfiability problem for relational CFDs is NP-complete [21]. A close examination reveals that it is intractable only under a database schema that requires attributes to have a finite domain, *e.g.*, Boolean [21]. It is in

PTIME in the absence of finite-domain attributes. As remarked in Section 3, while GEDs can express CFDs when relations are represented as graphs, they cannot enforce an attribute to have a finite domain. That is, the satisfiability problem for GEDs is intractable in the absence of finite-domain attributes. Hence its intractability is not inherited from CFDs, as indicated by coNP-complete vs. NP-complete.

Proof: We give an NP algorithm to check whether a set Σ of GEDs is not satisfiable, based on Theorem 2. This is possible because of the bound on terminal chasing sequences by GEDs given in the proof of Theorem 1.

In particular, when Σ consists of GFD$_\text{x}$s, chase(G_Σ, Σ) is always consistent. Indeed, in the absence of constant and id literals, no chase step can result in conflicts.

For the lower bounds, we show that the problem is coNP-hard for (a) GFDs, and (b) GKeys without constant literals; these suffice since such GKeys are a special case of GED$_\text{x}$s and GEDs. We prove (a) and (b) by (different) reductions from the complement of the 3-colorability problem. The 3-colorability problem is to decide, given an undirected graph G, whether there exists a proper 3-coloring ν of G such that for each edge (u, v) in G, $\nu(u) \neq \nu(v)$. The problem is NP-complete even when G is connected [25].

The proof for (a) uses two GFDs of the form $Q[\bar{x}](\emptyset \rightarrow Y)$, where Y consists of variable and constant literals. It is different from the one given in [23], where GFDs are interpreted via subgraph isomorphism, while we adopt graph homomorphism here. For (b) we use three GKeys of the form $Q[\bar{x}](\emptyset \rightarrow x.\text{id} = y.\text{id})$ without constant literals. □

5.2 The Implication Problem

A set Σ of GEDs *implies* another GED φ, denoted by $\Sigma \models \varphi$, if for all graphs G, if $G \models \Sigma$ then $G \models \varphi$.

The *implication* problem for GEDs is as follows:

- Input: A finite set Σ of GEDs and another GED φ.
- Question: Does $\Sigma \models \varphi$?

The implication analysis helps us optimize data quality rules and graph pattern queries, among other things.

Characterization. We characterize the implication $\Sigma \models \varphi$ as follows. Assume $\varphi = Q[\bar{x}](X \rightarrow Y)$, where pattern $Q = (V_Q, E_Q, L_Q)$. We use the following notations.

(a) The *canonical graph* of Q is $G_Q = (V_Q, E_Q, L_Q, F_A)$, where F_A is empty, along the same lines as G_Σ.

(b) We use Eq_X to denote *the equivalence relation of X in* G_Q, such that for any literal l in X, $v \in [u]_{\text{Eq}}$, where l is $u = v$, denoting $x.A = c$, $x.A = y.B$ or $x.\text{id} = y.\text{id}$. Moreover, Eq_X contains $[x]_{\text{Eq}_X} = \{x\}$ for each $x \in V_Q$.

(c) We use chase(G_Q, Eq_X, Σ) to denote the result of the chase of G_Q by Σ starting with Eq_X. Note that it is inconsistent if Eq_X is inconsistent (see Section 4).

(d) We say that a literal l can be *deduced* from an equivalence relation Eq if $v \in [u]_{\text{Eq}}$, where l is $u = v$. That is, the equality specified by l can be deduced from the transitivity of equality literals, and the semantics of id literals in Eq.

We say that a set Y of literals can be *deduced* from Eq if each literal of Y can be deduced from Eq.

Theorem 4: *For a set Σ of* GEDs *and $\varphi = Q[\bar{x}](X \rightarrow Y)$, $\Sigma \models \varphi$ if and only if either (1)* chase(G_Q, Eq_X, Σ) *is inconsistent; or (2)* chase(G_Q, Eq_X, Σ) *is consistent and Y can be deduced from* chase(G_Q, Eq_X, Σ). □

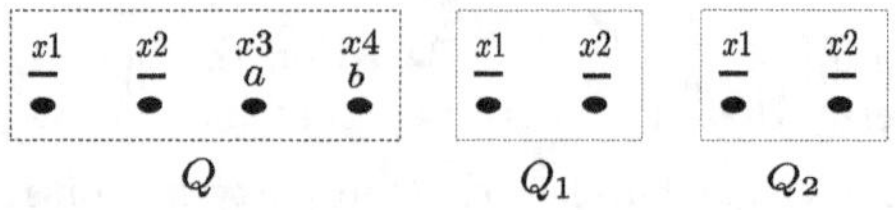

Figure 4: The implication of GEDs

Intuitively, if chase(G_Q, Eq_X, Σ) is inconsistent, then for all graphs $G \models \Sigma$ and for all matches $h(\bar{x})$ of pattern Q in G, $h(\bar{x}) \not\models X$. Condition (1) covers this case. Otherwise, if chase(G_Q, Eq_X, Σ) is consistent, condition (2) ensures that Y is a logical consequence of Σ, Q and X.

Example 7: Consider a set $\Sigma_1 = \{\phi_1, \phi_2\}$ and φ:

$\phi_1 = Q_1[x_1, x_2](x_1.A = x_2.A \rightarrow x_1.\text{id} = x_2.\text{id})$,
$\phi_2 = Q_2[x_1, x_2](x_1.B = x_2.B \rightarrow x_1.A = x_1.B)$,
$\varphi \ = Q[x_1, x_2, x_3, x_4](X \rightarrow Y)$,

where Q, Q_1 and Q_2 are shown in Fig. 4, X is $x_1.A = x_3.A \wedge x_2.B = x_4.B$, and Y is $x_1.\text{id} = x_3.\text{id} \wedge x_2.\text{id} = x_4.\text{id}$. Canonical graph G_Q has the same form as Q of Fig. 4. Then chase(G_Q, Eq_X, Σ) yields all literals in Y, and $\Sigma \models \varphi$.

Note that x_3 and x_4 have distinct labels, and each is identified with a node labeled '_': $x_3 \in [x_1]_{\text{Eq}}$ and $x_4 \in [x_2]_{\text{Eq}}$, where Eq is the result of the chase. This explains why we use $\asymp$ when comparing labels (see Section 4). □

Theorem 4 tells us that to decide whether $\Sigma \models \varphi$, it suffices to chase the canonical graph G_Q of pattern Q.

Proof: We verify conditions (1) and (2) of Theorem 4 by using Lemmas (a) and (b) below. Consider a terminal chasing sequence $\text{Eq}_X, \text{Eq}_1, \ldots, \text{Eq}_k$ of G_Q by Σ starting with Eq_X, valid or not. We show the following lemmas.

(a) For any graph G and pattern $Q[\bar{x}]$, if $G \models \Sigma$, $h(\bar{x})$ is a match of Q in G and $h(\bar{x}) \models X$, then $h(\bar{x}) \models \text{Eq}_k$.

(b) For consistent chase(G_Q, Eq_X, Σ), Y can be deduced from chase(G_Q, Eq_X, Σ) if and only if for any graph G and match $h(\bar{x})$ of Q in G, $h(\bar{x}) \models \text{Eq}_k$ implies $h(\bar{x}) \models Y$. □

Complexity. Based on the characterization, we settle the complexity of the implication analysis of GEDs.

Theorem 5: *The implication problem is* NP*-complete for* GEDs, GFDs, GKeys, GFD$_\text{x}$s *and* GED$_\text{x}$s. □

As opposed to Theorem 3, the implication analysis for GFD$_\text{x}$s is NP-hard, in the absence of constant and id literals, although chase(G_Q, Eq_X, Σ) is always consistent in this case. This is because to check whether Y can be deduced from chase(G_Q, Eq_X, Σ), we need to examine all possible homomorphic mappings of patterns of Σ in G_Q. The intractability remains intact even when Σ consists of a single GED.

The lower bound for GEDs does not follow from its counterpart for CFDs, which is coNP-complete [21], for the same reason as for the satisfiability analysis. While the implication problem for EGDs is NP-complete [8], the proofs are quite different, especially for the upper bound for GEDs and lower bound for GKeys, in the presence of id literals.

Proof: We give an NP algorithm to check $\Sigma \models \varphi$ based on the characterization of Theorem 4 and the bound given in the proof of Theorem 1. For the lower bounds, we show that the problem is NP-hard for GFD$_\text{x}$s and GKeys, since GEDs, GFDs and GED$_\text{x}$s subsume GFD$_\text{x}$s. We prove these by (different) reductions from the 3-colorability problem, capitalizing on Theorem 4. In the reductions, we use Σ consisting of a single $\mathsf{GFD_x}$ ϕ (resp. GKey ψ), where ϕ and φ have the form $Q[\bar{x}](\emptyset \rightarrow Y)$ and Y consists of variable literals only (resp. $Q[\bar{x}](\emptyset \rightarrow x.\mathsf{id} = y.\mathsf{id})$ for GKeys ψ and φ). □

5.3 The Validation Problem

The *validation problem* for GEDs is stated as follows.

- Input: A finite set Σ of GEDs and a graph G.
- Question: Does $G \models \Sigma$?

As remarked earlier, the validation analysis is the basis of inconsistency and spam detection, to find violations of GEDs in a knowledge base or a social graph.

Recall that validations of relational FDs and CFDs are in PTIME. It is harder for GEDs unless P = NP.

Theorem 6: *The validation problem is* coNP*-complete for* GEDs, GFDs, GKeys, $\mathsf{GFD_x}$s *and* $\mathsf{GED_x}$s. □

As for the implication problem, the validation analysis is intractable even for $\mathsf{GFD_x}$s, which is an extension of relational FDs that carries neither constant literals nor id literals. The intractability remains intact when Σ consists of a single $\mathsf{GFD_x}$ or a single GKey. The proof is quite different from the validation analysis of relational EGDs [8].

Proof: We provide an NP algorithm to check whether $G \not\models \Sigma$, for GEDs. We show the lower bounds for GKeys and $\mathsf{GFD_x}$s by (different) reductions from the complement of the 3-colorability problem. These suffice since $\mathsf{GFD_x}$s are a special case of GFDs, $\mathsf{GED_x}$s and GEDs.

In the reductions, we use Σ consisting of only a single $\mathsf{GFD_x}$ $Q[\bar{x}](X \rightarrow Y)$ (resp. GKeys), where $X = \emptyset$ and Y consists of a single variable literal (resp. id literal). □

Tractable cases. The main conclusion of this section is that the intractability of the analyses of GEDs is quite robust. In fact, even for GEDs defined in terms of tree patterns, the satisfiability, implication and validation problems remain intractable. This is because the analyses require to enumerate and examine all matches of a pattern Q in a graph G in the worst case, not just to check whether there exists a match of Q in G. We defer the proof to a latter publication.

Nonetheless, there are tractable cases that allow us to make effective use of GEDs. For example, one may consider a set Σ of GEDs in which graph patterns have a size at most k, for a predefined bound k. This is practical. Indeed, real-life graph patterns often have a small size: 98% of SPARQL queries have no more than 4 nodes and 5 edges, and single-triple patterns account for 97.25% of patterns in SWDF and 66.41% of DBPedia [24]. One can readily verify that the satisfiability, implication and validation problems for GEDs are in PTIME when patterns have a bounded size k.

6. FINITE AXIOMATIZABILITY

We next study the finite axiomatizability of GEDs.

We naturally want a finite set $\mathcal{A}$ of inference rules to characterize GED implication, along the same lines as Armstrong's axioms for relational FDs [5]. As observed in [1], the finite axiomatizability of a dependency class is a stronger property than the existence of an algorithm for testing its implication. An axiom system reveals insight of logical implication, and can be used to generate symbolic proofs.

$\mathsf{GED_1}$	$\Sigma \vdash Q[\bar{x}](X \rightarrow X \wedge X_{\mathsf{id}})$, where X_{id} is $\bigwedge_{i\in[1,n]}(x_i.\mathsf{id} = x_i.\mathsf{id})$, and $\bar{x}$ consists of x_i for all $i \in [1, n]$.
$\mathsf{GED_2}$	If $\Sigma \vdash Q[\bar{x}](X \rightarrow Y)$ and literal $(u.\mathsf{id} = v.\mathsf{id}) \in Y$, then $\Sigma \vdash Q[\bar{x}](X \rightarrow u.A = v.A)$ for all attributes $u.A$ that appear in Y.
$\mathsf{GED_3}$	If $\Sigma \vdash Q[\bar{x}](X \rightarrow Y)$ and $(u = v) \in Y$, then $\Sigma \vdash Q[\bar{x}](X \rightarrow v = u)$.
$\mathsf{GED_4}$	If $\Sigma \vdash Q[\bar{x}](X \rightarrow Y)$, $(u_1 = v) \in Y$ and $(v = u_2) \in Y$, then $\Sigma \vdash Q[\bar{x}](X \rightarrow u_1 = u_2)$.
$\mathsf{GED_5}$	If $\Sigma \vdash Q[\bar{x}](X \rightarrow Y)$ and $\mathsf{Eq}_X \cup \mathsf{Eq}_Y$ is inconsistent, then $\Sigma \vdash Q[\bar{x}](X \rightarrow Y_1)$ for any set Y_1 of literals of $\bar{x}$.
$\mathsf{GED_6}$	If $\Sigma \vdash Q[\bar{x}](X \rightarrow Y)$, $\mathsf{Eq}_X \cup \mathsf{Eq}_Y$ is consistent, $\Sigma \vdash Q_1[\bar{x}_1](X_1 \rightarrow Y_1)$, and if there exists a match h of Q_1 in $(G_Q)_{\mathsf{Eq}_X \cup \mathsf{Eq}_Y}$ such that $h(\bar{x}_1) \models X_1$, then $\Sigma \vdash Q[\bar{x}](X \rightarrow Y \wedge h(Y_1))$.

Table 2: Axiom system $\mathcal{A}_{\mathsf{GED}}$ for GEDs

For a set Σ of GEDs and a GED φ, *a proof of* φ *from* Σ *using inference rules of* $\mathcal{A}$ is a sequence of GEDs

$$\varphi_1, \ \ldots, \ \varphi_n = \varphi,$$

such that each φ_i either is a GED in Σ, or can be deduced from φ_j's by applying an inference rule (or axiom) in $\mathcal{A}$, for $j < i$ (see [1] for details about proofs).

We say that φ is *provable from* Σ *using* $\mathcal{A}$, denoted by $\Sigma \vdash_{\mathcal{A}} \varphi$, if there exists a proof of φ from Σ using $\mathcal{A}$. We write it as $\Sigma \vdash \varphi$ when $\mathcal{A}$ is clear from the context.

We say that for GEDs, an inference system $\mathcal{A}$ is

- *sound* if $\Sigma \vdash_{\mathcal{A}} \varphi$ implies $\Sigma \models \varphi$;
- *complete* if $\Sigma \models \varphi$ implies $\Sigma \vdash_{\mathcal{A}} \varphi$;

for all GED sets Σ and GEDs φ; and

- *independent* if for any rule $\mathsf{r} \in \mathcal{A}$, there exist GEDs Σ and φ such that $\Sigma \vdash_{\mathcal{A}} \varphi$ but $\Sigma \not\vdash_{\mathcal{A}\setminus \mathsf{r}} \varphi$.

Here $\mathcal{A}\setminus \mathsf{r}$ denotes $\mathcal{A}$ excluding r. That is, removing any rule from $\mathcal{A}$ would make it no longer complete. We remark that we focus on finite implication, considering finite graphs.

We refer to $\mathcal{A}$ as a *finite axiom system* or a *finite axiomatization* of GEDs if $\mathcal{A}$ is sound, complete and independent for GEDs. We say that GEDs are *finitely axiomatizable* if there exists a finite axiomatization of GEDs [1].

Inference rules. We give a set $\mathcal{A}_{\mathsf{GED}}$ of rules for GEDs in Table 2, in which we denote by (a) $Q[\bar{x}]$ a pattern; (b) X a set of literals of $\bar{x}$; (c) $h(X)$ the set of literals obtained by substituting $h(x)$ for all $x \in X$, for a match h of Q in a graph; (d) G_Q the canonical graph of pattern Q (Section 5.2); (e) Eq_X the equivalence relation of a set X of literals in G_Q; and (f) $(G_Q)_{\mathsf{Eq}}$ the coercion of Eq on G_Q (Section 4). The consistency of an equivalence relation Eq is defined in Section 4. To simplify the presentation, we allow $c = x.A$ as a literal in intermediate results of a proof, for constant c.

Recall that Armstrong's axioms consist of three rules for relational FDs: reflexivity, augmentation and transitivity [5]. Four rules are needed for CFDs [21] and EGDs [38]. In contrast, $\mathcal{A}_{\mathsf{GED}}$ has six rules for GEDs over graphs.

Example 8: (a) We first prove the following property: if $\Sigma \vdash \varphi$, $\varphi = Q[\bar{x}](X \rightarrow Y)$ and $Y_1 \subseteq Y$, then $\Sigma \vdash Q[\bar{x}](X \rightarrow Y_1)$, where Y_1 is a set $\{u_i = v_i \mid i \in [1, n]\}$ of literals that are also in Y. When $X \cup Y$ is consistent, we have

(1) $Q[\bar{x}](X \rightarrow Y)$	φ
(2) $Q[\bar{x}](X \rightarrow (v_1 = u_1))$	(1) and $\mathsf{GED_3}$
(3) $Q[\bar{x}](X \rightarrow (u_1 = v_1))$	(2) and $\mathsf{GED_3}$
...	
(2n+1) $Q[\bar{x}](X \rightarrow (u_n = v_n))$	(2n) and $\mathsf{GED_3}$

(2n+2) $Q[\bar{x}](X \to (u_1 = v_1)(u_2 = v_2))$ (3), (5) and GED_6

...

(3n) $Q[\bar{x}](X \to Y_1)$ (3n-1), (2n+1) and GED_6

It can also be proven for inconsistent $X \cup Y$. To simplify the presentation, we denote this property as GED_7 and apply it in proofs, although GED_7 is not in $\mathcal{A}_{\mathsf{GED}}$.

(b) Recall the augmentation rule of Armstrong's axioms: if $X \to Y$ then $XZ \to YZ$. Analogously, consider $\Sigma \vdash \varphi_1$, where $\varphi_1 = Q[\bar{x}](X \to Y)$, and GED $\varphi = Q[\bar{x}](XZ \to YZ)$. We show that $\Sigma \vdash \varphi$ using $\mathcal{A}_{\mathsf{GED}}$ as follows. First consider the case when $\mathsf{Eq}_X \cup \mathsf{Eq}_Z$ is consistent:

(1) $Q[\bar{x}](XZ \to XZ \wedge X_{\mathsf{id}})$	GED_1
(2) $Q[\bar{x}](XZ \to XZ)$	(1) and GED_7
(3) $Q[\bar{x}](X \to Y)$	φ_1
(4) $Q[\bar{x}](XZ \to XYZ)$	(2), (3) and GED_6
(5) $Q[\bar{x}](XZ \to YZ)$	(3) and GED_7

When $\mathsf{Eq}_X \cup \mathsf{Eq}_Z$ is inconsistent, the proof consists of steps (1) and (2) above, followed by:

(3) $Q[\bar{x}](XZ \to YZ)$	(2) and GED_5

(c) Let $\Sigma \vdash \varphi_1$ and $\Sigma \vdash \varphi_2$, where $\varphi_1 = Q[\bar{x}](X \to Y)$ and $\varphi_2 = Q[\bar{x}](Y \to Z)$. We show that $\Sigma \vdash Q[\bar{x}](X \to Z)$ using $\mathcal{A}_{\mathsf{GED}}$. When $\mathsf{Eq}_X \cup \mathsf{Eq}_Y$ is consistent, we have:

(1) $Q[\bar{x}](X \to X \wedge X_{\mathsf{id}})$	GED_1
(2) $Q[\bar{x}](X \to X)$	(1) and GED_7
(3) $Q[\bar{x}](X \to Y)$	φ_1
(4) $Q[\bar{x}](X \to XY)$	(2), (3) and GED_6
(5) $Q[\bar{x}](Y \to Z)$	φ_2
(6) $Q[\bar{x}](X \to XYZ)$	(4), (5) and GED_6
(7) $Q[\bar{x}](X \to Z)$	(6) and GED_7

If Eq_X is inconsistent, the proof has steps (1), (2) and

(3) $Q[\bar{x}](X \to Z)$	(2) and GED_5

If $\mathsf{Eq}_X \cup \mathsf{Eq}_Y$ is inconsistent, it has steps (1)–(3) and

(4) $Q[\bar{x}](X \to XY)$	(2), (3) and GED_6
(5) $Q[\bar{x}](X \to Z)$	(4) and GED_5

These prove the transitivity of Armstrong's axioms. □

Axiomatization. GEDs are finitely axiomatizable.

Theorem 7: *The set $\mathcal{A}_{\mathsf{GED}}$ of rules given in Table 2 is sound, complete and independent for* GEDs. □

Proof: We outline a proof, highlighting intuition.

(1) Soundness. The soundness is verified by induction on the length of proofs by using $\mathcal{A}_{\mathsf{GED}}$, based on the chase and Theorem 4. Below we illustrate each rule in $\mathcal{A}_{\mathsf{GED}}$.

(a) GED_1 extends the reflexivity of Armstrong's axioms to cover id literals. Similarly, GED_3 and GED_4 ensure that equality literals are symmetric and transitive.

(b) GED_2 enforces the semantics of id literals: if x and y refer to the same node, then they have the same sets of attributes with the same values $x.A = y.A$.

(c) If $\mathsf{Eq}_X \cup \mathsf{Eq}_Y$ is inconsistent, then $\mathsf{chase}(G_Q, \mathsf{Eq}_X, \Sigma)$ is inconsistent, since Eq_X and Eq_Y are included in its result. GED_5 says that if this happens, then any set Y_1 of literals of $\bar{x}$ is a "logical consequence" of the inconsistent X, Σ and Q, following condition (1) of Theorem 4.

(d) When $\mathsf{Eq}_X \cup \mathsf{Eq}_Y$ is consistent, Q_1 can be embedded in $(G_Q)_{\mathsf{Eq}_X \cup \mathsf{Eq}_Y}$ via a match h, and if $h(\bar{x}_1) \models X_1$, then one can verify that if $\mathsf{chase}(G_Q, \mathsf{Eq}_X, \Sigma)$ is consistent, then $h(Y_1)$ can be deduced from $\mathsf{chase}(G_Q, \mathsf{Eq}_X, \Sigma)$. Hence GED_6 follows from condition (2) of Theorem 4.

Observe that GED_2 and GED_6 are unique for graph dependencies, which are needed to handle id-based entity identification and embedding of graph patterns, respectively.

(2) Completeness. Assume that $\Sigma \models Q[\bar{x}](X \to Y)$. To prove that $\Sigma \vdash Q[\bar{x}](X \to Y)$, for a terminal chasing sequence ρ of G_Q by Σ, where ρ is $\mathsf{Eq}_1 = \mathsf{Eq}_X, \mathsf{Eq}_2, \ldots, \mathsf{Eq}_k$, we treat Eq_i as a set of equality literals. Then we show the following claims by induction on the length of ρ.

Claim 1: For each $1 \leq i \leq k$, $\Sigma \vdash Q[\bar{x}](X \to \mathsf{Eq}_i)$.

Claim 2: If there exist GED $\varphi \in \Sigma$ and match h of the pattern of φ such that $\mathsf{Eq}_k \Rightarrow_{(\varphi,h)} \mathsf{Eq}_{k+1}$ and Eq_{k+1} is inconsistent in G_{Eq_k}, then $\Sigma \vdash Q[\bar{x}](X \to \mathsf{Eq}_{k+1})$.

We can verify that $\Sigma \vdash Q[\bar{x}](X \to Y)$ using the claims as follows. By Theorem 4, if $\Sigma \models Q[\bar{x}](X \to Y)$, then we need to consider two cases: (a) $\mathsf{chase}(G_Q, \mathsf{Eq}_X, \Sigma)$ is inconsistent; and otherwise, (b) Y can be deduced from $\mathsf{chase}(G_Q, \mathsf{Eq}_X, \Sigma)$. In case (a), Claim 2 and GED_5 put together can derive $\Sigma \vdash Q[\bar{x}](X \to Y)$. In case (b), we can show that $\Sigma \vdash Q[\bar{x}](X \to Y)$ following Claim 1.

(3) Independence. For each rule GED_k in $\mathcal{A}_{\mathsf{GED}}$, we show that there exist a set Σ of GEDs and another GED φ, such that the proof of $\Sigma \vdash \varphi$ necessarily uses GED_k.

Take GED_5 as an example. Consider $\Sigma = \emptyset$ and $\varphi = Q_5[x]((x.A = 1) \wedge (x.A = 2) \to x.A = 3)$, where Q_5 consists of a single node x. We show by contradiction that without using GED_5, we cannot prove $\Sigma \vdash \varphi$. Indeed, no other rule allows us to deduce $Q[\bar{x}](X \to Y)$ when Y contains a constant that appears in neither X nor Σ. □

7. EXTENSIONS OF GEDS

We next extend GEDs by supporting built-in predicates (Section 7.1) or disjunctions (Section 7.2). We show that the extensions complicate the static analyses.

7.1 Denial Constraints for Graphs

We first extend GEDs with built-in predicates, referred to as *graph denial constraints*, denoted by GDCs.

GDCs. A GDC ϕ is defined as $Q[\bar{x}](X \to Y)$, where Q is a pattern, and X and Y are sets of literals of one of the following forms: (a) $x.A \oplus c$, (b) $x.A \oplus y.B$, for constant $c \in U$, and non-id attributes $A, B \in \Upsilon$, and (c) $x.\mathsf{id} = y.\mathsf{id}$; here $\oplus$ is one of built-in predicates $=, \neq, <, >, \leq, \geq$.

Along the same lines as GEDs, we define $G \models \phi$ for a graph G; similarly for other notions. Obviously GEDs are a special case of GDCs when $\oplus$ is equality '=' only. One can verify that GDCs can express denial constraints of [3] when relation tuples are represented as vertices in a graph.

Example 9: We can express "domain constraints" as GDCs, to enforce each node of "type" τ to have an attribute with a finite domain, *e.g.,* Boolean, as follows:

$$\phi_1: Q_e[x](\emptyset \to x.A = x.A),$$
$$\phi_2: Q_e[x](x.A \neq 0 \wedge x.A \neq 1 \to \mathsf{false}).$$

Here Q_e consists of a single node labeled τ, ϕ_1 is a GED that enforces each τ-node x to have an A-attribute, and ϕ_2 ensures that $x.A$ can only takes values 0 or 1. □

Complexity. The increased expressive power of GDCs comes with a price. Recall that the satisfiability, implication and validation problems for GEDs are coNP-complete,

NP-complete and coNP-complete, respectively. In contrast, the static analyses of GDCs have a higher complexity unless P = NP, although their validation problem gets no harder.

Theorem 8: *The satisfiability, implication and validation problems for* GDCs *are* Σ_2^p*-complete,* Π_2^p*-complete and* coNP*-complete, respectively.* □

The lower bounds of these problems remain intact when Σ consists of a fixed number of GDCs with variable and constant literals only. The proof of Theorem 8 is more involved than their counterpart for GEDs (Theorems 3, 5 and 6).

Proof: (1) To prove the upper bound of the satisfiability problem, we establish a small model property, as opposed to the proof of Theorem 3 that is based on the chase. We show that if a set Σ of GDCs has a model, then it has a model of size at most $4 \cdot |\Sigma|^3$. The proof requires attribute value normalization. Based on the property, we give an Σ_2^p algorithm to check whether a set of GDCs is satisfiable.

We show the lower bound by reduction from a generalized graph coloring problem (GGCP) [37, 40]. GGCP is to decide, given two undirected graphs $F = (V_F, E_F)$ and $G = (V_G, E_G)$, whether there exists a two-coloring of F such that G is not a monochromatic subgraph of F. A monochromatic subgraph of F is a subgraph in which nodes are assigned the same color. The problem is Σ_2^p-complete when G is a complete graph and F contains no self cycles [37].

The reduction is a little complicated. We use a set Σ of four GDCs to encode 2-coloring, monochromatic G and graph F. These GDCs use constant and variable literals with $\neq$ and $\leq$, but employ no id literals. One of them is a forbidding constraint of the form $Q[\bar{x}](X \rightarrow \text{false})$.

(2) For implication, we also show a small model property: if $\Sigma \not\models \varphi$, then there exists a graph G_h such that $|G_h| \leq 2 \cdot |\varphi| \cdot (|\varphi| + |\Sigma| + 1)^2$, $G_h \models \Sigma$ and $G_h \not\models \varphi$. Based on the property, we give an Σ_2^p algorithm to check $\Sigma \not\models \varphi$. The lower bound is verified by reduction from the complement of GGCP, using Σ of three GDCs of the form above.

(3) For validation, the lower bound follows from Theorem 6 since GEDs are a special case of GDCs. For the upper bound, we use the algorithm for checking $G \not\models \Sigma$ developed for GEDs in the proof of Theorem 6. We show that the algorithm also works for GDCs and better still, remains in NP. □

7.2 Adding Disjunction

We next extend GEDs by adding limited disjunctions.

GED$^\vee$s. A GED ψ *with disjunction*, denoted by GED$^\vee$, has the same syntactic form $Q[\bar{x}](X \rightarrow Y)$ as GEDs, but Y is interpreted as the disjunction of its literals. That is, for a match $h(\bar{x})$ of Q in a graph G, $h(\bar{x}) \models Y$ if *there exists* a literal $l \in Y$ such that $h(\bar{x}) \models l$. Hence we also write ψ as

$$Q[\bar{x}](\bigwedge_{l \in X} l \rightarrow \bigvee_{l' \in Y} l').$$

The other notions such as satisfiability and implication remain the same as their GED counterparts.

GED$^\vee$s subsume GEDs. Each GED $Q[\bar{x}](X \rightarrow Y)$ can be expressed as a set of $Q[\bar{x}](X \rightarrow l)$ of GED$^\vee$s, one for each $l \in Y$. In contrast, some GED$^\vee$s are not expressible as GEDs.

Example 10: Recall GDCs from Example 9 that enforce $x.A$ to be Boolean. It is expressible as a GED$^\vee$:

$$\psi\text{: } Q_e[x](\emptyset \rightarrow x.A = 0 \vee x.A = 1).$$

It specifies a domain constraint: each τ-node x has an A-attribute and that $x.A$ can only take Boolean values. □

Complexity. Disjunctions also complicate the static analyses but do not make the validation analysis harder. The lower bounds remain intact when Σ consists of a fixed number of GED$^\vee$s with constant and variable literals only.

Theorem 9: *The satisfiability, implication and validation problems for* GED$^\vee$s *are* Σ_2^p*-complete,* Π_2^p*-complete and* coNP*-complete, respectively.* □

Proof: The proof is similar to the one for Theorem 8. For satisfiability (resp. implication), the upper bound is also verified by means of a small model property, and the lower bound by reduction from (resp. the complement of) GGCP, by using a set Σ consisting of three GED$^\vee$s. □

8. RELATED WORK

We categorize related work as follows.

Relational dependencies. FDs were introduced in [15] and have been well studied for relations. Armstrong's axioms were proposed for FDs in [5], and the chase in [39]. EGDs and TGDs were introduced in [7]. There were also renewed interests in extending FDs to improve data quality, *e.g.,* denial constraints [3] and CFDs [21] (see [1,18,20] for surveys).

For relational FDs, the satisfiability, implication and validation problems are in $O(1)$, linear time and PTIME, respectively (cf. [1]). Similar to the strong notion of satisfiability studied in this work, a consistency problem was shown NP-complete and undecidable for EGDs and TGDs [26], respectively; their implication problems are also NP-complete and undecidable, respectively [8]; and the validation problem was shown coNP-complete for EGDs [8] and Π_2^p-complete for TGDs [36]. The satisfiability, implication and validation problems are NP-complete, coNP-complete and in PTIME for CFDs [21], respectively. The satisfiability and implication problems are NP-complete and coNP-complete for denial constraints [6], respectively. An axiom system of four rules was developed for EGDs in [38], while TGDs are not finitely axiomatizable for finite implication. A set of four rules was shown sound and complete for CFDs [21].

GEDs carry graph patterns and id literals. Their satisfiability, implication and validation problems are intractable. However, their static analyses bear complexity comparable to their counterparts for denial constraints, CFDs and EGDs. Moreover, GEDs have the finite axiomatizability and the Church-Rosser property of the chase, as for relational FDs.

One might want to encode GEDs as relational dependencies and employ relational techniques to reason about GEDs. However, (a) id literals and graph patterns with wildcard complicate the encoding; and (b) it is not clear what we can get from an encoding. To express GEDs we need both EGDs and limited TGDs. Reasoning about generic TGDs is beyond reach [8, 26]. While some special cases have been studied, *e.g.,* oblivious terminating TGDs and EGDs [33, 34], their syntactic characterization is not yet in place, and their fundamental problems such as satisfiability and validation are still open. It is not clear whether GEDs can be expressed in the special forms, and even so, what results can GEDs inherit from them. In light of this, we opt to give a clean native definition of GEDs and develop their proofs directly. (c) The chase and axiom system for GEDs are quite different from their counterparts in the relational setting. For instance, chasing with GEDs may expand a graph with new attributes and run into conflicts, in contrast to with EGDs.

FDs *for graphs.* Graph constraints are being investigated by W3C [31] and industry (*e.g.,* [35]). The constraints currently supported are quite simple, *e.g.,* uniqueness constraints, cardinality constraints and property paths; a "standard" form of FDs is not yet in place. However, there have been several research proposals for FDs on RDF graphs. This line of work started from [32]. It defines keys, foreign keys and FDs by extending relational methods to RDF, and interpreting the "scope" of an FD with a class type that represents a relation name. Using clustered values, [42] defines FDs with conjunctive path patterns, which were extended to CFDs [28]. FDs are also defined by mapping relations to RDF [13], with tree patterns in which nodes represent relation attributes. As opposed to class names [32], tree patterns [13] and path patterns [28, 42], GEDs are specified with (possibly cyclic) graph patterns with variables and node identities.

Closer to this work are [2, 16, 29, 30] for RDF. A class of EGDs was formulated in [2] in terms of RDF triple patterns with variables, which are interpreted with homomorphism and triple embedding. Along the same lines, a class of FDs, tuple-generating dependencies (TGDs) and forbidding dependencies were defined for RDF in [16]. The FDs were extended in [30] to support constants like CFDs [21]. Chasing algorithms were developed in [2, 29, 30] for the implication analysis of EGDs and FDs. The decidability of the implication and validation problems was established in [16] for the EGDs (and hence FDs), among other things. Finite axiom systems were provided for the EGDs, TGDs, and for EGDs and TGDs put together, consisting of 9, 5 and 16 rules, respectively [2, 16]. Several axiom systems were also provided for various classes of FDs over relations of an arbitrary arity [29, 30], with 13 rules for the general case.

This work differs from [2, 16, 29, 30] in the following.

(1) GEDs are defined for general property graphs, not limited to RDF. (a) GEDs distinguish node identity from value equality. Their id literals enforce that nodes identified have the same attributes and edges. (b) GEDs can uniformly express GFDs, keys of [19] and forbidding dependencies (Section 3). (c) GEDs support constant literals, beyond [2, 16, 29].

(2) Our revised chase differs from the prior work in the following. (a) We study the chase of a graph (pattern) by GEDs, not limited to the implication analysis. For instance, the chase also helps us characterize the satisfiability analysis. (b) Chasing with GEDs has to deal with id literals, a major cause of invalid steps. It may also add new attributes as enforced by GEDs. (c) We establish the Church-Rosser property of the chase, which was not considered in [2, 16, 29, 30].

(3) We provide characterizations of the static analyses of GEDs, and the complexity of the satisfiability, implication and validation problems for GEDs in various settings. The satisfiability problem was not studied for EGDs or FDs of [2, 16, 29, 30]. Moreover, the complexity bounds remain to be developed for their implication and validation problems.

(4) The axiom system $\mathcal{A}_{\text{GED}}$ differs from [2, 16, 29, 30] in the following. (a) Besides value-based reasoning, $\mathcal{A}_{\text{GED}}$ deals with id-based deduction to enforce the semantics of node identities. (b) It adopts graph pattern matching in property graphs, beyond RDF and relations. (c) $\mathcal{A}_{\text{GED}}$ allows attribute generation (Section 4), which is not supported by the axiom systems for EGDs and FDs [2, 16, 29, 30]. While this can be derived from TGDs and EGDs of [16] put together, the finite axiomatizability for finite implication of TGDs requires further investigation [8].

As remarked in Section 5, a class of keys was studied for RDF [19]. Over property graphs, a form of GFDs [23] was defined with a graph pattern Q that is interpreted via subgraph isomorphic mapping. These GFDs can express CFDs [21] when tuples are represented as vertices in a graph, but cannot express keys of [19]. The satisfiability, implication and validation problems are shown coNP-complete, NP-complete and coNP-complete, respectively, for GFDs of [23].

This work differs from our prior work [19, 23] as follows.

(1) GEDs extend GFDs [23] by supporting id literals, and can express the GFDs of [23]. Moreover, to simplify the definition of the keys of [19] and to reason about GFDs and GKeys in a uniform framework, GEDs adopt the graph homomorphism semantics for graph pattern matching, as opposed to subgraph isomorphism [19, 23] (see Section 3).

(2) We revise the chase for GEDs, which was not studied in [23]. A form of chase was studied for keys [19], which is a simple case of the general process studied here.

(3) We establish the complexity of the satisfiability, implication and validation problems for GEDs in various settings. These were not studied in [19], and were considered for GFDs of [23] only. As remarked earlier, we employ characterizations and proof techniques different from [23] to cope with different semantics of graph pattern matching, *e.g.,* the chase to prove upper bounds. We also give lower bounds for GKeys, GFD_xs and GED_xs, which were not studied before.

(4) We provide finite axiomatization for GEDs, which was not considered for GFDs and GKeys [19, 23].

(5) To the best of our knowledge, no previous work has studied graph dependencies defined in terms of built-in predicates or disjunction, including [19, 23].

The chase has also been studied for data exchange with relational (disjunctive) EGDs [11] or FDs [9], for ontology querying [12], and for optimizing SPARQL queries [41] with the constraints of [32]. In contrast, we study the chase of a graph by GEDs, and deal with id literals.

FDs *for XML.* Keys [10, 22] and FDs [4] have also been studied for XML, which are quite different from GEDs in formulation and semantics. As a consequence, the results on XML do not apply to GEDs and vice versa.

9. CONCLUSION

We have proposed GEDs, which can uniformly express GFDs and keys for graphs. For GEDs, we have revised the chase with the Church-Rosser property, provided characterizations for their static analyses, settled the complexity of their satisfiability, implication and validation problems in various settings (Table 1), and shown the finite axiomatizability of their finite implication. We have also studied extensions of GEDs with built-in predicates or disjunction.

One topic for future work is to identify practical special cases in which the static analyses and validation are tractable. Another topic is to develop parallel scalable algorithms for reasoning about GEDs, to warrant speedup with the increase of processors. It is also interesting to study other practical forms of graph dependencies, *e.g.,*TGDs.

10. REFERENCES

[1] S. Abiteboul, R. Hull, and V. Vianu. *Foundations of Databases*. Addison-Wesley, 1995.

[2] W. Akhtar, A. Cortés-Calabuig, and J. Paredaens. Constraints in RDF. In *SDKB*, pages 23–39, 2010.

[3] M. Arenas, L. Bertossi, and J. Chomicki. Consistent query answers in inconsistent databases. In *PODS*, 1999.

[4] M. Arenas and L. Libkin. A normal form for XML documents. In *PODS*, pages 85–96, 2002.

[5] W. W. Armstrong. Dependency structures of data base relationships. In *IFIP Congress*, pages 580–583, 1974.

[6] M. Baudinet, J. Chomicki, and P. Wolper. Constraint-generating dependencies. *JCSS*, 59(1):94–115, 1999.

[7] C. Beeri and M. Y. Vardi. The implication problem for data dependencies. In *Automata, Languages and Programming*, pages 73–85, 1981.

[8] C. Beeri and M. Y. Vardi. On the complexity of testing implications of data dependencies. Technical report, The Hebrew University of Jeruslem, 1981.

[9] A. Bonifati, I. Ileana, and M. Linardi. Functional dependencies unleashed for scalable data exchange. In *SSDBM*, pages 2:1–2:12, 2016.

[10] P. Buneman, S. B. Davidson, W. Fan, C. S. Hara, and W. C. Tan. Keys for XML. In *WWW*, pages 201–210, 2001.

[11] M. Calautti, S. Greco, C. Molinaro, and I. Trubitsyna. Exploiting equality generating dependencies in checking chase termination. *PVLDB*, 9(5):396–407, 2016.

[12] A. Calì and A. Pieris. On equality-generating dependencies in ontology querying - preliminary report. In *AMW*, 2011.

[13] D. Calvanese, W. Fischl, R. Pichler, E. Sallinger, and M. Simkus. Capturing relational schemas and functional dependencies in RDFS. In *AAAI*, 2014.

[14] Q. Cao, M. Sirivianos, X. Yang, and T. Pregueiro. Aiding the detection of fake accounts in large scale social online services. In *NSDI*, pages 197–210, 2012.

[15] E. F. Codd. Relational completeness of data base sublanguages. *In: R. Rustin (ed.): Database Systems: 65-98, Prentice Hall and IBM Research Report RJ 987, San Jose, California*, 1972.

[16] A. Cortés-Calabuig and J. Paredaens. Semantics of constraints in RDFS. In *AMW*, pages 75–90, 2012.

[17] R. Fagin, P. G. Kolaitis, R. J. Miller, and L. Popa. Data exchange: semantics and query answering. *Theoretical Computer Science*, pages 89–124, 2005.

[18] R. Fagin and M. Y. Vardi. The theory of data dependencies - an overview. In *ICALP*, pages 1–22, 1984.

[19] W. Fan, Z. Fan, C. Tian, and X. L. Dong. Keys for graphs. *PVLDB*, 8(12):1590–1601, 2015.

[20] W. Fan and F. Geerts. Foundations of data quality management. *Synthesis Lectures on Data Management*, 4(5):1–217, 2012.

[21] W. Fan, F. Geerts, X. Jia, and A. Kementsietsidis. Conditional functional dependencies for capturing data inconsistencies. *TODS*, 33(1), 2008.

[22] W. Fan and L. Libkin. On XML integrity constraints in the presence of DTDs. *J. ACM*, 49(3):368–406, 2002.

[23] W. Fan, Y. Wu, and J. Xu. Functional dependencies for graphs. In *SIGMOD*, 2016.

[24] M. A. Gallego, J. D. Fernández, M. A. Martínez-Prieto, and P. de la Fuente. An empirical study of real-world SPARQL queries. In *USEWOD workshop*, 2011.

[25] M. R. Garey, D. S. Johnson, and L. Stockmeyer. Some simplified NP-complete graph problems. *Theoretical computer science*, 1(3):237–267, 1976.

[26] M. H. Graham, A. O. Mendelzon, and M. Y. Vardi. Notions of dependency satisfaction. *Journal of the ACM (JACM)*, 33(1):105–129, 1986.

[27] I. Grujic, S. Bogdanovic-Dinic, and L. Stoimenov. Collecting and analyzing data from e-government Facebook pages. In *ICT Innovations*, 2014.

[28] B. He, L. Zou, and D. Zhao. Using conditional functional dependency to discover abnormal data in RDF graphs. In *SWIM*, pages 1–7, 2014.

[29] J. Hellings, M. Gyssens, J. Paredaens, and Y. Wu. Implication and axiomatization of functional constraints on patterns with an application to the RDF data model. In *FoIKS*, 2014.

[30] J. Hellings, M. Gyssens, J. Paredaens, and Y. Wu. Implication and axiomatization of functional and constant constraints. *Ann. Math. Artif. Intell.*, 76(3-4):251–279, 2016.

[31] H. Knublauch and D. Kontokostas. Shapes constraint language (SHACL). W3C Working Draft, Feb. 2017. *https://www.w3.org/TR/shacl/#dfn-shacl-instance*.

[32] G. Lausen, M. Meier, and M. Schmidt. SPARQLing constraints for RDF. In *EDBT*, pages 499–509, 2008.

[33] B. Marnette. Generalized schema-mappings: from termination to tractability. In *PODS*, pages 13–22, 2009.

[34] B. Marnette and F. Geerts. Static analysis of schema-mappings ensuring oblivious termination. In *ICDT*, pages 183–195, 2010.

[35] Neo4j Team. The Neo4j developer manual v3.1 (chapter 3.5.2: Constraints), 2017. *http://neo4j.com/docs/developer-manual/current/*.

[36] R. Pichler and S. Skritek. The complexity of evaluating tuple generating dependencies. In *ICDT*, pages 244–255, 2011.

[37] V. Rutenburg. Complexity of generalized graph coloring. In *MFCS*, pages 573–581, 1986.

[38] F. Sadri. *Data dependencies in the relational model of databases, a generalization.* PhD thesis, Princeton Unversity, 1980.

[39] F. Sadri and J. D. Ullman. The interaction between functional dependencies and template dependencies. In *SIGMOD*, pages 45–51, 1980.

[40] M. Schaefer and C. Umans. Completeness in the polynomial-time hierarchy: A compendium. *SIGACT news*, 33(3):32–49, 2002.

[41] M. Schmidt, M. Meier, and G. Lausen. Foundations of SPARQL query optimization. In *ICDT*, pages 4–33, 2010.

[42] Y. Yu and J. Heflin. Extending functional dependency to detect abnormal data in RDF graphs. In *ISWC*, 2011.

Acknowledgments. Fan and Lu are supported in part by ERC 652976, NSFC 61421003, 973 Program 2014CB340302, Beijing Advanced Innovation Center for Big Data and Brain Computing, EPSRC EP/M025268/1, Shenzhen Peacock Program 1105100030834361, Guangdong Innovative Research Team Program 2011D005, the Foundation for Innovative Research Groups of NSFC, and two Innovative Research Grants from Huawei Technologies. Lu is also supported in part by NSFC 61602023.

A Worst-Case Optimal Multi-Round Algorithm for Parallel Computation of Conjunctive Queries

Bas Ketsman[*]
Hasselt University &
transnational University of Limburg
bas.ketsman@uhasselt.be

Dan Suciu[†]
University of Washington
suciu@cs.washington.edu

ABSTRACT

We study the optimal communication cost for computing a full conjunctive query $\mathcal{Q}$ over p distributed servers. Two prior results were known. First, for one-round algorithms over skew-free data the optimal communication cost per server is $m/p^{1/\tau^*(\mathcal{Q})}$, where m is the size of the largest input relation, and τ^* is the fractional vertex covering number of the query hypergraph. Second, for multi-round algorithms and unrestricted database instances, it was shown that any algorithm requires at least $m/p^{1/\rho^*(\mathcal{Q})}$ communication cost per server, where $\rho^*(\mathcal{Q})$ is the fractional edge covering number of the query hypergraph; but no matching algorithms were known for this case (except for two restricted queries: chains and cycles).

In this paper we describe a multi-round algorithm that computes any query with load $m/p^{1/\rho^*(\mathcal{Q})}$ per server, in the case when all input relations are binary. Thus, we prove this to be the optimal load for all queries over binary input relations. Our algorithm represents a non-trivial extension of previous algorithms for chains and cycles, and exploits some unique properties of graphs, which no longer hold for hyper-graphs.

Keywords

Conjunctive queries, Multi-round, Worst-case optimal load

1. INTRODUCTION

In recent years, a new family of query evaluation algorithms has emerged with proven optimal cost. Traditional query engines choose a join order, then compute the joins one at a time, and, as a consequence, may compute intermediate results that are much larger than the final query output. This leads to suboptimal evaluation algorithms, even if the best join order is chosen by the optimizer. In contrast, the new class of algorithms achieve optimality by computing all joins at once, and thus avoiding to compute potentially large intermediate results. For complex queries on very large datasets, the new class of algorithms can be significantly more efficient than traditional query plans.

In the case of sequential algorithms, running on a single server, the complexity is given by the runtime. The optimal runtime for a full conjunctive query $\mathcal{Q}$ on a database instance where the largest relation has m tuples is given by the largest possible query output. Atserias, Grohe, and Marx [4] have shown that the query output has size $\leq m^{\rho^*(\mathcal{Q})}$, where $\rho^*(\mathcal{Q})$ is the optimal edge covering number of the query hypergraph and m is the size of the largest relation; this bound is referred to as the AGM bound. Several algorithms have been described in the literature that run within this bound: Leapfrog-trie-join [16], NPRR [13], and Generic Join [14].

In this paper we study distributed algorithms, which run on a cluster of p servers, usually called a *shared nothing* architecture. A formal model for a shared nothing architecture was described in [12] and is called the Massively Parallel Communication model, hence MPC. In this model the servers compute a query in several rounds, where each round consists of a local computation followed by a communication step where the entire data is reshuffled among the p servers. The complexity of an algorithm in the MPC model is given by the *communication cost*, defined as the largest amount of data received by any single server during any round of communication, and also called *load per server*. An ideal load is $\tilde{O}(m/p)$, with m the size of the largest relation, but often queries require a larger load.[1] Unlike the sequential setting, the optimal load for computing full conjunctive queries in the MPC model is open. However, two important partial results have been described recently.

First, Koutris et al. [6] consider the MPC model under two restrictions: there is only one round of communication, and the database instances are skew free. A simplified definition of a skew-free database is one where every data value occurs at most m/p times in any input relation. Under these restrictions, the authors showed that the optimal load is $O(m/p^{1/\tau^*(\mathcal{Q})})$, where $\tau^*(\mathcal{Q})$ is the optimal fractional vertex covering number of the query hypergraph.

A second result was shown by the same authors in [11]. They dropped both restrictions, and proved the following lower bound: any algorithm, with r number of rounds, must incur a communication cost that is at least $m/(r \cdot p^{1/\rho^*(\mathcal{Q})})$. They also gave matching algorithms, but only for cycles

*PhD Fellow of the Research Foundation - Flanders (FWO)
†Supported by NSF IIS-1247469 and NSF AiTF 1535565

PODS'17, May 14 - 19, 2017, Chicago, Illinois, USA

ISBN 978-1-4503-4198-1/17/05...$15.00
DOI: http://dx.doi.org/10.1145/3034786.3034788

[1]In this paper, $\tilde{O}$ hides a factor $\log^r(p)$, with r the largest arity of any relation.

and for chain queries: no matching algorithm is known in general. The proof of the lower bound relies on the AGM bound, and can be described informally as follows. Consider a worst-case database instance, on which the query's output is the AGM bound $m^{\rho^*(\mathcal{Q})}$. Assume an algorithm that computes the output of this query using a load L. Then, any server receives at most $r \cdot L$ tuples from each input relation, and thus it can output at most $(r \cdot L)^{\rho^*(\mathcal{Q})}$ tuples, by the AGM bound. Since the p servers must return all output tuples, $p \cdot (r \cdot L)^{\rho^*(\mathcal{Q})} \geq m^{\rho^*(\mathcal{Q})}$, and therefore the load is $\geq m/(r \cdot p^{1/\rho^*(\mathcal{Q})})$. We assume $O(1)$ rounds throughout this paper, and then the lower bound becomes $\Omega(m/p^{1/\rho^*(\mathcal{Q})})$.

These two lower bounds work under quite different assumptions. The first lower bound of $m/p^{1/\tau^*(\mathcal{Q})}$ works for one round of communication and holds even for databases where each value occurs at most once in any input relation (in particular, they are skew-free). Therefore, the query's output is no larger than m, the size of the largest input relation. The second lower bound, $m/p^{1/\rho^*(\mathcal{Q})}$, removes any restrictions on the number of rounds, and applies to databases where the query returns the largest output, in other words where the AGM bound is tight. The fractional vertex cover $\tau^*(\mathcal{Q})$ seems related to skew-free databases, where the output is small, while the fractional edge cover $\rho^*(\mathcal{Q})$ seems related to skewed databases where the output is large. Since no matching algorithm is known for the general case, it is open which of these two bounds, if any, will turn out to be optimal.

In this paper we prove that any full conjunctive query where the input relations are binary can be computed with load $\tilde{O}(m/p^{1/\rho^*(\mathcal{Q})})$. Since this matches the general lower bound, our algorithm is optimal, and proves that the optimal load is given by $\rho^*(\mathcal{Q})$ rather than $\tau^*(\mathcal{Q})$, when all input relations are binary.

Our techniques build upon, and extend in non-trivial ways, techniques introduced by Koutris et al. [11] for computing chain queries and cycle queries in multiple rounds with load $m/p^{1/\rho^*(\mathcal{Q})}$. Their main insight was a simple algorithm for computing the two-way semi-join query,

$$\mathrm{H}(x, y) \text{ :- } \mathrm{R}(x), \mathrm{S}(x, y), \mathrm{T}(y),$$

in two rounds, with load m/p. If we restrict the number of rounds to one, then any algorithm requires a load $\geq m/p^{1/2}$, because $\tau^*(\mathcal{Q}) = 2$. But in two rounds we can simply compute $\mathrm{R}(x), \mathrm{S}(x, y)$ first, with load m/p by hash-partitioning on x, then compute the second semi-join by hash-partitioning on y and using the fact that the intermediate result is no larger than the size of S. Thus, the two-way semi-join can be computed with load $m/p^{1/\rho^*(\mathcal{Q})}$, since $\rho^*(\mathcal{Q}) = 1$. The algorithm for chains and cycles in [11] consists of repeatedly separating the values in the database into light and heavy hitters, and handling the heavy hitters in multiple rounds, through semi-join reductions. The specific techniques however apply only to chains and cycles (and can be generalized to trees). The paper left open the optimal communication cost for queries beyond chains and cycles.

Our result represents a non-trivial generalization of the algorithms for chains and cycles. We use the same building blocks as in [11], namely splitting the input values into light and heavy hitters, then computing the query separately on the two sets, but we require several new ideas to compute arbitrary queries over binary relations. We use three key properties of graphs (which, in general, do not hold on arbitrary hypergraphs): $\rho^*(\mathcal{Q}) + \tau^*(\mathcal{Q})$ equals the number of nodes; $\tau^*(\mathcal{Q}) \leq \rho^*(\mathcal{Q})$; and the graph admits a half-integral optimal fractional edge packing. Our algorithm starts by computing an optimal half-integral edge packing f for the query's graph. Then the exact strategy depends on the structure of f. The easy case is when f is tight, meaning that f describes both an edge packing and edge cover. The general case is when f is non-tight, and here we identify fragments of the query having a tight edge packing and compute them as before.

Thus, our results show that, at least in the case of queries over binary relations, the communication cost for multi-round algorithms is given by $\rho^*(\mathcal{Q})$ rather than $\tau^*(\mathcal{Q})$. We leave open the optimal communication cost for queries over relations of arbitrary arity. In particular, it is not known what this bound might be for queries where $\tau^*(\mathcal{Q}) > \rho^*(\mathcal{Q})$. In general, the best algorithm we know to compute the query over skew-free database instances is the one-round algorithm with load $m/p^{1/\tau^*(\mathcal{Q})}$. (The two-way semi-join query is an exception where $\tau^*(\mathcal{Q}) > \rho^*(\mathcal{Q})$ and we happen to know how to compute it in two rounds with load given by $\rho^*(\mathcal{Q})$.) On the other hand, the best multi-round lower bound we know follows from the AGM bound and is $m/p^{1/\rho^*(\mathcal{Q})}$: to close the gap one needs to either design a new multi-round algorithm for skew-free databases, or prove a new multi-round bound that is stronger than that implied by the AGM bound.

Outline.

We introduce the necessary definitions in Section 2. Section 3 describes the MPC model. In Section 4 we introduce the basic building blocks which are used in Section 5 to describe our main result, a worst-case optimal multi-round algorithm for parallel-evaluation of conjunctive queries. In Section 6 we briefly relate to the external memory model. We conclude in Section 7.

2. DEFINITIONS

Instances and Queries.

For a set S and positive integer n we denote by $|S|$ the number of elements in S and by $[n]$ the set $\{1, \ldots, n\}$. Let **dom** be an infinite domain of data values. A *schema* σ is a finite set of relation symbols R with associated arities $ar(R)$. For relation symbol R and tuple $\mathbf{t} = (d_1, \ldots, d_n)$ over **dom**, we call $R(\mathbf{t})$ a fact if $n = ar(R)$. A fact $R(\mathbf{t})$ is said to be over database schema σ if $R \in \sigma$. An *instance* I over σ is a finite set of facts over σ. For relation name R we denote by R^I the tuples in instance I with relation symbol R, that is $R^I = \{\mathbf{t} \mid R(\mathbf{t}) \in I\}$. A *query* over input schema σ_1 and output schema σ_2 is a generic mapping from σ_1-instances to σ_2-instances.

Conjunctive Queries.

We assume an infinite set of variables **var** disjoint from **dom**. An *atom* over schema σ is of the form $R(\boldsymbol{x})$, where R is a relation symbol in σ and $\boldsymbol{x}$ is a tuple $(x_1, \ldots, x_n)$ of variables from **var** with $n = ar(R)$. A *conjunctive query* (CQ) $\mathcal{Q}$ over input schema σ is a query of the form

$$\mathrm{H}(\boldsymbol{x_0}) \text{ :- } \mathrm{S}_1(\boldsymbol{x_1}), \mathrm{S}_2(\boldsymbol{x_2}), \ldots, \mathrm{S}_\ell(\boldsymbol{x_\ell}),$$

where $\mathrm{S}_i(\boldsymbol{x_i})$ are atoms over σ and $\mathrm{H}(\boldsymbol{x_0})$ is an atom with

$H \notin \sigma$. Atom $\mathrm{H}(\boldsymbol{x_0})$ is called the *head* of $\mathcal{Q}$, and the set $\{\mathrm{S}_i(\boldsymbol{x_i}) \mid i \in [\ell]\}$ its *body*. We assume that every variable in the head of a query also occurs in its body. For conjunctive query $\mathcal{Q}$ and subset C of body atoms, we sometimes write $\mathcal{Q}_C$ to denote the query obtained by removing from $\mathcal{Q}$ all atoms not in C.

By *vars*($\mathcal{Q}$) we denote the variables of query $\mathcal{Q}$ and by *atoms*($\mathcal{Q}$) its body atoms. If *vars*($\mathcal{Q}$) $= \boldsymbol{x_0}$ we call $\mathcal{Q}$ *full*. If $\mathrm{S}_i \neq \mathrm{S}_j$ for all $i \neq j$, with $i, j \in [\ell]$, we say that $\mathcal{Q}$ is *without self-joins*. In the remainder of this document we only consider CQs that are full and without self-joins. For simplicity, we also assume each variable to occur at most once in every atom. We call a variable *isolated* if it occurs only in unary atoms.

The semantics of conjunctive queries is defined in terms of valuations. A *valuation* V for query $\mathcal{Q}$ is a mapping from the variables in $\mathcal{Q}$ to values in **dom**. A valuation V for $\mathcal{Q}$ *satisfies* on instance I if all the facts obtained by applying V over the body atoms of $\mathcal{Q}$ are in I. The output $\mathcal{Q}(I)$ of a conjunctive query $\mathcal{Q}$ over instance I is the set of facts obtained by applying satisfying valuations for $\mathcal{Q}$ on I over its head atom.

For query $\mathcal{Q}$, we define the degree of variable $x \in vars(\mathcal{Q})$ as the number of atoms containing x, and the *degree* of $\mathcal{Q}$, denoted $d(\mathcal{Q})$, as the maximum degree of any variable in $\mathcal{Q}$. For set of variables $X \subseteq vars(\mathcal{Q})$, the *residual query* $\mathcal{Q}[X]$ is the query obtained by removing variables X from $\mathcal{Q}$, and decreasing accordingly the arities of the relations that contain those variables.

Example 1. *For an example, consider the chain query,*

$$\mathrm{L2}(x_1, x_2, x_3, x_4) \text{ :- } \mathrm{S}_1(x_1, x_2), \mathrm{S}_2(x_2, x_3), \mathrm{S}_3(x_3, x_4).$$

The residual query $L2[\{x_2, x_3\}]$ *takes the form:*

$$\overline{\mathrm{L2}}(x_1, x_4) \text{ :- } \overline{\mathrm{S}}_1(x_1), \overline{\mathrm{S}}_2(), \overline{\mathrm{S}}_3(x_4).$$

Henceforth, we omit mentioning schemas for queries and instances when they are clear from the context.

Fractional Covers and Packings.

We recall the definition of fractional edge (vertex) packing and fractional vertex (edge) cover of a query's hypergraph. Let f be a mapping from the atoms in $\mathcal{Q}$ to positive weights; f is a *fractional edge packing* if

$$\sum_{a: x \in vars(a)} f(a) \leq 1, \text{ for every } x \in vars(\mathcal{Q}), \tag{1}$$

where a is over *atoms*($\mathcal{Q}$). If instead

$$\sum_{a: x \in vars(a)} f(a) \geq 1, \text{ for every } x \in vars(\mathcal{Q}), \tag{2}$$

where a is again over *atoms*($\mathcal{Q}$), then f is called a *fractional edge cover* for $\mathcal{Q}$. In both cases we refer to the sum $\sum_{a \in atoms(\mathcal{Q})} f(a)$ as the *value* of f for $\mathcal{Q}$, and are mostly interested in mappings f with optimal value. Optimal means maximum for fractional edge packings, and minimum for fractional edge covers.

Both LP-problems have a natural dual over the variables of $\mathcal{Q}$: A mapping f' from the variables in $\mathcal{Q}$ to positive weights is a *fractional vertex cover* if

$$\sum_{x \in vars(a)} f'(x) \geq 1, \text{ for every } a \in atoms(\mathcal{Q}), \tag{3}$$

and describes a *fractional vertex packing* if instead

$$\sum_{x \in vars(a)} f'(x) \leq 1, \text{ for every } a \in atoms(\mathcal{Q}). \tag{4}$$

Similar as before, for mappings f' we refer to the result of $\sum_{x \in vars(\mathcal{Q})} f'(x)$ as their *value* for $\mathcal{Q}$ and we are interested in finding fractional vertex covers with minimum value, and fractional vertex packings with maximum value. At optimality, the value of the fractional edge packing coincides with the value of the fractional vertex cover, and is called the *fractional vertex covering number* for $\mathcal{Q}$, denoted $\tau^*(\mathcal{Q})$. Similarly, at optimality the value of fractional edge cover coincides with the value of fractional vertex packing, and is called the *fractional edge covering number*, denoted $\rho^*(\mathcal{Q})$.

In general there is no clear relation between $\tau^*(\mathcal{Q})$ and $\rho^*(\mathcal{Q})$, unless f or f' are tight. We call f tight if the inequalities in conditions (1) and (2) are equalities. Similar for f' and conditions (3) and (4). A tight fractional edge packing is also a fractional edge cover, thus implying $\tau^*(\mathcal{Q}) \geq \rho^*(\mathcal{Q})$. Similarly, a tight fractional vertex cover is also a fractional vertex packing, thus $\tau^*(\mathcal{Q}) \leq \rho^*(\mathcal{Q})$.

Degree Information.

Let I be an input instance and S a relation symbol. For a value $c \in$ **dom**, and column i of relation S, $i \in [ar(S)]$, denote by $\deg_S(c, i)$ the frequency of value c in column i of relation S^I. When S is unary, $\deg_S(c, 1) = 1$ if $S(c) \in S^I$ and $\deg_S(c, 1) = 0$ if $S(c) \notin S^I$.

Given a query $\mathcal{Q}$, we are usually interested in the frequencies of values for variables, rather than relation columns. Therefore we introduce the following abbreviations: For this, consider value $c \in$ **dom**, variable $x \in vars(\mathcal{Q})$, and let a be a body atom of $\mathcal{Q}$ where x is incident to. By $\deg_S(c, x)$ we denote the frequency of value c in in the column of S^I corresponding to the position of x in atom a. For example, for atom $S(x, y)$, $\deg_S(c, x) = \deg_S(c, 1)$ and $\deg_S(c, y) = \deg_S(c, 2)$. Further, by $\deg(c, x)$ we denote the maximal frequency over all relations where x is incident to in $\mathcal{Q}$. The latter means that $\deg(c, x) = \max_R\{\deg_R(c, x)\}$, where R is over those relations incident to variable x in $\mathcal{Q}$.

3. THE MULTI-ROUND MPC MODEL

We study query evaluation in the *Massively Parallel Communication* model (MPC) [12, 5], which takes a number p of servers and allows to express large-scale data processing algorithms in a sequence of rounds. Each round consists of two phases: a global communication phase in which data is reshuffled; and a local computation phase in which each server processes its local data fragment. Servers are assumed to be part of a complete communication network and have unlimited computation power. For a given algorithm, the maximum load is expressed in number of tuples and denotes the maximum amount of tuples that a server receives during any of the communication rounds. Initially, the input instance is assumed to be uniformly partitioned over the available servers, thus yielding load m/p. The query's answer is also distributed over the p servers, and consists of the union of all output fragments on all servers.

Worst-Case Load.

In this paper we consider the same framework as in [11] and are interested in algorithms for computing conjunctive queries with worst-case optimal load. The latter particularly means that we place no restrictions on the input instance, which thus may have skew. Skew refers to the maximum frequency of values occurring in certain columns of instance relations.

Allowing p rounds enables servers to collect the entire input instance and thus generate the desired output for a given query with load at most m/p in a trivial way. To prevent this undesirable behaviour from happening, we consider only algorithms that run in a constant number of rounds. As our focus is on large-scale data we consider data complexity and additionally assume that the size of the data is significantly larger than the number of servers: $m > p^2$.

Lower Bound.

The following lower-bound was obtained recently:

Lemma 1 ([11]). *For any randomized algorithm computing a CQ $\mathcal{Q}$ over p servers in $O(1)$ rounds, there exists an input instance where all relations have size $\leq m$ such that the load is $\Omega\left(m/p^{1/\rho^*(\mathcal{Q})}\right)$ w.h.p. in the random choices of the algorithm.*

Henceforth we say that a CQ $\mathcal{Q}$ has an *X-load algorithm* if an algorithm exists to compute $\mathcal{Q}$ in the above described model using p servers in a constant number of rounds with load at most $\tilde{O}\left(m/p^{1/X}\right)$ w.h.p., where m denotes the size of the largest relation, and X is a non-negative number, usually $\rho^*(\mathcal{Q})$.

For specific classes of CQs, like chain queries and cycle queries, a $\rho^*(\mathcal{Q})$-load algorithm is given in [11], thus showing that for these queries the lower bound is tight.

4. BUILDING BLOCKS

In this section we set the stage by introducing the basic building blocks for our worst-case optimal multi-round algorithm, which is described in Section 5.

4.1 Hypercube

The hypercube algorithm was introduced by Afrati and Ullman [1] in the context of Mapreduce, where it is called *shares algorithm*, and has since then been intensively studied [5, 6, 3, 11]. For a conjunctive query $\mathcal{Q}$, the hypercube algorithm defines a reshuffling strategy based on hashing of data values allowing to compute $\mathcal{Q}$ through local evaluation on servers in parallel.

First, we assign to every variable x_i of $\mathcal{Q}$ a number p_i, which is called the *share* of x_i. Then, the p servers are conceptually ordered in a space $\mathcal{S} = [p_1] \times [p_2] \times \cdots \times [p_{|vars(\mathcal{Q})|}]$, where every coordinate in $\mathcal{S}$ points to a unique server. Here it is assumed that $\prod p_i \leq p$. Additionally, to every variable a randomly chosen hash function $h_i : \mathbf{dom} \rightarrow [p_i]$ is assigned which maps data values to a bucket in the associated share.

During its single communication round, the HC algorithm sends every fact $R(a_1, \ldots, a_n)$ over atom $R(x_{i_1}, \ldots, x_{i_n})$ to the set of servers agreeing on the partial coordinate defined by its values and associated hash functions. More concrete, it sends the fact to all servers with coordinates in the set

$$\{\mathbf{c} \in \mathcal{S} \mid \bigwedge_{j \in [n]} c_{i_j} = h_{i_j}(a_j)\}.$$

It has been shown that the HC algorithm can compute CQs in the one round setting with optimal load when values are light, as made precise in the following lemma:

Lemma 2 ([6]). *Let $\mathcal{Q}$ be a CQ, I an instance, m be the maximal size over all relations in I, and f a fractional vertex cover for $\mathcal{Q}$. Define $p_i = p^{f(x_i)/(\sum_j f(x_j))}$ for every variable x_i. Suppose that for every atom $a_j = S_j(\boldsymbol{x_j})$ in $\mathcal{Q}$, every subset of variables $\boldsymbol{y} \subseteq \boldsymbol{x_j}$, and every tuple $\boldsymbol{t}$ over $\boldsymbol{y}$: $deg_{S_j}(\boldsymbol{t}, \boldsymbol{y}) \leq m/\Pi_{x_i \in \boldsymbol{y}} p_i$ (when this condition holds we say the database is skew-free). Then the HC algorithm with shares $\mathbf{p} = (p_1, \ldots, p_k)$ has a load $\tilde{O}(m/p^{1/\sum_i f(x_i)})$ with high probability over the choices of the random hash functions.*

Here, $\deg_{S_j}(\boldsymbol{t}, \boldsymbol{y})$ is defined as the frequency of tuple $\boldsymbol{t}$ over the columns of relation S_j that correspond to variables $\boldsymbol{y}$.

By choosing f the optimal fractional vertex cover, we obtain a one round, $\tau^*(\mathcal{Q})$-load algorithm, but in this paper we will also use the HC algorithm with different, non-optimal fractional vertex cover. When each relation has arity at most two, the skew-free condition simplifies to the following: for every variable x_i and value $v \in \mathbf{dom}$, $\deg(v, x_i) \leq m/p^{f(x_i)/\sum_j f(x_j)}$.

4.2 Semi-Join Decompositions

It is a common strategy in distributed query evaluation to reduce relations using semi-joins before sending them over the network. Interestingly, it has been observed in [11] that semi-join queries can be computed in the multi-round MPC setting with significantly less load compared to single-round algorithms, even when instances have no skew. That technique extends to any *guarded* query $\mathcal{Q}$, which is a conjunctive query that has some atom $b \in atoms(\mathcal{Q})$ for which $vars(b) = vars(\mathcal{Q})$. We call b a *guard atom* for $\mathcal{Q}$.

Lemma 3 ([11]). *Let $\mathcal{Q}$ be a guarded query, then $\mathcal{Q}$ can be computed using a constant number of rounds with load $\tilde{O}(m/p)$ over p servers.*

The number of rounds depends on the number of non-guard atoms. If the guard has arity at most two (which we assume through the paper), only two rounds are needed.

Example 2. *We illustrate the underlying algorithm by an example. For this, consider the generalized semi-join query* H *from the introduction,* $\mathrm{H}(x, y)$:- $\mathrm{R}(x), \mathrm{S}(x, y), \mathrm{T}(y)$.

The algorithm takes only two rounds: the first round computes $\mathrm{S}'(x, y)$:- $\mathrm{R}(x), \mathrm{S}(x, y)$, *and the second round computes* $\mathrm{H}(x, y)$:- $\mathrm{S}'(x, y), \mathrm{T}(y)$. *We explain in detail the first round only: the second round is similar, since the size of* S' *is no larger than that of* S. *Call a value c in column x of $S(x, y)$ a light hitter if $deg_S(c, x) \leq m/p$: otherwise we call it a heavy hitter. The database has at most p heavy hitters and we may assume throughout the paper that all p servers know all heavy hitters c: this can be achieved in a preprocessing phase, using another round of communication. The algorithm treats separately the subsets of the relations* $\mathrm{R}(x)$ *and* $\mathrm{S}(x, y)$ *where x is a light hitter or a heavy hitter. For the light hitters, the algorithm uses a standard partitioned hash-join on the variable x: since all values are light, the maximum load per server is $\tilde{O}(m/p)$ w.h.p. For the heavy hitters, the algorithm uses a standard broadcast join: broadcast all heavy-hitter tuples in* $\mathrm{R}(x)$ *to all p servers, and* $\mathrm{S}(x, y)$ *is not reshuffled, then join the local fragment of* $\mathrm{S}(x, y)$ *with the entire relation* $\mathrm{R}(x)$. *Since there are $\leq p$ heavy hitters,* *the size of the broadcast relation* $\mathrm{R}(x)$ *is* $\leq p$*, hence the load per server is* $\leq m/p$ *because* $p^2 \leq m$.

Notice that the optimal load for computing H over instances without skew in the one-round MPC setting requires load $m/p^{1/2}$, by Lemma 2, which is significantly higher than load m/p.

Definition 1. Let $\mathcal{Q}$ be a query. A *semi-join decomposition for* $\mathcal{Q}$ is a minimal subset of atoms $\mathcal{V} \subseteq atoms(\mathcal{Q})$ such that every atom $a \notin \mathcal{V}$ is contained in some atom $b \in \mathcal{V}$, more precisely $vars(a) \subseteq vars(b)$. Given a semi-join decomposition $\mathcal{V}$ of $\mathcal{Q}$, the *reduced query* $\mathcal{Q}_{\mathcal{V}}$ is defined as the query consisting of all atoms in $\mathcal{V}$.

If S is a relation symbol in $\mathcal{V}$ we sometimes denote $S^{\mathcal{V}}$ its occurrence in $\mathcal{Q}_{\mathcal{V}}$. The *semi-join reduction* consists of $|\mathcal{V}|$ queries of the form

$$\mathrm{S}^{\mathcal{V}}(\boldsymbol{x}) \text{ :- } \mathrm{S}(\boldsymbol{x}), \mathrm{R}_1(\boldsymbol{x}_1), \mathrm{R}_2(\boldsymbol{x}_2), \ldots, \mathrm{R}_k(\boldsymbol{x}_k),$$

where R_i are all atoms with $\boldsymbol{x}_i \subseteq \boldsymbol{x}$. It is straightforward to check that any algorithm for computing $\mathcal{Q}_{\mathcal{V}}$ can be used to compute $\mathcal{Q}$ in two steps: (1) compute all semi-join reductions to obtain reduced relations $\mathrm{S}^{\mathcal{V}}$, and (2) compute $\mathcal{Q}_{\mathcal{V}}$ on the reduced relations $\mathrm{S}^{\mathcal{V}}$.

A semi-join decomposition is not necessarily unique (e.g., when two atoms have $vars(a) = vars(b)$), but always exists. We can easily obtain one by iteratively removing atoms from $\mathcal{Q}$ that are variable-contained in other atoms. The remaining atoms form a semi-join decomposition $\mathcal{V}$ for $\mathcal{Q}$.

Example 3. *For an example consider query* $\mathcal{Q}$*,*

$$\mathrm{H}(x, y, z) \text{ :- } \mathrm{R}(x, y), \mathrm{S}(y, z), \mathrm{T}(y).$$

Then, the semi-join decomposition $\mathcal{V}$ *for* $\mathcal{Q}$ *is the set* $\{\mathrm{R}(x, y), \mathrm{S}(y, z)\}$. *The semi-join reduction consists of queries:*

$$\mathrm{R}^{\mathcal{V}}(x, y) \text{ :- } \mathrm{R}(x, y), \mathrm{T}(y) \text{ and } \mathrm{S}^{\mathcal{V}}(y, z) \text{ :- } \mathrm{S}(y, z), \mathrm{T}(y),$$

and the reduced query $\mathcal{Q}_{\mathcal{V}}$ *takes the form:*

$$\mathrm{H}(x, y, z) \text{ :- } \mathrm{R}^{\mathcal{V}}(x, y), \mathrm{S}^{\mathcal{V}}(y, z).$$

We have the following generalization of Lemma 3:

Lemma 4. *Let* $\mathcal{Q}$ *be a CQ over relations with arity at most two and* $\mathcal{V}$ *a semi-join decomposition for* $\mathcal{Q}$*. All queries in the semi-join reduction can be computed in two rounds using* p *servers with load at most* $\tilde{O}(m/p)$*, where* m *is the maximal size of relations.*

4.3 Heavy-Hitter Configurations

Finally, we introduce the notion heavy-hitter configuration, which allows to partition instances based on where heavy hitters are located in the query structure. A similar technique is used in [11].

For an instance I, query $\mathcal{Q}$, and given threshold value $\delta \in [0, 1]$, we call a value c for variable x *heavy* (w.r.t. δ) if $\deg(c, x) > m/p^{\delta}$, with m the number of tuples in the largest relation of I; and *light* otherwise. Notice that our definition of heavy and light is relation independent, therefore a variable x may have up to $k \cdot p^{\delta}$ many heavy hitters, with k the number of distinct atoms where x is incident to.

A *heavy-hitter configuration* Ψ for query $\mathcal{Q}$ is a pair (H, δ) with δ a threshold value and H a subset of the variables in $\mathcal{Q}$. For any atom $S(x_1, \ldots, x_k)$ in $\mathcal{Q}$, we call a fact $S(c_1, \ldots, c_k)$ (from instance I) compatible with Ψ if for all variables x_i and corresponding values c_i: $\deg(c_i, x_i) > m/p^{\delta}$ if $x_i \in H$, and $\deg(c_i, x_i) \leq m/p^{\delta}$ if $x_i \notin H$. By $I|_{\Psi}$ we denote the subset of instance I containing all facts compatible with configuration Ψ. We call I_{Ψ} the Ψ*-compatible* instance (w.r.t I). It is straightforward to check that $\bigcup_{H \subseteq vars(\mathcal{Q})} I|_{(H,\delta)} = I$, for every $\delta \in [0, 1]$.

A case of special interest is when $H = \emptyset$. Then we call a tuple in I_{Ψ} a *light hitter*, and call I_{Ψ} the *skew-free subinstance* of I, with respect to chosen threshold value δ. In particular, if $\delta = 0$ then $I_{\Psi} = I$, and if $\delta = 1$ then I_{Ψ} contains only values with degree $\leq m/p$.

Example 4. *For an example, let* $p = 4$ *and consider the join query* $R(x, y), S(y, z)$ *over instance* I*,*

$$I = \{\mathrm{R}(a, d), \mathrm{R}(b, d), \mathrm{R}(c, e), \mathrm{S}(d, a), \mathrm{S}(e, b), \mathrm{S}(c, d)\}.$$

Thus, $m = 3$*. For threshold value* $\delta = 1/2$*, we have* $m/p^{\delta} = 3/2$ *and we distinguish the following heavy-hitter configurations:*

$$I|_{(\{y\},\delta)} = \{\mathrm{R}(a, d), \mathrm{R}(b, d), \mathrm{S}(d, a)\},$$
$$I|_{(\emptyset,\delta)} = \{\mathrm{R}(c, e), \mathrm{S}(e, b), \mathrm{S}(c, d)\}.$$

For all other sets $H \subseteq vars(\mathcal{Q})$*:* $I|_{(H,\delta)} = \emptyset$.

Sometimes we want to express a subinstance in which certain values are fixed. For this, let $\mathcal{Q}$ be a query, I an instance, and $X \subseteq vars(\mathcal{Q})$. Let $\boldsymbol{t} = (c_1, \ldots, c_n)$ be a sequence of values from **dom**, denoting exactly one value for each variable in $X = \{x_1, \ldots, x_n\}$. Then, by $I_{\boldsymbol{t},X}$ we denote the subinstance of I consisting of all facts from I that are compatible with choice $\boldsymbol{t}$ for variables X in $\mathcal{Q}$. More specifically, $I|_{\boldsymbol{t},X}$ consists of all relations $R^{I|_{\boldsymbol{t},X}}$ defined as follows: if $R(y_1, \ldots, y_k)$ is an atom in the query, then $R^{I|_{\boldsymbol{t},X}} = \{R(d_1, \ldots, d_k) \in I \mid \forall y_i, x_j : y_i = x_j \Rightarrow d_i = c_j\}$. For example, recall instance I and query $\mathcal{Q}$ from Example 4, in which we want to express the subinstance of I compatible with value c on the position of variable x. Then $I_{c,x} = \{\mathrm{R}(c, e), \mathrm{S}(d, a), \mathrm{S}(e, b), \mathrm{S}(c, d)\}$. In other words, $I_{c,x}$ restricts the values of $R(x, y)$, but leaves the values of $S(y, z)$ unrestricted since this atom does not contain x.

A CQ $\mathcal{Q}$ can be computed over an instance I by fixing a threshold value and evaluating $\mathcal{Q}$ over each Ψ-compatible subinstance of I separately:

Lemma 5. *For CQ* $\mathcal{Q}$*, threshold value* δ*, and* $X \subseteq vars(\mathcal{Q})$*:*

1. $\mathcal{Q}(I) = \bigcup_{H \subseteq vars(\mathcal{Q})} \mathcal{Q}(I|_{H,\delta})$*; and*
2. $\mathcal{Q}(I) = \bigcup_{\boldsymbol{t} \in \boldsymbol{dom}^{|X|}} \mathcal{Q}(I_{\boldsymbol{t},X})$.

By the assumption that degree information is known for every value in the considered input instance, servers can recognize Ψ-compatible facts autonomously for specified configurations.

5. A WORST-CASE OPTIMAL LOAD ALGORITHM

In this section we present our main result:

Theorem 3. *Every CQ* $\mathcal{Q}$ *over relations with arity at most two can be computed with a* $\rho^*(\mathcal{Q})$*-load algorithm using at most seven rounds.*

We assume that all heavy hitters are known by all servers. If that is not the case, then one additional round of computation is required to compute and broadcast all heavy hitters. In a nutshell, our strategy is to first identify structural properties of the target query and then attack each heavy-hitter configuration in parallel using customized algorithms. More precise, we focus on a distraction-free subset of conjunctive queries, called simple queries, defined in Section 5.1. Here we also show that algorithms for simple queries can be generalized to the more general class of queries considered in Theorem 3. We then gradually provide algorithms for simple queries with desired load: for queries with tight edge packing first, in Section 5.3, then for queries without such packing in Section 5.4.

5.1 Simple and Connected Queries

We introduce the class of connected CQs first, then proceed to simple queries.

Connected Queries

A CQ is called *connected* when its query graph is connected, meaning that for every pair of variables $x, y \in vars(\mathcal{Q})$ there is a sequence of atoms $a_1, \ldots, a_n$ such that $x \in vars(a_1)$, $y \in vars(a_n)$, and for every $i \in [1, n-1]$: $vars(a_i) \cap vars(a_{i+1}) \neq \emptyset$. A subset C of atoms in CQ $\mathcal{Q}$ is called a *connected-component* of $\mathcal{Q}$ if $\mathcal{Q}_C$ is connected and C is maximal with this property.

By definition, the edge covering number is additive, meaning that the sum of fractional edge covering numbers over the connected components of a query equals its fractional edge covering number. We use this observation in the following lemma:

Lemma 6. *Let $\mathcal{Q}$ be a CQ and A and B be disjoint subsets of atoms from $\mathcal{Q}$, with atoms($\mathcal{Q}$) $= A \cup B$ and vars(A) $\cap$ vars(B) $= \emptyset$. Then,*

1. *$\rho^*(\mathcal{Q}_A) + \rho^*(\mathcal{Q}_B) = \rho^*(\mathcal{Q})$; and*
2. *$\mathcal{Q}$ has a $\rho^*(\mathcal{Q})$-load algorithm if $\mathcal{Q}_A$ has a $\rho^*(\mathcal{Q}_A)$-load algorithm and $\mathcal{Q}_B$ has a $\rho^*(\mathcal{Q}_B)$-load algorithm.*

Simple Queries

We now introduce the class of simple CQs. A CQ $\mathcal{Q}$ is called *simple* if (*i*) $\mathcal{Q}$ has only binary atoms and (*ii*) there are no distinct atoms $a, b \in atoms(\mathcal{Q})$ for which $vars(a) \subseteq vars(b)$. Notice that simple queries denote exactly those CQs representing a simple graph without self-loops (i.e. edges $R(x, x)$). The following lemma shows that we can transform every query into a simple query by doing a semi-join decomposition, without affecting the fractional edge covering number.

Lemma 7. *Let $\mathcal{Q}$ be a connected CQ where each relation has arity at most 2, and let $\mathcal{V}$ be a semi-join decomposition for $\mathcal{Q}$ (see Def. 1). Then (1) the reduced query $\mathcal{Q}_\mathcal{V}$ is simple, and (2) $\rho^*(\mathcal{Q}) = \rho^*(\mathcal{Q}_\mathcal{V})$.*

Proof. (1) Since the query is connected, every atom that has only one variable has that variable occurring in at least one atom with two variables and, thus, will be eliminated by the semi-join decomposition. For (2), we show that (*i*) every fractional edge cover for $\mathcal{Q}_\mathcal{V}$ defines also a fractional edge cover for $\mathcal{Q}$ with same value, and that (*ii*) every fractional edge cover for $\mathcal{Q}$ can be transformed into a fractional edge cover for $\mathcal{Q}_\mathcal{V}$ with same value. The equality then follows.

For (*i*), observe that, by construction, every atom $b^\mathcal{V}$ in $\mathcal{Q}_\mathcal{V}$ corresponds to an atom b in $\mathcal{Q}$ which is a guard in $\mathcal{Q}_b$. Therefore, given fractional edge cover f for $\mathcal{Q}_\mathcal{V}$, fractional edge cover f', where $f'(b) = f(b^\mathcal{V})$ if $\mathcal{Q}_b$ exists and $f'(b) = 0$ otherwise, is as desired.

For (*ii*), let f be a fractional edge cover for $\mathcal{Q}$. Notice that for every atom $a \in atoms(\mathcal{Q})$ there is an atom $b \in \mathcal{V}$. Let π be the function mapping atoms a onto the corresponding atoms b, particularly their annotated versions, as described.[2] We define π so that $\pi(\emptyset)$ denotes the set of all atoms not in the range of π. Then, for every atom $b \in atoms(\mathcal{Q}_\mathcal{V})$, let $f'(b) = \sum_{a \in \pi^{-1}(b)} f(a)$. It now follows by construction that f' satisfies the LP-constraints for $\mathcal{Q}_\mathcal{V}$, and that f' has the same value for $\mathcal{Q}_\mathcal{V}$ as f for $\mathcal{Q}$. □

Example 5. *For an example we recall query $\mathcal{Q}$ and semi-join decomposition $\mathcal{V}$ from Example 3. Here, the optimal edge cover f for $\mathcal{Q}_\mathcal{V}$ is unique and assigns weight 1 to both its atoms. It is easy to observe that f describes also an optimal edge cover for $\mathcal{Q}$.*

By the above lemma, a similar result as for unconnected queries can be obtained for queries with a semi-join decomposition:

Lemma 8. *Let $\mathcal{Q}$ be a connected CQ where all relations have arity at most 2, and let $\mathcal{V}$ be a semi-join decomposition for $\mathcal{Q}$. If $\mathcal{Q}_\mathcal{V}$ has a $\rho^*(\mathcal{Q}_\mathcal{V})$-load algorithm in r rounds, then $\mathcal{Q}$ has a $\rho^*(\mathcal{Q})$-load algorithm in $r+2$ rounds.*

Proof. Let p be the number of available servers and m the size of the largest considered relation.

First, compute the semi-join reductions for $\mathcal{V}$, in two rounds, following the strategy in Lemma 4, with load at most $\tilde{O}(m/p)$. Next, compute $\mathcal{Q}_\mathcal{V}$ over the reduced relations using the algorithm assumed by the lemma. Notice that the size of the semi-join reduced relations is at most m, and $\rho^*(\mathcal{Q}') = \rho^*(\mathcal{Q})$, thus the load is as desired. □

5.2 Light Hitters

At a very high level, our strategy for computing $\mathcal{Q}(I)$ is to consider all configurations of heavy hitters, and compute the query separately for each such configuration. We start by discussing the case when all variables are light: here, we compute the query using a particular choice of fractional vertex cover in Lemma 2. To explain it, we review a couple of nice properties from graph theory.

Of particular interest in this context is the result that, for simple graphs, every optimal fractional edge packing has a half-integral equivalent. The latter means a fractional edge packing with optimal value, and over range $\{0, 1/2, 1\}$. As shown in [15], one can obtain such packing by searching for an optimal fractional edge packing that also maximizes the number of 0-weight edges. Interestingly, these packings have a very particular structure, in which 1/2-weight edges express variable-disjoint odd-length cycles. Henceforth we denote the set of atoms in $\mathcal{Q}$ with weight 1/2 under fractional edge packing f by $\mathcal{C}_f(\mathcal{Q})$. Translated to conjunctive queries, we now have the following property:

[2] Notice that π exists but is not necessarily unique, as multiple atoms b may exist. Then one can arbitrarily choose one of the available options.

Lemma 9 ([15]). *Let $\mathcal{Q}$ be a simple CQ. Then $\mathcal{Q}$ has a half-integral fractional edge packing with value $\tau^*(\mathcal{Q})$, and set $C_f(\mathcal{Q})$ contains only disjoint odd-length cycles.*

In the case of simple graphs, there exists a simple relationship between the fractional vertex covering number and fractional edge covering number, which does not hold in general on hypergraphs:

Lemma 10 ([15]). *For any simple CQ $\mathcal{Q}$,*

1. $\tau^*(\mathcal{Q}) \leq |vars(\mathcal{Q})|/2 \leq \rho^*(\mathcal{Q})$; *and*
2. $\tau^*(\mathcal{Q}) + \rho^*(\mathcal{Q}) = |vars(\mathcal{Q})|$.

The proof of Lemma 10.1 follows by considering the assignment $f(x) = 1/2$ to every variable x. Since f is both a fractional vertex packing and a fractional vertex cover ($\mathcal{Q}$ is simple, hence every edge $R(x, y)$ connects two distinct nodes x, y and thus is covered, $f(x) + f(y) = 1$), with value is $\sum_x f(x) = |vars(\mathcal{Q})|/2$, it implies $\tau^*(\mathcal{Q}) \leq |vars(\mathcal{Q})|/2 \leq \rho^*(\mathcal{Q})$. The proof of Lemma 10.2 follows by noting that f is a vertex packing iff f' is a vertex cover, where $f'(x) = 1-f(x)$, and furthermore $\sum_x f(x) + \sum_x f'(x) = |vars(\mathcal{Q})|$.

Our algorithm computes the query on the light hitters by running the HC algorithm using the vertex cover $f(x) = 1/2$ for every variable x, implying:

Lemma 11. *Let $\mathcal{Q}$ be a simple CQ. Consider the heavy-hitter configuration $\Psi = (\emptyset, 1/|vars(\mathcal{Q})|)$. Then $\mathcal{Q}$ can be computed by a $2/|vars(\mathcal{Q})|$-load algorithm in one round on the instance I_Ψ. We call the tuples in I_Ψ* light hitters.

The proof follows by applying the HC algorithm in Lemma 2, and noting that $1/(\sum_j f(x_j)) = 2/|vars(\mathcal{Q})|$, and that the share of each variable x_i is $p^{f(x_i)/\sum_j f(x_j)} = p^{1/|vars(\mathcal{Q})|}$. In particular, the lemma gives a $\rho^*(\mathcal{Q})$-load algorithm for the subinstance I_Ψ.

Thus, our strategy for computing $\mathcal{Q}(I)$ is to consider all possible heavy-hitter configurations $\Psi = (H, \delta)$, for some δ (to be determined) and for all choices of heavy hitter variables $H \subseteq vars(\mathcal{Q})$ and compute the query separately on I_Ψ.

5.3 Tight Edge Packings

We show how to compute a conjunctive query under the assumption that it has a tight half-integral edge packing f; in the next section we remove this restriction. As observed before (Sec. 2), existence of a tight f implies $\rho^*(\mathcal{Q}) \leq \tau^*(\mathcal{Q})$, thus for simple CQs $\mathcal{Q}$ we have $\tau^*(\mathcal{Q}) = \rho^*(\mathcal{Q}) = |vars(\mathcal{Q})|/2$, by Lemma 10. Throughout this section we denote $L = vars(\mathcal{Q}) \setminus H = vars(\mathcal{Q}[H])$. To start, we show how to handle a simple case, when $\mathcal{Q}[H]$ has no binary atoms.

Lemma 12. *Let $\mathcal{Q}$ be a simple CQ. Assume that $\mathcal{Q}$ admits a tight edge packing f, and let $\Psi = (H, 1/|vars(\mathcal{Q})|)$ be a heavy-hitter configuration, where $\mathcal{Q}[H]$ has no binary atoms. Then $\mathcal{Q}$ can be computed over the Ψ-compatible instance by a $\rho^*(\mathcal{Q})$-load algorithm in two rounds.*

Proof. Let I be the Ψ-compatible instance. (Recall that I is the subset of some instance J with maximal-relation size m.) If $|vars(\mathcal{Q})| \leq 2$ the result follows trivially, as then $\mathcal{Q}$ consists of either a single atom (nothing needs to be done), or two disjoint unary atoms (Lemma 6 applies). Henceforth we assume $|vars(\mathcal{Q})| > 2$, which implies $\rho^*(\mathcal{Q}) \geq 3/2$ (with $\rho^*(\mathcal{Q}) = 3/2$ when $\mathcal{Q}$ is the triangle query).

Let I be an arbitrary Ψ-compatible instance. For the computation of $\mathcal{Q}(I)$ we consider a different threshold value, namely $\delta' = 2/|vars(\mathcal{Q})|$ and split instance I in $I_{\Psi'}$ for each heavy-hitter configuration $\Psi' = (H', \delta')$. Notice that heavy-hitters under δ remain heavy under δ', particularly because $m/p^{1/|vars(\mathcal{Q})|} > m/p^{2/|vars(\mathcal{Q})|}$. We now compute $\mathcal{Q}$ for every subinstance $I_{\Psi'}$ over the p servers in parallel. For this let $L' = vars(\mathcal{Q}) \setminus H'$.

We first show the case $L' = \emptyset$. Then instance $I_{\Psi'}$ is very small. More precise $|I'_\Psi| \leq O(p^{4/vars(\mathcal{Q})})$. Thus, we can send all facts in $I_{\Psi'}$ to a single server and compute $\mathcal{Q}(I_{\Psi'})$ locally. The load is as desired by assumption $m > p^2$, $|vars(\mathcal{Q})| \geq 3$, and $\rho^*(\mathcal{Q}) = vars(\mathcal{Q})/2$.

If $|L'| \geq 1$. We observe $|L'| \leq |vars(\mathcal{Q})|/2$. Indeed, every variable in L' is incident to a set of relations with 1 as the sum of weights (due to tightness of the packing), and no variables in L' share a relation, thus $|L'| \leq \rho^*(\mathcal{Q}) = |vars(\mathcal{Q})|/2$. Further, by the assumption that $\mathcal{Q}[H]$ has no binary atoms, it follows that $\mathcal{Q}[H']$ has no binary atoms either.

Now, to compute $\mathcal{Q}$, let $\mathcal{Q}'$ be the query obtained by removing from $\mathcal{Q}$ all atoms not incident to a variable in L'. Then $\mathcal{Q}'$ consists of unconnected components all representing a star with variable from L' in its center.

For $\mathcal{Q}(I_{\Psi'})$ we hash-partition the tuples over relations in $\mathcal{Q}'$ as for computing $\mathcal{Q}'(I_{\Psi'})$ using the HC-algorithm over $p^{2|L|/|vars(\mathcal{Q})|}$ servers, by allocating weight 1 for all variables from L' and weight 0 to all others. The load is at most $m/p^{2/|vars(\mathcal{Q})|}$ by Lemma 2.

Tuples over relations not in $\mathcal{Q}'$ are broadcast to all servers. As all these tuples are heavy, this does not affect the load (the analysis is analogous to case $L' = \emptyset$). Then the final output is obtained by computing $\mathcal{Q}'$ on every server. □

By Lemma 12, in the remainder of the section we assume $\mathcal{Q}[H]$ has at least one binary atom, thus $|L| \geq 2$. As a warm-up towards the general case, where $\mathcal{Q}[H]$ may generate unary and binary atoms, we first show the case where heavy-hitter configurations do not generate isolated variables: in that case semi-join decomposition $\mathcal{Q}_v$ of $\mathcal{Q}[H]$ is also simple (because the only unary relation symbols that can remain in the semi-join decomposition contain isolated variables).

Lemma 13. *Let $\mathcal{Q}$ be a simple CQ. Assume that $\mathcal{Q}$ admits a tight edge packing f, and let $\Psi = (H, 1/|vars(\mathcal{Q})|)$ be a heavy-hitter configuration, such that $\mathcal{Q}[H]$ is without isolated variables. Then $\mathcal{Q}$ can be computed over the Ψ-compatible instance by a $\rho^*(\mathcal{Q})$-load algorithm using three rounds.*

Proof. Let p be the number of available servers and I the Ψ-compatible instance. We use item 2 of Lemma 5 and write:

$$\mathcal{Q}(I) = \bigcup_{\boldsymbol{h}} \mathcal{Q}(I_{\boldsymbol{h},H}) \tag{5}$$

where $\boldsymbol{h}$ ranges over all heavy-hitter tuples. The algorithm proceeds by allocating for every heavy-hitter tuple a group of $p' = c \cdot p^{|L|/|vars(\mathcal{Q})|}$ exclusive servers, where $c = 1/d(\mathcal{Q})^{|H|}$ is a constant (recall that $d(\mathcal{Q})$ denotes the degree of the query graph). Then for every heavy-hitter tuple $\boldsymbol{h}$, $\mathcal{Q}(I_{\boldsymbol{h},H})$ is computed over its assigned set of servers.

Before giving the details, notice that the number of heavy-hitter tuples is at most $p^{|H|/|vars(\mathcal{Q})|}/c$ and $|L| + |H| =$

$|vars(\mathcal{Q})|$, thus we use a total number of servers $\leq p' \cdot p^{|H|/|vars(\mathcal{Q})|}/c = p$.

Next, we show how to compute $\mathcal{Q}(I_{\boldsymbol{h},H})$ over its p' servers. Consider an atom $R(x,y)$ that has a variable $x \in H$. If also $y \in H$, then, for the purpose of computing $\mathcal{Q}(I_{\boldsymbol{h},H})$, $R(x,y)$ is a single Boolean value (true or false), which we broadcast to all servers. Assume $y \in L$. Then R becomes a unary relation $R(y)$. To compute $\mathcal{Q}(I_{\boldsymbol{h},H})$ it thus suffices to compute $\mathcal{Q}[H]$, where the unary relations depend on the particular heavy-hitter tuple $\boldsymbol{h}$. To obtain the final output, output facts for $\mathcal{Q}[H]$ are augmented with values $\boldsymbol{h}$ and are in the output for $\mathcal{Q}$ only if the required booleans are present.

To show the computation of $\mathcal{Q}[H]$, let $\mathcal{V}$ be a semi-join decomposition for $\mathcal{Q}[H]$. The computation proceeds as follows:

Step 1: Compute the semi-join reductions for $\mathcal{V}$ in two rounds, using load m/p' (see Lemma 4). We note that $m/p' = m/(c \cdot p^{|L|/|vars(\mathcal{Q})|}) \leq m/(c \cdot p^{2/|vars(\mathcal{Q})|}) = m/(c \cdot p^{1/\rho^*(\mathcal{Q})})$, because $|L| \geq 2$.

Step 2: Compute the reduced query $\mathcal{Q}_\mathcal{V}$ of $\mathcal{Q}[H]$, on the semi-join reduction from the previous step, in one round, using the $2/|vars(\mathcal{Q}_\mathcal{V})| = 2/|L|$-load algorithm in Lemma 11; recall that $\mathcal{Q}_\mathcal{V}$ is simple, hence Lemma 11 applies.

We still need to prove *(1)* all tuples in $I_{\boldsymbol{h},H}$ are "light" (as per Lemma 11) for the residual query $\mathcal{Q}[H]$, hence the application of HC in Lemma 11 is correct, and *(2)* the load is within our budget. For *(1)* note that, by assumption, I is a $(H, 1/|vars(\mathcal{Q})|)$-compatible instance, hence every value of a variable $\notin H$ has degree $\leq m/p^{1/|vars(\mathcal{Q})|}$. Since $L = vars(\mathcal{Q}_\mathcal{V})$, it follows that its degree is also $\leq m/(p')^{1/|L|}$, proving that it is light according to Lemma 11. For *(2)*, we note that the load of the HC algorithm given by Lemma 11 is $m/(p')^{2/|vars(\mathcal{Q}_\mathcal{V})|} = m/(p')^{2/|L|} = m/p^{1/\rho^*(\mathcal{Q})}$, proving that this is a $\rho^*(\mathcal{Q})$-load algorithm. □

Example 6. *For an example illustrating the above algorithm, consider query $\mathcal{Q}$,*

$$\begin{aligned}\mathrm{H}(\boldsymbol{x}) \text{ :- } & \mathrm{R}_1(x_1,x_2), \mathrm{R}_2(x_2,x_3), \mathrm{R}_3(x_3,x_4), \mathrm{R}_4(x_4,x_5), \\ & \mathrm{R}_5(x_5,x_6), \mathrm{R}_6(x_6,x_1), \mathrm{R}_7(x_2,x_5), \mathrm{R}_8(x_3,x_6)\end{aligned}$$

and heavy-hitter configuration $\Psi = (H, 1/6)$ with $H = \{x_1, x_4\}$. For $\mathcal{Q}$, $\tau^*(\mathcal{Q}) = \rho^*(\mathcal{Q}) = 3$, and $\tau^*(\mathcal{Q}[H]) = 4$, which shows at least two rounds are necessary to compute $\mathcal{Q}$ with desired load over a Ψ-compatible instance. Residual query $\mathcal{Q}[H]$ takes the form:

$$\begin{aligned}\overline{\mathrm{H}}(\boldsymbol{x}') \text{ :- } & \overline{\mathrm{R}}_1(x_2), \overline{\mathrm{R}}_2(x_2,x_3), \overline{\mathrm{R}}_3(x_3), \overline{\mathrm{R}}_4(x_5), \\ & \overline{\mathrm{R}}_5(x_5,x_6), \overline{\mathrm{R}}_6(x_6), \overline{\mathrm{R}}_7(x_2,x_5), \overline{\mathrm{R}}_8(x_3,x_6).\end{aligned}$$

Semi-join decomposition $\mathcal{V}$ for $\mathcal{Q}[H]$ has the following semi-join reductions:

$$\overline{\mathrm{R}}_2^{\mathcal{V}}(x_2,x_3) \text{ :- } \overline{\mathrm{R}}_2(x_2,x_3), \overline{\mathrm{R}}_1(x_2), \overline{\mathrm{R}}_3(x_3).$$

$$\overline{\mathrm{R}}_5^{\mathcal{V}}(x_5,x_6) \text{ :- } \overline{\mathrm{R}}_5(x_5,x_6), \overline{\mathrm{R}}_4(x_5), \overline{\mathrm{R}}_6(x_6).$$

$$\overline{\mathrm{R}}_7^{\mathcal{V}}(x_2,x_5) \text{ :- } \overline{\mathrm{R}}_7(x_2,x_5).$$

$$\overline{\mathrm{R}}_8^{\mathcal{V}}(x_3,x_6) \text{ :- } \overline{\mathrm{R}}_8(x_3,x_6).$$

As there are only $4 \cdot p^{1/3}$ heavy-hitter tuples for x_1 and x_4, we can compute $\mathcal{Q}$ for every heavy-hitter tuple h_1, h_4 separately over the remaining $p^{2/3}$ servers.[3] *The semi-joins can be computed with load $m/p^{2/3}$. Then, it remains to compute reduced query $\mathcal{Q}_\mathcal{V}$,*

$$\begin{aligned}\mathrm{H}^{\mathcal{V}}(x_2,x_3,x_5,x_6) \text{ :- } & \overline{\mathrm{R}}_2^{\mathcal{V}}(x_2,x_3), \overline{\mathrm{R}}_5^{\mathcal{V}}(x_5,x_6), \\ & \overline{\mathrm{R}}_7^{\mathcal{V}}(x_2,x_5), \overline{\mathrm{R}}_8^{\mathcal{V}}(x_3,x_6),\end{aligned}$$

using the HC algorithm, which can be done with load $m/p^{1/3}$ in one round over the assigned fraction of $p^{2/3}$ servers. Finally, we need to compute the cross product of the locally found tuples for $\mathcal{Q}_\mathcal{V}$ with the output for query $\mathcal{Q}[vars(\mathcal{Q}) \setminus H]$ over the broadcast facts.

[3]Notice that both x_1 and x_4 are incident to two atoms, thus each have at most $2p^{1/6}$ many heavy-hitters.

In the next lemma we drop the restriction that $\mathcal{Q}[H]$ can have no isolated variables. When the semi-join decomposition $\mathcal{Q}_\mathcal{V}$ is the cartesian product of a simple query, and several isolated unary predicates, the above strategies no longer work. While we could use Lemma 6 to compute separately the connected components of $\mathcal{Q}_\mathcal{V}$, the problem is that $\rho^*(\mathcal{Q}_\mathcal{V})$ (which is $\leq \rho^*(\mathcal{Q}[H])$) is too high. In Lemma 13 we used implicitly the fact that $\rho^*(\mathcal{Q}) = |H|/2 + \rho^*(\mathcal{Q}_\mathcal{V})$: this holds because the tight fractional edge packing for $\mathcal{Q}$ is also a tight fractional edge packing for $\mathcal{Q}[H]$ *and* the fact that $\mathcal{Q}_\mathcal{V}$ is simple, which implies $\rho^*(\mathcal{Q}[H]) = \rho^*(\mathcal{Q}_\mathcal{V}) = |L|/2$. But when $\mathcal{Q}_\mathcal{V}$ is not simple, then $\rho^*(\mathcal{Q}_\mathcal{V})$ can be as high as $\rho^*(\mathcal{Q})$ (for example $\mathcal{Q} = H(\boldsymbol{x})$:- $R(x,y), S(y,z), T(z,u), U(u,w), W(w,z)$ has the tight packing $f(R) = 1$, $f(T) = f(U) = f(W) = 1/2$, $f(S) = 0$ and $\rho^*(\mathcal{Q}) = 5/2$, but when $H = \{y\}$ then $\mathcal{Q}[H] = R(x), S(z), T(z,u), U(u,w), W(w,z)$ and $\mathcal{Q}_\mathcal{V} = R(x), T(z,u), U(u,w), W(w,z)$ thus $\rho^*(\mathcal{Q}[H]) = 5/2$). Notice that also the technique from Lemma 12 does not help for the example query. To overcome this issue a more rigorous share-allocation technique is needed. Here, we need to assume that the tight fractional edge packing is half integral, and distinguish two cases: when $vars(\mathcal{C}_f(\mathcal{Q})) \cap H$ is $= \emptyset$ or $\neq \emptyset$. (recall that $\mathcal{C}_f(\mathcal{Q})$ is the set of atoms with weight 1/2).

Lemma 14. *Let $\mathcal{Q}$ be a simple CQ. Assume that $\mathcal{Q}$ admits a tight, half-integral edge packing f, and $\Psi = (H, 1/|vars(\mathcal{Q})|)$ is a heavy hitter configuration, where $vars(\mathcal{C}_f(\mathcal{Q})) \cap H = \emptyset$ and $\mathcal{Q}[H]$ has at least one binary atom. ($\mathcal{Q}[H]$ may have isolated variables.) Then $\mathcal{Q}$ can be computed over the Ψ-compatible instance by a $\rho^*(\mathcal{Q})$-load algorithm in three rounds.*

Proof. Let I be the Ψ-compatible instance. The definition of L and $\mathcal{Q}[H]$ are as before. Now let $L_1 = \{x_1, \ldots, x_k\}$ be the set of isolated variables in $\mathcal{Q}[H]$. Recall that $vars(\mathcal{Q}[H]) = L$, thus $L_1 \subseteq L$. Let $L_2 = L \setminus L_1$. We have $|L_2| \geq 2$, because $\mathcal{Q}[H]$ has at least one binary atom.

By the assumption that all variables in $\mathcal{C}_f(\mathcal{Q})$ are light it follows that $vars(\mathcal{C}_f(\mathcal{Q})) \subseteq L_2$, and particularly that every variable $x_i \in L_1$ is incident to an atom $R_i(x_i, y_i)$ of $\mathcal{Q}$ with weight 1 under f. Denote $H_1 = \{y_i \mid f(R_i(x_i,y_i)) = 1 \text{ and } x_i \in L_1\}$: thus, each $x_i \in L_1$ chooses a unique $y_i \in H_1$ based on the matching f. $H_1 \subseteq H$ (since x_i became isolated) and $|H_1| = |L_1|$ (because of the matching). Further, define $H_2 = H \setminus H_1$. Denote:

$$p' = c \cdot p^{|L_2|/|vars(\mathcal{Q})|}, \text{ and}$$

$$p_{i,h} = p^{2/|vars(\mathcal{Q})|} \cdot \deg_{R_i}(h, y_i)/m, \text{ for } i \in [k],$$

with $y_i \in H_1$, h a heavy-hitter value for y_i, and $c = 1/d(\mathcal{Q})^{|H_2|}$ a constant. Notice that $\sum_h p_{i,h} \leq p^{2/|vars(\mathcal{Q})|}$. Further, denote $p_{\boldsymbol{h}} = p' \cdot \prod_{i \in [k]} p_{i,h_i}$, with $\boldsymbol{h} = (h_1, \ldots, h_k)$.

As in Lemma 13, we compute $\mathcal{Q}$ for every heavy-hitter tuple for variables H separately, using item 2 of Lemma 5.

Only now we make a distinction between the heavy-hitter tuples $\boldsymbol{h}$ for H_1 and $\boldsymbol{g}$ for H_2. To compute $\mathcal{Q}(I|_{\boldsymbol{h},\boldsymbol{g}})$, we need to compute the residual query $\mathcal{Q}[H]$, whose semi-join decomposition we denote $\mathcal{Q}_{\mathcal{V}}$: we will compute this query using $p_{\boldsymbol{h}}$ exclusive servers (note that this number depends on $\boldsymbol{h}$ but not on $\boldsymbol{g}$). We do not exceed budget p, because

$$\sum_{\boldsymbol{h}} p_{\boldsymbol{h}} = p' \prod_{i\in[k]} (\sum_{h_i} p_{i,h_i}) \leq p' \cdot p^{2|H_1|/|vars(\mathcal{Q})|}$$
$$= c \cdot p^{(|H_1|+|L_1|+|L_2|)/|vars(\mathcal{Q})|},$$

there are at most $p^{|H_2|/|vars(\mathcal{Q})|}/c$ heavy-hitter tuples $\boldsymbol{g}$, and $|L_1| + |H_1| + |H_2| + |L_2| = |vars(\mathcal{Q})|$.

We can compute the semi-join reductions for $\mathcal{V}$ over the assigned $p_{\boldsymbol{h}}$ servers using Lemma 4. The latter is with desired load because $p' \geq p^{2/|vars(\mathcal{Q})|}$ (due to $|L_2| \geq 2$). It remains to show how to compute $\mathcal{Q}_{\mathcal{V}}$ using $p_{\boldsymbol{h}}$ servers. The query $\mathcal{Q}_{\mathcal{V}}$ consists of the cross product:

$$\mathcal{Q}_{\mathcal{V}} = \mathcal{Q}'_{\mathcal{V}} \times \overline{\mathrm{R}}^{\mathcal{V}}_1(x_1) \times \cdots \times \overline{\mathrm{R}}^{\mathcal{V}}_k(x_k) \tag{6}$$

where $\mathcal{Q}'_{\mathcal{V}}$ is a semi-join decomposition for $\mathcal{Q}[H \cup L_1]$, and $\overline{\mathrm{R}}^{\mathcal{V}}_i(x_i)$, $i \in [k]$ are the isolated unary relations obtained from the binary relations $R_i(x_i, y_i)$ with $x_i \in L_1$ and $y_i \in H_1$; notice that the size of $\overline{\mathrm{R}}^{\mathcal{V}}_i(x_i)$ is $\deg_{R_i}(h_i, y_i)$. To compute this cross product, we organize the $p_{\boldsymbol{h}}$ servers into a $(k+1)$-dimensional hypercube, of sizes $p' \cdot \prod_{i\in[k]} p_{i,h_i}$: we compute the query $\mathcal{Q}'_{\mathcal{V}}$ using the p' servers of the first dimension, and hash-partition $\overline{\mathrm{R}}^{\mathcal{V}}_i(x_i)$ to the p_{i,h_i} servers in its dimension: the load is as desired because $\tilde{O}\left(|\overline{\mathrm{R}}^{\mathcal{V}I_{\boldsymbol{h},\boldsymbol{g}}}_i|/p_{i,h_i}\right) = \tilde{O}\left(\deg_{R_i}(h_i, y_i)/p_{i,h_i}\right) \leq \tilde{O}\left(m/p^{2/|vars(\mathcal{Q})|}\right)$.

Notice that the query $\mathcal{Q}'_{\mathcal{V}}$ is computed repeatedly, namely $\prod_{i\in[k]} p_{i,h_i}$ times, while each relation $\overline{\mathrm{R}}^{\mathcal{V}}_i(x_i)$ is replicated $p' \cdot \prod_{j\in[k], j\neq i} p_{j,h_j}$ times.

It remains to show how to compute $\mathcal{Q}'_{\mathcal{V}}$ using p' servers. $\mathcal{Q}_{\mathcal{V}'}$ is a simple query (since it is obtained by removing isolated unary relations from $\mathcal{Q}_{\mathcal{V}}$) and all tuples in $I_{\boldsymbol{h},H}$ over the modified schema of $\mathcal{Q}_{\mathcal{V}'}$ are "light", thus we can use the algorithm of Lemma 11. Particularly, the load of the HC algorithm given by Lemma 11 is $m/(p')^{2/|vars(\mathcal{Q}_{\mathcal{V}'})|} = m/(p')^{2/|L_2|} = m/p^{2/|vars(\mathcal{Q})|} = m/p^{1/\rho^*(\mathcal{Q})}$, proving that this is a $\rho^*(\mathcal{Q})$-load algorithm.

To summarize, the algorithm is the following. For each heavy-hitter tuple $\boldsymbol{h}$ for H_1 and $\boldsymbol{g}$ for H_2, use $p_{\boldsymbol{h}}$ exclusive servers to compute $\mathcal{Q}(I|_{\boldsymbol{h},\boldsymbol{g}})$ as follows:

Step 1: Compute the semi-join reductions for $\mathcal{V}$ in two rounds over instance $I|_{\boldsymbol{h},\boldsymbol{g}}$ as in Lemma 4.

Step 2: Compute the cross product in Eq.(6) by organizing the $p_{\boldsymbol{h}}$ servers into a $(k+1)$-dimensional hypercube. Along the first dimension, compute the query $\mathcal{Q}'_{\mathcal{V}}$ (the result of the semi-join reduction in the first step) using p' servers using the algorithm of Lemma 11, by assigning a weight $f(x) = 1/2$ to each variable. Along all other dimensions, hash partition $\overline{\mathrm{R}}^{\mathcal{V}}_i(x_i)$ (the result of the semi-join reduction in the first step). □

Lemma 14 provides an alternative to the strategy in [11] to compute even-length cycles.

Example 7. *For an example consider the even-length cycle* $C_8 = \{R_i(x_i, x_{(i \bmod 8)+1}) \mid i \in [8]\}$ *and heavy-hitter configuration* $\Psi = (H, 1/8)$, *and* $H = \{x_1, x_2, x_3, x_6, x_7\}$. *There is one isolated variable,* $L_1 = \{x_8\}$ *and, assuming* $f(R_i) = (i \bmod 2)$, *we pair* x_8 *with* $H_1 = \{x_7\}$. *Partition the p available servers in groups of size* $p_{\boldsymbol{h}} = p^{4/8} \cdot deg_{R_7}(h, x_7)/m$, *one group for each heavy-hitter tuple* $\boldsymbol{h}$ *over* H, *where* h *denotes the value for variable* $x_7 \in H$ *in* $\boldsymbol{h}$. *Let semi-join decomposition for* $\mathcal{Q}[H]$ *be:*

$$\overline{\mathrm{R}}^{\mathcal{V}}_7(x_8) \text{ :- } \overline{\mathrm{R}}_8(x_8), \overline{\mathrm{R}}_7(x_8).$$
$$\overline{\mathrm{R}}^{\mathcal{V}}_4(x_4, x_5) \text{ :- } \overline{\mathrm{R}}_4(x_4, x_5), \overline{\mathrm{R}}_3(x_4), \overline{\mathrm{R}}_5(x_5).$$

Query $\mathcal{Q}_{\mathcal{V}}$ *takes the form:*

$$\mathrm{H}^{\mathcal{V}}(x_4, x_5, x_8) \text{ :- } \overline{\mathrm{R}}^{\mathcal{V}}_4(x_4, x_5), \overline{\mathrm{R}}^{\mathcal{V}}_7(x_8).$$

Compute for each heavy-hitter tuple $\boldsymbol{h}$ *the respective semi-joins in* $\mathcal{V}$ *for* $I|_{\boldsymbol{h}}$ *over its fragment of* $p_{\boldsymbol{h}}$ *servers. Hereafter, hash-partition the tuples in* $R^{\mathcal{V}}_4$ *over a fragment of* $p^{2/8}$ *servers and hash-partition the tuples in* $\overline{R}'^{\mathcal{V}}_7$ *over the remaining fragment of* $p^{2/8} \cdot deg_{R_7}(h, x_7)/m$ *servers. Further broadcast all heavy-hitter tuples in* $I|_{\boldsymbol{h}}$. *Then by computing* $\mathcal{Q}_{\mathcal{V}}$ *locally on every server and taking the cross product with the locally computed output for* $\mathcal{Q}[vars(C_8) \setminus H]$ *over the broadcast heavy-hitter tuples, we obtain the output for* $\mathcal{Q}$.

Finally, we generalize Lemma 14 to the case where some variables in $\mathcal{C}_f(\mathcal{Q})$ may be heavy.

Lemma 15. *Let* $\mathcal{Q}$ *be a simple CQ. Assume* $\mathcal{Q}$ *admits a tight, half-integral edge packing* f, *and* $\Psi = (H, 1/|vars(\mathcal{Q})|)$ *is a heavy hitter-configuration, where* $\mathcal{Q}[H]$ *has at least one binary atom. (*$vars(\mathcal{C}_f(\mathcal{Q})) \cap H$ *may be* $\neq \emptyset$ *and* $\mathcal{Q}[H]$ *may have isolated variables.) Then* $\mathcal{Q}$ *can be computed over the* Ψ*-compatible instance by a* $\rho^*(\mathcal{Q})$*-load algorithm using five rounds.*

Proof. Let $C_1, \ldots, C_\ell$ be the odd-length cycles in $\mathcal{C}_f(\mathcal{Q})$ with heavy variables. For every cycle C_i we (arbitrarily) choose one of its heavy variables and call it x_i. Let H' be the set of selected variables and let $\mathcal{Q}[H']$ be the residual query obtained by removing these variables from $\mathcal{Q}$. Let $L' = vars(\mathcal{Q}) \setminus H' = vars(\mathcal{Q}[H'])$.

To compute $\mathcal{Q}$ we again make use of item 2 of Lemma 5, by computing $\mathcal{Q}$ for every heavy-hitter tuple $\boldsymbol{h}$ for H' separately over an exclusive group of $p' = c \cdot p^{|L'|/|vars(\mathcal{Q})|}$ servers, with p the total number of available servers and $c = 1/d(\mathcal{Q})^{|H'|}$ a constant. There are at most $p^{|H'|/|vars(\mathcal{Q})|}/c$ many heavy tuples over H', and $p' \cdot p^{|H'|/|vars(\mathcal{Q})|}/c = p$, thus the number of used servers is within budget.

Interestingly, for the semi-join decomposition $\mathcal{V}$ of $\mathcal{Q}[H']$, query $\mathcal{Q}_{\mathcal{V}}$ satisfies the conditions of Lemma 14. For this to see let f' be the fractional edge packing obtained from f by updating all interrupted 1/2-weighted cycles in $\mathcal{Q}_{\mathcal{V}}$ to paths with alternating weights 1 and 0. More formally, for each cycle $C_i = a_1, \ldots, a_k$ where a_1 and a_k denote the atoms involving variable x_i, define $f'(a^{\mathcal{V}}_i) = 0$ if i is odd, and $f'(a^{\mathcal{V}}_i) = 1$ if i is even. For all other atoms $a^{\mathcal{V}} \in \mathcal{Q}_{\mathcal{V}}$, let $f'(a^{\mathcal{V}}) = f(a)$. Notice that all atoms $a^{\mathcal{V}}_i$ are in $\mathcal{Q}_{\mathcal{V}}$ except for $a^{\mathcal{V}}_1$ and $a^{\mathcal{V}}_k$. From $\{a \mid a^{\mathcal{V}} \in atoms(\mathcal{Q}_{\mathcal{V}})\} \subseteq atoms(\mathcal{Q})$ it follows that f' describes a fractional edge packing for $\mathcal{Q}_{\mathcal{V}}$. By construction, f' is tight for $\mathcal{Q}_{\mathcal{V}}$ and thus $\tau^*(\mathcal{Q}_{\mathcal{V}}) = \rho^*(\mathcal{Q}_{\mathcal{V}}) = |vars(\mathcal{Q}_{\mathcal{V}})|/2 = \rho^*(\mathcal{Q}) - |H'|/2$.

The computation of $\mathcal{Q}[H']$ now proceeds by first computing the semi-join reductions for $\mathcal{V}$ over relations where $\mathcal{Q}[H]$ is based on heavy-hitter tuple $\boldsymbol{h}$ and then computing $\mathcal{Q}_{\mathcal{V}}$ over the semi-join reduced relations for configuration

$(H', 1/|L'|)$ using the algorithm from Lemma 14 and 6 over the assigned p' servers. Notice that the semi-join reductions can be computed with desired load, as $p' \geq p^{1/\rho^*(\mathcal{Q})}$ (because there is at least one cycle C_i, with $|vars(C_i)| \geq 3$, and only one of its variables is removed). Further notice that $m/(p')^{2/|L'|} = m/p^{2/|vars(\mathcal{Q})|}$. □

Example 8. *For an example consider the query $\mathcal{Q}$,*

$$\mathrm{H}(\boldsymbol{x}) \text{ :- } \mathrm{R}_1(x_1, x_2), \mathrm{R}_2(x_2, x_3), \mathrm{R}_3(x_3, x_4), \mathrm{R}_4(x_4, x_5), \mathrm{R}_5(x_5, x_3),$$

and heavy-hitter configuration $\Psi = (H, \delta)$ with $H = \{x_4\}$ and $\delta = 1/5$. To compute $\mathcal{Q}$ assign to every heavy-hitter value h a unique fraction of $p' = p^{4/5}$ servers. As there at most $p^{1/5}$ many values h, [4] *we do not exceed budget p. To compute $\mathcal{Q}$ first consider the residual query $\mathcal{Q}[H]$ and semi-join reduce the relations accordingly, with $\mathcal{Q}[H]$ as below:*

$$\overline{\mathrm{H}}(\boldsymbol{x}') \text{ :- } \overline{\mathrm{R}}_1(x_1, x_2), \overline{\mathrm{R}}_2(x_2, x_3), \overline{\mathrm{R}}_3(x_3), \overline{\mathrm{R}}_4(x_5), \overline{\mathrm{R}}_5(x_5, x_3),$$

which is simplified to query $\mathcal{Q}_\nu$ by use of a semi-join decomposition. Here $\mathcal{Q}_\nu$ takes the form:

$$\mathrm{H}^\nu(\boldsymbol{x}') \text{ :- } \overline{\mathrm{R}}_1^\nu(x_1, x_2), \overline{\mathrm{R}}_2^\nu(x_2, x_3), \overline{\mathrm{R}}_5^\nu(x_5, x_3).$$

Now we have $\rho^*(\mathcal{Q}) = 5/2$ and $\rho^*(\mathcal{Q}_\nu) = 2$. For $\mathcal{Q}_\nu$ we know how to compute it with load $m/p^{1/2}$, thus over a fraction p' of the servers we obtain load $m/p^{2/5}$ as desired.

Combining the above Lemmas we obtain:

Theorem 1. *Let $\mathcal{Q}$ be a simple CQ that admits a tight, half-integral fractional edge packing. Then $\mathcal{Q}$ can be computed by a $\rho^*(\mathcal{Q})$-load algorithm using five rounds.*

Proof. To compute query $\mathcal{Q}$ over arbitrary instance I, one can simply compute $\mathcal{Q}$ for each heavy-hitter configuration $\Psi = (H, 1/|vars(\mathcal{Q})|)$ separately, with $H \subseteq vars(\mathcal{Q})$, over instance I_Ψ following the algorithms in Lemma 12 and 15. Correctness follows from Lemma 5. Particularly notice that the load increases only by constant $2^{|vars(\mathcal{Q})|}$, which corresponds to the number of possible heavy-hitter configurations. □

5.4 Non-Tight Edge Packings

For CQ $\mathcal{Q}$, let $\mathcal{N}_f(\mathcal{Q})$ denote the set of variables in $\mathcal{Q}$ incident to only 0-weighted predicates under fractional edge packing f. Given that f is optimal and maximizes the number of 0-weighted predicates, $\mathcal{N}_f(\mathcal{Q})$ denotes exactly those variables witnessing non-tightness of f.

Example 9. *For an example consider query $\mathcal{Q}$,*

$$\mathrm{H}(\boldsymbol{x}) \text{ :- } \mathrm{R}_1(x_1, x_2), \mathrm{R}_2(x_2, x_3), \mathrm{R}_3(x_3, x_4), \mathrm{R}_4(x_4, x_5), \mathrm{R}_5(x_5, x_3), \mathrm{R}_6(x_6, x_2),$$

which is essentially the same query as in Example 8 except for additional atom R_6. Query $\mathcal{Q}$ has no tight fractional edge packing due to predicates R_1 and R_6. Here, $\tau^*(\mathcal{Q}) = 5/2$, and $\rho^*(\mathcal{Q}) = 7/2$. We divide the p servers in shares $p_1 = p^{2/7}$ and $p_2 = p^{5/7}$. Now hash-partition the tuples for R_6 over share p_1 and proceed the computation of $\mathcal{Q}$ without predicate R_6 over share p_2. Notice that the latter query now has a tight edge packing, we can thus proceed as in Example 8.

We first show the case where none of the variables in $\mathcal{N}_f(\mathcal{Q})$ are heavy. Notice that we now consider a different threshold value.

Lemma 16. *Let $\mathcal{Q}$ be a simple CQ $\mathcal{Q}$ with non-tight half-integral edge packing f, and heavy-hitter configuration $\Psi = (H, 1/\rho^*(\mathcal{Q}))$, satisfying $\mathcal{N}_f(\mathcal{Q}) \cap H = \emptyset$. Then, $\mathcal{Q}$ can be computed over the Ψ-compatible instance by a $\rho^*(\mathcal{Q})$-load algorithm using five rounds.*

Proof. As before, let $L = vars(\mathcal{Q}) \setminus H$. By assumption, $\mathcal{N}_f(\mathcal{Q}) \subseteq L$ and $\mathcal{N}_f(\mathcal{Q}) \neq \emptyset$, as otherwise f is tight.

Notice that all atoms in $\mathcal{Q}$ have at least some variable not in $\mathcal{N}_f(\mathcal{Q})$, as otherwise f cannot be optimal. Indeed, then one can obtain a fractional edge packing with higher value by simply assigning weight 1 to the selected predicate.

We partition the atoms of $\mathcal{Q}$ in two sets A and B. Set A contains all the atoms from $\mathcal{Q}$ where variables in $\mathcal{N}_f(\mathcal{Q})$ are incident to, and $B = atoms(\mathcal{Q}) \setminus A$.

Now compute $\mathcal{Q}$ by computing the cross product $\mathcal{Q}' = \mathcal{Q}_A \times \mathcal{Q}_B$, and then post process the answer by selecting only those tuples where values for variables of $\mathcal{Q}_A$ equal the values for corresponding variables in $\mathcal{Q}_B$. Observe that this indeed provides us the desired output result.

To compute $\mathcal{Q}_A$ and $\mathcal{Q}_B$, consider share definitions:

$$p_1 = p^{\tau^*(\mathcal{Q}_1)/\rho^*(\mathcal{Q})}$$
$$p_2 = p^{\rho^*(\mathcal{Q}_2)/\rho^*(\mathcal{Q})}.$$

We first argue $p_1 \cdot p_2 = p$. For this, notice that $\tau^*(\mathcal{Q}_A) = |\mathcal{N}_f(\mathcal{Q})|$, which is because $\mathcal{N}_f(\mathcal{Q})$ defines an (integral) vertex cover for $\mathcal{Q}_A$, and one can easily obtain an edge packing with same value by selecting for each variable in $\mathcal{N}_f(\mathcal{Q})$ exactly one incident atom.[5] Further notice that $\tau^*(\mathcal{Q}) = |\mathcal{C}_f(\mathcal{Q})|/2 + (|vars(\mathcal{Q})| - |\mathcal{C}_f(\mathcal{Q})| - |\mathcal{N}_f(\mathcal{Q})|)/2$, thus from Lemma 10 we obtain $\rho^*(\mathcal{Q}) = |vars(\mathcal{Q})|/2 + |\mathcal{N}_f(\mathcal{Q})|/2$. The result now follows by the additional observation that $\rho^*(\mathcal{Q}_B) = vars(\mathcal{Q}_B)/2$ due to tightness of f for $\mathcal{Q}_B$, where $vars(\mathcal{Q}_B) = vars(\mathcal{Q}) \setminus \mathcal{N}_f(\mathcal{Q})$.

We compute $\mathcal{Q}_A$ over a share of p_1 servers by allocating to all the variables in $\mathcal{N}_f(\mathcal{Q})$ a weight of 1 and to all others a weight 0. This strategy works as desired because I_Ψ is light for all variables in $\mathcal{N}_f(\mathcal{Q})$, and the meaning of light is not affected by considering only p_1 servers. Indeed,

$$m/p^{1/\rho^*(\mathcal{Q})} = m/p_1^{1/\tau^*(\mathcal{Q}_1)}$$

and $\tau^*(\mathcal{Q}_A) = |\mathcal{N}_f(\mathcal{Q})|$. Following Lemma 2 the load is as desired and requires only one round.

The computation of $\mathcal{Q}_B$ over I_Ψ relies on Theorem 1 using a share of p_2 servers. This algorithm uses at most five rounds, and by choice of p_2 the load is as desired. □

Finally, in Lemma 17 we deal with the case where variables in $\mathcal{N}_f(\mathcal{Q})$ are heavy:

Lemma 17. *Let $\mathcal{Q}$ be a simple CQ with heavy-hitter configuration $\Psi = (H, 1/\rho^*(\mathcal{Q}))$. Let f be a non-tight half-integral edge packing for $\mathcal{Q}$ with $\mathcal{N}_f(\mathcal{Q}) \cap H \neq \emptyset$. Then $\mathcal{Q}$ can be*

[4]Technically there can be $2 \cdot p^{1/5}$ heavy values, which we ignore, as this influences the load only by a constant factor.

[5]This strategy works because A consists of disjoint star-queries, one for each variable in $\mathcal{N}_f(\mathcal{Q})$.

computed over the Ψ-compatible instance by a $\rho^*(\mathcal{Q})$-load algorithm using seven rounds.

Proof. Let I be an arbitrary Ψ-compatible instance. Let $H' = \mathcal{N}_f(\mathcal{Q}) \cap H$, and $\mathcal{Q}[H']$ be the residual query obtained by removing from $\mathcal{Q}$ the variables in H', and $L' = vars(\mathcal{Q}) \setminus H'$.

Let $\mathcal{V}$ be a semi-join decomposition for $\mathcal{Q}[H']$. Fractional edge packing f describes a fractional edge packing for $\mathcal{Q}_\mathcal{V}$ when ignoring the annotation of relation symbols. Particularly, then f is also maximal for $\mathcal{Q}_\mathcal{V}$, as only 0-weight atoms are removed from $\mathcal{Q}$ to obtain $\mathcal{Q}_\mathcal{V}$, and non-optimality would thus contradict the assumed optimality of f for $\mathcal{Q}$. Therefore $\tau^*(\mathcal{Q}_\mathcal{V}) = \tau^*(\mathcal{Q})$.

Similar as before we compute $\mathcal{Q}$ for every heavy hitter tuple $\boldsymbol{h}$ over H' separately over a unique set of p' servers, where $p' = c \cdot p^{\rho^*(\mathcal{Q}_\mathcal{V})/\rho^*(\mathcal{Q})}$, and $c = 1/d(\mathcal{Q})^{|H'|}$ a constant. As there are only $p^{|vars(H')|/\rho^*(\mathcal{Q})}/c$ many such tuples we remain within budget. Indeed, $\rho^*(\mathcal{Q}) = |vars(\mathcal{Q})| - \tau^*(\mathcal{Q}_\mathcal{V}) = \rho^*(\mathcal{Q}_\mathcal{V}) + |H'|$, following Lemma 10, $|vars(\mathcal{Q})| = |vars(\mathcal{Q}_\mathcal{V})| + |H'|$, and the earlier made observation $\tau^*(\mathcal{Q}) = \tau^*(\mathcal{Q}_\mathcal{V})$. The computation then proceeds in two steps:

Step 1: Compute the semi-join reductions defined by $\mathcal{V}$ over instance $I|_{\boldsymbol{h},H'}$ using the strategy in Lemma 4.

Step 2: Reshuffle the semi-join reduced relations from the previous step to compute $\mathcal{Q}_\mathcal{V}$ by following the algorithm in Lemma 16. Then broadcast heavy-hitter tuples in $I|_{\boldsymbol{h},H'}$ over the schema of $\mathcal{Q}[L']$, and compute locally on every server the crossproduct $\mathcal{Q}[L'] \times \mathcal{Q}_\mathcal{V}$ to obtain the desired output.

Completeness of the output follows from Lemma 16 and Lemma 5. Step 1 is done in two rounds with desired load because $p' \geq c \cdot p^{1/\rho^*(\mathcal{Q})}$. The latter particularly follows from the fact that $\mathcal{Q}_\mathcal{V}$ does not contain isolated variables and cannot be empty, as both would contradict the assumed optimality of f for $\mathcal{Q}$.

For Step 2, notice that $\mathcal{Q}_\mathcal{V}$ and f indeed satisfy the conditions of Lemma 16 and thus the obtained load using at most five rounds is $\tilde{O}\left(m/p^{1/\rho^*(\mathcal{Q})}\right)$. □

Similar to Theorem 1, for conjunctive queries with non-tight half-integral edge packing we now obtain the following result:

Theorem 2. *Let $\mathcal{Q}$ be a simple CQ and f a non-tight half-integral edge packing. Then $\mathcal{Q}$ can be computed by a $\rho^*(\mathcal{Q})$-load algorithm using seven rounds.*

Proof. for every heavy-hitter configuration $(H, 1/\rho^*(\mathcal{Q}))$ in parallel, using Lemma 16 if $vars(\mathcal{N}_f(\mathcal{Q})) \cap H = \emptyset$, and the algorithm in Lemma 17 otherwise. □

5.5 Wrap-Up

By combining the two theorems we obtain a general algorithm for computing conjunctive queries over relations with arity at most two: first simplify the query by considering a semi-join decomposition $\mathcal{V}$ for $\mathcal{Q}$.

Step 1: Compute a semi-join decomposition $\mathcal{Q}_\mathcal{V}$ using the algorithm in Lemma 8.

Step 2: Compute a half-integral fractional edge packing f for $\mathcal{Q}_\mathcal{V}$. If f is tight then use the algorithm in Theorem 1; if f is non-tight use the algorithm in Theorem 2.

Hence our main result:

Theorem 3. *Every CQ $\mathcal{Q}$ over relations with arity at most two can be computed with a $\rho^*(\mathcal{Q})$-load algorithm using at most nine rounds.*

As our algorithm takes a fractional edge packing as parameter, notice that, in contrast to finding a maximum vertex cover for a given graph, which is well-known to be NP-complete, the problem of finding maximum (integral) edge packings (i.e., maximum matchings), is solvable in polynomial time. Interestingly, finding optimal half-integral edge packings for a graph (or simple query) with the properties of Lemma 9 is comparably easy. For a polynomial time algorithm based on iteratively finding augmenting paths (i.e., paths with alternating assignment of weight 0 and 1 to its edges) and blossoms (i.e., odd-length cycles) we refer to [7].

When a query has multiple optimal fractional edge packings satisfying the conditions of Lemma 9, then one of the packings may yield a preferred evaluation strategy over the other:

Example 10. *For an example consider query $\mathcal{Q}$,*

$$\mathrm{H}(\bar{x}) \text{ :- } \mathrm{R}_1(x_1,x_2), \mathrm{R}_2(x_2,x_3), \mathrm{R}_3(x_3,x_1), \mathrm{R}_4(x_3,x_4), \mathrm{R}_5(x_4,x_5), \mathrm{R}_6(x_5,x_6), \mathrm{R}_7(x_6,x_4),$$

which represents two triangles connected by an edge. Here $\rho^*(\mathcal{Q}) = \tau^*(\mathcal{Q}) = 3$. We can consider the fractional edge packing assigning weight $1/2$ to predicates R_1, R_2, R_3, R_5, R_6, R_7 and 0 to predicate R_4, or alternatively the edge packing assigning weight 1 to predicates R_1, R_4, R_6, and 0 to all others. The latter seems beneficial as Lemma 14 guarantees three rounds in contrast to five for Lemma 15, particularly if certain variables are heavy.

Notice that disallowing multiple occurrences of the same variable in a single atom is without loss of generality. Indeed, given a query that violates this condition, we can simply ignore duplicates variable occurrences by implementing a preprocessing step in which each server autonomously discards those tuples not satisfying the by the query implied equality types.

Finally, notice that our algorithm can be generalized to conjunctive queries with existential quantification (projections) and self-joins in the usual way by duplicating the self-joined relations and implementing projections as a post processing step. Then, however, we inevitably lose optimality as the AGM bound is no longer the right notion to express the worst-case output size [8].

5.6 Higher-Arity Relations

Unfortunately it is unclear how to generalize our techniques to higher-arity relations, as the graph properties we rely on do not generalize to hypergraphs. More specifically, they fail already for ternary relations. First, in general the inequality $\tau^*(\mathcal{Q}) \leq \rho^*(\mathcal{Q})$ does not hold.

Example 11. *For an example of a query $\mathcal{Q}$, where $\tau^*(\mathcal{Q}) > \rho^*(\mathcal{Q})$, consider*

$$\mathrm{H}(\boldsymbol{x}) \text{ :- } \mathrm{R}(x_1,y_1,z_1), \mathrm{T}(x_2,y_2,z_2), \mathrm{S}_1(x_1,x_2), \mathrm{S}_2(y_1,y_2), \mathrm{S}_3(z_1,z_2).$$

Here, $\tau^*(\mathcal{Q}) = 3$, which is easy to see as all three predicates S_1, S_2, S_3 need to be covered, and do not share variables. On the other hand, $\rho^*(\mathcal{Q}) = 2$ is witnessed by the cover containing predicates R and T.

Therefore, taking the HC algorithm as a building block seems to not work in general for higher-arity relations. Particularly for query $\mathcal{Q}$ from Example 11, it is even unclear how to compute $\mathcal{Q}$ with $\rho^*(\mathcal{Q})$-based load over instances without skew. Unless, for example, in the special case where all columns of relations are keys, as then intermediate join outputs can grow only by a constant factor with respect to the input (the factor is caused by the arity of the output relation). In fact, the only class of queries over higher-arity relations that is currently known to be computable with $\rho^*(\mathcal{Q})$-load algorithm are those having a guard atom, as in Lemma 4.

Second, $\rho^*(\mathcal{Q}) + \tau^*(\mathcal{Q}) = |vars(\mathcal{Q})|$ in general does not hold for hypergraphs either. Again, this can be observed by considering query $\mathcal{Q}$ from Example 11. There, $\rho^*(\mathcal{Q}) + \tau^*(\mathcal{Q}) = 5 < |vars(\mathcal{Q})|$.

6. EXTERNAL MEMORY MODEL

Recently, much attention went also to worst-case I/O-optimal algorithms for computing join queries in the external memory model [9, 10]. The external memory model is a sequential computation model in which a distinction is made between space for data storing (external memory) and processing (internal memory). The former is unbounded, the latter is bounded by parameter w, which expresses its size in number of disc blocks: a disc block is the amount of data, denoted B, moved from external to internal memory (or vice versa) in a single I/O operation. For a more comprehensive description of the model we refer to [2].

In [11] it was observed that algorithms for the MPC model can be simulated straightforwardly in the external memory model, given that they are tuple-based, and that the internal memory is at least as large as the maximal amount of space needed by any of the individual servers (i.e., $w \geq r \cdot L/B$).

The tuple-based MPC model is the MPC model, as described in Section 3, where additionally only tuples from subqueries of $\mathcal{Q}$ are communicated, and the communication depends only on the data statistics that are initially available to the algorithm. As the algorithm from Section 5 satisfies these conditions, the following Corollary follows steadily from the results in [11].

Corollary 1. *For every CQ $\mathcal{Q}$ over relations with arity at most two, an external memory algorithm exists that, for any $w > m^{\rho^*(\mathcal{Q})/(\rho^*(\mathcal{Q})+1)}$, computes Q with $\tilde{O}\left(\frac{m^{\rho^*(\mathcal{Q})}}{w^{\rho^*(\mathcal{Q})-1} \cdot B}\right)$ I/O cost, by simulating the algorithm from Section 5 with $p = (m/w)^{\rho^*(\mathcal{Q})}$.*

7. CONCLUSION

In this paper we introduced an algorithm for computing conjunctive queries over binary atoms in parallel shared-nothing settings. Our algorithm runs with load $m/p^{1/\rho^*(\mathcal{Q})}$, and therefore obtains the worst-case optimal load when relations have the same size m. In combination with the lower bound given in [11], it shows that the load in this setting is given by the fractional edge covering number $\rho^*(\mathcal{Q})$ rather than the fractional vertex covering number $\tau^*(\mathcal{Q})$, at least when relations are binary.

Our techniques build upon, and extend in a non-trivial way, techniques introduced in [11] computing chain queries and cycle queries in multiple rounds with worst-case optimal load. Our result critically relies on key properties from graphs, which in general do not hold for hypergraphs, already for arity three. Therefore we leave open the optimal communication cost for queries over relations of arbitrary arity. Particularly it is unclear what the bound might be for queries where $\tau^*(\mathcal{Q}) > \rho^*(\mathcal{Q})$, as in general, the best algorithm we know to compute queries over skew-free database instances is the one-round HC algorithm with load $m/p^{1/\tau^*(\mathcal{Q})}$. On the other hand, the best multi-round lower bound we know follows from the AGM bound and is $m/p^{1/\rho^*(\mathcal{Q})}$. To close the gap one needs to either design a new multi-round algorithm for skew-free databases, or prove a new multi-round bound that is stronger than that implied by the AGM bound.

8. REFERENCES

[1] F. N. Afrati and J. D. Ullman. Optimizing joins in a map-reduce environment. In *EDBT*, pages 99–110, 2010.

[2] A. Aggarwal and J. S. Vitter. The input/output complexity of sorting and related problems. *Commun. ACM*, 31(9):1116–1127, 1988.

[3] T. J. Ameloot, G. Geck, B. Ketsman, F. Neven, and T. Schwentick. Parallel-correctness and transferability for conjunctive queries. In *PODS*, pages 47–58, 2015.

[4] A. Atserias, M. Grohe, and D. Marx. Size bounds and query plans for relational joins. *SIAM J. Comput.*, 42(4):1737–1767, 2013.

[5] P. Beame, P. Koutris, and D. Suciu. Communication steps for parallel query processing. In *PODS*, pages 273–284, 2013.

[6] P. Beame, P. Koutris, and D. Suciu. Skew in parallel query processing. In *PODS*, pages 212–223, 2014.

[7] J. Bourjolly and W. R. Pulleyblank. König-egerváry graphs, 2-bicritical graphs and fractional matchings. *Discrete Applied Mathematics*, 24(1-3):63–82, 1989.

[8] G. Gottlob, S. Tien Lee, G. Valiant, and P. Valiant. Size and treewidth bounds for conjunctive queries. *J. ACM*, 59(3):16, 2012.

[9] X. Hu, Y. Tao, and C. Chung. Massive graph triangulation. In *SIGMOD*, pages 325–336, 2013.

[10] X. Hu and K. Yi. Towards a worst-case I/O-optimal algorithm for acyclic joins. In *PODS*, pages 135–150, 2016.

[11] P. Koutris, P. Beame, and D. Suciu. Worst-case optimal algorithms for parallel query processing. In *ICDT*, pages 8:1–8:18, 2016.

[12] P. Koutris and D. Suciu. Parallel evaluation of conjunctive queries. In *PODS*, pages 223–234, 2011.

[13] H. Q. Ngo, E. Porat, C. Ré, and A. Rudra. Worst-case optimal join algorithms: [extended abstract]. In *PODS*, pages 37–48, 2012.

[14] H. Q. Ngo, C. Ré, and A. Rudra. Skew strikes back: new developments in the theory of join algorithms. *SIGMOD Record*, 42(4):5–16, 2013.

[15] E. R. Scheinerman and D. H. Ullman. *Fractional graph theory: a rational approach to the theory of graphs.* Wiley, New York, 1997.

[16] T. L. Veldhuizen. Triejoin: A simple, worst-case optimal join algorithm. In *ICDT*, pages 96–106, 2014.

What do Shannon-type Inequalities, Submodular Width, and Disjunctive Datalog have to do with one another?

Mahmoud Abo Khamis
LogicBlox Inc.

Hung Q. Ngo
LogicBlox Inc.

Dan Suciu
LogicBlox Inc. and
University of Washington

ABSTRACT

Recent works on bounding the output size of a conjunctive query with functional dependencies and degree bounds have shown a deep connection between fundamental questions in information theory and database theory. We prove analogous output bounds for *disjunctive datalog rules*, and answer several open questions regarding the tightness and looseness of these bounds along the way. The bounds are intimately related to Shannon-type information inequalities. We devise the notion of a "proof sequence" of a specific class of Shannon-type information inequalities called "Shannon flow inequalities". We then show how a proof sequence can be used as symbolic instructions to guide an algorithm called PANDA, which answers disjunctive datalog rules within the size bound predicted. We show that PANDA can be used as a black-box to devise algorithms matching precisely the fractional hypertree width and the submodular width runtimes for aggregate and conjunctive queries *with* functional dependencies and degree bounds.

Our results improve upon known results in three ways. First, our bounds and algorithms are for the much more general class of disjunctive datalog rules, of which conjunctive queries are a special case. Second, the runtime of PANDA matches precisely the submodular width bound, while the previous algorithm by Marx has a runtime that is polynomial in this bound. Third, our bounds and algorithms work for queries with input cardinality bounds, functional dependencies, *and* degree bounds.

Overall, our results showed a deep connection between three seemingly unrelated lines of research; and, our results on proof sequences for Shannon flow inequalities might be of independent interest.

Keywords

Submodular width; Disjunctive datalog; Shannon-type inequalities; Entropy; Functional dependencies; Restricted access patterns; Degree bounds; Join algorithms

PODS'17, May 14 - 19, 2017, Chicago, IL, USA

ISBN 978-1-4503-4198-1/17/05...\$15.00

DOI: http://dx.doi.org/10.1145/3034786.3056105

1. INTRODUCTION

In this paper we answer four major questions that resulted from four different research threads, and establish new connections between those threads.

1.1 Size Bound for Full Conjunctive Queries

Grohe and Marx [30], Atserias, Grohe, and Marx [13], and Gottlob, Lee, Valiant and Valiant [27] developed a deep connection between the output size bound of a conjunctive query with (or without) functional dependencies (FD) and information theory. Our first problem is to extend this bound to degree constraints, and to study whether the bound is tight.

We associate a full conjunctive query Q to a hypergraph $\mathcal{H} = ([n], \mathcal{E})$, $\mathcal{E} \subseteq 2^{[n]}$. The query's variables are A_i, $i \in [n]$. Its atoms are $R_F, F \in \mathcal{E}$. The query is:

$$Q(\mathbf{A}_{[n]}) \text{ :- } \bigwedge_{F \in \mathcal{E}} R_F(\mathbf{A}_F), \tag{1}$$

where $\mathbf{A}_J$ denotes the set $\{A_j \mid j \in J\}$, for $J \subseteq [n]$. Our goal is to compute an upper bound on the output size, when the input database satisfies a set of *degree constraints*. Define $\deg_F(\mathbf{A}_Y|\mathbf{A}_X) \stackrel{\text{def}}{=} \max_{\mathbf{t}} |\Pi_{\mathbf{A}_Y}(\sigma_{\mathbf{A}_X=\mathbf{t}}(R_F))|$; then, a degree constraint is an assertion of the form $\deg_F(\mathbf{A}_Y|\mathbf{A}_X) \leq N_{Y|X}$, for $X \subset Y \subseteq F$, A *cardinality constraint* is an assertion of the form $|R_F| \leq N_F$, for some $F \in \mathcal{E}$; it is exactly the degree constraint $\deg_F(\mathbf{A}_F|\emptyset) \leq N_{F|\emptyset} \stackrel{\text{def}}{=} N_F$. A *functional dependency* $\mathbf{A}_X \to \mathbf{A}_Y$ is a degree constraint with $N_{X\cup Y|X} = 1$. Thus, degree constraints strictly generalize both cardinality constraints and FDs.

The first output size upper bound was pioneered in [13,30], who established a tight bound, for cardinality constraints only, known today as the AGM bound. Extensions to FDs and degree constraints were discussed in [27] and [3], respectively, who left open the question whether these bounds are tight. Handling queries with degree constraints has a strong practical motivation. Armbrust et al. [10–12], described a new approach to query evaluation, called *scale-independent query processing*, which guarantees a fixed runtime even when the size of the database increases without bound; this guarantee is provided by asking developers to write explicit degree constraints, then using heuristics to derive upper bounds on the query output. Thus, improved upper bounds on the size of the query answer have immediate applications to scale-independent query processing. Several complexity results on the associated decision problem ("is the output size of the query bounded?") were considered in [15–17].

Our first question is whether the upper bounds for FDs or degree constraints are tight. To set the technical context for this question, we briefly describe how the bound was derived. Fix an input database $\mathbf{D}$ and consider the joint distribution on random variables $\mathbf{A}_{[n]}$ where each output tuple $\mathbf{t} \in Q(\mathbf{D})$ is selected uniformly with probability $1/|Q(\mathbf{D})|$. Let $h(\mathbf{A}_S)$ denote the marginal entropy on the variables $\mathbf{A}_S$. Then[1], by uniformity $h(\mathbf{A}_{[n]}) = \log |Q(\mathbf{D})|$, and $h(\mathbf{A}_Y|\mathbf{A}_X) \leq \log N_{Y|X}$ for every degree constraint. A function $h : 2^{\mathbf{A}_{[n]}} \to \mathbb{R}_+$ is said to be *entropic* if there is a joint distribution on $\mathbf{A}_{[n]}$ such that $h(\mathbf{A}_S)$ is the marginal entropy on $\mathbf{A}_S$, $S \subseteq [n]$. The *entropic bound* of a query is $\log |Q| \leq \max_h h(\mathbf{A}_{[n]})$, where h ranges over all entropic functions satisfying the given constraints. Recently, Gogacz and Toruńczyk [25] showed that the entropic bound is tight even in the presence of FDs. However, they did not address general degree constraints.

The problem with the entropic bound is that we do not know how to compute it (except for the special case when all degree constraints are cardinality constraints), because the entropic cone is characterized by infinitely many *non-Shannon-type inequalities* [33, 38]. To overcome this limitation, Gottlob et al. [27] replace entropic functions (which are difficult) with polymatroids (which are easier). A *polymatroid* is a set function $h : 2^{[n]} \to \mathbb{R}_+$ that is non-negative, monotone, and submodular, with $h(\emptyset) = 0$ (see Sec 2). Every entropic function h is also a polymatroid, if we write $h(S)$ for $h(\mathbf{A}_S)$. (We will use $h(S)$ and $h(\mathbf{A}_S)$ interchangeably in this paper, depending on context.) Linear inequalities satisfied by all polymatroids are called *Shannon-type inequalities* [38]. The *polymatroid bound* of a full conjunctive query is $\log |Q| \leq \max_h h(\mathbf{A}_{[n]})$, where h ranges over all polymatroids satisfying the given constraints. The polymatroid bound, while at least as large as the entropic bound, is known to be tight for cardinality constraints, because the AGM bound is a polymatroid bound for cardinality constraints (see Prop. B.1) and it is tight [13]. The polymatroid bound is also tight for cardinality constraints with certain sets of FDs [3]. We ask whether it is tight in more general settings:

Question 1. Is the polymatroid bound tight for general degree constraints? Or, at least for queries with both cardinality and FD constraints?

Example 1.1. Consider the query:

$$Q(A_1, A_2, A_3, A_4) \text{ :- } R_{12}(A_1, A_2), R_{23}(A_2, A_3), R_{34}(A_3, A_4), R_{41}(A_4, A_1) \quad (2)$$

Assuming all input relations have size $\leq N$, then (a) the AGM bound is $|Q| \leq N^2$, (b) if we add the degree constraints $\deg_{12}(A_1A_2|A_1) \leq D$ and $\deg_{12}(A_1A_2|A_2) \leq D$ for some integer $D \leq \sqrt{N}$ then $|Q| \leq D \cdot N^{3/2}$, and (c) if we replace the degree constraints with FDs $A_1 \to A_2$ and $A_2 \to A_1$ the bound reduces further to $|Q| \leq N^{3/2}$. These bounds can be proven using only Shannon inequalities, thus they are polymatroid bounds. They are also asymptotically tight (see [4]).

Answer 1. The polymatroid bound is *not* tight! By adding a variable to a non-Shannon inequality by Zhang-Yeung [39] and constructing accordingly a database instance, we prove in Appendix A the following.

[1] All logs are in base 2, unless otherwise stated.

Theorem 1.2. *For any integer $s > 0$, there exists a query Q of size $\Theta(s)$, with cardinality and FD constraints, such that the ratio between the polymatroid bound and the entropic bound is $\geq N^s$, where N is the size of the database.*

1.2 Size Bound for Disjunctive Datalog Rules

Disjunctive datalog [9, 21] is a powerful extension of datalog. In this paper we are interested in a single disjunctive-datalog rule:

$$P: \quad \bigvee_{B \in \mathcal{B}} T_B(\mathbf{A}_B) \text{ :- } \bigwedge_{F \in \mathcal{E}} R_F(\mathbf{A}_F) \quad (3)$$

The body is similar to that of a conjunctive query, while the head is a disjunction of output predicates T_B, which we call *targets*. Given a database instance $\mathbf{D}$, a *model* of P is a tuple $\mathbf{T} = (T_B)_{B \in \mathcal{B}}$ of relations, one for each target, such that the logical implication indicated by the rule holds. More precisely, for any tuple $\mathbf{t}$, if $\pi_F(\mathbf{t}) \in R_F$ for every input relation R_F, then there exists a target $T_B \in \mathbf{T}$ such that $\pi_B(\mathbf{t}) \in T_B$. We write $\mathbf{T} \models P$ to denote the fact that $\mathbf{T}$ is a model. Define the size of a model to be $\max_B |T_B|$, and define the *output size* of P to be the minimum size over all models:

$$|P(\mathbf{D})| \stackrel{\text{def}}{=} \min_{\mathbf{T}:\mathbf{T} \models P} \max_{B \in \mathcal{B}} |T_B| \quad (4)$$

Our second question is to find an output size upper bound for a disjunctive datalog rule. If the rule has a single target then it becomes a conjunctive query: a model is any superset of the answer, and the output size is the standard size of the query's answer. We thus expect the upper bound to come in two flavors, entropic and polymatroid, as for full conjunctive queries.

Question 2. Find the entropic and polymatroid output size bounds of a disjunctive datalog rule, under given cardinality constraints, and more generally under degree constraints. Determine if it is tight.

Example 1.3. Consider the disjunctive datalog rule:

$$P: \; T_{123}(A_1, A_2, A_3) \vee T_{234}(A_2, A_3, A_4) \text{ :- } R_{12}(A_1, A_2), R_{23}(A_2, A_3), R_{34}(A_3, A_4), R_{41}(A_4, A_1)$$

A model of size N^3 can be obtained by populating the target T_{123} with all triples obtained from the active domain, but we will show that $|P(\mathbf{D})| \leq N^{3/2}$, $\forall \mathbf{D}$.

Answer 2. To describe the answer to the second question, we recall some standard notations [38]. We identify set-functions $h : 2^{[n]} \to \mathbb{R}_+$ with vectors in $\mathbb{R}_+^{2^n}$, and we use both $h(\mathbf{A}_S)$ and $h(S)$ to denote h_S, where $A_1, A_2, \ldots$ are (random) variables. (The reason being, $h(\mathbf{A}_S)$ is more apt for marginal entropies, and $h(S)$ is more apt for polymatroids.) The sets $\Gamma_n^* \subset \overline{\Gamma}_n^* \subset \Gamma_n \subset \mathbb{R}_+^{2^n}$ denote the set of entropic functions, its topological closure, and the set of polymatroids. We encode degree constraints by a set DC of triples $(X, Y, N_{Y|X})$, specifying $\deg_F(\mathbf{A}_Y|\mathbf{A}_X) \leq N_{Y|X}$. Define

$$\mathsf{HDC} \stackrel{\text{def}}{=} \left\{ h \mid \bigwedge_{(X,Y,N_{Y|X}) \in \mathsf{DC}} h(Y|X) \leq \log N_{Y|X} \right\} \quad (5)$$

to be the collection of set functions satisfying those constraints, where $h(Y|X) \stackrel{\text{def}}{=} h(Y) - h(X)$. Fix a closed subset

$\mathcal{F} \subseteq \mathbb{R}_+^{2^n}$. Define the log-*size-bound* of a disjunctive datalog rule P w.r.t. $\mathcal{F}$ to be the quantity:

$$\mathsf{LogSizeBound}_{\mathcal{F}}(P) \stackrel{\text{def}}{=} \max_{h \in \mathcal{F}} \min_{B \in \mathcal{B}} h(B). \tag{6}$$

The following is our second result, whose proof can be found Appendix A and [4].

Theorem 1.4. *Let P be any disjunctive datalog rule (3), and DC be given degree constraints.*

(i) For any database instance $\mathbf{D}$ satisfying all constraints in DC, the following holds:

$$\log |P(\mathbf{D})| \leq \underbrace{\mathsf{LogSizeBound}_{\bar{\Gamma}_n^* \cap HDC}(P)}_{\textit{entropic bound}} \tag{7}$$

$$\leq \underbrace{\mathsf{LogSizeBound}_{\Gamma_n \cap HDC}(P)}_{\textit{polymatroid bound}} \tag{8}$$

(ii) The entropic bound above is asymptotically tight.

Eq.(7) and (8) generalize the entropic and polymatroid bounds from full conjunctive queries to arbitrary disjunctive datalog rules (see Prop. B.1). The tightness result *(ii)* generalizes the main result in [25], which states that the entropic bound is asymptotically tight for full conjunctive queries under FDs.

1.3 Worst-case Optimal Algorithms

A *worst-case optimal algorithm* is an algorithm for computing a query in time bounded by its size bound. Such algorithms are known for full conjunctive queries under cardinality constraints [1, 34, 35, 37] and FDs [3]. Our next problem is finding a worst-case optimal algorithm for a disjunctive datalog rule P, under degree constraints. More precisely, given an input database $\mathbf{D}$ satisfying the given constraints, compute a model $\mathbf{T}$ in time no larger than the worst-case bound for $|P(\mathbf{D})|$ under those constraints. Notice that we allow the algorithm to compute *any* model. A conjunctive query Q is a single-target disjunctive datalog rule P_Q. If Q is full, then from any model $\mathbf{T}$ of P_Q we can answer Q by semijoin-reducing $\mathbf{T}$ with each input relation. Thus, any algorithm evaluating disjunctive rules can also be used to answer a full conjunctive query. However, this does not hold for non-full queries. For example, if Q is Boolean, then P_Q has a single target $T_\emptyset()$, and can be answered trivially by simply returning $T_\emptyset = \{()\}$, since this is always a model, but this does not help us answer Q. Our third problem is:

Question 3. Design a worst-case optimal algorithm for disjunctive datalog rules under degree constraints.

Answer 3. Details are presented in Sections 3 and 4. We summarize the ideas here. We present an algorithm called PANDA (**P**roof-**A**ssisted e**N**tropic **D**egree-**A**ware), which computes a model of a disjunctive datalog rule P within the runtime predicted by the bound (8). PANDA is derived using a novel principle that we introduced in [3]. First, one has to provide "evidence", called *proof sequence*, that the polymatroid bound is correct. Second, each step in the sequence is interpreted as a relational operator (one of: join, horizontal partition, union), leading to a model of P.

The polymatroid bound (8) is difficult to handle. While the feasible region $\Gamma_n \cap \mathsf{HDC}$ is polyhedral, the objective of (6) is non-linear. We start by proving in Lemma 3.2 that it is equivalent to a linear program: there exist constants $\lambda_B \geq 0$, for $B \in \mathcal{B}$ for which:

$$\max_{h \in \Gamma_n \cap \mathsf{HDC}} \min_{B \in \mathcal{B}} h(B) = \max_{h \in \Gamma_n \cap \mathsf{HDC}} \sum_{B \in \mathcal{B}} \lambda_B h(B) \tag{9}$$

The RHS of (9) is simpler to deal with. To prove an upper bound for it, one has to prove an inequality of the following form, which we call a *Shannon-flow inequality*:

$$\sum_{B \in \mathcal{B}} \lambda_B \cdot h(B) \leq \sum_{(X,Y,N_{Y|X}) \in \mathsf{DC}} \delta_{Y|X} \cdot h(Y|X) \tag{10}$$

This is a (vast) generalization of Shearer's lemma [18]. The inequality (10) implies $\log |P| \leq \sum \delta_{Y|X} \log N_{Y|X}$, and we show in the paper how to choose the coefficients $\delta_{Y|X}$ such that the last expression is precisely (8). Thus, the first task is to prove (i.e. provide evidence for) the inequality (10).

A key technical result in the paper is Theorem 3.8 which, stated informally, says that Eq.(10) can be proved using a sequence of rules of one of the following four types, where $X \subseteq Y$:

Submodularity	$h(Y\vert X) \to h(Y \cup Z\vert X \cup Z)$
Monotonicity	$h(Y) \to h(X)$,
Composition	$h(X) + h(Y\vert X) \to h(Y)$,
Decomposition	$h(Y) \to h(X) + h(Y\vert X)$.

To explain the theorem, assume for the sake of discussion that all coefficients in (10) are natural numbers. Then both sides can be seen as bags of terms, and the theorem says that there exists a sequence of rewritings that transform the bag on the RHS to the bag on the LHS. Obviously, if such a sequence exists, then Eq.(10) holds, because each rewriting replaces a term (or sum of two terms) with a smaller or equal term (or sum of two terms). The converse statement is non-obvious. For example in our prior work [3] we found that, without the decomposition rule, the remaining three rules are *not* complete: there exists a Shannon-flow inequality without a proof sequence.

Finally, PANDA consists of interpreting each step in the proof sequence as a relational operation, leading to:

Theorem 1.5. *PANDA computes a model of a disjunctive datalog rule P under degree constraints DC in time*

$$\tilde{O}\left(N + \text{poly}(\log N) \cdot \prod_{(X,Y,N_{Y|X}) \in DC} N_{Y|X}^{\delta_{Y|X}}\right),$$

where $\displaystyle\sum_{(X,Y,N_{Y|X}) \in DC} \delta_{Y|X} \log N_{Y|X} = \mathsf{LogSizeBound}_{\Gamma_n \cap HDC}(P)$.

1.4 Towards Optimal Algorithms

What is an optimal runtime to compute a given conjunctive query? A common belief is that its cost is of the form $\tilde{O}(N^d + |\mathsf{output}|)$, where N is the size of the input database, N^d represents the "intrinsic" cost of the query, and $|\mathsf{output}|$ is the unavoidable cost of reporting the output.[2] Worst-case optimal algorithms are not optimal in this sense. They are only good for inputs whose intrinsic cost is about the same

[2]In this paper, the big-O notation is in data-complexity, hiding a factor that is query-dependent and data-independent. The big-$\tilde{O}$ hides a single log-factor in data-complexity.

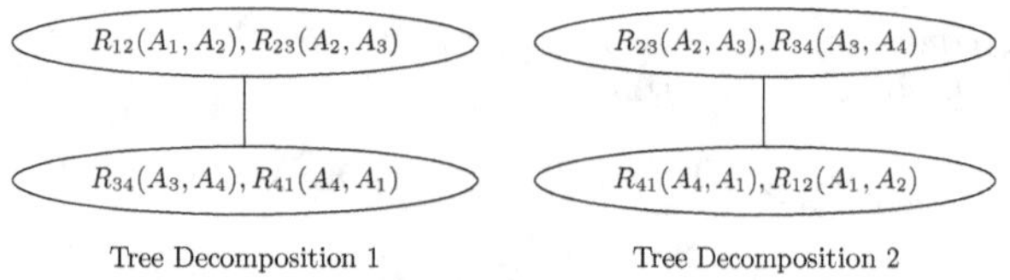

Figure 1: Two tree decompositions for the query in Example 1.1. Normally, each tree node is labeled with a set of variables, e.g. $\chi(t) = \{A_1, A_2, A_3\}$; for convenience we also show the atoms contained in those variables, i.e. $R_{12}(A_1, A_2), R_{23}(A_2, A_3)$.

as the worst-case output size. As described below, there are algorithms whose runtimes are more output-sensitive. If the query is Boolean, then the output size is always 1, and the cost is totally dominated by the intrinsic cost of the query; for simplicity we discuss here only Boolean queries, but our discussion extends to other conjunctive and aggregate queries [2]. Thus, an optimal algorithm should compute a Boolean query in time $\tilde{O}(N^d)$, with an exponent d as small as possible. Generalizing to degree constraints, it should compute the query in time $\tilde{O}(\prod N_{Y|X}^{\delta_{Y|X}})$, where $N_{Y|X}$ are the degree bounds, and the product is minimized.

In search of a yardstick for optimality, we borrow from the long history of research on fixed-parameter tractability. A class $\mathcal{C}$ of Boolean conjunctive queries (equivalently, CSP instances) is *fixed-parameter tractable* (FPT, with parameter $\mathcal{H}$, the query's hypergraph) if there is an algorithm solving every $\mathcal{C}$-instance in time $f(|\mathcal{H}|) \cdot N^d$ for some fixed constant d, where f is any computable function, and N is the data size. In a beautiful paper, Marx [32] showed that $\mathcal{C}$ is FPT iff it has a bounded submodular width. His results suggest to us using the submodular width, $\mathsf{subw}(Q)$, as a yardstick for optimality. In order to prove that bounded submodular width implies FPT, Marx described a query evaluation algorithm that runs in time $O(\text{poly}(N^{\mathsf{subw}(Q)}))$.[3] We define an algorithm to be *optimal* if its runtime is $\tilde{O}(N^{\mathsf{subw}(Q)})$. While no lower bounds are known to date to rule out faster algorithms for a specific query, Marx's dichotomy theorem ruled out faster algorithms for any recursively enumerable class of queries (see [4,32]). Our fourth problem is:

Question 4. Design an algorithm evaluating a Boolean conjunctive query Q in $\tilde{O}(N^{\mathsf{subw}(Q)})$-time. Extend the notion of submodular width, and the algorithm, to handle arbitrary degree constraints, to full conjunctive and aggregate queries.

We briefly review the notion of submodular width, and its relationship to other width notions. Note that all known width parameters considered only cardinality constraints. A polymatroid h is *edge-dominated* if $h(F) \leq 1, \forall F \in \mathcal{E}$. Edge domination is a normalized version of cardinality constraints. The submodular width is defined to be $\mathsf{subw}(Q) \stackrel{\text{def}}{=} \max_h \min_{(T,\chi)} \max_{t \in V(T)} h(\chi(t))$, where h ranges over edge-dominated polymatroids, and (T, χ) over tree decompositions of Q (see Defn. 2.2). Prior notions of width such as tree-width [23], generalized- [28] and fractional- hypertree width [30] (see [26] for a nice survey) are defined by first defining the width of a tree decomposition, then choosing the decomposition that minimizes this width. Thus, there is always a *best* tree decomposition (T, χ), and a query evaluation algorithm runs on that (T, χ); e.g., the fractional hypertree width is $\mathsf{fhtw}(Q) \stackrel{\text{def}}{=} \min_{(T,\chi)} \max_{t \in V(T)} \rho^*(\chi(t))$, where ρ^* is the fractional edge cover number of the set $\chi(t)$. In the submodular width, we are allowed to choose the tree T *after* we see the polymatroid h. Marx showed that $\mathsf{subw}(Q) \leq \mathsf{fhtw}(Q)$, for all Q, and there are classes of queries for which the gap is unbounded. (See also a simple example in [4].)

[3]It is not clear what the exact runtime of Marx's algorithm is. His theorem states that it is $O(\text{poly}(N^{\mathsf{subw}(Q)}))$. Our best interpretation of Lemma 4.3 and Lemma 4.5 of [32] is that Marx's algorithm runs in time at least $O(N^{2 \cdot \mathsf{subw}(Q)})$.

Example 1.6. Fig. 1 shows the only non-trivial tree decompositions of the query Q in Example 1.1. Each tree has a fhtw of 2, hence $\mathsf{fhtw}(Q) = 2$. In contrast, we will show later that $\mathsf{subw}(Q) = 3/2$. For the Boolean version of the query, an algorithm with runtime $O(N^{\mathsf{subw}(Q)})$ will match the best known $O(N^{3/2})$-time algorithm for detecting a 4-cycle in a graph with N edges described by Alon et al. [8].

Answer 4. Our answer is presented in Section 5. Briefly, we generalize the notion of submodular width $\mathsf{subw}(Q)$ to account for arbitrary degree constraints, and call it *degree-aware submodular width*, $\mathsf{da\text{-}subw}(Q)$. In fact, we describe a very general framework that captures virtually all previously defined width-parameters, *and* extends them to degree constraints. We then show how to use PANDA to compute a query in time whose exponent is $\mathsf{da\text{-}subw}(Q)$, using the same earlier principle: from a proof of the bound of $\mathsf{da\text{-}subw}(Q)$, we derive an algorithm that computes Q in that bound:

Theorem 1.7. *PANDA computes any full, Boolean conjunctive, or aggregate query Q in time $\tilde{O}(N + \text{poly}(\log N) \cdot 2^{\mathsf{da\text{-}subw}(Q)} + |\mathsf{output}|)$.*

2. BACKGROUND

Throughout the paper, we use the following convention. The non-negative reals, rationals, and integers are denoted by $\mathbb{R}_+$, $\mathbb{Q}_+$, and $\mathbb{N}$ respectively. Uppercase A_i denotes a variable/attribute, and lowercase a_i denotes a value in the discrete domain $\mathsf{Dom}(A_i)$ of the variable. For any subset $S \subseteq [n]$, define $\mathbf{A}_S = (A_i)_{i \in S}$, $\mathbf{a}_S = (a_i)_{i \in S} \in \prod_{i \in S} \mathsf{Dom}(A_i)$. In particular, $\mathbf{A}_S$ is a tuple of variables and $\mathbf{a}_S$ is a tuple of specific values with support S. Occasionally we use $\mathbf{t}_S$ to denote a tuple with support S.

We will work on multi-hypergraphs $\mathcal{H} = ([n], \mathcal{E})$ (i.e. a hyperedge may occur multiple times in $\mathcal{E}$). A function $f : 2^{[n]} \to \mathbb{R}_+$ is called a (non-negative) *set function* on $\mathcal{H}$. A set function f on $\mathcal{H}$ is *modular* if $f(S) = \sum_{v \in S} f(\{v\})$ for all $S \subseteq [n]$, is *monotone* if $f(X) \leq f(Y)$ whenever $X \subseteq Y$, is *subadditive* if $f(X \cup Y) \leq f(X) + f(Y)$ for all $X, Y \subseteq [n]$, and is *submodular* if $f(X \cup Y) + f(X \cap Y) \leq f(X) + f(Y)$ for all $X, Y \subseteq [n]$. Unless specified otherwise, we will only consider *non-negative* and *monotone* set functions f for which $f(\emptyset) = 0$; this assumption will be implicit in the entire paper. Let M_n, SA_n, and Γ_n denote the set of all (non-negative and monotone) modular, subadditive, and submodular set functions on $[n]$, respectively.

Definition 2.1. Given a hypergraph $\mathcal{H} = ([n], \mathcal{E})$, define the following two set functions:

$$\mathsf{ED} \stackrel{\text{def}}{=} \{h \mid h : 2^{[n]} \to \mathbb{R}_+, h(F) \leq 1, \forall F \in \mathcal{E}\} \tag{11}$$

$$\mathsf{VD} \stackrel{\text{def}}{=} \{h \mid h : 2^{[n]} \to \mathbb{R}_+, h(\{v\}) \leq 1, \forall v \in [n]\} \quad (12)$$

ED stands for *edge-dominated* and VD stands for *vertex-dominated.*

Given a set function h and a scalar s, we will use $s \cdot h$ to denote h scaled by s. (Specifically, we will be interested in $\log N \cdot \mathsf{ED}$ and $\log N \cdot \mathsf{VD}$.)

For any two finite sets S and T, let S^T denote the collection of all maps $f : T \to S$. Such a map f is also viewed as a vector whose coordinates are indexed by members of T and whose coordinate values are members of S.

For the sake of clarity, this section focuses on a full conjunctive query $Q(\mathbf{A}_{[n]}) = \bigwedge_{F \in \mathcal{E}} R_F(A_F)$, whose hypergraph is $\mathcal{H} = ([n], \mathcal{E})$, as discussed in Section 1. For each $F \in \mathcal{E}$, let $N_F \stackrel{\text{def}}{=} |R_F|$, where $N_F \in \mathbb{N} \cup \{\infty\}$. We set $N_F = \infty$ if R_F is not a materialized predicate, a negation of a predicate, or if its size is not known. Throughout this paper, let

$$N = \max_{F \in \mathcal{E}, |R_F| < \infty} N_F. \quad (13)$$

(The full version [4] explains how we deal with Boolean, count, or aggregate queries.)

2.1 Queries without FDs nor degree-bounds

Bounds on the worst-case output size. Bounding the worst-case output size $|Q|$ of a natural join query Q is a well-studied problem. There is a hierarchy of such bounds.

A trivial bound is the *vertex bound* $|Q| \leq \mathsf{VB}(Q) \stackrel{\text{def}}{=} N^n$. A slightly less trivial bound is the *integral edge cover* bound, described as follows. Define the edge cover polytope

$$\mathsf{EC} \stackrel{\text{def}}{=} \left\{ \boldsymbol{\lambda} \mid \boldsymbol{\lambda} \in \mathbb{R}_+^{\mathcal{E}}, \sum_{\substack{F \in \mathcal{E} \\ v \in F}} \lambda_F \geq 1, \forall v \in [n] \right\}.$$

The integral edge cover bound is

$$\log |Q| \leq \rho(Q, (N_F)_{F \in \mathcal{E}}) \stackrel{\text{def}}{=} \log \left(\prod_{F \in \mathcal{E}} N_F^{\lambda_F} \right) \quad (14)$$

where $\boldsymbol{\lambda} = \operatorname{argmin} \left\{ \sum_{F \in \mathcal{E}} \lambda_F \log N_F \mid \boldsymbol{\lambda} \in \mathsf{EC} \cap \{0,1\}^{\mathcal{E}} \right\}$. This bound is dependent on the input relations' sizes. Often, to state a bound that is independent of the input size, researchers use a cruder approximation of the bound: $\rho(Q) = \rho(Q, (N_F = 1)_{F \in \mathcal{E}})$, which is called the *integral edge cover number* of $\mathcal{H}$.

Building on earlier works [7, 18, 24, 29], Atserias, Grohe, and Marx [13] observed that the rational relaxation of (14) still holds, leading to the *AGM-bound*:

$$\log |Q| \leq \log \mathsf{AGM}(Q, (N_F)_{F \in \mathcal{E}}) \stackrel{\text{def}}{=} \log \left(\prod_{F \in \mathcal{E}} N_F^{\lambda_F} \right) \quad (15)$$

where $\boldsymbol{\lambda} = \operatorname{argmin} \left\{ \sum_{F \in \mathcal{E}} \lambda_F \log N_F \mid \boldsymbol{\lambda} \in \mathsf{EC} \right\}$. The relaxation $\rho^*(Q) \stackrel{\text{def}}{=} \log \mathsf{AGM}(Q, (N_F = 1)_{F \in \mathcal{E}})$ is called the *fractional edge cover number.*

One remarkable property of the AGM-bound is that it is asymptotically tight. There are known algorithms [1, 34, 35, 37] with runtime $\tilde{O}(\mathsf{AGM}(Q))$: they are *worst-case optimal.*

Tree decompositions and their widths. Tree decompositions capture conditional independence among variables in a query, facilitating dynamic-programming. We refer the reader to the recent survey by Gottlob et al. [26] for more details on historical contexts, technical descriptions, and open problems thereof. We are necessarily brief in this section.

Definition 2.2. A *tree decomposition* of a hypergraph $\mathcal{H} = ([n], \mathcal{E})$ is a pair (T, χ), where T is a tree and $\chi : V(T) \to 2^{[n]}$ maps each node t of the tree to a subset $\chi(t)$ of vertices such that (1) Every hyperedge $F \in \mathcal{E}$ is a subset of some $\chi(t)$, $t \in V(T)$, (2) For every vertex $v \in [n]$, the set $\{t \mid v \in \chi(t)\}$ is a non-empty (connected) sub-tree of T. Somewhat confusingly, the sets $\chi(t)$ are often called the *bags* of the tree decomposition.

The common method of defining width parameters is the framework introduced by Adler [5]. Let $\mathcal{H} = ([n], \mathcal{E})$ be a hypergraph. Let $g : 2^{[n]} \to \mathbb{R}_+$ be a function that assigns a non-negative real number to each subset of $[n]$. Then, the *g-width* of a tree decomposition (T, χ) is $\max_{t \in V(T)} g(\chi(t))$. The *g-width of* $\mathcal{H}$ is the *minimum* g-width over all tree decompositions of $\mathcal{H}$. Note that the g-width of a hypergraph is a *minimax* function.

For any subset of vertices $B \subseteq [n]$, define $s(B) = |B| - 1$, $\rho(B)$ the integral edge cover number of the set B using edges in $\mathcal{H}$, and $\rho^*(B)$ the fractional edge cover number. Then, the *treewidth* of $\mathcal{H}$, denoted by $\mathsf{tw}(\mathcal{H})$, is the s-width of $\mathcal{H}$. The *generalized hypertree width* of $\mathcal{H}$, denoted by $\mathsf{ghtw}(\mathcal{H})$ is the ρ-width of $\mathcal{H}$. And, the *fractional hypertree width* of $\mathcal{H}$, denoted by $\mathsf{fhtw}(\mathcal{H})$, is the ρ^*-width of $\mathcal{H}$. Very recently, Fischl et al. [22] showed that, checking whether a given hypergraph has a fractional hypertree width or a generalized hypertree width at most 2 is NP-hard, settling two important open questions.

The above three width parameters are based on the same idea: we decompose the query into sub-queries in a dynamic-programming algorithm, and the runtime is dominated by the worst bag size bound of the tree decomposition. It is known [2, 6, 14, 19] that a vast number of problems in graphical model inference, database query computation, constraint satisfaction, and logic can be solved using this strategy. However, this tree-decomposition-first strategy has a drawback that once we stick with a tree decomposition we are forced to suffer the worst-case instance for that tree decomposition. Marx [31, 32] had a wonderful observation: we can partition the data first, and then use a different tree decomposition for each part of the data, then we can in some cases significantly improve the runtime. This idea leads to the notions of *adaptive width* and *submodular width* of a query, where in essence data partitioning and query decomposition are used in an interleaving way.

Definition 2.3. Recall the notion of edge domination from Defn. 11. Then, the *adaptive width* $\mathsf{adw}(\mathcal{H})$ of $\mathcal{H}$ and the *submodular width* $\mathsf{subw}(\mathcal{H})$ of $\mathcal{H}$ are defined by

$$\mathsf{adw}(\mathcal{H}) \stackrel{\text{def}}{=} \max_{f \in \mathsf{ED} \cap \mathsf{M}_n} \min_{(T,\chi)} \max_{t \in V(T)} f(\chi(t)), \quad (16)$$

$$\mathsf{subw}(\mathcal{H}) \stackrel{\text{def}}{=} \max_{f \in \mathsf{ED} \cap \Gamma_n} \min_{(T,\chi)} \max_{t \in V(T)} f(\chi(t)). \quad (17)$$

2.2 FD and degree constraints

The above series of bounds and width parameters were based on a single class of statistics on the input relations: their sizes. In practice we very often encounter queries with functional dependency (FD) and degree bound information. The FDs come from two main sources: primary keys and builtin predicates (such as $A_1 + A_2 = A_3$). The degree constraints come from more refined statistics of the input (materialized) predicates.

Definition 2.4. A *degree constraint* is a triple $(X, Y, N_{Y|X})$ where $X \subset Y \subseteq [n]$ and $N_{Y|X} \in \mathbb{N} \cup \{\infty\}$. A relation R_F is said to *guard* the degree constraint $(X, Y, N_{Y|X})$ if $X \subset Y \subseteq F$ and for every tuple $\mathbf{t}_X$ we have

$$\deg_{R_F}(Y|\mathbf{t}_X) \stackrel{\text{def}}{=} |\Pi_Y(\sigma_{\mathbf{A}_X=\mathbf{t}_X}(R_F)| \leq N_{Y|X}. \quad (18)$$

The quantity on the left hand side is called the *degree of* $\mathbf{t}_X$ with respect to Y in relation R_F. Note that a relation may guard multiple degree constraints.

To avoid writing $\log_2$ in many places, define $n_{Y|X} \stackrel{\text{def}}{=} \log_2 N_{Y|X}$. We use DC to denote a set of degree constraints. A cardinality constraint is a triple $(\emptyset, F, N_F)$. We use CC to denote a set of cardinality constraints. Similar to HDC defined by (5), let HCC denote the set of functions h satisfying cardinality constraints CC.

For example, consider an input relation $R(A_1, A_2, A_3)$ satisfying the following conditions: for every value a_1 in the active domain of A_1, there are at most D different values $a_2 \in \mathsf{Dom}(A_2)$ such that $(a_1, a_2) \in \Pi_{A_1A_2}(R)$. Then, R guards the degree constraint $(\{A_1\}, \{A_1, A_2\}, D)$.

The output size of $Q(\mathbf{A}_{[n]})$ can be bounded by

$$\log_2 |Q| \leq \underbrace{\max_{h \in \mathsf{HDC} \cap \bar{\Gamma}^*_n} h([n])}_{\mathsf{DAEB}(Q)} \leq \underbrace{\max_{h \in \mathsf{HDC} \cap \Gamma_n} h([n])}_{\mathsf{DAPB}(Q)} \quad (19)$$

(DAEB and DAPB are "degree-aware" entropic and polymatroid bounds, respectively. Note that (19) is a special case of (7) and (8).) The CSMA algorithm from [3] can solve a join query Q with known degree constraints in time $\tilde{O}(N + \text{poly}(\log N) \cdot 2^{\mathsf{DAPB}(Q)})$.

3. SHANNON FLOW INEQUALITIES

The PANDA algorithm is built on the notion of a "proof sequence" for a class of Shannon-type inequalities called the *Shannon flow inequalities*.

Definition 3.1. Let $\mathcal{B} \subseteq 2^{[n]}$ denote a collection of subsets of $[n]$. Let $\mathcal{C} \subseteq 2^{[n]} \times 2^{[n]}$ denote a collection of pairs (X, Y) such that $\emptyset \neq X \subset Y \subseteq [n]$. Let $\boldsymbol{\lambda}_\mathcal{B} = (\lambda_F)_{F \in \mathcal{B}} \in \mathbb{Q}^{\mathcal{B}}_+$ and $\boldsymbol{\delta}_\mathcal{C} = (\delta_{Y|X})_{(X,Y)\in\mathcal{C}} \in \mathbb{Q}^{\mathcal{C}}_+$ denote two vectors of non-negative rationals. For any polymatroid h, let $h(Y|X)$ denote $h(Y) - h(X)$.[4] If the following inequality

$$\sum_{B \in \mathcal{B}} \lambda_B \cdot h(B) \leq \sum_{(X,Y)\in\mathcal{C}} \delta_{Y|X} \cdot h(Y|X) \quad (20)$$

holds for all $h \in \Gamma_n$ (i.e. for all polymatroids), then it is called a *Shannon flow inequality*. The set $\mathcal{B}$ is called the set of *targets* of the flow inequality.

Section 3.1 motivates the study of these inequalities. Section 3.2 explains why they are called "flow" inequalities.

3.1 Motivations

Fix a disjunctive datalog rule P of the form (3) with degree constraints DC. Abusing notations, we write $(X, Y) \in \mathsf{DC}$ whenever $(X, Y, N_{Y|X}) \in \mathsf{DC}$. In particular the set DC can play the role of the generic set $\mathcal{C}$ in the definition of Shannon flow inequality. To explain where the Shannon flow inequalities come from, we study the (log) polymatroid bound (8) for P, which was defined by (6) with $\mathcal{F}$ chosen to be $\Gamma_n \cap \mathsf{HDC}$. Appendix C.1 contains the proof of the following reformulation: the maximin optimization problem (6) (with $\mathcal{F} = \Gamma_n \cap \mathsf{HDC}$) has precisely the same objective value as a linear program.

Lemma 3.2. *There exists a non-negative vector* $\boldsymbol{\lambda} = (\lambda_B)_{B\in\mathcal{B}}$, *with* $\|\boldsymbol{\lambda}\|_1 = 1$, *such that*

$$\mathsf{LogSizeBound}_{\Gamma_n \cap HDC}(P) = \max_{h \in \Gamma_n \cap HDC} \sum_{B\in\mathcal{B}} \lambda_B \cdot h(B). \quad (21)$$

This linear program along with Farkas lemma give rise to Shannon flow inequalities. We first need the dual LP of (21). Associate a dual variable $\delta_{Y|X}$ to each degree constraint, a variable $\sigma_{I,J}$ to each submodularity constraint, and a variable $\mu_{X,Y}$ to each monotonicity constraint. For any $Z \in 2^{[n]}$, define the quantity

$$\begin{aligned}\mathsf{inflow}(Z) \stackrel{\text{def}}{=} & \sum_{X:(X,Z)\in\mathsf{DC}} \delta_{Z|X} - \sum_{Y:(Z,Y)\in\mathsf{DC}} \delta_{Y|Z} + \sum_{\substack{I \perp J \\ I\cap J=Z}} \sigma_{I,J} \\ & + \sum_{\substack{I \perp J \\ I\cup J=Z}} \sigma_{I,J} - \sum_{J:J\perp Z} \sigma_{Z,J} - \sum_{X:X\subset Z} \mu_{X,Z} + \sum_{Y:Z\subset Y} \mu_{Z,Y}.\end{aligned}$$

Here, $I \perp J$ means $I \not\subseteq J$ and $J \not\subseteq I$. Note that the function $\mathsf{inflow} : 2^{[n]} \to \mathbb{Q}_+$ is also a function of the dual variables $(\boldsymbol{\delta}, \boldsymbol{\sigma}, \boldsymbol{\mu})$. However, we do not explicitly write down this dependency to avoid heavy-loading notations. The dual of the RHS of (21) is

$$\begin{aligned} \min \quad & \textstyle\sum_{(X,Y)\in\mathsf{DC}} n_{Y|X} \cdot \delta_{Y|X} & & (22)\\ \text{s.t.} \quad & \mathsf{inflow}(B) \geq \lambda_B, & & \forall B \in \mathcal{B}\\ & \mathsf{inflow}(Z) \geq 0, & & \emptyset \neq Z \subseteq [n].\\ & (\boldsymbol{\delta}, \boldsymbol{\sigma}, \boldsymbol{\mu}) \geq \mathbf{0}. \end{aligned}$$

(Recall that $n_{Y|X} \stackrel{\text{def}}{=} \log_2 N_{Y|X}$.) Let $\mathbf{h}^* = (h^*_Z)_{Z\subseteq[n]}$ denote an optimal solution to (21), then its objective value $h^*([n])$ is the same as the objective value of (22) due to strong duality. In particular, let $(\boldsymbol{\delta}^*, \boldsymbol{\sigma}^*, \boldsymbol{\mu}^*)$ denote an optimal solution to (22), then $\sum_{B\in\mathcal{B}} \lambda_B \cdot h^*(B) = \sum_{(X,Y)\in\mathsf{DC}} \delta^*_{Y|X} \cdot n_{Y|X}$. One way to characterize *any* dual feasible solution $(\boldsymbol{\delta}, \boldsymbol{\sigma}, \boldsymbol{\mu})$, is to use Farkas' lemma [36], which in our context takes the following form (see Appendix C.1 for a proof):

Proposition 3.3. *Given* $\boldsymbol{\lambda}$ *and* $\boldsymbol{\delta}$, *the inequality*

$$\sum_{B\in\mathcal{B}} \lambda_B \cdot h(B) \leq \sum_{(X,Y)\in DC} \delta_{Y|X} \cdot h(Y|X) \quad (23)$$

is a Shannon flow inequality if and only if there exist $\boldsymbol{\sigma}$ *and* $\boldsymbol{\mu}$ *such that* $(\boldsymbol{\delta}, \boldsymbol{\sigma}, \boldsymbol{\mu})$ *is feasible to the dual LP* (22).

3.2 Proof sequences

A key observation from Abo Khamis et al. [3] was that we can turn a proof of a special case of inequality (23) into an algorithm. The proof has to be performed in a sequential manner; and this brings us to the concept of a proof sequence. In this paper, we refine the proof sequence notion from [3] in four significant ways. First, the definition

[4]The quantity $h(Y|X)$ is the polymatroid-analog of the conditional entropy $H[Y|X] = H[Y] - H[X]$.

of the proof sequence is different, allowing for a simpler algorithm (PANDA) than CSMA in [3]. Second, in [3] we left open whether proof sequences are a complete proof system, even for special Shannon-flow inequalities; the CSMA algorithm used a specific workaround to achieve optimality even without proving completeness of proof sequences. Our most important contribution here is to prove completeness of our new proof sequence. Third, we are able to bound the length of the proof sequence to be polynomial in the size of the linear program (22), as opposed to the doubly exponential length in [3]. Fourth, new technical ideas are introduced so that we can construct proof sequences for the much more general Shannon flow inequality (23) (as opposed to the special case of "output inequality" in [3]).

Definition 3.4. Let $\mathcal{P} \subseteq 2^{[n]} \times 2^{[n]}$ denote the set of all pairs (X,Y) such that $\emptyset \subseteq X \subset Y \subseteq [n]$. A vector $\mathbf{f} \in \mathbb{R}_+^{\mathcal{P}}$ has coordinates indexed by pairs $(X,Y) \in \mathcal{P}$. We denote the corresponding coordinate value of $\mathbf{f}$ by $f(Y|X)$. The vector $\mathbf{f}$ is called a *conditional polymatroid* iff there exists a polymatroid h such that $f(Y|X) = h(Y) - h(X)$; and, we say h defines the conditional polymatroid $\mathbf{f}$. Abusing notation somewhat, the conditional polymatroid defined by the polymatroid h is denoted by $\mathbf{h}$. In particular, $\mathbf{h} = (h(Y|X))_{(X,Y)\in\mathcal{P}}$. If h is a polymatroid then $h(\emptyset) = 0$, in which case we write $h(Y)$ instead of $h(Y|\emptyset)$.

To formally define the notion of a proof sequence, we rewrite the Shannon flow inequality (20) as an inequality on conditional polymatroids in the $\mathbb{Q}_+^{\mathcal{P}}$ space. We extend the vectors $\boldsymbol{\lambda}_{\mathcal{B}} \in \mathbb{Q}_+^{\mathcal{B}}$ and $\boldsymbol{\delta}_{\mathcal{C}} \in \mathbb{Q}_+^{\mathcal{C}}$ to become vectors $\boldsymbol{\lambda}, \boldsymbol{\delta}$ in the $\mathbb{Q}_+^{\mathcal{P}}$ space in the obvious way:

$$\lambda(Y|X) \stackrel{\text{def}}{=} \begin{cases} \lambda_{\mathcal{B}}(B) & \text{when } Y = B, X = \emptyset \\ 0 & \text{otherwise.} \end{cases}$$

$$\delta(Y|X) \stackrel{\text{def}}{=} \begin{cases} \delta_{\mathcal{C}}(Y|X) & \text{when } (X,Y) \in \mathcal{C} \\ 0 & \text{otherwise.} \end{cases}$$

Then, inequality (20) can be written simply as $\langle \boldsymbol{\lambda}, \mathbf{h} \rangle \leq \langle \boldsymbol{\delta}, \mathbf{h} \rangle$. Note the crucial fact that, even though $\boldsymbol{\lambda} \in \mathbb{Q}_+^{\mathcal{P}}$, for it to be part of a Shannon flow inequality only the entries $\lambda_{B|\emptyset}$ can be positive. We will often write λ_B instead of $\lambda_{B|\emptyset}$. These assumptions are implicit henceforth. Prop. 3.3 can now be written simply as:

Proposition 3.5. *Given any $\boldsymbol{\lambda}, \boldsymbol{\delta} \in \mathbb{Q}_+^{\mathcal{P}}$, where $\lambda_{Y|X} > 0$ implies $X = \emptyset$, the inequality $\langle \boldsymbol{\lambda}, \mathbf{h} \rangle \leq \langle \boldsymbol{\delta}, \mathbf{h} \rangle$ is a Shannon flow inequality if and only if there exist $\boldsymbol{\sigma}$ and $\boldsymbol{\mu}$ such that $(\boldsymbol{\delta}, \boldsymbol{\sigma}, \boldsymbol{\mu})$ satisfy the constraints*

$$\mathsf{inflow}(Z) \geq \lambda_Z, \emptyset \neq Z \subseteq [n] \text{ and } (\boldsymbol{\delta}, \boldsymbol{\sigma}, \boldsymbol{\mu}) \geq \mathbf{0} \tag{24}$$

The conditional polymatroids satisfy four basic laws:

$$\begin{aligned} h(I \cup J|J) - h(I|I \cap J) &\leq 0, \quad I \perp J \text{ (submodularity)} \\ -h(Y|\emptyset) + h(X|\emptyset) &\leq 0, \quad X \subset Y \text{ (monotonicity)} \\ h(Y|\emptyset) - h(Y|X) - h(X|\emptyset) &\leq 0, \quad X \subset Y \text{ (composition)} \\ -h(Y|\emptyset) + h(Y|X) + h(X|\emptyset) &\leq 0, \quad X \subset Y \text{ (decomposition)} \end{aligned}$$

For every $I \perp J$, define a vector $\mathbf{s}_{I,J} \in \mathbb{Q}_+^{\mathcal{P}}$, and for every $X \subset Y$, define three vectors $\mathbf{m}_{X,Y}, \mathbf{c}_{X,Y}, \mathbf{d}_{Y,X} \in \mathbb{Q}_+^{\mathcal{P}}$ such that the laws above can be written correspondingly in dot-product form:

$$\langle \mathbf{s}_{I,J}, \mathbf{h} \rangle \leq 0, \quad I \perp J \text{ (submodularity)} \tag{25}$$

$$\langle \mathbf{m}_{X,Y}, \mathbf{h} \rangle \leq 0, \quad X \subset Y \text{ (monotonicity)} \tag{26}$$

$$\langle \mathbf{c}_{X,Y}, \mathbf{h} \rangle \leq 0, \quad X \subset Y \text{ (composition)} \tag{27}$$

$$\langle \mathbf{d}_{Y,X}, \mathbf{h} \rangle \leq 0, \quad X \subset Y \text{ (decomposition)} \tag{28}$$

Definition 3.6. A *proof sequence* of a Shannon flow inequality $\langle \boldsymbol{\lambda}, \mathbf{h} \rangle \leq \langle \boldsymbol{\delta}, \mathbf{h} \rangle$, is a sequence $(w_1\mathbf{f}_1, \dots, w_\ell \mathbf{f}_\ell)$ satisfying the following: (1) $\mathbf{f}_i \in \{ \mathbf{s}_{I,J}, \mathbf{m}_{X,Y}, \mathbf{c}_{X,Y}, \mathbf{d}_{Y,X}\}$ for all $i \in [\ell]$. The $\mathbf{f}_i$ are called *proof steps.* (2) $w_i \in \mathbb{R}_+$, $i \in [\ell]$ are the corresponding *weights* of the proof steps. (3) All the vectors $\boldsymbol{\delta}_0 \stackrel{\text{def}}{=} \boldsymbol{\delta}, \boldsymbol{\delta}_1, \dots, \boldsymbol{\delta}_\ell$ defined by $\boldsymbol{\delta}_i = \boldsymbol{\delta}_{i-1} + w_i \cdot \mathbf{f}_i$, $i \in [\ell]$ are non-negative. (4) Furthermore, $\boldsymbol{\delta}_\ell \geq \boldsymbol{\lambda}$.

Note that $\langle \boldsymbol{\delta}_{i-1}, \mathbf{h} \rangle \geq \langle \boldsymbol{\delta}_i, \mathbf{h} \rangle$ for every conditional polymatroid $\mathbf{h}$, and every $i \in [\ell]$. The proof step $\mathbf{s}_{I,J}$ is called a *submodularity step*, $\mathbf{m}_{X,Y}$ a *monotonicity step*, $\mathbf{d}_{Y,X}$ a *decomposition step*, and $\mathbf{c}_{X,Y}$ a *composition step.*

Definition 3.7. Let $\langle \boldsymbol{\lambda}, \mathbf{h} \rangle \leq \langle \boldsymbol{\delta}, \mathbf{h} \rangle$ be a Shannon flow inequality. From Prop. 3.3 there exists $(\boldsymbol{\sigma}, \boldsymbol{\mu})$ such that $(\boldsymbol{\delta}, \boldsymbol{\sigma}, \boldsymbol{\mu})$ belongs to the polyhedron (24). We call $(\boldsymbol{\sigma}, \boldsymbol{\mu})$ a *witness* for the Shannon flow inequality.

We present here one construction of a proof sequence for a Shannon flow inequality. See [4] for more advanced constructions of shorter sequences.

Theorem 3.8. *Let $\langle \boldsymbol{\lambda}, \mathbf{h} \rangle \leq \langle \boldsymbol{\delta}, \mathbf{h} \rangle$ be a Shannon flow inequality with witness $(\boldsymbol{\sigma}, \boldsymbol{\mu})$. There exists a proof sequence for the inequality $\langle \boldsymbol{\lambda}, \mathbf{h} \rangle \leq \langle \boldsymbol{\delta}, \mathbf{h} \rangle$ with length at most $D(3\|\boldsymbol{\sigma}\|_1 + \|\boldsymbol{\delta}\|_1 + \|\boldsymbol{\mu}\|_1)$, where D is the minimum common denominator of all entries in $(\boldsymbol{\lambda}, \boldsymbol{\delta}, \boldsymbol{\sigma}, \boldsymbol{\mu})$.*

Proof. We induct on the quantity

$$\ell(\boldsymbol{\lambda}, \boldsymbol{\delta}, \boldsymbol{\sigma}, \boldsymbol{\mu}) \stackrel{\text{def}}{=} D\left(\|\boldsymbol{\lambda}\|_1 + 2\|\boldsymbol{\sigma}\|_1 + \|\boldsymbol{\delta}\|_1 + \|\boldsymbol{\mu}\|_1\right),$$

which is an integer. The base case is when $\|\boldsymbol{\lambda}\|_1 = 0$, which is trivial because the inequality has a proof sequence of length 0. In the inductive step, assume $\|\boldsymbol{\lambda}\|_1 > 0$, meaning there must be some $B \subseteq [n]$ for which $\lambda_B > 0$. We will produce a Shannon flow inequality $\langle \boldsymbol{\lambda}', \mathbf{h} \rangle \leq \langle \boldsymbol{\delta}', \mathbf{h} \rangle$ witnessed by $(\boldsymbol{\sigma}', \boldsymbol{\mu}')$ such that $\ell(\boldsymbol{\lambda}', \boldsymbol{\delta}', \boldsymbol{\sigma}', \boldsymbol{\mu}') < \ell(\boldsymbol{\lambda}, \boldsymbol{\delta}, \boldsymbol{\sigma}, \boldsymbol{\mu})$. From the induction hypothesis we obtain a proof sequence $\mathsf{ProofSeq}'$ for $\langle \boldsymbol{\lambda}', \mathbf{h} \rangle \leq \langle \boldsymbol{\delta}', \mathbf{h} \rangle$. Finally the proof sequence $\mathsf{ProofSeq}$ for $\langle \boldsymbol{\lambda}, \mathbf{h} \rangle \leq \langle \boldsymbol{\delta}, \mathbf{h} \rangle$ is constructed from $\mathsf{ProofSeq}'$ by appending to the beginning one or two proof steps.

From Prop. 3.5, we know $\sum_{\emptyset \neq W \subseteq [n]} \mathsf{inflow}(W) \geq \lambda_B > 0$. Consequently, there must exist $Z \neq \emptyset$ for which $\delta_{Z|\emptyset} > 0$; otherwise, all variables $\delta_{Y|X}, \sigma_{I,J}, \mu_{X,Y}$ contribute a non-positive amount to the sum $\sum_{\emptyset \neq W \subseteq [n]} \mathsf{inflow}(W)$. Let $w \stackrel{\text{def}}{=} 1/D$, and fix an arbitrary $Z \neq \emptyset$ where $\delta_{Z|\emptyset} > 0$. We initially set $(\boldsymbol{\lambda}', \boldsymbol{\delta}', \boldsymbol{\sigma}', \boldsymbol{\mu}') = (\boldsymbol{\lambda}, \boldsymbol{\delta}, \boldsymbol{\sigma}, \boldsymbol{\mu})$; then we modify $(\boldsymbol{\lambda}', \boldsymbol{\delta}', \boldsymbol{\sigma}', \boldsymbol{\mu}')$ slightly depending on the cases below.

Case 1: $\lambda_Z > 0$. Reduce both λ'_Z and $\delta'_{Z|\emptyset}$ by w. From Prop. 3.5, we can verify that $\langle \boldsymbol{\lambda}', \mathbf{h} \rangle \leq \langle \boldsymbol{\delta}', \mathbf{h} \rangle$ is a Shannon flow inequality witnessed by $(\boldsymbol{\sigma}', \boldsymbol{\mu}') = (\boldsymbol{\sigma}, \boldsymbol{\mu})$. By induction hypothesis, $\langle \boldsymbol{\lambda}', \mathbf{h} \rangle \leq \langle \boldsymbol{\delta}', \mathbf{h} \rangle$ has a proof sequence $\mathsf{ProofSeq}'$ of length at most $D(3\|\boldsymbol{\sigma}\|_1 + \|\boldsymbol{\delta}'\|_1 + \|\boldsymbol{\mu}\|_1)$. Furthermore, the $\mathsf{ProofSeq}'$ *is* also a proof sequence for $\langle \boldsymbol{\lambda}, \mathbf{h} \rangle \leq \langle \boldsymbol{\delta}, \mathbf{h} \rangle$.

Case 2: $\lambda_Z = 0$ *and* $\mathsf{inflow}(Z) > 0$. Reduce $\delta'_{Z|\emptyset}$ by w. Then, from Prop. 3.5, we can verify that $\langle \boldsymbol{\lambda}, \mathbf{h} \rangle \leq \langle \boldsymbol{\delta}', \mathbf{h} \rangle$ is a Shannon flow inequality witnessed by $(\boldsymbol{\sigma}, \boldsymbol{\mu})$. The inductive step is now identical to that of Case 1.

Case 3: $\mathsf{inflow}(Z) = 0$. Since $\delta_{Z|\emptyset} > 0$, there must be some dual variable that is contributing a negative amount to $\mathsf{inflow}(Z)$. In particular, one of the following three cases must hold:

(1) There is some $X \subset Z$ such that $\mu_{X,Z} \geq w$. Define $\boldsymbol{\delta}' = \boldsymbol{\delta} + w \cdot \mathbf{m}_{X,Z}$ and reduce $\mu'_{X,Z}$ by w. Note that $\|\boldsymbol{\delta}'\|_1 = \|\boldsymbol{\delta}\|_1$, $\|\boldsymbol{\mu}'\|_1 = \|\boldsymbol{\mu}\|_1 - w$, and $\langle \boldsymbol{\lambda}, \mathbf{h}\rangle \leq \langle \boldsymbol{\delta}', \mathbf{h}\rangle$ is a Shannon flow inequality. witnessed by $(\boldsymbol{\sigma}, \boldsymbol{\mu}')$. By induction hypothesis, $\langle \boldsymbol{\lambda}, \mathbf{h}\rangle \leq \langle \boldsymbol{\delta}', \mathbf{h}\rangle$ has a proof sequence $\mathsf{ProofSeq}'$ of length at most $D(3\|\boldsymbol{\sigma}\|_1 + \|\boldsymbol{\delta}'\|_1 + \|\boldsymbol{\mu}'\|_1)$. It follows that $\mathsf{ProofSeq} = (w \cdot \mathbf{m}_{X,Z}, \mathsf{ProofSeq}')$ is a proof sequence for $\langle \boldsymbol{\lambda}, \mathbf{h}\rangle \leq \langle \boldsymbol{\delta}, \mathbf{h}\rangle$ of length at most $D(3\|\boldsymbol{\sigma}\|_1 + \|\boldsymbol{\delta}\|_1 + \|\boldsymbol{\mu}\|_1)$.

(2) There is some $Y \supset Z$ such that $\delta_{Y|Z} \geq w$. Define $\boldsymbol{\delta}' = \boldsymbol{\delta} + w \cdot \mathbf{c}_{Z,Y}$. Note that $\|\boldsymbol{\delta}'\|_1 = \|\boldsymbol{\delta}\|_1 - w$ and $\langle \boldsymbol{\lambda}, \mathbf{h}\rangle \leq \langle \boldsymbol{\delta}', \mathbf{h}\rangle$ is a Shannon flow inequality witnessed by $(\boldsymbol{\sigma}, \boldsymbol{\mu})$. From the proof sequence $\mathsf{ProofSeq}'$ for $\langle \boldsymbol{\lambda}, \mathbf{h}\rangle \leq \langle \boldsymbol{\delta}', \mathbf{h}\rangle$ we obtain the proof sequence $\mathsf{ProofSeq} = (w \cdot \mathbf{c}_{Z,Y}, \mathsf{ProofSeq}')$ for $\langle \boldsymbol{\lambda}, \mathbf{h}\rangle \leq \langle \boldsymbol{\delta}, \mathbf{h}\rangle$ of the desired length.

(3) There is some $J \perp Z$ such that $\sigma_{Z,J} \geq w$. Define $\boldsymbol{\delta}' = \boldsymbol{\delta} + w \cdot \mathbf{d}_{Z,Z\cap J} + w \cdot \mathbf{s}_{Z,J}$, and reduce $\sigma'_{Z,J}$ by w. In this case, $\|\boldsymbol{\delta}'\|_1 = \|\boldsymbol{\delta}\|_1 + w$, $\|\boldsymbol{\sigma}'\|_1 = \|\boldsymbol{\sigma}\|_1 - w$, and $\langle \boldsymbol{\lambda}, \mathbf{h}\rangle \leq \langle \boldsymbol{\delta}', \mathbf{h}\rangle$ is a Shannon flow inequality witnessed by $(\boldsymbol{\sigma}', \boldsymbol{\mu})$. By induction hypothesis, $\langle \boldsymbol{\lambda}, \mathbf{h}\rangle \leq \langle \boldsymbol{\delta}', \mathbf{h}\rangle$ has a proof sequence $\mathsf{ProofSeq}'$ of length at most $D(3\|\boldsymbol{\sigma}'\|_1 + \|\boldsymbol{\delta}'\|_1 + \|\boldsymbol{\mu}\|_1)$. It follows that $\mathsf{ProofSeq} = (w \cdot \mathbf{d}_{Z,Z\cap J}, w \cdot \mathbf{s}_{Z,J}, \mathsf{ProofSeq}')$ is a proof sequence for $\langle \boldsymbol{\lambda}, \mathbf{h}\rangle \leq \langle \boldsymbol{\delta}, \mathbf{h}\rangle$ of length at most $D(3\|\boldsymbol{\sigma}\|_1 + \|\boldsymbol{\delta}\|_1 + \|\boldsymbol{\mu}\|_1)$. □

The PANDA algorithm needs another technical lemma. (See Appendix C.2 for its proof.)

Lemma 3.9. *Let $\langle \boldsymbol{\lambda}, \mathbf{h}\rangle \leq \langle \boldsymbol{\delta}, \mathbf{h}\rangle$ be a Shannon flow inequality with witness $(\boldsymbol{\sigma}, \boldsymbol{\mu})$. Let D be a common denominator of all entries in $(\boldsymbol{\lambda}, \boldsymbol{\delta}, \boldsymbol{\sigma}, \boldsymbol{\mu})$, and $w = 1/D$. Suppose $\|\boldsymbol{\lambda}\|_1 > 0$ and $\delta_{Y|\emptyset} > 0$. Then, there are two vectors $\boldsymbol{\lambda}', \boldsymbol{\delta}'$ satisfying the following conditions:*

(a) $\langle \boldsymbol{\lambda}', \mathbf{h}\rangle \leq \langle \boldsymbol{\delta}', \mathbf{h}\rangle$ is a Shannon flow inequality (with witness $(\boldsymbol{\sigma}', \boldsymbol{\mu}')$).

(b) $\boldsymbol{\lambda}' \leq \boldsymbol{\lambda}$ and $\boldsymbol{\delta}' \leq \boldsymbol{\delta}$ (component-wise comparisons).

(c) $\|\boldsymbol{\lambda}'\|_1 \geq \|\boldsymbol{\lambda}\|_1 - w$ and $\delta'_{Y|\emptyset} \leq \delta_{Y|\emptyset} - w$.

(d) D is a common denominator of all entries in the vector $(\boldsymbol{\lambda}', \boldsymbol{\delta}', \boldsymbol{\sigma}', \boldsymbol{\mu}')$.

4. THE PANDA ALGORITHM

This section presents an algorithm called PANDA that computes a model of a disjunctive datalog rule P in time predicted by its polymatroid bound (defined by (8)):

$$\tilde{O}(N + \text{poly}(\log N) \cdot 2^{\mathsf{LogSizeBound}_{\Gamma_n \cap \mathsf{HDC}}(P)}).$$

(Recall the definition of N in (13).) The main result of this section is Theorem 1.5, whose proof is in Appendix D. We start with a simple example illustrating how one might turn a proof sequence into an algorithm.

Example 4.1. We illustrate PANDA on the disjunctive rule P in Example 1.3. First we prove $|P| \leq N^{3/2}$. This follows from

$$\begin{aligned}\log |P| &\leq \min(h(A_1A_2A_3), h(A_2A_3A_4)) \\ &\leq \frac{1}{2}(h(A_1A_2A_3) + h(A_2A_3A_4)),\end{aligned}$$

and from this Shannon-flow inequality:

$$h(A_1A_2A_3) + h(A_2A_3A_4) \leq h(A_1A_2) + h(A_2A_3) + h(A_3A_4)$$

The inequality implies $\log |P| \leq \frac{3}{2}\log N$, because each of $h(A_1A_2)$, $h(A_2A_3)$, $h(A_3A_4)$ is $\leq \log N$. It remains to prove the Shannon-flow inequality above, and for that we use this proof sequence:

$$\begin{aligned}h(A_1A_2) + h(A_2A_3) + h(A_3A_4) &\overset{(1)}{\to} \\ h(A_1A_2) + h(A_2A_3) + [h(A_4|A_3) + h(A_3)] &\overset{(2)}{\to} \\ h(A_1A_2|A_3) + h(A_2A_3) + [h(A_4|A_2A_3) + h(A_3)] &= \\ [h(A_1A_2|A_3) + h(A_3)] + [h(A_2A_3) + h(A_4|A_2A_3)] &\overset{(3)}{\to} \\ h(A_1A_2A_3) + h(A_2A_3A_4)\end{aligned}$$

PANDA interprets these steps as relational operators. (1) is a decomposition step: we partition $R_{34}(A_3, A_4)$ horizontally into $R'_3(A_3)$ and $R'_{34}(A_3, A_4)$, where R'_3 contains all values a_3 that are "heavy hitters", meaning that $|\sigma_{A_3=a_3}(R_{34})| \geq \sqrt{N}$, and R'_{34} consists of all pairs (a_3, a_4) with a_3 being "light hitters". (2) are two submodularity steps: PANDA does nothing, but keeps track that the term $h(A_1A_2|A_3)$ refers to $R_{12}(A_1, A_2)$ and $h(A_4|A_2A_3)$ refers to $R'_{34}(A_3, A_4)$. (3) are two composition steps, interpreted as joins. PANDA computes the first target $T_{123}(A_1, A_2, A_3) = R_{12}(A_1, A_2) \bowtie R'_3(A_3)$, and the second target $T_{234}(A_2, A_3, A_4) = R_{23}(A_2, A_3) \bowtie R'_{34}(A_3, A_4)$. Both joins take time $\tilde{O}(N^{3/2})$, because $|R'_3| \leq \sqrt{N}$ and $\deg_{R'_{34}}(A_3A_4|A_3) \leq \sqrt{N}$.

The above example has the nice property that the two terms $h(A_4|A_3)$ and $h(A_3)$ resulting from the decomposition (1) *diverged*, i.e. were used in different targets. This allowed PANDA to place each tuple from R_{34} in either R'_3 or R'_{34}: no need to place in both, since these relations are not joined later. However, we could neither prove nor disprove the divergence property in general. Instead, PANDA conservatively places each tuple in *both* relations, yet it must ensure $|R'_3(A_3)| \cdot \deg_{R'_{34}}(A_3A_4|A_3) \leq |R_{34}|$. For that it creates $\log N$ bins, with tuples whose degree is in $[2^i, 2^{i+1})$, for $i = 0, \ldots, \lfloor \log N \rfloor$, and processes each bin separately. This needs to be repeated at each non-divergent decomposition step, hence the additional $\text{poly}(\log N)$ factor in the runtime.

In general, PANDA takes as input the collection of input relations $\mathcal{R}$, the degree constraints DC, a Shannon flow inequality and its proof sequence. The Shannon flow inequality is constructed by solving the optimization problem (6) where $\mathcal{F}$ is $\Gamma_n \cap \mathsf{HDC}$. From Lemma 3.2, we can find a vector $\boldsymbol{\lambda}_{\mathcal{B}}$ with $\|\boldsymbol{\lambda}\|_1 = 1$ such that the problem has the same optimal objective value as the linear program $\max_{h \in \Gamma_n \cap \mathsf{HDC}} \langle \boldsymbol{\lambda}, \mathbf{h}\rangle$. Recall from Section 3.2 that, when we extend $\boldsymbol{\lambda}_{\mathcal{B}}$ to the (conditional polymatroid) space $\boldsymbol{\lambda} \in \mathbb{Q}_+^{\mathcal{P}}$, only the entries $\lambda_{B|\emptyset}$ for $B \in \mathcal{B}$ can be positive. Let $(\boldsymbol{\delta}, \boldsymbol{\sigma}, \boldsymbol{\mu})$ denote an optimal dual solution to this LP, then by strong duality

$$\sum_{(X,Y) \in \mathsf{DC}} n_{Y|X} \cdot \delta_{Y|X} = \mathsf{LogSizeBound}_{\Gamma_n \cap \mathsf{HDC}}(P) \qquad (29)$$

Moreover, from Proposition 3.3 we know $\langle \boldsymbol{\lambda}, \mathbf{h}\rangle \leq \langle \boldsymbol{\delta}, \mathbf{h}\rangle$ is a Shannon flow inequality. For inductive purposes, we will assume a slightly more general condition that the guiding Shannon flow inequality satisfies $0 < \|\boldsymbol{\lambda}\|_1 \leq 1$. From Theorem 3.8, we obtain a proof sequence for the Shannon flow inequality. Also for inductive purposes, the following invariant is maintained throughout:

Definition 4.2 (Degree-support invariant)**.** The guiding Shannon flow inequality is promised to satisfy the following invariant: if $\delta_{Y|X} > 0$ then there exist $Z \subseteq X$, $W \subseteq Y$ such that $W - Z = Y - X$ and $(Z, W, N_{W|Z}) \in \mathsf{DC}$. (Note that, if $X = \emptyset$ then $W = Y$ and $Z = \emptyset$.) The degree constraint $(Z, W, N_{W|Z})$ is said to *support* the positive $\delta_{Y|X}$. (If there are multiple constraints $(Z, W, N_{W|Z})$ supporting $\delta_{Y|X}$, then the one with the minimum $N_{W|Z}$ is always chosen to be *the* constraint that supports $\delta_{Y|X}$, where ties are broken arbitrarily.)

Invariant 4.2 is certainly satisfied at the very beginning. A very high-level description of the algorithm is as follows. Recall from Definition 3.6 that a proof sequence $\mathsf{ProofSeq}$ is a series of proof steps, which are used by PANDA as "symbolic instructions". For each instruction, PANDA does some computation, spawns a number of subproblem(s) all of which are disjunctive datalog rules, and creates new (intermediate) relations to become input of the subproblems if necessary. The output of the ith subproblem is a set of tables $T_B^{(i)}$ for $B \in \mathcal{B}$. The overall output is the set of tables $T_B = \bigcup_i T_B^{(i)}$, $B \in \mathcal{B}$; namely for each $B \in \mathcal{B}$ we take the union of the corresponding tables from the subproblems's outputs. The number of subproblems will be shown to be polylogarithmic in the input size.

We now walk the reader step-by-step through the algorithm. Define a "budget" quantity of

$$\mathsf{OBJ} \stackrel{\text{def}}{=} \sum_{(X,Y)} n(\delta_{Y|X}), \tag{30}$$

where

$$n(\delta_{Y|X}) \stackrel{\text{def}}{=} \begin{cases} \delta_{Y|X} \cdot n_{W|Z} & \text{if } \delta_{Y|X} > 0 \text{ and} \\ & (Z, W, N_{W|X}) \text{ supports it} \\ 0 & \text{if } \delta_{Y|X} = 0. \end{cases}$$

From (29), $\mathsf{OBJ} = \mathsf{LogSizeBound}_{\Gamma_n \cap \mathsf{HDC}}(P)$. We assume that the input size is within the budget, i.e. $N \leq 2^{\mathsf{OBJ}}$. (We will see later how to enforce this assumption when it is not satisfied.) We will keep every step of the algorithm to run within the budget of $\tilde{O}(2^{\mathsf{OBJ}})$. Specifically, we will keep every intermediate relation the algorithm computes of size $\leq 2^{\mathsf{OBJ}}$. In the base case, the algorithm stops as soon as there is a relation $R \in \mathcal{R}$ with attribute set $\mathbf{A}_B$ where $B \in \mathcal{B}$, in which case R is a target relation. Otherwise, the algorithm takes steps which are modeled after the proof steps. Let $\mathbf{f}$ be the first proof step (instruction) with weight w, i.e. $\mathsf{ProofSeq} = (w{\cdot}\mathbf{f}, \mathsf{ProofSeq}')$ where $\mathsf{ProofSeq}'$ contains the rest of the instructions.

Case 1: $\mathbf{f} = \mathbf{s}_{I,J}$ is a submodularity step. By definition of proof sequence, $\boldsymbol{\delta} + w \cdot \mathbf{s}_{I,J} \geq \mathbf{0}$, and thus $\delta_{I|I\cap J} \geq w > 0$. Let $(Z, W, N_{W|Z}) \in \mathsf{DC}$ be the degree constraint supporting $\delta_{I|I\cap J}$; then $Z \subseteq I \cap J$, $W \subseteq I$, and $W - Z = I - I \cap J$. The algorithm proceeds by setting $\boldsymbol{\delta}' = \boldsymbol{\delta} + w \cdot \mathbf{s}_{I,J}$. Note that $\delta'_{I\cup J|J}$ is now positive, and so it needs a supporting degree constraint. From the fact that $W - Z = I - I \cap J = I \cup J - J$, $(Z, W, N_{W|Z})$ can support $\delta'_{I\cup J|J}$. Since $\mathbf{f}$ was the next step in the proof sequence, $\langle \boldsymbol{\lambda}, \mathbf{h}\rangle \leq \langle \boldsymbol{\delta}', \mathbf{h}\rangle$ is a Shannon flow inequality with proof sequence $\mathsf{ProofSeq}'$.

Case 2: $\mathbf{f} = \mathbf{m}_{X,Y}$ is a monotonicity step. By definition of proof sequence, $\boldsymbol{\delta} + w \cdot \mathbf{m}_{X,Y} \geq \mathbf{0}$, and thus $\delta_{Y|\emptyset} \geq w > 0$. Let $(\emptyset, Y, N_{Y|\emptyset}) \in \mathsf{DC}$ be the degree constraint supporting $\delta_{Y|\emptyset}$, and $R \in \mathcal{R}$ be a guard for this degree constraint (hence $|\Pi_Y(R)| \leq N_{Y|\emptyset}$). Then, we proceed by setting $\boldsymbol{\delta}' = \boldsymbol{\delta} + w \cdot \mathbf{m}_{X,Y}$. Note that $\delta'_{X|\emptyset}$ is positive, and so it needs a supporting degree constraint, which is the newly added degree constraint $(\emptyset, X, N_{X|\emptyset})$, guarded by R, where $N_{X|\emptyset} \stackrel{\text{def}}{=} |\Pi_X(R)| \leq |R| \leq 2^{\mathsf{OBJ}}$.

Case 3: $\mathbf{f} = \mathbf{d}_{Y,X}$ is a decomposition step with weight w. From $\boldsymbol{\delta} + w \cdot \mathbf{d}_{Y,X} \geq \mathbf{0}$, it follows that $\delta_{Y|\emptyset} \geq w > 0$. From the guarantee that $\delta_{Y|\emptyset}$ has a supporting degree constraint, it follows that there is a relation $R \in \mathcal{R}$ guarding $(\emptyset, Y, N_{Y|\emptyset})$, which means $|\Pi_Y(R)| \leq N_{Y|\emptyset}$. We showed in [3] that R can be partitioned into at most ($k = 2\log_2|R| \leq 2 \cdot \mathsf{OBJ}$) sub-tables $R^{(1)}, \ldots, R^{(k)}$ such that $N^{(j)}_{Y|X} N^{(j)}_{X|\emptyset} \leq N_{Y|\emptyset}$, for all $j \in [k]$, where

$$N^{(j)}_{Y|X} \stackrel{\text{def}}{=} \max_{\mathbf{t}_X \in \Pi_X(R^{(j)})} \deg_{R^{(j)}}(Y|\mathbf{t}_X), \tag{31}$$

$$N^{(j)}_{X|\emptyset} \stackrel{\text{def}}{=} |\Pi_X(R^{(j)})|.$$

(See (18) in Definition 2.4.) For each of these sub-tables $R^{(j)}$ of R, we create a subproblem with the same input tables but with R replaced by $R^{(j)}$. The jth subproblem has degree constraints $\mathsf{DC}^{(j)}$ where

$$\mathsf{DC}^{(j)} = \mathsf{DC} \cup \{(\emptyset, X, N^{(j)}_{X|\emptyset}), (X, Y, N^{(j)}_{Y|X})\}.$$

The table $R^{(j)}$ guards both of the new degree constraints. Set $\boldsymbol{\delta} = \boldsymbol{\delta} + w \cdot \mathbf{d}_{Y,X}$. The jth subproblem is on the Shannon flow inequality $\langle \boldsymbol{\lambda}, \mathbf{h}\rangle \leq \langle \boldsymbol{\delta}, \mathbf{h}\rangle$ with proof sequence $\mathsf{ProofSeq}'$.

Case 4: $\mathbf{f} = \mathbf{c}_{X,Y}$ is a composition step with weight w. By definition of proof sequence, $\boldsymbol{\delta} + w \cdot \mathbf{c}_{X,Y} \geq \mathbf{0}$, and thus $\delta_{Y|X} \geq w > 0$ and $\delta_{X|\emptyset} \geq w > 0$. From the facts that $\delta_{Y|X}$ and $\delta_{X|\emptyset}$ have supports, there must be two sets $Z \subseteq X$ and $W \subseteq Y$ for which $W - Z = Y - X$ and $(Z, W, N_{W|Z}) \in \mathsf{DC}$ which is guarded by an input relation R; and an input relation S for which $|\Pi_X(S)| \leq N_{X|\emptyset}$. Note that $X \cup (W - Z) = X \cup (Y - X) = Y$. We consider two cases:

(Case 4a) If $N_{X|\emptyset} \cdot N_{W|Z} \leq 2^{\mathsf{OBJ}}$, then we can compute the table $T(\mathbf{A}_Y) \stackrel{\text{def}}{=} \Pi_X(S) \bowtie \Pi_W(R)$ by going over all tuples in $\Pi_X(S)$ and expanding them using matching tuples in $\Pi_W(R)$. The runtime of the join is $\tilde{O}(N_{X|\emptyset} \cdot N_{W|Z}) = \tilde{O}(2^{\mathsf{OBJ}})$, and the size of T is $\leq 2^{\mathsf{OBJ}}$. The Shannon flow inequality is modified by setting $\boldsymbol{\delta} = \boldsymbol{\delta} + w \cdot \mathbf{c}_{X,Y}$, with the the proof sequence $\mathsf{ProofSeq}'$, and the set of degree constraints is extended by adding the constraint $(\emptyset, Y, N_{Y|\emptyset} \stackrel{\text{def}}{=} |T|)$, guarded by T.

(Case 4b) If $N_{X|\emptyset} \cdot N_{W|Z} > 2^{\mathsf{OBJ}}$, then we *will not* perform this join. Instead, we *restart* the subproblem with a fresh inequality. In particular, set $\boldsymbol{\delta} = \boldsymbol{\delta} + w \cdot \mathbf{c}_{X,Y}$. Now we have $\delta_{Y|\emptyset} \geq w$. We restart the problem with the inequality $\langle \boldsymbol{\lambda}', \mathbf{h}\rangle \leq \langle \boldsymbol{\delta}', \mathbf{h}\rangle$ satisfying the conditions stated in Lemma 3.9. We show in the proof of Theorem 1.5 (in Appendix D) that in this case $\|\boldsymbol{\lambda}\|_1 > w$, and the new inequality is a Shannon flow inequality with a smaller upper bound on the proof sequence length.

5. DEGREE-AWARE WIDTH PARAMETERS

5.1 Minimax and maximin widths

We slightly reformulate existing width parameters under a common framework. Recall from Section 2 that there are two classes of width parameters: the first class captures the class of algorithms which seek the best tree decomposition with the worst bag runtime, while the second class captures the class of algorithms which adapt the tree decomposition to the instance at hand. In the definitions below, the maximin width notion is from Marx [31, 32].

Definition 5.1. Let $\mathcal{F}$ denote a topologically closed class of non-negative set functions on $[n]$. The *$\mathcal{F}$-minimax width* and *$\mathcal{F}$-maximin width* of a query Q are defined by

$$\mathsf{Minimaxwidth}_{\mathcal{F}}(Q) \stackrel{\text{def}}{=} \min_{(T,\chi)} \max_{t\in V(T)} \max_{h\in\mathcal{F}} h(\chi(t)), \quad (32)$$

$$\mathsf{Maximinwidth}_{\mathcal{F}}(Q) \stackrel{\text{def}}{=} \max_{h\in\mathcal{F}} \min_{(T,\chi)} \max_{t\in V(T)} h(\chi(t)). \quad (33)$$

These width notions are used by specializing $\mathcal{F}$ to capture two aspects of the input. The first aspect is either the entropic functions or some relaxation, coming from the chain of inclusion $\mathsf{M}_n \subset \overline{\Gamma}^*_n \subset \Gamma_n \subset \mathsf{SA}_n$. The second aspect models the granularity level of statistics we know from the input database instance, with the following inclusion chain

$$\mathsf{HDC} \subset \mathsf{HCC} \subset \mathsf{ED}\cdot\log N \subset \mathsf{VD}\cdot\log N. \quad (34)$$

Note that the bounds in the constraints HDC are not normalized as in the sets ED or VD in the traditional width parameters. This is because normalizing makes it less general than it can be, and it does not make practical sense to assume that all degree bounds are the same! (For example, the FD-based degree bounds are always 0, while the relation-size-based degree bounds are $\log_2 N_F$.) Consequently, we used the $\log_2 N$ scaled up versions of the traditional width parameters to compare with our new width parameters.

From these specializations, the minimax and maximin widths capture all width parameters we discussed in Section 2, summarized in the following proposition. (See [4] for the proof.)

Proposition 5.2. *Let Q be a conjunctive query with no FDs whose hypergraph is $\mathcal{H} = ([n], \mathcal{E})$. Then the followings hold (Recall notation from Section 2):*

$$\begin{aligned}
1+\mathsf{tw}(\mathcal{H}) &= \mathsf{Minimaxwidth}_{\mathcal{F}\cap\mathsf{VD}}(Q)\\
&= \mathsf{Maximinwidth}_{\mathcal{F}\cap\mathsf{VD}}(Q)\\
&\qquad \forall\mathcal{F}\in\{\mathsf{M}_n, \overline{\Gamma}^*_n, \Gamma_n, \mathsf{SA}_n\} && (35)\\
\mathsf{ghtw}(\mathcal{H}) &= \mathsf{Minimaxwidth}_{\mathsf{SA}_n\cap\mathsf{ED}}(Q)\\
&= \mathsf{Maximinwidth}_{\mathsf{SA}_n\cap\mathsf{ED}}(Q) && (36)\\
\mathsf{fhtw}(\mathcal{H}) &= \mathsf{Minimaxwidth}_{\mathcal{F}\cap\mathsf{ED}}(Q)\\
&\qquad \forall\mathcal{F}\in\{\mathsf{M}_n, \overline{\Gamma}^*_n, \Gamma_n\} && (37)\\
\mathsf{subw}(\mathcal{H}) &= \mathsf{Maximinwidth}_{\Gamma_n\cap\mathsf{ED}}(Q) && (38)\\
\mathsf{adw}(\mathcal{H}) &= \mathsf{Maximinwidth}_{\mathsf{M}_n\cap\mathsf{ED}}(Q). && (39)
\end{aligned}$$

While SA_n yields too large of an upperbound, and M_n only yields a lowerbound, depending on the constraints we want to impose, some parts of the hierarchy collapse. The following observation is straightforward:

Lemma 5.3. *If $\mathcal{G} \subseteq \mathcal{F}$ are two classes of functions,*

$$\begin{aligned}
\mathsf{Minimaxwidth}_{\mathcal{G}}(\mathcal{H}) &\le \mathsf{Minimaxwidth}_{\mathcal{F}}(\mathcal{H})\\
\mathsf{Maximinwidth}_{\mathcal{G}}(\mathcal{H}) &\le \mathsf{Maximinwidth}_{\mathcal{F}}(\mathcal{H}).
\end{aligned}$$

For a fixed class $\mathcal{F}$ of functions, we have

$$\mathsf{Maximinwidth}_{\mathcal{F}}(\mathcal{H}) \le \mathsf{Minimaxwidth}_{\mathcal{F}}(\mathcal{H}).$$

5.2 New width parameters

Using the maximin and minimax formalism, we extend the traditional width parameters to handle general degree constraints. As shown by Theorem 1.2 we know that there is a gap between the polymatroid bound and the entropic bound; and hence it is natural to use $\overline{\Gamma}^*_n$ itself instead of some approximation of it.

Definition 5.4. We define the following width parameters for queries Q with degree constraints DC. The first two parameters are generalizations of fhtw and subw under degree constraints, and the last two are their entropic versions:

$$\begin{aligned}
\mathsf{da\text{-}fhtw}(Q) &\stackrel{\text{def}}{=} \mathsf{Minimaxwidth}_{\Gamma_n\cap\mathsf{HDC}}(Q) && (40)\\
\mathsf{da\text{-}subw}(Q) &\stackrel{\text{def}}{=} \mathsf{Maximinwidth}_{\Gamma_n\cap\mathsf{HDC}}(Q) && (41)\\
\mathsf{eda\text{-}fhtw}(Q) &\stackrel{\text{def}}{=} \mathsf{Minimaxwidth}_{\overline{\Gamma}^*_n\cap\mathsf{HDC}}(Q) && (42)\\
\mathsf{eda\text{-}subw}(Q) &\stackrel{\text{def}}{=} \mathsf{Maximinwidth}_{\overline{\Gamma}^*_n\cap\mathsf{HDC}}(Q). && (43)
\end{aligned}$$

(da stands for "degree-aware", and eda for "entropic degree-aware".) The following relationships hold between these four quantities.

Proposition 5.5. *For any query Q with degree constraints*

$$\begin{array}{ccc}
\mathsf{eda\text{-}subw}(Q) & \le & \mathsf{eda\text{-}fhtw}(Q)\\
\text{\rotatebox{90}{$\le$}} & & \text{\rotatebox{90}{$\le$}}\\
\mathsf{da\text{-}subw}(Q) & \le & \mathsf{da\text{-}fhtw}(Q).
\end{array}$$

The quantities $\mathsf{eda\text{-}fhtw}(Q)$ and $\mathsf{da\text{-}subw}(Q)$ are not comparable. The gap between the two sides of any of the above four inequalities can be made arbitrarily large by some input.

Due to the fact that every non-negative modular set function is entropic, we have

Corollary 5.6. *When Q has only edge domination constraints ED (i.e. no FD nor proper degree bounds), we have $\mathsf{adw}(Q) \le \mathsf{eda\text{-}subw}(Q)$.*

Following Marx [31, 32], for these queries $\mathsf{da\text{-}subw}(Q) = \mathsf{subw}(Q) = O(\mathsf{adw}^4(Q)) = O(\mathsf{eda\text{-}subw}^4(Q))$. Thus, when there is no FD nor proper degree bounds, if a class of queries has bounded eda-subw, then it has bounded da-subw. It is open whether or not the same relationship holds when Q has FDs and/or degree bounds.

We have mentioned quite a few known and proved new bounds in this paper. The bounds can be summarized systematically as follows. Each bound is identified by coordinates (X, Y, Z). The X-axis represents the entropy approximation that is being used: one starts from the desired target $\overline{\Gamma}^*_n$, then relaxes it to Γ_n and SA_n. The inclusion chain is $\overline{\Gamma}^*_n \subset \Gamma_n \subset \mathsf{SA}_n$. The Y-axis represents the constraints we can extract from the input database instance, where we can go from bounding domain sizes, relation sizes, to incorporating more refined degree bounds and functional dependencies. One chain of inclusion was given by (34). The Z-axis represents the level of sophistication of the query plan that is being considered in this bound. The simplest query plan just joins everything together without computing any tree decomposition – or, equivalently, this is the plan that uses the trivial tree decomposition with one bag containing all attributes. (Recall the bounds DAEB(Q) and DAPB(Q) from (19).) Then, one can get more sophisticated with computing a tree decomposition before computing the bags.

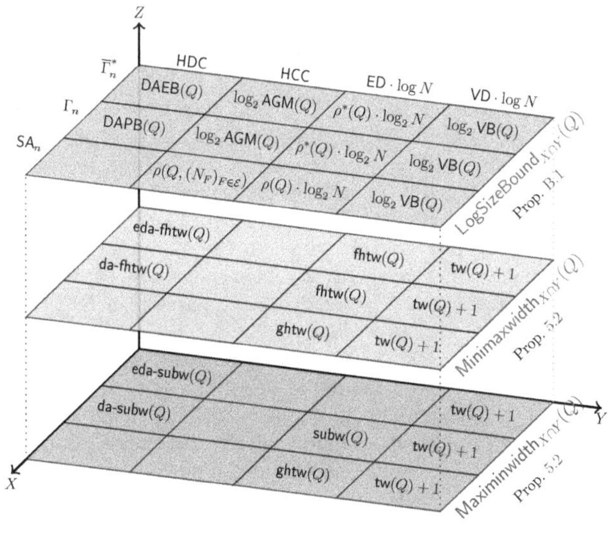

Figure 2: A hierarchy of bounds

And, lastly the query plan can also be adaptive to the input instance, yielding the submodular-width style of complexity. The bounds are summarized in Figure 2. If bound A has coordinates (X_1, Y_1, Z_1) that are smaller than the coordinates (X_2, Y_2, Z_2) of bound B (i.e. $X_1 \leq X_2 \wedge Y_1 \leq Y_2 \wedge Z_1 \leq Z_2$), then bound $A \leq$ bound B.

5.3 Achieving degree-aware width parameters

With increasing levels of complexity, the corollaries below explain how PANDA can be used to evaluate a (full or Boolean) conjunctive query achieving the degree-aware polymatroid size bound defined in (19), the degree-aware version of the fractional hypertree width defined in (40), and the degree-aware version of the submodular width defined in (41). Then, going beyond conjunctive queries, we show that PANDA can be used to solve aggregate queries by combining PANDA with the FAQ framework. The missing proofs can be found in the full version [4].

We start with two straightforward corollaries.

Corollary 5.7. *A full or Boolean conjunctive query Q with degree constraints can be solved by PANDA in time*

$$\tilde{O}(N + \text{poly}(\log N) \cdot 2^{\mathsf{DAPB}(Q)}).$$

Corollary 5.8. *A full or Boolean conjunctive query Q with degree constraints can be solved by PANDA in time*

$$\tilde{O}(N + \text{poly}(\log N) \cdot 2^{\mathsf{da\text{-}fhtw}(Q)} + |\mathsf{output}|).$$

The third corollary is on achieving the the degree-aware submodular width. Unlike the first two corollaries, proving this requires a couple of new ideas. In order to compute da-subw, even in a bruteforce manner, we need an auxiliary lemma, which is somewhat related to Neumann's minimax theorem [20].

Lemma 5.9. *Let A and B be two finite sets, and $f : A \times B \to \mathbb{R}$ be any function. Let B^A denote the set of all maps from A to B. Then, the following holds:*

$$\min_{a \in A} \max_{b \in B} f(a, b) = \max_{\beta \in B^A} \min_{a \in A} f(a, \beta(a)).$$

Intuitively, on the LHS we select for each $a \in A$ a neighbor b for which $f(a, b)$ is maximized; call such neighbor a's "representative". Then, we select the a with the least-weight representative. On the RHS, we have a "representative selector" β; we pick the a-value with the least-weight selected representative, and then maximize over all selectors.

Corollary 5.10. *A full or Boolean conjunctive query Q with degree constraints DC can be solved by PANDA in time*

$$\tilde{O}(N + \text{poly}(\log N) \cdot 2^{\mathsf{da\text{-}subw}(Q)} + |\mathsf{output}|).$$

Proof. We first apply Lemma 5.9 to reformulate (41). To this end, we need a few notations. Let $\mathcal{M}$ be the set of all maps $\beta : \mathsf{TD} \to 2^{[n]}$, such that $\beta(T, \chi) = \chi(t)$ for some $t \in V(T)$. In English, β is a "bag selector" map that picks out a bag from each tree decomposition (T, χ). Let $\mathbf{B}$ be the collection of images of all $\beta \in \mathcal{M}$, i.e.

$$\mathbf{B} = \{\mathcal{B} \mid \mathcal{B} = \mathsf{image}(\beta) \text{ for some } \beta \in \mathcal{M}\}. \quad (44)$$

Using Lemma 5.9, we can rewrite (41) as follows.

$$\begin{aligned}
\mathsf{da\text{-}subw}(\mathcal{H}) &= \max_{h \in \Gamma_n \cap \mathsf{HDC}} \min_{(T,\chi) \in \mathsf{TD}} \max_{t \in V(T)} h(\chi(t)) \\
\text{(Lemma 5.9)} &= \max_{h \in \Gamma_n \cap \mathsf{HDC}} \max_{\beta \in \mathcal{M}} \min_{(T,\chi)} h(\beta(T, \chi)) \\
&= \max_{h \in \Gamma_n \cap \mathsf{HDC}} \max_{\beta \in \mathcal{M}} \min_{B \in \mathsf{image}(\beta)} h(B) \\
&= \max_{\beta \in \mathcal{M}} \max_{h \in \Gamma_n \cap \mathsf{HDC}} \min_{B \in \mathsf{image}(\beta)} h(B) \\
&= \max_{\mathcal{B} \in \mathbf{B}} \max_{h \in \Gamma_n \cap \mathsf{HDC}} \min_{B \in \mathcal{B}} h(B) \\
\text{(Lemma 3.2)} &= \max_{\mathcal{B} \in \mathbf{B}} \underbrace{\max_{h \in \Gamma_n \cap \mathsf{HDC}} \left\{ \sum_{B \in \mathcal{B}} \lambda_B h(B) \right\}}_{\text{Linear program (21)}} \quad (45)
\end{aligned}$$

In (45), for a fixed $\mathcal{B} \in \mathbf{B}$ the inner max is exactly LP (21) whose dual is (22). In particular, to compute the da-subw(Q), we can solve a collection of linear programs and take the maximum solution among them. Since there is a different linear program for each valid choice of $\mathcal{B}$, the total number of linear programs is $\leq 2^{2^n}$.

In order to compute Q in the desired time, we mimic this strategy in the algorithm. For each $\mathcal{B} \in \mathbf{B}$, we solve the LP (21). Let $(\boldsymbol{\delta}^*, \boldsymbol{\sigma}^*, \boldsymbol{\mu}^*)$ denote a dual optimal solution. From Proposition 3.3, $\langle \boldsymbol{\lambda}, \mathbf{h} \rangle \leq \langle \boldsymbol{\delta}^*, \mathbf{h} \rangle$ is a Shannon flow inequality. On this input PANDA computes a tuple $\mathbf{T}_{\mathcal{B}} = (T_B)_{B \in \mathcal{B}}$ of tables such that, for every $\mathbf{a} \in Q$ there exists a $B \in \mathcal{B}$ for which $\Pi_B(\mathbf{a}) \in T_B$.

Let $M = |\mathbf{B}|$ and suppose $\mathbf{B} = \{\mathcal{B}_1, \dots, \mathcal{B}_M\}$. We prove the following claims:

Claim 1: for every $(B_1, \dots, B_M) \in \prod_{i=1}^M \mathcal{B}_i$, there is a tree decomposition $(T, \chi) \in \mathsf{TD}(Q)$ such that, for every tree node $t \in V(T)$, $\chi(t) = B_j$ for some $j \in [M]$. Breaking ties arbitrarily, we call this tree decomposition *the* tree decomposition (of Q) associated with the tuple $(B_1, \dots, B_M)$.

Claim 2: for any tuple $(B_1, \dots, B_M) \in \prod_{i=1}^M \mathcal{B}_i$ with associated tree decomposition (T, χ), define

$$J(B_1, \dots, B_M) \stackrel{\text{def}}{=} \Join_{t \in V(T)} T_{\chi(t)}.$$

Then,

$$Q \subseteq \left(\bigcup_{(B_1,\dots,B_M) \in \prod_{i=1}^M \mathcal{B}_i} \Join_{j=1}^M T_{B_j} \right) , \quad (46)$$

$$\subseteq \left(\bigcup_{(B_1,\ldots,B_M)\in\prod_{i=1}^M \mathcal{B}_i} J(B_1,\ldots,B_M) \right). \quad (47)$$

Assuming the claims, the query can be computed by running Yannakakis algorithm to compute all the relations $J(B_1,\ldots,B_M)$ within a runtime of $\tilde{O}(2^{\text{da-subw}(Q)} + |J(B_1,\ldots,B_M)\cap Q|)$. If we apply Yannakakis's algorithm straight up on $J(B_1,\ldots,B_M)$, then we can attain the runtime $\tilde{O}(2^{\text{da-subw}(Q)}+|J(B_1,\ldots,B_M)|)$, because every table T_{B_j} has size bounded by $2^{\text{da-subw}(Q)}$. To reduce the runtime to $\tilde{O}(2^{\text{da-subw}(Q)} + |J(B_1,\ldots,B_M)\cap Q|)$, we semijoin-reduce every table T_{B_j} with every input relation. There are $\prod_{i=1}^M |\mathcal{B}_i|$ such problems, which is a query-complexity quantity.

We next prove Claim 1. Fix a tuple $(B_1,\ldots,B_M) \in \prod_{i=1}^M \mathcal{B}_i$. Suppose to the contrary that for *every* tree decomposition (T,χ) there is a tree node $t \in V(T)$ such that $\chi(t) \neq B_j$ for every $j \in [M]$. Call the bag $\chi(t)$ a *missed* bag of the tree decomposition. Consider a bag selector $\beta : \mathsf{TD}(Q) \to 2^{[n]}$ where $\beta(T,\chi)$ is exactly the missed bag of the tree decomposition (T,χ). Note that by definition of $\mathbf{B}$ we have $\mathsf{image}(\beta) = \mathcal{B}_k$ for some $k \in [M]$. This is a contradiction because B_k must then be the missed bag of some tree decomposition, but it is not missed anymore.

Finally, we prove Claim 2. Consider an output tuple $\mathbf{a} \in Q$. For each $j \in [M]$, let B_j denote the bag for which $\Pi_{B_j}(\mathbf{a}) \in T_{B_j}$. Then, obviously $\mathbf{a} \in J(B_1,\ldots,B_M)$. This proves the first inclusion in (47). The second inclusion is obvious because the join $J(B_1,\ldots,B_M)$ drops some tables from the join $\Join_{j=1}^M T_{B_j}$. □

Example 5.11. We illustrate how PANDA computes the query Q in Example 1.1 in time $\tilde{O}(N^{\text{subw}(Q)})$. We use Marx' original definition of submodular width which, recall, corresponds to using base N for the logarithm, hence the expression $N^{\text{subw}(Q)}$ instead of our $2^{\text{da-subw}(Q)}$. We prove first that $\text{subw}(Q) \leq 3/2$. Since Q has two tree decompositions, shown in Fig. 1, we need to prove:

$$\begin{aligned}\min(&\max(h(A_1A_2A_3), h(A_3A_4A_1)),\\ &\max(h(A_2A_3A_4), h(A_4A_1A_2))) \leq 3/2\end{aligned}$$

where h is any edge-dominated polymatroid h. (The first max corresponds to the first tree, the second max to the second tree.) Using the distributivity law of min over max, we convert the inequality from min(max) $\leq 3/2$ into max(min) $\leq 3/2$, which is equivalent to the conjunction of four inequalities:

$$\begin{aligned}\min(h(A_1A_2A_3), h(A_2A_3A_4)) &\leq 3/2\\ \min(h(A_1A_2A_3), h(A_4A_1A_2)) &\leq 3/2\\ \min(h(A_3A_4A_1), h(A_2A_3A_4)) &\leq 3/2\\ \min(h(A_3A_4A_1), h(A_4A_1A_2)) &\leq 3/2\end{aligned}$$

The first inequality follows from $h(A_1A_2A_3)+h(A_2A_3A_4) \leq h(A_1A_2)+h(A_2A_3)+h(A_3A_4)$ (Example 4.1) and the latter is ≤ 3 because h is edge-dominated. The others are similar. This concludes $\text{subw}(Q) \leq 3/2$.

At this point PANDA converts each of the four Shannon-flow inequalities that it has just proven, into a disjunctive datalog rule. For example, the first inequality becomes precisely the disjunctive datalog rule P in Example 1.3. Then, it evaluates each of these four rules, obtaining four target relations $T_{123}, T_{234}, T_{341}, T_{412}$ (since each target occurs in two rules, PANDA takes their union; it also semi-joins each target with the input relations, to remove spurious tuples, e.g. it semi-joins T_{123} with R_{12} and R_{23}). Each of the four targets has size $\leq N^{3/2}$ and the runtime so far is $\tilde{O}(N^{3/2})$. Finally, PANDA runs Yannakakis' algorithm for acyclic queries on the first tree (in essence, joining T_{123} with T_{341}) then separately on the second tree, and returns the union of the two results. We need to prove that it returns the correct output, and for that we use the following subtle argument. Let $\mathbf{a} = (a_1, a_2, a_3, a_4)$ be any tuple. We show that, if $\pi_F(\mathbf{a}) \in R_F$ for every input relation R_F, then at least one of the two trees contains (the projection of) $\mathbf{a}$ in both its targets. Suppose the contrary: some tuple $\mathbf{a}$ fails this property. For example, $\pi_{123}(\mathbf{a}) \notin T_{123}$ in the first tree, and $\pi_{412}(\mathbf{a}) \notin T_{412}$ in the second tree. That implies that $T_{123} \vee T_{412}$ is not a model of the disjunctive datalog rule corresponding to the second inequality above, contradiction. Thus, each tuple $\mathbf{a}$ is fully included in some tree, and by taking the union PANDA returns all answers to Q.

Our final corollary concerns aggregate queries. By an aggregate query we mean a FAQ-query under one semiring (also called SumProd or FAQ-SS, see [2,6]).

Corollary 5.12. *An* FAQ-SS *query Q without free variables and with degree constraints DC can be solved by* PANDA *in time*

$$\tilde{O}(N + \text{poly}(\log N) \cdot 2^{\text{da-subw}(Q)} + |\text{output}|).$$

The last two corollaries prove Theorem 1.7. It is possible to handle FAQ-SS queries *with* free variables and degree constraints using our framework and algorithm; however, the result is slightly messy to state and explain, and thus we skip stating this simple observation here.

6. CONCLUDING REMARKS

Our negative answer to question 1 leads to a natural question: can we design an algorithm whose runtime matches the entropic bound under the presence of FDs or degree constraints? Worst-case optimal join algorithms [1, 34, 35, 37] were able to achieve this when there are no FDs. And, as shown in [3] there are classes of queries with FDs for which the answer is positive (using the chain algorithm). A natural direction is to extend the class of queries with FDs where the entropic bound can be met, beyond what was shown in [3]. Along the same line, the next natural open question is to design algorithms to evaluate disjunctive datalog queries matching the bound $\text{LogSizeBound}_{\bar{\Gamma}^*_n \cap \text{HDC}}(P)$. From there, the possibility of achieving eda-subw and/or eda-fhtw is within reach. We already have an example where PANDA was able to achieve eda-subw and eda-fhtw: the 4-cycle example. In general, the inner-most column of Figure 2 contains open algorithmic questions: we do not know of algorithms meeting bounds involving both $\bar{\Gamma}^*_n$ and HDC. Another big open question is to remove the polylog factor from the runtime of PANDA.

Acknowledgements

This work is partly supported by NSF grants 1535565 and 1614738, and by DARPA under agreement #FA8750-15-2-0009. The U.S. Government is authorized to reproduce and distribute reprints for Governmental purposes notwithstanding any copyright thereon.

7. REFERENCES

[1] M. Abo Khamis, H. Q. Ngo, C. Ré, and A. Rudra. Joins via geometric resolutions: Worst-case and beyond. In *PODS 2015*, pages 213–228, New York, NY, USA, 2015. ACM.

[2] M. Abo Khamis, H. Q. Ngo, and A. Rudra. FAQ: questions asked frequently. In *PODS 2016*, pages 13–28, 2016.

[3] M. Abo Khamis, H. Q. Ngo, and D. Suciu. Computing join queries with functional dependencies. In *PODS 2016*, pages 327–342, 2016.

[4] M. Abo Khamis, H. Q. Ngo, and D. Suciu. What do shannon-type inequalities, submodular width, and disjunctive datalog have to do with one another? *CoRR*, abs/1612.02503, 2016.

[5] I. Adler. *Width functions for hypertree decompositions.* 2006. Ph.D. Dissertation, Albert-Ludwigs-Universität Freiburg. 2006.

[6] S. M. Aji and R. J. McEliece. The generalized distributive law. *IEEE Transactions on Information Theory*, 46(2):325–343, 2000.

[7] N. Alon. On the number of subgraphs of prescribed type of graphs with a given number of edges. *Israel J. Math.*, 38(1-2):116–130, 1981.

[8] N. Alon, R. Yuster, and U. Zwick. Finding and counting given length cycles. *Algorithmica*, 17(3):209–223, 1997.

[9] M. Alviano, W. Faber, N. Leone, S. Perri, G. Pfeifer, and G. Terracina. The disjunctive datalog system DLV. In O. de Moor, G. Gottlob, T. Furche, and A. J. Sellers, editors, *Datalog Reloaded - First International Workshop, Datalog 2010, Oxford, UK, March 16-19, 2010. Revised Selected Papers*, volume 6702 of *Lecture Notes in Computer Science*, pages 282–301. Springer, 2010.

[10] M. Armbrust, K. Curtis, T. Kraska, A. Fox, M. J. Franklin, and D. A. Patterson. PIQL: success-tolerant query processing in the cloud. *PVLDB*, 5(3):181–192, 2011.

[11] M. Armbrust, A. Fox, D. A. Patterson, N. Lanham, B. Trushkowsky, J. Trutna, and H. Oh. SCADS: scale-independent storage for social computing applications. In *CIDR 2009, Fourth Biennial Conference on Innovative Data Systems Research, Asilomar, CA, USA, January 4-7, 2009, Online Proceedings*, 2009.

[12] M. Armbrust, E. Liang, T. Kraska, A. Fox, M. J. Franklin, and D. A. Patterson. Generalized scale independence through incremental precomputation. In *SIGMOD 2013*, pages 625–636, 2013.

[13] A. Atserias, M. Grohe, and D. Marx. Size bounds and query plans for relational joins. In *FOCS*, pages 739–748. IEEE Computer Society, 2008.

[14] N. Bakibayev, T. Kociský, D. Olteanu, and J. Zavodny. Aggregation and ordering in factorised databases. *PVLDB*, 6(14):1990–2001, 2013.

[15] M. Benedikt, J. Leblay, and E. Tsamoura. Querying with access patterns and integrity constraints. *PVLDB*, 8(6):690–701, 2015.

[16] M. Benedikt, B. ten Cate, and E. Tsamoura. Generating plans from proofs. *ACM Trans. Database Syst.*, 40(4):22, 2016.

[17] Y. Cao, W. Fan, T. Wo, and W. Yu. Bounded conjunctive queries. *PVLDB*, 7(12):1231–1242, 2014.

[18] F. R. K. Chung, R. L. Graham, P. Frankl, and J. B. Shearer. Some intersection theorems for ordered sets and graphs. *J. Combin. Theory Ser. A*, 43(1):23–37, 1986.

[19] R. Dechter. Bucket elimination: A unifying framework for reasoning. *Artif. Intell.*, 113(1-2):41–85, 1999.

[20] D. Du and P. Pardalos. *Minimax and Applications.* Nonconvex Optimization and Its Applications. Springer US, 1995.

[21] T. Eiter, G. Gottlob, and H. Mannila. Disjunctive datalog. *ACM Trans. Database Syst.*, 22(3):364–418, 1997.

[22] W. Fischl, G. Gottlob, and R. Pichler. General and Fractional Hypertree Decompositions: Hard and Easy Cases. *ArXiv e-prints*, Nov. 2016.

[23] E. C. Freuder. Complexity of k-tree structured constraint satisfaction problems. In H. E. Shrobe, T. G. Dietterich, and W. R. Swartout, editors, *Proceedings of the 8th National Conference on Artificial Intelligence. Boston, Massachusetts, July 29 - August 3, 1990, 2 Volumes.*, pages 4–9. AAAI Press / The MIT Press, 1990.

[24] E. Friedgut and J. Kahn. On the number of copies of one hypergraph in another. *Israel J. Math.*, 105:251–256, 1998.

[25] T. Gogacz and S. Toruńczyk. Entropy bounds for conjunctive queries with functional dependencies. In *Proc. 20th International Conference on Database Theory (ICDT)*, 2017.

[26] G. Gottlob, G. Greco, N. Leone, and F. Scarcello. Hypertree decompositions: Questions and answers. In *Proceedings of the 35th ACM SIGMOD-SIGACT-SIGAI Symposium on Principles of Database Systems, PODS 2016, San Francisco, CA, USA, June 26 - July 01, 2016*, pages 57–74, 2016.

[27] G. Gottlob, S. T. Lee, G. Valiant, and P. Valiant. Size and treewidth bounds for conjunctive queries. *J. ACM*, 59(3):16, 2012.

[28] G. Gottlob, N. Leone, and F. Scarcello. Hypertree decompositions and tractable queries. *J. Comput. Syst. Sci.*, 64(3):579–627, 2002.

[29] M. Grohe and D. Marx. Constraint solving via fractional edge covers. In *SODA*, pages 289–298. ACM Press, 2006.

[30] M. Grohe and D. Marx. Constraint solving via fractional edge covers. *ACM Transactions on Algorithms*, 11(1):4, 2014.

[31] D. Marx. Tractable structures for constraint satisfaction with truth tables. *Theory Comput. Syst.*, 48(3):444–464, 2011.

[32] D. Marx. Tractable hypergraph properties for constraint satisfaction and conjunctive queries. *J. ACM*, 60(6):Art. 42, 51, 2013.

[33] F. Matus. Infinitely many information inequalities. In *2007 IEEE International Symposium on Information Theory*, pages 41–44. IEEE, 2007.

[34] H. Q. Ngo, E. Porat, C. Ré, and A. Rudra. Worst-case optimal join algorithms: [extended abstract]. In *PODS*, pages 37–48, 2012.

[35] H. Q. Ngo, C. Ré, and A. Rudra. Skew strikes back: new developments in the theory of join algorithms. *SIGMOD Record*, 42(4):5–16, 2013.

[36] A. Schrijver. *Theory of linear and integer programming*. Wiley-Interscience Series in Discrete Mathematics. John Wiley & Sons Ltd., Chichester, 1986. A Wiley-Interscience Publication.

[37] T. L. Veldhuizen. Triejoin: A simple, worst-case optimal join algorithm. In N. Schweikardt, V. Christophides, and V. Leroy, editors, *Proc. 17th International Conference on Database Theory (ICDT), Athens, Greece, March 24-28, 2014.*, pages 96–106. OpenProceedings.org, 2014.

[38] R. W. Yeung. *Information Theory and Network Coding*. Springer Publishing Company, Incorporated, 1 edition, 2008.

[39] Z. Zhang and R. W. Yeung. On characterization of entropy function via information inequalities. *IEEE Transactions on Information Theory*, 44(4):1440–1452, 1998.

APPENDIX

A. MISSING DETAILS FROM SECTION 1

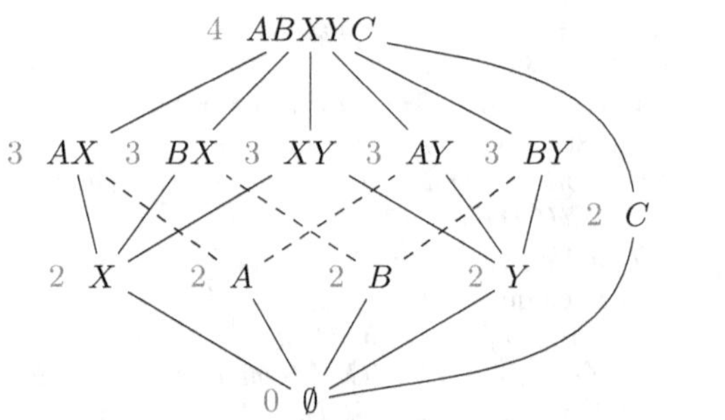

Figure 3: A polymatroid h (shown in green).

Proof of Theorem 1.2. Consider the following query:

$$Q(A,B,X,Y,C) \text{ :- } K(A,B,X,Y,C),$$
$$R(X,Y),S(A,X),T(A,Y),U(B,X),V(B,Y),W(C)$$

with given cardinality constraints $|R|,|S|,|T|,|U|,|V| \le N^3$, $|W| \le N^2$ (none on K), and the following keys in K: AB, AXY, BXY, AC, XC, YC. We show that the entropic bound is $\le N^{43/11}$ while the polymatroid bound is N^4. This statement follows from two claims. First, the following non-Shannon inequality holds for all entropic functions:

$$11h(ABXYC) \le 3h(XY)+3h(AX)+3h(AY)+h(BX) +h(BY)+5h(C)+(h(ABXYC|AB)+4h(ABXYC|AXY) +h(ABXYC|BXY))+(h(ABXYC|AC)+2h(ABXYC|XC) +2h(ABXYC|YC)). \quad (48)$$

The first claim implies $11\log|Q| \le 11\log N^3 + 5\log N^2 = 43\log N$. Second, there exists a polymatroid h satisfying all cardinality and FD constraints such that $h(ABXYC) = 4\log N$. The two claims show a ratio of $N^{1/11}$ between the two bounds.

We now prove the first claim. Let $I(\mathbf{X};\mathbf{Y}|\mathbf{Z}) := H(\mathbf{XZ})+H(\mathbf{YZ})-H(\mathbf{XYZ})-H(\mathbf{Z})$ denote the conditional mutual information between random variables $\mathbf{X}$ and $\mathbf{Y}$ conditioned on random variables $\mathbf{Z}$. In a breakthrough paper in information theory, Zhang and Yeung [39] proved that $\overline{\Gamma}_4^* \subsetneq \Gamma_4$ by proving that the following inequality is a non-Shannon-type inequality (see [38, Th.15.7]):

$$2I(X;Y) \le I(A;B)+I(A;XY)+3I(X;Y|A)+I(X;Y|B).$$

We expand and rearrange it, obtaining

$$h(AB)+4h(AXY)+h(BXY) \le 3h(XY)+3h(AX) +3h(AY)+h(BX)+h(BY)-(h(A)+2h(X)+2h(Y))$$

Add $h(ABXYC|AB)+4h(ABXYC|AXY)+h(ABXYC|BXY)$ to both sides:

$$6h(ABXYC) \le 3h(XY)+3h(AX)+3h(AY)+h(BX)+h(BY) -(h(A)+2h(X)+2h(Y))+(h(ABXYC|AB)+ 4h(ABXYC|AXY)+h(ABXYC|BXY)) \quad (49)$$

From these three Shannon-type inequalities $h(A)+h(C) \ge h(AC)$, $h(X)+h(C) \ge h(XC)$, and $h(Y)+h(C) \ge h(YC)$ we derive the following:

$$5h(ABXYC) \le h(A)+2h(X)+2h(Y)+5h(C)+ (h(ABXYC|AC)+2h(ABXYC|XC)+2h(ABXYC|YC)) \quad (50)$$

By adding Eq.(49) and (50) we obtain (48).

The second claim is shown in Fig. 3. The figure shows a polymatroid h on the five variables A,B,X,Y,C. For each missing set of variables $\mathbf{Z}$, $h(\mathbf{Z}) \stackrel{\text{def}}{=} h(\mathbf{Z}^+)$, where $\mathbf{Z}^+$ is the smallest set shown in the figure that contains $\mathbf{Z}$: in other words, the figure shows the closed sets of a closure on $\{A,B,X,Y,C\}$. For example, $h(AB) \stackrel{\text{def}}{=} h(AB^+) = h(ABXYC) = 4$, etc. One can check that h satisfies all cardinality constraints and functional dependencies (using base N for the logarithm): for example $h(XY)=3$, $h(AX)=3$, and $AB \to XYC$ (because $h(AB)=h(ABXYC)$) etc.

Finally, to construct a query Q with an amplified gap between the two bounds, consider a query Q which is a cross-product of $11s$ independent copies of ZY. □

Due to space limitation, We prove only the first part of Theorem 1.4, leaving the second part in the full version [4].

Proof of part (i) of Theorem 1.4. Since $\overline{\Gamma}_n^* \subseteq \Gamma_n$, the second inequality is trivial. To show the first inequality, let T denote the set of all tuples $\mathbf{t}$ satisfying the body of P; construct a set $\overline{T}$ of tuples as follows. We scan though tuples $\mathbf{t} \in T$ one at a time, and either add $\mathbf{t}$ to $\overline{T}$ or ignore $\mathbf{t}$. To decide whether to add $\mathbf{t}$ to $\overline{T}$, we also keep a collection of tables $\mathbf{T} = (\overline{T}_B)_{B\in\mathcal{B}}$. These tables shall form a model of the disjunctive datalog rule P. Initially $\overline{T}$ and all the $\overline{T}_B$ are empty. Consider the next tuple $\mathbf{t}$ taken from T. If $\Pi_B(\mathbf{t}) \in \overline{T}_B$ for *any* $B \in \mathcal{B}$, then we ignore $\mathbf{t}$. Otherwise, we add $\Pi_B(\mathbf{t})$ to $\overline{T}_B$ for *every* $B \in \mathcal{B}$, and add $\mathbf{t}$ to $\overline{T}$. In the end, obviously the collection $(\overline{T}_B)_{B\in\mathcal{B}}$ is a model of the disjunctive datalog rule. Furthermore, by construction the tuples $\mathbf{t} \in \overline{T}$ satisfy the property that: for every two different tuples $\mathbf{t},\mathbf{t}' \in \overline{T}$, every $B \in \mathcal{B}$, we have $\Pi_B(\mathbf{t}) \ne \Pi_B(\mathbf{t}')$ and both $\Pi_B(\mathbf{t})$ and $\Pi_B(\mathbf{t}')$ are in $\overline{T}_B$.

Now, construct a joint probability distribution on n variables by picking uniformly a tuple from $\overline{T}$. Let $\overline{h}$ denote the entropy function of this distribution, then, from the above property

$$\log_2 |\overline{T}| = \overline{h}([n]) = \overline{h}(B), \forall B \in \mathcal{B}. \quad (51)$$

Furthermore, $\overline{h} \in \overline{\Gamma}^*_n$ by definition, and $\overline{h} \in \mathsf{HDC}$ because T was a set of tuples satisfying all input degree constraints. Consequently,

$$\begin{aligned}
\min_{(T_B)_{B\in\mathcal{B}}} \max_{B\in\mathcal{B}} \log_2 |T_B| &\leq \max_{B\in\mathcal{B}} \log_2 |\overline{T}_B| \\
\text{(due to (51))} &= \max_{B\in\mathcal{B}} \overline{h}(B) \\
\text{(due to (51))} &= \min_{B\in\mathcal{B}} \overline{h}(B) \\
\text{(because } \overline{h} \in \overline{\Gamma}^*_n \cap \mathsf{HDC}) &\leq \max_{h\in\overline{\Gamma}^*_n\cap\mathsf{HDC}} \min_{B\in\mathcal{B}} h(B) \\
&= \mathsf{LogSizeBound}_{\overline{\Gamma}^*_n\cap\mathsf{HDC}}(P).
\end{aligned}$$

□

B. MISSING DETAILS FROM SECTION 2

Here we revisit known output size bounds for conjunctive queries without FDs nor degree bounds, and we reformulate them from the perspective of our framework. Recall that a full conjunctive query is a special case of a disjunctive datalog rule: It is a disjunctive datalog rule with only one target $B = [n]$. Hence for a full conjunctive query Q, the log-size-bound given by (6) simplifies to

$$\mathsf{LogSizeBound}_{\mathcal{F}}(Q) \stackrel{\text{def}}{=} \max_{h\in\mathcal{F}} h([n]).$$

The full version [4] proves the following simple proposition which recaps the major known bounds under one umbrella. Since the proposition is restricted to full conjunctive queries rather than the more general disjunctive datalog rules, it makes stronger claims about size bounds: In particular, some bounds collapse part of the hierarchy of function classes: $\mathsf{M}_n \subset \overline{\Gamma}^*_n \subset \Gamma_n \subset \mathsf{SA}_n$. (Review notation in Section 2.)

Proposition B.1. *Let Q be a full conjunctive query with no FDs whose hypergraph is $\mathcal{H} = ([n], \mathcal{E})$. Then the followings hold:*

$$\begin{aligned}
\log_2 \mathsf{VB}(Q) &= \mathsf{LogSizeBound}_{\mathcal{F}\cap(\mathsf{VD}\cdot\log N)}(Q), \\
&\quad \forall \mathcal{F} \in \{\mathsf{M}_n, \overline{\Gamma}^*_n, \Gamma_n, \mathsf{SA}_n\} \quad (52)\\
\rho(Q, (N_F)_{F\in\mathcal{E}}) &= \mathsf{LogSizeBound}_{\mathsf{SA}_n\cap \mathit{HCC}}(Q) \quad (53)\\
\rho^*(Q)\cdot \log_2 N &= \mathsf{LogSizeBound}_{\mathcal{F}\cap(\mathsf{ED}\cdot\log N)}(Q), \\
&\quad \forall \mathcal{F} \in \{\mathsf{M}_n, \overline{\Gamma}^*_n, \Gamma_n\} \quad (54)\\
\log_2 \mathit{AGM}(Q) &= \mathsf{LogSizeBound}_{\mathcal{F}\cap \mathit{HCC}}(Q), \\
&\quad \forall \mathcal{F} \in \{\mathsf{M}_n, \overline{\Gamma}^*_n, \Gamma_n\} \quad (55)
\end{aligned}$$

The top part of Figure 2 depicts all the bounds in Proposition B.1. Regarding the AGM-bound, the fact that the size bound on Γ_n is equal to the size bound on M_n allows us to compute the bound efficiently (polynomial time in query complexity). By contrast, computing the integral edge cover bound is NP-hard in query complexity, despite being the worse bound: over the more relaxed function class SA_n. From the above proposition and the chains of inclusion $M_n \subset \overline{\Gamma}^*_n \subset \Gamma_n \subset \mathsf{SA}_n$ and $\mathsf{HCC} \subset \mathsf{VD}\cdot\log N$, we have $\mathsf{VB}(Q) \geq 2^{\rho(Q,(N_F)_{F\in\mathcal{E}})} \geq \mathsf{AGM}(Q)$ for any Q.

C. MISSING DETAILS FROM SECTION 3

C.1 Details from Section 3.1

The bound $\mathsf{LogSizeBound}_{\Gamma_n\cap\mathsf{HDC}}(P)$ is the optimal objective value of the following optimization problem:

$$\begin{array}{lll}
\max & \min_{B\in\mathcal{B}} h(B) & (56)\\
s.t. & h(Y) - h(X) \leq n_{Y|X}, & (X, Y, N_{Y|X}) \in \mathsf{DC}\\
& h(I\cup J|J) - h(I|I\cap J) \leq 0, & I \perp J\\
& h(Y) - h(X) \geq 0, & \emptyset \neq X \subset Y \subseteq [n]\\
& h(Z) \geq 0, & \emptyset \neq Z \subseteq [n].
\end{array}$$

(Recall that implicitly we have $h(\emptyset) = 0$, and that $n_{Y|X} \stackrel{\text{def}}{=} \log_2 N_{Y|X}$.) Here, $X \perp Y$ means $X \not\subseteq Y$ and $Y \not\subseteq X$. The optimization problem above is not easy to handle. Lemma 3.2 allows us to reformulate it into an LP. Lemma 3.2 is a special case of the following lemma.

Lemma C.1 (A generalization of Lemma 3.2). *Let $\mathbf{A} \in \mathbb{Q}^{\ell\times m}, \mathbf{b} \in \mathbb{R}^\ell$, and $\mathbf{C} \in \mathbb{Q}^{m\times p}_+$ be a matrix with columns $\mathbf{c}_1, \dots, \mathbf{c}_p$. Consider the following maximin optimization problem:*

$$\max\{\min_{k\in[p]} \mathbf{c}_k^T\mathbf{x} \mid \mathbf{A}\mathbf{x} \leq \mathbf{b}, \mathbf{x} \geq \mathbf{0}\} \quad (57)$$

If problem (57)'s objective value is positive and bounded, then there exists a vector $\boldsymbol{\lambda} \in \mathbb{Q}^p_+$ satisfying the following conditions:

(a) $\|\boldsymbol{\lambda}\|_1 = 1$

(b) The problem (57) has the same optimal objective value as the following linear program:

$$\max\{(\mathbf{C}\boldsymbol{\lambda})^T\mathbf{x} \mid \mathbf{A}\mathbf{x} \leq \mathbf{b}, \mathbf{x} \geq \mathbf{0}\} \quad (58)$$

Proof of Lemma C.1. The dual of (58) can be written as

$$\min\{\mathbf{b}^T\mathbf{y} \mid \mathbf{A}^T\mathbf{y} \geq \mathbf{C}\boldsymbol{\lambda}, \mathbf{y} \geq \mathbf{0}\} \quad (59)$$

Let $\mathbf{1}_p \in \mathbb{R}^p$ be the all-1 vector. The LP (57) can be rewritten as

$$\max\{w \mid \mathbf{A}\mathbf{x} \leq \mathbf{b}, \mathbf{1}_p w - \mathbf{C}^T\mathbf{x} \leq \mathbf{0}, \mathbf{x} \geq \mathbf{0}, \quad w \geq 0\} \quad (60)$$

The dual of (60) is

$$\min\{\mathbf{b}^T\mathbf{y} \mid \mathbf{A}^T\mathbf{y} \geq \mathbf{C}\mathbf{z}, \mathbf{1}_p^T\mathbf{z} \geq 1, \mathbf{y} \geq \mathbf{0}, \quad \mathbf{z} \geq 0\} \quad (61)$$

Let $(w^*, \mathbf{x}^*)$ and $(\mathbf{z}^*, \mathbf{y}^*)$ be a pair of primal-optimal and dual-optimal solutions to (60) and (61). Define $\boldsymbol{\lambda} = \mathbf{z}^*$. To show that (57) is equivalent to (58), we show that (60) is equivalent to (58). In particular, we claim that $\mathbf{x}^*$ and $\mathbf{y}^*$ are a pair of primal-optimal and dual-optimal solution to (60) and (59), and that the objective values of (58) and (60) are identical. The fact that $\mathbf{x}^*$ and $\mathbf{y}^*$ are feasible to (58) and (59) is trivial. We are left to verify that they have the same objective value. Due to complementary slackness of the (60) and (61) pair, note that $w^* > 0$ implies $\mathbf{1}_p^T\mathbf{z}^* = 1$ and $(\mathbf{1}_p^T w^* - \mathbf{C}^T\mathbf{x}^*)^T\mathbf{z}^* = 0$. It follows that $\mathbf{b}^T\mathbf{y}^* = w^* = (\mathbf{1}_p^T\mathbf{z}^*)\cdot w^* = (\mathbf{C}^T\mathbf{x}^*)^T\cdot\mathbf{z}^* = (\mathbf{C}\mathbf{z}^*)^T\cdot\mathbf{x}^* = (\mathbf{C}\boldsymbol{\lambda})^T\cdot\mathbf{x}^*$. □

Proof of Proposition 3.3. The proposition is a simple consequence of Farkas' lemma. There are *many* variants of Farkas' lemma [36]. We use a version whose proof we also reproduce here because the proof is very short.

Let $\mathbf{A} \in \mathbb{R}^{m\times n}$ be a matrix and $\mathbf{c} \in \mathbb{R}^n$ be a vector. Let $P = \{\mathbf{x} \mid \mathbf{A}\mathbf{x} \leq \mathbf{0}, \mathbf{x} \geq \mathbf{0}\}$ be a polyhedron and $D =$

$\{\mathbf{y} \mid \mathbf{A}^T\mathbf{y} \geq \mathbf{c}, \mathbf{y} \geq \mathbf{0}\}$ be a dual polyhedron. Then, a variant of Farkas' lemma states that D is non-empty if and only if there is *no* $\mathbf{x} \in P$ such that $\mathbf{c}^T\mathbf{x} > 0$. To see this, note that the system $\{\mathbf{c}^T\mathbf{x} > 0, \mathbf{x} \in P\}$ is infeasible iff $\max\{\mathbf{c}^T\mathbf{x} \mid \mathbf{x} \in P\} = 0$, which by strong duality is equivalent to $\min\{\mathbf{0}^T\mathbf{y} \mid \mathbf{y} \in D\}$ is feasible, which is the same as D is non-empty.

Now, to see why the above variant of Farkas' lemma implies Proposition 3.3, we note that (23) holds for all polymatroids iff $\{(\boldsymbol{\lambda}_{\mathcal{B}} - \boldsymbol{\delta}_{\mathsf{DC}})^T\mathbf{h} > 0 \mid \mathbf{h} \in \Gamma_n\}$ is infeasible; now we are in the exact setting of the above variant of Farkas' lemma and the rest follows trivially. □

C.2 Details from Section 3.2

Definition C.2 (Tight witness). A witness is said to be *tight* if $\mathsf{inflow}(Z) = \lambda_Z$ for all Z.

We remark that, if $\mathsf{inflow}(Z) > \lambda_Z$, we can always increase $\mu_{\emptyset,Z}$ by the amount $\mathsf{inflow}(Z) - \lambda_Z$ so that $\mathsf{inflow}(Z) = \lambda_Z$. In particular, it is easy to turn any witness into a tight witness. The proof of Lemma 3.9 below follows the same strategy as in the proof of Theorem 3.8, but with some subtle differences.

Proof of Lemma 3.9. W.L.O.G. we can assume that $(\boldsymbol{\sigma}, \boldsymbol{\mu})$ is a tight witness. We construct $(\boldsymbol{\lambda}', \boldsymbol{\delta}', \boldsymbol{\sigma}', \boldsymbol{\mu}')$ from $(\boldsymbol{\lambda}, \boldsymbol{\delta}, \boldsymbol{\sigma}, \boldsymbol{\mu})$ as follows. Initially we set $(\boldsymbol{\lambda}', \boldsymbol{\delta}', \boldsymbol{\sigma}', \boldsymbol{\mu}') = (\boldsymbol{\lambda}, \boldsymbol{\delta}, \boldsymbol{\sigma}, \boldsymbol{\mu})$. Let $\mathsf{inflow}'(Z)$ denote the quantity $\mathsf{inflow}(Z)$ measured on the vector $(\boldsymbol{\lambda}', \boldsymbol{\delta}', \boldsymbol{\sigma}', \boldsymbol{\mu}')$. Due to tightness of the witness, at this point $\mathsf{inflow}'(Z) - \lambda'_Z = 0$ for every Z.

Now, we start disturbing the flow balance equations starting from $Z = Y$ by setting $\delta'_{Z|\emptyset} = \delta'_{Z|\emptyset} - w$ which means $\mathsf{inflow}'(Z)$ was reduced by w. Note that Z is the only point for which $\mathsf{inflow}'(Z) - \lambda'_Z \neq 0$ (it is negative). If $\lambda'_Z > 0$, then we simply reduce λ'_Z by w and terminate. If $\lambda'_Z = 0$, then either (1) there is some $X \subset Z$ such that $\mu'_{X,Z} \geq w$, (2) there is some $Y \supset Z$ such that $\delta'_{Y|Z} \geq w$, or (3) there is some $J \perp Z$ such that $\sigma'_{Z,J} \geq w$. Cases (1) and (2) are handled in a similar way to the proof of Theorem 3.8 while case (3) is handled differently. In particular, if (1) holds, then we reduce $\mu'_{X,Z}$ by w and set $Z = X$. If (2) holds, then we reduce $\delta'_{Y|Z}$ by w and set $Z = Y$. If (3) holds, then we reduce $\sigma'_{Z,J}$ by w, *increase* $\mu'_{Z\cap J,J}$ by w, and set $Z = Z \cup J$. In all three cases, (the new) Z is the only point where $\mathsf{inflow}'(Z) - \lambda'_Z$ has a deficit, and the process continues if the new Z is not $\emptyset$.

The above process terminates because every time we move Z to a new deficit point, the quantity $2\|\boldsymbol{\sigma}\|_1 + \|\boldsymbol{\delta}\|_1 + \|\boldsymbol{\mu}\|_1$ is reduced by w. When the process terminates, all quantities $\mathsf{inflow}'(Z) - \lambda'(Z) = 0$ and thus $\langle \boldsymbol{\lambda}', \mathbf{h}\rangle \leq \langle \boldsymbol{\delta}', \mathbf{h}\rangle$ is a Shannon flow inequality witnessed by $(\boldsymbol{\sigma}', \boldsymbol{\mu}')$ by Proposition 3.5. Property (b) holds because we only reduce the $\boldsymbol{\sigma}'$ and $\boldsymbol{\delta}'$ entries. Properties (c) and (d) hold trivially. □

D. MISSING DETAILS FROM SECTION 4

Proof of Theorem 1.5. Consider an input proof sequence of length $\ell \leq D(3\|\boldsymbol{\sigma}\|_1 + \|\boldsymbol{\delta}\|_1 + \|\boldsymbol{\mu}\|_1)$, thanks to Theorem 3.8. If we do not hit Case 4b, then there will be at most ℓ steps in the algorithm, where each step either takes $\tilde{O}(2^{\mathsf{OBJ}})$ time or spawns $O(\mathsf{OBJ})$ subproblems, for a total of $\tilde{O}(\text{poly}(\mathsf{OBJ}) \cdot 2^{\mathsf{OBJ}})$-time. A subproblem will terminate at producing a relation $T(\mathbf{A}_B)$ for some $B \in \mathcal{B}$ because the proof sequence will, by definition, reach a point where $\delta_{B|\emptyset} \geq w > 0$ for some $B \in \mathcal{B}$.

The worst case is obtained when the algorithm branches as far as possible only to have to restart at Case 4b with a slightly shorter proof sequence of length at most $D(3\|\boldsymbol{\sigma}\|_1 + \|\boldsymbol{\delta}\|_1 + \|\boldsymbol{\mu}\|_1) - 1$. Thus, overall the exponent of OBJ (in $\text{poly}(\mathsf{OBJ})$) will be $\leq \frac{1}{2}D^2(3\|\boldsymbol{\sigma}\|_1 + \|\boldsymbol{\delta}\|_1 + \|\boldsymbol{\mu}\|_1)^2$. (Note that this constant is data-independent because the optimal dual solution $(\boldsymbol{\delta}, \boldsymbol{\sigma}, \boldsymbol{\mu})$ can be taken to be an extreme point of the dual polyhedron (24), whose constraints are only on the input query.) Since OBJ equals the polymatroid bound $\mathsf{LogSizeBound}_{\Gamma_n \cap \mathsf{HDC}}(P)$, which is bounded by the vertex bound $\log(N^n)$, and n is a constant in data complexity, we have $\mathsf{OBJ} = O(\log N)$, and the runtime is $\tilde{O}(\text{poly}(\log N) \cdot 2^{\mathsf{LogSizeBound}_{\Gamma_n \cap \mathsf{HDC}}(P)})$, as desired.

The last bit we have to verify is that every subproblem has a proof sequence that can eventually reach $\delta_{B|\emptyset} \geq w$ for some $B \in \mathcal{B}$. Since we start with a proof sequence and in Cases 1, 2, 3, and 4a we continue with the remaining steps of the input proof sequence, the only case where we have to worry about proving the existence of a proof sequence reaching $\delta_{B|\emptyset} \geq w$ is Case 4b. In this case we restart with inequality $\langle \boldsymbol{\lambda}', \mathbf{h}\rangle \leq \langle \boldsymbol{\delta}', \mathbf{h}\rangle$. Lemma 3.9 guarantees that $\lambda'_B > 0$ implies $\lambda_B > 0$. Hence, we will be done if we can show that $\|\boldsymbol{\lambda}'\|_1 > 0$. To this end, we show that the algorithm maintains another invariant, that for every subproblem it always holds that

$$\sum_{(X,Y)} n(\delta_{Y|X}) \leq \|\boldsymbol{\lambda}\|_1 \cdot \mathsf{OBJ}. \tag{62}$$

We call the quantity $\sum_{(X,Y)} n(\delta_{Y|X})$ the "potential" of the subproblem at that point in time. At the initial iteration, the potential of the input problem was exactly the budget. When Case 1 applies, the potential is unchanged because $\delta_{I|I\cap J}$ was reduced by w, $\delta_{I\cup J|J}$ was increased by w, and they have the same support. When Case 2 applies, the potential does not increase because we subtracted $w \cdot n_{Y|\emptyset}$ from the potential and added $w \cdot n_{X|\emptyset} \leq w \cdot n_{Y|\emptyset}$ instead. Similarly in Case 3, we subtracted $w \cdot n_{Y|\emptyset}$ from the potential, and added $w \cdot (n^{(j)}_{X|\emptyset} + n^{(j)}_{Y|X}) \leq w \cdot n_{Y|\emptyset}$ to the potential. In Case 4a, we subtracted $w \cdot (n_{X|\emptyset} + n_{W|Z})$ and added at most the same amount to the potential. In Case 4b, since $\boldsymbol{\delta}' \leq \boldsymbol{\delta}$ and $\delta'_{Y|\emptyset} = \delta_{Y|\emptyset} - w$, the potential is reduced by strictly more than $w \cdot \mathsf{OBJ}$ because we subtracted $w \cdot (n_{X|\emptyset} + n_{W|Z}) > w \cdot \mathsf{OBJ}$ from the potential. Since $\|\boldsymbol{\lambda}\|_1$ was reduced by at most w, invariant (62) still holds. This also proves that $\|\boldsymbol{\lambda}\|_1 > w$, because the residual potential, which is non-negative, is strictly smaller than $(\|\boldsymbol{\lambda}\|_1 - w)\mathsf{OBJ} \leq \|\boldsymbol{\lambda}'\|_1\mathsf{OBJ}$.

Finally, we get back to the assumption that $N \leq 2^{\mathsf{OBJ}}$ and how to enforce it in case it is not initially satisfied. Suppose there is an input relation $T(\mathbf{A}_Y)$ where $n_{Y|\emptyset} \stackrel{\text{def}}{=} \log_2 |T| > \mathsf{OBJ}$. If $\delta_{Y|\emptyset} = 0$, then T does not contribute to the bound nor the proof sequence and can be ignored. If $\delta_{Y|\emptyset} > 0$, then we could have replaced the original inequality with a new one $\langle \boldsymbol{\lambda}', \mathbf{h}\rangle \leq \langle \boldsymbol{\delta}', \mathbf{h}\rangle$ satisfying the conditions stated in Lemma 3.9, in the same way we handled Case 4b above. However, since the new inequality has $\mathsf{OBJ}' < \mathsf{OBJ}$ and OBJ is already the optimal (i.e. lowest) bound possible, this scenario is impossible. □

Author Index

www.ingramcontent.com/pod-product-compliance
Lightning Source LLC
LaVergne TN
LVHW080007210926
848481LV00011B/2961
* 9 7 8 1 4 5 0 3 5 4 7 5 2 *